Contemporary
Literary Criticism

Guide to Gale Literary Criticism Series

For criticism on	Consult these Gale series
Authors now living or who died after December 31, 1999	*CONTEMPORARY LITERARY CRITICISM (CLC)*
Authors who died between 1900 and 1999	*TWENTIETH-CENTURY LITERARY CRITICISM (TCLC)*
Authors who died between 1800 and 1899	*NINETEENTH-CENTURY LITERATURE CRITICISM (NCLC)*
Authors who died between 1400 and 1799	*LITERATURE CRITICISM FROM 1400 TO 1800 (LC)* *SHAKESPEAREAN CRITICISM (SC)*
Authors who died before 1400	*CLASSICAL AND MEDIEVAL LITERATURE CRITICISM (CMLC)*
Authors of books for children and young adults	*CHILDREN'S LITERATURE REVIEW (CLR)*
Dramatists	*DRAMA CRITICISM (DC)*
Poets	*POETRY CRITICISM (PC)*
Short story writers	*SHORT STORY CRITICISM (SSC)*
Literary topics and movements	*HARLEM RENAISSANCE: A GALE CRITICAL COMPANION (HR)* *THE BEAT GENERATION: A GALE CRITICAL COMPANION (BG)*
Asian American writers of the last two hundred years	*ASIAN AMERICAN LITERATURE (AAL)*
Black writers of the past two hundred years	*BLACK LITERATURE CRITICISM (BLC)* *BLACK LITERATURE CRITICISM SUPPLEMENT (BLCS)*
Hispanic writers of the late nineteenth and twentieth centuries	*HISPANIC LITERATURE CRITICISM (HLC)* *HISPANIC LITERATURE CRITICISM SUPPLEMENT (HLCS)*
Native North American writers and orators of the eighteenth, nineteenth, and twentieth centuries	*NATIVE NORTH AMERICAN LITERATURE (NNAL)*
Major authors from the Renaissance to the present	*WORLD LITERATURE CRITICISM, 1500 TO THE PRESENT (WLC)* *WORLD LITERATURE CRITICISM SUPPLEMENT (WLCS)*

ISSN 0091-3421

Volume 209

Contemporary Literary Criticism

Criticism of the Works
of Today's Novelists, Poets, Playwrights,
Short Story Writers, Scriptwriters, and
Other Creative Writers

Jeffrey W. Hunter
PROJECT EDITOR

THOMSON

GALE

Detroit • New York • San Francisco • San Diego • New Haven, Conn. • Waterville, Maine • London • Munich

Contemporary Literary Criticism, Vol. 209

Project Editor
Jeffrey W. Hunter

Editorial
Jessica Bomarito, Kathy D. Darrow, Jelena O. Krstović, Michelle Lee, Thomas J. Schoenberg, Noah Schusterbauer, Lawrence J. Trudeau, Russel Whitaker

Data Capture
Francis Monroe, Gwen Tucker

Indexing Services
Laurie Andriot

Rights and Acquisitions
Margaret Chamberlain-Gaston, Jacqueline Key, Lisa Kincade, Shalice Shah-Caldwell

Imaging and Multimedia
Dean Dauphinais, Leitha Etheridge-Sims, Lezlie Light, Mike Logusz, Dan Newell, Christine O'Bryan, Kelly A. Quin, Denay Wilding, Robyn Young

Composition and Electronic Prepress
Kathy Sauer

Manufacturing
Rhonda Dover

Associate Product Manager
Marc Cormier

LIBRARY OF CONGRESS CATALOG CARD NUMBER 76-46132

ISBN 0-7876-7979-8
ISSN 0091-3421

Printed in the United States of America
10 9 8 7 6 5 4 3 2 1

Contents

Preface vii

Acknowledgments xi

Literary Criticism Series Advisory Board xv

Preface

Named "one of the twenty-five most distinguished reference titles published during the past twenty-five years" by *Reference Quarterly,* the *Contemporary Literary Criticism* (*CLC*) series provides readers with critical commentary and general information on more than 2,000 authors now living or who died after December 31, 1999. Volumes published from 1973 through 1999 include authors who died after December 31, 1959. Previous to the publication of the first volume of *CLC* in 1973, there was no ongoing digest monitoring scholarly and popular sources of critical opinion and explication of modern literature. *CLC,* therefore, has fulfilled an essential need, particularly since the complexity and variety of contemporary literature makes the function of criticism especially important to today's reader.

Scope of the Series

CLC provides significant passages from published criticism of works by creative writers. Since many of the authors covered in *CLC* inspire continual critical commentary, writers are often represented in more than one volume. There is, of course, no duplication of reprinted criticism.

Authors are selected for inclusion for a variety of reasons, among them the publication or dramatic production of a critically acclaimed new work, the reception of a major literary award, revival of interest in past writings, or the adaptation of a literary work to film or television.

Attention is also given to several other groups of writers—authors of considerable public interest—about whose work criticism is often difficult to locate. These include mystery and science fiction writers, literary and social critics, foreign authors, and authors who represent particular ethnic groups.

Each *CLC* volume contains individual essays and reviews taken from hundreds of book review periodicals, general magazines, scholarly journals, monographs, and books. Entries include critical evaluations spanning from the beginning of an author's career to the most current commentary. Interviews, feature articles, and other published writings that offer insight into the author's works are also presented. Students, teachers, librarians, and researchers will find that the general critical and biographical material in *CLC* provides them with vital information required to write a term paper, analyze a poem, or lead a book discussion group. In addition, complete bibliographical citations note the original source and all of the information necessary for a term paper footnote or bibliography.

Organization of the Book

A *CLC* entry consists of the following elements:

- The **Author Heading** cites the name under which the author most commonly wrote, followed by birth and death dates. Also located here are any name variations under which an author wrote, including transliterated forms for authors whose native languages use nonroman alphabets. If the author wrote consistently under a pseudonym, the pseudonym will be listed in the author heading and the author's actual name given in parenthesis on the first line of the biographical and critical information. Uncertain birth or death dates are indicated by question marks. Single-work entries are preceded by a heading that consists of the most common form of the title in English translation (if applicable) and the original date of composition.

- A **Portrait of the Author** is included when available.

- The **Introduction** contains background information that introduces the reader to the author, work, or topic that is the subject of the entry.

- The list of **Principal Works** is ordered chronologically by date of first publication and lists the most important works by the author. The genre and publication date of each work is given. In the case of foreign authors whose works have been translated into English, the English-language version of the title follows in brackets. Unless otherwise indicated, dramas are dated by first performance, not first publication.

- Reprinted **Criticism** is arranged chronologically in each entry to provide a useful perspective on changes in critical evaluation over time. The critic's name and the date of composition or publication of the critical work are given at the beginning of each piece of criticism. Unsigned criticism is preceded by the title of the source in which it appeared. All titles by the author featured in the text are printed in boldface type. Footnotes are reprinted at the end of each essay or excerpt. In the case of excerpted criticism, only those footnotes that pertain to the excerpted texts are included.

- A complete **Bibliographical Citation** of the original essay or book precedes each piece of criticism. Source citations in the Literary Criticism Series follow University of Chicago Press style, as outlined in *The Chicago Manual of Style,* 14th ed. (Chicago: The University of Chicago Press, 1993).

- Critical essays are prefaced by brief **Annotations** explicating each piece.

- Whenever possible, a recent **Author Interview** accompanies each entry.

- An annotated bibliography of **Further Reading** appears at the end of each entry and suggests resources for additional study. In some cases, significant essays for which the editors could not obtain reprint rights are included here. Boxed material following the further reading list provides references to other biographical and critical sources on the author in series published by Thomson Gale.

Indexes

A **Cumulative Author Index** lists all of the authors that appear in a wide variety of reference sources published by Thomson Gale, including *CLC*. A complete list of these sources is found facing the first page of the Author Index. The index also includes birth and death dates and cross references between pseudonyms and actual names.

A **Cumulative Nationality Index** lists all authors featured in *CLC* by nationality, followed by the number of the *CLC* volume in which their entry appears.

A **Cumulative Topic Index** lists the literary themes and topics treated in the series as well as in *Literature Criticism from 1400 to 1800, Nineteenth-Century Literature Criticism, Twentieth-Century Literary Criticism,* and the *Contemporary Literary Criticism* Yearbook, which was discontinued in 1998.

An alphabetical **Title Index** accompanies each volume of *CLC*. Listings of titles by authors covered in the given volume are followed by the author's name and the corresponding page numbers where the titles are discussed. English translations of foreign titles and variations of titles are cross-referenced to the title under which a work was originally published. Titles of novels, dramas, nonfiction books, and poetry, short story, or essay collections are printed in italics, while individual poems, short stories, and essays are printed in roman type within quotation marks.

In response to numerous suggestions from librarians, Thomson Gale also produces an annual cumulative title index that alphabetically lists all titles reviewed in *CLC* and is available to all customers. Additional copies of this index are available upon request. Librarians and patrons will welcome this separate index; it saves shelf space, is easy to use, and is recyclable upon receipt of the next edition.

Citing *Contemporary Literary Criticism*

When citing criticism reprinted in the Literary Criticism Series, students should provide complete bibliographic information so that the cited essay can be located in the original print or electronic source. Students who quote directly from reprinted criticism may use any accepted bibliographic format, such as University of Chicago Press style or Modern Language Association (MLA) style. Both the MLA and the University of Chicago formats are acceptable and recognized as being the current standards for citations. It is important, however, to choose one format for all citations; do not mix the two formats within a list of citations.

The examples below follow recommendations for preparing a bibliography set forth in *The Chicago Manual of Style,* 14th ed. (Chicago: The University of Chicago Press, 1993); the first example pertains to material drawn from periodicals, the second to material reprinted from books:

Morrison, Jago. "Narration and Unease in Ian McEwan's Later Fiction." *Critique* 42, no. 3 (spring 2001): 253-68. Reprinted in *Contemporary Literary Criticism.* Vol. 169, edited by Janet Witalec, 212-20. Detroit: Gale, 2003.

Brossard, Nicole. "Poetic Politics." In *The Politics of Poetic Form: Poetry and Public Policy,* edited by Charles Bernstein, 73-82. New York: Roof Books, 1990. Reprinted in *Contemporary Literary Criticism.* Vol. 169, edited by Janet Witalec, 3-8. Detroit: Gale, 2003.

The examples below follow recommendations for preparing a works cited list set forth in the *MLA Handbook for Writers of Research Papers,* 5th ed. (New York: The Modern Language Association of America, 1999); the first example pertains to material drawn from periodicals, the second to material reprinted from books:

Morrison, Jago. "Narration and Unease in Ian McEwan's Later Fiction." *Critique* 42.3 (spring 2001): 253-68. Reprinted in *Contemporary Literary Criticism.* Ed. Janet Witalec. Vol. 169. Detroit: Gale, 2003. 212-20.

Brossard, Nicole. "Poetic Politics." *The Politics of Poetic Form: Poetry and Public Policy.* Ed. Charles Bernstein. New York: Roof Books, 1990. 73-82. Reprinted in *Contemporary Literary Criticism.* Ed. Janet Witalec. Vol. 169. Detroit: Gale, 2003. 3-8.

Suggestions are Welcome

Readers who wish to suggest new features, topics, or authors to appear in future volumes, or who have other suggestions or comments are cordially invited to call, write, or fax the Associate Product Manager:

Associate Product Manager, Literary Criticism Series
Thomson Gale
27500 Drake Road
Farmington Hills, MI 48331-3535
1-800-347-4253 (GALE)
Fax: 248-699-8983

Acknowledgments

The editors wish to thank the copyright holders of the criticism included in this volume and the permissions managers of many book and magazine publishing companies for assisting us in securing reproduction rights. We are also grateful to the staffs of the Detroit Public Library, the Library of Congress, the University of Detroit Mercy Library, Wayne State University Purdy/Kresge Library Complex, and the University of Michigan Libraries for making their resources available to us. Following is a list of the copyright holders who have granted us permission to reproduce material in this volume of *CLC*. Every effort has been made to trace copyright, but if omissions have been made, please let us know.

COPYRIGHTED MATERIAL IN *CLC*, VOLUME 209, WAS REPRODUCED FROM THE FOLLOWING PERIODICALS:

America, v. 189, December 15, 2003. Copyright © 2003 www.americamagazine.org. All rights reserved. Reproduced by permission of America Press. For subscription information, visit www.americamagazine.com.—*The American Enterprise,* v. 6, March-April , 1995; v. 10, May-June, 1999. Copyright © 1995, 1999 American Enterprise Institute for Public Policy Research. Both reproduced with permission of The American Enterprise, a magazine of Politics, Business, and Culture. On the web at www.TAEmag.com.—*The American Spectator,* v. 20, September, 1987; v. 24, September, 1991; v. 32, January, 1999 Copyright © *The American Spectator* 1987, 1991, 1999. All reproduced by permission.—*Artforum,* v. 37, January, 1999 for "Flights and Fancies" by Brooks Adams. Copyright © Artforum, January 1999. Reproduced by permission of the publisher and author.—*Book Page,* April, 2003. Copyright © 2003 ProMotion, Inc. Reproduced by permission.—*Book World-The Washington Post,* v. 21, June 2, 1991 for "With Malice Towards All" by Landon Parvin. Copyright © 1991, Washington Post Book World Service/Washington Post Writers Group. Reproduced by permission of the author.—*Booklist,* v. 94, January 1, 1998; January 1, 2003 Copyright © 1998, 2003 by the American Library Association. Both reproduced by permission.—*Book Reporter.com,* February 10, 2004 for a review of *The Da Vinci Code* by Roz Shea. Reproduced by permission of The Book Report Network.—*Boston Herald,* August 8, 2003. Copyright © 2003 Boston Herald. Reprinted with permission of the Boston Herald.—*Commonweal,* v. 130, September 12, 2003. Copyright © 2003 Commonweal Publishing Co., Inc. Reproduced by permission of Commonweal Foundation.—*Contemporary Literature,* v. 35, fall, 1994. Copyright © 1994 by the Board of Regents of the University of Wisconsin System. Reproduced by permission.—*Crisis (online journal),* September 1, 2003. Copyright © 2003 by Morley Publishing Group, Inc, the publisher of CRISIS Magazine. Reproduced by permission.—*Critical Quarterly,* v. 36, summer, 1994. Copyright © 1994 Basil Blackwell Ltd. Reproduced by permission of Blackwell Publishers.—*Dissent,* v. 31, fall, 1984. Copyright © 1984 by Dissent Publishing Corporation. Reproduced by permission.—*Essays in Criticism,* v. 38, January, 1988 for "Irishry" by Margaret O'Brien. Copyright © 1988 Oxford University Press. Reproduced by permission of Oxford University Press and the author.—*ETC: A Review of General Semantics,* v. 56, spring, 1999. Reproduced by permission.—*Far Eastern Economic Review,* v. 444, June 8, 1989. Republished with permission of *Far Eastern Economic Review,* conveyed through Copyright Clearance Center, Inc.—*The Guardian,* December 7, 2002, for a review of P. J. O'Rourke's *The CEO of the Sofa* by John Dugdale. Copyright © 2002 by Guardian Publications Ltd. Reproduced by permission of the author.—*Hollins Critic,* v. 40, October, 2003. Copyright © 2003 by Hollins College. Reproduced by permission.—*Hudson Review,* v. 19, spring, 1966; v. 23, autumn, 1970; v. 34, winter, 1981/82; v. 37, autumn, 1984. Copyright © 1966, 1970,1981/82,1984 by The Hudson Review, Inc. All reproduced by permission.—*Kirkus Reviews,* v. 72, April 15, 2004. Copyright © 2004 by The Kirkus Service, Inc. All rights reserved. Reproduced by permission of the publisher, Kirkus Reviews and Kirkus Associates, L.P.—*Library Journal,* v. 125, November 15, 2000; v. 128, June 1, 2003. Copyright © 2000 by Reed Elsevier, USA. Both reprinted by permission of the publisher.—*Literature and History,* v. 9, October, 2000 for "Out of the East: James Fenton and Contemporary History" by Joe Moran, 2000, Manchester University Press, Manchester, UK. Reproduced by permission.—*London Review of Books,* v. 4, March 4, 1982; v. 9, February 19, 1987; December 10, 1987; v. 13, March 21, 1991; v. 17, August 24, 1995; v. 23, November 1, 2001. Copyright © *The London Review of Books.* All appears here by permission of the *London Review of Books.*—*Maclean's,* v. 111, November 16, 1998. Copyright © 1998 by Maclean's Magazine. Reproduced by permission.—*The Nation,* v. 259, June 22, 1992. Copyright © 1992 by The Nation Magazine/ The Nation Company, Inc. Reproduced by permission.—*National Catholic Reporter,* v. 39, October 3, 2003 for "*Da Vinci Code* is More Fantasy than Fact" by Andrew Greeley. Reproduced by permission of the author.—*National Review,* v. 39, June 5, 1987; v. 43, August 26, 1991; v. 55, December 8, 2003 Copyright © 1987, 1991, 2003 by National Review, Inc, 215 Lexington Avenue, New York, NY 10016. All reproduced by permission.—*New Criterion,* v. 6, October, 1987 for "Reading Denis Donoghue" by Bruce Bawer; v. 13, May, 1995 for "Art vs. Aestheticism: The Case of Walter Pater" by Roger Kimball. Copyright © 1987, 1995 by The Foundation for Cultural Review. Both reproduced by permission of the authors.—

COPYRIGHTED MATERIAL IN *CLC*, VOLUME 209, WAS REPRODUCED FROM THE FOLLOWING BOOKS:

PHOTOGRAPHS AND ILLUSTRATIONS APPEARING IN *CLC*, VOLUME 209, WERE RECEIVED FROM THE FOLLOWING SOURCES:

Thomson Gale Literature Product Advisory Board

The members of the Thomson Gale Literature Product Advisory Board—reference librarians from public and academic library systems—represent a cross-section of our customer base and offer a variety of informed perspectives on both the presentation and content of our literature products. Advisory board members assess and define such quality issues as the relevance, currency, and usefulness of the author coverage, critical content, and literary topics included in our series; evaluate the layout, presentation, and general quality of our printed volumes; provide feedback on the criteria used for selecting authors and topics covered in our series; provide suggestions for potential enhancements to our series; identify any gaps in our coverage of authors or literary topics, recommending authors or topics for inclusion; analyze the appropriateness of our content and presentation for various user audiences, such as high school students, undergraduates, graduate students, librarians, and educators; and offer feedback on any proposed changes/enhancements to our series. We wish to thank the following advisors for their advice throughout the year.

Dan Brown
1964-

American novelist.

The following entry presents an overview of Brown's career through 2005.

INTRODUCTION

Brown is the author of four bestselling mystery-thriller novels, all of which combine extensive research, complex, intricate plotting, and intriguing conspiracy theories with breathless, edge-of-the-seat action. His runaway best-selling religious mystery-thriller, *The Da Vinci Code* (2003), sparked heated controversy over its representation of the Catholic Church as well as enthusiastic reviews as a "brainy," exciting thriller. "I am fascinated with the gray area between right and wrong and good and evil," Brown told *Bookpage* interviewer Edward Morris; "Every novel I've written so far has explored that gray area."

BIOGRAPHICAL INFORMATION

Brown was born June 22, 1964, in Exeter, New Hampshire. His father was a math professor and his mother a musician specializing in sacred music. Brown thus grew up in an environment enriched by the intermingling of scientific and religious discourse. In an interview with the online journal *Bookreporter.com,* Brown observed that his interest in secret societies, which are a central element of his novels, "sparks from growing up in New England, surrounded by the clandestine clubs of Ivy League universities, the Masonic lodges of our Founding Fathers, and the hidden hallways of early government power. New England has a long tradition of elite private clubs, fraternities, and secrecy." Brown attended Phillips Exeter Academy, a private school located in his hometown. He graduated with a B.A. from Amherst College in 1986 and studied art history at the University of Seville in Spain. In 1993 Brown returned to New Hampshire and began teaching English at Phillips Exeter; in 1996 he turned to full-time writing. While teaching, Brown got the idea for his first novel, *Digital Fortress* (1998). One of his students had been tracked down and briefly detained by the U.S. Secret Service agency, which somehow discovered that the teenager had made hostile political comments via e-mail to a friend. This incident inspired

Brown to further research government computer intelligence, which led him to write *Digital Fortress*. This bestselling debut novel was soon followed by *Angels & Demons* (2000), *Deception Point* (2001), and *The Da Vinci Code,* all of which spent months at the top of best-seller lists. "One of the aspects that I try very hard to incorporate in my books is that of learning," Brown told Morris; "When you finish [*The Da Vinci Code*]— like it or not—you've learned a ton." In an interview with *Bookreporter.com,* Brown commented, "In many ways, editing yourself is the most important part of being a novelist . . . carving away superfluous text until your story stands crystal clear before your reader." Brown lives in New Hampshire with his wife, Blythe Brown, an artist and art historian.

MAJOR WORKS

Digital Fortress concerns an attack on TRANSLTR, a government computer decoding system that monitors potential terrorist activities on the internet and e-mail.

Its plot reveals the workings of a secret government organization, the National Security Agency (NSA), the foundations of which are threatened by a mysterious code-writing formula known as Digital Fortress. Susan Fletcher, an NSA cryptographer and brilliant mathematician, is assigned to investigate a secret code, created by Digital Fortress, which TRANSLTR is unable to break. In the process, she discovers a conspiracy that threatens to undermine the national stability of America. *Angels & Demons,* Brown's second novel, is an intricately plotted international mystery thriller. It introduces the character Robert Langdon, a Harvard professor of iconography and religious art who returns in *The Da Vinci Code.* In *Angels and Demons* Langdon is asked to decipher the mysterious word "Illuminati," branded onto the body of a physicist who has been murdered in Switzerland. Langdon's investigations take him to Vatican City, where he teams up with Vittoria Vetra, an Italian scientist, and is drawn into the machinations of a terrorist plot against a group of Roman Catholic cardinals on the eve of the election of a new pope. Together, Langdon and Vetra learn of an ancient secret brotherhood, calling themselves the Illuminati, whose mission is to seek revenge against the Roman Catholic Church for the oppression of such scientists as Galileo Galilei and Nicolaus Copernicus. Langdon and Vetra find themselves in an action-packed race against time to prevent the detonation of an anti-matter time bomb set to explode in the Vatican. Brown's third novel, *Deception Point,* concerns the discovery of a meteor embedded in the Arctic Circle that may contain evidence of extraterrestrial insect life. The activities of NASA concerning this discovery become entangled with the mysterious death of a government scientist and the political machinations of a presidential election. White House Intelligence analyst Rachel Sexton and oceanographer Michael Tolland are sent to investigate the mysterious phenomenon, which leads them to the heart of a political conspiracy and possible scientific fraud. Rachel and Michael must fight for their lives in this harsh arctic environment against a team of assassins working for a mysterious organization that wishes to prevent them from reporting their findings to the public.

The Da Vinci Code, Brown's fourth novel, (being adapted to film by Columbia Pictures), reintroduces the character Robert Langdon, this time involved in an investigation of the murder of the chief curator at the Louvre museum in Paris. A mysterious coded message found at the site of the body leads Langdon, teamed up with French cryptologist Sophie Neveu, on an international quest to solve an increasingly complex puzzle surrounding the murder. The serpentine plot of *The Da Vinci Code* makes use of Brown's extensive research of art history, ancient secret societies, age-old conspiracy theories, and controversial historical studies of the development of Christianity. Langdon and Neveu are led to investigate the Priory of Sion, an historically real secret brotherhood whose members are said to have included such famous men as the scientist Sir Isaac Newton, the artist Andrea Botticelli, the writer Victor Hugo, and the painter Leonardo da Vinci. Langdon and Neveu further find themselves dealing with members of Opus Dei, a strict Catholic sect involved in the mystery. Their investigations ultimately lead them on a quest for the Holy Grail and to a shocking solution to its centuries-old riddle. "I had to do an enormous amount of research" for *The Da Vinci Code,* Brown told Morris; "It involved numerous trips to Europe, study at the Louvre, some in-depth study about the Priory of Sion and Opus Dei and about the art of Da Vinci." *The Da Vinci Code* is based on the premise that the Catholic Church intentionally suppressed elements of the "feminine sacred" that were an integral part of early Christianity. In an interview with *Bookreporter.com,* Brown asserted, "Two thousand years ago, we lived in a world of Gods and Goddesses. Today, we live in a world solely of Gods. Women in most cultures have been stripped of their spiritual power. [*The Da Vinci Code*] touches on questions of how and why this shift occurred . . . and on what lessons we might learn from it regarding our future."

CRITICAL RECEPTION

All four of Brown's bestselling novels have been lauded as entertaining, intricately plotted, fast-paced, suspenseful thrillers with riveting conclusions. While some reviewers have noted that Brown's narrative premises and conspiracy theories are not always plausible and that his action sequences can be over the top, others have found the circumstances of his stories convincing and believable. Sybil Steinberg called *Digital Fortress* an inventive and clever debut thriller, commenting, "In this fast-paced, plausible tale, Brown blurs the line between good and evil enough to delight patriots and paranoids alike." In a review of *Angels & Demons,* Steinberg observed, "Though its premises strain credulity, Brown's tale is laced with twists and shocks that keep the reader wired right up to the last minute." Nancy Pearl called *Angels & Demons* "one of the best international thrillers of recent years," commenting that Brown's second novel is "both literate and extremely well researched, mixing physics with religion." Andy Plonka noted, "*Angels & Demons* should appeal to readers of widely ranging interests. The thriller devotees will be pleased, the information junkies content, the intricate puzzle enthusiasts satisfied, and the historical buffs appeased with a bit of church history and art history to contain their appetites." Jeff Zaleski described *Deception Point* as "a finely polished amalgam of action and intrigue," concluding that it is "an excellent thriller—a big yet believable story unfolding at breakneck pace, with convincing settings and just the right blend of likable and hateful characters." Zaleski added that Brown has "also done his research, folding in sophisticated scientific and military details that make his plot far more fulfilling than the norm." Several reviewers have commented on Brown's thematic treatment of the conflict between science and religion in his novels. Janet Maslin of *The New York Times* observed that in both *Angels & Demons* and *The Da Vinci Code*, Brown "is drawn to the place where empirical evidence and religious faith collide. And he creates a bracing exploration of this realm."

The Da Vinci Code is Brown's most popular and most critically acclaimed—as well as his most controversial—work to date. Many reviewers have described *The Da Vinci Code* as a "brainy" thriller, combining erudite factual research with international intrigue and age-old conspiracy theories. Reviewers were impressed with Brown's ability to weave extensive historical information into his narrative while maintaining a highly entertaining storyline. Charles Taylor described *The Da Vinci Code* as "an ingenious mixture of paranoid thriller, art history lesson, chase story, religious symbology lecture and anti-clerical screed." Taylor further observed that Brown, "for all the facts he throws around, operates squarely in the territory of the pop bestseller." David Lazarus observed, "Brown does a terrific job of spooling out the controversial history lesson without ever lapsing into pedantry or preachiness." Annie C. Bond similarly applauded Brown's ability to integrate factual information with a compelling storyline, noting, "Brown demonstrates not only knowledge of art, art history, and architecture but also a talent at weaving it all together into such an intricate tapestry that it becomes difficult to determine what is his imagination at work and what is actually a mini-lesson in history." Many critics, however, have debated Brown's claim to factual accuracy in the book's representation of art history and the history of Christianity. While some were impressed by the author's extensive research, others disdainfully found that the novel is marred by historical inaccuracies and factual distortions. Maurice Timothy Reidy, for example, described *The Da Vinci Code* as "an incredibly simplistic reading of both history and theology." Critics have specifically questioned Brown's representation of Christianity and the Catholic Church. While some found his revisionist history of Christianity to be a compelling perspective on the Catholic Church, others found the novel anti-Catholic in its message. A number of reviewers have also commented on Brown's feminist theological perspective on Christianity in *The Da Vinci Code*. Some agree with Brown's premise that the Catholic Church has historically repressed the "feminine sacred" element of early Christianity, while others find this assertion unconvincing. Patrick McCormick, reviewing *The Da Vinci Code* in *The U.S. Catholic*, observed, "a great deal of the novel's appeal is its feminist sensibility, particularly its translation of feminist critiques of Christianity and Catholicism into

popular fiction. . . . The book suggests—as some feminist scholars have been arguing for a while—that the original Jesus movement was much more welcoming to women, marriage, and sexuality than the church Constantine and Augustine handed on to us." McCormick concluded, "In the end Brown's novel is a vastly entertaining read that mixes the thrill of a high-speed chase with the magical pleasures of a quest through an enchanted forest of art, literature, and history. . . . But, in its own popularizing way, it also gives voice to a growing feminist critique of a patriarchal church and secrets it keeps about the goodness and godliness of women." Cynthia Grenier, on the other hand, observed that, while *The Da Vinci Code* expresses "a deeply, profoundly feminist view of the Catholic faith," it ultimately shows "disregard for historical accuracy and a marked hostility to the Catholic Church."

PRINCIPAL WORKS

Digital Fortress (novel) 1998
Angels & Demons (novel) 2000
Deception Point (novel) 2001
The Da Vinci Code (novel) 2003

CRITICISM

Sybil Steinberg (review date 22 December 1997)

SOURCE: Steinberg, Sybil. Review of *Digital Fortress,* by Dan Brown. *Publishers Weekly* 244, no. 52 (22 December 1997): 39-40.

[*In the following review, Steinberg describes Brown's* Digital Fortress *as an inventive, fast-paced, and plausible debut thriller. Steinberg comments that the villain, Ensei Tankado, is the most interesting character in the novel.*]

Information Age terrorism is the topical subject of Brown's inventive debut thriller [*Digital Fortress*] about a virtual attack on the National Security Agency's top-secret super computer, TRANSLTR. Although TRANSLTR is meant to monitor and decode e-mail between terrorists, the computer can also covertly intercept e-mail between private citizens. The latter capability drives former NSA programmer Ensei Tankado to paralyze TRANSLTR with Digital Fortress, a devious mathematical formula with an unbreakable code. Tankado then demands that the NSA publicly admit TRANSLTR's existence or he will auction Digital Fortress's pass-key to the highest bidder. Brown cleverly makes ironic, mischievous Tankado (who dies in the first chapter) the most interesting character in the book and its real protagonist, as the programmer posthumously outmaneuvers his dull-witted opposition, countering their obsessive quest for complex solutions with brilliant simplicity. His favorite saying, "Who will guard the guards?" stands in noble contrast to the NSA agents' self-righteous insistence that they always know what is best for America. Tankado's bland opposition includes Susan Fletcher, the head of NSA's Cryptography Division, her oddly credulous boss, Commander Strathmore, and her academic fiancé, who is dispatched to Seville on a quest for Tankado's secret decoder ring. In this fast-paced, plausible tale, Brown blurs the line between good and evil enough to delight patriots and paranoids alike.

Gilbert Taylor (review date 1 January 1998)

SOURCE: Taylor, Gilbert. Review of *Digital Fortress,* by Dan Brown. *Booklist* 94, nos. 9-10 (1 January 1998): 780.

[*In the following review, Taylor describes Brown's* Digital Fortress *as an exciting thriller.*]

The National Security Agency (NSA) is one setting for this exciting thriller [*Digital Fortress*]; the other is Seville, where on page 1 the protagonist, lately dismissed from NSA, drops dead of a supposed heart attack. Though dead, he enjoys a dramaturgical afterlife in the form of his computer program. Digital Fortress creates unbreakable codes, which could render useless NSA's code-cracking supercomputer called TRANS-LTR, but the deceased programmer slyly embossed a decryption key on a ring he wore. Pursuit of this ring is the engine of the plot. NSA cryptology boss Trevor Strathmore dispatches linguist Dave Becker to recover the ring, while he and Becker's lover, senior code-cracker Susan Fletcher, ponder the vulnerability of TRANSLTR. In Seville, over-the-top chase scenes abound, meanwhile, the critical events unfold at NSA. In a crescendo of murder, infernos, and explosions, it emerges that Strathmore has as agenda that goes beyond breaching Digital Fortress, and Brown's skill at hinting and concealing Strathmore's deceit will rivet cyber-minded readers.

Sybil S. Steinberg (review date 1 May 2000)

SOURCE: Steinberg, Sybil S. Review of *Angels & Demons,* by Dan Brown. *Publishers Weekly* 247, no. 18 (1 May 2000): 51.

[*In the following review, Steinberg asserts that Brown's* Angels & Demons *is a gripping, well-plotted thriller,*

although the premise strains credulity and the action is sometimes over the top.]

Pitting scientific terrorists against the cardinals of Vatican City, this well-plotted if over-the-top thriller [*Angels & Demons*] is crammed with Vatican intrigue and high-tech drama. Robert Langdon, a Harvard specialist on religious symbolism, is called in by a Swiss research lab when Dr. Vetra, the scientist who discovered antimatter, is found murdered with the cryptic word "Illuminati" branded on his chest. These Illuminati were a group of Renaissance scientists, including Galileo, who met secretly in Rome to discuss new ideas in safety from papal threat; what the long-defunct association has to do with Dr. Vetra's death is far from clear. Vetra's daughter, Vittoria, makes a frightening discovery: a lethal amount of antimatter, sealed in a vacuum flask that will explode in six hours unless its batteries are recharged, is missing. Almost immediately, the Swiss Guard discover that the flask is hidden beneath Vatican City, where the conclave to elect a new pope has just begun. Vittoria and Langdon rush to recover the canister, but they aren't allowed into the Vatican until it is discovered that the four principal papal candidates are missing. The terrorists who are holding the cardinals call in regarding their pending murders, offering clues tied to ancient Illuminati meeting sites and runes. Meanwhile, it becomes clear that a sinister Vatican entity with messianic delusions is in league with the terrorists. Packing the novel with sinister figures worthy of a Medici, Brown (*Digital Fortress*) sets an explosive pace as Langdon and Vittoria race through a Michelin-perfect Rome to try to save the cardinals and find the antimatter before it explodes. Though its premises strain credulity, Brown's tale is laced with twists and shocks that keep the reader wired right up to the last revelation.

Nancy Pearl (review date 15 November 2000)

SOURCE: Pearl, Nancy. "Cheap Thrills: Novels of Suspense." *Library Journal* 125, no. 19 (15 November 2000): 124.

[*In the following review, Pearl asserts that Brown's* Angels & Demons *is one of the best international thrillers in recent years. Pearl comments that the novel is literate and well researched, and finds its conclusion riveting.*]

One of the best international thrillers of recent years, Dan Brown's *Angels & Demons* is both literate and extremely well researched, mixing physics with religion. Robert Langdon, a renowned Harvard symbologist, is asked to help decipher a symbol branded on the mutilated corpse of a prominent scientist who had recently discovered antimatter, a sample of which has been stolen. As Langdon becomes drawn into the authorities' global search for the unstable and dangerous material, he discovers additional murder scenes with similar mysterious symbols that lead to an ancient secret society with a grudge against the Catholic Church. Right up to the riveting conclusion, Brown clearly knows how to deliver the goods.

Jeff Zaleski (review date 10 September 2001)

SOURCE: Zaleski, Jeff. Review of *Deception Point,* by Dan Brown. *Publishers Weekly* 248, no. 37 (10 September 2001): 56-7.

[*In the following review, Zaleski describes* Deception Point *as an excellent thriller that skillfully combines action with intrigue.*]

Struggling to rebound from a series of embarrassing blunders that have jeopardized its political life at the start of this lively thriller [*Deception Point*], NASA makes an astounding discovery: there is a meteor embedded deep within the arctic ice. And it isn't just any meteor. Inside the huge rock, which crashed to earth in 1716, are fossils of giant insects—proof of extraterrestrial life. Yet, given NASA's slipping reputation, the question arises: Is the meteor real or a fake? That uncertainty dogs NASA and its supporters in Brown's latest page-flipper, a finely polished amalgam of action and intrigue. Trying to determine the truth are intelligence agent Rachel Sexton and popular oceanographer Michael Tolland, both among the first to suspect something is amiss when the meteor is pulled from the ice. Their doubts quickly make them the targets of a mysterious death squad controlled by someone or something that doesn't want the public to hear the meteor may be a fraud. Together, Sexton and Tolland scramble across arctic glaciers, take refuge on ice floes, are rescued by a nuclear submarine, then find themselves trapped aboard a small research vessel off the coast of New Jersey. All the while, the nation's capital is buzzing as to whether NASA has engaged in deception. Or is NASA just a dupe for aerospace companies that have long wanted a bigger share of space contracts? Brown (*Angels & Demons*) moves into new territory with his latest. It's an excellent thriller—a big yet believable story unfolding at breakneck pace, with convincing settings and just the right blend of likable and hateful characters. He's also done his research, folding in sophisticated scientific and military details that make his plot far more fulfilling than the norm.

Janet Maslin (review date 17 March 2003)

SOURCE: Maslin, Janet. "Spinning a Thriller from a Gallery at the Louvre." *New York Times* (17 March 2003): E8.

[*In the following review, Maslin enthusiastically recommends Brown's* The Da Vinci Code, *calling it an erudite, exhilarating, "brainy" thriller-suspense novel.*]

The word for *The Da Vinci Code* is a rare invertible palindrome. Rotated 180 degrees on a horizontal axis so that it is upside down, it denotes the maternal essence that is sometimes linked to the sport of soccer. Read right side up, it concisely conveys the kind of extreme enthusiasm with which this riddle-filled, code-breaking, exhilaratingly brainy thriller can be recommended.

That word is wow.

The author is Dan Brown (a name you will want to remember). In this gleefully erudite suspense novel, Mr. Brown takes the format he has been developing through three earlier novels and fine-tunes it to blockbuster perfection. Not since the advent of Harry Potter has an author so flagrantly delighted in leading readers on a breathless chase and coaxing them through hoops.

The first book by this onetime teacher, the 1998 *Digital Fortress,* had a foxy heroine named Susan Fletcher who was the National Security Agency's head cryptographer. The second, *Deception Point,* involved NASA, a scientific ruse in the Arctic and Rachel Sexton, an intelligence analyst with a hairdo "long enough to be sexy, but short enough to remind you she was probably smarter than you."

With *Angels & Demons,* Mr. Brown introduced Robert Langdon, a Harvard professor of art history and religious symbology who is loaded with "what his female colleagues referred to as an 'erudite' appeal." No wonder: the new book finds the enormously likable Langdon pondering antimatter, the big-bang theory, the cult of the Illuminati and a threat to the Vatican, among other things. Yet this is merely a warm-up for the mind-boggling trickery that *The Da Vinci Code* has in store.

Consider the new book's prologue, set in the Grand Gallery of the Louvre. (This is the kind of book that notices that this one gallery's length is three times that of the Washington Monument.) It embroils a Caravaggio, an albino monk and a curator in a fight to the death. That's a scene leaving little doubt that the author knows how to pique interest, as the curator, Jacques Saunière, fights for his life.

Desperately seizing the painting in order to activate the museum's alarm system, Saunière succeeds in buying some time. And he uses these stolen moments—which are his last—to take off his clothes, draw a circle and arrange himself like the figure in Leonardo's most famous drawing, "The Vitruvian Man." And to leave behind an anagram and Fibonacci's famous numerical series as clues.

Whatever this is about, it is enough to summon Langdon, who by now, he blushes to recall, has been described in an adoring magazine article as "Harrison Ford in Harris tweed." Langdon's latest manuscript, which "proposed some very unconventional interpretations of established religious iconography which would certainly be controversial," is definitely germane.

Also soon on the scene is the cryptologist Sophie Neveu, a chip off the author's earlier prototypes: "Unlike the waifish, cookie-cutter blondes that adorned Harvard dorm room walls, this woman was healthy with an unembellished beauty and genuineness that radiated a striking personal confidence." Even if he had not contrived this entire story as a hunt for the Lost Sacred Feminine essence, women in particular would love Mr. Brown.

With Leonardo as co-conspirator, since his life and work were so fraught with symbols and secrets, Mr. Brown is off to the races. Google away: you may want to investigate the same matters that Langdon and Agent Neveu pursue as they tap into a mother lode of religious conspiracy theory. The Priory of Sion, the Knights Templar and the controversial Vatican prelature called Opus Dei are all invoked, as is the pentacle, the Divine Proportion, the strange sex rites glimpsed in the film *Eyes Wide Shut* and the Holy Grail. If you think the Grail is a cup, then Mr. Brown—drawing upon earlier controversial Grail theories involving 19th-century discoveries by a real Saunière—would like you to think again.

As in his **Angels & Demons,** this author is drawn to the place where empirical evidence and religious faith collide. And he creates a bracing exploration of this realm, one that is by no means sacrilegious, though it sharply challenges Vatican policy. As Langdon and Sophie follow clues planted by Leonardo, they arrive at some jaw-dropping suppositions, some of which bring **The Da Vinci Code** to the brink of overkill. But in the end Mr. Brown gracefully lays to rest all the questions he has raised.

The book moves at a breakneck pace, with the author seeming thoroughly to enjoy his contrivances. Virtually every chapter ends with a cliffhanger: not easy, considering the amount of plain old talking that gets done. And Sophie and Langdon are sent on the run, the better to churn up a thriller atmosphere. To their credit, they evade their pursuers as ingeniously as they do most everything else.

When being followed via a global positioning system, for instance, it is smart to send the sensor flying out a 40-foot window and lead pursuers to think you have done the same. Somehow the book manages to reconcile such derring-do with remarks like, "And did you know that if you divide the number of female bees by the number of male bees in any beehive in the world, you always get the same number?"

The Da Vinci Code is breezy enough even to make fun of its characters' own cleverness. At one point Langdon is asked by his host whether he has hidden a sought-after treasure carefully enough. "Actually," Langdon says, unable to hide his grin, "that depends on how often you dust under your couch."

Charles Taylor (review date 27 March 2003)

SOURCE: Taylor, Charles. Review of *The Da Vinci Code,* by Dan Brown. *Salon.com* http://archive.salon.com/books/review/2003/03/27/da_vinci/ (27 March 2003).

[*In the following review, Taylor calls Brown's* The Da Vinci Code *a fantastic new thriller.*]

Trust me.

Sometime in the next few weeks, someone you know is going to tell you they've read this fantastic new thriller called **The Da Vinci Code,** and before you can stop them they will have launched into a breathless description of the plot. Carried away by the pleasure of reliving each twist and turn, every narrow escape, they'll spill all the book's secrets and stare at you expectantly, as if to say they'll forgive you for leaving them in the lurch and dashing right out to the bookstore to buy it.

When that happens, you should cut them off quickly—and then dash right out to the bookstore and buy it. Dan Brown's novel is an ingenious mixture of paranoid thriller, art history lesson, chase story, religious symbology lecture and anti-clerical screed, and it's the most fun you can have between the sort of covers that aren't 300-count Egyptian cotton.

If the idea of a mystery that draws on the history of religion and art sounds like the kind of "must read" you've picked up before only to find yourself bored silly (i.e., Umberto Eco's *The Name of the Rose*), let me hasten to reassure you that Brown, for all the facts he throws around, operates squarely in the territory of the pop bestseller. *The Da Vinci Code* doesn't offer the kind of solid descriptive writing you find in the work of the best practitioners of crime fiction. Brown appears to be the kind of writer who hits on a snazzy gimmick and then mines it for all it's worth. And it's one hell of a gimmick.

Brown's hero is Robert Langdon, a Harvard professor of religious symbolism who, after a lecture in Paris, is awakened in his hotel room in the middle of the night by a member of the Police Judiciare. After being spirited away to the Louvre, he finds that the museum's curator, whom he was scheduled to meet with earlier in the evening, is dead of a bullet to the stomach. In the time before his death, the curator has managed to leave a trail of clues, the most visible of which is that he has arranged his body in emulation of Leonardo da Vinci's "The Vitruvian Man." He has also drawn a pentacle on his chest in his own blood, and scrawled another cryptic message—"O, Draconian devil! Oh, lame saint!"—beside his body in black-light pen.

No sooner has Langdon begun to unravel the possible meanings of the dead man's clues than he discovers that the grandstanding police captain (whom Brown has given the great name of Bezu Fache) suspects him of the murder. Langdon's temporary salvation comes in the form of Sophie Neveu, a police cryptologist summoned to the scene who knows Langdon is being set up as the fall guy. Their only chance of following the trail left for them is to go on the lam.

If all that sounds insanely complicated, consider that I haven't even mentioned the assassin, an albino giant who is also a devout member of the Catholic secret society Opus Dei. Or that the bishop who heads Opus Dei is summoned to a secret meeting with Vatican officials. Or that, like Leonardo himself (and Botticelli and Isaac Newton and Victor Hugo and Jean Cocteau), the dead curator was a member of another secret society, the Priory of Sion. Or the fact that Sophie Neveu is the dead man's granddaughter.

The fun of *The Da Vinci Code* is that things get even more complicated than that. As in his previous novel, *Angels & Demons* (which also featured Robert Langdon), Brown has written the story in real time. The book is one continuous chase—by car and plane, from Paris to London and back to Paris—with Langdon and Sophie in one "Beat the Clock" situation after another, putting their prodigious noggins to work on the coded clues they've been left while staying out of the clutches of Bezu Fache.

Edward Morris (review date April 2003)

SOURCE: Morris, Edward. "Explosive New Thriller Explores Secrets of the Church." *Book Page* (April 2003): 11.

[*In the following review, Morris describes Brown's* The Da Vinci Code *as an absorbing, action-packed story, narrated within a factually rich context.*]

What if a secret society possessed indisputable proof that Christianity in general—and the Catholic Church in particular—are built on historical error? To what extremes might zealous defenders of the faith go to find and destroy such potentially catastrophic evidence? These are the premises that set Dan Brown's absorbing new novel, *The Da Vinci Code,* in motion and then send it pinballing through a labyrinth of intricate schemes, sidetracks and deceptions.

Threaded through the story are plot-related codes and cryptograms that impel the reader to brainstorm with the protagonists, Harvard symbologist Robert Langdon (introduced in *Angels & Demons*) and French police cryptologist Sophie Neveu. An after-hours murder at the Louvre swirls these two strangers into the middle of an ongoing combat between the Priory of Sion, a shadowy order that dates back to the Crusades, and Opus Dei, a relatively new bastion of Catholic conservatism.

"I first learned of [Leonardo] Da Vinci's affiliation with the Priory of Sion when I was studying art history at the University of Seville," Brown says in a telephone interview from his home in New Hampshire. "One day, the professor showed us a slide of *The Last Supper* and began to outline all the strange anomalies in the painting. My awareness of Opus Dei came through an entirely different route and much later in my life. After studying the Vatican to write *Angels & Demons,* I became interested in the secrecy of the Vatican and some of the unseen hierarchy. Through that, I also became interested in Opus Dei and met some of the people in it."

While the characters and storylines of *The Da Vinci Code* are manifestly his own contrivances, Brown stresses that all the contextual details about history, biography, location and art are true. "One of the aspects that I try very hard to incorporate in my books is that of learning," he says. "When you finish the book—like it or not—you've learned a ton. I had to do an enormous amount of research [for this book]. My wife is an art historian and a Da Vinci fanatic. So I had a leg up on a lot of this, but it involved numerous trips to Europe, study at the Louvre, some in-depth study about the Priory of Sion and Opus Dei and about the art of Da Vinci."

Weighty as it is, Brown's scholarship never slows down the sizzling action. Robert and Sophie stay on the run at a breathless pace as menacing characters pop up in their flight path like silhouettes in a shooting gallery. Unlike a conventional mystery, in which clues become clear only in hindsight, many of the clues here are presented as such: a dying murder victim who arranges his body a particular way, a slip of paper with a phrase scribbled on it that may be a light-shedding anagram, a line of seemingly random numbers.

"For some reason, I was a good math student," Brown says, explaining his involvement with codes and symbols. "And language came easily. Cryptology and symbology are really fusions of math and language. My father is a well-known mathematician. I grew up around codes and ciphers. In *The Da Vinci Code,* there's a flashback where Sophie recalls her grandfather creating this treasure hunt through the house for a birthday present. That's what my father did for us."

Beyond spinning a good yarn within a richly factual context, Brown admits to yet another aim. "I am fascinated with the gray area between right and wrong and good and evil. Every novel I've written so far has explored that gray area." He reveals that his next novel will deal with "the oldest and largest secret society on earth" and with "the secret history of our nation's capital."

Brown concedes that turning Christianity's most fiercely held beliefs into fictional fodder may spark some controversy. But he says it's a risk worth taking. "I worked very, very hard to make the book fair to all parties. Yes, it's explosive. I think there will be people for whom this book will be—well, 'offensive,' may be too strong a word. But it will probably raise some eyebrows."

Jo Ann Heydron (review date July-August 2003)

SOURCE: Heydron, Jo Ann. "Literary Art." *Sojourners* 32, no. 4 (July-August 2003): 58-9.

[*In the following review, Heydron describes Brown's* The Da Vinci Code *as a brainy, fascinating book with remarkable narrative drive.*]

I avoid movies with car chases and wish more television heroes were not both handsome and single. In my reading, however, I tend to be more open-minded. And that's lucky, since I might otherwise have missed this fascinating book. Dan Brown's new novel, *The Da Vinci Code,* may sport a handsome, single hero and be loaded with car chases, but it will also drive the reader to look around her, in Western art and church history, for what she may well have missed: evidence of her own sanctity.

One of the two main plot lines we alternately follow involves discovering who is ultimately responsible for a murder in the Louvre, committed on page one by an albino monk. The other traces the solution of far more interesting puzzles by (handsome and single) Harvard professor of religious symbology Robert Langdon—accused by the French police of having committed the murder—and his newly acquired colleague, French cryptologist Sophie Neveu. (Neveu, at least, has some counter-cultural appeal: Her beauty is not "waifish" but "healthy" and "unembellished.") Written in short, suspenseful chapters, the book's narrative drive is all the more remarkable because it contains a skeletal history of a real secret society, of which Leonardo da Vinci and other icons of Western culture are said to have been members. Langdon believes that the secret this society has guarded since its inception is the nature and location of a legendary Christian relic.

A late-night novel for the brainy, *The Da Vinci Code* is more accessible than *The Flanders Panel* and *The Club Dumas*—similar puzzle-centered thrillers by Arturo Pérez-Reverte—and it offers far more to chew on than an Indiana Jones movie. I'd like to say Langdon is nothing like Indiana Jones, but this wouldn't be entirely true: He resists driving getaway cars because he can't use a clutch, and, for the most part, he leaves gun-handling to others. But at crucial moments he comes up with quick-draw answers to the book's many ciphers and riddles, and, of course, Neveu is inevitably drawn to him.

Brown's several references to important works of art had me leafing through prints at the library. It is quite true, for example, that the man seated at Jesus' right hand in da Vinci's "The Last Supper" is not a man at all. The book may encourage you to rent Stanley Kubrick's last film, *Eyes Wide Shut,* so you can take a closer look at the sexual rites. (So far I have resisted the impulse.) I wonder, too, if *The Da Vinci Code* will swell the crowds at the Louvre in the same way that Marion Zimmer Bradley's *The Mists of Avalon* sent a new crop of pilgrims to Glastonbury.

There's enough fact in this book that you'll want to find the line where fiction begins. That exact location still eludes me, even after I spent an uncharacteristic amount of time on the Internet looking for information. For example, there appears to be no field or professor of religious symbology at Harvard. Opus Dei, the Catholic sect to which our murderous—and masochistic—albino monk belongs, seems on its home page (for what that's worth) to be about as dangerous as a women's auxiliary or Rotary Club (though many would disagree). At a time when official announcements inspire immediate doubt, and conspiracy theorists begin to look like the only sane people around, Brown's book will touch a nerve.

Here's one fact of which I'm sure: While at my local library in April looking at art books, I noted that 50 holds had already been placed on *The Da Vinci Code.*

Stephanie Schorow (review date 8 August 2003)

SOURCE: Schorow, Stephanie. "*Code* Read: Author Weaves Medieval Art, Mysticism, Murder in a Fascinating Best-selling Tale." *Boston Herald* (8 August 2003): E29.

[*In the following review, Schorow examines the line between fact and fiction in Brown's* The Da Vinci Code, *which she describes as a fascinating tale.*]

This summer's blockbuster beach book reads like the Gospel according to Fox Mulder.

The author of ***The Da Vinci Code*** apparently hasn't met a conspiracy theory he doesn't like. Dan Brown has stuffed his latest novel with enough coverups to put Oliver Stone on a bender and the Internet on anagram overload.

Still, the mix of art history, mathematics, medieval mysticism—with heaping helpings of murder, car chases and riddles—has pushed the novel toward its 19th week on *The New York Times* bestseller list. Readers are scrutinizing Leonardo da Vinci's *The Last Supper* and *Mona Lisa* for secret codes just as Beatles fans once hunted for "Paul is Dead" clues on album covers.

"It's a thriller, it's a real page turner," said Jen Hirsch, Brookline Booksmith assistant manager. Moreover, "it's really pretty intelligent for that kind of genre."

In *Code,* the Exeter, N.H., author blurs historical fact and historians' speculation. Although he insists "all descriptions of artwork, architecture, documents and secret rituals in this novel are accurate," Leonardo da Vinci scholars are harrumphing over Brown's portrayal of the Renaissance artist and inventor as a sort of trickster leading Holy Grail seekers through a Middle Ages matrix.

Da Vinci didn't load his work with secret messages, said James Ackerman, Harvard emeritus professor of fine arts.

"In some loose sheets Leonardo did play around with words and numbers, but he is not known to have seriously attempted to make a code or to have injected any code messages in paintings," Ackerman said.

But there's no denying the book taps into our deep fascination with the masterful painter and scientific genius. Although he didn't produce many paintings, and

he never published (or finished) many treatises on his scientific theories, "he seemed to define what we mean by Renaissance man," said Owen Gingerich, Harvard history of science professor. Da Vinci had "little influence on the science of the day," but "his reputation has grown to legendary proportions."

Da Vinci certainly intrigues *Code* protagonist Robert Langdon, a Harvard professor of "symbology" who is drawn into the investigation of the murder of a curator inside Paris' Louvre museum. The dying man arranged his naked dying body to mimic one of Leonardo's famous drawings and left a trail of clues to a staggering secret.

Faster than you can say "Sacre bleu," Langdon is joined by the beautiful and brainy French cryptographer Sophia Neveu, the curator's granddaughter. The pair embark on a quest that involves the Holy Grail, the Knights Templar, Mary Magdalene, the real Catholic group Opus Dei (www.opusdei.com) and a reputed secret society, the Priory of Scion.

A clue involves the figure seated to Christ's right in *The Last Supper.* The "Code" identifies the feminine figure with the long hair and demure gaze as Mary Magdalene. The outline of her and Jesus forms both a V and an M, Da Vinci's Holy Grail clues.

But Ackerman said, the figure is really that of St. John, who was often depicted with feminine features. "For Mary Magdalene to appear has no scriptural foundation," Ackerman said. "It's kind of heretical, in fact."

Da Vinci's work does have an aura of mystery because he wrote his notes in a cryptic, backward script. But "there's hardly anything to be cracked," Gingerich said. "As soon as you understand the mirror-image writing, you can read it with reasonable accuracy; it's so legible compared to so many of the scrolls" of his contemporaries.

A mystery thriller "can stand on its own presumptions," Ackerman said. "I don't think that fiction writers have any obligation to stick to the historical documents."

Sandra Miesel (essay date 1 September 2003)

SOURCE: Miesel, Sandra. "Dismantling *The Da Vinci Code*." *Crisis* http://www.crisismagazine.com/september 2003/feature1.htm (1 September 2003).

[*In the following essay, Miesel argues that Brown's* The Da Vinci Code *is based on numerous historical inaccuracies, distorted facts, false claims, unreliable sources, specious reasoning, and outlandish claims.*]

"The Grail," Langdon said, "is symbolic of the lost goddess. When Christianity came along, the old pagan religions did not die easily. Legends of chivalric quests for the Holy Grail were in fact stories of forbidden quests to find the lost sacred feminine. Knights who claimed to be "searching for the chalice" were speaking in code as a way to protect themselves from a Church that had subjugated women, banished the Goddess, burned non-believers, and forbidden the pagan reverence for the sacred feminine." (*The Da Vinci Code*, pages 238-239).

The Holy Grail is a favorite metaphor for a desirable but difficult-to-attain goal, from the map of the human genome to Lord Stanley's Cup. While the original Grail—the cup Jesus allegedly used at the Last Supper—normally inhabits the pages of Arthurian romance, Dan Brown's recent mega-best-seller, *The Da Vinci Code,* rips it away to the realm of esoteric history.

But his book is more than just the story of a quest for the Grail—he *wholly* reinterprets the Grail legend. In doing so, Brown inverts the insight that a woman's body is symbolically a container and makes a container symbolically a woman's body. And that container has a name every Christian will recognize, for Brown claims that the Holy Grail was actually Mary Magdalene. She was the vessel that held the blood of Jesus Christ in her womb while bearing his children.

Over the centuries, the Grail-keepers have been guarding the true (and continuing) bloodline of Christ and the relics of the Magdalen, *not* a material vessel. Therefore Brown claims that "the quest for the Holy Grail is the quest to kneel before the bones of Mary Magdalene," a conclusion that would surely have surprised Sir Galahad and the other Grail knights who thought they were searching for the Chalice of the Last Supper.

The Da Vinci Code opens with the grisly murder of the Louvre's curator inside the museum. The crime enmeshes hero Robert Langdon, a tweedy professor of symbolism from Harvard, and the victim's grand-daughter, burgundy-haired cryptologist Sophie Neveu. Together with crippled millionaire historian Leigh Teabing, they flee Paris for London one step ahead of the police and a mad albino Opus Dei "monk" named Silas who will stop at nothing to prevent them from finding the "Grail."

But despite the frenetic pacing, at no point is action allowed to interfere with a good lecture. Before the story comes full circle back to the Louvre, readers face a barrage of codes, puzzles, mysteries, and conspiracies.

With his twice-stated principle, "Everybody loves a conspiracy," Brown is reminiscent of the famous author who crafted her product by studying the features of ten earlier bestsellers. It would be too easy to criticize him for characters thin as plastic wrap, undistinguished prose, and improbable action. But Brown isn't so much writing badly as writing in a particular way best calculated to attract a female audience. (Women, after all, buy most of the nation's books.) He has married a thriller plot to a romance-novel technique. Notice how each character is an extreme type . . . effortlessly brilliant, smarmy, sinister, or psychotic as needed, moving against luxurious but curiously flat backdrops. Avoiding gore and bedroom gymnastics, he shows only one brief kiss and a sexual ritual performed by a married couple. The risqué allusions are fleeting although the text lingers over some bloody Opus Dei mortifications. In short, Brown has fabricated a novel perfect for a ladies' book club.

Brown's lack of seriousness shows in the games he plays with his character names—Robert Langdon, "bright fame long don" (distinguished and virile); Sophie Nevue, "wisdom New Eve"; the irascible taurine detective Bezu Fache, "zebu anger." The servant who leads the police to them is Legaludec, "legal duce." The murdered curator takes his surname, Saunière, from a real Catholic priest whose occult antics sparked interest in the Grail secret. As an inside joke, Brown even writes in his real-life editor (Faukman is Kaufman).

While his extensive use of fictional formulas may be the secret to Brown's stardom, his anti-Christian message can't have hurt him in publishing circles: *The Da Vinci Code* debuted atop the *New York Times* best-seller list. By manipulating his audience through the conventions of romance-writing, Brown invites readers to identify with his smart, glamorous characters who've seen through the impostures of the clerics who hide the "truth" about Jesus and his wife. Blasphemy is delivered in a soft voice with a knowing chuckle: "[E]very faith in the world is based on fabrication."

But even Brown has his limits. To dodge charges of outright bigotry, he includes a climactic twist in the story that absolves the Church of assassination. And although he presents Christianity as a false root and branch, he's willing to tolerate it for its charitable works.

(Of course, Catholic Christianity will become even more tolerable once the new liberal pope elected in Brown's previous Langdon novel, *Angels & Demons,* abandons outmoded teachings. "Third-century laws cannot be applied to the modern followers of Christ," says one of the book's progressive cardinals.)

WHERE IS HE GETTING ALL OF THIS?

Brown actually cites his principal sources within the text of his novel. One is a specimen of academic feminist scholarship: *The Gnostic Gospels* by Elaine

Pagels. The others are popular esoteric histories: *The Templar Revelation: Secret Guardians of the True Identity of Christ* by Lynn Picknett and Clive Prince; *Holy Blood, Holy Grail* by Michael Baigent, Richard Leigh, and Henry Lincoln; *The Goddess in the Gospels: Reclaiming the Sacred Feminine* and *The Woman with the Alabaster Jar: Mary Magdalen and the Holy Grail,* both by Margaret Starbird. (Starbird, a self-identified Catholic, has her books published by Matthew Fox's outfit, Bear & Co.) Another influence, at least at second remove, is *The Woman's Encyclopedia of Myths and Secrets* by Barbara G. Walker.

The use of such unreliable sources belies Brown's pretensions to intellectuality. But the act has apparently fooled at least some of his readers—the *New York Daily News* book reviewer trumpeted, "His research is impeccable."

But despite Brown's scholarly airs, a writer who thinks the Merovingians founded Paris and forgets that the popes once lived in Avignon is hardly a model researcher. And for him to state that the Church burned five million women as witches shows a willful—and *malicious*—ignorance of the historical record. The latest figures for deaths during the European witch craze are between 30,000 to 50,000 victims. Not all were executed by the Church, not all were women, and not all were burned. Brown's claim that educated women, priestesses, and midwives were singled out by witch-hunters is not only false, it betrays his goddess-friendly sources.

A MULTITUDE OF ERRORS

So error-laden is *The Da Vinci Code* that the educated reader actually applauds those rare occasions where Brown stumbles (despite himself) into the truth. A few examples of his "impeccable" research: He claims that the motions of the planet Venus trace a pentacle (the so-called Ishtar pentagram) symbolizing the goddess. But it isn't a perfect figure and has nothing to do with the length of the Olympiad. The ancient Olympic games were celebrated in honor of Zeus Olympias, *not* Aphrodite, and occurred every four years.

Brown's contention that the five linked rings of the modern Olympic Games are a secret tribute to the goddess is also wrong—each set of games was supposed to add a ring to the design but the organizers stopped at five. And his efforts to read goddess propaganda into art, literature, and even Disney cartoons are simply ridiculous.

No datum is too dubious for inclusion, and reality falls quickly by the wayside. For instance, the Opus Dei bishop encourages his albino assassin by telling him that Noah was also an albino (a notion drawn from the non-canonical 1 Enoch 106:2). Yet albinism somehow fails to interfere with the man's eyesight as it physiologically would.

But a far more important example is Brown's treatment of Gothic architecture as a style full of goddess-worshipping symbols and coded messages to confound the uninitiated. Building on Barbara Walker's claim that "like a pagan temple, the Gothic cathedral represented the body of the Goddess," *The Templar Revelation* asserts: "Sexual symbolism is found in the great Gothic cathedrals which were masterminded by the Knights Templar . . . both of which represent intimate female anatomy: the arch, which draws the worshipper into the body of Mother Church, evokes the vulva." In *The Da Vinci Code,* these sentiments are transformed into a character's description of "a cathedral's long hollow nave as a secret tribute to a woman's womb . . . complete with receding labial ridges and a nice little cinquefoil clitoris above the doorway."

These remarks cannot be brushed aside as opinions of the villain; Langdon, the book's hero, refers to his own lectures about goddess-symbolism at Chartres.

These bizarre interpretations betray no acquaintance with the actual development or construction of Gothic architecture, and correcting the countless errors becomes a tiresome exercise: The Templars had *nothing* to do with the cathedrals of their time, which were commissioned by bishops and their canons throughout Europe. They were unlettered men with no arcane knowledge of "sacred geometry" passed down from the pyramid builders. They did not wield tools themselves on their own projects, nor did they found masons' guilds to build for others. Not all their churches were round, nor was roundness a defiant insult to the Church. Rather than being a tribute to the divine feminine, their round churches honored the Church of the Holy Sepulchre.

Actually looking at Gothic churches and their predecessors deflates the idea of female symbolism. Large medieval churches typically had three front doors on the west plus triple entrances to their transepts on the north and south. (What part of a woman's anatomy does a transept represent? Or the kink in Chartres's main aisle?) Romanesque churches—including ones that *predate* the founding of the Templars—have similar bands of decoration arching over their entrances. Both Gothic and Romanesque churches have the long, rectangular nave inherited from Late Antique basilicas, ultimately derived from Roman public buildings. Neither Brown nor his sources consider what symbolism medieval churchmen such as Suger of St.-Denis or William Durandus read in church design. It certainly wasn't goddess-worship.

FALSE CLAIMS

If the above seems like a pile driver applied to a gnat, the blows are necessary to demonstrate the utter falseness of Brown's material. His willful distortions of documented history are more than matched by his outlandish claims about controversial subjects. But to a postmodernist, one construct of reality is as good as any other.

Brown's approach seems to consist of grabbing large chunks of his stated sources and tossing them together in a salad of a story. From *Holy Blood, Holy Grail,* Brown lifts the concept of the Grail as a metaphor for a sacred lineage by arbitrarily breaking a medieval French term, *Sangraal* (Holy Grail), into *sang* (blood) and *raal* (royal). This holy blood, according to Brown, descended from Jesus and his wife, Mary Magdalene, to the Merovingian dynasty in Dark Ages France, surviving its fall to persist in several modern French families, including that of Pierre Plantard, a leader of the mysterious Priory of Sion. The Priory—an actual organization officially registered with the French government in 1956—makes extraordinary claims of antiquity as the "real" power behind the Knights Templar. It most likely originated after World War II and was first brought to public notice in 1962. With the exception of filmmaker Jean Cocteau, its illustrious list of Grand Masters—which include Leonardo da Vinci, Isaac Newton, and Victor Hugo—is not credible, although it's presented as true by Brown.

Brown doesn't accept a political motivation for the Priory's activities. Instead he picks up *The Templar Revelation*'s view of the organization as a cult of secret goddess-worshippers who have preserved ancient Gnostic wisdom and records of Christ's true mission, which would completely overturn Christianity if released. Significantly, Brown omits the rest of the book's thesis that makes Christ and Mary Magdalene unmarried sex partners performing the erotic mysteries of Isis. Perhaps even a gullible mass-market audience has its limits.

From both *Holy Blood, Holy Grail* and *The Templar Revelation,* Brown takes a negative view of the Bible and a grossly distorted image of Jesus. He's neither the Messiah nor a humble carpenter but a wealthy, trained religious teacher bent on regaining the throne of David. His credentials are amplified by his relationship with the rich Magdalen who carries the royal blood of Benjamin: "Almost everything our fathers taught us about Christ is false," laments one of Brown's characters.

Yet it's Brown's Christology that's false—and *blindingly* so. He requires the present New Testament to be a post-Constantinian fabrication that displaced true accounts now represented only by surviving Gnostic texts. He claims that Christ wasn't considered divine until the Council of Nicea voted him so in 325 at the behest of the emperor. Then Constantine—a lifelong sun worshipper—ordered all older scriptural texts destroyed, which is why no complete set of Gospels predates the fourth century. Christians somehow failed to notice the sudden and drastic change in their doctrine.

But by Brown's specious reasoning, the Old Testament can't be authentic either because complete Hebrew Scriptures are no more than a thousand years old. And yet the texts were transmitted so accurately that they *do* match well with the Dead Sea Scrolls from a thousand years earlier. Analysis of textual families, comparison with fragments and quotations, plus historical correlations securely date the orthodox Gospels to the first century and indicate that they're *earlier* than the Gnostic forgeries. (The Epistles of St. Paul are, of course, even earlier than the Gospels.)

Primitive Church documents and the testimony of the ante-Nicean Fathers confirm that Christians have *always* believed Jesus to be Lord, God, and Savior—even when that faith meant death. The earliest partial canon of Scripture dates from the late second century and already rejected Gnostic writings. For Brown, it isn't enough to credit Constantine with the divinization of Jesus. The emperor's old adherence to the cult of the Invincible Sun also meant repackaging sun worship as the new faith. Brown drags out old (and long-discredited) charges by virulent anti-Catholics like Alexander Hislop who accused the Church of perpetuating Babylonian mysteries, as well as 19th-century rationalists who regarded Christ as just another dying savior-god.

Unsurprisingly, Brown misses no opportunity to criticize Christianity and its pitiable adherents. (The church in question is always the Catholic Church, though his villain does sneer once at Anglicans—for their grimness, of all things.) He routinely and anachronistically refers to the Church as "the Vatican," even when popes weren't in residence there. He systematically portrays it throughout history as deceitful, power-crazed, crafty, and murderous: "The Church may no longer employ crusades to slaughter, but their influence is no less persuasive. No less insidious."

GODDESS WORSHIP AND THE MAGDALEN

Worst of all, in Brown's eyes, is the fact that the pleasure-hating, sex-hating, woman-hating Church suppressed goddess worship and eliminated the divine feminine. He claims that goddess worship universally dominated pre-Christian paganism with the *hieros gamos* (sacred marriage) as its central rite. His enthusiasm for fertility rites is enthusiasm for sexuality, not procreation. What else would one expect of a Cathar sympathizer?

Astonishingly, Brown claims that Jews in Solomon's Temple adored Yahweh and his feminine counterpart, the Shekinah, via the services of sacred prostitutes—possibly a twisted version of the Temple's corruption after Solomon (1 Kings 14:24 and 2 Kings 23:4-15). Moreover, he says that the tetragrammaton YHWH derives from "Jehovah, an androgynous physical union between the masculine Jah and the pre-Hebraic name for Eve, Havah."

But as any first-year Scripture student could tell you, Jehovah is actually a 16th-century rendering of Yahweh using the vowels of Adonai ("Lord"). In fact, goddesses did *not* dominate the pre-Christian world—not in the religions of Rome, her barbarian subjects, Egypt, or even Semitic lands where the *hieros gamos* was an ancient practice. Nor did the Hellenized cult of Isis appear to have included sex in its secret rites.

Contrary to yet another of Brown's claims, Tarot cards do *not* teach goddess doctrine. They were invented for innocent gaming purposes in the 15th century and didn't acquire occult associations until the late 18th. Playing-card suites carry no Grail symbolism. The notion of diamonds symbolizing pentacles is a deliberate misrepresentation by British occultist A. E. Waite. And the number five—so crucial to Brown's puzzles—has some connections with the protective goddess but myriad others besides, including human life, the five senses, and the Five Wounds of Christ.

Brown's treatment of Mary Magdalene is sheer delusion. In *The Da Vinci Code,* she's no penitent whore but Christ's royal consort and the intended head of His Church, supplanted by Peter and defamed by churchmen. She fled west with her offspring to Provence, where medieval Cathars would keep the original teachings of Jesus alive. The Priory of Sion still guards her relics and records, excavated by the Templars from the subterranean Holy of Holies. It also protects her descendants—including Brown's heroine.

Although many people still picture the Magdalen as a sinful woman who anointed Jesus and equate her with Mary of Bethany, that conflation is actually the later work of Pope St. Gregory the Great. The East has always kept them separate and said that the Magdalen, "apostle to the apostles," died in Ephesus. The legend of her voyage to Provence is no earlier than the ninth century, and her relics weren't reported there until the 13th. Catholic critics, including the Bollandists, have been debunking the legend and distinguishing the three ladies since the 17th century.

Brown uses two Gnostic documents, the Gospel of Philip and the Gospel of Mary, to prove that the Magdalen was Christ's "companion," meaning sexual partner. The apostles were jealous that Jesus used to "kiss her on the mouth" and favored her over them. He cites exactly the same passages quoted in *Holy Blood, Holy Grail* and *The Templar Revelation* and even picks up the latter's reference to *The Last Temptation of Christ*. What these books neglect to mention is the infamous final verse of the Gospel of Thomas. When Peter sneers that "women are not worthy of Life," Jesus responds, "I myself shall lead her in order to make her male. . . . For every woman who will make herself male will enter the Kingdom of Heaven."

That's certainly an odd way to "honor" one's spouse or exalt the status of women.

THE KNIGHTS TEMPLAR

Brown likewise misrepresents the history of the Knights Templar. The oldest of the military-religious orders, the Knights were founded in 1118 to protect pilgrims in the Holy Land. Their rule, attributed to St. Bernard of Clairvaux, was approved in 1128 and generous donors granted them numerous properties in Europe for support. Rendered redundant after the last Crusader stronghold fell in 1291, the Templars' pride and wealth—they were also bankers—earned them keen hostility.

Brown maliciously ascribes the suppression of the Templars to "Machiavellian" Pope Clement V, whom they were blackmailing with the Grail secret. His "ingeniously planned sting operation" had his soldiers suddenly arrest all Templars. Charged with Satanism, sodomy, and blasphemy, they were tortured into confessing and burned as heretics, their ashes "tossed unceremoniously into the Tiber."

But in reality, the initiative for crushing the Templars came from King Philip the Fair of France, whose royal officials did the arresting in 1307. About 120 Templars were burned by local Inquisitorial courts in France for not confessing or retracting a confession, as happened with Grand Master Jacques de Molay. Few Templars suffered death elsewhere although their order was abolished in 1312. Clement, a weak, sickly Frenchman manipulated by his king, burned no one in Rome inasmuch as he was the first pope to reign from Avignon (so much for the ashes in the Tiber).

Moreover, the mysterious stone idol that the Templars were accused of worshiping is associated with fertility in only *one* of more than a hundred confessions. Sodomy was the scandalous—and possibly true—charge against the order, *not* ritual fornication. The Templars have been darlings of occultism since their myth as masters of secret wisdom and fabulous treasure began to coalesce in the late 18th century. Freemasons and even Nazis have hailed them as brothers. Now it's the turn of neo-Gnostics.

Twisting da Vinci

Brown's revisionist interpretations of da Vinci are as distorted as the rest of his information. He claims to have first run across these views "while I was studying art history in Seville," but they correspond point for point to material in *The Templar Revelation*. A writer who sees a pointed finger as a throat-cutting gesture, who says the Madonna of the Rocks was painted for nuns instead of a lay confraternity of men, who claims that da Vinci received "hundreds of lucrative Vatican commissions" (actually, it was just one . . . and it was never executed) is simply unreliable.

Brown's analysis of da Vinci's work is just as ridiculous. He presents the *Mona Lisa* as an androgynous self-portrait when it's widely known to portray a real woman, Madonna Lisa, wife of Francesco di Bartolomeo del Giocondo. The name is certainly not—as Brown claims—a mocking anagram of two Egyptian fertility deities Amon and L'Isa (Italian for Isis). How did he miss the theory, propounded by the authors of *The Templar Revelation,* that the Shroud of Turin is a photographed self-portrait of da Vinci?

Much of Brown's argument centers around da Vinci's *Last Supper,* a painting the author considers a coded message that reveals the truth about Jesus and the Grail. Brown points to the lack of a central chalice on the table as proof that the Grail *isn't* a material vessel. But da Vinci's painting specifically dramatizes the moment when Jesus warns, "One of you will betray me" (John 13:21). There is no Institution Narrative in St. John's Gospel. The Eucharist is not shown there. And the person sitting next to Jesus is *not* Mary Magdalene (as Brown claims) but St. John, portrayed as the usual effeminate da Vinci youth, comparable to his St. John the Baptist. Jesus is in the exact center of the painting, with two pyramidal groups of three apostles on each side. Although da Vinci was a spiritually troubled homosexual, Brown's contention that he coded his paintings with anti-Christian messages simply can't be sustained.

Brown's Mess

In the end, Dan Brown has penned a poorly written, atrociously researched mess. So, why bother with such a close reading of a worthless novel? The answer is simple: *The Da Vinci Code* takes esoterica mainstream. It may well do for Gnosticism what *The Mists of Avalon* did for paganism—gain it popular acceptance. After all, how many lay readers will see the blazing inaccuracies put forward as buried truths?

What's more, in making phony claims of scholarship, Brown's book infects readers with a virulent hostility toward Catholicism. Dozens of occult history books, conveniently cross-linked by Amazon.com, are following in its wake. And booksellers' shelves now bulge with falsehoods few would be buying without *The Da Vinci Code* connection. While Brown's assault on the Catholic Church may be a backhanded compliment, it's one we would have happily done without.

Maurice Timothy Reidy (review date 12 September 2003)

SOURCE: Reidy, Maurice Timothy. "Breaking the Code." *Commonweal* 130, no. 15 (12 September 2003): 46.

[*In the following review, Reidy asserts that Brown's use of history and theology in* The Da Vinci Code *is inaccurate and extremely problematic.*]

The publishing hit of the summer wasn't written by J. K. Rowling or a certain well-compensated senator from New York. That distinction belongs to Dan Brown, the previously unknown author of **The Da Vinci Code,** a fast-paced thriller set amid the museums and cathedrals of Europe. The book is that rarest of birds: a critical and commercial success. *New York Times* book critic Janet Maslin called it "an exhilarating brainy thriller" and at one point this summer, it was on top of every bestseller list in the country.

Yet it's a strange sort of hit. Consider these reviews from Amazon.com readers. "Completely turned my opinion of the Bible and the Catholic Church upside down," wrote one. "This is one of the best books (if not the best book) I've ever read," added another. "Appropriately, there are many who would remind me that it's the second best book, after the Bible. Well, **The Da Vinci Code** is, in many ways, a further exploration of the Bible."

Some plot summary: The book begins with the murder of a curator at the Louvre. A Harvard symbologist named Robert Langdon is called in to interpret the clues left by the dying man. Before long, Langdon is fleeing the police with a female cryptologist, on the trail of a mystery involving Leonardo Da Vinci, an ancient secret society, Opus Dei, and (you guessed it) the Holy Grail.

Spoiler alert: the book's big secret is that the Holy Grail isn't a cup, but a code, of sorts, for the lineage of Jesus and Mary Magdalene. Magdalene, it turns out, wasn't a prostitute, but a close companion of Jesus. Her real identity was concealed by early church leaders who feared the truth would undermine church teaching on celibacy (which, of course, hasn't been questioned since). "The church, in order to defend itself against the Magdalene's power, perpetuated her image as a whore and buried evidence of Christ's marriage to her," one character explains breathlessly, "thereby defusing any potential claims that Christ had a surviving bloodline and was a mortal prophet."

This may sound like *Last Temptation Redux,* but **The Da Vinci Code** is a great read, despite its theories. I bought a copy at the airport and finished it on the flight home. Some have taken offense at its religious content: on her Web site, Amy Welborn called it a "pretentious, bigoted, tendentious mess." It is tendentious, but I didn't find it bigoted. I was particularly surprised by the sympathetic portrait of the Opus Dei bishop charged with making sure the Magdalene secret isn't revealed.

The problem, it seems, is that some people have taken the story to be *true.* Indeed, Brown has encouraged this confusion by insisting upon the book's historical accuracy. Asked in an interview how much of the novel is based on fact, he replied: "All of it."

At least one expert disagrees. Writing in the *New York Times* last month, Bruce Boucher, a curator at the Art Institute of Chicago, disputed several facts in the book, including Brown's contention that Mary Magdalene was pictured in Da Vinci's *Last Supper,* disguised as the Apostle John. (Brown offers this as partial proof of her relationship with Jesus.) It's true that no one would mistake Da Vinci's John for a linebacker. Still, Brown seems guilty of confusing art with fact.

Less has been written about the book's theology, but it's just as problematic. Brown relies heavily on the Gnostic Gospels, predictably presenting them as secret texts that reveal the real "truth" about Jesus' life and teachings. This is familiar stuff: Elaine Pagels for the Robert Ludlum set. But it also an incredibly simplistic reading of both history and theology.

More troublesome is Brown's reliance on *Holy Blood, Holy Grail* by Michael Baigent and Richard Leigh. Published in 1983, the book centers on the Prieure de Sion, a secret society founded in the twelfth century, and a nineteenth-century French priest who argued that French Merovingian dynasty of the seventh century carried the royal blood of Jesus and Mary Magdalene. At one point in **The Da Vinci Code,** Leigh Teabing, a character named for Leigh and Baigent, pulls their book from his shelf and declares: "To my taste, the authors made some dubious leaps of faith in their analysis, but their fundamental premise is sound." Really?

Back in 1990, University of Chicago Professor Martin E. Marty called *Holy Blood* "sensationally misguiding." "I saw nothing at all in the earlier book—absolutely hokey," he told me via e-mail. "I've not read **The Da Vinci Code** but know it's built on the same kind of thing. There's no hint of a clue of [a] whisper of

evidence in any documents from the time. . . . These things come and go every few years and this one will pass, too. Good entertainment, but 'ungrounded.'"

Brown has argued that historical arguments are themselves suspect because history is written "by those societies and belief systems that conquered and survived." This is a cop-out. It is disingenuous for Brown to present his book as factual and then hide behind questions like "how historically accurate is history itself?" He should stick to fiction.

Annie C. Bond (review date fall 2003)

SOURCE: Bond, Annie C. Review of *The Da Vinci Code,* by Dan Brown. *Phi Kappa Phi Forum* 83, no. 4 (fall 2003): 42-3.

[*In the following review, Bond describes Brown's* The Da Vinci Code *as an engaging, enjoyable, and well-plotted novel that is also historically accurate.*]

When I initially learned that a book, a novel, had been written using some of Christianity's more, shall we say, esoteric subject matter, I was more than a little wary of the accuracy of the book. But I was refreshingly surprised by Dan Brown's fourth venture into the realm of fiction.

While I was not familiar with his previous works, the hubbub that his fourth was causing warranted reading **The Da Vinci Code** for myself. I had not yet met the work's main character, Robert Langdon, an Oxford-trained Harvard professor of symbology, but as I began reading I was drawn into a tightly woven tale of murder, mystery, and puzzles as quickly as Langdon was.

The novel begins with the gruesome murder of the Louvre's curator, Jacques Sauniere, and with the even more bizarre clues that the victim leaves in the museum's most famous wing. It is these cryptic clues that lead to Langdon's involvement, as well as that of Sophie Neveu, a police cryptologist.

Before delving deeper into the twisted plot of this work of fiction, I must mention that much of the symbolism and details relates to the existence of a certain secret group known as the Priory of Sion. Those who have even a passing knowledge of the organization's history must have recognized the importance of the names that Brown devised for his characters.

Jacques Sauniere was actually a real person who played a pivotal role in the events in which the Priory has been involved since the end of the nineteenth century, and indeed continues to be involved in to this day. The "real" Sauniere was a priest in the south of France who made an interesting discovery when remodeling his church. What exactly was discovered remains unclear, but it is rumored to involve the Merovingian dynasty and the quest for the Holy Grail. I realize this sounds a bit far-fetched, but bear with me. A little background on this subject brings a whole new dimension to this book.

The name Sophie pays tribute to the knowledge that is bestowed upon the heroine at the end of the book. But more on that later.

While the Priory of Sion does exist and may have connections with the Knights Templar and the Freemasons, what this organization is sworn to protect is the knowledge that there are among us, in this day and age, descendants of Christ scattered throughout the world. What is interesting is the idea that Jesus was not a celibate rabbi, as is the image portrayed in the New Testament, but that he was also a man who had fathered children of his own. As you can see, that belief, if it is not just a belief but a distinct possibility, would rock the very foundation of Christianity as it exists today.

Back to the book itself, Brown demonstrates not only knowledge of art, art history, and architecture but also a talent at weaving it all together into such an intricate tapestry that it becomes difficult to determine what is his imagination at work and what is actually a mini-lesson in history.

In the bizarre scene that Sauniere leaves for the authorities to find at the Louvre, Langdon is labeled the prime suspect of the murder of the elderly curator, as the gentleman made a point to ensure that Langdon would be involved with Neveu, so that as a team the two of them would be able to decipher the clues properly.

As the pair begins to unravel bits and pieces of the mystery, the number of pieces of the elaborate jigsaw puzzle seems to expand exponentially. Once one piece is uncovered and its true meaning is discovered, the action truly begins.

The race against time leads the couple from the murder scene at the Louvre to a Swiss Bank on the outskirts of Paris. The information gleaned there from a bank official then leads Langdon and Neveu on a mad dash to an expert on the Sion and in Holy Grail lore, who conveniently resides in a chateau not far from Paris. When this character enters the game, once again a puzzle piece is found. The path then leads the now-trio to London.

It is here that Brown again showcases his knowledge of this subject matter when the next crucial piece of information is revealed. At an out-of-the-way church, Langdon and Neveu discover another treasure that Sauniere and the Priory have left for them. The story then leads them to still another landmark of importance, and the truth of the Holy Grail is finally revealed.

Brown's in-depth study of the body of literature and research that has come out in the last twenty years is extensive, and for the most part accurate. His style is certainly unique, and as this is only his fourth book, I look forward to his next venture onto the literary scene. If you read and enjoyed his work, I would be remiss to mention that of his other works I have since read, I have found them as interesting, as accurate, and as enjoyable as *The Da Vinci Code.*

Andrew Greeley (review date 3 October 2003)

SOURCE: Greeley, Andrew. "*Da Vinci Code* Is More Fantasy than Fact." *National Catholic Reporter* 39, no. 42 (3 October 2003): 18.

[*In the following review, Greeley criticizes Brown's representation of history and the Catholic Church in* The Da Vinci Code, *asserting that Brown's novel is filled with historical inaccuracies and represents an anti-Catholic perspective.*]

Dan Brown's fast-paced, intricately plotted second novel [*The Da Vinci Code*] deserves to be on *The New York Times* bestseller list. It is a skillfully written read, complete with secret codes, anagrams, elaborate technology, pagan sex orgies, sudden reversals of fortune, age-old conspiracies, pre-Christian fertility cults, the Knights Templar, Gnostic gospels, corrupt cops, brutal murders, feminist "theory" and frantic midnight rides through Paris. The battle over control of the Holy Grail in which the two protagonists (a Harvard professor and a French police cryptologist) are caught up is between the "Priory of Sion" and Opus Dei. The former has been given charge of the Holy Grail, which might reveal secrets that will severely damage Christianity. The latter has been charged by the Vatican with destroying the priory and the secrets of the Grail.

The priory struggles to keep alive a religion of balance between male and female (celebrated in ritual intercourse) which Constantine crushed out of Christianity to strengthen male power. The Holy Grail is not a chalice but the memory of Mary Magdalene who was the consort of Jesus and the mother of his daughter, Sarah, whose descendents are still alive.

Opus has assigned one of its supernumeraries to kill the leaders of the priory and he does so with a holy zeal, after he has scourged himself according to the customs of the group. In a secret meeting at Castel Gandolfo the Vatican has given the Opus prelate 20 million euros in bearer bonds to finance the killings. It also promised that a planned suppression of Opus would be cancelled. The hit man kills the four top officials in the priory and a nun who tries to prevent him from opening a secret compartment in the Church of San Sulpice. A captain of the judiciary police and certain other folks seem to be involved on the side of Opus.

All of this is rich material, guaranteed to keep one turning the pages till the story is finished. Still, the reader must wonder how much of it is fantasy. The answer, I would argue, is that practically all of it is fantasy. Every couple of years a book comes along that promises to tell you who Jesus really was and/or how the church has hidden the "real" Jesus for 19 centuries. Somehow they do not stand up to serious historical examination.

I am hardly a defender of Opus Dei, but I cannot imagine them setting a killer loose in a struggle against a group it considers dangerous. Nor can I imagine the Vatican picking up the tab for serial killings. As usual in such stories, the Roman curia is pictured as smooth, sophisticated schemers who will stop at nothing to preserve the power of the church.

The curia is hardly all that deft and devious, save in its internal plots and conniving—like getting rid of a colleague or undoing an ecumenical council. It is in fact a fractionalized bureaucracy whose heavy-handed personnel would have a hard time conspiring themselves out of a wet paper bag. Poison and daggers were abandoned long ago.

Is all this stuff anti-Catholic? In a sense it is, and I am waiting for the voice of the indefatigable Bill Donahue of the Catholic League to cry boycott. However, the worst the book will do is upset some dedicated Catholics who won't leave the church anyhow and feed the bigotry of some hard-line anti-Catholics.

For the record, the book is filled with historical inaccuracies. Bruce Boucher of Chicago's Art Institute in an article in *The New York Times* Aug. 3 tore apart Dan Brown's knowledge of Leonardo Da Vinci. Moreover, Brown's use of the term "Vatican" is woefully inaccurate. He depicts the "Vatican" as conspiring with Constantine to suppress the Gnostic gospels in the early 4th century. However, the Vatican Hill was a disorderly cemetery at that time. The "Vatican" is also involved in the suppression of the Templars, though the headquarters of the pope at that time was the Lateran Palace (and the pope was in Avignon anyway). Brown also refers to an individual he calls the Secretariat Vaticana who has charge of papal finances. Presumably he means the secretary of state, though that official does not in fact control Vatican finances. Brown knows little about Leonardo, little about the Catholic church, and little about history.

Yet something must be said about the Grail legend whose origins are not Christian and whose ambience is more heretical than Catholic. Back in the dim prehistory of Ireland, there was a spring fertility ritual (enacted on Beltane, usually May 1) in which animal blood was poured into a concave stone altar to represent the union of the male and female in the process of generating life. Later tales grew up to explain the rite,

the best known of which is the story of Art MacConn. Memories of the ritual and the story floated around in the collective preconscious of the Celtic lands in company with folk tales, myths, bits of history and cycles of legends about such folk as Arthur, Merlin, Parsifal and Tristan. Later writers like Geoffrey of Monmouth, Chretien de Troyes, Thomas Mallory, and Wolfram von Eschenbach combined this bricolage of images and myths into more systematic stories with an overlay of Christianity. However, these storytellers (excepting von Eschenbach) were tainted by the perspectives of Catharist heresy and the results were dreamy, flesh-denying, life-denying legends that violated the older, if pagan, Irish tales. The Grail is always to be sought and never found. This version persists in the work of such disparate artists as Richard Wagner, Alfred Tennyson, Fritz Lowe and Robert Bresson. In the Irish story, Art gets the magic cup and the magic princess, though, more realistically she, being an Irish woman, gets him—a happy ending! (see Jean Markale, *Women of the Celts*).

Finally, Brown and his Harvard "symbologist" (semioticist?) are apparently unaware of the most powerful religious symbol of the mother love of God in the last 1,500 years of history, one with a profound impact on painting, music, sculpture, architecture and poetry. Surveys tell us Mary, the mother of Jesus, is one of the four key elements of Catholic religious identity among young people in the United States (along with concern for the poor, the action of God in the sacraments and the presence of Jesus in the Eucharist). Some feminist theologians reject the Mary symbol on the grounds that it was patriarchal in its origin. Granted that like all symbols, the Mary symbol can be and has been misused, the efforts of some writers to cancel out a millennium and a half of rich religious imagery with the shibboleth "patriarchal" (instead of purifying it) can most charitably be described as heroic. How many medieval cathedrals do they propose to destroy? One wonders nevertheless what Dan Brown's reasons were for ignoring the Mary symbol.

Patrick McCormick (review date November 2003)

SOURCE: McCormick, Patrick. "Painted Out of the Picture." *U.S. Catholic* 68, no. 11 (November 2003): 36-8.

[*In the following review, McCormick describes Brown's* The Da Vinci Code *as a fun, brainy, erudite thriller. McCormick emphasizes the book's element of feminist theology.*]

The good news for Catholics this summer was that the runaway bestseller about church officials embroiled in a conspiracy of silence was a work of fiction. After being pummeled for more than a year with headlines about bishops and cardinals covering up sexual abuse of minors by clerics, it seemed like a vacation to curl up with a wicked tale about a Vatican conspiracy to protect early Christianity's biggest sexual secrets and realize it was only a novel.

Dan Brown's brainy thriller, *The Da Vinci Code* (Doubleday), which since March has been sitting atop the *New York Times* bestseller list, has something to please every taste. It's a murder mystery with enough clues and puzzles to keep Nero Wolfe and Hercule Poirot's little grey cells spinning. It's an international man (and woman) hunt that makes Tommy Lee Jones' pursuit of *The Fugitive* look like bumblings of the Keystone Cops. It's a high-speed chase for the Holy Grail that laps Indiana Jones and his pop three times before they're even out of the gate. And it's a battle royal between secret societies over stakes that dwarf *The Lord of the Rings*. What's more, this potboiler with more cliffhangers than a six-pack of Saturday afternoon serials is just plain fun to read.

Brown's tale gets off to a flying start when an albino-monk-henchman-assassin (working for Opus Dei, no less) breaks into the Louvre one starry night and mortally wounds the museum's chief curator, Jacques Saunier. Managing to escape his killer's grasp, however, Saunier uses the last few moments of his life to transform his own naked corpse into a body of evidence richly inscribed with clues and codes that will help the novel's protagonists uncover and defeat his enemies.

Before you can say "Mona Lisa" or "The Last Supper" Harvard art historian and religious symbol expert Robert Langdon (think Indiana Jones with a better tailor) and police inspector and cryptologist Sophie Neveu (Saunier's brilliant and fetching granddaughter) are on the scene and the scent of a murder mystery that will lead them across Europe and into some of Christianity's oldest and best kept secrets. But they are also being hunted by Saunier's assassin and a small army of French police pursuing them as murder suspects.

Together the intrepid investigators use their talents to move through a maze of artistic, linguistic, and mathematical codes and puzzles, unraveling the mystery of Saunier's murder and uncovering the greater mystery of his identity as the head of an ancient secret society entrusted with a secret about Christianity's founder and origins. This is a secret, Langdon and Neveu learn, that Christianity has kept from the faithful for nearly 2,000 years, a secret that church officials have tried to extinguish time and time again, and that members of Saunier's society (including Da Vinci, whose art is chock-full of clues about this secret) have protected and passed on to successive generations. It is the secret of the Holy Grail.

And so the murder investigation and manhunt become a quest to uncover the mystery of the Grail, and our protagonists soon discover that they are not looking for a golden cup but for a person whose story and identity have been buried far beneath the surface of Christianity's official teachings, a person whose importance to Christ and early Christianity is suppressed and distorted by tradition and only hinted at obliquely in Christian art and legend.

Without giving away the whole game, let's just say that anyone with feminist sensibilities would be amused to learn who this novel says the Holy Grail was and what this person's connection to Jesus and the early church may have been. Such a reader would also see why a patriarchal hierarchy committed to a celibate male clergy might be willing to move heaven and earth to keep this person's identity and marital status a secret. (OK, I gave some of it away.) To be fair, some of these notions have been suggested before, and some scholars have previously argued that the person in question has gotten a raw deal from official Christian tradition.

Why has a murder mystery about a Vatican conspiracy to cover up early Christianity's biggest sexual secret become this year's runaway blockbuster? In large part because Brown has crafted a great thriller with the sort of smart, resourceful hero who could easily go Hollywood (imagine Jack Ryan with a doctorate in art history). With the breakneck pacing, serpentine plotting and conspiratorial tone of the best of Tom Clancy or Michael Crichton, *The Da Vinci Code* has all the stuff for a major blockbuster.

But Brown's erudite thriller also has a Harry Potterish appeal. The author may describe his art historian hero as "Harrison Ford in Harris tweed," but like young Master Potter, Robert Langdon launches readers into the arcane world of religious symbols, mathematical puzzles, and linguistic codes that are as challenging as a fast game of quiddich.

And like Potter, Langdon's adventure draws us into a magical and parallel universe of secret societies, mystical rituals, and ancient texts with indecipherable codes protecting mysteries long kept secret from ordinary folks. While appealing to a slightly older audience, Brown's thriller lets readers slip through the same looking glass as Lewis Carroll and J. K. Rowling. A Da Vinci painting is no longer a landscape or a portrait, but a portal to a strange and secret world.

Still, a great deal of the novel's appeal is its feminist sensibility, particularly its translation of feminist critiques of Christianity and Catholicism into popular fiction. The book suggests—as some feminist scholars have been arguing for a while—that the original Jesus movement was much more welcoming to women, marriage, and sexuality than the church Constantine and Augustine handed on to us.

Jesus embraced women as friends, colleagues, and disciples, and the earliest Christian community accepted women as apostles, priests, and the heads of local churches. Indeed, one of those women (Brown suggests) was Jesus' preeminent disciple and the first apostle. Sadly, however, the early church soon lost its feminist nerve, and a patriarchal spirit and theology supplanted and suppressed an appreciation of the divine feminine, leaving only a small secret sect to protect and pass on the secret of the Holy Grail.

Unfortunately—as in any novel—it's tough to know where fact ends and fiction begins, and few serious scholars would make or support the sweeping sort of claims found here. Still, many feminist academics have argued that official Catholic teaching misreads the history of the early church and has passed on a "man-itized" tradition that has stripped away the voices, perspectives, and stories of women who were disciples, apostles, and colleagues of Christ—and silenced the feminine dimension of God herself.

Biblical scholar Elisabeth Schüssler Fiorenza's modern classic *In Memory of Her: A Feminist Theological Reconstruction of Christian Origins* (Crossroad) reread the standard reports of early Christianity with a feminist eye, and found the overlooked and forgotten women who co-founded Christianity.

Elizabeth Johnson's equally ground-breaking *She Who Is* (Crossroad) recovered feminine language and symbols to speak of God and gave the whole Christian community ways to speak of and to the God in whose image we are made, male and female. And Karen Jo Torjesen's *When Women Were Priests* (HarperSanFrancisco) uncovers evidence of women's leadership in the early church and the scandal of their subordination in the rise of Christianity.

In the end Brown's novel is a vastly entertaining read that mixes the thrill of a high-speed chase with the magical pleasures of a quest through an enchanted forest of art, literature, and history. And that is reason enough to recommend any book as a beach or bedstand companion. But, in its own popularizing way, it also gives voice to a growing feminist critique of a patriarchal church and secrets it keeps about the goodness and godliness of women. And that's good news, too.

Charles McGrath (essay date 23 November 2003)

SOURCE: McGrath, Charles. "Another Holy Mystery." *New York Times Magazine* (23 November 2003): 23-4.

[*In the following essay, McGrath discusses the representation of Christianity in Brown's* The Da Vinci Code.]

QUESTIONS OF FAITH:

Would you consider yourself a conspiracy theorist?

Absolutely not. . . . I see no truth whatsoever in stories of extraterrestrial visitors, crop circles, the Bermuda Triangle or many of the other "mysteries" that permeate pop culture. However, the secret behind *The Da Vinci Code* was too well documented and significant for me to dismiss.

This novel unearths some surprising Christian history. Are you a Christian?

I am, although perhaps not in the most traditional sense of the word. . . . I consider myself a student of many religions. The more I learn, the more questions I have. For me, the spiritual quest will be a lifelong work in progress.

Interview with Dan Brown, from his Web site,
www.danbrown.com

What would Jesus do, people sometimes ask themselves in these perplexing times. What would Jesus drive? What would Jesus read, I wonder. The Bible presumably. And if he wanted to be current, Dan Brown's thriller, *The Da Vinci Code,* which shot to the tops of the best-seller lists within weeks of publication last spring and has remained there ever since—even though Brown's prose veers toward the clunky, Tom Clancy end of the thriller spectrum (as opposed to the more stylish end, represented by, say, Alan Furst). The book, while a gripping read, is not exactly an easy one: it's full of puzzles and anagrams to be solved, not to mention several minilectures on art history and iconography. Sales of *The Da Vinci Code* have been propelled, as is so often the case, by word of mouth. From the publicity and advertising and, indeed, from many of the reviews, you would never know what the book was about.

I won't disclose too much here, for the sake of those who have yet to dip into *The Code,* but it's fair to say that the novel is in part a pro-feminist, anti-Catholic polemic. It presumes that the church has been engaged in a centuries-old cover-up to suppress an extremely embarrassing theological detail: that Jesus, far from being celibate, was actually married—to Mary Magdalene, no less—and that he fathered a child, who went on to found the Merovingian dynasty. (This, in fact, is the most disquieting part of Brown's hypothesis—that the direct descendants of Jesus are most likely to be found in France, where they don't even go to church anymore.) The Vatican comes in for considerable bashing in the book, and so does Opus Dei, the right-wing Catholic organization known to be a particular favorite of the current pope.

Where was the hair-triggered William Donohue, head of the Catholic League for Religious and Civil Rights and normally so quick to pounce at even a suggestion of bias or unfair criticism, when this was coming out?

He may have been stamping out fires elsewhere, or perhaps he thought the whole business too silly to merit attention. *The Da Vinci Code* is a novel, after all—even though Brown claims in a note at the beginning that "all descriptions" of "documents and secret rituals . . . are accurate."

Recently, however, the Brown hypothesis was elevated into news, of a sort, by ABC, which broadcast an hour-long special, called "Jesus, Mary and Da Vinci," based on the book. The show, which was an unholy mish-mash—part "Unsolved Mysteries," part PBS documentary, featuring samplings from both soft rock and Gregorian chant and an assortment of talking heads ranging from the eminent (Umberto Eco, Elaine Pagels) to the eccentric—left out much of the really racy stuff in Brown's book: the discussion of ancient goddess cults, for example, and of the masked sex orgies held in honor of the "sacred feminine." (The book claims that this is what Tom Cruise stumbled into in the middle of *Eyes Wide Shut.* How much more proof do you need?) Instead, "Jesus, Mary and Da Vinci" focused on the Mary Magdalene aspect, which is not really news. That Mary Magdalene was not a prostitute is something that even the church acknowledges now, and Pagels and others have amply documented a tradition of Gnostic gospels in which Mary plays a far greater role than she does in the canonic ones. According to this tradition, in fact, she was the most important of the disciples—the one closest to Jesus and the one upon whom he conferred special, esoteric wisdom. But whether she and Jesus married, much less conceived a child, is something else again, and at the end of the program, the host, Elizabeth Vargas, sadly concluded, "We didn't find any proof." All we know, she added, is that "this is a love story."

Actually, it's a conspiracy story. The real point, understated in the television show but explicit in the book, is not so much what's true or false, but the vast web of people who don't want you to find out; and the surprising message in the success of *The Da Vinci Code* is that at the very same time when religious fundamentalism is on the rise in this country, there are apparently millions of us who—either genuinely or for the sake of entertainment—are willing to bring to organized religion the same skepticism and distrust we bring to government.

In some cases, the fundamentalists and the skeptics may even be the same; at least that's what you could conclude from the best-selling "Left Behind" thrillers, by Tim LaHaye and his collaborator, Jerry B. Jenkins. There are 11 installments so far, and they all take place after the Rapture, when all the true believers have been assumed into heaven, leaving everyone else to deal with the Antichrist and his minions, who sometimes take the shape of liberals and advocates of global government. There are deceivers everywhere.

You could argue that this is nothing more than the continuation of an authentic religious tradition in America, where we have always been suspicious of orthodoxies—and of Rome, in particular—and where we believe that everyone has the right to discover and interpret the truth for himself. But what seems different in the thriller theology is the element of paranoia and distrust, and the sense that even personal virtue may not be a sufficient bulwark against being duped. Religion, in this formulation, turns out to be less about revelation than about plots.

On the other hand, at least in the Brown version, there's that welcome notion of a sexy, uxorious Jesus; Jesus the family man. What would he read? *People* magazine probably. What would he drive? A van, of course—one big enough for all the kids.

David Klinghoffer (review date 8 December 2003)

SOURCE: Klinghoffer, David. "Religious Fiction . . ." *National Review* 55, no. 23 (8 December 2003): 48-9.

[*In the following review, Klinghoffer asserts that the greatest strength of Brown's* The Da Vinci Code *lies in his treatment of a historically real conspiracy theory.*]

When a novel has stuck around the top of the *New York Times* bestseller list for half a year, there is something interesting going on. Such a book has set off a pretty loud pealing of the electric chimes at the front door of the culture. In the case of Dan Brown's *The Da Vinci Code,* what's so special exactly? That depends on what makes conspiracy theories so fascinating.

Brown starts out with the bizarre murder of a curator at the Louvre by an albino assassin sent, it would seem, by the Catholic religious order Opus Dei. From there we're off like a bottle rocket, as a Harvard professor of "religious symbology," Robert Langdon, who happens to be visiting Paris, is called in for a consultation with the police. For the curator, before he succumbed to his wounds, had taken off all his clothes, arranged himself and some of the nearby artwork in a most curious fashion, and daubed a cryptic message in his own blood, mentioning Langdon's name.

I don't have to tell you that a book like this needs a love interest for protagonist Langdon, whom Brown supplies in the person of Sophie Neveu, a beautiful police cryptologist. Pretty soon Langdon is himself a suspect in the murder and he and Sophie are on the run from the French law. As we learn, a mysterious group of unknown individuals is trying to keep uncomfortable historical truths a secret, and the albino assassin is mixed up in it.

The conspiracy theory at the heart of Dan Brown's huge bestseller was not invented by him (it has been kicking around for years), but it's a juicy one and he's made the most of it, creating a story with a very effective cliffhanger at the end of almost every one of his 105 chapters. You are pulled along relentlessly—a feat of narrative art that really does deserve to be called art, no matter what Yale literary critic Harold Bloom said recently in mocking the "immensely inadequate" Stephen King (a similarly gifted writer) when the latter won a lifetime literary prize. If you don't believe writing in this vein merits appreciation, try thinking up a plot like the one in *The Da Vinci Code* yourself.

Since Brown's novel *is* a novel, it can more forthrightly take advantage of the tension inherent in unlocking ancient doors that perhaps should never be opened. He's witty, succinct, and smart—though the reader will have to be prepared to encounter the phrase "the sacred feminine" more than once, and if that makes you extremely queasy, you had better leave this book alone.

But the best thing about *The Da Vinci Code* is that the conspiracy is just an awfully neat one. What makes for an outstanding conspiracy? It doesn't have to be real, as this one is surely not, despite Brown's inclusion of a preface boldly headlined "FACT." One requirement is a complex array of lore. Brown has that: He provides many fascinating historical and quasi-historical tidbits—like the symbolic significance of the figure of a rose, the mathematical phenomenon called the Fibonacci sequence, the ancient Hebrew coding sequence called *atbash,* and much more, with an emphasis on the cryptic meanings of the paintings and drawings of Leonardo da Vinci, all artfully woven into the plot.

Above all, a worthwhile conspiracy needs to explain something that previously you didn't know needed explaining, something also that links to a truth, or at least a pseudo-truth, of deep significance. Again, pseudo-depth will do fine—we're talking about entertainment, after all. *The Da Vinci Code* has this.

But this book is certainly not for everyone, for the following reason. In this sort of thriller, there has to be something urgently important at stake should the conspiracy be revealed. What's at stake in *The Da Vinci Code* is nothing less than traditional Christianity itself. The Holy Grail, we are told, is not a holy cup but rather holy blood, the lineage of Jesus of Nazareth: The founder of Christianity had a daughter, Sarah, by Mary Magdalene. If true, this theory would overturn some of the central beliefs of Christians.

As a believing Jew, I certainly can't be accused of special pleading on behalf of Christian dogma. This should give me credibility when I say that this "Holy Blood" theory—of Jesus having descendants—is too

nutty to merit serious consideration; any suggestion that such a fact could have been kept secret for two millennia is absurd. Brown does acknowledge that there is some merit—some truth and beauty—in Christianity; but such merit as he sees is very far from the faith of actual Christian believers. Any Christian who is offended by fiction that directly contradicts his faith should certainly avoid this book.

If I were a Christian, though, I think I would find it a little disturbing that some fellow Christians do in fact view this novel as a threat to their faith. Some Catholic magazines have published detailed refutations of *The Da Vinci Code*; that they believe this is necessary indicates that many Catholics, and many in the general reading public, are taking this book far more seriously than they ought to. This also suggests that the problems in Catholic religious education are every bit as severe as Catholic conservatives have been alleging for some time now. If the professional educators were doing their job, any believing Catholic past elementary-school age would know that Brown's book is—a total falsehood.

What about the book's influence in the broader culture? Here, I am calmed by the reflection that there's something profoundly religious about conspiracies in the first place, even fictitious ones. Think about this next time you are at the beach in chilly weather. Though the sky is cloudy and a cold wind is up, you'll see people sitting on blankets in the sand just staring out to sea. Why? Because when you look at the ocean you get the intuition that just under the surface resides a vast hidden world of exotic, usually unseen creatures. The realization that there's all that life underneath—in some ways a mirror of our own world on dry land but in others dramatically different—is simply thrilling. It's what keeps people's eyes glued to the ocean even when there is ostensibly nothing going on out there.

This, too, is what makes a conspiracy thrilling, the revelation of concealed complexity all around. Likewise, it's what attracts many of us to thinking about spiritual matters—the gut-level perception, powerful if unproven, of an existence beyond the one of our mundane daily lives. *The Da Vinci Code* may be silly; but in its fashion, it's also thrilling. If its popularity means people are thinking about invisible realities, that's good news.

Gerald O'Collins (review date 15 December 2003)

SOURCE: O'Collins, Gerald. "Sensational Secrets." *America* 189, no. 20 (15 December 2003): 15-17.

[*In the following review, O'Collins finds that* The Da Vinci Code *contains many inaccuracies about the history of Christianity.*]

Dan Brown's *The Da Vinci Code* is a fast-paced, well-plotted murder mystery that takes the reader through the Louvre, a long night of murders and a police chase out of Paris to a wet morning in London. There the identity of the evil "Teacher" who masterminded the killings is revealed in the Chapter House of Westminster Abbey.

Using as his prime piece of evidence Leonardo Da Vinci's *Last Supper*, Brown proposes that the figure on Christ's right is not the beloved disciple but Mary Magdalene, who married Jesus and bore him a child. She was the Holy Grail for his blood and Jesus wanted her to succeed him in leading his followers. The official church suppressed the truth about Mary's relationship with Jesus and did its best to belittle her as a prostitute. So much for the tributes Church Fathers like Hippolytus, Gregory the Great and Leo the Great paid to her as "the apostle of the apostles," "the representative of the church" and "the new Eve announcing not death but life" to the male disciples!

Since the 12th century, a secret society called the Priory of Sion, which practices sex orgies, has safeguarded the "real," explosive secret of the Holy Grail: that Jesus was married to Mary Magdalene and that their bloodline continues today. Threatened with the loss of their personal prelature at the hands of a new, liberal pope, the bishop who leads Opus Dei promises help to the secretary of state, curiously called the "Secretariat Vaticana," who is the head of "the Secretariat Council" (a group that does not exist in the Roman Curia). A numerary of Opus Dei, a reformed killer, is set loose to recover from the leaders of the Prior of Sion the cryptex that contains the sensational secret about Jesus and Mary Magdalene.

There is to be no killing, but the plan goes astray. The mysterious Teacher provides the numerary with a gun and prompts him to kill four top officials of the priory and a nun who tries to defend a hiding place in the Church of Saint-Sulpice.

High on suspense, the novel concentrates on six major characters: a fanatical but ingenuous bishop of Opus Dei; Robert Langdon, a Harvard professor; Sophie Neveu, an attractive French cryptologist who turns out to be descended from Jesus and Mary Magdalene; Silas, a huge albino killer; Sir Leigh Teabing, an immensely wealthy seeker of the Holy Grail; and a brilliant French detective whose toughness conceals a heart of gold. A love affair develops between Robert and Sophie. But before they enjoy a week together in Florence, Robert returns to Paris to locate the resting place of Mary Magdalene, now disclosed as being under the Louvre Pyramid.

In *The New York Times* (8/3), Bruce Boucher exposed the eccentric nonsense about Leonardo that masquerades as new expertise. But there is more to be said about the effort to discredit mainstream Christianity and exalt the sacred feminine, and even goddess worship that was supposedly driven underground by orthodox church leaders.

Quite a few earlier writers have tried their hand at "proving" a liaison between Jesus and Mary Magdalene—notoriously Michael Baigent, Richard Leigh and Henry Lincoln in *Holy Blood, Holy Grail* (1982). They alleged that several royal families of Europe (but not the Windsors) are descended from Jesus and Mary. Brown is more cautious and names only the ancient Merovingians as belonging to Jesus' bloodline. His case rests on cracking the code of Leonardo's painting. But his interpretation, as Boucher shows, is "extremely eccentric" and, frankly, misinformed.

The Da Vinci Code teems with historical misinformation. The claim that the Emperor Constantine shifted the Christian day of worship to Sunday (p. 232) is simply false. Evidence from St. Paul and the Acts of the Apostles shows that right from the start of the Christian movement Christians replaced Saturday with Sunday as their day of worship. Sunday was the day when Jesus rose from the dead. What Constantine did on March 3, 321, was to decree Sunday to be a day of rest from work. He did not make Sunday the day of worship for Christians; it had been that from the first century.

Brown tells us that under pressure from Constantine, Christ was declared to be divine at the Council of Nicaea in 325. "Until that moment in his history Jesus was viewed by his followers as a mortal prophet . . . a great and powerful man, but a man nonetheless." Would Brown please read St John's Gospel, which has St. Thomas calling Jesus "My Lord and my God" and expresses Christ's divinity in many other passages. Decades before John's Gospel was finished, St. Paul's letters repeatedly affirm faith in Christ as divine. The Council of Nicaea did not invent faith in Christ's divinity but added another (semi-philosophical) way of confessing it—declaring his "being of one substance with the Father."

When pleading his case for the eternal feminine and goddess worship, Brown ignores recent scholarship and belittles the Jewish roots of Christianity. He assures us that "virtually all the elements of Catholic ritual—the miter, the altar, the doxology and communion, the act of 'God-eating'—were taken directly from earlier pagan mystery religions." Doesn't Brown know about the use of altars in Jewish worship, in which much of Christian ritual has its roots? The wearing of the miter by patriarchs and then by other bishops in Eastern Christianity originated from the emperor's crown. In the West the use of miters can be traced back to the 11th century, when the pagan mystery religions had long disappeared. The Christian doxology ("Glory be to the Father and to the Son and to the Holy Spirit") is based on some of the Jewish psalms (e.g., Psalms 8, 66, 150). Holy Communion has its origins in the Jewish Passover, celebrated by Jesus and his disciples on the night before he died.

Apropos of Judaism, Brown introduces some stunning errors about ritualistic sex and God. Old Testament scholars agree that prostitution was sometimes used to obtain money for the temple. But there is no convincing evidence for sacred or ritual prostitution, and none at all for Israelite men coming to the temple to experience the divine and achieve spiritual wholeness by having sex with priestesses (p. 309). On the same page, Brown explains that the Holy of Holies "housed not only God but also His powerful female equal, Shekinah." A word not found as such in the Bible but in later rabbinic writings, *Shekinah* refers to the nearness of God to his people and not to some female consort.

It is also breathtaking nonsense to assert as a "fact" that the sacred tetragrammaton, YHWH, was "derived from Jehovah, an androgynous physical union between the masculine *Jah* and the pre-Hebraic name for Eve, *Havah*." YHWH is written in Hebrew without any vowel signs. Jews did not pronounce the sacred name, but "Yahweh" was apparently the correct vocalization of the four consonants. In the 16th century some Christian writers introduced Jehovah, under the mistaken notion that the vowels they used were the correct ones. Jehovah is an artificial name created less than 500 years ago, and certainly not an ancient, androgynous name from which YHWH derived.

One could go on and on, pointing out the historical errors in *The Da Vinci Code.* One last example. Killing so-called witches was a horrible crime in the story of Christianity. But the idea that the Catholic Church burned at the stake "five *million* women" (p. 125) is bizarre. Savagery of that extent would have depopulated Europe. Experts give instead the figure of around 50,000 victims over the three centuries when witch hunts were carried out by Catholics and Protestants. But it suits the tenor of Brown's book to multiply the figure by 100.

The historical misinformation is put in the mouth of the villainous Sir Leigh Teabing, a former British Royal Historian (is there such a post?), and in the mouth of the hero, Robert Langdon, a "professor of symbology" (a new field to me). On their performance, I would not have given either of them their jobs, let alone voted for Langdon's tenure.

In short, enjoy the read, but discount the history. Dan Brown adds no new evidence to previous, discredited attempts to establish that Jesus was married to Mary Magdalene and fathered children by her.

Roz Shea (review date 10 February 2004)

SOURCE: Shea, Roz. Review of *The Da Vinci Code,* by Dan Brown. *Bookreporter.com* http://bookreporter.com/reviews/0385504209.asp (access date 10 February 2004).

[*In the following review, Shea calls* The Da Vinci Code *a stunning thriller that offers a new perspective on the legend of the Holy Grail. Shea asserts that Brown's extensive historical research adds intellectual depth to his story.*]

The search for the Holy Grail is one of the most intriguing enigmas of history, art and fiction. Speculation as to its location, its meaning, even its existence have fueled the imaginations of artists, writers, rulers and clerics for centuries. Dan Brown's **The Da Vinci Code** is a stunning new thriller that presents a new slant on the meaning of the very nature of this vessel, which was purported to hold the blood of Christ.

Harvard symbologist Robert Langdon is in Paris on business when he receives an urgent midnight call at his hotel from the Paris Judicial Police. The man he had planned to meet with the next day, a curator of the Louvre, has been found murdered in the Grand Gallery of the world's most famous art museum. Langdon has been summoned apparently because of his connection to the victim and his knowledge of ancient symbols.

He is rushed to the scene to find Jacques Sauniere's body lying spread-eagled and naked with a pentagram painted on his torso. He is told that Sauniere apparently painted the symbol on his own chest and arranged his body in the bizarre position before he died of a gunshot wound to the abdomen. Langdon's expertise in symbology and his acquaintance with the curator are called upon to help decipher the motive and help police find the killer.

Police detective Sophie Neveu from the Paris police cryptology division arrives on the scene; she and Langdon embark on a dangerous and frantic search for the murderer. They soon discover that Sauniere's message was not a clue to the identity of his killer, which is what the police believe, but instead holds a much deeper and significant message to mankind. The connections to the murderer reach into the very depths of some of the highest authorities of Europe.

Langdon and Neveu are ensnared in the ever-tightening mesh of this deadly triangle of power, as Langdon seeks to clear himself of suspicion of his colleague's murder. The desperate battle between The Priory of Sion, Opus Dei and the Vatican in the search for the Holy Grail airs one of the most fascinating theories on the Holy of Holies published in a very long time.

Dan Brown's extensive research on secret societies and symbology (he wrote *Angels & Demons,* a bestseller about secret Italian religious societies) adds intellectual depth to this page-turning thriller. His surprising revelations on Da Vinci's penchant for hiding codes in his paintings will lead the reader to search out renowned artistic icons as The Mona Lisa, The Madonna of the Rocks and The Last Supper. The Last Supper holds the most astonishing coded secrets of all and, after reading *The Da Vinci Code,* you will never see this famous painting in quite the same way again.

Brown has given us a controversial subject wrapped in thriller clothing that will provoke debate in the circles of religious and secret societies—and among readers. Curl up on the couch and dive into a title filled with speculation, action and intrigue.

Doris L. Eder (essay date 2004)

SOURCE: Eder, Doris L. "The Formula: The Novels of Dan Brown." *Contemporary Literary Criticism* 209, edited by Jeffrey W. Hunter. Farmington Hills, Mich.: Thomson Gale, 2005.

[*In the following essay, originally written in 2004, Eder examines the themes, style, and plot of Brown's novels.*]

THE FORMULA.

All Dan Brown's novels open with a prologue in which a corpse is found in an extraordinary position. The murdered man embodies a riddle that generates the plot or body of each novel. Successive murder victims are Ensei Tankado of *Digital Fortress*[1]—the Canadian geologist hurled from a helicopter to his death at the opening of *Deception Point*;[2] Leonardo Vetra, the scientist discovered dead in his lab in *Angels & Demons*;[3] and Jacques Saunière, curator at the Louvre, in *The Da Vinci Code.*[4] Similarly, each of Brown's novels concludes with an epilogue that brings each novel full circle, the epilogue following upon a tryst between hero and heroine. In the first novel, *Digital Fortress,* the romantic encounter in the Smoky Mountains between David Becker and Susan Fletcher has been postponed since the opening chapter. It precedes an epilogue linking Tankado to his estranged father, Japanese magnate Numakata, on the other side of the globe. The preternaturally symmetrical thriller *Deception Point* closes with its male and female protagonists, Michael Tolland and Rachel Sexton, guests of President Zach Herney in the White House, completing a tryst in the Lincoln Bedroom, preceding an epilogue in which Ekstrom, NASA's administrator, consigns his fake meteorite to the ocean whence it came. In *Angels & Demons,* the tryst between Vittoria Vetra and Robert Langdon itself constitutes the epilogue to the novel, whereas in *The Da Vinci Code,* a subtler work, there is just a promise of a future assignation between Langdon and Sophie Neveu. *The Da Vinci Code*'s epilogue brings Langdon back to the prologue's setting of the Louvre, where Langdon is at last able to solve the final riddle posed by Sophie's grandfather, Jacques Saunière. In each novel Brown tackles a different world, but he constantly refines an almost identical narrative formula.

PREEMINENCE OF PLOT.

Brown's plots are extremely complex and ingenious, each being woven of several strands—double, triple, multiple. In *Deception Point,* as many as six narrative strands intertwine. The plots of the three most recent novels are particularly symmetrical—*Deception Point* in its line-up of opposing agencies and individual political opponents; *Angels & Demons* in its array of ambigrams,[5] and its ritual brandings and murders; and *The Da Vinci Code* with its repetitive planting and solving of Saunière's clues and riddles. Both *Angels & Demons* and *The Da Vinci Code,* the two Robert Langdon thrillers to date, begin with Langdon being summoned at night by an unknown individual to help solve a murder case. For the most part Brown handles exposition adroitly. Instead of inserting it en bloc at the outset—or, worse, at the end of the action—it is interwoven with it, offered in doses, as required. One particularly admires how exposition is handled in *Deception Point* by a bevy of experts chosen by the president to authenticate and explain NASA's latest discovery to the world. Similarly, having a Harvard professor of symbology (Robert Langdon) discourse on the esoterica with which *The Da Vinci Code* is crammed makes sense.

E. M. Forster held that the tapeworm of plot "is the lowest or simplest of literary organisms," as also the highest common factor present in the novel. As Forster says, if plot is isolated from everything else, the sole measure of its success—or failure—is that it should make the reader want to know what happens next.[6] Certainly, Brown is a master at keeping the reader turning the page to find out exactly that. However, when you have marveled at his razzle-dazzle plots, you will find other elements in Brown's novels, such as setting, characterization, and style, very much wanting.

These novels all feature secret societies, ancient and modern: the National Security Agency in *Digital Fortress*; the National Reconnaissance Office (NRO), the National Aeronautics and Space Administration (NASA), and the Delta Force in *Deception Point*; CERN (Centre Européen de Recherche Nucléaire), the Vatican, and the *Illuminati* in *Angels & Demons,* and, in *The Da Vinci Code,* the Catholic Church, *Opus Dei,* and the Priory of Sion. The author has shed light on his interest in cryptography and secret societies by remarking, "I grew up around codes and ciphers."[7] Asked why he is obsessed with secret societies, Brown says this "interest sparks from growing up in New England, surrounded by clandestine clubs of Ivy League universities, the Masonic lodges of our Founding Fathers, and the hidden hallways of early government power. New England has a long tradition of elite clubs, private fraternities, and secrecy."[8] As for his attempts to build bridges between science and art or religion and science, Dan Brown is the son of a national award-winning professor of mathematics and a professional sacred musician, so he grew up inhabiting different cultures. His wife, Blythe, is a painter and art historian who helps with his research, accompanying him on travels on which Brown collects data and carries out novelistic research.

All Brown's novels have apocalyptic climaxes: the destruction of TRANSLTR, the world's most powerful secret supercomputer because of the introduction of an impregnable code in *Digital Fortress*; the thrilling sequences on the Milne Glacier and aboard the *Goya,* when the magma dome explodes in *Deception Point*; the explosion of the canister of antimatter and the brief subsequent apotheosis of Carlo Ventresca in *Angels & Demons*; and, in *The Da Vinci Code,* the climactic scene near Sir Isaac Newton's tomb in Westminster Abbey. A more intriguing aspect of his formula, however, are the reversals the author brings about, whereby a seemingly benign father figure, who may even appear to be a savior, is instead revealed to be a villain. (Conversely, the seeming villain or nemesis may ultimately be found to nurture the best possible motives.) Such reversals center on the figures of Commander Trevor Strathmore and his opponent, Ensei Tankado, of *Digital Fortress*; on William Pickering in *Deception Point*; on the saintly Carlo Ventresca in *Angels & Demons,* and on Sir Leigh Teabing in *The Da Vinci Code.* They are generally well-managed, the exception being the reversal in *Angels & Demons,* for it is utterly implausible that Ventresca would have gone through the conspiratorial machinations depicted, which endanger everything dear to him—the Catholic Church, Vatican City, and the City of Rome—not to mention himself.

Settings.

Brown revels in exotic settings, distant in time and place. He advises fellow writers to expose their readers to new worlds.[9] The setting in a Brown novel is concrete and specific without being particularly evocative or atmospheric. He does better with Old World settings such as Rome and Vatican City in *Angels & Demons* or Paris in *The Da Vinci Code* than he does with the colossal, aseptic governmental agencies that loom large in *Digital Fortress* and *Deception Point*—although the Arctic chase in the latter is full of chills, thrills, and

spills. The international mystery-thrillers are therefore more seductive than the others. This author has been praised for the scope of his research—geographic, historical, scientific, and religio-mythic—and for the accuracy of his settings. In line with a contemporary love affair with virtual reality, there is now a vogue for *Da Vinci Code* European tours through which readers may validate the many buildings and monuments that figure in his final novel's labyrinthine plot. However, topographical details in these two novels, like some of their topics and themes, are pop, schlock, or superficial, containing little not to be found in standard guidebooks, handbooks, and encyclopedias.

Brown's main and subplots characteristically take place in alternating locales. In *Digital Fortress* the principal action involving protagonist Susan Fletcher centers on the National Security Agency in Fort Meade, while her lover David Becker, a language teacher from Georgetown University, is dispatched to Seville to track down Tankado's assassin, and there participates in a series of cat-and-mouse adventures, improbably preserving himself through a series of close brushes with death. (The Seville sequence is utterly implausible.) In *Deception Point,* the action alternates between Washington, D.C. and the Milne Ice Shelf, to which certain experts have been dispatched to testify to the authenticity of NASA's latest find. In *Angels & Demons* the ultramodern metal, glass, plastic, and chrome facility at CERN (European Council for Nuclear Research) contrasts with the age-old buildings and monuments and the colorful Renaissance costumes of Rome, Vatican City, and the Swiss Guard. *The Da Vinci Code* is set primarily in Paris and its environs, although towards the end of the novel the principal characters move to London and Scotland.

Time-scheme.

Action in a Brown novel proceeds at a breathless pace. Again, in his advice to writers on how to get published, Dan Brown urges that a novel's action be subjected to a ticking clock, since "nothing intensifies dramatic tension like time pressure," which compels characters to act.[10] Sometimes Brown observes an almost Aristotelian dramatic unity, arranging that the action of an entire novel takes place on a single day. Aside from a few flashbacks to fill in background and establish characters and their relationships, *Digital Fortress*'s main action takes place over a Saturday and Sunday, in split-screen mode, in the United States capital and in Spain. It is difficult to trace how much time passes between Rachel's power breakfast with her father, Senator Sexton, and her final romantic encounter with Michael Tolland in the Lincoln Bedroom in *Deception Point* because this novel's action is both extended and many-stranded, but one senses its clock ticking throughout. In *Angels & Demons,* whose action covers a little over twenty-four hours, time and place are charted with pinpoint accuracy. Langdon is awoken at 5:18 a.m. by Maximilian Kohler, a little over an hour later he is winging his way toward Geneva at 11,000 m.p.h.; later that afternoon, accompanied by Vittoria Vetra, he arrives in Rome aboard the papal helicopter. A warning call seemingly from the *Illuminati* to the Vatican about the forthcoming ritual murders of the four cardinals most eligible to become pope is issued an hour and a half before the first murder is to take place—at 8 p.m. Three more murder-brandings duly take place on the point of each successive hour, with Vatican City predicted to blow up at midnight. At four minutes to midnight, Ventresca and Langdon fly the canister of antimatter up into the heavens. Next day, Vittoria and Robert Langdon meet at the Hotel Bernini, destruction having been averted and another pope elected.

The action of *The Da Vinci Code* also takes place over two days; its time scheme is more persuasive or credible than that of *Angels & Demons.* One can imagine Brown assuring one that Langdon and Vittoria could make their way in the time allotted from the Vatican Library to the Pantheon to the Chigi Chapel to St. Peter's Square to Santa Maria della Vittoria and to the Piazza Navona. But the frantic pace of this novel allows for neither contingency nor delay; Langdon and Vittoria do not have nearly enough time to solve the many riddles and codes confronting them. And the drastic nature of the actions portrayed—particularly Langdon's plummeting into the Tiber with only a homemade parachute and still living to tell the tale—would have taken up much more time than Dan Brown allows.

CHARACTERS.

It is worth examining the three types of character who people a Brown thriller. Least satisfactory are his villainous hit men or professional killers, uniformly cardboard figures, who speak and act in a way that defies belief. Among their ranks are Hulohot, the Portuguese mercenary in *Digital Fortress*; the stage Arab Hassassin of *Angels & Demons*; and the self-mortifying albino monk Silas, henchman of Opus Dei in *The Da Vinci Code.* The three Delta Force operatives of *Deception Point* are not meant to be human, and because they lack humanity, readers are not tempted to judge or evaluate their credibility as human beings.

Then there are the lead characters, paired male and female protagonists: Susan Fletcher and David Becker (in *Digital Fortress*); Rachel Sexton and Michael Tolland (in *Deception Point*); Robert Langdon and Vittoria Vetra (in *Angels & Demons*), and Langdon and Sophie Neveu (in *The Da Vinci Code*). Brown's heroines are all brainy and beautiful, quick-witted, courageous, and resourceful, but also vulnerable. His plots truly center

on them and his novels have a feminist aura and a measure of political correctness that sorts oddly with the genre's traditionally male chauvinist cast. One sees steady character development in the female leads, from the first through the last novels. Rachel, daughter of smooth con man Senator Sedgewick Sexton, is an improvement on Susan Fletcher, while Vittoria Vetra, the epitome of Mediterranean beauty, is more complex, earthy, and interesting than either. Finally, Sophie Neveu is the most engaging young woman of all, various and complex.

Brown's male protagonists also develop, from Becker through Tolland to Langdon, and Robert Langdon gains in complexity between the thrillers set in Rome and Paris, respectively. Langdon is a real find, in fact—a clever expository device for presenting complex ideas plausibly, since he is a professor of symbology, and so able to hold forth on complex topics, yet remain in character. By the time he appears in *The Da Vinci Code,* he has a recognizable, distinct personality, erudite but a good sportsman, empathetic yet with a wry sense of humor. And Brown even equips his heroes and heroines with flaws or physical failings: Langdon suffers from claustrophobia because he fell down a well as a small boy, while Rachel has a horror of icy water because she almost drowned in any icy pond when a little girl.

Brown's arch villains are most interesting of all, for they initially present themselves in the guise of benign father figures or saviors. This is particularly true of Trevor Strathmore of *Digital Fortress* and of Carlo Ventresca, the *camerlengo* of *The Da Vinci Code*; to a lesser extent, it applies to William Pickering of *Deception Point,* and certainly to the intriguing figure of Leigh Teabing in the final novel. Outside these categories, Brown is capable of creating some well-rounded stereotypes—consider, for instance, Senator Sexton and Marjorie Tench of *Deception Point.*

THEMES.

Blockbuster thrillers need not have themes. However, the motto engraved on Ensei Tankado's ring in *Digital Fortress, Quis custodiet ipsos custodes?* might well stand as an epigraph to all Brown's novels and might also be construed as their common theme. Juvenal first posed the question "But who is to guard the guards themselves?" In Brown's first novel, Commander Strathmore of the NSA is convinced that the most important thing in the universe is United States security, and thus believes himself ordained to spy on all and sundry with impunity. Similarly, in *Deception Point,* William Pickering, director of the National Reconnaissance Office, convinced that the end justifies the means, assures his employee Rachel that it was essential to save NASA and to preserve it as a government agency: that he did so by perpetrating a colossal fraud, that he deceived his president and brought about the deaths of half a dozen people is of little consequence beside this. The ultimate authority in *Angels & Demons* resides in the Catholic Church. The seemingly saintly chamberlain to the late pope is not only a parricide who has murdered him; he is also guilty of the deaths of two eminent scientists and of those of the four most eligible future candidates for the papacy. In addition, he endangers Vatican City and Rome, with all their treasures, sacred and temporal, by having antimatter smuggled into St. Peter's—and for what? Because he hates the soulless onward march of science/technology. Ventresca/Janus ascribes his crimes to the Church's inveterate enemy, the *Illuminati,* an ancient brotherhood of enlightened scientists who opposed the Church's attempts to quash scientific investigation of the universe but who still believed religion and science might be reconciled. In *The Da Vinci Code* a three-cornered conspiracy exists between the Priory of Sion, the Catholic Church, and its most militant offshoot, Opus Dei, concerning the two-thousand-year-old secret of the Holy Grail (*Sangreal* or *Sang Real*).[11] Saunière is murdered because he was the grandmaster of the Priory of Sion who kept this secret. Opus Dei seek to expose it, and the Catholic Church to keep it hidden.

Several reviewers see Brown's real subject as the thin line or grey area separating individual privacy and freedom from public investigation and scrutiny. He records what happens when, as Michelle Delio puts it, "personal privacy slams up against national security or institutional interests."[12]

GENRE.

Brown's genre is the mystery or techno-thriller. He is most often compared with Tom Clancy, although David Lazarus, in a review for the *San Francisco Chronicle,* thinks of him as "Umberto Eco on steroids."[13] Science, technology, and gadgetry play a significant role in Brown's thrillers, particularly in *Digital Fortress* and *Deception Point.* What Clancy and Brown have in common is ingenious plotting, a penchant for conspiracy theories, a complete grasp of the specifics of whatever world they choose to write about, and stereotypical, rather wooden characters. Clancy's novels demonstrate greater mastery of technical detail than Brown's, but Brown's dialogue is superior—which is not difficult, for Clancy's people all seem to speak with one voice.

STYLE.

Brown's style improves over the course of four novels, the writing in *The Da Vinci Code* being more integrated and subtle and less peppered with egregious errors than it is in the preceding novels. A modicum of humor even plays about the figure of Robert Langdon that is not present in *Angels & Demons. The Da Vinci Code*'s

opening page nonetheless offers a sample of what Dan Brown's readers must contend with. Like other writers of techno- and mystery thrillers, this author revels in dynamic, supercharged verbs—the opening page offers "staggered, collapsed, tore, thundering, barricading, gasping, froze." Brown's verb choices can go way over the top, as in the following two examples: "a devastating loss whose emotional scars still raked at Rachel's heart" (*DP* [*Deception Point*], 10) or "Langdon wondered if the intense chill now raking through his body was the air-conditioning or his utter amazement with the significance of what he was now staring at." (*A&D* [*Angels & Demons*], 38). The latter sentence also shows Brown's characteristically inept, unidiomatic handling of prepositions. And how about this? "As the grief strafed her heart, a new emotion surged into Vittoria's consciousness" (*A&D,* 117). Brown's metaphors are too concrete and his reference can be ambiguous, as in "Langdon's thoughts were a blur as they raced toward the edifice." (*A&D,* 340)

Metaphors are not just mixed, but piled one upon another to such an extent they result in absurdity. Examples: "Then, like a snake uncoiling, he heaved a long sigh and picked up the pace." (This is a most inapt description of Ekstrom, head of NASA, since Ekstrom has been described as a Viking of a man—*DP,* 79) Or there is this evocation of Langdon's response to the murder that opens *Angels & Demons*: "The sun helped dissolve the image of the empty eye socket emblazoned into his mind." (*A&D,* 62)

Angels & Demons introduces Robert Langdon for the first time. The professor of symbology from Harvard is a middle-aged hunk with "erudite appeal." Introducing him, Brown writes, "A dark stubble was shrouding his strong jaw and dimpled chin." (*DVC* [*Da Vinci Code*], 8). And behold Mediterranean siren Vittoria Vetra: "Her limbs were strong and toned, radiating the healthy luminescence of Mediterranean flesh that had enjoyed long hours in the sun." (*A&D,* 65) These descriptions are typical of true romance or bodice rippers. That of the French police chief Bezu Fache, or le Taureau, is like an animated cartoon, reminding one of Ferdinand the Bull: "As he advanced, his dark eyes seemed to scorch the earth before him, radiating a fierce clarity that forecast his reputation for unblinking severity in all matters." (*DVC,* 21)

A besetting fault is Brown's failure to get the simplest sensory details right. Here is a sample of the kind of technical prose the author handles with ease: "Runs on slush hydrogen. The shell's a titanium matrix with silicon carbide filters. She packs a 20:1 thrust/weight ratio; most jets run at 7:1." (*A&D,* 13) But in something as simple as an account of how Langdon is dressed, the author trips up: "A crisp breeze rustled the lapels of his tweed jacket." (*A&D,* 19) What price rustling tweed?

As a former English teacher, it is astonishing how many grammatical errors and solecisms Brown is guilty of. Perhaps some bloopers are caused by a habit of writing down to his audience but their prevalence can only be attributed to sloppy editing, though Brown claims to edit himself assiduously. On his Website, he declares that "editing yourself is the most important part of being a novelist. . . . For every page in *The Da Vinci Code,* I wrote ten that ended up in the trash."[14]

Certainly, there is little evidence of external editing except in his final novel, *The Da Vinci Code.* Even so, the following failures to edit are drawn from that novel: "Equally as bizarre was the series of numbers" (of Saunière's cryptic death message—43). "Saunière had apparently lay down . . ." for lain down (44). "She was finally feeling like she could breathe normally again" (139).

Certain stylistic quirks stem from vocabulary—there are a few words Brown loves to use but whose exact meaning remains obscure to him. Among these are the verbs "to burgeon," the past participle "wrought," and the noun "indignity," mistaken for indignation. In *Deception Point* (187) a government official hands someone a "burgeoning manila folder." (The file might have burgeoned before or after it was handed over but could not do so during the transfer. Presumably "bulging" is what was intended.) *The Da Vinci Code* also offers this grandiloquent description of Westminster Abbey: "The colossal stone interior burgeons with the remains of kings, statesmen, scientists, poets, and musicians." (395) In *Deception Point,* a project is "wrought with failure" and in another novel "the man's voice was wrought with conviction" (*A&D,* 498). William Pickering assures Marjorie Tench in *Deception Point*: "Your indignity has no resonance with me, so save it." (338)

This is not to say there is not some good writing to be found, but it is the exception rather than the norm. In *The Da Vinci Code,* the inside knowledge of the museum world is intriguing, the evocation of the Louvre at night, felicitous: "Langdon followed, his vision slowly adjusting to the dark. All around large-format oils began to materialize like photos developing before him in an enormous darkroom . . . their eyes following as he moved through the rooms." (25) For once, an apt simile is found.

PUBLISHING PHENOMENON.

The Da Vinci Code has been at or close to the top of *The New York Times* best-seller list for over a year and has sold over seven million copies. It has been translated into forty languages and the film rights have been sold. It should make a fine movie, for Brown's technique is intrinsically cinematic. At the time of writing, *Angels & Demons, Deception Point,* and *Digital*

Fortress are all on *The Times*'s list of mass-market paperback best sellers. The author did not achieve blockbuster success until he moved, along with his editor, Jason Kaufman, from Pocket Books to Doubleday in 2001. Doubleday were extremely generous in sending out advance copies of *The Da Vinci Code.*[15]

It has not hurt sales that the novel has stirred protest and controversy among the religious, while a body of ingenuous readers have been deluded into taking its versions of sacred goddess worship, the Holy Grail, the Knights Templar, the Priory of Sion, Christianity, Mary Magdalene, and other matters as gospel. Such literal readers swallow whole Brown's statement that the only fictional elements in his book are "the characters and the action that takes place. All of the locations, the paintings, the ancient history, the secret documents, the rituals, all of this is factual."[16] Although places and events, secret organizations and beliefs prominent in the fiction have left traces in history and found expression in diverse works of art and literature (from Leonardo da Vinci to Walt Disney, according to Brown), some of the sources are dubious, to say the least. In an article entitled "The Last Word: The Da Vinci Con," Laura Miller remarks that the phenomenal success of Brown's final novel "has lifted some pretty odd boats," and points to a spurious source. *The Da Vinci Code* shows indebtedness to Michael Baigent, Richard Leigh, and Henry Lincoln's *Holy Blood, Holy Grail,* another book about the Priory of Sion, published in 1983 and a best seller twenty years ago. Miller sums this up as a bogus but impressive pop pseudohistory.[17] Curiously, it closely resembles Teabing's exposition to Sophie in *The Da Vinci Code* of the history of the Holy Grail. And interestingly, for an author fond of anagrams, the name Teabing turns out to be an anagram of Baigent, while the name Saunière appears also to derive from *Holy Blood, Holy Grail.*[18] Meantime, other new boats are bobbing on the swell raised by Brown's blockbuster. *The Da Vinci Code*'s success has prompted publication of a slew of related titles such as Darrell L. Bock's *Breaking the Da Vinci Code,* Dan Burstein's *Secrets of the Code: The Unauthorized Guide to the Mysteries behind "The Da Vinci Code,"* James L. Garlow and Peter Jones's *Cracking Da Vinci's Code,* and Betsy Eble's *Depth & Details: A Reader's Guide to Dan Brown's "The Da Vinci Code."*

Notes

1. This novel was first published by St. Martin's Press in 1998. The edition referred to throughout this essay is the paperback issued by the same publisher in 2004. Further references throughout the text are abbreviated *DF.*

2. This novel was first published by Pocket Books in 2001. The edition referred to throughout was published by Atria Books in 2001. All references to

this edition are abbreviated *DP.* Although *Deception Point* was published after *Angels & Demons,* the two techno-thrillers, *Digital Fortress* and *Deception Point,* are discussed together and the two international mysteries, *Angels & Demons* and *The Da Vinci Code,* are also paired for consideration because they have certain affinities. The novels are therefore not discussed in order of publication.

3. This novel was first published by Pocket Books in 2000. The edition referred to throughout is the large-print edition issued by Random House the same year. References are abbreviated *A&D.*

4. This novel was first published by Doubleday in 2003, which is the edition referred to throughout. Further references are abbreviated *DVC.*

5. The ambigrams are words like vertical palindromes—i.e. they read the same from above or from below. In his acknowledgments, Brown thanks artist John Langdon—note the name—for producing a series of these throughout the novel.

6. *Aspects of the Novel* (New York: Harcourt, Brace & World 1954, pp. 27-28.

7. In an interview with Edward Morris—see his review for *BookPage,* April 2003—www.bookpage.com.

8. Consult FAQs under *The Da Vinci Code* on Dan Brown's own Website—http://www.danbrown.com/novels/davinci_code/faqs.html.

9. See Brown's "Getting Published: Seven Powerful Tips," www.danbrown.com/tips.htm.

10. Ibid.

11. *The Da Vinci Code* is about the search for the Holy Grail, not as symbolized by the traditional chalice with which Christ instituted the Eucharist but rather as epitomized by a woman who represents, in Brown's terms, "the lost sacred feminine." Other terms for the Holy Grail are *Sangreal* or *Sang Real,* the latter referring to the idea that Christ was not divine but mortal, that he married Mary Magdalene and established with her a mortal bloodline traceable to the Merovingian kings of France. See also fn. 17.

12. See "Da Vinci: Father of Cryptography?" http://www.wired/com.

13. This review, dated April 6, 2003, may be found at www.reviewsofbooks.com/da_vinci_code/.

14. http://www.danbrown.com/novels/davinci_code/faqs.html.

15. Valerie MacEwan "Try Putting This Book Down," *PopMatters Magazine*—http://www.popmatters.com/books/reviews/d/da-vinci-code/shtml.

16. See Dan Brown's interview with Linda Wertheimer for NPR on April 26, 2003, available at http://elibrary.bigchalk.com/.

17. Sunday *New York Times,* February 22, 2003, late ed., sect. 7, col. 1, p. 23.

18. For this anagrammatic insight, see Roxanne Roberts's review for the *Washington Post,* July 20, 2003, also available at http://elibrary.bigchalk.com/.

Bruce Allen (essay date 2005)

SOURCE: Allen, Bruce. "Decoding Dan Brown's Success." In *Contemporary Literary Criticism* 209, edited by Jeffrey W. Hunter. Farmington Hills, Mich.: Thomson Gale, 2005.

[*In the following essay, Allen discusses Brown's oeuvre, commenting on plot, characterization, and other elements within* Angels & Demons, Deception Point, *and* The Da Vinci Code.]

Rafael Sabatini, of course. Nathaniel Hawthorne has the right ring, Gabriel Garcia Marquez, an irresistible lilting rhythm. But "Dan Brown"?

Unprepossessing handle aside, this hardworking native of the smallish non-metropolis of Exeter, New Hampshire (renowned nevertheless as the home of one of the nation's oldest and best preparatory schools) has become a "name" such as—and, arguably, even more commercially potent than that of—Stephen King.

Brown's four hefty best-sellers, all published within the brief five-year period 1998-2003, have earned him accolades as a "new master of smart thrills" (*People Magazine*), "a more astute storyteller than most of his brethren in the thriller vein" (*Kirkus Reviews*), and "one of the best, smartest, and most accomplished writers in the country" (fellow best-selling author Nelson De Mille).

And, with his most recent blockbuster **The Da Vinci Code,** Brown reached unprecedented heights of commercial success. As of this writing (almost exactly two years after its publication), this engagingly intricate tale of globe- and time-hopping intrigue has spent (count 'em) 114 weeks on the *New York Times Book Review*'s hardcover best seller list (in both its original edition and the special illustrated one, priced at a cool $35, which appeared in October, 2004), resting serenely in sixth place.

In addition to this novel's 18 million copies sold, the softcover edition of Brown's second novel **Angels & Demons** presently occupies fifth place on the *NYTBR*'s paperback best seller list (97 weeks, and counting), trailed by **Code**'s immediate predecessor **Deception Point** (a paltry 55 weeks).

Dan Brown's rapid acquisition of fame and fortune may well have been (pardon the expression) encoded in his genes. He grew up in Exeter, the son of a highly respected (now retired) professor of mathematics and author of several standard math textbooks (as well as a 1989 recipient of a Presidential Medal for Excellence in Science and Mathematics Teaching) and a mother who is a professional musician.

Dan, who was born in 1964 and is the eldest of this accomplished couple's three children, attended Phillips Exeter Academy (graduating in 1982)—to which he would return, to teach English, following a brief (not unsuccessful) career in California as a songwriter and pianist. A tour of Spain, during which he studied art history, ensued, as did Brown's marriage to Blythe, an art historian and painter who doubles—or, if you will, triples—as her husband's research partner.

(A few sparse further biographical facts are available on Brown's rather Spartan website www.danbrown.com, which really isn't much more than a vehicle for drawing attention to his spectacularly successful fiction.)

In any case, whatever plans Brown might have had for either a musical career or an academic one as extensive and distinguished as his father's, began to fade in 1998 with the publication of his first novel *Digital Fortress.* This fast-paced caper, about a threat to the security and integrity of a (fictional) code-breaking branch of the United States Intelligence Agency, was an immediate financial (and, to a slightly lesser degree, critical) success. It sold formidably well, and was hailed as a "crisp and pungent first thriller (and designated as an Amazon-.com Recommended Book) and a "disturbing, cutting-edge techno-thriller which should galvanize everyone who sends or receives e-mail or even dreams of navigating the Web" (genre author John J. Nance).

Considering the fact that it was written while its author was employed as a full-time teacher, *Digital Fortress* is an impressively tightly woven piece of work. In short, punchy chapters that convey information (and ratchet up suspense) quite economically, Brown conflates several interconnected plots, all spun from the suspicious death of a Japanese computer genius (whose body is found in Seville) and connected to the branch of the United States's National Security Agency by which the dead man (Ensei Tankado) had been employed, and from which he had been "dismissed."

Brown's title denotes a mathematical construct and computer program created by Tankado that challenges the "wits" of the NSA's super computer TRANSLTR, heretofore capable of unscrambling any code pertaining to terrorist activity or other threats to U.S. internal security. Enter statuesque cryptographer and NSA operative Susan Fletcher, her equally brainy and beautiful fiancé, civilian college professor and foreign language

specialist David Becker (a sometime NSA operative), and the transcontinental race is on—to retrieve the "kill code" that can deactivate Digital Fortress, prevent the theft and misuse of top national secrets affiliated with and protected by TRANSLTR, and soothe the compromised nerves of Susan's boss and fellow genius, Commander Trevor Strathmore.

It's all great fun, reaching a series of staggered climaxes in the troubled bowels of the NSA's top-secret main building. And strict credibility isn't really the issue. Crises multiply exponentially, new villains pop up at judiciously spaced intervals, and dialogue is dedicated more to the purpose of explicating complex technical information than in the service of creating characters who think and talk like recognizable human beings. Characterization is in fact quite minimal. Susan Fletcher is an intrepid Amazon, David Becker an erudite GQ model, Commander Strathmore a conventionally conflicted upper-echelon bureaucrat. Interestingly enough, the character invested with the most life is the dead man Tankado, whose personal history is expertly linked to the book's surrounding plot, and disclosed, piecemeal, with considerable skill.

The success of *Digital Fortress* enabled Brown to become a full-time writer, and led to the publication (in 2000) of the novel the author himself has called "the prologue to *The Da Vinci Code.*" *Angels & Demons* introduces the character who is essentially a refinement of *Digital Fortress*'s David Becker: Harvard professor of Religious Iconology and Art History Robert Langdon.

The novel begins smashingly (so to speak), in a late-night phone call to Langdon placed by research scientist Maximilian Kohler, who informs Langdon that one of the world's leading physicists, Leonardo Vetra (who was also a Catholic priest), has been brutally murdered, his body mutilated, the word "Illuminati" branded onto his chest.

Langdon is of course an expert on the history of the sinister ancient society thus anatomically evoked: a gathering of intellectuals who prized the unrestricted pursuit of secular learning above the restraints of formal religion, thus incurring the enmity of the Catholic church and resulting in the persecution and execution of various offending Illuminati.

Therefore, Langdon is whisked off to Switzerland, where Kohler presides as director of CERN (the "Conseile Européen pour la Recherche Nucléaire"), a globally important think-tank where the late Vetra had recently conducted some explosively innovative research.

Kohler, a wheelchair-bound character who evokes instant memories of Peter Sellers as Dr. Strangelove, introduces Langdon to Vetra's inexcusably beautiful and brilliant adopted daughter Vittoria (herself an accomplished physicist)—and to the unsettling information that Vetra, bent on re-creating the "big bang" whereby (in the majority of modern scientific information) the universe was created, by producing "antimatter" (roughly, a substance composed of atoms whose particles are in effect mirror images of matter's components—whose electrical properties are thus the reverse of matter's electrical properties). The problem: should matter and antimatter ever "meet," their collision would create an explosion of unthinkably catastrophic proportions.

The antimatter that Vetra had concocted (with Vittoria's assistance—so that she may fill Langdon, and us, in on relevant recondite information) was of course safely stored ("suspended" in a sealed container), but has gone missing.

Juxtaposed brief chapters introduce a nameless "assassin" who pursues the criminal agenda of pseudonymous arch-bad guy "Janus"—and lead the plot to Rome, and thence Vatican City, where a conclave is in progress, charged with choosing a successor to the recently deceased Holy Father.

Langdon and Vittoria manage to keep their minds off each other's physical perfections (she's a young Sophia Loren, he's a gracefully aging Harrison Ford) and on the danger at hand (a time bomb planted in the Vatican), as Brown's plot uncoils—again, in quick, vivid chapters, virtually each of which has its own cliffhanger ending.

As he did in *Digital Fortress,* Brown fills the novel with highly specific information. You'll come away from this book entertained, but you'll also know a little more about the process of choosing a new pope, the history of the Illuminati, and even the rarefied field of atomic physics. The presence of several endangered Cardinals, and the concept of a logical proof "that Genesis is a scientific possibility," among other intricacies, season the mix agreeably. The sheer exuberant inventiveness of *Angels & Demons* goes a long way toward obliterating readers' memories of its generic characters, Hollywood ending, and continual recourse to summary clichés (e.g., "Nothing captured human interest like human tragedy").

The reading audience captured, and captivated by Brown's boffo second novel was more than ready when his third, *Deception Point,* was published in 2001. This is a racy combination of science, politics, and recent history—a venture into territory patrolled in recent years by Tom Clancy, and another noteworthy example of Brown's ability to absorb complex technical information and reshape it into absorbing narrative.

Once again, paired adventurers of both genders undertake a dangerous mission, as White House Intelligence analyst Rachel Sexton is sent by the U.S.

President (who's under siege in an election year, trailing his challenger in the polls) to the Arctic, where the discovery of an ancient meteorite beneath the icy terrain of far northern Ellesmere Island strongly suggests the possibility of intelligent life on other planets.

Rachel's mission is interrupted and complicated by communications with an increasingly embattled and paranoid administration, the bickering priorities of various federal agencies, and the presence of a charismatic marine scientist and television personality who plays Robert Langdon to her Vittoria Vetra, David Becker to her Susan Fletcher.

The villain this time is a vicious powerbroker aided by a team of highly skilled assassins, all of whom will Stop at Nothing to Hide the Truth about what the discovery on Ellesmere Island signifies. (It's as if the Wizard of Oz had eschewed mere mystification, and moved on to the more complex satisfactions of genocide.)

Deception Point speaks confidently to the paranoid in all of us, positing a world in which government officials are perfectly willing, in fact eager, to commit any number of atrocious crimes in the name of national security. Prominent among this novel's chief pleasures are its delayed revelations of who's guilty of what and is or are colluding with whom. The rapid jump-cuts among its several intersecting plots are handled with genuine skill, in what may well be Brown's single most artful narrative construction thus far. Its characters aren't exactly real people, and one does upon reflection despair for the future of a planet whose survival presumably depends upon the selfless dedication of impossibly beautiful, accomplished, and fearless people. Nevertheless, if you buy Brown's blithely unrealistic premises, *Deception Point* delivers the goods.

By the time his third successive best seller had made Dan Brown's name a word in households around the world, we might have been prepared for the phenomenon of *The Da Vinci Code.* Published in June, 2003, it began its conquest of the *New York Times*'s fiction best seller list in the number one spot, and the rest has been publishing history.

It's the adult equivalent of J. K. Rowling's Harry Potter novels. More than 25 million copies in print. Hundreds of thousands of copies of its audio version sold. Rave reviews calling it "Blockbuster perfection" (the *New York Times*), a "masterpiece" (*Library Journal*), and "an ingenious mixture of paranoid thriller, art history lesson, chase story, religious symbology lecture, and anticlerical screed (*Salon.com*).

A feature film version, directed by Academy Award winner Ron Howard and starring double Oscar winner Tom Hanks is scheduled for release in 2006. The book is on sale *everywhere*: at airports, in drugstores, "super stores" like Walton's, and so on. *Code*'s success has undoubtedly inspired and paved the way for such history- and information-laden literary thrillers as Matthew Pearl's *The Dante Club,* Jon Fasman's *The Geographer's Library, The Rule of Four* by Ian Caldwell and Dustin Thomason, and Elizabeth Kostova's lavish reworking of the Dracula legend, *The Historian.*

Besides creating this coattail effect, Brown's pop masterpiece has provoked a number of attacks and exposés of its historical "inaccuracies" (e.g., *The Da Vinci Hoax, Truth and Fiction in "The Da Vinci Code"*): examples of a fine frenzy of scholarly overreaction not un-akin to former Vice President Dan Quayle's umbrageous chastising of fictional TV character Murphy Brown).

And, in a further illustration of the erudition that seems to run (as hair or eye color does in other families) in the Brown family, Dan's father Richard is reportedly devising a lecture and slide-show explaining the role of "Mathematics in *The Da Vinci Code.*"

While the world may indeed welcome such audio-visual explication, the last thing it needs is a fully detailed summary of this already legendary novel's plot. Suffice it to say that Harvard's own Robert Langdon is once again engaged to decipher mysterious images, this time related to the murder of the elderly curator of Paris's Louvre Museum. The unfortunate victim, you see, had the presence of mind, during his agonizing dying moments, to make of his demise a tableau that incorporated a classic Renaissance image (that of the human figure in Leonardo Da Vinci's celebrated drawing "The Vitruvian Man"), and comprised a series of clues pointing to a conspiracy that had spanned several centuries and involved such major historical figures as Sir Isaac Newton, painter Sandro Botticelli, and poet-novelist Victor Hugo, as well as the versatile genius Leonardo himself.

As he did in *Angels & Demons,* Brown pits the commercial and political exigencies of secular organizations against the vested interests of a tradition-bound church. A hoard of secret documents, we gradually learn, contains information regarding a story (not original with Brown) that Jesus did not die on the cross, instead surviving to marry Mary Magdalene, and father a line of kings.

Brown's twist on this tale is the supposition that the secret history of Jesus has been guarded through the centuries by an underground society known as the Priory of Sion (of which Da Vinci was a member), and that clues to this history are encoded in Da Vinci's famous painting of *The Last Supper* and elsewhere in his work.

It's a very fertile idea, from which Brown constructs a series of (literal) puzzles that challenge the ingenuity of the increasingly bedazzled Langdon, his female companion sleuth du jour (smoldering police cryptologist Sophie Neveu), the conservative Catholic organization Opus Dei, a devious Cardinal and his pouting catamite, and the inevitable preening, conscience-challenged Villain behind the Scenes.

What distinguishes *The Da Vinci Code* from standard-issue Ludlum or Clancy or Cussler is its nervy iconoclasm (devoutly religious readers have responded with predictable surprise and disapproval to its melodramatic rearrangements of firmly entrenched doctrine), and Brown's increasing skill in keeping the reader's attention riveted to the page. Almost every one of this fat book's 105 chapters ends poised on a question or a threat or a new development hinted at and yet to be revealed in full. The nail-biting never ends, and even those readers least willing to suspend their disbelief will find that they're hooked for this dazzling story's duration.

Though its conclusion will surely satisfy the most jaded thriller reader's expectations, the end of *The Da Vinci Code*'s story is very probably not yet in sight. The aforementioned movie version will of course be a megasuccess long before it shows up in theaters. Brown, whose high visibility seems to increase almost daily (numerous radio and television interviews, anointment by *Time Magazine* as one of The World's 100 Most Influential People), works steadily away at the next installment of his Robert Langdon franchise. All we know at present is that the fifth Brown novel is conceived as a sequel to *The Da Vinci Code* and has something to do with the concealed history of Washington, D.C.

Though it's easy to envy Dan Brown his success, it's hard to deny that he deserves it as much as any writer can. An arduous researcher and a hard worker (who has recently disclosed that he begins his usual working day at 4 AM), he's a very American success story—even more like Stephen King, one suspects, than his vast wealth and celebrity indicate.

He has all the tools and he's had luck to match them: a solid formal education, and a disciplined mind that enables him to perform the exhaustive research his widely ranging novels demand. And—never let it be forgotten—his early success and consequent deep pockets have made possible all the traveling that has expanded his horizons to such even more remunerative effect.

One might say furthermore that Brown has mastered the technique pioneered by James Michener—of simultaneously entertaining and educating his readers. Whether or not he can be considered a skilled literary craftsman, he surely deserves some credit for reawakening contemporary readers' interest in the cultural legacy of the Renaissance. And, on the level of more visceral and immediate considerations, he has exploited with impressive cleverness both the contemporary fear that the world is a perpetually dangerous enigma whose meaning we cannot quite grasp, and the human desire to break down codes, solve puzzles, and uncover secrets. (See his website, for further examples of this literary prestidigitator's . . . well, mathematical ingenuity.)

Finally, there's no denying that his characters (however thinly they're drawn) persuasively stand as attractive images of the kind of people we'd like to be: intelligent, committed to good causes and humane values, resolute and courageous citizens of a world that needs as many of their kind as it can get. It's no accident that Tom Hanks was enlisted to play Robert Langdon on film. In an earlier age, the part might well have gone to James Stewart: an average guy who seems as approachable as your next-door neighbor, but just may be—underneath his aw-shucks exterior—as accomplished and remarkable fellow as the estimable Dan Brown.

FURTHER READING

Criticism

Abbott, Charlotte. "Code Word: Breakout." *Publishers Weekly* 250, no. 4 (27 January 2003): 117.
    Review of *The Da Vinci Code.*

Brown, Dan, and *Bookreporter.com.* "Author Talk: Dan Brown." *Bookreporter.com* http://bookreporter.com/authors/talk-brown-dan.asp (20 March 2003).
    Brown discusses how he researched and wrote *The Da Vinci Code.*

Cornier, Nadia. Review of *The Da Vinci Code,* by Dan Brown. *Mystery Reader* http://www.themysteryreader.com/brown-davinci.html (access date 17 December 2003).
    Asserts that Brown is a masterful storyteller, and that *The Da Vinci Code* is a superb thriller.

Falsani, Cathleen. "Cardinal Takes a Crack at *The Da Vinci Code.*" *Chicago Sun-Times* (9 January 2004): 24.
    Falsani recounts her conversation with a Catholic Cardinal regarding the level of historical accuracy about the Catholic Church in *The Da Vinci Code.*

Grenier, Cynthia. "Novel Gods." *Weekly Standard* 9, no. 2 (22 September 2003): 32-4.
    Compares the representation of religion in Brown's *The Da Vinci Code* with that of *The Lovely Bones,* by Alice Sebold. Asserts that both novels put forth a problematic feminist theology which is essentially godless.

Kulman, Linda, and Jay Tolson. "Jesus in America." *U.S. News and World Report* 135, no. 22 (22 December 2003): 44-9.
    Cover story assessing the representation of Christianity in *The Da Vinci Code.*

Lawson, Mark. "Signs for the Times." *Guardian* (26 July 2003): 23.
    Highly critical of *The Da Vinci Code,* asserting that the narrative is "preposterous and sloppy."

Lazarus, David. "*Da Vinci Code* a Heart-Racing Thriller." *San Francisco Chronicle* (6 April 2003): M4.
    Describes *The Da Vinci Code* as a fun, exciting, fast-paced novel, with numerous satisfying, unexpected plot twists.

Mnookin, Seth. "Page-Turner." *Newsweek* 141, no. 23 (9 June 2003): 57.
    Coverage of the legal case in which author Lewis Perdue accused Brown of plagiarism. The claim asserted that many of the ideas in *The Da Vinci Code* were taken from Perdue's novel *Daughter of God.*

"Decoding *The Da Vinci Code.*" *Newsweek* 142, no. 23 (8 December 2003): 54.
    Discusses Brown's representation of Christianity in *The Da Vinci Code.*

Plonka, Andy. Review of *Angels & Demons,* by Dan Brown. *Mystery Reader* http://www.themysteryreader.com/brown-angels.html (access date 17 December 2003).
    Asserts that *Angels & Demons* is exceedingly well written and has a wide-ranging appeal.

Safire, William. "The Etymon Code." *New York Times Magazine* (28 September 2003): 26.
    Discusses the etymology of some of the words that appear in *The Da Vinci Code.*

Additional coverage of Brown's life and career is contained in the following sources published by **Thomson Gale**: *Authors and Artists for Young Adults,* Vol. 55; *Contemporary Authors,* Vol. 217; *Literature Resource Center*; and *Major 21st-Century Writers* (e-book), 2005.

Contemporary Crime Fiction

The following entry presents an overview of contemporary crime fiction through 2002.

INTRODUCTION

Contemporary crime fiction is rooted in a long history. In its earliest form, crime literature can be traced back to the sixteenth and seventeenth centuries, when pamphlets and essays detailing murderous deeds were popular reading among the general public. The trend continued in the eighteenth and nineteenth centuries, with crimes fueling the plots of major works by such authors as Charles Dickens and Fyodor Dostoevsky. Edgar Allan Poe and Sherlock Holmes creator Sir Arthur Conan Doyle paved the way for many twentieth-century crime fiction styles. In England, the early twentieth century is considered the "golden age" of crime writing, with authors Agatha Christie and Dorothy Sayers establishing a new sub-genre in crime fiction featuring a domestic, amateur detective as its protagonist. In America, hardboiled fiction works by Dashiell Hammett and Raymond Chandler featured the now-stock figure of the strong male private eye who works alone and heroically to achieve justice. In the latter part of the twentieth century, the nature and scope of crime fiction changed yet again; most significantly, contemporary crime writers frequently began incorporating social, urban, environmental, political, and racial issues into their stories. While crime fiction continues to use established formulas, the genre is identified by critics as being most closely aligned with mainstream realism.

In his introduction to an anthology on modern crime fiction, Peter Messent writes about the genre's evolution, noting that while early-twentieth-century crime novels were mostly dominated by "white heroes" and a largely male perspective, contemporary crime novelists have expanded their horizons to include female and non-white perspectives that were absent in the hardboiled detective fiction or even the domestic, amateur detective novels of the early twentieth century. Within crime fiction itself, several sub-genres have appeared, including revised versions of hardboiled detective fiction and noir thrillers, regional murder mysteries, and professional crime thrillers such as lawyer and police procedurals. The romantic individualism associated with the character of the alienated private eye is now viewed by critics and writers alike as somewhat marginal and limited in perspective. Instead, they favor authors who focus more openly on the conflict between authority and the individual, centrality versus marginality in terms of gender and ethnicity, and the law and its limits in a social system that is itself often viewed as corrupt.

Yet the traditions established by the father-figures of hardboiled American crime fiction continue to be utilized by such authors as Robert B. Parker in his *Perchance to Dream* (1991) and *Paper Doll* (1993), both of which use confessional, first-person narrative. Stock attributes of crime fiction including a heavy focus on detailed descriptions of surroundings, food, and dress continue to be integral to the realism portrayed by crime novels, but this familiar narrative style is also modified somewhat, and authors such as Sara Paretsky and Sue Grafton are notable for the way their investigative characters' narrative voices reveal a personal side to the characters, in addition to an awareness of the social milieu in which they operate. This new awareness and recognition of the social impact and import of detection of crime is considered by many critics the most significant difference between contemporary and early twentieth century crime fiction.

The sense of alienation that was an integral part of the private-eye characters of earlier crime fiction has now morphed into a broader sense of conflict, including doubts about both the society and legal system within which these characters operate. Michael Connelly's *The Black Ice* (1993), James Ellroy's *L.A. Confidential* (1990), and Thomas Harris's *The Silence of the Lambs* (1988) are all cited as examples of crime fiction in which the main characters are viewed as outsiders, like their early-twentieth-century counterparts, but in addition to their own sense of individual isolation, these detectives also contend with the conflict of operating within the social, economic, and political bodies whose corruption they expose. One of the most significant changes in contemporary crime fiction has been in the role of female detectives. Female crime writers take the sense of conflict a step further, often using the social context of their characters to convey the complexities of the society and systems in which they operate. In contrast to the domestic and amateur sphere occupied by such characters as Christie's Miss Marple, modern-day female detectives function as professionals, operating as experts in their particular field. It is noteworthy that the social and professional progress made by women in the twentieth century is reflected in the way female characters are portrayed in these novels.

Other social factors have also impacted the development of crime fiction. In particular, the multiculturalism of the 1990s resulted in the prominent acceptance of many "minority" crime writers such as Walter Mosley, Tony Hillerman, Barbara Neely, Laura Joh Rowland and Dale Furutani. Mosley's detective protagonist, Easy Rawlins, is viewed by many critics as the epitome of the modern private eye, torn between his status as a Black American and as a detective, often put in positions where he has to compromise his own code of justice. Other non-white authors often feature characters who, like Mosley's Rawlins, highlight the bitter and often irreconcilable differences that exist in contemporary society. Although not generally regarded as part of the minority crime fiction group, women crime writers identify more closely with non-white crime writers than with traditional crime thrillers. Unlike their traditional male counterparts, Paretsky and Grafton's female detectives often identify themselves, in fact even define themselves, very clearly in relation to their families, backgrounds, and memories. In addition, female protagonists in crime fiction seem to display a unified sense of female identity and community.

Continuing to draw their narrative strengths from established formulas of crime narratives, popular crime novels often follow a similar progression of events: an initial set-up, where the main characters and setting are introduced; the commission of the crime; the investigation; and final resolution. The predictability of this set of actions is regarded by critics as extremely appealing to audiences due to its promise of a restoration of order at the conclusion of the story. Many contemporary authors have used these formulas to diversify and expand the scope of their fiction, often using stock storylines to explore social and cultural issues more openly than ever before. In his study of modern crime fiction, Samuel Coale points to such works as Elizabeth George's *A Great Deliverance* (1988) as a fine example of this kind of deviation. In a novel that follows the typical detective cycle, George deals sensitively and openly with the subject of emotional abuse. According to Coale, this blending of formula with innovative expansion of the norms is what has come to dominate the genre, lending a great sense of moral seriousness to many contemporary crime fiction novels.

REPRESENTATIVE WORKS

Peter Ackroyd
Hawksmoor (novel) 1985
Dan Leno and the Limehouse Golem (novel) 1994; also published as *The Trial of Elizabeth Cree: A Novel of the Limehouse Murders,* 1995

Paul Auster
City of Glass (novel) 1985

Lawrence Block
A Dance at the Slaughterhouse (novel) 1991
Everybody Dies (novel) 1998
Tanner on Ice (novel) 1998

Edward Bunker
No Beast So Fierce (novel) 1972
Little Boy Blue (novel) 1981

James Lee Burke
A Stained White Radiance (novel) 1992
Dixie City Jam (novel) 1994

John Camp
The Fool's Run (novel) 1989
The Empress File (novel) 1991
Secret Prey [as John Sandford] (novel) 1998
Certain Prey [as John Sandford] (novel) 1999

Caleb Carr
The Alienist (novel) 1994
The Angel of Darkness (novel) 1997

Jerome Charyn
The Education of Patrick Silver (novel) 1976
The Good Policeman (novel) 1990
Maria's Girls (novel) 1992

Michael Connelly
The Black Ice (novel) 1993
The Concrete Blonde (novel) 1994
Blood Work (novel) 1998
Angels Flight (novel) 1999
The Narrows (novel) 2004

Patricia Cornwell
Postmortem (novel) 1990
Cruel and Unusual (novel) 1993
Unnatural Exposure (novel) 1997
Blow Fly (novel) 2003
Trace (novel) 2004

James Crumley
Bordersnakes (novel) 1996

Philip K. Dick
Do Androids Dream of Electric Sheep? (novel) 1968; also published as *Blade Runner,* 1982

James Ellroy
L.A. Confidential (novel) 1990
My Dark Places: An L.A. Crime Memoir (novel) 1996
The Cold Six Thousand (novel) 2001

Janet Evanovich
One for the Money (novel) 1994
High Five (novel) 1999

Dick Francis
Nerve (novel) 1964
High Stakes (novel) 1975

Dale Furutani
Death in Little Tokyo (novel) 1996
The Toyotomi Blades (novel) 1997

Elizabeth George
A Great Deliverance (novel) 1988
Payment in Blood (novel) 1989
For the Sake of Elena (novel) 1992
In the Presence of the Enemy (novel) 1996
In Pursuit of the Proper Sinner (novel) 1999

William Gibson
Neuromancer (novel) 1984
Mona Lisa Overdrive (novel) 1988
Virtual Light (novel) 1993

Sue Grafton
'F' Is for Fugitive (novel) 1989
'H' Is for Homicide (novel) 1991
'K' Is for Killer (novel) 1994
'M' Is for Malice (novel) 1996
'O' Is for Outlaw (novel) 1999
'R' Is for Ricochet (novel) 2004

Martha Grimes
The Anodyne Necklace (novel) 1983
Rainbow's End (novel) 1995
The Case Has Altered (novel) 1997

John Grisham
A Time to Kill (novel) 1989
The Firm (novel) 1991
The Pelican Brief (novel) 1992
The Client (novel) 1993
The Chamber (novel) 1994
The Runaway Jury (novel) 1996
The Summons (novel) 2002
King of Torts (novel) 2003

Thomas Harris
Black Sunday (novel) 1975
The Silence of the Lambs (novel) 1988
Hannibal (novel) 1999

Carolyn G. Heilbrun (Amanda Cross)
Death in a Tenured Position (novel) 1981; also
　　published as *A Death in the Faculty,* 1982
The Players Come Again (novel) 1990
The Puzzled Heart (novel) 1998

Tony Hillerman
The Blessing Way (novel) 1970
Dance Hall of the Dead (novel) 1973
The Ghostway (novel) 1985
Coyote Waits (novel) 1990
The First Eagle (novel) 1998
Sinister Pig (novel) 2003

William Hjortsberg
Falling Angel (novel) 1978

P. D. James
An Unsuitable Job for a Woman (novel) 1972
The Black Tower (novel) 1975
Death of an Expert Witness (novel) 1977
Innocent Blood (novel) 1980
A Taste for Death (novel) 1986
The Children of Men (novel) 1993

Faye Kellerman
The Ritual Bath (novel) 1986
Day of Atonement (novel) 1991
Serpent's Tooth (novel) 1997
Jupiter's Bones (novel) 1999

Carole laFavor
Along the Journey River (novel) 1996
Evil Dead Center (novel) 1997

Mary J. Latsis and Martha Hennissart (Emma Lathen)
Murder without Icing (novel) 1973
Double, Double, Oil and Trouble (novel) 1978
Something in the Air (novel) 1988

Elmore Leonard
Fifty-two Pickup (novel) 1974
Stick (novel) 1983
Killshot (novel) 1989
Get Shorty (novel) 1990
Out of Sight (novel) 1996
Be Cool (novel) 1999
When the Women Come out to Dance (short stories)
　　2002
Mr. Paradise (novel) 2004

Thomas McCall
A Wide and Capable Revenge (novel) 1993
Beyond Ice, Beyond Death (novel) 1995

Walter Mosley
Devil in a Blue Dress (novel) 1990
A Red Death (novel) 1991
Black Betty (novel) 1994
Gone Fishin' (novel) 1997

Michael Nava
The Hidden Law (novel) 1992

Barbara Neely

Blanche on the Lam (novel) 1992
Blanche Among the Talented Tenth (novel) 1994
Blanche Cleans Up (novel) 1998
Blanche Passes Go (novel) 2000

Jack O'Connell

The Skin Palace (novel) 1996
Word Made Flesh (novel) 1999

Sarah Paretsky

Indemnity Only (novel) 1982
Deadlock (novel) 1984
Blood Shot (novel) 1988; also published as *Toxic Shock*
Tunnel Vision (novel) 1994
Total Recall (novel) 2001

Barbara J. Parker

Suspicion of Innocence (novel) 1994
Suspicion of Betrayal (novel) 1999
Suspicion of Malice (novel) 2000

Robert B. Parker

Perchance to Dream: Robert B. Parker's Sequel to Raymond Chandler's The Big Sleep (novel) 1991
Paper Doll (novel) 1993
Shrink Rap (novel) 2002

Mike Phillips

Point of Darkness (novel) 1995

Laura Joh Rowland

Shinjū (novel) 1994

Lisa Scottoline

Moment of Truth (novel) 2000

Robert Skinner

Skin Deep, Blood Red (novel) 1997

Scott Turow

Presumed Innocent (novel) 1987
The Burden of Proof (novel) 1990
Pleading Guilty (novel) 1993
Reversible Errors (novel) 2002

Don Winslow

The Death and Life of Bobby Z (novel) 1997
California Fire and Life (novel) 1999

Jack Womack

Random Acts of Senseless Violence (novel) 1994

OVERVIEWS

Peter Messent (essay date 1997)

SOURCE: Messent, Peter. "Introduction: From Private Eye to Police Procedural—The Logic of Contemporary Crime Fiction." In *Criminal Proceedings: The Contemporary American Crime Novel,* edited by Peter Messent, pp. 1-21. London: Pluto Press, 1997.

[*In the following essay, Messent reviews various types of crime fiction, starting with a brief background of American crime fiction at the beginning of the twentieth century, and drawing a parallel between modern crime fiction and mainstream realism.*]

This volume [*Criminal Proceedings*] is both a response to the variety of contemporary crime fiction in America and an illustration of the flexibility of its generic boundaries. Hard-boiled fiction usually deals with criminal activity in a modern urban environment, a world of disconnected signs and anonymous strangers. Crime acts as a connective tissue within this world, and it is the detective's job to trace the hidden relationships crime both indicates yet conceals, to bring them to the surface, and show the way the city works.[1] This helps to account for the common association made between crime fiction and the mainstream of American twentieth-century realism,[2] for in its engagement with the urban social ground and the problems to be found there, crime fiction tackles head-on territory which other literary forms seem often to evade.

Hard-boiled fiction in America has conventionally been filtered through a 'white, heterosexual, male' perspective.[3] Thus, for instance, Marty Roth writes that 'in detective fiction gender is genre and genre is male' with women only figuring to 'flesh out male desire and shadow male sexual fear'.[4] One of the most interesting developments in contemporary crime fiction is the way such limits have been challenged as 'racial and gendered minorities have found voice and visibility',[5] and have used the genre for their own particular ideological ends. A significant number of the chapters in this volume address this issue.

Other chapters suggest some of the different forms that contemporary crime fiction takes. Thus John Harvey, the British crime writer, moves beyond the environment of the city to discuss James Crumley's Western detective novels, while Barry Taylor explores the unsettling landscape of Elmore Leonard's crime fictions and the different (criminal, legal, and paralegal) 'modes of power and practice' they dramatise. Rather than charting the contents of this collection, however, I start by outlining one of the most noticeable changes in crime fiction over recent years: the move from private-eye novel to police procedural. I discuss the implications of the term, private eye, and what it says about the detective's agency and role. Thus one of the strands of my chapter focuses on the sense of authoritative subjectivity within the genre, and the questions that it raises. For recent criticism recognises that the romantic individualism commonly associated with the private eye, and the related sense of alienation from her or his surrounding environment, is a falsification of the actual nature of her or his social role and position. I suggest that, despite the continuing production and popularity of the private-eye story, the generic shift to police procedural has been prompted by a recognition that the marginal position and limited perspective of the PI hero or heroine makes for an ineffectual, and even irrelevant, figure as far as the representation of criminal activity and its containment goes. At this stage, I should say that Barry Taylor's chapter, which follows mine, contains material pointing to a sharp counter-argument, and interrogates the clear sense of generic development (and its relation to issues of social authority and panopticism) which I delineate. The critical dialogues which take place in this collection are intended not to give final answers to the way the genre works, but both to indicate some of the different ways in which its current practitioners are using, and pushing against, its formal constraints, and to suggest the importance and ongoing vitality of the debate about authority and individual agency, centrality and marginality, the law and its limits, and social system and individual criminal act, which it has inspired. All the chapters in this collection, in one way or another, engage this debate.

In the later part of my own chapter I discuss in some detail one novel closely related to the police procedural, Patricia Cornwell's *Postmortem* (1990). I choose this particular text to discuss, not only because it illustrates key features of this sub-genre, but also for its illustration of another tendency increasingly evident in a number of recent American crime novels. There has traditionally been an ambiguity at the heart of the private-eye form that renders it (in the majority of cases) inevitably conservative, in the genre's endorsement of the social status quo whatever the failures in the fabric of American economic and political life it reveals. However, I see in such fictions as Cornwell's an even more conservative turn: for they both endorse the status quo and, in addition, consign crime to the realm of the morally 'monstrous'. The popularity of her Scarpetta novels, and the more general prevalence of such a tactic, may be symptomatic of a deep-rooted need for social reassurance on the part of the contemporary audience for which such texts are written. I end my chapter by briefly suggesting how, in the fiction of James Ellroy, the police procedural can take a very different shape than this.

The two acknowledged father figures of hard-boiled American crime fiction are Dashiell Hammett and Raymond Chandler. Both Sam Spade and Philip Marlowe, their most famous protagonists, are private investigators, PIs, private eyes—the three terms linked in connective chain to one another. Hard-boiled private-eye fiction is certainly still alive and well in America. Robert B. Parker's *Perchance to Dream* (1991) is a sequel and a homage to Chandler's *The Big Sleep* (1939), and indicates the latter writer's powerful influence on his successor. Little sign of the anxiety of influence is apparent here as Parker recreates the sardonic voice and sentimental undertone of his predecessor, and manages similarly to combine 'the epigrammatic flourish of Oscar Wilde with the moral environment of "The Killers"'.[6]

Sara Paretsky's detective heroine, V. I. Warshawski, makes the kind of intertextual reference so common within the genre, when she self-consciously distances herself from Chandler's protagonist. Warshawski does this both in terms of her unwillingness to resort to violence and the nature of her emotional sensibility: 'I'm no Philip Marlowe forever pulling guns out of armpits or glove compartments. Marlowe probably never fainted, either, from the sight of a dead woman's splintered skull.'[7] Nonetheless, as Evelyne Keitel indicates, in her heroine's 'downwardly mobile' quality, her knowledge of the 'mean streets' of (in this case) Chicago, and in her social marginality marked by financial and emotional independence and an unprofitable sense of moral integrity in a corrupt public world, Paretsky also clearly follows in Chandler's footsteps.[8]

Parker, Paretsky, and Sue Grafton too, use—like Chandler—the first-person voice: a device which signals a certain sense of authority on the part of the narrating subject in her or his negotiations with the surrounding world. The use of the wisecrack and the one-liner, distinctive features of hard-boiled language, reinforce such an impression. 'A stylized demonstration of knowledge' expressing 'an irreverence toward . . . institutional power', the wisecrack signals 'an assertion of autonomy, a defiant refusal to be brow-beaten', and introduces 'an unsettling element in the interplay of discourses so the chances of the truth gradually unfolding become greater'.[9] Contemporary private-eye fiction takes up where Hammett and Chandler leave off in its reliance on this particular stylistic tactic. Thus Spenser responds to a police fist in the stomach in Robert B. Parker's *Paper Doll* (1993) with the retort:

> 'Who's your trainer?' I said. 'Mary Baker Eddy?'
>
> He didn't know who Mary Baker Eddy was, but he tried not to let it show.[10]

While V. I. Warshawski, in *Tunnel Vision* (1993), physically barred from entering Jasper Heccomb's office by his assistant, Tish, reacts by saying:

'What's he doing in there?' I asked mildly. 'Holding an orgy?'

Her face flooded with color. 'How can you say things like that?'[11]

Similarly, wittily ironic descriptive language works for Marlowe's successors as it did for him, as a sign both of alienation from the environment through which they move, and of a verbal control over it.[12] Kinsey Millhone describes the young girl with 'a ruby drilled into the side of her nose' in charge of a high school library reference desk in *F Is for Fugitive* (1989):

> She had apparently been seized by a fit of self-puncturing because both ears had been pierced repeatedly from the lobe to the helix. In lieu of earrings, she was sporting the sort of items you'd find in my junk drawer at home: paper clips, screws, safety pins, shoelaces, wing nuts. She was perched on a stool with a copy of *Rolling Stone* open on her lap. Mick Jagger was on the cover, looking sixty if a day.[13]

As this quotation suggests, perceptual and verbal control run together in such American crime fictions to assert both individualism and autonomy. The critic Rosemary Jackson relates the idea of the stable self to the seeing eye. Implicit in the ability to see clearly, and the sense of command that comes with the dominance of the eye over a perceptual field, is that sense of authority and comprehension associated with the sovereign subject. From such a perspective, '"I see" . . . [is] synonymous with "I understand". Knowledge, comprehension, reason, are established through the power of the *look,* through the "*eye*" and the "*I*" of the human subject.' Accordingly, so Jackson suggests, a loss of the sense of visual control introduces a deep uncertainty concerning identity, the authority of the self, and the relation between self and world.[14]

Private-eye fiction is generally marked by exactly this former stress on the power of the eye/I. Walter Benjamin saw 'the figure of the detective . . . prefigured in that of the flaneur',[15] the walker of the streets and appreciative watcher of the varieties of urban life. The detective genre, in such a reading, becomes 'symptomatic of the experience of modernity'. For the detective operates as a transformed version of the flaneur—the idler now become the searcher, 'dig[ging] into the "discontinuous structure of the [city] world"' (one of arbitrary connections and of temporal and spatial fragmentation) to find the clues which allow a way 'behind the facade and beneath the veils of the metropolitan exterior'.[16]

The detective, then, sifts and sorts, using her or his reasoning powers to penetrate below the surface of things, entering the labyrinth or underworld of the city to do so. She or he rebuilds 'synchronic . . . [and] diachronic continuity', both filling in a spatial and temporal gap in a narrative (who was where and when) and restoring the sense of coherence to a community or family history ruptured by a crime.[17] The power of the I/eye enables this process. So detective fiction stresses over and over again the authority that comes from close, continual, and apparently detached observation (the magnifying glass has become an icon of the genre, or at least one branch of it).

Sequences which show the authoritative seeing eye of the detective at work are a repeated and primary feature of the private-eye novel. Kinsey Millhone stares at photos of the dead body of Lorna Kepler in *K Is for Killer* (1994) as, somewhat late in the day as far as the committing of this particular crime is concerned, she uses the only means at hand to mimic 'the spiral method of a crime scene search':

> I was frustrated by the flat, two-dimensional images. I wanted to crawl into the frame, examine all the items on the tabletops . . . I found myself squinting, moving pictures closer to my face and then back again, as if the subject matter might suddenly leap into sharper focus. I would stare at the body, scanning the background, taking in items through my peripheral vision.[18]

Spenser's initial search to find Pam Shephard in *Promised Land* (1976) is more immediately successful and again depends on the power of the detective's eye:

> What to do now? . . . I could stake [the house] out and see what happened . . . The safest thing was to stand around and watch. I liked to know as much as I could before I went in where I hadn't been before. . . . At four-fifteen Pam Shephard came out of the shabby house with another woman . . . and I swung along behind. Pam Shephard and her friend went into a supermarket and I . . . watched them through the plate-glass window . . . I followed them back to the house on Centre Street and watched them disappear inside. Well, at least I knew where she was.[19]

This process of seeing is paradigmatic to the genre, where the detective acts (so it would appear) as knowledgeable and autonomous subject, restoring order to society through his clear-sightedness at the narrative end. The image of Sherlock Holmes, the model of the classic British detective, as 'the great *doctor* of Victorian society' whose 'spectacular' diagnosis causes social disease to be cured,[20] suggests something of this authoritative role.

But things are never quite this simple in the hard-boiled crime novel. The American private-eye hero differs considerably from Holmes, most particularly in the personal vulnerability that comes from an immersion within the violent world being investigated, in the recognition that corruption is not just confined to this criminal underclass but pervades the entire social fabric, and in the (romantic) sense of alienation and isolation from the social body that accompanies that recognition.

The hard-boiled genre is commonly associated with realism in its use of a terse, tough, and coolly descriptive style.[21] The apparent clear-sightedness of the detective (with the reader's view commonly filtered through her or his perception) seems to exist at one remove from any 'official' version of events. But the private eye by no means provides an unproblematic representation of the way things 'really' are. What the detective sees cannot exist in an ideological vacuum. Though the hard-boiled hero usually appears an ironically detached and objective figure who exists on the *margins* of society (thus again differing from the classic British detective), Bethany Ogdon argues that his values—for it is the male protagonist on whom she focuses—mirror dominant social prejudices, emerging directly as a result of the 'hyper-masculine identity' he would project,[22] and metaphorising women, homosexual or weak male figures, and non-white males, all (variously) in terms of the polluting Other.

Ogdon's argument is one-sided, her description of homophobia, racism and misogyny implying a type of ideological unity and consistency to the genre which this volume would contradict. But her challenge to the apparent transparency and independence of the hard-boiled detective's view, his representation as a solitary individual able to stand free of the normal social bonds and restraints, is to the point. For the clarity of perception which the focused eye of the private investigator seems to bring with it is misleading. It conceals a peculiarly ambivalent relationship to the dominant social codes and values, and accordingly raises questions about the range and nature of the detective's agency itself. For the detective may generally present her or himself as a liminal figure but, in the last analysis, she or he serves the interests of the dominant social order, however repressive and unjust that order might be. Her or his way of seeing reality (and the apparent detachment and autonomy it appears to suggest) cannot, in other words, finally be separated out from that of the official custodians of the state (the police, the FBI, etc.). Dennis Porter writes that 'in a detective story . . . the law itself is never put on trial' and points to the 'generic "conservatism"' of a form that defends the established social system even as it reveals widespread corruption both in leading citizens and in public officialdom.[23] Franco Moretti puts this in a different, but connected, way when he discusses the act of theft, as it is normally represented in detective fictions, in terms of the criminal's 'individualistic ethic' rather than of the larger economic order where it originally (from his political perspective) belongs:

> What, indeed, is theft, if not the redistribution of social wealth? . . . But theft is crucial for yet another reason. Money is always the motive of crime in detective fiction, yet the genre is wholly silent about *production*: that unequal exchange between labour-power and wages which is the true source of social wealth. Like

popular economics, detective fiction incites people to seek the profit in the sphere of circulation, where it cannot be found—but in compensation, one finds thefts, con-jobs, false pretences, and so on. The indignation against what is rotten and immoral in the economy must concentrate on these phenomena. As for the factory—it is innocent, and thus free to carry on.

Moretti's comments here, and his statement that 'the detective is the figure of the state in the guise of "night watchman", who limits himself to assuring respect for laws',[24] are primarily directed toward classic English detective fiction. Yet they have considerable implication for American hard-boiled fiction too. For the paradox to which Dennis Porter points—that the detective reveals corruption at all levels of the social system but, in doing so, helps to preserve the status quo (her or his authoritative eye and agency subject to its requirements)—is central to the genre. In *Tunnel Vision,* Sara Paretsky, in a typical narrative tactic, uses an act of individual violence, and (again typically) the murder of a woman—Deirdre Messenger—to engage larger issues both of economic injustice (the cut-rate employment of illegal Romanian workers in the American construction industry) and political and financial corruption (resulting from the violation of a grain embargo against Iraq and the consequent laundering of money back in America). The result, however, of all Warshawski's investigations and discoveries, and her solving of the original crime, is 'one giant motherfucking cover-up' (p. 477) in the public sphere, with her only real success coming in the domestic one: the final removal of Emily Messenger from the home of her sexually abusive father. An individual crime is solved, but nothing changes in the larger social scheme of things. As Ralph Willett puts it:

> The challenge offered to the corporate rich—to big medicine, big business, big shipping, etc.—sustains the populism found in much hard-boiled fiction and also its contradictions. The social criticisms of the Warshawski novels are constrained by the nature of the genre. As Paretsky conceded, V. I. is only capable of doing 'some very small things' for individuals.[25]

Paretsky's protagonist directly interrogates the existing social order but cannot finally affect it. Warshawski, like the majority of hard-boiled private-eye protagonists, is caught finally in a kind of in-between world: seeing corruption in, and disliking many aspects of, the environment through which she moves, but serving the interests of the law and the status quo in solving the individual crime and repairing the rent in the social fabric that has occurred. Indeed the very form of the detective novel re-enacts this process. Preserving 'the lost authority of narrative in a chaotic modernist culture', the detective (like the psychoanalyst) 'must produce continuous narrative from a lost narrative as a means of promoting [community] health'.[26] The genre is 'radically anti-novelistic' in the way it operates to restore the social status quo, for 'detective fiction's object is to *return to the beginning . . .* [to] reinstate a previous situation' as it was (or almost as it was) before 'disturbing forces broke loose'.[27]

The private eye, then, may appear to see and act from an individualistic and autonomous perspective, but the detective's agency is in fact subordinated to larger forms of social monitoring and control, and her or his vision is limited by the 'private' basis on which she or he operates. In terms of the power and authority of the *Public Eye,* the PI's position might be seen as both marginal and (even) self-deluding. Dashiell Hammett's 'Continental Op' novels (of which *Red Harvest,* published in 1929, is perhaps the best known) start to hint at another route that hard-boiled crime novels can take in their representation of the relationship between the individual detective, criminality, and the larger social system. For the Continental Detective Agency which employs the Op is loosely modelled on the Pinkerton National Detective Agency, for which Hammett himself worked. Founded in 1850, the Pinkertons came to be identified with the icon of the wide-open eye and the motto, 'We Never Sleep'. The Agency was associated with forms of hegemonic authority at the time of the American Civil War, when it acted as a Union spy service, and in its later interventions on behalf of well-regulated American capitalist development, most conspicuously in the late 1870s (The Molly Maguires) and 1892 (the Homestead Strike).

The all-seeing eye of the Pinkertons can be taken to stand, then, as a metonymic representation of a larger and increasingly invasive monitoring on behalf of the state of anything threatening to upset the established social order. Dennis Porter talks of the role of bureaucracy and technology in such a process in terms of the image of the 'unseen seer, who stands at the centre of the social Panopticon and employs his "science" to make all things visible'—or at least who attempts to do so—'on behalf of the forces of order'.[28] The detective operative working for the Pinkertons was more directly linked with such forces than the conventional private eye. And the police procedural is in many ways the logical end-point to which the Pinkerton detective stories (the fictionalised versions of Agency cases published from 1874 onward) point. The real meaning of detection and its relation to the larger social order can be seen more clearly when the links between the detective and the hegemonic order (and the powers of investigation conferred by that order) are revealed without any of the mystification which the private-eye novel introduces.[29]

Though the latter form still flourishes, the growing turn on the part of practitioners of the detective genre to the police procedural might be seen to constitute a recognition of the social meanings of detection previously

rendered opaque. Its popularity, though, can be seen more simply, and perhaps more accurately, as an acknowledgement of the fact that, in a contemporary world where the making visible of crime has come to depend more and more on sophisticated scientific techniques and the ability to collate information quickly and on a large-scale and official basis, the private eye is increasingly irrelevant to, and necessarily blinkered in, this process. James Ellroy captures something of this feeling when, speaking of his own fiction, he says:

> I consciously abandoned the private-eye tradition that formally jazzed me. Evan Hunter wrote, 'the last time a private eye investigated a homicide was never'. The private eye is an iconic totem spawned by pure fiction, romantic moonshine. . . . The American cop was the real goods from the gate.[30]

Joyce Carol Oates, in her analysis of the shift from the private-eye novel to the police procedural, also focuses on the element of fantasy in the former (she is writing specifically about Chandler here but her comments can be taken as paradigmatic):

> Private investigator, private 'eye': the fantasy figure of Chandler's detective is not unlike that of an 'invisible' man or a supernatural being with fairy-like powers of observation, intuition, mobility, survival. Philip Marlowe is repeatedly 'sapped' on the head with blackjacks or gun barrels, shot at, beaten, kicked, choked, drugged, trussed up and left for dead, yet he invariably recovers, and sometimes within the space of a few minutes takes his 'dispassionate' revenge on one or another of the caricatured thugs and bit players who populate, like vermin, the Los Angeles/'Bay City' sets of [his] novels.

She, too, points to the irrelevance of the figure of the PI in contemporary criminal investigations: 'private detectives are rarely involved in authentic crime cases, and would have no access, in contemporary times, to the findings of forensics experts'.[31]

The police procedural, then, seems to be supplanting the private-eye novel as 'realistic' crime fiction.[32] While the latter relies on a model of rule-bending individualism, the former puts its emphasis precisely on procedure and *collective* agency. A fantasy of extra-systemic freedom and authenticity gives way to a more problematic vision of individual detectives operating through systemic procedures.[33] If police detectives, like their unofficial counterpart, tend both to reveal widespread social corruption and to preserve the status quo, here the possibility of romantic alienation is held far more firmly in check, for the relationship between the detective's role and the agency of the state is necessarily foregrounded.[34] However, there are (as suggested above, and as one would expect) clear crossovers between these two generic variants, and the police procedural, *despite* the bureaucratic machinery it engages, is not necessarily any more sceptical about individual agency and the power of the I/eye of the detective. In Patricia Cornwell's fiction, for instance, this is far from being the case.

Cornwell's *Postmortem* belongs to one branch of the police procedural category. Her protagonist, Kay Scarpetta, is in fact a forensic pathologist and Virginia's chief medical examiner, but she works to solve crimes with, and uses the resources of, both the local police force and the FBI (though her relationships with both groups are not always comfortable). Oates says that: 'The clue-crammed mystery [of the Ellery Queen type] is currently enjoying a spectacular resuscitation . . . as a consequence of recent discoveries in forensic science, including DNA tracing.' Cornwell's novels rely on such 'scientific detection',[35] the type of detective work which depends on her heroine having the ready access to local and national information and surveillance services that her official status brings.

Scarpetta's investigation of *Postmortem*'s serial murders depends on the technological resources at hand. Thus the initial suspect for the most recent of these crimes (the one with which the novel begins) is identified by fingerprints on the victim's skin, revealed by laser wand. Scarpetta's knowledge and skill with the high-tech tools of her trade give her authority, and allow her finally to see through to the crime's solution. She becomes, like Poe's Dupin, the one with the superior understanding necessary to solve the puzzles challenging her, though, in her case, this comes predominantly from her forensic abilities.

This account of the novel is somewhat reductive, for, like most successful practitioners of the hard-boiled genre, Cornwell takes her reader into a more complicated world than this, where the autonomy and self-confidence of her heroine is threatened, and where the line between a criminal underclass and public official-dom is not as firm as might initially be supposed. For Scarpetta is both a detective rationally investigating a case and also a woman haunted by subconscious fears. The book starts with her dreaming of the 'formless and inhuman . . . white face'[36] of the unknown murderer outside her bedroom window, and she refers later to the 'dark areas where I did not want to go' (p. 58). Her very sense of autonomy and selfhood is threatened by the invasive sexual threat that this figure constitutes. Scarpetta identifies with the female victims she examines. They are all young professional women, and Lori Petersen, whose death is the main focus of the narrative, is a doctor: in the words of Scarpetta's niece, Lucy, 'just like you' (p. 37). The investigator in fact ends up as fear-wracked victim, screaming with terror (p. 313) as the murderer finally enters her bedroom— only for the threat to be dispelled as he is shot dead by Marino, the cop who (unknown to Scarpetta) has recognised her danger and is keeping her under surveillance.

If the detective's sense of herself as authoritative and objective subject is challenged in the text, so too are boundaries blurred between criminal exceptionality and apparent social normality and respectability (within the official world in which Scarpetta works). The criminal works with cops, even if he is not one of them: a communications officer hired by the city, he has chosen his victims when hearing their voices on the emergency calls he has processed. When Marino appears in the climactic scene, wearing the same kind of black police jump suit as the murderer, Scarpetta, 'for a paralysing second . . . didn't know who was the killer and who was the cop' (p. 317).

This suggestion of collapsed polarities takes more overt form as the sexual aggression the murderer shows his female victims is mirrored by Bill Boltz, the Commonwealth's attorney for Richmond. Scarpetta's relationship with the latter stalls as a result of the 'sudden aggression . . . raw brute force' (p. 220) of his sexual hunger. Boltz, it is discovered, has previously sexually assaulted the journalist, Abby Turnbull, after spiking her drink, and both this, and his general attitude toward her, carry echoes of McCorkle's (the murderer's) responses to his victims. The extent of Boltz's responsibility for his wife's suicide, using his gun soon after they have made love, is also subject to Scarpetta's speculation (pp. 196-7).

Boltz, then, is an unconvicted rapist and perhaps, indirectly, a type of murderer. And Commissioner Amburgey tampers with criminal evidence because of his 'hatred' (p. 325) for Scarpetta, who has, through no fault of her own, publicly humiliated him during an earlier case (p. 127). Amburgey, it is indicated, will resign his job as a result of the pressure Abby can bring to bear on him as a journalist, but Boltz remains untouchable. Criminality extends beyond the boundaries of the underworld and remains, in part, finally publicly unrevealed and unpunished.

But this is rendered, if not irrelevant, then secondary to the main business of the text: Scarpetta's solving of the serial murders. Her eventual success here is ensured, even before the criminal's last move against her, by her scientific skill and deductive abilities (together with an unexpected connection which comes about as a result of the thoroughness of her investigative work).[37] For her forensic activities and use of information technology are major elements in her discovery and proof of Mc-Corkle's criminality. DNA coding, access to the resources of the FBI computer to trace related crimes, reliance on the laser to identify the traces of a glittery substance (the borax in soap powder) left by the murderer on his victims' bodies, and the medical knowledge to identify the enzyme defect which affects him—all these help her literally and metaphorically (to refer back to Moretti) to doctor the social disease she encounters. With the withdrawal of the threat to her psychic security on McCorkle's death, and the defeat of Amburgey, her scientific objectivity and personal authority and autonomy is pretty much restored at the novel's end.

Despite the anomalous position of Boltz, then, it is the return to the status quo, both in terms of Scarpetta's sense of her own identity and of the established social order, which is the dominant factor as the novel ends. This restoration is eased and aided by the existence of a strong thematic strand that runs throughout the text and which evasively counters both that blurring of the borders between criminality and normality on which I have previously commented and the possibility of significant social analysis which the novel starts, on occasion, to imply. For the investigation into serial killing seems to lead in just such a latter direction. In Scarpetta's America, the reader is told, 'there were more stranger killings as opposed to crimes of passion' (p. 82). That this is so signals the loss of affect which is so noted a feature of the recent social landscape: the collapse of that web of domestic and community relationships that have conventionally located the subject and which have, in past times, aided the detective in her or his reconstruction of narrative legibility (the rebuilding of a clearly evident causal chain of relationships). Here the logical and direct connections between the criminal and his victim have evaporated almost to the point of complete invisibility.[38] Scarpetta's search for a connection in the chain of victims finally takes her to the 911 calls as the faint and only link between the victims and their killer.

Any discussion of the social causes of crime is, however, largely stifled here by its consignment to the category of the monstrous moral exception to the general rule. This categorisation cuts against other aspects of the relationship between criminality and legality in the text; against the more disturbing aspects of Cornwall's representation of the nature of the social body, and of the stability and authority of the female subject within it. Images of pollution, disease and infection are recurrent in hard-boiled fiction, but that of monstrosity has become especially prevalent in the recent period. Thus, in James Patterson's *Kiss the Girls* (1995), for example, the terms 'monster' and 'bogeyman' are used to describe the two serial killers that homicide detective and psychologist, Alex Cross, attempts to hunt down.[39] To consign crime to the realm of pure evil and individual moral monstrosity is a way of isolating it from all social, political or economic causes, and 'explaining' it as a freakish and psychopathic exception to all that we know to be normal. This is exactly what Cornwell does throughout *Postmortem*. The serial killer is 'the monster' (p. 23). Scarpetta explains to Lucy that he is one of those 'people who are evil . . . Like dogs . . . Some dogs bite people for

no reason. There's something wrong with them. They're bad and will always be bad', and when Lucy replies 'Like Hitler' (p. 39), the simile is allowed to stand unchallenged. This kind of discourse runs throughout the text ('He isn't *sick* . . . He's antisocial, he's evil . . .' p. 92) and returns the reader to a black-and-white world where evil stands as pure 'other', finally abolished with the return to social 'normality' brought about by the (mostly) rational, analytic, and commanding figure of the female detective.

Scarpetta's restoration of the status quo, the heroic qualities with which she is associated, and the identification between criminality and moral monstrosity, suggest we can find in this version of the police procedural much of the same 'conservative' tactics (to recall Dennis Porter's earlier comments) to be found in the private-eye novel: indeed, if anything, in exaggerated form. Even the criminal acts committed by members of the ruling Richmond establishment are seen as individual blemishes—sexual passion, a personal grudge—rather than symptoms of systemic corruption. The eventual restoration of Scarpetta's individual authority as scientific investigator (necessary of course for Cornwell's sequence of novels to continue) thus goes together, despite some earlier signs to the contrary, with a continuing confidence in the 'goodness' and efficacy of the law, and a complete acceptance of the social order which it defends.

I am not attempting to lay down absolute rules for the detective novel with the patterns I have identified in this chapter, but to suggest one line of development, and the prominence of a certain set of relationships, within the hard-boiled tradition. The genre is one which, especially in recent years, has been developed in many different directions, and the representation of the relationship between the individual detective and the existing social order *can* be used (as both lesbian detective fiction, and that by members of ethnic and racial minority groups, illustrate) to challenge dominant values and stereotypes. The more effective the nature of that challenge, I would suggest, though, the further the writer must depart from the basic generic model.

That the detective novel, both private-eye and police procedural, is able to contain widely divergent social and political visions can be suggested by brief reference to James Ellroy's work within the latter sub-genre. Ellroy's fictions offer a far more disturbing conception both of the subject and her or his relation to the larger social system than that found in Cornwell. The disorienting narrative tactics he uses (as compared to the majority of detective fictions) challenge standard generic expectations. For the confusing landscape of his novels—the moves between different locations, events, and narrative perspectives, the rapid-fire movement of his elliptic prose, and the sheer number of his characters—works at a textual level to suggest the problematic nature of any authoritative negotiation of the complex and labyrinthine city world he depicts. And, in the thoroughgoing nature of his destabilising of the agency and identity of his detective subjects, he radically challenges the sense of individual autonomy, objectivity and authority on which the detective genre has tended traditionally to rely.[40] Ellroy's fictional refigurations of the history and geography of Los Angeles of the late 1940s and 1950s serve as entry points to a fictional world of collapsing boundaries, uncanny doublings and identity slippage, where political, economic and media interests powerfully combine in the suppression of any version of the 'truth', and where the law (and the investigative actions of his cop protagonists) are always subordinate to such interests. In his later chapter in this collection, Josh Cohen suggests how:

> Ellroy's shift of narrative perspective from the Chandlerian private eye to the waged cop constitutes a critique of the romanticised and historically inaccurate figuration of crime as existential conflict between alienated individual and urban modernity, and consequently marks the progressive cooption of *flaneurie* by the state.

The logic of my own chapter is, then, in many ways continued in his. Ellroy's is a grim and one-sided picture but it is one that cuts through the romantic and existentialist elements of the private-eye genre. And, if his vision of the deep-seated corruption of the public world (and the collapse of the boundaries between criminality and legality) is standard hard-boiled fare, and if his narratives (as one might also expect) conclude with the continuation and restoration of the social status quo, they provide, nonetheless, an effective counterbalance to the less provocative and more conformist fictions of some of his hard-boiled peers. The detective novel, as my final comments suggest, is a generic house with many different rooms. The intent, in the chapters which follow, is critically to unlock and explore at least some of these rooms.[41]

Notes

1. See Marty Roth, *Foul & Fair Play: Reading Genre in Classic Detective Fiction* (Athens: University of Georgia Press, 1995), pp. 158, 176, 185 et al.

2. See Dennis Porter, *The Pursuit of Crime: Art and Ideology in Detective Fiction* (New Haven: Yale University Press, 1981), p. 41. The start of my second paragraph begins to imply, however, the problematic nature of 'realism' as a term.

3. Bethany Ogdon, 'Hard-boiled Ideology', *Critical Quarterly,* vol. 34, no. 1 (Spring, 1992), p. 84.

4. Roth, *Foul & Fair Play,* pp. xiv, 113.

5. Ralph Willett, *Hard-Boiled Detective Fiction, BAAS Pamphlets in American Studies 23* (Halifax: Ryburn, 1992), p. 5.

6. See Porter, *The Pursuit of Crime,* p. 68.

7. Sara Paretsky, *Tunnel Vision* (London: QPD, 1994 [1993]), p. 103.

8. Evelyne Keitel, 'The Woman's Private Eye View', *Amerikastudien: Eine Vierteljahresschrift,* vol. 39 (1994), pp. 170-1. See too Keitel's comments on Sue Grafton's Kinsey Millhone.

9. Willett, *Hard-Boiled Detective Fiction,* pp. 8-9.

10. Robert B. Parker, *Paper Doll* (New York: Berkley, 1994 [1993]), p. 130.

11. Paretsky, *Tunnel Vision,* p. 182.

12. Such control is often in fact illusory, the province merely of the verbal.

13. Sue Grafton, *F Is for Fugitive* (New York: Bantam, 1990 [1989]), p. 47.

14. Rosemary Jackson, *Fantasy: The Literature of Subversion* (London: Methuen, 1981), pp. 45, 44-6. James Ellroy's fictions continually metaphorically insist on the loss of such visual control. See, for instance, the play on the idea of Danny Upshaw as 'Man Camera' in *The Big Nowhere* (London: Arrow, 1994 [1989]), pp. 5, 94, 134, 166-7 et al.

15. Quoted in David Frisby's incisive essay, 'Walter Benjamin and Detection', *German Politics and Society,* issue 32 (Summer, 1994), p. 95.

16. See Frisby, 'Walter Benjamin and Detection', pp. 94, 93, 97. For discussion of the difference between 'evidence' and 'clue', and of the concept of 'relatedness', see Roth, *Foul & Fair Play,* pp. 186-92. Roth's comments on the way the detective sifts through '*dirt* or *garbage*' (p. 199) connects with Benjamin's flaneur/detective, searching 'among the refuse . . . for secrets among the confusion of things' (Frisby, p. 95).

17. See Roth, *Foul & Fair Play,* p. 164.

18. Sue Grafton, *K Is for Killer* (London: Macmillan, 1994), p. 141.

19. Robert B. Parker, *Promised Land* (Harmondsworth, Middlesex: Penguin, 1978 [1976]), pp. 41-2.

20. See Franco Moretti's essay 'Clues', in his *Signs Taken for Wonders: Essays in the Sociology of Literary Forms,* trans. Susan Fischer, David Forgacs, David Miller (London: Verso, 1983). This is one of the most useful and stimulating essays on detective fiction, though it mainly focuses on the classical rather than the hard-boiled model.

21. See Ogdon, 'Hard-boiled Ideology', pp. 74-5.

22. Ibid., p. 76.

23. Porter, *The Pursuit of Crime,* pp. 122, 125.

24. Moretti, *Signs Taken for Wonders,* pp. 139, 154-5. David Murray repeats the former quote in his chapter on Tony Hillerman. This suggests its importance to any discussion of the detective genre and its social implications.

25. Willett, *Hard-Boiled Detective Fiction,* p. 54. See, too, the section on Paretsky in the same author's *The Naked City: Urban Crime Fiction in the USA* (Manchester: Manchester University Press, 1996), pp. 110-15.

26. Roth, *Foul & Fair Play,* pp. 61, 170.

27. Moretti, *Signs Taken for Wonders,* p. 137.

28. Porter, *The Pursuit of Crime,* p. 125.

29. Though, again, see Barry Taylor's chapter for a counter-argument.

30. James Ellroy, *The American Cop, without Walls,* Channel 4 (British) TV programme, 29 November, 1994.

31. Joyce Carol Oates, 'The Simple Art of Murder', *The New York Review of Books,* vol. 42, no. 20 (21 December 1995), pp. 34-5.

32. Oates, 'The Simple Art of Murder', p. 34.

33. One place the individualist fantasy has migrated is into the right-wing populism of the *Dirty Harry* and vigilante sub-genres, with their vision of procedure as liberal evasion and obfuscation. This is suggestive of some of the political ambivalences behind the Chandler model itself. I am indebted to Barry Taylor's comments on the draft version of my chapter for my argument here. My thanks to him, and to Dave Murray, for their very helpful advice at this stage.

34. This is not to say that such a sense of alienation and apartness does not exist in such fiction: see, for instance, James Lee Burke's fictional detective, Dave Robicheaux.

35. Oates, 'The Simple Art of Murder', p. 34.

36. Patricia Cornwell, *Postmortem* (New York: Avon, 1991 [1990]), p. 1. Henceforth, page references to follow quotes.

37. Intuition also plays its part here. Later chapters in this collection return to the question of the relationship between reason and intuition.

38. I acknowledge my debt here to a paper given by Barry Taylor on Thomas Harris' *The Silence of the Lambs* (1988) at the British Association for American Studies conference in April 1991. See also his 'The Violence of the Event: Hannibal Lecter in the Lyotardian Sublime', in Steven Earnshaw (ed.), *Postmodern Surroundings* (Amsterdam and Atlanta, Georgia: Editions Rodopi, 1994), pp. 215-30.

39. See James Patterson, *Kiss the Girls* (London: HarperCollins, 1995), pp. 161, 237, 332 et al.

40. Ever since Hammett, the matter of the identity and role of the hard-boiled detective has been far from unproblematic. See, for instance, John Whitley, 'Stirring Things Up: Dashiell Hammett's Continental Op', *Journal of American Studies,* vol. 14, no. 3 (December, 1980), pp. 443-556. In Ellroy, though, this concern is taken to its furthest limits.

41. I dedicate this chapter to the memory of Tony Sycamore. His enthusiasm for detective fiction was contagious.

Hans Bertens and Theo D'haen (essay date 2001)

SOURCE: Bertens, Hans, and Theo D'haen. Introduction to *Contemporary American Crime Fiction,* pp. 1-16. Houndmills, England: Palgrave, 2001.

[*In the following essay, Bertens and D'haen trace the origins of modern crime fiction in the works of nineteenth-century authors, reflecting on the changes in style and focus of crime fiction as it has evolved into the twentieth century.*]

Crime writing, in the sense of 'writing about crime', predates the rise of the detective story. We already find it in the sixteenth and seventeenth centuries in the numerous pamphlets and broadsheets detailing the heinous deeds of murderers, robbers, and highwaymen. In the eighteenth century, Daniel Defoe, next to his many other writings, not only turned out numerous 'true crime' stories; he also turned them into literature, for instance *Moll Flanders* (1721). In the nineteenth century, crime fuels the plot of some of the best known works of Honoré de Balzac, Edward Bulwer-Lytton, Charles Dickens, and the great Russian writers, first and foremost Fyodor Dostoevsky.

It is also to the nineteenth century that we can trace the origins of the two main streams in detective fiction. In Edgar Allan Poe's 'tales of ratiocination' and Arthur Conan Doyle's Sherlock Holmes stories, we encounter the gifted amateur detective. He is the forerunner of the heroes of Agatha Christie, Dorothy Sayers, Margery Allingham, and numerous other practitioners of the genre in the period that is now commonly referred to as the 'Golden Age' of British detective writing—a period that begins after the First World War and ends with the outbreak of the Second World War. In the same period the amateur detective develops into the American 'hard-boiled' private investigator, the 'private eye' who detects for a living. The nineteenth century also announced what would eventually become the police procedural in novels by Charles Dickens and Wilkie Collins (*The Moonstone* (1869)), and, on the European Continent, in the work of French writers such as Emile Gaboriau. These precursors would seem to have been inspired by the actual activities of the then newly created police forces or detective departments.

The British Golden Age mystery typically features a closed setting (a country manor, a university college, a library, a train, a cruise ship, a country village), a middle to upper class milieu (from the modest means of Agatha Christie's Miss Marple to the nobility of Dorothy Sayers's Lord Peter Wimsey and the near-royalty of Margery Allingham's Albert Campion), and a usually eccentric detective. The detective's task is to repair an individual violation of a social order that embodies a collective and unchanging ideal of 'Britain' (or perhaps even only 'England', as few Golden Age mysteries seem to bother with what is felt or thought beyond the home counties). In the 1990s, a number of American crime writers, particularly Martha Grimes and Elizabeth George, have shown remarkable skill updating this essentially British interbellum mystery mode. In a different vein Peter J. Heck has his American mysteries—featuring Mark Twain—echo Agatha Christie.

In contrast to the classic English 'whodunit', the setting and form of the American private investigator novel are open. The setting is urban. Even where some scenes are set in the country, as in Chandler's *The Lady in the Lake* (1945), the story starts and ends in the big city with emphasis placed on the continual movement of the protagonist, especially by car. The private investigators of Dashiell Hammett, Raymond Chandler, and Ross Macdonald stand for a certain idea of decency, honor, comradeship, in short, for what it means to be 'an American', particularly a male American. The world that Sam Spade, Philip Marlowe, and Lew Archer operate in, though, is rotten at the core. The private eye has to break or bend the law himself in order to reassert an ideal 'America' founded on equality, justice, and the right to life, liberty, and the pursuit of happiness. However, that reassertion always remains both incidental and temporary. The private eye remains incapable of structurally righting his world. The British-style Golden Age detective guarantees a reassuring return to a well ordered and closed universe. The American-style hard-boiled private eye, on the contrary, leaves us with a sprawling urban jungle pressing in on us, and no guarantees whatsoever—or, to put it another way, with many questions but no answers.

The alienation that results from the fundamental incompatibility between the private eye's moral ideal and the unruly reality of the world he lives in only deepens as the twentieth century wears on. Raymond Chandler's *The Big Sleep* (1939) indicts the ecological, social, and moral waste occasioned by the oil industry. Ross Macdonald's *The Moving Target* (1949) denounces the exploitation of Mexican illegal immigrant labor in California's postwar agricultural industry. To take an example from the 1990s, James Crumley's *Border-snakes* (1996) focuses on the absolute and arbitrary use of power by Texan ranchers along the Mexican border, and on the morally corrupting army background of the wealthiest of these. In novels featuring ethnic private eyes, such as Walter Mosley's 'Easy' Rawlins series, the exploitative nature of white-dominated America with regard to its non-white citizens is simply a given.

Though the private eye is still going strong—if not without some modifications to the original formula—it may well be that the police procedural is much better suited to our age than private eye fiction. As Peter Messent puts it in *Criminal Proceedings,*

> the police procedural . . . seems to be supplanting the private-eye novel as 'realistic' crime fiction . . . while the latter relies on a model of rule-bending individualism, the former puts its emphasis precisely on procedure and *collective agency* . . . a fantasy of extra-systemic freedom and authenticity gives way to a more problematic vision of individual detectives operating through systemic procedures.
>
> (Messent, 1997, 12)

As such the police procedural more accurately reflects the increasingly complex and organized nature of present day society. The private investigator, then, has to move over. In fact, in much 1990s crime fiction the protagonist, if male, no longer is a professional private investigator, but rather someone who drifts into 'detecting' almost by accident, and often against the grain. Such an investigator of sorts often is, or at least starts out as, a marginal down-but-not-quite-out—a former lawyer or newspaperman who has fallen on hard times. John Lescroart's Dismas Hardy, Steven Womack's Harry James Denton, Doug J. Swanson's Jack Flippo, and John Morgan Wilson's Benjamin Justice fit this category. Eventually, such characters may apply for a legitimate private eye license. For instance, Lescroart's hero, when we first meet him in *Dead Irish* (1989), is an ex-marine, ex-cop, ex-lawyer, ex-husband, who now works as a bartender in San Francisco. The other novels in the Dismas Hardy series, *The Vig* (1990), *Hard Evidence* (1993), *The 13th Juror* (1994), and *The Mercy Rule* (1998), see Hardy mount the social ladder again. He rejoins the DA's office, then sets up as a defense lawyer. These later books more and more turn into courtroom dramas or legal thrillers.

Female private eyes of the 1990s, in contrast, more often have a past within the police force and usually immediately set up as private eyes after leaving the force, though in true hard-boiled fashion they, too, have to struggle to make ends meet: Valerie Wilson Wesley's Tamara Hayle, Grace F. Edwards's Mali Anderson, and Kathy Hogan Trocheck's Callahan Garrity all fit this bill.

Some recent private eyes, such as George P. Pelecanos's Nick Stefanos, verge on the grotesque. Others combine the roles of private eye and heroine of a screwball comedy, as, for instance, Janet Evanovich's Stephanie Plum. Or they completely cross over into zany humor, as in the case of Groucho Marx look-alike (and talk-alike) Kinky Friedman. Those that remain on the serious side, like Dennis Lehane's Kenzie and Gennaro, and Harlan Coben's Myron Bolitar, often end up openly despairing at the final ineffectualness of the present day private eye. Rare indeed seems to be the private investigator who comes across as absolutely credible and simultaneously conveys a reasonably optimistic message. In the last fifteen years, only Robert Crais's Elvis Cole fits this category, even though Crais only succeeds by ironizing his classic hard-boiled predecessors.

However effectual private investigators may be, in the final analysis they always remain outsiders to the social, economic, and political bodies whose corruption and decay they expose. The police procedural allows for detailing such corruption and decay from *within* the very institutions that theoretically should safeguard America's ideal order. In the 1990s, especially James Ellroy and Michael Connelly have fully exploited the possibilities of this subgenre in linking the themes of individual, institutional, and social corruption. James Ellroy focuses on the moral decay of political, big crime, economic, and media America in *L.A. Confidential* (1990) and *American Tabloid* (1996). In Michael Connelly's Harry Bosch novels, society's official guardians themselves turn into criminals often as the result of injustices or humiliations they suffered at the hands of that same society. *The Black Ice* (1993) explicitly traces the turning into a drug baron of an LA detective, and the resulting string of brutal murders, to the exploitation of Mexican and Asian immigrant labor along the US-Mexican border during the early part of the twentieth century. In the same writer's debut, *The Black Echo* (1992), a high-ranking FBI official, who was once on the staff of the US embassy in Saigon, turns into the leader of a gang of bank robbers composed of Vietnam veterans. More in general, even when the criminals in recent police procedurals are psychopathic monsters, they have been made that way by society, witness the serial murderers of James Ellroy's *Blood on the Moon* (1984) and *The Black Dahlia* (1987), Thomas Harris's *Silence of the Lambs* (1988), or Caleb Carr's *The Alienist* (1994).

Not surprisingly, given the 1990s climate of political correctness, racism, ethnicity, and gender feature prominently on the agenda of much present day crime writing. However, outspoken critique largely remains the province of ethnic and female detective writing. The mainstream white male detective—both the private investigator and the police detective—has largely moved into the realm of the personal and psychological—see for instance Lawrence Block's Matthew Scudder and Connelly's Harry Bosch—or of the grotesque and the horrible, as in Harris's *Silence of the Lambs,* and much of Ellroy's fiction. This is not to say that the latter

works do not reflect on society. It is rather that in these novels that social dimension is to be inferred from the situations, actions, and characters they present us with. In fact, the result can politically be very powerful, as in Ellroy's *American Tabloid,* or T. Jefferson Parker's *The Triggerman's Dance* (1996), where the protagonist is pressured by the FBI into infiltrating a rightwing outfit financed by a wealthy businessman intent on keeping America white. Another rightwing conspiracy drives the plot of James Lee Burke's *Dixie City Jam* (1994), in which Louisiana Cajun detective Dave Robicheaux is up against a band of neo-Nazis that threaten not only the life of his wife, but also the fabric of American society.

The rise of multiculturalism in the 1980s and 1990s has led to a veritable explosion of 'ethnic minority' crime writing. Of course, even well before the advent of multiculturalism, non-white protagonists were not unfamiliar in American detective fiction. From the 1920s on at least, African American detectives have held a place in American crime writing, and Chester Himes's Coffin Ed Johnson and Grave Digger Jones played a prominent role in 1950s and 1960s crime fiction. In the 1920s and 1930s, the ethnically Chinese Honolulu Police detective Charlie Chan featured in a popular series of novels by Earl Derr Biggers, and subsequently in a long string of even more popular movies. The early 1970s saw the introduction of a native American detective in the figure of Tony Hillerman's Lieutenant Joe Leaphorn of the Navajo Tribal Police, who in the course of the 1980s was seconded by Sergeant Jim Chee who later went on to replace him. Hillerman gained both early and lasting recognition for this series, winning the Edgar Award for *Dance Hall of the Dead* (1973), an Anthony Award for *Skinwalkers* (1986), and a Macavity for *A Thief of Time* (1988). In 1991 The Mystery Writers of America named Hillerman Grand Master. However, although their protagonists are non-caucasian, Biggers and Hillerman themselves were, or are, definitely Anglo. Until recently only African American authors seem to have featured detectives representative of their own ethnic minority.

In the 1990s, however, there has been a very definite change, as we can gather from the increasing recognition on the part of award-granting bodies of writers with non-caucasian backgrounds. In 1994 Chinese-Korean American Laura Joh Rowland's *Shinjū* (1994) was nominated for a Hammett Award. With *Death in Little Tokyo* (1996), starring a Japanese-American computer executive who turns into an amateur detective, Dale Furutani was co-winner of an Anthony for Best First Novel. The novel also won a Macavity for Best First Mystery, and was nominated for an Agatha for Best First Mystery Novel. If we look at African American authors we see that Walter Mosley won a Shamus for Best First Novel with *Devil in a Blue Dress* (1990), and a Hammett Award nomination with *White*

Butterfly (1992), while Barbara Neely's 1992 *Blanche on the Lam* won Anthony, Macavity, and Agatha awards for Best First Novel of the year—a feat almost repeated by Terris McMahan Grimes's *Somebody Else's Child* (1996).

Regardless of ethnic or gender background, we find that social issues dominating public discussion at the time of writing increasingly filter into crime writing. This is very clear in Sara Paretsky's Vic Warshawski mysteries. *Tunnel Vision* (1994), for instance, addresses incest, single parent families, the housing conditions of the poor, and their attendant health problems. Pornography, snuff movies, and the sexual exploitation of youth set the themes of Lawrence Block's *A Dance at the Slaughterhouse* (1992). In different ways, some of these same issues also inform Grace F. Edwards' *If I Should Die* (1997), Valerie Wilson Wesley's *When Death Comes Stealing* (1994), Dennis Lehane's *Gone, Baby, Gone* (1998), and Michael Nava's *The Burning Plain* (1999) —a motley crew comprising two African American women writers, one white male, and one gay Chicano. It is worth noting that these 1990s crime writers sometimes cast doubt on the socially and legally correct solution to the issue they raise in a particular novel. Lehane's *Gone, Baby, Gone,* for instance, which seems at least partly inspired by the dismal string of child abductions and murders that came to light with the arrest of Marc Dutroux in the summer of 1997 in Belgium, takes an unexpected turn when the four-year old whom the PI duo of Kenzie and Gennaro are eventually able to return home, might really have been better off with her kidnappers, who actually were trying to rescue her from her irresponsible mother.

New, also, is that the social issues just mentioned heavily impinge on the private life of 1990s detectives. The fact that detectives have a private life is of course in itself already a major departure from the hard-boiled tradition. Since the 1980s, and especially in the 1990s, characters increasingly develop over the series in which they feature. Personal and family relationships may influence the progress of the detective's case. Lehane's Patrick Kenzie and Angela Gennaro novels, the first of which, *A Drink Before the War* (1994), won a Shamus Award in 1995, are set in Dorchester, a south Boston Irish-Italian, and increasingly also African American, working-class suburb where both PIs also grew up. Kenzie and Gennaro's familiarity with the neighborhood, its people, its cops, its smalltime hoods as well as local mafia bosses, is vital to their ability to solve the cases they get involved in. At the same time, these cases also have a strange way of taking them back to their own youth or childhood.

An author who gleefully exposes his private investigator's very personal life, and does so in an inimitably idiosyncratic way, is Kinky Friedman, whose series features a New York-based 'Texas Jew boy' named after his author. The Friedman novels offer pungent social commentary, but unlike for instance Lehane's Kenzie and Gennaro novels, they do not do so by way of their plot, but rather in the form of acerbic asides to the reader. In fact, in a 1990 interview in *Clues* Friedman (the author) stated in the tongue-in-cheek tone typical of his work that 'plots are cemeteries . . . if you get a plot in a Kinky book, you can consider it gravy . . . basically, they evolve . . . I deal in loops more than in plots' (Friedman, 1990, 5). To say that the Kinky Friedman novels have no plot at all is perhaps an exaggeration. What plot there is, though, is usually quirky, and driven by verbal pyrotechnics rather than what one would call narrative logic. Here, for instance, is part of a telephone conversation between the 'Kinkster' and a prospective client in *God Bless John Wayne* (1995)— Friedman's cat has just knocked his 'large, Texas-shaped ashtray' upside down onto his crotch:

> 'Get off the goddamn desk', I said to the cat in a stage whisper.
>
> 'I beg your pardon?'
>
> 'Nothing,' I said. 'Domestic problem.'
>
> 'There will, of course', she continued, 'be a very handsome retainer.'
>
> 'My teeth are fine', I said. 'God's my orthodontist.'
>
> There was a fairly long silence on the line. The woman, obviously, was not amused. I looked up at the cat and saw that the cat, obviously, was not amused either. If you always spent your time trying to entertain women and cats, I reflected, life could be a hard room to work.
>
> *(Wayne, 2-3)*

Still, while the series in question is undoubtedly interesting in its own right, and a welcome addition to the varied landscape of 1990s American crime writing, Friedman's handling of the conventions of the detective genre is so idiosyncratic that it is difficult to see how anyone else could build on his particular achievement.

A number of stock attributes of the hard-boiled private eye—the weather, drinking, smoking, music, cars, clothes, literary quotations and references—continue to play a role in 1990s crime writing, though often they are used tongue-in-cheek to playfully reflect on the genre itself. For instance, in Hammett's *The Maltese Falcon* (1930) it rains heavily throughout most of the action; Joe Lansdale's *The Two-Bear Mambo* (1995) takes this device to its logical limit when constant rain brings about a flood with grotesque consequences for the plot of the novel. In Vicky Hendricks's *Miami Purity* (1995) the sweltering heat that weighs down the characters is only one of many pointers to James M. Cain's *The Postman Always Rings Twice* of 1934 (with the novel's title recalling the popular 1980s television series *Miami Vice*).

The 'thick' description of details of dress, food, drink, and cars typical for crime writing undoubtedly has something to do with the reality effect that crime fiction typically strives for. Beyond this, though, and particularly in 1990s crime fiction, description also serves to signal certain qualities about the characters and their world. The only car that will work for Evanovich's Stephanie Plum, for instance, is a 1950s Buick. In *Bordersnakes,* James Crumley's Milo Milodragovitch drives a superb Cadillac El Dorado, whereas the Mexican drugs dealers go around in Japanese jeeps. Michael Ventura, in *The Death of Frank Sinatra* (1996), has his private eye Mike Rose enjoy the Las Vegas air in a fabulous white 1972 Cadillac convertible. In general, good guys drive American makes, bad guys Japanese cars (even if built in the United States) or (less frequently) expensive foreign imports. Connelly's Harry Bosch drives a Ford Caprice (police issue), just as he drinks domestic brand beers, and smokes domestic brand cigarettes. Rock music from the 1970s and 1980s draws the line between 'us' and 'them' for Pelecanos's Nick Stefanos, while jazz serves that function for Connelly's Bosch and for Grace F. Edwards' Mali Anderson in *If I Should Die.*

Particularly noteworthy in the crime fiction of the late 1980s and the 1990s is the fascination with serial killers—undoubtedly sparked off by a number of notorious real-life instances. Probably the best known novel in question remains Thomas Harris's *The Silence of the Lambs* (1988), not least because of the highly successful movie version. Beyond this, though, certain plots and themes regarding serial killers seem to take on a life of their own in this period, and particularly so in white male crime writing. In Ellroy's *Blood on the Moon* (1984), the killer sends the woman he eventually intends to be his final victim a red rose after each murder. To taunt the detective investigating the case the killer each time sends a poem. In Parker's *Crimson Joy* (1988), a serial murderer leaves a red rose at the scene of each crime. The killer in Philip Margolin's *Gone, but Not Forgotten* (1993) leaves a (black) rose at each murder scene, and writes poems to the detectives on the case, as does the killer in Connelly's *The Concrete Blonde* (1994).

In what follows it is our aim to survey the work of some of the groundbreaking crime writers of the 1990s. Before we start on our tour, it is necessary that we first say something about what has probably been the most remarkable development of all, namely the astonishingly prominent role of women writers on the contemporary American crime fiction scene.

Given the prominence of women writers on the American popular fiction scene of the second half of the nineteenth century, it is not surprising that American women writers were among the first to explore the pos-

sibilities offered by the then still brand-new genre of detective fiction. Anna Katherine Green, for instance, published her first mystery in 1878, thus preceding Arthur Conan Doyle by ten years, and remained active well into the 1920s. Moreover, some of these early female mystery writers achieved massive popularity. Mary Roberts Rinehart, who can rightfully be seen as Green's literary heiress, and who published books from 1908 until the early 1950s, was at one point in her career the highest paid author in the United States.

However, while in the 1920s and 1930s British women authors succeeded in establishing themselves as major contributors to the mystery, their American counterparts, for all their success in terms of sales, were slow in finding similar recognition. When in 1930 the doyen of British mystery writers, Arthur Conan Doyle, died, a whole range of female successors had either already made a name for themselves (Agatha Christie, Dorothy Sayers, Patricia Wentworth), had just started doing so (Margery Allingham, Josephine Tey), or was waiting in the wings (Ngaio Marsh, who was born and bred in New Zealand, but would firmly situate herself in the British tradition). By the time the Second World War broke out the great names in British detective writing were female rather than male. In the United States critical success was almost exclusively reserved for men. Rinehart may have been the biggest seller, but for the critics the pace was set by her much younger male colleagues. As a matter of fact, in the crime fiction canon of the American interbellum women are still virtually invisible.

In retrospect, we can see that the (male) American crime writers who started their careers in the second half of the 1920s and the early 1930s were, in some cases perhaps unwittingly, engaged in masculinizing a genre that in the USA maintained up until that point strong links with the 'women's novel' of the second half of the nineteenth century; the novel whose widespread popularity had so aggravated not exactly bestselling contemporary writers like Nathaniel Hawthorne. Although the romance-cum-suspense mysteries of Rinehart, who at the time easily outsold all of her young male colleagues, are of course not a straight continuation of the 'women's novel', their setting, manipulation of gothic themes, and 'romance' character, have strong affinities with the genre. The masculinization of American crime writing took several forms. From the mid-1920s on, S. S. Van Dine and, a little later, Ellery Queen and John Dickson Carr (who in spite of his utterly British detectives, Dr Fell and Sir Henry Merrivale must be unconditionally claimed for the United States) took their cue from Conan Doyle and intellectualized the genre, presenting ingenious puzzles, often involving arcane information, and what seemed to be rigorous exercises in logic on the part of a superior mind. In 1933 Erle Stanley Gardner published the first of his countless Perry Mason books, bringing the macho clash of personalities and wits of the American courtroom into the genre. The following year James M. Cain's *The Postman Always Rings Twice* brought a new, and what at the time seemed a stark and unsentimental realism to crime writing. Cain held a seedy world of sorry and almost accidental criminals up for anxious but spell-bound examination. Last but not least, between 1929 and 1934 Dashiell Hammett published the five novels that for all practical purposes established the field of private eye fiction, a field whose tough-guy masculinity seemed almost designed to keep out female writers, let alone female protagonists. Even if the private eye preferred a strictly regulated and sedentary life style to the usual fast and unpredictable action, as did Rex Stout's beer-swilling Nero Wolfe who made his first appearance in the 1934 *Fer-de-Lance,* his masculinity and, in this particular case, hostility to women, was strongly emphasized.

This masculinization of American crime writing (or detective and mystery fiction as most of it was until recently called) marginalized its female practitioners. It was not until the 1950s, thirty years after their British colleagues, that American women began to be a real force on the American scene. Dorothy B. Hughes, Margaret Millar, Charlotte Armstrong (who all had started publishing in the early 1940s) and Patricia Highsmith (whose first novel appeared in 1950) won the respect of their peers that had been denied to their predecessors. In 1956 the Edgar Award was won by Margaret Millar's *Beast in View,* while Patricia Highsmith's *The Talented Mr Ripley* featured on the short-list, and the next year the Edgar went to Charlotte Armstrong, for her *A Dram of Poison.* A few years before, Dorothy Salisbury Davis's *A Gentle Murder* (1951) had already won her a reputation as a highly skilful writer of suspense tales, a status that was confirmed by the Edgar nomination for her 1959 *A Gentleman Called.* Still, if one looks at the history of the Mystery Writers of America's Grand Master Award—surely the most prestigious and coveted award in the field of crime writing—it is hard to avoid the conclusion that critical recognition of the achievement of the older generations of female American crime writers has been rather slow in coming. While the first ever Grand Master Award went to Agatha Christie, in 1955, in was not until 1971 that the honor was conferred upon the first American woman, Mignon Eberhart. Interestingly, Eberhart's election as a Grand Master may be interpreted as a sort of breakthrough. Eberhart, who had produced a steady stream of novels since her debut in 1929—coincidentally also the year of Queen's and Hammett's first novels—owed a good deal to Mary Roberts Rinehart and borrowed liberally from the gothic romance whose influence her male contemporaries had sought to remove from the crime writing scene. With hindsight, then, Eberhart's election to crime writing's Hall of Fame may be construed as a belated re-evaluation of one particular strand of crime fiction that had earlier been ignored because of its links with women's fiction. And perhaps we may see John Dickson Carr's flirtation with the gothic in the later part of his career in the same light.

Still, Eberhart's election was something of a fluke. It took seven years until the next woman, Dorothy B. Hughes, was similarly honored. Hughes, however, had to share the honor with Daphne du Maurier and Ngaio Marsh in what seems a transparent attempt to right a historical wrong. This triple election was in any case rather insulting: 1978 is the only year in which three Grand Masters were created in one single swoop, so that for once the honor conferred was unpleasantly diluted. It is only since the early 1980s that the female contribution to American crime writing has been more adequately recognized. Between 1983 and 1990 Margaret Millar, Dorothy Salisbury Davis, Phyllis A. Whitney (another writer heavily indebted to the romance and gothic traditions) and Helen McCloy (who had started her career as early as 1938) were added to the roster of Grand Masters.

It is tempting to think that this belated reappraisal is related to similar reappraisals of female achievement that have taken place under the pressure of feminist scholarship in a whole range of artistic and semi-artistic disciplines. Another reason may well be that the vitality and strength of recent female crime writing have contributed to the substantially increased visibility of the work of earlier generations of women writers. The female boom of the last two decades—see Walton and Jones for detailed figures and charts (1999, 27-30 and 41-3)—is of course part of the more general revitalization of crime writing that we have witnessed since the early 1970s (and for which Patricia Highsmith and her British colleagues P. D. James and Ruth Rendell had helped to pave the way).

Tony Hillerman published his first Joe Leaphorn book, *The Blessing Way,* in 1970; two years later George V. Higgins started his series of talkative crime novels with *The Friends of Eddie Coyle;* Robert B. Parker introduced Spenser, heir apparent to Philip Marlowe and Lew Archer, in the 1973 *The Godwulf Manuscript;* Elmore Leonard abandoned the Western for taut, ironical, and streetwise crime stories; Lawrence Block's Matt Scudder made a first, tentative, appearance in three mid-1970s paperbacks; Martin Cruz Smith was flexing his muscles (meanwhile making a living as Nick Carter and Simon Quinn) for the smash hit *Gorky Park* (1981), and so on and so forth. But even if we take that general renaissance, in which women crime writers begin to fully participate in the early 1980s, into account, we must still conclude that in the second Golden Age of crime writing that we are still witnessing, female crime writing stands out because of its power, its breadth, its innovation, and even its irreverence, no matter if that irreverence at times takes the form of a somewhat childish mischievousness (but Thomas Harris's unpleasant Hannibal Lecter stuff did deserve the awful parody in the title of Jill Churchill's *Silence of the Hams* (1996)).

Women writers are prominent in every subgenre crime writing has produced and have in fact recently added some. Patricia Cornwell has pioneered the forensic medicine novel, her debut *Postmortem* (1990) winning the Edgar, Anthony, Macavity, and John Creasey awards for Best First Novel plus the *Prix de Roman d'Aventure* in an unprecedented triumphal march that points both to the novel's groundbreaking qualities and the fact that women writers are now fully visible to award-granting juries and committees. Furthermore, since the publication of *Postmortem,* multiple awards have also gone to Nancy Pickard's *I.O.U.* (1991), Barbara Neely's *Blanche on the Lam* (1992), Margaret Maron's *Bootlegger's Daughter* (1992), Nevada Barr's *Track of the Cat* (1993), Sharyn McCrumb's *She Walks These Hills* (1994), Mary Willis Walker's *Under the Beetle's Cellar* (1995), and Terris McMahan Grimes's *Somebody Else's Child* (1996), to mention only those books that will be discussed in the following chapters. Nevada Barr, whose fascinating first novel *Track of the Cat* has just been mentioned, Judith Van Gieson, Karin McQuillan and others have developed what one might call ecological mysteries, with Barr specializing in National Parks, Van Gieson in endangered species, and McQuillan in Africa's wildlife.

We may add to this the meteoric rise of crime fiction with a lesbian protagonist. Initially limited to small specialized presses (Seal, Naiad), lesbian detectives have since the early 1990s found mainstream publishers in what must be seen as a major emancipatory breakthrough, even if the stance of their creators (Sandra Scoppettone, Ellen Hart, Katherine V. Forrest) is middle-of-the-road rather than radical. And then there is of course that most visible of all female subgenres: the private eye novel featuring a female investigator. Female private investigators were not absolutely unheard of before the early 1980s, when the current female PI boom took off. However, they were very rare and very hard to take seriously. Erle Stanley Gardner's Bertha Cool and G. G. Fickling's Honey West are equally implausible, even if they could not be more different. Unfortunately, the male hand of their creators is all too obvious (since 'G. G. Fickling' presented the combined creative efforts of Gloria and Forrest E. Fickling the hand is only half male in the case of Honey West). It is the new wave of women writers that began publishing in the late 1970s and early 1980s that gave us the credible and intelligent female private eye that now seems to have been around forever.

The late arrival of what are now the most visible subgenres within female crime writing—the police procedural (with its variations such as Cornwell's series featuring a medical examiner and Barr's series featuring a park ranger), and the PI novel—of course finds it explanation in social circumstances. Until well into the 1960s, the world of professional investigators, either salaried by a law enforcement agency or self-employed, was practically off-limits to women. They were employed to type up reports and to bring around coffee, but were only rarely allowed to do detective work. Moreover, the few women who were admitted to the sacred halls of actual investigation met with stubborn resistance. The career of Dorothy Uhnak, whose Christie Opara, police officer in New York City, is a very early female professional (her Edgar-winning first novel *The Bait* was published in 1968), illustrates the odds that female professionals faced even after their admission to the force. Having joined the New York City Transit Police Department in 1953, she became a detective in 1955, but left in disillusionment twelve years later: "'. . . I wasn't allowed to take the examination for promotion, so that after fourteen years, I left the department and returned to college . . .'" (Budd, 1986, 116). (See also Uhnak's account of such routinely discriminatory practices in her *Policewoman: A Young Woman's Initiation into the Realities of Justice,* 1964.) As a result, female crime writers who wanted to work with a realistically embedded female protagonist had to opt for the amateur formula. It is only in the last twenty-odd years that female professional investigators have been accepted by their superiors and colleagues, and often with great reluctance, so that fiction featuring a professional female detective could claim that it indeed reflected an emerging social reality.

Implicit in this is that certainly during the 1970s and 1980s crime fiction featuring a female professional almost inevitably possessed emancipatory qualities. With regard to the police procedural this emancipatory dimension consisted first of all in the simple, but very important, fact that women were shown as serious participants in law enforcement and in the bringing to justice of criminal offenders. But the police procedural was also perfectly equipped to show how one of society's most important institutions resisted such integration because of its masculinist nature. Bringing women into police departments almost invariably made the institution show its true, thoroughly masculinist colors and thereby undermined its supposed neutrality. If one does not see the female police procedural as a form of betrayal—with women defecting from their group and identifying with the masculinist State—then the genre quietly empowers its protagonists in their efforts to hold their own in a sometimes inimical and often condescending environment.

This empowerment is far more outspoken in the case of the female private investigator, especially if she is modeled after the classic male PI with his masculinist language and behavior but retains her own identifiably female perspective. (It is of course even more outspoken if the female investigator also adopts the classic PI's masculinist outlook. However, since a major aim of female empowerment is to detach power and gender from each other, adopting a masculinist stance that implicitly confirms the identification of power with masculinity is counterproductive. We will look at some examples of that counterproductiveness later in this book.) The female PI, then, is most effective if she simultaneously affirms and undermines the tradition because both strategies are means of self-empowerment. That empowerment begins with her self-employment and its corollary: her economic independence. Female PI's often emphasize that their independence is hard-won and difficult to maintain, which of course only adds to its symbolic value. A second, extremely important means of self-empowerment is the characteristic PI voice, wisecracking, ironic, self-mocking, sometimes conspirational (in the sense that the reader is made to feel an insider who is granted the privilege of sharing the PI's thoughts) and always irreverent and resolutely anti-hierarchical. Since the male PI already uses the style to empower himself, with female PI's the classic voice has a double impact: it signals that they are aware of one important source of power and that they are willing and able to cross gender lines in order to make it available to themselves. Female PI's can deploy this masculinist idiom and the accompanying attitude very effectively because its socially leveling thrust is in their case hooked up with the undermining of traditional gender roles, in particular if it is used against powerful males. (They must of course be on their guard against genuinely adopting the wilfully unemotional and detached stance that so often comes with the PI voice.) Moreover, the female PI novel, with its first-person female narrator, breaks with the format in which we have men looking at women (subjecting them to the power of the 'gaze', as modern literary theory would call it). Instead, we have women looking at men, or, even better, narrators who are aware of their narratorial power and subject it to scrutiny.

I should immediately add that very few female PI writers get around to such theoretical subtleties. The feminism of crime writing by women is almost invariably liberal rather than radical, so that the acts of resistance of their detectives get a personal rather than a political coloring. In other words, they often do not seem to be up against an impersonal, systemic form of discrimination, but against incidental and personal slights. Except in a number of novels featuring lesbian investigators we do not find the sort of theoretical awareness or politics that characterizes much contemporary academic feminism. Female investigators give no indication of having read Derrida or Lacan or of seeing the true phallocentric nature of things. However, even if its social origins remain obscure, there is no denying that they are aware of the inequality and the unequal power-sharing that confronts them wherever they go, or that they work consistently to resist and change the roles that Western society has traditionally reserved for women.

Dedicated readers of crime fiction know that female investigators do so consistently because they have been able to follow many of them through a whole series of novels. Since a series offers writers much more scope for developing a character or a group of characters than single novels which invariably lead to closure (especially in crime fiction), our focus will be on series and series protagonists. In discussing these series characters we will largely forgo theoretical exposition. This is not to deny the importance of theory, but it would be silly to pretend that crime writing is under-theorized and needs another book with a heavily theoretical approach. Anyone interested in theoretical perspectives can easily find them. Among such publications, we can especially recommend Sally Munt's *Murder by the Book? Feminism and the Crime Novel* (1994), some of the essays (including his own) in Peter Messent's collection *Criminal Proceedings: The Contemporary American Crime Novel* (1997), and Priscilla L. Walton and Manina Jones's *Detective Agency: Women Rewriting the Hard-Boiled Tradition* (1999). We will primarily, and from an openly evaluative point of view, look at the novels themselves.

Bibliography

Primary

Block, Lawrence. *A Dance at the Slaughterhouse.* New York: Avon, 1992.

Burke, James Lee. *Dixie City Jam.* New York: Hyperion, 1994.

Carr, Caleb. *The Alienist.* New York: Bantam, 1995 [1994].

———. *The Angel of Darkness.* New York: Ballantine, 1998 [1997].

Chandler, Raymond. *The Big Sleep.* Harmondsworth: Penguin, 1948 [1939].

Connelly, Michael. *The Black Echo.* New York: St. Martin's, 1993 [1992].

———. *The Black Ice.* London: Phoenix, 1996 [1993].

———. *The Concrete Blonde.* New York: St. Martin's, 1995 [1994].

———. *The Last Coyote.* New York: St. Martin's, 1996 [1995].

———. *The Poet*. New York: Warner Books, 1997 [1996].

———. *Trunk Music*. London: Orion, 1997.

———. *Blood Work*. London: Orion, 1998.

———. *Angels Flight*. Boston: Little, Brown, 1999.

Edwards, Grace F. *If I Should Die*. New York: Bantam, 1998 [1997].

Ellroy, James. *Brown's Requiem*. London: Arrow, 1995 [1981].

———. *Clandestine*. London: Arrow, 1996 [1982].

———. *Blood on the Moon*. In *L.A. Noir* [1984].

———. *Because the Night*. In *L.A. Noir* [1984].

———. *Suicide Hill*. In *L.A. Noir* [1986].

———. *The Black Dahlia*. London: Arrow, 1993 [1987].

———. *The Big Nowhere*. New York: Mysterious Press, 1989 [1988].

———. *L.A. Confidential*. New York: Warner, 1997 [1990].

———. *White Jazz*. London: Arrow, 1993 [1992].

———. *American Tabloid*. London: Arrow, 1995.

———. *My Dark Places*. London: Arrow, 1997 [1996].

———. *L.A. Noir: The Lloyd Hopkins Trilogy*. London: Arrow, 1997.

———. *The Cold Six Thousand*. New York: Knopf, 2001.

Friedman, Kinky. *God Bless John Wayne*. London and Boston: Faber and Faber, 1995.

Grimes, Terris McMahan. *Somebody Else's Child*. New York: Onyx, 1996.

———. *Blood Will Tell*. New York: Signet, 1997.

Harris, Thomas. *Red Dragon*. New York: Bantam 1998 [1981].

———. *The Silence of the Lambs*. New York: St. Martin's, 1991 [1988].

Hillerman, Tony. *The Blessing Way*. London: Macmillan, 1970.

———. *Dance Hall of the Dead*. New York: HarperPaperbacks, 1990 [1973].

———. *Skinwalkers*. New York: HarperPaperbacks, 1990 [1986].

———. *A Thief of Time*. New York: HarperPaperbacks, 1990 [1988].

———. *The First Eagle*. New York and London: HarperCollins, 1998.

Lansdale, Joe. *The Two-Bear Mambo*. London: Indigo, 1997 [1995].

Lehane, Dennis. *A Drink Before the War*. New York: Avon, 1996 [1994].

Lehane, Dennis. *Gone, Baby, Gone*. New York: Avon, 1999 [1998].

Lescroart, John. *Dead Irish*. London: Headline, 1996 [1989].

———. *The Vig*. London: Headline, 1996 [1990].

———. *Hard Evidence*. New York: Ivy, 1994 [1993].

———. *The 13th Juror*. New York: Island, 1995 [1994].

———. *The Mercy Rule*. London: Headline, 1999 [1998].

Margolin, Phillip. *Gone, but Not Forgotten*. New York: Bantam, 1994 [1984].

Mosley, Walter. *Devil in a Blue Dress*. London: Pan, 1992 [1990].

———. *A Red Death*. New York: Pocket Books, 1992 [1991].

———. *White Butterfly*. London: Pan, 1994 [1992].

———. *Black Betty*. London: Pan, 1995 [1994].

———. *A Little Yellow Dog*. London: Serpent's Tail, 1996.

———. *Gone Fishin'*. New York: Pocket Star, 1998 [1997].

Nava, Michael. *The Hidden Law*. New York: Ballantine, 1994 [1992].

———. *The Burning Plain*. New York: Bantam, 1999 [1997].

Neely, Barbara. *Blanche on the Lam*. New York: Penguin, 1993 [1992].

———. *Blanche Among the Talented Tenth*. New York and London: Penguin, 1995 [1994].

———. *Blanche Cleans Up*. New York: Viking Penguin, 1998.

Parker, T. Jefferson. *The Triggerman's Dance*. London: Headline, 1997 [1996].

Pickard, Nancy. *Generous Death*. New York: Pocket Books, 1987 [1984].

———. *I.O.U.* New York: Pocket Books, 1992 [1991].

Rowland, Laura Joh. *Shinjū*. New York: HarperPaperbacks, 1996 [1994].

————. *Bundori.* New York: HarperPaperbacks, 1997 [1996].

Ventura, Michael. *The Death of Frank Sinatra.* New York: St. Martin's, 1997 [1996].

Walker, Mary Willis. *Under the Beetle's Cellar.* London: HarperCollins, 1997 [1995].

Wesley, Valerie Wilson. *When Death Comes Stealing.* New York: Avon, 1995 [1994].

————. *No Hiding Place.* New York: Avon, 1998 [1997].

SELECT SECONDARY BIBLIOGRAPHY

Budd, Elaine. *13 Mistresses of Murder.* New York: Ungar, 1986.

Messent, Peter, ed. *Criminal Proceedings: The Contemporary American Crime Novel.* London and Chicago: Pluto, 1997.

Walton, Priscilla L. and Manina Jones. *Detective Agency: Women Rewriting the Hard-boiled Tradition.* Berkeley, Los Angeles, and London: University of California Press, 1999.

Lee Horsley (essay date 2001)

SOURCE: Horsley, Lee. "Part III: 1970-2000." In *The Noir Thriller,* pp. 184-95. Houndmills, England: Palgrave, 2001.

[*In the following essay, Horsley discusses the revival of literary noir fiction in the late-1900s, explaining that many authors of this genre draw inspiration from traditional noir literature of the mid-1900s and add a distinctly political and contemporary edge.*]

A voyeuristic private eye who faithfully follows a mass murderess, surreptitiously guarding her; a transsexual Mancunian hit woman; a Chicago psychopath who takes on the identity of the woman he kills; a pornographic film-maker who gets caught up in the Profumo affair; a commodity fetishist and modern cannibal; a detective searching for the man whose identity he has usurped and whose heart he has eaten; an addict in a hi-tech scramble suit that turns him into a blur who is given the job of hunting himself; a 12-year-old girl learning to survive and kill on the savage streets of a near-future New York:[1] in the last three decades, noir protagonists have appeared in many different guises, and their very diversity testifies to the vitality and contemporaneity of this form of crime fiction. But however aberrant, bizarre or grotesque his (or, increasingly, her) incarnations may be, these are still recognisably near relations of the hard-boiled investigators, victim-protagonists and killer-protagonists of earlier noir thrillers. In this final section,

my aim is to explore both the links between post-1970s and traditional literary noir and to illustrate something of the energy and variety of contemporary noir and of the growing body of mainstream fiction that has assimilated characteristic themes and techniques of the noir thriller.

Although literary noir has never altogether disappeared from the bookstands nor *film noir* from the screen,[2] there was arguably a period in the early sixties when the appeal of noirish fiction and films was somewhat diminished. The 'spirit of the times' tended towards optimism. In America, as we have seen, there was the continued growth of white suburban affluence and the mood of expectancy associated with the 'brave new rhetoric' of Kennedy's presidency.[3] In Britain there was a sense of moving towards the advanced economic and technological society that America already had, and the upbeat, 'joyful irreverence'[4] of the Swinging Sixties—a time more in tune with James Bond[5] than with the noir anti-hero. In both countries, however, there were at the same time many tensions, doubts, failures and signs of dissent that gathered force as the events of the sixties, from the assassination of Kennedy on, undermined confidence and strengthened the spirit of protest. As Mailer implies in *An American Dream,* after the trauma of the assassination the 'dream' turns to a vision of violence and murder.[6] At the end of the sixties and in the early seventies, American society was being shaken by riots in the black ghettos, the assassinations of Robert Kennedy and Martin Luther King, the growing opposition to the Vietnam War, higher crime and unemployment rates, Watergate and increasingly vociferous demonstrations of counter-culture discontent. Though the changes in British society were less dramatic, there was nevertheless a comparable movement away from the mood of the sixties. The early seventies saw bitter confrontations between government and unions, the collapse of the boom in the stock market and the property market, rising unemployment and inflation and worsening conflict with the IRA. 'Outbursts of militancy, violence, and terrorism, the revelations of corruption in high places, and the break-up of the optimistic consensus' led many to see the British seventies as a return to the gloom of the 'devil's decade' of the 1930s.[7]

Both America and Britain, then, were experiencing the kind of political and social malaise that made the cynicism and satiric edge of noir seem all too appropriate. Even during the sixties there were a number of films—some of which Silver and Ward group with canonical *film noir,* some with neo-noir[8]—that drew on the films and novels of earlier decades, and by the early seventies the phenomenon was attracting considerable critical attention. As Naremore writes, 'Whether classic noir ever existed, by 1974 a great many people believed in it.'[9] There was increased use of the 'noir' label by film critics and more 'consciously neo-noir' films began to appear (Walter Hill's 1978 film, *The Driver,* is singled out by Silver and Ward as one of the 'earliest and most stylised' examples).[10] Adaptations of literary noir were becoming more numerous: J. Lee Thompson's 1962 film of John D. MacDonald's *The Executioners* (*Cape Fear*); three adaptations of Chandler novels—Paul Bogart's 1969 *Marlowe* (an adaptation of *Little Sister*), Robert Altman's 1973 film of *The Long Goodbye* and the Dick Richards' remake of *Farewell, My Lovely* (1975); Altman's 1974 film of Anderson's *Thieves Like Us*; the adaptations of Ross Macdonald's early Lew Archer novels, *Harper* (Jack Smight, 1966) and *Drowning Pool* (Stuart Rosenberg, 1975—'the last vestiges of the classic gumshoe');[11] Burt Kennedy's 1976 adaptation of Thompson's *The Killer Inside Me;* and three separate American adaptations of the more nearly contemporary but equally noir Parker novels of Richard Stark (Donald Westlake): *Point Blank* (John Boorman, 1967), *The Split* (Gordon Flemyng, 1968) and *The Outfit* (John Flynn, 1973).

There were bound to be some changes in literary noir as the 'lurid era' of the 25-cent paperback originals drew to a close in the sixties. There was, however, no real watershed, and one's sense of continuity is strengthened by the fact that some of the most notable noir crime novelists of the fifties and sixties were still publishing in the seventies: amongst others, Stanley Ellin, John D. MacDonald, Ross Macdonald, Margaret Millar, Patricia Highsmith, Charles Willeford, Donald Westlake (under his own name and as Richard Stark) and James Hadley Chase. The influence of such mid-century novelists as Thompson, Goodis and Himes on contemporary writing was made possible by the reissue of their work from the 1980s on in Black Lizard and Vintage Crime editions in the United States, and, in late-eighties Britain, in Maxim Jakubowski's Black Box Thrillers and Blue Murder editions. Many of the new voices of the period offer striking revivifications of the traditional patterns of literary noir. Edward Bunker, for example, drawing on his own experiences, writes from the criminal's point of view about the effects of imprisonment, deprivation and exclusion in novels like *No Beast So Fierce* (1973) and *Little Boy Blue* (1981). The staple fare of gangland revenge and betrayal is given freshness and immediacy by the dialogue of George V. Higgins' first novel, *The Friends of Eddie Coyle* (1970), the film adaptation of which (directed by Peter Yates, 1973) is judged by Silver and Ward to be 'closer to the true noir cycle than the homage offered by such films as *Chinatown* and *Farewell, My Lovely*'.[12] A tough British version of these themes is developed in Ted Lewis' Carter novels of the seventies. Long-established noir themes have continued to exert their hold in more recent fiction. Craig Holden, in his first novel, *The River Sorrow* (1995), provides a distinctly modern (or postmodern) reworking of sexual obsession

and wrong man plots. James Ellroy, writing in the eighties and nineties, uses the more extreme possibilities of the crime novel to recreate the violence and corruption of post-World War Two Los Angeles, imaging the beginnings of 'half a century of tumult and change in America'.[13]

Other recent writers, particularly in Britain, have used basic noir plots for even more explicitly political purposes than those of Ellroy. As at the time of Greene and Ambler, British writers in particular have effectively assimilated thriller conventions with the serious treatment of wider historical conflicts. Philip Kerr, in his *Berlin Noir Trilogy,* locates the investigations of Bernie Gunther in a very fully realised European context, *March Violets* (1989) and *The Pale Criminal* (1990) being set in Berlin in the years immediately preceding World War Two and *A German Requiem* (1991) moving from Berlin to Vienna and the beginnings of the Cold War. Also set in Germany, Ian McEwan's *The Innocent* (1990) uses the murder committed as a result of an obsessive love triangle as a metaphor for the divisions and conflicts in Berlin during the 1950s. Colin Bateman, in *Cycle of Violence* (1995), makes similarly metaphoric use of a traditionally noir 'inescapable burden of the past' theme, weaving it together with the public tragedy of an Ireland in which it is equally true that '"What goes around comes around, eh?"' (241). As these examples might suggest, British literary noir has in recent years emerged as a much more distinctive phenomenon, with successive 'new waves' of writers creating novels that address contemporary issues and that are capable of appealing to a much wider audience.[14]

The last three decades have also seen the creation of a large number of new investigative series, some more noirish than others. The hard-boiled style was developed in an identifiably British way during the eighties by writers like Julian Barnes (writing as Dan Kavanagh, in a four-novel series relating the seedy but generally humorous and upbeat adventures of a bisexual private eye called Duffy), Mark Timlin (in his long-running Nick Sharman series) and Robin Cook (Derek Raymond, whose Factory novels are amongst the darker investigative series). In the United States the formula has been given a variety of strong regional identities.[15] Several series protagonists have contended with the crimes of northern cities: Lawrence Block, for example (who started in the sixties by writing paperback originals for Gold Medal), began, in the seventies, a series of novels featuring an ex-cop, Matt Scudder, a guilt-ridden, gloomy alcoholic (eventually ex-alcoholic) investigator of a New York in which it seems that 'people could adjust to one reality after another if they put their minds to it' (*A Stab in the Dark,* 137). In the eighties, Loren Estleman started to write his rather less noir series of Detroit-based Amos Walker novels, which tend to move towards detective-story resolutions, complete with penetrations of disguise and revelations of identity (for example, in *The Midnight Man* and *Downriver*). In the nineties, Sam Reaves introduced his cab-driving Vietnam veteran Cooper MacLeish, who first appears in *A Long Cold Fall* (1991), in which sentiment, human warmth and hearts of gold effectively counteract the noir potential of the pitiless Chicago cold and the 'blind universe' that grants Cooper 'the grace of survival' (14). Louisiana has been another location well served by tough investigators. At the more noir end of the scale, there is James Sallis' New Orleans detective, Lew Griffin, who, like many another investigator, is guilt-ridden and ex-alcoholic, but also a university teacher and a writer, postmodern and self-reflexive—and black (Sallis, who is white, says he was '20 or 30 pages in before I realised he was black').[16] Working nearby is James Lee Burke's Cajun detective, Dave Robicheaux, the protagonist of narratives in which the defeat of villainy is set against reminders not to accept 'the age-old presumption that the origins of social evil can be traced to villainous individuals' who can simply be locked away (*A Stained White Radiance*, 302)—a dark awareness that is in turn moderated by life-affirming contacts with a loved child (*A Stained White Radiance*) or an earthy dance (*Dixie City Jam*). Strongly positive elements, particularly the affirmative presence of family, also counterbalance the sense of a 'whole nother side of [American] life, a darker, semilawless, hillbilly side' (*Give Us a Kiss*, 6), in the 'country noir' novels of Daniel Woodrell, some of which (like *Under the Bright Lights*) feature another Cajun investigator, Rene Shade.

In series such as these the honourable ghost of Marlowe is often near at hand, encouraging the nobler possibilities within the hard-boiled tradition, bringing to the fore the moral integrity, the compassion and the tough-sentimental view of life that infuse the investigative narrative with a redemptive potential and make it less darkly noir. Contemporary writers both acknowledge Chandler's influence and try to differentiate themselves from him, as Ross Macdonald did in the late fifties, when he modified his 'heir to Chandler' role, declaring that *The Doomsters* (1958) marked 'a fairly clean break with the Chandler tradition'.[17] One way in which more recent crime writers have made the break has been to distance their protagonists from the identity and ethos of the lone white male, the crusader-knight of the mean streets. They have done this either by creating an investigator who is himself black, as in Sallis and Mosley, or by making the protagonist homosexual (as in Joseph Hansen's Dave Brandstetter novels) or part of a close-knit group of mixed race and gender. James Crumley, who introduced two hard-drinking, tough-talking protagonists—Milodragovitch and Sughrue—in the 1970s, is a self-declared heir to the Chandler tradition (describing himself as 'a bastard child of Raymond

Chandler'),[18] but emphasises that his is a much less traditional morality. He defines his own sensibility as conditioned by the disillusionments of the Vietnam War and his 'vision of justice' as in consequence less clear-cut. His protagonists are 'reverent towards the earth and its creatures'[19] and sustained by eccentric alliances with criminals and other misfits. In addition to male bonding, there are the beginnings of surrogate families—Sughrue, for example, holding 'Baby Lester laughing in my arms' at the end of *Mexican Tree Duck* (1993).

Like many other recent investigators, Crumley's protagonists, though retaining some of the romanticised qualities of the lone male, are no longer solitary defenders of macho values. What we see in novels of this kind is a 'softening' of the protagonist by allying him with others, often with a larger surrogate family that represents those marginalised by the dominant society (non-white characters, strong women, outcasts of all kinds). This is a widespread tendency, evident in the little family collected together by Easy Rawlins, in the bond between the white, straight Hap Collins and the black, gay Leonard Pine (in the comic noir novels of Joe Lansdale, such as *Savage Season* and *Two-Bear Mambo*) and in the representative sampling of minorities and misfits allied with Andrew Vachss' 'outlaw' private detective, Burke.[20] Even in the decidedly Chandleresque novels of Robert B. Parker (who wrote his Ph.D. thesis on Hammett, Chandler and Ross Macdonald), the protagonist, Spenser, develops strong ties both with an impressive black sidekick, Hawk, and with his Jewish psychiatrist-girlfriend, Susan Silverman.

With a few exceptions, most obviously Chandler himself, this study does not include detailed examinations of crime novels that develop series investigators. As the above discussion perhaps suggests, this is primarily because, whether traditional or contemporary, series characters tend to have 'non-noir' traits like integrity, loyalty and compassion—qualities that make them more positive and resilient figures than other types of noir protagonist, often sentimentalising them and allowing them to attain more reassuring narrative resolutions and redemptive human attachments. The changing nature of private eyes and other investigative series characters is, however, closely related to developments that can also be seen in the more obviously noir narratives of recent decades. The alternative family offers the investigative protagonist a real human connection, a hedge against what Ballard, in *High-Rise* (1975), calls 'a new kind of late twentieth-century life' that thrives on 'the rapid turnover of acquaintances, the lack of involvement with others' (36). It provides a way of belonging that does not involve acquiescence in a wider society which, whatever its underlying disorders, has an almost irresistible surface allure. As will be seen in Chapter 7, it has been increasingly the case in the noir thriller that various kinds of 'belonging'—assimilation, complicity, dependency—have become nightmares as disturbing as deprivation and exclusion. In post-eighties noir, as America and Britain moved into the Thatcher-Reagan years, there is a marked emphasis on tedious homogeneity and on the threat posed by the erasure of difference consequent on an addiction to the pleasures and games of a consumer society. In novels in which this kind of dependency is a source of anxiety, what often distinguishes the more positive characters is an ability to form individual bonds in a society that seems to be losing its capacity for genuine social relationships. Particularly in American noir, there are fewer of the isolated figures who withstood the conformist pressures of a small community in the literary noir of the fifties and sixties; instead of existential loners, there are protagonists who demonstrate that communal ties need not mean loss of individual identity.

In recent critical debate, one question frequently raised is whether the fashionable trappings of neo-noir are themselves symptomatic of an acquiescence in slickly commercial postmodern nostalgia. The sense that 'noir' created in the seventies and eighties was a 'retro' and nostalgic avoidance of contemporary experience has been encouraged by the often cited essay, 'Postmodernism and Consumer Society', in which Jameson gives *film noir* 'a central role in the vocabulary of ludic commercialized postmodernism'.[21] Referring to *Body Heat* (Lawrence Kasdan, 1981), Jameson notes the film's 'faintly archaic feel' and its small-town setting, which 'has a crucial strategic function: it allows the film to do without most of the signals and references which we might associate with the contemporary world, with consumer society—the appliances and artefacts, the high rises, the object world of late capitalism'.[22] Leaving aside for the moment the matter of nostalgic pastiche, the most important question is whether self-consciously 'noir' contemporary narratives are to be seen as escaping from or as engaging with contemporary issues. One of my central arguments in Part III of this study is that the literary noir of recent decades, even when its settings are retro, has been as concerned with exposing the nature of contemporary consumer society as earlier noir was with satirising, for example, the conformist ethos of small-town America in the fifties.

Whether it is 'reality' or just our perception of it that has changed, contemporary debate has been dominated by the writings of 'cultural specialists' (academic critics, for example) who produce models and interpretations of consumer culture,[23] thereby modifying the rhetoric and themes of social-political analysis. The view of contemporary society as a culture of consumption, consuming not just commodities but performances and spectacles—and consuming the consumer—has come to the fore, increasingly in the eighties and nineties, as one of the dominant themes of literary noir,

shaping the representation of protagonists as well as the content and structure of narratives. In America, consumerism was clearly well established in the years following World War Two. As John Updike recalls the fifties in 'When Everyone Was Pregnant', 'Romance of consumption at its height. . . . Purchasing power: young, newly powerful, born to consume.'[24] Reagan's presidency, however, was even more closely associated with encouragement of a commodity culture and the entrepreneurial spirit, with the promotion of selfishness, greed, a get-rich-quick mentality and the rise of the yuppie.[25] In Britain, the Thatcherite eighties, during which personal wealth rose 'by 80 per cent in real terms',[26] were similarly a time of rapidly expanding personal consumption. Although 'all the totems of an advanced consumerist society' had been present in the seventies, it was really only in the eighties that the consumer paradise arrived. As Peter York says,

> . . . the eighties effect took quite a lot of things coming together; the right time, right place, right people, right feelings, right fistfuls of cash. This wasn't *just* a consumer boom. Yes, we did go out and buy more—more TVs, more VCRs, state-of-the-art hi-fis, etc.—but it was really a new generation of consumerism with changes in advertising, retailing, financing, attitudes and expectations. And it's *still with us*: it set the pattern for the next ten or fifteen years.[27]

Britain, then, was 'all getting a bit . . . yes, *American, really*'[28], and this applied not only to the consumer boom but to all the attendant emphasis on presentation, performance, the celebrity culture and 'personal projection'. There was a huge expansion in the amount of electronic space available for the projection of images: 'We were starting to sell ourselves, now, in a way we'd never even dreamt of before.'[29]

Just as thirties thrillers took deprivation as their theme, the noir films and novels of more recent decades have turned their attention to the excesses and dependencies of the society of the media, the spectacle, the consumer. Consumerism is obviously not an element new to noir. The thirties gangsters, characterised by stylish consumption, 'swell clothes', penthouses, high-powered cars, expensive restaurants, were used as a means of exploring the growth of American consumerism, often with an anti-consumerist subtext that equated vulgar display with moral disorder.[30] Close attention to fetishistic detail (hats, guns, shoes and other accessories) and a general fascination with fashion (for example, the 'to-be-looked-at-ness' signified by the clothing of fashionably dressed women) were part and parcel of classic noir.[31] In neo-noir films with a retro look, the incorporation of such things can be seen as a consumer society indulgence, 'a kind of window-shopping through the past'.[32] And there are unquestionably neo-noir films of which this is a fair enough criticism—*Mulholland Falls* (Lee Tamahori, 1996), for example, in which 'the chief function of these four tough guys is to light cigarettes with Zippos and model a peacock collection of suits and accessories'.[33]

Even retro noir, however, often engages seriously not only with the historical period it represents but with issues that are of contemporary relevance, and the detailed observation of consumption, style and decor can be part of the critical thrust of the film. In Ulu Grosbard's 1981 film, *True Confessions,* for example, a thoroughly noir tale of two brothers set in mid-forties LA,[34] the whole style of life of the priest (Robert De Niro)—his surroundings, his dining out, his golf clothes and clubs—is used to establish him in opposition to his brother, a detective (Robert Duvall). The detective's single brown suit and modest apartment help to confirm his status as a figure who will pursue the corrupt regardless of the consequences. They are also, however, no guarantee of his own incorruptibility, and his conspicuous non-consumption is in part an ironic reference back to the integrity of the shabby private eye. This is a detective who has been a bagman and who does not 'give a shit' that Jack Amsterdam did not kill the 'virgin tramp'. He will go after him anyway. *True Confessions* is not, then, an exercise in nostalgic reincarnation, but instead uses retro evocation of the forties private eye films both to demythologise the traditional genre and to raise complex questions about moral responsibility and complicity in a corrupt society.[35]

In films and novels not aiming to evoke the styles of the forties and fifties, fashions and commodities even more obviously constitute part of what is being satirised. In literary noir, this is apparent in the work of writers like James Hall, James Ellroy and Bret Easton Ellis in the United States and the left-wing nineties noir of, for example, Christopher Brookmyre and Iain Banks in the United Kingdom—amongst several others who have contributed to the development of genuinely British forms of noir. In a large body of contemporary noir, the representation of consumerism does much more than simply establish the 'texture of life' that constitutes the background to the narrative. Characters are (as in *True Confessions*) defined in relation to consumerism. The attack on those who 'consume' the natural world emerges strongly, for example, in Ross Macdonald's 1971 novel, *The Underground Man,* in which the greed of the destructive rich, careless of the land on which they build their extravagant houses, is juxtaposed with the simple integrity of Lew Archer, identified from the opening scene with the natural simplicity implied by feeding peanuts to his 'scrub jays' (1-2). In a nineties novel like Hall's *Buzz Cut* (1996), there is a similar opposition between simplicity and rampant consumerism, epitomised in the contrast between Thorn, with his 'trial and error' handmade fishing canoe on the one hand and, on the other, Morton Sampson, with a cruise ship that is the ultimate in consumerist luxury. In the comic 'noir

grotesque'[36] of Carl Hiaasen, which takes the commercial exploitation of South Florida as a recurrent theme, the good guys are the reclusive drop-outs from the consumer society, like 'the guy at the lake' who lives in a cabin that 'looks like a glorified outhouse' (Skink, in *Double Whammy* [1988]) or Stranahan, in *Skin Tight* (1989), who lives in solitude in a 'dirt cheap' stilt house, 'delighted to be the only soul living in Stiltsville' (713-14). Plots follow the rise and fall of Thatcherite yuppies in pursuit of the 'fistfuls of cash' that will buy them state-of-the-art commodities (Huggins, Brookmyre), consumer greed acts as a metaphor for moral bankruptcy (Leonard, Willeford), cannibalism acts as a metaphor for ungovernable and dehumanising consumer urges (Ellis). In addition to elaborating the image of the consumer, many contemporary noir thrillers have explored the closely related images of the player and the voyeur, adding new dimensions to character types (victim turned gambler, gangster, investigator) familiar from more traditional narratives.

The concept of the player has become prominent in discourse ranging from street argot (the player as, for example, pimp and pusher) to sober academic theorising (the player as any participant in the many conflicts of interest that can be modelled as games).[37] In all of these uses of the term, the underlying assumption is that players can influence events and that, whatever their environment, people must be players in order to be part of the games that determine pleasure and profit. Acting as a player has become a prime metaphor for moving from the status of victim to that of an active agent of domination and change. As in much earlier noir,[38] one of the prominent themes is the hidden connection between criminality and supposed respectability, and the lies and false narratives that contrive to conceal the fact that politicians are just gangsters in positions of power. But whereas this connection was, in earlier decades, linked to a quite specific nexus of crime, business and politics, to an interrelated control structure with crooks running the show, the metaphor of the player and the game is generally used to suggest that everyone is playing their own game and that, in contrast to the gamblers of earlier narratives, they stand at least some chance of influencing their fates.

The figure of the voyeur has similarly been given an increasingly pivotal role in both film and fiction. In *film noir,* as has often been observed, 'the male prerogative of the look' is much in evidence, though there are examples of films in which a woman appropriates this prerogative, as Carol does, say, in Siodmak's *Phantom Lady* (1944) when she unnerves a barman by staring at him until he finally cracks.[39] In more recent films and novels, 'looking' is complicated in ways that act to disrupt the traditionally male activity of voyeurism[40] by representing the female appropriation of the power of the look, by questioning the extent to which the role of the voyeur can be equated with masculine dominance and by exploring the ways in which a woman in the role of 'passive actor' (the one seen) can simultaneously be an active agent. Contemporary novels have also, of course, paid increasing attention to the implications of a highly developed technology of voyeurism, with its wider network of seeing, controlling and commodifying. What we find here, then, is the breakdown of dichotomies between user/used, active/passive, actor/acted upon, watcher/watched, both because of role reversals and because of the network of relationships in which, for example, the watcher is watched by others who are observing and perhaps manipulating his (or her) reactions.

In the cinema this has become, naturally enough, a recurrent theme. As a male activity it is epitomised in a film like *The Osterman Weekend* (Sam Peckinpah, 1983), in which the devious surveillance associated with political scheming and paranoia becomes indistinguishable from sexual voyeurism. The watcher is watched, and each watcher observes the sexual activities of the other, including the snuff-movie-like scene of the wife of one being killed whilst naked in bed. The whole activity is so pervasive a part of the television-centred life being led that it passes unnoticed even when one 'watcher' is accidentally stranded on the kitchen television screen. The cinema of the eighties and nineties also provides many examples of the appropriation and reversal of male voyeurism: for example, there is the placing of a man as a sexual object, as when Dorothy makes Jeffrey undress in David Lynch's *Blue Velvet* (1986), or the casting of Gina Gershon in the sort of role that would once have gone, say, to Robert Mitchum, admiring the physical charms of Jennifer Tilly in *Bound* (Larry and Andy Wachowski, 1997). In crime novels, this kind of appropriation is frequently found in the (non-noir) lesbian-feminist crime novels that began appearing in the late 1970s and early 1980s, for example, M. F. Beal's *Angel Dance* (1977) and Vicki P. McConnell's *Mrs Porter's Letter* (1982),[41] and, more recently, in decidedly noirish novels by writers like Stella Duffy, Susanna Moore, Helen Zahavi and Vicki Hendricks.

Game-playing, voyeurism and consumption have not supplanted more traditional themes, but have become increasingly predominant in a range of noir narratives, including the Gothic and future noir variants discussed in the final chapter. This contemporary refashioning of noir themes is a manifestation of the flexibility and responsiveness to social change that have characterised noir from its inception and of the continued vitality of the form. There has been considerable cross-fertilisation between the noir thriller and related genres. Crime writers have written for a more broadly based audience and mainstream writers have adapted noir characters, plots

and motifs. There have also been changes in the way books are promoted and marketed. In Britain, for example, there has been a 'deliberate and commendable move by many publishers to promote good fiction with a criminal element outside the straightjacket of a fixed crime "list" or imprint. . . .'[42] Arguably the various remodellings indicate that the idea of noir has spread so widely that it has become difficult to pin down. At the same time, however, transformations help to clarify some of the constant, recognisable elements of 'the noir vision': the unsettling subjectivity of the point of view, the unstable role and moral ambivalence of the protagonist, and the ill-fated relationship between the protagonist and a wider society that itself is guilty of corruption and criminality. In the mid-fifties, Borde and Chaumeton drew the conclusion that the 'moral ambiguity, the criminal violence, and the contradictory complexity of events and motives' worked together in *film noir* 'to give the spectator the same feeling of anxiety and insecurity', and that this was 'the distinguishing feature of *film noir* in our time'.[43] Their summary captures some of the identifying traits of noir, but the persistence of this 'network of ideas'[44] from the 1920s through to the end of the 1990s suggests the necessity of revising the Borde and Chaumeton argument regarding the historical specificity of noir: 'The noir of dark film is dark *for us*,' they wrote, 'that is, for European and American viewers in the 1950s.'[45] What is true of *film noir* (as studies such as Naremore's have demonstrated) is true to an even greater extent of literary noir. If noir is 'the reflex of a particular kind of sensibility . . . unique in time as in space',[46] then the historical limits set must correspond to the greater part of the twentieth century—and extend, perhaps, to 'the near future'.

Notes

1. The novels referred to are, respectively: Behm, *Eye of the Beholder*; Blincoe, *Acid Casuals*; Theroux, *Chicago Loop*; Frewin, *London Blues*; Ellis, *American Psycho*; Hjortsberg, *Angel Heart*; Dick, *A Scanner Darkly*; and Womack, *Random Acts of Senseless Violence*.

2. Alain Silver and Elizabeth Ward (eds), *Film Noir* (London: Secker and Warburg, 1979, 1992), p. 398.

3. Malcolm Bradbury and Howard Temperley, *Introduction to American Studies* (London: Longman, 1981, 1998), p. 269.

4. Arthur Marwick, *British Society since 1945* (Harmondsworth, Middx.: Penguin, 1982, 1996), pp. 121 and 174.

5. See the analysis of Bond as *the* Swinging Sixties hero in Michael Denning, *Mechanic Accents: Dime Novels and Working-Class Culture in America* (London: Verso, 1987), pp. 91-2.

6. Norman Mailer, *An American Dream* ([1965] London: Flamingo, 1994); Mailer's post-seventies

noir crime novel, *Tough Guys Don't Dance* (London: Abacus, 1997), written at speed in 1984, is a less serious and less successful use of the form.

7. Marwick, p. 184.

8. Silver and Ward, pp. 336 and 440-3.

9. James Naremore, *More Than Night: Film Noir in Its Contexts* (Berkeley: University of California Press, 1998), p. 37.

10. Silver and Ward, p. 398.

11. See Silver and Ward, p. 414.

12. Silver and Ward, pp. 108-9.

13. Ellroy, in an unpublished interview with Lee Horsley, London, 7 October 1995, quoted in Lee Horsley, 'Founding Fathers: "Genealogies of Violence" in James Ellroy's L. A. Quartet', *Clues,* 19, No. 2 (1998), pp. 139-40.

14. For discussions of recent developments in British noir, see: Mike Ripley and Maxim Jakubowski, 'Fresh Blood: British Neo-Noir', in Lee Server, Ed Gorman and Martin H. Greenberg (eds), *The Big Book of Noir* (New York: Carroll and Graf Publishers, 1998), pp. 317-22; Paul Duncan, 'It's Raining Violence: a Brief History of British Noir', *Crime Time,* 2, No. 3 (1999); and two recent Nicholas Blincoe articles, 'The Same Mean Streets Seen from a Fresh Angle', in *Murder, They Write* (*The Times,* 18 April 1998), p. 17; and 'British Hardboiled', in Nick Rennison and Richard Shephard (eds), *Waterstone's Guide to Crime Fiction* (Brentford, Middx.: Waterstone's Booksellers Ltd, 1997), pp. 11-13.

15. The settings of literary noir and *film noir* are discussed, respectively, by Ralph Willett, *The Naked City: Urban Crime Fiction in the USA* (Manchester: Manchester University Press, 1996), and Nicholas Christopher, *Somewhere in the Night: Film Noir and the American City* (New York: The Free Press, 1997).

16. James Sallis, 'In the Black', *Time Out,* 4-11 September 1996, p. 50, quoted in Woody Haut, *Neon Noir: Contemporary American Crime Fiction* (London: Serpent's Tail, 1999), p. 112.

17. John M. Reilly (ed.), *Twentieth-Century Crime and Mystery Writers* (New York: St Martin's Press, 1980, rev. edn 1985), p. 589.

18. Reilly, p. 227.

19. Reilly, p. 228.

20. For example in *Blue Belle* ([1988] London: Pan, 1989).

21. Naremore, p. 39.

22. Fredric Jameson, 'Postmodernism and Consumer Society', in Peter Brooker (ed.), *Modernism/Postmodernism* (London: Longman, 1992), pp. 170-1.

23. Mike Featherstone, *Consumer Culture and Postmodernism* (London: Sage Publications, 1991, 1998), pp. viii-ix.

24. John Updike, 'When Everyone Was Pregnant', in *Museums and Women* (1973), quoted in Malcolm Bradbury, *The Modern American Novel* (Oxford: Oxford University Press, 1983, 1992), p. 158.

25. Richard Martin, *Mean Streets and Raging Bulls: The Legacy of Film Noir in Contemporary American Cinema* (Lanham, Md: The Scarecrow Press, 1997), pp. 52-3.

26. Peter York and Charles Jennings, *Peter York's Eighties* (London: BBC Books, 1995), p. 42.

27. York and Jennings, p. 40.

28. York and Jennings, p. 150.

29. York and Jennings, pp. 153-60.

30. David E. Ruth, *Inventing the Public Enemy: The Gangster in American Culture* (Chicago: The University of Chicago Press, 1996), pp. 63-81.

31. Laura Mulvey quoted by Naremore, pp. 196-7.

32. Naremore discusses this line of criticism, pp. 211-12, and refers readers to Anne Friedberg, *Window Shopping: Cinema and the Postmodern Condition* (Berkeley: University of California Press, 1993) for a fuller discussion of postmodern spectatorship and consumerism.

33. Naremore, p. 212.

34. The film is an adaptation of a John Gregory Dunne novel, *True Confessions* (1977), which is based on the Black Dahlia murder case (in LA in the 1940s). The novel and film (scripted by Dunne and his wife, Joan Didion) are compared in an article by Jon L. Breen, 'True Confessions', in Server *et al.,* *The Big Book of Noir,* pp. 149-52. Breen rightly classes *True Confessions* as 'one of the great films of the eighties, a classic of latter-day film noir' (149).

35. See John G. Cawelti, '*Chinatown* and Generic Transformation', in Gerald Mast and Marshall Cohen (eds), *Film Theory and Criticism* (New York: Oxford University Press, 1985), pp. 503-20, on nostalgic evocation not as an end in itself but as a means of ironically undercutting the generic experience.

36. 'Noir grotesque' is a useful category suggested by Rennison and Shephard (eds), *Waterstone's Guide,* p. 167: in addition to Hiaasen, it includes Ferrigno, Hjorstberg and Lansdale; see also Julie Sloan Brannon, 'The Rules Are Different Here: South Florida Noir and the Grotesque', in Steve Glassman and Maurice O'Sullivan (eds), *Crime Fiction and Film in the Sunshine State: Florida Noir* (Bowling Green, Ohio: Popular Press, 1997), pp. 47-64, which centres on the work of Carl Hiaasen and Charles Willeford.

37. See, for example, L. C. Thomas, *Games, Theory and Applications* (Chichester: Ellis Horwood, 1984), pp. 15-21.

38. For example, in the novels of Hammett and Paul Cain.

39. Michael Walker, 'Film Noir: Introduction', in Ian Cameron (ed.), *The Movie Book of Film Noir* (London: Studio Vista, 1992), p. 113.

40. See, for example, the discussion in Linda Hutcheon, *The Politics of Postmodernism* (London: Routledge, 1989), pp. 134-40.

41. See Sally R. Munt, *Murder by the Book? Feminism and the Crime Novel* (New York and London: Harvester Wheatsheaf, 1994), pp. 120-46, for a detailed discussion of lesbian crime fiction.

42. Ripley and Jakubowski, 'Fresh Blood', in Server *et al.* (eds), *Big Book of Noir,* p. 321.

43. Raymond Borde and Etienne Chaumeton, 'Toward the Definition of Film Noir', in R. Barton Palmer (ed.), *Perspectives on Film Noir* (New York: G. K. Hall & Co., 1996), p. 65.

44. Naremore, p. 276.

45. Borde and Chaumeton, in Palmer (ed.), *Perspectives,* p. 59.

46. Ibid.

ETHNICITY AND RACE IN CRIME FICTION

Madelyn Jablon (essay date 1996)

SOURCE: Jablon, Madelyn. "'Making the Faces Black': The African-American Detective Novel." In *Changing Representations of Minorities East and West: Selected Essays,* edited by Larry E. Smith and John Rieder, pp. 26-40. Honolulu: College of Languages, Linguistics, and Literature, University of Hawaii, and the East-West Center, 1996.

[*In the following essay, Jablon surveys the development of African American detective fiction in the twentieth century, specifically commenting on the works of Walter Mosley and Barbara Neely.*]

Chester Himes aspired to be a writer of serious fiction, but his ambitions were forgotten when Marcel Duhamel, editor of La Série Noire, offered him a thousand-dollar advance for a detective story. In less than two weeks, Himes submitted the manuscript for *Five-Cornered Square* [*La Reine des Pommes*]. This was the beginning of the Harlem Detective Series: eight novels each written in a month's time or less.[1]

When Duhamel first approached Himes with the idea of writing detective fiction, Himes was reluctant. Although the advance was attractive, Himes had no experience with this kind of writing. When he confessed his insecurities to Duhamel, the editor suggested that Himes read the works of several writers of detective fiction and copy what they did. He suggested Himes read Peter Cheney, Raymond Chandler and Dashiell Hammett for an "idea" of how it is done. Himes may have been recalling Duhamel's advice and his efforts to "copy" the work of others fifteen years later when he observed that he hadn't "created anything whatsoever . . . just made the faces black."[2] Although Himes saw his work as imitative, fans of detective fiction have insisted on his originality. By "making the faces black" he transfigured the genre, laying the foundation for a subsequent generation of African-American detective writers who would continue the tradition of innovation Himes began.

The significance of Himes' contribution to the genre of hard-boiled detective fiction is most apparent in his creation of the Harlem detectives. Grave Digger and Coffin Ed were unique in the community of hard-boiled detectives. Unlike the Chandlerian hero, an isolationist and loner, the Harlem detectives needed each other. They worked as a pair, restoring order to police precincts and jook joints with a routine which depends on their rapport for its success: "Straighten up!" Grave Digger shouts. "Count off!" Coffin Ed yells. They draw their pistols in unison and shoot at the ceilings of the precinct house and jook joint, or on either side of a crowd of moviegoers. Order is restored and the detectives depart with Grave Digger signaling the conclusion of the performance with a final word of warning: "Don't make graves."[3] The intensity of this friendship is best measured by the reader's foreboding when Grave Digger finds the person who threw acid in Coffin Ed's face. When Coffin Ed is blinded, Grave Digger demands the police release the criminal in his custody, and we along with the police fear for her.

The friendship which sets these detectives apart is a necessity for cops who are alienated from the Harlem community because they represent the law. Paradoxically they are alienated from their fellow police officers as well: as the only black men on the force they are perceived as representing lawlessness. They have neither the fraternity of their fellow police officers nor the friendship and goodwill of the citizens of Harlem.[4] They depend on each other for the emotional support needed when they receive the bad news that their services are no longer needed by the Harlem police force, and when their all-too casual handling of their weapons earns them a reprimand by their senior officers. "Making the faces black" necessitates a recasting of the detective, transforming him from a mystery man—aloof and reserved—into a person dependent on others.

The next generation of African-American writers of detective fiction follow Himes' lead. Walter Mosley and Barbara Neely create detectives who rely on the assistance of others at work and at home. They are dependent on family, friends and co-workers to fulfill a variety of needs. More importantly their participation in family and community represents a choice made by Easy and Blanche who have neither spouse nor biological offspring. Although Easy is divorced and Blanche refuses to marry, both choose to parent children. Blanche parents Taifa and Malik, the children of a deceased sister. When the children return home from their private school in Boston with the wrong ideas about color (they suggest she straighten her hair and avoid the sun), Blanche who has financed their education by her employment as a domestic realizes that "she loved them too much to even complain about having to put up with their bullshit."[5] A reoccurring dream reflects her anxiety about when the children are on their own and the old folks "she was lucky enough to have in her life" are gone (211). Easy's family is comprised of Jesus or "Juice," a boy he rescued from the streets and a life of prostitution and Feather, a girl whose white mother was murdered by her father for bearing a black child.[6] Easy is such a proud father, he brags that his family is superior to biologically-determined ones because according to Easy, "the only agreement between us was love and mutual need" (32). He boasts of his relationship with Juice as mutually desirable: "He was my son. A son of preference. We weren't blood, but he wanted to live with me and I wanted to have him—how many fathers and sons can say that?" (51) Driving his truck with a ten-inch knife in his back, Easy worries about his children's dinner. His concern for their safety has him considering giving up the profession of detective, but his children approve and respect him for the work he does. When he arrives home, his son pulls the knife out of his back and tends his wound. Blanche's concern for her children leads her to the mystery and the scene of its occurrence. Troubled by their "hincty" ideas about color, she joins them and their friends on a vacation at Amber Cove, a resort on the coast of Maine catering to affluent light-skinned black people (8). At Amber Cove, her suspicions that "well-off blacks were even more color prejudice than the everyday folks who'd tormented Blanche everyday of her life" proves true (21).

Both detectives develop romantic interests, but neither enters into a serious relationship. In his search for Elizabeth Eady, otherwise known as "Black Betty," Easy falls in love with Gwen, Elizabeth's daughter, but this romance comes to an abrupt end when Gwen is murdered by the criminals as part of their strategy to destroy Betty. Blanche is attracted to Stu, the resident pharmacist in the town outside Amber Cove, but this attraction is tempered by his negative reaction to her line of work. Blanche's amorous feelings for Stu blind her to his guilt and make him the least likely suspect because he courts the sleuth. Both detectives escape serious attachment through the death or discovery of the criminal identity of their prospective partner. In this way, both are able to have a variety of interpersonal relationships without compromising the autonomy and independence characteristic of hard-boiled detectives.[7]

In addition to family and romantic interests, Easy and Blanche have friends who help them solve the crime. Easy's relationships with Saul Lynx is a modern-day recasting of that of Grave Digger and Coffin Ed's. Saul Lynx appears on the opening page of the novel, interrupting Easy's sleep with an offer of $200.00 for finding Elizabeth Eady. Saul tells Easy he is needed because he is "known for finding people in the colored part of town" (15). White cops and private detectives enlist the assistance of men like Grave Digger, Coffin Ed and Easy Rawlins to act as tour guides in black neighborhoods and locate people. Hence the black neighborhoods of Los Angeles in the 1960's are portrayed like Harlem of the preceding decade. Easy is wary of Saul and suspicious of his motives. His initial interactions with Saul show him to be an astute observer of his own behavior when he generalizes: "back then any white person had to prove themselves to me before I considered trusting them" (115). Saul "proves himself" by taking a bullet intended for Easy. At the hospital, Easy meets Mrs. Lynx and their infant son about whom he notes: "there was very little of Saul in his dark features but you could tell by the hair, a little" (252). This experience tempers Easy's distrust of white people. Blanche is the spinster-detective refashioned as the feminist or womanist detective. In the nineteenth century, the spinster detective's penchant for crime and mystery was imagined to fill the void created by the absence of children and husband. This predecessor of the feminist detective was a lonely woman pitied because she was undesirable and never married. Feminist and womanist detectives provide a vivid contrast with their literary antecedents. They are desirable women who choose not to marry. Blanche has been asked twice but "both times she'd been overcome by the same feeling she'd first experienced at the age of twelve while stuck in a small elevator for three hours" (12). She cannot have her freedom compromised, not even by a well-intentioned well-meaning man like Leo. Although loneliness makes Blanche occasionally regret her decision not to marry, her girlfriend, Ardell, assists her with advice on parenting, plays Watson to Blanche's

Sherlock by assisting in the unraveling of the mystery, and, most importantly, keeps Blanche's well-being the foremost concern of every circumstance.

Blanche is a womanist detective and this determines her relationships with others and the world around her.[8] She appreciates Ardell's friendship. When she is not speaking to her on the phone, she is thinking about calling her. Blanche takes pleasure in assisting younger women make decisions about their future. In addition to guiding her niece, Taifa, through adolescence and teaching her nephew, Malik, to "treat girls and women with fairness and respect," she helps Tina deal with her future mother-in-law's stubborn preference for a light-skinned daughter-in-law (185). Blanche helps Tina recognize her own value and self-respect when everyone else is criticizing her for her color. Blanche is reading Octavia Butler's novel, *Dawn,* and singles out the famous black feminist writer, Mattie, to call "girlfriend" at Amber Cove. She prays to her ancestors, and understands her "urge to hug trees, talk to the ocean and lean on the dark as though it were a mother's welcoming arms" as the spiritual inheritance of black women (60). She prays to "Mother Water" and seeks spiritual advice from Madame Rosa who sends her to the ocean "to find the answer to her dream" (610). As one of the first African-American women detectives, Blanche combines the independence and intelligence of her literary foremother, the spinster, with the concern for family and community that Walker characterizes as womanist.[9]

Bethany Ogdon argues that female detectives do not exhibit a "hard-boiled ideological orientation."[10] She notes that though detectives "'from the margins' (any detective who is not white, male and heterosexual) may appear in stories that have been defined by critics and publishers as hard-boiled, these stories always implicitly critique elements of the hard-boiled ideology even as they incorporate some elements of the traditional hard-boiled detective story" (71). Ogdon's argument gains credence through comparison of the descriptions of violence and gore in classic hard-boiled fiction and the *Freikorps* novels published during the interwar years in Germany. Although Ogdon's observation concerning the different degrees of violence in fiction featuring men is astute, she might describe the advent of women detectives as a evolution in the genre rather than existing outside the genre. Violence is one solution, but Blanche introduces nurturing as another, equally powerful remedy:

> Blanche immediately knew how she could help. She pulled her hand away from his and wrapped her arms as tightly around him as she could. Al J. hugged her to him so hard she thought she'd explode. His tears were hot on her shoulder. His sobs were deep and silent and almost made her glad she had never loved enough to generate this kind of pain. She remembered hugging Tina yesterday and wondered if hugging was one of the things Madame Rosa had sent her here to do.
>
> (142)

Interestingly her hugging has her wondering if she should be thankful for never loving someone this much. This "never loving someone" puts her in the tradition of the hard-boiled detective who has compassion for others but is, himself, strangely detached from the deepest emotional connections.[11]

Their decisions to parent are an extension of Blanche's and Easy's concerns for the community. This is easily recognizable in the story Easy tells which reveals that he does indeed know everyone as Saul surmises. Moreover he also recognizes the importance of talking to people: "Most days, no matter what I was working on, I would have stopped and talked awhile. That's what made me different from the cops and from other people, black and white, trying to find out something down in black L.A. The people down there were country folks and they liked it when you stopped for a few minutes or so" (91). Easy's relationship to the victim deviates from the pattern of most hard-boiled detective novels because the victim is no stranger. He remembers Elizabeth as the source of adolescent fantasies while growing up in Houston. While he searches for her, he will assist Mouse in finding the friend who tattled his crime to the police. He will assist Mofass to regain control over the real estate business wrangled by a turncoat secretary. Finally he will assist Martin, a friend stricken with cancer, find relief from his suffering by euthanasia. Easy's involvement in the Los Angeles community goes beyond that of the Harlem detectives who resemble jealous watchdogs who allow a select group of familiar people to enter, exit and move about unharmed while they bark and bare their fangs to strangers. Blanche's commitment to the community extends beyond the boundaries of the black Boston suburb where she lives and the beach resort where she vacations. Her commitment is evident in her ambition to help eliminate the color syndrome which has divided the black community for so long: "She wondered how soon after the first baby was born of the rape of a black woman by a white man did some slaver decide that light-skinned slaves were smarter and better by virtue of white blood? And how long after that had some black people decided to take advantage of that myth?" (67) As Rabinowitz notes, for the African-American detectives, "Chanderian heroism is not an option."[12] The second generation of African-American detectives is immersed in the community that Himes founded in his pairing of Grave Digger and Coffin Ed. Easy and Blanche are rooted in their respective communities. This makes for a second distinction among the generations of black detectives, for unlike Grave Digger and Coffin Ed, Easy and Blanche are not the "tools" of a white police force to be used and discarded when their usefulness is done. As private investigators, they are at liberty to accept and reject cases, decline and accept remuneration, and determine the method of investigation and the plan into which it fits.

While Grave Digger and Coffin Ed are part of the justice systems, Easy and Blanche are outsiders who use their own discretion when it comes to dealing with criminals and the authorities. They don't just find criminals or solve mysteries, they also administer punishment and restore justice. Whereas the Harlem detectives cannot choose to keep information from the authorities (as officers they are the authorities), Easy and Blanche often choose to keep their discoveries from the police. Like most hard-boiled detectives they know that "the law is just the other side of the coin from the crime, that they're both the same and interchangeable" (197). This cynical view of the police and the law is one of several reasons for not choosing to call in the authorities. A second is that Easy and Blanche fear that they will be dismissed, ignored or thrown in jail for their efforts. Easy speculates: "I knew the police mind (at least I thought I did). If I had told them about the house he was going to they would have put me in jail. They wouldn't have gone straight to the address because they never listen to criminal cant; and all blacks were criminals" (248). Blanche expresses similar sentiments when Tina urges her to call the police. She says such action is useless not because the authorities won't book the criminal, but because they won't believe her: "How seriously do you think the police would take me? It scares me half to death to think of ever having someone do something to me that I can't avoid going to the police to get fixed" (229).

Both detectives take the law into their own hands, recognizing this as the only means of achieving justice. Easy turns the criminals over to the authorities, but as he watches the trial from a back seat in the courtroom, he is not surprised that wealth and social standing are all the evidence the defense needs to acquit those whose greed prompted a series of cold-blooded murders. The people responsible for the murder of Elizabeth's brother and two children are tried and released. After the trial, Easy signs-on with the construction crew to build the shopping mall that he and Mofass had hoped to build. He retaliates for the city's confiscation of their property and resale of it to a white contractor. "No one ever suspected that it was me who put the extra sand in the cement that made it crumble only one year after the opening ceremonies" (255). Hence Easy takes justice into his own hands, doing what he can to revenge the wrongs done to him. He proffers this philosophy like a street vendor advertising his wares or soapbox orator espousing his beliefs: "One of the problems with so may oppressed people is that they don't have the stomach to give what they get" (42). Blanche also

pursues her own ideas of punishment and revenge. Following the age-old adage that you don't call the police on a brother (something we see operating repeatedly in Himes), she assumes the role of judge and jury. Following the eye-for-an-eye and tooth-for-a-tooth definition of justice, she repays the criminal for smacking her on the head by kicking him in the chest. More importantly, she believes his guilt and remorse are all the punishment required, and this proves true enough when the criminal commits suicide several days after the discovery of his crime. The African-American detective who "takes the law into his or her own hands" exemplifies what Richard Slotkins identifies as the synthesizing of the roles of outlaw and detective in the modern hard-boiled detective:

> The detective and outlaw . . . begin to inhabit the same space and finally begin to swap roles. And this, for me, is the root of the modern hard-boiled detective story. It is the combination, in a single figure, of the outlaw and detective. The inner life of the figure is that of the outlaw, whose perspective is that of a victim of social injustice. He has seen the underside of American democracy and capitalism and can tell the difference between law and justice and he knows that society lives more by law than by justice. Yet he also embodies the politics of the police detective, the belief that we need order, some kind of code to live by if we are to keep from degenerating into a government of pure muscle and money. And he is willing to use force to impose order and strike a proper balance between law and justice.[13]

This description of the modern-day hard-boiled detective seems an especially accurate reflection of the African-American detective depicted by Himes, Mosley and Neely. Grave Digger, Coffin Ed, Easy and Blanche are victims of racial injustices. They know that society lives more by law than by justice, and they know that racism persists in spite of the laws intended for its demise. Nevertheless they believe in order and justice. Wrongdoings are uncovered; criminals are found-out and punished even if their economic and social positions shelter them from the punishment their crimes warrant. The difference, though, between the white modern-day detective characterized by Slotkin and the African-American detective is the extent to which they believe they can control or limit the degeneration and corruption. For the detective described above, a descendant of Natty Bumppo and the Western hero, it's a show-down between good and evil. The possibility exists that justice and good will prevail. The African-American detective entertains no such illusion. And while his successes may represent the triumph of the working class, a home-run against the team of the affluent who monopolize business and government, it is an ineffectual strike against the wrong and injustice imbedded in the fabric of society, the racism and sexism for which there is no antidote. Unlike the dreamers who can imagine justice even if they imagine it a long way off in the distance, the black detectives proffer tidbits of advice for combating one wrong among a myriad of wrongs. While Mosley advocates treating others as they treat you as a means of fighting racism, Blanche recommends a different course of action for women:

> ". . . what if every woman in the country refused to make dinner Thursday evening. Just the thought of it makes our power clear. And what if every secretary or waitress in the world decided to take the same day off. We don't need other people to know our power, we need ourselves, ourselves."

> "You mean organize," Tina said.

> "Exactly, my dear, exactly. That's when the change will come, when women organize and declare it time for the boys to make way. I don't mean the insipid women's organizations out there today, fooling around trying to reform the system using the boy's rules. Ridiculous. No risk, no gain. We want equality, but we're no longer willing to get hurt in order to get it. Today's national movements, women's and blacks', seem more interested in being players in the white male club than challenging the white male patriarchy."

> (189)

This acknowledgment of wrong and the suggestion for its remedy occurs in several instances in *Blanche and the Talented Tenth* and *Black Betty* when the detective becomes a mouthpiece for the author. Both deviate from the prototypical tight-lipped reserved detective when they speak passionately about ideology and reform.

Race defines these detectives. It makes them realize that the police don't want to hear their story or help them. Instead these detectives jeopardize their own safety when they go to the police for assistance as does Easy who is illegally detained in a jail cell. Race determines relationships with others at every step of the investigation. Easy will have to fight every white person he meets. He walks into a gas station for directions and a soda, but the man behind the counter greets him with a pistol poised and ready. When Saul arrives at Easy's house, the half-asleep detective instinctually covers himself with a sheet explaining that he feels "vulnerable" when people see his skin (12). Easy's investigation takes him into the desert where is conscious of himself as "a black spot on a white background" (41).

While race may make Easy feel "that feeling of anger wrapped tight under my skin," class is an equally important contribution to his identity (60). Unable to meet the mortgage payments, Easy has lost his home and is worried about having enough money to care for his children. His first-person narrative generalizes about the lives and experiences of poor black men. As such it fits Peter Freese's definition of a "cultural mediator," "providing readers with exciting introductions to unknown cultures."[14] In this instance, Easy introduces a middle-class white audience to the culture of improver-

ished black men. Relying on understatement and the objective style of speech typical of the hard-boiled detective, Easy describes the lives of poor black men: "The first thing a black man and a poor man learns is that trouble is all he's got so that's what he has to work with" (106); ". . . behind every poor man there's a line of death. Siblings and children, lovers and wives. There's disease and no doctor. There's war, and war eats poor men like an aardvark licking up ants" (92-93); and "Poor men are always ready to die. We always expect that there is somebody out there who wants to kill us. That's why I never questioned that a white man would pull out his gun when he saw a Negro coming. That's just the way it is in America" (44). Elsewhere he makes the comparison between the lives of white and black explicit:

> John's bar didn't open until noon but I would have found him there even if we hadn't had that appointment. Men like John and me didn't have lives like the white men on TV had. We didn't roll out of bed for an eight-hour job and then come home in the evening for *The Honeymooners* and a beer.

> We didn't do one thing at a time.

> We were men who came from poor stock. We had to be cooks and tailors and plumbers and electricians. We had to be our own cops and our own counsel because there wasn't anything for us down at City Hall.

> We worked until the job was done or until we couldn't work anymore. And even when we'd done everything we could, that didn't mean we'd get a paycheck or a vacation. It didn't mean a damn thing.

> (188)

Easy's working class status differs from the affluence associated with the first detectives. Marty Roth observes that these detectives were usually aristocrats who had the leisure to pursue an investigation. He suggests that this class status originated in British detective fiction and continued in early American detective novels.[15] Easy's working class status also represents a break with the formula created by Himes. In keeping with the examples by Chandler and Hammett, the Harlem detectives are middle-class men who commute from their homes in Queens to their jobs in Harlem. Always in the third person, Himes' descriptions make Harlem a "country unto itself" where exotic people have experiences remote from those of the readers. The reader is a passive spectator of a drama which increases the gaping void between white middle class experience and the experiences of poor black people. Unlike Mosley, Himes never invites readers to imagine what it is like to be poor and black. Instead his writing has the effects of the photographs in Richard Wright's *Twelve Million Black Voices,* objectifying and dehumanizing the experiences of the subjects. The following excerpt from *A Rage in Harlem* has this effect:

> There were more bars on his itinerary than any other comparable distance on earth. In every one the

jukeboxes blared honeysuckle-blues voices dripped stickily through jungle cries of wailing saxophones, screaming trumpets and buckdancing piano-notes; someone was either fighting, or had just stopped fighting, or was just starting to fight, or drinking ruckus-juice and talking about fighting.

(36)

While Mosley explains the life of the bartender with an implicit request for reader's sympathy, Himes portrays the Harlem bar. Even though Goldy, the person visiting, is familiar with these surrounding, the experience is defamiliarized through its rendering.

Barbara Neely is also concerned with issues of class. In her mystery series, the sleuth's working class background provides the skills necessary for investigative work:

> Blanche looked around the lobby again. Despite the quiet and calm, there was an echo in the air of something not so serene. Something unpleasant had happened here, and not too long ago. She was sure she was right. She was good at sensing buildings, picking up the mood and personality of place. She thought of this sixth sense as a skill she'd developed from years of cleaning and cooking in houses, apartments and offices of all types.

(15)

Blanche's experiences as a domestic provide her with the skills for solving the mystery. They also provide the impetus for her visit to Amber Cove: "She wanted a glimpse of how and why being among people who had everything could make a child or a fool look down on those who didn't have a pot" (18). Her children have developed a class and color consciousness which Blanche is determined to stifle at its roots. As someone content with her own dark-skin color, she sees herself as "race representative" at Amber Cove: "the only guest present with any true color" (40). She observes the lives of the talented tenth and is reminded of the lives portrayed in television soap operas (25). The Amber Coveites fascination with secrecy and intrigue reminds her of the white people:

> WCP—Whitefolks Curdled Passion—a kind of lumpy rolling stew on which the lid was always kept until the pot exploded. At which point, the kind of people Blanche worked for usually had a migraine; visited a therapist; went off to Aspen for R & R; or retired into a whiskey bottle or coke spoon. She wasn't accustomed to black people who let things fester and go unsaid. In her world, people got in each other's faces and talked loud about each other's bad behavior. But it looked like she'd been wrong about the Whitefolks part of WCP. Maybe Curdled Passion had more to do with believing in a white bread world than being white—in believing that emotions were nasty habits that needed to be hidden, if not destroyed.

(49)

Blanche White is not ashamed of her color or her working class background. Instead she regards both as good fortune. She "tests" prospective romantic involvements by telling them that she is employed as a domestic, and she gauges their interesting by measuring their shock and discomfort. She speaks her mind to a rich woman who had a child she "didn't have the courage to claim" by telling her: "There's more than one way to be poor, more than one kind of education and a whole lot of ways to be ignorant. And you honey, with your books, pictures and money, your cottage and so forth are poorer, dumber and more ignorant than I'll ever be" (221-22). Blanche represents the black working class and shares their values and beliefs. She is suspicious of people with money. She suspects them of wrongdoing and immorality.

The detective's integration into the community and family change the nature of the detective process. These detectives integrate their work into complex, busy lives. Easy interrupts whatever he is doing to return home and prepare lunch for his children. Every moment he is away, he thinks of the neighbors who keep an eye on Juice and Feather. The detective process is not a beeline from discovery to punishment of the criminal. Instead it follows the pattern made by stitches in a crazy quilt, a random zigzagging which seems to have no direction or destination. The detective process is different for Blanche whose discovery of the crime and pursuit of the criminal originate with her concern for her children. She worries about dinner and is equally concerned with the kids' sand castles and hair braiding as she is with the mysterious deaths taking place. Here, too, the solution to the mystery is not the shortest distance between two points but a circuitous one that detours to include the other parts of the detective's life. Unlike the Harlem detectives, Easy and Blanche are more than detectives. They have multiple roles and the detective work is portrayed as only one piece in the mosaic of their lives.

In his discussion of the detective fiction, Peter Hühn examines the detective process as an allegory of reading and writing. The detective is a reader who analyzes the environment for clues and reconstructs the story written by the suspects. The suspects, on the other hand, are writers who "tamper with the text of everyday reality, changing or rearranging signs so as to conceal or transform."[16] In addition to his role as reader of the text authored by the suspect, the detective is the writer of the mystery presented to the reading audience. Hühn illustrates how "entangled writing and reading contests ultimately only serve to demonstrate the superior power of *writing*."[17] In African-American detective novels, this contest between reading and writing is complicated by the introduction of the vernacular or "speakerly" text, a third category which undermines the efficacy and power of reading and writing.[18]

In Himes' *A Rage in Harlem,* Grave Digger and Coffin Ed read the mystery to discover that three con men have come to Harlem with a trunk of imitation gold ore and a story about the discovery of a gold mine in New Mexico. These men tell their story to unsuspecting Harlemites, preying on their allegiance and commitment to black enterprise. The con men explain that the discoverers of the mine, several black men, want their discovery to benefit black people, so they have sent scouts to Harlem to recruit sponsors and investors. Those who are conned mistake the samples of fake gold ore for real gold ore, and the con men's lies for the truth. Reading the suspect's story as a lie enables the detectives to write a story which leads to the discovery and punishment of the criminals. As authors, the detectives construct the plot or sequence of events that leads to the criminals. This story is told by a third-person narrator who usurps the detective's power. The narrator's distance from the experiences he describes has already been noted.[19] This narrator's power as a writer is limited by two characters—twins—Goldy and Jackson, who write competing narratives told from the perspective of participants. The twins rely on African-American storytelling and folk traditions to narrate their stories and determine the course of events. Goldy maintains this control by disguising himself as a Sister of Mercy who walks the streets of Harlem attracting little attention except from passerbys who drop a coin in his tin cup and receive a card assuring their admittance to heaven. Goldy's speech is also a disguise, incomprehensible to all but those he intends to address. To onlookers, he sounds possessed, for he seems to be speaking in tongues or babbling incomprehensibly.[20] Taxi cab drivers put money on the numbers which punctuate his speech, for they believe that he is a prophet. Disguised as Sister Gabriel, Goldy greets Grave Digger with "And I saw three unclean spirits like frogs come out of the mouth of the dragon" (44). Although onlookers laugh, Grave Digger understands Goldy's message about a suspect and prods for more information: "I hear you, Sister. And what makes those three frogs hop?" (44) Goldy responds "For they are the spirits of devils working miracles" (44-45). When he sees Jackson (who has been set up with a fat bankroll to lure the suspects) walking down the street with one of the con men, Goldy says to his brother: "Ye have found the Spirit" (60). However when the police approach him and ask if he is riding with the hearse (which contains gold ore instead of a casket) his response is enigmatic: "Yes, sir, in the service of the Lord. To take that which is left of him who hath been taken in the first death, praise the Lord, to wait in the endless river until he shall be taken in the second death" (91). Upon hearing this response, the confused white policemen cease their interrogation and by so doing believe they have shown respect for a religion they don't understand.

Jackson demonstrates the power of storytelling as it issues from the oral tradition. At the novel's close, he tells Reverend Gaines the story thereby usurping the narrator's power as writer. His role as master writer is evident when he initiates the story's action by asking his twin brother, Goldy, to assist him in his search for Imabelle. Jackson's love for Imabelle recounts a classic blues theme: he will do anything to find his woman: ". . . cut throats, crack skulls, dodge police, steal hearses, drink muddy water, live in a hollow log, and take any rape-fiend chance to be once more in the arms of his high-yellow heart" (96). Allusions to Jackson's folk origin appear in descriptions of his walk—as though "picking his way through a briarpatch" (121)—and descriptions of his physical demise as nothing less than the work of John Henry (85). When in trouble, he sings folk songs (73), blues songs he remembers his mother singing (107), spirituals (137) and his own improvisational "lowdown blues" (120). Like Brer Rabbit, he doesn't seem formidable, but Jackson controls the reading and writing of criminals and detectives. Like his twin brother, Goldy, he issues from the vernacular tradition. Together they represent the metaphorical nature of language and its inherent multiplicity of meaning. As storytellers and tricksters, they control experience thereby escaping the control of writers and readers—criminals and detectives alike.

The power of the vernacular is also evident in Mosley's fiction. In his study of *Devil in a Blue Dress* and *A Red Death,* Theodore O. Mason, Jr. identifies the detective, Easy Rawlins, as a "cultural transgressor."[21] Mason says "usurping white language resembles owning a house, insofar as both acts move one into the realm of transgression, the zone of dangerous instability."[22] Language also serves as a means of transgression in *Black Betty.* For example, Easy observes that "all black policemen who want to rise in the ranks have to learn how to speak like half-educated white men" (196). He also knows that speaking dialect can serve as a disguise which allows him to use racist assumptions to his advantage. Easy says "I spoke in dialect that they would expect. If I gave them what they expected then they wouldn't suspect me of being any kind of real threat" (72). He can use dialect to his advantage by playing "dumb" and taking advantage of white people's erroneous assumptions about intelligence. But in the exchange which follows, Mosley enlarges his perspective of the vernacular beyond its possibilities as an act of transgression or even a means of disguise:

> "Did you ever get that degree from UCLA?"
>
> "Shit. Motherfuckers wanted me to study some kind of language. Uh-uh, man. I walk on the ground an' I talk like my people talk."
>
> "But you could do somethin', Jackson. You're smart."
>
> "Naw, Easy, I cain't do nuthin'."

"Why not? Of course you could."

"Naw, man. I been a niggah too long." He said it as if he were proud of the fact.

"You think that Martin Luther King is down south marchin' an' takin' his life in his hands just so you could be gamblin' and actin' like a niggah?"

"I ain't got nuthin' to do wit' him, Easy. You know I be livin' my life the onliest way I can."

"But Jackson, we can't be runnin' in the streets bettin' on each other's lives. We got to be men. We got to stand up for ours."

Jackson pulled off his big hat. Sweat was running down his face. It was one of the few times I ever looked him in the eye that he didn't smile.

(134-35)

Jackson chooses not to transgress boundaries. Why should he? He prefers to stay in the black community and to speak only Black English. His preference empowers the Black vernacular and his authoring of his own story. Easy must wrestle whites for control over the black vernacular. He confronts Sarah Cain for wanting him to be her "niggah" (124). He threatens LaMone, the white realtor who purchases Mofass' confiscated property from the city with ". . . if you insist on makin' me out a nigger I ain't got no choice but to be one" (174). Easy's transgressive acts diminish his ability to write his own story. Instead, he becomes a character in the story written by the suspects. His first-person narrative becomes a necessary means of undermining their control. The novel, *Black Betty,* is the result of this effort.

Blanche is a naive reader, unaware that she is also a character whose actions are controlled by the criminal in his story. Stu, the criminal, and Blanche, the detective, wrestle for authorship. Her romantic feelings for him presents the possibility that they will collaborate in the writing of the story, but he retreats from this possibility by killing himself. She remains to tell the story, to rewrite DuBois' *The Talented Tenth* by inserting herself into the story and re-naming it *Blanche Among the Talented Tenth.* In this story, Blanche and the vernacular take precedence. Blanche does a lot of "dissing." She invents words and expressions and uses the black vernacular. Free indirect discourse has this language consistent with the language used by the narrator. There is no conflict between the character and narrator for control of the story.

Although Himes describes his writing as imitative of established writers of detective fiction, he made substantial contributions to the genre. The experimentation he began is being continued by writers such as Walter Mosley and Barbara Neely, the next generation of African-American writers of detective fiction. Although Hurston identified imitation as one of the characteristics of Negro expression, it has been studied by theorists of the African-American vernacular who point out that the imitation to which Hurston refers always implies difference. This is one among several definitions Henry Louis Gates, Jr. gives to signifying. He describes it as imitation with a signal difference.[23] Maybe it was this kind of imitating Himes had in mind when he described his contribution to the genre as just "making the faces black."

Notes

1. I am indebted to Peter Freese for this information. In *The Ethic Detective* (Essen, Germany: Verlag Die Blaue Eule, 1992), Freese reproduces excerpts of this conversation between Himes and Duhamel as quoted in Stephen F. Milliken's *Chester Himes: A Critical Appraisal* (Columbia: U of Missouri P, 1976), p. 208f. Freese, 22-23.

2. Freese, 15. Quoted from John A. Williams, "My Man Himes: An Interview with Chester Himes," in John A. Williams and Charles F. Harris, eds. *Amistad 1* (NY: Random House, 1970), p. 49.

3. Chester Himes, *A Rage in Harlem* (NY: Vintage/ Black Lizard Edition, 1991), p. 51. Originally published in the U.S.A. as *For Love of Imabelle* (1957). All further references to this work will be included parenthetically in the text.

4. In "Chandler Comes to Harlem: Racial Politics in the Thrillers of Chester Himes," Peter J. Rabinowitz discusses the "contradiction in their position" as an "explanation for the rage and violence that characterizes their actions. . . ." Barbara A. Rader and Howard G. Zettler, eds. *The Sleuth and the Scholar: Origins, Evolution, and Current Trends in Detective Fiction* (Westport, CT: Greenwood P, 1988), p. 24.

5. Barbara Neely, *Blanche Among the Talented Tenth* (NY: St. Martin's P, 1994), p. 8. All further references to this work will be included parenthetically in the text.

6. Walter Mosley, *Black Betty* (NY: Norton, 1994), p. 19. All further references to this work will be included parenthetically in the text.

7. See Richard Slotkin's "The Hard-Boiled Detective Story: From the Open Range to the Mean Streets" for a discussion of the detective's character and its origins. Barbara A. Rader and Howard G. Zetter, eds. *The Sleuth and the Scholar: Origins, Evolution and Current Trends in Detective Fiction* (Westport, CT: Greenwood P., 1988), p. 93.

8. I coin this term, "womanist detective," by borrowing the term "womanist" from its inventor, Alice Walker, who defines "womanist" as "a black feminist or feminist of color" and "a woman who loves other women, sexually and/or nonsexually, and one who appreciates and prefers women's culture, women's

emotional flexibility, and women's strength." For the complete definition see Walker's *In Search of Our Mothers' Gardens* (NY: HBJ, 1983), p. xi.

9. For another example of African-American feminist detective fiction see Valerie Wilson Wesley's *When Death Comes Stealing* (NY: G. P. Putnam's Sons, 1994).

10. Bethany Ogdon, "Hard-boiled ideology," *Critical Inquiry* 34.2 (Summer 1992): p. 71.

11. For a discussion of the emotional detachment which characterizes the detective see Richard Alewyn, "The Origins of the Detective Novel," Glenn W. Most and William W. Stowe, eds. *The Poetics of Murder: Detective Fiction and Literary Theory* (NY: HBJ, 1983), p. 67.

12. Rabinowitz, p. 21.

13. Slotkins, p. 99.

14. Freese, pp. 9-10.

15. For a discussion of the class origins of the detective see Marty Roth's *Foul & Fair Play: Reading Genre in Classic Detective Fiction* (Athens, GA: U of Georgia P, 1995), p. 72.

16. Peter Hühn, "The Detective as Reader: Narrativity and Reading Concepts in Detective Fiction." *Modern Fiction Studies* 33.3 (Autumn 1987): p. 456.

17. Ibid., p. 459.

18. According to Henry Louis Gates, Jr. "speakerly texts privilege the representation of the speaking black voice. . . ." For a fuller definition see Gates, *The Signifying Monkey: A Theory of African-American Literary Criticism* (NY: Oxford, 1988), p. 112.

19. This narrator is the objective reporter, an outsider whose distance from his subject is evident in his descriptions of it. For example, he describes Harlem as "a city of black people who are convulsed in desperate living, like the voracious churning of millions of hungry cannibal fish. Blind mouths eating their own guts. Stick in a hand and draw back a nub" (93).

20. For a fuller discussion of Goldy see Nora M. Alter's "Chester Himes: Black Guns and Words." Warren Motte and Gerald Prince, eds. *Alternatives* (Lexington, KY: French Forum Pubs, 1993), p. 14.

21. Theodore O. Mason, Jr., "Walter Mosley's Easy Rawlins: The Detective and Afro-American Fiction." *The Kenyon Review* 14.4 (Fall 1992): p. 174.

22. Ibid., p. 180.

23. "Repetition and revision are fundamental to black artistic forms . . . I decided to analyze the nature and function of Signifyin(g) precisely because it *is* repetition and revision or repetition with a signal difference." Gates, xxiv.

Andrew Pepper (essay date 1999)

SOURCE: Pepper, Andrew. "Bridges and Boundaries: Race, Ethnicity, and the Contemporary American Crime Novel." In *Diversity and Detective Fiction,* edited by Kathleen Gregory Klein, pp. 240-59. Bowling Green, Ohio: Bowling Green State University Popular Press, 1999.

[*In the following essay, Pepper explores the differences between white and Native American fictional detectives, pointing out that readers tend to identify more fully with white characters and view ethnically diverse detectives as more fragmented and alienated from both established law enforcement and the society in which they operate.*]

The arrival in the United States of millions of immigrants from non-European countries since changes in the Immigration Act in 1965 has radically altered the social composition, particularly of the American urban population. Cities, it seems, are fast becoming home to a bewildering range of different nationalities and ethnic groups. In New York, formerly dominant Euro-centric groups have been dramatically superseded by arrivals from China, Korea, Jamaica, the Dominican Republic, Colombia, Cuba, and Russia; the city now boasts churches, cultural events, political associations, festivals, shops, and restaurants for all the different groups, together with dozens of foreign-language newspapers and cable TV stations. Los Angeles, its streets dotted with Iranian coffee shops, Korean supermarkets, and Chinese laundromats, and entire neighborhoods where nothing but Cantonese or Spanish is spoken, seems truly to be a multi-ethnic "babylon." As David Rieff notes, "Along Wilshire Boulevard and Melrose Avenue the faces behind the counter were Han and Dravidian, Korean, Persian, Mixtec and Ethiopian, anything, it seemed, except black and white" (144).

On paper, at least, cities like New York and Los Angeles do seem to possess a genuinely multiethnic character. However recent high-profile events, such as the beating of Rodney King and subsequent rioting in Los Angeles, police corruption in New Orleans, the O. J. Simpson trial and more importantly the verdict, and the Million Man March in Washington, DC, have conspired to give the impression that the United States, far from being a kind of multicultural utopia, remains fundamentally split down some kind of racial middle and that cities like New York or Los Angeles, despite their apparent polyethnic character, are in fact organized primarily along black/white faultlines.

This debate has raged with particular intensity in the academy. Scholars like Andrew Hacker, whose book *Two Nations: Black and White, Separate, Unequal, Hostile* highlights the extent of specifically racial divisions in the United States, point out that because race *has* been the fundamental axis of social organization in American society and because the experiences of non-European immigrants have been significantly different to those of European descent, race as a concept cannot be meaningfully discussed under the broader heading of ethnicity. Other scholars, however, like Werner Sollors, while acknowledging the continuing persistence of racially motivated divisions in U.S. society, nevertheless, seek to depict African-Americans merely as "one of many different *ethnic* groups," and race, as "one of the dimensions of the larger cultural and historical phenomenon of ethnicity" (35).

This essay, however, will argue that neither position offers a particularly satisfying portrait of the nature of relationships between different ethnic and racial groups in the United States, because neither offers a suitably complex and flexible model for (group *and* individual) identity formation. To claim that race is indeed the principle axis of social organization and that U.S. society is split down a racial middle leads one towards the inherently dangerous conclusion that black and white necessarily represent something homogeneous, and that in a nation undergoing such a rapid metamorphosis, the population remains simply white- or black-identified. However to deny the claim outright would be to risk trivializing significant divisions in American society that *are* racially determined, and to overlook the simple fact that having dark rather than light skin or certain set of heritable characteristics, as Kwame Anthony Appiah notes, can have very profound social, political and economic consequences (Lentricchia 285).

What is needed, therefore, is an account that is able to entertain at least two apparently conflicting perspectives at the same time, but sociology is, perhaps, less able to offer such an account than fiction, because the novel, as the Russian critic Bakhtin argues, is "heteroglot" and therefore embraces many different voices or languages. Whereas sociology, in Bakhtin's terms, aspires towards a unitary language or an overall perspective that is arguably noncontradictory, the novel welcomes diversity. In fact, the contemporary American detective novel, in particular, has sought to depict society in all its diversity—as the detective attempts to discover who has done what, he or she necessarily comes into contact with individuals drawn from different backgrounds and cultures. And while there might ultimately be only one "language of truth," that of the hard-boiled investigator, his or her voice, according to Bakhtin at least, will necessarily reflect the full diversity of his or her social milieu because language is constructed via a process of what he calls "dialogics" (whereby each voice or utterance only takes its meaning in relation to other voices or utterances and therefore reflects all the voices in a given society).

The article will ask, and at least start to answer, why detective fiction in which the usually alienated, disaffected *Anglo* detective is replaced by an investigator who is part of a socially marginalized group is particularly suitable for this kind of usage. In general, the hard-boiled detective has been perceived to be a positive figure. This does not mean that he or she functions like some kind of morally pure state-sponsored henchman, but simply that in his or her refusal to capitulate to authority and in his or her dogged determination to uncover what has really happened, he or she usually comes across as an attractive figure or at least someone with whom readers can in part identify. This view of the detective has in the past led to one viewing him in dangerously essential and transcendent terms, a man like Chandler's Phillip Marlowe entirely in control of his actions and language. This is not the case with a black or Native American detective, however. In fact, precisely because he or she has traditionally been forced to live in *at least* two worlds (that of his or her culture, which itself needs to be seen in fragmented terms, and that of the so-called "dominant" culture, be it white, Western or Anglo in orientation), he or she will automatically possess an appropriately fractured sense of self; appropriately, because it necessarily problematizes a straightforward model of identity formation. Moreover, such a detective, because he or she understands the kinds of frustration that, to varying extents, define the experiences of all non-white Europeans (ie. having to operate in a white-controlled world) but can also detect differences between various groups and individuals, is arguably better able to view the polyethnic environment in suitably ambiguous terms.

"Race" and "Ethnicity" as Overlapping Yet Diverging Categories

If the "self, as Stuart Hall argues, needs to be conceptualized not in coherent, unitary terms but as a "moveable feast" of usually overlapping and contradictory identities, then what are the implications for different so-called "minority" groups? For just at a time when, for example, Chicanos and blacks in the United States are successfully contesting the perceived dominance of Anglo/white/western culture and promoting or retrieving a sense of their own (previously marginalized) cultures, they are told that the type of coherent and universal identities which might seem attractive are no longer possible. Should one, therefore, be wary of such "post-modern" critiques of the self and simply view this particular challenge as another example of cultural revisionism on the part of a Euro-centric culture intent on maintaining its apparent dominance via blatant divide and rule tactics? Or can this kind of thinking open up our understanding of different African American (and by implication Chicano, Cuban, Jamaican, etc.) experiences and force us to see each group in necessarily heterogeneous, multiplicitous terms?

Again, it seems, this question can be partly answered if one adopts a deliberately self-conscious, flexible approach to the notion of identity construction and before we move onto a more detailed exploration of the crime fiction itself, it is necessary to pause for a moment and consider what this phrase actually means. Terms like race and ethnicity no longer refer to categories that are fixed and stable but to ones that are best seen as fluid and relational, reflecting a growing awareness of the temporary and socially constructed nature of all identities. Yet the temptation to entirely collapse race and ethnicity on top of one another needs to be resisted. One needs to remember that having dark and not light skin can affect what kind of job you have, where you can or cannot live, who your friends are, and that in very many cases, the experiences of non-white European immigrants in the United States *have* been significantly different from those of their Europeans counterparts. Mary Waters makes the point that while an Italian-American might seek to equate the experiences of being black in the United States to being Italian American,

> [T]he reality is that white ethnics have a lot more choice and room for maneuvering than they themselves think they do. [But] the situation is very different for members of racial minorities whose lives are strongly influenced by their race or national origins regardless of how much they may not choose to identify themselves in either ethnic or racial terms.
>
> (157)

Here the question of how a person defines him or herself, and perhaps more importantly, is defined by the rest of his or her society is crucial. When a fourth generation Italian American tries to be "Italian," where does his or her notion of being "Italian" come from? From an understanding of rituals, traditions, and history, or from family, or even just from watching films and televisions shows? And is it the same for an African American? Benjamin Ringer and Elinor Lawless argue that an ethnic group is besieged by two sets of forces that are in opposition to each other—an internal set that serves to establish a group's cultural distinctiveness or "we-ness" and an external set that serves to establish its "they-ness." Ringer and Lawless, moreover, contend that the latter process is far more pervasive and more actively influences and shapes the character of a particular group if that group is also racially distinctive. Thus, whereas Italian Americans might enjoy considerable choice in selecting which bits of their ethnicity or ethnic heritage to make a part of their lives (because the internal force that serves to establish his or her "we-ness" is stronger than the external force that serves to establish his or her "they-ness"), individuals of non-European descent do not enjoy the same levels of choice when it comes to deciding how to identify themselves. A Jamaican or African American, for example, might similarly try to choose which parts of their ethnicity to make a part of their lives, there is an equal, if not greater, external force that seeks to categorize them merely as black.

The implication, here, is not that American society itself is inherently determined by a black/white model of categorization and the various ethnic groups neatly fit into either category, but rather, there exists a *tendency* to view the United States in this manner; a tendency, primarily on the part of those who have been ascribed a white identity, to want to collapse all differences into the inadequate but dangerously seductive categories of "black" and "white." What I mean is best explained by the African American poet and novelist, Ishmael Reed. Stressing what Sollors calls the "disturbing ability of the categories of 'black' and 'white,' despite their blatant inadequacies to describe a highly miscegenated, polyethnic culture to devour all ethnic differences" (*Invention* xix), Reed argues that despite widespread racial mixing, people have actively sought to retain the racial divide because it serves a useful purpose—to convince blacks not only that they are somehow inferior to whites but also that they are responsible for everything which has gone wrong with American society:

> By blaming all of its problems on blacks, the political and cultural leadership are able to present the United States as a veritable utopia for those who aren't afraid of "hard work." . . . And so, instead of being condemned as a problem, the traditional view of the black presence, the presence of "blacks" should be viewed as a blessing. Without blacks taking the brunt of the system's failures, where would our great republic be?
>
> (Sollors, *Invention* 229)

If we need to be careful about viewing race and ethnicity as entirely overlapping categories, we should also be aware that neither are they entirely diverging categories. Despite the simple fact that being black in America is *not* the same as being Polish or Italian, scholars have sought to demonstrate that the lines which bind and divide different ethnic and racial groups are not as rigid or as natural as some people might have argued or in fact hoped. William Peterson points out that the terms ethnic and racial have at various times been used to describe the same thing (i.e., the Irish race and the Irish as an ethnicity) and argues that since the word *ethnos* (from which our word ethnicity is derived) "originally pertained to a biological grouping, it was closer to our definition of 'race' (which probably derived from the word *ratio* which, in medieval Latin, was used to designate species)" (Thernstrom 235). He also argues that the separation of the two terms has been inhibited and undermined by confusion in real life between physiological and cultural criteria; an African American, to this extent, can be defined in both ethnic and racial terms—as an individual who belongs to a specific cultural group with its own distinct history, and someone who possesses certain physiological features (Thernstrom 236).

There is pressing evidence, furthermore, to show that racial and indeed ethnic exclusivity in the United States is a falsehood. Writers like Ishmael Reed, Walter Mosley, Henry Louis Gates and Paul Gilroy have strenuously argued that terms like black or African American can no longer be theorized as self-evident but rather as entities whose *essential* character is in fact fluid, fragmented, and defined via a process of negative differentiation (A is an X because he isn't a Y or A is an African American because he isn't Mexican American). Theorists and critics have asked how one can even begin to talk about ethnic and racial groups in essential or transcendent terms given the extent of miscegenation and the growth in crosscultural relationships. If someone is one-fifth Jewish, four-fifths Irish American, half Puerto Rican, or half-African American how does one categorize him? Is it possible? Just as Walter Mosley, a half Jewish, half African American novelist declared, "There's no such thing as a pure black race. We are so intermixed that there is no race. That is, no pure race" (Oxford 4). Ishmael Reed similarly contends that blacks in the United States have a multi-ethnic heritage and argued that "[I]f Alex Haley had traced his father's bloodline, he would have travelled twelve generations back—not to Gambia, but to Ireland" (Sollors, *Invention* 227).

The destabilization of apparently fixed terms like African American or black is perhaps more useful than anything else in helping us to better understand the overlapping and yet diverging relationship between race and ethnicity not least because it asks for, if not demands, a far less rigid approach to the idea of boundary formation. Of course, it is very tempting to view race as some kind of special objective category, not least because having dark skin can affect, in a very real sense, how one is treated, where one can or cannot live and so forth. Furthermore the desire, from within black cultures, to construct some kind of transcendent racial identity in order to counterbalance perceived attacks from "outside" has, according to Paul Gilroy, never been stronger. Yet we must resist this temptation to universalize black or African American experience in unitary terms because such a practice is not only untenable in the light of postmodernist critiques of coherent subjectivities: it also denies or glosses over differences that can, as this essay will demonstrate in the next section, be profoundly liberating.

WALTER MOSLEY'S EASY RAWLINS: THE
DETECTIVE AS CULTURAL MEDIATOR

To some extent, Mosley's surrogate detective Ezekiel "Easy" Rawlins comes across in the five novels (to date) as a tough and adept character in the mould of, say, Phillip Marlowe—he takes punishment without backing down, isn't afraid of what might happen to him, pursues the truth with a dogged determination, and usually finds out exactly who did what during the course of each novel. Yet his status as African American means that he is constantly torn between what he must do in order to survive and what he feels might be in the best interest of his specific community. Typically, the fact that the hard-boiled detective allows himself to become personally involved in his investigation and adopt some kind of moral position in relation to the crime itself is a key feature of hard-boiled detective fiction. Easy, however, cannot afford to assume such a position because as a black man living in a white-controlled world, he is necessarily forced to compromise his private code of justice (if he has such a code) just to keep his head above water. Rugged individualism, Mouse tells Easy in *Devil in a Blue Dress* is a just myth propagated by white culture in order to falsely valorize its achievements:

> "Nigger cain't pull his way out of the swamp wit'out no help, Easy. You wanna hole on t'this house and git some money . . . ? Alright. That's alright. But Easy, you gotta have somebody at yo' back, man. That's just a lie them white men give 'bout makin' it on they own. They always got they backs covered."

> (158)

One needs to be aware that just as Paretsky's V. I. Warshawski or Sue Grafton's Kinsey Millhone are different kinds of private detectives to, say, Chandler's Phillip Marlowe because they are female, Easy Rawlins is a different kind of private detective because he is African American. (Though one needs to be careful about conflating female and non-white detectives too closely simply on the grounds that they both, in some way, revise existing conventions.) Easy is both part of the dominant white culture, in so far as much of his work comes from white businessmen or families (i.e., Dewitt Albright in *Devil in a Blue Dress* or the Cain family in *Black Betty*), and part of a specific African American community in South Los Angeles. Furthermore he is both inside this particular community and culture (in so far as he has a family and relies on his community to sustain him) and outside it—as an African American struggling to survive in a white controlled world, he invariably finds that he is forced into situations that compromise friendships. In *A Red Death*, for example, he even admits that, "I was on everybody's side but my own" (221). This sense of ambiguity or "doubleness," Mosley suggests, is an inherent part of being African American in the United States. Precisely because Easy has been forced to live in at least two worlds (that of his own African American community, which itself needs to be seen in fragmented terms, and that of the so-called dominant culture, be it white or Western Anglo in orientation) also means that he possesses the kind of fractured identity or subjectivity that enables us to begin to frame black and indeed African American culture in appropriately fluid and fragmented terms.

Bakhtin argues that a single national language is composed of a multiplicity of competing languages, each struggling to assert itself in relation to each other and the dominant or official language. Language, he maintains, is a practice in which there are two forces constantly in conflict with one another; a centripetal force, "working towards a unified and static language" and a centrifugal force, "endlessly developing new forms which parody, criticize and generally undermine the pretensions of the ambitions towards a unitary language" (Tallack 119). This particular battle is an important feature of Mosley's work. Characters like Mrs. Keaton, an elderly librarian in *White Butterfly,* might seek to "colonize" Mosley's African American population and force them "to abandon their own language and stories to become part of her educated world" (56). However the African American characters themselves, specifically Easy, resist such pressures and deliberately choose to express themselves in dialect because to do otherwise would be to negate an entire oral tradition—"folk tales, riddles and stories colored folk had been telling for centuries" (56). Language, here, is not merely a vehicle for communications; it is also a means of connecting people to their history and culture and the fact that most if not all of Mosley's black characters speak in dialect signals the author's intention to challenge, undermine, and even overturn official values.

The centrifugal force in Mosley's writing, therefore, might be stronger, reflecting Easy's claim that he could only truly express himself "in the natural uneducated dialect of [his] upbringing" (*Devil* 17). Yet the impact of the centripetal force or that force which seeks to colonize or appropriate black languages and cultures, cannot be underestimated. Indeed, though Easy himself is proud of his cultural heritage, proud to be black, his identity is not simply constructed from that which is specifically African American. As Mosley starts to question what this kind of term actually means, we start to get a picture of his protagonist as someone whose sense of "self" has, in fact, been constructed from a dizzying range of sometimes conflicting and sometimes interlocking perspectives or subject-positions. Being African American, for Easy at least, is not merely about speaking in dialect and knowing where he came from, but also about holding opinions more often associated with, say, the white/Anglo middle class, or Mexicans or Jews—like a passion for education and reading that extends beyond wanting to know about his own culture (in *A Red Death* the reader learns that he is taking a night school class in English and European history) and a respect for home ownership, which is seen by some within his community as a specifically white value.

In his language, therefore, we find flexibility, not dogma: a single voice that also represents or reflects an entire spectrum of different perspectives, and utterances.

A brief list of examples taken from the novels themselves illustrates the point. In *Devil in a Blue Dress,* the reader discovers, on the one hand that "there were no real differences between the races" (62), and on the other, that no one with white skin actually "thought that we were really the same" (144). Furthermore, while Easy lives in the kind of unequal and racially segregated world where a black man could be arrested or assaulted just for looking at a white women, there are at least some points of overlap between the so-called black and white worlds. Easy might be quick to celebrate certain aspects of black culture(s), like music or storytelling, but he is both aware of its fragmented, heterogeneous nature and he makes friendships and associations with people from other groups and cultures. Moreover, while he can see from his own experiences that black and white America are hopelessly segregated and divided by massive inequalities in wealth and opportunity, he refuses to be ghettoized or isolated simply as a black man who has already been cast in the role of loser. What we find in his character, above all, is a model for boundary formation that is flexible and sophisticated enough to accept that borders, like skin color, exist and have real meaning but that doesn't merely categorize terms like white or black as homogeneous, unitary entities where no kind of interaction takes place.

In his representation of the wider environment—Los Angeles from the 1940s onwards—Mosley paints a similarly complicated picture of racial and ethnic relations. To some extent, I suppose, given that racially motivated segregation even now remains a fact of life in many LA neighborhoods, it is inevitable that Mosley should choose to depict a world where those with dark and light (or black and white) skin live in separate worlds. From *Devil in a Blue Dress* onwards, one is made acutely aware of the fact that just as whites or Anglos rarely venture into Watts, blacks or African Americans hardly ever venture out of Watts, other than for work. Furthermore, this situation seems, if anything, to actually worsen as the novels (and century) progress. By 1962, the temporal setting for the fourth novel of the series, *Black Betty,* Mosley's description of Mofass as being "someone from the old days when there was a black community almost completely sealed off from whites" (109), implies that events in the wider cultural forum like the election of J. F. K. and the rise of the Civil Rights movement have led to a partial relaxation of strict racial divisions. Yet ghettoization and its inevitable consequences appear to be that much more tangible. Watts, in the first novel of the series *Devil in a Blue Dress* is, to some extent, described as a mecca of opportunity for anyone willing to work—"the promise of getting rich pushed people to work two jobs in the week and do a little plumbing on the weekend" (55-56). However this sense of albeit false optimism has vanished by the 1960s and the same community is likened to a graveyard where hope for the future is little more than a bad joke:

> Most of them were black people . . . Women like Betty who'd lost too much to be silly or kind. And there were the children, like Spider and Terry T once were, with futures so bleak that it could make you cry just to hear them laugh. Because behind the music of their laughing, you knew there was the rattle of chains.

> (*Betty* 216)

Given the extent of social, political, and economic inequalities between black and white, Anglo and African American, in Mosley's fiction (a divide that is appropriately represented in *Black Betty* via a comparison between those described above and the fabulously wealthy Cain family of Beverly Hills), it is difficult not to think of Andrew Hacker's description of the United States in general as a nation fundamentally split down a racial or black/white centre. Yet the author, I think, also wants to suggest that a system of classification based around a straight-forward racial binary, cannot effectively come to terms with the extent of diversity in his city. Skin color might well be the most intransigent boundary in Mosley's fiction, but to suggest that race is the *only* axis of social organization would be to ignore other divisions (based on class, gender, and ethnicity, for example) and gloss over those areas where the experiences of those from different cultural backgrounds do, in fact, overlap.

Sole focus on black as a monolithic group, Mosley suggests, fails to take into account the huge diversity of skin color, and by implication miscegenation, within black culture(s). A quick glance though *Devil in a Blue Dress* and *A Red Death,* for example, bears this point out. In the former, just as Coretta James has "cherry brown" skin (44), Odell Jones is colored like a "red pecan" (42) and Jackson Blue is "so black that his skin glinted blue in the full sun" (120). Meanwhile in the latter, just as Etta Mae is described as "sepia-colored" (26), Mofass is "dark brown but bright" (13), Mouse is "dusky pecan" (72), Jackie Orr is "olive brown" (86) and Andre Lavender is "orange skinned" (120). No need, as Henry Louis Gates says of his similarly "multi-colored" family, to point out that those with lighter skin were part Irish or English because they wore "the complexity of their bloodline on their faces" (Gates 73).

The tendency to see the world in simplistic black/white terms also glosses over significant class and regional differentials within the so-called black community. Most of the black community in Watts, at least in the first three novels of the series (*Devil in a Blue Dress, A Red Death, White Butterfly*), seem to have migrated to the West coast from south Texas and Louisiana, and differ-

ences between people from those areas and, for example, African Americans from the northeastern cities, like LAPD officer Quentin Naylor from Philadelphia, are self-evident. There are even noticeable differences between people from Houston and New Orleans, at least in terms of social networks and circles of friends—as Easy explains in *A Red Death,* "Mofass was from New Orleans and though he spoke like me, he wasn't intimate with my friends from around Houston, Galveston and Lake Charles" (18). There are significant differences, too, between those African Americans who work in bars, factories, or who steal for a living, and professional or middle-class African Americans, like Quentin Naylor, who had "an educated way of talking" (*Red Death* 168). Within Watts itself, class differences also prevail. Those who live on Bell Street and "thought that their people and their block were too good for most of the rest of the Watts community" (*Red Death* 197) are part of what might be termed the lower-middle class and seek to foreground differences between their status and the rest of the Watts community as vociferously as possible. Yet it is important to remember that they are no less black for doing so. Countering the idea that black represents some kind of essential state of being that is itself inextricably linked to notions of suffering, "the blues," discrimination and poverty, bell hooks makes the point that while black people from the middle classes may well have been affected by racism in different ways but, "it is not productive to see them as enemies or dismiss them by labelling them not black enough." Rather, she points out, black people in America have multiple identities and that what needs to be stressed is that "our concept of black experience [in the past] has been too narrow and constricting" (37).

Mosley also suggests that an exclusive fixation on those factors which divide different groups, in fact, negates areas of common ground where the interests and experiences of blacks, working-class whites, Mexicans, and given in post-Second World War context, Jews, overlap. In *Black Betty,* for example, we learn that a poor white man called Alamo has forged some kind of allegiance with Easy based on their mutual dislike for the establishment. "He would have hated Negroes if it wasn't for World War One. [But] he felt that all those white politicians had set up the poor white trash the same way as black folks were set up" (30). Similarly, Easy states, in *Devil in a Blue Dress,* that before "ancestry" had been discovered "a Mexican and a Negro considered themselves the same" (182). In *A Red Death,* furthermore, he becomes friends with a Jewish communist activist called Chaim Wenzler. Chaim might have white or light skin, but as a Jew who fled to the United States from Nazi-occupied Europe, he can also understand the painful consequences of violent discrimination. In one passage, he tells Easy that whites [in this case meaning non-Jews] "don't understand being treated like this" (144), and in another, he declares, "Negroes in America have the same life as the Jew in Poland" (111).

This is not, however, a bland multiculturalism that Mosley is espousing, where differences between various minority cultures are, to some extent, collapsed and blacks in America are simply treated as one of many different groups. Discrimination, residential segregation, and racism—all with their roots in the institution of slavery—are a harsh fact of life, even for those with mixed parentage who perhaps do not easily fit into the category of black. Daphne Monet, the object of Easy's quest in *Devil in a Blue Dress,* might appear to have white skin and therefore possess a 'white' identity, but she cannot escape the consequences of her heritage. Her father was an African American and though she desperately wants to marry a powerful Anglo banker and political powerbroker, her concealed racial identity inevitably negates this possibility. "All them years people be tellin' her how she light-skinned and beautiful," Mouse tells Easy, "but all the time she knows that she can't have what people have" (209). Furthermore, though Wenzler's aim is to promote a sense of unity between blacks in the United States and American Jews, Mosley falls well short of exactly correlating their experiences. During the heyday of the 1950s "Red" scare, Easy is told about a list circulating in the business community that identifies not only blacks but also Jews who have been excluded from the work place due to political allegiances. This does not, however, signal some kind of parity—as Jackson Blue ruefully explains to him. "One day they gonna throw that list out. . . . Mosta these guys gonna have work again. . . . But you still gonna be a black niggah. An' niggah ain't got no union he could count on, an niggah ain't got no politician gonna work fo' him" (*Red Death* 230). Given the pre-Civil Rights context of Mosley's first three novels, the fact that Los Angeles is primarily organized along racial or black/white lines is not surprising. However anticipating and reflecting recent theories which dismiss the idea that races are simple expressions of biological or cultural sameness and highlight "the existence of a multiplicity of black tones and styles" (Gilroy 1-2), Mosley works to deconstruct blackness as a singular, monolithic trope.

ETHNIC AND RACIAL DIVISIONS IN MIKE PHILLIPS'S *POINT OF DARKNESS*

bell hooks suggests that there is a tendency within the black community in the United States to either essentialize black experience, or, at least, not critique essentialism since many fear "it will cause folks to lose sight of the special history and experience of African-Americans." Yet she stresses that blacks in America have many different identities and "when this diversity

is ignored, it is easy to see black folks as falling into two categories . . . black-identified and white-identified" (29). The arrival of blacks from various places in the Caribbean (Cuba and Jamaica, for example) has further accentuated the multiplicitous nature of black identity in the America. Literature and other art forms produced by black artists from these countries, hooks argues, work to deconstruct notions of universalism by affirming multiple black identities and challenging "the colonial imperialist paradigms of black identity that represent blackness one-dimensionally in ways that reinforce and sustain white supremacy" (hooks 28). Indeed, one can perhaps understand why crime novels written by, and about, individuals from, say, Jamaica or Cuba (who do not easily fit into categories like black or white or at least, not in the traditional sense), offer a more complex, flexible, and satisfactory model for identity construction, one that acknowledges both the extent of existing racial divisions and the inability of the old language of race relations to cope with the fragmented nature of black and white identities in the United States.

To claim that race has been, and still is, the fundamental axis of social organization in Mike Phillips's New York is tempting for his Jamaican-born, British-raised investigator, Sam Dean, in so far as the city's Caribbean population, like its African American one, is externally defined or misdefined simply on the basis of skin color. Indeed, the fact that black people in New York regardless of their background, culture, or class are, even superficially, lumped together and viewed by the dominant white European culture in singular terms is some basis for the kind of Pan Africanism that certain politicians want to promote. (Sam notes that blacks of different nationalities and cultures were starting to see the benefits of coming together and "finding common ground" in city politics.) Furthermore it reflects a popularly held desire among some of the city's black intellectuals for a kind of cross-cultural black identity. When Sam's cousin Bonnie, lecturer at a university in Queens, asks him to describe his dark-skinned Latino girlfriend Sophie, the choices she offers him reflect an apparently prevailing view built into many American racial/social attitudes. "You've got two choices," she tells him. "Black or white? Which one is it?" (Phillips 39).

Sam, however, rejects the kind of racial exclusivism that Bonnie is seeking to promote. Though, at the time, he falls into her trap and blurts out, "You'd definitely call her black," later on, he finds himself increasingly dissatisfied with his answer, not least because it fails to take into account the significant cultural differences between Bonnie and Sophie. Indeed, when the two women finally meet and Bonnie disparagingly declares that Sophie is not "one of us," Sam sets out his own position:

I'm loyal to my friends and my memories and want progress for the race. That's how we were brought up, you know that. That don't change. But there's no reason, whether its psychological or sociological or mystical or whatever, that's gonna make me join that exclusion shit.

(149)

Sam, then, might be fiercely loyal to what he sees as his race but he uses the term in its loosest possible sense. Just as Henry Louis Gates states in his autobiographical account of his family's history *Colored People,* "I want to be black, to know black, to luxuriate in whatever I might be calling blackness at any particular time—but to do so in order to come out of the other side, to experience a humanity that is neither colorless nor reducible to color" (xv), Sam self-consciously foregrounds his pride in being black but at the same time acknowledges its multiple style and meanings. After all, belief in a pure black identity is something of a misnomer, he suggests, because most black people outside Africa descend from a racial mixture. "Europeans, Indians, and Chinese, all of them at one point or the other stuck their fingers in the New World's black gene pool" (196).

Phillips's point, I think, is that it takes the knowing and perceptive eye of Sam Dean, the novel's investigator, to locate those areas where the interests, experiences, and histories of the different groups either overlap or diverge. As a detective, or surrogate detective, his generic function in *Point of Darkness* is to locate the daughter of an old friend who has gone missing in New York. Yet the plot, as such, I would argue, is something of a Trojan horse, concealing a secondary, perhaps more important agenda, whereby Sam must be able to move among the city's different groups, reading and deciphering people's characters "not only from the physiognomy of their faces but also via a social physiognomy of the streets" (Willet 3). It is a job which he performs admirably. When he visits a Spanish-Caribbean cafe in Queens with Bonnie and Oscar, her African American boyfriend, though many of the faces are black, Sam senses their unease—"as if they were in enemy territory" (212). In another restaurant, Sam is able to precisely identify the identity of the waiters. To his trained eye, they are not simply black or even Caribbean but specifically Haitian—"That is to say, they looked a lot like Jamaicans, but with a kind of prissy smoothness to their style and movements" (139).

Where the lines that bind and divide individuals and individual groups, however, is practically impossible to work out, even for someone like Sam. Far from being a city organized along strictly racial lines Phillips' New York is more a teeming morass of sometimes conflicting, sometimes interlocking alliances. Though Jamaicans and other Caribbean blacks share a nominal racial identity with the city's African American population, differences are clearly foregrounded. The two groups speak differently, think differently and act differently. African Americans, Sam claims, are fixed to one country while Jamaicans, for example, "move comfortably between two countries" (222), and from a cultural point of view, seem to share more in common with the various Latin Americans. Ethnicity does act as a source of conflict between the two groups, especially when perceived Caribbean successes are compared to African American failures, but Phillips is careful to contextualize differences. Though many African American neighborhoods are portrayed as spoilt, rundown and dangerous, and Caribbean ones as dynamic and energetic, differences between the two groups, and the socioeconomic status, are shown to be temporal and based in specific historical circumstance. "African Americans," Sam explains, "had lost it in the grim struggles of the northern cities and then TV had taught them human worth could be measured by possessions and happiness was an escape capsule . . . [but] the Caribbeans still pulled together because that was part of their immigrant heritage" (138).

Ultimately Sam Dean, like Mosley's Easy Rawlins, acts as a kind of cultural mediator whose responsibility or function is as much observational as it is investigative; he moves among the city's different groups, deciphering what he hears and sees in order to decide for himself along what lines the city is divided. The point is that his "self" is not fixed or essentialized but fluid and representative of the fractured environment, as well as his chameleon-like ability to assume different roles and different identities depending on where he is and who he is talking to. In one scene, he is very much a black man, not only struggling to keep his head above water in a white-operated world but also proud of his racial identity and the sense of belonging it affords him as he moves between different black communities. In another scene, he is Caribbean and in another, he is specifically Jamaican—someone whose outlook and indeed entire character is in some way informed by the politics, culture, and climate of one particular place, or defined via a sense of what he is *not* (African American, Haitian, Cuban, etc.). Furthermore, in another scene, he is not so much Jamaican as English or someone who uses his "accent" to help him to elicit information from white or Anglo Americans: individuals who in similar circumstances "might've treated an African-American with a well-rehearsed suspicion" (269).

If Sam's identity cannot be seen to be fixed or "whole" do we view him as less of a man or less of a detective than, say, Chandler's Phillip Marlowe? And just at a time when, for example, Jamaicans and African Americans in the United States are successfully contesting the perceived dominance of Anglo/white culture and retrieving a sense of their own (previously marginalized) identities, can we simply write off attempts to discount or undermine their very existence as another example of cultural revisionism on the part of a Euro-centric culture intent on maintaining its apparent dominance via divide and rule tactics? The answer to both questions has to be an emphatic no. Sam, at least in this situation, is a more effective investigator than Phillip Marlowe could ever be precisely because he can assume different identities to suit different situations (arguably, Marlowe did this, too, but once he stepped outside the Anglo culture to which he belonged, he was always merely a white man). Moreover, to view boundaries (surrounding individual and group identities) in flexible, nonessential terms is liberating for Sam in so far as it allows him to both make connections with those from similar backgrounds and feel pride at the achievements of those who belong to his race and to his specific culture, and, at the same time, move beyond the rather limited essentialist position that dictates who he can and cannot forge friendships with and indeed trust. Once in New York, he inevitably gravitates towards those people who share a Jamaican identity and he feels pride at the dynamism and vitality of the different Caribbean communities, but, at the same time, discovers that a single group identity cannot function as some kind of broad umbrella under which all blacks, or all West Indians, or even all Jamaicans, regardless of outlook, class, and background, can take refuge. Moreover, such a view exactly mirrors a shift that has taken place in contemporary black cultural politics from a discourse of apparent unity, whereby black as a term was used as a means of somehow describing the collective experiences of so-called black people (often in relation and response to having to operate in a white-controlled world) to one of pluralism or fragmentation whereby the diverse and at times contradictory nature of different black experiences and identities has been foregrounded.

CONCLUSION: APPLICATIONS

Given that one key purpose of this collection in general is to show how different crime or detective novels can be used to teach cultural diversity both in the classroom and to the general reader, one needs to consider how we can best put some of the ideas outlined in this essay to work. How can they either help us to better understand the relationship between race and ethnicity in contemporary America or, given the extent to which the ethnic and racial composition of U.S. society has altered over the last 20 years, enable us to come to some kind of new appreciation of the American social mosaic? As a conclusion, then, I want to look at the 1992 Los Angeles riots and though such an important event needs a much wider discussion than I have the space to give it, I want to consider how one can *begin* to frame the various conflicts.

That the riots themselves caused widespread damage and loss of life is not in dispute. More than 50 people were killed and over 2,000 were injured. Plumes of thick-black smoke could be seen for miles around as some 4,000 individual buildings were razed to the ground, at an estimated cost of $1 to $2 billion. What does seem to be in dispute, though, is what the violence itself represented. Indeed, though the Watts riots some 25 years before were broadly understood to be a display of frustration and anger on the part of the community's mostly black population, people seemed to be divided as to what the violence in 1992 reflected. For many, the bloodletting was merely the most visible expression of the ever-widening gap between blacks and whites in America and proof that any advances made during the 1960s' Civil Rights upheavals had subsequently been lost. Others, however, saw the disturbances as a chance to attack the old language of race relations and call for a new appreciation of America's social mosaic. Ronald T. Takaki, for example, remarked soon afterwards that perhaps the most important lesson of the explosion was "the recognition of the fact that we are a multi-racial society and that race can no longer be defined in the binary terms of white and black" (Takaki, "Different" 5).

The temptation to view the disturbances in purely black/white terms is of course strong, not least because the initial trigger was undoubtedly the acquittal of four white police officers accused of assaulting a black motorist and the perceived injustice that it represented (especially when their actions had been openly caught by an amateur video cameraman). Yet if one also considers some of the following factors, it becomes increasingly difficult to settle for black/white conclusions. Blacks or African Americans constitute just 10 percent of the city's total population while the various Latino groups make up almost 40 percent; of the 5,000 people arrested during the course of the rioting, only 37 percent were black; blacks in South-Central seemed to vent their anger as much at Koreans as whites; poor whites joined in on the side of Latinos and blacks; blacks fought against other blacks; Koreans accused the mostly white LA police department of deliberately failing to protect them and their interests.

To suggest that American society is fragmented and that the lines which bind and divide various groups are determined not just by straightforward racial or ethnic allegiances but also by, say, class interests, background, and even religion is, of course, nothing new. Yet, in the context of the Angeleno riots, the notion that the black or African American or Caribbean detective operating in a fractured, multiracial environment can function as a kind of cultural bridge is highly relevant. This is not to suppose that Mosley's Easy Rawlins or Phillips's Sam Dean, if put into a hostile real-life environment like contemporary LA, could diffuse tension, successfully mediate between the different groups and bring about stability. It is simply to suggest that via their abilities to deconstruct differences that appear to be natural and, at the same time, to acknowledge those areas where differences cannot be collapsed, they offer some kind of way forward through the morass of U.S. racial and ethnic politics.

The Los Angeles riots, however one ultimately regards them, exposed deep fault lines in American society. Partly the product of specifically black frustration at apparent injustices handed out by the white-dominated judicial system, the riots reinforced the sense that racial divisions, particularly for those in society who are discriminated against and marginalized simply on the basis of where they come from or how they look, are frighteningly real. Indeed, just as it needs to be emphasized that being, say, Chicano and being Cuban are not the exactly same, one also needs to be remember that the predicaments of certain groups (i.e., African Americans), as Richard Rodriguez notes, should not be casually compared to the experiences of other Americans:

> My fear is that multiculturalism is going to further trivialize the distinct predicament of black Americans . . . It is my belief that there are two stories in American history that are singular and of such extraordinary magnitude that they should never be casually compared to the experiences of other Americans. One is the story of the American Indian; the other is the story of the black slave.
>
> (Takaki, *Different Shores* 281)

Of course, significant advances were made by many blacks as a result of Civil Rights, but the continuing impact of slavery and subsequent institutional discrimination in the job and housing market cannot be underestimated. At the same time, however, it is just as dangerous to erect semipermanent boundaries between the different groups; such a process only naturalizes differences which are often socially shaped and thereby glosses over those areas where the interests and experiences of different groups *do* overlap. As bell hooks argues, "other groups now share with black folks a sense of deep alienation, despair, uncertainty, loss of sense of grounding, even if it is not informed by shared circumstances." She concludes, "Radical postmodernism calls attention to those shared sensibilities which cross boundaries of class, gender, race, etc., that could be fertile ground for the construction of empathy—ties that would promote recognition of common commitments and serve as a base for solidarity and coalition" (27).

Whether or not Mosley's Easy Rawlins novels and Mike Phillips' *Point of Darkness* could ever be classified as radical postmodernist texts is not ultimately clear (and such a statement also depends on exactly where one

places the genre in relation to notions of high and low forms of writing). Yet insofar as both authors not only write from the margins but also construct, through their respective protagonists and portrait of the wider community, a fragmented and pluralistic model for black identity formation, their work fulfills two important criteria, as laid down by bell hooks. Such a model, I would go on to add, is useful in helping us to work through the kind of difficulties outlined in the previous paragraph, not just because it is flexible and sophisticated enough to entertain apparently contradictory perspectives; inherent in this kind of model too, is the sense that one can be proud of one's culture and race, as Easy Rawlins and Sam Dean are, but still see them as fractured and multiplicitous categories, and that one can draw sustenance from one's own community and culture, as Easy Rawlins and Sam Dean do, but never so completely immerse oneself in it that outsiders are automatically viewed as enemies. And such a position might be a useful starting point for reconsidering and recontextualizing the 1992 Los Angeles riots.

Works Cited

Gates, Henry Louis. *Colored People*. London: Penguin, 1995.

Gilroy, Paul. *Small Acts: Thoughts on the Politics of Black Cultures*. London: Serpents Tail, 1993.

Hacker, Andrew. *Two Nations: Black and White, Separate, Unequal, Hostile*. New York: Charles Scribners, 1992.

hooks, bell. *Yearning: Race, Gender and Cultural Politics*. London: Turnaround, 1991.

Lentricchia, Frank. *Critical Terms for Literary Study*. Chicago and London: University of Chicago Press, 1987.

Mosley, Walter. *Black Betty*. London: Serpents Tail, 1994.

———. *Devil in a Blue Dress*. London: Serpents Tail, 1991.

———. *A Red Death*. London: Serpents Tail, 1992.

———. *White Butterfly*. London: Serpents Tail, 1993.

Oxford, Esther. 'The Monday Interview: Walter Mosley,' *Independent* (UK), 9.10.95, 4.

Phillips, Mike. *Point of Darkness*. London: Michael Joseph, 1994.

Rieff, David. *Los Angeles: Capital of the Third World*. London: Phoenix, 1993.

Ringer, Benjamin. *Race-Ethnicity and Society*. London and New York: Routledge, 1989.

Sollors, Werner. *Beyond Ethnicity: Consent and Descent in American Culture*. New York and Oxford: Oxford University Press, 1986.

————. *The Invention of Ethnicity.* Oxford and New York: Oxford University Press, 1989.

Takaki, Ronald T. *A Different Mirror: A History of Multi-Cultural America.* Boston and London: Little Brown & Co., 1993.

————. *From Different Shores: Perspectives on Race and Ethnicity* ed. *in America,* 2nd ed. Oxford and New York: Oxford University Press, 1994.

Tallack, Douglas. *Literary Theory at Work: Three Texts.* London: BT Batsford, 1987.

Thernstrom, S. *The Harvard Encyclopedia of American Ethnic Groups.* Cambridge, MA: Harvard University Press, 1980.

Waters, Mary C. *Ethnic Options: Choosing Identities in America.* Berkeley: University of California Press, 1990.

Willett, Ralph. *The Naked City: Urban Crime Fiction in the USA.* Manchester and New York: University of Manchester Press, 1996.

Andrew Pepper (essay date 2000)

SOURCE: Pepper, Andrew. "America's Changing Colour: Towards a Multicultural Crime Fiction." In *The Contemporary American Crime Novel: Race, Ethnicity, Gender, Class,* pp. 140-79. Edinburgh: Edinburgh University Press, 2000.

[*In the following essay, Pepper offers a detailed account of race and its influence on American society, focusing on its impact on crime fiction written by several contemporary African-, Jewish-, Latin-, Native-, and Asian-American authors.*]

Like a magician who produces a rabbit from a top hat only to make it disappear, the logic of the book [*The Contemporary American Crime Novel*] so far has been to affirm the significance of the black/white racial binary in American life, if only by focusing on examples of 'black' and 'white' crime fiction, while simultaneously questioning its validity and existence. The idea that this kind of model reflects the full range of lived experiences in a nation whose city streets vibrate to the rhythms of diverse ethnic cultures and whose population can be traced back to every corner of the world from Laos and Cuba to El Salvador, Colombia, Korea, Armenia and China, is clearly misguided. Nonetheless, while the idea that 'blackness' and 'whiteness' ever described fixed, natural essences has been well and truly dismissed, the persistence of race and racism as a continuing blight on the American landscape has been noted. After all, who could have failed to notice the racial fault-lines exposed and opened up by the melee to condemn and explicate Mark Fuhrman or Louis Far-

rakhan in recent years? And who could assert, with any degree of conviction, that race in America is of no consequence, when much of the evidence points to the contrary. However unreal or problematic 'race' as a biological or scientific category might be, belief in the existence of race, like belief in the existence of witches, as Kwame Anthony Appiah notes, continues 'to have profound consequences for human life'.[1] Or as Howard Wincant puts it:

> As we watch the videotape of Rodney King being beaten up by Los Angeles police officers; compare real estate prices in different metropolitan neighbourhoods; select a radio channel to enjoy while we drive to work; size up a potential client, customer, neighbour, or teacher . . . we are compelled to think racially, to use the racial categories and meaning systems into which we have been socialised.[2]

Indeed, the continuing and pervasive influence of race in American life and concurrently, the problematisation of race as a viable method of classification is the structuring tension that will inform much of this final chapter. What follows, then, is an attempt to address and, if not to resolve then at least unpack, this contradiction, by opening up the generic frame of reference to include not just examples of 'black' and 'white' crime fiction, but also crime novels featuring and written by protagonists of Jewish, Cuban, Mexican, Ojibwa and Korean extraction.

Certainly this list speaks about the growing ethnic diversity in American life but what to make of this diversity is by no means self-evident. To those on the conservative right like Arthur Schlesinger Jr diversity begets fragmentation and fragmentation, of course, threatens the grand American project invoked by the Founding Fathers' maxim, *E Pluribus Unum.* 'The U.S. escaped the divisiveness of a multiethnic society by a brilliant solution: the creation of a brand new national identity', Schlesinger argues, with more than a passing reference to the 'melting pot' theory. 'The point of America was not to preserve old cultures but to forge a new, American culture'.[3] Other critics, however, like Lawrence Fuchs, have celebrated the diverse nature and origins of American society and conceived the United States as a 'kaleidoscope' or 'mosaic' of different-but-equal cultures and individuals whose interactions necessarily change but do not exactly transform one another.[4] This view, as we shall see, perhaps comes closer to informing my own treatment of the novels and novelists to be discussed in this chapter, but missing from both versions, nonetheless, is any idea of the way in which racial and ethnic identities have, and continue to be, constructed through, and in relation to, a hierarchical system of domination and subordination in which the role of the 'State' (or at least the institutional and legal apparatus established to regulate and order social relations) cannot be overlooked. Smith and Feagin helpfully illustrate how this process has functioned in the United States:

> State power has often been the object of the politics of racial representation; and state policies, the means to enforce relations of domination-subordination. In the American case, the archetypal foundations for centuries of subsequent racial-ethnic incorporation, negotiation and conflict began with the early colonial struggles between European settlers and Native Americans and between early colonial settlers and their imported African slaves. The latter involved a multi-layered construction of dominance and oppression that cut across all major institutions.[5]

To conceive of the 'State' as monolith and its power as all-pervasive, to the point where individual agency—the ability of individuals to define themselves—is extinguished, would be overstating the case. But who could deny that from its inception the United States has been founded upon principles, and legislation, which have explicitly excluded peoples of non-white, non-European descent from enjoying privileges and benefits extended to their white, Euro-American counterparts? Though the Declaration of Independence was rhetorically a 'colour-blind' document, the US Constitution amended the latter's claim that all men should be allowed to enjoy 'certain unalienable rights' to effectively define African-American slaves out of existence.[6] Subsequent legislation further reinforced the subordinate status of non-whites in the early Republic and gave institutional legitimacy to racist practices that would be replicated elsewhere, in the economy, education, housing and politics. The Naturalisation Act of 1790 extended citizenship only to 'free, white people'; Chief Justice John Marshall's ruling, in the case of *Cherokee Nation vs Georgia* (1831), that Indian tribes were to be seen as 'domestic, dependent nations' effectively placed Native Americans outside America's political and constitutional borders; and two Supreme Court rulings in the 1920s, *Ozawa vs United States* and *Thind vs United States,* underlined both the artificial, arbitrary nature of racial classification as well as the power of such classifications to determine (unequal) social, economic and political relations across all spectrums of American life.[7]

Takao Ozawa, a middle-class, University of California-educated immigrant from Japan, appealed to the Supreme Court that he should be considered for naturalisation on the ground not simply that he was a 'model' citizen who had severed all cultural and religious links with his 'home' country but more pertinently because his skin colour was 'white' or at least whiter than the average Spaniard or Italian. The Supreme Court rejected Ozawa's appeal, arguing that 'skin color does not correlate well with racial identity',[8] and that 'the words "white person" are synonymous with the words "a person of the Caucasian race"',[9] which Ozawa was deemed not to be. However in arriv-

ing at this decision, the Court ignored the basic implications of Ozawa's argument—that scientific racial classifications were actually untenable—and thus opened the door to further citizenship applications from other non-white European immigrants. One such applicant, Bhagat Singh Thind, an Indian immigrant from the Punjab, argued that since anthropologists had classified certain Indians as 'Caucasian' rather than 'Mongolian', under the terms laid down by the earlier Supreme Court ruling, he was eligible for citizenship. In its 1923 ruling, however, the Court threw out his appeal arguing that a 'white person' and a 'Caucasian' were not, in fact, synonymous, and that the distinction between, say, an Indian and someone from north-west Europe was, quite simply, a matter of 'common sense':

> It is a matter of familiar observation and knowledge that the physical group characteristics of the Hindus render them readily distinguishable from the various groups of persons in this country commonly recognized as white. The children of English, French, German, Italian, Scandinavian and other European parentage quickly merge into the mass of our population and lose the distinctive hallmarks of their European origin. On the other hand, it cannot be doubted that the children born in this country of Hindu parents would retain indefinitely the clear evidence of their ancestry.[10]

Intentionally or otherwise, the Court's decisions exposed a gaping contradiction at the heart of the American system. On the one hand, racial classifications, at least in a specifically biological sense, were rejected for being too nebulous and inadequate for the purpose of distinguishing between persons with different physiological characteristics. On the other hand, differences between persons of white, European and non-white, non-European extraction were enshrined and legitimised with reference not just to their cultural background and in the case of Thind, his Hindu religion, but also to their visible, physical characteristics. 'Race', as Haney-Lopez points out, was shown *not* to be a matter of physical difference but rather 'what people believed about physical difference',[11] something which inevitably entailed not just physiological but also cultural factors—not just how a person looked but also what language he or she spoke or what religion he or she practised. In so doing the Court bowed to popular, or rather nativist, concerns about the cultural and physiological impact of wholesale mixing between persons of European and non-European descent. Mr Justice Sutherland's haughty summary that people 'intuitively recognize' racial difference and 'reject the thought of assimilation'[12] legitimised a hierarchical model of social relations, whose origins lay in the 'black/white' binary established in the popular imagination with the arrival of African slaves on American shores as early as the 1630s, and whose impact continues to be felt, despite the passage of civil rights legislation in the 1960s.

The conflation of 'race' and 'ethnicity' here, and implicitly in the Supreme Court's ruling in the case of *United States* vs *Thind,* raises important questions about the relationship between both terms. Indeed, given their intertwined historical associations, it is tempting to simply collapse 'race' and 'ethnicity' on top of one another. William Peterson observes that the terms 'ethnic' and 'racial' have at different times been used to describe similar properties or attributes (i.e. the Irish 'race' and Irish as an 'ethnic' category) and argues that since the Greek term ethnos (from which our word 'ethnicity' is derived) originally pertained to a biological grouping, it was perhaps closer to our definition of 'race' (a word most likely derived from the medieval Latin term ratio which was used to designate species). Peterson also states that separation between the two terms has been further undermined by the confusion in real life between cultural and physiological criteria; he points out, for example, that African-Americans have been defined in ethnic and racial terms—as belonging to a specific 'ethnic' group with its own distinct culture and history and possessing certain physiological features.[13]

Nomenclature may indicate a close historical inter-relationship between race and ethnicity but cultural critics have fiercely debated the relative significance of both terms, whether race or ethnicity should be the dominant paradigm through which the contemporary United States is read and understood; in other words, whether race, as Harold Abramson and latterly Werner Sollors argue, is merely 'one of the dimensions of the larger cultural and historical phenomenon of ethnicity',[14] or, as M. G. Smith and more recently Howard Wincant and E. San Juan Jr contend, whether race needs to be treated as a special 'objective' category on the grounds that racial, and not ethnic, categorisation 'became the principle of exclusion and inclusion that continues to inform and reinforce all other social antagonisms [in the United States]'.[15] Certainly it would be hard to deny that the historical experiences of immigrants from Europe and, say, Asia and Africa were not quantitatively and qualitatively different, but does this kind of acknowledgement necessarily involve the rearticulation of race as the only usable trope of difference (and the corresponding obliteration of ethnicity)? And what of all classifications in this brave new, post-structualist world, where 'essences' (racial and ethnic) have been exposed as subjective fictions?

My answer is admittedly circumspect. Rather than succumb to the temptation either to collapse race and ethnicity on top of one another, or to excessively privilege one at the expense of the other, what follows is underpinned by a discourse that is flexible enough to view race and ethnicity as overlapping and yet diverging categories, sophisticated enough to acknowledge that commonalities between and among individuals and communities do not necessarily override equally significant cultural, historical and physiological differences, and clear-headed enough to accept that the social, political and economic consequences not just for those with, say, dark as opposed to light coloured skin have been very profound. At its heart, this model embraces a definition of race and ethnicity which focuses on the mechanics of social power, or rather foregrounds the way in which differences are constructed to reinforce relations of domination-subordination. Significantly such a model does not preclude, but rather depends upon, the ambitions and efforts of individuals and communities to contest and even overturn such relations, so that race and ethnicity, ultimately, need to be theorised in suitably complex terms, as an unstable, 'decentred' set of historically diverse experiences situated within fluctuating but nonetheless hierarchical relations of social, political and economic power.

Those who conceive race as merely one of the dimensions of the larger cultural and historical phenomenon of ethnicity, who want to entirely subsume 'race' into the wider category of 'ethnicity', by implication, are either blind to, or do not properly account for the kind of historical and material forces of racial inequality responsible for the passage of the Naturalization Act of 1790. Disturbingly such a position informs and shapes a liberal but bland multiculturalism where similarly minded groups, communities and individuals exist as 'equal' component parts of a falsely utopian, pluralistic America. I say, disturbingly, because who could argue with any conviction that the historical experiences of African-Americans or Native-Americans differed from that of, say, Irish or Italian-Americans only in degree (of suffering, marginalisation)? Yet those who consider race as a special objective category that cannot be discussed under the heading ethnicity, who resist all attempts to subsume race into the category of ethnicity run a different kind of risk; that of essentialising racial difference and compartmentalising those who have been ascribed racial identities in the United States into hermetically pure enclaves. This position informs and shapes an equally disturbing multiculturalism built upon the rhetoric of essentialism, whereby the different racial and ethnic properties of Europeans and non-Europeans are naturalised and presented as being somehow fixed, unchanging.

To view race and ethnicity as overlapping and yet diverging categories, conceived and situated in relations of unequal power, however, frees us from the tyranny of both of these positions. Informing and shaping what Manning Marable has called a 'radical democratic multiculturalism' this model emphasises the distinctive properties of particular groups and communities, foregrounds differences within and among these same groups and communities, and forges links between different groups and communities. Crucially, though as

Marable notes, such interactions are conceived of and understood in relation to the functioning of power—'and the ways in which ideology and aesthetics are used to dominate or control oppressed people'.[16]

Significantly, a model that acknowledges the logic and history of patterns of racial and ethnic domination while simultaneously conceiving of race and ethnicity as fluid, dynamic, unfixed categories, corresponds with the prevailing view of the United States contained in and expressed by the crime novel; that of a nation in which the existence of a central power source and a dominant culture neither guarantees the loyalty nor ensures the oppositionality of the detective or his or her surrogate, but rather replicates, within his or her persona, the kind of dynamic struggle which characterises the process of identity formation at large. The logic and trajectory of this final chapter, therefore, extends out of what has come before; namely, an acknowledgement that whereas 'top-down' power seeks to bind, control and condition the fabric of people's lives, individual agency invariably challenges, transgresses and elides its ability to do so. In terms of the American crime novel, this contradiction manifests itself most visibly in the persona of the detective (or his or her surrogate) who is both an agent of the state and an *'agent provocateur'*; someone operating according to his or her own code or values, or values constructed within a broader community whose opposition to the 'dominant' culture has been forged along axes of, say, race, ethnicity, gender, or sexuality.

As the scope and framework of the book opens up not just to 'black' and 'white' voices and perspectives, but also to a whole spectrum of hyphenated American identities (Jewish, Cuban, Mexican, Korean), the question of what unites and divides groups and individuals in an age when the ideas or ideals 'of coherent communities and consistent subjectivities, of dominant centers and distant margins . . . no longer seem adequate'[17] is brought into sharper focus. The emerging portrait of a multi-ethnic, multiracial American society is a complex one—a society where changes are being fuelled by a cultural politics that recognises the fragmented, provisional nature of identities and the intersecting modalities of race, ethnicity, class, gender and sexuality that criss-cross and atomise individual subjectivities. Of course, shared properties inevitably connect crime novels, whatever the racial or gendered identity of the author or protagonist, but differences, as we shall see, are often more revealing. It would be far too trite to suggest that differences between, say, Burke's Dave Robicheaux novels and Mosley's Easy Rawlins series can be explicitly attributed to the ethnic or racial identity of the author or protagonist. After all, both writers, as we have already seen, skilfully open up tensions between competing values and ideologies at play in American society in order to challenge the 'preferred' view of the United States as harmonious and progressive. That said, as Feagin and Smith argue, internal differences within racial and ethnic groupings 'constitute an important form of resistance to the homogenization by dominant centers of power'.[18] In other words, differences—between ethnic and racial groupings and by implication their cultural artifacts (i.e. crime novels)—are not entirely arbitrary and require further investigation. If this is one starting point for the chapter, another is the recognition that 'internal differences within ethnic and racial groupings' manifest themselves not just along ethnic or racial lines, but also in terms of gender, class and sexuality. To this extent, the kind of 'radical democratic multiculturalism' to which Manning Marable refers, acknowledges the link between ideology, power and culture, in its broadest sense, and envisages a radical restructuring of the 'system of cultural and political power itself'.[19] The crime novel may not share such explicitly utopian goals, but as we have already seen, the maverick, dissenting detective is better placed than most to reveal links between existing political and cultural systems and the marginalisation and oppression of oppositional voices.

'TIES THAT FRAY BUT WON'T SNAP': RITUAL, TRADITION AND MEMORY IN JEWISH-AMERICAN CRIME FICTION

When Walter Mosley alluded, in *A Red Death,* to the discrimination and suffering experienced by Jews in Europe at the hands of the Nazis and African-Americans in the New World, he was making an implicit reference to the close, though often antagonistic, relationship that African-Americans have traditionally forged with their Jewish counterparts in the United States. Both Jews and Blacks, as Cornel West observes, have been, and to some extent, continue to be a 'pariah' people—'a people who had to make and remake themselves as outsiders on the margins of American society and culture'.[20] The brutal extremities of slavery in America and the Holocaust in Europe have given each group at least partial insight into the suffering and hardships experienced by the other, and opened up significant areas of common ground. Rather than succumbing to the cult of victimhood, moreover, both groups have responded with verve and imagination to the challenges of living in the United States; in a very real sense, their achievements have helped to define and characterise America in the twentieth century. 'A century that begins only a generation after the emancipation of penniless, illiterate enslaved Africans and the massive influx of poor Eastern European Jewish immigrants', West asserts, 'is unimaginable without the creative breakthroughs and monumental contributions of Blacks and Jews'.[21] And who could disagree, when the list of creative influence from both groups includes, among many others, Louis Armstrong and George Gershwin, Miles Davis and Irving Berlin, Bessie Smith and Leonard Bernstein, Charlie Parker and Jackson Pollack, August Wilson and

Arthur Miller, Richard Wright and Saul Bellow, Zora Neale Hurston and Phillip Roth, Amiri Baraka and Allan Ginsberg, James Baldwin and Harold Brodsky, Ralph Ellison and Joseph Heller?

Certainly, within the realm of culture at least, the achievements of blacks and Jews have made a mockery of attempts to define 'America' and American culture in anything but multi-ethnic terms. Yet this unanimity of success has not been replicated across the board. While Jewish-Americans, particularly in the post-World War Two era, have by and large moved en masse from working to middle and upper-class status, the disparity of wealth and opportunity for middle and working-class African-Americans has never been greater. Though the ranks of the black middle classes continues to grow, as David Theo Goldberg points out, 'nearly half of black American children now live in poverty . . . [and] in the public mind of America, "black" and "underclass" have tended to become synonymous'.[22] Such disparities have provoked many African-Americans to question the wisdom of comparing the experiences of blacks and Jews. Increasingly relations between the two groups have been defined by mutual distrust and hostility. Crown Heights and Williamsburg in Brooklyn have played host to violent confrontations between poor blacks and Hasidic Jews, while Louis Farrakhan's ill-concealed anti-Semitism has merely poured petrol on to the flames of discontent. While some Jewish-Americans have looked to their own experiences and set out to explain continuing African-American poverty in terms of the latter group's inability to make the most of opportunities, growing numbers of African-Americans have sought to explain so-called Jewish economic 'success' and their own so-called 'failure' in explicitly racial terms. In other words, Jewish-Americans, by their own volition and with the tacit approval of the dominant culture, have enjoyed and been allowed to enjoy 'white-skin privilege'—despite virulent claims by certain right-wing extremist thinkers that Jews constitute a distinctive race. This privilege, furthermore, has come at the expense of, or at least has been predicated upon, the presence of a 'polluting' blackness. Consequently, as Goldberg notes, in much black anti-Semitic rhetoric, the 'Jew' has come 'to stand metaphorically for the figure of the capitalist, of capitalism, of prevailing social power . . . of whiteness itself'. He concludes, 'Jews are perceived and now mainly perceive themselves as white'.[23]

Whether or not such claims stand up to closer scrutiny, however, is a debatable point. Certainly, precisely because of their 'light' skin colour, most Jews in the United States, have choices that most African-Americans, quite simply, do not have. The choice, that is, to blend or assimilate into the dominant American culture, to renunciate their Jewish heritage and learn to enjoy the fruits of being white in America. In these terms, or at least in terms of how individuals and groups identify themselves and are recognised or more pertinently *mis*-recognised by others, race and ethnicity need to be understood as diverging categories. Mary C. Waters makes the telling point that the choices available to someone defined in ethnic terms are often far greater than those defined in racial terms:

> The reality is that white ethnics have a lot more choice . . . than they themselves think they do. [But] the situation is different for members of racial minorities, whose lives are strongly influenced by their race or national origin, regardless of how much they may choose not to identify themselves in either ethnic or racial terms.[24]

That said, the apparently seamless conflation of 'whiteness' and 'Jewishness' has also been called into question. To be 'white' in America, Michael Lerner argues, is to fit into the social construct of the beneficiaries of European imperialism. Yet, Lerner continues, far from benefiting from this situation, Jews 'have been socially and legally discriminated against, have been the subject of racism and genocide, and in those terms . . . are not white'.[25] In this case, race and ethnicity need to be understood as overlapping categories, because discrimination against Jews in America and elsewhere, has assumed different forms; attacks based on both physiological properties (i.e. looks) and cultural and religious factors (i.e. different attire, religious rituals and beliefs, eating habits etc.). Consequently, many have argued that it has not been easy or straightforward for Jews to blend into the American mainstream, or rather that such a process comes at a heavy cost. As Lerner concludes, 'By and large, the way to get into this system is to take off your kippah, cut off your beard, hide your fringes; in other words, to reject your entire cultural and religious humanity'.[26]

The vexed question of what it means to be an American Jew or rather 'Jewish-American'[27] has occupied writers throughout the twentieth century. Leslie Fiedler once wrote that 'the very notion of a Jewish-American literature represents a dream of assimilation, and the process it envisages is bound to move towards a triumph (in terms of personal success) which is also a defeat (in terms of survival)'.[28] This tension is picked up upon and developed, as we shall see, by Faye Kellerman, Kinky Friedman and Jerome Charyn, three contemporary Jewish-American crime writers whose respective detective-protagonists (Peter Decker, Kinky Friedman and Isaac Sidel) reflect upon the difficulty of knowing what it means to be Jewish-American, or rather reflect upon the slipperiness and fluidity of Jewish-American identity in an uncertain age when the ties that bind them to their ancestors and co-religionists overseas have frayed but not snapped. This process of reflection, whereby each figure finds himself caught, figuratively, between America and Judaism, between an awareness of their ancestry and an acknowledgement of their 'Americanness', is mapped on to the generic framework of the crime novel, whereby the ambiguous cultural politics of the hard-boiled detective perfectly expresses or at least mirrors this atmosphere of anxiety and uncertainty. The tensions opened up as a result of the maverick detective's implication in the hegemonic practices of the state and the 'ethnic' detective's anxiety about being 'ethnic' *and* 'American' may not be as pronounced or violent as those characterising, say, Himes or Mosley's work but in so far as such tensions are never entirely closed off, Kellerman, Friedman and Charyn skilfully marshal the various component parts of the genre into fresh, illuminating patterns that speak about the ambiguities of contemporary life and the fractured nature of modern identities.

This question—in essence, 'how do you know who you are?'—constitutes an ongoing line of enquiry that runs through most, if not all, of Faye Kellerman's eleven (to date) crime novels, featuring LAPD detective, Peter Decker.[29] Decker, in many ways, is cut from a familiar generic mould. Embodying what Dennis Porter has called 'an ideal American-ness'[30] Kellerman's detective not only possesses many of the qualities the genre conventionally demands of its practitioners—toughness, determination, clarity of purpose and vision, humanity and a sense of self-reliance that is the product of the detective's awareness of the failings of the institution he or she serves. The ranch and horses Decker owns are also not-too-subtle signifiers of a mythic past where the kind of 'American' values Decker appears to possess were forged on the frontier. Yet Kellerman transforms Decker from cliched totem to complex, contemporaneous figure by giving him a Jewish ancestry which is brought into sharper focus as his relationship with Rina Lazarus, an attractive widow, develops throughout the series. Adopted and raised by Baptist parents, Decker has always known of his Jewish ancestry but has made little effort to investigate it, or come to terms with what it means, until he meets Rina, herself an orthodox Jew, in the first novel of the series, *The Ritual Bath*. There after, his curiosity and desire piqued, Decker's quest for self-knowledge, and Rina, compels him to embrace Judasim and as the series unfolds, Kellerman skilfully charts his attempts to come to terms with his fractured identity and bring its various constituent parts into albeit uneasy equilibrium.

Rina's anxiety about the conflicted nature of her own identity once precipitated a shift in her own religious beliefs and practices from the modern orthodox Judaism of her parents, where 'we were indistinguishable from the rest of the neighbourhood kids except that we kept kosher and observed Shabbos',[31] to the traditional orthodox Judaism of her first husband, Yitzchak, where the differences were more pronounced. In a clever mirroring device, it also anticipates and reflects Decker's

own quest for self-knowledge, at least in so far as it leads him in a similar direction; into an apparently secure, familial environment of ritual and tradition, to some extent shielded from the corrosive influences of a capitalist-fuelled modernity. Yet in both cases, this shift is not nearly as conclusive as it might appear. In Rina's case, the trajectory of the series leads her in precisely the opposite direction; from Kellerman's first novel, *The Ritual Bath,* where she is part of an enclosed, isolated, orthodox Jewish community built around a religious teaching institution and strictly adheres to its codes and values, Rina's relationship and eventual marriage to Decker compels her to open up to the modern world of which Decker, by the very nature of his job and his Christian/American upbringing, is inexorably a part.

In Decker's case, meanwhile, one if left to ponder upon the difficulty or even impossibility of transforming himself in line with the strictures of orthodox Judaism and, perhaps more pertinently, in Rina's image. In a later novel, *Serpent's Tooth,* Decker realises that he had become 'the type of Jew she wanted'[32] and acknowledges the value of prayer—if only because the ritual forces him to contemplate the nature of God and his own spiritual quest for 'twinkle of time' (p. 255). Still, his reasons for doing so are grounded just as much in the practical and romantic as the spiritual—failure to embrace orthodox Judaism on his part would have ended his relationship with Rina—and as a committed, long-serving police detective who has no intention of giving up his job, it is impossible to shield himself, or his family, from the brutal realities of life in contemporary Los Angeles.

Decker's quest for spirituality is both a signifier of his orthodox Judaic beliefs and a reaction against the grotesque excesses of degenerate late capitalist culture. Yet as a police detective who, to a great extent, defines himself through his work, Decker depends, and in a perverse way, thrives upon the presence of such excesses. This contradiction is played out through the structure of the novels. Decker's criminal or public investigations—into LA's pornographic industry in *Sacred and Profane* or a mass shooting in *Serpent's Tooth*—parallel but also clash with his private search for spiritual meaning. Diana Arbin Ben-Merre argues that Kellerman's double plots suggest both the 'difficulties of integrating Decker's public life as a detective with his private life as a . . . returning Jew' and the 'difficulties of trying to integrate the world of secular endeavors with the world of spiritual belief'.[33] That said, both worlds are marked, surprisingly perhaps, by a similar sense of indeterminacy. Throughout the series, the apparently rigid, unchanging properties of orthodox Judaism splinter to reveal a more ambiguous constitution; in *Sacred and Profane*, for example, Decker is told by Rabbi Schulman that 'uncertainty is a condition of belief'.[34] This ambiguity both mirrors and informs the trajectory of Decker's investigations and the character of the 'justice' he dispenses. Tensions that are the product of the detective's contradictory function as state-sponsored enforcer and subversive dissenter, to a lesser or greater degree, shape the structure of the American crime novel. Here, they perform a similar function, but also speak about the difficulties of 'knowing'—knowing in a ratiocinative and metaphysical sense. Decker's actions in *Day of Atonement* when he kills an adolescent delinquent in the line of fire, and then proceeds to fire 'a chamber and a clip' into the dead man's head, oversteps his function even as dispenser of 'alternative-sense' justice, and prefigures his anxiety about setting free the dead man's accomplice, Noam Levine, who may or may not have killed someone in a botched robbery, simply because he is repentant and is the teenage son of a close family friend. This anxiety, too, assumes an overtly religious character, both when Decker cannot quite reconcile his actions with the strictures and demands of orthodox Judaism, and when Noam seeks in vain for a forgiveness he knows is beyond his reach. As Ben-Merre concludes:

> [The novel] shows how one person becomes a victim, another a victimizer, and how both these categories begin to overlap. Even after the criminals are found and guilt is apportioned out, the final image is that of a victim who is also a victimizer praying to a God who does not answer.[35]

Jewish-American identities are multiple and forged through a myriad of political, economic, social and religious affiliations. Indeed, if one is struck in Kellerman's *The Ritual Bath* by the introspective, insular nature of the novel's orthodox Jewish community or in *Day of Atonement* by the similarly distinctive character of Brooklyn's Boro Park, with its Hebrew-emblazoned storefronts displaying black hats, wigs and kosher foods, then one only has to look at other Jewish figures in Kellerman's novels whose assimilation has been more pronounced or at the visible presence of liquor stores, pizza parlours and doughnut luncheonettes at the fringes of Boro Park, to realise that cultural or religious homogeneity is no longer a possibility. Which is not to pretend that the ability and will of the State, as refracted through the desires and ambitions of a 'dominant' culture, to determine and arrange social relations is negligible. Rather it is to suggest that the tangible changes and concessions that Decker and Rina make in respect to the other, ultimately, represents a perhaps albeit utopian hope that we can all speak from a particular position, voice or culture without being imprisoned inside an ethnic enclave whose imagined boundaries are policed from outside and within to maintain a purity that does not actually exist, at least in terms of the experiences of many Americans.

The dynamic configuration of perspectives, cultures, religions and voices is nicely expressed, too, in Kinky Friedman's many crime novellas, featuring the author's private detective alter-ego, also named Kinky Friedman. Friedman—the detective and by implication the author, too—is an eccentric, protean figure; he plays in a country and western band called the Texas Jewboys, who were Jewish 'by inspiration'[36] if not ancestry, and best known for deliciously named tracks like 'They Ain't Making Jews Like Jesus Anymore'. Friedman is a cigar-chomping New Yorker, a Greenwich village bohemian with a collection of oddball friends, a collection of cats and a penchant for the unconventional, someone whose sense of identity has been forged in the image of the vibrant, multi-ethnic, dangerous, intoxicating culture the city has spawned. Just as significantly he is also a private detective; an eclectic figure constructed with more than a passing reference to both Sherlock Holmes, the doyen of ratiocinative investigators, and action-orientated, hard-drinking 'gumshoes' like Raymond Chander's Phillip Marlowe. Friedman's eye for detail and razor-sharp intellect often leaves his close friends, and by implication the reader, astounded but he is not afraid to 'mix it up', physically speaking, with adversaries who cross his path. In *Frequent Flyer,* he is beaten, spat at, gassed, shot at and left for dead but still manages to triumph over his neo-Nazi antagonists.

In some respects, the satirical elements of Friedman's crime fiction manoeuvre and locate it outside of the kind of hard-edged, uncompromising vision of a racially divisive urban America in terminal, unremitting decline which increasingly characterise the genre. Perhaps for this reason, Friedman's detective is not affected to the same extent as, say, Himes' Coffin Ed and Grave Digger, by rage which is the product of their implication in a system predicated upon their own subordination. Perhaps, too, this is because Friedman, the detective, is able to pass as white or enjoy the benefits of white-skin privilege; as Mary Waters suggests, he is to some extent able to choose which constituent parts of his ancestry, his culture and his religion to make a part of his life, whether this means eating bagels or attending classes run by the Jewish Defence League. However, this situation by no means guarantees the eradication or non-existence of anti-Semitic prejudice, nor does the satirical tone of Friedman's writing necessarily blunt its political or oppositional ambitions. Friedman's quip about the rise of Germany in the post-World War Two world—'I understand they've come up with a new microwave oven; seats forty'[37]—may well be humorous but it masks a deep-seated concern about the terrible plight suffered by European Jews and Gypsies at the hands of Hitler's Nazis. In fact, the humour somehow makes the actions and ambitions of the Nazis that much more shocking, perhaps because one is disarmed by it and hence unprepared for revelations that follow.[38]

Being 'Jewish' in America is not entirely symbolic or without cost because the past cannot simply be sealed-off in a capsule and forgotten. As Friedman, the detective, acknowledges, about the Holocaust, 'I was too young to have been there at the time but I was a Jew. There would always be a piece of yesterday in my eye'.[39] Intrusions of the past into the present, moreover, do not only take the form of 'remembering'. A violent conspiracy hatched by neo-Nazis in *Frequent Flyer* to conceal the contemporary whereabouts of Josef Mengele, a Nazi doctor responsible for the death and torture of thousands of Jews in the Polish concentration camps, alludes to the continuing persistence of anti-Semitic sentiment and the marking of Jewish-Americans, in the eyes of extremists at least, as different. The sheer scale of the Nazis' crimes against people of Jewish extraction makes the detective's traditional task of restoring even a fragile, temporary 'order' that much more problematic. Of course, one of the features of hard-boiled American crime fiction has always been the provisional, incomplete nature of 'justice' and the problemisation of detection as a vehicle for social control. That said, the sheer enormity of the Holocaust renders even this paradigm unworkable and while Friedman, the detective, successfully thwarts the neo-Nazi conspiracy, at least on American soil, he can do nothing to prevent horrific images of Jewish suffering in World War Two from punctuating his fevered dreams.

Perhaps reflecting Jewish-American 'success' at being able to infiltrate or blend into the white mainstream, Jerome Charyn's detective fiction charts the meteoric rise of Isaac Sidel, during the course of six (to date) novels,[40] through the ranks of the New York Police Department to the eventual and dizzy heights of Commissioner, the city's premier policeman. Yet rather than signalling his implication in the hegemonic ambitions of a 'dominant' culture (which itself is something of a fiction because it is the Irish who hold the purse-strings of power) Sidel's lofty but precarious position in the hierarchy of the department is little more than a gift that others have bestowed upon him. Of particular concern to the Irish king-makers, who have seen their preferred candidates move on to the FBI and pastures outside New York, is relinquishing power to the growing African-American presence in the department. Indeed, though boundaries which are conceived of in racial terms (between the city's various white ethnic groups and, say, African-Americans or newly arrived Cuban immigrants) tend to be drawn as unyielding and fixed, those denoting differences between the city's white ethnic population are constantly on the verge of collapse. Patrick Silver, an ex-cop of Irish extraction who gives his name to the third instalment of the series, *The Education of Patrick Silver,* may affirm his 'Irishness' by drinking Guinness in the King of Munster saloon but he also runs an unofficial synagogue for

Jews and gentiles by pulling people off the streets, sticking a prayer shawl over their heads and including them in the 'minyan'.[41] Meanwhile Isadore Wasser, a Jewish 'melamed' or spiritual teacher in *The Good Policeman,* may speak perfect Yiddish but he is also 'an anarchist who didn't care about kosher things'[42] and acts as chief advisor or 'consigliori' to his Italian-American son-in-law, Jerry DiAngelis, a fearsome mafioso who nonetheless has a strong affinity for Judaism.

Like Friedman's novellas, Charyn's crime fiction flirts with satire and certainly the playfulness implicit in the idea of an Irish ex-cop running a synagogue or a Jewish 'melamed' advising an Italian gangster also manifests itself in Charyn's construction of Isaac Sidel himself. Sidel is a wildly unorthodox, improbable creation: a cultural hybrid, born of a Jewish father and Irish mother; a bohemian imbued with the spirit of artistic genius; a detective with a razor-sharp intellect and memory bank 'that could give you the size of a criminal's smelly sock';[43] a politician juggling allegiances and favours in order to remain afloat; and a reckless, renegade vigilante, cursed with a tapeworm and obsessed with bringing down the Guzmanns, a family of Peruvian immigrants from Marrano Jewish stock who operate a prostitution racket out of the Bronx. Still, the satirical elements of Sidel's character, and Charyn's novels, sit uncomfortably alongside the explicit and often disturbing violence exercised by Sidel and the Guzmanns in their ongoing struggle. The tension produced by this unease, moreover, opens up a space for Charyn to investigate the origins of Sidel's rage—rage that eventually drives him to deliberately maim one of Papa Guzmann's sons by running him down in his car. On the surface, the nature of Sidel's dispute with the Guzmann's is purely material. As pimps and murderers, it is perhaps understandable that they should be so firmly fixed in his sights, not least because they were responsible for killing his beloved son-in-law, Manfred Coen, in the second novel of the series, *Blue Eyes.*

Yet there is also an ethno-religious or spiritual element to their conflict. Though Sidel's identification with Judaism, in any shape or form, is severely strained, he cannot divorce himself entirely from its spiritual dimension. A self-confessed atheist and 'skeptical Jew',[44] Sidel's desire for forgiveness and spiritual salvation, nonetheless, is brought into sharper focus as the series develops. Concerned about the possible consequences of his violent ways, he starts to experience overdetermined ethno-religious hankerings—'[he] wished he could enter some little shul, cover his balding skull with a prayer shawl, and sing his way to God'.[45] Sidel's conflict with the Guzmanns assumes religious significance because Papa Guzmann's ancestry is founded upon a rejection of Judaism, at least in so far as Marrano Jews, during the time of the Spanish Inquisition, were forced to covert to Christianity, leave Spain or face execution. Sidel himself is convinced that Papa Guzmann's ability to cast spells in order to further his criminal ambitions is the product of this 'deviant' heritage. 'Only men who drank the boiling piss of Christian Jewish saints could be such strong magicians', he says, scathingly, about his arch-enemy. Guzmann, meanwhile, is equally convinced that Sidel is not merely a 'whore cop' but rather his own 'personal devil' who 'had been born into this world to plague [him]'.[46]

Charyn himself has suggested that the contemporary writer, like a destitute craftsman, 'has been left with little else than a sense of dislocation, a splintered reality, and the shards and bones of language'[47] to work with. The contemporary crime writer, too, has struggled to come to terms with a world in which answer, and meanings, are only ever subjective, provisional and incomplete. Sidel's anger, and the violence it spawns, could well relate to what he sees as a policeman or be the product of a more personal grievance against the Guzmanns and what they stand for, but conclusive answers are not forthcoming. Instead one is left to speculate on the perhaps more interesting thought that Sidel's antipathy towards his nemesis could also be antipathy towards himself; his ambition to destroy Papa Guzmann, a veiled attempt to destroy that side of his character founded upon the same principles of violence and intimidation that Papa Guzmann has used to establish his criminal empire. Guzmann's confused ethno-religious ancestry also mirrors Sidel's, as does his spiritual yearnings and quest for salvation. In a revealing essay on Charyn's fiction, Mike Woolf suggests that a key structuring tension of the Isaac Sidel series is the 'persistence of a notion of redemption in an ostensibly doomed and damned world'.[48] Such a notion remains only a possibility, but when Sidel visits a Rabbi in *The Good Policeman* and acknowledges his failings, the fact that he has often broken departmental rules, killed people when it wasn't his job or place to do so, the dynamic between crime, religion and the mechanics of city life is brought into albeit uneasy resolution. One could also say that Woolf's claim for Charyn, that he is 'reflective of contemporary fragmentation and responsive to the persistence of spiritual potential within the contemporary environment'[49] goes equally for Kellerman and Friedman too. Charyn himself playfully suggests that the legacy bestowed on New York, and by implication on America, by Jewish culture cannot be found in the concrete physicality of bricks and mortar but in the imaginative projections of its subjects. 'And the deepest, darkest thinkers are always criminals of one kind', he concludes, maybe a little too knowingly, 'There's an odd relationship between Jews, cities and the metaphysics of crime'.[50]

'THROUGH BARRIOS AND ACROSS BORDERLINES . . .': 'LATINOS' IN THE CITY OF ANGELS

If African-Americans, throughout the long and often bloody passage of American history, have been singled out and subjected to the most violent, inhumane punishments by the white-dominated majority in the United States, and Jewish-Americans, for an admittedly much shorter, less sustained period and to a less vitriolic extent, encountered prejudicial discrimination on the basis of an uneasy cocktail of ethno-religious and racial[51] factors, then white fears of Latino 'difference' has been brought into sharper focus by the mass influx of Mexican immigrants into the United States, and large number of so-called political exiles escaping from Castro's Cuba to the El Dorado of south Florida. Spurred on, in California at least, by fears of a Latino or Hispanic takeover, a fractured alliance of native-born voters, politicians and businessmen drawn from right across the racial and ethnic spectrum, came together to ensure the passage of Proposition 187, denying illegal immigrants access to emergency health-care and other public services. In doing so, they mobilised anti-immigration sentiment throughout the United States; sentiment whose origins in part relate to the large numbers of Asians and particularly Latinos arriving in America since changes to the immigration laws in 1965.

To a certain extent, the influx of large numbers of immigrants from countries throughout Latin America—not just Mexico but also Puerto Rico, Cuba, Guatemala, El Salvador, Honduras and Colombia—has further questioned the viability of binary racial caste in which a dominant white population is situated in opposition to a minority black one. Ethnic, class, gender and regional diversity makes this kind of model untenable in both a practical and theoretical sense. In part, too, Latinos themselves bridle at attempts to corral them on to either side of the binary divide, particularly the black side. Linda Chavez, president of the Center for Equal Opportunity and author of *Out of the Barrio* (1991) is quick to underline the differences between Latino- and African-Americans, arguing haughtily that, 'Most native-born Hispanics have leapt over blacks in achievement . . . [and] within one or two generations living in the United States, the great majority of Hispanics are integrated into the social and economic mainstream'.[52]

In fact Chavez's efforts to distance Hispanics from African-Americans, to position Hispanics within the social and economic mainstream, ends up reifying this binary mode of thought or at least implicitly suggesting that what happens when Hispanics arrive and settle in the United States is that they somehow cross this divide and march triumphantly into the promised land of whiteness. Smith and Feagin make a similar but also diametrically opposed point; namely that while Hispanics and other newcomers to the United States have often been 'able to negotiate a higher status for themselves entailing less discrimination than that faced by African-Americans', higher has not meant equal—'for equal political and economic citizenship . . . has not yet been effectively won by any groups of color'.[53] Furthermore the post-1960s' tendency to marshal previously disparate ethnic or national groups (Cuban, Puerto Rican, Mexican etc.) into the homogeneous categories of 'Latino' or 'Hispanic' suggests both the indeterminate and also impervious nature of racial divisions in America. As David Theo Goldberg argues, the category 'Latino' or 'Hispanic' problematises certain prevailing assumptions about racial formation in so far as it becomes 'not so much a third race . . . black and white melding into brown, as an evidencing that race is politically fabricated and contested'.[54] To this end, 'the 'Hispanic' is recognised by the ethno-racial technology of the census as white, but the nervous insecurity of this recognition is reflected in the qualifications about when to count 'Mexicans' or 'Hispanics' as 'black'.[55]

Anxieties over how to identify oneself, and the dynamic tensions between being able to define oneself and being defined by others, are played out in Alex Abella's *The Killing of the Saints* (1992), featuring Cuban-American court-appointed investigator Charlie Morell, and Michael Nava's *Goldenboy* (1989), *How Town* (1991) and *The Hidden Law* (1992), featuring Mexican-American lawyer and surrogate detective, Henry Rios. Moving freely but also awkwardly between 'centre' and 'margins', both in a physical sense, as their investigations transport them between the *barrios* of east Los Angeles and cocktail parties of west Los Angeles, and in a cultural sense, as their ancestry and physiology marks them as 'different' from whites who occupy most of the positions of power and privilege and blacks who do not, Morell and Rios cut across but also run up against traditional hierarchical designations.

In doing so, of course, they recall Raymond Chandler's prototype detective, Phillip Marlowe, who also trod an uneasy path between the 'centre' he unwillingly belonged to and the anonymity of the 'margins' he preferred, but their ability to do likewise, to choose, in a sense, is limited by a schizophrenic tendency on the part of the majority white culture to identify them as insiders and outsiders, often simultaneously. Moreover, while the latent anxieties in Chandler's fiction as a result of Marlowe's conflicted status and ambitions were usually reconciled, albeit problematically, at the end of each narrative, Abella's *The Killing of the Saints* in particular opens up and exploit the tensions produced by Morell's fractured identity as insider and outsider, in order to undermine if not explode one of the basic cornerstones of the genre; the retrieval of knowledge or the ability of the detective, and reader, to piece together

the fragments he or she come across in order to arrive at a rationally deduced 'answer' which might not punish the 'guilty' and exculpate the 'innocent' but which at least explains what has happened.

The generic ruptures are prefigured in the first pages of the novel when two Cuban immigrants walk into a jewellers in downtown Los Angeles, armed with a .357 Magnum, .45 Colt automatic, sawn-off Browning shotgun with retractable butt, black Sten machine pistol, gray Uzi sub-machine gun, six sticks of dynamite and two grenades, and apparently possessed by Oggun, 'the mighty warrior of the [Afro-Cuban] *santeria* religion',[56] proceed to murder six people, store employees and customers, during the course of a botched robbery attempt which is eventually foiled by battalions of armed police. The sheer scale of the carnage is unprecedented, even by Los Angeles' own violent standards, but even more disruptive, at least in generic terms, is the presence of *santeria* as a complicating factor in the subsequent investigation and trial. Hired by one of the defendants, Ramon Valdez, to be his legal representative, because of his own Cuban ancestry, Charlie Morell's official function is to gather information that could help to exonerate his client. Unofficially, as a detective defined in terms of his own private sense of justice, his job is to determine for himself, and by implication the reader, exactly what has happened and more significantly, who or what is to blame—and in the spirit of his generic antecedents, take action to rectify any perceived 'injustices'.

Yet throughout Morell's investigation, the politics of race and ethnicity, and his own ambivalence about his Cuban heritage and how this heritage manifests itself in lived experience, pollutes his judgement and renders him unable to perform this function. On the surface the case against his client, Ramon Valdez, is convincing. Valdez has been apprehended at the scene of the crime and there are witnesses to confirm his culpability in the jewellery store massacre. As a 'Marielito'[57] Cuban with a lengthy prison record, moreover, Valdez's fearsome reputation and penchant for violence, is confirmed by Morell's subsequent investigations when he is told that Valdez slit another man's throat in an argument. Still, this alone fails to guarantee his guilt and as Morell's investigation continues, another portrait of Valdez begins to emerge; that of an intelligent, cultured, well-educated man whose violent tendencies have been fuelled by a long history of racially motivated rejection and discrimination. His story is a distopic inversion of Horatio Alger's heroic tales of immigrant success. As a dark-skinned Cuban, Valdez is frustrated even by his plans to find menial work. His position as a salesman peddling kitchen appliances to South American housewives is terminated because his boss decides that his 'black' skin could scare off potential buyers. He is rejected by a number of Cuban entrepreneurs because of his status as a 'Marielito' and by an African-American businessman because he is 'too Hispanic', and in the end has to support himself by selling marijuana, a situation which sends him into a downward cycle of drug-taking and dependency which culminates in his discovery of *santeria* and his alleged transformation into violent sadist.

Emerging from Morell's fraught investigations into his client's past is a sophisticated picture of racial-ethnic relations in which the cheerful optimism of those like Ollin, a light-skinned Cuban-American television presenter, who declares, 'people of all colors and origins get to rise and prosper here' (p. 128) collides head-on with the bleak pessimism of those like Valdez whose apocalyptic musings have been shaped and informed by lived experience of race and class-based discrimination. In fact Valdez's response to Ollin's patriotic rhetoric is persuasive:

> You're white, educated, from the middle class. You have no idea what it's like to be brown or black and be treated like an idiot just because you are not fluent in the language . . . You don't know how it feels to be afraid of Immigration all the time, to be lost in a place where all you can hope is forty dollars a day if you can find the work. You don't know how it feels to know that you're not even second class, you're third class, that even American blacks are better than you.

(p. 128)

On the one hand, Valdez's appears to conceive of 'race' and 'ethnicity' as diverging categories, at least in so far as he distinguishes himself, as a dark-skinned Cuban, from 'American blacks' and elsewhere in the novel differences between immigrants from Cuba and Mexico—'Castro's children and the sons of Montezuma' (p. 13)—are emphasised. On the other hand, 'race' and 'ethnicity' are conceived of as overlapping categories, at least in so far as Valdez's views confirm the presence of a racial-ethnic cleavage where an albeit fluid, diverse white population (or those permitted to enjoy the privileges of whiteness) is set against an albeit fluid, diverse non-white population whose physiology marks them as 'different' (or different from a white European 'norm').

Morell's experiences in the United States both confirm and undermine the existence of such a cleavage. In many ways he is a model American citizen, someone who has chosen to shed his Cuban ancestry (and been allowed to do so) on his way to becoming a Porsche-driving lawyer with a degree from an Ivy League college. As a light-skinned Cuban who is able to 'pass' as white, discrimination has not prevented him from achieving wealth and status, but he is not blind to the prejudices that shape and inform social relations in his adopted home. In fact his awareness of the scope and extent of racial-ethnic divisions and his concerns that

Los Angeles might 'by some twist of fate [have] slipped into a big Johannesburg' (p. 149) mean that he is less quick to condemn Valdez's actions than figures from the white establishment. His ambivalence towards Valdez's culpability is underscored by an inability to dismiss, as his colleagues do, a key tenet of his client's defence; diminished responsibility on the grounds that he was acting under the influence of *santeria*. To blue-blooded Anglos like Clay Smith III, *santeria* is merely 'voodoo shit' but Morell is more circumspect, describing it as a 'mystery cult that claims millions of followers and powers beyond description' (p. 32). But circumspection dissolves into confusion and doubt and while Morell attempts to explode his client's posturing as hollow and without foundation, incidents which appear to have no rational explanation compel him to think otherwise. Morell can expose some of these, like the supposed 're-appearance' his late father, as cynical tricks played on him by his client in order to elicit his sympathy and support, but others elide and problematise notions of rational logic. So when a thunderbolt strikes the courtroom just as the trial is reaching its climax and sweeps Valdez's co-conspirator, Ramon Pimienta, out of the room in a dancing ball of fire 'never to be seen again' (p. 290), it is perhaps not surprising that Valdez himself is eventually found not guilty.

Abella skilfully maps the familiar tropes of hard-boiled crime fiction on to a perhaps more unfamiliar racial-ethnic landscape where the order and rationality upon which the former depends are fatally undercut by eruptions of spiritual excess. Santeria, here, is emblematic of a 'Cubanness' that Morell can neither fully embrace nor reject and caught between the Cuban world of his father and ancestry and the WASP-dominated American culture he has aspired to join, he finds himself drifting, unsure of who he is. As I have argued throughout the book, the identity of the (white) hard-boiled detective, despite assertions to the contrary, has never been fixed or secure but as we have seen, this liminality is compounded by the competing claims placed on the detective not just by his or her allegiance to state-sponsored and alternative notions of 'justice' but also by the inevitable 'colouring' of both terms along particular racial-ethic lines. Following Valdez's acquittal, Morell stumbles across evidence pointing towards his guilt and enraged by the cynical manner in which his clients has manipulated not just him but the entire legal system, he confronts him and when Valdez tries to escape, Morell attacks him and Valdez falls to his death. Justice is therefore served. Or is it? For however much Valdez's words and action expose him as a charlatan, one cannot dismiss his justifications out of hand, neither the ones relating to the effects of racial-ethnic discrimination nor the influence of *santeria*. Moreover while it may be tempting to conceive of Morell's final intervention in palliative or even heroic terms—a victory for justice—one could equally argue that his vigilante assault on Valdez is as much the product of rage, resentment and bitterness at his own inadequacies and failings as a detective.

In deliciously radical fashion, the trajectory or movement of Abella's narrative is not, to use Porter's reductive terms, one of 'perceptual de-familiarization' to 're-familiarization'[58] but rather one where an overall core of doubt remains. In the end, we do not know whether Valdez was possessed or not, nor what caused the disturbance in the courtroom and the earthquake which also disrupted the trial, nor even what happened to Valdez's partner Jose Pimienta after his 'disappearance' during the trial. Significantly 'not-knowing' in a generic context (i.e. not knowing why Valdez and Pimienta did what they did) becomes 'not-knowing' in a personal context (i.e. not knowing who you are). From apparently secure moorings at the start of the novel as a middle-class lawyer able to pass as white, Morell is soon forced to reassess the legitimacy of the identity he has chosen for himself. Identifications based on race-ethnicity, class, gender and sexuality project him like a pinball from 'centre' to 'margins' and in doing so undermine the fixity of this relationship and shatter the wholeness of his projected identity. At once an insider and outsider, Morell both rejects his Cuban ancestry, at least in so far as it connects him with poor dark-skinned 'Marielitos' like Valdez and embraces it because only by knowing where he has come from can he hope to know who he is—as he later acknowledges, while watching immigrant families from Central America picnicking in a local park, 'I wanted to know about these people and by doing so to come to know myself as well, the pieces of myself that were scattered among these Caribbean exiles like arms of a starfish' (p. 74).

Furthermore, while he might initially want to identify himself as white, and though he might drive a fancy car and move freely around the city cocooned by the privileges of class and skin colour, the invisible line that connects him to people like Clay Smith III and distinguishes him from people like Ramon Valdez is not nearly as secure as he imagines. At one of Smith's cocktail parties, Morell is made aware that his status is not a right but a privilege, something bestowed on him by others rather than earned by his own actions. After an argument between Morell and the host has turned ugly, Smith rounds on his former friend and spits, 'You fucking Cubans are all the same' (p. 226), and in doing so, confirms not just the existence but also the depth of exactly the kind of racial-ethnic schism which, as immigrant 'success' stories, Morell and other Cuban-Americans had once sought to dismiss as fiction.

Brief mention should also be made of Michael Nava's intriguing series of crime novels featuring Henry Rios, a lawyer of Mexican extraction, also located in Los Angeles. Arguably the best of these is *The Hidden Law,* in which Rios is called upon to investigate the death of a Chicano senator and in doing so opens up tensions and sometimes violent conflicts not just within the Latino community but also among different factions of Mexican immigrants. All, too, are interesting from the viewpoint of Rios' continuing struggle to assert his homosexuality in the face of hostility from both inside and outside his own neighbourhood, community and family. In some ways, Rios is too good to be true, someone whose humour, integrity and moral virtuosity remains in tact despite the vitriolic discrimination he faces and the often inhumane barbarity he is witness to as a legal defendant. Of course whether his homosexuality qualifies him as 'too good to be true' depends, to some extent, on one's point of view, but within the context of the novels, it functions to further disrupt the kind of cohesive group identity that politicians like the murdered Agustin Pena are keen to talk up, if only for reasons of personal advancement.

Rios lives, on and off, with Josh, an Anglo who is HIV-positive and, during *The Hidden Law,* finds his condition worsens. Apart from giving the books an added human dimension, their relationship, between a Chicano and white man, offends not just homophobics and whites but also Chicano 'activists' like college lecturer Tommy Ochoa, who in a veiled reference to his partner and career, accuses Rios of 'writing off [his] heritage'.[59] Still, Ochoa's remarks are misguided because they fail to acknowledge the extent to which diversity and also disunity is an inevitable feature of the Mexican-American community in Los Angeles—rich against poor, middle class against working class, straight against gay, the recently arrived against the long established. In Ochoa's eyes, Rios has sold out his ancestry in order to embrace the fruits (excuse the pun) of the United States, but as we learn in *The Hidden Law* he is simply trying to come to terms with the legacy of an alcoholic, abusive father. Furthermore, Henry comes to understand his father's action not simply in individual terms but rather as part of a larger cultural phenomenon of Chicano patriarchs venting their fury at their perceived marginalisation at the hands of white bosses on their wives and children.[60] In fact this is where the ambitions of Nava's novel Abella's *The Killing of the Saints* overlap because just when it appears that the cultural terrain has become so fragmented that it is practically unreadable, one is greeted by insights that point both to the existence and significance of what Dyson calls an 'enabling solidarity'—the idea in *The Hidden Law* that connections exist between Chicanos if only on the grounds that patterns of behaviour and cultural norms are replicated over generations—and the very real presence of a system built upon relations of racial-ethnic domination and subordination whose underlying logic has always, and continues, to privilege those of white European descent.

COLLIDING WORLDS AND THE NATIVE
AMERICAN SEARCH FOR ORDER: TONY
HILLERMAN, CAROLE LAFAVOR

The increasingly fraught collision between the bloated, rotten civilisation transported to the New World from Europe and the spiritually inclined, apparently harmonious one descended from the various Native American tribes already settled through the American continent is a characteristic feature of the work of Tony Hillerman and Carole laFavor. If the crime and violence that Hillerman's two tribal police detectives, Joe Leaphorn and Jim Chee, are called upon to investigate emanate from the self-serving, neo-colonial ambitions of white businessmen, mafiosi, politicians and even cultural anthropologists, then the manner in which these ruptures are dealt with owes as much to a Navajo-derived need to return the world to a state of harmony or 'hozhzo' as to either the ratiocinative methods of traditional detectives or the action-orientated approach of their hard-boiled cousins. Part of the Slow Talking clan and a trained shaman, Chee's outlook as a tribal police officer owes much to his belief and indeed participation in Navajo traditions, rituals and practices. Able to see that all living matter has two forms—'the form of the yei and . . . the outer form we see'[61] Chee's vision affords him an advantage over white police detectives who, particularly in their dealings with other Native Americans, tend to assume guilt where it does not exist. Hillerman's other detective, Joe Leaphorn is more sceptical and as an archetypal rationalist rejects traditional Navajo witchcraft beliefs, but his investigative methodology, too, is shaped and informed by his cultural heritage. 'He used [a map of Indian land] in his endless hunt for patterns, sequences, order', Hillerman writes in *Coyote Waits*, 'something that would bring a semblance of Navajo hozhzo to the chaos of crime and violence' (p. 150).

This particular frame of reference opens up Hillerman's crime fiction to a number of generically subversive possibilities, not least the problematisation of rational thought as the touchstone of investigative practice. Disappointingly, though, Hillerman tends to close off such possibilities, at least in so far as incidents and potential transgressions which appear to have no rational basis are usually revealed to be attempts by aspiring white conspirators to conceal their culpability by exploiting particular Navajo mythologies. Hence the death of a tribal policeman who has strayed into an area haunted by witches in *Coyote Waits* is traced back to the desperate actions of an antiquities collector or the apparent violence wrought on the Reservation's population by a Navajo wolf in *The Blessing Way* ultimately implicates a crew of mafiosi who are using the Reservation's proximity to a US military base to illegally procure weapons. Furthermore his detectives' search for harmony or 'hozhzo' tends to function as a more general

palliative, particularly where relations between the Navajo and white population are concerned. Which is not to suggest that Hillerman entirely avoids exploring the impact of white cultural imperialism or the legacy of state-sanctioned genocide, just that these issues never become central to his narratives or their resolution. Unlike Welch's *The Death of Jim Loney* (1988) where the damaging effects of living in ghetto-like isolation and adopting white-derived demeaning identities are openly acknowledged, or James Lee Burke's *Black Cherry Blues* (1989) where institutional rather than individual malpractice lies at the heart of an attempt to steal mineral extraction rights from Montana's Native Americans, Hillerman's tendency to focus on the 'micro' rather than the 'macro' ends up obfuscating the state-sanctioned, racially determined foundations to social, political and economic inequalities.

Carole laFavor is certainly more vigorous about exposing the complicity of state-sanctioned institutions in damaging and subjugating the Ojibwa population on the Red Earth Reservation in northern Minnesota. Her second novel, *Evil Dead Center* (1997), features a conspiracy between the Red Earth Social Service agency and a local politician-cum-foster father to forcibly procure Ojibwa children to appear in crudely made pornographic films. Indeed this particular crime, for laFavor, is part of a much larger problem whereby Native American children, despite the apparent protections offered by the Indian Child Welfare Act, are forcibly removed from their Reservation homes on spurious grounds and relocated with white families, thereby separating them from their families and culture and inflicting on them untold damage. laFavor's idyllic portrait of family life, at least that of her Ojibwa protagonist Renee LaRoche, is a utopian antidote to this particular example of white cultural imperialism. LaRoche, a lesbian, lives in comfortable harmony on the Reservation with her Anglo partner Samantha and her daughter Jenny, and close by her aunt and grandmother, whose wisdom and spiritual knowledge attests to important cultural differences between her own Ojibwa culture and that of the white-dominated Minnesotan population. As she informs LaRoche, 'They came to this land and forget their original instructions. We haven't forgotten. The spirits, who live in every grove of trees, every turn in the river, every lakeshore of the north country, whisper to us not to forget'.[62]

Like Hillerman, laFavor avoids oversimplifying divisions, so that a 'good' Native American population is locked into inexorable conflict with a 'bad' white one. Her first novel, *Along the Journey River* (1996), exposes the corrupt practices of tribal chief Jed Morriseau, while *Evil Dead Center* implicates a number of Ojibwa men in the pornography ring. Like Hillerman, too, laFavor skilfully opens up tensions within the tribe itself. LaRoche is not an officially sanctioned officer with the tribal police, in part because her previous involvement in the politically radical American Indian Movement has made her distrustful of institutional agencies. The fact that LaRoche works, even on an informal basis, for the tribal police, however, potentially alienates her from former partners like Caroline Beltrain, an activist with the Movement being sought by the tribal police and FBI in connection with the bombing of a government building. LaRoche works closely with head of the tribal police, Bulieau Hobey, but in trusting him so much risks her relationship with Beltrain. Moreover as a lesbian, she is only too aware of the fascist implications of her official role and seeks both to emphasise her agency as a freelance, someone 'trying to save the world' (p. 54), and acknowledge the difficulties of having to keep a 'foot in each world' (p. 25).

laFavor may open up these tensions but she also closes them off so ruthlessly that *Evil Dead Center* at least mutates into a less interesting, more straightforward crime novel. Hobey, the model patriarch, and Beltrain, the political activist, become friends, and to sweeten the pill, Hobey persuades the FBI to drop their charges against her. Beltrain and LaRoche remain friends, despite initial tensions, and between them expose and capture Floyd Neuterbide, the pornography ringleader whose guilt is prefigured by the not-so-subtle references to framed photographs of Rush Limbaugh and Ronald Reagan on his wall. Order, or in Navajo-speak 'hozhzo', is restored and one ends up with the impression that LaRoche has sacrificed nothing and yet gained everything by her involvement in the investigative process. One also senses that whatever happened to her, she would be able to pick herself up off the floor, dust herself off and start afresh, not unaffected but undamaged by what she has seen and done.

'IS THIS MY ASSIMILATION, SO MANY YEARS IN THE MAKING?': CHANG-RAE LEE'S *NATIVE SPEAKER*

It would be fair to say that much of this book has been characterised by the meeting and uneasy conflation of two not altogether seamless methodological styles. On the one hand, its logic has been underwritten by an awareness, not always successfully articulated, of the multiplicity of meanings, an awareness that the critic or for that matter the author are not the sole guarantor of meaning, that meanings can also be constructed at the level of readership and that as a result, to put it bluntly, one person's nirvana can be another's purgatory. On the other hand, however, it would be a dishonest critic who failed to acknowledge that some books, some texts, some cultural artifacts are not necessarily 'better' than others—for such a word is too vague or too satiated with subjective connotations—but are certainly more innovative, challenging and therefore interesting than others. Who could deny, after all, that they do not have

a sneaking preference for, in this case, crime novels that do not merely meet and satisfy their expectations but challenge them, that compel them though aesthetic or political or thematic innovation make them look at the genre and the world in fresh, illuminating ways? So to quote Sinatra, as we face the final curtain, it is perhaps appropriate or fitting to end the book by focusing on Chang-Rae Lee's *Native Speaker* (1995) and in a flourish of daring academic panache, stepping off the fence, if only for a moment, to state right at the outset that Lee's spectacularly innovative, startlingly fresh novel does all of this and more.

It is perhaps also appropriate to re-ask a question posed right at the start of the book; namely, to what extent do crime novels, as part of that larger beast known collectively as popular culture, simply reaffirm existing, culturally dominant ways of looking at and thinking about the world? Because while one such way is undoubtedly satiated in the logic of white, male, heterosexual bias, it would perhaps be fair to say that an alternative and increasingly 'dominant' way of conceiving of and understanding the world, at least within the academy, is through the tropes of race, ethnicity, gender and class. To this end, loci of power are both easy and less to identify, and while relations of domination and subordination do end up privileging certain groups and individuals at the expense of others, they are never fixed or unchanging. The question that we perhaps need to pose, then, at least in relation to the contemporary American crime novel, is not simply whether or how particular examples 're-affirm existing, culturally dominant ways of looking at and thinking about the world' but rather how and to what extent particular crime novelists (whatever their race, ethnicity, class or gender) exploit the complexities and ambiguities of the form to challenge or problematise both a residual white, male, heterosexual elitism and an emerging doctrine of 'political correctness' whereby the 'good' white, male, heterosexual detective is merely replaced by the 'good' non-white, female, gay detective.

The question of character is crucial. A type of crime fiction from Chandler through to Sara Paretsky and arguably writers like Carole laFavor and Michael Nava has been predicated on the implicit assumption that the essentially 'good' character of the detective can if not overcome then at least counterbalance the moral emptiness and degeneracy inherent in contemporary American society, and emerge at the end of each novel not exactly unscathed but fundamentally unaltered by what he or she has seen and done. Comparing this particular variant of the hard-boiled detective with Jake Barnes, the irrevocably 'damaged' protagonist of Ernest Hemingway's *The Sun Also Rises,* John G. Cawelti argues:

> In the end the hard-boiled detective story represents an escape from the naturalistic consciousness of determin-

ism and meaningless death . . . Jake Barnes's insight and integrity, his freedom and false values, were forced upon him by his wound. He is as much a victim of the world as voluntary rebel. The hard-boiled detective has a few scratches, but no deep wounds spoil his function as fantasy hero. He is the man who has been able to say the hell with it, and yet to retain the world's most important benefits—self-esteem, popularity and respect.[63]

True enough, maybe, in relation to figures like Chandler's Phillip Marlowe, but could one apply this assessment to all hard-boiled detectives? To Dashiell Hammett's the Continental Op or Jim Thompson's Lou Ford? Because it is a fundamental assumption of this book that, perhaps evolving out of Hammett or Thompson's creations, there has been a growing interest in the type of crime fiction in which the detective or surrogate cannot simply brush off his or her 'few scratches' and unproblematically retain his or her 'self-esteem, popularity and respect'. Rather, he or she finds that the tensions caused by seeking to retain a degree of agency and yet having to operate within a larger system with usually antithetical ambitions, and the very nature of having to deal with crime, not merely 'crime' as a generic convention or plot device but as a tangible, messy, disruptive entity or force, seeing and having to cope with its effects, end up inflicting real damage— actual and psychological. Of course there are variations of this particular idea or model and it would be wrong to suggest that, say, Ellroy's protagonists are affected or damaged in the same way or even to the same extent as Himes' Coffin Ed and Grave Digger. Much of the book, to this end, has considered the different ways in which crime writers have transposed the kind of already problematised paradigm described above on to the contested, fractured terrain of cultural 'difference'; how being African-American or Chicano or female or working class or gay or a mixture of all these, and having to enforce or at least work towards restoring a *status quo* implicitly founded upon one's subordination, can have distressing consequences. Still, if a preference has been shown, it has been shown towards the kind of crime novel which foregrounds and explores these consequences—novels like Lee's *Native Speaker* whereby the figure of the detective and the conventions of the genre are transformed, brought into fresh, original configurations that acknowledge, implicitly or otherwise, the confusing, ambiguous and corrosive elements of crime and detection.

Set in contemporary New York City, *Native Speaker* tells the story of Henry Park, a second-generation Korean immigrant who is not exactly a detective but an undercover operative working for a covert surveillance agency that collects information for clients like multinational corporations or foreign governments on individuals working against their vested interests, 'Typically the subject was a well-to-do immigrant supporting

some potential insurgency in his old land, or else funding a fledgling trade union or radical student organisation'.[64] Despite a claim to neutrality that recalls Sam Spade's legendary snarl at the end of Hammett's *The Maltese Falcon*—so that Spade's 'I stick my neck out for no one', becomes Park's 'We pledged allegiance to no government' (p. 15)—it is almost impossible, for the reader and later for Park himself, not to see the fingerprints of a loosely connected, albeit fractured power elite peppered all over the directives that the investigators receive via Dennis Hoagland, the agency's faceless but ruthless dispatcher-cum-boss.

Peter Messent's claim that 'the police procedural . . . seems to be supplanting the private-eye novel as "realistic" crime fiction . . . [whereby] a fantasy of extra-systemic freedom and authenticity gives way to a more problematic vision of individual detectives operating through systemic procedures'[65] is, in part, borne out by the trajectory of this book and its interest in the tensions produced by the uneasy conflation of individual agency and institutional authority. *Native Speaker* is not a police procedural, as such, but in so far as Lee characterises Park as 'amiable' and with liberal sympathies, and yet simultaneously implicates him in the hegemonic ambitions of an unseen power elite, he seems to be only too aware of the dramatic possibilities implicit in this conflation. Any thoughts that Hoagland's organisation, replete with its impressively multi-ethnic collection of investigators, is a billboard poster for a celebratory multiculturalism are rendered untenable by the revelation that Koreans or Japanese or Filipinos are preferred simply because they stand a better chance of being able to elicit information from their compatriots. Ethnic bonding is but a strategic ruse, as Park discovers soon after his induction. Watching another investigator, Pete Ichibata, 'take apart' a Chinese dissident responsible for organising anti-Beijing protests outside the UN, Park acknowledges being 'thrilled' by the success of their mission—in detective speak, a job well done—but with some unease, seems dimly aware that their 'success' has, in effect, 'doomed' the student's girlfriend back home in China. As another agent surmises, 'A bad thing can happen in the world. We do what we're paid for and then who can tell what it means?' (p. 41).

Park shields his wife, Lelia, and also himself, from the more unpleasant aspects of his job by conceiving of it in professional, neutral terms. Traversing the margins of preferred anonymity and heeding his boss' advice to 'just stay in the background . . . [be] unapparent and flat' (p. 40), Park's coolly methodical approach manifests itself most visibly in the apparently objective style of his report writing. 'I am to be a clean writer, of the most reasonable eye, and present the subject in question like some sentient machine of transcription. I will know nothing of the craft of argument or narrative or drama. Nothing of beauty or art' (p. 189). Still, Park's ability to remain so detached is tested and found wanting, first of all in his dealings with a Filipino psychologist who manages to probe his implacable surface to reveal the schizophrenic nature of his ambitions and sympathies, and then with a Korean-American politician and aspiring Mayoral candidate, John Kwang. Having joined Kwang's grass-roots organisation and taken his place alongside legions of not just Korean but also Japanese, Indian, Vietnamese, Haitian, Colombian and Nigerian volunteers, Park finds it increasingly difficult to dispatch potentially incriminating reports to his boss not least because he can see the value in Kwang's work and comes to genuinely like and respect him.

The depth and extent of his conflicted loyalties, to Kwang and his function as 'detective' (or at least detached observer), slowly and silently tear him apart, shattering his pretence of objective detachment and forcing him into the damaging position whereby he must betray people who have come to trust and depend on him, and in doing so, betray himself. Fearing what Hoagland might do should he quit the organisation in mid-assignment, Park reluctantly hands him a list featuring the names of recently arrived immigrants who have contributed to a '*gghh*' or non-profit-making money club set up by Kwang in order to redistribute funds to members in greatest need. The list is then passed on to the Immigration and Naturalization Service who identify three dozen families on it as illegals, thereby condemning them to the fate of deportation and ruining Kwang's political ambitions in the process. 'My ugly immigrant's truth', as Park later acknowledges, 'is that I have exploited my own and those others who can be exploited. This forever is my burden to bear . . . Here is my American education' (p. 297).

For this failure, this damage, is an inevitable consequence not just of his conflicted status as a detective but also as an immigrant, as 'Korean' and 'American'. Indeed, throughout the novel, Lee skilfully brings these two subjects—immigrant and detective—and their attendant cultural baggage into fresh, illuminating configurations, both in order to explore the problematic nature of identity and undermine the apparently natural association between whiteness and detection. On the one hand, whereas folklore and tradition would have us believe that the most visible and effective detectives were always white, Hoagland, Park's boss, is adamant that their very visibility renders them unsuitable to do the job:

> He bemoaned the fact that Americans generally made the worst spies. Mostly he meant whites. Even with methodical training they were inclined to run off at the mouth, make unnecessary displays of themselves . . . They felt this subcutaneous aching to let everyone know they were a spook, they couldn't help it, it was like some charge or vanity of the culture.
>
> (p. 161)

Yet the very fact that non-whites are suitable, at least according to Hoagland, on the grounds on their invisibility, is not for Park at least a cause for celebration. Stalking the anonymous margins has conspired to rob Park of his sense of self, who he is. Lelia, his wife, is not even sure, and as their marriage begins to crumble, admits, 'I realised one day that I didn't know the first thing about what was going on inside your head' (p. 117). Being a detective and being an immigrant, to this extent, are joined because to succeed as either requires sacrifice—sacrificing one's 'vanity' in order to achieve invisibility and sacrificing one's immigrant identity in order to blend into the mainstream. 'Success' is thus bitter-sweet and Park's acknowledgement of his effectiveness as an investigator and his ability to fit in— 'It appears I can go anywhere I wish'—is immediately followed by the achingly poignant rhetoric question, 'Is this my assimilation, so many years in the making? Is this the long-sought sweetness?' (p. 188).

This is perhaps why his connection to Kwang runs so deep, because Kwang offers him a chance to reassess himself in the light of a broader socio-political project intent not just on emphasising the 'positive' aspects of Korean ancestry and culture but also on forging links between Korean immigrants and those from Southeast Asia, India, China and Japan, Central America and the Caribbean. Park's perception of Kwang, initially, is that of a skilful, 'consummate' politician, a barbed compliment that suggests slipperiness, manipulation and superficiality, and while this is an impression that he never quite manages to let go of, he is forced through what he sees and hears (as a detective but increasingly as a convert) to reassess its basic negative slant.

At the heart of Kwang's project appears to be not a cynical ploy to curry favour with minority groups in order to further his own political standing but a genuine desire to bind people from different cultures and ethnic-racial groups together in his own image of family and community—an image which in its most elemental version had 'nothing to do with blood' (p. 136). As Park later acknowledges, 'I know he never sought to be an ethnic politician. He didn't want them to vote for him solely because he was colored or Asian. He knew he'd never win anything that way. There aren't enough of you' (p. 302). Cast into a political system still dominated by an 'old syntax', in terms that barely acknowledge the extent of social and cultural transformation ushered in by successive waves of 'new' immigrants from Asia and Latin America, Kwang's ambitions are best articulated in the speech he makes to an audience of disgruntled blacks, Hispanics and Koreans, responding to the growing boycott by black customers of Korean-owned grocery stores following a series of incendiary encounters. 'That is not a black problem or a brown and yellow problem, that is not a problem of our peoples, that is not even ultimately a problem of mistrust or our ignorance', he tells the crowd, 'Let us think it is the problem of a self-hate . . . The problem is our acceptance of what we loathe and fear in ourselves' (pp. 140-1). In other words, as Charles Taylor argues, the issue of 'misrecognition', of being misrecognised by others and then transforming that distorted image into self-image, is crucial,[66] even or rather particularly if that distorted image is not exactly demeaning. 'When others construct you favorably, it's easy to let them keep at it, even if they start going off in ways that aren't immediately comfortable or right', Kwang tells Park, 'This is the challenge for us Asians in America' (p. 180).

Kwang's response to this problem is two-fold. He is quick to emphasise areas of common interest between blacks and Koreans—that 'what we have in common, the sadness and pain and injustice, will always be stronger than our differences' (p. 142)—but within a broader context which acknowledges how distinctive social and cultural forces have shaped their experiences (and relative 'successes' or 'failures') differently. Yet growing out of this concern over misrecognition, Kwang also argues that what needs to be tackled, at least in the public sphere is a prevailing (white) fear of difference and how this fear is seized upon and magnified by politicians and the media in order to further their own nativist agendas. As he remarks:

> But the more racial strife they can report, the more the public questions what good any of this diversity brings. The underlying sense of what's presented these days is that this country has difference that ails rather than strengthens and enriches. You can see what can happen from this, how the public may begin viewing anything outside mainstream experience and culture to be threatening or dangerous.
>
> (p. 256)

It is here, finally, that the form and content of *Native Speaker* come together—and beautifully. Formally, Lee interprets the generic structure of the crime novel in its most radical configuration, to position his detective both as self-determining individualist and subjugated, state-sponsored henchman, and to open up the subsequent tension in order to both problematise the idea of the detective as guarantor of knowledge and meaning, and reinforce the damaging, corrosive impact of his or her involvement in a situation whose full implications only become apparent during the course of the investigation. Thematically, this revelation is so powerfully realised because Park's betrayal of Kwang (by giving up the names on Kwang's 'money-club' list to Hoagland and the INS) not only shatters any remaining doubts over his agency or lack of, but also induces a media-frenzy of 'negative' coverage for Kwang and thus brings about exactly what Kwang, and latterly Park too, have struggled so valiantly to stem; fear of difference influencing the political agenda and impact-

ing upon the ability of non-white immigrants to define themselves. Success as a detective equals cultural annihilation as an immigrant. A bitter pill to swallow. But Lee cleverly sweetens it in the novel's concluding chapter without recourse to sentimentality or subterfuge. Because Park leaves the organisation and rescues his marriage, choosing instead to help Lelia, his wife, with the language classes she gives to non-English speaking children, and thus transforming himself from a 'false speaker of language' (p. 5) at the start of the novel, at least in so far as he cannot recognise what is distinctive about himself, voice and ancestry, into someone who is able to appreciate and even celebrate the diversity implicit in the visual and cultural landscape of New York City and in the richly evocative languages of Lelia's pupils. Thus *Native Speaker* concludes, '[Lelia] calls out each one as best she can, taking care of every last pitch and accent, and I hear her speaking a dozen lovely and native languages, calling all the difficult names of who we are' (p. 324).

Conclusions: Towards a Multicultural America?

Chang-Rae Lee's *Native Speaker* brings into focus what has always been a significant feature of American life; the sharp dichotomy between a nominal acceptance of diversity in all its guises—America, after all, has traditionally prided itself on its status as a 'nation of immigrants'—and a virulent anxiety that diversity begets fragmentation and dilutes the distinctive character of the nation, or at least the nation as conceived in white, European imaginations. Such anxieties have always characterised American life and from time to time, act as catalyst for more widespread, sustained attacks, not just on blacks and other non-white communities but at various times on women, gays, lesbians, Jews and the working class. Lee suggests that the nature and depth of current racially conceived anti-immigrant sentiment does not bode well for America's future and one cannot help but feel that as public optimism about the benefits of living in a diverse, multicultural society continues to abate and Americans retreat further into their own ethnic and racial groups, less afraid to voice their resentments and fears, their guilt and anger, further unrest seems depressingly inevitable.

Yet Lee's vision, and that of other crime writers discussed in this book, notably Abella, Kellerman, Mosley, Sallis and Phillips, is not resolutely apocalyptic and draws back from the politicised posturing of neo-conservative doom-mongers like Arthur Schlesinger Jr who talk about the Balkanisation of America and gaze longingly back at a largely mythic American past where unity of purpose and indeed character prevailed. Nor, though, is their vision excessively upbeat, a Disney-style celebration of diversity that flattens out cultural difference and overlooks the fact that different individuals and groups have not always co-existed in conditions of harmony and mutual respect. Writing in what I have defined as a 'popular-unpopular' genre (one with 'popular' appeal at least in so far as the basic parameters of the genre are, in Klein's words, 'well-known, widely accepted and easily accessible',[67] but whose protagonist is often confused, conflicted, violent, unsympathetic, or selfish, whose conception of 'morality' and 'justice' is deeply problematic) these writers have not shied away from showing the often bitter, irreconcilable differences that exist between, and significantly also among, particular groups, or been afraid to explore the way in which social power and its consolidation in the hands of a few has twisted and damaged people's lives, even in the case of the detective who in previous incarnations might well have shrugged off such difficulties with a slug of bourbon and a shrug of the shoulders.

These detectives are unable to transcend their circumstances, the materiality of their lives, in the same way as their generic predecessors or at least more overtly heroic figures like Chander's Phillip Marlowe or Ross Macdonald's Lew Archer. Yet damage does not necessarily correspond with defeat, and knowledge about 'the way things are' with nihilism. Not entirely estranged from their populist roots, these figures are made from sterner stuff and seen through their eyes, the world they inhabit, America on the cusp of a new century, is neither a utopian nor distopian one. Relations of domination and subordination may well be a fact of life but they do not necessarily preclude negotiation, dialogue and interaction. The contours of identity are clearly visible and yet elusively fluid. The contemporary American crime novel may not be what bell hooks describes as 'radical postmodernist practice' or that which calls attention to the 'shared, sensibilities which cross the boundaries of class, gender, race' and which could 'be fertile ground for the construction of empathy'[68] because the revolutionary possibilities inherent in the detective's anti-establishment mindset are often blunted or closed off by their implication in the hegemonic ambitions of their paymasters or the dominant culture. Still, multicultural detectives and multicultural crime fictions offer some hope that new relations between and among groups can be forged; straight, white, male traditions are in the process of being reconstituted while emerging African-American, female, gay, lesbian, Latino and Asian voices threaten old hierarchies and converse with one another, suspicious but also hopeful. America, as Nancy Abelmann and John Lie assert in their book *Blue Dreams* (1995), is irredeemably multicultural, 'frustrating the efforts of European-American suburbanites, African-American nationalists, and Korean American ethnic purists alike to find a place of their own'.[69] Whether a consensus can be constructed that deals with these frustrations, one not based on hierarchical domination of black over white, male over female, straight over gay, European over non-European, remains to be

seen but the various, not always uniform messages put forward by those American crime writers discussed in this volume seem to suggest that such a task is not entirely hopeless.

Notes

1. Kwame Anthony Appiah, 'Race', in Frank Lentricchia and Thomas McLaughlin (eds), *Critical Terms for Literary Study* (Chicago, IL and London: University of Chicago Press, 1987), p. 277.

2. Howard Wincant, 'Dictatorship, Democracy, and Difference: The Historical Construction of Racial Identity', in Michael Peter Smith and Joe R. Feagin (eds), *The Bubbling Cauldron: Race, Ethnicity and the Urban Crisis* (Minneapolis, MN: University of Minnesota Press, 1995), p. 31.

3. Arthur Schlesinger Jr, 'The Cult of Ethnicity, Good and Bad', *Time Magazine*, 8 July 1992, p. 52.

4. See Lawrence Fuchs, *The Ethnic Kaleidoscope: Race, Ethnicity and Civic Culture* (Hanover, NH: University of New England Press, 1990).

5. Michael Peter Smith and Joe R. Feagin, 'Putting "Race" in Its Place', in Smith and Feagin (eds), *The Bubbling Cauldron: Race, Ethnicity and the Urban Crisis*, p. 6.

6. Alluding to the status of black Americans without explicitly naming them, Article I, Section 2 of the US Constitution declared, 'Representatives and direct taxes shall be apportioned among the several States which may be included within this Union, according to their respective number, *which shall be determined by adding to the whole number of free persons, including those bound to service for a term of years and excluding Indians not taxed, three-fifths of all other persons*'.

7. See Ian Haney-Lopez, *White by Law: The Legal Construction of Race* (New York: New York University Press, 1996); extracts reprinted in Jon Gjerde (ed.), *Major Problems in American Immigration and Ethnic History* (full details below).

8. See Ian Haney-Lopez, 'The Evolution of Legal Constructions of Whiteness', in Gjerde (ed.), *Major Problems in American Immigration and Ethnic History* (New York: Houghton Mifflin, 1998), p. 300.

9. Haney-Lopez, *Major Problems in American Immigration and Ethnic History*, p. 302.

10. 'Thind vs. United States: "The United States Supreme Court Clarifies the Meaning of 'White', 1923", in Gjerde, *Major Problems in American Immigration and Ethnic History*, p. 290.

11. Haney-Lopez, *Major Problems in American Immigration and Ethnic History*, p. 305.

12. 'Thind vs. United States', in Gjerde, *Major Problems in American Immigration and Ethnic History*, p. 290.

13. William Peterson, 'Concepts of Ethnicity', in Stephen Thernstrom (ed.), *The Harvard Encyclopedia of American Ethnic Groups* (Cambridge, MA: Harvard University Press, 1980), pp. 235-6.

14. See Werner Sollors, *Beyond Ethnicity: Consent and Descent in American Culture* (Oxford and New York: Oxford University Press, 1986), p. 36.

15. E. San Juan Jr, *Racial Formations/Critical Transformations: Articulations of Power in Ethnic and Racial Studies in the United States* (London and New Jersey: Humanities Press, 1992), p. 5. Also see Michael Omi and Howard Wincant, *Racial Formation in the United States: From the 1960s to the 1990s* (London and New York: Routledge, 1994).

16. Manning Marable, *Beyond Black and White: Transforming African-American Politics* (London and New York: Verso, 1995), p. 124.

17. See Roger Rouse in Smith and Feagin, *The Bubbling Cauldron*, pp. 17-18.

18. Smith and Feagin, *The Bubbling Cauldron*, p. 23.

19. Marable, *Beyond Black and White*, p. 124

20. Cornel West, 'Introduction', in Michael Lerner and Cornel West, *Jews and Blacks: A Dialogue on Race, Religion and Culture in America* (New York: Plume, 1996), p. 2.

21. Ibid., p. 2.

22. David Theo Goldberg, *Racial Subjects: Writing on Race in America* (London and New York: Routledge, 1997), p. 130.

23. Goldberg, *Racial Subjects*, p. 132.

24. Mary C. Waters, *Ethnic Options: Choosing Identities in America* (Berkeley, CA: University of California Press, 1990), p. 157.

25. Michael Lerner in Michael Lerner and Cornel West, *Jews and Blacks: A Dialogue on Race, Religion and Culture in America*, p. 67.

26. Ibid., p. 67.

27. Even the use of names—American Jew or Jewish-American—is significant. David Theo Goldberg writes: 'Common usage speaks more readily in terms of "American Jews" than of "Jewish-Americans", revealing more like American Indians than . . . Italian-American . . . This suggests that Jewishness transcends Americanness, ethnic belonging subsumes national identity rather than vice versa', *Racial Subjects*, p. 138.

28. Leslie Fiedler, *Waiting for the End* (London: Jonathan Cape, 1965), p. 70.

29. *The Ritual Bath* (1986), *Sacred and Profane* (1987), *Milk and Honey* (1990), *Day of Atonement* (1991), *False Prophet* (1992), *Grievous Sin* (1993), *Sanctuary* (1994), *Justice* (1995), *Prayers for the Dead* (1996), *Serpent's Tooth* (1997) and *Jupiter's Bones* (1999).

30. Dennis Porter, *The Pursuit of Crime: Art and Ideology in Detective Fiction* (New Haven: Yale University Press, 1981), pp. 171-2.

31. Faye Kellerman, *Day of Atonement* (London: Headline, 1991), p. 250.

32. Faye Kellerman, *Serpent's Tooth* (London: Headline, 1997), p. 158.

33. Diana Arbin Ben-Merre, 'Murdering Traditional Assumptions: The Jewish-American Mystery', in Jerome H. Delameter and Ruth Prigozy (eds), *The Detective in Film, Fiction and Television* (Westport, CT: Greenwood, 1998), p. 63.

34. Ibid., p. 63.

35. Ibid., p. 65.

36. See Kinky Friedman, *Musical Chairs,* in *More Kinky Friedman* (London: Faber & Faber, 1993), p. 202.

37. Kinky Friedman, *Frequent Flyer,* in *More Kinky Friedman* (London: Faber & Faber, 1993), p. 100.

38. For example, in *Frequent Flyer* we are told how 'good German doctors would inject air, water, gasoline, or toxic chemicals into the veins of children' (p. 61).

39. Friedman, *Frequent Flyer,* p. 129.

40. *Marilyn the Wild* (1974), *Blues Eyes* (1975), *The Education of Patrick Silver* (1976), *Secret Isaac* (1978), *The Good Policeman* (1990) and *Maria's Girls* (1993).

41. Jerome Charyn, *The Education of Patrick Silver* (first published 1976) (London: Bloomsbury, 1992), p. 13.

42. Jerome Charyn, *The Good Policeman* (London: Bloomsbury, 1990), p. 70.

43. Charyn, *The Education of Patrick Silver,* p. 20.

44. Ibid., p. 97.

45. Charyn, *The Good Policeman,* p. 153.

46. Charyn, *The Education of Patrick Silver,* p. 10 and p. 33.

47. Mike Woolf, 'Exploding the Genre: The Crime Fiction of Jerome Charyn', in Brian Docherty (ed.), *American Crime Fiction* (London: Macmillan, 1988), p. 133.

48. Ibid., p. 142.

49. Ibid., p. 134.

50. Jerome Charyn, *Metropolis: New York as Myth, Marketplace and Magic Land* (London: Abacus, 1986), p. 267.

51. 'Race', here, is defined as a concept 'which signifies and symbolises social conflicts and interests by referring to different types of human bodies' (Omi and Wincant, *Racial Formations in the United States,* p. 55).

52. Linda Chavez, *Out of the Barrio: Towards a New Politics of Hispanic Assimilation* (London and New York: HarperCollins, 1991), p. 6.

53. Smith and Feagin, *The Bubbling Cauldron,* pp. 8-9.

54. Goldberg, *Racial Subjects,* p. 65.

55. Ibid., p. 66.

56. Alex Abella, *The Killing of the Saints* (London: Serpent's Tail, 1992), p. 5.

57. A name given to Cubans jailbirds and political enemies who were released from prison in 1980 on the condition that they left Cuba for the US from the port of Mariel.

58. Porter, *The Pursuit of Crime,* p. 245.

59. Michael Nava, *The Hidden Law* (New York: Ballantine, 1992), p. 86.

60. As Nava writes:

    Outside in the larger world, where they labored under the contemptuous eye of Anglo bosses, the fathers were social and political ciphers. No wonder, then, that in the families they tolerated no dissent from their wives and children. And they drank.

    (p. 169)

61. Tony Hillerman, *Coyote Waits* (New York: HarperCollins, 1991), p. 232.

62. Carole laFavor, *Evil Dead Center* (first published 1997) (London: The Women's Press, 1998), p. 32.

63. John G. Cawelti, *Adventure, Mystery, Romance: Formula Stories as Art and Popular Culture* (Chicago, IL: University of Chicago Press, 1976), p. 161.

64. Chang-Rae Lee, *Native Speaker* (first published 1995) (London: Granta, 1998), p. 16.

65. Peter Messent, 'From Private Eye to Police Procedural: The Logic of Contemporary Crime Fiction', in Messent (ed.), *Criminal Proceedings: The Contemporary American Crime Novel* (London: Pluto, 1997), p. 12.

66. See Charles Taylor and Amy Gutman (eds), *Multiculturalism and 'The Politics of Recognition'* (Princeton, NJ: Princeton University Press, 1992), pp. 25-6.

67. Kathleen G. Klein (ed.), 'Introduction', *Diversity and Detective Fiction* (Bowling Green: The Popular Press, 1999), p. 1.

68. bell hooks, *Yearning: Race, Gender and Cultural Politics* (London: Turnaround, 1991), p. 27.

69. Nancy Abelmann and John Lie, *Blue Dreams: Korean Americans and the Los Angeles Riots* (London and Cambridge, MA: Harvard University Press, 1995), p. 191.

Hans Bertens and Theo D'haen (essay date 2001)

SOURCE: Bertens, Hans, and Theo D'haen. "'Other' Detectives: The Emergence of Ethnic Crime Writing." In *Contemporary American Crime Fiction,* pp. 175-89. Houndmills, England: Palgrave, 2001.

[*In the following essay, Bertens and D'haen trace the development of ethnic detective fiction in the twentieth century, discussing such authors as Tony Hillerman, Walter Mosley, and Dale Furutani.*]

Popular literature often addresses hopes and fears affecting large sections of a nation's population, especially when in the throes of social, political, and economic change or upheaval. In the case of the detective this is very clear. The genre originated in early and mid-nineteenth-century France and England, closely upon the creation of the first modern and professional police services. This development itself marked the middle-classes's determination to safeguard its own only recently won hegemony *vis-à-vis* both the arrogant arbitrariness of aristocratic rule and the growing 'greed' of the have-nots (see, for instance, Knight 1980; Mandel 1984; Porter 1981).

In the classical ratiocinative detective novel, first codified by Edgar Allan Poe, the solution of the mystery signals the restoration of law and order, after which the world resumes its course and the body social and politic can return to business as usual. This kind of fiction, which had its 'Golden Age' between the wars in England, is typically set in middle-class milieus, from the rural modesty of the village of Agatha Christie's Miss Marple to the upperclass manors in which her Poirot performs. It equally typically features drawing-room mysteries bordering on intellectual games not unlike *The Times* crossword puzzle featured in so many samples of the genre. With its inevitable re-establishment of social and moral order this form of fiction served to counter the social and political threats of the interbellum by conjuring up an idyllic, unchanging, almost pastoral England. Implicitly it sought to perpetuate the political system enabling such a vision.

At the same time, the American hard-boiled private eye novel arose to serve a similar need, but tailored to American circumstances. Specifically, it addressed the fears of America's white middle class in a period when this felt itself threatened by a combination of developments both abroad and at home coming to a head during the two world wars: the rise of the Soviet Union leading to the first 'red scare' of the early 1920s, massive waves of immigration from southern and eastern Europe between 1880 and the First World War leading to the establishment of a quota system for future immigration, the Crash of 1929, and the outbreak of the Great Depression. It is especially in the pulp fiction of the period that these threats are openly identified. Yet, they also speak from some of the work we now consider as marking the high point of hard-boiled crime fiction, and written by authors who considered themselves—and are considered by others—as definitely on the left side of the political spectrum. In Dashiell Hammett's *The Maltese Falcon* (1930), for instance, white Anglo-Saxon Sam Spade is pitted against a homosexual oriental, a foreign moneyshark—British but with a German-Jewish name—an Irish immigrant hussy, and a low class gangster punk. In other words, Hammett, in spite of his political sympathies, presents a negative picture of what conservative middle America thought of as 'undesirables'.

At the same time, the interbellum also saw the creation of some ethnic detective series, though typically these were not written by writers who belonged to the ethnic minorities in question but by white writers. One of the most successful series was that featuring Honolulu-born Chinese American Charlie Chan, written by the Ohio-born and Harvard-educated Earl Derr Biggers (1884-1933). Because of his early death Biggers only completed six Chan novels. However, from 1926 on Chan starred in numerous movies, though always played by white actors. Rather predictably, in recent years the Charlie Chan series—the movies rather than the novels—has been decried as racist because of its alleged stereotyping of Asian Americans. The same charge has been brought against the Florian Slappey short story series, first serialized—like the early versions of the Charlie Chan novels—in the 1920s and 1930s in *The Saturday Evening Post,* and later collected as *Florian Slappey Goes Abroad* (1928) and *Florian Slappey* (1938). Slappey is an African American detective, created by white Charleston-born Octavus Roy Cohen (1891-1959), who also authored various other mystery series featuring white detectives.

CONTEMPORARY ETHNIC DETECTIVES

A more contemporary example of ethnic detective writing undertaken by a white author is the extremely successful Lieutenant Leaphorn and Detective Jim Chee series, featuring two Native Americans—one part, the other a full-blooded Navajo. The series author, Tony Hillerman, is definitely white, even if raised among native Americans. Hillerman is often considered the 'founding father' of 'serious' ethnic detective writing other than African American. Hillerman's example has been followed by a number of Native American crime writers. Unfortunately, none of these seem to share Hillerman's writing talent.

Aimée and David Thurlo's Ella Clah mysteries, for instance, are routinely compared to Hillerman's Leaphorn and Chee novels. They themselves explicitly dedicate the third Ella Clah mystery, *Blackening Song*

(1995), to Hillerman. In a sense they even try to outdo the master by making their FBI Special Agent Ella Clah not just a Navajo but also a woman. In the end, though, the Thurlos are merely weak epigones of the master. The characters in the Ella Clah mysteries are wooden, and so is the dialogue, which fails to distinguish the characters from one another. The descriptions of the majestic southwestern landscape are no match for those in Hillerman's novels. The plots are farfetched, and ultimately unconvincing, as they tend to rely excessively upon the supernatural. *Blackening Song,* for instance, prominently features the 'skinwalkers' that are a staple also of Hillerman's fiction. Hillerman, though, takes great care never to claim that these evil Navajo 'witches'—supposedly able to turn into coyotes—actually exist. With him, they are part of Navajo belief, and this belief can be exploited and manipulated with evil intent. Or, as in *The First Eagle* (1998), it can lead an old Navajo woman to erroneously interpret what she saw. With the Thurlos, in contrast, we find people literally changing into coyotes. We are even made to 'witness' a gathering of skinwalkers practising their rituals.

Much more interesting, yet less squarely within the detective genre, is Mardi Oakley Medawar's *Death at Rainy Mountain* (1996), the first of a series starring mid-nineteenth-century Kiowa investigator Tay-Bodal or 'Meat Carrier'. Frankly, the detective story here merely serves as a coathanger for the odd characters, and for a description of the customs of the Kiowa at the end of the American Civil War. This is also the avowed intention of Medawar, a Cherokee herself. In her 'author's note' to *Death at Rainy Mountain* she stresses the historical accuracy of much of what she writes about in this novel. 'During the course of telling a story', she claims, 'I can give my people back their heroes . . . I can restore to these heroes their names.' Via her detailed descriptions of her people's customs and rituals, she can write her people back into history. Medawar's intention is shared by many contemporary 'other' detectives. These detectives include a variety of ethnic and gay private eyes. We will begin our discussion of such 'other' detectives with African American crime fiction, arguably the earliest form of 'ethnic' crime writing.

AFRICAN AMERICAN CRIME WRITING: WALTER MOSLEY'S EASY RAWLINS

Until not long ago it was customary to label Chester Himes, with his hard-boiled Harlem detectives Grave Digger Jones and Coffin Ed Johnson, the first practitioner of African American crime fiction. More recently, however, research has unearthed various earlier black mystery writers. Paula L. Woods, in her introduction to *Spooks, Spies, and Private Eyes: Black Mystery, Crime, and Suspense Fiction of the 20th Century* (1995), credits Harlem Renaissance author Rudolph Fisher with being the first African American author of a mystery novel also featuring African American characters. With *The Conjure-Man Dies: A Mystery Tale of Dark Harlem* (1932), Woods claims, Fisher 'was the first [black mystery writer] to set his story in the black community and to address issues important to American negroes, including their relationship to their African ancestry, color prejudice, and superstition' (Woods, xv). Around the same time as Fisher, another Harlem Renaissance writer, George S. Schuyler, published some detective stories focusing on some of these same issues. Yet another Harlem Renaissance author, Alice Dunbar-Nelson, also ventured into the detective genre, but she concentrated on white characters. Woods credits Frank Bailey with having pushed, in *Out of the Woodpile: Black Characters in Crime and Detective Fiction* (1991), the genealogy of African American detective writing back to Jamaica-born W. Adolphe Roberts, who in the 1920s published several mystery novels. She herself unearths even earlier examples, such as a 1900 story by Pauline E. Hopkins (1859-1930), and a 1907 story by J. E. Bruce (1856-1924). None of these, however, featured African American detectives, or were set in African American communities. Still, 'Talma Gordon', the 1900 Pauline Hopkins's story anthologized in *Spooks, Spies, and Private Eyes,* clearly thematizes the issues of miscegenation and 'passing'.

In *The Blues Detective: A Study of African American Detective Fiction,* a critical study that appeared one year after Woods's *Spooks, Spies, and Private Eyes,* Stephen F. Soitos firmly grounds black detective fiction in Pauline Hopkins's *Hagar's Daughter,* a novel serialized in 1901-02 in the *Colored American Magazine,* of which Hopkins was one of the editors. *Hagar's Daughter* features not one, but two black detectives, one of them, and arguably the more important, a female, Venus Johnson. As with 'Talma Gordon', miscegenation and passing play important roles. J(ohn) E(dward) Bruce's novel with the telling title *The Black Sleuth* was serialized in 1907-09 in *McGirt's Magazine,* but remained unfinished. It features an African-born detective, Sadipe Okukenu, and the relationship to Africa and the African past looms large.

Both Hopkins and Bruce were active in movements for the advancement of African Americans and used their literary skills to support the black struggle. The same is true of Rudolph Fisher's *The Conjure-Man Dies,* the crime fiction of Chester Himes and, later, the postmodern anti-detective novels of both Ishmael Reed—particularly *Mumbo Jumbo* (1972) and *The Last Days of Louisiana Red* (1974)—and Clarence Major—specifically *Reflex and Bone Structure* (1975). It still is true of the most recent African American author to successfully enter the lists of hard-boiled detective fiction: Walter Mosley.

Mosley's 'Easy' (from Ezekiel) Rawlins series combines strands of the classic hard-boiled detective novel in the language and character of Rawlins himself, and in the intrigues he gets involved in, and of the adaptation of this tradition in African American fiction, as Soitos has outlined it. Soitos isolates four 'tropes of black detection'. First, 'the black detective's identity is directly connected to community' and black detectives 'are aware, and make their readers aware, of their place within the fabric of their black society' (Soitos, 29). They also always 'delineate the color line as primary in any case or social relation' (31). Second, black detectives, like all African Americans, operate from a typical double-consciousness background. This involves role-playing, the adopting of masks and disguises, and the assumption of a trickster identity. Then, there is what Soitos calls 'blackground'; the interweaving into the text of references to a number of 'black vernaculars' such as 'music/dance, black language, and black cuisine' (37). Finally, Soitos also lists the use of hoodoo, as the expression of specifically black religious and sociophilosophical beliefs, or of a specifically black world view, as distinctive of African American detective fiction.

Hoodoo is absent from Mosley's fiction. Soitos's other tropes, though, are certainly prominently present. There are frequent references to jazz, including the mention of famous performers, such as Billie Holiday, passing through the black bars of Los Angeles. Southern dishes are featured on Rawlins's visits to friends and acquaintances, most of whom, like Rawlins himself, originate from East Texas. The black vernacular is also very much in evidence, especially in the speech of Raymond 'Mouse' Alexander, Easy's boyhood friend. However, Mosley's Rawlins most conspicuously answers to Soitos's tropes one and two. Different from what Soitos claims with regard to black detective fiction, though, the Easy Rawlins novels are not third-person narratives. Easy tells his own story, in the typical hard-boiled idiom.

When we first meet him, in *Devil in a Blue Dress* (London: Pan, 1992 [1990]), Rawlins is a tough East Texas-born ex-GI, who after the Second World War has removed to California. The reasons for his move have to do with the labor market, and with the racial attitudes of the south. In this, the fictional Rawlins joins in a trend shared by many historical African Americans in the same period. However, Rawlins also has another motive for leaving his birthplace: through no fault of his own, he is implicated in a murder. His best friend 'Mouse' has shot and robbed his own stepfather, with Rawlins as an unwilling witness. Mouse is slight of build, but deadly. Rawlins, who has been involved with the woman Mouse wants to marry, and who fears he may now know one secret too many about Mouse, hops on the bus for California. This episode in Rawlins's life is regularly alluded to throughout the 'color' novels—*Devil in a Blue Dress, A Red Death* (1991), *White Butterfly* (1992), *Black Betty* (London: Pan, 1995 [1994]), and *A Little Yellow Dog* (1996)—making up the regular Rawlins-series, and is described at length in *Gone Fishin'* (1997). In each novel, Mouse makes an appearance, often as a deus ex machina saving Easy's life, committing the violence Easy himself is apparently incapable of, or which he is simply unwilling to perform. At the same time, Easy is never quite sure whether Mouse will not eventually turn on him.

'Color' not only features prominently in the titles of the Rawlins novels, it is also, though in a different sense, what the series is about. From its very opening sentence, *Devil in a Blue Dress* is literally all about the color line: 'I was surprised to see a white man walk into Joppy's bar.' The man in question is not just white of skin, he also wears a white suit and hat, has light-blond hair, and is called DeWitt Albright. He will become Rawlins's new employer. Rawlins used to be a mechanic at Champion aircraft, but has been fired by the white team boss, ostensibly for being lazy, but in reality because he dared to stand up for his rights. Albright will also almost become Rawlins's nemesis.

Albright wants Easy to find a beautiful white girl, Daphne Monet, who has a preference for 'dark meat' and is rumored to frequent black jazz bars. Here, as in most of the cases he reluctantly gets involved in, Easy's color allows him access where whites, including the police, dare not go, or would be ineffectual anyway: the black community of Watts, Los Angeles. In *A Red Death,* for instance, Rawlins is pressed by the FBI to infiltrate an alleged communist ring operating from a black church. In *White Butterfly* he is pressured into assisting the police with the investigation of the murder of a white girl. The trail leads to the black community, where similar murders have also been taking place. Hitherto, nobody very much cared about these murders, precisely because they happened among blacks. In *Devil in a Blue Dress,* Daphne's 'whiteness' is all-important—or, rather, the secret of her 'passing' for a white woman is all-important, since in reality she is the 'black' Ruby Hanks. As the fiancée of a rich white business tycoon with political ambitions, Daphne/Ruby and her ancestry have become pawns on the political chessboard.

At the end of *Devil in a Blue Dress,* Daphne/Ruby has disappeared from Easy's life, and DeWitt Albright, Joppy, and a host of other characters are dead, not least thanks to Mouse's interventions. When Easy accuses Mouse of committing murder unwarrantedly, Mouse teaches Easy a little lesson from the black point of view:

'You just like Ruby', Mouse said.

'What you say?'

'She wanna be white. All them years people be tellin' her how she light-skinned and beautiful but all the time she knows that she can't have what white people have. So she pretend and then she lose it all. She can love a white man but all he can love is the white girl he think she is.'

'What's that got to do with me?'

'That's just like you, Easy. You learn stuff and you be thinkin' like white men be thinkin'. You be thinkin' that what's right fo' them is right fo' you. She look like she white and you think like white. But brother you don't know that you both poor niggers. And a nigger ain't never gonna be happy 'less he accept what he is.'

(*Devil*, 209)

The lesson Mouse here teaches Easy trickles down through the entire Rawlins series. In *Devil in a Blue Dress* Easy tells himself, and his readers, that he is no longer afraid of white men. In fact, he has killed plenty of fair-skinned, blond-haired, blue-eyed German boys in Europe. In order to prove himself, both to himself and to his white fellow-GI's, he even volunteered for the Battle of the Bulge. At the end of the novel Easy bests the police, and the DA's office, by selling them an acceptable version of what happened, exonerating himself and everyone he cares about. He even is able to hold on to part of the small fortune Daphne/Ruby had stolen from her fiancée, and which Mouse divides between himself, Easy, and the girl. With the money, Easy sets up as the landlord of a small block of apartments. At the same time, he resorts to typical double-consciousness behavior when he hides his new status from the world, and especially the white civic authorities, foremost among them the IRS, and poses as merely the caretaker and janitor of his own property. Similarly, whereas Easy is perfectly capable of using 'standard' American English, both as to vocabulary and grammar, he resorts to 'black' speech in his dealings with whites, and strikes the pose of a 'dumb negro' as part of his trickster disguise.

The Easy Rawlins series is historical in conception, giving us an extended view of Rawlins's life in 1948 (*Devil in a Blue Dress*), 1953 (*A Red Death*), 1956 (*White Butterfly*), 1961 (*Black Betty*), and 1962 (*A Little Yellow Dog*). We follow both his own development as a character, and his changing relationship to American society. This relationship gradually darkens as Rawlins, outsmarted and outmaneuvered by white businessmen, over the years loses not only his block of flats, but even the little house he owned in *Devil in a Blue Dress.* The marriage he enters into breaks up in *White Butterfly,* when his wife, with their little daughter, leaves him for a friend and former colleague. In *A Red Death,* he adopts an orphan boy, Jesus, and in *White Butterfly* a little girl, Feather. With them he moves into another small house he buys in a black middle class neighborhood in West Los Angeles. In all, Rawlins finds that, as Mouse predicted, he has to curtail considerably his ambitions with regard to 'liberty, and the pursuit of happiness' if he wants to keep a 'life' in a world ruled by racial prejudice.

A Little Yellow Dog is perhaps the most entertaining Easy Rawlins novel as far as its action goes. At the same time, it also sees Rawlins reduced to bare essentials, with few illusions left. He now works as 'supervising senior head custodian' in a junior high school, and tries to lead as inconspicuous a life as possible with his two adopted children. Fate comes knocking in the form of Mrs Idabell Turner, a teacher, who seduces Rawlins one morning when she asks him to take care of her little yellow dog for just one day. Predictably, things spin out of control, and once again Mouse's little lesson from *Devil in a Blue Dress* proves only too true. In all previous Easy Rawlins novels shooting people was the job of Mouse. Now, Rawlins himself shoots several people, one of them being Mouse himself. Easy also gets romantically involved with a murderess, and ends up acknowledging the fact. Most importantly, *A Little Yellow Dog* ends after Kennedy has been assassinated, an event that spells the loss of hope for Rawlins and for the nation. In *Black Betty*, when having a nightmare, he still 'tried to think of better things . . . about our new young Irish president and Martin Luther King; about how the world was changing and a black man in America had the chance to be a man for the first time in hundreds of years' (*Black Betty*, 2). With hindsight, we know that Rawlins's high hopes for King too are to be dashed soon after the time in which *A Little Yellow Dog* is set. In interviews and articles Mosley himself has become increasingly sombre and militant about race in America.

DALE FURUTANI'S KEN TANAKA

Unlike Mosley's Easy Rawlins series, many other novels featuring ethnic detectives tend to avoid violence. In order to make their point, they often also provide extensive backgrounds to their stories. Hence, in some of these novels the emphasis partly shifts from plot and character to social and historical explanation. This is particularly the case in newer ethnic detective fiction, like Dale Furutani's Ken Tanaka mysteries. Indeed, in *Death in Little Tokyo* (1996), and even more so in its successor, *The Toyotomi Blades* (1997), the author regularly presents disquisitions on Japanese, and in particular Japanese American history, with specific emphasis on moments or instances of ethnic discrimination.

The pedigree of Asian American crime writing is much less firmly established than that of its African American counterpart. As a matter of fact, Ken Tanaka may well be the first Japanese American private eye, and Furutani may well be the first Japanese American detective author. In fact, Furutani's hero is a rather unlikely private eye. Tanaka is a 42-year-old Hawaiian-born computer programmer. He has a failed marriage to a caucasian behind him; so does his present girlfriend Mariko, an aspiring Japanese American actress in her 30s, and an ex-alcoholic. Tanaka and Mariko blame white racism for their failure to get ahead in their respective careers. Mariko invariably is cast in minor 'Asian' roles; Tanaka himself has been laid off in a recent 'downsizing' operation.

Tanaka and Mariko are both members of a mystery club. When it is Tanaka's turn to stage a fake crime for the benefit of his fellow club members, he does this so realistically that he snares an actual client. From there on, the plot of *Death in Little Tokyo* starts echoing Hammett's *The Maltese Falcon*. To be fair, Tanaka has in the first chapter announced that the mystery he will provide will take its cue from Hammett's novel. So when a woman calling herself Rita Newly presents herself to him with the request that he take delivery of a package for her, he at first assumes that someone is turning the tables on him. However, when the Japanese man Tanaka collected the package from is found murdered, things turn serious. In the end, both the murderer and his victim turn out to be Japanese Americans. The root of their murderous conflict lies in the period the two men spent in the 'relocation' camps the United States government set up for its citizens of Japanese descent during the Second World War, and in the division between those Japanese Americans that took the loyalty oath imposed upon them by the United States authorities, and those that did not. Ultimately, then, it is white prejudice and paranoia that are to blame for the tragedy that occurred.

The fame Ken Tanaka gains from solving his first case earns him an invitation to appear on a Tokyo talk show. In Japan, he is called upon to help investigate the mysterious disappearance, from museums and private collections around the world, of some famous seventeenth-century samurai swords: the Toyotomi blades that feature in the title of the second Ken Tanaka mystery. In fact, Tanaka himself owns one of the six blades in question—bought, perhaps somewhat implausibly, at a Los Angeles garage sale. The sword was featured in a photograph of his that has appeared in the Japanese press, and all at once a new light is thrown upon the invitation to come to Japan. The Toyotomi blades put together form a map pinpointing an ancient treasure. Tanaka, aided by Mariko and his own computer skills, of course succeeds in locating the treasure. However, he has been beaten to it first by ancient robbers, and more recently by the Japanese traditionalists who have been after the swords and who had hoped to use the treasure for their own purposes. In the end, the treasure turns out to consist of bales of silk and brocade—priceless at the time they were stored, but now rotting and turning to dust. *The Toyotomi Blades* really is one long meditation on what it means to be a Japanese American in terms of ancestry and loyalties, and on the relationship of Japan to the Western world and modernity in general, and to the United States in particular.

At the end of *The Toyotomi Blades* Tanaka decides to look into the possibility of applying for a legitimate private investigator license. It is difficult to see, though, how much further Furutani can take his protagonist without toughening him up considerably. After all, he is probably not always going to have the good fortune, as in *The Toyotomi Blades,* of having the disinterested assistance of a Hawaiian Sumo-wrestler. Admittedly, there is some enjoyable tongue-in-cheek reflection on the conventions of hard-boiled fiction and on how Tanaka's own exploits relate to this. There are also the regular references to Japanese cinema, especially Akira Kurosawa and Toshiro Mifune, and to American movie classics. In all, though, *The Toyotomi Blades* calls for an awful lot of coincidence to construe a workable plot. Perhaps that is why Furutani with his latest novels, *Death at the Crossroads* (1998) and *Jade Palace Vendetta* (1999), has turned to writing 'Samurai mysteries', featuring roaming samurai warrior Matsuyama Kaze, and set in the early seventeenth-century Japan of the making of the Toyotomi blades. With this, Furutani joins the vogue for historical detective fiction, and more in particular meets the interest in feudal Japan that we also see in Chinese-Korean American Laura Joh Rowland's highly successful *Shinjū* (1994) and *Bundori* (1996), which star a 'special investigator' of Edo (that is, Tokyo before the 1868 Meiji Restoration).

TWICE MARGINALIZED: ETHNICITY AND SEXUALITY

A particularly interesting example of non-mainstream crime writing is the pairing of ethnicity and sexual 'otherness' that we find in the Henry Rios novels of Michael Nava, five times winner of the Lambda award for Best Gay Men's Mystery, and in the first Benjamin Justice mystery of John Morgan Wilson. Nava is a Mexican American lawyer and a gay rights activist who, with Robert Davidoff, is the author of *Created Equal: Why Gay Rights Matter to America.* Not surprisingly the Rios novels feature a Mexican American lawyer and focus on ethnicity and homosexuality. *The Hidden Law* (1992) refers to the title of a W. H. Auden poem rather cryptically describing the workings of fate. Nava applies this theme to the Chicano community. Specifically, he details how the lives of fathers determine those of their sons. In spite of whatever success they may

achieve, minority fathers always remain aware that they continue to be second-class citizens in the Anglo world. Often, they take their hidden rage at that world out on their wives and children. They also tend to take it out on themselves in the form of self-destructive drugs or alcohol abuse. The sons revolt. Sexually, Nava seems to imply, they may do so by turning gay. Professionally, they try to turn themselves into what they think to be successful opposites of their fathers. Rios himself is a good example of this filial rebellion, because as a gay lawyer he champions all the 'permissive' causes his macho policeman father abhorred. His client Michael Ruiz finds himself in a similar position: he feels unloved by his successful Chicano parents, and is being over-protected by his Chicano grandmother. Partly as a result of the psycho-social pressure he experiences, Ruiz allows himself be to be put forward as the murderer of Gus Peña, a Chicano California state senator who perfectly answers to the type of minority father sketched.

Rios eventually finds out that the real murderer is Peña's son. The latter's mother and sister consented to the murder because of the domestic violence rampant in the Peña household, because of Peña's unrelenting alcoholism, and his forceful opposition to his son's relationship with an older Anglo woman. They are all speculating on Ruiz being acquitted for lack of evidence. As it turns out, Rios's intervention puts both Peña's son and Ruiz behind bars—they will have to face up to what they are. So will Rios himself. In the course of his investigation Rios has come to realize how 'the hidden law' rules his own life, and that of his community, and how his being gay relates to all this. In the end, Rios closes his law practice in order to take stock of his life and to finally do himself some good, as his psychologist had urgently counseled him to do.

The Hidden Law, like the Henry Rios novels in general, provides a panoramic picture of multi-ethnic Los Angeles. Curiously, Nava is exceedingly sparse with physical descriptions of Rios. Still, on the rare occasions when we do get a glimpse of Rios's appearance—often through the reactions of other characters—the emphasis invariably is on his mestizo, Mexican-Hispanic traits.

Next to the ethnic, there is the gay interest. In *The Burning Plain* (1997) Rios gets involved with a young actor in whom he sees Josh, his lover from the earlier novels in the series, reincarnated. The man is promptly found murdered. When a number of other gay young men about town are also killed, Rios himself becomes a prime suspect. Working to clear his name, Rios uncovers sexual depravity, corruption, blackmail, and murder rampant in the highest political offices, as well as in the movie studio boardrooms. A casual remark about a woman at a poetry reading comparing Los Angeles to the hell of Dante's *Inferno* reveals the full extent of Nava's ambitions. *The Burning Plain* is a rewriting, many times removed, of Dante's masterpiece. It was Dante who described the seventh circle of hell, the one to which homosexuals were assigned, as a 'burning plain'.

In *Simple Justice* (1996), which won an Edgar for best first novel, John Morgan Wilson likewise pictures gay Los Angeles as a contemporary hell. At the age of 17, Ben (Benjamin) Justice catches his father in the act of raping his 11-year-old sister. He kills his father, a police officer with a history of violence especially toward his wife and son. The incident destroys the family. Years later, when Justice is a star reporter on the *L.A. Times*, and his lover Jacques lies dying from Aids, a story that Justice writes on the disease wins him a Pulitzer Prize. However, when it is rumored that the gay couple he wrote about is fictional and he does not reveal their identity, he has to return the prize and loses his job. Now, after having almost drunk himself into the grave, Justice lives alone in his former lover's garage apartment, cultivating his memories.

Justice is invited by his former editor at the *L.A. Times*, who is now employed by the rival newspaper the *L.A. Sun*, to work as a gofer for one of the *Sun*'s crime reporters, Alex(andra) Templeton, who is preparing a story about a murder outside a gay bar. A Chicano boy, Gonzalo Albundo, with blood on his hands, was caught bent over a dead white boy, Lusk. Gonzalo readily confesses to the killing. In the course of his duties, Ben meets Paul Masterman Jr, a conservative senator's son, in whom he becomes sexually interested. Paul is orchestrating his father's bid for re-election and arranges a TV spot aimed at the votes of the gay electorate on the site of the Lusk killing.

As the story unfolds, Wilson deftly weaves in the ethnic theme. Justice is white. Templeton is African American, and so is Jefferson Bellworthy, a gay ex-football star who now is a bouncer and barman for the club in front of which Lusk was killed. Lusk himself was Jewish, and so is Derek Brunheim, Lusk's longtime lover. Gonzalo Albundo is Hispanic. Jim Jai-Sik, alias Jim Lee, and briefly Ben's lover, is Korean American. Wilson is equally skilful with regard to the psychological dimension of his characters. Paul Masterman, who turns out to be the real killer, but also Lusk and Ben himself—just like Nava's characters—at least partially seem to have become gay because of serious relational problems with their fathers. These problems intersect with social pressures specifically linked to their respective ethnic backgrounds.

A lot of the action and motivation of *Simple Justice* is fueled by the fear of coming out. Gonzalo Albundo rather confesses to a murder he did not commit than to

being gay. Paul Masterman rather commits murder than confess to a youthful homosexual one night stand. Ben himself, finally, preferred to return his Pulitzer Prize to 'coming out' with his own personal tragedy—the 'fictional' couple in his prize-winning story has, after all, been real enough: Ben himself and his lover Jacques. *Simple Justice* paints a heartbreaking picture of the gay community of Los Angeles, throbbing with sexual energy, but also with hurt and desperation. And always, in Nava's Henry Rios series as in Wilson's Benjamin Justice novels, the threat of Aids is palpably present, and the ravages the disease causes in the lives of the protagonists, and in the gay community at large, are movingly detailed.

THE PAST REVISITED: ROBERT SKINNER'S *SKIN DEEP, BLOOD RED*

An original perspective on the ethnic issue, and one that takes us right back to the beginnings of both ethnic and hard-boiled crime writing in the United States, is provided by Robert Skinner's *Skin Deep, Blood Red* (1997). The novel definitely claims a place in the Hammett tradition. In fact, it initially reads like a straightforward calque of *The Maltese Falcon*. There is the smuggling into the United States of a valuable item—a suitcase full of uncut diamonds fresh from South Africa. We meet an enticing blonde with an Irish surname, or at least alias, Miss Flynn. The villain is a highly cultivated but at the same time unspeakably evil and more than slightly sinister Jewish businessman: Mr Ganns. The hero is an unflappable, attractive, but playing hard-to-get investigator: Wesley Farrell. Even the physical description of Farrell reads like a cross between the Sam Spade of *The Maltese Falcon* and the Ned Beaumont of *The Glass Key*. Also the period in which *Skin Deep, Blood Red* is set is close enough: the late 1930s. Obviously, there are also some twists to the plot that distinguish Skinner's novel from its predecessor. To begin with, the locale is not San Francisco, but New Orleans. Then, the murder that sparks off the story is not that of the investigator's partner in detection, as in *The Maltese Falcon*, but rather that of a corrupt police officer. Farrell is not a professional private eye, anyway, but rather a nightclub owner accidentally drawn into sleuthing. The novelty of *Skin Deep, Blood Red*, however, and at the same time its main interest, lies in its treatment of race, and particularly 'passing'.

Farrell turns out to be part Creole, and therefore black in the eyes of 1930s America, particularly so in the south. He has passed as white for most of his life, and wants to keep it that way in order to safeguard his position both in the underworld of New Orleans and in the city's regular society. Over the course of the novel Farrell's past is gradually revealed, along with his acceptance of his mixed heritage and his final assumption of a Creole identity. In the process, he is transformed from a typical hard-boiled 'lone ranger' into a man assuming family responsibilities. To begin with, there is the re-established relationship with his long-lost father, the white New Orleans police detective Frank Casey. Ironically, the blame for the separation of Wesley's parents rests with his mother's upper-crust Creole family. They deemed Casey, though white, socially inferior because of his Irish immigrant origins. The social prejudice practised by Creole society proves to be just as devastating for the individuals caught up in it as the racial discrimination prevalent among whites. Skinner explicitly holds out an alternate model when he depicts how Casey and his Creole wife live the early years of their marriage in Cuban Havana, free of racial prejudice. However, Farrell also recognizes his love for the black singer he has been having an affair with for years. Finally, he assumes the guardianship of a young black cousin whose childhood experiences strongly resemble Farrell's own. Farrell's assumption of his Creole identity, with all the risks this implies, obviously amounts to a plea for hybridity and tolerance on the part of his creator. The second novel in the series, *Cat-Eyed Trouble* (1998), conveys a similar message.

If all this smacks of a particularly contemporary and modish political correctness, so be it. The fact remains that Skinner has succeeded in putting a novel spin on some of the oldest clichés in the genre, thereby proving their resilience and their usefulness in ever new circumstances. Specifically, by rewriting *The Maltese Falcon* for the 1990s, he has not only retuned one of the earliest classics in the hard-boiled tradition, but also has refashioned a story that originally conveyed white America's fear of 'undesirables' into an advertisement for ethnic and cultural tolerance.

Select Secondary Bibliography

Knight, Stephen. *Form and Ideology in Crime Fiction.* Bloomington: Indiana University Press, 1980.

Mandel, Ernest. *Delightful Murder: A Social History of the Crime Story.* London: Pluto, 1984.

Porter, Dennis. *The Pursuit of Crime: Art and Ideology in Detective Fiction.* New Haven and London: Yale University Press, 1981.

Soitos, Stephen F. *The Blues Detective: A Study of African American Detective Fiction.* Amherst: University of Massachusetts Press, 1996.

Woods, Paula L. *Spooks, Spies, and Private Eyes: Black Mystery, Crime, and Suspense Fiction of the 20th Century.* New York: Doubleday, 1995.

LITERARY TRADITIONS AND CRIME FICTION

Timothy Shuker-Haines and Martha M. Umphrey (essay date 1998)

SOURCE: Shuker-Haines, Timothy, and Martha M. Umphrey. "Gender (De)Mystified: Resistance and Recuperation in Hard-Boiled Female Detective Fiction." In *The Detective in American Fiction, Film, and Television,* edited by Jerome H. Delamater and Ruth Prigozy, pp. 71-82. Westport, Conn.: Greenwood Press, 1998.

[*In the following essay, Shuker-Haines and Umphrey analyze the female detective characters from the works of Sue Grafton and Sara Paretsky, noting that while there are vast differences among these detectives, gender is nonetheless a central component of their narratives.*]

What should we make of the recent emergence of the female hard-boiled detective? In a literary-historical sense she is an oxymoron, standing outside the gendered traditions of both the classic female detective and the tough-guy dick. The classic archetype, a Miss Marple or a Jessica Fletcher, generally operates within the domestic sphere, solving drawing-room crimes and reestablishing harmony through a combination of skillful listening, good sense, and intuitive judgment about character.[1] She uses her social knowledge and skills to identify the criminal and thus locate the source of social disruption, purifying and restabilizing society. The hard-boiled detective stands in stark opposition to this female figure. His locate is not the drawing room but the liminal zone of the criminal underworld, and his qualities are not intuition and social knowledge but violence and a personal code of honor. Whereas the classic detective novel presents a stable social order with an isolated crime, hard-boiled fiction presents a world filled with corruption, destabilized by the dangerous allure of female sexuality. With his strict code of honor and renunciation, the hard-boiled hero embodies a vision of righteousness and justice.[2]

The hard-boiled detective would thus appear to be a necessarily male figure, defined by his emphasis on violence, individuation, and horror of female sexuality. David Glover (1989) has argued that the hard-boiled tradition was developed as a masculine reclaiming of the detective novel, which was seen as overly feminized, dominated by detectives who were female (Miss Marple, Harriet Vane) or insufficiently masculine (Hercule Poirot, Peter Wimsey). Thus, the gender confusion inherent in the female hard-boiled detective has the potential to destabilize radically this gendered opposition between classic and hard-boiled detective fiction by problematizing both the construction of the detective and the socially restorative function of detection.

Yet these potentials are not consistently realized when the detective's sex is changed, as a comparison of Sue Grafton's *F Is for Fugitive* and Sara Paretsky's *Blood Shot* reveals. Each novel foregrounds gender as central to both the construction of the detective and the development of the narrative. Yet each writer uses gender differently. Grafton's Kinsey Millhone undermines the relation between gender and biological sex, emphasizing gender's performative nature, but she does so by leaving intact masculinity and femininity—and their hierarchical relation. Paretsky's V. I. Warshawski, on the other hand, presents a valorized female self that enables her to reject both traditional feminine and masculine positions and to offer a critique of male power formations from a feminist perspective, opening up the utopian possibility of community without gender hierarchy. Yet this very utopian vision is based on an uncritical acceptance of the concept of a unified "woman's" identity and community.

Gender relates to the figure of the female hard-boiled detective in complicated and contradictory ways. Initially, both Millhone and Warshawski identify themselves as autonomous and ungendered, and their names reflect this identity metonymically. "Kinsey," Millhone's mother's last name, is ambiguous in gender. "V. I.," on the other hand, stands for "Victoria Iphigenia," an explicitly feminized name that echoes V. I.'s Italian mother's side; yet V. I. rejects that name, allowing her friends to call her, if anything, "Vic." In contrast, hostile acquaintances who want her to circumscribe her activities and behave more like a proper woman (for example, Sergeant Mallory, an old family friend) call her "Vicki." Both "Kinsey" and "Vic" thus operate as ungendered and single-word identifiers that circulate as de facto masculine signifiers in a tough world off-limits to femininity.

At the same time, though, both Millhone and Warshawski identify themselves relationally, either positively or negatively, in a way that accords more with "the feminine" as socially defined.[3] Millhone describes herself in the opening pages of *F Is for Fugitive* as "thirty-two years old, twice married, no kids, currently unattached and likely to remain so given my disposition, which is cautious at best" (FF ['*F*' *Is for Fugitive*] 3).[4] This description both assumes the primacy of the relational (the male hard-boiled dick could omit his marital status because his bachelorhood would be taken for granted) and rejects it so as to emphasize autonomy.

Warshawski opens her narrative with memories—memories of her childhood in South Chicago and of the people who lived next door while she grew up, the

mother-daughter family of Djiaks. Throughout the book she thinks of herself in terms of this former context, especially as it evokes memories of her mother, Gabriella, who once defended the unmarried and pregnant Louisa Djiak from the righteous wrath of her neighbors. Thus, while not explicitly gendering herself, Warshawski is gendered feminine twice over: once as she is constituted in relation to others rather than as contextless and unbound, and again as she reads her identity through the lens of a female community.

In other words, both Millhone and Warshawski remain inscribed to some extent within categories of masculinity and femininity as they are socially constructed. Yet, the strategies mobilized by each to grapple with this gendering differ: Millhone operates independently and remains within a binary heterosexual economy, oscillating between masculine and feminine subject positions; Warshawski uses a mediating, homosocial network of female friends and family to redefine the paradigm of "femininity" via an implicit feminist critique. And just as Warshawski ruptures the heterosexual binary that Millhone caricatures but leaves intact, *Blood Shot* challenges the socially reconstitutive role of detective fiction that *F Is for Fugitive* ultimately accepts.

Kinsey Millhone's persona is gendered substantially as masculine. A woman who has few friends and lives for her work, she is self-consciously, almost parodically male-defined, as, for example, when she describes her tendency to amuse herself with the abridged California Penal code and textbooks on auto theft (FF, 209) rather than engaging in the teatime gossip of a Miss Marple. This masculine stylization and thus her identification with male hard-boiled dicks are perhaps clearest in relation to her gun: "I sat at the kitchen table, loaded seven cartridges in the clip and smacked it home. This was my new handgun. A Davis .32 chrome and walnut with a five-and-a-quarter inch barrel. . . . This one weighed a tidy twenty-two ounces and already felt like an old friend" (FF 149). The gun, described here in such loving detail, becomes a fetishized "old friend" with clear phallic overtones. Millhone's strong identification with her male precursors is further reinforced in this scene by the setting—vapor street-lights filtering through the window, the neon vacancy sign sputtering red light into the room—which has become associated with the hard-boiled tradition through film noir's visual conventions (Place and Peterson 1976; Schrader 1986; Hirsch 1981).

Yet, crucial to Millhone's construction is the psychological mutability of gender, its discontinuity and oscillation. "There was something enormously appealing," she remarks early in the book, "in the idea of setting one persona aside and constructing a second to take its place" (FF 19). She ably plays the feminine role when appropriate, particularly in the context of the heterosexual romance. When she and Dwight Shales, a potential suspect, have dinner for example, they discuss their leisure activities (his is backpacking, hers the penal code); but as the scene grows more intimate she quickly shifts gears: "I listened with both eyes and one ear trying to discern what was really going on. . . . While his mouth made noises . . . his eyes said something else. I disconnected my brain and fine-tuned my receiver, picking up his code. This man was emotionally available" (FF 209). Most notable about this passage is the extremity of the gender switch: She disconnects the "male" logic of her brain so as to engage her "female" sexual intuition; she moves from the penal code to sexual dalliance.[5] Thus, even as she refuses the biological "naturalness" of gender identity in this oscillation, she remains caught within a heterosexual economy that posits two distinct genders (so distinct as to be parodic), unwilling to escape or reimagine the gender roles that define them.

Just as Millhone's character is grounded in the heterosexual binary, so too is the narrative of *F Is for Fugitive,* which centers on the psychic dramas of two groups: Daughters yearning for paternal love and patriarchs succumbing to the temptations of illicit sex. Millhone is called into a small town to investigate the murder of Jean Timberlake, the promiscuous, illegitimate daughter of Shana Timberlake, "the town roundheel." The town's leading citizens (men, of course) come under suspicion as Millhone discovers that each was sexually involved with either Jean or Shana. Doctor Dunne, the town physician, turns out to have been Jean's father. Reverend Haws, the minister at the town's only church, had sex with Jean every week in his office before choir practice. Shales, the high school principal, had gotten Jean pregnant just before her death. With the pillars of society thus implicated in a young girl's demise, the way is open for a critique of the sexual oppression and abuse of women.

Yet, rather than condemning the men's behavior, Millhone forgives it. All these men had wives with failing bodies or minds—Mrs. Dunne had paranoid schizophrenia; Mrs. Shales, multiple sclerosis; Mrs. Haws, a serious skin condition. Millhone views these women as do their husbands—with pity, contempt, and revulsion. By pathologizing the female body, Millhone identifies with and forgives the men driven by such extreme circumstances to extramarital sex.

Male innocence is further reinforced by the overwhelming power of female promiscuity and sexual aggression. Millhone describes Shana, for example, as "exhibitionistic" when she dances in the local bar and notes how Shana has "no modesty at all" (FF 128). Jean is seen as the instigator in her affairs with both Haws and Shales and is described as "insatiable," driven by "a need to dominate." "We were at her mercy," one of her high school paramours says, "because we wanted her so

much" (FF 118). This focus on Jean's sexual power leads to the extraordinary implication that a high school principal's sexual affair with a student is a function not of his power, but of hers. There is no correlation between the social power of the men involved and their sexual activities; in the face of the dangerous and disruptive sexuality of Shana and Jean, they are helpless.

Here we find ourselves back in the traditional dynamics of the detective novel; female sexuality is a disruptive force that threatens the social order and must be punished.[6] This is hard-boiled with a twist, for at least the traditional femmes fatales—Brigid O'Shaughnessy in *The Maltese Falcon,* Phyllis Dietrichson in *Double Indemnity*—offered a thrilling vision of transforming their sexual charisma into material and personal power. Shana and Jean Timberlake, on the other hand, remain merely disruptive, reaping no such benefits.

This patriarchal vision of female desire as dangerous ties the revelations of social scandal to the family romance at the heart of the narrative. Millhone, originally hired by Royce Fowler to free his son Bailey, discovers that the murderer was neither Bailey nor any of the men sexually involved with Jean, but Ann Fowler, Bailey's sister. Ann, obsessively in love with Shales, kills Jean to prevent her pregnancy from ruining him and kills Shana because she believes, incorrectly, that Shana is involved with him.

Thus, the murders of the sexually dangerous women are tied not to men protecting their social standing, but to a jealous woman. The incestuous nature of Ann's jealousy is revealed by her third murder: that of her own mother. Deprived of the love of her stern father, who is interested only in his son Bailey, she both frames Bailey and kills her mother to claim her father's love. It thus becomes clear that Ann's desire for Shales was tied to his paternal function; he was the principal at the school where she was a counselor. Just as Shales's affair with his young student Jean had incestuous overtones, Ann's murder of Jean is meant to open a space she can occupy as the beloved of Shales, the father substitute.

Ultimately, the daughter's yearning for the father implicates Millhone, evoking memories of her sense of loss at the death of her own father when she was five. In the end, Millhone muses on her links with both Jean (who, before she died, was searching for her father) and Ann: "None of us had survived the wounds our fathers inflicted all those years ago. Did he love us? How would we ever know? He was gone and he'd never again be what he was to us in all his haunting perfection" (FF 306).

Yet, the book implies that women can, through self-denial, win a shred of this paternal love. When Ann shoots off her foot after struggling with her father over a gun, she cries, "You were never there for me. . . . You were never there" (FF 305); but at that moment she ends up in his arms. Both shooting off her foot and giving up the gun act as symbolic castrations; Ann relinquishes her claims to phallic power by handing the gun over to her father, and she cripples herself as a form of punishment. Rendered helpless and dependent, she finally gains the paternal embrace. Millhone takes this lesson to heart. While the book opens with Millhone's complaints that her elderly landlord, Henry Pitts, is too doting and threatens her independence, it closes with her determination to treasure him. "He may," she says, "be the closest thing to a father I'll ever have" (FF 307).

The book locates the source of disruption in the daughter's unreciprocated love for the father. The danger of incest, its threat to the patriarchal order, lies in the desires of the daughter and can be overcome only by curbing female desire and independence: Just as all the men must be protected or exonerated, so the women must be killed or imprisoned. On the one hand, Millhone could never identify with this threatening version of femininity and thus ensures that the women are punished and stability is restored; on the other, Millhone as daughter accepts her subordination within the father/daughter dyad. Thus, her primary identification with masculinity not only maintains gender as gender difference but also, in a contradictory and narratively conservative way, reinscribes gender as gender hierarchy. Even as she plays with gender difference by parodying both masculinity and (to a lesser extent) femininity, such playfulness fails as a disruptive strategy in the final analysis.

Where *F Is for Fugitive* defines gender in terms of individual psychology, *Blood Shot* locates it in social formations and resists rather than reinscribes gender hierarchy. The oppressive function of gender categories is clear in the way Warshawski is constructed by others—particularly the men she pursues—as an unnaturally unfeminine woman, a "bitch": mongrel bitch, cold-blooded bitch, meddlesome bitch. Such an epithet signals a need to reinforce femininity ("bitch" only applies to women) even as Warshawski's detective activities transgress the boundaries of proper femininity: Compliance, subservience, submission to the wills of men. It forcefully reinscribes Warshawski as female Other to the masculine Self, reasserting female inferiority through metaphors of animality even as the female detective acts to subvert and usurp male power.

Warshawski resists such constructions by locating an authentic and valorized female "Self" through her relations with strong female characters. Gabriella, Warshawski's deceased mother, exists in her memories as an accomplished opera singer and exemplary parent. Lotty, Warshawski's closest friend and mother-surrogate,

is a renowned doctor who runs a family clinic for impoverished women and children. And Ms. Chigwell is a seventy-eight-year-old, fearless woman whose medical career was blocked by her gender but who becomes Warshawski's partner in a daring rescue.

These women, whose strength is *not* represented as traditionally "masculine," function as a community, homosocial in character and intensity, that mediates Warshawski's relationship to a tough world in which femaleness can be, if not a liability, then certainly an anomaly—a world in which she must rely on deception in order to succeed. Warshawski relates to each of them without deception or bravado, describing Lotty, for example, as "the one person I never lie to. She's—not my conscience—the person who helps me see who I really am, I guess" (BS [*Blood Shot*] 339). This authentic Self, constructed as female but not feminine within Warshawski's community, in turn enables her to defy the psychologized heterosexual binary that condemns femininity in *F Is for Fugitive*. Such a community, a crucial departure from the radically individualist male hard-boiled tradition, empowers Warshawski on a social level as she attacks the abuses of male power.

Paretsky, as opposed to Grafton, views incest within this political frame of male power. For Paretsky, incest signifies not a female desire that threatens the social order, but a male desire that constitutes it. Paretsky makes this argument structurally by overlaying two narratives—the search for Caroline Djiak's father and an investigation of industrial poisoning. Originally hired by Caroline, a childhood friend, to discover the identity of her father, Warshawski tries to trace some friends of Caroline's mother Louisa, who used to work at the Xerxes solvent plant. But these friends had died as a result of the chemical's toxicity, and Warshawski finds herself investigating a massive corporate cover-up.

This investigation leads to three powerful men—Humboldt, wealthy financier and owner of Xerxes; Dresberg, an organized crime boss; and Jurshak, a corrupt South Chicago politician. These three figures represent bastions of power, and Warshawski topples them all. She also discovers that Jurshak is the father of Caroline, whose mother Louisa was Jurshak's niece. Whereas the symbolically incestuous acts in Grafton are blamed on the daughters, here Jurshak is clearly responsible for the rape of his niece, part of a systematic pattern of abuse begun with Louisa's older sister.

The theme of the powerful abusing the powerless unites these stories of incest and corporate greed. By superimposing a crime of gender and a crime of class, Paretsky brings together the tales of two rapes: The rape of the girl's body by her uncle and the rape of workers' bodies by their employer. Both are performed by leading citizens who veil their culpability by allowing their victims to be blamed for their suffering: The pregnant Louisa was thrown out of the house to avoid scandal while the workers' illnesses were attributed to their smoking rather than their work environment.

Warshawski uncovers the truth behind these lies. This truth-bearing function is, of course, a central part of the traditional detective story, but here that function is radicalized. Classic detective narratives cleanse society by locating the source of disorder in specific deviant individuals who can be identified and purged, with the truth acting simultaneously to expose the criminal and to clear society as a whole (Cawelti 1976, 80-105; Taylor 1989). Paretsky's novels locate society's evils not on the margins but in its most central, stable figures. Her villains make up the pantheon of a male elite—politicians, corporate executives, bankers, union bosses, religious leaders. Nor are these villains deranged. Their motivations are inevitably financial, and their movement into crime is simply an extension of the logic of business.

This corrupt power lies not only in the public realm of business and politics but also in the private realm of the family. Thus, Warshawski physically or financially ruins Dresberg, Jurshak, and Humboldt; she also confronts Louisa's parents about disowning her. When Louisa's mother finally acknowledges the incest, her husband slaps her. Warshawski punches him in return, initiating a full-scale fight. "I stood over him panting from fury, my gun in my hand barrel-first, ready to smash it into him if he started to get up. His face was glazed—none of his women-folk had ever fought back against him" (BS 273).

Most significant here is not that Warshawski gets into a fight, a standard trope in hard-boiled fiction, but that she fights on behalf of women. The gun, barrel-first, is no longer Millhone's fetishized phallus, but a threatening bludgeon. Warshawski fights not so much like a man as like a fury, an avenging spirit striking out against malevolent uses of male power; and with such a gesture she transforms detection into political resistance. Grafton, accepting both gender opposition and hierarchy, offers no such social model; her individualism leads to a maintenance of the gendered status quo rather than social transformation. Paretsky, on the other hand, rethinks the detective's inscription in both social and gender hierarchies and offers a utopian social model grounded in values of authenticity and egalitarianism, a model in which women (and some men) emerge as a unified political force with a single, clear response to women's oppression.

She does so, however, at the expense of a critical examination of the construction of Warshawski's identity. Just as Warshawski's political utopia is a fiction, so too is any sense of authentic and unified "self-

hood." Yet both fictions are necessary in the politics of Paretsky's work, which posits a feminist Archimedean point from which Warshawski can critique male power formations.

In this light, Grafton's epistemology of performance may be more politically useful in the long run, since her play with gender categories offers the possibility of their symbolic deconstruction. More recent works, Grafton's *H Is for Homicide* and the movie *V. I. Warshawski,* exhibit both the potential and the limitations of this more playful approach to gender.

Like *F Is for Fugitive, V. I. Warshawski,* a Disney film loosely based on two of Paretsky's novels, parodies gender categories and thus subverts Paretsky's more trenchant critiques of male power. In this film, Warshawski is firmly embedded in the heterosexual binary, her toughness treated as a cross-dressing joke. We first see her as she wakes up in her filthy apartment and sniffs her running clothes before putting them on; we then cut from the morning's jogging shoes to the evening's high heels. Clearly she occupies both masculine and feminine positions, but the borderline never blurs. The movie dispenses with Warshawski's female community while playing up her heterosexual attachments. Lottie is marginalized, while Murray Ryerson, Warshawski's reporter friend, becomes both central and romantic; and the narrative is set in motion when she picks up a man in a bar who is later murdered.

The plot of the film reinforces a conservative rather than an alternative social and familial vision. Warshawski seduces Boom-Boom Grafalk, a hockey star and part owner of a threatened shipping business; when he is murdered, she both takes care of his daughter Kat and investigates his death. The ultimate villain is Boom-Boom's ex-wife, now married to his dissolute brother. Identified by her loose morality (promiscuity, drug and alcohol dependency), she ultimately attempts to kill her own daughter to gain her inheritance. Warshawski thus is positioned on the side of the paternal bond against the bad mother, just as she is positioned on the side of corporate stability and inherited wealth against hedonistic criminals. Finally, Warshawski is established here on the side of mystification over truth. After killing Kat's mother, who is trying to drown her daughter, Warshawski asks Murray to print the report that the mother died trying to protect Kat. "You wouldn't want her growing up thinking her mother tried to kill her." In stark contrast to her decision to tell Caroline of her incestuous parentage, the filmic Warshawski lies to reinforce the ideology of the nuclear family. The film ends with the rebellious female detective reinserted in the family, as she and Murray take the place of Kat's now-dead parents.

Thus the film flips pronouns but ultimately maintains the structure and generic rules of the traditional thriller.

Its gender switch acts as a joke, easily laughed off as one returns to the comfortable position of the nuclear family by the end. Yet, this bifurcation between stable opposites, this fragmentation of gender subjectivity, however regressive in the film and in *F Is for Fugitive*, has the potential to open a conceptual space for destabilizing "femininity" as such. *H Is for Homicide,* one of Grafton's later novels, suggests (despite its use of class and ethnic stereotypes) the possibility—however fragile—of a politics that binds rather than divides women, a politics dependent upon the instability of bourgeois ideological constructions of "femininity." "Woman" becomes pluralized into "women," differentiated by ethnicity and class but linked by shifting alliances born of the performative quality of gender.

One first encounters Millhone as she returns from Los Angeles in her VW bug at 3:00 A.M. to her cozy home, recently rebuilt by her landlord Henry Pitts. "Life was good," Millhone muses. "I was female, single, with money in my pocket and enough gas to get home. I had nobody to answer to and no ties to speak of" (HH ['*H' Is for Homicide*] 3). Soon, however, this self-assured Millhone goes under cover for most of the book as "Hannah Moore"—skintight pants, ratted hair, inexpert makeup, and cheap perfume abounding. "What a vamp . . . what a tramp!" Millhone chirps. "I didn't know I had it in me" (HH 48). This literal performance, this parodic persona of the trashy woman, complicates Grafton's already-destabilized gender categories as class becomes a marker of difference *within* "femininity."

"Hannah Moore" accompanies Bibianna Diaz, a woman Millhone's been tailing for auto insurance fraud, back to Los Angeles. Both are more or less abducted by Raymond Maldonado, a kingpin in the fraud industry and Diaz's viciously self-appointed fiance. In her initial interactions with Maldonado, Millhone experiences a kind of exhilaration at the freedoms of her newfound persona. "I was making up Hannah's character as I went along, and it was liberating as hell. She was short-tempered, sarcastic, outspoken and crude. I could get used to this. License to misbehave" (HH 125). This impertinent femininity allies her across class lines with Diaz, whom she tries to protect from Maldonado's advances and abuses.

But Hannah Moore's exaggerated femininity shifts as the book progresses from sass and trash to the vulnerability that also marks Diaz's relationship with Maldonado. As she finds herself trapped in a rundown apartment, making dubious friends with a pit bull, guarded constantly by one of Maldonado's men, no gun and no telephone to call for help, such discursive freedom feels hollow. This disempowered feminine position vis-à-vis male violence provokes a rupture in the text, an intense moment of homesickness. "I felt a squeezing in my stomach," she says, "not an ache, but some process that was almost like grief" (HH 212). Her thoughts slip back to childhood and a child's memories of the horrors of the first moments away from home at summer camp.

This return to home, the safe and comfortable space of the bourgeois, signifies both Millhone's need to escape the suffocation of a specifically gendered class position that she has come dangerously close to adopting and the conventional detective story's need for closure. The return is thus a gesture that provides haven for the individual while leaving unequal social relations intact: Millhone has an out, while Diaz may not. Still, in spite of the conservatism of the resolution, "Hannah Moore's" friendship with Diaz suggests the utopian possibilities of a postmodern approach to identity. Gender in this scheme cannot be contained within stable binary oppositions (masculine and feminine) based on either biology or equally shared oppression; gender categories are themselves decentered, creating the possibility of alliance by exposing the fictionality of a unity based on the erasure of ethnic and class difference.

Complicated questions thus arise about the implications of the gender strategies employed by Paretsky and Grafton. Is Paretsky's vision of authentic truth and justice a function of the epistemology of the detective story, which is built around the masculine paradigm of uncovering the single truth and achieving closure? Does Grafton's poststructuralist destabilization of gender categories have the potential to break out of those narrative conventions? Or is some form of realist epistemology an essential foundation for any substantive political critique and ultimately more powerful than a focus on discursive instability?

The academic paper, like the detective novel, is conventionally structured around the search for evidence, the weighing of hypotheses, the investigation of causation. And like the detective novel, the academic paper climaxes with the privileged understanding, the story that makes all the details fall into place. This paper does not conclude that way. Instead of suppressing the contradictory moments in collaborative writing, we wish to foreground them by breaking into our individual voices for a final commentary:

Timothy Shuker-Haines: While acknowledging the tremendous power of poststructuralist critiques of representation, I want to defend Paretsky's project and ultimately the very concept of closure. Any social critique, including feminism, that is going to remain politically substantive and generative must ground itself, at least implicitly, on a vision of what the world is and what it should be. An exclusive focus on strategies of representation would condemn feminism to academicism, aestheticism, and marginality. To critique oppression we must believe in an alternative justice; to critique falsehood, we must believe in some form of an alternative truth. Such concepts as truth and justice sound hopelessly bourgeois and masculine and are clearly potentially oppressive, but I think we implicitly believe in them; and we are shackling ourselves if we do not articulate them, offer a critique of them, and ultimately fight for them. I see this as Paretsky's project; I think it's a noble one.

Martha Umphrey: Yet it seems to me that, in the realm of fiction, politics and representational strategies are inseparable. Warshawski's sense of identity (at least Paretsky's version of it) is the vehicle for and epistemologically equitable with the sense of closure and catharsis offered in the detective story's generic structure. Thus, it may well be that the conservative ideology of form inhering in the detective story serves to contain as much as to liberate Paretsky's feminist politics. One key insight in current feminist theory, informed by poststructuralism and, I think, more importantly by critiques of "mainstream" feminism offered by women of color, is that just as subjectivity itself is multiple and fragmented, so too is the category of "woman." Closing down the play of meaning by fixing it in the unproblematized identity of a single woman, a female detective, appears in that light as potentially regressive; and thus Grafton's strategies for destabilizing subjectivity appear at least potentially more promising as a means of politicizing the genre than Paretsky's. It's possible, as Gertrude Stein wrote of her own mystery *Blood on the Dining Room Floor,* that "on the whole a detective story does have to have an ending" (Stein 1982, 88) (and, one might add, a detective); but if so, then to perform feminist cultural work that is potentially liberating for all women, the very form of the detective narrative may have to dissolve, as has this essay, into non-resolution.

Notes

1. This figure is not the only type of classic female detective, but she remains one of the best known. For surveys of female detectives, see Kline (1988), Craig and Cadogan (1981), and Reddy (1988).

2. Cawelti (1986) remains a crucial work in analyzing classic and hard-boiled detective fiction.

3. For the most popularized, although problematic because potentially essentializing, analysis of femininity as relational, see Gilligan (1982).

4. Quotations from the novels are cited in the text using the following abbreviations:

   FF: Sue Grafton's *F Is for Fugitive* (1990)

   HH: Sue Grafton's *H Is for Homicide* (1991)

   BS: Sara Paretsky's *Blood Shot* (1988).

5. For an extended theoretical discussion of gender as performative, see Butler (1990).

6. For a summary of theory on the disruptiveness of female sexuality, see E. Ann Kaplan (1980).

References

Butler, Judith. *Gender Trouble: Feminism and the Subversion of Identity.* New York: Routledge, 1990.

Cawelti, John. *Adventure, Mystery, and Romance: Formula Stories as Art and Popular Culture.* Chicago: University of Chicago Press, 1976.

Craig, Patricia, and Mary Cadogan. *The Lady Investigates: Women Detectives and Spies in Fiction.* London: Victor Gollancz, 1981.

Gilligan, Carol. *In a Different Voice: Psychological Theory and Women's Development.* Cambridge, MA: Harvard University Press, 1982.

Glover, David. "The Stuff That Dreams Are Made of: Masculinity, Femininity and the Thriller." In *Gender, Genre, and Narrative Pleasure,* edited by Derek Longhurst, 67-83. London: Unwin Hyman, 1989.

Grafton, Sue. *F Is for Fugitive.* New York: Henry Holt and Company, 1989. Reprint. New York: Bantam, 1990.

———. *H Is for Homicide.* New York: Henry Holt and Company, 1991.

Hirsch, Foster. *The Dark Side of the Screen: Film Noir.* San Diego, CA: A. S. Barnes, 1981.

Kaplan, E. Ann. "Introduction." In *Women in Film Noir,* edited by E. Ann Kaplan, 1-5. London: British Film Institute Publishing, 1980.

Kline, Kathleen. *The Woman Detective: Gender and Genre.* Urbana: University of Illinois Press, 1988.

Paretsky, Sara. *Blood Shot.* New York: Delacorte, 1988. Reprint. New York: Dell, 1989.

Place, J. A., and L. S. Peterson. "Some Visual Motifs of Film Noir." In *Movies and Methods: An Anthology,* edited by Bill Nichols, 325-38. Berkeley: University of California Press, 1976.

Reddy, Maureen. *Sisters in Crime: Feminism and the Crime Novel.* New York: Continuum, 1988.

Schrader, Paul. "Notes on Film Noir." In *Film Genre Reader,* edited by Barry Keith Grant, 169-82. Austin: University of Texas Press, 1986.

Stein, Gertrude. *Blood on the Dining Room Floor.* Alice B. Toklas, 1948. Reprint. Berkeley, CA: Creative Arts Book Company, 1982.

Taylor, Barry. "*Gorky Park*: American Dreams in Siberia." In *Gender, Genre, and Narrative Pleasure,* edited by Derek Longhurst, 136-56. London: Unwin Hyman, 1989.

Samuel Coale (essay date 2000)

SOURCE: Coale, Samuel. "The Mystery of Mysteries: Rites, Reasons, and Resolutions." In *The Mystery of Mysteries: Cultural Differences and Designs,* pp. 1-34. Bowling Green, Ohio: Bowling Green State University Popular Press, 2000.

[*In the following essay, Coale traces the literary origins of the modern mystery novel through the works of such authors as Tony Hillerman, Amanda Cross, James Lee Burke, and Walter Mosley. Coale also speculates on the ways in which these particular authors have pursued social and cultural issues in their works, "which lie outside the usual landscape of the genre's formula."*]

It is the nature of mystery novels to perform their own demise. They must also serve a pre-conceived formula as they simultaneously self-destruct. The solution that usually concludes this process necessarily undermines it, since once it is discovered, the fiction is concluded. Such a structure presents a distinct chain of events in a horizontal sequence that purports to reflect and constitute the social and historical external world we inhabit (Bonnycastle). In doing so, however, any other "mysteries"—the nature of human choice, of evil, of circumstance and accident—must be intentionally marginalized and evaded, repressed and hidden for the self-eviscerating process to take place.

Popular mysteries rely on formula. The re-enactment of that formula and, therefore, the process of the narrative itself must include the initial set-up of the cast, the characters, and the context in which they operate; the crime that disrupts all of these; the discourse of investigation and inquiry, usually built upon a series of interviews and interrogations; and the final solution or recognition of the underlying truth of the crime and the culprit who performed it.

The appeal of the mystery formula is understandable—and profitable.[1] It creates a rational world amid an irrational or at the very least a non-rational world. It substitutes rational discourse for metaphysical speculation, which nevertheless relies on the metaphysical certainty that the truth is out there. It underscores faith in a systematic series of revelations in place of ultimate unknowns, and in doing so must marginalize that unknown territory as best it can so as not to sink the ship. The formula clearly supports and upholds the western belief and faith in objective discourse and careful analysis, or as Anne Williams has suggested, in the Patriarchal Symbolic order of language, logic, chronology, and genealogy, the organization of a male-oriented culture which provides "a relatively stable arrangement of chains of association . . . a basic structure of interpersonal relationships" (263).

All such literary formulae play to our sense of expectation within severe limitations at the same time that they reinforce our desire to believe that the world works in such a recognizable and reasonable manner. They replay our sense that this is the way the world always works, and that in our reading of these generic texts, we re-enact the similar situations and expectations of each of these formulaic stories. As Joyce Carol Oates suggests, "Readers of genre fiction, unlike readers of what we presume to call 'literary fiction,' assume a tacit contract between themselves and the writer: they understand that they will be manipulated, but the question is how? and when? and with what skill? and to what purpose? However plot-ridden, fantastical, or absurd, populated by whatever pseudo-characters, genre fiction is always resolved" (*New York Times* Book Review 31 Oct. 1996: 50). We experience not the shock but the comfort of recognition, knowing full well that genre fiction supports the status-quo of contemporary conventional opinion and does so by avoiding the ambiguity and the uncertainty of the more complex world in which we live. In submitting ourselves to the re-enactment of the formula, therefore, we preserve the present order of things.[2]

Such formulas play directly into the distinctions that Jacques Barzun has made between the tale and the novel in "The Novel Turns Tale" (131). While the novel "professes to illuminate life by pretending to be history," the tale "is a narrative too, but [it] appeals to curiosity, wonder and the love of ingenuity. If it 'studies' anything, it is the calculating mind rather than the spontaneous emotions, physical predicaments rather than spiritual." As John Fowles comments directly after this, writers like Conan Doyle belong "to the tale-tellers, in the long modern line from Poe to Ross Macdonald." As Barzun continues, "One goes to a tale because it is a marvellous invention, because it is ingenious, full of suspense and concentrated wisdom . . . and [because it] appeases the heart by its love of reason" (131). The mystery formula, then, springs more directly from the tale than from the more "literary" novel.

There are literally too many excellent mystery writers to choose from, but I have selected my own personal favorites to discuss, who by now have created a significant and diverse body of work and in doing so can stand as examples of many others: Tony Hillerman, Amanda Cross (Carolyn Heilbrun), James Lee Burke, and Walter Mosley. They pursue social and cultural differences in their mysteries, which lie outside the usual landscape of the genre's formula—Hillerman's Navajos, Cross' feminist academics, Burke's Cajun-Southern Louisianans, and Mosley's urban blacks. Often the confrontation between formula and content results in some very interesting twists and fictional situations. As Michiko Kakutani has suggested, "By manipulating the conventions of the detective story, writers are able to comment both on its formal limitations and on the limitations of its philosophical outlook" (37).

Nevertheless all four writers have chosen to write within the time-honored framework of the mystery formula. Thus, as Martin E. Marty might define them, they situate their tribal subjects and values within a popular totalizing perspective.[3] That choice necessarily demands various strategies, as they attempt to remain true to both cultural differences (which, in many cases, actually contradict the basic premises of the mystery) and the structure of popular fiction. It is this on-going process in their fiction that has led to this study.

These four authors and several previous and contemporary ones—such as Dashiell Hammett (who is one of the several members of the hard-boiled "school" of earlier American mystery writers), P. D. James (who probably spearheads the modern revival of the British Golden Age of such mystery writers as Dorothy Sayers and Agatha Christie), John Fowles, Tim O'Brien, and Joan Didion, among others—both subvert and maintain the mystery formula. The form has become so widespread that such very different writers as Gabriel Garcia Marquez and Paul Auster have also used it in their fiction in a calculated attempt to undermine its rational and linear construction of experience.

The linear structure of the mystery formula stems in part from the philosophy of Rene Descartes, certainly one of the best exemplars and founding patriarchs of the belief in rationalism. "Ever since Descartes and the Rationalists elevated humans above nature by emphasizing our ability to *think* rather than merely to act and *feel,* Western ideology has valued almost exclusively the ability to solve problems through rational, linear, conscious thought," suggests David L. Calof (13). Descartes' method, which preceded but proved to be a great influence upon the Enlightenment in the eighteenth and nineteenth centuries, initiates an empirical procedure in which he re-created a series of steps followed in a logical order based on his own immediate experience and observation often without due regard for system and theory. Such observations, he thought, could be verified or disproved by further observation or experiment. In this process he, like the mystery formula, had to repress certain "ultimate" or metaphysical mysteries, or at least try to finesse them, and at the same time to produce a methodology which relied upon cause and effect, the underlying faith of what came to be the belief in western progress heralded and upheld by the Enlightenment. In re-tracing Descartes' steps, we can see both what the analytical mystery formula can accomplish and what it must marginalize.

Descartes at first accepted what his senses revealed to him and then doubted them. His senses could obscure and confuse him in terms, for example, of how he actually saw the sun and what he knew about its real size and dimensions. He assumed that he had to be a thinking thing, that his own consciousness and his awareness of his very existence proved to be one and the same thing. Therefore his mind had to be separate from his senses. It must dominate the body, since it "is distinct from and superior to matter" (Descartes 19). In effect he recognized in his conscious self "the will to dominate, to control events, [and] to eliminate chance and the irrational" (21). By examining what his senses revealed to him, by using those senses, and by combining them with his memory and understanding, he could therefore "link and join present knowledge to past" and thereby unearth the causes of whatever errors he had made (168).

From this methodology Descartes arrived at the idea that the facts of consciousness and of the world, of subject and object, mind and matter, can be misinterpreted but once known are based solely on a strict causality and physical laws which lead inevitably to predictability (22). Every effect or consequence must have its agent or motive, every result its antecedent, every outcome its determinant, exactly in the same manner of his own conscious methodology. Thus, the cosmos reproduced his methodological approach: "The laws which govern the physical world and which will continue to govern it to the end of all time may be discovered and used by man for his own ends," and the facts of existence, based mathematically as they must be on extension and motion, must reflect "the notion of the unity of mathematics" (16). If outward signs suggest appearances only, these can be re-interpreted in the light of experience and understanding and the underlying, predictable prior cause known.

When it comes to the existence of God, however, and other metaphysical speculations, Descartes must fudge things a bit. First of all he makes it clear to himself that he can distinguish dream from reality, sleep from waking. When one is awake and only when one is awake, memory connects all things. Only when one is awake can one know the place from which memory comes, the present place in which one exists, and the time in which these appear and thus link all these perceptions to the rest of one's conscious life. Proof appears to reside in the belief that one can distinguish consciousness from the unconscious because of all of the above. Of course this is precisely what occurs in the mystery formula. Signs may reveal themselves as clues and not merely as mysteriously elusive icons in dreams, because the formula excludes the latter and focuses on the former.

In proving the existence of God, Descartes asserts that things outside the mind can project and imprint themselves upon it, producing ideas within it. There also exist very real differences between actual objects and the ideas generated or inaugurated by those objects in the form of ideas. God is obviously infinite in a way that the human mind and the physically visible world cannot possibly be. Therefore an infinite God, a first cause, must produce the objects which imprint themselves on the human mind, as the infinite can and must produce the finite. And the pictures, images, and ideas that the mind produces must themselves lead back to that first cause, as the finite must lead back by its very limitations to the infinite, which alone can contain all things. If one, therefore, has the idea of God, God must exist, for the idea must have been put there. That idea of infinite perfection can only come from an infinite being, since human imperfection itself could never conjure up such a thing: "I would not, nevertheless, have the idea of an infinite substance, since I am a finite being, unless the idea had been put into me by some substance which was truly infinite. . . . The idea, I say, of this supremely perfect and infinite being is entirely true" (Descartes 125). So Descartes' will to power must itself come from somewhere else, and he must submit to that infinite will that must exist to create his own. Therefore God as a first cause must exist. Such assumptions would crumble under Nietzschean scrutinies and contemporary skeptical strategies and would never make it into the mystery formula. While Descartes in his time felt the need to prove the existence of an infinite God, the mystery formula obviously does not. And Descartes' own methodology reveals its shortcomings in producing a logical but "bizarre" series of assumptions that belie his own formulaic procedures.

The nature of Descartes' God partakes of the nature of geometry: extension, cause, and effect have helped to produce him. But the assumptions Descartes must rely upon to make what we would call a leap of faith cannot stand up under the scrutiny of his own methodology and thus of course must be discarded from most Enlightenment thought. "It is very obvious that there must be at least as much reality in the cause as in its effect. . . . the cause must equally be a thinking thing, and possess within it the idea of all the perfections that I attribute to the divine cause" (Descartes 128, 131, 134). Obvious to whom? Attributions by whom? Descartes continues: "Everything I perceive clearly and distinctly cannot fail to be true. . . . I know already that I cannot be deceived in judgments the reasons of which I know clearly. . . . But even if I were asleep, everything which is presented to my mind clearly, is absolutely true" (149).

In accepting Descartes' analytical approach as one of the most influential within western scientific and Enlightenment thought, one must necessarily lop off those other parts of it which today strike us at best as clever and at worst absurd. But if one part can be doubted, the whole must be doubted as well. Descartes admits that his proof for the existence of God "is apprehended by the intuition rather than by deductive reasoning" (20) and yet at the same time confesses, "I notice further that this power of imagination which is in me, in so far as it differs from the power of conceiving,

is in no way necessary to my nature or essence . . . that is to say, to the essence of my mind; for, even if I did not have it, without doubt I should still remain the same as I am now, whence it seems that one can conclude that it depends on something different from my mind" (151). Thus, Descartes must marginalize and exclude those very speculations and uncertainties that the mystery formula must. In doing so he re-enacts the built-in marginalization and provides us with the limitations of his own analytical reasoning upon which the believer in western progressive thought and the reader of mysteries must depend. At the philosophical core of the modern method, then, rests the contradictions and assumptions that must be transcended or buried for that method to function as we popularly know it.

The Cartesian discourse at the heart of the western enlightened tradition of philosophical and analytical thought was, of course, preceded by certain religious and/or mythic patterns in western culture. W. H. Auden, for instance, in "The Guilty Vicarage," "saw detective fiction as the Christian morality play restated in modern dress" (95). C. Day Lewis described the pattern of the detective novel as formalized as a religious ritual, comparing the crime or murder to sin, the criminal to the high priest of this rite, and the detective to a yet higher power who appears on behalf of the victim of such rites (400). And of course in the very ritual of discovering, exorcizing, and expelling the scapegoat, the criminal, in the midst of normal society, the mystery formula performs an act of exorcizing all guilt and criminality, guilt being that universal psychological condition that underlies everything from Oedipus' crimes to Cain's. "In the beginning there was guilt: the basic motive for reading crime fiction," Julian Symons insists, "is the religious one of exorcizing the guilt of the individual or the group through ritual and symbolic sacrifice" (9). After all "victim, murder, investigation, all have a hieratic and ritual quality" (12).

As Peter Brooks makes clear, a certain psychological pattern, what he calls Freud's master plot, also underlies and supports the rites and patterns of the narrative in general, the mystery in particular, and the Cartesian discourse which parallels it (287-99). For Freud life ultimately desires death; the need for an ending is contained within the organism itself; ends are implicit in beginnings. Thus, the beginning of any narrative initiates desire and anticipation for what is to come. And the end results in a recognition or revelation which completes that initial desire and arousal: "What operates in the text through repetition is the death instinct, the drive toward the end. . . . the narrative must tend toward its end, seek illumination in its own death. Yet this must be the right death, the correct end" (Brooks 293-94). That end in the mystery, of course, involves the adding up of specific clues which, if done correctly, produces the final revelation and resolution. And the pursuit of those clues occupies the detective's consciousness with a vengeance. He or she is obsessed in terms of finding out exactly what has happened. The web of the text re-enacts this sense of demonic possession, this pursuit of the answer, just as clearly as does the detective himself or herself. Text and character, therefore, perform similar actions.

Unlike other more "open" or literary narratives, however, the mystery with its clues, its demonic drive within the text, and its detective to reveal, discover, master, and exhume what has already happened are themselves carefully enclosed within the mystery formula. The formula itself is a repetition of previous mystery formulas, welcoming the reader into its already known and recognized patterns. All the psychic drives toward repetition and death, including the narrative's own, are carefully embodied in the structure of the formula, thus encapsulating and making comfortable those very psychic drives that it so regularly unleashes and reins in. In a mystery the text and the reader return to the origins of the plot that the author has known from the beginning. We are reassured that things can be unearthed and spelled out. The return to origins usually does not involve a return of the repressed but sets us on our formulaic way to clear identities, verifiable explanations, and certain truths. Thus, mysteries are, at least, doubly repetitive, and they seal their own comforting fates.

Quasi-religious rites and psychological explanations, however, only parallel the formula that the mystery embodies. They allegorize the process and in a way substitute themselves for it, not finally explaining how the formula actually functions. As Barbara Johnson has said, psychological analysis is "capable of finding only itself wherever it looks. . . . [It is an] act . . . of mere *recognition* of the expected" (34). While it is true that "the theoretical frame of reference which governs recognition is a constitutive element in the blindness of any interpretive insight" (342), it is also true that narratives are more dynamic than static, more "operational" than "timeless," and it is to Brooks' credit that he points out the dynamics of narrative as well, viewing it as essentially sequential and successive, a re-enactment of a plot and story.

Every mystery also suggests a novel of manners, a creature of its own time and social milieu, both the author's and the reader's. We view the characters, as the author has created them, as visible products of their society, dominated by the manners of that society which "exert control [and are] a determinant upon [their] actions" (Tuttleton 10). Thus, these characters seem to be realistically drawn and representative of certain social classes, ethnic groups, economic backgrounds, and the like. And this sociological determinant encourages us to view the murder, say, as a "dramatic violation of com-

monly held ethical values" (Tuttleton 12), a disruption of conventional manners and taboos. No wonder so many mystery writers from Robert Barnard to Amanda Cross write satirically and ironically, since in effect they are criticizing certain social myths by reason of their mysteries and characters. Cross, for instance, attacks and undermines the American myth of homogeneity and political egalitarianism by revealing the clear stratification of social groups, the complexities of their customs, and the gender biases of their myths and outlooks. Barnard works similarly in satirizing the profound class consciousness of his English characters.

Much of this, of course, has contributed to the popularity of mysteries in the last one hundred and fifty years. The formula itself comforts and clarifies. As David S. Reynolds tells us about Poe and the invention of the detective story, the mystery re-enacts the "ultimate imaginary victory over the irrational. . . . [Poe's] invention of the modern detective story stems directly from . . . [his superimposition of] ideas from contemporary science or pseudoscience upon sensational situations. . . . In creating the brainy detective, Poe gained victory over the popular Subversive imagination" (247, 238, 248). Marcus Klein proves that the private eye was indeed the product of the Gilded Age and rapid urbanization in America, what he refers to as the "ghettoization of urban America" (5), and the growth of finance capitalism, the industrial revolution, and mass immigration. Klein's detective is obviously very different from the kind Julian Symons describes. Symons scrutinizes only British writers from the Golden Age, whose detectives are products "of a class in society that felt it had everything to lose by social change" (11). One thinks immediately of Dupin, Holmes, Lord Peter Wimsey, and Hercule Poirot. These white, upper-class, brainy fellows from the 1830s onwards reassured the reading public, members of a more privileged class which had the time to read such things, that "those who tried to disturb the established order were always discovered and punished" (Symons 11).

And yet part of the fascination with the mystery formula resides in what it both tries to exclude and marginalize and what it cannot. First of all, the formula must severely restrict its scope in order to function, and that restriction previously exists within the limitations of the Cartesian analytical point of view, itself restricted by what the mystery formula tends to ignore, i.e., Descartes' more metaphysical speculations, despite his attempts to embody them in his methodology. But it must also exclude other dimensions of the wider vision of mystery. The formula must marginalize inscrutable enigmas and problems, puzzles which perpetually baffle and perplex and remain inexplicable, existing beyond one's powers to discover, understand, or explain. It must exclude religious mysteries that can be known only by revelation and cannot fully be comprehended.

It must also skirt religious sacraments and the secret religious rites of certain mystery cults. The philosophical riddles involved with the (possible) freedom of human choice—why, for instance, does the murderer choose to murder? What entices one to cross the line?—the existence of all kinds and degrees of evil in the world, and (possible) pre-determined acts of hubris, fate, and even accident must be, in some way, ignored. Anything that may suggest the unknowable and the unfathomable, whether religious or otherwise, must be virtually and carefully excluded from the text for it to operate successfully within the boundaries of its formula. The mystery writer, as David I. Grossvogel suggests, "establishes surrogates for the beyond on this side of the divide . . . inviting a mock penetration of the unknown" and by inventing such incarnations hopes to short-circuit the larger issues he may stumble upon (13).

TRADITIONAL MYSTERIES: HAMMETT AND JAMES

The story of the invention and development of the detective and crime narrative has been told successfully in many other places. The line from Poe's Dupin to Doyle's Holmes, Sayers' Wimsey, and Christie's Poirot, among others, is clear and clean, and such diverse writers as the American Dashiell Hammett and the British P. D. James build on this tradition, the former by rejecting the "British country house" atmosphere and plots, the latter by extending and deepening them.

Hammett at one time worked as a Pinkerton detective. In the United States the first police force in New York was organized in the 1840s, and it led to Allan Pinkerton's founding the first detective agency in 1873. Interestingly enough the Pinkerton operative's main job was union-busting, infiltrating the labor unions as a spy to report on the radical agitators and their plans: "Labor spying was the main source of revenue for the agency" (Klein 176). Pinkerton agents were still actively involved in strike breaking during and after World War One. In the Ludlow Coal Strike in Colorado, they were deputized by the local sheriff and involved in the massacre of miners. Hammett fictionalizes the situation with his Continental Op in *Red Harvest.* History thus underscores the essentially conservative if not reactionary basis of what would become the mystery formula.

The real American breakthrough in the history of the mystery came in the 1920s and the 1930s in the rise of *Black Mask,* the most famous of the crime pulp magazines, which were themselves an outgrowth of the sensationalistic Dime Novels of the late nineteenth century. *Black Mask* and others created the stylistic frame for the hard-boiled short story and in doing so insisted on simplicity, realism, a terse and minimalist language, and "the classless, restless man of American democracy, who spoke the language of the street" (Klein

182), in the words of Ross Macdonald, the American mystery writer. Real detectives had been described as rogues, thieves, and deceivers, as lowlifes as much affected by the criminal world as trying to correct it. Wrote early critics of the trade, "the life of a detective is a living lie. . . . [he is] the outgrowth of a diseased and corrupted state of things, and is, consequently, morally diseased himself. His very existence is a satire upon society" (Klein 156, 158). Such creatures or operatives embodied no moral values themselves; they were close to the genuine secrets of how American society functioned in all its criminality and deception and were professionals in the fundamental sense of the word. The image of the tough, half-criminal detective preceded Hammett's apotheosis of him, but the manner of presentation of the *Black Mask* writers in general and Hammett in particular—he began by reviewing detective fiction in the magazine—created a "fundamentally American" type (Klein 193).

"We were trying to get murder away from the upper classes, the week-end house party and the vicar's rose-garden," wrote Raymond Chandler in 1944 in his famous essay, "The Gentle Art of Murder," "and back to the people who are really good at it" (Klein 180). Consequently the new breed of private eyes or policemen exuded a deliberate cynicism, proud of, as Marcus Klein has put it, the "integrity of their disenchantment," wearing their "civic despair as style" (179, 194). These characters opposed the dandified Holmeses and Poirots as hardened products of a tough urban milieu that surpassed the idealized country house and village in mystery fiction. Frederick Karl relates detective and western fiction to the combat novel in American fiction and suggests that these popular offshoots brought "back the sole frontier remaining to us and provide[d] an alternative to bourgeois society, which deals death to the instinctual life" (95). Such fiction reawakened these basic American themes, within which "violence establishes a purity with its own rules, its own field of force" (Karl 25).

The literary triumph of these tough-guy tales existed in the terse and minimalist style Hammett and others after him honed and perfected. For Claude-Edmonde Magny, Hammett employed "the aesthetics of the stenographic record," based on the aesthetics of American films. His sparse, objective prose relied upon the use of juxtaposition, ellipses, the change of camera angles, and the crosscuts that film relied upon to tell its story. Such a behaviorist approach in which "the psychological reality of a person . . . is limited to what can be perceived by a purely external observer [and is essentially] reduced to a succession of acts" (40), proved to be immensely successful in the rendering of a mystery, since the author worked "to conceal the essential fact from the reader in order to oblige him to reconstruct it, little by little, by conjectures and make it gradually emerge

116

from the matrix of mystery in which it was hidden" (Magny 49). Such a manner also hid characters' motives the way Hemingway managed to do in his best fictions and added to the aura of mystery and deceit. This style continued in the mysteries of Chandler, Macdonald, Robert B. Parker, George V. Higgins, Elmore Leonard, and James Lee Burke.

Sam Spade in Hammett's *The Maltese Falcon* (1929), of his five novels arguably his masterpiece, is one of the first and most famous tough-guy detectives. Calm, self-possessed, poised, wary, he speaks tersely and observes quietly. Nothing gets in the way of his investigations, and his values are relatively simple: "When a man's partner is killed he's supposed to do something about it. It doesn't make any difference what you thought of him" (Hammett 226). When it comes to the possibility of love, even that won't interfere. As he tells Brigid O'Shaughnessy, "All we've got is the fact that maybe you love me and maybe I love you. . . . I've been through it before" (227). And despite his wheeling and dealing and innate cynicism, "Don't be too sure I'm as crooked as I'm supposed to be" (227).

Spade is very resourceful when it comes to money. He takes $200 from Brigid early on, even though he doesn't believe her story. He takes $200 from Joel Cairo to search for the falcon, even though Cairo's interests may be different from O'Shaughnessy's. He takes $50 as a down-payment from another client on the side. He keeps $1,000 of the $10,000 Casper Gutman gives him for his trouble. And when Cairo offers him $5,000 for the bird, he tells Gutman it was $10,000, so that Gutman goes on to offer him $25,000 down, $25,000 later, and $500,000 when he gets and sells the falcon.

Gender roles are clearly drawn. The only other men who aspire to Spade's expertise are Sid Wise, Spade's sharp-eyed lawyer, and Casper Gutman who admires Spade's skills in the game as much as Spade admires his. The unskilled others include the homosexual Cairo, the young inexperienced thug named Wilmer Cook, and Spade's easy-going lout of a partner, Miles Archer. Both Wise and the clever but fat bulbous Gutman are aptly named.

Spade's attitude toward women is well known. They are either children, sisters, angels or babes. "God, you women" (107), Spade sputters to the whining jealous Iva Archer. To his sidekick, Effie Perrine, whose intuition proves to be false—she dislikes Iva and supports Brigid—he exclaims revealingly, "You're a damned good man, sister" (167). Brigid, of course, exudes sex appeal and cunning, both of which Spade finds impossible to resist despite or more likely because of her lies and deviousness. And Brigid even stoops to doping Gutman's seventeen-year-old daughter Rhea as part of his plan.

The social Darwinism of crude capitalism and the nightmarish accidents of life embody the world that Spade inhabits in the true tough-guy tradition. Falcon or no, everybody is a crook; everybody has an angle. The labyrinthine levels of double-cross and triple-cross boggle the mind. The history of the falcon itself is one long tale of greed and thievery, and despite the references to the Saracens, the Emperor Charles, and the Templars, Gutman insists, "We all know that the Holy Wars to them . . . were largely a matter of loot" (128). Spade would agree: "Most things in San Francisco can be bought, or taken" (56).

The story of Flitcraft, which Spade tells, points to the essential randomness of life, as well as the repetitious routines and habits that people rely upon to evade that darker vision. A beam falls and just misses Flitcraft, and he recognizes that "life could be ended for him at random. . . . [so] he would change his life at random by simply going away" (66). This he does, deserting his family and disappearing. But once away he re-establishes his old habits, now based on his developing vision of exactly what had happened to him: "He adjusted himself to beams falling, and then no more of them fell, and he adjusted himself to them not falling" (67). Within the intricate maze of Hammett's plot lies the irrational sudden event that can unhinge any attempt at constructing a life that appears to be clean, orderly, sane and responsible. That amoral eruption, a glimpse into the abyss, undercuts the binary morality of the mystery formula, which is still played out to the end, however battered and bruised, and calls attention to its very artifice. It's a fine balancing act on Hammett's part and lends Spade a certain philosophical perspective, in which he consistently expects the unexpected, trusts no one except his own instincts, and realizes the very gamesmanship of his career.

But it is Hammett's style that succeeds best of all and embodies his dark vision. The minimalist approach, swift and enigmatic, necessarily masks human motive and reflects Spade's self-possessed approach to things, as detail stands out to be observed and interpreted during the process of the investigation: "He talked in a steady matter-of-fact voice that was devoid of emphasis or pauses, though now and then he repeated a sentence slightly rearranged, as if it were important that each detail be related exactly as it had happened" (63). Hammett's emphasis on eyes reveals the nature of his method in which he focuses most often on characters gazing at one another, at cigarettes, at drinks, seeing and being seen:

> She *looked* at Spade again. He did not in any way respond to the appeal in her *eyes*. He leaned against the door-frame and *observed* the occupants of the room with the polite detached air of a disinterested *spectator*. The girl turned her *eyes* up to Dundy's. Her *eyes* were wide and dark and earnest.
>
> (77, italics mine)

Remarks Spade to Brigid: "You're good. You're very good. It's chiefly your eyes, I think" (36). "He stood beside the fireplace and looked at her with eyes that studied, weighed, judged her without pretense that they were not studying, weighing, judging her" (56).

Hammett conjures up his characters by using stark and telling physical details. Casper Gutman reveals "a great soft egg of a belly . . . with bulbous pink cheeks. . . . As he advanced to Spade all his bulbs rose and shook and fell separately with each step" (108). In contrast Spade is all sharp edges, "his chin a jutting v under the more flexible v of his mouth. . . . The v *motif* was picked up again by thickish brows rising outward" (3). Brigid reveals "cobalt-blue eyes that were both shy and probing. . . . She wore two shades of blue. . . . The hair curling from under her blue hat was darkly red, her full lips more brightly red" (3-4). Fight scenes are carefully detailed, gesture by gesture: "The elbow struck him beneath the cheek-bone. . . . Cairo let the pistol go the instant that Spade's fingers touched it. . . . The fist struck Cairo's face. . . . Cairo shut his eyes and was unconscious" (47, 48).

At the same time Hammett's terse dialogue suggests an almost Jamesian fascination with jockeying for position, keeping one's agenda hidden and masked, creating a pose that necessarily fits into the external situation, and playing a role crisply and succinctly. One thinks of Brigid's rhetorical plea to Spade in her use of repetitious phrases carefully cultivated: "I haven't lived a good life. . . . I've been bad. . . . You know I'm not all bad, don't you? . . . Help me, Mr. Spade. . . . You can help me. Help me" (36). Spade is quick to pick up on Brigid's set pieces: "You told me that this afternoon in the same words, same tone. It's a speech you've practiced" (57). And the dialogue between Spade and Gutman reveals two cunning men at the top of their craft.

To turn from the very American Hammett to the very British P. D. James is to leap from Spade's cynical one-liners to Adam Dalgliesh's more brooding and refined reveries. In fact in the eyes of most literary and popular critics, P. D. James in her full-bodied, richly detailed, and psychologically probing mysteries has extended and enhanced the tradition of Agatha Christie and Dorothy Sayers, as in many ways have Elizabeth George and Martha Grimes, American authors writing in the British tradition. James has not only continued "the novel of straight detection" (Symons xiv); "she has pushed, as a modernist must, against the boundaries of the classical detective story" and been "called a natural successor to Sayers [with] the same care in plotting . . . the accuracy of minor points . . . and like Sayers gives us dialogue that is convincing rather than entertaining" (Tuttleton 212, 211). At the same time she "persistently raise[s] questions that reflect such evidence

of ourselves as we have been able to gather, about honesty, duty, courage, and all those virtues" (Winks 97), thus deepening the psychological compulsions and moral issues her characters must face.

In James' case the tough-guy private eye in contemporary mystery fiction has been superseded by the more humane, more flawed detective. P. D. James' police detective, Adam Dalgliesh, for example, occupies a position similar to other modern detectives, in that he is given an interesting and intriguing personality, complete with his own self-doubts and contradictions: "He is introspective, brooding, mournful" (Symons 61). He is "the poet who no longer writes poetry. The lover who substitutes technique for commitment. The policeman disillusioned with policing" (61). As James herself has said, "I made my detective a very private and detached man who uses his job to save himself from involvement with other human beings because of tragedies in his own life" (Cooper-Clark 21). He would fit Glenn W. Most's interpretation that "the true mystery in a mystery novel is . . . the nature of the detective who solves it" (342). And Richard Alewyn's assessment that detectives are essentially romantic artists, "the ones who know how to read the clues and to interpret the signs which remain invisible or incomprehensible to normal men, [revealing as romantics do] an everyday and peaceful deceptive surface, with abysses of mystery and danger underneath" (77, 76).

For the most part James' mysteries—which include *A Taste for Death* (1986), *Devices and Desires* (1990), and *Original Sin* (1995)—have also been described as essentially novels of manners focusing on the professional upper-middle classes. Although she displays "an almost obsessional zest in describing furniture and fittings" (Symons 211), most critics have praised her innovative subjects and sites, such as a home for incurables, a publishing house, and a forensic research laboratory. Such a view suggests that readers see and assess her characters, as she has created them, as visible products of a particular society, dominated by the manners of that society. Such significant conflict and confrontation, therefore, arise from the clash between professional manner and personal distress.

But there is an even greater dimension to the mystery formula that James has pursued. As we have seen, certain religious and mythic patterns in western culture extend and deepen the Cartesian discourse at the heart of the western enlightened tradition of empirical and analytical thought, which itself was built upon Judeo-Christian traditions. The mystery can resemble a Christian morality play, as well as a novel of manners—one does not necessarily exclude the other and might, in fact, reinforce one another—with all its formal and ritualistic characteristics, complete with exorcism, expulsion, guilt, and a final scapegoat.[4]

As Dennis Porter has pointed out, P. D. James "clings to one central concept of Christian faith, namely Pauline caritas," a religion of love and self-sacrifice, in a world which seems to have outlived both, mired in its own evils and self-obsessions, and offers us "models of right conduct" which suggest that "to read one of her novels is to risk a kind of conversion."[5] Her novels reveal what Elaine Pagels has described as "the struggle within Christian tradition between the profoundly human view that 'otherness' is evil and the words of Jesus that reconciliation is divine" (184). And in doing so James capitalizes on the modernist interest in myth and psychology, in ritual and possible redemption, within the boundaries of the rationalistic formula of the traditional mystery.

For the rite of exorcism to take place, James creates a world that is pervaded by sin, guilt, human culpability, and complicity, a dark world full of the darker ambiguities of human choice and motive that always outlast and transcend the single apprehension of the murderer. Guilt spreads and stains the whole of her domain. "It isn't as simple as that to solve the problem," James has said. "The problem may be solved but other problems are left unsolved, because these are problems of the human heart and problems about which perhaps nothing effective can be done" (Cooper-Clark 19). In effect, as she continues, "Detective fiction may be a substitute for the old morality plays[, but] because the detective is increasingly becoming a human being, that part of his personality which is evil has to be shown. So, to an extent, this destroys the old ideas that you have the good and evil, the dark and the light" (18).

James' sense of a world stained by sin and guilt, within which love and self-sacrifice may be possible, a descent of grace in a world of evil, parallels in many ways Paul Ricoeur's ideas on the subject in *The Symbolism of Evil.* "It is in confession," Larry D. Bouchard suggests about Ricoeur's thought, "that we most closely approach the inward experience of evil," and the primary symbols "in the language of confession [are] stain, sin, and guilt" (39). According to Bouchard, Ricoeur believes that "the development from one symbol to the next—the turning from exteriority (stain) to interiority (guilt) through the broken relation of humanity 'before God' (sin)—is dialectical, not chronological" (39). In other words each interacts with the other. Murder provides the exterior stain, James pursues the interior guilt of her characters, and both participate, in the characters' estrangement from one another and from themselves, in the religious act of sin. The pervasive vision conjures up "the terrifying fact of the irreducibility of evil. . . . to the extent that original sin makes guilt inevitable and objective, there is a penultimate possibility of the tragic, but to the extent that the ultimate answer to the demonic is not heroic defiance but saving grace, the tragic is transcended" (Bouchard 46, 92). The mystery formula and

James' sense of caritas and love transcend the tragic in her novels, but the inevitable stain of guilt found there does not.

James' titles often suggest this religious and moral vision. *Devices and Desires* (1989) comes from the Anglican prayer of confession. *Original Sin* (1995) speaks for itself. And in discussing the final choice of the title, *Innocent Blood* (1980), James relates that choice directly to the Bible: "It immediately struck me as a very good title because it had this ambiguity about it as to whether the blood she had inherited [Philippa in the novel] was or was not innocent. And, of course, it ties up with the section in Ecclesiastes about it being an abomination to the Lord that one should shed innocent blood" (Cooper-Clark 32).

In short, in her mysteries James does not exclude or marginalize inscrutable enigmas and puzzles which perpetually baffle, perplex, and remain inexplicable. She often focuses on essential religious mysteries which involve a scapegoat and the exorcism of his/her crimes, some of which can be suggested only by revelation and cannot be fully comprehended. Essentially murder victimizes all of her characters, and that sense of victimhood pervades all of her novels. "It is, in short, no surprise," writes Dennis Porter, "if her plots recall both the bloody familial dramas of Greek myths and the tortured family romance of psychoanalytic theory" (16).

At first *The Children of Men* (1993), a dystopian novel in the tradition of Aldous Huxley's *Brave New World,* may seem an anomaly in James' fiction. It is not a mystery but a cautionary tale of the future in the year 2021. No baby has been born since 1995, and those that were born in that year, called Omegas, have become cruel, arrogant, and violent. England is run by the tyrant-warden, Xan Lyppiatt, who has organized private armies, a state security police, distant penal colonies, a system to import slaves known as Sojourners, and the Quietus ceremony which ritualizes the mass suicide of the old. The narrative is almost evenly divided between the diary entries of Theodore Faron, historian of the Victorian age, a self-declared, uncommitted, dispassionate observer (and cousin of the infamous, all-powerful Xan), and the third-person narrative which James writes to implicate him in the circumstances that come to surround and seduce him. The plot of this fable and Faron's decision to participate in it reveal that sense of self-sacrifice, love, and caritas—the jacket painting is a detail from Bartolomeo Schedone's "Christian Charity"—that James sees as the only possible way toward some kind of human if not traditionally religious redemption.

The text is saturated with religious imagery and yearnings. A revolutionary committee which opposes Xan's rule of terror and treachery calls itself the Five Fishes, an ancient Christian symbol, and at first pretends to be merely the Cranmer Club, interested in studying the old Book of Common Prayer.[6] The priest Luke performs a Eucharist later in the book. And at the very beginning Faron wonders if people will ever remember what deity St. Paul's Cathedral was built for: "Will they be curious about his nature, this deity who was worshipped with such pomp and splendour, intrigued by the mystery of his symbol, at once so simple, the two crossed sticks, ubiquitous in nature, yet laden with gold, gloriously jewelled and adorned?" (James, *Children* 4).

The fable itself, of course, reveals the answer. Theodore becomes involved with the Five Fishes and joins them when they attempt to flee Xan's spies and soldiers. His uncommitment turns to passionate conviction in the process. He abandons order for justice. James creates suspense with the flight of the revolutionaries, several of whom are grotesquely murdered along the way. Julian, one of the women in the group, has become pregnant by Luke, the priest, and Faron accompanies her deep into the forest to allow the birth to take place far from Xan's control. A boy is born, and Faron feels as if "he was both participant and spectator, isolated . . . in a limbo of time in which nothing mattered" (227). He describes the child as "the new Adam, begetter of the new race, the saviour of mankind" (66), Julian is described by Xan, who finds them in the forest, as "the most important woman in the world but she isn't the Virgin Mary" (238), and all have fled to prevent Xan's being able to announce the birth to the world as part of his regime: "There would be no simple shepherds at this cradle" (198). Theodore murders Xan, and he and Julian christen the baby at the novel's end.

It is helpful to trace this Christian vision briefly in several of James' other novels. In *Devices and Desires,* for instance, she conjures up the bleak Norfolk coast—she makes much of the fact that place often determines the tale she pursues[7]—because of its symbolic desolation which represents man's fallen state. Interestingly enough the victim and the murderer emerge from the long-standing mutual guilt shared by a brother and sister. This suggestively incestuous relationship between a brother and sister often appears in James' novels—one thinks of Alex and Alice Mair in this novel, Gabriel and Claudia Etienne in *Original Sin,* and Barbara Swayne Berowne and Dominic Swayne in *A Taste for Death.* Both Dominic Swayne and Alice Mair are murderers, and Gabriel Etienne is the primary victim of murder, a recognition perhaps of murder's earliest stirrings: "Crime stories certainly go back before the Bible. It is rather interesting, isn't it, that you get Cain and Abel in the first stories of the Bible and this is the story of a murder" (Cooper-Clark 20).

In any case in *Devices and Desires* the Mairs do not go for help when their father injures himself but wait until he dies. There are extenuating circumstances, but what survives longest is Alice's sense that "I've been made to feel guilty from childhood. And if at the heart of your being you feel that you've no right even to exist, then one more cause of guilt hardly matters" (413). She murders Alex's mistress to enhance his career, the guilty but devoted act of the single sister to prevent the mistress from continuing to blackmail him.

In *Innocent Blood,* in many ways more of a novel about the search for personal identity rather than a straightforward mystery, Philippa Rose Palfrey is mesmerized by the "whole mythology of identity" and sets out to discover who her real parents are in an effort to overcome or come to terms with once and for all "the loneliness of the self" (51, 95). In the course of the novel the self-absorbed and arrogant Philippa more or less encourages her real mother to commit suicide and exonerates the man, the father of the little girl her mother and father murdered years ago, who has come to kill her mother but instead stabs her when she is already dead. The tale of vengeance and revenge moves with the certainty of myth and ritual, even to the point where Philippa gives herself for one night to her adopted father.

James seems to praise High Anglicanism in *Innocent Blood* as "a satisfying compromise between reason and myth, justified by the beauty of its liturgy, a celebration of Englishness" (114). Her true vision comes at the end, where Philippa begins to realize that "it is only through learning to love that we find identity. . . . She hoped one day to find hers. She wished [the father of the murdered daughter] well. And perhaps to be able to wish him well with all that she could recognize of her unpracticed heart, to say a short, untutored prayer for him and his Violet [the blind woman he has decided to marry], was in itself a small accession of grace" (348-49).

In *Original Sin,* the river Thames underscores James' dark vision of the world as "a dark tide of horror," above which "a cluster of low cloud lay over London, stained pink like a lint bandage which had soaked up the city's blood" (71, 68). Peverell Press occupies Innocent House along its dark banks, and the murder victim is found with a toy snake wrapped around his neck. But the real horror and guilt of the book are embodied in a past murder at Innocent House and the Holocaust. Both permeate the entire atmosphere of the novel in a way that suggests all people are if not murderers capable of betrayal, treachery, and murder. Real snakes haunt a character's real nightmares.

Original Sin is very self-consciously a writer's book with its focus on the publishing world, on archives, diaries, letters, manuscripts, book-signings, even including Esme Carling, a failing mystery writer who ends up murdered. The titles of the five sections make this clear:

"Foreword to Murder," "Death of a Publisher," "Work in Progress," "Evidence in Writing," and "Final Proof." James seems to connect the art of writing mysteries with the very pervasive guilt that stains every one of her pages. Authors themselves, of course, are creators of the crime and share the villain's plot and ingenious strategies. In many ways the writer elevates the very outlawed powers she is pretending to denounce, thus participating in the dark rites that initiate the need for love and possible human redemption. As readers we, too, participate in these dark rites.

James' masterpiece is *A Taste for Death,* in which religious revelation becomes the driving force of the narrative, embodied in the victim, Sir Paul Berowne, which leads him to submit to his own murder. His accumulated guilt, involving his first wife's death, the abortion, suicide, and drowning of women in his employ, his marrying his dead older brother's fiance to carry on the line, and his disaffection with his ministerial post in Parliament, leads him to spend the night at St. Matthew's Church. There his brother-in-law, eager to keep the Berowne status and money that his pregnant sister, Berowne's second wife, clings to, as he must cling to her, kills him. Exclaims the murderer, Dominic Swayne, "He wanted to die. . . . He practically asked for it. He could have tried to stop me, pleaded, argued, put up a fight. He could have begged for mercy. . . . That's all I wanted from him. . . . But he knew what I'd come for. . . . As if I had no choice. Just an instrument. . . . But I did have a choice. And so did he. Christ, he could have stopped me. Why didn't he stop me?" (444).

The mystery that haunts the center of the novel is Berowne's passion for revelation, a passion that cannot be explained but that occupies the heart of darkness of the murder mystery. Whatever drives him "had been something more profound, less explicable, than disillusionment, midlife restlessness, the fear of a threatened scandal. Whatever had happened to him on that first night in St. Matthew's vestry had led him, the next day, to change the whole direction of his life. Had it also led him to his death?" (53). "He told me that he had had an experience of God," proclaims another character (264). In a world of greed, social status, and envy such experiences may necessarily lead only to death. In any case the mystery of Berowne's sudden conversion infects Dalgliesh, and his subordinates begin to see a likeness between the two. The revelation remains unrevealed, but it haunts all the pages of this novel and is not dissipated by the more rational mystery's solution. The novel concludes with a sermon: "If you find that you no longer believe, act as if you still do" (459). It seems to be James' ultimate advice.

At one point James takes us into Sarah Berowne's flat. She is a photographer and the left-leaning estranged daughter of Paul, and the reader is shown some of her work. One photograph in particular stands out at the end of the paragraph, that of "a buxom grandmother, noted for her detective stories, who gazed mournfully at the camera as if deploring either the bloodiness of her craft or the size of her advance" (216). One need not spend much time in guessing whose self-portrait this might be. Murder and the writing about murder fill the air with a certain madness: "To be part of a murder investigation [or to conjure one up?] was to be contaminated by a process which would leave few of their lives unchanged. Murder remained the unique crime. Peer and pauper stood equal before it" (260). This is the source and dark heart of P. D. James' art of fiction. And no amount of rational explanation can make it disappear.

Certainly this darker, more complex vision of things underscores James' strength as a writer of mysteries. The novel of bad manners, the atmosphere, and the furnishings serve only to anchor her wider and more moral, more human concerns and doubts. What James seeks is that essential man, a common humanity, however ambiguous and self-serving, in all its complexities and complicities: "Scrape away the carefully acquired patina of professional success, prestige, orthodox good manners, and the real man was there" (55). It is this pursuit which fuels her dark fictions. The manners and the essential human matter exist in an uncertain equilibrium in regard to one another. From the carnage of her vision, however, she pursues the conversion of her characters, readers, and probably herself, as she initiates the rites of mystery over and over again, playing out the ritual of exorcism and possible redemption, although she recognizes that blood is never innocent, that original sin contaminates our devices and desires, and that we all have a taste for death.

Clearly the mysteries of Dashiell Hammett and P. D. James are a world apart, not to mention the ocean between them, but they once again reveal the flexibility of the form. In renouncing the "British country house" plot, Hammett helped create the American hard-boiled mystery. In continuing the "country house" tradition, James reinvigorated that specifically British sub-genre. Both attest to the popularity of the mystery structure and suggest very distinct ways in how it can be both deepened and extended.

SUBVERTING THE FORMULA: FAULKNER, FOWLES, AND OTHERS

There are also many ways in which the mystery formula may be not only broadened and enriched, as James has done, but subverted from within. The formula rests upon its own certified binary oppositions, the good guy and the bad guy, the detective and the murderer, the recognition of clues and the resolution of the plot. Such oppositions can appear to be monolithic and hierarchical, producing a kind of master-slave structure; at first the murderer is the master, but the tables are turned when he and his crime are discovered by the detective. As we know from Jacques Derrida's theory of deconstruction, however, this binary scheme, inherent in western thought, can become notoriously unstable, once the functional relationships between them are revealed and exposed. The process of narrative itself thwarts such a monolithic structure. "Literature exists in and through the act by which it questions what at the same time it proposes," Richard Poirier insists (147-48). "One obvious characteristic of a literary text is that its words tend to destabilize one another and to fall into conflicted or contradictory relationships. . . . such contradictions are inherent to the mystery of human existence in time and to the very words by which we have imagined it" (Poirier 147-48). In another sense mystery writers are playing with fire. They are themselves the creators of the crime, and the villain thus shares their own sense of plot and ingenious strategies. In many ways these writers elevate the very outlawed powers they are pretending to denounce (Reynolds 109) and violate those very taboos their tales are advising us not to.

The identification between writer and villain extends to include the reader as well, a process within which the good and the bad are less clearly defined. "The true [mystery] addict," Symons asserts, "is a sort of Manichee and his spirits of light and darkness, the detective and the criminal, are fighting each other for ever" (9). This constant confrontation leads to questions concerning the relationship between good and evil and the coexistence of both in the same person. As Gabriel Sarrazin has described such conundrums, "It has remained to our century and to America to erect evil and good upon equal pedestals and read in them an equal purpose" (Reynolds 112). If such subversive elements and perspectives can be smuggled into the mystery text or themselves are the result of the self-contradictory powers of language and literature, then as Lehman acknowledges, "no solution, however convincing, can quite measure up to the riddle it unravels" (Symons 41). And we are left with Robin Winks, forced to recognize that "many mysterious elements relating to precise actions and precise motivations at precise times, as opposed to general explanations of motive, will almost certainly and properly be left unresolved" (Winks 105).

In many contemporary American mysteries, there is another element that destabilizes the traditional mystery formula. Several authors envision a world in which moral values no longer dictate the outcome of confrontations. Many re-enact their discovery of a violent chaotic society whose very exposure in their fiction undercuts any idea of a lasting ethical order. This recognition of a darker, wider, chaotic realm, akin as it

is to the nightmarish domain of gothic novels, threatens all possible frameworks of law and order and plunges both reader and characters into an unendingly visceral and savage "new world order." Things may threaten to remain unresolvable because they cannot be adequately comprehended, and we have therefore entered newer, darker, and uncharted territories of both the individual psyche and society.

The mystery formula has become such a popular genre in the twentieth century that several writers, including many who are neither American nor British, have toyed with it in their own literary fiction and have consciously chosen to subvert and undercut it. Examples include everything from William Faulkner's *Sanctuary* (1931) and Paul Auster's *City of Glass* (1985), from his *New York Trilogy* (the only one we could consider here as a "genuine" mystery writer), to more recent fiction such as Tim O'Brien's *In the Lake of the Woods* (1994) and Joan Didion's *The Last Thing He Wanted* (1996), among others. And of course other writers have taken aim at the formula as well, including John Fowles in his short story, "The Enigma" (1974), and Gabriel Garcia Marquez in *Chronicle of a Death Foretold* (1982). In each the standard mystery approach has either been subverted from within, terminally disrupted and dispatched, reversed, or transcended.

Andre Malraux referred to *Sanctuary* as "the infusion of Greek tragedy into the detective story." Faulkner conjures up such a corrupt and evil world that its demonic workings-out inevitably overwhelm all attempts to try and solve the complex case of Popeye's murder of Tommy and his rape with a corncob of Temple Drake. The lawyer, Horace Benbow, attempts to convict Popeye of both the murder and the rape, but Temple refuses to cooperate and, because she is either in awe or terrified of Popeye, confesses on the witness stand that it was Lee Goodwin who actually killed the defenseless Tommy in the barn at the Old Frenchman's Place. Benbow is so stunned by Temple's testimony that he lets his case collapse, and Popeye goes free—to be convicted and executed later for a crime he didn't commit, a kind of Flitcraft's revenge.

Faulkner builds his novel carefully, withholding the climactic scenes of rape and murder as in the most standard of mysteries. Readers, therefore, cannot discover what has actually happened until the conclusion. At the same time Faulkner creates a nightmarish realm of cryptic events, each gesture and action clearly recorded but lacking a discernible motive and explanation. Readers feel trapped in a kind of pure present in the first thirteen chapters, where people come and go, run in circles, and play a kind of hide-and-seek at the Old Frenchman's Place, where Gowan Stevens has stopped with Temple to pick up some bootleg liquor. Consequently the reader can see the actions but not understand exactly what is going on: "Motionless, facing one another like the first position of a dance, they stood in a mounting terrific muscular hiatus" (Faulkner 114). Hiatus gives way to cinematic blur and sudden ellipses in the narrative, as the meaning of events remains uncertain and undiscovered, "like sitting before a series of printed pages turned in furious snatches, leaving a series of cryptic, headless and tailless evocations on the mind" (Faulkner 204).

Throughout the novel Faulkner creates a corrupt world in which no sanctuary exists or exists only as mere mask and facade, whether it be social status and respectability, money, traditional gender roles, the gangster code of "ethics," or a belief in good and evil, right and wrong. Horace's sister Narcissa will do anything to keep her social position intact. Temple Drake half-enjoys the rape and her incarceration at the whorehouse in Memphis. Gowan Stevens, who is dating Narcissa, escapes from the Old Frenchman's Place, leaving Temple there on her own. Clarence Snopes, a local politician, trades payoffs for information and will sell anything to anyone if the price is right. Each family group is in some way distorted and dysfunctional. And even Horace Benbow's belief in the law and justice crumbles in the face of so many betrayals and lies.

Horace discovers that "there's a corruption about even looking upon evil, even by accident; you cannot haggle, traffic, with putrefaction" (152). He recognizes that it involves his own sexuality and his own yearning for his step-daughter, that he is as guilty of a possible violation of social codes as is Temple, and that "the Snake was there before Adam, because he was the first one thrown out of heaven; he was there all the time" (181):

> Perhaps it is upon the instant that we realise, admit, that there is a logical pattern to evil, that we die, he thought, thinking of the expression he had once seen in the eyes of a dead child, and of other dead: the cooling indignation, the shocked despair fading, leaving two empty globes in which the motionless world lurked profoundly in miniature.
>
> (266)

In such a world there can be no justice but only collapse, waste and enervation, in which the "monotonous pitch" of insects suggest "the chemical agony of a world left stark and dying above the tide-edge of the fluid in which it lived and breathed" (267). Eliot's wasteland overwhelms the mystery formula, all justice is betrayed, and the would-be detective story concludes with its vision of a "sullen and discontented" Temple Drake in the Luxemborg Gardens with her father the judge, who has engineered in part her exoneration, staring at "the dead tranquil queens . . . and on into the sky lying prone and vanquished in the embrace of the season of rain and death" (380).

Building perhaps on Faulkner's displacement of the mystery formula, such diverse authors as Paul Auster, Tim O'Brien, and Joan Didion radically eviscerate it, as their texts set up mysteries to be solved and then collapse, remaining open-ended and curiously incomplete. Auster, for instance, suggests that "in the good mystery there is nothing wasted. . . . nothing must be overlooked. Everything becomes essence; the center of the book shifts with each event that propels it forward" (15). But as *City of Glass* unfolds, characters vanish, clues proliferate, and the would-be detective, Daniel Quinn, unable to decipher these clues, fades away. Quinn explains that "what interested him about the stories he wrote was not their relation to the world but their relation to other stories" (14). He also writes mysteries under the pseudonym of William Wilson, creates a detective named Max Work, assumes the identity of "Paul Auster" when a would-be client calls the Auster Agency to seek advice, and pursues one of two look-alike men named Stillman he spies arriving at Grand Central Station.

For Edgar Allan Poe, to whom Auster refers several times in *City of Glass,* doubling always suggested dissolution, so much so that one necessarily includes the other. When a character meets his double in a final showdown, the result is inevitable death and destruction, as in "The Fall of the House of Usher." When Roderick Usher is confronted by his twin sister Madeline, whom he has buried alive, the two collapse one upon the other, and the entire house sinks into the dark tarn that reflects it. Similarly in "William Wilson" the narrator, William Wilson (which he admits is not his real name, so that the reader is never certain exactly who the narrator is), finally confronts his double (whether in reality or in his imagination Poe leaves provocatively ambiguous) and kills him. Thus William Wilson 1 kills William Wilson 2, but the actual event can be interpreted as either a suicide or a murder, and Poe leaves the final denouement problematic.

Likewise in *City of Glass,* Quinn discovers the "real" Paul Auster in New York, who of course is being invented by Paul Auster, the author. Quinn discovers that he and Auster's son are both named Daniel, that Quinn's dead son Peter has the same name as his client, Peter Stillman, and that his initials, DQ, are the same as *Don Quixote,* which Cervantes wrote as "an attack on the dangers of make-believe" and that "had to claim that it was real" (151). Quinn recalls that Poe's detective Dupin believed that it was necessary to identify "the reasoner's intellect with that of his opponent" (65), the detective's with the villain's. He also expresses his own pursuit of finding a place "where one could finally disappear" (167), "by flooding himself with externals, by drowning himself out of himself" (98) like Melville's Bartleby or Poe's A. Gordon Pym. The upshot results in the complete undermining of the mystery's faith in closely observed details which will inevitably lead to a solution: "The implication was that human behavior could be understood, that beneath the infinite facade of gestures, tics, and silences, there was finally a coherence, an order, a source of motivation" (105). *City of Glass* conducts the reader into a realm of reflective mirrors, which finally reflect only absence and the abandoned red notebook in a dark empty room where Quinn has been hiding out. "What will happen when there are no more pages in the red notebook?" (200). All will vanish. And the nameless narrator can only admit, "[Quinn] will be with me always. And wherever he may have disappeared to, I wish him luck" (203).

Auster, like O'Brien and Didion, is writing in a postmodern world in which the very nature of language has been questioned. Does it illuminate or imprison, reveal or re-veil, connect us to the world or isolate us in our own solipsistic imaginings? Auster focuses on the apparent collapse of language in contemporary times, that deconstructionist and post-structuralist vision that "names became detached from things; words devolved into a collection of arbitrary signs; language had been severed from God" (70). In such a world, as the character Stillman suggests, all has fallen into ambiguity and contradiction, which also involves "a knowledge of evil" (70). Evil in *Sanctuary* destroyed common morality and justice; in *City of Glass* it destroys or at least eviscerates language and the detective as well. The mystery beckons to Quinn and to us and then dissolves before our eyes, as if analogy (this tale is like one of Poe's) breeds causation. It also comments upon Poe's fiction, which leads to an ultimate identification, duplicating Poe's use of doubles that results in dissolution and death.

Tim O'Brien, who has written several stunning novels on his experiences in Vietnam, delights in confronting the mystery formula with ultimate metaphysical mysteries, a dialectic he reveals in his numerous footnotes to *In the Lake of the Woods*: "There are certain mysteries that weave through life itself, human motive and human desire. Even much of what might appear to be fact in this narrative—action, word, thought—must ultimately be viewed as a diligent but still imaginative reconstruction of events" (30). The impossibility of ultimately knowing anything about human motive and desire builds throughout the footnotes: "The man's soul remains for me an absolute and impenetrable unknown. . . . We are fascinated, all of us, by the implacable otherness of others. . . . they are all beyond us" (103). Perhaps his justification lies in the necessity "to bear witness to the mystery of evil" (203). Perhaps the book exists "to remind me. To give me back my vanished life" (301). Or perhaps he is mesmerized by "our love of enigma. . . . No answers, yet mystery itself carries me on" (269). Ultimately

there *is* no end. . . . Nothing is fixed, nothing is solved. . . . Mystery finally claims us. . . . One way or another, it seems, we all perform vanishing tricks, effacing history, locking up our lives and slipping day by day into the graying shadows. Our whereabouts are uncertain. All secrets lead to the dark, and beyond the dark there is only maybe.

(304)

O'Brien has discovered that mysterious void at the center of all human experience, motive, and desire. Faulkner remarked that he wrote about "the human heart in conflict with itself," Hawthorne about the unfathomable mystery of the human heart. We can hear echoes of their words in O'Brien's: "Blame it on the human heart," the line which precedes the quotation above which begins, "One way or another, it seems, we all perform vanishing tricks" (304). And O'Brien has made very clear that the convoluted and inexplicable human heart has always been his first concern:

Writing fiction . . . display[s] in concrete terms the actions and reactions of human beings contesting problems of the heart. . . . The heart *is* dark. We gape into the tangle of this man's soul, which has the quality of a huge black hole, ever widening, ever mysterious, its gravity sucking us back into the book itself. . . . To reach into one's own heart, down into that place where the stories are, bringing up the mystery of oneself.

("Magic" ["The Magic Show"] 176, 182-83)

John Wade, the boy-magician turned politician in *In the Lake of the Woods,* has deleted his own dark deeds from the Army records of the My Lai massacre in March 1968, in Vietnam and decides to run in a Democratic primary for the United States Senate. He thinks he can evade his past mistakes and dazzle his constituents with his charismatic personality and flair. The records, however, are discovered, and their publication in the press destroys his political career. He had believed that he could conjure up a self of his own choosing and devising and is one more representative in American fiction of those willfully self-made male American "heroes" like Ahab, Jay Gatsby, and Thomas Sutpen who spring from the Platonic conceptions of themselves. Wade's nickname is "Sorcerer," which is the perfect name for such a character—as is "Wade": the human condition can wade in darker waters but forever skirts the ultimate seas. He does it with smoke and mirrors. O'Brien himself admits to loving magic tricks as a child: "I liked the aloneness, as God and other miracle workers must also like it. . . . I liked shaping the universe around me. I liked the power" ("Magic" 175).

Of course what happens to such a self is that not only must it self-destruct, but its past exploits and history must inevitably catch up with it. When Wade loses the primary for the United States Senate, his political career is finished, as is the Sorcerer's ability to keep pulling rabbits out of the hat: "Wade felt an estrangement from the actuality of the world, its basic nowness, and in the end all he could conjure up was an image of illusion itself, a head full of mirrors" (Lake 281). No wonder O'Brien quotes Hawthorne's description of Wakefield near the very end of the novel: "He had happened to dissever himself from the world—to vanish—to give up his place and privilege with living men, without being admitted among the dead" (Lake 297).

History in *In the Lake of the Woods* does not just correct Wade's image of himself as Sorcerer and successful politician; it annihilates it. The wilderness swallows him whole, and he literally vanishes in the novel, as has his wife Kathy a few weeks before him. We never know what has happened to them. The mystery remains insoluble. But of course this is exactly what has attracted O'Brien: "Mystery everywhere—permeating mystery—even in the most ordinary objects of the world . . . infinite and inexplicable. Anything was possible" (2). Ultimate mystery has devoured the mystery formula, revealing its artifice and structure, and leaves us "in the deep unbroken solitude, age to age, [where] Lake of the Woods gazes back on itself like a great liquid eye. Nothing adds or subtracts. Everything is present, everything is missing. . . . [it is] where the vanished things go" (290, 243).[8]

In Joan Didion's latest novel, *The Last Thing He Wanted,* things such as facts do not vanish, but they remain virtually unexplained. We get them all but not within any final resolution. As in both Auster's and O'Brien's novels, the text participates in its own demise and becomes a mystery in its own right, a gathering of facts and possibilities, a fluid pursuit of answers with none to give, so that the reader finds herself imprisoned in the process of revelation that is never satisfied. We eventually discover that Elena McMahon, daughter of an arms-dealer, has been assassinated on a Caribbean island in 1984, that she had become involved with a "crisis junkie," Treat Morrison, from the State Department or CIA, and that she was shot by the local police, who are connected to the Salvadoran and counterterrorist Colonel Alvaro Garcia Steiner. He may have also tried to kill Morrison and blame it on Elena, whose father had been selling arms to the Sandinistas in the Nicaraguan civil war. Didion clearly takes government bureaucracy and secrecy to task and wants to expose the incestuous corruption that underscored the American support for the Contras in Nicaragua in the 1980s, but her narrative method, with her use of ellipses, flashbacks, sudden epiphanies and flashforwards—all of them fractured and splintered in terms of memory and monologue—just as clearly reveals the ultimate inability of understanding exactly what has gone on. She is aware

finally of "a momentary phantasmagoria in which everyone focused on some different aspect and nobody at all saw the whole" (Didion 203).

Didion's famously obsessive fragmentary style—she circles, repeats, and juxtaposes tales and events with speculations, rumors, asides, and incomplete memoirs—destroys any possibility of continuity, of cause and effect, and thus sabotages the clear investigatory path of the mystery formula. Like O'Brien she senses a larger mystery, a yawning dread, in the world, a heart of darkness Joseph Conrad would have appreciated. And therefore in her pursuit of connecting "every moment . . . to every other moment, every act to have logical if obscure consequences, an unbroken narrative of vivid complexity" (56), she realizes that government policy in our information age creates "entire layers of bureaucracy dedicated to the principle that self-perpetuation depended on the ability not to elucidate but to obscure," that everything can be "obfuscated by acronym" (169, 91). Consequently these "glimpses of life on the far frontier of the Monroe Doctrine" (10) lack an ultimate coherence or solution. Mystery becomes a way of life, a mode of technical mastery, and Elena McMahon, one of its more prominent victims, "remained remote most of all to herself, a clandestine agent who had so successfully compartmentalized her operation as to have lost access to her own cutouts" (152).

The true price of such overwhelming obfuscation and loss of direction results in what Jerzy Kosinski, author of such novels as *The Painted Bird* and *Being There,* has called the theft of the self. The real mystery is that that self can never be retrieved and thus never "solved." Motives vanish in "Elena's apparently impenetrable performances in the various roles assigned her" (Didion 154), and the reader is left desperately trying to "correct or clarify whatever misunderstandings or erroneous impressions might or might not have been left" (170). We are left with Didion's own "half-mad gaze" (47) in which no mystery formula, at least in its more popular guise, can appease us or survive.

There are so many other writers, who are not American, who have played with and re-fashioned the mystery formula in contemporary fiction, and these include John Fowles and Gabriel Garcia Marquez. Fowles' *The Magus* offers solution after solution to the mysterious rites that Nicholas Urfe has gotten himself into, but in each and every instance, the solution at hand is seen to be a ploy, a fake, a staged theatrical display which leads to further mysteries. Eventually Urfe must face himself alone in Fowles' existential climax, freed from all preordained scripts, left with the ultimate mystery that life itself provides without explanation. Fowles is a superbly seductive writer, building his plot of Chinese boxes carefully and then, as in *The French Lieutenant's*

Woman, offering multiple solutions or endings. The idea is to keep the process and the pursuit open, as it is in life, and leave the reader to face the tantalizing void of no answers or all possible ones.

In "The Enigma" 57-year-old John Marcus Fielding—family man, happily married, rich, a Conservative Member of Parliament, owner of a magnificent Elizabethan manor house in the country—vanishes. There are few clues to pursue, but Michael Jennings, the police sergeant who comes from a family of fine policemen and who essentially "saw life as a game, which one played principally for oneself and only incidentally out of some sense of duty" (Fowles, *Ebony* 213), is convinced that he can solve the case. In fact he makes two lists of possible solutions, the first he calls "*State of Play,*" the second, which is more speculative, "*Wild Ones.*" He finally interviews Isobel Dodgson, the former French girlfriend of Peter Fielding, the missing minister's son, and slowly falls in love with her. During the interview Isobel speculates about the nature of John Fielding and suggests but offers no proof whatsoever of what might have happened to him. In doing so Fowles eviscerates the mystery formula, claiming that it is truer to life to do so, since "the unreal literary rules" (239) of the mystery do not exist in the real world of mind and matter.

Isobel describes the entire Fielding household as more or less a decorous masquerade, in which each member of the family believes in or questions their facade of propriety and status but does nothing to change it. Some may be hypocritical; others may fit their appropriate roles easily; "someone alive" may be "playing dead" (224). According to Isobel, Fielding may have thought that "there was an author in his life. In a way. Not a man. A system, a view of things? Something that had written him. Had really made him just a character in a book" (240). And so on the spur of the moment he decides to opt out, to vanish. It is his way of achieving immortality, of performing "God's trick . . . Deus absconditus . . . Walking out" (242). In doing so he will remain forever an unsolved mystery which, as Isobel points out (certainly to Fowles' eternal delight), is "the one thing people never forget . . . the unsolved. Nothing lasts like a mystery" (242).

On this point Faulkner, O'Brien, Didion, and Fowles would all agree, and to assure that the mystery remains unsolved and therefore open-ended and seductive, they create their fictions accordingly. When Jennings and Dodgson discover their mutual attraction, they realize, as has Fowles before them, that "the tender pragmatisms of flesh have poetries no enigma, human or divine, can diminish or demean—indeed, it can only cause them, and then walk out" (247).

Gabriel Garcia Marquez pursues such pragmatisms of flesh by standing the mystery formula on its head. He

reveals the crime, the killers, and the victim early on in *Chronicle of a Death Foretold* and in doing so pursues the human motives and complex cultural reasons that have participated in and initiated this murder. "There had never been a death more foretold" (57), explains the narrator, and he wants to reconstruct the events that led up to it not "from an urge to clear up mysteries but because none of us could go on living without an exact knowledge of the place and the mission assigned to us by fate" (113). The mystery of fate and why it seems to rule everyone in the Caribbean backwater village is exactly what Marquez and the narrator are pursuing twenty-seven years after the fact: "I returned to this forgotten village, trying to put the broken mirror of memory back together from so many scattered shards" (5).

What Marquez discovers is that racism, social codes no longer believed in but maintained at all costs, notions of traditional gender-based honor, and the community's submerged longing for a scapegoat help to account for the murder of the Arab, Santiago Nasar, by the twins, Pedro and Pablo Vicario, who have heard that Nasar deflowered their sister Angela, a desecration that is discovered on her wedding night by her husband, the mysterious Bayardo San Roman. Never in the novel do we find out that Nasar is indeed the culprit. Angela has said that he was, but there is no proof. Thus, at the center of the mystery lurks the unresolved issue of why she selected him as her lover in the first place. Why did she point the finger at him?

Marquez offers suggestive cultural clues. First of all, brothers must defend the virginal honor of their sisters. Explains Pablo's fiance, Prudencia Cotes, "I never would have married him if he hadn't done what a man should do" (72). Elaborates the narrator, "Most of those who could have done something to prevent the crime and did not consoled themselves with the pretext that affairs of honor are sacred monopolies, giving access only to those who are part of the drama" (114). In fact at one point the Vicario twins decide not to kill Nasar. It seems that only human inertia and a misguided belief in fate egg them on toward the final denouement. The machismo code of honor permeates the entire culture, as the narrator reveals by describing the several relationships between men and women, bachelors and whores, married men and mistresses, owners and servants, all of which reinforces it. The Vicarios are justified in killing Nasar, according to them, because the code demands it.

At the same time the narrator realizes how many people are "dominated then by so many linear habits" (113). They don't so much believe these habits as let them stand unassailed. The investigating magistrate in a marginal note on his report scrawls, "*Give me a prejudice and I will move the world*" (117). In another marginal note he writes, "*Fatality makes us invisible*"

(133), thus suggesting that fate is the perfect smoke-screen, excuse, and justification for people's actions or the lack of them. Fate embodies the cultural past, the religious need for an occasional scapegoat, the code of honor. It can be relied upon to act out its own premeditated drama with no personal need or desire to consider otherwise. If no one is responsible, then no one can prevent the crime. Each can only vaguely fathom "their part of the destiny that life had assigned them" (96). All view themselves as mere witnesses to a *fait accompli,* and the killers, as they cut and slaughter Santiago Nasar at the front door of his house, "didn't hear the shouts of the whole town, frightened by its own crime" (140). Marquez has upended the typical mystery formula to grapple with wider mysteries and his own more social and metaphysical speculations.

Faulkner, Auster, O'Brien, Didion, Fowles, and Marquez, in formally subverting the mystery formula, have revealed the power of that totalistic structure by its very calculated absence and yet at the same time have pursued in their different ways the framework of detective fiction, complete with investigations, interviews, and the detective himself or herself. Martin Marty's description of totalism and tribalism, as mentioned above, suggests the difference between what these authors have done and what Tony Hillerman, James Lee Burke, Amanda Cross, and Walter Mosley have accomplished. For Marty, totalism indicates a "'totalist ideology' [that] refers to any doctrine which attempts a complete, unified explanation of world and society" (12), as the mystery formula does. Tribalism, on the other hand, in challenging that idea of totalism, demonstrates that "only the peoples and groups to which one naturally belongs, or chooses to belong, or even invents as new constructs, can provide coherence. Only these can give people an identity and then empower them" (11).

"Perhaps the most potent mode of subversion is that which can speak directly to a 'conventional' reader," suggests Linda Hutcheon (202). Hillerman, Cross, Burke, and Mosley employ the mystery conventions to grapple with certain peoples and/or cultural and social differences that are not usually found in the typical formulaic structure, but they also transform it because of these differences. In each case the question about such formulaic and popular literature remains: Does it merely support conventional ideologies, or can it resist them and in doing so challenge them? What exactly is the relationship between a marginal perspective, landscape, or group of people and the conventional center? Does the mystery formula stunt or empower its native American, feminist, southern, and black subjects? How does this affect Hillerman's Navajos and Mosley's Blacks? Whether or not these issues can be fully resolved, they certainly raise, what Brook Thomas has described as the ultimate "questions of power, domina-tion, exclusion, *and* emancipation in conjunction with the study of [popular] literature" (ix).

Although the following chapters appear in no specific order—older writers appear first—each does grapple with certain literary issues. All four writers confront the difficulties associated with the nature of literary representation and with the presentation and construction of their own particular ideological points of view. Each faces the dilemma of sacrificing some of his or her concerns to the demands of the mystery genre, at the same time trying to create a recognizable mystery that remains true to its popular roots.

Hillerman, for example, must encounter both the mimetic and performative act of literary representation in terms of the Navajos in his fiction. The reader must observe them as Navajos within a distinctly recognizable and different cultural milieu of their own making and traditions and as performing within the mystery formula.

Likewise in his creation of Navajo policeman Jim Chee, Hillerman uses both Navajo and Hopi myths and ceremonies not merely as a smokescreen for the necessary mechanics of the mystery formula but also as a way of creating a new sense of order and harmony that can help to heal the very oppositional and confrontational (good versus evil) aspects of the formula itself. Chee's on-going battle with himself between his policeman's role in a white world and his Navajo consciousness transforms the usually straightforward world of the well-crafted mystery into an exploration of different but not necessarily incompatible cultures. In effect the "white" mystery has been purified by Native American traditions. Changing Woman has had her way with, in this case, the male-dominated structure that can only succumb to Her cyclical patterns.

In a similar manner Amanda Cross has revitalized the popular mystery tradition by investing it with a decidedly feminist heroine and perspective. In *The Players Come Again* (1990) Cross re-tells the myth of Ariadne in such a way that Ariadne determines her own destiny, as opposed to being the helpless female at the mercy of and who must rely solely upon the whims of Theseus. In the novel the revised version of the ancient myth clearly undercuts the patriarchal roots of literary modernism—the mystery revolves around early novels in the 1920s produced by the famous Emmanuel Foxx (a kind of Joyce-Eliot-Faulkner) and the one secretly written by his wife Gabrielle—refashions the underpinnings and assumptions of Greek myths as opposed to the more matriarchal Cretan ones, and helps Kate Fansler solve the mystery at hand.

When Cross employs the mystery formula, however, with its clear reflection of rational and linear plotlines, themselves a product of Cartesian logic and the patriarchal, male-dominated, objective plot, the reader may wonder whether she in any way challenges this trajectory or merely reoccupies it from the different perspective of her feminist heroine within it.

With James Lee Burke, the issue is more of a generic one. His earlier non-mystery novels clearly certify him as a Southern writer with their re-enactments of gothic curses, their descriptions of the weight and burden of the historical past, their pervading sense of unrelenting guilt, and their Poesque fascination with hauntings and horrors. The observant reader should consider the possible consequences when such a recognizable genre is re-shaped by or incorporated into the more straightforward mystery formula. Perhaps it is one reason why Burke's endings often appear to be more complex and blurred than the typical conclusions of mysteries.

With all these writers there remains the continuing problem of relating a marginal group—the Navajos, academic feminists, Southern Louisiana Cajuns, blacks—to the center and including them in mainstream popular fiction, but with Walter Mosley there is also the linguistic issue. Henry Louis Gates, Jr., has discussed in great detail the role and use of oral expression in black culture, in particular both with the process of signifying and in the essential foundation of much written black literature. Can that particular style survive within the confines of the traditional mystery? Or must it be modified and abandoned in some way?

The interviews with the writers took place after each chapter was practically complete. They serve to comment upon the analyses but are not, for the most part, incorporated into them. In all cases all four writers have introduced new perspectives into and broadened the male-oriented formulaic shape of the mystery formula and have opened up the genre to newer visions of restoration, order, and harmony.

The process is still continuing with newer writers, such as Rudolfo Anaya in *Zia Summer* (1995) and *Rio Grande Fall* (1996). The first mystery is overstuffed with Chicano lore, Aztec rites, and New Mexican history and social hierarchies. All of this conflicts with Anaya's more realistic and brutally raw prose when it comes to describing characters and their crimes. In this the novel suggests Hillerman's first, *The Blessing Way*. Anaya, however, integrates all of these things smoothly and swiftly in his more vigorous and incantatory *Rio Grande Fall*.

A quote at the beginning of *Zia Summer* by Sandra West Prowell, author of *The Killing of Monday Brown*, describes Anaya in "his rightful place beside Walter Mosley, Tony Hillerman, and James Lee Burke as a master of the cultural mystery." This is the first place where I have come across their names so publicly linked. It is a noble lineage this book will examine and explore.

Notes

1. "No American literary genre is more commercially profitable than the mystery, of which millions of hard-cover novels are sold annually, and yet more millions in soft-cover, in flourishing sections in bookstores and in 180 independent 'mystery' stores." Joyce Carol Oates, "Inside the Locked Room," a review of *A Certain Justice* by P. D. James, *The New York Review of Books*, 2 Feb. 1998: 20.

2. In discussing "context control and domination" in his work on the postmodern condition, Jean-Francois Lyotard, in effect, explains what it is the mystery formula accomplishes: "it excludes in principle adherence to a metaphysical discourse. . . . it demands clear minds and cold wills; it replaces the definition of essences with the calculation of interactions; it makes the 'players' assume responsibility not only for the statements they propose, but also for the rules to which they submit those statements in order to render them acceptable. It brings the pragmatic functions of knowledge clearly to light, to the extent that they seem to relate to the criterion of efficiency: the pragmatics of argumentation [and] of the production of proof." Jean-Francois Lyotard, *The Postmodern Condition: A Report on Knowledge* (Minneapolis: University of Minnesota Press, 1984) 62.

3. Martin E. Marty, *The One and the Many: America's Struggle for the Common Good* (Cambridge: Harvard University Press, 1997) 10, 11. In Marty's terms, "*totalism* is the name assigned to the idea that a nation-state can and should be organized around a single and easily definable ideology or creed," which in my use of the word suggests the ideology of the mystery formula in its totalistic formulaic patterns. *Tribalism*, Marty suggests, opposes totalism in that it assumes that "only the peoples and groups to which one naturally belongs, or chooses to belong, or even invents as new constructs, can provide coherence." Hillerman, Cross, Burke, and Mosley integrate their "tribalist" or cultural focus into the "totalizing" agenda and design of the mystery. In text as *One*.

4. This is discussed in more detail in the first chapter in terms of the detective novel as a religious ritual, in which the murder becomes the sin, the criminal is the high priest of this rite, and the detective suggests an even higher power who appears on behalf of the victim of such rites. The sin is exorcized, the criminal punished and expelled, guilt has yet again been assuaged, and normal Christian society is once again restored. Most mysteries work in a similar manner, but James' more visible link to such an exorcism suggests Amanda Cross' fiction in the third chapter.

5. Dennis Porter, "Detection and Ethics: The Case of P. D. James." *The Sleuth and the Scholar: Origins, Evolution, and Current Trends in Detective Fiction*, ed. Barbara A. Rader and Howard G. Zettler (New

York: Greenwood Press, 1988) 16, 17. In text as *Sleuth.* For James "caritas" suggests a benevolent goodwill toward all of humanity, a kind of general public benevolence with its more lenient judgment of others. Love describes a more passionate attachment between individuals and can lead to murder in the way "caritas" usually does not.

6. Thomas Cranmer (1489-1556) was the archbishop of Canterbury (1533-1556) who revised the Book of Common Prayer in the Anglican Church in England.

7. "There nearly always is a 'place' first, and to an extent, that dictates what one is writing about. . . . Characters come very quickly afterwards" (*Interview* 27).

8. O'Brien is writing in the Hawthorne-Melville-Faulkner-Morrison tradition of American dark romance, a complex subject which deserves much more attention than I can give it here. For an in-depth discussion of this "mesmerized" fiction with its sense of ultimate mystery and haunted domain, I suggest my own *Mesmerism and Hawthorne: Mediums of American Romance* (Tuscaloosa: University of Alabama Press, 1998).

Works Cited

PRIMARY SOURCES

Auster, Paul. *City of Glass.* New York: Penguin Books, 1985.

Cross, Amanda. *The Players Come Again.* New York: Ballantine Books, 1990.

Didion, Joan. *The Last Thing He Wanted.* New York: Knopf, 1996.

Faulkner, William. *Sanctuary.* New York: Modern Library, 1931/1958.

Fowles, John. *The Ebony Tower.* Boston: Little, Brown, 1974.

Hammett, Dashiell. *The Maltese Falcon.* New York: Random House, 1972.

James, P. D. *The Children of Men.* New York: Knopf, 1993.

———. *Devices and Desires.* New York: Knopf, 1990.

———. *Innocent Blood.* New York: Warner Books, 1980.

———. Interview by Dina Cooper-Clark. *Interviews.*

———. *Original Sin.* New York: Knopf, 1995.

———. *A Taste for Death.* New York: Knopf, 1986.

Marquez, Gabriel Garcia. *Chronicles of a Death Foretold.* New York: Ballantine Books, 1982.

O'Brien, Tim. *In the Lake of the Woods.* Boston: Houghton Mifflin, 1994.

———. "The Magic Show." *Writers on Writing.* Ed. Robert Pack and Jay Parini. Hanover, NH: UP of New England, 1992.

SECONDARY SOURCES

Bonnycastle, Stephen. *In Search of Authority: An Introductory Guide to Literary Theory.* 2nd ed. Canada: Broadview P, 1996.

Bouchard, Larry D. *Tragic Method and Tragic Theology: Evil in Contemporary Drama and Religious Thought.* University Park, PA: Pennsylvania State UP, 1989.

Brooks, Peter. "Freud's Masterplot." *Contemporary Literary Criticism: Literary and Cultural Studies.* Ed. Con Robert Davis and Ronald Schleifer. New York: Longman, 1989.

Descartes, Rene. *Discourse on Method and the Meditations.* Trans. and introduction by F. E. Sutcliffe. London: Penguin, 1968.

Karl, Frederick. *American Fictions: 1940-1980.* New York: Harper and Row, 1983.

Klein, Marcus. *Easterns, Westerns and Private Eyes: American Matters, 1870-1900.* Madison: U of Wisconsin P, 1994.

Magny, Claude-Edmonde. *The Age of the American Novel: The Film Aesthetic of Fiction between the Two Wars.* New York: Frederick Ungar, 1972.

Oates, Joyce Carol. "H. P. Lovecraft: The King of Weird." *New York Times* 31 Oct. 1996: 50.

———. "Inside the Locked Room." Review of *A Certain Justice* by P. D. James. *New York Review of Books* 5 Feb. 1998: 19-21.

———. "The Simple Art of Murder." Review of *Stories and Early Novels* and *Later Novels and Other Writings* by Raymond Chandler. *New York Review of Books* 21 Dec. 1995: 32-40.

Reynolds, David S. *Beneath the American Renaissance: The Subversive Imagination in the Age of Emerson and Melville.* New York: Knopf, 1988.

Symons, Julian. *Bloody Murder: From the Detective Story to the Crime Novel.* 3rd ed. New York: Mysterious P, 1992.

Tuttleton, James. *The Novel of Manners in America.* New York: Norton, 1972.

Winks, Robin. *Modus Operandi: An Excursion into Detective Fiction.* Boston: David R. Godine, 1982.

Hans Bertens and Theo D'haen (essay date 2001)

SOURCE: Bertens, Hans, and Theo D'haen. "The 'English Tradition' in Contemporary American Crime Fiction." In *Contemporary American Crime Fiction,* pp. 129-45. Houndmills, England: Palgrave, 2001.

[*In the following essay, Bertens and D'haen investigate the revival of the English mystery tradition, beginning with the works of P. D. James and others, and concluding with a review of more contemporary authors such as Martha Grimes and Elizabeth George.*]

When in 1962 P. D. James published her first novel, *Cover Her Face,* few readers will have suspected that James's work would give a new lease on life to the, at that point, moribund genre of the classic English mystery novel. *Cover Her Face* is not exceptional, and neither is its police protagonist, Adam Dalgliesh. That is to say, he *is* rather exceptional—tall, dark, moody, a published poet—but not compared to most Golden Age detectives created by the women writers who in this first novel are clearly James's inspiration. Reminiscent of Ngaio Marsh's Roderick Alleyn, Dalgliesh does as far as exceptionality goes not particularly stand out in the company of Dorothy Sayers' Peter Wimsey, Margery Allingham's Albert Campion, or, for that matter, Alleyn himself. As we can see now, however, James's mysteries developed into complex meditations on deception, guilt, and retribution—occasionally at the expense of their mystery element—while Dalgliesh became more enigmatic and reminded us less and less of his Golden Age precursors.

That an Englishwoman who had come of age in the aftermath of the Depression (James was born in 1920), and who had worked as a Red Cross nurse during the Second World War, would set the classic mystery on a new, more serious and darker course, is with hindsight perhaps not so surprising. What does come as a surprise is that since the early 1980s a number of American women writers have followed James's lead in revitalizing this particular genre, although not necessarily along her lines. I should emphasize that what I have in mind here is not the revitalization of the classic mystery *per se,* such as the donnish mysteries featuring Amanda Cross's Columbia-based professor Kate Fansler, but contributions to the revitalization of the specifically *English* version of the mystery, complete with English characters and English settings. If successful, or at least mostly successful, as is the case with the English mystery series developed by, for instance, Martha Grimes and Elizabeth George, such contributions are genuine *tours de force* that derive added interest from the fact that they have been created, so to speak, from outside. Whatever else they may be, because of their non-English origin they are inevitably self-conscious constructs that built upon a deep familiarity with the conventions of the genre.

MARTHA GRIMES, LONG PIDDLETON, AND THE TWELFTH VISCOUNT ARDRY

Martha Grimes, who published her first mystery in 1981, makes no attempt to hide her intimate knowledge of the classics of mystery and detective writing: references abound to both the male tradition—from Poe to Chandler—and the female one—Sayers, Christie, Josephine Tey, and the highly rated P. D. James. More in general, and in keeping with a prominent strand of the classic English mystery, Grimes's crime fiction is intensely literary. It invites us to revisit that pleasant realm of the English literary mystery created by Michael Innes, Nicholas Blake, Edmund Crispin and other highly literate writers in whose work literary history is never far away and who more than their less well-read colleagues emphasize the 'comedy' part of the comedy of manners that the classic mystery so often is. Especially Crispin's sense of comedy echoes in Grimes's novels, in which, as I have already suggested, literary allusions abound. We come across Shakespeare, Rimbaud, Marlowe, Browning, Trollope, Coleridge, Henry James, Grahame's *The Wind in the Willows,* and so on, in an impressive range of references, some of which are structurally functional. In Grimes's debut, *The Man with a Load of Mischief* (1981), a murder is made possible by the way a specific scene from *Othello* is staged. In *The Horse You Came In On* (1993) an early reference to Chatterton (which will resurface at various points in the novel) introduces a story that hinges on forgery. *Horse* is more generally a good example of Grimes's literariness: the novel contains fragments from a novel in progress by one of the characters (somewhat reminiscent of Djuna Barnes's *Nightwood*), offers a fake Poe story (which cleverly announces its own fakeness), and throws in an aborted scene from a mystery two other characters are trying to cook up. As if this is not enough, for the more academically oriented connoisseur Grimes presents a deconstructionist poet who is appropriately self-serving and talentless (Elizabeth George gives a similarly dismissive treatment to a Marxist literary critic in one of her novels), next to references to such unfrequented nooks in literary history as the Algonquin Round Table. Part of the pleasure of reading Grimes, then, is the pleasure of recognition: we encounter familiar themes, familiar locales—the village of Long Piddleton which returns in all the novels is of standard 'postcard' picturesqueness—familiar references, and familiar conventions. Clearly counting on our familiarity with the genre, Grimes conspirationally draws us into the game she is playing: her first novel, *The Man with a Load of Mischief* comes complete with the sort of map of Long Piddleton—not wholly appropriately designed in Tolkien-like fashion—that we associate with the heyday of the classic mystery.

Grimes's two main detectives are true to the classic convention. Like P. D. James's Adam Dalgliesh, her Superintendent Richard Jury reminds us of Roderick Alleyn: good-looking, tall, formidable in an unassuming, contemplative way, and yet compassionate and attentive. In many ways Jury, although a professional, resembles the highly literate and cultured amateur detective: there are books all over his apartment and, being a gentleman, he is essentially without ambition. His collaborator Melrose Plant, former twelfth Viscount Ardry and eighth Earl of Caverness, is a wealthy, fastidious, and somewhat diffident aristocrat who combines elements of Sayers's Peter Wimsey (the sartorial finesse and general knowledgeability), Allingham's Albert Campion (the diffident manner), and Crispin's Gervase Fen (the professorship in literature), even if Plant, unlike Wimsey, is always reluctant to leave his impressive country estate for the delights of the metropolis. But he comes complete with a gentleman's gentleman and the taste in cars we expect from his kind ('"Will you be requiring the Flying Spur or the Rolls, sir?"'). Even some of the comedy—one aspect in which Grimes easily outdoes her female predecessors—seems familiar: Jury's relationship with his formidable, and formidably attractive, co-tenant Carole-anne Pulatski reminds one increasingly, as the series develops, of the curious relationship between Albert Campion and the improbable Magersfontein Lugg. Like Lugg, she does not have a wholly reputable background, which includes a stint as a topless dancer, goes in for a sort of possessive mothering that includes the usual attempts at emotional blackmail, and treats her charge's possessions and rooms as if they are joint property: 'Carole-anne had decided three months ago that her favorite policeman should have [his flat] redecorated and (naturally without his knowledge) had called Decors, one of the swankiest outfits in London, to come round with their swatches' (*I Am Only the Running Footman*, 170).

In most of Grimes's novels the light mood that results from this sort of comedy, and that gives a self-conscious twist to the tradition, is never far away. In Jury's private life we have Carole-anne, in his professional existence there is the hypochondriacal Sergeant Wiggins and the feud between the cat Cyril and Jury's chief Racer, who is exactly as inferior to Jury as superiors are supposed to be, while in Melrose Plant's entourage there is the cast of Long Piddleton characters and the constant if not always convincing fuss they create. These novels are more than averagely entertaining: the comedy is woven into (sometimes too) ingenious, suspenseful plots. Grimes moves like a fencer around scenes and characters, offering a heady succession of angles and perspectives, and the language sparkles, the more so since the reader is always aware that here we have an American writer impeccably reproducing British idioms and accents. The odd ones out are *The Horse You Came In On* and *Rainbow's End* (1995) in which Grimes

decides to use American settings: Baltimore and New Mexico, respectively.

Curiously, with American settings Grimes is out of her element. Although, just as Elizabeth George, she is good on American stereotypes like the awful Baltimore cabbie in *The Horse You Came In On,* she is inexplicably weak in imagining how the American cityscape must strike a fairly reclusive and utterly English upperclass character like Melrose Plant who finds it 'so difficult . . . to make a trip, to bestir himself, to drag himself away from hearth and home and the Jack and Hammer' (*Horse,* 75). We never get the feeling of amazed and uneasy estrangement that we expect from Plant's confrontation with Baltimore. On the contrary, on his way from the airport to the city he reflects that 'there was nothing much to see on this typical airport-to-centre-city trip which could have been in London, Baltimore, New York, or anywhere except possibly Calcutta' (112). America simply does not register on Plant's consciousness. The best (and most implausible) example of this incomprehensible blindness on the part of Plant, who is otherwise fastidious enough, is his almost thoughtless putting on of the presumably not utterly clean clothes and cap of a dead bum. Perhaps we must conclude that while as an American Grimes is perfectly attuned to the 'strangeness' of England, and can, therefore, create a convincing fictional representation, she is too familiar with the American scene to imagine how 'strange' it still is in European eyes.

While in *The Five Bells and Bladebone* (1987) Grimes had already almost violated her readers' expectations by creating serious confusion with regard to a killer's identity, in a recent Jury and Plant novel, *The Case Has Altered* (1997), Grimes more fundamentally transcends both her own earlier novels and the limits of the classic English mystery. We have the usual comedy, although more low-key than usual, we have the usual problem of getting Plant convincingly into the action (at Jury's request he poses as a connoisseur of antiques), and we have the sly fun that Grimes in her more recent novels is fond of poking at her characters. Curiously, the narrator's irony at times strongly reminds us of Henry James's late novels: 'Plant's smile was, well, *dapper*'. (*Case,* 224)

Although no one would describe *The Case Has Altered* as the sort of mystery the late Henry James might have produced, the novel certainly shows us what Grimes can do in the way of serious writing. Arresting and precise descriptions abound: 'out in the distant pastures, the rime-caked sheep looked as if they were dressed in glass coats' (11); a house sits 'behind tall, thin trees that looked more like bars than trees, straight and evenly spaced' (21); a barmaid vigorously starts 'wiping down the bar. Having been left in charge, she was going to exert her limited authority and flaunt whatever sexuality she could muster.' (213) Melrose Plant, in the earlier novels often not much more than an observing consciousness, is given convincing insights into other characters:

> . . . Melrose thought this must be the source of [Parker's] magnetism. . . . He did not waste time in small talk; he plunged right into the way he felt about life. Unlike many who gave the impression of divided attention—whose minds, you knew, were elsewhere—Parker's attention was wholly concentrated on the person he was with; he projected a sense of immediacy. He was not afraid to reveal things about himself, which invited whoever he was with to do the same. This was the source of the comfort Parker unknowingly and unselfconsciously offered. One felt at home.
>
> (183)

Grimes is also quite good on the complicated and delicate relationship between Jury and the defendant, the Jenny Kennington he has first met in *The Anodyne Necklace* (1983), a relationship that here founders on a mutual lack of trust and on the woman's secretiveness. Grimes catches all the strains and the subtle emotional shifts. We find the same subtle appreciation of mood and tensions in the interrogations that Jury conducts, that of the murdered girl's family, for instance, and in the novel's dialogues. On top of this, Grimes perfectly captures the desolate and wind-swept Lincolnshire Fens in winter.

In *The Case Has Altered* Grimes almost closes the gap with the serious novel. That she is well capable of this had already been illustrated by a non-series novel, the 1996 *Hotel Paradise* which, although driven by a number of mysteries and a sort of investigation, is only marginally a mystery. We have the enigmatic drowning of a young girl, over 40 years ago; a murder, some 20 years ago, of which the man who was found guilty is probably innocent; an unsolved murder in the present, and the unexplained appearances of a mysterious young woman; but the heart of the novel is its recreation of *temps perdu*. Central to *Hotel Paradise* is a strangely muted and innocent 1950s in an unidentifiable small town locale somewhere in the US—we may be in northern Pennsylvania or upstate New York, but Grimes is careful not to give away any definite clues. Television plays no role, there are no fast food franchises, and the local sheriff on his daily rounds slots dimes into parking meters to keep his flock from breaking the law. The magical hush that plays over everything and that gives the novel its timeless quality has to do with the voice and the limited perspective of its narrator, the 12-year-old Emma, whose discovery of who and what she is and of a wider world in which old loyalties must inevitably be redefined, is the foreground for Grimes's fascinating picture of small town life in the 1950s.

ELIZABETH GEORGE, THE EIGHTH EARL OF ASHERTON, AND ACTON, NORTH LONDON

Martha Grimes has done interesting things with the classic English mystery. Still, Elizabeth George (1949) must be considered the best of the writers who in the last two decades have revitalized the genre. Moreover, judging by the number of reprintings of her books—more than a dozen for her first novel—she is also the most successful, so that for once critical acclaim and popular success are not at odds with one another.

That first book, *A Great Deliverance* (1988), is a virtuoso performance. However, that is not what the reader expects after all the necessary introductions have been made. In fact, George's CID Detective Inspector Lynley, who will dominate the series that will develop from *A Great Deliverance,* initially has all the earmarks of a Lord Peter Wimsey replay, and his entourage is not much more promising. Our first glimpse of Lynley is that of a 'tall man who managed to look as if somehow he'd been born wearing morning dress.' In keeping with this, '[h]is movements [are] graceful, fluid, like a cat's' (31). Lynley is not only the Eighth Earl of Asherton, with an Eton and Oxford background, he is also rich, living in posh Belgravia and with a Bentley to take him to the ancestral estate in Cornwall if he is so inclined. As we will find out in George's fourth novel, *A Suitable Vengeance* (1991), the estate comes complete with a smuggler's cove, an abandoned mine, and an old mill. He excels, moreover, at his job. In short, as policewoman Barbara Havers, who is assigned to work with him early in the novel—a partnership that will turn out to be a major variation upon the male/female partnership convention—tells herself somewhat sourly, 'He was the golden boy in more ways than one' (48). Lynley's inner circle reflects the exceptional (and improbable) qualities of the man himself. His close friend Simon Allcourt-St James is a brilliant forensic scientist and has in his early 30s 'known too much pain and sorrow at far too young an age' (36) and the women—St James's bride Deborah and Lynley's friend Lady Helen Clyde—are as impossibly attractive as the girls featuring in many classic mysteries (those of John Dickson Carr, for instance). After this, it cannot come as a surprise that Lynley easily matches his female companions in the looks department: he is 'the handsomest man' Havers has ever seen. But with Barbara Havers George has already laid a potential bomb under this paragon of looks and breeding and introduced a perspective to which Dorothy Sayers never exposed Lord Peter Wimsey: 'She loathed him.' (31)

Barbara Havers, who will become Lynley's permanent partner in the series, is in virtually everything his opposite. Her background and accent are definitely working class, her education is of the grammar-school kind, she is plain and dumpy and is, moreover, well aware of it. In her late 20s, she still lives with her parents in a 'wrong' street in Acton, North London, and fights an utterly depressing daily battle with her mother's at this point still rather serene madness and her father's addiction to betting and snuff—a habit which his doctor has expressly forbidden. As if this is not enough, the father has an aversion to bathing and has the equally unsettling, although less offensive, habit of referring to himself in the third person. Apart from the mental condition of her parents, but surely related to it, the most disturbing element in the Havers household is the shrine devoted to Barbara's long dead younger brother who died of leukemia at the age of ten: an elaborate, sick construction placed in such a way that the boy's picture can watch the 'telly'. Given such circumstances, we are not surprised to find that Havers has a more than average chip on her shoulder, the more so since her one experience with a man (as we learn in a later novel) has not even included the morning after. But, as Lynley realizes in *A Great Deliverance,* 'There was no question of angry virginity here. It was something else.' (118) It is this something else that has dogged Havers's police career so far. At one point promoted to Criminal Investigation she 'has proved herself incapable of getting along with a single DI for her entire tenure in CID' (24). As a result she has been demoted, a decision that has led her 'termagant personality' to explode in a memorable way. When *A Great Deliverance* opens, her superiors, aware of her undeniable ability, agree to give her one more chance, coupling her with the infallibly courteous and ever-patient Lynley, a gamble that unexpectedly pays off. This particular partnership is a brilliant innovation. While Grimes sticks to the standard combination of two males (who, in a minor deviation from tradition, are each other's equals), George makes a very uneasy male-female relationship part of her reworking of the classic format.

The Lynley-Havers relationship is a subtheme in all of George's books, but in *A Great Deliverance,* where its foundations are laid, it plays an exceptionally important role. George brilliantly creates correspondences between the case Lynley and Havers are sent out to investigate in the imaginary Yorkshire Dales village of Keldale and Havers's personal life, sometimes even in a literal sense, as when the shrine to her deceased brother in her parents' living room is mirrored by the shrine that a murdered Yorkshire farmer has apparently devoted to his long disappeared spouse. Inexplicably, George totally implausibly arranges for Allcourt-St James and his wife—with whom, to complicate matters, Lynley is in love—to be honeymooning in the same village. In fact, Allcourt-St James, like Lynley presumably the product of an infatuation on the author's part with either a certain type of Golden Age detective novel or with a certain sector of English society, will never find a natural place in George's novels, his presence usually unnecessary and always forced. Only Lady Helen Clyde,

who gradually replaces Deborah Allcourt-St James in Lynley's affections and finally, after intense heart-to-heart talks in *For the Sake of Elena* (1992) consents to marry him (and actually does so in *In the Presence of the Enemy,* 1996), will become more or less integrated in the series.

But to return to Lynley and Havers. The case that takes them to Yorkshire is one in which a young woman has been found next to her father's decapitated body and has confessed to the crime only to completely shut up afterwards. The case is, however, by no means as straightforward as it seems. For one thing, the murder weapon has gone missing; for another, there seems to be no motive. Lynley and Havers succeed in unravelling an extraordinarily complicated mystery, in which one discovery leads to another. In a technique that she also uses to great effect in her other novels, and that suggests a parallel with archeological excavation, George allows her detectives to strip away layer after layer of deceptions and falsehoods until finally the terrible truth stands revealed.

In *A Great Deliverance* that truth is incestuous abuse, the systematic and prolonged abuse by a religious fanatic of his two young daughters, one of whom has years ago run away to save herself. This older sister, who is now in her mid-20s, is in the course of the investigation tracked down by Havers and is subsequently confronted with the sister she has last seen as a little girl. In the harrowing scene that follows she succeeds in breaking through the stupor that has overtaken her younger sister since their father's death. Her detailed description of the father's sexual demands provokes a response from the younger sister who in so doing finally returns to speech. It also has an enormous impact on Havers, who with Lynley and some others is watching the scene from behind a one-way glass panel. Havers crashes blindly from the room to find a restroom and is violently sick. The terrible form of abuse that has just been revealed to her and the overwhelming feelings of guilt experienced by the sisters—the younger turns out indeed to have murdered her father—forcibly bring home the total inadequacy of her own parents and confront her with her own feelings of guilt. We learn that Havers's parents never visited their ten-year-old son in hospital because they could not cope with his illness, leaving the daily visits to his sister, the emotionally vulnerable teenager Barbara, who has never forgiven herself for not being there when he actually died and who has ever since taken a subtle, insidious and rather disturbing revenge: the shrine in the Havers's living room is of her making, a way to daily remind her parents of their inadequacy and guilt, just as the shrine in the farm probably has been created by the older sister to remind her father of his failure as the husband of a runaway wife and mother. Confronting the fact that she has substantially contributed to the misery of her parents' lives and possibly even to her mother's feeble-mindedness, Havers 'put her head down on the porcelain and wept. She wept for the hate that had filled her life, for the guilt and the jealousy that had been her companions, for the loneliness that she had brought upon herself, for the contempt and disgust she had directed towards others.' When Lynley, who has followed her, 'wordlessly [takes] her in his arms', she weeps 'against his chest, mourning most of all the death of the friendship that could have lived between them.' (308)

As this makes clear, Havers's view of Lynley has dramatically changed. From slick, loathsome, and impossibly aristocratic womanizer Lynley has become a potential friend, a development made possible by the mutual respect that has grown in the course of the novel and by a shared sense of humour. But Havers is also aware that an earlier and ugly personal attack, triggered by the class bias and personal unhappiness that consistently lead her to completely misconstrue his behavior and feelings, may very well have destroyed that potential friendship.

This, however, is not the case. Lynley has not only in the meantime realized that Havers's unreasonable aggressiveness has more to do with her personal problems than with anything he might do or not do, he also knows that her anger, although totally off its immediate target, is not wholly misplaced: '. . . beyond Havers there was truth. For underneath her bitter, unfounded accusations, her ugliness and hurt, the words she spoke rang with veracity.' (243) Lynley, who in the later novels repeatedly shows an intense self-awareness, is willing to redirect Havers's anger and to hook it up with his real shortcomings: his sexual encounter with a Keldale witness that Havers has overheard and, more mysteriously, sins that are only hinted at when he briefly reflects on his reasons for having chosen this particular profession: '*It's a penance . . . an expiation for sins committed. . . .*' (128) Considering that he is not in a position to cast the first stone—the reasons for which are spelled out in *A Suitable Vengeance*—Lynley is able to make allowances for Havers's personal demons and ends by giving her a chance to redeem herself and by offering the moral support that she now has come to appreciate. Fully aware of the limitations of Havers's social graces and of the fact that easy personal relationships will probably be forever beyond her, he has also come to value her honesty, her courage, her ability, and her devotion to the job.

With its unexpected twists and revelations, *A Great Deliverance* is a wholly satisfying mystery in the Golden Age tradition. But it is more than that. George gives an unprecedented depth to the conventional figure of the aristocratic detective, who in her hands, unlike earlier versions like Albert Campion and Peter Wimsey,

loses every trace of P. G. Wodehouse's Bertie Wooster. Lynley is a man of great seriousness who has his own demons—which are spelled out in *A Suitable Vengeance*—and who occasionally, as in an ugly scene in *In the Presence of the Enemy*, allows his anger to run away with him. This seriousness is not limited to Lynley. *A Great Deliverance* is more generally a serious book. Havers's pain and guilt are terribly serious and so is the series of interlocking crimes that is revealed. What is perhaps worse is that there is no real deliverance. A daughter is reunited with her long lost mother but will never forget that she has been betrayed and deserted, just like she herself has deserted her younger sister. The priest who, through the confessional, was aware of the abuse, must live with the knowledge that his silence has effectively condoned the practice and has ultimately led to murder. The woman who seduces Lynley stands accused of what within the context of this novel almost constitutes a crime: a wilful superficiality that must serve to protect her against responsibility. *A Great Deliverance* is about the evasion of moral responsibility, an evasion so general and so diffuse that no character fully transcends it. Only Lynley, who is atoning for earlier evasions and Havers, in her painful recognition of what she has done to her awful parents, come close.

It is this moral seriousness that marks George's distance from the classic tradition. We are of course meant to recognize her borrowings: the brother suspected, and cleared, of murder in *A Suitable Vengeance* reminds us of how Sayers has Peter Wimsey exonerate his brother Denver; we have the murder in the isolated country house (in *Payment in Blood* (1989), in which, incidentally, the relationship between Lynley and Havers is already a good deal more balanced); we have the world of Cambridge colleges in *For the Sake of Elena* (1992), and so on. George's novels, however, always convey a moral judgment that goes much further than anything the classics ever offered. The widespread moral irresponsibility that is inevitably revealed, and of which the actual culprit is occasionally less guilty than a good many others who will get off scot-free, reminds one of the bleak world of the classic private eye. Whereas in classic private eye fiction much of that irresponsibility is suggested, a result of metaphors and mood rather than detection, in George's fiction it is actually shown, an effect of her habit of offering a variety of characters and multiple points of view. On the other side of the spectrum we find characters who, with equally disastrous results, more or less monopolize responsibility, who are unwilling to share their burden either out of pride or out of love—as in the more recent *In Pursuit of the Proper Sinner* (1999) in which a husband commits suicide to keep hidden from his wife what she is already fully aware of.

Apart from her complex plots, this panoramic strategy, reminiscent of mid-nineteenth-century realist fiction, is George's great strength, not in the least because it also allows her to maintain a constant level of suspense by switching perspectives (and thus cutting off the flow of information) at exactly the right cliff-hanging moment. Still, in her more recent fiction, this strength begins to develop into a weakness, paradoxically because she sets her sights too high. Although *A Great Deliverance* is very good on its Yorkshire setting, it focuses almost exclusively on the investigation. The result is a taut novel—in spite of its considerable length—that has the reader walking an emotional tightrope. With *For the Sake of Elena* we arrive at something of a turning point. The novel is very good on the cowardly self-centeredness of the Cambridge don who is the father of the main victim; on the relationship between Lynley and Lady Helen Clyde; on the depressing sexism of a number of minor male characters; and on the hatred an ex-wife feels for her former husband and his new wife. It is even better on Havers, who after the death of her father is now solely responsible for a mother who has slid into dementia and can no longer take care of herself. Especially chilling is the scene in which Havers's mother has 'messed' herself because she is too scared of the hose of the vacuum cleaner—which she takes to be a snake—to leave the sofa. Livid with the woman who is supposed to look after her mother and who has deliberately left the hose on the floor to make sure that her charge would not wander off, Havers fires her and, racked by guilt, finally decides to place her mother in a home. This is what the 'literary' George—the George giving us material that is not related to an investigation—does brilliantly: relatively brief scenes of great emotional intensity and power that substantially contribute to the seriousness of her fiction.

In her most recent novels George's affinity with realism is both a liability and an asset. What works against her is her desire to provide too many minor characters with a believable perspective and a matching psycho-social background. As a result *In the Presence of the Enemy,* published in 1996, runs to 630 pages while the 1997 *Deception on His Mind* in which, interestingly, Havers is given a solo performance, adds another 120 to clock in at 750 pages. Keeping the reader's interest alive for such marathon runs would tax any novelist. George does not quite bring it off because not all of the perspectives that she offers are equally interesting; in fact, with regard to some she would seem to be on automatic pilot, working out stereotypes along all too predictable lines, sometimes even to the point of caricature. (In *Deception* we have a German whose English is quite good, but who yet begins every other sentence with '*Ja*'. Germans do not have this particular affliction, not even when they speak German.)

A positive development in the recent novels is their overt interest in politics, an interest that is of course wholly absent from the classical tradition. Right from the start George has been a political writer in the sense that the personal in her novels always has had political overtones. Although she is obviously not a radical feminist novelist, there is always a feminist undercurrent in her fiction. Even in those cases where the criminal is a woman there is a strong suggestion that the fact that this is a world in which males still dominate virtually everything has either directly or indirectly contributed to the crime. This is not to say that all of George's women are blameless victims. It is clear, however, that they must cope with both individual and social pressures that the male characters who are the instruments of these forces are largely ignorant of. Lynley is one of George's few males who at a certain point becomes aware of this. As he puts it in a conversation with his future wife: "'All I can say right now is that I finally understand that no matter how the load is shifted between partners, or divided or shared, the woman's burden will always be greater. I do know that.'" (*Elena*, 382)

In *In the Presence of the Enemy* and even more so in *Deception on His Mind* the major crimes, although as personally motivated as the murder in her first novel, are embedded in a much larger political framework. *Presence,* published when John Major still headed a British Conservative government, pits a junior minister who with her espousal of family values, her limitless ambition and uncompromising inflexibility (with regard to the IRA, for instance) is roughly modelled on Margaret Thatcher, against the editor of a leftist tabloid with whom she once had a brief and exclusively physical affair. This set-up enables George to bring in the hypocritical and sleazy dealings of a number of Conservative politicians and the equally unsavory practices of British tabloids. (The only indication that her sympathy lies with Labour is that her tabloid editor wakes up to his basic immorality while the Minister does not: 'One couldn't walk the path he'd chosen so many years ago upon coming to London and still remain a sentient creature. If he hadn't known that before, he knew now that it was an impossibility. He'd never been so lost.' (*Presence,* 442)) Unfortunately, the novel is marred by a wholly superfluous first part in which Allcourt-St James, his wife Deborah and Lady Helen Clyde try to trace a missing child. For whatever reason, George, for all her realism, finds it hard to cut this particular tie with the Golden Age. (Lady Helen tells Deborah, "'Darling . . . just think of Miss Marple. Or Tuppence. Think of Tuppence. Or Harriet Vane.'" (163) Unfortunately, neither Deborah Allcourt nor Helen Clyde come close to Harriet Vane in terms of intrinsic interest.) Lacking the anger and drive of Barbara Havers, Deborah and Helen are plucky girls in the young Tuppence mold rather than the mature and serious women that one expects a mature and serious version of Peter Wimsey to associate himself with.

It is the political factor plus the absence of the Lynley entourage—even more than the absence of Lynley himself—that makes *Deception on his Mind* so convincing, even if here, too, George errs on the side of comprehensiveness: we simply get too many perspectives, not all of which are relevant to the story that she is telling and with regard to some of which her imagination lets her down. But that story is gripping enough, beginning with the discovery of a dead Pakistani on the beach just north of Balford-le-Nez, an Essex seaside resort not too far from Clacton-on-Sea (the Nez in question looks suspiciously like the real-life Naze—also not too far from Clacton—in the map that George provides with a tongue-in-cheek reference to the classic tradition). To the local Pakistani community, led by a firebrand political activist, the murderer must have been motivated by racial hatred. Since this implies a white murderer the Pakistanis, whose anger explodes in a small-scale riot, suspect a cover-up. At this point Detective Chief Inspector Emily Barstow, in charge of the investigation, invites Barbara Havers, who has rather implausibly come to Balford to keep an eye on a Pakistani neighbor and his little girl, to liaise between the Pakistani community—represented by the activist and Barbara's London neighbor—and the investigating officers. Before long Barbara drifts into the investigation itself, allowed to do so by Barstow, whom she has met at a police course and for whom she has immense admiration. Emily Barstow openly defies convention with her 'jet black hair, dyed punk and cut punk', is as matter of fact about sex (which is 'a regular bonk with a willing bloke' (*Deception*, 84)) as about anything else, has the figure of the 'dedicated triathlete' that she is, and is in Barbara's eyes dazzlingly good at her job: 'nowhere was there a woman more competent, more suited to criminal investigations, and more gifted in the politics of policework than Emily Barlow' (66).

What she is definitely not good at, however, is race relations. There is a good deal of racism in the novel, even if, as Barbara at one point tells herself, by no means all of her compatriots are racists. We have the almost intangible segregation in Barbara's hotel, for example, but also shockingly crude and mean incidents of overt racism. Gradually, Barbara's hero is exposed as a hardline racist. For a while, Barbara is able to ignore Emily's references to 'those people' and her derogatory generalizations: '"none of these yobbos can be trusted half an inch"' (609). But when Emily is fully prepared to let a '"Paki brat"'—the ten-year-old daughter of Barbara's neighbor—drown in order to catch a Pakistani criminal who is trying to make his way across the North Sea to Germany and has thrown the child overboard, Barbara is squarely confronted with Emily's refusal to see Pakistanis in human terms. Holding a gun on Emily,

she tells her to turn the boat in which they are chasing the fleeing Pakistani and to pick up the foundering child. When Emily does not immediately respond she fires the gun but fortunately misses after which a badly shaken Emily allows her and the (male) detective who is also on board, and who clearly sides with Barbara, to save the child's life.

Race and the differences between Pakistani and English culture constitute the dominant themes of the novel. Race determines the relations between the Pakistani community and the police (ironically, and in typical George fashion, the activist turns out to be right with regard to Barstow's racism, while she is right concerning his criminal activities), while the enormous cultural differences greatly complicate the investigation and for a long time divert the suspicion from the actual murderer. It is Barbara, who is a good deal more attuned to these differences than her temporary superior who is blinded by her own prejudices, who finally tumbles to the truth. Moreover, the issue of race is instrumental in Barbara's unprecedented pulling of a gun on a superior officer. They seem to hold each other hostage: Emily may report Barbara's insubordination leading to attempted murder while Barbara, as she is well aware, is in a position to report Emily's racism and willingness to sacrifice the life of a child to the pursuit of a personal vengeance. But there is no doubt that Emily holds all the cards: she not only outranks Barbara but she is also completely ruthless and unforgiving where Barbara is willing to make allowances. It is the fact that Barbara finally sees through Emily's 'professionalism'—built to a considerable extent on self-deception and the resolute denial of personal relationships—that allows her to see that Emily's apparent strength is her major weakness and that topples Emily from her intimidating pedestal: 'Don't think [your solution of the murder] changes a thing between us, Emily was telling her. You're finished as a cop if I have my way. Do what you have to do, was Barbara's silent reply. And for the first time since meeting Emily Barlow, she actually felt free.' (740)

In the course of the novels Barbara Havers gradually overcomes her crippling insecurity and pathological and often aggressive defensiveness. She frees herself first of all from Lynley. When they start working together, in *A Great Deliverance,* she tries to hang on to her instinctive loathing of him in order to protect her cut-and-dried, class-based view of everything he stands for. Eventually Lynley's competence and compassion break down her defenses and force her to revaluate her prejudices. Equally important is that Lynley, for all his easy superiority, is not infallible and occasionally allows his judgment to be affected by emotional involvement. '"Stop lying to yourself"', Havers tells him in *In the Presence of the Enemy*. '"You're not after facts. You're after vengeance. It's written all over you."' (261)

And when he does not see reason, she adds for good measure: "'Holy hell . . . You can be a real prick.'" (262) Because Lynley encourages her to speak her mind, instead of pulling rank as Emily Barstow does when Barbara sins against police hierarchy—"'You're out of line, Sergeant'"—Barbara can be her prickly, outspoken self.

In a parallel development, Barbara learns to cope with her suffocating feelings of guilt, which is to say that she finds a balance between her responsibilities with regard to her parents and, more in particular, her increasingly demented mother, and her responsibilities with regard to herself as an adult woman with a life of her own. Although she never overcomes her guilt—not to be confused with responsibility—she finally realizes her wish to go and live by herself. Finally, in *Deception on His Mind,* she learns to see through another false image: that of Emily Barstow, female supercop. Like Eve Bowen, the Conservative junior minister in *Presence,* Barstow stands for the female who has adopted the worst male traits: ruthless ambition, emotional distance, complete self-sufficiency, sexuality without affection. Realizing that Barstow's limitations far outweigh her own, Barbara is free to be her competent and compassionate, if dumpy and rather unprepossessing self.

With Barbara Havers, we are a long way from the classic tradition. And even if Lynley is closer to some of his Golden Age predecessors, there is an awareness of human frailty and of man's self-serving stupidity that is almost wholly absent from the tradition (Dorothy Sayers's *Gaudy Night* in which, appropriately, Harriet Vane plays the leading role, comes to mind as an exception). In one of the last scenes of *Presence,* watching the murderer and 'casting the observation into the light of what he'd learned about his background, Lynley fe[els] only a tremendous defeat' (620). Here the mood fuses with that of the more serious version of the private eye novel, just as it does at the end of *Deception* when Barbara feels equally 'weighted down by the case' (746)—a phrase one associates with Philip Marlowe or Lew Archer rather than with an English policewoman. But, then, that policewoman has in *Presence* been badly battered by the killer she attacks to save a young boy's life and has only a couple of weeks later, still hurting from her bruises and broken ribs, fired a gun at her superior officer to save another child from drowning. Not only the mood of the private eye novel, including its inevitable defiance of authority, but also its dramatic action and the self-sacrificial interventions of the classic PI, have entered George's reworking of the tradition.

Primary Bibliography

Friedman, Kinky. *God Bless John Wayne.* London and Boston: Faber and Faber, 1995.

George, Elizabeth. *A Suitable Vengeance.* New York: Bantam, 1991.

———. *For the Sake of Elena.* New York: Bantam, 1992.

———. *In the Presence of the Enemy.* New York: Bantam, 1996.

———. *In Pursuit of the Proper Sinner.* New York: Bantam, 1999.

Grimes, Martha. *The Horse You Came In On.* London: Headline, 1993.

———. *The Case Has Altered.* London: Headline, 1997.

Richard B. Schwartz (essay date 2002)

SOURCE: Schwartz, Richard B. "Live and Learn." In *Nice and Noir: Contemporary American Crime Fiction,* pp. 114-26. Columbia: University of Missouri Press, 2002.

[*In the following essay, Schwartz appraises contemporary crime fiction as a genre that draws on several sources for inspiration, including established literary traditions and folktales, as well as real-life experiences by the authors themselves.*]

The other half of the Horatian dyad, teaching, has not been neglected by crime writers. Indeed, given the journalistic dimensions of this craft, the teaching may sometimes come easier than the pleasing. Richard Price's above-mentioned *Clockers,* an account of the details of urban drug dealing (do they really drink Yoo-Hoo to calm their nervous stomachs?), is a good example of the practice. Both Mitchell Smith's *Stone City* and Tim Willocks's *Green River Rising* are extended meditations on penology, with many reflections on both the sociology of the maximum-security prison and the theoretical underpinnings of particular penological experiments. Ellroy's "L.A. Quartet," with its meticulous attention to correct details and its intercut clips from *Hush-Hush* magazine, the *Times, Mirror-News,* and *Examiner,* recalls Dos Passos's *U.S.A.* trilogy and its journalistic approach to historiography.

There is overlap here between crime fiction and the English mystery. In fact, some collectors assemble books based on subject rather than author, period, or genre. For example, there are collections of books involving murders employing poisons from specific geographical areas. A number of mystery series focus on historical periods and personages and offer details concerning the daily life and material culture of those periods. (This is rarer in crime fiction, though the work of Caleb Carr is a good counterexample. His success is encouraging others, and we can expect to see the historical crime novel become a major growth area.)

The procedural is a subgenre that focuses on detection techniques and technologies. The Mystery Writers of America association sponsors seminars and issues materials on such matters, so that its members can display the erudition expected by their readership. Real-life connections with actual practices and practitioners are points of discussion for jacket copy. Patricia Cornwell's experiences in this regard are often noted (and somewhat exaggerated), while Carl Hiaasen's, Edna Buchanan's, Thomas Harris's, and Michael Connelly's journalistic backgrounds are duly mentioned. Jonathan Kellerman, like his protagonist Alex Delaware, *is* a child psychologist, and Andrew Vachss *is* a practicing attorney, specializing in cases of abuse and, hence, looking into the abyss on a daily basis.

The endless semesters spent in the school of hard knocks often serve writers well when they finally break free of their daytime jobs. James Lee Burke, for example, worked on the oil rigs he often describes, and Charles Willeford (who worked as a painter, prizefighter, and soldier, among other things) had a rich enough experience to fill two volumes of autobiography (and those dealing only with his early life). Chandler's life did not include detective work, but it did include a gothic family history, military service, British education, and work in the oil industry (all very ably charted in an excellent recent biography by Tom Hiney).

Joseph Wambaugh was a police department insider as well as a chronicler of department experience, and Gerald Petievich worked for the secret service, which has responsibility for the forgery cases of which Petievich has written. Hammett was a Pinkerton operative, and Steve Martini was originally a trial lawyer, experience that is evident in his accounts of courtroom procedure, particularly in the ways and means of cross-examination. John Grisham and Scott Turow, of course, have also worked as attorneys as well as become highly successful crime novelists. Parenthetically, one of the few areas of crime writing in which supply falls short of demand is courtroom drama. This is a popular subgenre, and fanzines sometimes report on the percentage of a given novel devoted to actual courtroom scenes and procedures.

We have recently been treated to two exceptional novels that depict aspects of criminal experience in professional detail. The first is by Don Winslow. Winslow began his writing career with a series character named Neal Carey. Carey is, interestingly enough, a Columbia University graduate student. The challenge of getting such a protagonist out of the library and onto the crime scene offers intriguing opportunities for plotlines. In

1997 Winslow published his breakout book, *The Death and Life of Bobby Z,* a switched-identity-scam narrative that found a wide and appreciative audience.

In 1999 Winslow followed *The Death and Life of Bobby Z* with *California Fire and Life,* an elaborate tale of arson and the investigation thereof, featuring a protagonist named Jack Wade. Winslow knows whereof he speaks, for in addition to working as a private investigator both in Europe and in America he also worked as an arson investigator in Los Angeles for more than fifteen years. The film *Backdraft* (directed by Ron Howard, 1991) may have stolen a bit of Winslow's thunder, but *California Fire and Life* is a strong novel built upon strong facts and a professional knowledge of authentic techniques.

Robert Crais has followed this course with his recent novel, *Demolition Angel,* an elaborate account of explosives and their detonation and defusing, complete with accounts of air pressures, shock waves, detonation rates, and countermeasures. The acknowledgments section includes a statement expressing the concerns of Crais's technical consultants, who were worried that the book could prove to be instructional. As a result, Crais altered certain facts and procedures and included fictional elements, lest the criminals among his readership understand the full range of techniques and equipment at the disposal of modern law enforcement.

As the title suggests, *Demolition Angel* is a departure from Crais's Elvis Cole series, one featuring a female protagonist named Carol Starkey, one of the more memorable followers in Clarice Starling's wake. One might also mention in this regard Merci Rayborn, the excellent protagonist of T. Jefferson Parker's *The Blue Hour* and more recent *Red Light. Demolition Angel*'s movie rights brought top dollar, suggesting that there is still the occasional good role for women actors and an abiding audience interest in procedural detail.

The master here, on both counts, is Thomas Harris, and Harris's masterpiece is *The Silence of the Lambs.* While this is not the first novel dealing with a serial killer, it is the most prominent of such books. It is also the most prominent book to capitalize on the expertise of the FBI's profiling unit, particularly the expertise of the individual who coined the phrase *serial killer*: Robert K. Ressler. It was Ressler who introduced Harris to the sole female agent then in residence and Ressler who discussed cases with Harris such as that of Ed Gein, the terribly disturbed resident of Wisconsin upon whose activities *The Silence of the Lambs* is partially based.

Gein's name has passed into the realm of legend in Wisconsin, where stories à la those of the urban legend "hook man" are still told. (James Ellroy has acknowledged a particular interest in Ed Gein, given the fact that his mother, Geneva Hilliker Ellroy, was originally from Wisconsin.) Ressler also profiled such well-known individuals as Richard Trenton Chase, the Sacramento "Vampire Killer," William Heirens, Charles Manson, Richard Speck, Ted Bundy, John Joubert, Gerard Schaefer, John W. Hinckley, Duane Samples, Harvey Murray Glatman, John Wayne Gacy, Edmund Kemper, Monte Rissell, and Jeffrey Dahmer.

To date, Ressler has written three true crime books on his efforts, the most important of which is *Whoever Fights Monsters,* which he wrote with Tom Shachtman. This book contains the accounts of the above-mentioned cases and includes a summary of Ressler's profile of the archetypal serial killer and of his meetings with Thomas Harris. (Ressler admires Harris's work but objects to specific details; an agent-in-training such as Clarice Starling would never, Ressler says, be given the responsibilities that she was given or be put in such a dangerous position.)

While Evan Hunter, writing as Ed McBain, may be the master of the police procedural, Harris was shrewd enough to realize that an FBI procedural would offer greater range and opportunity. The FBI operates across state lines, has bigger databases and better toys, and provides the film director the opportunity for lush Washington establishing shots and cuts between them and the stark settings in "the field." Each of Harris's four novels has resulted in a movie *sale* as well as a successful *movie,* and he is closely attuned to cinematic opportunities.

In addition to the use of FBI profiling procedure, Harris includes other technical details. He explains how one takes the fingerprints from a corpse that has spent a great deal of time in the water. He instructs us as to the substance used by the FBI to counter the smells of rotting corpses (Vicks VapoRub). We receive a tour of the Anthropology and Entomology section of the Smithsonian, learn how to position a body when conducting a recreational flaying, and, of course, gain an appreciation of the difficulties involved in making a garment of human skin.

Even some of the novel's best jokes involve scientific detail, such as the chemical formula for bilirubin. For all that, however, the use of technical detail is handled with a very light touch. This is not an elongated class; it is a novel with characters and plot, both of which stay firmly in the narrative foreground. Harris realizes the risks of allowing these elements to be subsumed by procedure and maintains the balance neatly. He does so, in part, by building his narrative upon a time-honored structure.

First and foremost, *The Silence of the Lambs* is a beauty-and-the-beast tale. In finding leverage in Madame Le Prince de Beaumont's 1756 classic, Harris

has ridden a tidal wave of contemporary beauty-and-the-beast stories, including the Disney animated film, the Catherine and Vincent television series, Andrew Lloyd Weber's *Phantom of the Opera,* and such film and television titles as *Darkman, Swamp Thing, Terminator II,* and *Twin Peaks.*

The best-known, eighteenth-century version of the tale (and its faithful cinematic reproduction by Jean Cocteau in 1946) is part of a larger category of fairy tales—the animal-groom story. The de Beaumont rendering tells of a merchant with three daughters, one of whom is especially lovely. The merchant suffers financial reversals, loses his wealth, and undertakes a voyage in an attempt to recoup. While his other daughters request expensive gifts upon his return, Beauty asks for nothing beyond a single rose.

The journey fails, and in the course of the return voyage the merchant's ship is lost in a storm. He stumbles upon a magic palace, sees a rose in the palace garden, and plucks it for his daughter Beauty. This angers the beast who inhabits the palace, who demands either the life of the merchant or the hand of one of his daughters in marriage.

Beauty reciprocates her father's love by volunteering to serve as his substitute. However, once inside the palace of which she is now mistress she develops respect for the beast who is its master. Missing her father, who has become ill, she returns to his home but stays too long. Then, missing the beast, she returns to find him at the brink of death, grieving over what he has taken to be her loss. When Beauty tells the beast of her love for him he is turned into a prince and the two marry.

The Disney version also focuses on the relationship between Beauty (Belle) and her father (Maurice) and forces her to come to terms with the nature of loyalty as well as the nature of fear. The rose figures in the story, but in a different way than in the de Beaumont version. Instead of functioning symbolically as an emblem of Belle's virginity, the rose here is a magic one, given to the prince by an enchantress who he turned away in a storm and who punished him for his selfishness and meanness of spirit by turning him into a beast. Unless he finds love before the last rose petal falls, he will remain a beast forever. There is also a subplot involving a rival suitor, a handsome but oafish village figure named Gaston, and of course the requisite Disneyisms (talking objects and such) suitable for sale as merchandising tie-ins.

One of the Disney studio's clear intentions in the project is to present a very contemporary Belle, one who represents a conscious departure from the characteristics of earlier Disney heroines. Belle is an intellectual, bored in her small French village. She is also curious and independent and fully capable of charming, taming, and managing the Beast. She is also drawn with a woman's body, unlike, for example, her immediate predecessor in the Disney animated pantheon, Ariel of *The Little Mermaid.*

The Disney version's moral is made explicit in the lyrics of the title song, whose shelf life has been immeasurably extended now that Celine Dion has covered it on a "best of" record. The song indicates that love occurs when each lover is prepared to "bend" and realize that each has been wrong. That takes us several steps beyond the realization that beauty and beastliness are only skin-deep; there is also the need for cooperation and compromise and a willingness to relinquish control. Again, this is noticeably contemporary.

This is quite different from the *Beauty and the Beast* television series, which plunges us into melodrama with the romantic saga of Catherine and Vincent, the professional woman in Gotham and the lion-faced man in medieval garb who dwells within the tunnels below the city. Whenever called, Vincent leaves his idyllic world to protect Catherine in hers. He also has a tendency to pop in for soulful, seemingly endless chats. Vincent is the confidant extraordinaire, the man who will talk and share and love without ever posing a sexual threat. He demonstrates the cultural acceptance of Deborah Tannen's view of men, women, and communication by representing something approaching the female ideal—an extension of the best friend from a woman's youth, that special person with whom she bonded while the boys were busy establishing dominance relationships and playing contact sports.

"Although we can never be together we will never be apart," Catherine says, suggesting that the ultimate source for the program is not an animal-groom story but rather something like *Wuthering Heights,* that most passionate and violent of sexless love stories. If the Disney story answers Freud's question by saying that what women want is a man who will defend them from wolves but also take them dancing, the television story adds, "and talk, emotionally and endlessly."

The Silence of the Lambs is quite different. It plays off the key notion in the de Beaumont tale by focusing on the relationship between a young woman and her father. (There are no mothers in these stories.) Clarice Starling has become an FBI cadet out of loyalty to the memory of her father—a policeman killed years earlier in the line of duty. Her career is advanced by Jack Crawford, chief of the behavioral sciences unit at Quantico, but also by a psychotic psychiatrist, Dr. Hannibal Lecter. This is a modern story about a career woman in search of a mentor. This particular career woman has two.

In the de Beaumont story the plot is precipitated not by the appearance of the beast but by the separation from the father. It is an account of human development

susceptible to an aggressive Freudian reading. Beauty cannot mature without leaving home and hearth and embracing a man who at first appears beastly but who turns out to be rather princely. The rose represents Beauty's sexuality, and what Frye would term the mythos of the tale is a battle with demons that are far more psychological than bestial. The id—as frightening as it might be in its early manifestations—is still a terrible thing to waste.

In giving his story a professional-woman spin, Harris also avoids the "girly men" princes who turn up in these fairy tales, looking like they have just come from either central casting or the stage of a Sigmund Romberg operetta. He offers us instead a sweet but hardened FBI agent, whose wife is dying (this gets far more attention in the book than in the film), and a cannibalistic serial killer.

He has, in short, departed very far from our conventional sense of the prince beneath the beast, but still leveraged some of the initial energy and point of the tale. He has also leveraged some parallel aspects of the beast figure. Looking more closely at Dr. Lecter we see some familiar traits and trappings. Both Disney's Beast and Cocteau's (like TV's Vincent) sport capes, as does that other most famous of beastly mentors, the Phantom of the Opera. The Phantom (like Dr. Henry Jekyll with his Mr. Hyde) represents the monster as aesthete, the ur-figure here being, perhaps, the aristocratic aesthete, Count Dracula. (Certainly the academic version of the aesthete who has passed over to the dark side is Professor Moriarty.)

Hannibal Lecter is a great aesthete, using nothing less than the Goldberg Variations as background music for two of his murders. His cell is decorated with personal artwork—not of naked women or previous victims, but rather of the Duomo and Florence, the city in which we encounter him in the first section of the sequel, *Hannibal.* He is an individual with impeccable manners. He is, indeed, quite courtly in his behaviors. After some initial tilting he systematically treats Clarice with respect. He also pays her the supreme compliment in telling her that the world is a more interesting place with her in it. He wants to understand her and her experience; the high point in the arc of their relationship (in *The Silence of the Lambs*) is Clarice's account of the episode in her own life that is the basis for the novel's, and the film's, title. The moment of high intimacy, in effect, is one of extended, soulful talk.

I have spent some time on this particular novel to highlight the nature and effectiveness of Harris's strategy. His putative intention is to inform, and to inform with regard to a matter of great contemporary interest: serial killers and the complex procedures used by law enforcement agencies to bring them to justice.

The lessons taught and learned, however, are embedded in the most primal of forms, the traditional fairy tale, but a fairy tale given the most contemporary of spins, with the focus on the modern career woman, her need for assistance, but also her need for independence and respect.

Neither Clarice nor her close friend and fellow cadet Ardelia Mapp has time for any significant social life. Their places in their academy class are prized above all else. These are modern women. At the same time, the novel's values are exceedingly traditional. The post-Hoover, post-Patrick Gray FBI is presented as a successful organization whose members function as a coherent, cooperative team. In contrast to the Chandler loner, Clarice has individuals and resources at her disposal, and her celebratory graduation (in the film) proceeds without any irony or cynicism, just as her meeting with Crawford (in the novel) and his final words, "Starling, your father sees you," are uttered with total seriousness and carry all of the emotional freight that Crawford intends.

In short, this novel brings together old and new, the traditional and the contemporary, and it does so with an excellent sense of setting, though it is exceeded in this regard by *Hannibal*. The sequel novel has brought mixed reactions, though it has been a great commercial success. For one thing, the sequel is far closer in genre to the horror novel than to the crime novel; this has not been appreciated by all readers, some of whom have seen it as a simple extension of *The Silence of the Lambs* that seems too violent and too graphic. *Hannibal* is actually the kind of book that David Martin (not David Lozell Martin) has been writing.

There is general consensus that the Florentine section of the novel is brilliantly realized, but there have been concerns expressed about later sections and particularly about the book's ending. The fact that Jonathan Demme passed on directing the film and Jodie Foster passed on reprising the role of Clarice has suggested to some that the book is too violent, the facts of the ending and some of its details legitimately too difficult to accept. While the meal shared by Hannibal and Clarice at the end of the novel (and designed to be shared by them at the end of the film) presents directorial challenges when depicted in a visual medium, it flows naturally from all that we know of the characters. This is, after all, the woman who caught Buffalo Bill and earned the respect of Hannibal Lecter, not some frail flower. Moreover, the romantic relationship between the two (established in the novel, but altered for the film) flows not just naturally but absolutely from the beauty-and-the-beast tale. "Read Marcus Aurelius," Hannibal is fond of saying. "Read Madame Le Prince de Beaumont" is the proper rejoinder to Harris's critics.

The two books are simply different. The plot of *Hannibal* is looser and more episodic than that of *The Silence of the Lambs,* but the same can be said of the novel preceding *Silence, Red Dragon,* which is also a very fine book. Also, Clarice's travails in the bureau in *Hannibal* restore some of the Chandlerian distaste for large organizations and are sufficient to mute any criticism of *The Silence of the Lambs* as being too trusting or even sentimentally patriotic.

We should remember that Harris is an innovator. He does not take ten years writing a book in order to give us just what we expect. In *Hannibal* he gives us just what we would expect if we only knew where to look—the beast rushing to beauty's defense and then embracing her as his mate. Since that apparently was not expected, he has succeeded in the most difficult of the crime writer's tasks: surprising and outsmarting the reader after honestly giving that reader all of the clues required to solve the case.

Of course, he does that brilliantly in *The Silence of the Lambs* as well. It is striking to the point of embarrassment to realize how obvious and consistent the clues are, and still the narrative unfolds with great suspense along with ruthless logic. That is not easy to do, and making it look easy is harder still.

Harris's skill and success raise the whole issue of the level of quality we might reasonably expect from the form and the extent to which these works' subject matter can contribute to or detract from that quality. It is a fact, for example, that many individuals go to mystery and crime fiction to learn of exotic details and technical procedures. These matters can take precedence over the usual expectations of the novel reader: strong plots, rounded characters, significant themes, fully realized settings, and solid prose.

One hears great praise, for example, for Tony Hillerman and his ability to secure the trust of Native Americans, trust that runs sufficiently deep that these individuals will divulge secrets (for example, concerning tribal ceremonies) that no white man has ever known. The cynic might ask how trustworthy the material is if its confidentiality compromises our ability to confirm its accuracy, but that is not the point. The point is that Hillerman is being praised as a researcher rather than as a writer and that in valuing the facts in particular we are turning his mystery novels into anthropology texts.

One can, of course, have both: highly polished novels that also convey unique information. That is the desire, but with an audience that can sometimes fixate on the quality of the fact over the quality of the narrative there are potential dangers. Many of the most interesting crime novels have been crossover books—the subject of our next chapter—and they have been able to reach far broader audiences than conventional category fiction. Fresh and expansive views of the genre are, in my judgment, to be encouraged. At the same time, the stress on subject over craft can narrow the sights of writers and result in pap for the undiscriminating. We all know readers of shlock mysteries and romances who read them purely to pass time or feed an undernourished fantasy life. There are people, for example, who read Regency romances in order to "understand England during that period," people for whom the essence of the English seventeenth century is captured in *Forever Amber* or that of the American civil war in *Gone with the Wind.*

It is not the case that bestselling books must be pitched to a middlebrow audience, but it is the case that lowered expectations often result in the publication of commercial writing geared to those expectations. In this regard there is something of a disconnect between writers and readers. In one poll of crime writers, for example, the individual chosen as the contemporary master of the form was James Crumley, a wonderful writer, but one with a small and scattered output and a relatively small audience, certainly compared with that of writers such as Turow and Grisham. Many mystery and crime readers are not familiar with all of his work, and the vast majority of readers of bestsellers will not have heard of Crumley at all.

The writers of bestsellers are often scorned by the crime fiction fanzines. I was probably not the only reader to make audible sounds of disappointment at the ending of *Presumed Innocent*. As the master says, "When you have eliminated the impossible, whatever remains, however improbable, must be the truth." The ending was thus telegraphed from the very beginning. My pat quotation in cases such as these is, "Elmore Leonard would never do this."

Turow, however, is a far better writer than some who have achieved commercial success. The author of a book on the first year of law school, *One L,* he was a publisher's dream for the writing of courtroom fiction. Here, the argument would go, is an individual who is both a practicing attorney and the author of a book on law school. Hence, his legal audience will follow him and support him in his new endeavor.

Some of this thinking mirrors Hollywood's. Readers will recall the buzz concerning Johnny Carson's successor and the touting of Pat Sajack as a logical choice. Since Carson's prior role was as a successful game show host with *Who Do You Trust?* the logical person to succeed him would be the host of a currently successful game show. Talk shows are different from game shows, however, and books about law school experiences are different from novels, but then the publisher was right after all and *Presumed Innocent* was huge,

both as a novel and as a film. John Grisham's *A Time to Kill* has been criticized as a knockoff of *To Kill a Mockingbird,* but very few would turn down Grisham's royalties.

The fact is that mainstream novelists often plow very familiar territory, while writers of category fiction (social melodrama, for example, à la Arthur Hailey) are expected to take on grand subjects and instruct as well as titillate and divert. The development of strong plots, vivid settings, compelling characters, and substantial themes is already a tall order; to ask for unique material as well is asking a lot. As readers we are often forced to compromise.

One of the writers whose work I always read is Steve Martini. Martini's plots often stretch credulity. His most recent book, *The Attorney,* for example, features an individual named Jonah Hale who is raising his granddaughter because her mother—Jonah's daughter—is a drug addict. Jonah has the good fortune to win millions in the state lottery, whereupon his daughter attempts to trade the custody of Jonah's granddaughter for a big-money payoff. She enlists an obnoxious feminist activist named Zo Suade to help her. Zo turns up dead; Jonah is arrested, and Martini's series character, Paul Madriani, is called upon to defend him.

It is not quite as preposterous as it sounds in a brief summary, but the sentence-by-sentence writing is crude and often clichéd. Steve Martini, however, understands courts, he understands trials, and he understands California statutes. The legal material in his books is exquisite, and his depiction of lawyerthink and courtroom strategies is masterful. Other writers do everything at a slightly higher level of skill (J. F. Freedman, for example, Stephen Hunter, Peter Blauner, Robert Ferrigno, Lawrence Block, of course, or T. Jefferson Parker) and I read (and would recommend) them as well, but you can't always get all that you want in a form that makes such varied demands.

Genre writing enjoys a ready audience, but it also brings with it constraints. The last great age of such writing—the English eighteenth century—offers readers an uncommonly high level of average writing, but few peaks and masterworks. In our own time there are few writers on a par with Ellroy, Harris, Burke, and Leonard, but there are still many writers of uncommon competence. One writer, for example, who delivers bestsellers that include interesting characters, solid plots, and a highly developed sense of setting is Michael Connelly.

Connelly began as a crime journalist and turned to full-time novel writing after a series of early successes. His setting is Los Angeles and his series protagonist a crusty figure named Harry (short for Hieronymus) Bosch. The implicit notion that Harry's Los Angeles bears some striking similarities to the subjects of his namesake's paintings is frequently reinforced. His novels often deal with contemporary subjects; in *Angels Flight,* for example, he takes us to a Los Angeles landmark and offers us a murder victim who is suspiciously similar to the prominent local attorney Johnny Cochrane.

Connelly may, however, be overly constrained by his series character. His very best books, in my judgment, have been *The Poet,* a freestanding book written on a very broad canvas, and his most recent novel, *Void Moon.* The latter has an effective female protagonist named Cassidy "Cassie" Black and pivotal scenes in that most American of crime-novel settings, Las Vegas.

This young writer has all of the right tools, and he uses them in all of the right ways. He demonstrates that writers of true craft can also produce bestsellers for a broad audience. In this regard he may be compared with Jonathan Kellerman, who has been demonstrating that ability for years. Kellerman also occasionally writes freestanding books that do not focus on his series protagonist, Alex Delaware. An early and effective example is *The Butcher's Theater,* a serial-killer novel set, interestingly, in Jerusalem. Kellerman's masterpiece, however, is the more recent *Billy Straight,* a novel about a young boy who witnesses a crime that recalls the O. J. Simpson case. He then must protect himself from those who would do him harm and, as an unfortunate side result, from those who are actually seeking to protect him. Billy is the quintessential survivor in the contemporary urban jungle and acquits himself well.

Alex Delaware makes a brief appearance in the book; the setting, after all, is Los Angeles, and he is a top (if fictional) child psychologist there. However, the center of the stage belongs to Billy, an exceptionally well developed character, and LAPD detective Petra Connor, another effective female character, who investigates the case.

Just as the presence of constraint does not insure failure, its absence does not guarantee success. Conventions have a way of freeing writers as well as circumscribing them, since they offer a host of tools and a set of prior agreements recognized by the audience. Hence the frequent desire on the part of publishers for both a recognizable genre and a series character. At the same time, however, publishers seek books that "transcend genre." While this may seem a difficult or even contradictory ideal, writers such as Kellerman and Connelly are able to flourish within its terms.

Note

Three other historical novels worthy of mention (treating the fourteenth, sixteenth, and eighteenth centuries respectively) are Umberto Eco's *The Name of the Rose* (1983), Iain Pears's *An Instance of the Fingerpost* (1998), and David Liss's *A Conspiracy of Paper* (2000).

Willeford's *Something about a Soldier* and *I Was Looking for a Street* have recently been reissued (2000) in a single volume. Both are highly recommended.

See Deborah Tannen's *You Just Don't Understand: Women and Men in Conversation* (1990).

Whether Harris will follow the plot line established at the conclusion of the novel *Hannibal* or instead follow the direction established by the film is a most interesting question at this point. While the novel brings the two central characters together, the film splits them apart, maintaining the outlines of the original relationship between Clarice and Hannibal rather than envisioning them as a retired couple or active duo. There are ways out of this narrative box, but Harris's perfectionism is likely to be tested by them. At the same time, the pressures generated by the film's vast commercial success may prove overwhelming. At this point Harris's audience has in effect become split between those who know the novel and those who know only the film. The manner in which he eventually sustains his novelistic integrity without ignoring commercial blandishments should prove to be a textbook case for those studying the relationship between art and commerce in contemporary society. A remake of Harris's *Red Dragon* (shot earlier by Michael Mann under the title *Manhunter* with Brian Cox playing Lecter) is now in preproduction with Brett Ratner directing and Hopkins playing Lecter.

Holmes's comment on the far-fetched truth appears in *The Sign of Four* (1890), chap. 6.

THEMES

Robert S. Paul (essay date 1991)

SOURCE: Paul, Robert S. "Realism Turns to Religion." In *Whatever Happened to Sherlock Holmes: Detective Fiction, Popular Theology, and Society,* pp. 195-226. Carbondale: Southern Illinois University Press, 1991.

[*In the following essay, Paul addresses religion and ethics as they are dealt with in contemporary crime fiction.*]

> As he crossed the bridge and looked away down the lake toward Lausanne, Henry knew that his life could never be quite the same again. Old, unquestioned

values had been turned upside down. The black-and-white view of morality which he had accepted as his middle-class heritage had gone forever. He forced his mind to consider the facts, clearly and brutally, so that they might have their full, salutary impact.

—Patricia Moyes, *Death on the Agenda*

Not all the attempts to reflect the new ethos of realism in detective fiction can be dismissed as simply following the fashions: the permissive society is a fact that cannot be ignored, but there is a discernible mood in modern writing that makes it different both from the classic detective fiction of earlier times and from the patterns discussed in the previous chapter. We would call it "chastened conservatism" or "chastened realism": some writers, while accepting the ethical and religious skepticism of recent decades, indicate that they are not altogether happy with the trend and would welcome a return to clearer ethical norms. This is indicated either in terms of nostalgia or by calling for a new basis on which ethics can be established and rooted in civilized society.

THE CONSCIOUSLY RELIGIOUS PERSPECTIVE

This may explain the appearance of detective stories written from a consciously religious perspective such as the work of the Jewish writer, Harry Kemelman, and the Protestant, Charles Merrill Smith, but some of the most striking examples have been written from a Roman Catholic position; Jane Dentinger's Jocelyn O'Roarke describes herself as "mentally flagellating herself as only an ex-Catholic can," and her friend, Lieutenant Phillip Gerrard, remarks to her that "for a self-professed agnostic, your Catholic guilt reflex is still pretty sharp."[1] That is true not only in regard to feelings of guilt but also in her respect for the old-fashioned institution of marriage, and perhaps even more significantly, her philosophical belief—shared by Gerrard—in an essentially rational universe.[2]

A similar conservative stance may be seen in the struggles of Ralph McInerny's Father Dowling, Leonard Holton's Father Joseph Bredder, O.S.M., and William X. Kienzle's Father Koesler to relate themselves to the world since Vatican II.[3] This viewpoint is also expressed in the struggle of Lawrence Sanders' earthy ex-chief of detectives, Edward X. Delaney, to operate with integrity in the changing conditions of the New York City streets that he has loved and served:

> It was the freedom, Delaney said somberly to Monica [his wife]. It was partly the drugs, he agreed, but mostly it was the freedom. Complete, without any restraint. There were no rules, no laws, no prohibitions. Moral anarchy. The kid was really surprised, Delaney said [of a young culprit], when he finally realized he was going to be punished for what he had done. He couldn't understand it. It didn't seem to him all that big a deal.

The Chief told Monica that it frequently happened that way with people who couldn't handle freedom. They didn't know self-discipline. They acted on whim, impulse. They couldn't sacrifice the pleasure of today for the satisfaction of tomorrow.[4]

His first wife Barbara, who had died, thought he had become a cop because "he saw beauty in order, and wanted to maintain order in the world."[5] This is confirmed a little later when we read, "In fact he found a curious satisfaction in this task of 'putting things in order.' That's what a cop's job was all about, wasn't it? To restore and maintain order in a disordered world. Not only in society, but in the individual as well. Even in the cop himself."[6]

For Delaney, beauty is to be revealed only in truth. He realizes this when he reflects on the quality that makes certain paintings so attractive to him. Technique is not enough. "To be truly satisfying, the painting had to move him, to cause a flopover inside him when he looked upon life revealed. A painting did not have to be beautiful; it had to be true. Then it was beautiful."[7]

Obviously Delaney still accepts the older ethics. We read that his sympathy disturbs him because a cop is not paid to be compassionate:

> A cop had to see things in black and white. *Had* to. Explanations and justification were the work of doctors, psychiatrists, sociologists, judges, and juries. They were paid to see the shades of grey, to understand and dole out truth.

> But a cop had to go by Yes or No. Because . . . well, because there had to be a rock standard, an iron law. A cop went by that and couldn't allow himself to murmur comfort, pat shoulders, and shake tears from his eyes. This was important, because all those other people— the ruth-givers—they modified the standard, smoothed the rock, melted the law. But if there was no standard at all, if cops surrendered their task, there would be nothing but modifying, smoothing, melting. All sweet reasonableness. Then society would dissolve into a kind of warm mush: no rock, no iron, and who could live in a world like that? Anarchy. Jungle.[8]

When Detective Sergeant Boone expresses doubts about the way in which the investigation is going, Delaney has no doubts because "our cause is just."[9]

Father Joseph Bredder is explicit in his support of traditional values. During a discussion with a fellow priest about the modern movement away from spiritual concepts, we read,

> "Why do they [scientists] shy away from the word 'spiritual'?" he [Bredder] asked.

> "Bigotry, my dear fellow," replied Father Armstrong cheerfully. "Pure bigotry parading as learning . . . as it always does. We have entered the spiritual Dark Ages. Or perhaps we never really got out of them. Six

hundred years ago people used to recite little rhymes to ward off the Devil, and now they recite little equations, and with the same objective. What is called Science had replaced God and the Devil, and men's souls are reckoned as non-existent because they cannot be found with photoelectrical equipment."[10]

So later, in a conversation with his friend, Lieutenant Minardi of the L.A.P.D., Bredder declares, "Reality demands eternity. Without eternity there is no significance to anything," and Minardi responds,

> "Well, the significance of a crime is that a law has been broken and it is the job of the police to discover who broke the law and punish him to discourage others."

> "The significance of a crime is that a law of God, exemplified in the formation of society, has been broken and the crime remains until the offender repents," said Father Bredder. "The state will pass away. God will not."[11]

These are all Roman Catholic sentiments grounded in traditional theology.

The questioning of the sixties and seventies in Britain is illustrated in the writing of James Fraser. It belongs to the permissive society, but the change of style is profound. Ingeborg Cattell, a young woman with whom Detective Inspector Bill Aveyard gets involved, confesses, "I'm just not certain about the marriage thing. I don't go for drugs, protest marches, the Civil Liberties bit, but a lot of things are changing. You'd be surprised, even in these dull backwaters, how much we keep in touch with what's going on. It seems to me two of our institutions need redefining. One's the Church, and the other's marriage."[12] The point is reinforced by the appearance of an unattractive clergyman, but we see both the recognition of a new kind of society and a demand for the revision of—but not the total rejection of—older institutions. In the same story, Detective Sergeant Bruton is forced to reflect on the depths to which human nature can sink:

> Thinking men refuse to accept the depth to which the human ethos can sink. "How can they do that?" they ask, but it's a futile question. Bruton knew, and Aveyard eventually would come to know, for it was the nature of their job, that the human mind has been created with an infinite capacity for good and evil, in equal amounts, and though the good men do is often transcendental, the evil can wallow hog-like in inconceivable mire.[13]

The loosening hold of religion may in part account for the rapid rise of the spy story as a separate genre, for in the story of espionage, we do not need to make any attempt to follow absolutes of 'truth' or 'justice', because the distinction between right and wrong may be very simply resolved in terms of "them" and "us."[14]

Although Peter Dickinson's story of a tiny "Livonian" government-in-exile in London may not be dismissed simply as a spy story, it accepts many of the values and reflects the more blasé attitudes that are common to that genre. Because there seems to be so little purpose in life, the young prostitute, Procne Newbury, is far from shocked at the murder of her mother, and observes:

> "He [the murderer] did her a good turn, I been thinking. I mean, where she is now, if she knows it'll be a big thrill, won't it, being a murder victim; even up there there's not a lot of them can say that. And if she don't know, it's no skin off *her* nose, is it? She'd had a smashing life, her way. I mean there wasn't much to it, but she made it smashing, didn't she?"

> "Yes. I suppose that's what matters." [says Lydia.]

> "Course it is."[15]

That expresses a common mood: if there is anything beyond this life, fine; but if not, there's not much you can do about it, and it is "no skin off *your* nose," so "live it up!"

Lydia (Lady Timms) is the owner of the decaying boardinghouse where the Livonians have their headquarters, and she discusses the political issues between free societies and communism with Mr. Diarghi, of the Russian embassy.[16] But at the end of the story she expresses the political disillusionment of many of her contemporaries as she muses that

> all governments, to her, were abominable, but not equally so. She didn't care whether there was any logic in her instinct to support the tiny and defunct government upstairs against the vast and far-reaching neo-Stalinist engine in the Kremlin. She simply knew that their smallness made them incapable of more than little lies and minor mischiefs, whereas in Russia there were probably ten thousand Aakus and a million Mrs. Newburys. . . . Her dealings with Superintendent Austen confirmed her belief that the government of Britain was only marginally better than that of Russia, because an historical accident had left the individual citizen with a little more power against it; but the police state was there, waiting to be released into domination, like a djinn in a bottle.[17]

On the other hand, the continuation of traditional values may be seen in the ongoing popularity of older writers such as Edmund Crispin (Bruce Montgomery) with his stories of Gervase Fen.[18] Crispin is profoundly influenced by the Christian history of England and the morality associated with it. As far as we know religion never obtrudes in the exuberant career of Gervase Fen, but he always treats it with respect, if not affection. On one occasion, in dealing compassionately with the sorrow of a young girl who has learned of the suicide of her friend, he comes close to an expression of Christian doctrine that would have done credit to Father Brown. Fen brushes aside rather brusquely her hope that the death of her friend was not suicide. "Then seeing that the headlong gallop towards a nerve-storm was for the time being arrested, he added more gently: 'It's distressing and horrible, I know, but there's nothing you or any of us can do about it.' And half to himself he murmured: 'We owe God a death.'"[19]

Undoubtedly, the traditional position taken by Gervase Fen represents the basic position of his creator, but it is a position with which his readership had some sympathy. Although a freer attitude towards moral and ethical questions rapidly developed after World War II, it did not suddenly win the support of the whole population, for there were still many whose preferences and even prejudices were still largely influenced by the standards of the past. Fen's personal conduct was wholly traditional; we read that "he is—unlike so many other detectives of current fiction. . . . entirely faithful in his marriage," and although Dolly, his wife, disappears from the later books, "a divorce seems in highest degree improbable."[20]

Fen also represents the older values in his detective motivation. In *The Case of the Gilded Fly,* the first of the Crispin stories about Fen, which appeared in 1944, we hear of Fen's reaction to the death of an innocent bystander that had been an act of brutal murder:

> That wanton, useless act roused in Fen something which was neither heroism, nor sentimentality, not righteous indignation, nor even instinctive revulsion; and having stated the negative side, it is difficult to put into words, what, actually, it was, since it is not a common emotion in mankind, and since it lies at the basis of Fen's personality. I suppose that as near as anything would be to say that it was a kind of passionless sense of justice and of proportion, a deeply rooted objection to waste.[21]

The austere ethical residue of older attitudes and of the societies supported by them may not be as pronounced as in Crispin but it is still discernible in many British writers of the last half of this century such as Michael Innes (J. I. M. Stewart), Catherine Aird, Elizabeth Lemarchand, John R. L. Anderson, Ruth Rendell and others, but a few examples will suffice. W. J. Burley's Detective Chief Superintendent Wycliffe, on a Sunday morning, feels dissatisfied with his life and his job and points out to his wife that police officers, like other people, "want to do their Sunday thing: gardening, fishing, sleeping, taking the kids and dogs for walks, even going to church."[22] Going to church may now be the last of the options, but at least it is still a possibility. Elizabeth Lemarchand's Detective Chief Superintendent Pollard reflects on the change that has taken place in the English village and observes, "It's unfortunate that both old Bellamy and the former vicar are dead. There's nobody with recognised status and long inside knowledge of the community that one can talk to about

people's reliability and moral calibre."[23] Michael Innes' Sir John Appleby still holds an old-fashioned attitude to truth and evidence. In conversation with a shady art dealer, Egon Raphaello, he says,

> "My technique is quite simple. It consists in persuading people that it's to their advantage to tell the truth. The graver the crime, the more obvious surely, that is. I don't suppose people often get convicted of murders they didn't commit as a consequence of being insufficiently candid about precious little enterprises of their own, but it can land them in a very awkward situation."[24]

In contrast with American society, in which the secular orthodoxy makes it distasteful, if not dangerous, to recognize any official place for the Church in society, English society has been built on the recognition that the Church has an indispensable place and is at its center. In Lemarchand's *Nothing to Do with the Case,* the role of the Church is implicit: "The ground sloped up gently to the church, and she stood for a few moments looking at the tower. It was sturdy rather than lofty, and had an air of watching protectively over the village."[25]

"WHAT IS TRUTH?" PILATE'S QUESTION RECONSIDERED

However, we have the impression that few writers in the second half of the twentieth century could afford to ignore that there have been radical changes from the traditional view of society.

One of the first changes was the appearance of a different kind of detective. When a writer or his or her readers have difficulty in believing in God, or in any eternal and immutable principles of justice and truth, there is little need for these qualities to be personified in an omniscient detective or promoted in the doctrine of the character's infallibility. Truth today is a much more tentative matter than our immediate forefathers believed, and when we have ceased to "walk humbly with" our God, it often seems easier to love mercy than to do justice (Cf. Mic. 6.8).

Typical of the change of fashion in detectives is Richard Lockridge's Jewish detective, Lieutenant "Nate" Shapiro of Homicide South in New York City. In contrast to the sublime omniscience of Hercule Poirot and Nero Wolfe, and even to the omnicompetence of Peter Wimsey and Perry Mason, Lockridge's sad-faced hero makes a decisive break with the Sherlock Holmes tradition of the great detective: for Shapiro *nothing* is elementary. Captain William Weigand, his immediate superior officer, insists on sending him into cases for which Shapiro protests that he has absolutely no aptitude or competence, such as the world of avant-garde art (*Murder for Art's Sake,* 1967), fundamentalist evangelism (*Preach No More,* 1971), or that of literary best-sellers (*Write Murder Down,* 1972). Shapiro's typical reaction as he surveys the scene of the crime is to declare that he is completely out of his depth, and when he ultimately solves a mystery that has baffled everyone else, he is likely to say that he has only reached the truth by accident and that any number of people could have solved the problem more quickly than he had.

The Appearance of Violence and Terror

A further characteristic of our age is the appearance of terrorism and violence. This is not so much the terror caused by Mickey Spillane and other representatives of gore and violence who try to establish their own ideas of reality by means of brute force, but rather the violence of those hostage takers and others who seriously represent terror and cruelty as part of modern life.

A most striking example is David L. Lindsey's *Heat from Another Sun,* which indicates the traumatic effect of the Vietnam experience on the American public.[26] It is not a book for the squeamish, but it is a book in which the writer uses four-letter words, scatological references, and violence in such a way that they are necessary to the action and to the development of his characters.

At several levels, it is concerned with the twentieth-century obsession with violence in its most obscene forms. This appears in the frightening obsession of the financier Roeg at the heart of the story. But it is also present in a more sophisticated way as the hero, Detective Stuart Haydon, wrestles with his own past and with the circumstances involved in his job as a homicide detective. It raises some acute theological questions for our society, but they are handled at a far different level from the simplistic treatment of earlier writings. Lieutenant Robert Dystal, who may be regarded as typical of twentieth-century American society, is described as not given to much soul-searching:

> Questions of ethics and morality, problems of theodicy that teetered on the sharp edges of philosophical deliberations and could not be resolved by the useful exercise of good common sense, were of no value to him. He quietly believed that the consideration of such questions was nothing more than pretentious posturing, of no use to himself and with no practical application to the living of life. The truth, Haydon thought, would be as uncomfortable for Dystal as it was for him, though certainly for different reasons.[27]

What sets Lindsey's work apart from most of the other realistic writing of our period is that he is consciously a writer with religious faith, plumbing the depths of the potential for evil in ordinary people and "trying to set the reader's mind on fire with the obscenity of violence."[28] Yet the story ends, "Haydon inhaled deeply of the night air, which carried the sounds and smells of a

world both ancient and newborn, a world no better and no worse than the best and worst of men could make it."[29] It leaves the reader with a memory of creation that contains the hope of re-creation.

It is ironic that the American trend to toughness and violence should have appeared originally as a protest against British writers of the genteel, country-house, cerebral type of murder mystery, since recently, some of the toughest and most violent examples of realism in detection have come from the pens of British writers: the stories of Peter Alding's detective from the north of England, Inspector Fusil; William McIlvanney's Jack Laidlaw; and the horse-racing milieu of Dick Francis or the writings of Desmond Cory. However, for all the recourse to violence and the frank secularity, this style of writing can come close to religious feeling and theological expression. Detective Inspector Fusil, regarded by many of his contemporaries and neighbors as "a reet bastard," is obviously moved when he visits a cheap boardinghouse that caters to some of life's derelicts: "How many of the blasted lives had once appeared so promising? Was fate the villain, or each man his own? He hated criminals with the sharpness of someone who believed in the Old Testament's unforgiving definitions of good and evil, but for wrecked lives like these, he had a deep compassion in which good and evil could often not be separated."[30] This is reminiscent of Desmond Cory's *Circe Complex,* and the same tone is found in Cory's *Bit of a Shunt up the River,* which is worth a more extended comment.[31]

It is the story of an English loser—a racing driver divorced from his wife, who has given up racing to become an unsuccessful proprietor of a garage in Brighton. Tracy—he is known by his surname as his Christian names are Cuthbert Delamere—recognizes himself as a failure. He never quite made it to the top in racing, is unsuccessful in marriage and business, and never has any luck with women. Also, he is completely happy only when he is working with machinery.

A mysterious Mr. Green hires him to deliver a Lamborghini as a birthday present to his daughter, Bernadette, and Tracy is to take her to Wales where she will discuss divorce with her husband, Tommy Pope. In the course of this excursion, Tracy becomes involved in a murder and with its perpetrator, "Bony" Wright, a convicted murderer who has escaped from prison with the full intention of adding a few more corpses to his tally. Tracy is responsible for frustrating Bony's plans against Tommy and is instrumental in bringing the convict to his death. The poignancy comes from the curious empathy that Tracy and Bony share from their love of cars and racing. The story, with its language that would have been frowned upon in the Sunday School I knew as a lad, and the sexual angle of the trip with Bernadette, has all the makings of a hard, fast-moving, realistic yarn that is thoroughly modern and secular. The basic attitude toward life in these hedonistic times is suggested by Tracy as he thinks covetously about Ferraris, Corniches, Maseratis, and other exotic automobiles that were his stock-in-trade. "Nice cars, really. If you were lucky, you could get one for a birthday present. Just as if you were unlucky, you could get some part of a racing car all mixed up with your brains. You had to believe in luck. What else was there? Money."[32]

But at a deeper level, Tracy has to face the contemporary uncertainty about ethics. Can we still accept the easy distinctions that we have been in the habit of making between the respectable (good) and the disreputable (bad)? Is cruelty to be found only in people like Bony Wright? As Tracy is held at knife-point by Bony, he is forced to listen to a strong denunciation of the sadism that sometimes animates members of the judicial bench.[33]

At a deeper level still, the empathy that Tracy has with Bony leads him to new insights about his own personal destiny and identity. At the end of the action, there is a shoot-out in which Tracy is wounded and Bony is killed, but we are left questioning whether Bony deliberately allows himself to be shot so that Tracy could escape. Then while Tracy is lying in bed, in the curious state between consciousness and dreaming, he imagines that Bony has come to tell him that in death you have all the possibilities that were denied you in life. "I mean, I'm infinite. Everybody's infinite. They just don't realize it."[34] That is a new thought for Tracy who is only too conscious of his own finitude and failure in this life:

> A million Tracys, all too tired to. . . . No, that wasn't right. All the others had to be asleep already, because Bony hadn't talked to any of the others. Or had he . . . ? Sleep itself is a turning, anyway. Like death. You'd have of course an infinite number of deaths, and presumably only one of them was perfect—the one that rounded off the perfect life. . . . Had anyone ever *lived* that perfect life before dying that perfect death? There was supposed to be an answer to that one, wasn't there? That, when you thought about it, was the whole point about him. But then he was God. That had to be different.[35]

Well, there it is, and we are obviously close to a religious statement. Perhaps we are too close to religion for the average reader, because the end of the story surfaces in our normal greedy world, with Tracy taking the offer of "five hundred jimmy o'goblins" (pounds sterling) for keeping his mouth shut. He then disappears from the story as he began, "this wifeless, friendless, impecunious, none-too-bright Tracy," but with the curious hope that "what *hadn't* been just possibly had been, too."[36]

Unrepentant Conservatives in a Religionless Society

But where shall we place the work of Emma Lathen, the corporate nom de plume of the American team, Mary Jane Latsis, the economist, and Martha Henissart, the lawyer?

It is clearly in a class of its own.

The two began writing in 1960 and therefore the books, whether written under the name of Emma Lathen or of R. B. Dominic, belong unquestionably to the post—World War II era, a fact that is reemphasized in the comprehensive review of contemporary social and political issues that appears in the stories. But in relation to style and even to content, they belong to the classical period. It has been recorded that Lord C. P. Snow, in a review of one of the Emma Lathen books, observed: "She is probably the best living writer of American detective stories. . . . The detail . . . is investigated with the enthusiasm of Balzac. . . . She is very witty, in a wry and downbeat manner. The whole of her writing is in fact exactly what in our vanity we like to think of as proprietorially English."[37]

In an informative interview which the two writers granted to John C. Carr, they pointed out that they were prepared for their career in writing by their own early immersion in Victorian novels, "everything from Jane Austen through Sherlock Holmes."[38] They claimed that this influenced their writing in several ways, from the structure of their syntax to their ability to populate the world they described with believable characters.

Emma Lathen, according to Carr, "has preserved the benign and therefore highly entertaining aspects of the tradition: technical knowledge; unity of character and action and time, if not always of place; and the avoidance of the quotidian banalities of life, and of graphic descriptions of sex and violence."[39] In these ways Emma Lathen's works are unrepentantly conservative and at times, she seems to have had Dorothy Sayers consciously in mind—if not as a pattern to be copied, then certainly as a standard to be maintained or possibly surpassed.[40]

On the other hand, the books are uncompromisingly contemporary. They invariably employ contemporary institutions as their subject matter: the Emma Lathen books are set in the context of banking and the high finance of Wall Street, while the R. B. Dominic stories center in the politics of Washington, D.C. The writings of Emma Lathen, featuring John Putnam Thatcher, senior vice president of the Sloan Guaranty Trust, provide a running commentary on the social and political issues that have involved the American public since the 1960s.

A Place for Murder (1963) explores issues that were alive at that time in tax writeoffs among the very wealthy with their Connecticut "farms"; *Accounting for Murder* (1964) is about finagling in high financial circles in the matter of army contracts, but by 1967, when *Murder Against the Grain* appeared, we are in the midst of the United States—Russia wheat deal. *Death Shall Overcome* (1966) revolves around the relationship of big business to the ethnic issue and the Civil Rights movement. *A Stitch in Time* (1968) involves shady medicine and *Murder to Go* (1969), the questionable possibilities in large-scale, mass-produced food franchises. *When in Greece* (1969) reflects the political troubles in that country, and *The Longer the Thread* (1971) wrestles with the problem of American political and industrial interests in Puerto Rico. *Pick Up Sticks* (1970) revolves around land sales promotions in New England, and *Ashes to Ashes* (1970), the post—Vatican II problems in the Roman Catholic Church. By 1973, in *Murder without Icing,* we are in the bright world of sports (ice-hockey) franchises. In *Sweet and Low* (1974), we are introduced to the chocolate industry and to cocoa futures in view of unstable conditions in Africa, and in *Double, Double, Oil and Trouble* (1979), to the involvement of Texan oil companies in British offshore North Sea oil exploration. *Going for Gold* (1981) features a financial swindle during the winter Olympics, and *Something in the Air* (1988) is involved with expansion and takeover bids in commuter airlines.

Lathen's stories are set firmly within the context of contemporary American society and the issues in which it is involved—"money is the name of the game." It is in the urbane pursuit of *cui bono* that John Putnam Thatcher owes his success as an amateur detective. This is the basic realism that excludes all secondary motives:

> Wall Street transcends the short, narrow thoroughfare in the Borough of Manhattan. Wall Street is a creed, linking true believers on the Rue de la Bourse and the Paseo de la Castellana. Every noncollective onion sold in Moscow proves that the Real Presence can materialize anywhere.
>
> John Putnam Thatcher of the Sloan Guaranty Trust knew this very well. Unlike many people, he also knew that the best place to exploit his knowledge was on Wall Street proper, the Borough of Manhattan, the City of New York.[41]

But this theme occurs time and time again. We read that

> as senior vice-president of the third largest bank in the world, Thatcher had file cabinets bulging with evidence of an incontrovertible truth. Initialing contracts, programming computers, and underwriting pilot programs are occasionally arduous, often inconvenient, and always insufficient to extirpate the Old Ned lurking below.
>
> In fact, Thatcher had long since decided that Wall Street saw more of the real man than most other locales. With all deference to Sigmund Freud and the animal ap-

petites, Wall Street—and the world it serves—proves that sex is not the only outlet for deep-rooted, life-shaping forces. There are also buying and selling.[42]

This acceptance of the money motive at the center of modern society is the unchangeable article of faith that enables John Putnam Thatcher to cut through all the obfuscations of racial prejudice, ill-placed patriotism, or sexual infatuation to get to the central problem in every story. And yet one has the feeling that all the time he regards himself somewhat ironically, or even with slight distaste; but the reality of life in our society forces him to accept the primacy of the cash motive although that does not mean that he necessarily approves. He may believe that capitalism provides the best possible form of economics, but even though his loyalty to the Sloan is devoted, it is not uncritical. Rather like the deep but passionless commitment that many Britons have to the monarchy—while not uncritical of certain features—it would be difficult to imagine a livable world where it did not exist.

This underlines the most important reason for considering the works of Emma Lathen here: their complete absence of conventional religion as stimulating any kind of personal commitment; or rather, the tacit admission that Western society has made a religion of its secularity—it has become openly idolatrous. The Church is considered as an institution, particularly in *Ashes to Ashes,* which involves John Putnam Thatcher and the Sloan in the social turmoil that afflicted the Roman Catholic Church after Vatican II. In the novel, neither Thatcher nor any of his colleagues makes any remark that indicates any religious commitment or any reflection that can be interpreted as theological. However, in introducing the birth control question that erupted in *Ashes to Ashes,* Emma Lathen includes the following reflection:

> Man proposes, God disposes.
>
> For many centuries it was widely accepted that the course of human events was shaped by this division of labor. Then one of the bolder spirits of the Middle Ages put faith to the test. Does man propose? Hundreds of succeeding years were spent debating the proposition.
>
> Then, probably because Charles Darwin and Sigmund Freud between them made man uninteresting, attention was returned to the second member of the partnership. How can God dispose, somebody wondered in print, when God is dead? The subsequent outpouring of intellectual thought strained library facilities throughout the world.[43]

That is outrageously Chestertonian and simplistic. One might reflect upon some of the bolder spirits of the Middle Ages like Mirandola, who saucily hinted that humankind might be able to do some of the disposing; and if Charles Darwin and Sigmund Freud made humanity uninteresting, they did at any rate strip away some of the false mystery with which human nature had been surrounded.

However, Emma Lathen went on to describe something of the new humanism that was disrupting the equanimity of the Church and society in the comment, "Between man, whatever he is, and God, if He exists, there had erupted a new and frightening entity—the crowd. Flensburg, New York, was about to bear witness to the consequences of this interposition."[44] That suggests the characteristically agnostic attitude of people in the second half of the twentieth century. We live in an increasingly secular society.

If detective fiction during the earlier classical period drew its readers mainly from supporters of the bourgeois values in Middle America and from those in Europe who were nostalgic for the certainties of the past, and if the procedurals and more flamboyant writings drew support from the campuses and from those who felt alienated from Western society, perhaps Emma Lathen/R. B. Dominic derive support from those who live in a society that they recognize as blatantly secular, whatever the conventional beliefs of some of their contemporaries. This writing represents the realistic world of finance and high-pressure politics for an upwardly mobile society and for those who have to make their way in it and have to give some obeisance to its gods.

CHASTENED CONSERVATIVES IN A RELIGIONLESS SOCIETY: BETWEEN UNBELIEF AND FAITH

With the books of Dick Francis, the Welsh ex-professional jockey, we are back closer to the writings of authors like Desmond Cory and to the recasting of the crime novel during the second half of this century in Britain. For despite the fact that Dick Francis claims affiliation, at least on a formal, conventional basis, with the established Church of England, his world is thoroughly secular and his stories often contain elements of violence that are not for those with weak stomachs.[45] John C. Carr, in the introduction to his interview with Francis, observed that "some of the pain the heroes must have inflicted on them is just a little too much. Past the gag limit at times."[46] On the other hand, it has been pointed out that pain (and the recognition that it exists and has to be faced by practically everyone) has a significant part to play in Francis' writing. By using characters who have been hurt, sometimes physically, but more often emotionally, Francis enables his characters to develop, and this gives his stories added depth.

At first sight, Francis appears to operate within a somewhat limited circle of experience, since his plots are all set within the restricted area of horse racing (usually British). There is a recognizable "Francis formula" in which a narrator (first-person hero), who has been hurt in some way in the past, triumphs over those who are determined to make money out of the "sport of kings" and who are totally unscrupulous about crushing any who get in their way. This normal pattern means that the stories fall into the indeterminate area between detection and thriller, because the antagonists are known early in the story, and the quest remaining is how the hero will discover their plans and win against all the odds that seem to be stacked against him. As John C. Carr recognized, this is very English and is an adult version of the kind of encouraging schoolboy literature that used to grace the pages of the *Boys' Own Paper.*[47]

But it is adult in the sense that the suffering of Francis' characters is a necessary part of their development into maturity. Francis endows his characters with a richness of interest that goes beyond conventional requirements. As Michael Stanton pointed out:

> Emotionally starved or physically damaged (or both) as his protagonists are, it is not too much to say that Francis's fiction is about learning to love. One function of the plot or action is to teach people (often but not always the hero) to be fully human. Exciting as the action is, its end is not itself—its end is to show characters how to open their closed hearts.[48]

This is a perceptive comment because, although Francis' characters often engage in actions that earlier cultures would have regarded as immoral, the reason for such action arises directly out of the situation that is being portrayed and the insight that concerns Francis—tracing love in human relationships—carries us close to the humanism noted in other modern writers. In *The Craft of Crime,* John Carr also wrote, "Francis's realism about violence can be refreshing. His kicked around heroes take the whole novel to recover from a good beating and that certainly adds, rather than detracts, if we are to have sympathy for them—and Francis's heroes uniquely command our sympathy."[49]

Basically, the insight that "it is not too much to say that Francis's fiction is about learning to love" and "to teach people . . . to be fully human" means that the writer is reaffirming the fundamental and potential goodness of the human spirit and its need for love in relationship to others. In *Bonecrack* (1971), we see the fundamental need for human love reflected in father-and-son relationships—first between the protagonist Neil Griffon and his own father and then in the unhealthy relationship between Enso Rivera and his son Alessandro.

A further trait of the books is our innate need for justice, and not simply for legality. As Stanton observed, "The struggle is not simply between legal and illegal; it is between right and wrong, or good and evil. A moral polarity exists in Francis's novels—a polarity which is not exactly simple but is usually very clear."[50] Dick Francis' stories illustrate the basic need not simply for the justice of the courts, but for a justice that will be open and appropriate. Some of his heroes could have echoed the sentiments of W. S. Gilbert's *Mikado*:

> *My object all sublime*
> *I shall achieve in time—*
> *To let the punishment fit the crime—*
> *The punishment fit the crime.*

Although it should be added that the retribution meted out by Francis' heroes goes considerably beyond causing the guilty party to become a source of "innocent merriment." So Steven Scott plots his counterattack on the "bad guys":

> "Gee, dammit," said Allie, finally and explosively, "I just don't see why that guy should be allowed to rob you and make people despise you and get away with it."
>
> "Give me time," I said mildly, "and he won't."
>
> "Time?"
>
> "For thinking," I explained. "If a frontal assault would land me straight into a lawsuit for slander, which it would, I'll have to come up with a sneaky scheme which will creep up on him from the rear."[51]

And *Nerve* ends in a classic tale of revenge. In this case, Rob Finn takes his revenge against the embittered journalist who has brought about the end of his career and that of several other jockeys.[52]

Dick Francis points us back to an understanding of society that is basically ethical and maybe even theological. If "learning to live fully means learning to love" then we are close to the anthropological center that is to be found in a great deal of modern theology.[53] For the rest, Michael Stanton's comment sums it up, when he suggests that the satisfaction from reading Francis' novels "really comes not through their adherence to a formula but through their adherence to a set of values: the price of learning to need, the value of being vulnerable, the inestimable worth of human love."[54]

CRI DE COEUR

In their attempt to place literary detection fully within the setting of a "post-Christian" society, some writers probe even more deeply. They recognize the confused mixture of faith and agnosticism characteristic of our time, and they seem to reveal in their dealing with social and ethical matters an odd mixture of nostalgia and wistful longing—*Sehnsucht*—that may lie beneath so much of the professed realism and the open hedonism of the modern mood. Of no writer is this more true than of P. D. James (Phyllis Dorothy James White), an

English writer of whom it has been said that she is "one of the few authors who deserves a permanent place on the bookshelves of all those who treasure literary craftsmanship."[55]

The relationship between theology and the society she describes in her stories is illustrated in one of her earlier books, *An Unsuitable Job for a Woman*. This novel has a British setting, and in common with the feminist interests of the seventies, the detection is by Ms. Cordelia Gray, who after the suicide of her partner (formerly of the C.I.D.), suddenly finds herself the proprietor of Pryde's Detective Agency but possessing very little else. Cordelia's education illustrates the religious/social mix of British society. Her education was catholic if not eclectic, for although she was the daughter of a peripatetic Socialist lecturer with professed atheist leanings, she was raised in at least one foster home run by a woman who was a strong Protestant Nonconformist. She had been educated almost by accident, however, in a Roman Catholic convent school. In a later book, Cordelia says that she was never converted to Catholicism, but she had liked the convent because "I suppose it was the first time I felt secure. Life wasn't messy any more."[56] She explains her own personality as "the result of having an atheist father, a convent education, and a nonconformist conscience."[57] This shows how the different religious influences in English history affect society and leave Britain with a social conscience, a background of morality, and also a nostalgic feeling towards the ancient faith.

But there is also the skepticism of the modern age. This is particularly illustrated in Cordelia's thoughts when she suddenly finds the body of her former partner, Bernard Pryde; she reflects that since Bernard was dead he could not know anything:

> Her second fostermother, Mrs. Wilkes, would have said that Bernie did know, that there was a moment of indescribable glory, shining towers, limitless singing, skies of triumph. Poor Mrs. Wilkes! Widowed, her only son dead in the war, her small house perpetually noisy with foster children who were her livelihood, she had needed her dreams. She had lived her life by comfortable maxims stored like nuggets of coal against the winter. Cordelia thought of her now for the first time in years and heard again the tired, determinedly cheerful voice "If the Lord doesn't call on his way out, He'll call on his way back." Well, going or coming, He hadn't called on Bernie.[58]

Oh? How do you know that, Cordelia? The writer has already lined up Cordelia—albeit regretfully—on the side of contemporary agnosticism. After these doubting reflections, however, we read that "she said a brief convent-taught prayer to the God she wasn't sure existed for the soul which Bernie had never believed he possessed and waited quietly for the police."[59] But perhaps like most reluctant unbelievers in the Western world and certainly a large part of the British public, Cordelia has doubts even about her doubts; she wonders about the propriety of her willingness to take the oath in court. "There were moments, usually on a sunny Easter morning, when she wished that she could with sincerity call herself a Christian; but for the rest of the year she knew herself to be what she was—incurably agnostic but prone to unpredictable relapses into faith."[60]

These reflections underline themes that permeate almost all of P. D. James' stories—we live in a time when religious faith is difficult and agnosticism must be acknowledged; we have no answer for the evil and suffering that exist in the world. On the other hand, because of these doubts, we have little comfort in the face of death; and ethically we can only do the best we can. But there seems to run through the whole of the corporate consciousness a feeling of nostalgia, a wistfulness for a time when the laws that govern our life were accepted as absolute.

There is an incident in *Death of an Expert Witness* where Commander Dalgliesh of Scotland Yard finds it necessary to interview the teenage daughter of a suspect and they find themselves discussing what happens to people convicted of murder. That in turn leads to a discussion of crime and punishment and Eleanor Kerrison, the girl, says she thinks it is wrong of the state to punish a person for many years when his or her victim might have lived only a week. She goes on to say, "I suppose it was different when people believed in God. Then the murdered person might have died in mortal sin and gone to hell. The seven days could have made a difference then. He might have repented and had time for absolution." To this Dalgliesh replies, "All these problems are easier for people who believe in God. Those of us who don't or can't have to do the best we can. That's what the law is, the best we can do. Human justice is imperfect, but it's the only justice we have."[61]

Here is the uncertainty of the modern mood and the relativity of the world view that is common throughout Western civilization; there are no longer any absolutes. and where there is no belief in God, there can be no reason for absolutes. One may compare this with the certainties of the past, as Dalgliesh reflects on them in the work of a parish priest in *The Black Tower,* "Of the more corrosive, petty, mean-minded delinquencies in all their sad but limited variety, he, like any other parish priest, would have had his fill. He had his answer ready, compassionate but inexorable, offered . . . with all the gentle arrogance of absolute certainty."[62]

The agnosticism also comes through in Cordelia's dealings with Clarissa Lisle, the central figure in *The Skull Beneath the Skin.* Clarissa frankly admits that she cannot believe in God, and perhaps it is not surprising that

she has handed on her unbelief to her adopted son, Simon, who "found himself praying, petitioning the God in whom he no longer believed, with all the desperate urgency, all the artless importunity, of a child."[63]

Similarly, in *The Black Tower,* we see that it is possible for unbelief to be passed from one partner to another in marriage. The invalid Ursula Hollis, shunted by her husband into Wilfred Anstey's communal settlement where she is unable to interfere in his interests and preoccupations in London, reflects on her Catholic training:

> He [her husband] had forgotten that he had taught her to do without God. Her religion had been one of those possessions that, casually, neither understanding them nor valuing them, he had taken from her. They hadn't really been important to her, those consoling substitutes for sex, for love. She couldn't pretend that she had relinquished them with much of a struggle, those comforting illusions taught in St. Matthew's Primary School, assimilated behind the draped terylene curtains of her aunt's front sitting-room in Alma Terrace, Middlesborough, with its holy pictures, its photographs of Pope John, its framed papal blessing of her aunt and uncle's wedding. All were part of that orphaned, uneventful, not unhappy childhood which was as remote now as a distant, once-visited alien shore. She couldn't return because she no longer knew the way.[64]

The unbelief is here, but clearly also, the nostalgia.

This skepticism is also the attitude of one of the victims in *Innocent Blood:*

> Mavis had lost her God. Like all other believers she had made Him in her own image, a Methodist God, benign, suburban in his tastes, appreciative of cheerful singing and mildly academic sermons, not demanding more than she could give. The Sunday morning chapel had been more a comfortable routine than an imperative to worship. Mavis had been brought up a Methodist, and she was not a woman to reject early orthodoxies. But she had never forgiven God for letting Julie die.[65]

Wilfred Anstey, in *The Black Tower,* seems to personalize the problems of the Church. He has established his philanthropic work by deluding himself that he received a miracle at Lourdes, although he never really suffered from disseminated sclerosis, but only from a form of hysterical paralysis. However, he saw himself as a kind of medieval abbot dispensing good works and hospitality in an atmosphere of asceticism and spiritual discipline while making sure that his own cell had every little comfort. When Dalgliesh met Wilfred, Dalgliesh's first thought

> was that he looked like a bit-player acting with practised conviction the part of an ascetic bishop. The brown monk's habit suited him so well that it was impossible to imagine him in any other garb. . . . The

gentle questioning eyes with their suggestion of other people's suffering meekly borne were young eyes, the blue irises very clear, the whites opaque as milk. He smiled, a singularly sweet lopsided smile spoilt by the display of uneven and discoloured teeth. Dalgliesh wondered why it was that philanthropists so often had a reluctance to visit their dentist.[66]

Even more devastating in its implied criticism is Dorothy Moxon's disenchantment with Wilfred Anstey. When she remonstrates with him for handing over his work to another authority, without regard to those who had supported him in the venture, he says:

> "Dot dear, you and I have to accept that we cannot always choose the way in which we are called to serve."

> She wondered how she had never noticed it before, that irritating note of unctuous reproof in his voice. She turned abruptly away. The hand, thus rejected, slipped heavily from her shoulders. She remembered suddenly what he reminded her of: the sugar Father Christmas on her first Christmas tree, so desirable, so passionately desired. And you bit into nothingness; a trace of sweetness on the tongue and then an empty cavity grained with white sand.[67]

P. D. James probably had no conscious intention of making that a commentary on twentieth-century religion, but the figure of Wilfred Anstey is appropriate for the religion of our time, particularly a liberal, unrooted Protestantism intent on good works and determined to carry them through in a way that best meets its own need for spiritual satisfaction—often hanging on to the trappings of the ancient faith but without any real commitment to its discipline.

The problem of evil remains the unanswerable theological enigma. It is put forcibly by the embittered former science teacher, Victor Holroyd, in an exchange with one of the crippled patients in Wilfred Anstey's community of medical misfits. He dismisses "dull, repressed, religious" Grace Willison's habitual good humour as simply a condition of her disease.[68] Grace, very much hurt, declares that she does not claim her happiness as a virtue but says that even if it were only a symptom, she could still give thanks for it. Victor retorts acidly:

> As long as you don't expect the rest of us to join in, give thanks by all means. Thank God for the privilege of being no bloody use to yourself or anyone else. And while you're about it, thank Him for some of the other blessings of His creation; the millions toiling to get a living out of barren soil swept by flood, burnt by drought; for pot-bellied children; for tortured prisoners; for the whole doomed, bloody, pointless mess.[69]

Skepticism raises the basic problem of how we are to view our own death. Cordelia Gray, in *The Skull Beneath the Skin,* thinks it is interesting

> the way in which death had replaced sex as the great unmentionable, to be denied in prospect, endured in decent privacy, preferably behind the drawn curtains of

a hospital bed, and followed by discreet, embarrassed, uncomforted mourning. There was this to be said about the Convent of the Holy Child: the views of the sisters on death had been explicit, firmly held, and not altogether reassuring; but at least they hadn't regarded it as in poor taste.[70]

Clarissa Lisle is almost unhinged by fear of her own death, and she makes an interesting comment that probably indicates lack of faith even among professedly religious people:

> I've noticed that about the God people. They're just as frightened as the rest of us. They cling on just as long. They're supposed to have a heaven waiting but they're in no hurry to get there. Perhaps it's worse for them: judgments and hell and damnation. At least I'm only afraid of death. Isn't everyone? Aren't you?[71]

Of course, in a murder mystery, the participants are bound to be brought face to face with the reality of death, so after the death of Father Michael Baddeley, the sybaritic Julius Court, the epitome of cynical unbelief, observes:

> We were alike in one thing. Neither of us feared death. I didn't know where Baddeley thought he was going as he just had time to make that last archaic sign of his allegiance [he had put on his stole], but wherever it was he apparently saw nothing to fear. Neither do I. I know just as certainly as he did what will follow my death. Annihilation. It would be unreasonable to fear that.[72]

As Dalgliesh tells Eleanor Kerrison, in a world where there are no longer any absolutes, we can only do the best we can and human justice, although it is imperfect, is the only justice we have. The theme is repeated in a different set of circumstances in the same story on the question of the ambiguity of evidence. A group of the staff at Hoggatt's Forensic Science Laboratory has been discussing evidence given in court by expert witnesses, but the conclusion is drawn that, despite all the susceptibilities of jurors, it is the best we can do. As one of the characters remarks, "It's the same as democracy. A fallible system but the best we've got."[73]

But the most striking characteristic of P. D. James' books is her recognition that with loss of religious faith, society itself has lost something vital at its heart. There is a sense in which Ursula Hollis' experience of "lostness" cited above might be taken as a parable for the whole of society. A passage in *Innocent Blood* puts this into an illustrative figure when Philippa contemplates the east window of a church:

> She had bought a cheese and tomato roll for her lunch, and found herself suddenly hungry, but was reluctant to offend the susceptibilities of other visitors by eating it there. Instead she fixed her gaze where God the Father sat in majesty among His creation, glorified in the splendour of medieval stained glass. Before him was an open book. *Ego sum alpha et omega.* How simple

life must be for those who could both lose and find identity in that magnificent assurance. But for herself that way was closed. Hers was a bleaker and more presumptuous creed; but it was not without its comfort, and she had no other.[74]

There is something of regretful nostalgia in the attitude of Dalgliesh as he contemplates the basic decent honesty of Grace Willison: "Ruefully, he recognized in Miss Willison the type of unusually honest witness whom he had always found difficult. Paradoxically, this old-fashioned rectitude, this sensitivity of conscience, were more difficult to cope with than the prevarications, evasions or flamboyant lying which were part of a normal interrogation."[75]

The foregoing suggests that P. D. James' detective stories, at a deeper level, may represent the search of our hell-bent twentieth-century society for solid ethical grounds on which to reestablish itself. This is brought together in a remarkable way in *A Taste for Death.*

If we grant the possibility of this extended parable form, it is significant that the story begins and ends in the vestry of a shabby London church, which in its Anglo-Catholic orientation suggests the Western Catholic roots from which our culture has sprung. The story itself seems to pose the unspoken question of whether, in order to survive, that is where we should return.

The theme is repeated at several levels. The story begins with Commander Dalgliesh's disillusionment with police work and his disgust with the horror of death, but at least it ends with the solution of the death of Sir Paul Berowne.[76] It also starts with the discouragement of the parish priest, Father Barnes, and the declining authority of the Church of England in the inner city; but at length, Father Barnes experiences a new sense of purpose and has reason for encouragement.[77] But the paradox can point in the opposite direction, because at the beginning there is the devotion of Miss Emily Wharton to the parish of St. Matthew's, Paddington, and her love for the waif, Darren Wilkes, but the story ends with her disillusionment.

There is also the intriguing puzzle of Paul Berowne's religious experience which had begun in the conventional Anglicanism of his social class but which had brought him close to the beatific vision. His mother, Lady Ursula, regards his search to find meaning for existence as a fruitless quest.[78] Throughout the story there is an undercurrent of agnosticism represented in the conventional attitudes of Lady Ursula, the open medical skepticism of Stephen Lampart, the virtually total alienation of Lady Barbara Berowne from her husband and such casual references to the modern mood as the reflection that the use of the word *God* as an answer will always put a stopper to rational conversation.[79]

This change with regard to religion is strengthened and maintained in incidental references: in the recognition that divorce is no longer any final obstacle to the ambitions of a modern politician; in Mrs. Minns' recognition that she does not expect to see Sir Paul Berowne in any future world; in Inspector Kate Miskin's frank admission that she does not understand religious experience and finds no need for it.[80] There is also the expressed unwillingness of the twentieth-century person to accept some of the horrors of earlier orthodoxy—hell and damnation—because, as Teresa's mother says: "God can't be less merciful than I am. I can't believe that."[81]

When all this is added together, it presents a fairly comprehensive picture of religion in decline and documentation of the claim that "the world is full of people who have lost faith." But the context in which that statement is made shows that the malaise is much wider than simply a concern with religion and the articles of Christian orthodoxy. As Lady Ursula observes:

> The world is full of people who have lost faith: politicians who have lost faith in politics, social workers who have lost faith in social work, schoolteachers who have lost faith in teaching and, for all I know, policemen who have lost faith in policing and poets who have lost faith in poetry. It's a condition of faith that it gets lost from time to time, or at least mislaid.[82]

That which is at stake in the loss of religious faith affects the whole of society so that Dalgliesh is able to liken the Church to the preparation of evidence for a criminal case. Of the case in hand, he says, "You could say it's like the church, an ingenious edifice erected on an unproved supposition, logical within its terms, but only valid if one can accept the basic premise, the existence of God."[83]

This suggests that, for P. D. James, the issue is not an unrelieved indictment of religious faith; it is much more complex because, although we may be skeptical about religious experience and its hope for a world beyond this life, we cannot altogether discount the testimony of those who have experienced faith.[84] And perhaps the only sensible advice the writer would give to modern society is the advice given in a sermon recalled by Emily Wharton: "If you find that you no longer believe, act as if you still do. If you feel that you can't pray, go on saying the words."[85]

P. D. James' parable of Western civilization may be indicated when the culprit uncharacteristically spares the life of the boy, Darren, and he "sprang to his feet then almost ran to the tunnel end suddenly desperate to gain that half-moon of light before the darkness closed in on him for ever."[86]

What a pity he did not reach that light.

Notes

1. Jane Dentinger, *First Hit of the Season* (New York: Dell, 1984), 73.

2. Ibid., 37, 88.

3. E.g., Ralph McInerny, *Her Death of Cold* (New York: Viking, 1977), 112; Leonard Holton, *Out of the Depths* (New York: Dodd, Mead & Co. 1966).

4. Lawrence Sanders, *The Second Deadly Sin* (New York: G. P. Putnam, 1977), 256-57.

5. Ibid., 11.

6. Ibid., 40-41.

7. Ibid., 66.

8. Ibid., 134.

9. Ibid., 295.

10. Holton, *Out of the Depths,* 23.

11. Ibid., 43-44.

12. James Fraser, *Deadly Nightshade* (New York: Harcourt, Brace & World, 1970), 84-85.

13. Ibid., 185.

14. Cf. William Bradley, "The Ethics of James Bond," 35-46.

15. Peter Dickinson, *The Lively Dead,* 192.

16. Ibid., 88.

17. Ibid., 127-28.

18. Cf. the article by William A. S. Sarjeant, "Obsequies about Oxford: The Investigations and Eccentricities of Gervase Fen," *TAD* 14 (Summer 1981): 196-209.

19. Edmund Crispin, *Frequent Hearses* (1950; reprint, Harmondsworth, Eng.: Penguin, 1982), 48.

20. Sarjeant, "Obsequies about Oxford," 202.

21. Ibid., 204.

22. W. J. Burley, *Wycliffe's Wild Goose Chase* (Garden City, N.Y.: Doubleday, 1982), 12.

23. Elizabeth Lemarchand, *Nothing to Do with the Case* (New York: Walker & Co., 1981), 122.

24. Michael Innes, *Appleby's Other Story* (New York: Dodd, Mead & Co., 1974), 113.

25. Lemarchand, *Nothing to Do with the Case,* 48-49.

26. David L. Lindsey, *Heat from Another Sun* (New York: Harper & Row, 1984).

27. Ibid., 25.

28. David Lindsey in an interview reported in "Works in Progress," *Bookstop Shopper* (an occasional publication of the Bookstop, a bookstore in Austin, Texas), n.d. [1984?].

29. Lindsey, *Heat from Another Sun,* 296.

30. Peter Alding, *Ransom Town* (New York: Walker & Co., 1983), 60.

31. Cory, *The Circe Complex,* 223-26, and *A Bit of a Shunt up the River.*

32. *A Bit of a Shunt Up the River,* 15.

33. Cf. ibid., 117.

34. Ibid., 176.

35. Ibid., 177-78.

36. Cf. ibid., 187.

37. Lord C. P. Snow, quoted from John C. Carr, *The Craft of Crime: Conversations with Crime Writers* (Boston: Houghton Mifflin, 1983), 176. The quote first appeared in *Financial Times* of London, May 1970.

38. Mary Jane Latsis and Martha Henissart, quoted in Carr's *Craft of Crime,* 176-201. See particularly 184-89.

39. Carr, *Craft of Crime,* 176-77.

40. Ibid., 197.

41. Emma Lathen, *Double, Double, Oil and Trouble* (London: Gollancz, 1979), 7.

42. Emma Lathen, *Sweet and Low* (1974; reprint, New York: Pocket Books, 1975), 7-8.

43. Emma Lathen, *Ashes to Ashes* (1971; reprint, New York: Pocket Books, 1972), 97.

44. Ibid.

45. Michael N. Stanton, "Dick Francis: The Worth of Human Love," *TAD* 15 (1982): 137-43.

46. Carr, *Craft of Crime,* 204.

47. Ibid., 205.

48. Stanton, "Dick Francis," 140.

49. Carr, *Craft of Crime,* 204-5.

50. Stanton, "Dick Francis," 139.

51. Dick Francis, *High Stakes* (1975; reprint, New York: Pocket Books, 1977), 99.

52. Dick Francis, *Nerve* (New York: Harper & Row, 1964).

53. Stanton, "Dick Francis," 142.

54. Ibid., 143.

55. John Braine, quoted on the book jacket of James' *Taste for Death.*

56. P. D. James, *The Skull beneath the Skin* (New York: Scribner's, 1982), 86-87.

57. Ibid., 106.

58. P. D. James, *An Unsuitable Job for a Woman* (1972; reprint, New York: Popular Library, n.d.), 13.

59. Ibid., 15.

60. Ibid., 247.

61. P. D. James, *Death of an Expert Witness* (New York: Popular Library, 1977), 251-52.

62. P. D. James, *The Black Tower* (New York: Popular Library, 1976), 97.

63. James, *The Skull*, 110, 46.

64. James, *Black Tower*, 39-40.

65. P. D. James, *Innocent Blood* (New York: Scribner's, 1980), 67.

66. James, *Black Tower*, 45-46.

67. Ibid., 238-39.

68. Ibid., 41.

69. Ibid., 42.

70. *The Skull*, 107.

71. Ibid., 110.

72. *Black Tower*, 263.

73. *Death of an Expert Witness*, 97.

74. *Innocent Blood*, 70.

75. *Black Tower*, 61.

76. *A Taste for Death*, cf. 33, 38.

77. Ibid., 87; cf. 385, 447-48.

78. Ibid., 105-6.

79. Cf. ibid., 183, 189, 249, 332-33.

80. Cf. ibid., 267, 275, 284.

81. Ibid., 295.

82. Ibid., 335-36.

83. Ibid., 345.

84. Ibid., 351.

85. Ibid., 454.

86. Ibid., 403.

Lee Horsley (essay date 2001)

SOURCE: Horsley, Lee. "Pasts and Futures." In *The Noir Thriller*, pp. 228-50. Houndmills, England: Palgrave, 2001.

[*In the following essay, Horsley examines the themes of identity and the past in modern works of noir literature and film, including Peter Ackroyd's* Hawksmoor, *William Gibson's* Neuromancer, *Ridley Scott's film* Blade Runner, *and numerous others.*]

In Gibson's *Neuromancer* (1984), the protagonist, Case, exiled from cyberspace, sleeps in 'the cheapest coffins' and roams the streets of Night City, a place that is 'like a deranged experiment in social Darwinism': 'Stop hustling and you sink without a trace.' Isolated and self-destructive, worn down until 'the street itself [has come] to seem an externalisation of some death wish' (13-15), Case is hired to go on a virtual reality quest, 'the Straylight run'. His goal, Villa Straylight, belongs to a family that controls the world's two most powerful artificial intelligences; it is also, however, the highly wrought product of minds that in many ways seem remote from the era of hypertech and cyberspace. '"The Villa Straylight," said a jewelled thing on the pedestal, in a voice like music, "is a body grown in upon itself, a Gothic folly."' Its proliferating structures rise towards 'a solid core of microcircuitry', but are at the same time the emblems of an old family that has grown rich by exploiting others, 'growing inward' into a 'ragged tangle of fears' (242). As Ratz, the Chatsubo bartender, says, 'what grotesque props . . . castles hermetically sealed, the rarest rots of old Europe . . .' (278).

Gibson's novel, 'the quintessential cyberpunk novel',[1] is a fusion of the noir thriller, science fiction and the Gothic. Its computerised data matrix, Gothic castle and crazed aristocratic family merge entertainingly with its hard-boiled protagonist living precariously and immorally on the seedy margins of a corrupt world. A debt to Chandler is often suggested, though Case is in fact closer to Kells, the protagonist of Paul Cain's *Fast One*, an utterly cynical convicted criminal with a history of rash behaviour and drug addiction. In recent decades, particularly in the eighties and nineties, the label 'noir' has been applied to texts and films that combine elements of the noir thriller with future world and Gothic fantasies. Arguably this development is a return to origins. The hard-boiled tradition so inextricably bound up with noir is in part defined by the gritty realism of its style, its faithful representation of contemporary life and its hard-bitten response to socio-political corruption. In many respects, however, both literary and cinematic noir also have strong affinities with the literature of fantasy and romance, blending realistic representation with non-realistic and expressionist elements that are heightened, distorted, stylised and excessive—the knight of romance in Chandler, the mythic dimensions of Hammett's Poisonville, the supernatural suggestiveness of Woolrich's prose,[2] the monstrous satiric grotesques of Thompson's psychopath-narrator novels.[3] Indeed, it is often this pull towards excess which gives noir its unsettling power, its savage intensity and its haunting sense of irreversible fate, and, in novels that centre on a protagonist like Chandler's knight of the mean streets, it is the essentially romantic figure of the tarnished hero who is the 'last man standing' against this mood of fatality.

'One can imagine', James Naremore says, 'a large video store where examples of [*film noir*] would be shelved somewhere between gothic horror and dystopian science fiction: in the center would be *Double Indemnity,* and at either extreme *Cat People* and *Invasion of the Body Snatchers*.'⁴ The family resemblances to be found amongst noir, Gothic and science fiction are rooted in their shared history. The origins of science fiction are often seen to lie in later romance genres such as the Gothic novel.⁵ Old terrors are newly imagined, and, in cyberpunk, an old vocabulary (castles, romancers, ghosts, gods, voodoo) is coupled with a vocabulary of AIs (artificial intelligences), cranial jacks, the deck and the matrix. Gibson's fiction, especially *Count Zero* (1986) and *Mona Lisa Overdrive* (1988), repeatedly moves between technological 'magic' and the supernatural.⁶ The questing cyberpunk hacker is routinely haunted by past evils, by age-old forms of exploitation, superstitious horrors and decadent aristocratic cruelty. The cyberpunk text is as likely to be analysed in a critical study called *Gothic* as it is in one called *Cyberia*,⁷ and the same is true for such recent films as *Terminator, Alien* and *Blade Runner.* It is not only recent texts, of course, that can be located and discussed within both genres: *Frankenstein* (1818) can be credited with creating one of the most powerful and enduring Gothic 'terror-symbols' but is also widely accepted as 'the first real science fiction novel'; *Jekyll and Hyde* (1886) occupies a central place in the Gothic tradition and is at the same time one of the most important early examples of 'science fantasy'.⁸

The noir thriller is very often, like both *Frankenstein* and *Jekyll and Hyde,* a fantasy of duality, and *Jekyll and Hyde,* in particular, is a form of doppelgänger narrative rewritten countless times in the literary noir of the twentieth century. An apparently respectable protagonist's dark side surfaces, cannot be controlled, commits murder and brings ruin and destruction. Other elements in *Jekyll and Hyde*—sinister locations, darkness and decay, the fragmentary narrative, the suggestions of psychological monstrosity and regression to barbarity—are also familiar ingredients of the noir thriller. What sets Stevenson's novel apart from traditional noir, of course, is the admixture of fantasy. In recent decades, however, the stylistic and iconic aspects of non-fantastic literary noir (the tough style, the hard-boiled investigator, the gangster and the small-time crook, the femme fatale) have been reunited with literary forms in which there is a higher level of permissible fantasy, whether that fantasy is given a plausible scientific basis or involves blurring the distinctions between natural and supernatural. This kind of cross-breeding is to be seen in cyberpunk from Gibson's *Neuromancer* trilogy in the eighties to such recent novels as K. W. Jeter's *Noir* (1998), as well as in other near-future narratives, such as the Ballard and Womack novels analysed at the end of this chapter. It is also

seen in modern Gothic novels like those of Hjortsberg, Ackroyd and O'Connell.

If we think in terms of the defining features of literary noir, what we see in 'fantastic noir' is the intensification of two centrally important noir themes, the destabilising of identity and the inescapable presence of the past. As the comparison with *Jekyll and Hyde* suggests, divided identity is one of the shared preoccupations of the noir thriller and the Gothic novel. It is also frequently one of the underlying themes in the strand of science fiction which explores the interrelationship between the human and the technological. In non-fantastic noir, alienation from self can be evident in the fragmented narrative of a psychotic mind and in the confused or fearful responses of characters who encounter symptoms of this psychosis. In Gothic noir self-division can be literalised. So, for example, in Hjortsberg's *Falling Angel* (1978), Johnny Faithful has actually devoured the heart of Harry Angel. In Ackroyd's *Hawksmoor* (1985), the twentieth-century detective figure is haunted by his ghostly double, a late seventeenth- early eighteenth-century murderer.

Science fiction, too, has its dark doubles from *Frankenstein* on, but the distinctive science fictional means of destabilising our sense of unified character and human identity is by combining man with machine, or by challenging our perception of a human-mechanical divide. Man-machine symbiosis or brain-computer interfaces, the creation of artificial intelligences and biological engineering all disrupt our sense of the unity and integrity of individual bodies and minds. Bruce Sterling, for example in *Schismatrix* (1985), populates his future world with divergent species, the 'Mechs', enhanced by such things as brain-computer interfaces, and the 'Shapers', produced by the methods of bioengineering. In Rudy Rucker's *Software* (1982), giant artificial intelligences, 'boppers', extract the protagonist's 'software' (the information in his brain) and put it into a robot body. The sources of anxiety in fantasies of this kind are most often to do with external control (socio-political fatality) rather than inescapable inner demons (psychological fatality). The boundaries between inner and outer worlds are breached, producing fragmentation and the dissolution of a coherent self and raising radical questions about the nature of being (what is the essence of the human?). The intersection with the noir thriller, however, is more evident in the way this metamorphosis into the 'posthuman' foregrounds the issue of agency, bringing protagonists to wonder, not without cause, whether they retain free will and individual autonomy. For Gibson's Case, when he is trapped in the matrix by Neuromancer, the question is whether he has simply become a second-order electronic construct manipulated as an image by more powerful entities. Cobb Anderson, in Rucker's *Software,* asks himself what built-in programs are now a part of him: 'Were the boppers in a position to control him on a real-time basis? Would he notice the difference?' (120).

This apprehension about loss of control is closely analogous to the noir sense of fatality found in those novels which associate fate with the machinations of determinedly corrupt, possibly conspiratorial political and economic powers. A familiar figure in traditional noir is the man who does not realise that his actions are being externally controlled. In Hammett's *Glass Key,* for example, Ned Beaumont is unwittingly used by Paul Madvig, who is in turn under the sway of Senator Henry and his daughter, to whom Paul is a lower form of life, 'fair game for any kind of treatment' (780). The manipulating forces in the world of cyberpunk are generally less modest in their ambitions than the local if representative power brokers of traditional noir. Cyberspace transcends all local and national boundaries, and paranoia is on a correspondingly large scale, involving gigantic multinationals and omniscient intelligence organisations. This future-world projection, however, is not perceived as a fundamental departure from the more local forms of political and socio-economic control. Rather, it is the continuation of an old struggle by other means. Cyberpunk fiction moves away from the speculative dominant of 1960s science fiction, with its dramatic temporal and spatial dislocations, and turns instead to extrapolative world-building.[9] Its 'near-future' narratives imply inextricable connections between the past (our present) and a future in which both the streets and cyberspace replicate and satirically distort the structures and corruptions of contemporary corporate capitalism.

This diminution of temporal distance is also a characteristic of the Gothic noir narratives of Hjortsberg, Ackroyd and O'Connell. One of the distinguishing features of the Gothic is a 'fearful sense of inheritance in time', combining with a claustrophobic sense of enclosure in space to produce 'an impression of sickening descent into disintegration'.[10] The infernal cities of these writers are New York, London and the imaginary New England factory town of Quinsigasmond. They are all repositories of shadowy, ancient forces, but these dark powers are symbolically linked to the mechanisms, the buildings and the inescapable boundaries of the modern city. In the almost present futures of Ballard and Womack, the past is equally determinate, leaving the characters of the narrative with buried fears, hatreds and desires, begetters of a future that is in essence a reversion to the past—an encounter with the Conradian 'heart of darkness' that no noir protagonist ever manages to leave wholly behind.

A HELL OF A CITY

The themes of self-division and the inescapable past dominate William Hjortsberg's *Falling Angel,* which was filmed by Alan Parker as *Angel Heart* in 1987. The Faustian story of a satanic pact is grafted on to what at first appears to be a hard-boiled detective story, beginning with a phone call to the Crossroads Detective Agency, 'satisfaction guaranteed' at reasonable rates. It is possible to see the surprises of the narrative as the result of a generic switch from crime fiction to the Gothic novel. In a sense, however, the Gothic is heavily present from the opening sentence: 'It was Friday the thirteenth and yesterday's snowstorm lingered in the streets like a leftover curse' (1). Hjortsberg's skill lies in using throughout the language of superstition, curses, diabolic forces and evil incarnate to intensify and give horrifying substance to a noir narrative that centres on the investigation of dark secrets. It is a potent combination because we know that at bottom these narratives are the same. The hunter is indistinguishable from the hunted, and damnation is never negotiable.

'Harry Angel the famous shaman' (45) falls into a city in which there seems to be no way to evade the omnipresent Louis Cyphre. Ranging the city from its heights to its depths, Angel sees diabolical happenings at every level, though the real movement of the narrative is towards a recognition that evil is inescapable because it belongs to Harry's inner as well as his outer world. This is not just a matter of 'another bunch of crooks' in both high and demonic places (253). Harry's deficient self-knowledge is, of course, traditionally noir. Many a noir protagonist feels himself, like the amnesiac protagonist of John D. MacDonald's *ManTrap,* to be plunging through a long tunnel in which lights whip by 'illuminating fragments I could not understand' (152). When he finally recognises his true self he sees how deeply implicated he is and understands his fate. Like Angel, the noir investigator often finds that he has been somewhat careless in his choice of employer and fails to grasp why people keep dying around him. The noir amnesiac may all too effectively repress the memories that surface to give him nightmares—in Angel's case, of pursuer and pursued changing places and an evil twin embracing him with a savage kiss. What Angel adds to the noir thriller's scepticism about the possibility of goodness and innocence is a literalisation of devouring ambition ('Poor old Harry Angel . . . I killed him and ate his heart') and of the hidden self, Johnny Favourite, who has already earned damnation. The detective narrative's 'de-ciphering' has ironically revealed only a different sort of cipher, the true inner emptiness of Johnny Favourite. 'Where do you search for a guy who was never there to begin with?' (51). And alongside the satirically edged representation of the hollowness of the ambitious man is the final stress on the inevitability of death itself, the cipher as the 'zero' point that Louis Cyphre says is '"a portal through which every man must eventually pass"' (212).

Like Hjortsberg's novel, Peter Ackroyd's *Hawksmoor* subverts the rational confidence of classic Holmesian detection by imagining a connection that is only supernaturally explicable between pursuer and pursued, detective and murderer. However, where Hjortsberg provides a neatly dark resolution (the terrible truth of self-recognition), Ackroyd is more concerned with retaining a sense of ultimate, irresolvable mysteries, and thus moves towards a conclusion that is much more ambiguous than Johnny Favourite's incontrovertible failure to cheat the devil of his due. In Ackroyd's novel, this carefully preserved ambiguity serves the mainstream ambitiousness of metaphysical themes that are not fused with the kind of satirical observation to be found in *Falling Angel*. What Ackroyd presents in *Hawksmoor* are two mysteriously connected series of murders separated, in historical time, by about 250 years, the modern murders coinciding in almost every detail with the sacrificial murders long ago committed or 'willed' by Nicholas Dyer, who has been given the approximate historical niche of the architect, Nicholas Hawksmoor. The twentieth-century investigator has only baffling, haunting glimpses of the past that has created his present. His name, Nicholas Hawksmoor, suggests something of the doppelgänger relationship between investigator and murderer: as characters move through the novel, they repeatedly encounter their own inexplicable union with other human beings and experience the loss or dissolution of their own identities. The whole novel is structured in such a way that we as readers experience the viewpoints of several different characters—the minds of the murderer, the victims and the detective. The main murderer in *Hawksmoor* has been given a name which suggests a victim (a 'dyer') rather than a murderer; he begins life during the years of Plague and Fire as an orphaned child, outcast, terrified, drawn in amongst others who live on the margins of society. The detective is denied his traditional role of explaining a comprehensible crime and achieving neat closure. Ackroyd plays with the idea of the detective story that as a form moves towards an end which is really a discovery of the beginning (that is, of the origin of the crime), driving home the point that as metaphysical questions our speculations about origins and ends are unending and 'unbeginning', leading us back into an infinite regress of questions about where we came from and towards the equally unresolvable question of where we are going. We would like to think of ourselves as progressing, but instead only repeat the patterns of past ages. The crimes in *Hawksmoor* are part of a cycle, not specific acts pertaining to and resolvable at a particular time, but part of an endless repetition, and the investigator is himself constituted by the past, not detached from it.

Hawksmoor uses what seem to be supernatural events to undermine confidence that the evidence will be susceptible to empirical enquiry. Ackroyd's *Dan Leno and the Limehouse Golem* (1994) develops a similar theme, the power of the irrational within the human

mind, by creating a narrative in which superstition, prejudice and terror lead people to identify the Gothic monster, the golem, as the perpetrator of horrific crimes, but in which the actual source is something equally dark, mysterious and unknowable within the mind of a murderess (who is herself a victim). As in *Hawksmoor*, there is a 'gothic' rapport between characters and the places they inhabit, with London providing a topography of dark spaces and fear-laden enclosures. Both books echo De Quincey's 'On Murder Considered as One of the Fine Arts', with its account of the Ratcliffe Highway slaughter.[11] In *Dan Leno*, these murders are central to a plot which involves both performance and repetition of past crimes—the 'fine art' of re-enacting 'the immortal Ratcliffe Highway murders of 1812 . . . silently dispatched into eternity by an artist whose exploits will be preserved for ever in the pages of Thomas De Quincey' (25).

Like O'Connell's novels, *Dan Leno* is dominated by the themes of performance and spectatorship which are central to many contemporary noir thrillers. The Gothic, associated as it is with excess, the violation of taboos and the expression of violent emotion, lends itself to an exploration of the acting out and witnessing of transgressive performances in which players and spectators alike exceed the boundaries of the permissible. What Ackroyd builds on in *Dan Leno* is the association between Gothic heightening and our equivocal enjoyment, as audience, of the gruesome spectacle of murder. Like the post-seventies noir thriller generally, this is written to appeal to our appetite for sensational crime and then to make us reflect on the nature of that appetite, on our uncertainty about the relationship of fantasy to act and on violence which is 'inseparable from its reproduction as spectacle'.[12] *Dan Leno* is closer than *Hawksmoor* to the structure of the generic thriller. Much of the fragmented and deceptive narrative is seen through the eyes of a murderer whose identity we do not know until the very end. The combination of concealment and spectacle leads us to focus on the tension between secret deeds and a compulsion to display, to assert oneself publicly through dramatically violent acts.

The final revelation of the murderer's identity adds to *Dan Leno* a preoccupation that is more commonly present in the work of contemporary female crime writers. That is, Ackroyd emphasises the need felt by a woman both to author her own story and to be able to act and perform as a man can. For Elizabeth Cree, who is on stage with Dan Leno, the theatre offers the means of transforming herself from a repressed and powerless girl: 'My old self was dead and the new Lizzie . . . had been born at last' (106). Lizzie feels that she attains the status of the Romantic male outlaw hero made famous by De Quincey, 'an outcast who enjoys a secret power . . . transformed into an avenger whose bright yellow hair and chalk-white countenance afforded him the significance of some primeval deity' (37). Although her genius for performance, her imaginative and mimetic powers, are perverted into the 'fine art' of murder, she is nevertheless remarkable for her inventiveness. She escapes herself by triumphantly taking on other roles, cross-dressing, developing a male 'slanguage' and writing an incriminating diary for her husband John Cree, on his 'tyro' aspirations to the artistry of the Ratcliffe Highway murders: 'I must admit that I applauded my own work' (24-30, 62).

The popular invention of the Limehouse Golem, widely supposed to be the perpetrator of Lizzie's crimes, raises other questions about the way the human imagination works. Rather than structuring the novel around the supernatural connections established in *Hawksmoor,* Ackroyd uses *Dan Leno* to explore people's need for supernatural explanations. The golem is a Gothic conceptualising of the persistence of evil, 'as if some primeval force had erupted in Limehouse . . . Some dark spirit' for which London itself is responsible (83, 162). By incorporating George Gissing and Babbage's Analytical Engine in his narrative, Ackroyd suggests, as he does in *Hawksmoor,* that basic fears and needs will inevitably connect the human future with the past. Technology will not eradicate evil and indeed, ironically, will itself be blamed for ancient forces within man himself. The golem, like the computer, invokes 'the horror of an artificial life and a form without spirit', an 'automaton' (88, 269).

In exploring the need for explanatory myths, Ackroyd captures the atmosphere of avid bloodthirstiness and voyeurism that prevails as the public gossip about the murders. He is not, however, equally concerned with analysing the nature of such spectatorship or the implications of being the audience of violence. Jack O'Connell, on the other hand, responding in an oblique fashion to a society in which there is growing pressure for censorship, is much more intent on understanding the act of viewing transgressive behaviour than he is with the performance of the acts themselves. Novels like *The Skin Palace* (1996) and *Word Made Flesh* (1999) are an idiosyncratic mixture of thriller plots, Gothic atmosphere and the science fiction topos of the alternative or parallel world. Within Quinsigamond many of the more disturbing aspects of twentieth-century life are replicated in heightened, grotesque, often surreal ways and reflected in the fun-house mirror of satire. The invention of Quinsigamond removes recent history to a fantasy world. O'Connell is also, however, the most directly satirical of all the writers discussed in this chapter and he brings his novels very close to the climate of contemporary debate about the representation of sex and violence (pornography is a central issue in *The Skin Palace,* violence in *Word Made Flesh*). The Gothic scene-setting functions to make strange a very familiar set of conflicting views on the

justification of such representation and on 'the Preservation of Dangerous Art' (286). Quinsigamond itself is like a stage. The streets, O'Connell says, 'seem to exist to be pure spectacle'. Sex and violence alike are filmed and fictionalised by the inhabitants, the images stored in subway tunnels and labyrinthine underground libraries and killed for by powerful individuals.

The Skin Palace centres on the clash between different myths of America. It is a land of criminal opportunity on the one hand, a land of free artistic expression on the other. Jakob Kinsky, the son of a powerful gangster, nurses his ambition to become a director of 'hyperreal' *films noirs*: '"Give me some crime, cynicism, claustrophobia. . . . City grime. As much shadow as you can manage . . ."' (196-7). The novel is dominated by images of screens—from drive-in cinema screens and gigantic projections of multiple images to the television next to the couch. Characters define themselves in relation to the roles of creator, actor or spectator. Both of the main characters (Jakob and an aspiring photographer, Sylvia Krafft) are obsessed by the cinematic image, and, through their experiences, O'Connell poses the questions of risks and benefits. O'Connell suggests the excessiveness of the pornographic and voyeuristic compulsion, especially in his descriptions of Herzog's Erotic Palace, which is like a 'textbook example' authored by 'a visionary egomaniac living on hallucinogens and gothic novels . . . theatrical to the point of self-parody . . .' (67-8). Nevertheless he insists on the relationship between this compulsion and an appetite for understanding which is denied only by the dense (Sylvia's unsatisfactory mate Perry), the criminal (the gangster Kinsky) or the mindlessly censorious crusader (the Women's American Resistance and Families United for Decency).

The most recent of the Quinsigamond novels, *Word Made Flesh,* is another extended meditation on the themes of voyeurism, violence and bearing witness. Here, it is violence rather than eroticism that is mainly at issue. The novel confronts readers with the question of what it means to be spectators of violent acts, and how you differentiate voyeurism from 'witnessing' in a fully human and responsible way. The first horrifying spectacle, a man being flayed alive, draws us in as audience, buttonholed by the conspiratorial, queasy patter of a narrator who only wishes that we could hold the blades ourselves; he sees us flinch, but we do not close our eyes, 'and that will make all the difference'; he encourages us to view the victim 'as more object than person. This has worked for others in the past' (11-17). The narrative contains both spectators and players, and the most pressing issue is whether you can try to understand the world of the players without yourself being corrupted, and without anaesthetising your sensibilities.

As in *The Skin Palace,* O'Connell's narrative sustains the idea that image and story have transforming power. The object on which the plot turns is a book that contains the story written by a teenage girl who has made 'a weapon of her epiphany' after witnessing the July Sweep, a pogrom in which her whole world 'was summarily destroyed and, literally, shredded into pulp' (179f.). The power of her words in evoking a horrifying spectacle can be read as a demonstration of the sinister fascination of violence: the man responsible for the July Sweep wants to possess the book because in it he finds his deeds elevated to a legend. But the book is also a testament, a proof that words can transmute events into something that could convey the meaning of the 'Erasure' across 'space and time and culture' (310). *Word Made Flesh,* like *The Maltese Falcon* or Gibson's *Virtual Light,* is a quest narrative, but the object sought is more important than the falcon (an empty signifier of commodity fetishism) or the glasses of *Virtual Light* (offering a template of a future world that corrupt commercial forces aim to create). The fabulous manuscript of O'Connell's novel embodies the power of fiction itself to represent the past and shape the future.

THE MEAN STREETS OF THE METAVERSE

As the aspiring noir director in O'Connell's *Skin Palace* scouts for locations 'that agree with the images already screened in the skull-camera', he points an actual camera at scenes very like those in Ridley Scott's *Blade Runner* (1982), looking down on Gompers Station, with its 'indiscriminate tangles' of 'recombinant junk' (367). For O'Connell this sort of scene signifies a European past of pogroms and dictators, the violence of which continues to haunt the New World. In *Blade Runner* the urban decay and detritus of the late twentieth century, dominating the look of the film's cityscape, are a visual reminder of the determining force of present corruptions (the evolving present-as-past) in a dystopian future world. Although neither *Blade Runner* nor the novel on which it was based—Philip K. Dick's *Do Androids Dream of Electric Sheep?* (1968)—open into a parallel world of cyberspace, Scott's visual reminders of the mean streets of the classic noir cycle have become an identifying feature of the aesthetic of cyberpunk. The inner-city spaces of *Blade Runner* merge past and future. Images of urban alienation and corporate power structures in a sleazy, threatening metropolis are combined with modern 'add-ons'. In the making of the film, a 1920s set used for gangster films and *films noirs* was 'retrofitted' with 'a variety of mechanical stuff'; ducts, rewirings, video monitors, matte-paintings were used to incorporate looming towers, so that the city resembled 'a vast, boundless refinery'. The remorseless pressures of consumerism were embodied in flying billboards and loudspeakers blaring commercials.[13]

In Philip K. Dick's novel, dust and 'kipple' (junk) rather than vertiginous darkness characterise the future-world cityscape, suggesting ghost towns more than *films noirs.* But the sense of estrangement and dislocation, of loss of bearings, is equally strong. This is reinforced in the novel by the creation of a parallel world (not dissimilar to cyberspace in its disorienting effects), when Deckard is taken by a patrolman to a complicated modern building that he has never seen before. He is accused of being an android himself and told that he comes from a phantom police department. In fact, he has been arrested by an android-dominated police department which inhabits a 'closed loop' cut off from the rest of San Francisco—an alter-world interlude that, like cyberspace, acts to bring different levels of reality together in disquieting ways and to loosen the protagonist's belief in his ability to distinguish real worlds from false ones. Deckard's crisis of confidence deepens when Phil Resch, whom he associates with android 'inhumanity', passes the Voigt-Kampff test: '"Do you have your ideology formed,"' Resch asks, '"that would explain me as part of the human race?"' (108). This is at bottom a very traditional moral question, and one that has repeatedly been raised in the noir thriller: that is, at what point does one cross the line that separates humanity from inhumanity? Deckard admits to himself at the end, having killed the androids, that what he has done has 'become alien to me' (172).

As cyberpunk develops the ideas of manufactured or augmented selves and invasive technology, the more pessimistic implications are readily apparent. The protagonist, by coming into a closer relationship with the non-human, sacrifices a coherent sense of self, of human values and confident agency; or, in other plot patterns, humans themselves are programmable and thus susceptible to the control of external powers. It is not necessarily characteristic of cyberpunk, however, to give expression to such doubts. Writers like Mark Laidlaw and Rudy Rucker, for example, celebrate the competence of the surfers and hackers who adventure through cyberspace, like Rucker's Jerzy Rugby, who walks away from *The Hackers and the Ants* (1994) as 'a free man with a dynamite story' (305). Many recent films that share something of the 'future noir' look of *Blade Runner* are similarly upbeat, in the sense that individual action defeats those who abuse technological powers. So, for example, in *Total Recall* (Paul Verhoeven, 1990), which is also based on a Philip K. Dick story ('We Can Remember It for You Wholesale'), there are many noirish features, not just visually but in the theme of split identity and 'a really sophisticated mindfuck'. In noir, however, the crucial discovery that Quaid is the 'bad' Hauser would be of decisive importance, and Quaid would exist only, as Cohaagen says, as 'just a stupid dream'. In fact, however, by the exertion of the sheer physical strength generally associated with Schwarzenegger action-hero roles, the protagonist is able to break away to become Quaid. The noir possibility hovers behind the 'open' end ('Kiss me before we wake up'), but it is the kiss and the 'dream' Quaid that carry conviction, and the end of the film functions to confirm the romantic possibility of action and of a clean break with an old, bad self. This pressure towards achieving mastery, whether by traditional heroic resolve (analogous to the masculine competence of action-oriented hard-boiled fiction) or by technological virtuosity, is strongly present in much cyberpunk, modifying the 'future noir' mood, bringing it closer to 'cyberian' optimism than to dystopian pessimism.[14]

The filming of *Blade Runner* itself might be taken to demonstrate the tension within future noir between optimistic and pessimistic forms of closure. Dogged as it was by production and post-production disagreements, *Blade Runner* emerged in its well-known variant forms. The version that was first screened in 1982, though characterised neither by technophilia nor by the romantic sweep of, say, the *Star Wars* trilogy, did move towards reasonably positive closure, with the voice-over and the last scene, moving out of the grimy city towards togetherness without a termination date, bringing the film nearer to the upbeat ending of *Total Recall*. The Director's Cut, on the other hand, released in 1992, approaches the ambivalence of the more disturbing noir visions, not only resisting romantic closure but implying that Deckard himself may, after all, be a replicant. To open the film to the possibility of such a reading is to suggest comparison with those bleakly ironic noir narratives in which a protagonist finds that he is hunting himself or (here) his own kind. Although Dick's *Electric Sheep* does not reinforce its moral ambiguities with this kind of doubling, some of his other fiction shares this destabilising ambiguity, particularly *A Scanner Darkly* (1977). This is a novel that develops in an uncompromising way a narrative pattern that implies the existence of a dark, unrecognised inner self. The consequent disabling of the individual's capacity for independent action creates a closed loop from which there is no escape.

One of Dick's most compelling near-future novels, *A Scanner Darkly* is also the most despairingly personal. His painful experience of drug abuse in the sixties becomes the basis for a science fiction world in which other forms of control combine with addiction to produce a nightmare of noir entrapment. In his 'Author's Note' at the end, Dick argues that he is representing nemesis rather than fate, since any potential addict has the power to choose, but the punishment is conceived in terms of deterministic cause and effect: that is, once addiction has taken place, fatality takes over. Within the narrative choice is only really present in a Flitcraft-like episode in which Dick's protagonist, Bob Arctor, suffers a blow to the head that jars him into a rejection of bourgeois stability and tedium. Ironically, like many protagonists in the traditional noir thriller, Arctor finds not freedom but a worse-than-bourgeois entrapment.

Within the context of a high-surveillance science fiction world, forms of entrapment are, of course, sufficiently thoroughgoing to make ordinary paranoia pale into insignificance. Like *Blade Runner, A Scanner Darkly* creates a hunter character reminiscent of the private eye, but here with a much stronger sense that he is a victim. He 'didn't volunteer' and 'never did know' (234). Those in control of the splitting of personality are entirely willing to sacrifice Arctor to get the information they need about the illegal growing of the plants that produce Substance D, 'the flower of the future', the substance that affects users by bringing 'death of the spirit, the identity' (250-1, 233). *A Scanner Darkly* is the narrative of an assault on the protagonist's sense of self, with name changes (he is Bob and Fred and Bruce), his transformation by a hi-tech scramble suit into a 'blur', his splitting into hunter and hunted (when Fred is assigned the job of observing Bob Arctor), and his final loss of all grasp of who he is. Arctor is 'repeating doomed patterns', going through the same thing over and over like 'a closed loop of tape' (62-3). There is a stage in the narrative at which Arctor, giving a speech, deviates from his script, and he seems at this point capable both of ironising his role as 'the vague blur' and of a coherent critique of life in southern California—a commercial for itself, endlessly replayed, as if 'the automatic factory' cranks out indistinguishable objects (31-2). This lucidity, however, is short-lived. The anxiety underlying *Blade Runner* is the humanistic fear of dehumanisation through violence. In *A Scanner Darkly,* the anxiety is centred on becoming another sort of replicant, simply a manufactured object incapable of breaking away from the master script of his society—'Actor, Arctor . . . Bob the Actor who is being hunted . . .' (125).

The cyberpunk writers influenced by *Blade Runner* and Philip K. Dick are seldom so enclosed within doomed patterns, even when the protagonist (as in Jeter's *Noir*) is named 'McNihil'. The technology which can close the circle of fatality—mechanisms of total control and omniscient surveillance—can also be pressed into the service of the action hero, and in so far as it envisages effective action cyberpunk moves closer to the traditions of male romance. Given its strong links with tough-guy fiction, traditional noir has, of course, often crossed over into action heroics, retaining a distinctly noir character only if the action hero is ultimately unsuccessful or if, in victory, he is thoroughly tainted by the world of violence and corruption with which he is involved (Paul Cain's Gerry Kells rather than Daly's Race Williams; Hammett's Continental Op rather than Chandler's Marlowe). However noir the future world he traverses, the cyberpunk 'cowboy' tends to have something in common with the two-fisted (anti-)hero. High technology, like the Colt .45, can serve any ends, whether repressive or rebellious. William Gibson and Bruce Sterling are regarded as amongst the more pessimistic of cyberpunk writers. Their 'doomed vision' is characterised as a 'dark and hopeless' refusal to see 'technology as inherently liberating'; they harbour a belief in human programmability and create protagonists who allow themselves to be exploited by higher powers.[15] Even Gibson's Case, however, shows himself capable of appropriating effective technologies and stepping outside of the closed loop of the addict's dependency, the consumer's passivity or the subservience of the player who is confined to one game board.

At the end of *A Scanner Darkly,* the corpse-like protagonist can no longer act. He can 'react' (233), but his reflex programmed reaction in secreting one of the 'flowers of the future' leaves us with only a glimmer of hope in the final paragraph. Gibson's anti-heroes, on the other hand, are not totally in the power of the anachronistic rich or of the interdimensional corporations, or even of the giant artificial intelligences. They are tinged with the rebellious glamour of Burroughs' wild boys, '. . . glider boys with bows and laser guns, roller-skate boys, . . . slingshot boys, knife throwers, . . . bare-hand fighters, shaman boys who ride the wind . . .' (*The Wild Boys,* 147). Case, at the end of *Neuromancer,* fuelled by suicidal impulse and self-loathing, has no clear knowledge of what he is trying to achieve and no way of guessing the outcome. He is, however, capable of choice: '"Give us the fucking code. . . . If you don't, what'll change?"' (307). Exhilarating action is still a possibility, as it often is in the hard-boiled strand of the noir thriller, even if the change effected in *Neuromancer* is left open to question and the 'posthumanist' bias of cyberpunk is evident in the fact that the main result of Case's endeavours takes place on a wholly non-human level, with Wintermute having 'meshed somehow' with Neuromancer, thus freeing itself to talk to its own kind. In *Count Zero* and *Mona Lisa Overdrive,* however, there are elements of a more traditionally humanistic closure, with nature playing a redemptive role (Turner and the squirrel wood) and some positive human, or at least modified human, connections. Gibson's move away from the 'posthuman' perspectives of *Neuromancer* can also be seen in *Virtual Light* (1993), in which the central contrast is between an attempt to achieve a closed, coercive system and the opposing force of 'play' and unpredictable desire.

Michael Hutchinson, speaking of the dependence of authoritarian systems on citizens who can be counted on to act predictably, quotes George Bush's dictum, 'The only enemy we have is unpredictability.'[16] It is precisely this unpredictability in the exploitation of high tech that typifies the key players in *Virtual Light*. The computer becomes less of a character in its own right and more an instrument which can be used either to oppress ('fate' in the hands of the mega-corps) or to liberate, the means to realise desire. One of Gibson's most prominent themes here is an immobilising,

paranoid sense of fatality. The presence of the Death Star, an all-seeing techno-equivalent to fate, and the interconnected mega-corporation leave no question about the sheer size of what the individual is up against: '"You don't know shit about shit. . . . It's just too *big* for someone like you to understand"' (229). But there is also the possibility of tricking fate. Help comes from the Republic of Desire, an organisation (or disorganisation) demonstrating that the interconnectedness of computers may facilitate mega-corporational control, but that it can also be empowering, preserving space for anarchic desires. The plot turns on the revelation of the fact that the corporate powers intend to 'do' San Francisco 'like they're doing Tokyo' (270), with the Republic of Desire aiding the protagonist, Rydell, because they hate the idea of a rebuilt San Francisco and a controlled, designed future. The existing San Francisco, full of hidden depths, forbidden zones and hard-to-grasp interactions, stands for the mystery, randomness and unknowability that act as some kind of guarantee of old-fashioned human warmth and connection. The bridge, central to this world, is an emblem of the carnivalised city. Gibson's hard-boiled protagonist is appropriately disorderly and unpredictable. Rydell fits the noir pattern of the wandering adventurer, questing across boundaries in pursuit of the woman carrying a fabulous object (the virtual light glasses, containing the plans for the new San Francisco) that signifies greed and the unscrupulous pursuit of wealth. Gibson has a nicely ironic way of achieving closure, with Rydell in such deep trouble that he is ideally suited to a programme called Cops in Trouble ('in deep, spectacular, and . . . clearly *heroic* shit' [290]). But the emphasis on 'heroic' is real as well as comically incongruous. The values that Rydell has helped to preserve are as positive as those defended by Marlowe, but, as in much other contemporary noir, his strength is less a matter of lonely integrity in mean streets than of energy sustained by spontaneous communal street life.

A 'Gibson for the 1990s',[17] Neal Stephenson, in *Snow Crash* (1992), invented the word 'Metaverse', and, like Gibson, he uses proliferating realities to satirise consumerism and the addiction to spectacle as well as to celebrate possibilities for the anarchic expression of desire. The 'heroic shit' model of the player-narrative is immediately established in *Snow Crash* by the naming of the central figure: Hiro Protagonist. In a contemporary version of the noir ethic, Hiro uses the weapons of corruption against the corrupt—advertising (when he defeats the scrolls), programming, violence. He shares with the hard-boiled detective an alienated, counterculture persona, being someone who 'needs to work harder on his co-operation skills' (3). He is half-black and half-Asian and lacks a firm class orientation; intelligent and tough, a resourceful outsider, he is his own man, willing and able to kill if necessary. As his name suggests, however, he is less developed, less vulnerable and less beaten down than the true noir protagonist. When we learn of his spectacular competence as the last of the freelance hackers and the greatest sword-fighter, we begin to suspect him of having more of an action-hero lineage. He is a resourceful player who is ultimately successful, defeating with a hacker's ingenuity a plot for world domination.

'Snow crash' is a drug/computer virus premised on the mind/machine interface: "'Does it fuck up your brain? . . . Or your computer?" "Both. Neither. What's the difference?"' (41). Like other standard cyberpunk dangers, it evokes such dystopian fears as totalitarian control, loss of identity and loss of personal autonomy. The virus is metaphorically linked with the franchise. That is, what thrives in one place will thrive in another, and both are associated with an ethos of 'no surprises', comforting uniformity and an end to adventure. As in *Virtual Light,* the central theme hinges on the traditional humanistic opposition between individual randomness and the metaphysical and ideological certainties of religion and politics; also as in *Virtual Light,* without deploying any techniques that are strikingly Gothic, the narrative suggests the inter-penetration of past and future, confronting Hiro Protagonist with a threat that is at once very ancient and very up-to-the-minute. Snow crash produces a culture-wide version of the kind of assault on individual identity that, in traditional noir, destabilises an effective individual sense of self. An underlying myth of language formation carries the argument that the tendency of languages to diverge (post-'Infocalypse') acts as a kind of guarantee of independence, conferring immunity to 'viral infections' that bypass 'higher language functions' and tie into 'the deep structures', thus enabling 'viral ideas', from Nazism to 'crackpot religions', to establish themselves (369-76). The generally sympathetic criminality of the various factions in the novel (including the Mafia and a mutant member of the Aleuts) is set against the apparent normality and virtue of televangelists, consumerist society and mass culture.

Again, then, this is the characteristic cyberpunk mix of the archaic with the hi-tech, blending pasts (ancient forces, age-old iniquities, buried evils) with futures (whether of technological empowerment or dystopian repression). This mixture has become a staple element of youth culture, whether in manga (the legendary Akira kept long dormant under Neo-Tokyo, 'a city in the wild grip of technology gone mad'), video games, virtual nightclubs and virtual reality (VR) theme parks.[18] Recent future noir includes the 'cyber noir' or 'cybershock' novels, *neoAddix* (1997) and *Lucifer's Dragon* (1998), by the British writer Jon Courtenay Grimwood, a freelance journalist who writes regularly, amongst other things, for the Japanese film magazine *Manga Mania.* As in the cyberpunk of Gibson and Stephenson, dark forces are met by technological efforts to defy fatality.

In *neoAddix,* for example, biotech resurrection is one answer to an old order that seemed to have a monopoly of special powers: their trope is vampirism, that of the protagonists is technological enhancement. Grimwood's plot brings together the world of ancient aristocratic degeneracy (a sinister vampiric 800-year-old Prince) with the modern world of corporate corruption. The heir to the psychopathic Prince will be drawn from competing and thoroughly corrupt tycoons, and battle is waged by means both supernatural and technological. 'Tek', magic, the subconscious, the ghost world, dream time and astral travel are all just a difference of perspective on powers of the mind that have evolved only in terms of the way in which information is accessed. Grimwood's protagonists, Alex and the cyber-jockey, Johnnie T., appear to die and are resurrected by techno-wizardry: "'Do you remember who you are? . . . Doesn't matter. You'll be someone else when you wake up anyway'" (220). More than anything, it is this desta-bilisation of identity that justifies the label 'cyber noir', along with Grimwood's creation of dark doubles. Alex becomes that which he fights. Darker than Gibson or Stephenson, Grimwood ends *neoAddix* with an ultimate contest in which Alex must call on and accept 'the help of the Prince, and every other Grand Master who howled and gibbered in the wasteland of his brain', after which he recognises that he is 'no longer remotely human', and in the aftermath is more damaged and isolated than are most cyberpunk protagonists. Believing himself hideously scarred, with scars no one else can see, he lives in almost total isolation, 'the anchorite of San Lorenzo' (357).

The science fiction/Gothic/noir combination is by no means confined to novels that use cyberspace as the parallel dimension in which alternative identities can be created. The balance easily shifts towards the Gothic/supernatural, with the more dreamlike and grotesque elements coming to the fore. Michael Marshall Smith, whose subsequent novels, *Spares* (1996) and *One of Us* (1998) also involve cloning and memory implantation, published his first novel, entitled *Only Forward,* in 1994—a whimsical, funny and often macabre form of future noir in which the fantastic dimension is located in dream time, or dream accessed waking. The narrator, Stark, is a 'strong dreamer' who, like the hacker or cyberspace jockey, is a guide to a future world, a troubleshooter, a fixer and finder, and the epitome of hard-boiled cool. He is able to go into a tough neighbourhood, for example, because 'I look like the kind of guy who pimps for his sister not just for the money, but because he hates her. I can look like a guy who belongs' (18). At the same time, he always feels he has to play the hero and works less for the money than for what interests him or what is right. This private-eye-like integrity, however, is broken down by the exposure of his own dark side: he is himself the source of the evil he is tracking, and must confess both his unreliability as a narrator and his current sense of disorientation ('I'm not myself. Or maybe I am. It's been so long I can't remember' [254]). The nightmare that initiates the troubles of the narrative turns out to have been his own, and at the macabre, horror-novel climax, Stark recognises his guilt. The truth, finally, is not just 'more stark' but 'more Stark' (289). As this punning revelation suggests, Smith's tone mixes the blackly comic with the lightly jokey, and his playfulness extends as well to the noir sense of fatality: 'If there's anything I really hate, it's things going better than I expected. . . . Things turning out well fills me with nameless dread . . .' (62). *Only Forward* is throughout a tongue-in-cheek narrative of a postmodern tough guy brooding on the persistence of his modernist anxieties: 'The rough beast doesn't just visit me occasionally: there's a regular fucking bus route' (67).

INVITATIONS TO THE UNDERWORLD

Future noir has also developed in directions quite different from the elaborately fantastic world of cyberpunk. Two of the most genuinely and disturbingly noir near-future visions, both published in the mid-nineties, are Jack Womack's *Random Acts of Senseless Violence* (1993) and J. G. Ballard's *Cocaine Nights* (1996), the first American, the second British. These are novels that have a clear place in mainstream fiction, though bookstores also shelve them with genre fiction, either with science fiction (Ballard on the strength of his niche as a science fiction writer) or with crime fiction. Both are first-person narratives of guilt and violence, patterned in ways very familiar from the noir thrillers we have examined. Ballard's is a story of the narrator's investigation of a horrific crime in an effort to clear his brother. It is an investigation that ends not only with a recognition that there is a sense in which his brother is guilty, but with him taking guilt upon himself (the investigator thereby being transformed into a man seen at the end as a malefactor). The Womack novel is in the tradition of narratives that involve an innocent narrator drawn into a world of deprivation and violence and crossing the line by committing an act of murder which leads irrevocably to utter isolation in savage surroundings. But the use of a young girl in the narrator's role makes *Random Acts* a striking departure from the tradition. Ballard and Womack are both imagining a semi-contemporary future, with the present sliding almost imperceptibly into near future. Ballard sets his novel in a leisured, privileged retirement community, Womack sets his in a desperately poor urban environment, but both use traditional elements of the thriller to explore the movement of a society towards violence. Womack's explanations have more in common with those of much earlier noir thrillers. Deprivation and casual injustice are shown to be irrevocably shaping the life of a girl who is not dissimilar to Ellson's *Tomboy*—young, tough and doomed to take her place in a disintegrating urban

environment. Ballard's novel, on the other hand, imagines a world without economic deprivation, sheltered from all of the destructive forces abroad in Womack's New York, and asks whether under such conditions violence would in fact disappear. Each is in a way an Edenic fable. In *Random Acts,* the former life of the nuclear family is the innocent, sheltered childhood world of an intelligent middle-class family living apart from the encroaching darkness. *Cocaine Nights* presents us with a Johnsonian Happy Valley in which all is supplied, but in which the spectacle of violence is required (though this, too, might be said to have an element of social determinism, with changes caused by economic satiation rather than economic need). What the deprivation and the boredom release is, in each case, something within—Conradian hearts of darkness revealed at the end of symbolic journeys.

Ballard's science fiction novels, from *The Drowned World* (1961) on, made him the 'idolised role model' for cyberpunk writers, admired for pushing to the limits 'the bizarre, the surreal, the formerly unthinkable . . .'[19] *Cocaine Nights,* which seems at first glance to be a realistic novel of Mediterranean retirement, is in fact very closely related to the bizarre and surreal body of his science fiction, its deceptive surface so strongly reinforcing our sense of the conventional and mundane that the emerging 'future' is all the more disturbing in its coupling of banality and violence. As in much contemporary noir, crime is conceived as a combination of spectacle and game, fascinating, addictive and more dangerous than the participants realise. Conrad's *Heart of Darkness* is an unmistakable presence behind Ballard's evocations of savage joy and frenzy that are, like the 'certain midnight dances', inextricably bound up with a savage violence not that far removed from the cannibalism, heads on stakes and 'unspeakable rites' with which Kurtz's midnight dances end. In his earlier novels (*The Drowned World, The Crystal World*) Ballard often created narrative patterns that led critics to think, in spite of his denials, in terms of Conradian journeys into the interior, though with the Conradian theme modified (for example in *The Crystal World*) by imagining a journey towards the inner self, the core of the unconscious that contains brightness as well as darkness, a zone of transformation in which imaginative free play flourishes in opposition to the symbolic order, the world outside where the return of unconscious desire is suppressed.

In *Cocaine Nights,* Ballard uses a different structure: Dionysus on tour, rather than a journey to a forbidden zone, contained within an investigative framework that ends by revealing shared guilt. Ballard's Bobby Crawford parallels the 'mysterious stranger' in *The Bacchae*—'the god himself', the spirit of the instinctive group-personality and 'the ambiguous master-magician of pleasure and pain, beauty and cruelty'.[20] When the protagonist, Charles, comes to the Costa del Sol it is because his brother Frank is accused of the murder of five people. He begins by thinking that Frank must be pleading guilty as 'part of some bizarre game he was playing against himself', but the 'game' is quite other than he imagines, and he is drawn into staying by an attempt on his life, which is not so much a warning as an attempt to integrate him into the inner life of Estrella de Mar, '"a kind of invitation. Almost an invitation to . . ." "The underworld? The real Estrella de Mar?"' (174). It is for Charles, as it clearly also was for his brother, a liminal experience. On the face of it, all he does is fly to the present-day Costa del Sol, but even in the opening paragraph there is a sly insinuation of his affinities with Ballard's future-world protagonists, an implication both that he is crossing into an alien zone and that he is carrying with him his own repressed, forbidden repository of guilts and desires:

> Crossing frontiers is my profession. Those strips of no-man's land between the checkpoints always seem such zones of promise. . . . At the same time they set off a reflex of unease that I have never been able to repress. As the customs officials rummage through my suitcases I sense them trying to unpack my mind and reveal a contraband of forbidden dreams and memories. And even then there are the special pleasures of being exposed. . . .
>
> (9)

The phrases here establish the most important terms of the following narrative: crossing frontiers, zones of promise, able to repress, forbidden dreams and guilty memories. The Costa del Sol, like other strange zones of Ballard's science fiction, is both a realm of the imagination (a place that 'doesn't really exist. That's why I like the coast . . .' [17]) and a preview of the future: 'It's Europe's future. Everywhere will be like this soon'; '. . . It's the *fourth* world. . . . The one waiting to take over everything . . .' (23, 215-16).

Until it is touched by the Dionysiac spirit of Bobby Crawford, the Costa del Sol is completely null. This is more than just a picture of a world of moneyed leisure. Ballard heightens the descriptions enough so that they become surreal and dystopian: the 'memory-erasing' cubist architecture of the houses and apartments with white facades 'like blocks of time that had crystallised beside the road'; the residents, preternaturally still, holding unread books and watching television with the sound off (34-5, 75, 215-16). Into this 'walled limbo' (34), Bobby Crawford brings his youthful good looks (looking like 'a handsome and affable gangster' [68]) and, above all, his extraordinary fluidity and energy. He is capable of changing everyone's lives but also full of 'dark, lurking violence' (205). Having stumbled on to the truth that crime and creativity go together, Crawford puts people in touch with 'dormant areas' of their minds, making them fascinated by the 'other world' of crime

'where everything is possible', where they can break the rules and sidestep the taboos (245), 'leaving behind a treasure of incitement and desire' (263). Fires, speedboat chases, explosions, rapes all become communal spectacles: 'Crime at Estrella de Mar had become one of the performance arts. . . . Brutal, but great fun' (146). This, then, becomes an alternative vision of the future. Communal life is energised by transgressive behaviour: 'One of the modern world's pagan rites was taking place, the torching of the automobile, witnessed by the young women from the disco, their sequinned dresses trembling in the flames . . . a premonition of the carnival blaze that would one day consume Estrella de Mar' (158-60).

Estrella de Mar is first seen as 'a place without shadow', secure on its handsome peninsula, the 'private paradise' of 'a happier twentieth century' (65-6). Jack Womack's New York, on the other hand, is a place close to the world of urban noir. *Random Acts*[21] depicts a savage cityscape, the future of an America in which all urban centres are disintegrating into rioting, destitution and gang warfare. As their circumstances decline, the family of Womack's young narrator, Lola, is forced to move to the more marginal and dangerous parts of the city, journeying away from civilised security to live on the margins of West Harlem. Lola endures a Conradian journey not just to the 'worst' that the city contains but to a forced reassessment of her own identity, a reduction to a primitive level of being: 'I can't remember what I used to be like . . . it fears me' (231). She, is, like Marlow, shocked by how rapidly one accommodates oneself to appalling things: 'It was weird though that you could adjust to something so quick' (125). Feeling that all that is left to her is her 'rack and rage' (241), she at last beats to death her father's cruel employer, in what seems to her 'dreamtime': 'There's no denying I was mindlost' (251-2). Her capacity for murder is only one of the horrors discovered by Lola, who in the end commits herself to the world beyond all that is familiar, 'with the DCons' (256), the emblem of everything savage.

Random Acts is science fiction as extrapolation. The element of fantasy consists entirely of an extension of all the worst possibilities of urban American life. The jacket claims 'cyberpunk intensity' for the style, and the novel has in common with cyberpunk a strong sense of counter-cultural aggression. It is, however, far more genuinely noir than most cyberpunk, in part because it does not open up the possible alter-worlds of virtual space and imagined cityscapes, but instead presents the remorseless pressure of events which seem all too real, and which Lola increasingly finds herself unequipped to express: 'There's no wording proper what downed last night. The world brutalises however you live it whatever you do' (221). As everything, including her own language, breaks down, Lola's questions about the future echo the anxiety, fear and overwhelming sense of fatality that have recurrently been at the core of the noir narrative: "'How'll we endtime Iz?" I asked. "What's meant?" "Unknown" Iz said. "Spilling tomorrow into today's suited sometime but not once it darkens. Nada's changeable come nightside . . .'" (233).

Notes

1. Bruce Sterling (ed.), *Mirrorshades: The Cyberpunk Anthology* (London: Harper-Collins, 1986, 1994), p. xii.

2. As, for example, in *Night Has a Thousand Eyes*, published under the name of George Hopley in 1945.

3. On *film noir* as a fusion of fantasy and realism, see J. P. Telotte, 'The Fantastic-Realism of *Film Noir— Kiss Me Deadly*', *Wide Angle,* 14, No. 1 (1992), pp. 4-18: 'Thanks to [a] style that calls attention to itself . . . the film noir can seem a nearly schizophrenic form, powerfully pulled in different directions by both realistic and fantastic impulses' (7).

4. James Naremore, *More Than Night: Film Noir in Its Contexts* (Berkeley: University of California Press, 1998), p. 9.

5. See, for example, Brian Aldiss, *Trillion Year Spree* (London: Paladin, 1973, 1988): Aldiss argues that science fiction, poised between romance and realism, shares with the Gothic novel a reliance on suspense, mystery and 'a limited number of startling props', that it transforms standard Gothic character types (cruel father into scientist; seducing monk into alien) and reworks plot patterns, such as the descent into 'inferno or incarceration', where the protagonist must go to complete his search for secret knowledge. See also Mark Rose, *Alien Encounters: Anatomy of Science Fiction* (Cambridge, Mass.: Harvard University Press, 1981) and Fred Botting, *Gothic* (London: Routledge, New Critical Idiom, 1996).

6. This is, in part, simply a process of creating metaphoric representations of the various aspects of computer technology. A 'ghost self', say, is just a computer-simulated self. But it is also a way of investing cyberspace with a spiritual dimension. As Samuel Delany says, Gibson's cyberspace 'is haunted by creatures just a step away from Godhead'. Samuel Delany, *Mississippi Review.* Nos 2 and 3, p. 33, quoted in Jenny Wolmark, *Aliens and Others: Science Fiction, Feminism and Postmodernism* (Hemel Hempstead, Herts.: Harvester Wheatsheaf, 1993), p. 119.

7. *Neuromancer,* for example, is discussed both by Douglas Rushkoff, *Cyberia: Life in the Trenches of Cyberspace* (London: Flamingo, 1994), pp. 225-31 and Botting, p. 163.

8. David Punter, *The Literature of Terror: A History of Gothic Fictions from 1965 to the Present Day* (London: Longman, 1980), p. 121; Rose, p. 5; Aldiss, pp. 42-56; and Edward James, *Science Fiction in the 20th Century* (Oxford: Oxford University Press, 1994), p. 110.

9. See Wolmark, pp. 111-14.

10. Chris Baldick, 'Introduction' to Chris Baldick (ed.), *The Oxford Book of Gothic Tales* (Oxford: Oxford University Press, 1992, 1993), p. xix.

11. In the significance it attaches to Hawksmoor's churches, Ackroyd's earlier novel draws heavily on Iain Sinclair's *Lud Heat*. Sinclair incorporates De Quincey's detailing of the Ratcliffe Highway murders and takes as his epigraph De Quincey's line, 'All perils, specially malignant, are recurrent', which is also one of Ackroyd's central themes.

12. Mark Seltzer, *Serial Killers: Death and Life in America's Wound Culture* (New York: Routledge, 1998), p. 186.

13. Scott Bukatman, *Blade Runner* (London: British Film Institute, 1997), pp. 19-21; J. P. Telotte, 'The Doubles of Fantasy and the Space of Desire', in Annette Kuhn (ed.), *Alien Zone: Cultural Theory and Contemporary Science Fiction Cinema* (London: Verso, 1990), pp. 154-5.

14. See Rushkoff, pp. 223-32.

15. Rushkoff, pp. 225-9.

16. Michael Hutchinson, quoted by Rushkoff, pp. 287-8.

17. *Observer Life,* 10 September 1995.

18. *Manga Video,* 1995, p. 13; Bob Cotton and Richard Oliver, *The Cyberspace Lexicon* (London: Phaidon, 1994), p. 52.

19. Sterling, *Mirrorshades,* p. xii.

20. Michael Grant, *Myths of the Greeks and Romans* (New York: Mentor, 1962), pp. 248-51. As Paglia says, Dionysus is 'the return of the repressed', appealing to the 'salacious voyeurism' of an audience that looks 'directly into daemonic fantasy, the hellish nightscape of dream and creative imagination'. Camille Paglia, *Sexual Personae: Art and Decadence from Nefertiti to Emily Dickinson* (Harmondsworth, Middx.: Penguin, 1990), pp. 5, 102-3.

21. *Random Acts* is part of Womack's New York quintet, the other novels being *Ambient* (1987), *Heathern* (1990) and *Elvissey* (1993), which take place in twenty-first-century New York; and *Terraplane* (1988), an alternate-world version of thirties New York. *Random Acts* is the final novel of the series and the one closest to our own time.

Bibliography

Ackroyd, Peter, *Hawksmoor* (1985), London: Hamish Hamilton, 1986; *Dan Leno and the Limehouse Golem* (1994), London: Minerva, 1995.

Ballard, J. G., *High-Rise* (1975), London: Panther, 1985; *Running Wild* (London: Flamingo, 1988); *Cocaine Nights* (1996), London: Flamingo, 1997.

Cain, Paul [pseud. George Carrol Sims], *Fast One* (1932), Harpenden, Herts.: No Exit Press, 1989; *Seven Slayers* (1933-36, 1946), Los Angeles: Blood and Guts Press, 1987.

Dick, Philip K., *Do Androids Dream of Electric Sheep?* [*Blade Runner*] (1968), London: Grafton, 1990; *A Scanner Darkly* (1977), London: HarperCollins, 1996.

Gibson, William, *Neuromancer* (1984), London: HarperCollins, 1993; *Count Zero* (1986), London: HarperCollins, 1993; *Mona Lisa Overdrive* (1988), London: HarperCollins, 1994; *Virtual Light* (1993), Harmondsworth, Middx.: Penguin, 1994.

Grimwood, Jon Courtenay, *neoAddix* (London: New English Library, 1997); *Lucifer's Dragon* (London: New English Library, 1998).

Hammett, Dashiell, *The Big Knockover and Other Stories* (1923-29, 1966), Harmondsworth, Middx.: Penguin, 1969; *The Continental Op* (1923-30, 1974), New York: Vintage Crime, 1992; *The Four Great Novels* (London: Picador, 1982): including *Red Harvest* (1929), *The Dain Curse* (1929), *The Maltese Falcon* (1930) and *The Glass Key* (1931); *The Thin Man* (1932), Harmondsworth, Middx.: Penguin, 1974; *Woman in the Dark* (1933), New York: Vintage Crime, 1989.

Hjortsberg, William, *Falling Angel* (1978), Harpenden, Herts.: No Exit Press, 1996.

Jeter, K. W., *Noir* (London: Orion, 1998).

MacDonald, John D., *The Damned* (1952), Manchester: Fawcett (Gold Medal), 1964; *The Neon Jungle* (Greenwich, Conn.: Gold Medal, 1953); *April Evil* (1957), London: Pan, 1960; *Death Trap* (1958), London: Pan, 1964; *Soft Touch* [*Man-Trap*] (1958), London: Pan, 1961; *The Crossroads* (1959), London: Pan, 1965; *The Executioners* [*Cape Fear*] (1959), London: Pan, 1961; *The Deep Blue Good-by* (1964), Greenwich, Conn.: Gold Medal, 1964; *The Girl in the Plain Brown Wrapper* (1968), New York: Fawcett Crest, 1995.

O'Connell, Jack, *The Skin Palace* (1996), London: Pan, 1997; *Word Made Flesh* (1998), Harpenden, Herts.: No Exit Press, 1999.

Rucker, Rudy, *Software* (1982), Harmondsworth, Middx.: Penguin, 1985; *The Hacker and the Ants* (1994), New York: AvoNova, 1995.

Smith, Michael Marshall, *Only Forward* (1994), London: HarperCollins, 1998.

Stephenson, Neal, *Snow Crash* (1992), London: Roc (Penguin), 1993.

Sterling, Bruce, *Schismatrix* (1985), Harmondsworth, Middx.: Penguin, 1986.

Womack, Jack, *Random Acts of Senseless Violence* (1993), New York: Grove Press, 1995.

Christine A. Jackson (essay date 2002)

SOURCE: Jackson, Christine A. "Blood Dues: Rites of Initiation in Career Thrillers." In *Myth and Ritual in Women's Detective Fiction,* pp. 90-113. Jefferson, N.C.: McFarland & Company, 2002.

[*In the following essay, Jackson proposes that career thrillers by women writers tend to focus on the resolution of personal challenges faced by their female characters as much as on the actual action of a crime thriller.*]

The 1990s gave us television's gavel-to-gavel coverage of high-profile trials. This comprehensive media treatment whipped up audience eagerness to view every shadowy courthouse corridor. The phenomenon netted even higher book sales for novelists like John Grisham, Scott Turow, and Steve Martini. If the story included a legal proceeding, it warranted the label of "legal thriller." Works highlighting lawyer protagonists and dramatizing issues of justice still mean very big business for the publishing world.

Many more women are trying the case in this subgenre of detective fiction. Instead of limiting proceedings to the courtroom, women writers show us sleuths testing the edge of justice in classroom and newsroom settings. In many ways, academics and journalists belong to the same category as lawyers. Mysteries featuring these protagonists follow a similar narrative pattern. As one strand of the narrative, the sleuth, who could be an academic or journalist as well as a lawyer, nails the wrong-doer/killer. As another accompanying story strand, this very smart, well-educated main character must go back to school. As she moves from not knowing to knowing about the killer's identity, she also understands more about herself.

To accommodate the various occupations of protagonists, the label "legal thriller" could be changed to "career thriller." The object of the quest is somewhat different depending on the sleuth's job, but the narrative structure for all is the same. The plots of these thrillers rest on rites of initiation. To be allowed entry into these select secrets, the sleuth pays a very high dues—heartache, loss of a loved one, professional failure, or sometimes even a literal wound resulting in spilled blood.

The searcher is a professional in a high-pressure career. In addition to solving the murder or crime, she seeks a Grail of idealistic perfection through her profession.

The ritual action of passing tests and finding herself worthy plays out repeatedly over the narrative. This protagonist, already a well-educated practitioner in a highly specialized occupation, must re-learn her profession from the inside.

To complete a successful run of the initiation gauntlet, the main character confronts a series of difficult, even painful challenges. The professor becomes a student. The journalist writes her own story. The lawyer experiences guilt. To move from innocence to experience, the questing professional measures the distance between the world perceived as ideal and the world as it is.

Career thrillers provide a high degree of realistic backdrop for the crime. Most of the authors have extensive resumes in the same occupation as the sleuth. Carolyn Heilbrun has for many years been a professor at Columbia University. Edna Buchanan and Elaine Viets are professional journalists. Lisa Scottoline held clerkships at state and federal levels and worked as a trial lawyer. Barbara Parker began her professional life as a prosecutor with the state attorney's office in Miami-Dade County, Florida.

The world of the professional mystery is representational, but it is also metaphysical. The quest for transcendence takes the searcher through a tense struggle between and through opposites. Joseph Campbell amplifies the Grail search in *Transformations of Myth Through Time*.

To illustrate this concept of "going beyond," Campbell calls upon medieval Grail legend tradition and Percival or Parzival, one of the Knights of the Round Table. The name "Parzival" is emblematic of the direction that the search for the Ideal takes. Campbell notes that the name is related to the French, "*perce a val,* the one piercing through the middle of the valley, going between the pair of opposites" (TOMT [*Transformations of Myth Through Time*] 247). Despite the searcher's capability and professional expertise, she approaches this configured mystery as a neophyte.

Ritual initiation gives proof to the human experience that education of the spirit continues throughout life. The purpose of painful suffering is that suffering and falling short reveals secrets. It gives the protagonists "the courage to be at one in their wanting and their doing, their knowing and their telling" (Campbell, *Creative Mythology,* 85).

As professionals, these candidates sleuthing toward initiation already belong to an exclusive club. The ones who do not pass have already been burned away. The searcher must survive tests toward wisdom, truth, and justice. "Heroes emerge from their Ordeals to be recognized as special and different, part of a select few who have outwitted death" (Vogler 186). Through the typically reversed logic of myth, the expert becomes a learner.

"Initiation" usually refers to an individual's change from childhood to adulthood. Some psychologists have used the concept to explain physical and psychological development well into adulthood, as in Gail Sheehy's *Passages* (1976) and the more recent *New Passages: Mapping Your Life Across Time* (with Joelle Delbourgo, 1996). In fact, organized initiation appears in numerous facets of American public life. In the political realm, voter primaries serve as concentric rings of initiation, with the Presidency as the highly coveted prize at the center. The currently popular television show *Survivor* illustrates the same process in action. Thousands of potential contestants submit applications for the show. These applicants are winnowed down to people who actually appear on the episodes. Then the show presents viewers with an intensified view of the final tests.

Inevitably, the contestants endure failures. Again, through the reverse logic of myth, one achieves success only through failure and facing limits. The structure of overcoming obstacles and moving ever closer to a prized goal is deeply etched in our collective experience.

As she passes each test, the searcher is incrementally rewarded. New perceptions, the ability to pierce the veil of deception, and clairvoyance comprise this reward package (Vogler 187). The searcher finds clues, locates missing witnesses, or breaks free from being captured. Through this process, the searcher finds the murderer, but she also finds an inside truth. With this realization, the searcher becomes worthy of proceeding in her profession.

What makes professional life so amenable to a mystery novel plot? Every person's life is a journey in its own way. Bureaucracies on the job make modern employment more complex. Campbell mentions that in the past the purpose of mythology was to stamp the individual with the values of the group. Now professional organizations have evolved into "an increasingly officious array of ostensibly permissive, but actually coercive, demythologized secular institutions" (CM [*Creative Mythology*] 86). Educational preparation for these professions encourages individuality but may fail to alert students to more restrictive conditions on the job.

Fiction about unsolved death fits these professions in particular for several reasons. Academe, journalism, and law sit atop a solid tradition of possibly ambiguous linguistic constructions. They are also professions in flux. Academe is changing in terms of more claims on the time of students, concepts of students as education consumers, and online delivery systems. Today's newsrooms deal with high production costs, changes in readership, internet competition of news coverage, and publishing monopolies. The law likewise is changing in terms of publicity and an ever-shifting balance of power between defender and defended.

Start with an intractable tradition, add the impulse toward sweeping change, mix with a dose of interpretation, and stand back. The outcome is bound to be an uncontrollable situation for which mystery fiction poses an appealing forum for resolution.

Through a series of harrowing tests the protagonist relearns the profession. The process, ultimately, is what is important. The detective sleuth stretches the bounds of experience by rediscovering what caused her to become a professor, journalist, or lawyer in the first place. The experience leads the sleuth to recommit to the profession and reaffirm ideals.

Dorothy Sayers's *Gaudy Night* (1935), in which Harriet Vane uncovers skullduggery at Oxford, is among the earliest novels in this genre. Since then, there has been open admission on academic mysteries. Even a partial list of authors with academics or retired academics as sleuths forms a lengthy roster.

The academic world is a prime setting for crime. College life proceeds in a closed, regulated community, but conflicts and human frailties abound. The professor, teacher, or student sleuth possesses the highly refined skills of observation and cognition to draw conclusions others miss.

Our highly alert sleuth looks for the murderer in residence halls, classroom buildings, graduate seminars, and along campus walkways. In some ways, academe is on a different calendar from the rest of the world. The entire university community subscribes to the same schedule. Professors have office hours and regular class times. Students live mostly in a communal setting, with set schedules. The clock on the ivy-covered hall helps investigators keeps close tabs on alibis.

A university sets an environment ripe for murder. By definition, it is a place where people from different social and educational levels clash. Academics often have meetings with students or peers in high-pressure situations. These meetings provide an opportunity for embarrassment, humiliation, and worse. Frequently, the person killed is a horrible professor, student, or administrator exerting power inappropriately. We don't shed tears for the victim and may even sympathize with the murderer. With tenure and fatly endowed research positions in short supply, academe is a hotbed of greed, politics, and ambition. Where ambition builds, motives

for murder soon follow. Despite the passion of the crime, the murder often occurs in a context of the system ridding itself of evil.

A university can perpetuate the disparity between a searcher's outer world and inner reality. Campbell pinpoints a few reasons for the toppling of the ivory tower.

> There is no time, no place, no permission—let alone encouragement—for experience. And to make things even worse, along now come those possessed socio-political maniacs with their campus rallies, picket-line slogans, journalistic ballyhoo, and summonses to action in the name of causes of which their callow flocks had scarcely heard six months before—and even those marginal hours that might have been left from study for inward growth are invaded, wrecked, and strewn with daily rubbish.
>
> [CM 374]

A university must blend polarized goals. It has traditions to uphold while at the same time fostering independent inquiry. The result can be a split between experience and inner truth.

Academic mysteries highlight the sleuth's method of investigation. Critics have drawn lengthy comparisons between the research skills of an academic and the skills of the murder investigator. "Research skills make good sleuths" (Leonardi 113). The process of locating and combining evidence to formulate theories parallels more general paths toward knowledge. Israeli author Batya Gur teaches literature in Jerusalem. The homicide investigator for most of her mysteries is Michael Ohayon. Ohayon has an historian's background.

In Gur's *Saturday Morning Murder* (1988), Dr. Eva Neidorf, renowned psychologist, professor, and lecturer has been found shot in the head at an office in Jerusalem's Psychoanalytic Institute. Ohayon lays out his method for interviewing a witness. He needs to "get onto the wavelength of the person sitting opposite him and pick up on those ostensibly trivial things, the things people said between the lines and sometimes never said at all, that in the last analysis provided the master key to solving the mystery" (Gur 51). Ohayon gains his best clues from silences in between words.

Ohayon also uses his keen interest in history to reconstruct the crime and determine motive.

> And there was also what he privately referred to as "my historical need." In other words, the historian's need to obtain a full picture, to see everything concerning human beings as part of an overall process, like a historical process processing laws of its own, which—he never tired of explaining—if only we are able to grasp their meaning, provide us with the tools for going right to the heart of the problem.
>
> [Gur 51]

Here Gur presents the mystery as a larger objective reality that lies ahead of Ohayon. Being an astute detective and researcher, he digs out the information necessary to reach the correct conclusion. The words themselves are only tools, signs pointing beyond themselves to a meaning out there.

Like Gur, author Carolyn Heilbrun (*aka* Amanda Cross) is herself an academic. Cross's sleuth is literature professor Kate Fansler. Kate is a crusader, but inevitably, Cross arranges the quest so that the development of Kate's personal life parallels the mystery's solution. Because Cross so often places the reader in Kate's head, the most deeply scored line of the narrative involves Professor Fansler's own education.

For *Death in a Tenured Position* (1982), Cross structures the narrative so Kate's investigation into her colleague's suicide mirrors the sleuth's own indecision over whether she should become more involved with Reed. To marry would give away her ideals. For her, the marriage could be her own death in a "tenured position." The permanence of tenure is similar to being a wife. She runs the risk of losing herself. Why should she marry Reed? She is already married to Reading.

In *The Puzzled Heart* (1998), Cross sets up a similar "dual track" narrative. The case challenges Kate on a personal level. Reed is now Kate's husband, and he has been kidnapped. Kate receives an unusual ransom note. The note asks for no money, but it is blackmail, nonetheless. To obey it, Kate must undergo a drastic personality change: "publicly recant your insane feminist position" (12). This request upsets Kate almost as much as if Reed were threatened with bodily harm. As she sees it, the worst that could happen to Reed is that the kidnappers will "try to brainwash him and make him see the point of view of his captors" (26). This is basically the same threat the kidnappers hold against Kate. What she fears most for herself is that she could be forced to consider another point of view as valid. This order tests Kate's principles as an educator, her strength of mind, concepts of learning and being fair, and achieving Wisdom.

The first note about Reed's kidnapping knocks Kate sideways, and she needs strong tea to bring her out of the shock. She takes the second note more in stride. The note reads, "Neither the police nor any government agency must be contacted" (14). Here she remembers who she is and summons her superior knowledge of language to counter the unseen villains. "'I hate people who use *contact* as a verb,' Kate said" (15).

Despite her considerable sleuthing experience, Kate is too emotionally involved with this case to work it by herself. To pass the first hurdle, she calls in professional help, her friend and retired law professor Harriet.

The professional quester is essentially alone in undergoing rites of initiation. Still, kind souls along the way serve as guides. In *The Hero with a Thousand Faces*, Campbell describes the "wise guide," a mentor "whose words assist the hero through the trials and terrors to the weird adventure. He is the one who appears and points to the magic shining sword that will kill the dragon-terror" (8-9).

Although still new at this detective biz, Harriet is Kate's wise guide. Her age is a plus in the detective agency, because she is so unlikely a P. I. Like the wise old man, Harriet is enlisted to "conduct people across those difficult thresholds of transformation that demand a change in the patterns not only of conscious but also of unconscious life" (HTF [*The Hero with a Thousand Faces*] 9). She attempts to ease Kate's mind by telling a humorous anecdote about the first time she used a gun.

Kate's next obstacle is meeting with Harriet's partner at the detective agency to formulate a plan. This encounter lends Kate's interaction with the agency a more official status. Thanks to Harriet, Kate's meeting with Toni happens in a setting completely familiar to Kate, her office. Toni comes in undercover as one of the students. Having student conferences is a usual part of Kate's job. Only this time, the student conference ritual is turned on its head, because a student educates Kate, not the other way around.

Kate is more used to giving tests than taking them, but she has more to pass. Her third test involves the dog that Harriet and Toni have arranged to give Kate a cover story for contacting a suspect, owner of a kennel. The idea throws her for a loop. "She realized that for the first time she felt her life to be completely out of her control. That she might have a dog foisted on her seemed as likely as anything else that had been happening" (32-33).

The dog is a Saint Bernard puppy, well suited to her role as a rescuer. The dog is named "Banny," after Anne Bancroft. The sudden changes in Kate's life render her nearly speechless. Named after an Award-winning actress, the puppy exudes more articulate expression than Kate.

The professor is so tied to her schedule, she cannot imagine getting out to interview people outside the university. Banny's rescue of Kate comes just in time. The dog uses Kate's hall as a bathroom and refuses to stay in the car's backseat. Banny represents the uncontrolled, natural world, a world not defined by books or reading.

Kate is amazed by the next move Harriet and Tony suggest. To move closer to the suspect, Kate has to enroll in a dog training class. She is aghast by the way the desks are turned. Not only does the class expose the professor's ignorance, but Dorothy the kennel owner finds Kate's academic curiosity wanting. Dorothy says, "'You have not asked a single question, intelligent or not.' 'I'm an observer,' Kate said, rather defensively" (42).

Dorothy, the key to Reed's kidnappers, sees through Kate right away. Placed in this role as a student, Kate questions her own skills as a researcher and amateur detective. Her very identity as an assertive professional is at stake. "She had never felt so powerless and devoid of personality in her life" (44). However, little by little, she is drawn by the woman's knowledge and becomes capable of new insights. "I am certainly learning something about the dog world I wouldn't have dreamed of knowing a few days ago, Kate thought" (47). She even comes to admire Dorothy. If she were paying attention to her detective's instincts, she would certainly know better. However, a reverence for knowledge wins out. "Kate thought how nice it must be to know absolutely everything there was to know about one subject, even dogs" (48).

This segment in the dog training class tests Kate's willingness to be a student and revives her spirit of theorizing. She wakes up about her own passivity as she's waiting in line to pay the toll to cross the Henry Hudson Bridge (53).

> "I know you said not to call," Kate explained to an outraged Harriet, "but that is an order I've decided not to obey. You are working for me, you and Toni, and I want to see you tonight. Here, I don't care if someone is watching me, or if they see you visiting, or if they wonder whether you're visiting as friends or detectives. We've got to talk."
>
> [54-55]

Thus, she lays out her theory of who could have kidnapped Reed and why.

Before long, Kate and Banny rescue Reed, and he walks away from his kidnappers suffering few ill effects. His first words upon seeing Banny are "And where's the brandy?" (71). But Kate has yet to identify the reason for the kidnapping.

Who could have the most vengeful feelings for her? She finds the answer in her family's past and in her professional life. Kate's efforts to forestall yet another marriage ceremony turns out to be the motive of hatred against her. Kate arrives at a conclusion about herself.

> Her life had held, it seemed to her, fewer turmoils than most. What had threatened her, if indeed she had ever felt truly threatened, had been not violent emotions, but from time to time a sense of the purposelessness of existence, of the lack of reason for much that occurred. It was a sin of the spirit, she knew: a failure of faith in the rightness of the universe—of God, in short.
>
> [175]

Another failed exam involves a "student" who turns on Kate. "They lie in wait sometimes . . ." (204). The student figure emerges first as a savior, then as a double agent. It is the worst humiliation for Kate as an educator. She cannot see the student's attempts for what they were, manipulation and a false education. Kate takes her failing grade to heart, imagining all kinds of hellish punishments.

> "I am simply going to die or to become a fugitive like Lord Jim, lurking about in hot climates. I hate hot climates. Oh, God!" It was a cry worthy of someone without faith actually calling upon an exalted deity.
>
> [251]

The phrase "Puzzled Heart" comes from a poem by Emily Dickinson, which Cross uses as an opening epigram for the book: "to contemplate the journey with an unpuzzled heart." By the novel's end, Kate has clearly fallen short of this view of the journey. Her heart remains frustrated and troubled by life. But it appears that Cross looks askance at the unpuzzled heart. The most evil woman at the center of this mystery proceeds without puzzlement or question. This figure of evil has the certainty of a zealot, living in an ambiguous world with an unambiguous agenda. Cross gives Harriet the last word about what the puzzled hearts of the world can do in the face of such certainty: "We mustn't give up" (257).

Like the academic, the journalist detective absorbs clues and attempts to forge new meaning. Instead of reaching the Holy Grail of Wisdom, the journalist wields the Word. The journalist dwells in a landscape where words and meanings are separated. People are the story. Through an accurate re-creation of these stories, the journalist enacts change for good and unifies inner and outer worlds. She has spoken the Word Beyond Words.

"Word" as a word carries several potent meanings. The original Old English "wyrd" is connected to fate, which is Shakespeare's meaning for the "three weird sisters" in *Macbeth*. It also is a form of the verb "to be," and related to "worth," as in the Old English "weorth" (Moore and Knott). Speaking the Word Beyond Words is a very powerful secret, connected with destiny and worthiness. It has value beyond measure.

> And so, proceeding, we come to the problem of communication: the opening, that is to say, of one's own truth and depth to the depth and truth of another in such as way as to establish an authentic community of existence.
>
> [Campbell, CM 84]

Edna Buchanan's journalist sleuth Britt Montero learns the worth of this elusive word. As police reporter for the *Miami Times,* Britt walks the sun-steamed sidewalks of Miami. She has many opportunities for reporting that makes a difference. In *Contents Under Pressure* (1992), Britt has an in-box crammed with stories: a hostage crisis defused outside an elementary school and a former pro football player dead of a car accident due to a police chase. After Miami boils over from simmering tensions, Britt has the chance to write the story of her career, but she learns a more valuable lesson.

The elementary school story ends happily. Britt sounds more than a bit cynical as she writes it up: "A hero, a satisfying ending, readers happy at getting their money's worth from a dedicated public servant, cops happy at getting good press. . . . What more could a reporter ask for?" (10).

In the past, Britt has expected more from herself as a professional. A luncheon with her mother brings out the old idealism. Fed up with her mother's constant carping, Britt re-articulates what drives her as a journalist. "'Mom, you know how I feel about my job.' My stomach was beginning to churn. 'The world is full of poverty, ignorance, crime, and corruption. I do what I do because I think I can help change things'" (49).

The usual stories that run across the police blotter will not help change things, but Britt re-traces the cop chase of the pro football player. She uncovers a story of double-dealing and abuse of power. This story could indeed make a difference. Britt passes the first series of tests. She is willing to risk everything to write these words. She is threatened, stalked, and wounded, but she refuses to back down. She watches a good friend die in her arms. When tropical paradise explodes into a confusing nightmare, Britt nearly loses her own life. Still she navigates through broken glass and Molotov cocktails to live the complete story. She is not the only one proud of the effort.

> As we pieced together the stories of destruction, terror, and confusion, the managing editor emerged from his carpeted office in shirtsleeves, smiled at me, nodded and said, "Good work, Britt."
>
> I sat there numb as he walked away but his words stayed with me. Exhaustion, deadlines, and breaking stories suppressed my conflicting emotions and guilt for a time.
>
> [282]

Unfortunately, these words from her editor are the only reward she has. Due to the editors' decision to spare the city more violence, the story Britt writes about evil in the top ranks of the police department fails to make it into print.

> As soon as the riot coverage ended and the city was under control, I began putting together my story about the truth, what really happened. I worked hard on it, for two days. It explained everything. It was never published.
>
> [284]

Britt knows that her story can never exist on its own. It has to fit into the context of everything else that happened in the city. "The best things cannot be told" (Campbell, CM 84). The most Britt can achieve is to understand the secret about truth—that she can never tell it. She has reached the Word Beyond Words.

Elaine Viets's mystery series headlines journalist Francesca Vierling. Set in St. Louis, the series features Francesca's story-writing as an instrument of social justice and her wise-cracking wit as editorial cartoons that keep the creeps at bay. Francesca's rites of initiation also end with her entrance to an important secret territory. She comprehends the limits of the word in reporting the depths of human experience.

In *Doc in the Box* (2000), Francesca has to pass many tests. She is without love, having broken up with her long-term squeeze Lyle. She learns that her dear friend and professional mentor Georgia has breast cancer. These two trials end in the worst conviction of all for a reporter. She is having a hard time writing.

Francesca can handle her balding managing editor, Charlie of the bad comb-over and petty power plays. He assigns her to write a human interest story about a stripper's life. Francesca opts for a male stripper, Leo D. Nardo, a major drawstring at the Heart's Desire club.

Not so easy is knowing her own heart's desire. Deep down, Francesca suffers without Lyle. Even Leo D. Nardo's well-oiled, sculpted body pales by comparison. "The only book Leo had opened since he flunked out of school was the Yellow Pages. I liked my men smart. Like Lyle" (9).

Both love and writing leave Francesca's world. Her descent into the realm of male strippers essentially strips her. The next day at the newsroom brings a crisis of self-confidence:

> Something was wrong with my column, the one in today's paper. I knew it. I just didn't know what it was. Had I misspelled a name? Misquoted someone? Gotten some obvious fact wrong? Did someone call the paper and complain?
>
> [17]

Something is indeed wrong with her column. Charlie has replaced it.

Francesca has difficulty recapturing her usual breeziness. Her promise to be a "model columnist" doesn't last long. When she sits down to pound out the article on Leo, she realizes that she forgot to ask him two key questions (32). There among the hard bodies, her interview skills dissolved. She cannot finish the story, because Leo, like her column, has also vanished.

At this point, Francesca can barely manage the rough draft of a recipe. Charlie presses her to contribute to a St. Louis recipe collection. The non-cooking journalist contemplates giving him "Francesca's Top Five Food Delivery Numbers" (43).

Francesca passes a crucial test, however, when she makes a correct choice. She knows that her loss of writing ability takes a back seat to serious illness. Francesca helps transport Georgia to the hospital for treatment. Cancer and chemo are bad enough. Slick hospital floors and greasy cafeteria food add insult to injury. First Francesca summons all her word power to buoy up Georgia. She jokes that God is God "because he couldn't get into medical school" (29). Then she stops a huffy receptionist with her own patented South Side glare. Francesca chants, "I am a witch, and I curse you and your curse is that you will be treated the same way you treat these cancer patients" (31).

While the two wait in Radiation Oncology, an intruder shoots a receptionist and a doctor in an adjacent office. It's as if Francesca's word power has summoned strength and taken action of its own accord. Then the journalist learns that Doc in the Box, an office building crammed with physicians, is also on the killer's list. More doctors die. One kindly doctor victim is Dr. Jolley. The murdered doctors represent revenge for all the patients they rob of love, joy, and humor. The murders, then, are not random aberrations, but logical necessities. The narrative follows the reverse logic of rites of passage. The doctors, ordinarily healers and life-givers, must die to bring the dead to life.

The pressure is on Francesca to prevent more murders, but is she really trying? Given the pain Georgia has endured at the hands of the medical community, Francesca takes more than a little perverse satisfaction in the killing spree. She shocks her fellow journalist Tina by admitting aloud that "I've always wanted to give the killer a list of people who should be shot" (113). The murderer is only doing a public service, which is a refracted image of the journalist. Francesca's friend Valerie the chemo nurse has a theory reinforcing this tie. She tells Francesca, "For all I know, you're doing it. You could be using Georgia as a cover to get in these doctors' offices" (120). Could it be?

Like the murderer, Francesca seeks revenge as a way to regain love and creativity. She still whips out her trademark snappy comebacks. She deflects one slimy creep with "If I spent six months in a lighthouse, I wouldn't call you" (86). She admires the widow of one murdered doctor: "She was as tough as a two-dollar sirloin" (106). But part of the difficulty of initiation is following its reverse logic. Francesca thinks that by writing an award-winning story, she can regain her stride. "I wanted that prize. I wanted it like a lover. In

place of the lover I'd lost" (114). She does not yet fathom the secret that only failure is winning.

Francesca can still speak truth, but she can't write it. Searching through words should be a journalist's forte. In hunting the doctor killer, Francesca must pore over medical files. In better days, she could have invented some way to track these clues herself. We understand the depth of Francesca's impotence when her friend, pathologist "Cut up Katie," becomes a surrogate search engine (154).

Francesca's personal and professional sorrows continue to mute her responses to the world. She has no personal life (139). She senses her distance from the world of light and love (140). She has a hard time writing even the simplest 50th wedding anniversary story.

The couple had courted, half a century ago, at a famous St. Louis landmark, the Whispering Arch. The semicircle holds the secret that whatever is whispered at one end can be heard very far away at the other. With Francesca looking on, the couple exchanges loving words through the Arch.

When Francesca interviews the "bride," she admires the woman's courage and finds herself lacking. "'If you don't take chances, you don't live,' she said. Her words were like an ice pick in my heart" (149). Francesca goes through the same ritual of listening at the Whispering Arch. Instead of words of love, she hears something else. "Die, bitch, die!" (150).

By the reverse logic of initiation rites, Francesca will find life only by searching the land of the dead. Down is up, and vice versa. In a final test, Francesca chases the murderer up the Down ramp of a parking garage.

> Our pursuit took on a dreamlike quality, one of those dreams where you run and run and nothing happens. I saw a constantly shifting collage of car fenders and hoods and brake lights, heard my own hard breathing and the drivers' furious honking. Then suddenly, we were in blinding sunlight on the open upper deck.
>
> [220]

Only by falling through the looking glass can Francesca land before the door to the Word Beyond Words. She hears the killer's story "in the long silence" (237) that she can never completely write. Only after suffering comes the promise of love and life. The Heart's Desire club, Leo's employer, sits at the end of a road to a St. Louis chemical plant. She wades through the toxic puddles to reach it.

Both Britt and Francesca complete their initiation rites toward the Word Beyond Words. Telling the story the best way, interviewing the witness closest to the scene are techniques each reporter hopes will have an impact on the world. But each journalist must earn her stripes by discovering the Holy Grail in a truth that can't be written.

To say and understand The Word Beyond Words is to discern the difference between life and death. As Joseph Campbell points out, the concept as articulated by religions and mythologies around the world and through the ages is contained in the syllable *AUM*. This utterance is sometimes written as the *Om* of chanting rituals or the *Amen* of prayers and hymns. *AUM* has been called the quintessential sacred word, because it contains the building blocks of all words. To say it is to vocalize all sounds, from the open sound in the back of the throat to the *mmm* sound ending with the lips coming together. All vowels are contained in *AUM* (Campbell *Power of Myth* 230-31).

In addition, *AUM* stands for one other concept. Campbell says, "*AUM* is called the 'four-element syllable.' A-U-M—and what is the fourth element? The silence out of which *AUM* arises, and back into which it goes, and which underlies it" (PM [*Power of Myth*] 231). All the words a person says over a lifetime can be summed up in AUM, but its silence represents the eternal. So *AUM* combines the mortal, all sounds, with the immortal, silence. Being able to understand this Word Beyond Words is to distinguish between the "mortal aspect and the immortal aspect of one's own existence" (PM 231).

How does *AUM* fit into the sleuthing professional's quest for the Ideal? The sleuth sees, feels, and is shaken by the recognition of what lasts and what doesn't, what is mortal and what is immortal. Britt Montero comes to find value in the story that is not written. Francesca listens to the silence of her love for Lyle.

> It's been said that poetry consists of letting the word be heard beyond words. . . . But when you really realize the sound, "AUM" the sound of the mystery of the word everywhere, then you don't have to go out and die for anything because it's right there all around.
>
> [Campbell, PM 230]

The final sentence of *Doc in the Box* shows that Francesca understands *AUM*. She declares her love for Lyle. "The words that had been so hard to say slipped out so easily now." Then she, the perpetual word-generating machine, is finally silent. "For once, I listened to my editor" (Viets 243).

Law is another intense profession that lends itself to mystery. Legal thrillers generally feature a trial. A classic work such as *To Kill a Mockingbird* sets the premise. Atticus Finch is a moral wise attorney. He fights for forces of good, defending the underdog and attempting to bring justice to a corrupt land. As we know, the ef-

forts of Atticus are less than successful. "But the fact that Atticus cannot single-handedly defeat racism in no way detracts from his hero status" (Denvir 150). Atticus is Good, through and through.

Today's legal thriller has evolved into a new phase. The lawyer sleuth also seeks to close the gap between what may be legal and what is right. Unlike Atticus Finch, the protagonist may be forced to stand outside the "prosecution versus defense" structure of the courtroom drama to question the very premises that make that structure possible. At the same time, the sleuth questions himself and his ideals. This model adds the very human need for retribution and revenge onto the scales of Lady Justice. From this perspective, the world is a complicated place. It poses a series of tests to shape the character's belief in Ethos, a fairness and morality beyond technical justice.

In an article examining the success of legal thrillers, John Grisham summarizes the basis for plots in his books: "You throw an innocent person in there, get 'em caught up in a conspiracy, and you get 'em out" (1992). While Grisham's formula captures the idea of the character moving from one dilemma to the next, it fails to address how these changes affect the character. How does the lawyer progress from initial innocence to experience?

Grisham's *The Firm* (1991) sets a model for this narrative type. The title contrasts the decidedly "unfirm," even immoral, law partnership with "the firm" ideals of the young attorney who will test them and himself.

The idealistic hero fresh out of law school rockets to the top of his profession. For a brief time, he feels that he has it made, only to discover to his horror that the very organization he had idealized is itself corrupt. The young professional works his way through hidden motives of his colleagues, double-dealings, and his own temptations toward that same corruption. Often he finds that the corruption comes very close to home. For instance, in *The Firm,* Mitch's wife had been his mainstay, the one person he could trust. However, she too yields to temptation, being seduced by one of Mitch's senior colleagues. After a series of setbacks, the protagonist begins to fight back. He uses the same chicanery or semi-legal maneuvers to turn the tables on the evildoers. He pushes to a point where his need for retribution places him on the same moral level as the corrupt members of The Firm. Should he sink to their level?

In the end, he fights for a just resolution. This generally occurs in a different arena, a different version of the institution he had originally imagined. Even as Mitch learns that The Firm is anything but, the value of the overall prize has been ratcheted up several degrees.

This justice is better because it has been hard-won. He takes steps to unify outer reality with his renewed inner awareness of what justice, or Ethos, really means. The way to this insight is not easy.

Greek mythology presents several stories of humanity discovering the difficulty in deciding between what is right and what is just. The tale of Orestes dramatizes the cycle of retribution and the human cost of yielding to it.

Agamemnon and his wife Clytemnestra have three children, two daughters and a son. To win favorable winds from the gods so he can sail to Troy, Agamemnon sacrifices one of his daughters, Iphigenia. "A father's hands / Stained with dark streams flowing / From blood of a girl / Slaughtered before the altar" (Hamilton 182). Agamemnon returns home ten years later, triumphant from war, but a spirit of vengeance is in the air: "every sin causes fresh sin; every wrong brings another in its train" (Hamilton 241).

That night, the warriors hear their leader cry out. His wife Clytemnestra comes out into the square streaked with blood. She is strangely calm. Hamilton says of her demeanor, "She saw no reason to explain the act or excuse it. She was not a murderer in her own eyes, she was an executioner. She had punished a murderer, the murderer of his own child" (243).

Young blood comes onto the scene. Orestes, son of Agamemnon, brother of the slain girl, has a dilemma. He hears Apollo's order that he must act "to appease the angry dead." In addition, his surviving sister, Electra, has a request: "Electra frequently reminded her brother by messengers of the duty of avenging his father's death . . ." (Bulfinch 186).

Orestes is torn. If he lets his mother live, his father's murderer goes free. "But yet—but yet / The deed is to be done and I must do it" (Hamilton 245). Orestes kills his mother. "Atone for death by death. / Shed blood for old blood shed (244).

He emerges from the murder seeing hallucinations of women whose eyes drip blood. They are dressed in black, with hair like snakes. These are the Furies, spirits of Vengeance sent by his murdered mother. He wanders the world but the Furies never leave him. "I have been taught by misery," he says. After many years "the black stain of his guilt had grown fainter and fainter through his years of lonely wandering and pain" (246).

Orestes asks for a trial, at which he takes sole responsibility for the murder. Athena releases Orestes from his suffering. She persuades the avenging goddesses also to accept it. "From the Furies of frightful aspect they became the Benignant Ones, the Eumenides, protectors of the suppliant. They acquitted Orestes. And with the words of acquittal the spirit of evil which had haunted his house for so long was banished." (248)

Orestes pays a high price for his law degree, his knowledge of justice. Through long suffering, he achieves the strength to accept responsibility. This step of transcendence has a valuable reward in ending a cycle of retribution. Lisa Scottoline and Barbara Parker write about women lawyers searching to solve both professional and personal dilemmas. The legal tangle is resolved on one level. The evildoer is captured or identified and either killed or punished through the system. Yet on the character's personal level, Oresteian suffering over paying the blood dues of initiation comes into play.

Scottoline's protagonists work in an all-female law firm, Rosato and Associates. Parker's sleuth Gail Connor is in corporate law. The characters are drawn into a cycle of murder and retribution, an eye for an eye. They move through increasingly intensified initiation rites from innocence to understanding. They must then renounce sharing the motives of hatred that drive a murderer to seek retribution. Frequently, the narrative arc draws up short before the characters' complete redemption. Ostensibly this occurs so the series may continue with these characters. But at the end of each novel, the lawyer protagonist perceives the duality of weak against strong, unfairness against fairness, to enter the sphere of merciful law and forgiveness celebrated by the myth of Orestes.

Scottoline's *Rough Justice* (1997) features defense attorney Marta Richter. Marta is wealthy, high-profile and knows her way around a courtroom. As the novel begins, she is bringing a murder trial to what she had thought to be a successful close. She worked to free her client Elliot Steere. She had even bragged to the press: "*I just win boys. I leave the details to you*" (6). Now with the jury in deliberations, Marta's client drops the mask of Mister Nice Guy. Marta realizes that her client is indeed guilty of murdering a homeless man. To forestall Marta taking action, Steere sends a hit man to take out Marta. In turn, Marta becomes a hit woman and must unearth, literally, evidence that will send her client to prison.

Marta wants to report Steere to authorities, not from any altruistic motives, but out of hatred for him. Steere had manipulated her with an unstated promise of seduction. Marta goes after him as a woman scorned.

> In the split second she realized it, Marta's fury became unreasoning. She could have sworn he wanted her. He'd given every signal. He'd lean too close at counsel table, look too long at her legs. Once he'd touched her knee . . . and her response had been so immediate it

surprised even her. The memory made her feel crazy, unhinged. Unleashed. "I'm going to Judge Rudolph with this," she said.

[6]

At this point, Steere's role in the murder bothers her less than the fact that Steere had played her for a sap.

Later, Marta has the opportunity to wield the same technique. She capitalizes on sexual vibes from a member of the jury. During the blizzard delaying the jury's verdict, she sweet-talks her way into the man's hotel room. She needs Christopher's help in proving Steere guilty before the snow lets up. Christopher makes an open plea to her. Does she have feelings for him? Will she also use sex to manipulate, falling to the same level as Steere?

> Every instinct told her to lead him on, lie to him, even take him to bed if it got her what she wanted. Marta couldn't imagine telling the truth with the stakes this high. Then she looked at Christopher's rugged, open face and couldn't imagine not. He was a decent, kind man, and she was asking him to do something that could get him thrown in prison. He deserved a straight answer. "No. Not at all," she answered.

[201]

Marta later becomes a killer, essentially guilty of the same crime as Steere. The murder is a ritual acted out in the hot-blood of self defense. Still, from that act, she comes to understand guilt from the inside and knows that despite being tested, her value system has emerged intact.

Scottoline's *Moment of Truth* (2000) directly addresses the death of Honor, both literally and as a symbol. Main character defense attorney Mary DiNunzio searches for Ethos, the meaning of truth. Like Marta, Mary works in the all-female law practice of Rosato and Associates. Mary's search is cast in terms of an initiation. The values of the justice system are overturned, and Mary's task is to right them again.

Jack Newlin is head attorney for estates and trusts at Tribe & Wright, a high-profile Philadelphia law firm. He confesses to the murder of his wife, Honor. The problem is that Jack's confession is a lie. Jack's motive in getting himself arrested for murder is to shield his daughter, Paige, who he believes actually did have a hand in the murder.

As an attorney, Jack knows what the police will ask, so he arranges his story to fit the facts. Prosecutor Dwight Davis plans to ask for the death penalty.

> Davis scowled. A lawyer, killing for money. It brought shame on all of them. Davis had always been proud of his profession and hated Newlin for his crime. On his own behalf, and on behalf of the people for the Com-

monwealth. There was only justice to protect all of us. It sounded corny, but anything worth believing in ultimately sounded corny. Davis believed in justice; Newlin believed in money.

[91-92]

Davis makes the words sound good to himself. The dreadful fact is that the prosecutor knows Newlin is lying, and he does not care. He is really the one who believes in money. He sees this case as a way to advance his own reputation. Again, Scottoline reveals the hollowness at the core of people in the justice system.

The initiation narrative kickstarts with Jack's choice of an attorney, Mary DiNunzio. As a contrast to Jack and Marta, Mary is decidedly low-profile. "I don't have much experience with homicide cases, not as much as Bennie Rosato or lots of other lawyers in town" (29). Basically, this is why Jack has chosen her. He expects her to fail.

Mary is an alumna of Catholic parochial school. Her beliefs are formed but untested. She thinks of herself as a lapsed Catholic. Although convinced of her own venial sins that disappointed the nuns, she is basically innocent. She has a prim way of seeing the world, a way some would call "old-fashioned." Basically, Mary believes in her job and has faith that the cards of truth and justice will fall the right way. Her faith is soon put on trial.

Mary has an insight about Jack's fatherly sacrifice, because Mary's own father, Mariano, says he also would take a murder rap for his daughter. Mary is impressed with Jack's sense of duty. He will follow the correct path. After all, Jack is a member of Tribe & Wright. The name of the law firm carries connotations that Jack will do what's "right" according to the "tribe," or morality derived from the group. Still, Mary's values will be challenged. After interviewing her client, she tells Jack not to worry, "without understanding why" (34). She carries around only a shell of morality.

Mary clings to her world because it is seemingly fixed and impermeable. When she visits her home, she revels in its permanence. "The DiNunzios still used a percolator to make coffee, its bottom dent the only signs of wear in thirty-odd years. Progress was something that came to other households. Thank God" (81). But change is coming. Mariano suffers constant back pain. He puts on a brave front, but he brings deception into Mary's life and worse, a foreshadowing of death. Through a series of tests, she must move herself to a deeper understanding of the ambiguous choices necessary to reach Ethos.

Mary faces her first tough challenge when she informs Paige, Jack's daughter, that Honor is dead, and Jack has confessed to the killing. Mary questions her own career choice. "She needed a job with less emotional involvement. Emergency room doctor perhaps. Or child cancer specialist" (45).

As Mary toughens, she finds ways to combine her training from the nuns with her newly acquired skepticism. She suspects that Jack is shielding Paige because something about the girl is wrong. Jack's daughter is so offhand, nervous, and impolite. Her fellow lawyer, the more worldly Judy, tries to set her straight. "Bad manners aren't against the law" (132). However, as Mary proceeds with the case, she finds more evidence for her theory. Her eyes open to a world that fails to conform to her original ideas of truth and justice.

Professor Kate Fansler has Harriet the law professor as a wise guide. Mary's mentor on this quest is Lou, a retired investigator sometimes hired by Rosato and Associates. While Scottoline presents him as a comic figure at times, he sums up some useful thoughts about moral lapses:

> Lou didn't get up from his chair, even though it was his chance to slip out of the place. He felt tired suddenly. He didn't know when kids had changed, but they had, in his lifetime. They got to be empty inside; they didn't care about anything . . . they collected guns and shot each other . . . it had happened to Paige Newlin, too. There was something missing at her heart, and Lou worried that there was nothing in the world that could set it right.
>
> [184]

At one point, Lou's world-weary ways help Mary overcome her squeamishness. Mary and Lou have been following Paige, Jack's daughter. They locate the sixteen-year-old and her boyfriend at a motel. Mary has a strong reaction.

> Her mouth dropped open. She didn't know she was such a prude. Well, she kind of did. "They tried to get a room together?"
>
> "No, separate," Lou snorted. "Of course, together."
>
> "That's disgusting. They're way too young for that."
>
> "Not possible. Anyway, the hotel was booked and they didn't have a reservation. The room is beside the point, anyway."
>
> "It is? Why?"
>
> "Because they're having sex in the cloakroom."
>
> [158]

Mary eventually overcomes her disdain for Paige. They are both, after all, daughters of honorable men, and Mary is finding Jack more honorable by the minute. Her personal attachment to him is another assault against her professional ethics. Mary's next challenge involves saving Paige from a masked gunman. The faceless threat sends the two women on a long chase down

an alley. "She ran straight for the door with Paige, threw open the screen, and darted inside, fumbling for the main door and slamming it closed behind them" (283).

By saving Paige the daughter, Mary adds another dimension to herself as a worthy daughter, as a woman with love to give, and as a lawyer. Mary's willingness to place everything on the line for Paige wins her passage to the next level.

The final challenge remains. To prepare for battle, Mary visits the shadows of her church and finds light and tears of renewal. She thinks of the permanence of prayer. She is nearly to the Word Beyond Words, her own Moment of Truth. "The words summoned themselves from a place in her brain she didn't know existed . . . The words were the same as they always had been, as were their rhythms, falling softly on her ears" (336-37).

Armed with a strengthened sense of her own values, Mary confronts the source of evil, where it dwells among the offices of Tribe & Wright. There she faces the masked gunman, and for Mary, he wears the face of her own mortality. "Mary stiffened with terror. She couldn't speak. She didn't know who he was. She didn't know what to do. She couldn't believe it was happening. She didn't want to die" (341). In a frantic rush to escape, Mary flees down the stairwell of the skyscraper containing Tribe & Wright. She cries for help, "but even she couldn't hear it over the din" (345).

Like Francesca the journalist, Mary's confrontation with evil traces a symbolic path down the ladder at the center of established truth. With each of the floors passing in turn, she basically relives her initiation process. The descending floors represent a paring away of her various levels of ethical constructions. The process continues until she speaks into a realm where she can't hear her own voice. Then her descent ends. She lets go of light and drowns in the "sound of a siren that hadn't brought help" (344-45). She realizes that established order, represented by the siren, is of no value. She must find the way herself.

Mary's initiation ritual nearly kills her, but she reappears bedecked with flowers, a figure resurrected by her Moment of Truth.

Barbara Parker's series features attorney Gail Connor. All the novels present the image of a questing novice in search of fairness. Major players in this series include Gail, a divorced corporate attorney, and Gail's love interest, Anthony Quintana, a defense attorney from a well-established Cuban family. Gail's mother Irene is from an old Miami family and a bastion of WASP respectability. While the growing love affair between Gail and Anthony measures the strength of Gail's heart in balancing personal and professional ethics, she faces other tests. She is a pivotal character between ex-husband and daughter, between Irene and memories of her dead sister, and between the Cuban and Anglo communities in Miami.

The first book of the series, *Suspicion of Innocence* (1994), knocks justice off the bench. Gail's sister is found dead, and Gail is one of the suspects. She has faith that the system will exonerate her, but her release is long in coming. The accusation also launches Gail onto a quest of self-scrutiny. She examines all the ways she has been guilty or sought retribution. Final revelations about Renee's murder essentially destroy Gail's version of her own past and question the values of people shaping the city's entire legal system.

Suspicion of Betrayal (1999) conflates several themes in Gail's struggle to balance the scales of justice. The narrative takes on tones of a Gothic thriller in which Anthony is the dark figure Rochester and his home in Miami, surrounded by a fence with spikes, is both protective fortress and prison. This duality is not lost on Gail, as she imagines herself there as mistress of the manor.

A stalker theme reinforces the novel's Gothic cast. Gail keeps receiving threatening phone calls, hate mail, and death threats. Graphic photos suggest that her daughter Karen is in danger. These threats compound Gail's guilt from the past. She has regrets over her divorce from Dave, the light-haired ex-husband, and over being a professional woman instead of a full-time mom.

This is only part of the story, however. Gail's struggle toward a sense of fairness lifts the novel out of the Gothic genre. Gail must prove herself worthy of being called a lawyer and she is not willing to compromise in this struggle.

Throughout the Gail Connor series, Parker uses houses to reflect Gail's inner life. In *Betrayal,* to escape influence from the Pedrosa homestead, Gail and Anthony buy a house together. It is on the "bad side" of Coconut Grove. This house needs new wiring, landscaping, and a major plan to encourage rat evacuation. Time, decay, and a horrible handyman nibble away at this house, as if at Gail's attempts at starting a new life. While problems with property are very real for a divorced woman, Gail herself needs a corporate lawyer to help her manage her own shifts in property. The house changes are reflective of Gail's psyche. She is certain in some areas and very confused about others.

One of Gail's initiation rites involves buying a dress for her wedding to Anthony. She meets with her prospective women in-laws at Lola Benitez's exclusive dress shop. The shop is so exclusive that even Gail's mother belongs to the inner circle of clients. The shop unites Irene with the Cuban women from Anthony's family. Karen, Gail's rebellious eleven-year old, feels comfortable with this group and finds a dress she likes at the shop.

The only one finding this whole process of feminine bonding unsatisfactory is Gail. In a sincere gesture, Anthony's relative Elena welcomes Gail to the family:

> "I just wanted to tell you how happy I am that you're going to be part of our family. I've sensed sometimes that you don't feel comfortable with us. I hope I'm wrong."
>
> Gail turned her back to be zipped up. "I don't know why you should think that. I'm very fond of you all."
>
> [204]

Gail knows enough about shady dealings in Anthony's family to wonder if marriage to him would essentially mean being "married to the mob." The Cuban women represent a female chorus, affirming the values of marriage and traditional obedience to the husband's will. In response, Gail enacts a self-imposed exile from their group.

Parker sets up a complex moral universe, however. Gail is really in no position to judge the values of others, and she knows it. Her own ethics in dealing with clients are questionable. Financial shortfalls have prompted her to play fast and loose with a client's money, using it to finance her ex-husband's business deal. She tries to help a battered woman leave her husband. However, that woman continuously returns to her husband. Given Gail's rocky relationship with Anthony, she is hardly qualified to offer advice to smooth out a marital relationship.

Another case from Gail's past returns for retribution. Gail had played a central role in a house foreclosure. This is especially ironic, given her own difficulties with real estate deals. She knew at the time that the foreclosure was legally right, even if it was not fair or moral. The foreclosure has tragic consequences. The client returns bent on revenge. This woman, crazed with grief over losing her husband and children, reflects in some measure Gail's own situation. Through her clients, Gail comes face to face with the weaknesses of her own ethics.

In the myth of Orestes, the House of Atreus is cursed. Similarly, caught up in a cycle of retribution, the power of Anthony's family is on the wane. "The house of Pedrosa was falling" (419). Gail seeks a middle ground between her house in Coconut Grove and that of Anthony's family. Gail lands at her mother's home, where she had grown up. In doing so, Gail leads the spirit of retribution to the house of Irene.

Gail's own actions have set this revenge drama in motion. The murderer is indeed a kind of Fury. The spirit of vengeance stalks Gail as it did Orestes. The dead must be avenged.

The two are locked in a struggle, each condemning each other to hell, until the final demonic scene. The murderer prepares to kill Gail, and her mother and daughter, but the plan backfires. Murderer becomes victim.

> Orange tongues licked across her body, down her legs. Her eyes opened wide in agonized terror, and a scream tore from her lungs. Hair burned and crackled. Gail stood immobilized, horrified. The knife clanged on the terrace. Shimmering, dancing, the flames ate into the darkness and leapt up, outlining the aluminum frame supporting the screen. The fire spun and beat at itself, mouth agape in a soundless cry. Its image flickered on the surface of the water. Then image and fire came together. Flesh hissed. Water surged upward and fell back.
>
> [414]

Once the figure is extinguished in fire, the immediate danger is gone. Still, Gail's crime had its origin on paper. "Bits of curled, blackened paper floated on the surface" (414). The pieces are evidence of her guilt, a final recrimination.

In many ways, the figure in flames is Gail's double. Gail Connor has similarly demanded retribution against the unseen stalker, against Anthony, and many other wrongs. Gail must move, sometime, to that unstrained quality of mercy, but not yet. She is doomed to wander, like Orestes, an outcast from the human community.

At novel's end, Gail is away from most of the people she cares about. Her ex-husband and daughter take a sailing trip without her. Anthony, her future husband, is out of the country and has left strict instructions that he will accept nothing from her. Gail's pain over the trauma has started to fade, but it has not ended. As Gail and her mother prune trees, Irene asks about her plans. Gail asserts that without Anthony, she feels truly free, but she shows little joy in the discovery. She has fallen short of experience. "Don't I even get to have *my* life, imperfect as it may be? That's all I want" (422).

In *Suspicion of Malice* (2000), the fifth novel of Parker's "Suspicion" series, attorney Gail Connor is drawn yet again into a murder investigation. During the case, she travels farther along the halls of justice as she is more successful in blending personal and professional values for an inner Truth. However, she has a way to go. "Unfortunately for the truth, too much of it would remain with the dead" (340).

So far in the "Suspicion" series, Connor has not yet reached the point in her Oresteian saga where the Furies wield power as Beneficent Ones. That may change with the publication of *Suspicion of Vengeance* (2001), which promises an in-depth exploration of retribution and forgiveness.

Vengeance focuses on the death penalty. Anthony Quintana takes on the case of death row inmate Kenny Ray Clark. Clark plans to appeal his conviction with new evidence through DNA testing available through the Innocence Project. Familiar with the community originally shaken by the murder, Gail approaches this case with a cynicism about the justice system's power to right past wrongs. In a sense, the entire "Suspicion" series has been Gail's own Innocence Project. However, it is possible that in this adventure she will move to another plane in her understanding of Justice, with a capital "J."

Charles Rosenberg, law professor and a frequent television commentator during the O. J. Simpson criminal trial, writes, "The stone structures of ancient Greece are mostly dust. Even the Parthenon lies in near-ruin. Greek dramatic structures, by contrast, are alive and well and living in your television set" (Jarvis and Joseph ix). For "your television set," we might substitute "the pages of mystery fiction." Many mystery novels work out a conflict between people doing good and people committing crimes. "Where you have opposites of good and evil, you are simply in the field of ethics." (Campbell, *Transformations* 247). The more intense novels do not stop there. Like the Greeks, detective writers combine moral drama with the main character's struggle to understand the meaning of the drama, to solve a spiritual mystery. Its solution demands a high price. To learn this secret, the questing protagonist must "seek beyond the tumult of the state, in the silences of earth and sea and the silence of his heart, the Word beyond words of the mystery of nature and his own potentiality" (Campbell, CM 88). The reward is that the reader along with the sleuth has the opportunity to feel the spark of genuine experience.

Works Cited

Bulfinch, Thomas. *Bulfinch's Mythology: A Modern Abridgment by Edmund Fuller.* New York: Dell Publishing, 1959.

Campbell, Joseph. *Creative Mythology: The Masks of God.* New York: Penguin Books, 1968.

———. *The Hero with a Thousand Faces.* 2nd ed. Princeton: Princeton UP, 1968.

———. *Transformations of Myth Through Time.* New York: Harper Perennial, 1999.

Campbell, Joseph, with Bill Moyers. *The Power of Myth,* New York: Doubleday, 1988.

Cross, Amanda. *Death in a Tenured Position.* New York: Ballantine Books, 1981.

————. *The Puzzled Heart.* New York: Ballantine Books, 1998.

Denvir, John. "Rumpole of the Bailey." *Prime Time Law.* Eds. Robert M. Jarvis and Paul R. Joseph. Durham, NC: Carolina Academic Press, 1998. 145-154.

Grisham, John. *The Firm.* New York: Doubleday, 1991.

————. "The Rise of the Legal Thriller: Why Lawyers Are Throwing the Books at Us." *New York Times,* Book Review Section, 33, Oct. 18, 1992.

Gur, Batya. *The Saturday Morning Murder: A Psycho-analytic Case.* New York: HarperPerennial, 1993.

Hamilton, Edith. *Mythology: Timeless Tales of Gods and Heroes.* New York: New American Library, 1969.

Leonardi, Susan J. "Murders Academic: Women Professors and the Crimes of Gender." Irons 112-126.

Moore, Samuel, and Thomas A. Knott. *The Elements of Old English.* Ann Arbor, MI: The George Wahr Publishing Co., 1972.

Parker, Barbara. *Suspicion of Betrayal.* New York: Signet, 2000.

————. *Suspicion of Innocence.* New York: Signet, 1994.

————. *Suspicion of Malice.* New York: Dutton, 2000.

Rosenberg, Charles B. "Foreword" to *Prime Time Law.* Jarvis and Joseph ix-xii.

Scottoline, Lisa. *Rough Justice.* New York: HarperCollins, 1997.

Viets, Elaine. *Doc in the Box.* New York: Dell Books, 2000.

Vogler, Christopher. *The Writer's Journey: Mythic Structure for Writers,* 2nd ed. Studio City, CA: Michael Wiese Productions, 1998.

REPRESENTATIVE AUTHORS

Nick Heffernan (essay date 1997)

SOURCE: Heffernan, Nick. "Law Crimes: The Legal Fictions of John Grisham and Scott Turow." In *Criminal Proceedings: The Contemporary American Crime Novel,* edited by Peter Messent, pp. 187-213. London: Pluto Press, 1997.

[*In the following essay, Heffernan outlines the characteristics of the lawyer-procedural through the works of John Grisham and Scott Turow.*]

Q: What's black and brown and looks good on a lawyer?

A: A Dobermann Pinscher.

There is a deeply rooted ambivalence in American culture towards the law and, especially, lawyers. Historically, American political and cultural elites have to a notable degree been dominated by lawyers and those of a legalistic cast of mind. Thomas Jefferson announced the American colonies' rejection of British rule by issuing a 'declaration'—a legal document traditionally lodged with a court to justify self-help—reflecting both his own training as a lawyer and the pervasive legalism of his class. Along with his famous invocation of 'the laws of nature' in the opening paragraph of the Declaration of Independence, this illustrates the extent to which, from its very inception, American nationhood has been bound up with notions of the law and legality. As Jefferson's more forthright revolutionary comrade Tom Paine put it, America had no need of monarchs for 'in America law is king'.[1]

The substitution of the rule of law (and, many Americans would increasingly begin to observe, of lawyers) for the rule of kings gave rise to a culture in which democracy was understood and interpreted in terms of the law and in which the law furnished the popular concepts and vocabulary through which democracy operated. In the 1820s Alexis de Tocqueville was struck by the propensity of even the most lowly Americans to seek legal solutions to all kinds of problem, from the smallest personal dispute to the largest political issue. 'The language of the law', he remarked, had become 'a vulgar tongue' through which the masses pressed their claims and jockeyed for position in a society without traditional forms of entrenched hierarchy.[2] Even the personifications, symbols and secular icons of the Republic were lawyers (Jefferson, Lincoln) or legal documents (the Declaration, the Constitution).

But the American passion and reverence for the law was never unproblematic. The Declaration charged the new nation with the task of embodying the laws of nature in man-made statutes and institutions. These latter, it was feared, might prove more responsive to the material influence of money and power than to the abstract claims of natural justice and the rights of man. The hard facts of Indian slaughter and removal in the West, of chattel slavery followed by racial apartheid in the South, and of the concentration of class power in the industrialising North suggested to some that the rule of law was in fact at variance with natural rights and an impediment to the reign of justice in society.[3] And the adoption by ordinary Americans of the law as a kind *lingua franca* of democracy did not preclude a growing populist hostility toward the legal profession. Lawyers were variously perceived as arrogant demagogues, as overweening and overcharging experts, as puppets of undemocratic vested interests, or as unprincipled hacks willing to argue any case for a fee. Most of all, they came to be viewed as crafty manipulators of language and logic in whose system, at one time or another, persons had been transformed into property (in the case of slaves) and property into persons (in the case of corporations).

Popular culture is the arena in which Americans have articulated and explored this fascinated mixture of attraction and repulsion with which they regard lawyers and the law. Typically, the stock figure of the venal, self-seeking and conniving shyster lawyer has had to compete for popular attention with unimpeachable lawyer-heroes such as Perry Mason and the protagonists of *The Defenders,* stalwart guardians of truth, justice and the rights of the individual. Contemporary representations like *LA Law* have attempted to show lawyers in operation beyond the ready-made adversarial dramatics of the courtroom (the staple of any lawyer narrative) where they embody and act out the contradictions of modern professionalism so resonant in a society whose chief collective goods—including healthcare, education, science and technology as well as justice—are managed and administered, if not owned, by professionals. Chief among these contradictions is the question about the ends to which specialised knowledge and expertise should be put. Lawyers, to a greater degree perhaps than other modern professionals, find themselves placed between the powerful logic of market forces on the one hand, with its temptations of self-aggrandisement in a comfortable accommodation with power, and an ethical imperative of independent and disinterested service in the name of some higher ideal on the other.[4]

The current surge of popular hostility towards the profession, however, would seem to suggest that most Americans now regard lawyers as incapable of recognising, let alone responding to, such dilemmas of conscience. Books with titles like *Dead Lawyers and Other Pleasant Thoughts* or *What to Do with a Dead Lawyer,* as well as a rash of anti-lawyer jokes, have provoked the American Bar Association to call for an end to 'lawyer bashing' and to seek to have such forms of invective classified as 'hate speech'.[5] Yet such attempts to defend the public image of the profession are undermined by the way in which the line between popular culture and the court system has steadily been erased in the last decade. Court TV and media show trials such as the O. J. Simpson case, while feeding a popular hunger for 'real life' courtroom drama, have only eroded public confidence in judicial processes and caused lawyers (and judges too, in many cases) to be perceived as a class of petulant would-be celebrities. Topics such as 'litigation abuse' are debated on the Oprah Winfrey Show where, it is argued, lawyers hooked on the commission from massive compensation

awards are creating a log-jam of speculative corporate liability and medical malpractice suits that is strangling American industrial enterprise and impeding the progress of medical science.

The attacks have also come from within the profession. In a 1982 article in the *American Bar Association Journal,* Chief Justice Warren Burger drew attention to the dangers of what he saw as an unprecedented 'legal explosion', the result of a culture-wide tendency to call on lawyers and the law to resolve questions that were in fact raised by the decline in other, more traditional social and cultural institutions and structures, such as the family, the church and the neighbourhood.[6] Law could not function as a substitute for community, Burger implied. But the massive increase in the number of lawyers and laws since his warning (from 541,000 lawyers in 1980 to about one million in 1995) only testifies to the continuing decline of community and the increasing appeal of the law as a lucrative career choice. Other law professionals have echoed Burger's notions, diagnosing a condition of 'hyperlexis' in which the compulsion to produce new laws and new lawyers has reached the level of 'national disease'.[7] This contention that an impenetrable thicket of overcomplex laws and overpaid lawyers is somehow obscuring and compromising the basic principles of American life is summed up in the title of a recent book, *The Death of Common Sense: How Law Is Suffocating America,* with its populist championing of honest, down-to-earth 'common sense' against the self-serving sophistry and manipulations of legal experts and judicial elites.[8]

It is perhaps no accident that this late twentieth-century legal explosion has been accompanied by the rise of a hitherto little-noticed sub-genre of the crime thriller—the lawyer-procedural. While traditional courtroom drama may comprise an element of any lawyer-procedural, the form is actually distinguished by its focus on lawyers *outside* the courtroom, by the way in which it makes lawyers themselves (rather than their clients) the protagonists and bearers of suspense, and by the way in which the narrative draws the reader into the professional and occupational culture of lawyers. In the hands of its principal exponents, Scott Turow (whose *Presumed Innocent* gave the form its breakthrough to bestsellerdom in 1987) and John Grisham (whose formulaic reductions have kept it there ever since), the lawyer-procedural exploits the current fascination with lawyers and the legal apparatus, trades on the historic ambivalence noted above, and offers within the framework of a suspense narrative a set of meditations on American hyperlexis and the status of the lawyer as American hero or hate figure.

The startling publishing success of the lawyer-procedural since the late 1980s (and the relative lack of success of such outstanding forerunners of Turow and

Grisham as George V. Higgins) can be related to massive changes in the historical conditions which underpin the production and consumption of suspense fiction. The collapse of the Soviet Union, the disintegration of the Eastern bloc and the end of the Cold War made the old-style NATO spy thriller obsolete. The lawyer-procedural stepped into this vacant niche in the market, placing the thrills now in a domestic rather than international setting and capturing what commentators identified as a new national mood of introspection brought on by the loss of the ideological certainties associated with the old twin-superpower world system.

The form is also well positioned to register other key economic, cultural and political developments of the last decade and a half, in particular the glorification of wealth and unashamed selfishness in post-Reaganite America. For both Grisham and Turow, the law has been invaded by, and is now a principal vehicle for, this late twentieth-century spirit of aggressive materialism. In their work, law firms are portrayed as the running dogs of capitalist business enterprise; legal expertise as overwhelmingly dedicated to the protection and extension of corporate power; and lawyers themselves as archetypal yuppies, embodiments of contemporary acquisitiveness dedicated to the pursuit of a super-affluent, individualistic lifestyle legitimated by conspicuous workaholism. The lawyer-procedural's focus on the corporate culture of law firms and the lifestyles of well-compensated professionals makes it therefore a key literary reflection of late capitalist, yuppie America. Indeed, Grisham's stock-in-trade is the yuppie-protagonist-in-danger plot (brilliant young lawyer must decide whether to use knowledge/expertise for personal enrichment or public good); while Turow's is the older lawyer responding under duress to the encroachments of the yuppie ethos of competition, ambition and individualistic self-realisation. The pleasure offered to the reader here is one of simultaneous immersion in and implicit criticism of the lifestyles of affluent, upwardly mobile, middle-class professionals.

The post-Reagan Republican years have also created a political context which intensifies the resonance of the lawyer-procedural. The campaign to reinterpret the Constitution according to fundamentalist conservative dogma and to load the federal court system with right-wing judges has made the law into an ideological battlefield where the broadly liberal, redistributionist drift of American society since the 1930s can be arrested and reversed.[9] This overt political manipulation of the law in many ways complements its annexation by powerful economic interests. The law has become a central tool in engineering the historic shift away from American welfare capitalism towards a more volatile, nakedly competitive and socially divisive multinational finance capitalism. The lawyer-procedural dramatises what might be at stake in this contemporary struggle over the meaning and use of the law.[10] Grisham and Turow write about the law as an index of the wider political, cultural and moral health of the nation. The choices and decisions their characters make from within the law stand for the various responses individuals might make to the culture of late capitalist America at large. Their work capitalises on the popular sense that the law is at once the most exalted and compromised of American institutions, the embodiment of founding American ideals and the instrument of their betrayal, and that it is the fulcrum for the economic, cultural and political reshaping of American society. Above all, it cleverly positions the audience at once inside and outside the legal profession, maximising the play of attraction and repulsion that Americans have traditionally felt for lawyers.

POPULISM, PROFESSIONALISM, INDIVIDUALISM: JOHN GRISHAM

In the introduction to his first novel, *A Time to Kill* (1989), Grisham states that in ten years as a lawyer he 'represented people, never banks or insurance companies or big corporations. I was a street lawyer.'[11] This eagerness to present himself to his audience as a man of the people, rather than a hireling of powerful vested interests, illustrates Grisham's sensitivity to populist resentment of the legal profession. Indeed, populist attitudes towards professional elites of all kinds are very deliberately and overtly built into his fiction which, beneath the formulaic crime plotting and one-dimensional legal and political intrigue which are its selling points, can be read as a sustained attempt to balance the antagonistic claims of populism and professionalism in a society dominated by the ideology of possessive individualism.

The Firm (1991), Grisham's second novel and breakthrough bestseller, sets out this agenda very clearly. Brilliant and 'hungry' young Harvard Law School graduate, Mitch McDeere, is lured to work in a Memphis law firm specialising in securities and tax by the $80,000 starting salary, the company car (a BMW), the low-interest mortgage and the pension plan that will make him a millionaire at 45. However, the yuppie fantasy quickly becomes a nightmare as Mitch discovers that the firm is in fact a Mafia-owned money laundering operation and that conscience-stricken lawyers who attempt either to bail out or blow the whistle meet untimely ends. Mitch must seek either to forget his complicity by working the 100-hour weeks, pocketing the salary and enjoying the lifestyle, or honour his responsibilities as a professional and a citizen, a predicament that is sharpened when he is covertly approached by the FBI to testify against the firm and supply evidence that will bring down the Mob's evil Morolto family.

Populist resentment of urban professionals is catered to by the narrative's presentation of yuppie materialism as a Faustian pact with the criminal underworld. Indeed, the firm's senior partner, Nathan Locke, is marked out as none other than Mephistopheles himself by his 'ominous, evil presence', and Mitch knows it is time seriously to review his career choice when, during a particularly heavy week at the office, his secretary tells him that his eyes are beginning to resemble Nathan Locke's.[12] Professionals are referred to as deracinated 'transplants', severed from meaningful ties to local community and even family by selfish dedication to yuppie lifestyles and career development; while the portrayal of lawyers as nothing more than gangsters in brogues and button-downs literalises the populist view of the legal profession as itself a kind of diploma-wielding mafia (*TF* [*The Firm*], p. 23).

However, it is important to note that the firm also symbolises the operations of multinational finance capitalism. Through it the Moroltos have created an impenetrable network of corporations and banks that relays illicit money around the globe faster than the authorities can trace it. This equation of the Mafia with the corporate and financial structure of American capitalism links the populist hostility to lawyers with a wider populist distrust of big business or 'the money power'. But it also opens up a debate about the nature of professionalism as seen from within, so to speak, in which a 'bad' version of the professional as pliant servant of unprincipled power (the Mob, the corporations) is played off against a 'good' version of the professional as fiercely independent embodiment of a vocational ideal of selfless commitment to the public good.[13]

The ethical and ideological ambiguities of professionalism are distilled by a colleague, who tells Mitch soon after his arrival at the firm how:

> When you were in law school you had some noble idea of what a lawyer should be. A champion of individual rights; a defender of the Constitution; a guardian of the oppressed; an advocate for your client's principles. Then after you practice for six months you realize we're nothing but hired guns. Mouthpieces for sale to the highest bidder, available to anybody, any crook, any sleazebag with enough money to pay our outrageous fees . . . It's supposed to be an honourable profession, but you'll meet so many crooked lawyers you'll want to quit and find an honest job.

> (*TF*, pp. 57-8)

Mitch rejects his colleague's 'bad' professionalism in which the salary compensates for the loss of integrity, a position linked in the narrative to prostitution, the archetype of 'bad' professionalism, through the hooker (the 'pro', as she is called) hired by the firm to seduce Mitch during a business trip. (*TF*, p. 150). He resolves to extract himself from the firm and provide the FBI with evidence for its indictment. Thus while serving as a focus for Grisham's expression of populist hostility

towards professionals, Mitch also becomes a figure through whom Grisham can rehabilitate professionalism and restore it to a position of respectability and social responsibility.

Accordingly, Mitch mutates from callow yuppie careerist into a combination of populist hero and principled but hardened professional. His conversion to an ethical, 'good' professionalism is defined in terms of commitment to a cause larger than his own material well-being. 'Committed [is] the word', the Director of the FBI tells Mitch when he signs up to become the agent of the Morolto family's destruction. It is no accident that Mitch's conversion is sealed in the shadow of the Washington Monument and the Vietnam Veterans Memorial as this ethical professionalism is linked to the patriotic and martial ideals of honour, duty and sacrifice. And when the FBI's Director tells Mitch that he has been selected for this task because he is 'self-reliant and independent', it is as though Grisham wants to suggest that the 'good' professional is a blend of the classic Republican virtues with traditional American rugged individualism (*TF*, pp. 204-5). Indeed, Mitch's ability to discharge his civic and professional duty is conditional upon his development of physical and mental courage, cunning and street-smarts. Ethical professionalism is therefore also attached to the qualities of the pragmatic, unsentimental, tough 'pro', a narrative manoeuvre that glosses the image of the white-collar professional with the more appealing codes of the American male action hero.

But Mitch's decision to take on the Mafia from within also makes him into a populist hero, the 'little guy' standing up to the combined might of the criminal and corporate establishments (the firm, as we have seen, stands for both) and, it transpires, of the state to whose service he has just pledged himself. (In one Grisham novel someone observes sagely: 'David pulled it off, but the best bet is always on Goliath.'[14] But Grisham's world is one in which the little guy routinely kicks the giant's ass.) For, Mitch is quick to realise, too close an association with the FBI will arouse suspicion and get him killed: unquestioning service of the state is as dangerous and undesirable as any other kind of unquestioning service—Grisham's moral for all professionals. Thus, in having Mitch go it absolutely alone, Grisham transforms the Ivy League yuppie into an unlikely populist hero who, at the same time, can embody a rehabilitated professionalism based on independence, moral courage and the dedication of expertise to the public good.

Of this uneasy balance of contradictory ideologies that Mitch represents, it is in fact neither populism nor professionalism that Grisham appears ultimately to affirm but, surprisingly, the materialistic individualism that *The Firm* apparently sets out to satirise and critique.

Mitch applies his tax lawyer's knowledge of international banking systems not only to the project of incriminating the firm but also to the secret accumulation of eight million of its illegally gained dollars in his own untraceable bank accounts. This, in addition to the three million he extracts from the government in exchange for the provision of evidence, constitutes a personal fortune which enables Mitch and his beautiful young wife to retreat at the end of the novel into a life of luxurious leisure and world travel. Ethical professionalism and populist heroics are therefore not so much positive alternatives to Mitch's original selfish yuppie materialism as they are mere vehicles for its fulfilment. They enable Mitch to achieve his original goal of making a million dollars and retiring early quicker than continuing to work for the firm would.

The Firm's efforts to negotiate a path between populism and professionalism are supervened by a resolution drawn straight out of traditional American success mythology and fables of upward mobility (Grisham makes much of Mitch's childhood poverty and consequent 'hunger' for success). But the novel is also a fantasy of absolute extrication in which the hero's final liberation from every kind of social commitment and connection (save the romantic/erotic one of marriage) and his assumption of a new and completely 'free' identity are as important as his financial reward. In many ways Mitch's story is a curiously prescient allegory of the dramatic change of career path and personal fortune enjoyed by Grisham himself with the success of *The Firm*: disillusioned lawyer 'rats' on profession, makes several million bucks and retires. Subsequent Grisham novels have tended not only to deliver similar fantasies of extrication but also to utilise plots that are virtually identical to *The Firm*'s, while repeating that novel's attempts to do equal justice to the antagonistic claims of populism and professionalism.

In Grisham's next novel, *The Pelican Brief* (1992), a brilliant young law student uncovers a conspiracy including the assassination of two Supreme Court justices that involves a Howard Hughes-type corporate monomaniac, Arab terrorists, and top-level political and legal corruption. For Darby Shaw, as for Mitch in *The Firm*, the exercise of professional expertise and career ambition leads unexpectedly to a terrible and life-threatening knowledge which presents a moral dilemma: should that knowledge be withheld in the name of self-preservation, or communicated at great personal risk in the name of the public interest? Also, as with Mitch before her, Darby's decision to serve the public interest means that she can be a representative of ethical professionalism while also serving as a populist 'little guy', who must stand alone against the corporate, legal and political establishments in order to ensure that justice is done.

Like *The Firm, The Pelican Brief* is full of instances of 'bad' professionalism which counterbalance Darby's ethical stance and through which populist resentments can be expressed. The earlier novel's archetype of the 'bad' professional was the prostitute; the latter's is the mercenary, personified by Khamel, the Arab assassin who kills for anyone as long as the price is right and of whose consummate 'professionalism' Grisham constantly reminds us. While Khamel and his fellow mercenaries are always referred to as 'professionals', Darby's integrity and populist credibility are bound up with the fact that, as we are told, 'she's not a pro' (*PB* [*The Pelican Brief*], pp. 76, 137). And if the connections between the figure of the mercenary, professionals in general, and lawyers in particular were suggested by the description of the latter as 'hired guns' in the passage from *The Firm* quoted earlier, they are cemented by the incident in *The Pelican Brief* in which Khamel assumes the identity of a lawyer in order to attempt to kill Darby.

Despite not being a 'pro' in this particular sense, Darby is nonetheless a vehicle for the rehabilitation of professionalism as a legitimate calling. As with Mitch before her, this requires that she prove herself more of a street-wise, courageous and independently resourceful 'pro' at the art of survival than anyone could reasonably expect of a middle-class, pink-collar heroine. It also requires that, like Mitch, she give voice to Grisham's habitual qualms about the morality of the legal profession. Lawyers might claim to be motivated, Darby remarks, by 'idealism and money', by a desire to 'change the world and get paid for it'. But in fact, she explains, 'It's greed. They want BMWs and gold credit cards.' And despite the self-disgust that sets in, 'they can't leave [the profession] because of the money' (*PB* [*Pelican Brief*], pp. 305-6). Conveniently for Darby, she can: her unravelling of the conspiracy has put her in possession of a story that, with the aid of her journalist boyfriend, will make her 'rich and famous' (*PB*, p. 335). Again, the defence of an ethical professionalism in the service of truth and justice becomes a stepping-stone to individual wealth, and the narrative culminates in another fantasy of extrication from all social ties and commitments as Darby abandons law school for an indefinite period of leisured luxury with her lover. The extent of Grisham's ambivalence about his former profession is revealed by the way in which his heroes quit the law the instant they have completed their appointed task of redeeming the integrity of lawyers. Professionalism is rehabilitated and abandoned in the same gesture, while any lingering questions about the possibility of a sustained and socially engaged ethical professionalism are obviated by the escapist endings which lift the protagonists out of social relations altogether.

Grisham's next two novels can be read as attempts to deal with this problem, to produce resolutions that still cater to the antithetical claims of populism and professionalism, but allow greater scope for sustainable social and moral commitment without completely jettisoning the escapist individualism so integral to his two previous blockbusters. This involves making clearer narrative distinctions between populism and professionalism in order to permit them to follow ultimately different trajectories. In *The Firm* and *The Pelican Brief*, populist and professional attributes are uneasily combined in a single lawyer-hero figure. In *The Client* (1993) and *The Chamber* (1994), they are split and attached to two separate characters. For example, 'good' professionalism in *The Client* is represented by Reggie Love, an aptly named and selfless fighter for the rights of the poor and defenceless; while in her client, Mark Sway, Grisham gives us his most literal embodiment of the populist 'little guy' thus far. For Mark is just that—an eleven-year-old working-class kid from a broken home who has become privy to the details of a Mafia political assassination and who is under threat not only from the Mob, but also from the FBI and an aggressively ambitious US District Attorney, both of whom strive to compel Mark to testify with callous disregard for the little guy's safety.

Reggie's function is to protect Mark from the impersonal and forbidding machinery of the law enforcement agencies and the legal system itself in the name of compassion for, and commitment to, the weak and the vulnerable. Ethical professionalism here is presented as a kind of socialised version of devoted parenting, a notion reinforced by the novel's running theme of maternal suffering and self-sacrifice, as well as by the prominence given to a noble Juvenile Court judge who acts as surrogate legal father to Mark, complementing Reggie's role of legal mother (or mother-in-law). Mark's function, on the other hand, is to provide the streetwise anti-lawyer jibes ('She's a lawyer and she doesn't want money?' he asks incredulously of Reggie) and the obligatory populist heroics by outsmarting the Mob, the cops and the legal establishment using native wit and common sense. Just as important, though, is the way Mark comes to stand for the sense of intimidated mystification any ordinary American at the mercy of the specialised complexities of the legal system might feel. As the various legal authorities argue over Mark's fate, Grisham gives us this passage:

> There was something unfair about a system in which a little kid was brought into a courtroom and surrounded by lawyers sniping at each other under the scornful eye of a judge, the referee, and somehow in the midst of this barrage of laws and code sections and motions and legal talk the kid was supposed to know what was happening to him. It was hopelessly unfair.[15]

Here the populist resentments are not so much directed at lawyers as at a legal system which has grown so complex and labyrinthine that it renders ordinary citizens into helplessly bewildered 'little kids' dependent upon a professional 'parent' to protect them. All the more important, therefore, that the ethical and compassionate lawyer remain within the profession to ensure the provision of such protection. Thus, at the novel's end, as Mark departs for Australia to begin a new life funded by the federal witness protection programme, Reggie returns to her humble office to continue to defend the rights of the underprivileged for a one-dollar retainer. *The Client*'s projection of populism and professionalism onto separate characters therefore allows Grisham to deliver the escapist fantasy ending of extrication from social ties and commitments while at the same time suggesting that an ethical professionalism might possibly be sustainable within the law.

The Chamber employs a similar narrative structure, though perhaps embarrassed at having used the same plot for three novels in succession and finding difficulty in coming up with another, Grisham here offers us not really a thriller at all but what appears to be a novel of psychology and ideas, without much of either. As in *The Client,* populist and professional characteristics are attributed separately to the two main protagonists. Adam Hall is the idealistic young lawyer dissatisfied with his firm's expectation that he be a 'young cutthroat just eager to work eighteen hours a day and bill twenty'. As an embodiment of ethical professionalism, Adam wants 'to do public interest work . . . [not] spend my career representing wealthy crooks and wayward corporations'.[16] Sam Cayhall, whom Adam seeks to defend from the gas chamber, is Adam's estranged grandfather, a Mississippi redneck and Klansman awaiting execution on death row for his part in a racist bombing campaign in the 1960s.

Like Mark Sway in *The Client,* Sam is a figure for the ordinary 'little guy' at the mercy of the vast, impersonal machinery of the legal apparatus, though, unlike Mark, he is not an innocent but an unregenerate sinner. Yet he is no less a populist hero, for he has taken on the professionals on their home turf, having taught himself the law and conducted his own appeals procedure for a number of years. He becomes a kind of 'people's lawyer', providing legal expertise to his fellow death row inmates, and is able to voice a critique of lawyers and the law that combines an insider's knowledge with the external perspective of populist 'common sense'. 'I was taught by the same learned souls who provided your instruction', he tells his grandson, 'Dead judges. Honorable justices. Windy lawyers. Tedious professors. I've read the same garbage you've read.' Sam is thus in a position to demystify the law—previously portrayed by Grisham as mystifying and intimidating for the ordinary American—with this kind of populist relish:

> Why do lawyers practice? Why can't they just work like everyone else? Do plumbers practice? Do truck

drivers practice? No, they simply work. But not lawyers . . . They're special, and they practice. With all their damned practicing you'd think they'd know what the hell they were doing. You'd think they'd eventually become good at something.[17]

Sam also directs his populist 'common sense' against what he perceives to be the elitist cant of politically correct speech, taunting Adam's liberal convictions and testing his tolerance. That Adam remains loyal to Sam in spite of his bitterness, racism and awful crimes is of course an index of his compassion and commitment to defend the weak and the vulnerable. Though unable to save Sam from the gas chamber, the experience of defending him reveals to Adam the full horror of the death penalty and the pathos of death row prisoners. He quits lucrative private practice to devote himself to their cause and, simultaneously, that of a socially committed, ethical professionalism. Meanwhile, Sam's execution can be understood as a variant of the typical Grisham escapist fantasy of extrication: Sam welcomes death as a release from his guilt and his violent past, as the final liberation from the racist culture of the poor-white South which, it is suggested, is ultimately responsible for his crimes.

That negative overtones are given to populism in *The Chamber* by its association with a racist murderer points to the emergence of a new series of concerns in Grisham's more recent work. It reflects a more cautious and critical attitude towards the populism his books so assiduously court and address, an acknowledgement that the resentment of urban intellectual and professional elites can be based in ignorance and intolerance as much as in a folksy 'traditional Americanism' or a nobly plebeian 'common sense'. Grisham seems to have become particularly preoccupied by the dangers that the manipulation of populism's appeal for reactionary political ends might hold. Since *The Pelican Brief,* his most vilified models of 'bad' professionalism have been opportunistic politicians who exploit a populist rhetoric of prejudice for personal and ideological advantage. There is, for example, that novel's sinister White House chief-of-staff, a yuppie-from-hell, whose manipulation of the President's populist image serves his own ambition and ultra-conservative agenda. There is *The Client*'s overweening District Attorney, whose intimidation of poor Mark Sway is part and parcel of the populist, tough-on-crime posturing he hopes will see him elected to Senator. And there is *The Chamber*'s State Governor whose decision to implement the death penalty is a calculated part of his re-election campaign. These figures represent Grisham's fears about the cynical appropriation of populist impulses by an unprincipled professional political elite.

Here again, Grisham could be accused of biting the hand that once fed him, for during his law-practising days he was elected for a short period to the Missis-

sippi State legislature as a Democrat. Interestingly, however, whilst populist hostility in his novels has shifted decisively from lawyers to politicians, an increasingly explicit party political partisanship has marked his writing. Grisham villains now tend exclusively to be Republicans (they are explicitly labelled as such within his texts) and his recent themes impeccably liberal: corporate despoliation of the environment (*Pelican Brief, Client*); conservative political manipulation of the Supreme Court (*Pelican Brief, Chamber*); the plight of single working mothers (*Client*); the inhumanity of the death penalty and the rise of neo-Nazi groups (*Chamber*). This overtly pro-Democratic inclination is distilled in *The Client*'s mini-portrait of a crusading, paternalistic black judge, significantly called Roosevelt, who defends children—the emblematic 'little guys'—and delights in belittling any 'silk-stocking, blue-blooded Republican mouthpieces' that might enter his court seeking to defend vested interests or the money power.[18]

While it is not surprising, therefore, that Grisham—a self-confessed 'political junkie'—has been befriended by those other baby-boomer Southern Democrat lawyers, Bill and Hillary Clinton, the political turn of his recent work marks more than just the surfacing of his own well-known party loyalties.[19] It can be read as symptomatic of deeper ideological ambiguities that beset not just the Democratic party but liberal politics in the US as a whole. For, despite an historic connection to the idea of standing for the 'little guy' against elites and vested interests, liberalism in the US is increasingly the province of middle-class professionals and intellectuals (like Grisham and the Clintons), who are ever more distanced from the experiences and concerns of ordinary working Americans. Grisham's juggling of the claims of populism and professionalism reflects this social and political contradiction. Indeed, the tactic in recent books of using two central characters—one a populist 'little guy', the other a 'good' professional upon whose expertise and integrity the little guy comes to depend (true even of his most pessimistic book, *The Chamber*)—must be understood as an attempt to arrive at an imaginary resolution of it.[20] That the 'little guy' is typically assigned to a subordinate, client position in the relationship with his or her professional guardian suggests that existing social hierarchies will persist even within this idealised resolution. And the novels' projection of 'bad' professionalism onto Republican politicians who pander to populist attitudes for private advantage betrays perhaps a sense of bad faith on Grisham's part—one that is neatly displaced onto his political opponents. Notwithstanding his anxious parading of populist credentials in prefaces and interviews, then, Grisham's fiction articulates the world-view of a modern, liberal, professional elite whose understanding of itself as a model of responsible social leadership exists in tension with a guilty sense of privileged exclusivity and a healthy regard for the individual social mobility and lifestyle benefits that expertise brings with it.

UNJUST DESERTS: SCOTT TUROW

If Grisham's novels increasingly strive to rehabilitate professionalism in their depiction of the law, Turow's, by contrast, subtly subvert it. They do so by calling into question not just the dispassionate objectivity of legal professionals, but by interrogating the very notion of rationality upon which codes of professional conduct and the modern understanding of the law itself rest. Max Weber's distinction between the modern, '"rational" interpretation of the law on the basis of strictly formal conceptions' and more traditional, non-rational methods of dispensing justice is one which inhabits Turow's work.[21] His narratives typically revolve around this tension or opposition between reason and unreason: on the one hand, there is the modern democratic view of the law as a rational system based on formal rules which embody the abstract principles of right and wrong; on the other is an atavistic sense of the fundamentally irrational nature of human conduct and motivation, and of the determining role of passion and appetite in public, as well as personal, life. Whereas Grisham more and more tends to present his lawyer protagonists as bulwarks against the seductions of appetite and irrational desire, Turow presents his as battlegrounds for this contest between the rational and the irrational. For Turow, lawyers are representatives of a rational system of abstract justice, embodiments of 'the social world's realm of ultimate restraint', whose daily currency nonetheless is the passion of human conflict.[22] They are therefore placed most suggestively within this contest, and can serve as ideal figures through which Weber's definition of the modern professional as 'the personally detached and strictly objective expert' can be explored and tested.[23]

Rusty Sabich, the protagonist of *Presumed Innocent* (1987), sees himself as 'a person of values', values which he defines in opposition to his father—a fireman who, in his son's eyes, abused his position of civic trust by stealing from the buildings he was supposed to be protecting. As chief assistant to the State Prosecuting Attorney, Sabich feels that he likewise holds a position of civic trust, one in which the subordination of personal interest and ego to the rational administration of justice is paramount. He therefore describes himself as 'a functionary of our only universally recognized system of telling wrong from right, a bureaucrat of good and evil'. His duty is to arrive at the truth through rational processes for, as he habitually asks of his juries: 'If we cannot find the truth, what is our hope of justice?'[24] The narrative, however, strips away these rationalist pretensions. From the moment he lets his professional and ethical restraint slip by embarking on an illicit affair

with a colleague, Sabich's assumptions about the law and about himself as a 'person of values' are relentlessly undermined. The colleague is brutally murdered. Sabich is put in charge of the criminal investigation, the success of which is crucial to his boss's re-election as State Prosecuting Attorney. After stumbling across evidence of systematic corruption among his superiors, Sabich, in Kafkaesque fashion, finds himself accused of the murder by a political opponent, abandoned by his erstwhile colleagues and forced to stand trial. By clever manipulation of his knowledge of high-level judicial corruption, he is able not only to secure his acquittal but also to destroy the credibility and careers of his political opponents. He is publicly rehabilitated, rewarded with the post of State Prosecuting Attorney and promised promotion to judge, all the time harbouring the secret knowledge that in fact it was his jealous wife who committed the murder, with the strong possibility that she deliberately set Sabich himself up as fall-guy.

Turow implies, of course, that Sabich's professional code of restraint, detachment and objectivity in the name of truth and public service is after all nothing more than a flimsy fiction glossing over the deeply irrational impulses and desires that inhabit the self and determine public life. Sabich's ability to conspire in and coolly profit from a major perversion of justice reveals to him the existence of another, deeply irrational and instinctual self diametrically opposed to—and far more powerful than—his carefully cultivated 'professional' identity. As he confesses, 'until this happened, I really thought I was Joe College' (*PI* [*Presumed Innocent*], p. 288). The real lesson, however, is not that this makes him unusual, but rather that it makes him just like everyone else—a slave to jealousy, ambition, greed, lust and the instinct of self-preservation, passions that are revealed to be at the heart of the law, not its antitheses. Indeed, Turow cleverly allows for the possibility that Sabich himself (whose name, we are told, is derived from the Serbian for 'savage') has committed the murder and has constructed the scenario of his wife's guilt as a fail-safe, lest he be unable to manoeuvre his own trial judge into dismissing the case against him. The novel thus concludes in ambiguity and irony with a lawyer who is possibly guilty of murder (his innocence on this charge, as the title suggests, can at best only be 'presumed'), is certainly guilty of perverting the course of justice, and is set to be elevated to judge—the highest embodiment of the law as a rational system of dispassionate adjudication.

Presumed Innocent seems to offer an almost metaphysical argument for the triumph of nature over culture, for the futility of reason (and its social forms such as the law and professionalism) in the face of the 'natural' passions and irrationality that pervade private and public life. The protagonist of Turow's next novel, *The Burden of Proof* (1990), is a fictional mouthpiece for this position. 'In human affairs', observes mandarin Jewish defence lawyer Sandy Stern, 'reason would never fully triumph'; and while he allows that human beings are not innately 'evil', they are through 'self-interest, impulse, anger, lust, or greed . . . inclined that way . . . [and] know this can never change'.[25] Despite these convictions Stern's calling is to be reason's 'champion' (*BP* [*The Burden of Proof*], p. 227), to stand for those principles, embodied in the law, that he believes keep us 'decent, civilized' (*BP*, p. 152). And this commitment to reason is what has determined his decision never to act in the capacity of prosecutor, a role that would necessarily demand that he work to 'excite a jury's ugly passions' (*BP*, p. 151). Accordingly, Stern has developed a persona that reflects his commitment to reason and rationality as the benchmarks of civilised life; one that, as his name suggests, is defined above all by unbending propriety and self-restraint. As in *Presumed Innocent,* the thrust of the narrative is to deconstruct this persona and to reveal to Stern the extent to which the irrational determines not so much the life around him (he knew this already) as it does the life *within* him.

The emergence of the impulsive, irrational, passionate Stern is precipitated by his wife's unexpected suicide and is linked to his professional attachment to his brother-in-law and client, the bullish entrepreneur and capitalist Dixon Hartnell. These figures represent the opposing poles of self-restraint and self-gratification respectively, between which Stern himself oscillates. Clara Stern has killed herself out of shame, in part for a single and long-past infidelity (with Dixon Hartnell) which has left her with a recurring genital infection, and in part due to the discovery of her daughter and son-in-law's involvement in illegal and ruinous financial speculations. The novel codes Clara's suicide-from-shame as an extreme instance of that ethos of self-abnegating honour to which Stern himself is committed and which he believes is concomitant with the function of the law in civilised society. Dixon Hartnell, on the other hand, is an embodiment of the lawlessness of impulsive desire, a creature of license and unrestrained appetite, both in his frequently dubious business dealings and his energetic pursuit of sensual gratification. As Stern strives to uncover the circumstances of his wife's death while defending Dixon from federal charges of financial misdemeanour (the two prove to be linked by more than Dixon and Clara's affair), he is drawn into the realm of irrational desire above which he had previously so magisterially floated.

The extent of Stern's 'fall' is marked by the fact that within mere weeks of his wife's death he has had two affairs, bathed naked in a hot-tub with Dixon's (female) prosecutor, and enjoyed an anonymous grope with a perfect stranger in an elevator. This erosion of self-restraint and surrender to the baser instincts is presented

as in part a consequence of Stern's increasing closeness to Dixon Hartnell's dubiously acquired fortune (symbolised by Stern's agreeing to 'hide' Dixon's safe from federal investigators in his own office). If the law represents restraint then the free-market represents unbridled appetite, with Dixon the capitalist combining lust and greed in equal measure. As he becomes guardian of Dixon's corporate wealth, Stern's closeness to his client in other, even sexual, matters is emphasised: a dismayed Stern discovers that Dixon has enjoyed relations with every one of his, Stern's, sexual partners (including Clara), even contriving to expire *in flagrante* with the woman who is to become Stern's second wife.

Turow is not concerned here to endorse only one side in this opposition between the rationality of the law and the irrationality of the free market. For while Stern's dalliance with the volatile impulses of the financial and sexual marketplaces embodied in Dixon Hartnell undermines his pose of professional restraint, the new self that emerges is in many ways a more attractive and humane one. Stern discovers that his absolute commitment to the formal and abstract principles of the law has made him cold, judgemental and inaccessible, has excluded him not only from mundane sensual pleasures but also from the turbulent inner life of his own family. Indeed, this family, which Stern had supposed to be the model of restrained bourgeois propriety and rational conduct, is revealed to be a seething hotbed of irrational impulses and transgressions to which Stern had remained oblivious. The lawless Dixon Hartnell, on the other hand, emerges as a curiously honourable figure of noble self-sacrifice, carrying through his promise to Clara Stern to protect her son-in-law and daughter from prosecution for financial crimes even to the extent of taking their guilt on his shoulders. The degree to which Stern has been transformed, humanised, by this new acquaintance with irrational impulse and desire—his own as well as others'—is marked by his willingness not only to accept but to collude in a resolution of affairs in which formal justice is not done. Dixon's example has taught him that other, more visceral attachments—such as a lover's promise—can take precedence over a commitment to the abstract principles of the law. Like Rusty Sabich, who keeps his wife's guilt secret, Stern is prepared to see the dispensation of unjust deserts in the name of non-rational, 'blood' or family ties that prove stronger than professional codes. 'There are no disembodied principles in the practice of law', he muses toward the novel's end. 'There are human beings in every role, every case' (*BP*, p. 559).

While Turow uses the law in these novels to stage a metaphysical contest between reason and unreason portrayed as 'eternally' or 'naturally' opposed forces, there is also a strong current of Darwinism in his writing. This is evident in the way that his protagonists, projected into an environment characterised by relentless struggle, typically shed their civilised veneer of professionalism to reveal the almost savage, instinctual self beneath. This Darwinist current becomes especially pronounced in Turow's third novel, *Pleading Guilty* (1993), where it provides an extra dimension to the 'eternal' contest of reason and unreason, historicising—even politicising—what had heretofore been largely presented as a metaphysical condition.

For Mack Molloy, the novel's narrator, the law is a rational instrument for regulating the Darwinian struggle of modern commercial, urban life:

> come into the teeming city, with so many souls scream-ing, I want, I need, where most social planning amounts to figuring out how to keep them all at bay—come and try to imagine the ways that the vast unruly community can be kept in touch with the deeper aspirations of humankind for the overall improvement of the species, the good of the many and the rights of the few. That I always figured was the task of the law.
>
> (*PG* [*Pleading Guilty*], p. 174)

However, what is disclosed to Mack in the course of the narrative is the fundamental irrationality of rational-ity. Far from being a force that regulates the competi-tive anarchy of contemporary capitalism, the law in late twentieth-century America is an extension of it. Mack's law firm is, in effect, no more than a subsidiary of a gigantic multinational corporation, Trans National, whose global drive for profit-by-any-means ('the corporate version of manifest destiny', (*PG,* p. 257) exemplifies the modern perversion of rational means for irrational ends. The law, Mack observes, 'is devoted to making the world safe for airlines, banks, and insurance companies' (*PG,* p. 19); legal skills are applied to cases he characterises as 'my robber baron's better than your robber baron' (*PG,* p. 201); and the ultimate inversion of reason and unreason comes when Trans National—among whose major assets is an airline—stands to profit, rather than lose money, by being legally bound to compensate the victims of an air disaster.

Mack's decision to abscond with this money is a further example of the self's 'lower' appetites and impulses shattering the veneer of professional restraint which constitutes the 'higher, better Mack' (*PG,* p. 386). But it is important to note that among these impulses is a kind of class-conscious anger which stirs in Mack a thirst for 'popular', even 'natural' justice, as opposed to the mystifications of the official legal system which can conjure multi-million dollar profits from corporate li-ability. Mack is from a blue-collar background, an outsider riven by working-class resentment for what he calls 'your corporate types' who, he claims, 'are soon going to be a stateless superclass, people who live for deals and golf dates and care a lot more about where you got your MBA than the country you were raised in' (p. 149). It is this resentment that prompts him not

simply to take the money but to 'pass out just deserts' (p. 319) by incriminating the corporate hierarchy and effectively destroying the relationship between his firm and Trans National. Moreover, Mack sees himself as a victim of the competitive system, a loser in the economic and sexual marketplace (his career is on the slide; his wife has left him for another woman), whose last resort is to turn that system's logic against itself. 'Why', he asks, are 'the people the market fucks over . . . supposed to let the tea party continue for everyone else'; and he rationalises his behaviour by asserting that 'I showed some initiative, entrepreneurship, self-reliance. I helped myself. Those are free market concepts too' (*PG,* p. 376).

Pleading Guilty therefore suggests that the forces of ir-rationality are historically incarnated in the structures of multinational capitalism, and that the ostensibly rational principles of the law are entirely annexed to those structures, operating simply to administer the socially unjust and unequal deserts of the market system. There is no ideal space, as there is in Grisham's more recent novels, beyond this institutionalised irrationality in which an ethical professionalism might flourish and serve the cause of reason and social justice. This is the lesson all Turow's protagonists learn. As first- or second-generation immigrants, they embrace the law as their means of assimilation, their ladder of social mobil-ity and Americanisation. But each has ultimately to decide whether being an American consists in unwaver-ing respect for, and service of, the law or the pursuit of happiness in spite of the law. The culture's elevation of self-gratification through the marketplace into a universal principle, and the subordination of the law to the marketplace's corporate imperatives, make any such choice impossible.

That these characters remain sympathetic even as they let their better selves lapse (in Grisham, this would be cause to demonise them as models of 'bad' professionalism) stems from Turow's view of the law and the codes of professionalism alike as rationalist fic-tions concealing the fundamental irrationality of human life. But the circumstances in which they surrender to impulse and appetite also suggest that the law and codes of professionalism are ideological fictions that legitimate corporate greed and class hegemony and serve social and economic injustice. A metaphysical perspective on the law co-exists here with a political grasp of its social and ideological biases. In this respect, Turow, like Gr-isham, registers and articulates a populist resentment of the law and of legal professionals. But, unlike Grisham, he does not seek to co-opt or defuse it by rendering it subservient in his narratives to a cleaned-up, ethical professionalism through which the social leadership of a class of affluent, upwardly mobile professionals and managers can be legitimated.

Notes

1. See Kermit L. Hall, *The Magic Mirror: Law in American History* (New York: Oxford University Press, 1989); Robert A. Ferguson, *Law and Letters in American Culture* (Cambridge, Mass.: Harvard University Press, 1984); David Ray Papke, 'Law in American Culture: An Overview', *Journal of American Culture,* vol. 15, no. 1 (Spring 1992), pp. 3-14; and Carl S. Smith, John P. McWilliams and Maxwell Bloomfield, *Law and American Literature: A Collection of Essays* (New York: Knopf, 1983). The Thomas Paine remark is taken from *Common Sense,* quoted in Papke, p. 4.

2. Alexis de Tocqueville, *Democracy in America,* Andrew Hacker (ed.), (New York: Washington Square Press, 1964), p. 106.

3. The tension between natural and social law has been a major theme in classic American literature, as Brook Thomas points out in his *Cross Examinations of Law and Literature: Cooper, Hawthorne, Stowe and Melville* (Cambridge: Cambridge University Press, 1987).

4. Max Weber established this connection between modernity and the rise of the bureaucratic professional: 'The more complicated and specialised modern culture becomes, the more its external supporting apparatus demands the personally detached and strictly "objective" expert.' Max Weber, 'Bureaucracy', in *From Max Weber: Essays in Sociology,* H. H. Gerth and C. Wright Mills (eds), (London: Routledge, 1991), p. 216. On the ethical and ideological contradictions of modern professionalism, see Bruce Robbins, *Secular Vocations: Intellectuals, Professionalism, Culture* (London: Verso, 1993). Pioneering work on the way in which formula fiction of many kinds (including crime fiction) serves as a vehicle for exploring and interrogating the increasingly important and complex nature of professionalism and the role of professionals in modern societies was done by John G. Cawelti, *Adventure, Mystery and Romance: Formula Stories as Art and Popular Culture* (Chicago: University of Chicago Press, 1976) and Will Wright, *Sixguns and Society: A Structural Study of the Western* (Berkeley: University of California Press, 1975).

5. *The Times,* 7 July, 1993.

6. Quoted in Hall, *The Magic Mirror,* p. 308.

7. Bayless Manning, 'Hyperlexis: Our National Disease', cited in Papke, 'Law in American Culture', p. 13.

8. Philip K. Howard, *The Death of Common Sense: How Law Is Suffocating America* (New York: Random House, 1995).

9. See Herman Schwartz, *Packing the Courts: The Conservative Campaign to Rewrite the Constitution* (New York: Scribners, 1988); Ronald Dworkin, 'The Reagan Revolution and the Supreme Court', *New York Review of Books,* 18 July 1991, pp. 23-8; and, on the controversy surrounding President Bush's nomination of Clarence Thomas to the Supreme Court, the volume edited by Toni Morrison, *Race-ing Justice, En-gendering Power: Essays on Anita Hill, Clarence Thomas and the Social Construction of Reality* (London: Chatto and Windus, 1993).

10. On the economic and political restructuring of American capitalism in the 1980s, see Mike Davis, *Prisoners of the American Dream: Politics and Economy in the History of the US Working Class* (London: Verso, 1986). For an illuminating account of the role played by the law in the construction of the modern American corporate political and economic order at the beginning of this century see Martin Sklar, *The Corporate Reconstruction of America 1890-1916: The Market, The Law and Politics* (Cambridge: Cambridge University Press, 1988).

11. John Grisham, *A Time to Kill* (London: Arrow, 1992), p. xi.

12. John Grisham, *The Firm* (London: Arrow, 1991), pp. 61, 100. Henceforth *TF,* page references to follow quotes.

13. On the centrality of notions of independence, occupational autonomy and dispassionate public service to codes of professionalism see Robbins, *Secular Vocations*; Terence J. Johnson, *Professions and Power* (London: Macmillan, 1972); John and Barbara Ehrenreich, 'The Professional-Managerial Class' in Pat Walker (ed.), *Between Labor and Capital* (Boston: South End Press, 1979), pp. 5-45; and Alvin Gouldner, *The Future of Intellectuals and the Rise of the New Class* (New York: Oxford University Press, 1979).

14. John Grisham, *The Pelican Brief* (London: Arrow, 1992), p. 223. Henceforth, *PB.*

15. John Grisham, *The Client* (London: Arrow, 1993), pp. 167, 275.

16. John Grisham, *The Chamber* (London: Arrow, 1994), pp. 38, 39.

17. Ibid., p. 151.

18. Grisham, *The Client,* p. 332.

19. *Guardian,* 30 May 1994.

20. For a theoretical account of the way narratives function to provide symbolic resolutions of real social contradictions, see Fredric Jameson, *The Political Unconscious: Narrative as a Socially Symbolic Act* (London: Methuen, 1980).

21. Weber, 'Bureaucracy', p. 216.

22. Scott Turow, *Pleading Guilty* (Harmondsworth, Middlesex: Viking, 1993), p. 118. Henceforth, *PG.*

23. Weber, 'Bureaucracy', p. 216.

24. Scott Turow, *Presumed Innocent* (Harmondsworth, Middlesex: Penguin, 1988), pp. 378. Henceforth, *PI.*

25. Scott Turow, *The Burden of Proof* (Harmondsworth, Middlesex: Penguin, 1991), pp. 227 and 581. Henceforth, *BP.*

FURTHER READING

Criticism

Brannon, Julie Sloan. "The Rules Are Different Here: South Florida Noir and the Grotesque." In *Crime Fiction and Film in the Sunshine State: Florida Noir,* edited by Steve Glassman and Maurice O'Sullivan, pp. 47-66. Bowling Green, Ohio: Bowling Green State University Popular Press, 1997.

> Examines representations of South Florida in the works of Charles Willeford and Carl Hiaasen.

Browne, Ray B. "The Questions of Justifiable Homicide." *Clues* 18, no. 1 (spring-summer 1997): 25-38.

> Reviews Thomas McCall's *A Wide and Capable Revenge* as a crime novel that focuses on the theme of personal revenge.

Calhoun-French, Diane M. "Of Love and Death: Murder and Mayhem Meet the Romance." *Clues* 21, no. 1 (spring-summer 2000): 1-18.

> Discusses the hybridization of the murder mystery and romance genres.

Chapman, G. Clarke. "Tony Hillerman's Fiction: Crime and Common Grace." *Christianity and Literature* 48, no. 4 (summer 1999): 473-86.

> Highlights some features of Hillerman's fiction, such as the combination of implicitly religious themes with crime fiction.

Finkle, David. "John Camp/John Sandford: The Award-Winning Journalist Mines His Experiences for Background to His Pseudonymous Novels." *Publishers Weekly* 237, no. 26 (29 June 1990): 83.

> Sandford discusses his experiences as a reporter, his hobbies and interests, and the success of his mystery novels.

Frumkes, Lewis Burke. "A Conversation with John Sandford." *Writer* 113, no. 9 (September 2000): 26.

> Sandford discusses his mystery novels and his experiences as a writer.

Hubbell, Gary. "All You Have Left in the End: Conclusions and the Series Character in Sue Grafton's 'Alphabet Series'." *Clues* 18, no. 1 (spring-summer 1997): 15-24.

> Examines the character of Kinsey Millhone, protagonist of Sue Grafton's "alphabet series."

Meier, Robert H. "Getting Away with Murder." *Armchair Detective* 21, no. 2 (spring 1988): 150-52.

> Review and summary of Scott Turow's *Presumed Innocent.*

Messent, Peter. "Patricia Cornwell's *Unnatural Exposure* and the Representation of Space: Changing Patterns in Crime Fiction." *Clues* 21, no. 2 (fall-winter 2000): 37-45.

> Examines Patricia Cornwell's *Unnatural Exposure* as an example of a modern crime fiction novel that incorporates changes imposed on the genre by modern, urban settings and new technology.

Priestman, Martin. *The Cambridge Companion to Crime Fiction.* Cambridge, England: Cambridge University Press, 2003, 287 p.

> Anthology of essays on crime fiction from the 1800s to the present.

Pyrhönen, Heta. *Mayhem and Murder: Narrative and Moral Problems in the Detective Story.* Toronto, Canada: University of Toronto Press, 1999, 338 p.

> Collection of essays focusing on major crime authors of the twentieth century.

Wesley, Marilyn C. "Power and Knowledge in Walter Mosley's *Devil in a Blue Dress.*" *African American Review* 35, no. 1 (spring 2001): 110-16.

> Reviews *Devil in a Blue Dress* in the context of violence as it is explored in contemporary fiction by male authors.

Yarbrough, Trisha. "The Cultural Work of Regional Mysteries." *Clues* 22, no. 1 (spring-summer 2001): 13-20.

> Reviews characteristics of regional mysteries, focusing on works set in Oklahoma.

Denis Donoghue
1928-

Irish critic, essayist, editor, biographer, and memoirist.

The following entry presents an overview of Donoghue's career through 2004.

INTRODUCTION

Donoghue is a widely respected scholar of contemporary British and American literature. In contrast to current trends in post-modernist and post-structuralist critical theory, Donoghue stands out as a champion of Modernist literature and criticism. Advocating the revival of interest in such Modernist poets as T. S. Eliot, W. B. Yeats, and others, Donoghue passionately upholds the values of humanism, the imagination, and religious belief in literature. Rooted in the New Criticism of the early twentieth century, Donoghue advocates close readings of literary texts with special attention to aesthetics, as opposed to the interpretation of texts as constructions reflecting social and political ideologies.

BIOGRAPHICAL INFORMATION

Donoghue was born December 1, 1928, into a Catholic family in Tullow, Ireland. He grew up in the seaside town of Warrenpoint in Northern Ireland, where his father worked as a police sergeant. Donoghue attended the National University of Ireland, from which he earned a B.A. in 1950, an M.A. in 1953, and a Ph.D. in 1956. In 1951 he married Frances P. Rutledge, with whom he has eight children. Donoghue has worked as a scholar, lecturer, and professor at the National University of Ireland and University College, both in Dublin, and Cambridge University in Cambridge, England. Since 1979, he has held the post of Henry James Professor of Letters at New York University. His memoir, *Warrenpoint* (1990), recounts his experiences growing up in a Catholic family in Northern Ireland, with particular focus on his loving relationship with his father.

MAJOR WORKS

Donoghue has written and edited some twenty-five books of literary criticism and literary biography. Many of his books are collections of previously published essays and reviews, as well as the texts of lectures and radio broadcasts. In *Ferocious Alphabets* (1981), Donoghue offers perspective on the ongoing "ideological strife among modern critics." He provides a critique of critical theory through seventeen short essays on such poets as Gerard Manley Hopkins, Stephane Mallarmé, and T. S. Eliot, as well as such critics as Harold Bloom, Paul De Man, and Jacques Derrida. *The Arts without Mystery* (1983) is a compilation of essays based on six lectures broadcast over BBC Radio in 1982, in which Donoghue argues for the importance of a sense of mystery and sacredness in art and literature. *We Irish* (1986) comprises essays on Irish literature and culture, with particular focus on Yeats and James Joyce. *Reading America* (1987), essays on American literature and the American imagination, is divided into two sections, the first containing lengthy commentaries and the second containing seventeen short book reviews. *Being Modern Together* (1991) is a collection of essays on literature and theory in which Donoghue puts forth his defense of the Modernist aesthetic. In *Walter Pater* (1995), a critical biography, Donoghue argues that nineteenth-century critic and essayist Pater was a key precursor to Modernism and that his ideas exerted a crucial influence on such Modernist writers as Joyce and Eliot. Donoghue thus sets out to demonstrate that Pater's influence prevails as "a shade or trace in virtually every writer of significance from Hopkins to Wilde to Ashbery." In the fifteen essays of *The Practice of Reading* (1998), Donoghue argues for the close reading of literary texts with special attention to aesthetics and criticizes current trends in critical theory that focus on the sociological and political nature of literature. In *Words Alone* (2000), Donoghue offers a critical assessment of the poetry of Eliot through a personal account of the role of Eliot's poetry in his own intellectual development as a young man. Donoghue emphasizes the importance in Eliot's poetry of both a sense of the musicality of language and the expression of deeply held Christian faith. The seven lectures included in *Adam's Curse* (2001), with such titles as "God without Thunder," "Beyond Belief," and "The Death of Satan," address the theme of literature and religious faith. In *Speaking of Beauty* (2003), Donoghue explores the concept of beauty through an examination of critical, literary, and cultural texts that attempt to define beauty.

CRITICAL RECEPTION

Donoghue is among the most highly respected scholars of British and American literature. As Timothy Peltason, in a review of *The Practice of Reading*, observed,

"Donoghue is on the short list of critics from whom one always expects intelligent guidance of a high order about particular works of literature." Critics admire Donoghue's erudition in situating his arguments within a broad context of literary history and scholarship and his body of criticism advocating a return to Modernist aesthetics is regarded as an important intervention in the prevailing discourse of poststructuralist literary theory. He has been applauded for his fresh, insightful readings of the works of such Modernist poets as Eliot, Yeats, and others. Margaret O'Brien, in a review of *We Irish,* noted, "Donoghue's special skill is . . . the individualistic and humanistic one of acute perception rendered in lucid, supple prose." Donoghue has sometimes been criticized for lacking a central focus or strongly stated, well-developed line of argument in his essays. Some reviewers have also noted that his erudition tends to result in lengthy digressions and numerous citations that distract from his central ideas and defuse the impact of his arguments.

PRINCIPAL WORKS

The Third Voice: Modern British and American Verse Drama (criticism) 1959

Connoisseurs of Chaos: Ideas of Order in Modern American Poetry (criticism) 1965

An Honoured Guest: New Essays on W. B. Yeats [editor; with J. R. Mulryne] (essays) 1965

The Ordinary Universe: Soundings in Modern Literature (criticism) 1968

Swift Revisited [editor] (lectures) 1968

Jonathan Swift: A Critical Introduction (criticism) 1969

William Butler Yeats (criticism) 1971

Memoirs: W. B. Yeats [editor] (autobiography) 1972

Thieves of Fire (criticism) 1974

Seven American Poets from MacLeish to Nemerov: An Introduction [editor] (essays) 1975

The Sovereign Ghost: Studies in Imagination (criticism) 1976

Ferocious Alphabets (criticism) 1981

The Arts without Mystery (essays) 1983

Selected Essays of R. P. Blackmur [editor] (essays) 1986

We Irish: Essays on Irish Literature and Society (essays) 1986

Reading America: Essays on American Literature (essays) 1987

America in Theory [editor; with Leslie Berlowitz and Louis Menand] (essays) 1988

Warrenpoint (memoir) 1990

Being Modern Together (criticism) 1991

The Pure Good of Theory: The Bucknell Lectures in Literary Theory (lectures) 1992

The Old Moderns: Essays on Literature and Theory (essays) 1994

Walter Pater: Lover of Strange Souls (biography) 1995

The Practice of Reading (criticism) 1998

Words Alone: The Poet, T. S. Eliot (criticism) 2000

Adam's Curse: Reflections on Religion and Literature (essays) 2001

Speaking of Beauty (criticism) 2003

CRITICISM

Laurence Lieberman (review date spring 1966)

SOURCE: Lieberman, Laurence. "Wisdom and Wilderness." *Hudson Review* 19, no. 1 (spring 1966): 156-60.

[*In the following review of* Connoisseurs of Chaos, *Lieberman applauds Donoghue's focus on the "humanness" of poetry.*]

> Wisdom and wilderness are here at poise,
> Ocean and forest are the mind's device
> But still I feel the presence of thy will.
>
> —Yvor Winters (on Melville)

I have often felt (and who hasn't?) that modern American poetry needs the severest taskmaster it can find. For many poets, the staunch exemplar of discipline today is Mr. Yvor Winters. As much as any teacher of poets, perhaps more than any other, he has taken a hand in the shaping of today's craftsmen in verse. His influence has made its way into the contemporary British ear principally through the poems of Thom Gunn, a onetime pupil. I recall with pleasure Gunn's affectionate poem in *The Sense of Movement* likening Mr. Winters to the stern keeper of a dog kennel. I should guess that every poet who has worked with him has been shaken into a tougher grip on the tools of his craft.

In his books of criticism, Mr. Winters often presented an unpopularly harsh view of poets in vogue, and he grew to be regarded by many as a sort of literary curmudgeon of his age. The following categorical remarks in a new book on modern American poetry [*Connoisseurs of Chaos*] seems to echo the voice of Yvor Winters:

(1) Stevens, who ceased to believe in the God of Christianity and found that there was nothing left to believe, filled the void with his own inventions.

(2) Robert Frost discovered at an early age that he had an engaging personality. The discovery was unfortunate . . .

(3) He [Frost] is happy enough that the mind should be there, but he takes care never to extend it or put it under strain.

(4) Love was clearly a principle of order in Roethke's poems, but it never established itself as a relation beyond the bedroom.

(5) But when we read Whitman with our own scruples—such as they are—we often feel that a more scrupulous poet would have made more of what was there . . . he scants the verifiable past, and the loss to his own poetry is grievous.

(6) Robinson at an early age came to know certain things, and he thought that there was nothing else to know.

(7) Emily Dickinson carried very little theological freight. . . . She moved very lightly in matters of religion. It is unlikely that she had what Yeats called 'a talent for conviction.'

The critic laments Whitman's neglect of history, Stevens's preference for aesthetics over Christianity, Dickinson's laxity—and even deliberate heresy—in her approach to the Puritan tradition, Robinson's indifference to "Eliot's revolutionary poems," Frost's lack of intellectual rigor and his failure to rise above "the middle style," and Roethke's scarcity of human protagonists. He seems perplexed that so much great poetry could have been nourished in a wilderness. It would seem that in the wilderness of American tradition, he often cannot see the trees for the woods.

Denis Donoghue is an Irishman who brings to his studies in American poetry a rare set of qualifications. He has written an excellent book on modern British and American verse drama and a collection of critical essays on Yeats. It is not surprising that such a man would make uncompromising demands of the modern poets. Moreover, there is another factor that very likely carries much weight in accounting for his stern expectations from poetry. In an article on Hannah Arendt published in a special British Number of *Poetry* (May, 1962), Mr. Donoghue reveals his *Weltschmerz* in regard to contemporary poets:

> . . . while reading Hannah Arendt I had the disturbing impression that she had far more to say—more of humane relevance—than any ten contemporary poets. In comparison with her mind most of the literary minds on current exhibition seemed thin, slack, frivolous. This impression came more in sorrow and dismay than in anger.

At another point in the article, it becomes apparent that his sorrow is not so much a matter of his disillusionment with poets, or poetry; rather, he has suffered a crushing blow to his faith in the imagination:

> . . . there are facts, situations, events with which the human imagination cannot cope. I had always assumed that the imagination was good enough for anything, and I had been delighted by Stevens's picture of reality and the imagination in dynamic poise, the violence within *grappling with* [italics mine—L. L.] that other violence which is its occasion, its challenge. . . . But Hannah Arendt is right; the human imagination is dazed by the reality of the concentration camps: it staggers, doubts its own evidence, lurches in torpor or hysteria. It cannot disclose the real.

In *Connoisseurs of Chaos,* Mr. Donoghue returns again and again to the favorite recipe from Wallace Stevens noticed above, but with a difference. As we can see, the two violences in Stevens are reality and the imagination. In the new collection of essays, reality and the imagination usually have an altered relation. Instead of "grappling with" each other, imagination is seen to be "holding," "pressing back against," or "defending against" reality. Mr. Donoghue continues to have affection for the concept, and to find it useful, but he applies it with less conviction.

The altered phraseology implies the view that poetry in our time retreats from the terrible facts of our lives. Imagination becomes a way *out,* not a way *in.* Poetry, ideally a way of embracing even the most painful reality, becomes a protection, a form of escape. For Donoghue, this abuse of poetry reaches a ghastly limit in poems by Stevens and Frost which touch on the subject of war. Frost is guilty of "complacency," and Stevens pushes his handsome theory "to the strange conclusion that the mind's defense against the terror might well be successful—even in the case of war."

Mr. Donoghue gives a very high estimate of the achievement of each of the poets dealt with at length in this book, and he demonstrates an evident grasp of their uncommon beauties. The samples of criticism presented early in my discussion were the severest examples I could find, extreme random statements pointing to Mr. Donoghue's strongest reservation about each poet, finally. I think the hidden source of all of these negative statements is his longing for a completely humane poetry, as revealed in the essay on Hannah Arendt ("if they [contemporary poets] have any contribution to make to human survival then please hurry up"). Though I must take exception with some of his specific complaints, I think he is chiefly right in his feeling that there is a serious gap between the concerns of our best poets and the most important experiences of our time, and this is a major source of strength in his criticism. Further, when Donoghue insists that poems must not be content to remain "essays in self-indulgence," but must grapple with the terrors of the concentration camps, it is his faith in poetry that is speaking, not his disillusionment.

Nearly every poet in the collection is viewed, at one point or another, as an instance of Stevens's idea that all art is a fortress that the imagination constructs to fend off the chaos of experience, or in Winters's phrase, wisdom is matched against the wilderness. For much of the book, Donoghue, in his affection for the art of poetry, seems to become satisfied, and to forget our deepest trouble. In the introduction to the book, he even takes refuge (and we join him!) in poetry's escape-hatch: "Literature helps us to live our lives, by offering us instances of the productive imagination at work." But in the essay on Hannah Arendt, Mr. Donoghue is unwilling to settle for any indirect or second-hand solution to the disease of modern man's spirit. The imagination must cope directly with the most terrible facts.

Perhaps it must draw the "violence without" into itself and transform it into a quantity that the mind of man can apprehend, or perhaps it must fortify the mind to a degree of toughness that can withstand that violence (those facts) without turning away from it in defeat.

I think there are at least two modern poems in English that achieve this for a reader, Yeats's "The Second Coming" and Frost's "The Most of It." Though it may well be that Frost is guilty of complacency about war in other poems, he is certainly guiltless in this one. It is true that the poems refract the terrible facts of experience through symbols, the "rough beast" in the one, and the "great buck" in the other. But in both the refraction takes place without loss of intensity. The raw facts *are* disclosed. Direct references in art to the bomb, to Auschwitz, always seem to call up the sort of numb disbelief that we have come to adopt as a protection against terror. In the poems by Frost and Yeats, the symbol surprises us into the terror of the inhumane in all its original force, reminding us that we have suppressed the humane impulse to indignation that atrocity should always arouse. For me, as a reader, these poems achieve this effect more powerfully than do the writings of Hannah Arendt.

I have pursued these considerations at such length because I feel they are central to the author's point of view in all of his recent essays. It is precisely his struggle to plumb the depths of each poet's capacity for humaneness that makes *Connoisseurs of Chaos* an enormously valuable book.

But I must quarrel with a couple of Mr. Donoghue's critical methods. While he chides the best American poets for ignoring the mainstays of poetry in the Anglo-American tradition—the Past, Christianity, earnest commitment to ideas, humane social awareness—he overpraises poets like Frederick Goddard Tuckerman and Herman Melville for undermining the "sentimental" traditions of the Nineteenth Century from within.

Tuckerman was a connoisseur of silence in an age of noise. He created a quiet splendor out of his refusal to sound the trumpet of metaphor, analogy, correspondence. Theoretically, he might have followed Whitman's lead, making a clean break with the genteel tradition. But he was not fitted by temperament to enter a new world expanding without limit. Instead, he settled for less and less, remaining within that tradition and rejecting most of its favorite tools with a deepening honesty and sorrow. And towards the end of his life, he made better and better poetry out of less and less, identifying finally with the cricket in his greatest poem—"each a fretful, noisy being, speaking to deaf ears." (The quotation is from Mr. Donoghue.)

Tuckerman was ignored for several generations. Only recently has his work begun to elicit the attention and interest it deserves. Like many a late literary find, his importance will be exaggerated by at least one generation of scholars. In the end, we will probably have to look to Mr. Yvor Winters for a balanced judgment of Tuckerman's work. Mr. Winters, in his quiet way, has been introducing Tuckerman's poetry to his students at Stanford for many years. He has tested his growing awareness and appreciation of Tuckerman's achievement in the classroom, while most of his colleagues seemed but remotely aware that Tuckerman had ever lived. Now Mr. Donoghue has done the best job to date (to my knowledge) of defining Tuckerman's place in the tradition. It becomes doubly clear why Tuckerman did not win an audience for his work. He could not hope to earn the admiration of the audience for the old guard of the genteel tradition (Emerson, Longfellow, etc.), since he repudiated the "entire myth of correspondence" that engaged their interest. Nor could he share the new audience that had become intoxicated with Whitman's vast inclusiveness. Since he had no public life as an artist, he would become more and more arrested by the virtues of private life, and he would achieve art from a keenly honest examination of the condition of loneliness. I have taken some liberties in interpreting Mr. Donoghue's text, connecting a few circuits where he had installed loose wiring of implication. Certainly, he has helped me to see Mr. Tuckerman's position in American letters better than I had ever seen it before. But it is evident that the claim he makes for Tuckerman is too high.

He assesses this poet's value largely in an aesthetic vacuum. He lifts the exacting strictures that he apparently reserves for poets of the first rank (Whitman, Dickinson, Frost, Stevens, Roethke). He does not examine the texture or language of the poetry. There is less tendency to compare this poet with others, to classify, to rank—to fit him into a sort of hierarchy of saints. Mr. Donoghue is more willing to inspect Tuckerman's talents exclusively in their own backyard, so to speak. If one considers this essay alone, one appreciates the justice of it, the judicious fairness to a poet who has been so underrated, rather overlooked, for so many years. But as a part of the collection of articles, one is struck by a certain disproportion: Tuckerman is the only American poet considered at some length whose genius is not subjected to severe qualifications of one kind or another.

The sort of contradiction that becomes apparent here is, in a way, central to the collection of essays, and perhaps to modern criticism, in general. There is a certain impish pleasure in taking pot shots at authors of established reputation—the snow ball aimed at the top hat—and a commensurate pleasure in disclosing the hidden virtues of consistently underrated authors. The clearest evidence of this tendency in *Connoisseurs of Chaos* is a contradiction in the opening pages of the essay on Melville's poetry. The essay begins:

It is the common understanding that Melville was a great poet only in his prose. I have no wish to disturb that view. . . .

Three pages later, he is capable of the following:

. . . he (Melville) wrote hundreds of poor poems and about fifteen poems of the first order that give him a place in American poetry beside Whitman and Emily Dickinson.

Melville's best poems are so very superior to the rest of his work, they seem better than they are. Comparative ranking, whether of poets or of poems by a single poet, often falls into this trap.

Robert Martin Adams (review date autumn 1970)

SOURCE: Adams, Robert Martin. "The State of the Dean." *Hudson Review* 23, no. 3 (autumn 1970): 578-84.

[*In the following review, Adams comments that Donoghue's* Jonathan Swift *offers a fresh, insightful perspective.*]

What good is the apparatus of humanistic scholarship, where in the world does it get us? Editions pile up on editions, monographs and studies and biographies and bibliographies and autographs and holographs and variants and influences and parallels and backgrounds and foregrounds and patterns and insights and outlooks and interpretations, interpretations, interpretations—and footnotes! the very thought of the footnotes sets our head swimming through a milky way of six-point superscripts, *cf.*'s and *op. cit*'s. Through which we peer myopically at the shimmering distant outline of the man who stirred up all this fuss by once writing something. The recent bibliography of scholarship concerning Jonathan Swift is a case in point. He was a public figure and the subject of intense interest, commentary, and gossip for the last forty years of his life; there has never been a period since when he was not being scrutinized, analyzed, criticized. Yet in the last twenty years alone, it seems likely that the total volume of things written about him has at least quadrupled. And not only things written about him—things written *by* him. A scholar resident in Australia or Manitoba can know more about him today than any of his most intimate contemporaries could conceivably have known. Any good research library has, for instance, the full text of his private diaries, all his correspondence, all his widely scattered poetry, all his fugitive papers, all his private annotations on various books, a full and careful listing of everything he did and didn't write. Hardly any of his major prose has not been the subject of at least one full-length study, and the commentary on some of them (not always the

most interesting) is at least a hundred times more voluminous than the original text. The quantity of critical discussion involving this detail of his writing, or that, is absolutely overwhelming; a man could read in the published Swift-literature from year's end to year's end without coming in sight of the end of it, and probably without advancing himself appreciably toward a coherent view of Swift's mind and art. Perhaps, if he had a coherent view of Swift's mind and art to start with, he might get out of his reading some evidence to support or modify it—but only at the cost of working his way through an enormous amount of irrelevant and extraneous material, overlapping and blurring patterns, interpretive muddle. He would have to fight every inch of the way. Synthesizing the many particular things we now know about Swift, without watering them down to obtuse or flatulent platitudes is clearly a major problem, and so far the synthesizing books haven't handled it at all well.

Interpretive problems advance upon us in heavy armor as we venture into Mr. John Clark's lamentably-titled volume on *A Tale of a Tub*;[1] and, as it represents a critical *Iliad* in a labyrinthine nutshell, perhaps we'd better concentrate on its first chapter. Mr. Clark is here concerned with interpreting two paragraphs in Section IX of the *Tale* (the "Digression on Madness"), those in which the subtle knaves who look beneath the surface of things are contrasted with the superficial idiots who remain complacently content with surface appearances. Four possibilities occur among the conceivable arrangements of value in this scene; either the reader is supposed to see the superficial approach as preferable to the subtle; or the subtle as preferable to the superficial; or both alternatives as equally undesirable, *tout court*; or both alternatives as undesirable, but with an implication that some third alternative is more desirable than either. The problem is one of evidence. It is confused by the fact that Swift in this passage is speaking through the mask of a "Hack" who is both superficial and subtle—that is, he pretends to be unspeakably profound and is actually appallingly obvious. So the question is, how and where does Swift propound the "third alternative" that Mr. Clark finds in the passage? When we read Mr. Clark, we are by no means at a loss to define this third alternative: it is an option in which the sane mind "elects to pass its life in adherence to the 'common forms' which compose 'the pattern of human learning'— the vast accumulation of value and experience that distinguishes the historical sense, and, indeed, that renders any sort of civilization possible" (p. 17). Now the quoted sections of this passage are in fact part of the two paragraphs that Mr. Clark is trying to explain: they are part of the description of the superficial man, who adheres to the common forms. In other words, the "third alternative" which Swift is said to recommend and represent is indistinguishable from one of the two alternatives that he is said to reject—except for the addition of numerous honorific extrapolations on the part of the critic. Let any doubtful reader inspect the original passage in the *Tale* for himself, and see if he can find a "third alternative" expressed. Perhaps Swift meant it to be inferred, or thought it so obvious that a reader would supply it for himself; quite certainly he did not mean to recommend "seriously" either superficiality (which he thought superficial) or deep learning (which he thought pretentious and fraudulent). The point is that he didn't *represent* this middle view or third alternative at all, the view that Mr. Clark, like all the conventionally-minded critical moralists, thinks he ought to have represented, must have represented, and therefore—somehow—did represent. It isn't there, just as the intelligent, moderate *via media* which Martin is supposed to represent in the *Tale* proper, by contrast with the assorted knaveries of Jack and Peter, doesn't really get dramatized, or incarnated, or—in fact—represented. I'm not questioning that Swift, as the mind controlling for its own ends the *Tale of a Tub,* believed in the values of the Church of England, and intended to celebrate them; it's just that his special way of celebrating them was to assail satirically Rome and Geneva, with such vehemence that some people felt he was effectually assailing Christianity itself. They were doubtless wrong; but they were not wrong at all in feeling that this author and this book offered less positive affirmation than they were used to. And Mr. Clark is not right (as the present reader judges the matter) in puffing up a middle-of-the-road position to be attributed to Swift as a positive affirmation—when in fact the text yields little or nothing of the sort.

Mr. Clark goes on to say not only that Swift in Section IX of the *Tale* endorses a mean between reason and passion (I think he would be embarrassed to say just where Jonathan Swift signed on *that* dotted line), but that this mean represents a higher social and ethical value which numerous critics (fifteen are cited on p. 8 alone) were somehow unable to perceive. "At their very heart, the credulous and curious man function alike—dependent upon a basic subjectivism and selfishness that spreads both in the mind and the state like a stain. . . . Credulous and curious man alike are ignorant: what they ignore is precisely that social and moral sense of responsibility to something outside themselves embodied in the more classic view of man" (p. 33). I don't think this construction will stand up long enough for a second look. To be sure, superficiality and pretension to "deep" learning are both "modern" failings, and so to be contrasted with the authenticity of the ancients; and if the passage made that connection, we should not find the slightest difficulty in it. But it doesn't. The classic virtues may be virtues, as true Christianity is indeed an authentic solution to the problems of eighteenth-century England; but they are so remote, so impractical, so incompatible with present schemes of wealth, power, and value, as not even to enter the picture.

I've thought it worth while to hack out the interpretive details of a passage like this only because it illustrates how Mr. Clark has allowed scholarship and commentary to encroach upon, and almost suffocate, his text. Swift's passage says nothing whatever about the "social and moral sense of responsibility to something outside themselves embodied in the more classic view of man." As a matter of fact, Swift would have dropped dead of thundering apoplexy before permitting himself to pen a phrase like that. But the critic extracts it from some other parts of the book, ekes it out with conventional wisdom, and applies it here, in this particularly cotton-wool form, to interpret a tough passage into a suitable soft one. Or again, he reminds us in a long excursus that the Theophrastian character-collections often included portraits of a credulous and a curious man, drawing from this fact the implication that these characters are related to one another in the *Tale* in the same way and to the same effect as they were in the Theophrastian tradition. But of course they clearly aren't; Swift uses them in a specially taut and working way which entices the reader into thinking he's siding with sanity and good sound sense (as against eccentric, esoteric subtlety), and then pulls the rug out from under him by equating this sound sense with stupidity. The critic's erudition in secondary sources and peripheral materials has been used to obscure his text.

It wouldn't be fair to say or imply that this obfuscation is altogether characteristic of Mr. Clark's procedures; his second chapter works much closer to the text, and in effect endorses a view of the book which his first chapter denied, i.e., that the *Tale*'s characteristic action is an inconclusive struggle between opposed absurdities, a foolish flight followed by a ridiculous fall, inflation and collapse. And increasingly, as he gets away from the scholarship, the analogues, and the background materials, Mr. Clark is able to see the work itself more clearly. There is, perhaps, a little more fancy terminology, a little more agon, persona, mimesis, and peripety than will be to everyone's taste. But our critic has many bright and useful things to say about the operation of Swift's glittering, edged machinery. Writing about only a single book, as he has undertaken to do, and digging himself deep into the secondary literature that has overgrown it, Mr. Clark has perhaps allowed himself too little access to some of Swift's short-range targets. Locke, Toland, Tindal, and the participants in the "Socinian" controversy have a relevance to Swift's satire that one would never guess from reading Mr. Clark's analysis; and Swift's very peculiar standing in the ancients-versus-moderns quarrel (knowing little or no Greek, he was engaged in defending the ancients from the supreme classical scholar of his day) could have been used to point up more sharply certain distinctive qualities and commitments of his mind. Mr. Clark, like most of his authorities, is more concerned to put the book in a philosophical milieu than a polemical one;

perhaps this is why he gives us, in the end, a more middle-of-the-road Swift, writing a less angled and nasty book, than some of us feel entitled to.

Denis Donoghue's new introductory study [*Jonathan Swift*][2] is of a precisely contrary disposition; it is one of those "fresh looks" at an author which are achieved by reading a relatively few critics in balance with, or even in opposition to, the basic texts, and assessing the character of one's author's mind decisively and anew. I don't suppose anyone can read Mr. Donoghue's rapid, rippling first chapter without a striking sense of renewal and rediscovery. It isn't precisely that he contradicts positions taken by Mr. Clark, for he expressly concedes that the *Tale* is one of the works in which ironic use of a mask-figure predominates. Yet he begins with the blunt and practical assumption that Swift doesn't have a very elaborate or interesting philosophical position— that his mind (in terms of belief) is limited, practical, literal, and quite short-range. His account of the *Tale* is built much less on "what it says" than on the verbal pattern of saying it—and I think this approach gets us much closer much quicker to the ways in which the book is distinctive. The play that the *Tale* makes with the very form of a book, the way in which its speech slithers into and out of the mouth of a conscious spokesman (inconsistently!), its knack for making us sense the disintegrative and dissociative power of wit—all these are deftly caught; while at the same time this gift for appreciating Swiftian irony is finely balanced against a sense that Swift frequently is not an ironic, not a satiric author at all. He was in fact (though Mr. Donoghue doesn't put it exactly this way) untouched by romantic expectations, and didn't think that a widened field of consciousness or a subtle balance of ironic equivocations was necessarily a Good Thing in itself. When he praises limitation = stupidity, he isn't necessarily kidding.

Mr. Donoghue's style being agile, informed, and contemporary, he handles Swift's mind like an Amsterdam jeweler displaying a gem—turning it over and over, putting it under different lights, pointing to its characteristic fires, patterns, colors, and flaws. When he talks of Swift's passion for negation, or the way in which he manages the concept of *getting rid of things,* a reader who knows the texts will be refreshed by the way in which a lot of disparate observations fall into a clear pattern, a lucid model. Summary criticism can do this; it tells you enough about the author so you can key in on him and find out a lot more on your own. And Mr. Donoghue is a marvel at this sort of work.

Occasionally, I confess, his argument seems to get a little loose in the weave. This happens mostly when he's applying someone else's insights to his own readings of the texts. Just as an instance, it may be true, as Marshall McLuhan has said, that until late in the seventeenth-century a point of view in prose was impossible. Mr. Donoghue not only accepts this dictum, he builds on it, to the effect that Swift's prudence in advancing from one point of view to another, comparing as he goes, is somehow related to the fixity of the printed word. Well, now. I think if we're going to have arguments like this at all, they have to be made more thoroughly. Is there anyone in the vicinity who *doesn't* advance prudently from one point of view to another? Let's say Sterne, just for the sake of argument. (A grumbling little voice in the back of my mind keeps saying why, why, why doesn't Apuleius or St. Augustine or Montaigne make use of a point of view in prose? but we'll crush it down.) At any rate, if Sterne is somehow unlike Swift in this respect, is it because of a different attitude toward the fixity of the printed word? Wasn't the printed word just as fixed for Sterne as for Swift? Was there anybody around who didn't write for printers, against whom the generalizations could be checked? (Maybe Thomas Traherne, whose writings didn't undergo Gutenberg's contraption till the twentieth century.) To be perfectly plain, I'm not saying the argument is specious or the observation about Swift wrong; just that, to be convincing, the discussion needs filling out. It is, of course, clearly labelled a speculation. But if we're speculating, I'd just as soon speculate that the history of the seventeenth century (the rise of nonconformity, Erastianism, and free-thinking, the incorporation of them into an alliance under the name of Whiggery) was more responsible than movable type for Swift's special cold *méfiance.* You couldn't very well be an Anglican clergyman after 1688 without a suspicion that in the new society the Lord's prayer could be converted into a club to beat you, and the beatitudes into a social engine to dispossess you, at a moment's notice. The rising tide of purse-proud bourgeois with their stockjobber's jargon and commercial morality, their sectarian cant and restless, projecting spirit, drove Swift back on an empty, arrogant ecclesiasticism from which he maneuvered, not so much cautiously as desperately, and within a very short range indeed (as Mr. Donoghue observes). There was a great scene in the old movie *Beau Geste* that reminds me a bit of Swift's strategy of desperation; it occurred when the last surviving defenders of Fort Zinfandel propped up their dead comrades in the embrasures to give the impression of a full garrison, and then rushed from corpse to corpse, firing over the shoulder now of one and now of another.

So there are details in Mr. Donoghue's book, as in anyone's, where the impulse makes itself felt to stop and carp; but there are plenty of other passages where a quick phrase, a sudden gesture of compression, makes one want to stop and applaud. When he points out, almost in passing, how precious for Swift is the distance between subject and object, he is brilliantly right; and his book is studded with insights that put Swift in sharp profile. Socially, psychologically, linguistically, stylistically, he emphasizes the hard, clear, limited quality of Swift's mind. Perhaps the best thing one can say about Mr. Donoghue's little book is that a student who has read and understood it will be equipped to plunge into the ever-flowing stream of "the literature" and make some sense out of it. There aren't many books about Jonathan Swift of which one could say as much.

Matthew Hodgart's little April-fool joke, based on the Cornell student riots of 1969, takes the form of a return voyage by Gulliver to the land of the Houyhnhnms, in the course of which the captain discovers a new state of liberal horses and revolting Yahoos.[3] Mr. Hodgart has, in other words, used Swift's Houyhnhnms as stalking-horses for his own view of the American student movement. It's a remarkably dim view, though surely not as dim as Jonathan Swift's would have been. Professor Hodgart's low estimate of the new campus styles won't come as much of a surprise to guilty faculty liberals, who are always eager for someone to spank them with a good stiff hairbrush, but it may startle a few of the sweet kids whose radical innocence is proof against the very suspicion that a noble savage can look, in certain eyes, like a dirty ape. One wonders how much of this pseudo-innocence is due to the assumption, happily fostered by the "social sciences," that life consists of a set of "problems" which can be quickly and permanently solved without knowing any history. Formulas as trite as "love," "freedom," or "justice"—the moral categories—apparently entitle one to ignore both the tangled roots of the past and one's own hideous intent. But there's so little else for a self-respecting person to be these days, except reactionary, that I forbear developing the argument. Mr. Hodgart's little booklet is, I think, weakened as an entertainment by the circumstance that his horses are as vicious as his apes. This gives Gulliver a somewhat righteous tone which Swift was able to avoid. There's also a flavor of the arch about his quotation-games which falls short of our sense that, in Swift at any rate, serious stakes were being played for. But he has followed Swift's own example in shooting at any target that moves and in disdaining no joke, however low, that presents itself. As an antediluvian Cornellian myself, I think I recognize (under allusive pseudonyms) several of the victims of Mr. Hodgart's poisoned arrows, though wild horses—or, for that matter, wild Yahoos—wouldn't get me to talk about them in public. Scholarship, literary scholarship, however, is a different matter; an annotated edition of the Fifth Book of *Gulliver* may not be as far off as we think, and it wouldn't be hard to fill in certain blanks at that time. On the other hand, the self-esteem of a lot of people is involved; no doubt they all have their ways of reading the new fable, so that they look good and the others bad. If Mr. Hodgart doesn't want his little joke to be festooned with false interpretations, esoteric allusions, and "background" studies of dubious relevance, he'd

better deposit an annotated copy of his own in the British Museum, with a notarized affidavit in sextuplicate, and a triple whammy on the wretched scholar who presumes to go against his intent.

Notes

1. *Form and Frenzy in Swift's Tale of a Tub,* by John R. Clark, Cornell University Press.

2. *Jonathan Swift: A Critical Introduction,* by Denis Donoghue, Cambridge University Press.

3. *A New Voyage to the Country of the Houyhnhnms, being the Fifth Part of the Travels into Several Remote Parts of the World by Lemuel Gulliver,* edited from an unpublished manuscript by Matthew Hodgart, M. A. Putnam's.

Howard Nemerov (review date January-March 1975)

SOURCE: Nemerov, Howard. "Figures of Thought." *Sewanee Review* 83, no. 1 (January-March 1975): 161-71.

[*In the following review, Nemerov compares Donoghue's* Thieves of Fire *to Harold Bloom's* The Anxiety of Influence.]

Thought is the strangest game of all. The players are the Nominalists vs. the Realists. Realists wear colorless jerseys and are numbered One, Many, and All. Nominalists wear crazy quilts instead of uniforms, and their numerals tend to be such things as the square root of minus one. This figure conceals two important circumstances: that there are not in truth Nominalists and Realists, but only the nominalism and realism of each player, who happens to be alone on the field where he plays himself; and that by the tacit pregame move of dividing into Nominalist and Realist he has made it impossible to win or even finish the game, although—and it is not a little—he has made it possible to play.

Thought proceeds to create the world by dividing it—what? the world, of course—into opposites, as in the initial Yin and Yang of the *Tao Te Ching,* the series of divisions in the first chapter of *Genesis,* the Love and Strife that Yeats took from Empedocles to be the base for the sequent complications of *A Vision,* and so on. Once there are the opposites, a mere two tricks make game. The first is that the opposites will have to bear on one and the other hand the whole weight of the much and many of the world as experienced: every leaf and every star must join one team or the other. The second is that, since a world of opposites is impossible, intolerable, the opposites must be mediated and shown to be one; because, of course, in the world as experienced they *are* one. That was where we began.

A productive model for the enterprise is map-making. Projecting a spherical world on a plane surface involves the cartographer in several distortions for every accuracy, beginning with the creative and mythological decree that there shall be two opposites named East and West; not quite truth, not quite fiction, this prevents any absolute or metaphysical arrivals, or even destinations; on the other hand, it makes—nor is this a little— navigation possible.

The opposites at first embody themselves in stories. How stories got started is as unknown and likely to remain so as how language did (they got together and talked it over among themselves?). With interpretation, whether exegesis or eisegesis, we are in a little better case: Edwin Honig tells us in his lovely book *Dark Conceit* that the behavior of the gods in Homer and in Hesiod was so scandalous it couldn't possibly mean what it plainly said it meant and had to be allegorized; hence scholiast, who begat rhapsode (like Ion) who begat exegete who begat theologian who begat literary critic who so far has begat nothing but more literary critic; an entire and respectable industry raised upon the strange mythological ordinance that things, in addition to being themselves, hence uninformative enough, had to mean something . . . else.

A splendid instance of how all this works except when it doesn't is Lord Bacon's procedure in dealing with the wisdom of the Ancients. Having first decreed that the figures of Greek myth *meant* something esoteric and wise and opened only to initiates but dark to all the rest of the world, and having then decided, or decreed, that the Sphinx *meant,* of all things, Science, he goes about with equal enthusiasm and ingenuity to translate term for term out of story and into thought, and is able to tell you why Science should have talons, why Science should appropriately be thought of as carried to Thebes on the back of an ass, and so on and so on, not at all indefinitely.

A main consideration to emerge is this: there is a plenty of ways to be wrong in our interpretations, and no way at all to be sure of being right. It is in this respect that the story—the novel, play, poem—is, as Northrop Frye said, silent; and it is in this respect that the story resembles Nature. That is, I may identify a certain tree by as many characteristics as the handbook affords me, but it will never up and say, "You guessed it, I am indeed a box elder." What we know is never the object, but only our knowledge. Though Milton might well have wanted to condemn Dr. Johnson and approve John Crowe Ransom for what they wrote about *Lycidas,* the poem itself will never do either. What we know is not it, but only our knowledge of it. That may be sad, but it does make navigation possible.

How then do we, even tentatively and provisionally, approve one interpretation above another? One possible

answer, a humble one concealing, as so often happens, titanic pride: We just like one interpretation better than another, and as soon as we do that we find reasons plentiful as blackberries, just as Lord Bacon did in demonstrating that the Sphinx was, or meant, or represented, Science. We may, and often do, try to recommend ourselves, our interpretations and the reasons for them to some not quite identifiable community of our fellows, involving ourselves in some risk of tautology, not to mention snobbery—this is the sort of thing you'll like if you're the sort that likes things of this sort, as I do—and an infinite regress, which will probably, however, be put a stop to by a change in Fashion, that last and most pervasive and secret of mythologies.

II

Harold Bloom's *The Anxiety of Influence* is offered as a Theory of Poetry. It is praised by no less sufficient an authority than Morris Dickstein as "the most provocative and original piece of literary theory in English since Frye's *Anatomy of Criticism.*" I can agree to provocative; I was provoked. And to original as well, but only in the sense of Dr. Johnson's saying that when the cow ran dry you could always milk the bull. But my trouble with the book may merely have been that it was too difficult for me, as I am afraid my brief description of its contents must inevitably show.

Bloom begins with the beguiling simplicity—but it is the last one we are to meet—of his premise: poets are influenced by the poets who have gone before them. His figurative way of describing the situation also looks simple at first: the problems of poets in dealing with the influence of past poets, or with the anxiety attendant upon it, are comparable with the problems people have in growing up, or dealing with the influence of the parents (though to Bloom the Father alone seems important), so that the model in both instances is what Freud called, "with grandly desperate wit," the family romance. Upon this base the author quickly erects a large rhapsodic apparatus of specialized terms and perhaps too many characters.

The ways in which the new poet (ephebe) copes with the old poet (precursor) are six in number, and their names are: Clinamen, Tessera, Kenosis, Daemonization, Askesis, and Apophrades. These Six Revisionary Ratios, as Bloom calls them, are summarized in an introduction. One example will be fair to give, and as it must stand for all I rolled a die and came up with

> *Askesis,* or a movement of self-purgation which intends
> the attainment of a state of solitude; I take the term,
> general as it is, particularly from the practice of pre-
> Socratic shamans like Empedocles. The later poet does
> not, as in *Kenosis,* undergo a revisionary movement of
> emptying, but of curtailing; he yields up part of his

own human and imaginative endowment, so as to separate himself from others, including the precursor, and he does this in his poem by so stationing it in regard to the parent-poem as to make that poem undergo an *askesis* too; the precursor's endowment is also truncated.

Rating the above for difficulty, I should say it is harder than Clinamen, much easier than Apophrades, and about the same as the other three.

These titles head up the six main chapters, to which are added a prologue, an interchapter called "A Manifesto for Antithetical Criticism," and an epilogue. Prologue and epilogue are about the Fullness, the Father, the Path, and sound enough like a statement of faith that I may excuse myself from dealing with them; the Manifesto, however, is criticism, and I cite a few provocative and original sayings from it:

> Every poem is a misinterpretation of a parent poem.

> There are no interpretations, but only misinterpretations, and so all criticism is prose poetry.

> The best critics of our time remain Empson and Wilson Knight, for they have misinterpreted more antithetically than all others.

> Criticism is the discourse of the deep tautology . . . the art of knowing the hidden roads that go from poem to poem.

Alas, I do not know whether these things are so or no. If I too admire Empson and Wilson Knight I have evidently been doing so for thirty years for the wrong reasons. Bloom is unflinching about accepting the consequences of his axioms: he really does believe that his book is a poem: "A theory of poetry that presents itself as a severe poem." It doesn't *look* like a poem. And it doesn't *sound* like a poem. But if he says it's a poem? He ought to know: he wrote it, didn't he?

While he limits himself to assertion, Bloom is on privileged ground. But the two brief appearances of reasoned argument in what I have quoted—"and so" in the second sentence and "for" in the third—don't at all appear to me to connect, and I am tempted to think of Bloom that his form is logic but his essence is confusion. Nor is it at all easy to improve one's opinion as to whether these things are so or not by applying to the six main chapters, for Bloom's explanations routinely seem to make things worse, as in, e.g., a paragraph about "Binswangerian *Versteigenheit* (or 'Extravagance,' as Jacob Needleman wittily translates it)," about the middle of which my bewilderment is not resolved by being told that "Binswanger's summary is useful if we read it backwards." Maybe my problems with Bloom's thoughts are problems merely of style; but what's so *mere* about that?

One minor nuisance. Bloom improves his quotations from the masters by adding their intentions, tones of voice, and even probably facial expressions, as in

"Freud, with grandly desperate wit," above, and "Kierkegaard . . . announces, with magnificently but absurdly apocalyptic confidence." And he can go further along this line, not only reading Binswanger backwards but telling us what Nietzsche might have thought had he lived to read Freud. But there are greater difficulties than that.

Bloom writes a literary and allusive shorthand which is, moreover, almost entirely associative; one thing reminds him of another and he can't stop, so that he is sometimes nothing but ellipsis, all beads and no string. On a single page he names, not merely in a catalogue but in what is proposed as a series of related relations, Goethe, Nietzsche, Mann, Emerson, Thoreau, Blake, Lawrence, Pascal, Rousseau, Hugo, Montaigne, Johnson, Aristotle, Homer, Arnold, Keats, Kierkegaard, several of them more than once. Not counting the repetitions, this amounts to one name every two lines, and is very hard to understand. To the formidably learned author each use of each of these names no doubt stands for something he could identify far more precisely; but to the reader the game becomes merely bewildering in a short while. Finally I thought to recognize the source of this idiom as the graduate seminar; just to have done the required reading is not enough, you have to have done it in the last twenty minutes.

Bloom has too many hypostases, too many noncecharacters, more terms than he has work for them to do. The principal ones are the Six Revisionary Ratios, which are held to be *the* six ways in which poets may handle—or fail to—the anxiety of influence. After being summarily described, these terms are treated throughout as unquestionably distinct clinical entities, as real as if each one had been abstracted from hundreds or thousands of cases, when in fact the whole field of observation contains not many more than half a dozen major instances from Milton on, and maybe a dozen more fleetingly alluded to.

In addition to the six principal terms and the anxiety of influence itself there are ephebe and precursor (he doesn't always capitalize his characters), the Covering Cherub (by Blake out of Genesis and Ezekiel), the Idiot Questioner (Blake, in *Milton*), a bald gnome called Error and his two little cousins, Swerve and Completion (the feeling of having strayed into a comic book grows stronger here), and as many more as you can or care to identify by the mode of their generation and decay, of which the following gives an instance:

> Chomsky remarks that when one speaks a language, one knows a great deal that was never learned. The effort of criticism is to teach a language, for what is never learned but comes as the gift of a language is a poetry already written—an insight I derive from Shelley's remark that every language is the relic of an abandoned cyclic poem. I mean that criticism teaches not a language of criticism (a formalist view still held

in common by archetypalists, structuralists, and phenomenologists) but a language in which poetry already is written, the language of influence, of the dialectic that governs the relations between poets *as poets.* The poet *in every reader* does not experience the same disjunction from what he reads that the critic in every reader necessarily feels. What gives pleasure to the critic in a reader may give anxiety to the poet in him, an anxiety we have learned, as readers, to neglect, to our own loss and peril. This anxiety, this mode of melancholy, is the anxiety of influence, the dark and daemonic ground upon which we now enter.

Chomsky's remark *is* an illuminating one; indeed it is a key to his work. But what save rhapsodic association governs its relation with the ensuing sentences? Unless Bloom has some other source of Shelley's remark than the celebrated place in the *Defence,* the remark is really quite different: "Every original language near to its source is in itself the chaos of a cyclic poem." I don't know that the difference makes much difference to the argument, for I'm not at all certain what the argument is, though Bloom's misremembering suits his theme of melancholy declension, influence, and anxiety better than Shelley's romantic fervor about origin and source. Further I am aware that there are these three ways of reading—as reader, as poet, as critic. But the hypostasis of them as three distinct persons together with the permutations mentioned—and those not mentioned but which the reader trying to negotiate the sentence to its end may already be fearfully anticipating—makes hash of what sense may be intended.

If you took the key sentence beginning with what he means ("I mean . . .") and removed that parenthesis during which you spent three weeks in the stacks, you would still be not quite out of the woods: "I mean that criticism teaches not a language of criticism . . . but a language in which poetry is already written, the language of influence." Reader, this statement is made by the same fellow who has just handed out his half-dozen Revisionist Ratios, holding them to be the nub of the matter, and now declares that criticism does not teach a language of criticism. My ho head halls. What criticism teaches, he says, is a language in which poetry is already written—e.g. finding the Emerson in Stevens, the Milton in practically everyone? No doubt this is a rich territory for scholarship; but criticism? When I dreamed long ago about an art critic who went to the museum to measure the distance between paintings I thought it was hyperbole, but now it turns out to be Bloom.

He does admit at least once to a doubt about the enterprise, ascribing it to his own Idiot Questioner: "What is the use of such a principle, whether the argument it informs be true or not?" "Is it useful to be told that poets are not common readers, and particularly are not critics, in the true sense of critics, common readers raised to the highest power? And what *is* Poetic Influ-

ence anyway? Can the study of it really be anything more than the wearisome industry of source-hunting, of allusion-counting?" And he develops the doubt for another ten lines citing Eliot, Emerson, Frye, and Arnold. But he overcomes it.

Such doubts as may occur to a reader, however, or as did occur to a poet, Wallace Stevens, get the usual short Freudian shrift. There are two devices which may be appropriate to the analytic session, as from doctor to patient, but which, when used in discourse between supposed equals, turn brutal and vulgar. One is to say that if the reader is not conscious of the problem then he must be *unconscious* of it. Bloom's example is Stevens. The other is to say that if the reader thinks an idea inapplicable, inaccurate, or plain not true, he has a *resistance* to it. Bloom's example is Stevens. And the final flip is to say that one's denial is an example of what one is denying; thus Bloom, after quoting Stevens (including "I am not conscious of having been influenced by anybody"): "This view, that poetic influence scarcely exists, except in furiously active pedants, is itself an illustration of one way in which poetic influence is a variety of melancholy or an anxiety-principle."

As for the Six Revisionary Ratios themselves, I cannot tell the reader whether they are so or no, whether they exist or not. In *Attitudes toward History* Kenneth Burke quoted C. S. Peirce on the usefulness of "words so unattractive that loose thinkers are not tempted to use them," with this sequel: "It is vital for science that he who introduces a new conception should be held to have a *duty* imposed upon him to invent a sufficiently disagreeable series of words to express it." Peirce called this "the moral aspect of terminology," and surely Bloom has done his moral duty. But though the terms are sufficiently disagreeable, are they science? These ways of being influenced, or of showing it, exist only for so long as enough of us agree with Bloom that they do; built into the nature of things they are not. Even in science, alas, if the new conception you introduced happened to be phlogiston or dormitive virtue or the luminiferous ether, you would no doubt do well to distinguish a half-dozen varieties of each by wonderful names.

I've a good few more quarrels with Bloom, both style and substance. But sufficient unto the day. I guess the main one is that though I agree to influence as a fact, and agree that the project of Coriolanus ("as if a man were author of himself and knew no other kin") is unlikely to work for any of us, I hold to the belief that you do at last grow up and stand there on your own, as what Philip Rieff called "the healthy hypochondriac who rightly expects to survive all interpretation" in *The Triumph of the Therapeutic.* When you begin, you write: "The grass is green," and everyone says, "Aha! Wallace Stevens." Twenty years later you write: "The grass is green," and it sounds just like you. This is a mystery, with which relation durst never meddle. But Bloom, as far as I make him out, doesn't believe it. Even his "strong poets" (he's very high on poets being *strong*), the ones whose poems "most move me"—the only statement made independently of apparatus that I found in the whole book, a touching moment indeed—even those poets, A. R. Ammons and John Ashbery, are much diminished in comparison of the former times:

> And as in lasting, so in length is man
> Contracted to an inch, who was a span.

The world just is degenerate from Milton's day, that's all. The myth latent in Bloom's book is perhaps the oldest one of all, an inheritance already aeons old in the Hindu tradition when the anxiety of its influence affected Daniel and Hesiod, Ovid, Dante, Peacock . . . and Bloom. It is the Myth of the Four Ages, of which the first three range from paradisal to endurable but happen to be mythological, while the fourth miserable one is perfectly real and happens to be home to us. Bloom doesn't appear to notice this, but he states the sequence plainly enough. Shakespeare is out of it; he "belongs to the giant age before the flood" (and Marlowe his precursor just wasn't big enough to matter). So the four ages are: Milton, the Enlightenment, Romanticism, and "a further decline in its Modernist and post-Modernist heirs."

From Bloom's book I derive three melancholy lessons or laws: 1) That the life of the institutionalized intelligence, as by its own sort of entropy, grows ever more difficult and never less so; 2) That intelligence itself, which is responsible for so much of the small freedom we have or can use, is intrinsically committed to determinism. That is one way of expressing the curse on knowledge; 3) That the effort to render English unintelligible is proceeding vigorously at the highest levels of learning. It is the more reassuring, then, to have Denis Donoghue's *Thieves of Fire* as a moving demonstration that none of the three is necessarily true.

III

There are a few ways in which the two books are alike, and the comparison is illuminating as to the differences as well. Both are short, both are about interpretation, the principle of action in both is the application of a myth to several writers, Milton being the one they have in common and the one they begin with in principle as well as in time. Beyond this, though, they resemble each other mainly as opposites might be thought to do; in the terms of Pascal's famous antithesis Bloom is geometry and Donoghue is finesse.

Donoghue's myth is that of Prometheus, and because his book began as the T. S. Eliot Memorial Lectures for 1972 at the University of Kent the author must have faced a pretty problem in manners right at the start, for not only was Eliot himself the least promethean of poets—he also had the most serious and grave reserva-

tions, however now and again qualified, about all Donoghue's Prometheans: Milton, Blake, Melville, Lawrence. I am glad to say Donoghue's solution is as elegantly courteous as his problem may have been shrewd, as time after time Eliot is brought in to have his say from the shades, reminding the author and his readers that the promethean is not the only kind of literature, and certainly not the only one worth having.

Thieves of Fire seems to me a beautiful example of thought at its work of creating by dividing, of the use of myth as an instrument or figure of thought: "The myth of Prometheus begins as a story, an anecdote of transgression, but because many generations have found it significant it has become a category, one of the available forms of feeling." In Donoghue's deep and sensitive reading, the story of the theft of fire, with the associated stories of cheating Zeus out of the sacrifice and of Epimetheus and Pandora, becomes the story of the Fall which is also the Rise: the fire is not only what broils the flesh and forges the sword—it is also thought, consciousness, conscience, guilt; our first benefactor being also the first great thief, and we ourselves uneasy with the gift because we are connivers and receivers of stolen goods. "Prometheus provided men with consciousness as the transformational grammar of experience."

From the story, too, come the figure and character of Prometheus as an identifiable type of mind, or imagination:

> There is no evidence that Zeus thought any the better of men for their new skills. The imagination has always been a contentious power, as a result, so far as men are concerned in their relations with the gods. A typology of the imagination would be an explication of the several ways in which men have risen above themselves by the possession of consciousness. The Promethean imagination is only the most extreme gesture in that account, and it is not alone in featuring arbitrary defiance in men, a show of force in the gods answered by a show of blasphemy in men. The predicament remains: imagination, the divine power in men, falsely acquired, stolen from the gods in the first of many similar outrages. Since then, the Promethean imagination has always been defiant: it starts with an incorrigible sense of its own power, and seeks in nature only the means of its fulfilment.

Thought of this kind delights me by its clarity and serviceableness; and an integral part of the delight is Donoghue's modesty, tact, and sense of limits: simplification is a necessity of thought, but all simplification is oversimplification: "There is no thought which embraces all our thought," he says, quoting Merleau-Ponty and going on to his own equally engaging formula for the tragedy of mind: "One of the deficiencies of anything is that it is not also something else."

Out of this balanced good sense emerges not only the promethean imagination with its titanic powers and devastations, its sense of destiny's being, as Rilke said, *always against,* but its antitype, the imagination receptive and obedient; "content with ready procedures and with the range of feeling which they allow . . . he hands his feeling over to the language, and is happy to abide by its determination." That is said in description of Herbert's "Decay" as over against Milton's sonnet "On the Late Massacre in Piedmont," and a similar balance obtains between Wordsworth and Blake.

Donoghue is especially convincing about the consistency of his related relations as to their characterizing presence in attitudes to language, nature, and God or the gods: his poets are compared as "prescriptive" or "descriptive," as modelers imposing their own thought upon the material and even upon its recalcitrance, or as carvers concerned to release from the material significance felt to be already present in it.

The feeling I got over and over from *Thieves of Fire* is that its author is making his cuts through reality just at the joints, and that is why it looks so easy. I am sadly conscious of having given much more time to saying why I don't like Harold Bloom's book than I am able to give to saying why I do like Denis Donoghue's book; a matter of the squeaky axle getting the grease. And I suppose it may be said that my likes and dislikes are, after all, arbitrary. But I would add one criterion for "liking" that may be thought to relieve it of its absolute subjectivity, wilfulness, or capriciousness, though it too must, I suppose, depend ultimately on my feeling that it is so. That criterion is the production of insight, the power conferred on the author by his metaphor, or myth, of producing one observation after another about literary works and about the imagination that impresses his reader as fresh, useful, true (remembering always that interpretation is misinterpretation, or, as Augustine put it, "What I am telling you is true in a way *because* it is false in a way"). I think Donoghue has had great and merited good luck in this respect; time after time I find him making remarks, whether he is interpreting the story of Prometheus itself or using it to illuminate certain traits in his authors and their books, that arouse my warmest admiration—together with, of course, that bare edge of envy that alone guarantees my feeling that he is getting things right: "Yes, of course, why couldn't I have thought of that myself?" Donoghue's interpretations, in detail as in the large, bring conviction because they illuminate. I can't bring the two sides of criticism's tautological equation any closer together than that, and had best stop right there.

Steven Helmling (review date winter 1981-82)

SOURCE: Helmling, Steven. Review of *Ferocious Alphabets,* by Denis Donoghue. *Hudson Review* 34, no. 4 (winter 1981-82): 631-35.

[*In the following review, Helmling describes Donoghue's* Ferocious Alphabets *as a sensible, humanistic critique of current trends in literary criticism. Helmling comments that the quality of the essays is uneven, "ranging from brilliant to routine."*]

The impasse between professors of literature and the public at large, even that subset of it called the reading public, has been evident for some time now; more recent—and, according to your beholding eye, either more disturbing or more laughable—are the fissures opening between the professors, too, under the impact of a handful of European philosophers and literary theorists. Once upon a time, when the doctors disagreed, they did so in a common language; nowadays, the very vocabularies heard on either side of the rift are the first objects of dispute, one side closing its ears to the corrupt platitudes of a bourgeois humanism, the other turning up its nose at a barbaric "scientistic" jargon. Under such conditions, views are not exchanged in measured and accommodating words; rather, allegiances are signalled by code words waved like red flags before bulls. We have not a debate, but a sort of war of religion. And all blasting away without attracting the slightest interest from non-professionals—until someone was denied tenure at Cambridge was it? That got some press. "Tempest in a teapot" was the predictable formula; the public was stroked once again, thank you Dr. Pavlov, to the view that the response properly elicited by the word "professor" is a display of amusement of some faint sort. On the facing page, a more positive reinforcement: an ad for status jeans, say, or "fun furs." Cowboy boots are big in New York just now. In desperate moods it can seem that if our better advertised academic literati are the hierophants of an unapprehended futurity, we're in trouble. How much more comforting to think that they and their venom-filled teapots are just what they seem, a trivial and contemptible irrelevancy. But of course such comfort is no comfort at all. "More substance in our enmities / Than in our loves": that's always a sobering accusation, but in the case of enmities so vain and so petty, the expense of spirit seems especially pointless.

Denis Donoghue's new book, *Ferocious Alphabets,*[1] addresses itself with widely-informed reasonableness, patience, and generosity to the present situation of highbrow literary criticism and theory. Simply to praise the book in these terms is to announce what side of the fight it's on; add that in its pages you will find words like "will," "faith," "truth," soul," and "wisdom," and you've declared only the most provocative items in Donoghue's emphatically humanistic baggage. The book's provocations are deliberate, of course, but not at all gratuitous. Donoghue is no cheerleader; he earns his language, and his motives are severally admirable: to establish some common ground from which to address all the parties in dispute; to accommodate the new continental criticism to the concerns of recent Anglo-American critics; to show the acolytes of *la nouvelle critique* that if one hasn't been converted, it isn't necessarily because one hasn't read (or has read but hasn't understood) Messieurs Barthes, Derrida, Foucault, etc. I haven't been able to help making *Ferocious Alphabets* sound belligerent, but it aims to be a peace-making book. One can only wish it luck in an arena where "peace" is a fighting word.

A blurb on the cover pronounces *Ferocious Alphabets* "extraordinarily available to the average reader," and Donoghue announces at the outset that he wants to allow "elbowroom to a figure commonly despised, the naive realist." The table of contents discloses that the book consists principally of short essays, seventeen of them, on figures ranging from Hopkins, Mallarmé and T. S. Eliot to Harold Bloom, Paul De Man, and Jacques Derrida. But the "average reader" would be mistaken to suppose that *Ferocious Alphabets* is a handbook, or a survey. Some of the essays could plausibly serve as introductions to the critics they treat, but most plunge immediately into discussions that assume an already initiated reader. Nor, despite the generally chronological arrangement of the seventeen figures, is the book in any sense a history of how we've arrived at our present pass. The seventeen essays are discrete; connections between one critic and another are suggested only incidentally if at all. Some of the essays are brilliant—the one on Bloom is the best thing I've read on Bloom—but others can be rather routine. Some take up matters that seem peripheral to the particular critic as well as to the arguments of *Ferocious Alphabets* itself, and a couple of the critics included are simply lightweights, about whom nothing Donoghue finds to say removes an initial sense that they just don't belong here.

The book's studied casualness is deliberate, and pays off: in discussing critics so diverse, Donoghue quite rightly wants to be able to say whatever seems most to need saying at a given moment, without obligations to some proposed thesis or scheme. But having read the book twice, I'll say that it's neither so casual as it seemed on first reading, nor quite so deliberate as, on a second reading, it seemed to me it ought to be. The first time through it seemed a very miscellaneous collection of things indeed; it begins by transcribing six brief radio talks Donoghue gave for the BBC about language, its decline, its oddities, and so on. I initially took these as a gesture toward that "average reader," an Antaeus-like touching of earth before grappling with a subject sure to bear discussion very quickly aloft. The six talks have charm, and they're unblighted by that public-spirited self-congratulation that makes American workouts in the genre so repellent but they're basically the same sort of performance. Suffice it to say that this was the part of the book that John Simon, in his review for the *Atlantic,* liked best. After the six talks comes a fifteen page **"Commentary on the Foregoing,"** in which Donoghue uses his own talks, and his difficulties

composing them, as instances of the rhetorical awkwardness of addressing an audience that one can only imagine, an audience not actually present, and offering no feedback or response. The point of the exercise, of course, is that this awkwardness is much like—but also unlike—that of a writer composing a text to be read by persons unknown at some future time. Here opens what some folks like to call "the radical problematic of writing": Donoghue would like to close this aperture, but is properly unsure how, or whether, it can be done. He begins the next section of his book, "Communication, Communion, Conversation," by insisting firmly that speech and print are distinct, that "print is a silent medium" and "does not expect to be answered. No eccentricity is involved in a page of written words or print, there is a decorum ready to receive such things . . . ." I take this to mean that what Derrida calls *différance*—the irony by which, necessarily, writing "defers" the presence it aims to summon, and simultaneously alters, makes "different," what it's meant to transcribe exactly—is sufficiently mediated by conventions any sophisticated reader has thought through. The "absence of presence" that is the post-structuralist's new-found scandal is really quite an old story, and can seem novel only to those who naively literalize conventions of literary address, who don't realize that the convention that writing summons the presence of the living voice has always been self-conscious.

Writing is not speech then; but within a page Donoghue seems to be saying what amounts to the same thing: "I want," he writes, "to replace a theory of communication by a theory of communion, and to argue that what writers want is the system of exchange which I [call] conversation." No Derridean would pause for breath before attacking this as yet another rhetoric of "presence." But the point of Donoghue's contrast between "communication" and "communion" or "conversation," a point so casually implied that if I hadn't been reading with a reviewer's eye I'd have missed it, is that the Derridean assault is mounted against linguistic theories of communication, like DeSaussure's or Jacobson's, that lay stress on the transitivity of the message: a datum transmitted intact (ideally) from source to destination. "Conversation" promotes instead an intransitive "communion," in which words are exchanged not for the sake of the meanings or messages they bear, but rather to enact and celebrate the affection and participation that is producing and produced by them.[2] Very well; still for the solitary writer brooding over a mute page, that "radical problematic" is still, arguably, at work, as Donoghue concedes in his next section, "Style as Compensation." Here Donoghue examines passages from half a dozen critics, discerning in them traces of the awkwardness of addressing an audience the writer must imagine, even in a sense create. That awkwardness is what "style" acts as "compensation" for.

Here, and in this tentative state, Donoghue abandons his book's most suggestive—and, of course, most troublesome—theme. The next two sections, "Epireading" and "Graphireading," are less than the culminating statement the book seems to lead to: if the two very useful neologisms are original with Donoghue, still the distinction they help us name has long been evident. "Epireaders" are those like Donoghue, who look in their reading for communion with a voice, an authorial presence. "Graphireaders" are those who insist that all is text, that voice, presence, author, and so on, are bourgeois impositions sponsoring the perpetuation of all things corrupt and contemptible. Donoghue identifies, as the ur-fathers respectively of these two schools, Hopkins and Mallarmé; the more contemporary representatives are Georges Poulet and, of course, Derrida.

The Poulet-Derrida polarity Donoghue would mediate with the notion of "conversation." Observe that what used to be called New Criticism is given no role to play here. When Donoghue does discuss critics of that now very unfashionable persuasion, it is only as examples of "Style as Compensation"; his fondness, even nostalgia, for their work is evident, but once the talk turns philosophic, they are bid a firm farewell. I wonder how much of the current embarrassment over New Criticism is due to the tendency, which I associate with M. H. Abrams and Frank Lentricchia, to regard it as a species of Kantianism (shameful stuff, that!) rather than as what it was, a compound of English skepticism and American pragmatism. (What is taken to be its Kantianism is a mere garnish, an entirely artificial fideism, very much an efflorescence of that "humanism" T. S. Eliot couldn't quite disown.) Certainly New Criticism, if that must mean Wimsattian dogmatisms or interminable "close readings," is long gone. But the awareness it had, stemming from Oscar Wilde and the Augustans, of conventions and their self-consciousness, is just what current discussion lacks. "Deconstruction" exposes just what the fictiveness of self-conscious literary conventions has always acknowledged; its attraction for some is that it does so from a posture of alienation from, rather than communion with, the texts (and by extension, the tradition) it examines. This pose is, from Donoghue's vantage point, a failure, even a deliberate abortion, of sympathy and (forgotten word) "imagination." "The conflict among the alphabets of criticism today turns upon the question of imagination," he concludes; "Graphireaders want to get along without acknowledging the creative imagination; because if they acknowledged it, they could not stop short of acknowledging a complete humanism of mind, consciousness, and genius. Is it still a question of Romanticism, then? Yes; but of Romanticism as a permanent category, not as something to be defined by renewing the old paper-war with Classicism."

I conclude with that last quote because its energy, at once so casual and so high-rolling, is a feature of *Ferocious Alphabets* that I haven't at all so far done justice to. I have seemed to complain that Donoghue's book is too casual for its own good, that its arguments don't quite tie up loose ends; I have apologized for making it sound belligerent, then seemed to chide it for being less belligerent than it should be. All of which is to say that I have responded here to *Ferocious Alphabets* as an argument or a complex of arguments, reviewed it, that is, under the category Donoghue has disdained as "communication": as a set of messages to be transmitted, whole if possible, to the receiving *tabulae rasae* of its intended readers. My criticisms on that score, though, don't begin to suggest what the reader will have to experience, after all, at first hand: the charm and intimacy with which Donoghue's prose enacts its own celebration of "conversation." Its geniality and ease, its vigor and scope, prompted me to reach for the word "humane," and to remember that the theory-ridden and increasingly acrimonious discipline of literary study is still called one of the "humanities." The value of the book is not in its larger arguments, but in the fluency and large-mindedness, page by page, of its broodings. Few books of literary criticism—fewer and fewer all the time—are at all pleasurable to read, or converse with. *Ferocious Alphabets* is both, and I've much enjoyed talking back.

Notes

1. *Ferocious Alphabets*, by Denis Donoghue. Little, Brown.

2. The transitive-intransitive figure is not Donoghue's; I borrow it from Roland Barthes, whose notion of the reader's "pleasure" is a response to the same linguistic scientism that has prompted Donoghue's "conversation" and "communion."

Claude Rawson (review date 4-17 March 1982)

SOURCE: Rawson, Claude. "Epireading." *London Review of Books* 4, no. 4 (4-17 March 1982): 23-4.

[*In the following review of* Ferocious Alphabets, *Rawson asserts that Donoghue's argument is honorable, but remarks that it lacks a sense of urgency and "concentration of purpose."*]

Denis Donoghue begins [*Ferocious Alphabets*], a little self-indulgently, by reprinting six short BBC talks on 'Words'. The excuse is that such radio talks offer a simple if incomplete model for Donoghue's conception of literary discourse: as an address to an invisible audience, or dialogue for ever aborted by the absence of a second party. Print, unlike radio, is silent. But the writer also seeks a 'communion' which is never achieved, and 'style' is his compensation for the lack, as 'culture is a compensation for the frustrations attendant upon biological life.'

These reflections emerge in two chapters of self-observation in a neo-Romantic mode of which Poe's 'The Philosophy of Composition' and Allen Tate's coyly named imitation of Poe, 'Narcissus as Narcissus', are well-known exemplars. Where Poe and Tate look back at themselves writing a poem, Donoghue contemplates the composition of five-minute literary causeries: an unintended concession to that current orthodoxy which sees 'literature' as no more important or special than any secondary discourse about it, so that a tertiary discourse about the secondary may be undertaken without inhibition. There is no trace of the irony of Tate's title, and a good deal of Shandean buttonholing: 'I found it impossible to avoid sounding smug . . .'

Donoghue's sense of art as perennially subjected to biological and circumstantial frustration belongs to a similar Romantic tradition. It has many forms: Shandy for ever trying to synchronise his writing with what the writing is about, and seeking thereby a total and impossible intimacy with his reader; or Poe worrying about the impossibility of a long poem because it cannot be read at one sitting, so that 'the affairs of the world interfere' with the integrity of poetic effect. Poe calculated that 100 lines was about the right length and gave exactly 108 to 'The Raven'. Donoghue ponders the possibilities of the five-minute as against the twenty or thirty-minute radio talk. A romantic self-consciousness couples strangely with the exactitudes of arithmetic. Poe claimed to pursue poetic 'intensity' with 'the precision . . . of a mathematical problem', and there is a whole Shandean mathematics of empathy.

Donoghue's conception of the interactions between author and invisible reader implies Wordsworthian notions of the poet as 'a man speaking to men', augmented by a later and sophisticated awareness of the written text as a formal (and fictive) occasion for the encounter. Donoghue rejects the 'communication' models of Jakobson or Richards, with their idea of message or signal passing from 'addresser' to 'addressee' or 'source' to 'destination', and offers instead a model based on the traditional image of 'conversation'.

This 'conversation' is a play of uncompleted intimacies, an effort of 'communion' rather than 'communication'. There is no finality of content but an ever-unfulfilled desire to share the experience behind the words. It differs from the Augustan idea of literature as conversation, where intimacy is discouraged, and where discretion, reticence, the hauteurs and urbanities proper to worldly exchanges among gentlemanly equals, probably approximate to 'communication' in Donoghue's terms:

to signals of status, and (in the literary ideal if not in the social practice) to the imparting of information and wisdom. Empson's bluff clubbable mannerisms belong perhaps to that conception of 'conversation'. Donoghue notes phrases like 'in that age', or 'Macaulay complains somewhere', as examples of a gentlemanly affectation which pretends to be above minute precisions, in language reminiscent of Ford's complaint against Fielding's pretence of being too lofty to remember the name of a parish. For Fielding, such signals of status implied a decorum of conversational content: your claim to a reader's attention entails a duty to tell him substantial things and not to bore him with minutiae.

There is a Shandean parody of this which in effect creates an alternative model:

> Writing, when properly managed, (as you may be sure I think mine is) is but a different name for conversation: As no one, who knows what he is about in good company, would venture to talk all,—so no author, who understands the just boundaries of decorum and good breeding, would presume to think all: The truest respect which you can pay to the reader's understanding, is to halve this matter amicably, and leave him something to imagine, in his turn, as well as yourself.

Here 'intimacy' is forced on the reader. The very reticences are themselves invitations to mental activity and participation. The transaction proceeds, one might suppose, according to the Donoghue prescription, for ever unfinalised, made up of hints, suggestions, unrealised velleities, half-formed thoughts, broken-off sentences, and finally an unfinished book. Donoghue tells us that 'the best conversations never end; they are merely postponed', with 'the "I" and the "you" . . . constantly changing places' and 'the desire of communion' kept constantly 'mobile'. It is apposite to remember that Donoghue once wrote an excellent essay called **'Sterne, Our Contemporary'**.

But in fact Donoghue's unfinished 'conversation', unlike Sterne's, is controlled by a rather literal-minded ideal of good manners, in which 'definitive' statements are out of place, and where 'it is considered vulgar . . . to claim the last word' or to press your case too hard. The Shandean 'incompleteness' in no way precludes hectoring, cajoling, or the running of arguments into the ground. Where Sterne invokes codes of 'good-manners' it is in a spirit of jeering transgression and with no thought of that tactful politeness which underlies the Donoghue model and makes it, after all, closer in some ways to the Augustan ideal of conversation.

Of course, neither of the conversational models, Augustan or Shandean, is a reproduction of actual or probable talk, but a stylisation evoking the idea of conversation and creating its own fictive world. The unruly aggressions of Sterne's manner are as literary as the polished hauteurs of Fielding, and would indeed be found intolerable in any real conversation. Donoghue writes well on the gap between text and conversation, notably in the style of William Gass, which particularly depends on the page rather than the voice and couldn't be reproduced by the 'human voice . . . without embarrassment'. He tends to say this of styles he dislikes, but it applies to others. And because he is talking more about critics than writers, his *exempla* are sometimes simpler and even cosier than they might be. His principal model for that writing which compensates for the lack of an interlocutor by dividing itself into more than one mind is Eliot, not Sterne: the Eliot, it would seem, mainly of the critical writings, urbane and didactic, or perhaps of the *Four Quartets*.

'Ferocious alphabets', the title of this genial book, refers to 'ideological strife among modern critics'. It comes from Stevens's 'The Pure Good of Theory', which describes the transfiguration of discordant energies, 'Groaning in half-exploited gutturals', by imagination's momentary 'universal flare'. Those 'gutturals' are the harsh element in which the seductions of the interior paramour are consummated. 'Heavenly [the book oddly reads 'heavily'] labials in a world of gutturals' are what the girl in 'The Plot Against the Giant' will whisper to him and 'undo' him with. They come ultimately, I imagine, from Whitman's 'Whispers of heavenly death . . . Labial gossip of night, sibilant chorals', urgent beckoning sounds, oddly combining peace and shrillness. Stevens's line is cited by Donoghue to show that writers in English 'find the letter *s* troublesome' and that Stevens would not have called sibilants 'heavenly', or 'heavily'. But Whitman did, near enough. Stevens thought they had possibilities too, actually.

In modern criticism, Donoghue distinguishes between epireading (good) and graphireading (bad). Epireading extends the concept of compensation from writer to reader. It is the reader's way of making up for the 'tokens of absence . . . in written words', and of getting back to the primary utterance or *epos*. His 'object of discovery is not a message . . . but a person . . . From print to voice: that is the epireader's direction.' The heroes of this tradition are Hopkins (G. M.), Poulet, Burke (K.), Ricoeur, Poirier and Bloom (H.). They are described in brief, attractively idiosyncratic little essays. Graphireading, by contrast, is concerned with 'text' rather than 'person'. It has to do with the disappearing author and 'the obsolescence of the self'. Its heroes include Derrida, Barthes, Paul de Man. Here readers 'write' or 'produce' the text, in a dynamic proliferation of code-play and language-games. Graphireaders restore words 'to their virtuality'. They are, for example, hospitable to all puns, except those deriding Derrida. They believe that 'print is cool, unsentimental, unyearning', that 'interpretation is a bourgeois procedure', and that epireaders 'turn literature

into a sentimental tragedy, the most bourgeois form of literature, short of the realistic novel'.

We know whom Donoghue prefers. But he prefers even more to 'retain the opposition as rival forces within our minds'. He notes that we value such oppositions in Yeats, in Eliot, in Stevens, admiring 'in poetry what we inflict pains to suppress in criticism'. But Yeats's 'quarrel of self and soul' was a principle of live antagonism, not a liberal openness to plurality, a matter of tension, not accommodation. Donoghue's gentle path, I suspect, leads in the end to that place where the best lack all conviction, except in agreeing about the passionate intensity of the worst. Donoghue must be classed among the best. He does not lack all conviction, but sometimes seems to lack the courage of some of it. His healthy 'detestation' of the inhumane occasionally peters out in a cosy ecumenism.

Donoghue's book is animated by a principled and thoughtful resistance to critical 'theory'. He recognises its inevitability as a tendency of the human mind, and its potential or occasional value in the clarifying or refining of critical perceptions, but he is suspicious of it as a primary pursuit or an end in itself. One of his difficulties is that a principled argument against 'theory' has itself to be conducted in theoretical or quasi-theoretical terms. The alternative is to be accused, rightly or wrongly, of intellectual philistinism, since any summary dismissal of pretentiously elaborate structures of thought is likely to be construed as an attack on thought itself. David Lodge, accustomed to having it both ways in such matters, describes the typical British objector as Hopkins described Browning: as 'a man jumping up with his mouth full of bread and cheese shouting that he will stand no damned nonsense.' Donoghue is too civilised to carry on so: he has his cheese, if at all, fastidiously poised on the end of his fork, while he discourses tolerantly and with grace.

The result is an oddly half-hearted book. The five-minute word-talk gives it its essential structure, a cultivated informality, a conversational tone, a small-scale airing of concepts not pressed too far. The manner is carried over into the later chapters, with their brief introductory sketches of critical masters. The courtesy and fairness with which he expounds their thinking suggests that this might have made an admirable expository book. The polemical objective is humane and honourable, but it lacks urgency and concentration of purpose, so that the personal testament dilutes the expository matter, and vice versa. This is not the best of Donoghue's many good books, but it is serious, undogmatic and fair. If it avoids talking with its mouth full of cheese, it is largely free too of another and equally British virtue, that species of accommodationism known as 'working with' things one makes a show of admitting one doesn't really like.

Louis Menand (review date fall 1984)

SOURCE: Menand, Louis. "Rules for the Game." *Dissent* 31, no. 4 (fall 1984): 493-96.

[*In the following review, Menand compares Donoghue's* The Arts without Mystery *and Frank Lentricchia's* Criticism and Social Change.]

Frank Lentricchia has chosen a difficult problem for his new book, *Criticism and Social Change*. His ambition is to devise a Marxism responsive to the challenges posed for its theoretical foundations by the poststructuralist or deconstructionist critical theories that have been invading literary studies in the past decade and have more recently established footholds in philosophy and law.

These theories are threatening to traditional Marxism, as they are to any humanist philosophy. They refuse to consider the key terms of humanist discourse—"man," "freedom," "right," and so on—as anything more than ideological constructs. And they see language not as referring to the world, as a social theory that makes its claim on us by virtue of its truth-to-life must, but as referring simply to other language. Our interpretations "of the world," deconstructionism has it, are really interpretations of other interpretations, with no originating, preverbal ground in sight.

One way of putting the issue is to say that Lentricchia wants to rewrite Marx's 11th thesis on Feuerbach to read, "The philosophers have interpreted the world in various ways; by reinterpreting their interpretations, we can change it." And he is anxious to avoid the rewriting he thinks poststructuralism, in its current academic incarnation, would perform: "The philosophers have only interpreted the world in various ways; and that is all that philosophers—or anyone else—can hope to do."

Lentricchia's advice to leftist intellectuals is to seize the means of representation. "Literature is inherently nothing," he writes near the end of his book; "or it is inherently a body of rhetorical strategies waiting to be seized. And anybody can seize them." The best equipped "anybody" turns out to be the academic intellectual, who is institutionally situated to exert an interpretive power over society's essential texts. The literary intellectual can best undertake the socially transformative work of textual appropriation, Lentricchia argues, by conceiving of his or her scholarly practice as a social activity: "genuine political work for the Henry James scholar, as Henry James scholar, becomes possible when contact is made with the activity of James's writing, with all possible emphasis on *act*."

This program will sound familiar: it belongs to the line of Marxist social criticism that includes Antonio Gramsci, Herbert Marcuse, and Louis Althusser. It finds a popularized echo in the motto of a kind of leftism current here and in France since the 1960s: if we remake ourselves, we will remake society.

II

But Lentricchia complicates the argument by introducing into his discussion the skepticism post-structuralist thought has brought to bear on this optimistic view of society and the self. He thus undertakes to weigh the force of the questions contemporary critical theory has taught us to ask. How can any social theory justify its program without appealing to some essentialist view of history or human nature—without claiming to know what human beings "really are"? If society, as Michel Foucault would have it, is a totalization of power relations, how can intellectuals, socially accredited and institutionally integrated, stand apart from or outside these relations in order to criticize them? And how is the genuinely radical act, one that is not ironized by the determining pressures of an inescapable past, possible? If language, as Jacques Derrida would have it, is simply a deferral of meaning, signs referring us only to other signs, how can the text the leftist intellectual would appropriate be made to yield anything but evidence of its undecidability?

Lentricchia's designated spokesman for most of his discussion is Kenneth Burke, recommended here as a critic who since the 1930s has managed to sustain a socially astute criticism in full awareness of the complications that would be proposed, many years after the bulk of his criticism had been written, by such writers as Derrida and Foucault. And in the opposite corner, Lentricchia places Paul de Man, whose deconstructionist practice as a literary critic is understood to issue from the political quietism of a comfortable academic nihilism.

Lentricchia has shown himself to be a sharp critic of other people's theories in his well-known survey of contemporary theory, *After the New Criticism* (1980), and in a long essay on Foucault published two years ago in *Raritan*. Though he is, understandably, somewhat kinder to his own views, some readers may still find the poststructuralist counterarguments in *Criticism and Social Change* more compelling than the proposed critical program itself. Such is the force of deconstruction that all efforts to transcend its negations invariably end up looking like a tugging at the bootstraps.

Lentricchia's defense of Marxism against the critique implied by deconstructionist theories of language and by what he has called the "supermaterialism" of Foucault rests finally on a single theoretical move: a crossing of Marxism with pragmatism. The Marxist theory of history is valuable, he argues, not because it is the true description of how social change occurs, but for the pragmatist reason that it is good in the way of belief.

[I]s Marxism "true"? [he asks.] Does it "correspond" to social reality? The answer is that . . . Marx created a picture which Marxists and many non-Marxist intellectuals today in the West respond to as if it were true, as if in fact this is where we live, what our history at bottom is all about. Marx's picture, in other words, is true not in the reflectionist terms in which it is often posed . . . but in the pragmatist sense that it has put many intellectuals into active and rich commerce with their society.

The consequence of this pragmatist turn is that Marxism becomes for Lentricchia's argument simply the name for "that which we all desire in the way of social relations," a thing that never requires substantiation since it derives its authority not from any verifiable correspondence to social actuality but from its rhetorical persuasiveness. Lentricchia calls this "Marx without science." Readers who recall the cautionary example in the preface to *The German Ideology* of the man who thought to eliminate the problem of drowning by convincing people that the idea of gravity was a superstition, will perhaps wonder where the Marx is.

III

On the face of it, nothing could be more antipathetic to the theoretical orientation of Lentricchia's book than Denis Donoghue's Reith Lectures, delivered on BBC radio in 1982 and reprinted with lengthy commentaries as *The Arts without Mystery.*

In Donoghue's survey of the contemporary critical scene, *Ferocious Alphabets* (1981), which has recently been reissued by Columbia University Press, the bias clearly favors a kind of criticism that Derridean theory has declared obsolete. In this criticism the critic tries to come into contact, as in conversation, with the voice of the writer—as opposed to engaging in the free play of interpretation advocated by Derrida and Roland Barthes, for whom the notion of a coherent authorial voice in or behind the text constitutes a kind of metaphysical fraud. In Derridean criticism, Donoghue complained, "you must deprive the poem of its sacredness, its mystery. The critic must be a secularist."

Those who may have wondered whether Donoghue meant what he seemed to be implying in this sentence will, after *The Arts without Mystery,* wonder no more:

> The reason why modern critics are embarrassed by the mysteriousness of art is that it threatens the purity of their secular status [Donoghue writes in this new book]. . . . They insist upon the assurance that nothing escapes their consciousness. If they sense that the work of art is indeed occult, they get away from it as quickly as possible.

And a few pages later he speaks of contemporary criticism's "undisguised revulsion against the sacred object, the original work of art."

The function whose usefulness we have frittered away—through the commercialization of the art world, the dissemination of pop culture, the politicizing of the art experience, interpretive relativism, and all the other things that are supposed to have made things so hard for high culture (when were they ever easy?)—is unabashedly Kantian: "With the arts, people can make a space for themselves, and fill it with intimations of freedom and presence."

The kind of transcendental status Donoghue would have us attribute to the art object is indicated succinctly by a passage in his introduction:

> While I was working on the Reith Lectures, two passages, one from St. Augustine, the other from E. M. Cioran, kept coming into my mind. From Augustine: "Whatever is understood by knowledge is limited by the understanding of the knowledge: even what can be called ineffable is not ineffable." From Cioran: "The indigence of language renders the universe intelligible."

The only conclusion I can draw from this is that if art is neither a language nor a form of knowledge, and if it is inaccessible to my language and my ways of knowing, then either the arts are inhuman or there is something less than human about the rest of my life.

IV

Every theory posits a privileged position from which its operations, so to speak, can be directed; that position is always occupied by the intellectual who has created the theory. Everyone else's theory becomes either a corroborating statement of the master theory or a symptom of the condition that it proposes to explain. What these two seemingly disparate books have in common, and the reason they could both spring from the same theory-saturated intellectual milieu, is the extraordinary intolerance they exhibit toward the theories and tastes of other people.

For there is one theoretical point at which these writers meet. It emerges when we put Donoghue's description of the art object—"the most available sign of an alternative life, an adversary image if the official life is understood as enforced social practice"—together with his description of himself: "I am a member of the middle class; in some respects I coincide with its official [?] interest, in other respects I am an alien within it." Art, it is clear, is the name for those cultural products that reinforce Donoghue's sense of himself as someone who is both inside and, when he desires to be, outside the walls that confine everyone else.

The consequences of this view become apparent in Donoghue's discussion of cultural pluralism—the proliferation of cultural objects in the modern world and the critical relativism that is understood to have accompanied it.

The simultaneous order which Eliot invoked is a dream of order, and nothing more [Donoghue sadly acknowledges]. The proliferation of images from every known society can be felt as plenitude, but not as order. . . . Indeterminacy is an answer to proliferation; so is play; and so is the habit of voiding claims upon our attention by declaring them all equally arbitrary.

The flood of ersatz art experiences—art in galleries, photography, rock music, television, postmodernist art of "whatever happens"—is attributed to a failure of the critical will, the will to assert discriminations and make value judgments. True art does not simply announce itself (this is, of course, one of the odd habits of transcendental phenomena); it requires an act of critical authority to distinguish itself from the fake.

V

Since Lentricchia is concerned to correct the notion that intellectuals can assume a position outside the social formation they presume to explain, but since he needs to make an argument that does not issue in despair, his management of this problem is somewhat more intricate. His position is most readily observed in the argument he makes to distinguish his kind of pragmatism from the Jamesian and Deweyan kind recently revised and promoted in two influential books by Richard Rorty. Rorty is right, Lentricchia allows, in wanting to change the course of Western intellectual conversation by getting rid of the fiction of a natural standpoint, some ahistorical a priori on which the conversation can be grounded. But, for Lentricchia, Rorty's brand of pragmatism seems to be a promise of "cacophony, a Babel-like chorus of unconstrained and incommensurable interpretation. Rorty's conversation sounds like no conversation at all."

Lentricchia's preferred version of the pragmatist conversation can be read, for instance, in this argument:

> It is precisely the radical instability (and appropriability) of terms like "rights" or "the people" that makes for transformation in philosophical or social history . . . when ruling discourse is seized and, in the name of ruling discourse, turned against the rulers.

This is pragmatism in the mode developed by Nietzsche: interpretation as the will to power. It is therefore not surprising that the single literary example in *Criticism and Social Change* is *Mein Kampf*. That book's greatness as literature—here Lentricchia is summarizing Burke's essay on Hitler's rhetoric—comes from its having offered "as an alternative to the many-voiced confusion of [the German] parliament (a 'vocal diaspora'), [Hitler's] single, mastering voice and presence, a unifying center interchangeable with Munich."

The example of Hitler is adduced as a caution, of course, a reminder to the intellectual to remain alertly self-critical of his own interpretive will to power. But

nothing distinguishes Hitler's appropriation of the conversation from the sort Lentricchia would like leftist intellectuals to undertake except the consequences.

And what is the force that compels self-criticism, since it is the intellectual himself who is expected to exercise it? The answer is a strange one in this nonessentialist argument, and strangely familiar: the intellectual who fails to heal himself "will bring against [his] efforts the reactions of contempt which history always keeps waiting in the wings in readiness to expose false humanists." History, it turns out, has a dustbin.

VI

Donoghue and Lentricchia both want the conversation of criticism to continue—Donoghue on the old New Critical, neo-Kantian terms, Lentricchia in terms derived in explicit opposition to those of the New Criticism—but they want the vocabulary to be uniform and coherent, to be, in fact, their own. This is why in *Criticism and Social Change* everyone who is not a Marxist dialectician is an aesthetic trivializer or a "cultural dupe." And it is why Lentricchia and Donoghue both, with opposite ends in view, refer to the cultural history of the past 200 years as though its dominant figure were Walter Pater. If it can be made to appear that we have always submitted to a single shaping vocabulary in the past, perhaps we can be persuaded to submit to another in the future.

No matter which way the conversation goes, though, short of social disintegration, it will not become the Babel these critics fear. Ungrounded conversation is restricted by the same social actualities that restricted all the essentialist conversations in the past—the social actualities Lentricchia so often appeals to.

Cultural pluralism seems to me the best chance we have to insure, not that we get the society we want, but that we don't get the society someone else wants. Intellectuals might play a more positive role in the cultural life if, instead of exercising so much humility toward the objects of their cultural preference or the awesomeness of their historical task, they begin to exercise a little toward the preferences and tasks of their fellow women and men.

Jay Parini (review date autumn 1984)

SOURCE: Parini, Jay. "The Limits of Expression." *Hudson Review* 37, no. 3 (autumn 1984): 521-24.

[*In the following review of* The Arts without Mystery, *Parini comments that Donoghue's arguments are not sufficiently developed.*]

And the light shone in darkness and
Against the Word the unstilled world still whirled
About the centre of the silent Word.

                    —T. S. Eliot, *Ash-Wednesday*

The Arts without Mystery is an expanded version of
Denis Donoghue's Reith Lectures, broadcast over the
BBC in 1982. That Donoghue conceived of these essays as lectures to a wide (and potentially hostile) audience is evident throughout; their tone is informal but
combative, with the critic present as performing voice
at every turn. One can almost *feel* Donoghue's audience
taking shape as he probes its contours, finding resistance
here or there, anticipating counter-arguments well ahead
of time. Each lecture is accompanied by "shoulder
notes"—marginalia of an oddly digressive and sometimes irrelevant nature; added to these are lengthy commentaries in which the critic addresses his critics. One
gets the sense that Donoghue's listeners were waiting in
the wings to pounce on every word. (He was not
paranoid: they apparently were!) The final commentary,
which follows the sixth lecture, ends with the verbatim
reproduction of an essay published prior to the Reith
Lectures, **"On the Limits of a Language."** This essay,
in which Donoghue reviews the provocative question of
experiences that lie "beyond nature" and hence beyond
language, seems to have precipitated the Reith series as
a whole.

Given the format, it was perhaps inevitable that unevenness and superficiality should crop up. The unevenness
takes the form of a periodic unwillingness to press a
topic to its conclusion. In **"The Parade of Ideas,"** for
instance, he argues that political pluralism—a precondi-
tion of modern democracy—has led to the collapse of
the unified audience which the arts once enjoyed. Now,
he says, "There are hundreds of audiences, groups of
people linked by miscellaneous interests." He goes on
to discuss the effects of pluralism on the arts, as they
are taught in universities or practiced by avant-garde
specialists like John Cage. But one feels the topic sliding out from under him as he advances to the end (not
the conclusion) of the lecture hour. He complains about
dogmatism in the arts, taking a justified swipe at F. R.
Leavis, who refused even to discuss his silly dismissal
of Sterne's *Tristram Shandy* with Lionel Trilling; he
mentions that people get upset when boundaries of
expertise are crossed, and he talks about Roland Barthes's famous essay on the popular singer Dietrich
Fischer-Dieskau, restating Barthes's point that "Fischer-
Dieskau is flattering petit-bourgeois society by offering
it an image of its own perfection." Okay. But one would
love to see most of these points developed, grappled
with, taken to the mat. The margins of Donoghue's essay swarm invisibly with questions: Was there ever really such a thing as a "unified culture" or is that a myth
used (too often) by critics to denigrate the contemporary
world? Has the "politics of pluralism" hurt the teaching

of literature and, if so, how can you tell? Shouldn't the
canon of "great texts" undergo constant revision? And
so on. Donoghue seems to have answers to these and so
many other crucial questions; he doesn't have the space,
however, to work them out properly.

One aspect of Donoghue's superficiality is the overuse
of references. He is vastly learned. One knows this
already from the string of splendid books he has written. But too many names, book titles, and references of
all sorts, flicker through these lectures; they create an
irritating static that one has to *listen through* to hear the
real music of Donoghue's argument. The trouble would
hardly be worth it if Donoghue were less good. But he
is brilliant, one of our best critical minds, so we must
listen. At crucial moments in each of the six lectures,
he really bears down, bringing into lucid focus a point
worth waiting for. Moreover, Donoghue writes with a
firm sense of values, from an avowedly religious (but
not dogmatic) viewpoint. Our criticism is in such a
state these days that the mere possession of a viewpoint,
a place to stand, argues in favor of this work.

At the outset, Donoghue states his aim: "I want to talk
about the arts in relation to the mysteries that surround
them, not as a problem to be cleared up but as the very
condition in which they appear at all. In that sense
mystery is to be acknowledged, not resolved or
dispelled." He could not have chosen a more combative
theme. Critics now feel an obsessive need to explain
things—and explain them away. Mystery seems an
insult to the intelligent mind. In our post-Positivist
world, reality is reduced to "what can be said," and the
rest is ignored or denied. It is as if we have yet to catch
up to the later Wittgenstein, who probed the tragic limits
of language with the intensity of genius in the *Philosophical Investigations*. Donoghue nicely seizes Gabriel
Marcel's distinction between *problem* and *mystery*. "A
problem," says Marcel, "is something met with which
bars my passage. It is before me in its entirety. A
mystery, on the other hand, is something in which I find
myself caught up, and whose essence is therefore not to
be before me in its entirety." In short: problems demand
solutions, mysteries do not; you witness and attend a
mystery.

The unconscious project of society, in Donoghue's view,
is to remove mystery from the arts in order to defang
them. One sees this happening almost daily as a
President, say, quotes a line of poetry for his own political ends or a bank displays a revolutionary painting in
its lobby. Art is easily tamed, misread, appropriated for
ends the artist never dreamed of and would certainly
never condone. Donoghue points out that artists are
bought off by fame and money; they are brought "into
the system" by universities, all eager to own a "creative
staff." He makes a further obvious, but devastating,
point: "Serious artists don't think of themselves as

avant-garde, on the subversive margin of society, driven there by capitalism and the corruption of the market. The division of society into middle-class liberals and the rest has lost its meaning." What may loosely be called "bourgeois liberalism" has swept the board, and the old Romantic notions of the artist-as-rebel have largely faded. Andy Warhol is fodder for *People Magazine,* avant-garde architecture adorns our business districts, and Saul Bellow is a best-selling author. High culture has been assimilated, and this is mostly a good thing. A Beethoven symphony is no less magnificent because the performance is sponsored by Mobil Oil and available on a hundred million television sets. The downside of all this, however, is that art is often de-mystified, stripped of its elemental power to journey into "the heart of darkness." The mystery is lost in the mastery. Donoghue writes: "There isn't much point in having the arts at all unless we have them with all their interrogative power." He associates this interrogative power with the "mystery" that lies behind what words or paint or musical notes can express: "The artist and the priest know that there are mysteries beyond anything that can be done with words, sounds, or forms. If we want to live without this sense of mystery, we can of course, but we should be very suspicious of the feeling that everything coheres and that the arts, like everything else, fit comfortably into our lives."

Donoghue refers throughout to paintings, sculpture, and music, but he is uncomfortable on these topics and quickly scurries back onto native grounds—literature and criticism. As he proved in his last book, *Ferocious Alphabets,* he is a wily decoder of current literary theories. Not surprisingly, then, the best parts of this new book are where he deals with critics. He asks a pertinent question: "What kind of scruple would a critical disclosure observe, if it were to respect, rather than ignore, the mystery of the art it addresses?" He blasts Foucault, in particular, calling him "a moral terrorist" who meets the "anxious objects" of his criticism with "humanist categories designed specifically to take the force and the harm out of them." Unfortunately, Donoghue doesn't pursue his quarry in the bushes: he backs off, almost too politely. He might have, in these essays, mounted a major attack on the self-conceited, reductive, and amoral criticism now thought to constitute the "cutting edge," especially in Yale or Paris. Deconstruction and post-structuralism remain minority cults, but the few critics who actually practice them have intimidated or outflanked those still writing in what Susan Sontag has referred to, snidely, as "the Matthew Arnold tradition." The purpose of criticism from the time of ancient Greece to our own has been consistent: to understand, interpret, and evaluate the forms of human discourse. When this central truth is lost sight of, the culture as a whole is threatened.

In his final lecture, Donoghue laments the refusal to discriminate that seems rampant just now, when "pleasure is offered as a substitute for understanding, and value as a critical term has virtually disappeared." There is a general desire at large to describe the underlying system that makes the production of meaning possible—the essential Structuralist enterprise—what Barthes referred to as the empty meaning that sustains all meaning. This is in itself admirable. I would not want to argue for the withdrawal of criticism from epistemology, that branch of philosophy which investigates the origins, nature, methods, and limits of human knowing; in fact, one of the salutary aspects of the theoretical turn recent criticism has taken is the breaking down of disciplinary boundaries. But the fundamental critical act remains that of engagement with a particular aesthetic or cultural object. Donoghue agrees, calling for a criticism that moves beyond a mere "appreciation" of the art object to "a phase of cognition, analysis, and action." He quotes R. P. Blackmur, who said that the act of judgment is "the last act in bringing particular works of art to full performance." But that final term—*action.* What does Donoghue mean by it? It may have something to do with the fact that art is not without content, and content is translatable into action or response. Good words (or brush strokes or musical bars) are like promises that must be kept to be complete. Donoghue suggests as much, but he might well have been more expansive or explicit.

Yet *The Arts without Mystery* is an important book because it faces so many issues at the heart of our contemporary malaise: the unwillingness to acknowledge mystery, the way our culture domesticates and, thereby, defuses the mystery that generates art in the first place. More so than many, Donoghue shows a deep understanding of what the arts *do* mean when they function correctly: "With the arts, people can make a space for themselves, and fill it with intimations of freedom and presence." My guess is that Donoghue has found an opening here, and one looks forward to his next move.

Patricia Craig (review date 19 February 1987)

SOURCE: Craig, Patricia. "Green War." *London Review of Books* 9, no. 4 (19 February 1987): 22-3.

[*In the following review, Craig remarks that Donoghue's* We Irish *makes for pleasurable reading.*]

Wars and battles: these words, appearing prominently in the titles of two of the books under consideration, might give the impression that poetry, or criticism, or the criticism of poetry, is a belligerent business. It doesn't stop with the book titles, either: the chapter on Edna Longley in W. J. McCormack's short and contentious study of Irish cultural debate requires us to attend to 'the reaction from Ulster', and sums it up thus: 'Fighting or Writing?' This humorously echoes the famous anti-Home Rule poster with its caption, 'Ulster will fight and Ulster will be right,' while referring specifically to the critical reception of the 'Field Day' pamphlets (nine to date), which deal with questions—thorny questions—of identity and cultural heritage in Ireland. Edna Longley, McCormack says, 'has been the most consistent critic of the "Field Day" enterprise', taking issue, as she does, with its refusal to distinguish properly between poetry and politics (fusing the two, that is, instead of allowing them to interact productively).

'Poetry and Politics in Northern Ireland' is the title of the essay (the penultimate one in *Poetry in the Wars*) in which Edna Longley gets to grips with 'Field Day'. One of her objections to the 'Field Day' standpoint has already been mooted in the essay on Seamus Heaney's *North*: she dislikes the practice of equating one set of circumstances with another, without sufficiently allowing for the differences between the two. Hence, she says, Heaney's Iron Age Danish excavations yield up material so alien to contemporary Ireland that the two can't be linked without a measure of falsification, even if the purpose is emblematic. Seamus Deane likewise comes in for criticism when he traces a line of continuity (in his first 'Field Day' publication, 'Civilians and Barbarians') from Spenser's slurs on the Irish ('stern and savage') to certain terms bandied about today: 'terrorist', 'bomber'. Brian Friel, another of the 'Field Day' directors, does something similar in his play, *Translations,* which isn't only about the act of translating place-names from Irish to English, but also 'translates' a typical British battalion in the Belfast or Derry of the 1970s, back into a pungent era of the past. Friel manages this translation very well, Edna Longley admits, but falls short in his aim of recharging certain historical images, because, in the play, 'no perspective discriminates between past and present, 19th-century Ireland and 20th-century Northern Ireland. There is simply equation . . .'

If such equations don't come out right, neither can a case be made out for division of the kind propounded by Tom Paulin, when he tries, in his poetry, to reinstate some idiosyncratic words: so Edna Longley contends. 'Paulin creates division where unities [i.e. a common language, standard English] already exist.' In fact, it is hard to see what the objection is to Paulin's rather sparing insertion into his poems of words like 'sheugh' (ditch) and 'clabbery' (muddy). This is just a way of asserting local singularity, and a perfectly reasonable poetic strategy. As Seamus Deane has noted, Paulin's blending of 'a kind of academic surrealism' and the tones of darkest Ulster has an ironic ring to it; it doesn't seem to me at all affected or patronising, as it does to

Edna Longley. And it's wrong to say of Paulin's 1983 collection, *Liberty Tree*—as she does—that it 'attacks contemporary Unionism for betraying the French and Irish Republican principles of '98'. You can't 'betray' what you never subscribed to, and Unionism evolved in direct opposition to those enlightened principles. What Paulin is deploring, in this book, is one kind of discontinuity, the 'snapped connection' which occurred after 1798, when Presbyterian and free-thinking Republicanism came to an end. That particular way of jettisoning a sectarian mentality was itself jettisoned. Throughout the 19th century, religious intolerance thrived in Ulster, culminating in the kind of arid conviction forcefully evoked by Tom Paulin in his poem 'Desertmartin':

> This bitter village shows the flag
> in a baked absolute September light.
> Here the Word has withered to a few
> Parched certainties, and the charred stubble
> Tightens like a black belt, a crop of Bibles.

Odd to find Edna Longley dismissing these lines as 'cliché'd, external impression of the Protestant community'.

The Protestant imagination, as expressed in literature, has never allied itself with sectarianism: this is one of the points underlined in the collection of essays *Across a Roaring Hill* (subtitled *The Protestant Imagination in Modern Ireland*), which Edna Longley co-edited in 1985. Some of the contributors to this book sought to distinguish between the imaginations of certain Protestant writers, and a Protestant, or Catholic, cast of mind, both of which may occur in people professing either, or neither, religion. The book also upheld the claims to Irishness of those whose Ireland, non-Gaelic or not, is every bit as valid as any other. Its aim, you might say, was the opposite of sectarian: yet the word 'Protestant' in the subtitle got up the noses of a good many egalitarian critics, W. J. McCormack among them. McCormack, who was himself a contributor to the book, now sees it as perpetuating what he calls 'a sectarian sociology of art'. In his *Roaring Hill* essay, he made out a case for not considering Anglo-Irish literature in isolation: internationalism, the argument goes, will soon make short work of sectarianism. Intellectual developments in Europe in the last quarter of the 19th century, which opened the way for a scientific approach to 'the interaction of religion and economics, class and culture, regional and metropolitan forces', unfortunately bypassed Ireland, McCormack says in *The Battle of the Books,* leaving a vacuum into which—we may suppose—a lot of hot air has rushed. As part of his effort to do away with the type of insularity which fosters conservatism, McCormack raises the matter of 'Field Day's' insufficient attention (so far) to various forms of 'experimental' writing, as well as questioning the 'conventional' critic's emphasis on the individual imagination, when it comes to appraising literature, at the expense of whatever 'social entity' can lay claim to it.

The strong line taken by both Edna Longley and W. J. McCormack—who are sometimes in accord, but more often at loggerheads—testifies to the ebullience of Irish letters, in which things often get very heated indeed. Not invariably, it's true: a level-headed approach is exemplified in the Irish essays of Denis Donoghue, in which sharpness of intelligence, a measure of asperity and an unfaltering lucidity can be found. McCormack's book (more a pamphlet really) arose out of a series of weekly exchanges with his publisher, and is in a sense an adjunct to his study of 1985, *Ascendancy and Tradition,* in that it enables him to get some complaints concerning the reception of that book off his chest. Some of its themes are reiterated too. We find him still harping on the provenance of the terms 'Anglo-Irish' and 'Protestant Ascendancy', and not giving an inch in his estimation of the importance of getting it right. He also urges us to be very clear about what we mean when we use such terms. McCormack is as doctrinaire as ever, in *The Battle of the Books,* but rather more showy and discursive, as befits the informal undertaking.

Denis Donoghue was one of the critics whose reactions to *Ascendancy and Tradition* didn't entirely please the author of the book, and McCormack goes to some lengths to persuade us that one or two of Donoghue's assertions are rather shakily based. However, it looks to me as if McCormack's objections amount to little more than quibbling—an indulgence of the argumentative faculty which seems highly developed in this critic. Donoghue's arguments are presented in a different tone—indeed, he applies the term 'latitudinarian' to himself, not at all complacently. It's a just designation, if we include tolerance and urbanity among its meanings. *We Irish,* judicious and unmalicious, is a joy to read. The title phrase, which may be traced back to Bishop Berkeley via Yeats, was quoted by Denis Donoghue in his *Crane Bag* essay (*LRB* [*London Review of Books*], 21 April-4 May 1983); the essay reappears here (slightly shortened), but with the phrase extracted and expanded into an opening article, in which it and its implications are forcefully scrutinised. 'We Irish'— declaration of allegiance, defining term, or, as Berkeley used it, a way of repudiating some *English* trait? ('We Irishmen cannot attain to these truths,' he wrote about some line of reasoning that struck him as absurd.) Donoghue, at any rate, dissociates himself from Yeats's idea that 'to be Irish was . . . to share a special mentality,' and notes, more than once, the present-day resentment aroused by Yeats's taking it on himself to speak for Ireland, an action which led to his sometimes appearing high-handed when he meant to be high-

minded. To experience such resentment, though, Donoghue reminds us, is to bring a political attitude to bear on poetry.

Elsewhere, he refers to the complex, and much pondered, condition of being Irish, while acknowledging that other varieties of national consciousness may be just as stimulating to their holders. The first two sections of the book deal with Yeats and Joyce, respectively; the third considers the literary consequences of exigencies occurring at one time or another; and the fourth contains spirited appraisals of literary figures like George Moore and James Stephens.

Poetry in the Wars is notable for its alertness and assiduity. Edna Longley is a formidable critic, and never better than when she's proposing a revaluation of someone wrongly discounted, like Edward Thomas. The first two essays in this book deal with Thomas, one relating him to Forst, the other to the English tradition—a sturdier strain of poetry than either the Georgian mode prevalent at the time Edward Thomas took to writing verse (1914-17) or the Modernism that displaced it. (A bit further on, there's another essay which pairs Thomas with Philip Larkin, and clears both of them of the charge of giving in to nostalgia.) The neglect of Thomas and Frost, Edna Longley believes, goes hand-in-hand with the 'overestimation' of Pound and Eliot: but I don't think it's necessary to discard Pound and Eliot in order to appreciate the other two. The 'Englishness' Thomas worked to preserve is exemplified in his poem 'Lob', which gets a striking exposition here. Lob is a will-o'-the-wispish figure who may materialise in folklore, legend, history, proverb, everyday country life ('Metamorphosis is the poem's message as well as its method,' says Edna Longley): 'Lob-lie-by-the-fire, Jack Cade / Jack Smith, Jack Moon, poor Jack of every trade.' With the line, 'One of the Lords of No Man's Land, good Lob', we get a topical piece of ambiguity: the poem was written in 1915, when Thomas had already enlisted (he was killed at Arras in 1917).

Thomas set out to shape his poetry in ways inevitably, rather than deliberately, English: he made the distinction himself, in a review he wrote in December 1914, when the concept of Englishness was being paraded for a propagandist purpose. 'Rhetorical bullets', Edna Longley calls those verses manufactured with militarism in mind, and says: 'Wilfred Owen's protest was also a form of literary criticism, correcting a false vocabulary, imagery and consciousness.' Poetry in the wars needs to guard against the partisan impulse. It is also, Thomas noted, likely to improve as it becomes retrospective, when the poet's understanding of the experience has had time to deepen. There's a place, though, for the unsettled response, especially if the author's temperament is a sceptical one.

Turning to a more recent war, or state of upheaval, we might question the generally disapproving attitude to the Heaney poem 'Whatever you say, say nothing'—it's as if Heaney's high poetic standing disqualifies him from resorting to playfulness, in the eyes of certain commentators. This poem puts on record some hasty, but none the less astute reactions to the current disruption in Northern Ireland, and also to the efforts of banal, would-be tolerant people to repudiate extremism: '"Oh, it's disgraceful, surely, I agree," / "Where's it going to end?" "It's getting worse . . ."' There is also the implicit point that the wish of such people to appear unbigoted is in conflict with the irrational loyalties they're lumbered with (the fly narrator doesn't exclude himself from this burden). 'Punishment' likewise—though in a more compressed and lyrical manner—acknowledges the power of inherited allegiances, while not exactly upholding them.

Edna Longley is a good interpreter of Heaney's poems, especially of those she finds praiseworthy, and she also acknowledges, in more general terms, his unique achievement: Heaney's 'poetic landscape receives a particular assent from all kinds of Ulster readers as an authentic common ground; almost, despite subterranean tensions, as a *de facto* imaginative recognition of the whole terrain'. (She takes the view, mistakenly I think, that *North* represents a wrong turning: a turning away from the profundity and sensuousness of the earlier books, towards a coarsening preoccupation—Northern politics.) She is excellent when it comes to specifying Louis MacNeice's verve, Keith Douglas's 'rich' economy of style, the poise and subtlety of Derek Mahon; and singularly illuminating when she turns her attention to the work of Paul Muldoon: the long Muldoon poems 'Immram' and 'The more a man has', in particular, come in for impressive elucidation. Throughout this collection of essays, in spite of a quota of things to carp at, like the faulty definition of 'aisling' and the wrong-headed denigration of certain departures in the work of one or two poets, we are conscious of the thoughtfulness, vigour and expertise of the author.

Mark Bence-Jones isn't bothered by any ambiguity in the term 'Ascendancy': in his book, the Ascendancy consists of people of a certain social standing, living in Ireland but keeping to an English intonation, Protestant as a rule but not to a man, Unionist likewise, and generally including an ancestral house among their assets. By the 1870s, when the book opens, such people were on the wane, though this as yet entailed no conspicuous deterioration, and no loss of self-assurance. Mark Bence-Jones starts with Irish hunting, and makes of it a daredevil and jovial business; next comes the sporty slaughter of many woodcock and pheasants. The Irish aristocracy acts true to type in this study, down to the display of eccentricities, which enables the author to assemble a good collection of anecdotes and *bon mots*. One Edwardian Co. Cork lady, for instance, was in the habit of sliding down the stairs on a tray, wearing pink tights, and the wife of a Louth baronet had a passion for donkeys. Boredom during a church service could be alleviated by jabbing with a hatpin at the people in front.

The crucial questions of the day, disaffection among the ordinary Irish, England's wars, the agitation for Home Rule, are tackled competently and straightforwardly in *The Twilight of the Ascendancy*: no ambivalence of attitude, or revisionist conscientiousness, to complicate things here. *Sang froid*—an attribute of the Ascendancy—was required after 1920, when the burning of great houses became a part of the republican programme, and economies for the upper classes didn't only entail the selling of a yacht. It was after this that the once grand, now unrepairable house, with shabby fittings and rain coming through the roof, acquired such a hold on Irish literary imaginations. One or two of these ruined or dilapidated houses, unbearably melancholy, stand out among the interesting photographs—family and official—with which the book is illustrated.

Seamus Heaney provides a foreword to *A Portrait of the Artist as a Young Girl*; one of the nine contributors to this book is Polly Devlin, whose autobiography *All of Us There* (1983) gets its title from Heaney's poem, 'The Seed Cutters'. There's another Heaney poem, 'The Ministry of Fear' ('Ireland made me' would have done as a subtitle), in which we find an allusion to the sense of inferiority foisted on Northern Irish Catholics ('Catholics, in general, don't speak / As well as students from the Protestant schools')—the grievance getting a stalwart and humorous airing. Polly Devlin has experienced this sense of imposed inferiority too, and has written about it, and about the need to overcome it, with flair and insight. The topic comes up again here, but in a muted way: the format doesn't conduce to thoroughness of approach. The material in this book started off as a series of radio broadcasts, with each of the nine authors discussing her Irish upbringing. What results is inevitably a bit unstudied—memories, and thoughts about the past, all jostling for a place. Touching quirks are well to the fore. Maeve Binchy remembers wanting to swop her sister for a rabbit. Edna O'Brien, at a young age, would talk to the trees surrounding her Clare home. One of Molly Keane's recollections is of horrid food. Joan Lingard can summon up a time when it wasn't foolhardy to walk the streets of Belfast after dark. All stress their luck in being born where they were. The effect of all this is a little bland, though animated—'I remember, I remember' more in the spirit of Hood than Larkin.

John Rees Moore (review date July-September 1987)

SOURCE: Moore, John Rees. "Irish Story." *Sewanee Review* 95, no. 3 (July-September 1987): 494-505.

[*In the following review, Moore compares Donoghue's* We Irish *and Seamus Deane's* A Short History of Irish Literature, *concluding that both books are useful to students of Irish literature.*]

The classic Irish tradition is as well marked as the American, although of course much older. The ancient saga material, going as far back as the eighth century, centers mainly around two heroes, Cuchulain and Finn MacCool. Until Standish O'Grady, Sir Samuel Ferguson, Douglas Hyde, and others began to make it available in the nineteenth century to English-speaking readers, it was inaccessible even to most Irish writers except scholars. Ireland had been almost a blank on the literary map of world literature. George Moore and Oscar Wilde helped gain a considerably wider audience in the English-speaking world. Earlier Irish writers like Farquhar, Swift, and Goldsmith were comfortably absorbed into the English tradition, just as Shaw was later. All that changed with the worldwide fame of the Abbey Theatre.

Though the same names recur in most accounts of modern Irish literature—Moore, Yeats, Synge, Lady Gregory, O'Casey, Joyce, O'Connor, O'Faolain, O'Flaherty, Flann O'Brien—many other writers of almost equal eminence could be mentioned. Maybe a hundred others have written memorable stories or poems or plays. Seamus Deane has succinctly surveyed the whole of Irish literature, but over half of his book is concerned with the last hundred years. (For a fuller account of the earlier period see Frank O'Connor's *A Short History of Irish Literature.*) Denis Donoghue's *We Irish* is a collection of essays on Irish literature and society, emphasizing Yeats and Joyce. Neither book is designed for the casual reader who comes to its subject unacquainted with Ireland and its culture. Both have much to offer the student of Irish literature. Donoghue, perhaps the most cosmopolitan and certainly the most productive of Irish critics, always has interesting things to say. Deane's book manages to be lively and incisive about a great many writers: it's hard to imagine a better book of its kind.

Yeats, Ireland's greatest literary patriot, wanted to raise a standard from Ireland's mythological past. Cuchulain was his chosen hero: he was made to embody the aristocratic virtues of courage, honor, and self-esteem. He is simple and passionate and beautiful, and women adore him. For over forty years he occupies a place in Yeats's work. In his last play, *The Death of Cuchulain,* Yeats pictures his hero's spirit surviving in a modern crisis:

> Are those things that men adore and loathe
> Their sole reality?
> What stood in the Post Office
> With Pearse and Connolly?
> What comes out of the mountain
> Where men first shed their blood?
> Who thought Cuchulain till it seemed
> He stood where they had stood?

Yet in his daylight moments Yeats knew that the old Irish heroism was doomed, that the violence that plagued the country in the twenties was a dirty business with little of terrible beauty about it. Sean O'Casey has most memorably demonstrated the irony of violence—how it brings out the worst in human nature while professing to bring out the best. In arguing against Conor Cruise O'Brien's idea that Easter 1916 was a deplorable mistake, creating a legacy of romantic foolishness, Donoghue says that there was no realistic third choice between surrender to England and active defiance. Today all except a small minority would accept partition. But "arm a few diehard Republicans and a few diehard Unionists, and you get today's killings." Yet, as Donoghue remarks, a visitor to Ireland is unlikely to be inconvenienced by violence. Yeats, like many others, seems to exalt symbolic violence, as well as its peaceful fruits; Joyce, on the other hand, though he admires intellectual pugnacity, abhors violence. No respected literary advocate now writes in support of the IRA.

Deane is very good on the strains in Anglo-Irish writing, particularly in the drama, between the natural and the artificial, the provincial and the metropolitan, the Irish and the English. From Farquhar's *The Beaux' Stratagem* to Goldsmith's *She Stoops to Conquer* and on to Sheridan's *The School for Scandal* both the authors and their Irish characters are outsiders in the English environment, and their reactions are ambivalent. The stage Irishman is a perpetrator of malapropisms and stupidities or an intelligent observer of English foibles, but all his manifestations "are symptomatic of the general vacillation . . . between the ideals of local particularity, however stereotyped, and the theme of universal rationality and humanism." Deane neatly and perceptively explains the shift from sentimental comedy to the witty and analytic plays of Wilde and Shaw, all plays usually relinquished to the English.

> The heroes and heroines of comedy, after Sheridan, became markedly more intelligent than the villains. Villainy, indeed, becomes identified with conventionality; virtue with a radical independence from convention. The way lay open to Wilde and Shaw. Much of what we have seen of eighteenth century comedy did, after all, stress the "vital Importance of Being Earnest." It was characteristic of the Irish contribution to this literature to express a profound ambivalence by converting its basic moral prescription into a pun.

In Shaw's *John Bull's Other Island* the situation is reversed in the sense that the Englishman is an outsider in Ireland. The stage-Englishman has changed places with the stage-Irishman, and we have, says Deane, "a culmination of two centuries of Anglo-Irish drama."

Wilde and Shaw became court jesters for the English, a role that Yeats refused. During the 1890s he had busied himself founding societies and editing four volumes of Irish folklore, but in 1900 he combined forces with George Moore to write the disastrous *Diarmuid and Grania,* which put an end to the Irish Literary Theatre. But when the Irish National Theatre Society produced Synge's *In the Shadow of the Glen,* this first in a series of unique folk plays set the tone for many to follow. Synge's masterpiece, *The Playboy of the Western World,* led to the famous row (later repeated in Philadelphia and Boston) that probably did almost as much for Irish drama as the play itself. Synge became one of Yeats's heroes, and Yeats wrote his eloquent defense of Synge's last (uncompleted) play, *Deirdre of the Sorrows,* in "The Tragic Theatre," in which Yeats declares that he "listened breathless [in the third act] to sentences that may never pass away."

Yeats, though a skillful director of plays quite different from his own, turned more and more to a drama more distanced from ordinary life (and from his audience). Deane comments acutely on Synge's language: "Like so many of the modern Irish writers, Synge created a language, which for all its power never quite escaped a tendency towards self-caricature. This is also true of Joyce, Flann O'Brien, O'Casey, and Beckett. It is only slightly less true of Yeats's prose and George Moore's reminiscences." At any rate Yeats found in the Japanese Noh drama a congenial model for experiment, and in his plays for dancers created dramatic poems that demand of the audience that it be at once entranced and alert. Later still a greater freedom and variety appear in his drama: *Words Upon the Window-Pane* encloses its climactic revelation in a cunningly realistic framework; *The Herne's Egg* indulges in almost Aristophanic fantasy; *Purgatory* has a folktale quality; and *Death of Cuchulain* is a miniature dramatic epic. Yeats is a symbolist (in opposition to realist), but differs from the French variety. "The true Symbolist," says Donoghue, "is content to live in a world purer, more spiritual, than the common one, but Yeats is not." "Lapis Lazuli," with its evocation of those Chinamen the poet delights to imagine as they gaze "on all the tragic scene," sums up Yeats in one of his most attractive older attitudes.

> One asks for mournful melodies;
> Accomplished fingers begin to play.
> Their eyes mid many wrinkles, their eyes,
> Their ancient, glittering eyes, are gay.

Lady Gregory, who deserves much of the credit for keeping the Abbey going, discovered a talent for comedy late in life. But her services went well beyond the writing of plays. Her two books retelling the Irish myths, *Cuchulain of Muirthemne* and *Gods and Fighting Men,* are considerable achievements. She is, however, overshadowed by her male compatriots. Sean O'Casey, along with Synge and Yeats, is the most famous of the Abbey writers. A figure of controversy from the first, he was championed by Yeats, not least during the uproar over *The Plough and the Stars.* Deane says of the mixture of styles in his plays: "When we hear in O'Casey's plays a strange mixture of music-hall voices, hell-fire preachers, phrases from Bunyan and the Authorized Version of the Bible, often deeply and naturally assimilated into colloquial speech, scraps of Shakespeare and Shelley, which remain unassimilated, and Shavian soliloquies masquerading as dialogue, we can appreciate just how dishevelled O'Casey's literary and cultural inheritance was." A Protestant member of the working class, O'Casey was bound to see history from an angle very different from Yeats's. The world was in a terrible state of "chassis" sustained only by its tragic and heroic women (the men, however amusing, are weak and irresponsible). As Deane remarks, the most nearly useless people are the best talkers. The contrast with Synge is enlightening: "Synge's people talk themselves out of inertia into action. O'Casey's people talk themselves into inertia for fear of action." Both playwrights endow the talk with vitality. But "the vitality intensifies as the community degenerates. As a result, we finally witness the emergence of a wonderful individual performance, a virtuoso display in the midst of dilapidation. That is one of the appropriate images for Irish writing between Wilde and Beckett." After *The Silver Tassie,* which O'Casey, in angrily replying to Yeats's rejection of the play for the Abbey, called greater than *The Plough and the Stars,* O'Casey's experiments in trying to find a theatrical form to fit his purposes were only sporadically successful. And unfortunately the irascible O'Casey carried his pugnacity, however gallant upon occasion, to degrading extremes. Donoghue calls him "the most quarrelsome writer in Ireland, a notoriously quarrelsome country."

George Moore, another quarrelsome Irishman, made an impact in England before he tackled Ireland. Deane credits him with four good novels: *A Modern Lover, A Mummer's Wife, A Drama in Muslim,* and (best of all) *Esther Waters. The Untilled Field* was a prototype of the book of short fictions in which the over-all design is more important than the individual stories. *Dubliners* and *More Pricks Than Kicks* owe something to Moore. The books share oft-repeated Irish themes: "exile and freedom, clerical despotism and the power of folk belief, repudiation of Ireland and attraction for it, sexual repression and sexual longing." Moore, of course, is less modern, being softer, more nostalgic, less bleak, and narrower in outlook. Having shown the English what he could do in his earlier work, Moore returned to Ireland and joined forces with Yeats and Martyn in an abortive attempt to create an Irish drama. The real fruit of this grotesque collaboration was *Hail and Farewell,* a masterpiece in what amounts to a new genre—part memoir, part novel, part comic epic.

Dublin is the center of Joyce's work from beginning to end, even in that most archetypal confabulation *Finnegans Wake.* Although *Portrait* shows us the young Stephen Dedalus leaving Ireland to forge the conscience of his race, to many readers with different ideas of conscience Joyce was taken to be an immoral writer. Like Moore, Joyce had a messianic complex and a strong artistic ego, but his artistry was subtler and deeper. Regarded as a book about language, *Portrait,* as Deane observes, shows the hero mastering his inherited languages until he can venture on a language of his own; but Joyce keeps such an ironic distance from his hero that many have taken the novel as a satirical portrait of the posturing esthete who has yet to prove his potential as an artist. But surely young readers are right to sympathize with Stephen. In *Ulysses* the young man is still trying to find his way, gnawed by remorse for his treatment of his dying mother, resentful of Buck Mulligan's mockery, and never truly finding the father he seeks (although Bloom, perhaps, is more successful in finding a surrogate son, if only temporarily). Deane says of the interwoven sojourns of the two that they "represent, among other things, an attempt on Joyce's part, to reintegrate the project of the artist hero with the spirit of the community, specifically that of Dublin but generally that of mankind, from which he has been separated." Joyce's work brings to a culmination Irish experiments in language form. "After it, the tremendous prestige of the English novel was never again so oppressive for Irish writers."

Oddly, as Joyce's work becomes more elitist in its linguistic acrobatics, it becomes mellower and more "democratic" in its sympathies. Deane is correct in observing that "in the *Wake,* the presence that moves behind the text is the presence of the ordinary workaday world and its workaday language." Deane cites the charming introduction to the Mookse and the Gripes episode to show how Joyce makes the old new. Joyce became more European in the sense that Donoghue, in a wide-ranging and allusive essay, persuasively argues for. Too proud to ally himself with the aims of the Irish literary revival, Joyce chose "the European way." Thus he became an artist "of European scope and grandeur, blood-brother to Dante, Shakespeare, Swift, Flaubert, Pater, Wagner and Ibsen." In struggling to disengage himself from the Irish condition, Joyce took Yeats as his chief antagonist. Donoghue says Joyce had to fight against the Yeatsian temptation: "Yeats is Joyce's chosen and fated precursor. Joyce had to swerve from Yeats's way of being a genius, and disown its forms to accomplish his own."

Of the epigones of Joyce, Samuel Beckett is the most famous. In a sense Beckett too revolted against his master, substituting a minimalist style for Joyce's linguistic opulence. (Beckett's first publication was an essay on Joyce.) Only after sending it to forty-three publishers did Beckett succeed in getting his first novel, *Murphy,* into print in 1937. And not until the appearance of *En attendant Godot* was a wider public aware of the author. What one could not have foreseen was the astonishing fecundity and inventiveness still to come. Though the wording is felicitous, I do not entirely agree with Deane that the Beckett heroes "all suffer from an apathy of sublime proportions. They recognize the futility of existence and regard with venom anyone who dares to gloss it otherwise." The trouble is that the apathy is spasmodically interrupted by cries of protest—if his people were that stoical or "oriental" they would not squirm so. They do have plenty of spleen, but it is frequently vented against themselves. Desire in them has never quite died out, and their frustration makes the drama. And the comic routines and obscenity only partially mask the rage and pity that lie behind Beckett's work. Deane's suggestion that "Beckett in his drama has more affinities with Yeats than with any other Irish writer" is true. A significant difference is that in the plays for dancers and later plays Yeats is still upholding something of the mystery of heroism and (frequently) finding something supernatural, as well as natural, in the power of feminine sexual attraction. Deane does not mention *Happy Days,* in some ways the most nearly perfect of Beckett's plays in its ingenious economy of means.

If, as Beckett is reported to have said, art is the bow tie about the throat of cancer, for Flann O'Brien the art of Joyce proved to be an albatross around his neck. His most ebulliently successful work, *At Swim-Two-Birds,* was praised by the master himself: "That's a real writer, with the true comic spirit. A really funny book." *At Swim* has a Joycean virtuosity but is nevertheless entirely original. It is simultaneously a demonstration and a demolition of the idea of a novel, but its delights are far from theoretical. To the "Joycean egotistical sublime" it offers an alternative radical freedom in which characters refuse to be compelled "to be uniformly good or bad or poor or rich. Each should be allowed a private life, self-determination and a decent standard of living." Deane's account of the comparative failure of O'Brien's later fiction is best put in his own words. "O'Brien's reaction to Joyce's work and, later, to Joyce's fame, is one of the most astonishing examples of the 'anxiety of influence' to be found, even in Ireland where the closeness of the small literary community stimulates fiction and friction of varied quality and unvaried regularity."

The contrast of an integrated past and a disintegrated present, so prevalent a theme in the literature of the

1920s, had reached the "point of exhaustion by the 1930s." Nevertheless, as late as the 40s Mervyn Wall was exploiting the theme in his two novels about a medieval Irish monk—*The Unfortunate Fursey* (1946) and *The Return of Fursey* (1948), which Deane praises as among the funniest and subtlest of modern Irish fantasies. But James Stephens is Deane's chief example of the combining of fantasy and realism. His fantasy world "is one of sunlit wisdom and instinctive happiness"; the social world "is dominated by the most unfeeling cruelties and selfishness."

Hostility toward Catholicism—Deane remarks how curious it is how few Irish writers show imaginative sympathy for it—and nostalgia for the culture that was represented by the Big House accounted for writings of an increasingly sinister tone. Somerville and Ross, best known for *The Irish R.M. and His Experiences,* wrote what V. S. Pritchett says is "the one outstanding Irish novel of the nineteenth century," *The Real Charlotte* (1894). It tells the story of an embittered old woman who destroys her young ward, a spirited and attractive girl who might have been saved by the heir of a Big House if he had had greater moral fiber and decisiveness. The theme—and image—of the ruined house also dominates, for instance, the horror stories of Sheridan Le Fanu and novels like Elizabeth Bowen's *The Last September,* as well as Yeats's "Ancestral Houses" and *Purgatory.*

If the ruined house was a frequent subject in Irish literature, it was also an Irish reality. Deane reminds us that "between 1921 and 1923, 192 Big Houses were destroyed." Despite the revolution that was supposed to have ushered in a new day, Republican writers of the 1930s and after—O'Connor, O'Flaherty, O'Donnell, O'Faolain—found the old divisions remained. So "everything seemed the same, the same utterly, only worse." By the time Eamon de Valera came to power (1932), a "holy" alliance of Church and State had occurred that isolated Ireland from the modern world. To be Irish and to be Christian was to be the enemy of everything modern.

A countercurrent is represented by Denis Devlin, whose *Lough Derg and Other Poems* (1946) displays a more European version of Catholicism, more tolerant in sexual matters and less heavy-handed politically. Poets of whatever persuasion had a hard time of it in the shadow of Yeats. As Donoghue shows, Austin Clarke took almost a generation to move out of the Yeatsian orbit, but in *Ancient Lights* (1955) he showed that he too had more enterprise in walking naked. Largely a poetry of statement, it takes a sour view of Church and State. But his rhetoric can rise to satirical eloquence:

> And all around the spires of Dublin
> Such swallowing in the air, such cowling

> To keep high offices pure: I heard
> From shore to shore, the iron gratings
> Take half our heavens with a roar.
>
> —"Ancient Lights"

Too often Clarke's obscurity seems willed. According to anecdote, he told Robert Frost (who had never heard of him), in answer to the question what kind of poetry did he write: "I load myself with chains and try to get out of them."

If Clarke became the "Angry Old Man of Irish Letters," as Deane dubs him, Patrick Kavanagh's *The Great Hunger* (1942) was the most impressive protest poem of its decade. Paddy Maguire, a peasant oppressed both physically and mentally by the grinding poverty of his life, dimly realizes that life is passing him by. "Watch him watch him, that man on a hill whose spirit / Is a wet sack flapping about the knees of time." The poet follows Maguire and catches him in a series of vignettes showing him at home, at work, and by himself. He has spent his passion on the land and sowed his seed on the ashes in the fire. Religion made a coward of him, and he missed his chance with a young girl. Year after year he comforts himself with the thought that everything will change. Finally he must ask "Who bent the coin of my destiny / That it stuck in the slot?" Maybe his fate was settled forty years ago. At any rate "O Christ! I am locked in a stable with pigs and cows forever."

Kavanagh's view is as far as possible from the Celtic Twilight of simple people having intercourse with fairies, and equally far from heroic tragedy. "But the weak, washy way of true tragedy— / A sick horse nosing around the meadow for a clean place to die." Later Kavanagh rejected *Hunger,* explaining: "*The Great Hunger* is concerned with the woes of the poor. A true poet is selfish and implacable. A poet merely states the position and does not care whether his words change anything or not. *The Great Hunger* is tragedy and Tragedy is underdeveloped Comedy, not fully born. Had I stuck to the tragic thing in *The Great Hunger* I would have found many powerful friends."

Denis Devlin's sophisticated poetry stands apart both from Clarke's narrowness and from Kavanagh's parochialism. A learned diplomat, Devlin successfully translated poems from the French, German, and Italian. Sometimes his linguistic virtuosity gets in the way of his vision and the result is an uncomfortable blur, but in his best poems he earns a place in the European as well as Irish tradition.

> White Moon, white moon, O grant us Artemis,
> Thy gift of lunacy lest bleed afresh
> The wound of separation of the flesh;
> Lest I relive, mature in swaddling clothes,
> That trauma between racket and repose,

Or see in the dark her corndusky hair
The breath held in, the foot upon the stair.

Deane aptly describes Devlin's poetry as "a metaphysical poetry in the symbolist mode." "Its uniqueness in Ireland emphasizes the rarity of a specifically Christian poetry in a country where the traditional modern relationship between poetry and belief has been fraught with tension and suspicion."

Of the poets of the next generation, Thomas Kinsella, Richard Murphy, and John Montague have all done notable work. Kinsella has lost part of his audience, as Deane points out, because of the obscure sources and experimental style in his later pamphlets, and only time will tell whether he will emerge as the major voice in Irish poetry of the latter twentieth century. To be sure, he has plenty of competition. Montague, one of several northern poets influenced by Kavanagh, and an admirer of Devlin, has in *The Rough Field* (1972) appointed himself the poetic guardian of a past, or passing, civilization. A poem like "The Source" combines elation, boyhood memories, a sense of speaking for the tribe, and the shock of present-day reality. Seamus Heaney has mined a similar vein. Deane puts the quality of Heaney's earlier verse effectively: "His fascination with the processes of decay and rot, with the simmering slime and mud and soil of his local farmland areas is reverential." In his more recent work, however, a more familiar human world emerges where Heaney balances "the play of his consciousness and the pain of his conscience against that of others." Many other fine contemporary poets deserve praise.

The Irish have done particularly well with the short story. The famous Christmas dinner in *Portrait* prefigures a continuing debate between opposing views on the relationship between nationalism and Catholicism. In O'Faolain's fiction we discover that there is no place for the heroic will in postrevolutionary Ireland. O'Connor, closer to the oral tradition, easily establishes a familiar relationship with his audience, but he is as alienated as O'Faolain. As Deane neatly phrases it, "he has the poise of a man who belongs and the pose of a man who is an outcast." O'Flaherty, perhaps best known for *The Informer,* celebrates the primitive will to survive against fearful odds. Of women writers Mary Lavin is one of the best. Her stories have a deceptive mildness; the implied criticism of life is usually severe. All the way from a story like James Stephens's "Desire," with its arctic nightmare, to Benedict Kiely's "Bluebell Meadow," with its nostalgia for the idyllic combined with its recognition of the destructive absurdity of religious intolerance, the intersection of fantasy and reality has a bittersweet flavor that is peculiarly Irish.

The bleakness of the early novels of Brian Moore and of John McGahern is almost unrelieved. Gradually Moore's central characters come up in the world at least financially, but they never succeed in finding the transcendent experience they are looking for. McGahern finally succeeds in showing a tenderness that convincingly holds its own in *The Pornographer.* Deane finds John Banville outstanding among the current crop of novelists. He says *Birchwood* (1973) is "one of the most startling of the century's varied achievements in Irish writing." Banville's theme in this and later novels is how writing itself both opens and bridges the gap between oneself and others. Banville belongs with Flann O'Brien and Beckett in his preoccupation with the "principle of radical doubt."

Two novelists who deserve more attention than they get are Aidan Higgins and Thomas Kilroy; another, Richard Power, is not mentioned by Deane. In 1960 Higgins made his debut with an extraordinary book of short stories, *Felo de Se.* In 1966 came *Langrishe, Go Down,* which in its description of a strange and painful love affair managed to combine the sordid and the lyrical in a very original way. Kilroy's *The Big Chapel,* retelling events of a hundred years ago, shows a talent for recreating history. Richard Power's *The Hungry Grass* (1969), published the year before its author's death at forty-two, gives, for once, a humorous, sympathetic, and extremely well observed novelistic account dramatizing the trials and tribulations of a parish priest in a village in the west of Ireland. Thomas Flanagan, a student of Irish culture, showed his powers as a historical novelist in *The Year of the French* (1979), but perhaps appeared too late for inclusion in Deane's book. The most extraordinary novels of the last few years that no reader of Irish fiction will want to miss are *Good Behaviour* and *Time After Time* (1981 and 1983) by Molly Keane, now in her eighties. She broke a literary silence of more than three decades in writing them—under the name of M. J. Farrell she had written ten novels and several plays. These two late novels deal with the Irish family as it has never been dealt with before. Funny, ironical, sad; precise and clear-eyed and never sentimental. The novel has never been as congenial an Irish genre as the short story, poetry, and the drama; nevertheless no mean harvest has been reaped in the years since *Ulysses.*

The pickings in recent drama, according to Deane, are relatively slender. Three playwrights dominate: Brian Friel, Thomas Murphy, and Thomas Kilroy. Friel's masterpiece, *Translations* (1981), examines the cultural effects of the displacement of Gaelic by English. Murphy's *The Gigli Concert* and Kilroy's *The Death and Resurrection of Mr. Roche* and *Talbot's Box* get Deane's nod as the best work of their respective authors.

Seamus Deane has done a rare thing: written a survey packed with reliable information in the lively and graceful style usually reserved for the personal essay.

Donoghue has collected his occasional Irish pieces under four headings: Yeats, Joyce, Contexts, and Occasions. His introductory essay, **"We Irish,"** plays with the idea at considerable length, using Yeats's haughty anti-English definition of Irishness and showing how it is partly based on a mistaken notion of Berkeley's position. "If there is a distinctive Irish experience," says Donoghue, "it is one of division, exacerbated by the fact that division in a country so small seems perverse. But the scale doesn't matter." His lengthy list of oppositions makes Ireland sound an impossibly schizophrenic country. Yet these divisions have provided the material for an art significant out of all proportion to the size of the country. And the major artists themselves have prompted controversy. Donoghue demonstrates why Yeats has been resented at home "not for his snobbery, his outlandish claim to the possession of Norman blood, or even for his evasion of history by appeal to two classes of people who existed only as shades—Gaelic Irish and Anglo-Irish—but because he claimed to speak in the name of the 'indomitable Irishry.'" Any Irishman who makes such a claim will meet an argument from another Irishman.

Whether discussing the details of a poem or considering the broad cultural implications of a political position, Donoghue brings an enviable arsenal of erudition to bear. (**"Bakhtin and *Finnegans Wake*"** is a case in point.) Donoghue can be witty and amusing when he gets his dander up, as he does in reviewing Hugh Kenner's *A Colder Eye*. Responding to Kenner's description of the Irish proclivity for violence, Donoghue writes: "Presumably the argument is that since we don't get enough sex, we have to have our ecstasies outside the bedroom. So that's what we have been up to since 1968, having our orgasms in public." But Donoghue, while resenting the smart-aleck cracks Kenner indulges in, also acknowledges his virtues: "In Kenner's book, silliness jostles with exactness of perception. . . . He can write like Swift or like a shamrock-toting tourist, prevented from knowing the difference by the Babel of discourses which surround the theme rather than by any defect in his extraordinary intelligence."

The Irish can be counted on to resent any foreign criticism (like other nationals), but among themselves they can also be severe. One of Donoghue's summings up is enough to dishearten all but the most stouthearted: "The past is another country: yes, but in Ireland it is the same country. It is hard to say what form a coherent life would take: coherent, in the sense of manifesting a decent relation between one's past and present, one's obligations and freedoms. Hard, and in Ireland becoming harder, because most people are finding that their lives are governed by immediacies: unemployment, the cost of daily living (inordinately high), taxation (ditto), the quality of government (abysmal), dependence on the charity of the EEC (shameful), and the wretchedness in the North." Life is short but art is long.

Bruce Bawer (review date October 1987)

SOURCE: Bawer, Bruce. "Reading Denis Donoghue." *New Criterion* 6, no. 2 (October 1987): 28-35.

[*In the following review of* Reading America, *Bawer is highly critical of Donoghue's arguments and writing style.*]

Denis Donoghue is one of that small company of transatlantic men of letters who have established reputations as distinguished critics of both English and American literature. An Irishman by birth, Donoghue has taught at University College, Dublin, at Cambridge University, and (currently) at New York University, where he occupies the Henry James Chair of Letters, and since 1959 has published a dozen volumes, including studies of Yeats, Swift, Emily Dickinson, modern verse drama, modern American poetry, and "the poetic imagination"; he is professionally concerned with the subject of Irishness (his last book, a selection of essays on his native land and literature, was entitled *We Irish*), and his new collection, *Reading America*—a gathering of twenty seven reviews and essays about American writers from Emerson to Ashbery—testifies to his equally serious interest in the question of just what it is that makes American literature American.

This question is most explicitly engaged in the book's opening essay, **"America in Theory,"** in which Donoghue discusses some of the more familiar critical conceptions of the nature of "the American experience" as it is rendered in the national literature. Examining the writings of such diverse critics as Tocqueville, D. H. Lawrence, Henry James, V. L. Parrington, Perry Miller, F. O. Matthiessen, W. H. Auden, Richard Chase, Leslie Fiedler, Leo Marx, Alfred Kazin, and Harold Bloom (Donoghue is nothing if not a compulsive scholar), he attempts to formulate a sort of unified field theory of American literature. But he never settles down quite long enough to state this theory succinctly and with finality; he seems unwilling to commit himself to any particular formulation, and thus throughout the essay is continually bringing in new quotations, new authorities.

For instance, Donoghue paraphrases Irving Howe to the effect that "the deepest desire in American literature is to be rid of every authority except that of the individual self," quotes Quentin Anderson's suggestion that American literature is designed to help readers "to fantasize a guiltless possession of the world," and apprises us of Nina Baym's argument that "the myth of the American experience . . . sets the hero free to disengage himself from a society he regards as embodied in women and the responsibilities of domestic life." At one point Donoghue seems to be subsuming all of these theories into the single (and well-put) observation that "[i]t is the moral and rhetorical aim of American literature . . . to separate essence from existence, and to protect essence—or call it selfhood—from the vulgarity imposed by mere conditions." In other words, American writers are more likely than their European counterparts to be essentialists, more likely to consider inner (or spiritual) existence to be separable from—if not more important or more interesting than—outer (or physical) reality. Having suggested this much, however, Donoghue proceeds to declare that "[a]n essentialist theory of American experience is . . . implausible," and to argue that "the American difference . . . arises from the incongruity between, on the one hand, a continent given over to commercial expansion and aggrandizement and, on the other, the promise of individualism and selfhood implicit in the once open expanse of virgin land."

What Donoghue seems to be saying here is that American literature tends to depict a tension between the forces of society and history and the lure of freedom, of unrestrained "selfhood." Many critics have observed this tension, though no two of them have described it in quite the same way, and different critics have convincingly emphasized different aspects of it; it is variously manifested as a conflict between city and wilderness, corruption and innocence, licit and illicit sexuality, marriage and bachelor-hood, the company of women and the company of men, Europe and America, East and West, acquisitiveness and affection, the temporal and the eternal, intelligence and ignorance. (Which of these elements proves to be stronger, more virtuous, or more attractive than the other, however, varies from author to author.) This characterization of American literature is a wonderfully catholic one: it embraces everything from *The Scarlet Letter, Daisy Miller,* and the Leatherstocking novels to *Main Street, The Great Gatsby,* and *The House of Mirth.* Yet Donoghue does not do an effective job of setting forth this version of his theory; indeed, he barely nods in its direction before moving on to the somewhat different observation that American literature is concerned with "self and space, or self and nature," and that it represents an "attempt to understand man as such, free of social and historical contingencies." "Free"? Suddenly it seems as if Donoghue has given up the notion that American literature depicts a tension, and has decided instead that social and historical contingencies—far from existing in conflict with the urge toward freedom and "self-hood"—are to all intents and purposes non-existent in American literature. Even this is not his final word on the subject, however. At the end of the essay—when he approvingly quotes Trilling's

declaration that, Parrington to the contrary, a nation's culture "is not truly figured in the image of current," but that (in Donoghue's paraphrase) "the form of its existence is struggle"—Donoghue seems to return to the notion that American literature tends to portray, not freedom from "social and historical contingencies," but a struggle between a longing for such freedom and a helplessness in the face of such contingencies.

In short, Donoghue's essay does not come to anything resembling a clear conclusion in regard to a theory of American literature. On the essay's penultimate page, in fact, he speaks with apparent disdain of "the ferocious lucidity of a theory," as if to say that it is fun to play around with theories, but to settle down with one—and to declare plainly one's allegiance to it—is positively beastly. This position, to the present critic's mind, seems a bit too close for comfort to the gamesmanship of Derrida & Co.

What is no less lamentable than Donoghue's theoretical tergiversation is his deviation into politics. He begins the essay's concluding paragraphs by posing a question that seems to appear—in more senses than one—from out of left field: "to what extent does our professional interest in American literature, and our participation in State Department cultural enterprises, commit us to general sympathy with the aims of an American administration?" Donoghue says that at the 1975 Salzburg conference on American Studies which inspired the piece, this question was not entertained, but adds that "[i]t would have to arise if we were to assemble at Salzburg now: April 12, 1986." The remaining sentences of the essay are so remarkable that I feel obliged to quote them in their entirety:

> We would have to find some courteous method [he continues] of indicating that while we remained professionally concerned with American literature, and therefore with the society it expresses, we do not feel bound to approve this official policy or that. It is clear that President Reagan's foreign policy, in its bearing upon Nicaragua, El Salvador, Libya, and other countries, arises with appalling directness from a vision of America's destiny in the world. It is impossible to distinguish a vision from a theory in this context. The President's private war with the duly elected government of Nicaragua is his version, righteous and unquestioning, of the theory of America as Redeemer Nation. It is not even necessary for him to say that he regards America's destiny as one of saving the world from Communism: it is a matter of course. His more immediate problem is to convince millions of Americans that their security is threatened by the existence of one form of government rather than another in Nicaragua.

> The easiest way, for a student of American literature, is to keep literature separate from a President's missionary zeal. I have no gift to set this statesman right. Perhaps it is enough to keep the political consequences of an inherited vision in mind, and to let it darken one's lucidity from time to time.

There are many things about the above passage that deserve comment, but I will confine myself to marveling at Donoghue's astonishing contradiction. If he genuinely does believe in keeping literature separate from politics, then what in heaven's name is this political jeremiad doing at the end of an essay on literary theory? The smug self-righteousness that is manifest here surfaces elsewhere in *Reading America*—and, for that matter, has surfaced not infrequently in Donoghue's other books. "I don't disavow an occasional inclination to set statesmen right," he admitted (note the similar phrasing) in the introduction to *We Irish,* but went on to claim that "[p]rofessionally, I am concerned with politics only when it invades literature and prescribes the gross conditions under which poems, plays, stories, and novels are written." May one be forgiven for finding this hard to believe?

But enough about **"America in Theory,"** which after all is only one of ten pieces included in the first of *Reading America*'s two sections, under the rubric "Essays." (As distinguished, that is, from the "Brevities"—a euphemism for "reviews"—that are collected in section two.) The other nine pieces in the section—one of them previously unpublished, two of them originally included in the *Times Literary Supplement,* and the remainder first published in *Festschriften* and in such small circulation journals as *Salmagundi, Nineteenth-Century Fiction,* and the *Sewanee Review*—take as their topics some of the major figures in American literature: Emerson, Thoreau, Whitman, Dickinson. Henry Adams, Henry James, T. S. Eliot, Wallace Stevens, and Lionel Trilling. As a rule, these pieces are overlong, stuffy, dull, pretentious, and a great deal more confusing than they need to be. **"Emerson at First,"** for instance, is a twenty page, chapter by-chapter synopsis of *Nature* in which Donoghue manages to work in references to Valéry, Stevens, Coleridge, Wordsworth, Schiller, Henry James, Yeats, Hegel, Winters, and Swedenborg, among others, most of which references seem designed less to illuminate Emerson (whom Donoghue, by the way, has discussed more interestingly, and more briefly, in his book *Connoisseurs of Chaos*) than to throw all but the most industrious, sympathetic, and intellectually agile readers off the track. (Donoghue is the sort of critic who likes to behave as if his readers are intimately familiar with materials that he *knows* they aren't intimately familiar with.) **"Thoreau"** (which appears to be an expanded version of a review of the Library of America's Thoreau volume and Sharon Cameron's 1985 study *Writing Nature: Henry Thoreau's Journal*) seems, for most of its length, to be little more than a collocation of biographical facts and critical quotations; it is not until the last paragraph that Donoghue makes it clear that he has indeed, in a roundabout way, been developing a thesis—namely, that "[i]t is only in language, and not

even in Nature, that Thoreau is content to reside." It is typical of Donoghue not to have put this sentence earlier in the piece, and saved us all a good deal of puzzlement.

"Whitman" is better. Though Donoghue devotes much of this thirty-page essay to a largely incoherent attempt to make Whitman's various metaphysical pronouncements cohere, he has some worthwhile things to say about Whitman's poetry. For example: "Whitman's favorite subject is movement, process, becoming: no wonder he loved bridges and ferries, which kept things moving while defining relationships, one thing with another." And: "To get the beauty of Whitman's poetry hot, one must read it in long, rolling stretches. No poet is less revealed in the single phrase, the image, or even the line. The unit of the verse is indeed the phrase, a loose limbed structure of several words easily held together and moving along because the cadence goes with the speaker's breath." Yet Donoghue grouses altogether too much about Whitman's self-centeredness, anti-intellectuality, and lack of interest in history and form—which is rather like complaining that Kareem Abdul-Jabbar is too tall to make a good jockey.

The remainder of the "Essays" section is a mixed bag. **"Emily Dickinson"** is a competent review of Richard Sewall's biography; **"On 'Gerontion'"** is an intelligent explication of Eliot's poem. In **"Henry Adams's Novels,"** however, Donoghue takes sixteen pages to make the admittedly correct but extremely simple point that Adams was too much of an ideologue on the subject of identity and power to be a good novelist; and in **"Henry James and *The Sense of the Past*"** he spends eight pages describing the various possible attitudes toward the past that one might assume, and then eight more pages describing the attitude that James adopts in his last, unfinished novel. This is provocatively if somewhat ploddingly accomplished, and the essay offers several examples of the way that Donoghue can at once impress with his insight and irritate with his manner of expressing it. Consider the following two sentences, for instance: "I assume, then, that James regarded 'the historic' as what pretends to be knowable, given a little rummaging around the archives and nothing much in the exercise of imagination. His chief sentiment, faced by the pretension, was resentment at the implication that there is a form of reality that makes the imagination redundant." This is very good, but badly put.

As for **"Stevens's Gibberish"** (published here for the first time, apparently), it is an extremely peculiar piece. It takes its cue from a couple of provocative lines in "Notes Toward a Supreme Fiction"—"The poem goes from the poet's gibberish to / The gibberish of the vulgate and back again"—but never settles upon anything resembling an intelligible thesis. At first Donoghue seems to be interested in demonstrating that "[i]n 'Notes

Toward a Supreme Fiction' the poet seeks a complete poetic speech by bringing together . . . 'the imagination's Latin' [and] 'the gibberish of the vulgate.'" But then he proceeds to twist the meaning of gibberish in all sorts of perverse and obscure ways, so that the essay eventually seems less a study of gibberish than an exercise in it. For instance, he speaks of a sort of gibberish "which corresponds not to words that fail but to words that drive meanings beyond their rational forms into a void or a vertigo," describes rhyme (for reasons that never become clear) as a form of gibberish, refers to "the gibberish of syntax," and wanders (critically speaking) into French airspace:

> If we transfer to the reader the faculty of gibberish hitherto ascribed to the poet, we offer him the latitude of reading which Roland Barthes proposed; not the duty of interpreting, moment by dutiful moment, the words on the page, but the pleasure that goes its own playful way. Barthes urged readers to act wilfully, running to excess in whatever directions they chose; anything, rather than accept the official rhetoric evidently enforced by a poem or novel. According to Barthes, there is no single privileged interpretation: the text is an occasion for being wilful.
>
> In this respect, Barthes's recommendation coincides with Derrida's. . . .

It takes a while, after this detour, for Donoghue to get back (or, as he puts it, "revert") to Stevens, and when he does, the discussion of Derrida and Barthes appears not to have gotten us anywhere. But then Donoghue's principal purpose in this essay seems to be to work in as many high-powered names as possible; consequently he leads us through references not only to Barthes and Derrida, but also to Valéry, Rimbaud, R. P. Blackmur, Frank Kermode, Harold Bloom, Hugh Kenner, Kenneth Burke, Alain Robbe Grillet, C. S. Peirce, E. M. Cioran, Anthony Hecht, and Michel Foucault, *et al.,* without ever making it very clear what our destination might be. What is frustrating is not that Donoghue is trying here to communicate some complicated ideas about language in poetry, but that rather than set these ideas forth as lucidly and coherently as possible, he presents them in unclear prose that abounds in gratuitous digressions and baffling transitions. This essay is followed by **"Trilling, Mind, and Society,"** a tiresomely elaborate examination of Lionel Trilling's attitudes toward the two subjects named in the title and his notion of their proper relation to one another.

The key word here, it should be noted, is *attitude.* For it might fairly be said that, in all of the essays in ***Reading America,*** Donoghue is concerned less with the literary value of these authors' productions than with their points of view; his is not a criticism of aesthetics, or even of ideas, but a criticism of attitudes—attitudes toward, say, life and literature, mind and matter, nature and man. Such attitudes are, of course, a legitimate field of critical inquiry, but Donoghue is so preoccupied

with them, in the first section of ***Reading America,*** that these supposedly literary essays read like studies in philosophy. He discusses the poetry of Whitman and Stevens in much the same way as he discusses the theories of Emerson and Trilling; to Donoghue, the *way* in which Stevens, say, wrote—the style, the form, the voice—seems to matter less than the attitudinal content of his poems.

It is no coincidence that the author whose name appears most frequently in these pages is Kenneth Burke—a man whom it does not seem quite proper to describe as a literary critic, a man of whom Donoghue himself observes, in a reverent review that appears in the second section of ***Reading America,*** that "[i]t is still not clear what kind of writer Burke is: it doesn't seem adequate to call him a literary critic, a poet, a novelist, a short story writer, a sociologist, or a philosopher of history." Donoghue's solution: "[p]erhaps we should simply call him a sage, and think of the latitude traditionally taken by such a mind." He proceeds to compare Burke—favorably—to Emerson ("No comparison nearer home suggests itself"), and to provide a useful summary of Burke's approach to literature—which, because it sheds light on the background of Donoghue's own method, seems worth rehearsing here.

Donoghue explains that during Burke's "second phase" (apparently his most important phase by far, at least to Donoghue), Burke proposed "to read literature 'as equipment for living'. . . . Poems, plays, and novels were approached as strategies for dealing with particular situations. One might find in a poem 'the dancing of an attitude.'" During this phase Burke worked out the theory of dramatism, which is based upon the notion that the most useful way to discuss human actions, whether in real life or in literature, is to do so in terms of five key words—act, scene, agent, agency, and purpose. "What Burke is offering," Donoghue writes, "is both a poetics of social life and a way of reading as an epitome of a way of living." What he is also offering, one might add, is a critical method that is impersonally clinical, that threatens to reduce literature to a blueprint of behavior, that slights the importance of style and ignores the obligation to make a critical judgment. It is a method whose influence is apparent on every page of Donoghue's essays, with their relative lack of attention to aesthetic questions and their virtual preoccupation with the concept of attitude—Emerson's and Thoreau's attitudes toward nature, Thoreau's and Stevens's attitudes toward language, Whitman's attitude toward self and history, Henry Adams's attitude toward identity and power, and Lionel Trilling's attitude toward mind and society.[1]

Burke's influence can also be observed in the frosty abstraction ridden style of Donoghue's essays. Like Burke's, moreover, Donoghue's diction is often perplexing (Hart Crane, he writes, "had misgivings about the exemplary figure of his poetry"), inexact (he describes Dickinson's withdrawal from the world as "a gradual sequence"), or just plain awkward (Marianne Moore "didn't regard herself as a critic in any systematic sense: for her, Kenneth Burke was superbly enough in that category"). He complains that R. W. B. Lewis, in a discussion of Crane's poem "Chaplinesque," "does not encourage the reader to think of other poems that might measure that poem's achievement": what he means, I think, is that Lewis does not encourage the reader to measure the poem's achievement against that of other poems. This passage about the quotations in Marianne Moore's reviews is typically infelicitous in its phrasing:

> She never doubts that the quoted words have a valid adjectival relation to the personality from which they have issued; nor does she concern herself with values embodied in the linguistic medium rather than in a personality deemed to precede it. Many theorists would deny the merit of positing a personality separate from its linguistic form. But Moore resorted to words to assure herself of a personal force as if behind them.

Donoghue is, furthermore, partial to highfalutin but murky phrases such as "[h]istory as the narrative form of meaning." He often seems to prefer to say something confusingly and at length when he might say it clearly and concisely. In his essay on Henry Adams, he perpetrates several baffling and pretentious sentences the whole point of which (as becomes clear after two or three readings) is that Adams was interested in writing novels not as a means of understanding patterns and forces but as a means of conveying an understanding of them which he'd already come to. And Donoghue has a fondness for "explaining" quotations by paraphrasing them in more elaborate language and then bringing in a gratuitous quotation from some critic. For example:

> In *The Dolphin,* Elizabeth Hardwick is quoted as saying to Lowell, "Why don't you lose yourself/and write a play about the fall of Japan?" I take this as meaning: "Why don't you forget about yourself for a while, suppress yourself, and write something 'objective,' remote from your private interests and circumstances?" Or, in Char's terms, why don't you expel yourself, in all your incompleteness, from the scene, and expel all the other people whom you are in the habit of dragging into your poems as functions of yourself; and wait, trust in the Lord, until you will all be ready, combining in genuine presence?

Finally, Donoghue employs the words *revert* and *advert* to distraction and has an unfortunate affection for such precious vocables as *prescind* and *betimes*; also, over the course of the book he describes a number of things as exorbitant, and misuses the noun form of the word at least once, writing that Eliot wrestles with "the exorbitance of emotion to any object that supposedly provokes and justifies it."

Donoghue is not, then, one of the major prose stylists of our time. Yet he is a man of considerable critical talents—which are, as it turns out, manifested far more engagingly in the second section of *Reading America* than in the first. This section consists of seventeen reviews—which originally appeared between 1967 and 1986, most of them in *The New York Times Book Review* or *The New York Review of Books*—of volumes by or about Conrad Aiken, Marianne Moore, Stevens, Ransom, Tate, H. D., Crane, Auden, Burke, Berryman, Lowell, Plath, and Ashbery. On the whole, these reviews are shorter, livelier, sharper, less abstract, and a good deal more witty and readable than the essays that precede them. Indeed, Donoghue's tone, in these pages, is often downright colloquial. He writes that Aiken's "narrative poems are interminable, as if Aiken wanted to get into some *Guinness Book of World Records* for the longest something-or-other in American poetry." In this section Donoghue is less blatantly concerned with the subject of attitude (though it does rear its head now and again; he carries on at length, for instance, about Lowell's "patience" and his attitude toward history). Nor does he lead us, in these reviews, on interminable detours through the thickets of theory. "Olson," he writes, "had a theory about space, that Space rather than Time is the American category. Enough of that." (Enough for a "brevity," perhaps, but not enough for a Donoghue essay; in section one of *Reading America* he devotes two paragraphs, no less, to Olson's eccentric theory of space.)

Patently, the review format obliges Donoghue to do something that he can avoid doing in scholarly essays: namely, to render critical opinions, and to do so succinctly. These opinions are often both cleverly phrased and wonderfully sensible. Of H. D., for instance, Donoghue says that her "theme was all she had, except for a small rare talent and a pale Greek face." Crane, he observes, "cultivated intensity at the expense of every other poetic value, as if he numbered only the hectic hours." Donoghue describes Plath's "Lady Lazarus" as a "big striptease, Lady doing her number and singing the blues"; and he remarks wisely of Plath's "Daddy"— with its Nazi death camp imagery—that "the thrill we get from such poems is something we have no good cause to admire in ourselves."

He observes at one point that Auden "is gifted in comparison and contrast, for the energy they release." So is Donoghue. If, in section one, his tendency to overindulge this talent—a talent, by the way, that he shares not only with Auden but with Burke—is responsible for many an irrelevant digression, in section two this same talent, more strictly disciplined, yields a number of provocative connections. Donoghue speaks, for instance, of Aiken's "night on the town with Edwin Arlington Robinson, another sprawling poet, incidentally, given to long narrative poems but a far more powerful because more dramatic poet than Aiken." And though his preoccupation with attitude is unfortunate, he does make an interesting distinction between Lowell's attitude toward history and Pound's. Needless to say, Donoghue more often thinks to compare writers' attitudes than their stylistic or formal choices; in **"Trilling, Mind, and Society,"** he writes that, in "Hawthorne and Our Time," Trilling "distinguished not so much between Hawthorne, James, and Kafka as between our diverse understanding of their tempers and achievement." This is much the sort of distinction that Donoghue tends to make, often—one must say—quite well.

Yet to read **Reading America** is to be woefully aware of Donoghue's relative indifference to the sort of distinctions—namely, aesthetic distinctions—that ultimately matter the most when one is speaking of a work of literature. To be sure, there are times—as I have indicated—when Donoghue does discuss aesthetic matters, and does so with a commendable discernment; but all too frequently, especially when one is reading the first section of the book, one feels the urge to remind him that a writer is not merely a bundle of attitudes, that a great novel or poem is something more than a document in behavioral psychology. All too frequently, in other words, Donoghue simply seems uninterested in the music of poetry, the rhythms of prose, all those ineffable aspects of literature that cannot be reduced, as it were, to one of the five categories of dramatism. To echo his own remark about Kenneth Burke, in short, it sometimes doesn't seem quite correct to describe Donoghue as a literary critic; in his more solemn, heavy-duty essays, he is really more of a textual diagnostician, a sort of NMR-spectrography technician in the laboratory of literature. If it is sad to have to say this sort of thing about a man of letters, it is particularly frustrating to have to say it about Denis Donoghue. For this man who at times doesn't look at all like a literary essayist has produced a small body of "brevities" which demonstrate that—all of his studied efforts to the contrary—he can be a very fine critic indeed.

Note

1. It is perhaps worth noting that Donoghue's admiration of Burke is far from a one sided affair. Burke has written about Donoghue—and very favorably, needless to say—more than once. In 1977, for example, Burke reviewed Donoghue's book *The Sovereign Ghost: Studies in Imagination* in *The New Republic*. The tenor of the review is expressed in its first sentence, which reads as follows: "Any text that deserves some measure of appreciation can consider itself lucky if Denis Donoghue chooses to write about it."

Margaret O'Brien (review date January 1988)

SOURCE: O'Brien, Margaret. "Irishry." *Essays in Criticism* 38, no. 1 (January 1988): 84-93.

[*In the following review of* We Irish, *O'Brien comments that Donoghue fails to express a coherent stance on Irish politics.*]

'Whatever You Say Say Nothing', the title of a poem by Seamus Heaney in *North,* is also a common admonition heard all over Ireland, not just that corner where a civil war is going on. Denis Donoghue [in *We Irish*] is trying to follow this racial wisdom. Beneath a polished surface of urbane prose there is a centre of unyielding ambiguity which keeps obfuscation and revelation in perfect, taut balance. Reading this collection means above all coping with the author's elegant but hermetic style. Conversely, it also means making sense of a few outbursts of unsubstantiated opinion, tiny, irrational explosions which appear to release a tension built up under the normal, stringent conditions of his style. The book's title is taken from Yeats's 'The Statues':

> We Irish, born into that ancient sect
> But thrown upon this filthy modern tide
> And by its formless spawning, fury wrecked,
> Climb to our proper dark, that we may trace
> The lineaments of a plummet-measured face.

Yeats's assertion of a racial homogeneity and superiority is, typically, both questioned and endorsed by Donoghue, who refuses to react simplistically, or perhaps respond positively, to the provocation in his title, for the attempt to define Irishness is what everything from Northern violence to the proliferation of literary-political debate on the island is about. Donoghue's book must be placed in this national context, particularly in relation to questions which impinge on the evaluation of literature and the delineation of a literary tradition.

Making a contribution to this argument, however, is emphatically not his main purpose here. The limited space he gives even to allusions to the controversy signals an intention to keep what Patrick Kavanagh calls, in the poem 'Epic', a 'local row' in its local place. Whereas Kavanagh allows the parochial to become the universal through the intervention of human imagination ('Homer's ghost came whispering to my mind / He said: I made the Iliad from such / A local row. Gods make their own importance'), Donoghue resists immersion in the politics of his parish. It may be that he is implicitly defending an important value for him which has to do with preserving the act of literary criticism from inordinate political or parochial influences. There is evidence to suggest, however, a less lofty motive, that the Northern identity of many of the most prominent spokesmen in the debate may contribute to Donoghue's preference to limit his participation. To locate his reasons it is necessary to probe beneath the surface of a quite resistant prose and one way to prise it open is to note its contradictions. Identifying a strand of modern Irish fiction, to which James Stephens belongs, Donoghue refers to a 'native product [which] tends to be runic, archaic, pedantic, a caprice of words . . . In such books the motto is: keep talking and it can't happen. Life is suffered only in the cracks between the words'. Donoghue reads Stephens in a way we have to read Donoghue.

As much as he has a penchant for pithy, nearly aphoristic statement, he also has a tendency toward the opposite, eloquent expansion. Characteristically, he dilates on the features of a literary phenomenon which others would label with a terse tag. For example, talking about evidence in *Dubliners* of what some critics might simply call free indirect speech, Donoghue lovingly explains, 'Often a sentence begins as if its sole business were to tell a disinterested truth, but within a few phrases it leans so far toward the character being described that it receives and accepts idioms he would use if he were managing the narrative'. He enjoys talking of language as if it were corporeal and animate (it 'leans', it 'receives'), never more than when he's tracing the 'lineaments of the plummet-measured face' of Yeats's syntax:

> We are discouraged from enquiring how the grammar works, or which verb goes with what noun; we are to allow ourselves to be entangled and to submit to a language in which the digressions are richer than the formal business, the sentence. I draw from this the conclusion that the sentence stands for the reality principle, and that to Yeats it is at best a necessary evil, a ball-and-chain, tolerable only to the extent to which its force is thwarted. The digressions, the subordinate clauses, are insubordinate, and they have the effect of depriving language of the nominative power in which empiricists delight; they turn the poem into a place of shadow and suggestion.

Donoghue too prefers to follow the syntactic pleasure principle, letting leisurely, sinewy clauses stretch into connotative oases of 'shadow and suggestion'. The problem with this penchant is that it is also linked to what he calls his 'latitudinarian' political posture and in these times in Ireland there is great demand precisely for 'nominative power'. Maybe Donoghue's style is an inspired passive resistance and several decades on will be appreciated for its sanity. Right now the reader who has a sense of urgency about certain Irish problems is going to feel impatient with Donoghue's walking or even strolling up to big questions and saying 'maybe' or 'either' or 'both'.

Donoghue is eminently qualified to influence his countrymen in the choices they are now making about their tradition, prominently the places that Yeats and Joyce should occupy in the canon. We see evidence everywhere of a lifetime's assiduous and sensitive reading of his own literature. The book is saturated with the humanism which has coexisted throughout his career with a trained scepticism; and there is no less intuition here about the Irish authors he has read than there is scholarship about Irish history and sophistication about critical method. Images of untutored literary experiences from childhood, like wheeling a newly-purchased radio on a tea-trolley down a village street in the North in order to hear Frank O'Connor read 'The Long Road to Ummerra', are interlaced with arguments based on Donoghue's latest theoretical investigations, such as his

application of Mikhail Bakhtin's distinction between monologism and dialogism to a reading of *Finnegans Wake*. But Donoghue's special skill is still the individualistic and humanistic one of acute perception rendered in lucid, supple prose. Many such moments occur in the book but the best probably crop up as unassuming comments about the second string of Irish writers. I cannot think of a more truthful and kind assessment of Frank O'Connor than to say that his 'strength . . . is his generosity. Knowing what duress means, and the penury of experience available to most people, he has always wanted to do the best for them, to show the quirky doggedness practiced by people who live on the margin'. A discerning insight about Sean O'Faolain, in relation to the story 'Fugue', is that the author 'on his hero's behalf, is trying to make me feel more, and more tenderly, than anything the story compels me to feel . . . The style is in excess of any event or sentiment he can remember or imagine for it'.

Donoghue's attraction to Yeats is exactly that his grand style matches the height of his desire, that there is in him sentiment so intense that no style could possibly exceed it. Commenting on Yeats's use of symbolism, Donoghue refers with approbation to 'an act of creation which subverts the original one'. The essays here on Yeats are much more impassioned than the more academic pieces on Joyce. Donoghue simply is not in sympathy with the new inspiration Joyce is providing for pluralistic, quotidian living and an art shaped by these ordinary contingencies. Although Donoghue shares with many Irishmen a time-honoured resentment against Yeats for his dismissal of middle-class, Catholic, urban culture as philistine, Donoghue hasn't joined forces with the major critics in Ireland today who have felt compelled to warn of the consequences for society and literature of Yeats's heroic-mythological poetic. Again, however, his views on the two great authors require extrapolating from some quite cryptic texts.

The Joyce essay, **'Bakhtin and *Finnegans Wake'*,** provides an example of the way ambiguity inevitably bubbles up in Donoghue's work, the spring here coming from a rift between head and heart. The author seems initially intrigued by the intellectual possibilities of placing Bakhtin's ideas on Joyce's text but ends discontented with the entire project, the reason being that neither Bakhtin nor even a more kindred critic, John Crowe Ransom, can account as well as Donoghue can on his own for what he perceives. Bakhtin can be used to explain the divergence between the root words of written language and the unutterable verbal amalgamations on the text's surface as an example of carnivalesque travesty of official culture; Ransom has seen the purposed fragmentation and polyvalence of the surface as a rebellion against logical positivist thinking. Donoghue finds these models too limiting and rigid. Ironically, as an author in his own right, he is rejecting at this closing moment the dialogism he previously demonstrated the effect of in Joyce, during the intellectual phase of his argument, when he was neutrally playing with the application of theory to text. His own instinctive behaviour at the end of the essay displays a strong personal preference for the values of monologism, as he defines it:

> A monologic artistic world is one which is controlled at every point by the artist who has projected it. In such a world, every thought is a function of the artist's consciousness: it either gravitates to him and becomes a sign of his power, or it is admitted only so that it can be degraded and repudiated.

This describes exactly his use and ultimate rejection of other critical voices. One might finally say that his uneasiness with Bakhtin, despite the elegance of his argument for heteroglossia in the *Wake,* is that he himself is committed to the cultivation of a single, authoritative voice, for the power that is in such a vehicle. It is very telling that in his individual reading of Joyce he appeals to Wallace Stevens, whom he has allowed to 'gravitate to him and become a sign of his power'; and that the interpretation he gives to the *Wake*'s 'gibberish' (a Stevens word, from 'Notes towards a Supreme Fiction') is a transcendent one, lifting the text and its author beyond the dualisms determined by Bakhtin's or Ransom's readings, since both predicate a comparison of one language with another: 'Isn't it possible that Joyce's gibberish is going behind the official Latins and Englishes not to make contact with some linguistic origin preceding history but, hastening the next Viconian phase, to place us in hieroglyphs, free before any law?'.

To locate an 'origin preceding history' is still to concede the existence of history as a subsequent fact. The critical point about Donoghue's reading of Joyce is his impulse to move him more toward Yeats on the spectrum that ranges from historical fact to artistic transcendence. The essay **'Yeats: The Question of Symbolism'** centres on the poet's use of symbol to manipulate time in a way that grants even greater autonomy, to be 'free before any law', or nearly. The difficulty in interpreting Donoghue on Yeats is a problem of voice: often it is hard to divide objective description of the poet's positions from the critic's personal involvement with them. Donoghue's empathy for Yeats is uncanny and total, such as saying with the sureness of intuitive, immediate insight, 'Rage kept him going when reasonableness would have brought him down'. As one receives a sense of identification from his tone here, this is also the case when he says, 'The aura we feel in the symbol marks for Yeats the presence of the supernatural in the natural: if he believed in anything, he believed in reincarnation'. While Denis Donoghue can't possibly be associated with theosophical notions, it does seem that he is in sympathy, however covertly, with Yeats's fight against time. The

triumphant point of his argument, a stunning one, is that Yeats found legend or myth to be the mediator between allegory, which represents the claims of history, and symbolism which asserts the priority of radiant timelessness.

What might have been a solution for Yeats, however, has become a severe problem for Irish poetry; and Donoghue, as much in sympathy with the compromise as the desire that prompted it, does not articulate the troubling consequences of the poetic. He begins his essay **'Romantic Ireland'** by distinguishing between myth and fiction, seeing both as fictive but myth as having a practical application in the world: men have been known to act on myths. Donoghue's tone is never harder to decipher than in this crucial section because one can't tell if he's paraphrasing Yeats or Stevens, whom he once again recruits to provide analogical buttressing, but the voice does seem Donoghue's own: 'And if there is any question of indigence of spirit, the indigence is now and in Ireland rather than then and in the other Ireland, the country sustained by the desire and need of it. Where Stevens speaks of gods and giants of a vivid time, Yeats speaks of Romantic Ireland, but the speech is continuous; it issues from the desire to be more and better than ourselves'. Yeats created a myth of Ireland to accommodate his desire, and if his use of actual legends anchored that desire in time, it also interpreted history, even warped it to the shape of desire. It is a warping akin to what memory does to the past, making it 'more and better'. Bakhtin is dedicated to the undermining of mythic hegemony, especially over language, through the agency of heteroglossia, the admission of diverse voices, an attitude antagonistic to Yeats as read by Donoghue. Opponents to Yeats in Ireland are not necessarily invoking Bakhtin but they are, through various arguments both individual in origin and inspired by thinkers from other cultures, attacking the central idea of cultural essentialism behind Yeats's stance.

Some of the most cogent arguments against cultural and literary essentialism have come from Seamus Deane, a Northern poet and critic. His essay, 'Heroic Styles: the Tradition of an Idea', attempts to expose how violence in the North has resulted from both sides pressing for the fulfilment of an heroic ideal by means of a univocal, tribal style. Deane's essay, while powerful, has the flaw of most highly polemical pieces: in the interests of persuasion it eliminates points that might impede the velocity and force of its argument. For example his rejection of Yeats as an exponent of univocalism is in some respects a reactive response which reduces the poet, ignoring his complexity, especially the self-questioning that modified most of his extreme, even obnoxious, stances. Donoghue, in this book, particularly the essay **'On "The Winding Stair"'**, does complete justice to the presence of continual conflict and difficult balances in Yeats. Because, however, of Donoghue's own temperament and deepest convictions about Yeats, he is precisely the person to confront Deane about the question of essentialism. This is particularly true because his defence of it is grounded in his sense of what the creative imagination requires, but a reader immersed in this debate is going to be disappointed at how little time Donoghue gives to the task of meeting this question head-on, particularly since what he does give is helpful, indeed enticing. He is right, for example, to say, as a corrective to the ironic hagiography now surrounding Joyce, as the supreme advocate of the ordinary, that Joyce too may have harbored a myth of essentialism. Miss Ivors in 'The Dead' may be taunting and ticking off Gabriel for his inability to embrace an ideal of Ireland, a failure of passion no less than that displayed in his marriage. I might add that Michael Furey, the passionate boy from Galway, may be an avatar of mythic values. Donoghue directly refers to Deane and begins an argument for essentialism with these few but significant words:

> If you say that essence precedes existence, you propose a quasi-historical relation which you are free to ignore or not. If you say that existence is predicated upon essence, you are proposing a logical rather than an historical relation. Either way, a mind does not show itself to be dizzy merely by assuming that the meaning of a particular historical existence issues from a situation which may be beyond the reach of historical scholarship. Nothing is gained, and only the satisfaction of ridicule is acquired, by scorning 'essence' as an object of interest and concern.

The beginning and end of these comments veer in two directions, one indicating where reasonable debate on the problem might go, the other suggesting what inflamed emotions have led to.

It is regrettable that in this book Donoghue himself has not held to a judicious, tolerant tone throughout. He is particularly hard on Heaney, the Northern poets generally (Mahon with his impeccable formalism and echoes of Stevens is exempt). The problem comes down to how one responds to violence in the North, generally to violence in the Republican tradition. Donoghue is extremely ambivalent on this sensitive subject because he can't decide just how violence may feed or impede imagination. He admits, in a rare moment of concord with Conor Cruise O'Brien, that Yeats may be more talk than action on violence. Donoghue uses Rilke to make a distinction between a naïve and sentimental poet, one of immediate emotional response, the other of self-conscious attitudes. Particularly in his relationship with violence Yeats seems to Donoghue a sentimental poet trying to be naïve. What Donoghue fails to appreciate about Heaney is that, being a Northerner and surrounded by actual violence, there is a social imperative not to be naïve, to worry and seek solutions that are responsible both to life and art. This has been costly and painful for Heaney and the poetry since *North* records the tiring process. Donoghue shows a puzzling

insensitivity to the sincerity of Heaney's struggle when he makes a sarcastic reference to the poet's bogus martyrdom, his air of 'sackcloth and ashes'. Donoghue doesn't seem to register that Heaney's persistent self-scrutiny registers the impossibility of being a naïve poet in Ireland now. So too the critical debate in large part spurred by 'Field Day', publishers based in Derry, irritates Donoghue, with his aesthetic sense of the shape the culture should have.

That his is an aesthetic rather than a political passion, however, becomes clear when he speaks of the uncouth but unmistakably authentic Patrick Kavanagh. Donoghue seems unable to fathom how the Monoghan poet has been a model for so many contemporary Irish writers. The way Kavanagh's example legitimates finding the origins of a voice in a local, specific culture rather than a received literary tradition is to Donoghue more incomprehensible than objectionable. He speaks with discernible envy of Larkin and Hughes and Hill as poets with a large, inexhaustible pap of uninterrupted cultural history to suck on; but Heaney's essay 'Englands of the Mind' perceives an insecurity in the post-colonial British identity and a diversity of voices in its contemporary literary expression that belies any monolithic impression. It can't be overstated how liberating an insight this is for an Irishman. It is consoling to think that nostalgia for a unified culture may not be available to anybody, whether they live at the centre or on the periphery—that, indeed, such distinct locations are now blurred. Donoghue registers more than anything in this book a reluctance to let go of a myth of unity perpetrated most consistently in art. He tells the anecdote of taking Frank Kermode around Dublin and the non-Irish critic observing that 'Ireland, more than most countries, is seen through a haze of allusion, mainly literary, musical and pictorial'. Donoghue adds, 'Kermode did not remark something equally true, that to see Ireland through its received artistic forms is mostly to see it as a lost cause . . . But when we give ourselves to a lost cause which we know to be lost, we do so from a different structure of desires and needs; perhaps because we dwell in impossibility and would not live elsewhere even if we could'. This could not better announce the nub of the problem. Donoghue doesn't appear to count himself among those Irishmen, from the plain people to the poets and politicians, who are tired of such graceful, transcendent suicide and are mustering the crude energy to 'live elsewhere', not knowing what shape this uncharted territory will take but being sure that it must make life possible for a various people, not a tribe.

Karl Miller (review date 21 March 1991)

SOURCE: Miller, Karl. "Literary Supplements." *London Review of Books* 13, no. 6 (21 March 1991): 6-7.

[*In the following review, Miller compares Donoghue's memoir* Warrenpoint *and William Styron's memoir* Darkness Visible. *Miller calls* Warrenpoint *a seductive and felicitous book.*]

Denis Donoghue has written a seductive book. Perhaps it could be said that he has spliced together two books, one of which is more seductive than the other. One of them narrates. The other contemplates. **Warrenpoint** is a series of passages, not unlike journal entries, some of which deal with his youth in the Northern Irish seaside town of that name, and in particular with his awareness, and acceptance, of his father, while the others consist of the annotations of the professor and man of letters. I don't mean to do as the Leavises did with *Daniel Deronda* and propose a Solomonic severance: let's just say that many readers would be very sorry to lose the memories if it were to come to a cut.

The father did not talk much, or read much, or go to the pictures. This was a Solomon whose wisdom did not propose things, or even say them. It was nevertheless a ruler's wisdom. He 'was the rock of ages'. When he was still he seems to have been very, very still, to have been his own statue, and when he moved he moved well. He was an exemplary walker towards undoubted destinations and the achievement of set purposes. A Catholic from the South, he was also a sergeant in the Royal Ulster Constabulary. Denis Donoghue communicates, but does not enlarge on, the possibility that there may have been a dilemma for his parent here. There was never any doubt in one way as to which side his father was on, together with all the other Catholics of the place—that of the South. But there was a duty that went with the job, and he did it. For this son, though not for his brother, their father was the law, and we are brought to feel that Denis Donoghue grew strong, and professorial, in responding to his father's strength of will. He accepted the regime at the police station, where the family lived in adjoining quarters; and he was later to be scornful of Freud's notion of a salutary resistance to fathers. It would have been hard for any son to resist the mother of the house, who is all but written out of the account—a state, however, which has an eloquence of its own. The mother, who was subject to 'attacks' of a medical nature, 'was a minor presence in comparison with my father'. Among relatives in the Republic 'it was taken for granted that whatever my mother did, she did badly.'

This is another dilemma about which little, but perhaps enough, is said. Denis Donoghue is interested in statements, and in sentences, and his own, when he touches on family matters, are in decisive, literal vein. They are delivered *de haut,* straight from the shoulder of someone who grew up to be six feet seven, and to be ill at ease in that long, 'wrong' body. His height seems to hover over the statements he makes on such subjects, and on some others. He, too, is the law, and we are inclined to take his word.

It was his 'instinct' to 'keep his distance' from Protestants. 'A Protestant was as alien to me as a Muslim, and Muslims had the merit that I didn't know any of them.' There's a Donoghue dying fall to that, and one imagines his lips moving to this effect up there in the snow-sphere of his six feet seven. 'A Protestant was someone who wasn't a Catholic.' But that wasn't all that a Protestant was. He was also an oppressor. That there were and are many sorts of Protestant, and that some Protestants have had no known wish to oppress Catholics, has very little potency for the book. Sergeant Donoghue strongly distinguished between family and others, while remaining instinctively on the side of those others who were Catholic. His son was at ease with his faith—'the existence of God wasn't a particular problem for me'—and he is its defender against the problems and misconceptions of others.

'Foreigners ask in dismay: How can Catholics and Protestants be killing one another since they're all supposed to be Christians? Not a telling point; there is often the most acute enmity between people who are similar but not the same.' He has also been calling them different. As for the telling point, some respect is surely due to the dismay of foreigners on this score, a feeling not remote from the historian Gibbon's less dismayed suggestion that there is a 'strange contradiction between the faith and practice of the Christian world'. Donoghue has 'never understood why people hate Christianity, especially people who express shock at the least trace of anti-semitism'—which distracts from the thought that anti-semitism has been, among other things, Christian. 'I could never understand how William Empson, a poet and critic I revere, could hate Christians and especially Catholics, thinking their religion nothing but a sordid cult of blood and sacrifice. Christ's blood was the form of this own suffering, he didn't recommend bloodletting for other people.' Did Empson hate Christians? If so, I wonder how many other Christians there are who believe this but are able to revere him. It has always been a particular problem that Christians have been bloodletters, and Denis Donoghue accepts that there are Irish people of the present century who have given their support to a cult of blood and sacrifice—which has included the blood and sacrifice of those who happened to be passing at the time.

The book is cold about those foreigners who are British. During the Second World War he sat by the wireless with his father listening to the News. 'I took it for granted that the British, unattractive as they were, spoke the truth, and that when the BBC announcer reported that Royal Air Force bombers had bombed some German city with great success, he was telling the truth. "All our aircraft returned home safely."' Censorship is a constraint which British politicians have shown an unattractive eagerness to impose. But this was a time when the country was in danger, which should count, as it doesn't here, for something. The book attends to Ireland's current troubles, but does not press for any solution. Ireland's prospects—which are thought likely to incorporate a Southern reluctance to join with the North—would appear to be no more agreeable to him than does its record in politics and government since independence. Unattractive Brits should not expect to discover that he backs the men of violence. But he argues against the revisionism which has been seeking to replace the myth of violence and revolution, blood and sacrifice, with a history of Ireland which speaks of class, social forces, economic determinants. His successor in the Chair of Modern English and American Literature at University College Dublin, Seamus Deane, has contributed to this work of revision, which is represented here as an un-Irish activity. Denis Donoghue's refusal to assist the work adds a dislike of Marx to his dislike of Freud.

'It is easy to denounce the Christian Brothers' to whom he listened to at school 'for teaching a dangerous version of Irish history, and to point to the renewed violence in Northern Ireland since 1968 as the inevitable fulfilment of that pedagogy.' The entry ends: 'Unfortunately, Ireland without its story is merely a member of the EC, the begging bowl our symbol.' This may disconcert some members of the EC, and some Irish-history revisionists. It is as if there were only the one story: but he has just been explaining that there is more than one, slow though the revisionist version may be to win adherents. The book ends with a news item reporting that Charlotte Street in Warrenpoint, along with his father's police station, had been blown up by the IRA.

Yeats is among the authors of the story he wants to preserve, the Yeats among others who wondered whether a play of his had caused certain Irishmen to be shot. Denis Donoghue concedes that stories and images may cause people to act and to die. He remarks that 'it would be fatuous to think that poetry is by definition without power of incitement.' On the next page he retracts, or balances, the suggestion: 'Above every poem or novel there should be a motto: "This road does not go through to action."' It may that all the claims about action and imagination which he makes at this stage, and which terminate in this motto, a motto employed, for a different purpose, in Frank Kermode's *Romantic Image*—it may that they are all true. But it may also be that he is at home with contradiction, growing up as he did in the shadow of that riven rock, the Catholic Protestant policeman. Some of his contradictions might be deemed mistakes by Protestants. Other might have seemed to deserve acceptance among the 'felicities' of life—this being a word he like to use and whose meaning he like to stretch. Not that such acceptance was always easy: 'For me, growing up involved reluctant assent to vacillation, coming to realise that there are occasions in life on which certitude is obnoxious.'

Meanwhile there were enough certitudes of another kind to be going on with, to take for granted.

Many of the entries which refer to adult experience refer to his reading, to words and sentences, and to his adult view of such features of his education as the practice of learning and memorising verse, a practice which may have served to promote a distinction between words and meaning, words and action, and which seems to have helped to shape his performance as a critic. The critic took to writing essays which were assemblies of words and thoughts and mottos—other people's and his own. The boy in question 'did not even try to write a poem or a story'. And yet the *Warrenpoint* assembly could be seen as a poem or a story, spliced, if you like, with a discursive supplement. Of his engagements with words—of the Irish Catholic Donoghue lexicon—he writes: 'Some words I can't use because, when I was a boy, they meant alien things. If you are a member of a choir, you are a chorister, but in Warrenpoint and, I suppose, in other places, too, a chorister was a member of a choir in a Protestant church. The Catholic version was choirboy.' Protestants talk about choirboys too. But we take his word for it that there was a difference for him, and we see that he is intent on a story of separation.

Soon after this he gets onto a sentence or semi-sentence which was interpreted for him in the classroom.

> It did not occur to me, in school, that sentences might not be the only form of statement or necessarily the best one. Not that I thought that they issued directly from nature or the hand of God, but I didn't question their being the entirely adequate expression of a perception. Nor did I think that there might be any other possibilities of the mind beyond that of perceiving. I knew that sometimes a part of the sentence could be left out; the omitted bit 'was understood', as Brother Cotter said. When Keats writes, in the 'Ode to a Nightingale', 'Already with thee!' we understood that he meant: I am now with thee. That was acceptable, because he had been talking of flying to the nightingale on the viewless wings of Poesy . . .

I have puzzled in the past over this exclamation mark in the Ode. The manuscript does not force you to read it as an aposiopesis, as the point at which a sentence breaks off; or indeed to read the three words that precede it as an exclamation. I think that the meaning is that where the bird is, perhaps (for all the poet knows) the Queen Moon is, and her starry court. Keats, however, remains on the ground: 'I cannot see what flowers are at my feet.' Haply he does complete a sentence at this turn in the Ode, whether or not the sentence has issued from nature or the hand of God, and it makes the poem less of an escape, and Keats less of an escape artist, if we think so.

Denis Donoghue says that he can't follow parts of some of the books he annotates, books such as *Totality and Infinity* by Emmanuel Levinas, but that he is sometimes able to respond to particular sentences in the parts that defeat him. The admission is unusual, and endearing. I am unable, as it happens, to follow some of his annotations—to persuade myself, for instance, that I know what he means by the singularity of existence and the plurality of the inner life. But here, too, there are sentences which elicit a response. This is a book which never loses the accepting reader for very long.

I believe that it will be thought a seductive book, a felicitous book, even by those who are unsettled by its ethnic and religious insistences and acceptances. There may be those for whom it is a jumble of memories and of the contingencies of the present, but I don't feel that way about it myself. The past is evoked in a manner which belies his sentences about an inability to write a poem or a story: but it also seems to me that the conjunction of the young Donoghue with the *savant* is among the attractions of the book. The alternation between what is going on now and what he now thinks was going on then might suggest some degree of attachment to a principle of randomness: at the same time, the two kinds of material could be thought to do something to explain one other. I'd hesitate to try to explain the explanation, but there are hints of a common interest in separation and acceptance, which can occasionally look like two faces of a single certitude— the certitude of someone who was to become the skilled reader of a sceptical and unstable modern literature. There he was and here he is, and what enters his mind in the present can sometimes resemble a version of what he was, out and about in his awkward body in the Warrenpoint of the Forties.

I went to University College Dublin once, after he had left for his Henry James Chair at New York University, and found the college echoing with the praises of the flown *savant,* with his sayings and with stories of his tenure. Two sorts of *ex cathedra* were apparent. He had made his mark, in the way that people hope for from professors. But few people would expect a memoir of this sweetness from a professor of English.

The American novelist William Styron has written a short book which describes how he came to grief at around the age of sixty, falling into a depression which nearly cost him his life. He felt, in romantic-confessional style, that he had to write it, and it is good to have it. I hope that it is not a disorder of the liberal conscience to suppose that the voices of those who have been through spells or seasons of mental trouble can now, with or without the sponsorship of romance, be heard with respect if they choose to write down what happened to them. Styron's account has several interesting features. His father had suffered from the same illness, and he lost his mother when he was 13. Throughout his life he had been dependent on alcohol, to which he here pays startling tribute: 'I did use it—often in conjunction with

music—as a means to let my mind conceive visions that the unaltered, sober brain has no access to. Alcohol was an invaluable senior partner of my intellect, besides being a friend whose ministrations I sought daily— sought also, I now see, as a means to calm the anxiety and incipient dread that I had hidden away for so long somewhere in the dungeons of my spirit.' Then quite suddenly he took a dislike to drink, and this threw him into a downward spiral, which was to be violently assisted by a psychiatrist's overprescription of the drug Halcion. Worries about his work—worries to which it is courageous of him to refer—made things worse, or were there at the start of his depression: part of the trouble could be termed writer's block writ hideously large. Last, but perhaps not least, he was brought round by being removed from his domestic surroundings, and from that lavish psychiatrist of his, and being placed in the seclusion of a hospital. Electro-convulsive therapy may have been mooted, but was avoided.

Darkness Visible has many vivid moments (one of which is Milton's). Two depressive onsets in particular lodge in the mind. On one occasion he is being awarded a prize in Paris. The ceremony is over, and he is counted on for lunch with the prize-giver's queenly widow and members of the Académie Française, at which point he tells this woman that he has to have lunch with his publisher. '*Alors!*' exclaims the queen as she turns her back on the author of *Lie down in darkness*: '*Au revoir!*' This yields the black humour of certain depressive illnesses, whose lightnings have a tendency to strike at literary parties. On another occasion he was seized with dread in a place where he had always felt at home: 'One bright day on a walk through the woods with my dog I heard a flock of Canada geese honking high above trees ablaze with foliage; ordinarily a sight and sound that would have exhilarated me, the flight of birds caused me to stop, riveted with fear . . .'

There are passages in the book which might have been written in the 19th century—some of them, give or take a word or two, by Poe: 'It may be more accurate to say that despair, owing to some evil trick played upon the sick brain by the inhabiting psyche, comes to resemble the diabolical discomfort of being imprisoned in a fiercely overheated room. And because no breeze stirs this cauldron, because there is no escape from this smothering confinement, it is entirely natural that the victim begins to think ceaselessly of oblivion.' Styron writes of the 'dungeons' of his 'spirit', of a 'long-beshrouded metaphysical truth'—language that belongs to the Gothic strain of certain of his fictions. To make remarks about the sometimes laboured and allusive style of the book feels like complaining in some pursed way of the 'more's' and the 'lessnesses' in the desolation-commemorating passage: 'I had suffered more and more from a general feeling of worthlessness as the malady had progressed. My dank joylessness was therefore all the more ironic because . . .' But to do so can hardly be beside the point; the book runs the risk of such objections, in the course of producing a style for the malady it recalls. This is a highly literary text, which is charged with references to other people's literary texts. The very name of his treacherous drug, Halcion, takes effect as an ironic allusion to the literary past. His novels, with their stress on suicide and gloom, could be said to find their afterword in the memoir, and the memoir abounds with references to other writers who suffered as he did—suicides and possible suicides, some of them his friends. Poe's pit and pendulum, Wordsworth's despondencies and madness, those enemies of promise, have shown up in Maine and Connecticut, as the lineaments of a present pain. Who would want to say that Styron is wearing a literary hat or a romantic mask, and who says they don't have dungeons in America any more?

George Core (review date April-June 1991)

SOURCE: Core, George. "Procrustes' Bed." *Sewanee Review* 99, no. 2 (April-June 1991): xxxix-xliv.

[*In the following review, Core compares several recent memoirs, calling* Warrenpoint *a "superb essay in reminiscence and meditation."*]

In *Necessary Lives: Biographical Reflections,* what would prove to be his last book, B. L. Reid presents a series of sharply etched meditations on what he deems the biographical trade. "Biography," he observes, "is not only a useful art but a necessary one: necessary precisely because it is useful. . . . Human psychology, human experience is a beautiful and awful mystery and . . . biography is one of the few efficient lights one can carry into the labyrinth." In turning to autobiography, which like biography he sees as a branch of history, he declares: "Every literate person who lives a notable life ought to write a memoir." And so Ben Reid did in *First Acts* (1988), a minor classic in that genre and a fascinating account of a hard life well lived to age twenty-eight. There, as in his lives of John Quinn and Roger Casement, he fulfills what he calls "biography's essential duty, its essential pleasure"—to tell us "in signal instances, illustrious or infamous, in any case exemplary, what it has meant to be human, to live a life." The memoirs and criticism in this issue can be measured by Reid's shrewd remarks, which apply equally well to John McCormick's essay on contemporary biography and the various essays in autobiography that follow as well as many of the reviews of biography and autobiography.

The title for this forum in the *SR* [*Sewanee Review*], "Islands of the Self," it happens quite by chance, was cribbed from a poem by Lawrence Durrell some months

before he died. The hope of the biographer and the autobiographer is that the islands of the self they discover and explore do not later drift uncharted in obscure seas of human experience but that they will be spotted and mapped by enterprising mariners and visited regularly by other adventuresome travelers.

The memoirs that I am glancing at here are devoted, for the most part, to the simple fact of growing up and the more complicated matter of growing into a world that becomes, to a certain extent, a world of one's own, even though that world, the everyday world of actuality and liability, is seldom of one's making. One makes the self but not the world around himself or herself, even if that world is intellectual and provides a place where fictions are invented and ideas are tested. That is one moral to be drawn from Denis Donoghue's **Warrenpoint,** a work written in an entirely different vein than we have long since grown to expect from this distinguished critic. The voice is much the same; the prose may be sharper. Professor Donoghue, unlike Professor Reid, does not explain his turn to memoir (Reid grew bored with criticism "as the literary vestment of opinion, and that too often pretentious and egotistical").

Mr. Donoghue is telling us not only what it means to grow up in northern Ireland as a Catholic and the son of a police sergeant, but he is recounting how his commitment to the life of the mind gradually took hold and finally possessed him. My only misgiving about this superb essay in reminiscence and meditation involves his insistence on presenting knotty ideas in contexts in which the appearance of idea is bizarre—startling. I hope that Denis Donoghue continues the story of this notable life, which is well worth the telling and the reading.

If Messrs. Reid and Donoghue overcame poverty so great that at times it meant a near-privation of mind and spirit, Leonard Kriegel has wrestled with an even heavier burden—the loss of the use of his legs that occurred when he was felled by polio at the age of eleven. The principal irony of this ironical situation is that he, after long months of painful therapy, finally had to learn how to fall—to protect himself when an inevitable spill occurred; but naturally he resisted, in part because falling meant "acceptance of defeat." Ultimately, however, he reports: "I found myself quite suddenly faced with a necessary fall—a fall into life."

This metaphor, like the most powerful metaphors drawn from literature and life, extends beyond a controlling image by its very nature as a hard ineluctable fact as well as an idea. Falling into life remains the controlling image of this collection of memoirs and meditations, essays in the self; but there are other dazzling metaphors as well, particularly the metaphor of Kafka's house that is announced in the title of the coda. In that essay Mr.

Kriegel says: "It is not, finally, the life one seeks to redeem—it is the disease. For it is the disease that challenges the self to be 'better' than it was." *Falling into Life* is published by North Point Press, whose own life as a publishing house is unfortunately ending.

The metaphor announced in the title of Richard Rhodes's memoir of his growing up in straitened circumstances—*A Hole in the World* (Simon and Schuster)—does not work nearly so well as falling into life because Rhodes's metaphor of loss, chiefly the loss of his mother (by suicide), is not so persuasive as Kriegel's—and because he overworks it. All the same this is a searing and convincing account of an American boyhood. If Sergeant Donoghue is the hero of **Warrenpoint,** the same applies to Rhodes's older brother, Stanley, who by going to the police saved himself and Richard from a monstrous stepmother who should have been the gate-keeper at Dachau or Buchenwald, not the wife of their hapless and feckless father—and their self-appointed scourge. It is no wonder that Rhodes chooses an epigraph from Kafka's "In the Penal Colony" for the long middle section of this splendid book, the part in which he presents a terrifying picture of the privations—physical, psychological, and spiritual—that he and Stanley suffered under their stepmother's brutal and unforgiving lash. In some respects life in a concentration camp would have been easier than the actual ordeal they survived. This was an expense of spirit in a waste of shame. The reader who is fascinated by what disease and abuse signify for the victim—and how the self is wrenched and reforged by such random privation—should read Kriegel and Rhodes, both of whom refused to be overwhelmed by circumstance but who continue to struggle with the effects.

The late Kate Simon surmounted other obstacles no less taxing than those endured by Messrs. Kriegel and Rhodes, as readers of *Bronx Primitive* (1982) and *A Wider World* (1986) know. *Etchings in an Hourglass* (Harper & Row) is a sequel to those remarkable portraits in autobiography. Altogether these three books of memoirs constitute one of the best autobiographies to appear in this century in our nation since Henry Adams privately published his own life history. Simon is a stylist of the first order, and nothing under the sun is too painful or disgusting or embarrassing for her to describe to us in her ironical and stark but sympathetic way, including the long debilitating illnesses of her first husband and their daughter, various affairs (casual and otherwise), and, at the end of her life, her own unflinching battle with cancer. These portraits and scenes add up, in a certain light, as notes for a picaresque novel, the history of a picaro's vicissitudes on the road of life. Randall Jarrell exhorted us to read at whim: fine—but read Kate Simon, whether or not at whim. Who else,

facing Death, would envision a "common African tableau" and then ask: "Would vulture, jackal, hyena be my funeral cortege?"

The fell shadow of Death looms large in *A Boy's War* (John F. Blair; illustrated), the sequel to *Being a Boy* (1988), Paxton Davis's splendid celebration of his boyhood in Winston-Salem during the 1930s. *Being a Boy* ends with a summer idyl at camp, a camp as seemingly perfect as that described by E. B. White in "Once More to the Lake." Mr. Davis's life as a cadet at VMI and an enlisted man during World War II did not prove so sunny and carefree, and he learned all too well the lesson of Melville's "March into Virginia": "All wars are boyish, and are fought by boys, / The champions and enthusiasts of the state." After a year at VMI as a rat (even at West Point freshmen are plebes), Davis decided that "it was mean and petty as well as archaic and useless"; but it was good training for boot camp in the army. The first quarter of the memoir is devoted to these chapters in Davis's life, which are told crisply, exactly, and humorously. The remainder of *A Boy's War* recounts Davis's singular experiences as a medical technician in Texas and then in Asia. The war ended for him, after a long stint in graves registration and the Typhus Commission, among other grim duties, in Calcutta in 1946. A fascinating history of an exotic and atypical life during World War II. I eagerly look forward to the publication of *A Boy No More,* the third and last memoir.

Hans Schmitt's *Lucky Victim: An Ordinary Life in Extraordinary Times* (LSU Press; illustrated) is a memoir that can be read profitably with *A Boy's War.* At the age of sixteen Schmitt, after stays in Holland and England, came to this country. He earned a B.A. at Washington and Lee and then an M.A. at the University of Chicago. (He has taught history for the past forty years.) By the end of the war Lieutenant Schmitt had returned to Germany and was dealing with German prisoners of war. The author carries this fascinating story up to the late 1940s, breaking it off a little later than does Paxton Davis, whose account ends when he is old enough to vote. Schmitt had to grow up more quickly than Davis: such was the difference in living under the Nazis and living in the United States, even in the Depression. One of the most engaging and valuable aspects of *Lucky Victim* for the reader is perceiving how Hans Schmitt changed from a refugee to an American citizen—the best part of his luck. What is more American than the fresh start and the changed life?

Carl Dawson's *November 1948* (University Press of Virginia) is another memoir devoted to the fresh start and the new life. Dawson came to Los Angeles, with his parents and siblings, from Yorkshire after the war. He recalls the trip to the U.S. and the first hard months in this country, punctuating his chronological narrative with memories of life in England. The story doesn't quite add up—in part because the author does not provide a large enough context for his brief tale, which is well written and sharply detailed, if curtailed.

By now nearly everyone knows the story, firsthand or second, that is told by Geoffrey Wolff in *The Duke of Deception* (Penguin), a book now over ten years old that remains well worth the reading or rereading. The author's father is the duke of deception, a scoundrel worthy to stand in the company of Mark Twain's Duke and Dauphin. My only misgiving about the memoir is that the author never makes it plain how the duke functioned while working as an engineer during World War II on projects that he wasn't equipped, by education or experience, to undertake.

In *This Boy's Life* (Perennial Library) Tobias Wolff, Geoffrey's younger brother, tells the other half of the story. When their parents were separated, Geoffrey stayed with his father; Tobias, with his mother—and both boys lost. The mother's pathology is almost as interesting as her deplorable spouse's—but is more pathetic. Tobias's story, so far as his own life and making his own way in disorderly circumstances, resembles Richard Rhodes's; and it is more engaging than his brother's and is equally well told and written. (The Wolffs' stories, like Carl Dawson's, often involve California, land of dreams and waywardness.)

Eavesdropping on a conversation going on among the Wolff brothers and Richard Rhodes about how they survived childhood and became responsible citizens as well as writers would yield material sufficient to keep a gaggle of psychologists and sociologists busy for years—were they acute enough to understand the implications of these searing experiences.

For the reader who is more inclined to idyl than mayhem when it comes to a boy's life—the kind of life lovingly recreated by Paxton Davis in *Being a Boy*—there is Robert S. Lancaster's *The Better Parts of a Life* (Proctor's Hall Press). The author is at his best in recalling his early life as he grew up in a large rollicking family in the Blue Ridge Mountains. His has been a varied life since—as a prep-school master, a practicing attorney in small towns, a college teacher and administrator, a cultural ambassador; but in no part of this wise and winning memoir is his memory fresher and his narrative more pointed than when he sharply recollects his wonderful boyhood, the life that the Wolffs and Richard Rhodes wanted for themselves. Being rooted in a family place, as Lancaster shows, is a gift so great as to be almost priceless.

Growing up is a theme not merely archetypal in a literary sense: the experience, if not the glittering idea, inevitably touches everyone, especially those, such as

Duke Wolff, who never grow up. Blessed or cursed, most of us, struggling or not, grow up. The memoir, even more than the bildungsroman, provides the natural mode for dealing with this universal subject and time, a time when life's possibilities seem infinite and inviting. Looking back, the author can find a shape and meaning to his or her early life that often remains obscure at later stages; and so writers of all sensibilities and stripes are inclined to calling up the memories of their early lives, lives misspent or fulfilled.

So it was with Frank O'Connor and V. S. Pritchett, two of B. L. Reid's exemplary figures in *Necessary Lives*; so it is with all the writers, including Reid himself, at whom I have glanced, all of whom have responded to his charge: "Every literate person who lives a notable life ought to write a memoir." His expectations of the author and for the form have in these instances been well met. Autobiography, like biography, is a form of life history. Both, as Ben Reid makes plain, tell us "in signal instances, illustrious or infamous, in any case exemplary, what it has meant to be human, to live a life."

Steven Helmling (review date April-June 1994)

SOURCE: Helmling, Steven. "Modernism Now." *Sewanee Review* 102, no. 2 (April-June 1994): 291-309.

[*In the following review, Helmling discusses several books engaged in the debate over Modernism and critical studies. Helmling asserts that Donoghue's* Being Modern Together *successfully argues for the continuing vitality of Modernism in literary criticism.*]

At a feminist workshop I attended not long ago, we were called upon to introduce ourselves and say a few words about our intellectual interests. Mine, I said, was modernism. "Oh," tittered a panelist; "the M—word!" That provoked the day's biggest laugh. Modernism has paid a heavy price for its implication in the New Criticism, and with the advent of "theory" in the last two decades, no other academic field has been so contested. Others have been equally or even more radically transformed; Victoria Kahn observed a few years ago that different theoretical "schools" seemed suited to different fields (deconstruction to romanticism, new historicism to the Renaissance); but such affinities flourish in an atmosphere of greater calm and sympathy than has yet seemed possible about modernism. It's my impression that in other fields the debate between old and new has achieved a measure of synthesis; in modernism studies, the norm has remained either acrimony across an abyss or a mutual turning of backs.

Perhaps that is changing, as "modernism" recedes further into the past and "theory" itself grows older. Of the books under review, some of the most interesting are by younger scholars for whom T. S. Eliot (1888-1965) or Ezra Pound (1885-1972) have never been anything but "history," and their (often new historicist) inquiries into problems that others among us still feel as contemporary are not coarsened by whatever partisan commitments they imply. Few authors of the books here throw down gauntlets, and some even confess an enthusiasm for modernist writing that their ideological biases would not long ago have disallowed.

Marianne DeKoven's *Rich and Strange: Gender, History, and Modernism* is a good example. For feminism, modernism (and its academic institutionalization) has been a prop of male privilege, a hero-worship of exclusively male figures, noting only condescendingly (if at all) Virginia Woolf, Marianne Moore, Gertrude Stein, etc., and "valorizing" such "phallocentric" virtues as impersonality, mastery, and control. Nevertheless DeKoven actually *likes* modernism, and wants to rehabilitate it for the modernism-bashing academy. She assumes that politics is very much at play in modernism's force-field, and that so far from being a cautionary example of how literature sells out to prevailing "ideology" ("false consciousness") by claiming to be apolitical, at least some modernist texts actually aimed to pioneer new ways in which literature might *be* "political"—by registering tensions from the world outside the text, and holding them in tension, pressing without resolving their contradictions.

To name this state of tension DeKoven borrows a term from Derrida, *sous-rature,* a condition of unstable stasis in which contradictory impulses coexist. (You can see the family resemblance of this version of *sous-rature* with Eliot's "medium" in which "varied feelings are at liberty to enter into new combinations," Pound's "vortex," I. A. Richards's "equipoise," Cleanth Brooks's "ambiguity," etc.) Thus DeKoven can admire Eliot, as Marx admired Balzac, for the style of his politics, even while deploring their content. DeKoven mentions class and race, but the politics most decisively at play here involve gender. Each of DeKoven's chapters juxtaposes a "canonical" male text with a neglected female one: in three (out of four) such chapters, the "male" is Conrad (which might seem to "heroize" *him* a bit unduly); the women are Gilman, Stein, Woolf, and Chopin. But the larger problem, the danger DeKoven doesn't quite evade, is that the "contradictions" she stages go too easily together. In Derrida *sous-rature* is a device for heightening (indeed exaggerating) the tensions between contradictory particulars; in DeKoven it is deployed to the opposite effect—to pacify differences prematurely.

Susan Rubin Suleiman's *Subversive Intent: Gender, Politics, and the Avant-Garde* manages this problem much better. She, too, juxtaposes conflicting things, but does so with a patient and lucid intelligence that brings every nuance of difference to life. Suleiman, too, writes

with obvious enthusiasm for the (mostly French) writings and paintings she discusses; in the process she illustrates another way of rehabilitating modernism, which is to take the parts you like and call them "avant-garde"—a strategy pioneered by Andreas Huyssen, Peter Bürger, and Thomas Crow, scholar-critics for whom "modernism" means T. S. Eliot, Thomas Mann, Stravinski (bad); "avant-garde" means dada, Marcel Duchamps, surrealism (good). At stake, again, is the question of political commitment—of (Suleiman's title) "subversive intent." The book keeps coming back to the question of whether the efforts of an aesthetic avant-garde can have a more-than-aesthetic (i.e., a political) effect.

Some styles of culture-criticism (perhaps the dominant ones) answer this question despairingly in the negative. Think of figures as different as T. S. Eliot, T. W. Adorno, Paul de Man, and Frederic Jameson: each writes a chastened, melancholy prose that requires (ideologically diverse styles of) pessimism as its (in the literary sense) "motivation"—such is the moral prerogative and the rhetorical need of any discourse of lost causes. An "oppositional criticism" whose project is actually going somewhere can conjure with the accents of hope, and feminism is a salient example. Suleiman echoes Craig Owens and others in suggesting that feminism is *the* key to a socially consequential "postmodernism" (the avant-garde *de nos jours*). But she remains alive to the dangers of "co-optation"; and adopts an ad hoc vigilance toward the texts she questions, and her own responses to them; she is also uncommonly alert (as so few academic critics are) to historical contexts. Along the way we get fine discussions of Robbe-Grillet, Duras, Angela Carter, Max Ernst, Duchamps, as well as the most illuminating (*and* briefest) comment I've seen on a text I'd thought thoroughly played out, Freud's "Dora."

Suleiman is also acute on how avant-gardes from surrealism to *Tel Quel* have so elided "the question of woman" as to vitiate their supposed sexual liberationism, as when the pornographic violence of a de Sade or a Bataille is read as an allegory about representation (etc.), rather than sex and gender relations. As you might expect from anyone who calls *Tel Quel* avant-garde, Suleiman is au courant with theory; as you might not expect, she writes, unfailingly, with complete lucidity. This, along with her intellectual reach and her playful sanity (the book opens with a hilarious and canny "metalogue" in the style of Geoffrey Bateson), makes *Subversive Intent* one of the two or three books I've enjoyed most in reading for this assignment.

In the same category is Michael Levenson's *Modernism and the Fate of Individuality: Character and Novelistic Form from Conrad to Woolf.* Levenson's *A Genealogy of Modernism: A Study of English Literary Doctrine, 1908-1922* (1984) is uncommonly intelligent and responsible; but the new book stakes much more on Levenson's own insights and the power of his writing—and the gamble pays off mightily. As you would expect from someone who reviews for the *New Republic,* Levenson writes with considerable flair; and he assembles his exhibits here with a sense of finely calculated, and illuminatingly original, provocation. His long opening chapter, for example, juxtaposes, to brilliant effect, *Heart of Darkness* with *The Ambassadors.* I can only call his pages on James (what I thought no "reading" of a canonized text could any longer possibly be) a tour de force. His comments on James's strategies of typification and metaphor tell us more about James and his art than any study of James I know. The performance is so exhilarating that I came down from it assuming that inevitably the rest of the book would have to proceed at a lower pitch. Some of it does, but the chapter on *Tarr* and the pages on *Ulysses* in the closing chapter (where it is contrasted with *To the Lighthouse*) are comparably penetrating. The account of Woolf's antagonism to Joyce makes a feminist case more subtle and convincing than I have read in any feminist revaluation of Woolf. Levenson's arguments are too fine and too forceful to summarize; I can only advise that here is a book shedding original light on material that you'd have thought overfamiliar (not to say stale), written in an exciting and eloquent prose. Highly recommended.

I thought at first I'd be saying something similar about Henry Sussman's *Afterimages of Modernity: Structure and Indifference in Twentieth-Century Literature.* It's a book full of bright and often brilliant ideas chasing each other's tails; but maddeningly the show never gets itself on the road. Page by page, even sentence by sentence, you swing from excitement to disappointment, the latter always proportional to the former. One chapter, for example, proposes an inquiry into modernity's extremities of (both literary and philosophical) style—the minimalism of Kafka and Wittgenstein versus the prolixity of Joyce and Derrida—an original, and once stated, self-evidently important access to a complicated and rich "period" problem. But the payoff is forgotten, as Sussman spends his wit haring off after grandiose bon mots ("AIDS may be regarded as a tragic physiological illustration of the Freudian thermodynamics of *Beyond the Pleasure Principle*"). It's not like reading a scholarly study but like encountering the commonplace book of some postmodern Herzog. As for what Sussman means by (his title's keywords) "afterimages," "structure," "indifference" . . . well, if you read it you'll see. And you may read it. It *is* a book well worth dipping around in, with plenty of acute asides about (beside the authors I've named) Beckett, Borges, Adorno, Freud, and about modernism, post-modernism, and other topics of the hour.

Judith Ryan's *The Vanishing Subject: Early Psychology and Literary Modernism* offers brief readings of several early modern figures (Pater, Huysmans, Rilke, Alice James and Henry James, Stein, Kafka, Hofmannsthal, Schnitzler, Joyce, Döblin, Broch, Proust, Woolf, Musil) by the light of the psychology of their time—that is, psychology before Freud. Ryan argues that Freud looms so large in our sense of "the modern" as to have eclipsed the psychologist-philosophers—Franz Brentano, Ernst Mach, William James—whose work was dominant through Freud's own generation. "The subject," the unitary Cartesian self as Europeans had conceived it since before Descartes, had been defined in opposition to its "objects"; now it was "vanishing" into those erstwhile "objects," themselves metamorphosing into this blurry postsubject's constituents (its "field of perception") and experience (its "stream of consciousness"). The subject/object distinction was (we would now say) being deconstructed. Ryan's restoration of this forgotten context is valuable (I was glad to be reading it more or less together with Levenson's workout on related themes), but the book is, and pretends to be, no more than an introduction: the psychologists themselves are dispatched in a short survey, and the separate chapters on individual writers (fifteen of them in under 200 pages) are brief, not to say perfunctory.

An emblem of the book's programmatic modesty is Ryan's resisting the temptation to link the "vanishing" of the pre-Freudian "subject" with the abuse that "the subject" is undergoing nowadays—a connection interesting in what it suggests about the place of Freud in relation to this whole theme, for while anti-Cartesian contemporary theory claims Freud as a precursor, fragmenting the self into its warring trio—id, ego, superego—his focus on this fragmented self was so exclusive as to restore some sense of its unitariness; moreover, the rigidity of the self, its impermeability to "outside" influences, its obdurate resistance to transformation—these were Freud's master themes, the key to his "pessimism." That pessimism hasn't sat well with Freud's heirs; even Lacan, who seems to keep the pessimism (if only in the form of *Schadenfreude*), nevertheless projects the self as an almost infinitely "sliding" effect, mere froth on the Heraclitean wave of signifiers—and this, please note, in the name of a scrupulous "return to Freud." Ryan also reminds us that in Europe, psychology as a discipline emerged under the aegis of academic philosophy—a circumstance that has made for amusing cross-purposes between European intellectuals and their would-be disciples in America. Consider one example: in Europe, "empiricism" means not a constant checking of speculation against observed fact, as it does in our tradition, but the conviction that the "facts" of consciousness, philosophically speaking, can be deduced from careful introspection. Husserl's transcendental phenomenology is thus an "empiricism."

(Naive Americans, thinking to throw out European bath-water, too often discard the Anglo-American baby as well.)

Perhaps this gives you some idea of the interest and stimulation of this book, even despite, or beyond, its way of circumscribing its own ambitions. Within that narrower scope it is the kind of book that teaches you little about the writers you know, but piques your interest in those you know little or not at all. The prose is accessible, too—which would make the book useful for students.

Leo Bersani's *The Culture of Redemption* indicts our culture's perennial "redemptive" impulse or fantasy, the need—Bersani associates it with the Freudian superego and its death impulse—to devalue reality in favor of some impossible idealization of it. In this cultural pathology, says Bersani, literature has seen a messianic opportunity, and has not resisted the temptation. This large and ambitious idea functions in the book more as a theme than a thesis. Bersani begins with readings of Freud and Melanie Klein, partly to sustain a psychoanalytic account of this redemptive hunger, partly to indict psychoanalysis as a symptom of it. "Redemption" itself remains a fuzzy notion: it can mean something impossibly grandiose, but also something as modest as the simple hope that things will get better. When Bersani announces that "the culture of redemption is the culture of death," the release from this "culture" that he's proposing itself seems, well, redemptive. And of course the largest interest of the writers he discusses—Baudelaire, Flaubert, Melville, Joyce, Pynchon—derives (as he well knows) precisely from their apocalyptic ambitions.

But never mind: Bersani's is a supple and resourceful intelligence that knows better than to get itself harnessed too confiningly to the program of an argument; and in this book the stated thesis matters less than the fineness of the readings of particular texts. In such books the readings I like best are usually the ones of writers I know least well; in this case, the reverse is true. I can't summarize any of his readings; suffice it to say that they are severally both bold and sensible, and (Bersani's saturation in "French Freud" and poststructuralism notwithstanding) salutarily at odds with present fashion. The chapter on *Ulysses,* in particular, is a much-needed antidote to the "poststructuralist Joyce" of plurisignificant *jouissance* that maintains what it pretends to supersede, the humanistically "affirmative" Joyce of a generation ago.

Mark Edmundson is a younger writer whose name I find myself looking for on the book-review pages. Well, here is his book, *Towards Reading Freud: Self-Creation in Milton, Wordsworth, Emerson, and Sigmund Freud.* It shows the same liveliness, the same deft touch with big themes, that make his reviews a pleasure; but the book, even as short as it is (only 168 pages of text), gives this airiness room to fall flat. The defect, I think, is that the book tells a story, and narrative logic cramps Edmundson's style of mind. The story is Freud's; Edmundson offers a biographical account of two of Freud's most creative periods, the late-1890s burst that culminated in *The Interpretation of Dreams* and the later, more protracted crisis spanning "On Narcissism" (1914) and "Mourning and Melancholia" (1917). Some readers will object that this narrative heroizes Freud, so involving us in Freud's private drama as to agitate those reflexes of "identification" denounced by Lacanians as "imaginary," by Marxists as "ideological," by poststructuralists as "subject-centered," etc. From elsewhere, the complaint will be that Edmundson scants the biographical evidence, making less of it than he could. Distrust of biographical criticism has been continuous from New Criticism to *nouvelle critique,* but Edmundson avoids the pitfalls, theoretically at least, neither making "the life" *explain* "the work" nor presenting "the work" as a keyhole on (that putatively more interesting thing) "the life," but rather reading the texts as acts in the life, the life as another of the author's in-progress texts.

Yet there is a narrative problem here—and a symptom is perhaps visible in the book's subtitle. Milton, Wordsworth, Emerson? Edmundson doesn't care whether Freud read any of them: they function as contrasting instances of "self-creation," of "textualizing" the self. The discussions of them could be considered an effort to "contextualize" Freud's effort, but they read rather as free-standing digressions, of great interest in their own right, but blurring the focus of the main narrative. Is narrative necessary? The words *self-creation* in the subtitle signal that Edmundson is reading Freud under the aegis of Richard Rorty, who recommends that we continue to think of communal hopes and private ironies narratively. But I don't want to reduce Edmundson to an instance of our postmodern ambivalences about narrative. I normally assume that we should read *against* rather than *with* an author—read suspiciously, critically; but what Edmundson has to offer makes it worth our while to read to his strength, rather than against his weakness—to read the book as an essay, rather than a story—even if he didn't (quite) write it that way. For what distracts from Edmundson's story is precisely his essayistic strength: his alertness to the chances and challenges of thinking on paper about the largest issues he can contrive for himself.

I wanted to like Tom Lutz's *American Nervousness, 1903: An Anecdotal History,* but by the time I'd finished the introduction, I couldn't. Not, that is, until, I'd read the first chapter—and so it went, all the way through. What I wanted to like is suggested by the title: a rich topic, an interesting episode in American cultural history, and an "anecdotal" approach. Reviewers complained of the book's academic jargon (discursive this, hegemonic that), but I'd read the complaints, after all, in places like the Sunday *New York Times Book Review,* which suggested an academic book reaching for a general audience. I dislike jargon myself, but if it pays its way, it can assist new understanding; Lutz makes it give money's worth as far as he takes it, but he routinely drops things short of where he should, giving us assertion where we want demonstration. But please note: these are the disappointments of my wanting *more*; note I do not turn my thumbs down.

Lutz's argument is that "nervousness" (or "neurasthenia") was a syndrome with tellingly cultural coordinates. *Historical*: first identified in the wake of the Civil War, it was epidemic by the Gilded Age, and *passé* by the 1920s, medically as well as socially. *Social*: it was a disease of the upper classes, a mark of status and refinement; the unwashed didn't suffer it, and one of the reasons Lutz makes 1903 the break-point of the syndrome's career is that in that year W. E. B. Du Bois's *The Souls of Black Folk* imaged the "double consciousness" of African Americans in neurasthenic terms—a sign that, thus democratized, indeed, *déclassé,* the syndrome's social or ideological uses were waning. (At just this time "the blues," which had meant leisure-class ennui, was beginning to mean a genre of melancholy African American song.) In his richest single reading Lutz considers the surprising extent to which James's *The Ambassadors,* also published in 1903, operates as a satire of "American nervousness." *Gender*: men presented symptoms (exhaustion, lethargy) complementary with women's (excessive "nervous" energy, hyperactivity), and their treatment regimes were similarly symmetrical (outdoors rough-and-tumble for men, forced bed rest for women). *Economic*: the disorder was ascribed to energies improperly "invested," "saved," or "wasted"; certainly the psychological self-management it prompted was conceived in economic terms. In this emotional economy the prime problem was management of surpluses, and Lutz coordinates "moral" self-helps of the period with economic treatises that first broached the problem of a "consumer economy" based on consumption (not production), on pleasurable expenditure (on mass-produced abundance) rather than saving against scarcity. (Lutz sees in "neurasthenic discourse" the beginning of Philip Rieff's "triumph of the therapeutic.") Conversely words connected with "neurasthenic discourse"—*asthenia, depression, panic*—were applied to the economy. *Political* (and more broadly *ideological*): in a chapter devoted to Theodore Roosevelt and William James, Lutz excavates the neurasthenic metaphors and paradigms common to the Rough Rider's imperialist foreign policy and the "pragmatism" of the anti-imperialist whose "radical pluralism" synthesized philosophy, psychology, and religion into a therapeutic for "sick souls," a secularized ethic of "healthymindedness." The "discourse of

neurasthenia" also sustained the racism of the period—in foreign policy, conjuring images of an overcivilized, i.e., "neurasthenic" white race beset by hordes of dangerously healthy blacks, browns, and yellows; in domestic policy, shaping debates about immigration, etc.

What makes this "nervousness" specifically American? What distinguishes it from European hypochondria? Lutz argues that "American nervousness" expressed and mediated the stresses of a new leisure class (not the same thing as a gentry, which we'd always had) emerging in a culture still founded on a work ethic. In *The Ambassadors* Strether's bewitchment with Europe begins when he notices that Europeans—and Europeanized Americans like the one he is supposed to "rescue"—seem *healthy,* seem to *thrive,* in moral circumstances his American training has moralized-medicalized as necessarily pathogenic.

Lutz's chapters focus on particular figures (Howells, Norris, Dreiser, Gilman, Freeman) or provocatively paired figures (William James and Teddy Roosevelt, Henry James and W. E. B. Du Bois), but his interest is less in "readings" of these figures than in setting them in the contexts of their milieux. Digression, quick cuts, "perspective by incongruity" are thus the book's expository norms; if this thins the "argument," it leavens the texture. And if Lutz's presentation seems too often hasty and superficial, his preparation certainly wasn't: he has saturated himself in an astonishing diversity of popular, medical, religious, economic, political and other "discourses" of the period, and deftly spices his account with amazing quotations, facts, *faits divers.* The "history" he offers is, after all, "anecdotal"—which makes for an interesting (and, I'd like to think, calculated) dissonance with the book's academic jargon, whose usual "motivation" (not to say "ideology") is to suggest system, science, the "methodology" of some putatively global view, as against the empiricism and impressionism of the "*merely* anecdotal." An eye-opening work of cultural history.

My reservations about Astradur Eysteinsson's *The Concept of Modernism* begin with his title. "Modernism" a *concept*? No: a word. A conceit, just maybe. Better yet (here, the new jargon actually helps), a "discursive formation." But Eysteinsson isn't borrowing high philosophic trouble, and neither should I. His subject is the contested history of various attempts to *make* "modernism" more than a mere word—the history of the chronic fight(s) over what the word can and cannot, should and should not, be made or allowed to mean. Eysteinsson confines himself to the Anglo-American setting; but his view of that setting is panoramic. Reading it, as a scholar-critic professionally concerned with modernism, I often felt as though my life was passing before me. You know you're getting old when your list of things to read is shorter than the list of what you *have* read—shorter, indeed, than what you've read and forgotten. Harry Levin? Joseph Frank? They're all here, knit into a seamlessly historical survey with Lukács and Adorno, John Barth and Susan Sontag, Renato Poggioli and Peter Bürger, Roger Shattuck and Fredric Jameson, Erich Auerbach and Jürgen Habermas, Frank Kermode and Andreas Huyssen. The uniform maleness of these names suggests one area that does get scanted, feminism; Eysteinsson attends to Gilbert and Gubar, and to Kristeva, but never so much as mentions Luce Irigaray, Hélène Cixous, Alice Jardine, Marjorie Perloff, Linda Hutcheon, even Elaine Showalter.

To every critic he does discuss, though, Eysteinsson brings an attention not only critical but polemical. I have graduate students badly in need of a history of the word *modernism,* but this book isn't quite it, because Eysteinsson means not merely to survey the debate, but to join in. It is intermittently interesting (and at moments faintly comical) to see long-dead bogies resurrected not as items of antiquarian interest but as errors still urgently in need of correction. Eysteinsson is sensible and very well-read; his relative conservativism is not a function of having ignored "theory." He makes many necessary and long-overdue discriminations in a field where political and other agendas have from the beginning multiplied contradiction, inconsistencies, confusion, and cross-purposes. You can't agree with all of his arguments, but he usefully surveys a lot of ground. His general pitch (as opposed to his "positions") reminds me of Gerald Graff's *Literature Against Itself;* it's that kind of book—moderate, measured, but certainly not toothless.

For me Herbert Schneidau will always be the author of *Sacred Discontent: The Bible and Western Tradition* (1976). It marked an epoch in my life, showing me not merely why and how to get interested in the Bible, but why I, a soreheaded counter-culture dissident from the sixties, raging at all the American idols, the Bible itself not least, was in fact not only an almost stereotypically biblical character, the prophet, but of a kind the Bible thought familiar (and silly) enough to satirize: Jonah, fuming at God when the brimstone doesn't fall. No other book has ever given me quite *that* kind of surprise. Schneidau's *Ezra Pound: The Image and the Real* (1969) was a prescient examination of what we would later know as "the problematic of representation"; it was ignored by the apostles of that problematic, for whom Pound and his cohorts were idols to be smashed, rather than precursors in iconoclasm. Schneidau's latest, *Waking Giants: The Presence of the Past in Modernism,* is more sedate than either of these books, its theme (see the subtitle) and contents (separate chapters on Hardy, Forster, Conrad, Anderson, and Pound) more diffuse. As in his other books, Schneidau here regards his chosen writers as prophets in the sense of culture-critics, intel-

ligences adversary to the cultural surround. His saturation in these writers and their historical backgrounds is deep and mature; the historical interest here displaces (rather than focusing, as in his other books) questions of "theory." A rich, reflective study, with something of an interim feel (his next book will be on the New Testament) from one of our most intellectually independent and adventurous scholar-critics.

Two collections of essays on T. S. Eliot memorialize the Eliot centenary in 1988. Jewels Spears Brooker's collection features many an éminence grise of Eliot studies (Grover Smith, James Olney, A. D. Moody, even Cleanth Brooks and Russell Kirk) with results ranging from the acute to the ceremonial. There is a fine piece by Cleo McNelly Kearns on Eliot and Buddhism—and a memoir by Michael Butler Yeats. The contributors mostly conduct themselves as if "theory" did not exist; the largest exception is Brooker's own introductory essay, explaining her title's keyword (*The Placing of T. S. Eliot*) by assimilating Eliot's sense of placelessness, of wandering "in between" (the Arnoldian "between two worlds" lament), to the *ni l'un, ni l'autre,* the nonspatial space, of Derridean *différance.* Ronald Bush's collection, *T. S. Eliot: The Modernist in History,* also features established figures (Walton Litz, Carol Christ), but makes room, too, for more recent scholarly styles. The prize goes to Lawrence Rainey, who has (amazingly, at this late date) unearthed, and prints in full, a previously unknown letter (February 26, 1922) in which Eliot advises a prospective publisher of *The Waste Land* to stay tuned for some notes he plans to add—a crucial document for the old question of how Eliot came to write the poem's notes, and what that imports for how we read it and them. For the Compleat Eliotiste this essay alone is worth the price of the ticket.

Rainey's book, however, *Ezra Pound and the Monument of Culture: Text, History, and the Malatesta Cantos,* is another kettle of fish—stinkier fish, I first thought. After a somewhat melodramatic introduction that coyly mixes its signals—Poundolatry and Poundoclasm, theory and antitheory, PC and anti-PC—its first chapter plunges into a minute examination of Pounds's misquotations, in one twelve-line passage of an early draft of what would become the Malatesta Cantos, of various esoteric sources. Had I not been reviewing the book, I'd have stopped reading right there. I'm glad I had to keep going; Rainey's eye is on much bigger game than pedantic source-sifting. In the event his contribution tells us little if anything new about the Malatesta Cantos themselves; there is no "reading" of them or any part of them. Instead the emphasis is on what Rainey calls the "sociomaterial" background: the particular texts Pound used in "researching" Malatesta, and the new late-nineteenth-century institutions that facilitated his interest—public-research libraries like the Bibliothèque Nationale (where, surviving call slips attest, Pound did much of his Malatesta reading), the extension of the railroad (which made Rimini and the Malatesta Tempio venues of "elite tourism"), the travel writing and guidebook industry (Baedeker, Tauchnitz), the vogue for historical novels (some of them fictionalized Malatesta) and popular histories of the Renaissance, the popularization of scholarship represented by, e.g., the *Encyclopedia Brittanica* (articles on Rimini, Malatesta, etc., were written by the same authors who produced or influenced the travel guides sold in railroad stations).

A central exhibit is the construction of the Malatesta legend or mystique (especially that of his relations with his third wife, Isotta), which began in Malatesta's own time with documents every one of which had political axes to grind—most famously Pope Pius II's diatribe charging Malatesta with murder, adultery, and sacrilege. Rainey traces the career of the legend to its resurgence in late nineteenth-century idealizing revaluations that served various political uses from nationalist anticlericalism, to northern Italian regionalist anticentralism, to dissident aestheticization of Burckhardtian-Nietzschean contempt of bourgeois culture (Pound belongs to this tradition), and Mussolini's statism (one of Mussolini's earliest idealizing biographers had previously authored an apologia for Malatesta).

Complementary to this excavation of the antecedent "background" of Pound's interests is Rainey's focus on their aftermath: how the *Cantos* themselves, and scholarship on them (Rainey traces a particular thread through the mimeographed *Analyst* of the mid-1950's, the Edwards-Vasse *Annotated Index* [1957], and the Carroll F. Terrell *Companion*), have now become not only a "foreground" for anyone approaching Malatesta, but also a link in the transmission of various sorts of mystifications and misinformation not only about Malatesta but about Pound, the *Cantos,* modernism, and other things. (In places the book becomes a satire of Pound scholars—names are named—who, subscribing too uncritically to Poundian notions of genius, replicate Pound's errors or caprices.) But Rainey passes beyond Pound scholarship to academic literary study in general, setting various fads and fashions, from the Lachmann school of textual editing to New Criticism and poststructuralism, in relevant "sociomaterial" contexts. Rainey pronounces a (well-informed) curse on all of criticism's houses for their "holocaust of 'fact,'" the tendency of literary "scholarship," whether in the name of yesterday's "text itself" or today's "linguistic turn," to dodge the grunt work of historical research into "the larger written environment." Rainey's critiques of, say, Wimsatt on the one hand, of Derrida on the other, are shrewd and fresh, giving the book a considerable interest beyond Pound studies.

Rainey's humor is sour, at times almost Malvolio-esque; he pointedly eschews ingratiating himself with any criti-

cal powers that be; even his reader is treated probationarily, force-fed pages of disagreeable minutiae—"fact"—before getting any taste of Rainey's bracing conclusions. (Each of the book's three long chapters follows the same organization, arguing from a mass of details to large principles.) The program can only be called "new historicist," though Rainey himself never uses that phrase, and his practice resembles that of no other "new historicist" I know of; his commitment to "fact" challenges the "textualization" of history in Greenblatt, Levinson, McGann, and others. This is a dogged, cranky, but very original and independent-minded book.

In *Pound's Epic Ambition: Dante and the Modern World* Stephen Sicari puts together two chestnuts of *Cantos* criticism: 1) that Pound's "epic" identifies Pound, as author-quester, with Homer's Odysseus; and 2) that Pound's "epic of judgment" (J. J. Wilhelm's phrase) also models its ambitions on Dante's *Commedia.* For Sicari these themes meet in Pound's appreciation of Dante's construction of a "wandering hero," the "Dante" *in* the poem, part of whose point is his "intertextual" relation to past epic protagonists. The book traces the fortunes of Pound's "wandering hero" (variously Odysseus, John Adams, Malatesta, Joseph Rock, Mussolini, etc.) through Pound's poem, in full-dress readings of several key cantos. Sicari acknowledges that his scheme risks over-tidying Pound's calculated fragmentation, a danger I can't say he has managed to avoid. (But who has?) And the intellectual orientation is old-fashioned—Étienne Gilson and Ernst Cassirer are the philosophers in residence—though in ways that serve Pound's "mystical" interests better than poststructuralism so far has. For the Pound scholar this is more a work of synthesis than a new contribution; but for the rare undergraduate bitten by the Pound bug, its accessibility and its provision of an overview of the *Cantos* put it among the books I'd recommend.

Pound's "mysticism" is also the focus of Akiko Miyake's *Ezra Pound and the Mysteries of Love.* Pound presented himself as a no-nonsense modern man, often in contrast to the Christian Eliot or the spiritualist Yeats. His interest in Neoplatonism, Eleusinian mysteries, courtly love and its philosophical apologists, etc. have always been acknowledged; but Pound seemed to take them metaphorically; to have suggested that his investment in them was less qualified, more literal, would have seemed, well, literal-minded. A turning point was James Longenbach's *Stone Cottage* (1988), which focuses the relations of Pound and Yeats from 1913 to 1916, when they spent winters as cotenants of a rural cottage—just the period when, supposedly, Pound was "modernizing" himself as Yeats sank ever deeper into séances, table-rapping, automatic writing, and whatnot. Longenbach couldn't help showing that Pound was deep into all this stuff, too; stumped for an explanation, he almost seemed to decide that Pound could only have been sucking up to Yeats.

Miyake sidesteps the question how seriously, or literally, Pound took these interests; her study will doubtless strike many readers as literal-minded itself, with the author's ascribing her own literal-mindedness to Pound. That said, it is the most comprehensive survey of these interests in Pound to date. She has discovered (apparently for the first time) that Pound in 1906 read an obscure 1840 tract by Gabriel Rossetti (father of the pre-Raphaelite) that tied ancient Greek mystery cults to Provençal and Tuscan courtly love poetry; she thence excavates every manifestation of this theme in all of Pound's work, including places we never thought to look for it, like the translations of Confucius. Miyake is more convincing on some things than on others, of course; and the material, alas, lends itself to what Erwin Panofsky called "homeosis," the danger of taking coincidental resemblances as signs of secret harmonies—a danger Pound flirted with, of course, but (we suppose, or hope) with some irony; Miyake takes him in earnest. And she leaves a few things out, most notably Pound's interest in Propertius, whom he explicitly ties to these interests. But her stupefyingly far-reaching researches (not just Aristotle, Aquinas, Dante, etc., but also Hegel, Buddhism, ancient Egypt, Confucius, and more, much of it conducted, it seems, in the original languages) leave no doubt of the extent of Pound's ambitions to synthesize a world culture with Eros as its ground bass. Anyone seeking light on these matters will need this book for years to come.

Miyake is Japanese; she holds a Ph.D. from Duke, and teaches at Kobe College in Japan. Her scholarly style is courtly, reverent, modest—not at all in tune with academic-cowboy decorums here—and her copyeditors have, agreeably, left an aura of foreignness on her prose. It is pleasant to imagine that this work of devoted scholarship might be an emblem of the peculiar irony that Pound, demonized at present in our anglophone academic subculture as a logocentric fascist and so forth, may in other times and places be hailed as the author of the first truly multicultural epic of what might (on the analogy of "world music") be called "world poetry."

Timothy Materer's *Selected Letters of Ezra Pound to John Quinn, 1915-1924* reprints in full "sixty seven of the approximately two hundred and thirty letters that Ezra Pound wrote to John Quinn"; Quinn's side of the correspondence is quoted only in editorial notes. Nine of the letters here, Materer advises, appeared in D. D. Paige's *Selected Letters of Ezra Pound* (1950); he doesn't mention that others (including some not collected here) have been excerpted in various places, most generously in Daniel Pearlman's *The Barb of Time* (1969), which is not listed in Materer's bibliography.

Apologies for this pedantry, but if you want Pound's letters to Quinn at all, you want to know about Pearlman. Materer's project needs no justification for the scholar, nor for the general reader who enjoys Pound's bodacious epistolary style. (Since Quinn died in 1924, the letters here do not yet evince the Uncle Remusization that marks the correspondence of Pound's later years.)

The articles in Derek Attridge's *Cambridge Companion to James Joyce* are addressed to the student rather than to the scholar of Joyce. (I'm surprised—and, why not, encouraged—that a publisher thinks a market of students for such books still exists. Not on *my* campus, I'm afraid.) The "Joyce" on offer here is, of course, the poststructuralist Joyce Attridge has sponsored before, but presented this time in user-friendly prose and in a surprisingly old-fashioned package. After Attridge's own orientation essay, the contributors take up "backgrounds" (Joyce as Irishman [Seamus Deane], as European [Klaus Reichert], as Parisian [J.-M. Rabaté]), works (J. P. Riquelme on *Dubliners, Stephen Hero* and the *Portrait*, Jennifer Levine on *Ulysses,* Margot Norris on the *Wake,* Vicki Mahaffey on the "shorter works"), and up-to-date themes (Karen Lawrence, "Joyce and Feminism" and Christopher Butler, "Joyce, Modernism and Postmodernism"). Hans Walter Gabler contributes a piece, "Joyce's Text In Progress," on Joyce's compositional practices. (No mention of John Kidd.) The putative student to whom it is addressed—if he/she exists—will find it useful.

The reading eye reads gestalts—word-groups, not words; words, not letters—and so I was into the text of Margaret Mills Harper's *The Aristocracy of Art in Joyce and Wolfe* before I realized that Joyce's foil here was Thomas, not Virginia: *Wolfe,* not *Woolf.* (An instance of the implication of socially constructed "canons" in the conditioning of the body: in the vicinity of "Joyce," the eye sooner confuses Thomas with Virginia than Thomas with Tom.) Harper's book is winningly modest (in our time of principled self-inflation)—but also surprisingly bold, after all, in linking the canonized Joyce with the all-but-forgotten Wolfe. Harper, a southerner, shrewdly makes her regionalism, and Wolfe's, a way of renewing our sense of Joyce's regionalism—an article of piety, of course, among the Joyceans, but often scanted in practice. Her common sense on such "problematic" questions as art and autobiography, or the artist and social class, implicitly reproaches the heavy weather of academic criticism as usual, even to the point of raising the question of the extent to which "canonization" distorts criticism of a writer—for why, exactly, are ways of dealing with these issues in Wolfe not acceptable for dealing with them in Joyce?

Harper herself is an obscure "provincial" professor, soldiering on far from the venues where the lions of her profession ramp. Jean-Michael Rabaté is one of the certified lions. He's a personable man to talk to, and has the considerable charm of Frenchness going for him; but in his book *James Joyce, Authorized Reader,* he stakes all—i.e., much too much—on the charisma of his style of the Derridean-Lacanian (et al.) *précieux.* Never mind the emperor's new clothes; grant that clothes are always imaginary, as much so as nakedness. Whether the spectacle of Rabaté's sensibility in action compels will depend on your beholding eye. For me Rabaté flops; for you he may soar (but I doubt it).

"Represent," "representing," "representation": in the past two decades these words have had a most excellent adventure (call it "Bill and Ted Go to Graduate School"); there are by now very few things you might confidently say that one of them could *not* possibly mean. In George Bornstein's volume of essays by various hands, *Representing Modernist Texts,* "representing" means "editing." (It's easy: re-presenting, in a, for once, quite literal sense.) But I don't mean to tax Bornstein with jumping the bandwagon of critical theory; on the contrary, as he reminds us, textual editors since Bowers have been insisting that theirs is the *real* bandwagon, deploring the failure of "critics" to get on board. What's more, as Michael Groden's contribution, "Contemporary Literary and Textual Theory," reminds us, this continued indifference of critics to textual problems is especially untenable now, since contemporary theory's revolt against New Criticism, its effort to see texts as contingent cultural products rather than autonomous ideal objects, belabors points that textual critics have been hammering at for years. Indeed: *author, text, work, intention*—no "theoretical" foray can "problematize" these notions as swiftly and totally as the nuts-and-bolts problems involved in establishing the text of the sheerest lyric poem.

None of textual editing's current big-gun theorists (McGann, Tanselle, Greetham) is, uhm, represented here; the larger issues are explored in Bornstein's introduction and Groden's concluding survey; the other contributors are either practicing editors writing from experience (Finneran on Yeats, Litz and MacGowan on Williams, Mendelson on Auden, Polk on Faulkner, Brenda Silver on Woolf), or critics offering arguments involving textual problems (Ronald Bush on Pound, Andrew Kappel on Marianne Moore, Lawrence Rainey on H. D.). Their reports fruitfully embarrass us with examples from practice, the shibboleths of every critical orthodoxy around; and their blend of gossip and anecdote about Yeats, Pound, or whomever, with the more abstractly conceived theoretical issues will doubtless help others besides myself to see fresh ways to be interested in textual problems. (An index would have assisted such an interest.) The focus on particular writers makes this an important collection of critical essays on modernism, not merely a casebook on narrow editorial problems. (Ronald Bush valuably reprints some

inaccessible early versions, with variants, of Canto VI.) In short it all adds up to the most persuasive case for, or invitation to, a greater rapprochement between editors and critics.

Saving the best for last? For reasons too many (and too obvious) to go into, I want to close with Denis Donoghue's ***Being Modern Together,*** which contains his three lectures in memory of Richard Ellmann that were delivered at Emory in April 1990. We expect "the lecture," generically, to be casual; we don't expect it to be an art form. Donoghue is a master of the seemingly casual lecture that leaves you chewing a good deal more than you thought he was biting off. As I began reading the first lecture, the most casual of the three, I caught myself thinking of Donoghue as some sort of descendant of Homer, improvising the themes, and beating time with the scepter, of his oral art—an academic medicine-tent wizard, a spellbinder, but with a conscience. There aren't many of these, and I suppose never have been; Donoghue's only rival in this department is Hugh Kenner. And it seems doubtful that in our (academic) precincts there will be any more forthcoming. (David Antin? I enjoy his highbrow postmodern stand-up, but it's a different schtick altogether.)

Of course, Donoghue's casual air of oral performance is an effect secured in the study; but I want to honor the contrast of Donoghue's difficult and subtle discriminations made as easy and lucid as they *can* legitimately be, as against the tendency of so many contemporary academic oracles—*Always problematize!* is evidently their motto—to make everything, however simple, maximally difficult. (Impossible, as in Derrida, is the announced ideal.) And another thing to admire in Donoghue's work, as against the grandiose omniportentousness that is our "postmodern" moment's period academic style, is a modesty, or better, a tact, a scruple, in delimiting the range of import of a given argument: Donoghue always knows, and lets you know, too, exactly what claim he is making, and just how far he means you to take it—a careful precision not only verbal but intellectual and moral as well, and achieved without preachiness or solemn-assery. Here, too, Donoghue's seeming casualness relieves, or freshens, his fundamental seriousness.

The effect of casualness also encourages an illusion of homogeneity, but in fact the book's three lectures are surprisingly different. The first, **"The Man of the Crowd,"** is a free-ranging scan of "modernity" considered as a response to the experience of masses of people in urban settings; the exhibits include Poe, Baudelaire, Hopkins, Walter Benjamin, and Simone Weil. The second, **"Beyond Culture,"** undertakes something much more focused: an effort to distinguish a peculiarly "modern" sense of the self *against* the very collective forms and forces culture proposes as the bases, or parameters, of "modern" identity—not, of course, a new idea; but what Donoghue does is to set some influential versions of it in fructive relation. The principal parties to the dialogue he sets in motion are Georg Simmel, who in *The Philosophy of Money* (1900) discerned the "modern" self withdrawing from, or eclipsed by, the instrumentalized social forms of a modernizing economic system, and Lionel Trilling, whose frequent theme, elaborated over the course of his career, was the "opposing self" in secession from, even active revolt against, the prevailing culture. Among the voices brought into this colloquy are Arnold, James, Pater, Yeats, Joyce, Eliot, Allen Tate, and Frederic Jameson. The discriminations achieve a fineness at which they broach the category of the ethical; and the concluding lecture, **"Ariel and His Poems,"** mounts an argument, ethical from the start, in defense of the imagination against those who would damn its operations as "idealist," as "false consciousness," as "ideological"; here the parties to the dispute include Wallace Stevens, Foucault, Habermas, Susanne Langer, Emmanuel Levinas, and Elizabeth Bishop.

I am perhaps giving the impression that Donoghue drops a lot of names; but readers who know his work will know that he doesn't drop them: he gets them into a conversation—even coerces them into it, insofar as some of them have made careers of refusing to have anything to say to one another. This ability to elicit exchange from interlocutors who usually prefer backbiting to talk is one of Donoghue's singular strengths. But Donoghue's mediations are not peace-making missions: when differences are sharp, he preserves the sharpness, and illuminates it, often rendering a subtler account of what is at stake in the dispute than the antagonists themselves. And consider also the range, the diversity of the figures he cites: some are current coin, of course, but others are names long out of circulation. (Susanne Langer? Simone Weil? In one throwaway aside Donoghue remembers Elizabeth Sewell's book on Valéry.) This breadth of allusion suggests not only the well-stocked mind of a man who has read everything and forgotten nothing; it also suggests a mind continually reassessing its stock, alert to the energies emitted when something read thirty years ago amalgamates with something read last month, or last night, or this morning.

As I write this, the mail brings galleys of another new book by Donoghue, *The Old Moderns: Essays in Literature and Theory.* Have I so far failed to mention Donoghue's energy and prolificness? Yes? Well, let me mention it now; and I'll try to resist all the old jokes about books coming too fast for reviewers to keep up. ("Have I read it yet? Why, I haven't even *reviewed* it yet," etc.) *The Old Moderns* reprints the three lectures of *Being Modern Together,* as well as four pieces gathered under the rubric *In Theory* (**"The Use and**

Abuse of Theory," "The Political Turn in Criticism," "The Sublime Blackmur," "Translation in Theory and in a Certain Practice"), and, under the heading *The Old Moderns,* ten essays on James, Yeats, Eliot, Joyce and Stevens. The closing essay, **"Is There a Perennial Literature?,"** is a ringing defense of imaginative literature against the "fanatics of a single idea" who would reduce it to some social or political effect; the energy of Donoghue's gesture here is presumably what secured the essay its place of honor at the volume's close, rather than where it more "naturally" fits, in the middle section, *In Theory.*

I have little space here to do more than commend *The Old Moderns* in the same terms I have already used for its predecessor; I'll only venture two thoughts that reading through it prompted. We see R. P. Blackmur is a near-constant presence, or point of reference, in this book and in Donoghue's work generally; yet Blackmur seems to me to embody the very type of the critical excess I have praised Donoghue for avoiding, the type who maximizes portentousness at every possible opportunity, too ready to risk fatuity for the sake of a grand phrase. Yet Donoghue recurs to Blackmur in ways that attest a large investment in what Blackmur was attempting. This seems to me an interesting crux well worth investigation for someone capable of withstanding the doses of Blackmur that would be required. The other point concerns Donoghue's awareness of and (generally speaking) resistance to contemporary theory. His resistance is well-informed, and attested by frequent reference to Habermas, Foucault, Derrida, et al. The names he mentions, though, are generally adversaries: only with Levinas does Donoghue make something like common cause. Yet I cannot help supposing that Donoghue would find much to admire, and much to use, in Paul Ricoeur and, especially, Hans Georg Gadamer, whom he nowhere mentions (so far as I can remember).

In most ways Donoghue would probably be judged the most old-fashioned of the critics under review here. His interrogatively allusive style of mind goes back at least to Matthew Arnold's essays and the "comparison and analysis" that T. S. Eliot recommended as the fundamental work of the critic; and, as we know, Arnold and Eliot are names no longer much deferred to in our neighborhood. Yet these two books more than make good on the implications of their titles, that "the old moderns" are still fully capable of being "made new," and that "being modern together" is still an option, perhaps an inevitability, in (please observe) the present tense. Many of the books under review here, by showing how much there is still to be made of modernism in "postmodern" styles of scholarship, attest to the continuing vitality of early twentieth-century writing even as they treat it as a thing of the past; Donoghue's demonstrates that the continuing vitality has by no means exhausted its own modes of intellectual-moral attention, criticism, discrimination, and inquiry.

Taken together—and how else can they be taken?—all these books add up to remarkable evidence of our continued implication, will we or nill we, in modernism now.

Roger Kimball (review date May 1995)

SOURCE: Kimball, Roger. "Art vs. Aestheticism: The Case of Walter Pater." *New Criterion* 13, no. 9 (May 1995): 11-18.

[*In the following review of* Walter Pater, *Kimball provides an overview of Donoghue's argument regarding Pater's role in the development of literary Modernism.*]

> *In an age when the lives of artists were full of adventure, his life is almost colourless.*
>
> —Walter Pater, "Sandro Botticelli"

> *If we had not welcomed the arts and invented this kind of cult of the untrue, then the realization of general untruth and mendaciousness that now comes to us through science—the realization that delusion and error are conditions of human knowledge and sensation—would be utterly unbearable. Honesty would lead us to nausea and suicide. But now there is a counter-force against our honesty that helps us avoid such consequences: art as the* good *will to appearance.*
>
> —Friedrich Nietzsche, *The Gay Science*

For most of us, the Victorian essayist Walter Pater survives chiefly as a kind of literary aroma punctuated by a handful of famous phrases. Having grown up with the astringent qualms of modernism—which ostentatiously defined itself in opposition to the earnest aestheticism of writers such as Pater—we are likely to find that aroma a bit cloying. Few serious modern writers indulged themselves in prose so effulgently purple as did Pater. His meticulous adumbrations of mortal things quickened into beauty by death will strike most contemporary readers as quaint, neurasthenic, or both. Perhaps the notion that "*All art constantly aspires towards the condition of music,*" as Pater wrote in "The School of Giorgione," is sufficiently abstract and elusive still to occasion productive meditation. But the idea—another of Pater's nuggets—that Leonardo's *Mona Lisa* "is older than the rocks among which she sits; like the vampire, she has been dead many times, and learned the secrets of the grave" seems little more than a set-piece of timid *fin-de-siècle* morbidity. Even the celebrated apothegm from the conclusion of *The Renaissance,* Pater's first and most famous book, is trouble-some: "To burn always with this hard, gem-like flame, to maintain this ecstasy, is success in life"—maybe, but for most of us the scintillations will long ago have been quenched by too-frequent repetition.

It is a matter of some curiosity, then, that the well-known literary critic Denis Donoghue should have undertaken [*Walter Pater*] a critical biography of Walter Pater.[1] Although he has written on a wide range of topics and figures, including Swift, Emily Dickinson, and the critic R. P. Blackmur, Mr. Donoghue is familiar to most of his readers as a champion of high modernism and its decidedly un-Pateresque ambitions.

At least, we might have thought them un-Pateresque. It is part of Mr. Donoghue's purpose in this book to restore Pater to his place as an important, though largely unacknowledged, precursor of modernism. "Pater," he writes, "gave modern literature its first act. The major writers achieved their second and third acts by dissenting from him and from their first selves." It is not, Mr. Donoghue thinks, so much a question of "influence" as of "presence." He sets out to show that Pater is "a shade or trace in virtually every writer of significance from Hopkins and Wilde to Ashbery."

In addition to those just named, his roster of Pater's literary heirs includes James, Yeats, Pound, Ford, Woolf, Joyce, Eliot, Aiken, Hart Crane, Fitzgerald, Forster, Borges, Stevens, and A. R. Ammons. The first "poem" in Yeats's eccentric edition of the *Oxford Book of Modern Verse* (1936) is a versified snippet from Pater's expostulation on the *Mona Lisa*. The mature T. S. Eliot would take sharp exception to Pater and everything he stood for; indeed, his essay "Arnold and Pater," from 1930, is a *locus classicus* in modernism's attack on Victorian aestheticism; but early works such as "Preludes," "Portrait of a Lady," and *The Love Song of J. Alfred Prufrock* are instinct with a Pateresque languor, brimming as they are with personages measuring out lives with coffee spoons while they come and go talking of Michelangelo.

Similarly, the early Stevens is full of Pateresque themes and aspirations. Pater certainly does not hold the copyright on the idea (as Stevens put it in "Sunday Morning") that "death is the mother of beauty." But taken in conjunction with complacent peignoirs, late coffee and oranges, and "the holy hush of ancient sacrifice," the identification of mortality as the condition of beauty assumes a distinctly Pateresque coloring. Again, Pater was hardly the first to favor evocation over declaration; but his *style* of embracing intimation echoes plainly in "Thirteen Ways of Looking at a Blackbird":

> I do not know which to prefer,
> The beauty of inflections

Or the beauty of innuendoes,
The blackbird whistling
Or just after.

If Mr. Donoghue is right, Pater's presence is more than a collection of echoes and insinuations. "Whatever we mean by modernity," he insists, Pater "is an irrefutable part of it." His first published essay, on Coleridge, in 1866 sounds the distinctive, disabused note: "Modern thought is distinguished from ancient by its cultivation of the 'relative' spirit in place of the 'absolute.' . . . To the modern spirit nothing is, or can be rightly known, except relatively and under certain conditions." Then, too, Pater's interest in French literature and German aesthetics helped to make English literature more cosmopolitan, more worldly. And the French element, especially, opened up exotic new avenues of feeling. In brief, Pater instigated for English letters something like what such writers as Baudelaire, Rimbaud, Verlaine, Huysmans, and Mallarmé did for the French. He made the forbidden, the outlandish, the silent a central literary preoccupation—though he did so quietly, with the greatest possible tact. If he was a "lover of strange souls" (Mr. Donoghue's subtitle comes from Pater's essay on Leonardo in *The Renaissance*), if "strangeness and beauty" was his "favorite conjunction," it was for him a matter of discriminating delectation not abandonment. In this respect, he betrays a kinship with Mallarmé, who advocated painting "not the thing itself, but the effect that it produces," and who once defined poetry as "a brief tearing of silence." Pater's route to exquisiteness was not through absinthe, hashish, sexual extravagance, or conscious blasphemy, but via a diffident voraciousness of appreciation.

Nevertheless, despite Pater's enormous reserve, there is a direct line of descent from *The Renaissance* (which was first published in 1873) to Oscar Wilde's *The Picture of Dorian Gray* (1890) and other such turn-of-the-century manifestations of arty decadence. Mario Praz was right (in *The Romantic Agony,* his classic study of the literature of decadence) to identify Pater as "the forerunner of the Decadent Movement in England." Not for nothing did Pater expatiate on the "fascination of corruption" and the poetic aspects of a countenance tinged with a deathly pallor. Algernon Swinburne was not only a friend but also a spiritual brother. Especially in his early years, Pater liked to think of himself as a champion of pagan virtues. But an underside of pagan vices clings firmly to Pater's prose. G. K. Chesterton perceptively noted the duality that accompanies the championship of paganism: "A man loves Nature in the morning for her innocence and amiability, and at nightfall, if he is loving her still, it is for her darkness and her cruelty. He washes at dawn in clear water as did the Wise Men of the Stoics, yet, somehow at the dark end of the day, he is bathing in hot bull's blood, as did Julian the Apostate."

Mr. Donoghue duly registers this aspect of Pater's legacy, but he shifts the emphasis: "It was Pater, more than Arnold, Tennyson, or Ruskin, who set modern literature upon its antithetical—he would have said its antinomian—course." That is to say, Mr. Donoghue highlights those elements of Pater's achievement that anticipate the critical, Romantic side of modernism: the side that exalted art as spiritual armor suited to a secular age and that found expression (for example) in Nietzsche's dictum that "we have art lest we perish from the truth." (Or—Nietzsche again—"Only as an aesthetic phenomenon is life and the world eternally justified.") As it happens, Pater claims us less through his ideas than through his sensibility, his style. He was not, Mr. Donoghue notes, really "learned in the history of art or in any of the subjects he took up—Greek myths, English poetry, Greek philosophy." Indeed,

> he was not an original thinker: virtually every idea he expressed can be traced to a source in English, French, or German writers. He is a force in the criticism of these subjects because he devised a distinctive style of writing about them: the Pateresque, a new color in the palette.

Mr. Donoghue's book is an effort to define and nurture that "new color," to recommend it anew as a compensation for the diminishments and losses of modernity. It is a measure of his eloquence that he succeeds in rendering the Pateresque at least momentarily plausible; it is a measure of the limitations of his chosen subject that that plausibility remains momentary, episodic.

Mr. Donoghue has segregated the biographical portion of his story in a "brief life" of some seventy pages at the beginning of the book. In some ways, it is remarkable that he was able to draw it out as long as he did. Pater extended his discretion even into the minutiae of his biography: his was a life notable above all for its lack of incident. We do, however, have the usual official signposts. We know that he was born Walter Horatio Pater near Stepney in 1839, the second son and third child of Richard and Maria Pater. A fourth child, Clara Ann, was born in 1841. Pater's father, a surgeon who catered to the poor, died shortly after Clara's birth at the age of forty-five. The family then moved to Enfield and, later, to Canterbury. In 1854, Pater's mother died, leaving the children in the care of their aunt Elizabeth. Pater was educated at the King's School, Canterbury, and then at Queen's College, Oxford, where he read widely but took an indifferent degree in 1862. While at Oxford he studied with the great Platonist Benjamin Jowett and came under the influence of Matthew Arnold and John Ruskin. He also, like so many university students then and later, used his college years as an opportunity to shed his religious faith. By 1859, Mr. Donoghue reports, Pater's attitude toward Christianity was "frivolous." He was, for example, overheard to say that it would be great fun to take Holy Orders without believing a word of Christian doctrine. His effort to put this scheme into effect was prevented by a friend who wrote to the Bishop of London, acquainting him with the state of Pater's beliefs.

In 1862, Pater's aunt Elizabeth died, and he set up house in London with Clara and his elder sister, Hester. In 1864, he won a provisional fellowship to Brasenose College, Oxford. The fellowship was confirmed the following year, and Pater settled into the pattern he would maintain for the rest of his life. Cared for by his maiden sisters, he shuttled quietly between Oxford and London, made occasional trips to the continent, and devoted himself to reading, writing, teaching, and aesthetic refinement. His circle of friends included Edmund Gosse, Mr. and Mrs. Humphry Ward, the classicist Ingram Bywater, as well as the influential Oxford don Mark Pattison and his young wife, twenty-seven years his junior, who are generally thought to have provided George Eliot with her models for Mr. Casaubon and Dorothea in *Middlemarch*. Pater's first visit to Italy, in the summer of 1865, was a revelation. He found in the Renaissance paintings he saw in Ravenna, Pisa, and Florence "the imagery of a richer, more daring sense of life than any to be seen in Oxford." It was then that he began "to associate the Italian Renaissance with freedom" and abundant sensuous life. In effect, "the Renaissance" for Pater named not a historical period but a state of mind, a promise of fulfillment.

It is here, just as Pater's career is about to begin, that things get difficult for the biographer. Like his image of Botticelli, Pater's life was "almost colourless." Mr. Donoghue notes that most people who write about Pater assume that "he must have had more life than appears, since otherwise he would have to be deemed a freak of nature." But the record shows that "by comparison with his grand contemporaries, he seems hardly to have lived." Thomas Hardy, meeting Pater in London in 1886, noted that his manner was "that of one carrying weighty ideas without spilling them." Deliquescence was as much a theme in his life as in his work. "There are," Mr. Donoghue notes, "weeks or even months in which he seems to have taken his favorite theme of evanescence and drifted away. We assume that he is still alive, but the evidence for his breathing is meagre."

Although he was clearly homosexual by disposition, Pater's fastidious nature—what Christopher Ricks called his "greed for fineness"—forbade anything so obvious as a love affair or a sex life. He was, as Edmund Wilson put it, "one of those semi-monastic types . . . that the English universities breed: vowed to an academic discipline but cherishing an intense originality, painfully repressed and incomplete but in the narrow field of their art somehow both sound and bold." In the event, Pater contented himself with a few passionate friendships and an ardent contemplation of youthful male

beauty wherever it chanced to present itself. It was a great sorrow to him, a lover of elegance, that he was himself physically unprepossessing: bald, bulky, and bushy in his formidable mustachios. Nonetheless, beginning in 1869 Pater dressed the part of a dandy. Mr. Donoghue equips him with top hat, black tailcoat, silk tie of apple green, dark-striped trousers, yellow gloves, and patent leather shoes. Pater appears as Mr. Rose in W. H. Mallock's satire *The New Republic* (1877): a "pale creature, with large moustache, looking out of the window at the sunset. . . . [H]e always speaks in an undertone, and his two topics are self-indulgence and art." In 1894, the last year of his life, Pater was invited to meet Mallarmé, who was then lecturing at Oxford. Mallarmé taught English in a *lycée*; Pater's French was excellent; but the two connoisseurs of intimation apparently thought it too vulgar actually to speak. According to one account, they "regarded each other in silence, and were satisfied."

Pater was not entirely without gumption; only he tended to hoard it for his imagination. The infamous Frank Harris—editor of the *Saturday Review,* sexual braggart, and author of the pornographic fantasy *My Life and Loves* (four volumes)—is notoriously an unreliable witness. But his anecdote about Pater has the ring of authenticity:

> He seemed at times half to realize his own deficiency. "Had I So-and-so's courage and hardihood," he cried once, "I'd have—." Suddenly the mood changed, the light in the eyes died out, the head drooped forward again, and with a half smile he added, "I might have been a criminal—he, he," and he moved with little careful steps across the room to his chair, and sat down.

The problem with Harris's anecdote is that it traps Pater in his caricature. It may be true; but it is not the whole truth. Such stories make it difficult to understand the genuine boldness of Pater's work: to appreciate, for example, the enormous scandal that *The Renaissance* caused when it was first published in 1873. Originally titled *Studies in the History of the Renaissance,* the slim volume consists of nine essays, some of which had been already published in one form or another, plus a brief preface and (in most editions) a conclusion. As Pater's friend Mrs. Mark Pattison noted in an otherwise friendly review of the book, the title is "misleading" because "the historical element is precisely that which is wanting. . . . [T]he work is in no wise a contribution to the history of the Renaissance." Pater took the point. In subsequent editions it was called by the title we know today, *The Renaissance: Studies in Art and Poetry.*

Not that the change of title really addressed Mrs. Pattison's criticism. "The book," another contemporary reviewer warned, "is not for any beginner to turn to in search of 'information.'" "Facts" and historical accuracy are not the coin in which Pater traded. For him, history was a mine to be worked for the *frisson* of insight; a certain amount of poetic license only aided the process.

Perhaps the chief instance of poetic license concerned the term "Renaissance." That Pater's conception of the Renaissance was idiosyncratic is clear first of all from the topics that he aggregated under the rubric. The book includes essays on such bona fide Renaissance figures as Pico della Mirandola, Leonardo, and Michelangelo; his essay on Botticelli did much to introduce the relatively unknown painter to the public. But the book also includes pieces on the medieval philosopher and ill-fated lover, Abelard, and the eighteenth-century art historian and impresario for "the glory that was Greece," Johann Winckelmann.

Pater notes that although interest in the Renaissance "mainly lies" in fifteenth-century Italy, he understands the term in "a much wider scope than was intended by those who originally used it to denote that revival of classical antiquity in the fifteenth century." For him, the Renaissance is a distinctive "outbreak of the human spirit" whose defining characteristics include "the care for physical beauty, the worship of the body, the breaking down of those limits which the religious system of the middle ages imposed on the heart and the imagination." Thus it is that although Winckelmann (who had long been one of Pater's culture heroes) was born in 1717, Pater concludes that he "really belongs in spirit to an earlier age" by virtue of "his enthusiasm for the things of the intellect and the imagination for their own sake, by his Hellenism, his life-long struggle to attain to the Greek spirit." For Pater, "Renaissance" was shorthand for a certain species of aesthetic vibrancy.

It was not necessarily a wholesome vibrancy. Part of what made Pater's debut scandalous was the hothouse atmosphere that he reveled in: the ripe, over-ripe sensorium that was so distant from the brisk admonitions of such pragmatic partisans of culture as Matthew Arnold. Pater's fascination with violence and death, with the interpenetration of death and beauty, was part of that ripeness. In his essay on Michelangelo, for example, Pater tells us that that great artist, like "all the nobler souls of Italy," "is much occupied with thoughts of the grave, and his true mistress is death—death at first as the worst of all sorrows and disgraces; . . . afterwards, death in its high distinction, its detachment from vulgar needs, the angry stains of life and action escaping fast." For Pater every genuine love was a kind of *Liebestod*.

But it was not only the atmosphere of Pater's book that shocked readers. Even more important was the blithe, aesthetic paganism that was implicit throughout *The Renaissance* and that Pater explicitly set forth in his conclusion. Dilating on "the splendour of our experience and its awful brevity," he recommended seizing the moment, regardless of the consequences: "Not the

fruit of experience, but experience itself, is the end." Since "a counted number of pulses only is given to us of a variegated, dramatic life," "our one chance" lay in "expanding that interval, in getting as many pulsations as possible into the given time." Neither morality nor religion figured in Pater's equation. What mattered was the intensity, the ecstasy of experience. Consequently, we must grasp "at any exquisite passion, or any contribution to knowledge that seems by a lifted horizon to set the spirit free for a moment, or any stirring of the senses, strange dyes, strange colours, and curious odours, or work of the artist's hands, or the face of one's friend." For Pater, the measure of life was not its adherence to an ideal but the perfection of self-satisfaction. "To burn always with this hard, gem-like flame, to maintain this ecstasy, is success in life." Pleasure, not duty, was the cardinal imperative, Life was not a continuously unfolding whole but a series of lyric moments: "In a sense it might even be said that our failure is to form habits."

Aesthetes embraced Pater's expostulation. The young Oscar Wilde declared that *The Renaissance* was "the golden book of spirit and sense, the holy writ of beauty." Others were not so enthusiastic. The Rev. John Wordsworth, a colleague of Pater's at Brasenose, acknowledged the book's "beauty of style" and "felicity of thought." But he objected that the fundamental message of the book was immoral: "I cannot disguise from myself," he wrote in a letter to Pater,

> that the concluding pages adequately sum up the philosophy of the whole; and that that philosophy is an assertion that no fixed principles either of religion or morality can be regarded as certain, that the only thing worth living for is momentary enjoyment and that probably or certainly the soul dissolves at death into elements which are destined never to reunite.

Nor were Christian clergymen the only critics of Pater's hedonism. The book was widely regarded as an invitation to moral frivolity. George Eliot spoke for many when she wrote that it was "quite poisonous in its false principles of criticism and false conceptions of life."

No one was more shocked by the scandal that *The Renaissance* precipitated than Pater himself. He did not abandon his aestheticism. But he did attempt to modulate it. In the second edition of *The Renaissance* he dropped the conclusion altogether. Later, he restored it, but with cosmetic modifications and a note informing readers that he had worried that "it might possibly mislead some of those young men into whose hands it might fall." When *The Picture of Dorian Gray* was published, Pater took the opportunity to distinguish his version of Epicureanism from Wilde's:

> A true Epicureanism aims at a complete though harmonious development of man's entire organism. To lose the moral sense therefore, for instance, the sense of sin and righteousness, as [does] Mr. Wilde's hero—

his heroes are bent on doing as speedily, as completely as they can—is to lose, or lower, organisation, to become less complex, to pass from a higher to a lower degree of development. . . . Lord Henry, and even more the, from the first, suicidal hero, loses too much in life to be a true Epicurean.

Pater attempted to provide a portrait of the "true Epicurean" in *Marius the Epicurean* (1885), an overwrought, somewhat ponderous autobiographical novel that describes the spiritual journey of its hero from paganism to the threshold of Christianity. (Pater much preferred hovering on the threshold of commitment to actually embracing any definite faith.) According to Mr. Donoghue, "the main reason [for writing the book] was to refute the charge, levelled against *Studies in the History of the Renaissance,* that he was a hedonist, an epicurean and—the implication was clear—that he instructed his undergraduates at Brasenose to live for pleasure alone." In fact, Pater did believe in living for pleasure alone. But he thought that careful discrimination among pleasures redeemed his aestheticism from vulgar hedonism or immorality.

Did it? In part. Pater would certainly have recoiled in horror from the crude narcissism and decadence that his work helped to inspire. But it is not at all clear that George Eliot was mistaken in castigating his "false principles of criticism and false conceptions of life." Mr. Donoghue wishes to resuscitate Pater partly because he thinks that a Pateresque aestheticism encourages readers to deal with art on its own terms, as affording an experience valuable in itself. "There are," he writes, "some experiences which are best approached on the assumption that their value is intrinsic." This is certainly true. And it may be that Pater's view of art, as Mr. Donoghue claims, can help to immunize art from ideology. Because he held that art "has no moral design upon us," Pater would have had no patience with efforts to subject aesthetic experience to politics—or any other "external" value. "In its primary aspect," he wrote in *The Renaissance,* "a great picture has no more definite message for us than an accidental play of sunlight and shadow for a few moments on the wall or floor."

Yet this is not the whole story. Mr. Donoghue writes that "the purpose of art is to offer the distressed soul release, however temporary." This is not a new theme for him. In his book *The Arts without Mystery* (1984), for example, Mr. Donoghue worried that our commitment to scientific rationality had drained the arts of their power to enchant and to kindle the imagination.[2] He sought to "reinstate mystery" into the arts while at the same time distinguishing mystery "from mere bewilderment or mystification." For Mr. Donoghue, the artist is most truly himself when he stands in an antagonistic or (one of his favorite words) "antinomian" attitude toward society. Yet this Romanticism is sharply qualified by prudence, the most un-Romantic of virtues. He understands that the main business of society cannot

countenance the extravagances that the artistic imagination furnishes.

> The arts are on the margin, and it doesn't bother me to say they are marginal. What bothers me are the absurd claims we make for them. I want to say the margin is the place for those feelings and intuitions which daily life doesn't have a place for, and mostly seems to suppress. . . . With the arts, people can make a space for themselves, and fill it with intimations of freedom and presence.

Pater would have agreed. "What modern art has to do in the service of culture," he wrote in his essay on Winckelmann,

> is so to rearrange the details of modern life, so to reflect it, that it may satisfy the spirit. And what does the spirit need in the face of modern life? The sense of freedom. . . . The chief factor in the thoughts of the modern mind concerning itself is the intricacy, the universality of natural law, even in the moral order. For us, necessity is . . . a magic web woven through and through us, like that magnetic system of which modern science speaks, penetrating us with a network, subtler than our subtlest nerves, yet bearing in it the central forces of the world. Can art represent men and women in these bewildering toils so as to give the spirit at least the equivalent for the sense of freedom?

The real question, for Mr. Donoghue as well as for Pater, is whether that "equivalent for the sense of freedom" is anything more than illusion. Does Pater's philosophy—does any thoroughgoing aestheticism—really leave room for "intrinsic value" as Mr. Donoghue claims?

In his preface to *The Renaissance,* Pater begins by *seeming* to agree with Matthew Arnold's famous definition of criticism, but he then slyly inverts Arnold's meaning:

> "To see the object as in itself it really is," has been justly said to be the aim of all true criticism whatever; and in aesthetic criticism the first step towards seeing one's object as it really is, is to know one's own impression as it really is, to discriminate it, to realise it distinctly. . . . What is this song or picture, this engaging personality presented in life or in a book, to *me?* . . . [T]he picture, the landscape, the engaging personality in life or in a book . . . are valuable for their virtues, as we say, in speaking of an herb, a wine, a gem; for the property each has of affecting one with a special, a unique, impression of pleasure.

For Pater, "one's own impression" trumps meaning. And it is a curious irony, as the critic Adam Phillips has observed, that although Pater insists on the value of discrimination and accurate identification of the critic's "impressions," his vocabulary is "notably vague." Thus it is that he "exploited the invitation of inexact words: 'sweet,' 'peculiar,' 'delicate,' and above all 'strange.'"

Mr. Donoghue rightly notes that Pater "looked at an object under the sign of pleasure, not of truth." He approvingly quotes another critic who spoke of "the disjunction of sensation from judgment" in Pater's work. The "Paterian imagination," he writes, seeks "relations" instead of "duties." "It follows that Pater practised consciousness not as a mode of knowledge but as an alternative to knowledge. . . . One of the ways in which Pater was antinomian was in his being ready to think that understanding wasn't everything." Indeed, his chief concern was "his pleasure in feeling alive." "Aesthetic criticism" in Pater's sense deals "not with objects, works of art, but with the types of feeling they embodied. . . . Ontology is displaced by psychology."

"Ontology is displaced by psychology": in other words, what matters for Pater are states of feeling, not truth. At the end of his book, Mr. Donoghue acknowledges the "risks" of aestheticism: "triviality, exquisiteness, solipsism." An additional risk is losing the weight or reality of one's experience. T. S. Eliot criticized Pater for propounding "a theory of ethics" in the guise of a theory of art. What he meant was that Pater's conception of "aesthetic criticism" offered not a principle of criticism but a way of life. At the center of that way of life is the imperative to regard all experience as an occasion for aesthetic delectation: a seemingly attractive proposition, perhaps, until one realizes that it depends upon a narcissistic self-absorption that renders every moral demand negotiable. "The sense of freedom" is indeed the essence of aestheticism; but it is the cold and lonely freedom of the isolated individual. This was something that Kierkegaard exposed with great clarity in his anatomy of "the aesthetic mode of life" in *Either/Or.* Mr. Donoghue tells us that "the part of Aestheticism which should now be recovered . . . is its concern for the particularity of form in every work of art." The problem is that although aestheticism begins by emphasizing form, it ends by dissolving form into the "pleasurable sensations" and "pulsations" that Pater so valued. In this sense, aestheticism is the enemy of the intrinsic. Mr. Donoghue criticized Eliot's essay on Pater as "extravagant" and "cruel." But Eliot was right: the theory of "art for art's sake" is "valid in so far as it can be taken as an exhortation to the artist to stick to his job; it never was and never can be valid for the spectator, reader or auditor."

Notes

1. *Walter Pater: Lover of Strange Souls,* by Denis Donoghue; Knopf, 361 pages.

2. See my review of the book in *The New Criterion* for September 1984.

Adam Phillips (review date 24 August 1995)

SOURCE: Phillips, Adam. "Provocation." *London Review of Books* 17, no. 16 (24 August 1995): 9-10.

[*In the following review, Phillips asserts that Donoghue's* Walter Pater *is a remarkable, engaging, often brilliant book.*]

In a contemporary review of *The Renaissance* in the *Pall Mall Gazette,* the critic Sidney Colvin wrote that 'the book is not one for any beginner to turn to in search of "information".' 'Information' was in inverted commas not because there were no facts or respectable opinions in the book, but because Pater did not seem to believe in information, as it was customarily understood in criticism of the arts. As most reviewers seemed to agree, he wasn't doing something new, he was doing something badly. 'In the matter of historical fact,' Denis Donoghue writes, joining in, as it were, 'Pater also took liberties, so many that it is a pity he did not derive more satisfaction from them.' But Pater was satisfied not by getting it wrong, but by not having to get it right. It was his style to affirm invention over accuracy and, indeed, satisfaction over argument.

Pater was neither scholarly nor overtly confessional; and he seemed unembarrassed by what a work of art could do to him, or how it tempted him to write about it. His approach tended to be, in Donoghue's arch but apt phrase, 'free of empirical duty'. Matthew Arnold and Modern Science could give you the object as in itself it really was; could give you the best, the most reliable, salutary truths. What Pater gave you were his impressions and his style. And his style unashamedly competed for attention with what he was apparently writing about ('Pater's sentences,' Donoghue writes, 'ask to be read as if they wanted to be looked at, not merely to be understood'). The real interest for Pater was in what the art, and the life of the artist, could evoke in him; what he could use it to become. Or rather, to write; because it was only in sentences that Pater became himself. He was, in other words, at least as interested in himself as he was in the art or artists he wrote about. For those keen to humble themselves in front of Great Art—or, more important, Great Religion—this was something of an affront.

The 'chief question', Pater wrote in *The Renaissance,* that the critic must ask of the artist is: 'What is the peculiar sensation, what is the peculiar quality of pleasure, which his work has the property of exciting in us, and which we cannot get elsewhere?' The critic was not asked to describe the formal qualities of the work, nor its historical context: he was invited to describe his pleasure. This, of course, was a question, and an invitation, calculated to appeal to those young enough, or bold enough, to have confidence in their possibilities for pleasure. Pater assumed, at least in his writing, that pleasure and sensation—not to mention the peculiar— were morally good. So when *The Renaissance* was published in 1873 it was a scandal, at least in Oxford. Pater was a homosexual Oxford don who lived with his two sisters, and scandal was anathema to him. The subjects that he treated—Pico della Mirandola, Botticelli, Leonardo, Du Bellay, Winckelmann, among others—seemed harmless enough. But the book that Wilde would notoriously refer to as his 'golden book' was too timely to be the work of an innocent. 'The' was the misleading word in the title; Pater was proposing a renaissance of aesthetic values—the renaissance, during the Renaissance, of pre-Christian values—that was manifestly antithetical to the official versions of itself that Victorian England was promoting.

In flagrant disregard for the responsibilities of his academic position, Pater seemed to be encouraging the natural paganism of youth at a time in their lives when those privileged undergraduates—the 'beginners' Colvin covertly refers to—were supposed to be consolidating their faith in Christianity and the Empire. ('Pater's England.' Donoghue writes, 'is not the country as given; on that he has little purchase.') Pater seemed to be suggesting in his infamous Conclusion that we have nothing to redeem but our moments of pleasure, and nothing to do beyond the having of special, pleasurable experiences. Life was about intensity and not achievement, about meaning and not profit; diligence was bad faith. His ideas, such as they were, were not original, nor did he claim that they were. An elegant confection of pre-Socratic philosophy, German Romanticism and French aestheticism, his writing mocked the grander ambitions of Late Victorian England as much by the oddity of its style as by the old beliefs it claimed were being recycled during the Renaissance. To the champions of moral and material progress—the scientists and the political idealists as much as the divines and the cultural critics—Pater had written a heretical text. 'Our failure is to form habits,' Pater had written. You couldn't make a society that was getting anywhere out of Pater's ideas.

The problem that every biographer of Pater has had is that Pater didn't make much of a life out of these ideas either. By all accounts he did not cut much of a dash in the world; there is more perplexity and distaste than affection or admiration in the reminiscences of him that Donoghue reports. And there was a dismal lack, at least from the spectator's point of view, of erotic or other adventures. He was physically unprepossessing, nice and rather remote: 'an ugly pig', as Arthur Symons put it, 'though learned and charming too'. Pater seems to have believed, perhaps like some of his biographers, that without looks you can't have a life. When Wilde was told that Pater had died, he replied that he did not know that he had lived. It was as though, even to his contemporaries, he was solely interesting for his writing. Unlike Flaubert, whom he admired, he had no Egypt. The style was the life, nothing else about him fascinated. Pater's peculiar sentences became his character, all that was left of him, it seems, even while he was alive. 'I think he has had—will have had—the most exquisite literary fortune.' Henry James wrote to Edmund Gosse when Pater died in 1894, 'i.e. to have taken it out all, wholly, exclusively, with the pen (the style, the genius) & absolutely not at all with the person. He is the mask without the face.' For James, Pater's

biography *is* his style. But for many other people the ridiculous thing about Pater was that he had a biography without a life, a grand, unusual style uninformed by experience. As a person, Pater was often considered an unappealing mixture of the preposterous and the feeble; his writing has a talent for making people supercilious. But the derision itself—from his earliest reviewers to Eliot's influential essay of 1930, 'Arnold and Pater', and even sometimes to Donoghue—is telling. So much animus spells some complicity. And some doubt about how to make sense of Pater, when he kept himself to his sentences.

Modern biographers, thwarted by the fact that nobody knows anymore what is of significance in a life, solve the problem by trying to include everything, though the contemporary fantasy of what everything is is rather predictable. Biographies are so long now not merely because we have more information, but because lives no longer have plots, they only have detail. Biography gives shape to a life, but a life doesn't. When it comes to Lives—as Pater clearly realised in his *Imaginary Portraits,* and his own autobiographical writing—less is more. But when it comes to Pater's life there has never been enough. Or no one has been sufficiently intrigued by the disparity that James, among others, remarked on.

For the critics of biography Pater would seem to be an ideal case: there is no discernible or apparently useful connection between what Pater did each day and what he wrote. He seems. Donoghue writes, 'sentence by sentence, a textual self in the art of becoming'; and this makes him grist for the modern mill. There is nothing outside the text, certainly not a man who sits down to breakfast. And yet, paradoxically, all of Pater's writing attests to the necessity and the enigma of the connection. All of Pater's writing about art is an idiosyncratic mixture of the biographical and the autobiographical, as though for him they were always inextricable. There is no biography, he implies, without autobiography; but also, and more interestingly, there is no autobiography without biography. We make our lives, though often hermetically, out of the lives of others. None of Pater's biographers have taken up his ironic, implicit invitation to join him to his sentences.

When it comes to biography—the connections, if any, between the man who suffers and the mind which creates, in Eliot's lurid terms—Donoghue prefers a mystery to a possible over-simplification. 'There is a relation between them . . .' be affirms, conceding nothing, 'but the relation is occult, it can't be specified. The best reason for evoking the creative imagination is that the phrase indicates our sense of this opacity.' As, one assumes, would the word 'God'. Pater, like all real artists, made things up, Donoghue asserts; that is what it is to have an imagination. But when people stand up for mystery you can never be sure which laws they are laying down. Indeed, one of the things that characterises a genuine mystery, one might think, is its resilience. A 'mind' and its work would be virtually profaned. Donoghue intimates, if they were 'explained or explained away by reciting the personal, domestic, social, economic and political conditions of its production'. Creative imagination or wholesale reduction seem implausible alternatives, calculated to pre-empt the interesting complexity of the issue. The imagination can also, of course, speculate without specifying, make useful or intriguing links without merely fixing the material. The injunction not to enquire into such matters seems pointlessly prohibitive. Good literary biographies, though rare, have been written. This is not one; but partly because, by Donoghue's own admission, it is 'a critical biography, a Brief Life'. But why include any Life at all if it merely gets in the way, if it is just an opportunity for false supposition?

As a biography of a person **Walter Pater** seems often cursory, and occasionally derisive of its subject. Pater, Donoghue writes, 'remained the don who got a poor second', lived in a 'bashful little house' with his 'spinster sisters'; and valued them 'for the civilised order they ensured while he entertained his undergraduates to hand-holding teas'. Donoghue makes as little as possible of Pater's homosexuality; and he reproves him, not infrequently, as though he were a boy. 'cheeky', 'insolent' and never bold enough. As an account of a style—though not quite a biography of a style—**Walter Pater** is often brilliant and always engaging, even when Donoghue's piety grates on one's own. Much like Pater himself. Donoghue uses his subject for his own purposes; not least of which is a spirited and eloquent contemporary defence of art for art's sake. Like all such defences it sometimes betrays the fastidious, precious enthusiasm that can make art sound like a monument to the most futile kind of moral superiority. At its best, though, Donoghue's eloquence shows us the good senses in which art might be better kept to itself; and what it loses when treated merely as a substitute or a symptom—viz. everything that makes it different from a substitute or a symptom.

For Donoghue, art represents the possibility of other (secular) worlds. But his misgivings about art as a substitute religion are as severe as his commitment to art as a haven. ('We should read literature in the spirit in which we enter a concert hall.') Pater is an important puzzle for Donoghue because he assumes the supreme value of art, but with a quasi-religious fervour; and his own art of aesthetic criticism seems often to level, and always to exploit, its subjects; to convert them, as it were, to his own style. Pater's writing celebrates idiosyncrasy, but avoids conflict—'Difference, yes, but not opposition' is Donoghue's motto for him. Pater's 'appreciations' show an obtrusive disregard for everything other than Pater's style. Irreverent towards conformities, his style consumes everything in its path. What he is interested in becomes an opportunity to

perform more Pater. For anyone concerned, as Donoghue is, about the ethics of a style—the imperiousness of certain kinds of writing—Pater is a provocation.

Like Swift, Yeats and Emily Dickinson—the other individual writers Donoghue has devoted books to—Pater unavoidably invites the questions that have always inspired Donoghue as a critic. Are writers people who, because they cannot bear the world, make it their own, in words; or are they people who so cherish the world that they want to show us the very different things it contains? Are they megalomaniacs or midwives? (The obvious answer is: usually both, like everybody else.) But this is the distinction—with its inevitable theological implications—that has been at the heart of Donoghue's remarkable critical project. What kind of god is the writer, an aesthetic narcissist or an aesthetic altruist? And what relationship, if any, does he have to God—competitive, complementary, humble etc? It is a question of 'the rivalry', as he put it in his Introduction to *The Ordinary Universe* nearly thirty years ago, 'between the persuasions of the natural world and the structure of one's own imagination, between Ordinary Things and Supreme Fictions'. In Pater the Supreme Fiction wins, but it is a style and not a myth.

Walter Pater becomes a remarkable book once Donoghue has got the determinedly Brief Life over with (it is a mere eighty pages in a book of over three hundred). What he calls 'Pater's quiet audacity' is like a foil for his own more abrasive refinement. Pater's shrewd refusals, his disavowal of the quotidian, confronts Donoghue with a new version of his own abiding aesthetic preoccupations. Though his writing has been impressively various, in successive books this conflict between the Ordinary Universe and the Supreme Fiction has been redescribed and theorised with a kind of stubborn eloquence. With Donoghue, unlike many other critics, passion has not shrunk to an obsession. His often brilliant close readings have been reassuringly unpredictable; but his surprises are always framed by an underlying contention. In **Yeats** [**William Butler Yeats**] (1971) he quoted Blackmur's distinction between the erotic poet and the sacramental poet. 'A sacramental poet,' Donoghue commented,

> respects the object for itself, but even more for the spirit which, however mysteriously, it contains . . . such a poet is always willing to 'let be', he is merely the spirit's celebrant. An erotic poet may respect the object in itself, but it is not characteristic of him to do so, and beyond the point of acknowledgment the only relevant spirit is his own and he is never willing to let be . . . the object has helped him to define his power, and he is tender toward it for that reason.

In his wonderful T. S. Eliot Lectures, **Thieves of Fire,** Donoghue borrowed Adrian Stokes's similar distinction between carving and modelling in sculpture, as a way of talking about both different ways of writing and different kinds of writer: 'Carving is concerned with the release of significance deemed already to exist, imprisoned in the stone, and modelling is a more plastic process by which the sculptor imposes his meaning upon the stone.' These are useful descriptions because they imply that the artist's relationship to his or her medium is also analogous to a person's relationship with others, indeed with everything that is not himself. The aesthetic, that is to say, becomes unavoidably ethical. The writer's relationship to language—to what he seems to want to do with words—is a picture of a form of life.

The carver (Blackmur's sacramental poet) says: 'I'm not telling you, I'm showing you.' Carvers are akin to scientists in so far as they claim simply to disclose what is already there. What they discover, though, is often something we then have to submit to (or worship) like a natural law or an essence. The risk for the carver is that he may be merely complying with the way things are supposed to be; by realising things as they are he leaves everything as it is. But then what could be more narcissistic, more grandiose, than the belief that one is in a position to recognise anything as it really is, the intrinsic essence of something (or someone)? The risk for the modeller (the erotic poet) is that he is an aesthetic entrepreneur: he can't leave anything alone because everything must be used for profit. Nothing is sufficiently real, or satisfying, until it is transfigured by his desire. The carver is always telling us, but sometimes under the guise of showing us. As a critic Donoghue has always been a carver trying not to be a modeller, and the critic as modeller is often one of Donoghue's targets (**Walter Pater** has a smack at Bloom). And yet it has been 'erotic poets' like Yeats and Stevens that Donoghue has been drawn to. Pater, the critic as artist, the modeller with the manners of a carver, is, therefore, a special case for him.

What exasperates Donoghue about Pater—and compels some of the finest criticism in this book—is that Pater tries to have it both ways; he has the shy modesty of the carver, and the arrogant obliviousness of the modeller. His modesty was a demand for submission. 'If a church, or any other object were completely itself,' Donoghue writes, 'it seemed stolid, impenetrable, opaque to the imagination. Pater liked to find its certitude a little ashamed of itself and willing to entertain at least an occasional doubt or misgiving. He wanted the imagination to have a chance of gaining access to any matter.' Donoghue is on the side of the imagination, but he is also mindful of what happens when nothing is acknowledged to resist the imagination, but he is also mindful of what happens when nothing is acknowledged to resist the imagination. If it gains access to everything there will be nothing left. What Donoghue cares for is the imagination that can love whatever resists it; or can, at least, notice that there is resistance somewhere. In **Walter Pater,** though, you

sometimes get the feeling that for Donoghue Pater would have been better off if he had just believed in original sin; as though he needed to locate recalcitrance somewhere, needed something to make a mockery of his wishes. When Donoghue writes that 'Pater's chief concern was his pleasure in feeling alive,' you feel Pater is being mysteriously admonished.

Donoghue wants Pater to come clean and get his axes out ('His tone was consistently urbane, as if the grinding of an axe was the last thing he intended'). On the one hand, Pater is 'a witness to the charm of the intrinsic', but only of moods and feelings and the transitions between them. On the other hand, and less to Donoghue's taste, in Pater's writing 'the object doesn't matter; what matters is the mind's experience of pleasure in lavishing attention upon it.' The indulgence of Pater's determined disregard makes Donoghue droll with exasperation ('One of the limitations of Pater's essay on Vézelay is that he knew virtually nothing about the iconography of church architecture'). There is, it should be said, virtually nothing that Pater writes about that Donoghue knows virtually nothing about: indeed, judging by his corrections of Pater, he often knows more. What Donoghue refers to as Pater's commitment to 'those visionary artists who refuse to transcribe the data before them and insist upon the privilege of their own vision' should have been a problem for him, as it is for Donoghue. It is clear that Donoghue wants Pater to be more troubled by his preferences and affinities, more bothered by his taken liberties ('Pater does not bother with meanings that may be established by scholarship'). He is continually dismayed by Pater's refusal of conflict, by the absence of drama in his writing. And yet when Donoghue's indignation about Pater's irresponsibility doesn't get the better of him—and there is some wonderful commentary in this book, particularly on *Diaphanéité, Plato and Platonism* and *Marius*—he defines better than anyone else the unique paradox of Pater's position: that he was antinomial without being oppositional. He found a way of being adversarial that wasn't merely a relish for conflict. Pater didn't go his own way because he was spoiling for a fight.

Donoghue's Pater is this 'antinomian'; he lived, Donoghue writes, 'by inflecting the official life offered him'. 'Inflecting' seems just right, as Donoghue often is in this puzzling and puzzled book; it catches the way Pater modifies rather than confronts, the way he can be radical without apparently having an argument. Pater's lack of reverence for antagonism—expressed in his almost total disregard for it—makes him, by definition as it were, difficult to place ('He claims for his refusals just as much respect as everyone gives to conflicts and causes'). Compared with the forthrightness of Carlyle, or Ruskin, or Arnold, or Wilde, Pater seems very hush-hush. But Donoghue is never quite sure in this book whether Pater is exemplary or just lazy. He is certainly an exemplary aesthete: 'An aesthete is an artist who considers what he can do by standing aside. What he does has its adversary merit in relation to the Victorian consensus on the moral value of work.' It is Donoghue's version of Pater as an asider—an insider as a middle-class Oxford don and an outsider as a uniquely bizarre writer, and a homosexual—that is the real interest of this book. 'He would prefer,' Donoghue writes, though he himself would not, 'to live without categories or definitions, or aside from them.' Pater is difficult to categorise as a writer because he was so uncategorical; so definitively vague.

It is almost as though Pater has allowed Donoghue to stand up for the virtues of aestheticism, while still being dismayed by its provenance, or even its necessity. He can only adopt Pater by resisting him, by making him out to be a slippery slope. 'Aestheticism,' he writes, 'was one expression of the premonition, sad indeed, that most of life, in the forms in which it presented itself, could not be understood and yet must be lived.' **Walter Pater,** among other things, is an irritated elegy for the contemporary death of aestheticism; and its severity is often as moving, and witty, as are its celebrations. Donoghue, though, does not tell us why it is quite so sad, nor why it should be otherwise.

For Pater, success in life was not to do with diligence or application: it was 'to burn always with this hard gem-like flame, to maintain this ecstasy' of secular epiphanies. No flame, of course, has ever been able to do this, let alone any person. But what Pater was repudiating with these bold assertions was, in a sense, as important as what he was affirming. Careerism and routine and transcendence were his targets, with objectivity as a necessary casualty (consensus, Pater implies, is just a way of making and enforcing new habits). The idea of genius was so crucial for Pater because geniuses are people who break our habits for us. If it is the distinctiveness, the achievement of a style that, as Donoghue asserts, 'is nearly all that literature from Pater to Stevens claims to achieve', then Pater may, indeed, have given 'modern literature its first act'. That style should be the thing that the erotic poets should triumph over the sacramental poets, is for Donoghue a mixed blessing. But it is because Donoghue won't let Pater be that he has written such an engaged, tetchy book.

David Wheatley (review date 1 November 2001)

SOURCE: Wheatley, David. "The Devilish God." *London Review of Books* 23, no. 21 (1 November 2001): 36-7.

[*In the following review, Wheatley discusses Donoghue's* Words Alone *and Adam's Curse, observing that both works focus on the importance of religious faith in art and literature.*]

Few presences were more imposing in postwar poetry than that of T. S. Eliot, but from his eminence as the Pope of Russell Square, Eliot has now shrunk to something more like a holy ghost. Pound's right-wing unpleasantness, because so deranged, seems somehow more forgivable, to the huddled ranks of Poundians at least. Critics unimpressed by the psychodrama of Eliot's Christianity, such as Harold Bloom and Helen Vendler, much prefer Yeats and Stevens. And as a glance at any anthology of 20th-century British poetry will show, the prewar voices most audible today belong to Auden and MacNeice. From the maudlin *Tom and Viv* to Peter Ackroyd's unauthorised Life and Carole Seymour-Jones's *Painted Shadow,* the collateral damage, too, has been heavy. Even now, much about Eliot remains opaque: 13 years after the first volume of this letters appeared, we can only speculate as to what continues to hold up publication of the second. Partisans of Anthony Julius's 1995 study, *T. S. Eliot, Anti-Semitism and Literary Form,* will have reached their own conclusions. The anti-semitic charge was squatting awkwardly on Eliot's reputation long before Julius's book, but old habits of deference died hard, even among his detractors. In 'T. S. Eliot at 101', Cynthia Ozick remembers swallowing 'without protest' the nasty bits of Eliot's poems as an undergraduate and the long, slow disenchantment that followed, but manages to end on a note of wistful nostalgia for the 'Age of Eliot': 'What we will probably go on missing for ever is that golden cape of our youth, the power and prestige of high art.' To Tom Paulin by contrast, post-Julius, Eliot is practically the devil incarnate, portrayed in Paulin's poem 'The Yellow Spot' gloating with Montgomery Belgion over the transportation of Jews and (could there be a connection here?) playing his favourite game of trying to find a rhyme for 'Ritz' ('no not Biarritz'). 'Resign resign resign,' screams the last line of Eliot's 'Difficulties of a Statesman'. With the catcalls from the terraces grown so strident, how much longer can Chairman Tom cling on?

Denis Donoghue was an admirer of Eliot's before Paulin was born, and brings the fruit of many decades' reading and rumination to **Words Alone: The Poet T. S. Eliot.** Donoghue begins by invoking his own 1990 memoir, **Warrenpoint,** which he had hoped to follow by writing something on literary Dublin in the 1940s and 1950s. Contemplating the slender yield of bohemian anecdotes from his time as a student and young lecturer at University College Dublin, he wisely decided to leave the field to Anthony Cronin's *Dead as Doornails*. The closest thing he could write to a memoir of those years, he realised, would be a book on Eliot, the writer whose work had left the deepest impression on him. As a lecturer he was by all accounts not without an Eliotian streak of his own: distant, Jesuitical, cosmopolitan. With titles like **The Sovereign Ghost, Ferocious Alphabets** and **Connoisseurs of Chaos,** his books flamboyantly advertised their distance from the local entanglements of Irish Studies. Though his remarks on Irish politics in *Warrenpoint* are firmly nationalist, there is something back-of-the-envelope about them, as though unable to conceal their author's impatience to move on to the very disparate subjects considered in *The Pure Good of Theory, The Old Moderns* and *Walter Pater: Lover of Strange Souls.*

Nevertheless, *Words Alone* contains a fair deal of straight autobiographical reminiscence. A vivid presence in Dublin in the 1950s was the 'morally intimidating' Donald Davie, then a fellow at Trinity College, where Donoghue would drop in on him to discuss modern poetry. 'He used the word "infidel",' Donoghue remembers, 'more freely and more deliberately than I supposed it had ever been used since the 17th century,' and risked taunts of 'infidel' himself by suggesting in a 1956 article that 'The Dry Salvages' was 'quite simply rather a bad poem' (Donoghue tends to agree). With his preference for the more lapidary Objectivist Pound, Davie grimaced at the concession that, yes. Eliot was indeed a great poet. Many years later the friendship ended when Donoghue described Davie's mind as having an 'experimental' relationship with its contents, which Davie took to mean that he didn't know how to think straight—and Donoghue does get Davie curiously wrong when he classes *Thomas Hardy and British Poetry* with Larkin's *Oxford Book of 20th-Century English Verse* as arguing that 'the Modernism of Eliot and Pound was a false trail,' when this was precisely the basis on which Davie attacked Larkin. Where Eliot was concerned, though, the young Donoghue's admiration was anything but experimental or tentative. Inspired by Eliot's 1953 lecture 'The Three Voices of Poetry' and interested in his plays, Donoghue produced his first academic book, *The Third Voice,* on modern verse drama, and his career was underway.

Reflections on Religion and Literature—the subtitle of *Adam's Curse*—could just as easily do duty for *Words Alone.* Discussing Eliot's 'Voices', Donoghue speculates on the enormous effort it must have required for a poet so subjective and idealist to turn towards tradition, classicism and impersonality, against the native 'urgings of his talent'; an effort comparable only to the effort of prayer. Hence the importance of all the untranslated fragments into which *The Waste Land* dissolves in its last few lines, and of writing 'Shantih shantih shantih' rather than a Christian platitude like 'the peace that passeth understanding'. It is the strangeness that counts, of the belief itself as much as of language, the insistence on something unrecognisable to set against the natural turpitude of the self. In his early years in England, Eliot liked to sign himself *metoikos* ('resident alien') in letters to journals, and was still calling himself a 'spirit unappeased and peregrine' by the time we get to 'Little Gidding', as if plain old 'wandering' weren't good enough. Donoghue devotes a useful passage in *Adam's Curse* to reminding us just how odd the whole business of belief could be for Eliot, to the point where he at-

tacked Bertrand Russell's amazing 'capacity for believing', and answered Russell's certainty that he would rot when dead with 'I cannot subscribe with that conviction to any belief.'

One of the attractive things about belief is the prospect of nothing being entirely your responsibility any more, and writing on the subject of evil, Donoghue cites a character in a *New Yorker* cartoon: 'With me it's neither nature nor nurture. It's Satan.' As Donoghue observes, it is hard to imagine a serious writer producing a book on the influence of the devil on contemporary literature, as Eliot did in *After Strange Gods.* There is something irresistible to Donoghue, as to Eliot, in the cosmic daring of such gestures, and their poke in the eye for the 'senile humanism' that both men hold in such evident disdain. In many ways *Words Alone,* no less than *Adam's Curse,* is Donoghue's defence of the institutional theistic imagination in an age of callow unbelief. That it should be institutional matters to him very much, and he looks closely at the stand-off between Eliot's Anglicanism and do-it-off yourself Emersonianism. 'Institutions are necessary,' Eliot wrote at the end of his essay on Baudelaire, before his reception into the Church of England in 1927. The key to this side of his personality, as William Empson was surely right to suggest, was the sloughing off of his boyhood Unitarianism, which he seems to have associated ever afterwards with his less than properly assertive father (though on the Christian-baiting Empson of *Milton's God,* Donoghue is predictably scathing). For religion as an inner light Eliot had nothing but contempt. 'The possessors of the inner voice,' he wrote, 'ride ten in a compartment to a football match at Swansea, listening to the inner voice, which breathes the eternal message of vanity, fear and lust'.

Donoghue bristles when poetry becomes self-sufficient, to the point of becoming a form of religion in its own right. The chief offender on this count in both *Words Alone* and *Adam's Curse* is Wallace Stevens, his distrust of whom is one thing at least he had in common with Donald Davie. Donoghue fairly wipes the floor with Stevens as a reader of Eliot. Most critics have agreed that 'X' in 'Extracts from Addresses to the Academy of Fine Ideas' seems to be Eliot, 'an obstruction, a man / Too exactly himself.' For Stevens, or Donoghue's Stevens, Christian belief was not to be countenanced, since it refused the Emersonian licence that 'all men are priests.' Stevens compares Eliot's acolytes to 'lean cats of the arches of the churches' and scoffs that 'They bear brightly the little beyond / Themselves, the slightly unjust drawing that is / Their genius: the exquisite errors of time.' The snigger is audible behind that line-break, 'the little beyond / Themselves'. In *Adam's Curse* Donoghue quotes Stevens again as a precursor of Hans Vaihinger's *The Philosophy of 'As If'*: 'The final belief is to believe in a fiction which you know to be a fiction, there being nothing else. The exquisite truth is to know that it is a fiction and that you believe in it willingly.' 'Believe', Donoghue retorts, is too strong a word here—'entertain' might be more appropriate. For Donoghue's Stevens it is 'as if' I may entertain the fiction that it's sunny outside when it's raining; but exquisite as my conviction may be, I'm really still getting wet. Then again, it's 'as if' I'm really still dry. None of which seems to me to refute Stevens any more than Dr Johnson kicking the stone refuted Berkeley; and it was Stevens, not Eliot, who wrote a poem called 'Not Ideas about the Thing but the Thing Itself'. Donoghue's Stevens fulfils his role of Emersonian fall-guy admirably, but should be classified under 'Ideas about the Thing' rather than 'the Thing Itself.'

Donoghue doesn't always come down on the side of belief for belief's sake, and he offers a spirited defence of Larkin's 'Aubade' against tut-tutting readings by Czeslaw Milosz and Seamus Heaney. On the charge of anti-semitism he is implacable, even reprieving the passage in *After Strange Gods* about too many 'free-thinking Jews' being 'undesirable in a Christian society'. It would be repressive of Jews, in Donoghue's gloss, to suggest that what they believe is a matter of indifference to society at large, the alternative being, presumably, a munificent disapproval (a line of argument that makes Eliot an unlikely forerunner of Marcuse and the theory of 'repressive tolerance'). Addressing another much picked-over poem, 'Burbank with a Baedeker: Bleistein with a Cigar', Donoghue enlists Gadamer to reclaim the word 'prejudice' (Eliot went further, refusing to demur at being called a 'bigot'). 'If I accept someone's authority,' Donoghue writes, 'and go along with his judgment of a particular issue because he knows more about it than I do, I act on a legitimate prejudice.' 'Because he knows more about it than I do': Donoghue is one of those rare critics who can manage to sound humble and lordly at the same time. Elsewhere he skimps on the humility, 'endless' though Eliot thought it was, to deliver the lordliness neat. 'I am assuming agreement that *The Waste Land* is fundamental to our sense of modern literature,' he announces at one point, while at the end of a chapter in **Adam's Curse** we are told: 'I have written of these exemplars in several books. There is no merit in going over the same ground again. *Papa locutus est.*'

In a much-quoted footnote to his review of *The Varieties of Metaphysical Poetry*, Geoffrey Hill complained about the decline of Eliot's poetry from the 'pitch' of 'Prufrock' to the 'tone' of *Four Quartets,* the former as thrillingly unstable as the latter is calculated and reassuring. Donoghue isn't having any of it, but it's hard to deny that something has got lost in the transition from the Shantih town of *The Waste Land* to the City of God in *Four Quartets*. Donoghue's insistence on taking seriously the question of belief doesn't come without some finger-drumming moments for those of us who remain

extra ecclesia: discussions in **Adam's Curse** of his boyhood study of Apologetics and Catholic Doctrine; of how well today's priests would do to face up to the 'hard sayings' of the Bible, and of the rights and wrongs of Vatican II (it's too early to say). It's notable, too, that he has little to say about the Christian Eliot in cruise-control mode, as in the late plays, unless those, too, count as ground already gone over all these years ago in *The Third Voice.*

Somebody else who has been defending the Christian legacy recently is Slavoj Zizek. In his most recent book, *Did Somebody Say Totalitarianism?,* he notes the inconsistency of *The Waste Land*'s gesture towards religious transcendence. Eliot may wish to replace the emptiness of secular life with the certainties of Christianity, but cannot help reinscribing it into 'the pagan myth of the renewed fecundity of the "waste land"', or, at the poem's conclusion, succumbing to a proto-Buddhist 'yearning for total annihilation rather than regeneration'. Like many apparent conservatives, in other words, Eliot secretly dreams not of conserving but of sweeping everything away. As St John of the Cross put it for him in the epigraph to *Sweeney Agonistes* (in English translation, for once): 'the soul cannot be possessed of the divine union, until it has divested itself of the love of created things.'

For the foreseeable future, Eliot's reputation will remain, like the Church in 'Choruses from "The Rock"', always decaying, and always being restored: a magnet for the self-righteously censorious, but also for those who continue to look for poetry, 'and not some other thing' instead, to answer their own needs. Were his reputation to sink altogether, though, the first group, as well as the second, stand to lose. As Stevens wrote in 'Esthetique du Mal': 'The death of Satan was a tragedy / For the imagination,' and even Emersonian liberals need to have someone to blame every now and then. And as Antoine de la Pérouse says in a passage from *The Counterfeiters,* quoted by Donoghue in the last chapter of **Adam's Curse**: 'No, no! . . . The devil and the Good God are one and the same; they work together. We try to believe that everything bad on earth comes from the devil, but it's because, if we didn't, we should never find strength to forgive God.' Eliot is the devilish God that contemporary poets find the hardest to forgive. Donoghue has written the apologia he needs. He deserves our gratitude for it, with a smidgen of forgiveness thrown in, too.

Igor Webb (review date spring 2002)

SOURCE: Webb, Igor. "T. S. Eliot's Achievements." *Partisan Review* 69, no. 2 (spring 2002): 302-06.

[*In the following review of* Words Alone, *Webb applauds Donoghue's focus on the elements of musicality and religious faith in Eliot's poetry.*]

Denis Donoghue's **Words Alone,** which he says is "partly a memoir, partly a study of [T. S.] Eliot's poetry," recounts Donoghue's young manhood in Dublin, mainly insofar as it was an educational/literary encounter with Eliot's poems. And yet, although that's about all we learn of the young Donoghue, there is an air of bildungsroman about the book, because its aim is to "describe the process by which a young student tries to gain access, however limited, to a book of poems. What is entailed in submitting oneself to a writer?"

This is a great, neglected, and (one fears) anachronistic subject: a young person's encounter with literature as an experience of awe, of dazzling discovery—something along the lines of Hazlitt's "My First Acquaintance with Poets." It would once have been common for higher education to be seen as an engagement, at worst illuminating and at best transformative, with books. In the U.S., this engagement would have been significantly *literary.* Today you can go through an entire course in college composition, which may be the only English course you take, without reading a single piece of literature.

For this very reason, Donoghue's autobiographical approach to Eliot's poetry is especially apt. For at least two or three decades, up to roughly the mid-1960s, Eliot was *the* figure with whom you began your "serious" education, and in relation to whom you measured your intellectual growth. You read "The Love Song of J. Alfred Prufrock" in freshman English. There was a kind of appropriate progression, not so much chronological as existential, from "Prufrock" to *The Waste Land* and later to *Four Quartets,* the poems read at different stages of one's college years.

That first encounter with "Prufrock," though, was the most stunning, was what knocked you back and buckled your knees. This was finally *it.* Just as it was for Donoghue, whose account of his first reading of Eliot is especially good. It is the music, Donoghue says, that drew him into Eliot's poetry, the music and his way with words, the displacement of words from their simple roles as signifiers into some other authority when rendered within a poem, an authority derived in part from *sound.* "Eliot's genius took the form of the auditory more than the visual imagination," Donoghue writes.

I, too, recall vividly that on first reading "Prufrock" one indeed had the sense of entering a sort of word-world, a world whose internal relations and cadences, whose quality of diction (rather than its referents) and incantatory music, were what one knew. I certainly did not know what the poem was about—its meaning. How many of us, in our freshman classrooms, could have said just what it meant to "wear the bottoms of [your] trousers rolled"? Or explained these lines: "I should have been a pair of ragged claws / Scuttling across the floor of silent seas"? But this was when one's education began. Donoghue shrewdly poses the question of what "submitting" oneself to a writer entails. In encountering Eliot for the first time you were so taken with the sensuous quality of this word-world that it came as an unexpected moral dilemma to ask whether you ought to submit to it, knowing that you could not hope to grasp the poem if you didn't. So you immediately faced the odd prospect, which Donoghue forefronts as a crucial aperture into Eliot's deeper purposes, that understanding might not always be gained in the usual intellectual ways, the ways of ratiocination. (It's the *music,* stupid, says Donoghue.) It was, of course, not until much later that it dawned on you how thoroughly that early, seductive reading experience—the experience of stumbling and chanting through "Prufrock"—foreshadowed Eliot's later, developed, religious conviction that reality depends upon faith.

When I first read "Prufrock" I had never read a word of Dante. I had not read *Hamlet,* either—or Baudelaire, John Webster, Ovid, Verlaine, Marvell, or Froude. Whatever else, following Eliot's allusions was a marvelous education in itself, even if you didn't follow each allusion to the whole work from which it was taken. Donoghue has exceptionally sensible and level-headed things to say about Eliot's allusions, which hardly seem to have given him any pause. But even for those of us who were less formidable students than Donoghue, following Eliot to his sources was also a marvelous education for two powerful reasons. First, Eliot's allusions established a coherent anthology that served as a dialectical reflection on the nature of civilization. Second, Eliot persuaded you that he was in deadly earnest, and that therefore the dilemmas posed through his anthology of allusions were themselves deadly serious. Donoghue is very good at delineating the implications and quandaries entailed by Eliot's reading, with its revealing glimpses of Eliot's religious quest. I remember this as being fairly intimidating: if you were not yourself on a religious quest, you felt, you were not a serious person.

Here, of course, is where the trouble starts. Donoghue's excellent little book, by beginning with music and by emphasizing Eliot's auditory mode of composition, hopes the reader can be moved along by the sheer force of Eliot's sounds—past Eliot's beliefs to appreciation of the poetry as poetry. It succeeds, at least in part. Even so, Donoghue feels he cannot help but take up the vexed questions of Eliot's anti-Semitism and his Christianity.

Donoghue, clearly at home with the literary and intellectual terrain of most of the book, seems uncomfortable, or at least less engaging, in his role as apologist for Eliot. He assumes this role self-consciously against the grain of contemporary opinion, which Donoghue sees as wrong-headed and intolerant. Donoghue thinks

Eliot is not anti-Semitic and has been badly misread. And he believes Eliot's effort to imagine a Christian society is reasonable and serious, and has been dismissed for shallow reasons.

For me, these are the weakest parts of this otherwise very fine book. Most of the time, Donoghue proceeds by applying the common sense of a learned and formidable intelligence to the poetry, and to the ideas within and around the poetry. He draws on an exceptionally wide set of references and does not lapse into pedantry. Hence he frequently settles for "Something along these lines is enough . . ."; and he does not shy away from saying, "I wish I knew more securely what Eliot means by. . . ." We welcome these apparently lax confessions because they are said by a widely read, even-handed, and distinguished reader. But in a few places the admirably relaxed Donoghue, on whom learning rests easily and who can sensibly take us through famously dense intellectual thickets, suddenly vanishes, and we find ourselves reading some other Donoghue, this one extremely picky and abruptly rigid.

This other Donoghue, for example, wants us to think that transferring "The rats are underneath the piles. / The Jew is underneath the lot. / Money in furs." from Eliot to Burbank would adequately rebut the charge of anti-Semitism. Or that the passage about "free-thinking Jews" in *After Strange Gods* should be understood as just a special case of the category "free thinkers." Donoghue's ear is usually acute, but this is not so when he says "I appreciate the fact that, since the Holocaust, Jews must be treated with particular tenderness." My point is that Eliot's references to Jews are offensive not because of some overt race-hatred on Eliot's part but because of both his tone and his blind use of Jews as examples of reprehensible behaviors or beliefs. I don't think this can be easily explained away. But neither can we damn everything Eliot ever wrote on this account alone, as if it were the very core of Eliot's writing.

Eliot's ideas about a Christian society, however, bear much more centrally on the poetry, especially his later poetry. According to Donoghue, Eliot objects to free-thinking Jews within a Christian society because any form of thought that affirms negatives, such as liberalism, rather than a particular end, in this case Salvation as Christians understand it, is reprehensible and divisive. Eliot valued cultural coherence and could not see that culture might be realized absent religion. Donoghue is certainly right to stress that this latter view deserves serious attention, and that it has been too easily dismissed and denigrated; but why people might not be wild about finding themselves once more the citizens of a Christian society surely is not obscure. The terrible weight of historical faith in *ends* has fallen brutally on those of other faiths, or of little faith, or without faith. Most of us are profoundly relieved, and grateful, to be able to live in a secular society—free of the despotism of absolute religious ends.

Eliot's religion—as Donoghue emphasizes—arises from and centers on his overwhelming dread of the void. It is his hypersensitivity in this respect, I think, that accounts for his lugubrious authority over so much literary judgment for so long, for his fixation on vulgarity, and for his disgust with life. I find it curious that those, like Eliot, who are overwhelmed by dread of the void never seem to consider that their hypersensitivity may be an unreliable guide to religious conviction, might itself lead them to sin or, in a lesser vein, intellectual error. Instead it is taken without scruple as token of one's superiority of sensibility and intellectual rigor.

Though Eliot's immense overemphasis on the void may make him a poor religious mentor, it's unquestionably a driving power in his poetry, the origin of his best and most moving writing. "The poetry," as Donoghue elegantly puts it, "does not depend upon a doctrine professed but upon a doctrine felt." And this is as true for Donoghue—and for me—in *Four Quartets* as in *The Waste Land*. The religious struggle of the poet is not, in these last poems, abstracted, but enacted through a form that Donoghue aptly speaks about in terms of music—that is, through a medium in which pattern and thought, feeling and meaning, are fused. Many readers have found these poems to be out of touch with flesh and earth, a disconnected ivory-tower kind of writing. Donoghue is responsive to this point of view, but argues ably against it. The poems take the form of a struggle between, as he puts it, ignorance and purpose. He conveys with delicacy and care the shifts and vagaries of this struggle—a struggle that, as he shows, takes a rugged, difficult route and ends with daunting renunciations. In Donoghue's account, the poems say that against the grip of meaninglessness or the moment's ecstatic glimpse of divinity we are all equally ill-equipped. Language—our best instrument of meaning-making—isn't up to the task, and yet has to do. What it can do, and does beautifully, makes its inadequacy all the more poignant. Here, at the penultimate moment, as it were, Donoghue's book-long tracking of the seductions and meanings of Eliot's music, with its comprehensive dependence on language and its equally comprehensive straining against language, pays off. The charge that the *Quartets* are abstract is refuted by the intense sensuousness of the language, a quality whose characteristics and meanings Donoghue has schooled us in for the whole book. And the charge, made by no less formidable a figure than Geoffrey Hill, that Eliot condescends to his readers in these poems is refuted by the palpable emotional cost of Eliot's ultimate abandonment of language, which for him is all. In the end, Donoghue dwells on Eliot's Christianity not for the sake of ideas, but for the sake of poetry. For those readers who do not share Eliot's beliefs, the poems "live,"

Donoghue says, alluding to a passage in William James, "by giving the sense of an existence with character and texture and power." In this way Donoghue ends strongly where he began, with the assertion that "submitting" to a writer is not a matter of agreeing with some line of argument or being overtaken by a particular philosophical statement, although these matter. Rather, he says the poems should be read as such. The point is far from trivial, and its significance is the animating motif of the book, carefully titled *Words Alone.*

Morris Hounion (review date 1 June 2003)

SOURCE: Hounion, Morris. Review of *Speaking of Beauty,* by Denis Donoghue. *Library Journal* 128, no. 10 (1 June 2003): 119.

[*In the following review, Hounion recommends Donoghue's* Speaking of Beauty *as a "gracefully written scholarly study."*]

In his latest endeavor [*Speaking of Beauty*], prolific critic and editor Donoghue (English, NYU) turns his attention to the language of beauty. As he explains in the introduction, he does not wish to define the concept of beauty but to examine it in its many social manifestations. Although he admits that he would prefer to showcase what other writers have written instead of advancing his own perspectives, he in fact manages to do both. Some examples are taken from popular culture, such as the evolution of screen beauty from Garbo to Audrey Hepburn to Julia Roberts, but Donoghue is primarily concerned with aesthetic critical theories. He challenges anyone who tries to relate beauty to social concerns, but on the whole he is tolerant of the many viewpoints he analyzes, including those of Henry James, Hawthorne, Yeats, Schiller, Adorno, Eliot, and Wallace Stevens. Especially strong is the final chapter on Ruskin's views of the decaying beauty of Venice. The appendix is a brief anthology of poems and prose excerpts that mention or define beauty. This gracefully written scholarly study is recommended for graduate-level academic collections, especially those with a strong emphasis on aesthetics.

William Pratt (review date January-April 2004)

SOURCE: Pratt, William. Review of *Speaking of Beauty,* by Denis Donoghue. *World Literature Today* 78, no. 1 (January-April 2004): 78-9.

[*In the following review, Pratt praises Donoghue's* Speaking of Beauty *as insightful and thought-provoking.*]

In the current intellectual climate, in which all ideas are regarded as political, it is an act of courage for a critic to write a book about beauty. Denis Donoghue is one critic who has such courage. He dared to speak openly about religion in an earlier book, stating in *Words Alone: The Poet T. S. Eliot* (2000) that "It is apparently necessary to say that Eliot's right to become a Christian is as clear as anyone's right not to be." His defiance of popular opinion is just as evident in this latest book [*Speaking of Beauty*], in which he declares, "I should note, to begin with, that it is easy not to think about beauty or 'the beautiful' or to talk about them." He not only discusses beauty and the beautiful but tries to define these elusive and unfashionable terms, taking his cues from writers as diverse as Shakespeare, Donne, Wordsworth, Arnold, Ruskin, Pater, Yeats, and Eliot—to mention only the more prominent of his quoted sources. He draws his epigraph from one of Pound's Pisan Cantos: "'Beauty is difficult, Yeats,' said Aubrey Beardsley." It is obvious that Donoghue the critic agrees with Pound the poet and Beardsley the painter. Beauty is indeed difficult, either for the artist to achieve or for the observer to define, and though he does not arrive at a final definition himself, he thoroughly explores the meaning of beauty at different times and in different places, assuming that to talk about art and literature at all is to have beauty in mind. For whether the word is spoken or not, art without beauty is meaningless, and Denis Donoghue is too good a critic to ignore it.

The author's range is wide, as in all his books, but his focus is clear. He quotes philosophers from Plato to Aquinas to Kant to Croce, but his central chapter is about a little-known story by Henry James, "The Beldonald Holbein," which deals brilliantly with the subject of beauty, and, by the time the critic has finished discussing the story, the reader becomes convinced that it is a masterpiece. Such is the power of genuine literary criticism that it can bring out meaning in a work a reader had missed though it was there all the time. James's story concerns a portrait painter whose trained eye sees beauty where others fail to see it. "The Beldonald Holbein" is the face of an older woman in which "every wrinkle was the touch of a master," in contrast to the more conventional beauty of a younger woman. However, the painter, who is English since the setting is London, needs a visiting French painter to help him recognize this subtle kind of beauty, which he would otherwise overlook. The women themselves are unaware that their beauty is being judged comparatively, until it is apparent that the artists are seeing a Holbein—meaning an understated but authentic beauty—where others see nothing remarkable. The artists can discern a strong human character behind the beauty that gives it substance, as in one of Holbein's realistic portraits of people whose plain looks mask a deeper attractiveness. Thus the story concerns different perceptions of beauty in life and art, but once the perception is made, all

London agrees with the painters that there is hidden beauty in a woman's face. Mrs. Brash, the older woman, comes to be seen as a "Holbein," while her patroness, Lady Beldonald, who has brought her to London from America to be a foil for what she thinks is her superior beauty, might be thought a "Titian"—but only in appearance, since her pretty face conceals vanity rather than strength of character. Donoghue extends the imaginative perception of beauty in James's story to the widely admired beauty of film actresses like Greta Garbo and Audrey Hepburn, whose glamor, like that of Lady Beldonald, was only skin deep.

The rest of **Speaking of Beauty** is interesting but more abstract, speculative, and argumentative than his discussion of the James story, indicating that Donoghue is better as a practical than as a philosophical critic. At his best, he demonstrates once again the value of real literary criticism—rare these days—that illuminates the work it discusses and resonates in the mind of the reader long after one has finished the book.

FURTHER READING

Criticism

ApRoberts, Ruth. Review of *Walter Pater,* by Denis Donoghue. *Nineteenth-Century Literature* 51, no. 3 (December 1996): 410-15.

> Remarks that Donoghue's *Walter Pater* is insightful but gives an unbalanced assessment of Pater's oeuvre.

Barth, J. Robert. Review of *Adam's Curse,* by Denis Donoghue. *Christianity and Literature* 51, no. 1 (autumn 2001): 119-22.

> Provides a brief summary of each of the seven lectures collected in *Adam's Curse.*

Birkerts, Sven. "Denis Donoghue's America." *Partisan Review* 56, no. 3 (1989): 495-98.

> Asserts that the first section of *Reading America,* containing lengthy essays, ultimately fails, while the second section of shorter reviews is successful in terms of both argument and prose style.

Burke, Kenneth. Review of *The Sovereign Ghost,* by Denis Donoghue. *New Republic* 177, no. 11 (10 September 1977): 29-31.

> Review of *The Sovereign Ghost,* focusing on Donoghue's treatment of the concept of the imagination in literature.

Cagle, Charles. Review of *The Old Moderns,* by Denis Donoghue. *Midwest Quarterly* 37, no. 2 (winter 1996): 228.

> Asserts that *The Old Moderns* lacks a strong central thesis.

Core, George. "Two Critics." *Virginia Quarterly Review* 65, no. 1 (winter 1989): 155-61.

> Comparison of Donoghue's *Reading America* and Monroe K. Spear's *American Ambitions.* Core offers praise for both authors, remarking that they are masters of the critical essay who successfully avoid following the latest trends in literary theory.

Countryman, Edward. Review of *America in Theory,* edited by Leslie Belowitz, Denis Donoghue, and Louis Menand, and *The American Revolution and the Politics of Liberty,* by Robert H. Webking. *History* 75, no. 245 (October 1990): 435-36.

> Review examining the common theme of the "'meaning' of the United States" in the two books.

Eagleton, Terry. "Is Theory What Other People Think?" *Times Literary Supplement,* no. 5000 (29 January 1999): 27.

> Review of *The Practice of Reading* which questions several of Donoghue's ideas about literary theory.

Jenkyns, Richard. "The Elements of Style." *New Republic* 212, no. 21 (22 May 1995): 34-7.

> Review of *Walter Pater*; asserts that Donoghue's argument lacks focus, is difficult to follow, and includes many inaccuracies and misinterpretations.

Leighton, Angela. "The Poet and the Religious Pose." *Times Literary Supplement,* no. 5145 (9 November 2001): 14-15.

> Review of *Words Alone,* asserting that the "root question" of the book is "belief."

Marcus, Steven. "Rekindling the Hard Gemlike Flame." *Partisan Review* 64, no. 1 (winter 1997): 147-55.

> Review of *Walter Pater,* asserting that Donoghue fails to put forth a cohesive central argument and seems to lose interest in his subject.

McGonigle, Thomas. "Portrait of the Critic as a Young Man." *Washington Post Book World* 20, no. 40 (7 October 1990): 3, 9.

> Review of *Warrenpoint,* praising Donoghue's portrayal of the father-son relationship.

Medcalf, Stephen. "The Dark Italics." *Times Literary Supplement,* no. 5153 (4 January 2002): 6, 7.

> Comparison of *Adam's Curse,* by Denis Donoghue, and *C. S. Lewis, Poet,* by Don W. King.

Olney, James. "Submitting Oneself to T. S. Eliot." *Southern Review* 37, no. 3 (summer 2001): 614-21.

Asserts that *Words Alone* is Donoghue's best and most interesting critical study to date.

Peltason, Timothy. Review of *The Practice of Reading,* by Denis Donoghue. *Comparative Literature* 52, no. 4 (fall 2000): 366-69.

    Review of *The Practice of Reading*; asserts that Donoghue's arguments are inconclusive and lack focus, and that he fails to fully engage in the debate over literary theory.

Pettingell, Phoebe. "Entering Eliot's Mind." *New Leader* 83, no. 5 (November-December 2000): 45-7.

    Review of *Words Alone,* praising Donoghue's fresh, passionate readings of Eliot's poetry.

Simon, John. "Pater Repatriated." *New Leader* 78, no. 5 (5-19 June 1995): 22-5.

    Offers praise for Donoghue's *Walter Pater.*

Spiegelman, Willard. "Criticism at Century's End." *Yale Review* 88, no. 1 (January 2000): 133-50.

    Comparison of *The Practice of Reading,* by Donoghue, *A Critic's Journey,* by Geoffrey Hartman, and *Trying It Out in America,* by Richard Poirer.

Wheatcroft, Geoffrey. "An Absence of Nostalgia." *Times Literary Supplement,* no. 4594 (19 April 1991): 25.

    Review of *Warrenpoint,* lauding the memoir as a fascinating book.

Additional coverage of Donoghue's life and career is contained in the following sources published by Thomson Gale: *Contemporary Authors,* **Vols. 17-20R;** *Contemporary Authors New Revision Series,* **Vols. 16, 102; and** *Literature Resource Center.*

James Fenton
1949-

(Full name James Martin Fenton) English poet, essayist, editor, playwright, librettist, nonfiction writer, and critic.

The following entry presents an overview of Fenton's career through 2003. For further information on his life and works, see *CLC,* Volume 32.

INTRODUCTION

Recognized as one of England's most prominent poets and critics, Fenton is known for his ability to transform difficult poetic forms and subject matter into interesting and entertaining verse that appeals to a wide range of readers. He is also commended for his sharp and entertaining essays on art and artists, literature and writers, and the devastating impact of war. Critics praise both his poems and prose for their range, skill, and perspicacity, and note his provocative use of historical events, such as the Tiananmen Square uprising in China and revolutions in Vietnam, South Korea, and the Philippines, in his work.

BIOGRAPHICAL INFORMATION

Fenton was born on April 25, 1949, in Lincoln, England. His father was an Anglican priest and theologian. At the age of nine, Fenton was sent to the musical preparatory school attached to the Durham cathedral. At thirteen, he began attending Repton, a public school in Derbyshire. While at Repton, Fenton discovered the poetry of W. H. Auden, who was to become a profound influence on his own poetry as well as a personal friend. Fenton began attending Oxford University, where he studied with the poet John Fuller, who became his mentor and close friend, in 1967. The following year, Fenton won the Newdigate Prize for his sonnet sequence *Our Western Furniture* (1968), a satirical, anti-imperialist poem about Commodore Perry's mission to Japan. The poem revealed Fenton's fascination with the history of Western imperialism in Asia and Indochina. After graduating from Oxford in 1970, Fenton decided to pursue a career in journalism. He began to write literary reviews and political commentary for the *New Statesman* in 1971. The following year, his first full-length collection of poetry, *Terminal Moraine,* was published to critical acclaim. The collection received an

Eric Gregory Award in 1973. For the next several years, Fenton worked as a foreign correspondent, traveling extensively in Indochina and Germany. In his work, he chronicled the collapse of the Non Lol regime in Cambodia and the Thieu regime in Saigon. In 1979 he was appointed theater critic for the London *Sunday Times*; several of his reviews were collected in *You Were Marvellous* (1983). Fenton collaborated with John Fuller to produce the poetry collection *Partingtime Hall* (1987). After a two-year stint as chief literary critic for the *Times,* he became the Far East correspondent for the *Independent,* which inspired his collection of essays *All the Wrong Places* (1988) and several of the poems comprising *Out of Danger* (1994). He became a professor at Oxford University in 1994.

MAJOR WORKS

Fenton's best-known verse explores the often violent contemporary political landscape. His war experiences provided much of the material for his later political poems and inspired many of the pieces in *The Memory of War* (1982), which includes poems from his entire career, and *Children in Exile* (1983), which contains only eight poems. In these verses, he often explores the physical and emotional toll of conflict, and communicates feelings of sorrow and desolation. For example, in "Dead Soldiers," which was first published in 1982, Fenton comments on the devastations of war by utilizing images of a feast that takes place on a battlefield. "Children in Exile," first published in pamphlet form, explores the misery of Cambodian refugee children who cannot escape nightmares of the horrors of the Pol Pot regime. *Out of Danger* signals a change in style; several reviewers note that many of the poems were conceived as songs. In "Manila Envelope," Fenton attacks the narrow state of American poetry and poetry criticism. In "Jerusalem," he contemplates Jerusalem as the center of centuries of violence and conflict. "Tiananmen" focuses on the failed insurrection of Chinese students against their repressive government. Other poems are ballads written from the point of view of such characters as a soldier in the Khmer Rouge, a Manila gang member, and a poor farmer.

Noted for his insight and wide-ranging knowledge, Fenton has also published several collections of prose and criticism. A selection of his theater reviews are collected in *You Were Marvellous. All the Wrong Places* includes several of Fenton's articles as a foreign correspondent. Through his eyewitness accounts of revolutions in Manila, South Korea, and Vietnam, he presents insights and vivid impressions of the massive social upheaval that accompany violent political change. Critics also find the volume highly autobiographical. *Leonardo's Nephew* (1998) collects fifteen essays focusing on the subject of art as well as several prominent artists, such as Edgar Degas, Jasper Johns, Pablo Picasso, Joseph Cornell, and Robert Rauschenberg. Reviewers praise the volume as entertaining and erudite. *The Strength of Poetry* (2001) is a collection of twelve of Fenton's lectures at Oxford, most of which analyze the lives and works of individual British, Irish, or American twentieth-century poets, such as W. H. Auden, Seamus Heaney, and Sylvia Plath. The collection features compelling anecdotes about its subjects. Published in 2002, *An Introduction to English Poetry* provides an overview of the history, scope, characteristics, and practice of English poetry.

CRITICAL RECEPTION

Since the publication of *The Memory of War,* Fenton has been regarded as one of England's most distinctive and accomplished poets: he was placed at the forefront of a new generation of English writers and quickly attained prominence in English literary circles. His essays

and criticism have elicited positive critical reviews, as commentators praise his insight, erudition, humor, and wide range of knowledge. Critics contend that his poetry reveals a proficiency in difficult and unusual English literary forms combined with exciting, frequently unexpected subject matter. Many critics compare Fenton with W. H. Auden, whom they have cited and analyzed as a major influence on his life and career. Reviewers have also found parallels between Fenton's poetry and that of W. B. Yeats and Joseph Brodsky. In tracing his poetic development, they analyze his use of historical events as well as his interest in Indochina and Asia in his poetic work. Viewing Fenton as a highly unique poet, commentators have also contemplated his work within the conventions of contemporary poetry and conclude that he is a talented, entertaining, and intelligent poet and critic who has made a valuable contribution to English literature.

PRINCIPAL WORKS

Our Western Furniture (poetry) 1968

Terminal Moraine (poetry) 1972

A Vacant Possession (poetry) 1978

Dead Soldiers (poetry) 1981

A German Requiem (poetry) 1981

The Memory of War: Poems, 1968-1982 (poetry) 1982

Rigoletto [adaptor; from the libretto by Francesco Maria Piave for a play by Victor Hugo] (play) 1982

Children in Exile (poetry) 1983

Memory of War; and, Children in Exile: Poems, 1968-1983 (poetry) 1983

You Were Marvellous: Theatre Reviews from the Sunday Times (essays) 1983

Children in Exile: Poems 1968-1984 (poetry) 1984

Simon Boccanegra [adaptor; from the libretto by Francesco Maria Piave for a play by Antonio García Gutíerrez] (play) 1985

Partingtime Hall [with John Fuller] (poetry) 1987

All the Wrong Places: Adrift in the Politics of the Pacific Rim (essays) 1988; also published as *All the Wrong Places: Adrift in the Politics of Asia,* 1989

Manila Envelope (poetry) 1989

Out of Danger (poetry) 1994

Leonardo's Nephew: Essays on Art and Artist (essays) 1998

The Strength of Poetry: Oxford Lectures (lectures) 2001

A Garden from a Hundred Packs of Seed (nonfiction) 2002

An Introduction to English Poetry (criticism) 2002

Love Bomb, and Other Musical Pieces (libretti) 2003

CRITICISM

Mark Ford (review date 10 December 1987)

SOURCE: Ford, Mark. "Out of the Blue." *London Review of Books* 9, no. 22 (10 December 1987): 20-1.

[*In the following excerpted review, Ford finds the poems in* Partingtime Hall *overly long and contends that many of the jokes fall flat.*]

[Paul] Muldoon gets a mention—along with just about everyone else they can think of—in Fenton and Fuller's collaborative book of light verse, **Partingtime Hall.** I especially enjoyed the public-school master Mountgracechurch MacDiarmid's taste in literature:

> Selected John Ashbery, Schuyler, O'Hara,
> *Gravity's Rainbow,* and *End as a Man,*
> *Young Torless,* Cavafy and others bizarrer,
> *Lord Weary, Das Schloss, Lady Windermere's Fan*
> . . .

The nymphomaniac pensioners in '**The Sexy Old Ladies of Havergo Hall**' are less discriminating in their pursuit of pleasure:

> If it breathes, and wears trousers, they move in for the
> kill.
> They've invited Karl Miller, but he's feeling ill.
> No wonder: his hostess knew John Stuart Mill
> And she's broken the bathroom lock.

Most of the poems are donnishly based on literary jokes like these, and probably the best in the book is a Geoffrey Hill parody which pictures Hill playing tennis against his devoted admirer Martin Dodsworth:

> Who crouches at the net, his mouth compressed
> Severely to a little Gothic slit?

On the whole, though, the book falls well short of its pre-match billing. Most of the poems are too long, and too many of the jokes fall flat. Humour supposed to be risqué, as in '**A Poem against Catholics**' and '**The Red Light District Nurse**', ends up as merely offensive. This is a puzzle, since both poets have written extremely successful light verse in the past—indeed, are almost the only serious English poets since Auden to have done so. A couple of poems—'**The Spectre**', '**The Dream within the Dream**'—attempt to get back to the zany, Lewis Carrollish fantasy-land Fenton built up so compellingly in '**The Kingfisher's Boxing-Gloves**' and the like, but neither really comes off. '**Partingtime Hall**' itself is a long narrative poem, full of atrocious rhymes, involving a love-affair that develops out of a suicide at a public school: parts of it are zesty enough, but it doesn't compare well with Fuller's own

novel in verse, *The Illusionists.* One of the book's best satires is a scabrous fantasy on Wendy Cope and Fiona Pitt-Kethley, who were each launched last year to huge popular acclaim.

Sean French (review date 3 March 1989)

SOURCE: French, Sean. "Being There." *New Statesman and Society* 2, no. 39 (3 March 1989): 44-5.

[*In the following review, French regards* All the Wrong Places *as an honest and fascinating reflection of Fenton's growing political consciousness.*]

When James Fenton won a literary prize for his first book of poems, **Terminal Moraine** (in 1973 when he was 24), he used the money to fly to Saigon. There was a touch of the early Auden about this trip. The duty of the poet was not just to diagnose historical turning points but, if possible, to be on the spot when they turned.

Thus Auden considered it his duty to head for Spain during the civil war. He never got near the front but he wrote the best-known poem to come out of the war with its extraordinary conclusion: "History to the defeated / May say Alas but cannot help or pardon".

As a fly on the chariot wheel of history, James Fenton has done far better [in **All the Wrong Places**]. He was aboard the first North Vietnamese tank to storm the presidential palace when Saigon fell in 1975 ("I was very, very excited"). And eleven years later when the Marcoses left Manila, he and his photographer were among the first to enter that presidential palace as well: "I caught up with Bing, who was looking through the remains of a box of monogrammed towels. We realised they had Imelda's initials. There were a couple left. They were irresistible."

Fenton's perspective is always that of an Englishman abroad, in the tradition of travel writers like Peter Fleming. He's not much concerned with the larger picture, with quoting expert spokesmen or commenting on economic matters. Instead he hangs around on the fringes and notices the details that accompany history being made. But he's not going to these places to be funny about them: the Vietnam section, in particular, is tinged with real horror.

There are three basic sections to this book, reporting on the revolutions that did happen in Vietnam and the Philippines and the revolution that didn't happen in South Korea. They have mostly already been published in *Granta* but they gain immensely from being in one volume.

Their cumulative effect is to change them from a collection of brilliant reports into a meditation on violent political change. The fall of Saigon was inevitable and Fenton has a haunting encounter with a group of South Vietnamese officers sitting in a cafe, knowing they can't escape and waiting for the Viet Cong to enter the city and kill them.

The revolution in Manila could quite easily not have happened but did, whereas in Seoul a revolution quite easily could have happened but didn't. More complicated still, the prospects for freedom and peace may well be better in South Korea, "that terrifying place".

There is a famous speech in David Edgar's play, *Maydays,* about the inevitable betrayals and disillusionments that follow revolutions. James Fenton went to Vietnam as a revolutionary socialist wanting to observe a revolution that everyone knew was going to happen. He observes the proceedings with a matchlessly light touch. But his account of Vietnam is, as he admits, only a fragment. He briefly visited Cambodia but the events there were beyond him. The Khmer Rouge didn't allow witty, dispassionate observers to stand on the sidelines—they killed them all.

The succeeding essays are less brilliant and perhaps less entertaining. The accounts of local politics are more detailed and more convoluted.

Auden became disgusted with his own attraction to violent change and withdrew from politics altogether. Fenton has done the opposite, and this book fascinatingly and honestly charts the shift of consciousness. He has moved *into* politics, into the minutiae of negotiation and compromise that keep apocalypse at bay. The results may be less dramatic and artistic but they are better to live in.

Richard West (review date 11 March 1989)

SOURCE: West, Richard. "The Scoops of a Wandering Poet." *Spectator* 262, no. 8383 (11 March 1989): 41-2.

[*In the following review, West maintains that* All the Wrong Places *"is a kind of notebook, a work in progress, but nevertheless enthralling, full of insight and often hilarious, in spite of its somber subject matter."*]

When the young poet James Fenton was offered a grant in 1973 to travel wherever he wanted, he chose Indo-China. He remained during the little-reported period between the US withdrawal from Vietnam and the Communist capture of Vietnam, Laos and Cambodia. Although he spent most of his time in Cambodia, the country he really loved, Mr Fenton was in Saigon at the death, and hitched a lift on the first tank into the President's Palace.

Going back to the East 11 years later, he pulled off another stroke of derring-do when he joined the mob looting the Malacanang Palace in Manila, just vacated by Ferdinand and Imelda Marcos. He accepted a job as the *Independent's* Far East correspondent, based in the Philippines, but taking special interest in South Korea. This book [*All the Wrong Places*] is a compilation of Mr Fenton's experiences in all these countries except Cambodia. He was so upset by the Khmer Rouge atrocities that he has not yet written what we, his admirers, believe will be the masterpiece on the Indo-China conflict.

The present volume is a kind of notebook, a work in progress, but nevertheless enthralling, full of insight and often hilarious, in spite of its sombre subject matter. Do not be put off by the title, which gives the impression that this is one of those trendy books about an innocent abroad. It is true that James Fenton was not a typical foreign correspondent. He travelled around Cambodia on a motorcycle, sandwiched between his chauffeur in the front, and his guide-cum-interpreter at the back. But he was not 'adrift in the politics of Asia' and very often he managed to be in the right places.

James Fenton's very personal, anecdotal style is less successful when writing of South Korea and the Philippines, where social unrest has not reached the proportions of civil war. The guerrillas he met in the Philippines have never come near to success in 40 years, and played no part in the overthrow of the Marcos couple. What I, for one, always want to read on the Philippines is less about current affairs and more on the character and history of those likeable but forlorn people.

Writing on Vietnam, Fenton is up in the league of Norman Lewis and Graham Greene. Because there were no more American troops in the country, and only a handful of foreign journalists, Fenton was able to concentrate his attention on the indigenous people, soldiers, peasants, students and monks. In contrast to books like *Dispatches,* by and about Americans, *All the Wrong Places,* has little about the foreign intruders.

James Fenton spent much time in the western part of the Mekong Delta, near the Cambodian border, across which he strayed (and was lucky to get back alive). He met there the Khmer Krom, Cambodians living in Vietnam, who hated the Khmer Rouge. In the winter of 1974-75, Fenton travelled around the Central Highlands, accompanied by an alarming French photographer, who was a communist of the Albanian faction, and used to make Marxist speeches in Vietnamese, accompanied by convulsive physical twitches. Although Fenton was at the time some kind of Trotskyist (I could not make head or tail of his views), he and Jean-Claude succeeded in getting to meet the communist forces.

After the journey, he wrote what ought to have been the finest scoop of the Vietnam War. He predicted the time and place of the final communist onslaught in 1975. By a mischance that would have blighted the life of most reporters, his story was held over till after the start of the final push.

His other triumph was having understood months, if not years, before other reporters just how abominable were the Khmer Rouge. The reasons for this had little to do with the US bombing and much to do with some darker side of the Khmer personality. The communist Vietnamese had suffered longer and worse from American bombing attacks, and yet they emerged from the war almost without vindictiveness. Among the many delights of this book is James Fenton's analysis of the difference between a Cambodian joke, which is all about sex, and a Vietnamese joke, which is all about tactics.

Reading this, I regretted again that Mr Fenton has not written his book about Cambodia. Only he could have made any sense of the wonderful Khmer-English phrasebook he discovered and lent me. Among the phrases were: Don't hiss at me! War is a rude reminder. Don't violate my virginity. He is surnamed a hunter of girls. I am thirstless of power.

When James Fenton got out of Vietnam, weeks after the communist takeover, the victors had already started to take the vanquished into 're-education camps'. The world was beginning to learn the horror of Cambodia. In *All the Wrong Places,* James Fenton says farewell to Indo-China in sorrowful mood. He should go back to see how much things are improving. The Khmer Rouge may still pose a threat to Cambodia. South Vietnam is still wretchedly poor, though swiftly improving. However, when I was in Saigon before Christmas I found the mood cheerful and more relaxed than in all the years I have known it. And for those, like myself, who always preferred Vietnam to Cambodia, a visit is pure delight.

Michael Leifer (review date 28 April-4 May 1989)

SOURCE: Leifer, Michael. "A Change of Personality." *Times Literary Supplement,* no. 4491 (28 April-4 May 1989): 465.

[*In the following excerpted review of* All the Wrong Places, *Leifer argues that Fenton's mix of journalism and travel writing "conveys the feeling of being there, at the expense perhaps of explaining exactly what is going on."*]

James Fenton's selection of past reportage is a mixture of good travel writing and of journalism. His insights and vivid impressions convey the chaos that is often the stuff of politics. Apart from his well-received descriptions of the last days of Marcos, Fenton includes here accounts of visits to Vietnam and South Korea, also at times of political change. *All the Wrong Places* is highly autobiographical, and seems to serve as a way of cleansing Fenton's own mind of political commitment. He went to Vietnam in order to see a war and the fall of a city, but he got more than he bargained for, as for example during a hair-raising visit to a smuggling and gambling village on the border with Cambodia. He captures the popular mood before the Spring offensive which led to the fall of Saigon and describes a journey to the critical highlands town of Ban Me Thuot. When Saigon fell, he rode on the tank which broke into the presidential palace. Fenton leaves Vietnam with mixed feelings as the euphoria of revolutionary change seeps away and he is confronted by the heavy hand of political censorship.

In Korea, he was a witness of a kind to the massacre in Kwangju in May 1980, and returned seven years later to observe the way in which Chun Du Hwan's hatchet man upstaged the opposition and won presidential office because of their political folly—Chun's fall from power had been influenced by that of Marcos. In the Philippines Fenton catches the atmosphere of the snap election and the last days of Marcos without becoming intoxicated by the Aquino phenomenon. He spends time with the New People's Army and agrees with Chapman in not being convinced that the revolution will prevail; he points out that "There is something enviably out of touch about the Filipino guerrilla". He also draws attention to the fear of informers, which has produced a self-destructive impulse within the Communist movement.

Fenton's writing well conveys the feeling of being there, at the expense perhaps of explaining exactly what is going on. In the case of the Philippines, he communicates the mixture of hope and hopelessness which is the national condition.

Derek Davies (review date 8 June 1989)

SOURCE: Davies, Derek. "Travels with My Angst." *Far Eastern Economic Review* 444, no. 23 (8 June 1989): 48.

[*In the following review, Davies examines Fenton's attitude toward journalism and deems* All the Wrong Places *a first-class journalistic work.*]

The title [of *All the Wrong Places*] sets the tone. The text is of current events—or at least the events which made up the headlines of the recent past in Indochina, the Philippines and Korea. But the writer, a poet, has some difficulty in coming to terms with his functions as a journalist. The result is a curious mixture of pride in his descriptions of his experiences and contempt for having experienced them.

Fenton plays the *faux naif*: he only went to Asia because he had won a poetry prize and even then it was a toss-up between Indochina or Africa. He chose the former because he liked the Vietcong and wanted to see a city fall, and responded to Saigon with abhorrence and nausea. He duly sees its fall, with less sympathy than felt by his despised colleagues, the hard-boiled journos. He was, at least to begin with, a "revolutionary social-ist": he wanted surgeon-like to watch the process carefully, not missing a detail. He takes the same I-am-a-camera angle to Cambodia, the Philippines and Korea.

His feelings appear to have been most engaged by the Philippines, with its politics of the theatre, its intoxication with words and fellowship, and its colonial history under the Spanish and the Americans—partly spent in a convent, partly in a brothel. As for Korea, it was terrifying, "a place to avoid." The poet is non-sentimental, if not at times full of hate. Unfortunately this does not prevent his book from frequent descents into almost Dickensian sentimentality.

Fenton dislikes his journalist colleagues. He watches pressmen rushing to cover a story "with superior detachment." He describes the horror of staying in a hotel favoured by pressmen, and the special kind of vigilance with which the competitive hacks observe each other, and the special look of those that have come back from a story: "See, I have come back sweating, covered with the dust of the road."

In his preface, Fenton attempts to equate his style of writing with the reporting which pre-dates journalism: the narrative accounts of a hazardous voyage by a ship's captain or a missionary's report of his tribulations to head office. He dedicates the book to Bill Burford who has made such a commercial success of the Cambridge undergraduate magazine *Granta,* partly because of the quality of writing and partly because it can publish everything from a short anecdote to something approaching the length of a novel (as it did with Fenton's Vietnam material).

Fenton despises conventional journalism, in which "form is length"—600 words, 1,200 words, 4,500 words—decided by "what space there is to be filled, who else is filing that day, how many ads there are, and so forth." Such rules were invented, Fenton claims, "decades ago, by horrible old men obsessed with the idea of stamping out good writing" who have passed their skills on to young men "who would never have become horrible without training." He tells of an American reporter who makes a ghastly sub-Saharan trip, but whose story of the experience lacks any personal touch, the writer mentioning himself once "as a Western observer." That may be in the American reporter's tradition, but the "horrible old men" of Fleet Street insisted that their correspondents always emphasised that they were on the spot. And passages in this book are embarrassingly reminiscent of the dispatches of William Boot to "The Beast" in Evelyn Waugh's skit *Scoop.*

It is a fair presumption that Fenton would include within his category of "terrible old men" such megalomaniacs as the late Lord Beaverbrook and the man who edited the *Daily Express* during the days of its greatest popularity, Arthur Christiansen. But together they published a number of talented writers, including regular columns from such wits as Tom Driberg, a leftwing, homosexualist parliamentarian (whose social attitudes hardly coincided with those of the proprietor or the editor), and Beachcomber (J. B. Morton), one of this century's great humorists.

Nevertheless, Fenton longs for "an elastic magazine, in which content can determine new forms." In fact, many magazines exist which are not as dominated as Fenton implies by space, which can and do publish items varying in length from a paragraph or two to very extended essays. The *New Yorker,* for example, was capable of dispatching its East Asia correspondent to Indonesia, say, for weeks on end, and printing the thousands of words that resulted, often over several issues. But the resulting wordage was often tough going, and the absence of deadline pressure did not mean either that the writer's reportage was more correct or that his judgments were more penetrating.

I wonder whether Fenton has read, for example, *Review* contributors Murray Sayle on the Japanese emperor or Bertil Lintner on the tribesmen of northern Burma. Both were written with far greater insight, background knowledge and sympathy than Fenton, the reluctant traveller from the dreaming spires of Oxford, brings to Asia.

The amateur approach, however, has its advantages. Fenton can report an anecdote, recounted to him by a vaguely involved third party, and charmingly confess he never did find out the truth of the matter, just as he charmingly describes how he failed to witness the massacre at Kwangju. Such a personal approach frees the writer not only from demands of space and deadlines, but of objectivity and balance.

The absence of discipline too often results in self-indulgence, plus the overall impression that Fenton feels he is the only journalist (sorry, poet) who is there, either writing or even witnessing the real story. The disguise often wears thin, as Fenton fails to maintain the "loner" image, just happens to be where stories are breaking or obeys editorial instructions to shift himself. And occasionally he falls into step with the very journalists he affects to despise.

He was off to Manila on holiday, glad that not much news was breaking there ("I would have leisure and space enough . . . not running after a story, not hunting with a pack of journalists"). But Marcos went on television and announced a snap election. This "smelt fishy" to Fenton (as indeed it smelt to the tired old hacks who had been covering the story day by day or week by week). So he panicked, and joined the pack in Manila. Once there, he is just as avid as they for the exclusive.

Generally however, Fenton justifies himself and his approach. All the editorial elasticity in the world does not guarantee writing of Fenton's quality. The eye he brings to bear may be jaundiced, viewing Asia through a British metropolitan lens, but it sees clearly and observes closely. That its owner was free from the slavery of deadlines has allowed him time to brighten up his metaphors and polish his prose. His reporting style does bring to life a group of monks in Cambodia, the demonstrators in Manila, the students of Kwangju. And the eye is clear: the ideological spectacles which he wore when he arrived are discarded.

Fenton does not enjoy his time in Asia. One feels throughout he would rather be back in Oxford, penning poems about plashy-footed, questing voles. Meanwhile, despite his gratuitous insults to the trade, he has written a first-class journalistic book.

Peter Forbes (review date 26 November 1993)

SOURCE: Forbes, Peter. "Out of Line." *New Statesman and Society* 6, no. 280 (26 November 1993): 41-3.

[*In the following excerpted review, Forbes argues that* Out of Danger *exhibits a radical change in Fenton's poetic style.*]

James Fenton used to be Auden-and-water—still more potent than most of our home-brewed verse. His first full collection in ten years, *Out of Danger,* shows a radical change of style. Only the fine **"The Milkfish Gatherers"** is in the usual bizarre-narrative mode. The new Fenton turns its back on the 20th-century obsession with the concrete particular, and aspires to the pure Blakean lyric. Many of the poems are simple songs woven around the great abstractions; the first, **"Beauty, Danger and Dismay"**, strikes the note.

There are huge risks in this, and I don't think Fenton faces up to them. The word "dismay", for example, appears at the crux of no less than three poems. One is

left with the uncomfortable feeling that Fenton wants us to take on trust the huge significance of the fact that *he* is dismayed. But why should we? A lengthy press release written by Fenton talks of "things which I admit are rather foolish but which *I couldn't bear to throw away*" [his italics]. If that's not the worst kind of invitation to the reader, I don't know what is.

Many of the poems were conceived as songs, and certainly **"In Paris with You"** is an acceptable Porterish lyric (Cole not Peter), complete with the jocular songwriter rhyme: "wounded/marooned". But all the magic would have to come from the unheard tune. The book contains manifesto poems that expound Fenton's current impatience with stylistic determinism. He demands the right to be various. Granted: but what the manifestos don't make explicit is his rejection of the 20th century.

Many of these poems dare the traditional flight of fancy: "Near as the rainbow to the rain, / The west wind to the windowpane, / As fire to hearth, as dawn to dew". Coming from such a cerebral poet, this apparent innocence is both startling and suspect. Isn't such alliterative rhetoric nullified by its palpable design on us, its attempt to mine the vein of received poeticisms? Early Fenton poems, such as the famous **"In a Notebook"**, use such traditional effects in a new way. He's walking a tightrope, but most of this book finds him thrashing around in the safety net.

Is there anything here to like unreservedly? (I admire Fenton's early work very much indeed.) **"The Mistake"**, one of the dismayed poems, will receive an echo in every breast; **"The Milkfish Gatherers"** is perfect poetic travel writing—about fishing rituals in the Philippines, where "They named the sea's inhabitants with style—The slapped vagina fish, the horse's dick". **"Jerusalem"**, written to the tune of Milton's "Hymn on Christ's Nativity", captures the terror and weight of symbolism impacted into one small city. But that's about it. . . .

Hilary Corke (review date 11 December 1993)

SOURCE: Corke, Hilary. "Part and Parcel of the Gallant Life." *Spectator* 271, no. 8631 (11 December 1993): 38.

[*In the following favorable review of* Out of Danger, *Corke traces Fenton's development as a poet.*]

I do not know if James Fenton is a tough guy, but I suppose he must be, since he does the things that tough guys do. He has presumably known extremities rather than just imagined them. That is not usual in our decades where the bravest thing the average poet ever does is argue with his publisher or speak without an introduction to A. N. Wilson. Some centuries ago it was otherwise. When the same person is a Vietnam war reporter and a master of the modern ballad, one has to struggle slightly to evade the dread epithet 'Renaissance Man'.

The Brigadier may of course indite triolets by the midnight candle in his tent; but Fenton's poems [in *Out of Danger*] are all part and parcel of the gallant life, not a private retreat carved out of it. His is a poetry of action, not of reflection. It is swift, thumpity in rhythm, very loose-jointed, laterally thought over the edge into surrealism. He doesn't on the surface appear too bothered about the number of stresses in a line, or to worry over switching his stanza-form in the course of a poem. He is regularly allegorical but rarely does he use a metaphor, and a simile never; nor does he seem concerned about naiveties and archaisms:

> A shrieking man stood in the square
> And he harangued the smart café
> In which a bowlered codger sat
> A-twirling of a fine moustache
> A-drinking of a fine Tokay.

Such features are, however, surely not inadvertencies: Fenton is actually very well instructed in metric, as *Ars Poetica,* his masterly series of seminars in the *Independent,* showed. He knows what he is doing. As there is an art that conceals art, so is there a deliberation in composition that painfully emerges in a construct of speed, lightness, brightness. When Fenton writes 'a-twirling' he is climbing up pastiche (of a broadside ballad) to rise to higher things, just as Betjeman (say) would flirt a cunning 'morn' in his ascent from Victorian *vers de société.*

The Betj is not invoked by the blurb, which inadequately cites only Auden. Certainly Auden used ballad-forms, but only rarely and to other effect. Certainly, too, both poets are 'political', in the broad non-party sense; but their personae could hardly be more different—Auden after all (who caught a cold when young in Iceland and clung to carpet-slippers ever after) was eminently a poet of reflection rather than action. Other names leap much more readily to hand: MacNeice for many of his rhythms; Edith Sitwell for her word-play—

> It's the same chalk on the blackboard!
> It's the same cheese on the sideboard!
> It's the same cat on the boardwalk!
> It's the same broad on the catwalk!

—Vachell Lindsay for his noise and nonsense:

> God that's glum, that glib Glob dig.
> 'Dig that bog!'

> 'Frag that frog.'
> 'Stap that chap, he snuck that cig.'

—Kipling, if you like, for much besides his *weltanschauung.*

About half these poems appeared earlier in **Manila Envelope,** but that was privately printed and not in general circulation. Some change seems apparent in some of the newer poems, which one might call more mature, provided one means by that no more than 'further down the line' and not 'wiser'. The language is less multicoloured, the texture still more spare and luminous, the language even more pared to essentials. He also seems to have been tunnelling out over the years a readier access to his own deeper personal feelings. There is, for example, more of 'love', even though he says:

> Don't talk to me of love. Let's talk of Paris.
> I'm in Paris with the slightest thing you do.
> I'm in Paris with your eyes, your mouth,
> I'm in Paris with . . . all points south.
> Am I embarrassing you?
> I'm in Paris with you.

A few years ago that passion seemed to be covered, or uncovered, by

> Jane meet John.
> John meet Jane.
> Take those jimjams off again.

—but now there emerges a less guarded Fenton, quite an old-fashioned gentleman in his way, who implies that, where 'love' is in question, Paris is the place for it and best turn out the light.

Let us be more serious. Here is a strong, fresh, pleasant wind blowing away the convoluted miasmas of most of his contemporaries; and the wind carries much clearer, cleaner, more complex and intensely memorable messages than the miasmas do.

Mick Imlah (review date 31 December 1993)

SOURCE: Imlah, Mick. "Pocket Musicals." *Times Literary Supplement,* no. 4755 (31 December 1993): 21.

[*In the following review, Imlah surveys the stylistic variety of the poems in* Out of Danger.]

[*Out of Danger*] is James Fenton's first full-size collection since **The Memory of War and Children in Exile** (1983), whose unwieldy title revealed his chosen pattern of publication: the release at intervals of single long poems or small groups in limited editions, gathered every ten years in high-profile collections from a bigger publisher (his first book, **Terminal Moraine,** came out in 1973). The bulk of this book is material from **Manila Envelope,** a privately printed package that was sent out in 1989 (reviewed in the *TLS* [*Times Literary Supplement*] of June 30 of that year). Only those who had the good fortune to get hold of that will be able to do Fenton the disservice of isolating the more recent work: sixteen poems which, in their lightness, simply bypass the high expectations that his intimidating reputation and slender output have combined to create.

Fenton's advantage over his contemporaries has had much to do with his rhetorical power, his technical resources, his imaginative and comic flair in the province between nonsense and nightmare; but more to do with his having gone, Kurtz-like, into horror-zones beyond the reach even of most front-line journalism: to Saigon as it was falling, Cambodia at its very worst, the Philippines at the overthrow of Marcos. What drew him to such experiences is a complicated question; but he couldn't have gone, and stayed, without a rare capacity, a will even, to be alone. (In none of his poetry of the Far East is there a gesture to folks back home, either friends or readers.) Now he has returned from the killing fields to grow roses in Oxfordshire, he appears disposed to surrender that distinction; as **"The Possibility"** puts it: "Solitude was beautiful / When I was sure that I was strong. / I thought it was a medium / In which to grow, but I was wrong."

This collection divides itself into two parts on either side of that realization, to both of which the title *Out of Danger* refers: on one side, horror-poems of Fenton's best sort; on the other, poems which spring from homecoming, from putting the land mines behind him, from embracing, for the first time in his work, the private safety and danger of love.

But "poems" begins to seem not quite the right word. Apart from **"The Manila Manifesto"**, a mixture of poems and little prose darts at Helen Vendler, which amusingly applies the language of agitprop in the place of critical debate ("We call on America to stop killing, torturing and imprisoning its poets"), this is really an album of songs: some highly sophisticated literary ballads, others seemingly pitched for Easy Listening. The second section, titled **"Out of the East"**, has the greater substance on the page, though it has actually been performed as "a pocket musical", and it is in performance that the best of it—the glorious nonsense medleys, **"The Ballad of the Shrieking Man"** and **"Here Come the Drum Majorettes!"**—would come fully to life. In each of these, the rhythms are the predominant idea, so that it seems almost any group of verbal ideas could be processed through them:

> The Coat
> The Tie

> The trouser clips
> The purple sergeant with the bugger-grips . . .

> **("The Ballad of the Shrieking Man")**

> It's the same scare with a crowbar!
> It's the same crow on the barstool!
> It's the same stool for the scarecrow!
> It's the same bar!

> **("Here Come the Drum Majorettes!")**

You may catch people after a Fenton reading improvising their own lines to the latter formula; that fits the spirit in which Fenton presents it. One is reminded of Kipling, composing with a stick before any verbal activity took place; and these ballads or chants elude most lines of criticism the way Kipling's baffled Eliot: "The critical tools which we are accustomed to use in analysing and criticising poetry do not seem to work."

Equally immune to criticism, in one sense, are the new love lyrics of the book's first section: things it isn't possible to dislike, which have some lovely touches between them. But where the nonsense ballads fill their moulds with unruly images, these seem governed by something like Swinburne's perverse instinct to purge his lines of "singularities", of "anything that strikes the eye, the ear, or the intellect as exceptional", in pursuit of a standard featureless rapture. It's roses, roses all the way—and rainbows:

> Stay true to me and I'll stay true to you—
> As true as you are new to me will do,
> New as the rainbow in the spray
> Utterly new in every way,
> New in the way that what you say is true.

But neither novelty nor truth is the point of a lyric like this—which, with its four stressed *oo*s in the second line, is less Cole Porter than Johnny Mercer. (And if someone told you that the lines "I'll be home again next winter / And I hope you'll write to me" were from the Teddy Bears' "Come Home for Christmas, Daddy", *c*1963, you might believe them.) And though it lays claim to a common idiom of delight, free of personal tripwires, such innocent would-be duetting can't really banish the mischief that roams the rest of the book; one which encourages the reader of this stanza to replace "true" and "new" with, say, "false" and "old", or "Filipino" and "French".

Some reflex of this sort seems to have gone on in the Noël Coward-like **"In Paris with You"**, where Fenton, as if fatigued by the repetitive white-writing of being "in love", lets being "In Paris" stand in for the phrase:

> Don't talk to me of love. Let's talk of Paris.
> I'm in Paris with the slightest thing you do.
> I'm in Paris with your eyes, your mouth,
> I'm in Paris with . . . all points south.

Am I embarrassing you?
I'm in Paris with you.

The only remarkable thing about this suave punning is that it's James Fenton doing it. From the poet of the bugger-grips, the coyness of those suspension points is a revelation.

Ellen Kreger Stark (essay date summer 1994)

SOURCE: Stark, Ellen Kreger. "An American's Confession: On Reading James Fenton's *Out of Danger.*" *Critical Quarterly* 36, no. 2 (summer 1994): 106-10.

[*In the following essay, Stark considers* Out of Danger *in relation to the recent trend of confessional poetry and assesses Fenton's poetic achievement.*]

These days, just about anyone in America can have his or her own talk show. (*Her* mostly, but that's another story.) One day of feeling poorly and sitting on your sofa will net you enough hours of Oprah, Ricki, Phil, Bertice, Montel, Vicki, Rolonda, Geraldo, Sally Jessy, Jenny, Regis and Kathie Lee to send you screaming back to work. Most of the shows centre around the *confession. I had a sex change operation and accidentally married my brother. A crazy teen-aged bitch tried to shoot me and steal my husband.* The most popular hosts are the ones who join in on the spirit of telling all. Oprah cried when she admitted she, too, had been molested as a child. And Jenny told us that yes, her breast implants had ruptured and it was nothing to be ashamed of.

So I suppose, as an American, I live in a culture of confession. The contemporary poetry scene in America is another kind of confession culture, although I can't begin to narrate the similarities and differences between these two modes of confession—a project someone will no doubt eagerly take up on the conference scene. Nearly every book of poetry I read these days tells a secret on every page. Many of us who are writing today do so in the tradition of confessionals like Sylvia Plath, Anne Sexton, and Robert Lowell. These are the poets who have been at the core of our reading and our education in our craft. We've been educated in the confession, in the narrative, in free verse (although since we haven't had any education in poetic form, the question arises, *what is our verse free from?*). While confession and free verse used to be considered to be radical gestures, nowadays, in poetry workshops, the conversation turns around not whether the poetry *is* confessional, because most of it is, but whether the confession is truly autobiographical, or fabricated. For example, one of the most respected American poets writing today is Sharon Olds, whose poetry is unrelenting in its telling of the most intimate and unspeakable details of family relationships. But unlike her confessional predecessors, Sexton and Plath, Olds is also unrelentingly guarded about her 'real-life' details and their intersection with her poetry. Her *I* may be telling all, but whether the *I* is Olds herself is another question.

So, I picked up James Fenton's latest collection of poetry [*Out of Danger*] expecting to read a confession, expecting to get to know James Fenton, or at least get to know intimately the story of an *I,* beginning, end, and in between. I must confess, it didn't happen. From the very first poem, I was introduced to the narrator—the *I,* but that *I* was not the transparently autobiographical *I* that I was used to. This *I* was to be many things—a lover, a witness, an observer, a participant—but never transparent. Fenton's narrator keeps moving. Early in the book, I thought I had gotten a hold on the narrator as he moved through two successive poems, **'The Possibility'** and **'The Mistake'**. In **'The Possibility'**, Fenton writes:

> I know that work is beautiful
> It is a boon. It is a good.
> Unless my working were a way
> Of squandering my solitude.

>   (p. 8)

Though the poem never names the possibility, it becomes more tangible in the trajectory followed through the next poem, **'The Mistake'**,

> And every nuance of your hypocrisy
> Towards yourself, and every excuse
> Stands solidly on the perspective lines
> And there is perfect visibility.

>   (p. 9)

Again, Fenton does not name the mistake, but we get the feeling as the details pile up, that the mistake is a missed possibility. Then, Fenton goes on to stop this momentum with **'I'll Explain'**. He does not explain or name the pain of **'The Possibility'**, or **'The Mistake'** as I had expected, but rather explains his inability (or reticence) to explain:

> It's what I was hoping to tell you.
> It's what I was hoping you'd guess.
> It's what I was hoping you *wouldn't* guess
> Or you wouldn't mind.
> It's a kind
> Of hopelessness.

>   (p. 11)

Is this the same narrator who appears in the next poem, the playful and amorous voice that rhymes 'wounded' with 'marooned' in **'I'm in Paris with You'**? As the narrator's voice shifts from poem to poem, my efforts to pin him down into telling me 'the whole story' were thwarted. Each time I thought I had captured the hidden story, I found *the possibility receded.* When I thought I had him caught in a confession, he moved himself out of danger. But what is this danger?

Confession can be a mask, a violence. This is what is so smart about Fenton's book, what Fenton's book shamed me into realising. Confession is a way of containing, controlling. By writing confessional poetry, we (those of us who practise the art) can lull ourselves into believing we've exposed the world's darkest secrets, we've revealed hopelessness, anguish, and our own inadequacies, we've done all we can, we've intervened. Then solving those problems becomes as easy as crossing out your final stanzas with a red pen. We pull our readers into this game as well. We convince them they *know,* that they're insiders in the story, that they have seen the underbelly of the world and have come through the other side. Fenton is masterful enough not to allow that—not to allow himself or his readers some falsely earned catharsis and not to allow his readers to get off the hook, over the edge so easily. In **'The Ballad of the Imam and the Shah'**, Fenton writes:

> The song is yours. Arrange it as you will.
> Remember where each word fits in the line
> And every combination will be true . . .
>
> (p. 37)

So I had been waiting for Fenton to tell me a story I could follow and could live with, one which would make me feel I am in-the-know yet exonerate me from responsibility. But this isn't something that any poetry can (or should) do. Indeed, how can we really *tell all* about anything? Perhaps my desire to read (and to write) the confessional is a desire to deny the fact that there are many things, love and war among them, that can't be told, a fact which Fenton's poetry bravely admits, even embraces. He writes:

> Why didn't they *say?* Oh, but they did indeed—
> Said with a murmur when the time was wrong
> Or by a mild refusal to assent
> Or told you plainly but you would not heed.
>
> (p. 9)

We, as Fenton's readers, are constantly implicated in the process of making meaning and reading some things and misreading others. So, perhaps the fault is mine for feeling something is missing, for feeling there is something Fenton will not *say*. Perhaps I am the one who wishes not to heed, who wishes not to feel, with him, emotions that can't be resolved, conflicts that can't be righted with words, or even deeds.

It is not only what Fenton says but how he says it that was a surprise to me. Most of these poems are in traditional forms, particularly the ballad, drawing atten-

tion to the poet's craft in a way that, for example, unrhymed syllabics or free verse would not. I hadn't thought before about how *form* relates to confession. The free-verse poet is able to cultivate the illusion of conversation, of an intimate, spur-of-the-moment spill, the kind of narratising we do among friends. But Fenton's form allows him to conceal and reveal in a way which can approach the intimate without seeming accidental or haphazard. These are not poems which tumble out in the moment of passion, they come rather from that emotional space, that lonely, sometimes helpless, sometimes exulted time of reflection when the emotions come into dialogue with one another. Thus, Fenton may conceal a certain type of abandon, but that in turn reveals other moments of intensely moving intimacy. For example, consider **'Out of the East'**, the volume's first war poem, a chilling fable which may well be the book's emotional centre. Fenton writes:

> You fought the way a hero fights—
> You had no head for fear
> My friend, but you are wounded now
> And I'm not allowed to leave you here
> Alive.
>
> (p. 28)

At this point in the book, I thought I knew Fenton's rules, I had come to rely on his controlled rhythms and intricate rhymes. But it was precisely because of that false comfort that my heart unexpectedly caught in my throat when I reached the word 'alive'. It interrupts, it hangs away from the rest of the book, like a marker, like a stone in a stream whose surface seemed deceptively smooth. 'Alive' is a relief, but an ironic one; it is a hook, an open wound, a loneliness. It is, in this place, *a cry for the war that can do this thing.* Similarly, in **'I Know What I'm Missing'**, each of the first two stanzas ends with the lines:

> And I stop to listen
> And forget what I've to do
> And I know what I'm missing—
> My friend
> My friend.
>
> (p. 61)

But the final stanza ends with these lines:

> . . . I'll know what I'm missing—
> My friend
> My friend
> I'm missing you.
>
> (p. 62)

Through the reversal of terms and changing patterns of repetition, the end of the poem becomes a private moment between two people that stands out against the more intellectual landscape of the rest of the poem, a moment which, in turn, stands out against the landscape of the book, coming as it does between the languages of love and war.

Fenton is a poet who also somehow manages to combine all these emotions with a great wit and playfulness with both his subject matter and his language, and he holds all these things in amazing balance in this book. I find myself drawn to reading it again and again for reasons I feel helpless to completely explain. I am in awe of it—the kind of awe felt in the presence of something strange and new, whose qualities are so enigmatic they elude evaluation. I also have a just beginning sense that my reading of this book will change my writing, though I cannot name or narrate the ways. There are some things which lie outside the realm of confession.

Arjuna Parakrama (review date summer 1994)

SOURCE: Parakrama, Arjuna. "The Art of (W)riting Oneself out of Danger: Review of *Out of Danger* by James Fenton." *Critical Quarterly* 36, no. 2 (summer 1994): 111-14.

[*In the following mixed review, Parakrama maintains that in* Out of Danger, *Fenton tends to oversimplify and distort political subjects.*]

Many of the poems in this selection [*Out of Danger*] are exquisite. The title poem **'Out of Danger'** remains my favourite. It's carefully crafted, strikingly original, yet deceptively simple because it has been shorn of all excess of emotion, of language, of description. The end-rhyme is not phoney, nor is it the determiner of meaning: where necessary (which is, in fact, every single case!) this rhyme has been vitiated in favour of sense. The emotion caught here is hardly esoteric, the pain is tangible and the desire to communicate forceful. The lyricism is in perfect balance with the tone of understatement and restraint. In our 'pre-critical' days, a test of good poetry was its ability to communicate a familiar emotion in an unfamiliar way, and thereby to throw some light on the emotion itself. Now emotions are suspect, so are tests, but I am still convinced that this is 'good' poetry, which means, I'm sure, that I am guilty of some classist-and-so-on assumptions!

In the first set of poems, then, Fenton is successful in seducing my sensibilities, whatever that means. The poetry describes painful, intimate relationships, and most notable is the radical absence of sentimentality of any kind. Unlike in much that passes for rhyming poetry, against which I harbour a bias, the complexity of the feeling has not been sacrificed here. Perhaps most important of all, Fenton has a sense of humour that takes in even himself, such a rare quality in contemporary writing especially when it doesn't trivialise its subject.

Fenton's surest skill is in these nuanced yet uncluttered pieces—notably **'Out of Danger'**, **'In Paris with You'**, **'Hinterhof'**, **'Serious'**, **'The Possibility'**, **'The Mistake'** and **'Beauty, Danger and Dismay'**—in which the reader is eavesdropping on one man's searingly honest attempt to deal with his and others' emotions, with his own failings and mistakes, with communication itself, with rationalisation of/after pain, with friendship, even death.

So much for the good stuff.

The poet's maleness and cultural specificity are, however, not subjected to this self-reflexivity and radical questioning that are part and parcel of the 'personal' poems. Is mere name-calling either necessary or sufficient here, then? Can the inevitable charge of sexism be made to stick even in the ironic pieces, or is irony and/or self-deprecation sufficient insurance against all such 'terrorist normative critic'al attacks? In **'The Journey'**, for example, the Freudian foreplay can hardly salvage the poem from being a trashing of female sexuality.

Yet, surely, in terms of Fenton's politics, his heart seems to be in the right place. He is very critical of US hegemony, he is strongly anti-war, he attacks fascism everywhere. Why, then, am I discomforted by the ambience (wrong word) of this collection? In the first section, **'Out of Danger'**, the tone is vaguely sad, the subject matter personal, the poetry lyrical. Only **'Jerusalem'** takes on an overtly political timbre. This, then, is the poet's life in England (the couple of pieces set elsewhere are self-consciously touristic since they are either purely descriptive and/or have been generated by brief visits)—no comment on the larger-than-personal dimension here. And yet, in the poems/songs set in the Philippines and in the commentary on the US, for instance, the poet arrogates to himself the right to political comment, to caustic criticism of social mores, and even to all-round satire. I'm not suggesting that Fenton is unsympathetic or ignorant of that which he describes, but, rather, that he's playing safe in taking on only 'non-home', and that he is, therefore, falling prey to the tendency to oversimplify and distort, which is the very devil to resist when one doesn't have to put one's money where one's mouth is.

Unless I can show this in terms of some examples I'm not going to convince you: rather than spread myself thin, I shall focus on one poem, reading it symptomatically. In **'Jerusalem'** written in December 1988, for instance, the first anniversary of the *intifadah* is completely obliterated by a poem that places the writer as one who has the luxury of being uninvolved, or, worse still, involved in an entirely different (touristic?) enterprise. Hence, the symmetry and 'poetic' tone of 'stone cries to stone, / Heart to heart, heart to stone' which surely trivialises the horror of Israel's response to the initial stone-throwing as symbolic protest. Wasn't it more a case of stone crying against sophisticated and deadly weaponry? By December 1988, over 70,000 (from 5,000 in 1987) military personnel were being deployed in the Occupied Territories with horrendous consequences, and yet it would seem that for Fenton the issue in Jerusalem is still Christian vs. Jew ('What was your mother's real name? / Would it be safe today to go to Bethlehem?') who are the 'us' and 'them', the protagonists; otherwise the final statement, 'I have destroyed your home. You have destroyed my home', is utterly disingenuous. Thus, the poet's ability to literally divorce and isolate Jerusalem from the urgent and catastrophic political realities of the area is symptomatic of the unquestioned privilege that he enjoys as classed-gendered-raced-regioned outsider.

There is criticism of both Jews and Christians in this piece, but nothing is either dismissive or snide: the conflict over Jerusalem as holy of holies is given the seriousness it deserves. Is there a hint of anti-Semitism, then, (I use this word in an unfashionable sense to mark prejudice against Arabs) in the trivialising reference to Islam: 'This hole is where the flying carpet dropped / The Prophet off to pray one night / And from here one hour later he resumed his flight'? Or in the troubling tone of 'Have you ever met an Arab? / Yes I am a scarab. / I am a worm. I am a thing of scorn'? The point is that the references themselves don't have a context in the poem that helps us to read them otherwise than as derogatory, dismissive and gimmicky. Perhaps the most problematic is a section that can only be an explicit take-off of the *intifadah*: 'I'll stone you. I shall break your every limb. / Oh I am not afraid of you / But maybe I should fear the things you make me do.' There can be no possibility of ignorance of the resonances here. Thus, the aggressor has been counter-factually predetermined as the Arab in the Occupied Territories which, willy nilly, favours the status quo, and real power relations have been turned on their head with no understanding of the gross inequalities on the ground. Compare, for instance, the poetic-sounding yet misleadingly vibrant and expansive metaphor in Fenton's 'Jerusalem itself is on the move. / It leaps and leaps from hill to hill / And as it makes its way it also makes its will', with the late Mouin Besseiso's devastating economy, writing in 1969: 'The country that was home / Has become an argument / Don't blame the rifle / When it died without leaving a will / On a cloud I wrote: / Down with censorship— / And they confiscated the sky' (trans. Ibrahim Abu-Nab and Martin Walker). Need I say more?

Another piece, **'On a Recent Indiscretion by a Certain Fulbright Fellow in Upper Egypt'**, is palpably guilty of racism, homophobia, insensitivity, bad taste, cultural stereotyping and so on and so forth, but the bigger indictment is perhaps that the poem is puerile, even silly. The weak attempts at self-deprecation and humour do not work here, as also in that strange exercise, **'Here Come the Drum Majorettes!'** (How can one justify the self-indulgence, let alone its extravagant racism, in the four lines which describe the 'Gleb on a steppe in a dacha', the 'Glubb in the sand (he's a pasha)', and 'a glib gammaglob in your backside'?)

In the rest of this collection there are two demeaningly ironic references to 'France', two fairly dismissive (and perhaps justified) invocations of US (though miscalled 'America' which conflates two continents with one 'superpower') poetry and fascism. All this would be fine if jolly old England got the same treatment, but it doesn't. In addition, cryptic, at least to me, salvos are fired at Boston, Los Angeles and New York, as is an obscure reference to Emily Dickinson's knees, which is interesting since at times Fenton's style is reminiscent of hers. You are never quite sure whether the poet is playing with you and this has its obvious strength in complicating the reader's response, but also its weakness because he can always get himself off the hook if challenged.

'Tiananmen' in Fenton's hands becomes simplistic ('The cruel men / Are old and deaf / Ready to kill / But short of breath'), and the rise of the Iranian brand of Islamic fundamentalism has been reduced to a caricature account of Khomeini's personal (psycho)biography ('The child who saw his father's killer killed / Has slaughtered half the children in the land'). And yet, this song ends with sixteen 'crimes' (felony, robbery, calumny, rivalry, tyranny, policy, malady etc.) which the reader ('first' world, of course) is invited to arrange at will because 'every combination will be true' and 'every permutation will be fine': this seems to be the bottom line with these other, marginal cultures for the poet—every permutation and combination is fine and true. What, one wonders, can be at stake in such a sweeping dismissal?

By locating the 'British' space firmly in the personal and therefore finessing/devaluing/siding-with-the-establishment in the current 'domestic' crises, by hitting all round the political (larger-than-personal) wicket in the pieces on other locations (Jerusalem, Manila, the USA, France, China, Vietnam, Iran, Turkey, Egypt, Fiji etc. etc.), by his utter amnesia towards the varied colonial heritages of these contexts and of the colonisers' culpability in some of the present predicaments, by his choice of Standard English throughout (the use of Tagalog or another *language* is less disruptive of hegemony than is a non-standard *dialect* or even colloquial forms. It is in the Philippine-based songs that slang and other non-standard structures are used, but, for instance, in **'Cut-Throat Christ'** the underworld is being described and hence slang becomes the *appropriate register.* In the largely unintelligible **'Here Come the Drum Majorettes!'** the nonsense words are prefigured and framed by the 'alienness' of Gleb (a

Russian) and Glubb ('a pasha')), and by his thoroughgoing maleness, Fenton has placed himself 'out of danger' from mainstream local (he's a jolly good fellow of the Royal Society) critique. He recuperates, therefore, in effect, a troubling Tory English nationalism without having to say one word about it.

Douglas Kerr (essay date fall 1994)

SOURCE: Kerr, Douglas. "Orientations: James Fenton and Indochina." *Contemporary Literature* 35, no. 3 (fall 1994): 476-91.

[*In the following essay, Kerr analyzes the issue of orientation in Fenton's Indochina poems and essays.*]

Opening a new book has something in common with arriving in a new country for the first time and can be attended by some of the same anxieties. Will I be able to find my way around? Are the natives friendly? Will I be bored? Can I cope with the language? For the traveler as for the reader, the first necessity is to orient yourself, to find out where you are and what's in store for you. One meaning of *orientation* is that of finding one's bearings; it can also mean finding and facing the east, or simply going eastward. For people interested in literary and cultural studies, the word should also evoke some of the difficult questions of attitude to and representation of the foreign, laid out in Edward Said's *Orientalism*.[1] In James Fenton's collection of poems called *The Memory of War* (1982), you travel through a sequence on a European theme, **"A German Requiem,"** and then come upon a little poem called **"Cambodia"** (23).[2] Here is an English poem on an Asian subject—an orientation, then. Where are its cardinal points? Does it help you find your bearings?

"Cambodia"

One man shall smile one day and say goodbye.
Two shall be left, two shall be left to die.

One man shall give his best advice.
Three men shall pay the price.

One man shall live, live to regret.
Four men shall meet the debt.

One man shall wake from terror to his bed.
Five men shall be dead.

One man to five. A million men to one.
And still they die. And still the war goes on.

The first impression is of a perhaps beguiling simplicity. This poem uses nothing but ordinary words, deployed in a prosodic form—end-stopped rhyming couplets—that is almost childish. It sounds like a playground counting chant: one two three four five— then a million. The poem's title at the beginning promised geography, but what is delivered in the end is history, a war. The place turns into an event. As John Pilger said of Cambodia's neighbor, "Vietnam was a war, not a country" (174). The imagery of Fenton's **"Cambodia"** is absolutely simple, yet it's absolutely undescriptive. It gives you some bare facts, and bare figures, but leaves you with a problem of orientation. Here we are, but just where are we? Who is the "one man" who keeps appearing? Is it the same man throughout? The subject of the poem is war: who is the one lucky man who escapes while a million and more do not? Or does he escape? Might he be a soldier, in the first stanza, going off to war? Is he a refugee who gets away, leaving his family to die? What is the relation between his well-meaning advice and the payment exacted from others? Could he be a so-called foreign adviser? Is it the poet himself? Why does he have nightmares? Why for that matter is almost all the poem, the first in a collection whose subject is supposed to be memory, couched in the future tense of prophecy rather than the past tense of history? Our arrival in **"Cambodia"** (the poem) has pitched us into an ambiguous, haunting, and frightening world, and we are already lost, disoriented. We are being underinformed and are not getting the help we need to find our bearings. We are threatened with the classic anxiety of the traveler: Is the guide lost?

James Fenton—a poet, English, middle class, white, in his twenties—traveled to Indochina in the summer of 1973 hoping to witness the end of a chapter in imperial history. He was to spend time in Vietnam, Cambodia, and Laos and was present in Saigon during and after the fall of the city to the Vietcong and the North Vietnamese army in 1975.[3] "I wanted to see a war, and I wanted to see a communist victory, which I presumed to be inevitable" (*Wrong Places* 4). He belonged to a generation that defined itself in its opposition to the involvement of the United States in Vietnam. He was disgusted with Western imperial interventions in the third world, which in Indochina stretched back to the middle of the nineteenth century.

How much sense does it make to describe a white English writer as postcolonial? We may be used to using *postcolonial* as a term for writing that emerges from the experience of imperialism, foregrounds a tension with the imperial center, and emphasizes constitutive differences from it.[4] The resort for the English postcolonial writer would seem to be to go abroad, to a place where Western imperialism is locked in struggle; to displace yourself from the center. Problematically for such a writer, these are also the very moves of the imperialist. In just the same way, the best-intentioned of Orientalists, in the professional or even honorific sense of the term, risks the charge of complicity in the discourse of Orientalism in the negative sense that we have learned from Edward Said. Being troped as Orientalists in this basically derogatory or suspect sense is an occupational hazard of Westerners orienting themselves in the East.

Fenton began his own displacement, intending to stay out of England for a long time, on the day (as it happens) after the death of W. H. Auden, the poet he most admired, and whose own *Journey to a War* (1939, with Christopher Isherwood) is an important intertext for Fenton's Indochina writing. He was going as a freelance, on the strength of some journalistic commissions and an award for the purpose of traveling and writing poetry. His political convictions, strongly but not religiously held, were socialist and internationalist:

> I wanted to see a communist victory because, as did many people, I believed that the Americans had not the slightest justification for their interference in Indochina. I admired the Vietcong and, by extension, the Khmer Rouge, but I subscribed to a philosophy that prided itself on taking a cool, critical look at the liberation movements of the Third World. We supported them against the ambitions of American foreign policy. We supported them as nationalist movements. We did not support their political character, which we perceived as Stalinist in the case of the Vietnamese, and in the case of the Cambodians . . . I don't know. The theory was, and is, that where a genuine movement of national liberation was fighting against imperialism, it received our unconditional support.
>
> (*Wrong Places* 4)

He was going as a witness to the struggle, but not an unbiased or "objectively" oriented one. A "genuine movement of national liberation" was afoot in Indochina, which deserved "unconditional support."

The unconditionality of that support was to be one kind of hostage to fortune. A more immediate difficulty, and a sometimes though never completely comic one, lay in the fact that Fenton, unconditional support or no, simply *looked* American (or French, or British) and was treated accordingly by Asian people. He describes being snarled at in Vientiane—"I mean really snarling, like a tiger"—by a Pathet Lao soldier standing behind a bush (*Wrong Places* 10). He finds himself constantly assimilated to a strong discourse of Americanism, which means he tends to be treated either as a colonialist enemy to be snarled at or else—for the third world has its stereotypes too—a naive tourist with more than is good for him in his wallet. The streets of Saigon were the theater for some tragic absurdities involving this latter figure. There was, for example, an implacable shoeshine boy, impossible to ignore ("You no give me money, you want I eat shit!"), eventually employed, overpaid, haggled with, finally paid more. "The next day, at the same time, he came into the bar; his eyes

were rolling back in their sockets and he staggered helplessly around the tables and chairs; I do not know what drug he had taken, but I know how he had bought it" (12). In another grotesque story told against himself, Fenton sets off on another act of intended charity—taking a beggar woman's apparently dying baby to the hospital, "on an errand of Western mercy" (14)—but is given such a runaround as to leave him (though the baby survives) disoriented to the point of first-world paranoia. "Suppose the old woman, the taxi driver, the man whose van stalled, the engine driver—suppose they were all now dividing out the proceeds and having a good laugh at my expense, congratulating the child on the way it had played its role?" (16). The beneficiaries of "unconditional support" have their own perceptions of, and ways of dealing with, the Western bearer of this commodity.

> I was disgusted, not just at what I saw around me, but at what I saw in myself. I saw how perilously thin was the line between the charitable and the murderous impulse, how strong the force of righteous indignation. . . . It was impossible in Saigon to be the passive observer. Saigon cast you, inevitably, into the role of the American.
>
> (16-17)

In some cases the would-be internationalist is saddled not only with a national identity but even with a covert function, which is the opposite of his intention. He spent time in the Kampuchea Krom, an area of Vietnam populated by ethnic Cambodians, which fascinated him precisely because of its marginality and fuzziness in matters of nationality and loyalties. Here the old men had fought for the French, their sons had fought for the Americans, and their grandsons were fighting for the Vietnamese: they treated the Vietnamese with distrust yet felt they were no longer Cambodians either. "And if they were not Cambodians, and not Vietnamese, what the hell were they?" (*Wrong Places* 39). In this national no man's land—it is in the war zone, the Vietcong control villages only a couple of miles away—Fenton spends some days in a monastery of friendly if eccentric Khmer monks. As he is leaving, one of the monks asks him if he is from the CIA.

> I laughed. "If I was from the CIA, I would be afraid to stay here. Besides, I'm not American." "That's what you say. But how do we know? This is an interesting area for you. You want to get information about the Vietcong." "I'm a journalist," I said, "and I hate the CIA." "But of course you'd *say* you hated the CIA." He was quite serious, and what he said destroyed, at a stroke, all the pleasure of the last days. Of course that's what they'd think. Why else would a foreigner come and spend such a time with them? What was worst of all was they didn't *mind*. They seemed almost to be used to it. I was an American spy doing my job; they were Cambodian monks, doing theirs. That was the world as they understood it. . . .
>
> (42)

Small wonder the international socialist is dismayed that it is assumed as a matter of course that he's a CIA agent and the embodiment of antisocialism; but of course the more he denies it the more he's behaving as such an agent would. He finds himself trapped, in other words, by the remorselessness of Indochina's history, in a discourse of binary oppositions. What has happened is that his own identity has been in a sense occupied, Americanized, in a manner without his consent and beyond his control. His anti-American socialism does not translate, in these circumstances and to these people. If he's not one of us, he must be one of them: this is how the monk orients himself to his visitor—to (as we say) where he's coming from. "Of course that's what they'd think"; and of course in a sense they are quite right to think it, as Fenton acknowledges. Where—in what orientation—could a foreigner in Indochina stand, to denounce the corrupting effect of foreigners in Indochina?

> Saigon was an addicted city, and we—the foreigners—were the drug. The corruption of children, the mutilation of young men, the prostitution of women, the humiliation of the old, the division of the family, the division of the country—it had all been done in our name. People looked back to the French Saigon with a sentimental warmth, as if the problem had begun with the Americans. But the French city, the "Saigon of the piastre" as Lucien Bodard called it, had represented the opium stage of the addiction. With the Americans had begun the heroin phase, and what I was seeing now were the first symptoms of withdrawal.
>
> (11)

For an English writer the metaphor of opium is of course very far from random, given the history of Britain's interventions in East Asia. He finds himself in the colonial trap, vested with the privilege and touched with the contagion of the system he has come to bury. Here, rather than Auden, the immediate precursor (as Fenton was to acknowledge ["**Journey**" 9]) is George Orwell, Inspector Eric Blair of the Indian Imperial Police.

That—what might be called the Orientalist bind—is one problem. But there is another dimension to the paradox of James Fenton's Indochina. He saw himself as an internationalist and was a member, in England, of the International Socialist party, as "a revolutionary socialist, of the kind who believe in no Fatherland of the Revolution; who have no cult hero (*Wrong Places* 6). This political philosophy was what brought him to Indochina, to bear witness in what the International Socialists saw as one of the most important battle-grounds of the revolution. But it also brought him into an inescapable and deepening paradox, for his internationalist convictions led him to align himself with a thoroughly nationalist liberation movement in Vietnam. The triumph of that nationalism (which he witnessed)

was to leave Saigon monologically bludgeoned—in countless banners and endless, maddening broadcasts over the PA system—by the slogans of the cult hero Ho Chi Minh. The grip of colonialism was replaced by the grip of Stalinism.

If the fate of Vietnam after 1975 was not one that an international socialist could unequivocally applaud, the fate of Cambodia in and after that year zero was, as everyone knows, quite another matter. Cambodia was to be given over for several years to the most paranoiac form of nationalism in the history of the world, under a regime that was to destroy a large minority of its own population, a number in seven figures. Some of these were victims of lunatic economic mismanagement, but many were killed for nationalistic reasons, for the crime of *not being Cambodian enough*. From the date of the fall of Phnom Penh, says John Pilger, "anybody who had owned cars and such 'luxuries,' anybody who had lived in a city or town, anybody with more than a basic education or who had acquired a modern skill, such as doctors, nurses, teachers, engineers, tradespeople and students, anybody who knew or worked for foreigners, such as travel agents, clerks, journalists and artists, was in danger; some were under sentence of death" (386). The Khmer Rouge policy was mad but not random. They were rooting out two things that were perceived as one: anything that was modern, anything that was foreign. It was the most extreme form of anti-internationalism ever put into practice.

Any foreigner who had worked or traveled in Cambodia before the Khmer Rouge victory would inevitably have formed friendships there. Now, any international contacts—on the part, for example, of locals employed by the foreign press corps—were seen as a contamination and a crime. The more friends outsiders had made, the more lives they had put in danger, although this was not immediately understood. Fenton himself remembers "discourag[ing] one [Cambodian] friend from leaving, in the belief that he could expect no decent future in a foreign country. . . . Some people indeed foresaw utter disaster, but a large body of opinion held that the end of the war would be a relief. For one reason or another, many of us mourn friends whom we could well have saved" (Introduction 12). The terrible dramatic irony of the truth about the Khmer Rouge, a truth only realized too late, hangs over Fenton's Cambodian poems in *The Memory of War*. One man may smile one day, and say goodbye.

Discursive hazards, then, as well as (sometimes) physical ones, littered the path of the international socialist journalist-poet in Indochina, and some of them were too deeply concealed to be avoided before the damage was done. That these problems were as next to nothing, compared to what the inhabitants were undergoing, was itself a problem if something, as opposed to nothing, was to be said about these places. Negotiating these paradoxes, as they emerged, makes the question of point of view problematic. Fenton's first gambit was to cast himself, as far as possible, as singular, even eccentric. He travels alone and light by preference, unencumbered by the obligations of official discourse (political orthodoxy, professional deadlines). Not so much is expected, after all, of the amateur, or the tourist. "The journey," he had promised himself at the outset, "was to be utterly selfish"; and if this sounds a bit disingenuous, it is the condition for what follows: "Everything was negotiable" (*Wrong Places* 6). He is talking here about political views, but in a wider sense what is constantly being negotiated in these writings is an orientation in and toward Indochina which is always provisional, a point of view that shifts like the needle of an unsteady compass.

Here a distinction might be drawn between the poems and the prose reporting. It would not be right to describe the poems as impersonal; nevertheless there is something distinctly elusive about the poet whose memory of war produces these poems. He tends to be found, if at all, somewhere near the edge of his composition, a detached or at least reserved onlooker: his only action is observation. If we think of poetry as traditionally a more subjective genre than reporting, it will be a surprise to find much more of James Fenton in the foreground of the journalistic writing than in that of *The Memory of War.* He refuses the conventional self-effacement of the reporter, which is actually a claim to the authority of objective truth. "I suppose that people like the story of a historical event told from a personal point of view"; this entails sharing your ignorance with the reader as well as your experience (**"Journey"** 13-14). So we see a lot of James Fenton as the often bewildered hero and *eiron* of the reportage, in the roles of tourist, dandy, adventurer, journalist, and fool.[5]

The "personal point of view," by contrast, is hard to identify in a poem like **"Lines for Translation into Any Language"** (29), where the first-person pronoun opens the poem with an observation—"1. I saw that the shanty town had grown over the graves and that the crowd lived among the memorials"—and then is never seen again, disappearing into the unexpected form of the narrative.[6] For to tell its story this poem adopts the form of the kind of schoolroom exercise—numbered lines for translation—you might find in a slightly old-fashioned language primer. The war reporting which is the theme of the discourse scrapes with a surreal incongruity against the conventions of the form—that the sentences in such exercises are self-contained without narrative or logical connection, that they are apparently authorless and without context, that their purpose is to test the understanding of the reader:

4. These people kept their supplies of gasoline in litre bottles, which their children sold at the cemetery gates.

5. That night the city was attacked with rockets.

6. The firebrigade bided its time.

7. The people dug for money beneath their beds, to pay the firemen.

8. The shanty town was destroyed, the cemetery restored.

In such exercises, the ability to translate—to transform the discourse of the other into one's own—would be proof of understanding. But in the circumstances this is an impossibility. The dark joke of the poem is that the experience of the Vietnamese is already only available to us in the language and through the point of view of the Western observer. Into which language should the reader of English translate these lines, as the title instructs? Into Vietnamese?

Point of view then—political and personal point of view—becomes an issue in these writings, especially in retrospect. It is in retrospect that the struggle against imperialism is understood to have carried the seeds of Stalinism and a kind of autogenocide (which does not mean that the struggle against imperialism was wrong). It is in retrospect that love for Cambodia—which Fenton says he greatly preferred to Vietnam—is seen to mean an endangering of the object of love, and contact itself turns out to have been in some cases a fatal contagion. It is the poems that confront some of the pain of getting it wrong (not that it was really possible to get it right) in this way; and among them **"In a Notebook"** (24-25) is a formal enactment of the way retrospect requires a reorientation.

The poem is in two parts, typographically distinct, and the first, italicized part evokes the life of a jungle village:

> There was a river overhung with trees
> With wooden houses built along its shallows
> From which the morning sun drew up a haze
> And the gyrations of the early swallows
> Paid no attention to the gentle breeze
> Which spoke discreetly from the weeping willows.
> There was a jetty by the forest clearing
> Where a small boat was tugging at its mooring.
>
> And night still lingered underneath the eaves.
> In the dark houseboats families were stirring
> And Chinese soup was cooked on charcoal stoves.
> Then one by one there came into the clearing
> Mothers and daughters bowed beneath their sheaves.
> The silent children gathered round me staring
> And the shy soldiers setting out for battle
> Asked for a cigarette and laughed a little.
>
> From low canoes old men laid out their nets
> While on the bank young boys with lines were fishing.
> The wicker traps were drawn up by their floats.
> The girls stood waist-deep in the river washing

> Or tossed the day's rice on enamel plates
> And I sat drinking bitter coffee wishing
> The tide would turn to bring me to my senses
> After the pleasant war and the evasive answers.

This is a version of pastoral idyll, a naturalized human scene, and realized without an orientalizing glamour. The rhyme scheme is that of a relaxed, dozy *ottava rima,* which keeps settling down to rest on substantives, or on those lulling participle forms which are not quite timeless (idyll's ideal) but suggest that history can have no very urgent business with the village. The poet himself is foreign here, an object of curiosity, yet accepted or tolerated as part of the peaceful scene, perhaps idly sketching his impressions in the notebook.

The second part of the poem is like a playback of this memory, but now the idyll gets rewritten as tragedy. Here many of the images and even lines of the first half are repeated, but seen now from a different vantage point, further away in space and time. Something terrible has intervened.

> There was a river overhung with trees.
> The girls stood waist-deep in the river washing,
> And night still lingered underneath the eaves
> While on the bank young boys with lines were fish-
>   ing.
> Mothers and daughters bowed beneath their sheaves
> While I sat drinking bitter coffee wishing—
> And the tide turned and brought me to my senses.
> The pleasant war brought the unpleasant answers.
>
> The villages are burnt, the cities void;
> The morning light has left the river view;
> The distant followers have been dismayed;
> And I'm afraid, reading this passage now,
> That everything I knew has been destroyed
> By those whom I admired but never knew;
> The laughing soldiers fought to their defeat
> And I'm afraid most of my friends are dead.

The poet who wrote of the village in a notebook in the past is reading those same lines, but now they mean something different; that scene of peace has now gone forever, destroyed by the people he most *admired.* The meaning of the experience has changed in memory. If we go back and read the first part again it's become ironic; there is a terrible discrepancy between the peacefulness of the scene and the war we now know is soon going to destroy it. The poet, now become his own reader, recollects not only the village but also himself, his own ignorance and self-deception, his willingness to believe that everything would be all right.

"Dead Soldiers" is another poem about being an observer, both in the picture and out of it. Fenton has described it as "plain memory, a little memoir" (**"Journey"** 14). Here the poet as reporter is invited by a warlord to a surreally luxurious outdoor banquet, at which the empty brandy bottles (in slang, "dead

soldiers") pile up at their feet. Lunch on the battlefield is a comic and grotesque scene. Only later does the reporter realize that the drunken officer who sat next to him was Pol Pot's brother. He has missed a good story: not only has he let slip the opportunity of interviewing the brother of the Khmer Rouge leader, he has also misjudged his host the Khmer prince, whom he seriously underestimates as a typical corrupt fat cat. Later he learns that the prince has not escaped to Europe with the loot but is still carrying on the struggle, "Somewhere in the Cardamoms or the Elephant Mountains." Behind the comedy of these drunken guzzlers there is a war which is about more than personal self-interest, just as the phrase "dead soldiers" does not refer only to empty bottles. It is easy to make the mistake of thinking that because the prince is a slob and his aide is boring, they can't be serious. But they are.

The comic and tragic perils of misreading account, I think, for the elusiveness of the first person in the poetry, which I have already mentioned. A certain reserve, and a perhaps rather English self-mockery, are erected to shield the first-person speaker from a genuine self-reproach. Graham Greene's novel *The Quiet American,* a story about an English reporter in Vietnam and about the difficulty of remaining merely an outsider, could have shown him that remorse, or at least mistakes, are not to be avoided by the gambit of aloofness. At this point the man whose journey was to be "entirely selfish," who prided himself on "taking a cool, critical look" at other people's struggles, turns out to have been looking in the wrong direction, and missing the point. His disorientation arguably proves him to have been an "Orientalist" after all, viewing the East as a spectacle, and misunderstanding an Eastern culture and history which he approaches from a privileged angle partly through trying to account for it in the terms of a Western political discourse (with its good guys to support and bad guys to condemn) which doesn't fit. I should say that I don't see disorientation as a flaw in the Cambodian poems (which I greatly admire) but as one of their important subjects. The poems of memory are about observing: as an observer, Fenton says, "I had the illusion that I was honest, and in many ways I was" (**Wrong Places** 106). He also admits, however, that he had intended to write a full prose account of his experiences in Cambodia. "But I found it too painful, during the years of the Khmer Rouge regime, to touch that subject, and by now it is too late" (xiv).[7]

Cambodia remained unfinished business; the later, longer poem **"Children in Exile"** (30-37) takes it up again. Here the subject is approached from the opposite orientation, focusing on a family of Cambodian refugees in Europe, and a kind of peace is made. To the young children, overeducated in horror ("Each heart bears a diploma like a scar"), the peaceful plains of Italy at first seem terrible and wild; they are afflicted by the fearful foreignness of their new home as well as by their awful memories of Pol Pot's Cambodia, when "they are called to report in dreams to their tormentors." The worst of the old nightmares and new culture shocks over, the children set about learning the West, an education that has its own frustrations.

> *La Normandie est renommée par ses falaises et ses*
> *fromages.*
>   What are Normandy, cliffs, cheeses and fame?
> Too many words on the look-out for too many mean-
>   ings.
>   Too many syllables for the tongue to frame.

It is a process of learning that is always untidy and clumsy and will always be incomplete. And meanwhile, untidily and incompletely, but with goodwill, a common ground is established in the household in Italy, a little international community with elements that are Italian, Cambodian, Vietnamese, American, and English. "Love is accommodating. It makes space." But no imaginable melting pot could, or should, boil away the difference of these young exiles, the foreignness of their provenance and history.

> I hear a child moan in the next room and I see
>   The nightmare spread like rain across his face
> And his limbs twitch in some vestigial combat
>   In some remembered place.

It is a haunting image of the irreducible otherness of a foreign experience, a gap which no amount of sympathy or imagination can bridge. This alterity can never be translated.

But if we have to remain in some ways tragically blind to foreign experience, it can also provide unexpected insights. Taken to visit the tourist sights at Pisa, the child who is a veteran of Pol Pot's Cambodia can bring an experienced eye to bear on all those martyrdoms and infernos depicted in Italian art. "[A] connoisseur among the graves" in the Campo Santo, in this context he is a foreign expert.

And it is not only his own cultural heritage that the poet can see afresh through the eyes of the children in exile. It is confusing, aggravating even, that these children now look forward to a future in America, a country with more than a measure of responsibility for their tragedy. But for the refugees, who have no choice, it's the future only that matters now.

> For it is we, not they, who cannot forgive America,
>   And it is we who travel, they who flee,
> We who may choose exile, they who are forced out,
>   Take to the hot roads, take to the sea, . . .
>   . . . . .
> It is they, it is they who put everything in hazard.
>   What we do decides whether they sink or swim.

Exile, like translation and tourism, is a mode of internationalism. "[I]t is we who travel, they who flee." Such internationalism may not be voluntary; in any case it can't abolish foreignness, nor should it. It is still a question of we and they, us and them. But in the end the pronouns of nationality matter less than the verbs of action. "What we do decides whether they sink or swim." The phrase echoes the words of the child at the start of the poem: "It is not what we are but what we do."

Exile requires reorientation. Orientation means finding yourself by finding the East. The children are a sort of inverted image of the poet-traveler. There was the Westerner, choosing his destination, in search of unfamiliar and exciting experience, and the confirmation of his views. Here is the East driven abroad, seeking a home, traumatized and then deracinated, to be reborn in Italy, the cradle of the modern West. Theirs is a more important displacement than that of the Western writer on his travels. But a stage of their journey also becomes another step, and in a sense an arrival, in his. Poet and children, needless to say, are luckier in their travels than the Cambodia they have left behind.

But the story does not end there; perhaps it has no end. Fenton's latest collection, *Out of Danger,* published in December 1993, contains a section of songs—a "pocket musical"—called **"Out of the East."** The title song, **"Out of the East"** (29), returns to the theme of the Indochina war.

> And it's a far cry from the cockpit
> To the foxhole in the clay
> And we were a
> Coordinate
> In a foreign land
> Far away
> And it's a far cry from the paddy track
> To the palace of the king
> And many try
> And they ask why
> It's a far cry.
> It's a war cry.
> Cry for the war that can do this thing.

The voice that speaks "out of danger," out of a lifetime of war, is both wounded and self-controlled, pitiful and menacing. It is the voice of a young Khmer Rouge soldier. Here, for the first time, Fenton has essayed a first-personal Cambodian voice. With this formal decision, opening a whole new set of possibilities and problems, Fenton's orientation is, perhaps, far from over.

Notes

"Cambodia" and "In a Notebook" are reprinted by permission of the Peters Fraser & Dunlop Group Ltd.

1. It can certainly be argued that both the thesis and the impact of Said's *Orientalism* (published in 1978) were in part a product of what had happened to the United States in Indochina.

2. The collection was also published, with additional material, as *The Memory of War and Children in Exile* (1983).

3. James Fenton's Asian travel writing is collected in the volume *All the Wrong Places* (1988).

4. See for example the discussion in Ashcroft and others, *The Empire Writes Back*, 1-37.

5. The foregrounding of this persona needs tact, of course, and carries its own risks. It earned Fenton's narrative "The Snap Revolution in the Philippines" (reprinted in *All the Wrong Places*) a withering rebuke from Benedict Anderson, in the *New Left Review*, as an example of "political tourism."

6. "Lines for Translation into Any Language" deals with an incident Fenton witnessed in Vietnam shortly before the fall of Saigon and later recorded in *All the Wrong Places* (74).

7. James Fenton did encourage and help Someth May to write the account of his experiences which became the extraordinary memoir *Cambodian Witness* (1986). "Watching [Someth May] plough through successive drafts," says Fenton in his introduction to this book, "I have sometimes wondered whether the pain of this effort has not been too great" (15). The double effort—learning to write in an unfamiliar language, and having to relive his terrible experience during the Khmer Rouge years—was a price Someth May was prepared to pay in order to tell the story of Cambodia in a Cambodian voice.

Works Cited

Anderson, Benedict. "James Fenton's Slideshow." *New Left Review* 158 (1986): 81-90.

Ashcroft, Bill, Gareth Griffiths, and Helen Tiffin. *The Empire Writes Back: Theory and Practice in Postcolonial Literatures*. London: Routledge, 1989.

Auden, W. H., and Christopher Isherwood. *Journey to a War*. London: Faber, 1939.

Fenton, James. *All the Wrong Places: Adrift in the Politics of Asia*. 1988. Harmondsworth: Penguin, 1990.

———. Introduction. *Cambodian Witness: The Autobiography of Someth May*. By Someth May. London: Faber, 1986. 11-16.

———. "Journey without Maps: An Interview with James Fenton." By Mark Wormald. *Oxford Poetry* 6.1 (1991): 9-16.

———. *The Memory of War and Children in Exile: Poems 1968-1983*. Harmondsworth: Penguin, 1983.

———. *Out of Danger*. Harmondsworth: Penguin, 1993.

May, Someth. *Cambodian Witness: The Autobiography of Someth May*. Ed. James Fenton. London: Faber, 1986.

Pilger, John. *Heroes*. Rev. ed. London: Pan, 1989.

Said, Edward W. *Orientalism*. 1978. Harmondsworth: Penguin, 1985.

Evelyn Joll (review date 12 December 1998)

SOURCE: Joll, Evelyn. "The Truth About Mummies and Sewers." *Spectator* 281, no. 8888 (12 December 1998): 38.

[*In the following review, Joll characterizes* Leonardo's Nephew *as "an unusual but fascinating book which is a pleasure to read."*]

All but two of these 15 essays [in ***Leonardo's Nephew***], which range from Egyptian mummies to Jasper Johns, first appeared in the *New York Review of Books* which allows its contributors generous space. This amplitude exactly suits Fenton who likes to address questions that crop up in mid-essay like mushrooms overnight, and then to follow them through. His style is refreshingly direct: one cannot envisage, for example, an article in the *Burlington Magazine* beginning thus: 'Gianlorenzo Bernini was not an entirely nice man, and nor was his little brother, Luigi.' A judgment which, if anything, seems understated as one reads on.

The title essay, '**Leonardo's Nephew**', was originally a talk given at the National Gallery in 1997. The nephew, Pierino Vinci, was born in 1529 but, having gained a reputation as a sculptor, died aged 22. Vasari records that Vinci made a statue of Bacchus, now lost, but James Holderbaum, an American scholar, has suggested that it appears in the background of Bronzino's *Portrait of a Young Man*, illustrated on the dust jacket here, and now on loan to the National Gallery. Holderbaum's theory, when reported by Fenton, evidently met with a frosty reception in Trafalgar Square.

'**Seurat and the Sewers**' has Fenton refuting T. J. Clark's claim in *The Painting of Modern Life* (1984) that in Seurat's great *Bathers at Asnières* in the National Gallery the bathers in the Seine are exactly where the Asnières collector-sewer debouched. Fenton proves that the bathers are fortunately several hundred yards upstream of the sewer. This required much research, hampered by the fact that, after the Franco-Prussian war, Parisians became aware that the new sewers made them vulnerable to enemy attack underground, so that when Fenton wanted to buy a sewer map at the sewer museum he was refused 'for reasons of the security of France'.

'**Who Was Thomas Jones?**' traces the unsuccessful career of the Welsh painter (1742-1803) who remained quite unknown until some beautiful small *plein-air* oil sketches on paper appeared at Christie's in 1954-55. Since then his works have been keenly collected, his reputation having been further enhanced by Lawrence Gowing's *The Originality of Thomas Jones* (1985). One of the two works illustrated here, the tiny but ravishing *Wall in Naples* (c. 1782), was sold by your reviewer, while at Agnew's in 1955 for 15 guineas, a figure multiplied 4,762 times when bought by the National Gallery in 1993.

In **'Johns: A Banner with a Strange Device'** we encounter young Jasper walking through a park in Savannah, Georgia with his father when they come upon a monument to a Sergeant William Jasper and the father tells the boy 'We were named for him.' Sergeant Jasper lost his life raising the American flag over a fort in an assault on the British lines in 1779, an episode thought to contain the genesis of Johns's *Flag,* the central image associated with him. In fact, Sergeant Jasper's flag was not the American flag, as Johns believed, but the colours of the South Carolina Continentals. This is the kind of detail that Fenton so enjoys relating.

'Degas in the Evening' describes the Degas sale in Paris in March 1918 when the National Gallery had £20,000 to spend, due to Maynard Keynes persuading the French to make this sum available against the huge debt they owed to Britain. The National Gallery director, Sir Charles Holmes, having shaved off his moustache and donned spectacles as cover, went to Paris with Keynes.

Soon after the sale began, German shells began to fall close by, which caused 'a considerable rush to the door, at least one prominent Parisian dealer being among the fugitives'. In two days Holmes acquired 27 items for £11,780, including the full-length portrait of Baron Schwiter by Delacroix. However, as the auctioneer did not keep to the catalogue order but dodged about, this confused Holmes into buying a few drawings by mistake. Keynes could not persuade Holmes to bid for a small Cézanne oil of apples so bought it himself. When Roger Fry saw it, he was in such a state of intoxication that Virginia Woolf described him as 'like a bee on a sunflower'.

There are also essays on Pisanello, Verrocchio, Maillol, Picasso, Joseph Cornell and Rauschenberg. As these are both erudite and entertaining, the result is an unusual but fascinating book which is a pleasure to read.

Brooks Adams (essay date January 1999)

SOURCE: Adams, Brooks. "Flights and Fancies." *Artforum* 37, no. 5 (January 1999): 17-18.

[*In the following positive assessment of* Leonardo's Nephew, *Adams praises Fenton's art criticism as plain-spoken, zesty, and insightful and argues that his essays on art denote "a gourmand's appetite for adventure, connoisseurship, and anecdote."*]

James Fenton, for better or worse, is one of the main reasons I still read *The New York Review of Books.* His art journalism is both plain-spoken and perverse, theory-free, zesty, and loose-limbed—at times, admittedly, to a fault. He ushers in a cavalcade of historical greats, from Pisanello to Rauschenberg. He locates many a gay skeleton in the closet. He's on the prowl for odd bits of arcana, both scholarly and scabrous, as well as fresh dish—dashing off, for instance, to Marbach, Germany, to consult the journals of the early-twentieth-century avant-garde patron Count Harry Kessler. Fenton gets good mileage out of his research: He uses this overripe Teutonic fruit, fairly dripping in anti-Semitic sentiment and homoerotic innuendo, in not one, but four different essays in this collection [*Leonardo's Nephew*]. The invaluable Kessler becomes somebody we feel we know after reading James Fenton.

This Britain-born poet and professor of poetry at Oxford, who is now nearing fifty, began his journalistic career as a stringer in Vietnam and Cambodia, also putting in some time in Germany for *The Guardian.* He later became a drama critic in London, for *The Sunday Times,* and chief book reviewer for *The Times.* As of this writing, there is even speculation that he will be named poet laureate of England. Like his compatriot the late Bruce Chatwin, he figures prominently in other people's books—for instance, Redmond O'Hanlon's 1984 travel memoir, *Into the Heart of Borneo,* in which the young Fenton, balding and Buddha-like, agitates for a grueling boat trip in search of a rare horned rhinoceros.

Fenton's art writing likewise denotes a gourmand's appetite for adventure, connoisseurship, and anecdote. His essays reenact the eighteenth- and nineteenth-century English gentleman's Grand Tour. When he writes about Verrocchio, for instance, Fenton goes to see every piece by the Renaissance sculptor on view in Europe and America and publishes his city-by-city account in **"Verrocchio: The New Cicerone."** With Picasso on his mind, Fenton is on his way to the Louisiana Museum in Denmark to catch an exhibition and symposium on "Picasso and the Mediterranean." For his Joseph Cornell piece, he feels it imperative to talk to Cornell collectors in Chicago and Washington, DC. (Was he able to work this in on the Verrocchio trip? Where does he find the time?) To some extent, these global mad dashes are the efforts of a (late) '60s person shooting for Eminent Post-Victorian.

When it comes to books and exhibitions, however, the purported subjects of his critical assignments, Fenton has trouble making hard calls. What specifically does he think of the unforgettable 1996 show "Degas:

Beyond Impressionism" alluded to in two of his essays? We'll never know, since in both **"Degas in Chicago"** and **"Degas in the Evening"** we get big, juicy chunks of historical narrative: the pungently incriminating story of a dinner involving Degas, Kessler, and Vollard, and then the brass-tacks story of the sale of Degas's collection after his death. Still, it might be nice to get some sense of the show or the book that goes with it.

In his review of the second volume of John Richardson's *A Life of Picasso,* Fenton writes glowingly (in **"Becoming Picasso"**) that Richardson "likes the story he is telling to be good, and if it contains bad, or monstrous, behavior, we are going to be let in on it." The same might be said of Fenton. What does our poet make of Deborah Solomon's biography of Joseph Cornell? Once again, it must remain a secret, because Fenton is so caught up in the history of the Renaissance *Wunderkammer.* After this learned digression, he arrives at the surprising conclusion that some of Cornell's miniature theaters were meant to be shaken. And he goes full tilt at the hyper-delicate matter of Cornell's sexuality: "He wanted to talk about Katherine Mansfield and Middleton Murry and Gurdjieff. And he wanted . . . well, oral sex."

Fenton is not above the bitchy tweak. Adam Gopnik, for instance, is lightly skewered in **"Becoming Picasso"** as "the man in the long skirt with the cloche hat, doling out these white feathers to the artists of the past, and hitting them over the head with his parasol." He is terribly polite to Jasper Johns in one essay, **"Johns: A Banner with a Strange Device"** (which is, I think, one of the best things written about the 1996-97 Johns retrospective at MOMA); then, in **"Becoming Picasso,"** he turns around and says that Johns deserves "a special lifetime award" in an imaginary exhibition to be called "A Century of Sucking Up," a show of artists' portraits of their dealers. Johns, he points out, "during the whole of his artistic career, appears to have represented only three recognizable faces: himself . . . , the Mona Lisa, and Leo Castelli."

Fenton has a vigilant (yet judicious) eye when it comes to suppressed homoerotic content. Pierino da Vinci, Leonardo's nephew (who died at twenty-two), had a patron, one Luca Martini, who was "perhaps" his lover. In **"The Secrets of Maillol,"** Fenton considers the recurring Kessler, an important patron of Maillol's, and gently concludes that "he was deeply queer, and most probably deeply repressed." On the other hand Rodin, who is also discussed in the Maillol essay, did not really, it seems, sleep with his male models: "It was a collaboration, not a seduction," Fenton carefully concludes. "To call it homoerotic would be to stretch the term beyond its useful meaning." If Fenton sometimes wisps out into anecdote and the merely interesting, well, *c'est la vie.*

This book is dedicated to the painter Howard Hodgkin (and his companion), and indeed the poet-critic and artist-collector share affinities. Like Hodgkin's painting, Fenton's writing is full of chromatic inflection. They have in common a slapdash surface that belies an underlying intensity that is almost overwrought. Each reflects the highest perquisites of British class and education. Both men readily invoke Lucullus, along with the pleasures of reading, looking, and sex.

For all the varied bounty on its shelves, Fenton's *kammer* nevertheless feels a bit close. The author's boa embrace of the connoisseur's creed produces its own kind of angst, and one finds oneself longing for some kind of acute present tense, some fresh blood, maybe a little barf material. Unfortunately, in Fenton's tireless quest for refinement and excellence, he doesn't quite bother to ask why his subjects matter—how, apart from the commendable exhumation of gay subtext, they might in the broadest sense be relevant to artistic praxis in the here and now.

John Russell (review date 23 April 1999)

SOURCE: Russell, John. "From the Clock Tower." *Times Literary Supplement,* no. 5012 (23 April 1999): 19.

[*In the following favorable review of* Leonardo's Nephew, *Russell commends Fenton as a master storyteller with a wide range of knowledge.*]

In **Leonardo's Nephew,** James Fenton does not discuss his principal calling, poetry. Two lines by Philip Larkin get in, by way of an epitaph for Edgar Degas, but, fundamentally, this is a book that starts from art and sticks with it, though room is made for many a digression. The title derives from a talk given by Fenton at the National Gallery in London in 1997. The Gallery has on loan a painting, "probably by Bronzino", which may or may not be a portrait of Leonardo da Vinci's nephew, Pierino. In the left-hand corner there is a statuette of Bacchus, which may or may not represent a signed and dated statuette by Pierino, which is in Venice. As Pierino never knew his uncle and died of fever when he was only twenty-two, his story is hardly a demanding one for Fenton. But it does summon up the gusto, and the delight in conflicting points of view, that make him a pleasure to read.

Grander by far is **"On Statues"**, a lecture given in 1996 at the invitation of the Institute for Psychoanalysis in London. It is a model of professorial practice. Fenton can set a scene in a line or two. He also has a gift for the unexpected cross-reference that carries his audience with him, and he knows how to round off lectures with a memorable sentence. In **"On Statues"**, Fenton the micro-dramatist takes us into the garden-room in Maresfield Gardens, Hampstead, on the day in September 1938, on which Siegmund Freud came to London to die. His son has set out for him, on his desk, the several hundred ancient statuettes that Freud had been allowed to bring with him from Vienna.

We feel for Freud as he pores over those statuettes, with death at his shoulder. Fenton roves freely throughout the long history of the roles of statue and statuette in human affairs. He reminds us of how, in the 1560s, the alabaster sculptures in the church of Saint-Jacob in Ghent were smashed by a boy aged fourteen or fifteen. He also recounts the story of a crowd of soldiers, who invaded Canterbury Cathedral in 1642 and "giant-like, began a fight with God himself". In the last sentence, Fenton returns movingly to Maresfield Gardens: "Death and delight were mingled there", he says, "among meanings and resonances we cannot hope to unravel, just as we will never unravel what all these statues mean, or what they once meant to those who delighted in them."

The remaining thirteen pieces in *Leonardo's Nephew* were all written for the *New York Review of Books*; their subjects range widely, from the sculptures of Andrea del Verrocchio to the conversation at dinner at Ambroise Vollard's in Paris in 1907. From there, they move to Seurat, Picasso, Joseph Cornell, Robert Rauschenberg and Jasper Johns. Fenton was for four years a drama critic in London (following three years as a foreign correspondent in South-East Asia). Only someone who had been to the theatre on business for 200 nights a year could have got the point, so neatly, of the plays that had been written, devised in every scenic detail and, on occasion, acted in by the great sculptor Gianlorenzo Bernini. (We are reminded that, one evening, John Milton was in the audience.)

Fenton likes to go and see things for himself. When he was researching the background of Seurat's great *Bathing-Party at Asnières,* he attempted to settle once and for all the exact configuration of the Parisian Cloaca Maxima, as it had been established by Baron Haussmann. Where others had relied on contemporary accounts, Fenton went to the authorities and asked if he could buy a map of the Parisian sewage system. "Certainly not", came the reply. The information was classified, and essential to the security of Paris in the event of a foreign invasion. (Such rebuffs are rare.)

In general, Fenton's fancy is piqued as much by the figure of Flinders Petrie in Egypt (working at night, naked, in an ancient tomb) as by Edgar Degas's use of what Walter Sickert called a "ball syringe" to fix and refix his pastels. He is, above all, a performer, with a feel for suspense, for surprise and for the unaffectedly majestic cadence. This is how he sums up the effect on

him of John Richardson's *Life of Picasso.* "As I read it", he says, "my education simply advanced by one great step. It is like being in a clock tower when one of the big cogwheels moves forward by one notch—a great, simple, fundamental event."

Joe Moran (essay date October 2000)

SOURCE: Moran, Joe. "Out of the East: James Fenton and Contemporary History." *Literature and History* 9, no. 2 (October 2000): 53-68.

[*In the following essay, Moran investigates the representation of contemporary history in Fenton's verse.*]

James Fenton is highly unusual among contemporary poets in not only writing about history but also participating in it, having been present at many of the major international wars and revolutions of the last twenty-five years. Fenton went to Indochina in 1973, travelling in and reporting from Vietnam, Cambodia and Laos. In 1975, he was evacuated from Phnom Penh just before the Khmer Rouge arrived, and moved to Saigon, where he famously rode on the first North Vietnamese tank to reach the Presidential Palace. Fenton was the *Guardian*'s correspondent in Germany in the late 1970s, witnessed the Kwangju massacre in Korea in May 1980, and in the mid-1980s reported from Mali, Ethiopia and the Philippines for the *New York Review of Books, Granta* and the *Independent*. Much of Fenton's work draws on these experiences, and this article seeks to examine some of the issues raised by the representation of contemporary history in his poetry. In his commitment to the rootedness of poetry in the concrete historical world, one of his major influences has clearly been the early work of W. H. Auden. Fenton's travels recall Auden's youthful tours of Germany, Iceland, Spain and China in the 1920s and 1930s, and indeed Fenton has written about the eerie synchronicity of hearing of the death of Auden—'the poet I most admired'—as he went through the passport check at Heathrow before his flight to Vietnam.[1] At the same time, Fenton does not quite fit into a 1930s notion of the poet as revolutionary witness, partly because of his own historically specific preoccupations. While Auden's context was a sense of impending crisis around the rise of Fascism in Europe, Fenton typically writes about the much more complex aftermath of colonialism and neo-colonialism in Asia and the Middle East.

Some of Fenton's interest in these issues is prefigured in two early poems written before his journey to Indochina, **'Our Western Furniture'** and **'The Pitt-Rivers Museum, Oxford'**. The first of these is a twenty-one sonnet sequence about the enforced ending to Japan's isolationist policy by an American expedition under the command of Commodore Matthew Perry in the 1850s. Fenton says that this was written in direct response to the highly specialized subject set by the judges of Oxford's Newdigate Prize for Poetry: 'The Opening of Japan, 1853-54'.[2] But writing in the year of the Tet offensive, Fenton clearly aims to use this early instance of American expansionism as a way of commenting on the United States' subsequent involvement in Southeast Asia. The poem's epigraph, in fact, quotes from Perry's report to Congress in 1856, in which he warns that America's main imperial rival will be Russia, as both seek to extend across Asia from different directions, clearly anticipating the domino theory formulated in the Cold War: 'The Saxon and the Cossack will meet . . . The antagonistic exponents of freedom and absolutism must thus meet at last and then will be fought the mighty battle on which the world will look with breathless interest.'[3] Fenton begins here a long-held opposition to American political and military ascendancy, as he has President Millard Fillmore justifying the United States' actions through the doctrine of manifest destiny: 'The striding centuries / Turn cities into dust as leaves to loam / And cause New Wonders from the dust to rise.' (*TM* [*Terminal Moraine*], 47).

But the poem also is not quite as simple as this, since it makes clear that there is nothing so obvious as gunboat diplomacy by the more powerful nation—although this is partly ironic, because America's appeal for 'friendship' in the diplomatic exchange of gifts and 'display of skills on either side' is still supported by a powerful squadron of ships ('Sensing your strengthening sinews with delight / You give us guns, and challenge us to fight.' (*TM*, 45)) Other Japanese voices in the poem are in favour of co-operating with the Americans, though, and the ill-effects of the seclusion policy—the famine and peasant discontent under the Tokugawa Shogunate, 'who steal the money that the rice-crop yields' (*TM*, 34)—are also described. The new American consul to Japan, Townsend Harris, reflects on how 'the frock coats of our motheaten urbanity' seem incongruous and unbecoming in their new home:

> Dumped in the temple garden in the sun
> Our western furniture looks out of place,
> It reeks of cities and a moneyed nation.
> What are we doing in this carapace?

> (*TM*, 48)

At a time (1968) when many of his contemporaries were engaged in more obviously strident protest poetry, it is clear that, even in this first published work, Fenton eschews the diagnostic, imperative tone of Auden's early poems ('Consider this and in our time') in favour of the more dialogic qualities of narrative. The narrator tells the story from different perspectives and personae whose 'views / Were less than partial glimpses of the

truth / Which worked unseen,' and finally concludes that he would not

> Presume to sit in judgment on the past
> Or to point out the baddies in the cast . . .
> Instead we offer you an almost-fiction
> Constructed on a grid of contradiction.

> (*TM*, 53)

Fenton also deals with the legacy of imperialism in another poem from his first collection, **'The Pitt-Rivers Museum, Oxford,'** which centres on the institutional efforts of a culture to read its own past. It again returns indirectly to a period of confident empire-building—although the visit to the museum in the poem is set in the present, the Pitt-Rivers still preserves its Victorian character, resembling 'with its dusty girders, / A vast gymnasium or barracks' (*TM*, 13). The huge expansion of museums in Britain in the late nineteenth century (about a hundred opened in the 1870s and 1880s, the Pitt-Rivers being founded in 1884) was clearly a response to the perceived need to narrativize and celebrate Britain's imperial dominance. The museum's exhibits in the poem are primarily the cultural treasures of Britain's colonial outposts: a Devil Doctor's mask, 'coolie' cigarettes, nut castanets, sistrums, whistling arrows and other hunting instruments, for instance. Moreover, the arrangement of these exhibits inscribes a Social Darwinist narrative of Anglo-Saxon hegemony—in fact, this was one of the principal innovations of General Pitt-Rivers himself, an anthropologist much influenced by Darwin and a friend of 'Darwin's bulldog,' T. H. Huxley. As Tony Bennett has pointed out, the displays here are arranged not geographically or culturally but according to Pitt-Rivers's widely copied 'typological' system, in which similar exhibits are displayed together in an evolutionary series in order to show the gradual cultivation of 'savage' peoples.[4] Fenton's poem clearly points to the pedagogic purpose of this account of the white man's burden, as his museum visitor encounters parties of schoolchildren with their teachers:

> For teachers the thesis is salutary
> And simple, a hierarchy of progress culminating
> In the Entrance Hall, but children are naturally
> Unaware of and unimpressed by this.

> (*TM*, 13)

The poem as a whole seems to undermine the museum's progressive narrative by siding with the disrespectful schoolchildren who 'giggle at curious finds,' fastening on the unassimilable strangeness of individual items like the 'withered hand' or the 'mutilated teeth' (*TM*, 13, 15). By making long lists of exhibits without presuming any connection between them and delighting in the objects in themselves, the poem treats the museum not as a site of cultural authority but as a 'chaotic pile of souvenirs' (*TM,* 14). But the poem historicizes and demystifies the Pitt-Rivers system of classification in more direct ways. Encountering the artefacts closer to home along with the 'primitive' art and idols—a jay's feather worn as a charm or a dowser's twig, for example—the poem concludes that '*We* cannot either feel that we have come / Far or in any particular direction.' (*TM,* 14). Although the narrator states sardonically that 'you have come upon the fabled lands where myths / Go when they die' (*TM,* 14), then, there is a recognition that the museum's aims are more momentous and sinister than the merely archaeological.

This concern about the ways in which different versions of the past can be written and rewritten is continued in Fenton's next full-length collection, **The Memory of War and Children in Exile,** where many of the poems use his own experiences as a foreign correspondent as raw material. Fenton's war reportage and travel writing from this period has received some sharp criticism. Benedict Anderson, for example, links Fenton with a slick, fashionable sphere of *Granta* celebrity journalism, accusing him of 'political tourism' and of being 'a creature of the media [whose] travels to exotic politics are aimed at the acquisition of slides which will be salable on the mass market for the vicarious *frissons* they offer to consumers'.[5] Douglas Kerr's more sympathetic evaluation of Fenton's prose writing concedes that Fenton is always 'the often bewildered hero and *eiron* of the reportage, in the roles of tourist, dandy, adventurer, journalist, and fool'.[6] In part, this is because Fenton uses New Journalism techniques which place him squarely at the centre of the action, employing sometimes humorous incidental detail—as in his description of the mass looting of the Presidential Palace in Manila, when he plays Bach's Prelude in C on Ferdinand Marcos's grand piano and steals Imelda's monogrammed towels—and an occasionally slick turn of phrase (in one dispatch, Fenton goes sightseeing in the Philippines because he is 'revolutioned out'[7]). As with Auden, a somewhat romanticized aura of the male, class-privileged Oxford eccentric surrounds Fenton the traveller, a persona reinforced by Redmond O'Hanlon's popular travel book, *Into the Heart of Borneo,* which positions Fenton as the unflappable Englishman abroad, engrossed in the works of Victor Hugo and Jonathan Swift as his canoe negotiates the rapids and the crocodiles in the tropical jungle interior.[8]

Fenton's poetry on these subjects, however, is markedly different. One of his early pieces, **'Letter to John Fuller',** slyly satirizes the confessional poetry of mainly American poets (Berryman, Lowell, Sexton), and its emphasis on suicidal states, championed by Al Alvarez in the 1960s and 1970s.[9] This distrust of what he sees as romantic self-absorption means that Fenton tends to steer clear of the uncomplicated first person in his poems. Another distinctive feature of his poetry is that,

while his war reportage is often consciously immediate and impressed with 'the weight of the moment, the privilege of being a witness,'[10] his war poetry (as the title of his second volume suggests) usually deals with the painful and inevitably more complex process of remembrance and mourning. A key poem is the one which opens the collection, **'A German Requiem',** which concerns the efforts of the vanquished power to come to terms with the experience of the Second World War. In fact, history here appears to be so traumatic as to be not only unspeakable but unthinkable, erased from the memory:

> It is not your memories which haunt you.
> It is not what you have written down.
> It is what you have forgotten, what you must forget.
> What you must go on forgetting all your life.
> And with any luck oblivion should discover a ritual.[11]

This 'solemn pact between the survivors' to 'forget the old times' is sanctioned by the post-war German political and religious establishment: 'The mayor has signed it on behalf of the freemasonry. / The priest has sealed it on behalf of all the rest.' (*MOW* [The Memory of War and Children in Exile], 13). But the poem is also about the persistence of historical memory, if only because the absence of victory parades and other symbolic forms of commemoration in Germany means that a necessary process of grieving has never taken place:

> But when so many had died, so many and at such
>   speed,
> There were no cities waiting for the victims.
> They unscrewed the name-plates from the shattered
>   doorways
> And carried them away with the coffins.
>
>   (*MOW,* 15)

The narrator thus concedes that 'Grief must have its term? Guilt too, then.' (*MOW,* 18). However, the ending of the poem, in which the narrator interviews an old German couple, reinforces its initial sense of 'the resourcefulness of recollection' (*MOW,* 18). These survivors from the war show him a priest-hole, and may thus be Jews who escaped from the concentration camps by hiding from the Nazis, but they are less than forthcoming about their experiences. The narrator is charmed by the 'secret smile' that 'passes from chair to chair' and 'forgets to pursue the point'. The poem thus concludes with a mirroring of the opening lines: 'It is not what he wants to know. / It is what he wants not to know.' (*MOW,* 19).

Fenton's poems about Southeast Asia, which form a sizeable portion of the collection, continue to develop these themes, although here the process of recollection tends to be privileged over the original experience of war. When Fenton arrived in Indochina in 1973, the situation there was tortuously convoluted: the regimes remaining in Phnom Penh and Saigon after the Paris Peace Conference were extremely fragile and each country had a complicated ethnic mix and fractious internal politics, largely as a consequence of a Byzantine colonial inheritance. (As Benedict Anderson points out, Southeast Asia is unusual in consisting of areas governed by virtually all the main colonial powers—Britain, France, Holland, Spain, Portugal and the US.[12]) In his introduction to his collected travel writing, Fenton admits to choosing Indochina 'partly on a whim', having read a few books but knowing little of the place, and suggests that his revolutionary politics merged with a more basic touristic urge: 'I wanted very much to see a communist victory [in Vietnam]. I wanted to see a war and the fall of a city because . . . because I wanted to see what such things are like.'[13] If this comment represents Fenton's views at the start of his travels around the war zone, many of his poems about Indochina concern the acquisition of new knowledges and the agonizing process of re-evaluation attendant upon them.

One example of this is found in **'Dead Soldiers,'** a piece of poetry-cum-reportage constructed (so the poem seems to suggest) from Fenton's own diary entries. It tells of a bizarre encounter in Cambodia in which the poet is invited by one of the Norodom family, a nephew of Prince Sihanouk, for 'lunch on the battlefield' (*MOW,* 26). Sat between Norodom and his aide, who turns out to be the estranged brother of Saloth Sar (alias Pol Pot), he is served a lavish meal of frogs' legs, pregnant turtles and banana salad, as the APCs 'fired into the sugar palms' (*MOW,* 27). The description of the frogs' thighs leaping one by one into the 'sad purple face' of the drunken aide, who everyone treats as the 'club bore' (*MOW,* 27), seems to encapsulate what Hannah Arendt has called 'the banality of evil'.[14] But this mimicking of colonial decadence—with orderlies carrying ice packs on their handlebars, and each diner attended by 'one of the other ranks / Whirling a table-napkin to keep off the flies' (*MOW,* 26)—deceives the narrator into believing that he knows how to read the situation. He fully expects these cliché-ridden figures to 'slip away with the swag' when the going gets tough and live out the rest of their days in reduced but still luxurious circumstances in the South of France. But these events and characters do not quite fit the interpretative framework his Western mindset has imposed on them:

> . . . we were always wrong in these predictions.
> It was a family war. Whatever happened,
> The principals were obliged to attend its issue.
>
> (*MOW,* 28)

The protagonists he imagines to be ordinarily corrupt and debauched turn out to be fanatically dedicated to their cause, and he proves even more misguided in his views of their enemies: of Pol Pot he remembers 'nothing more than an obscure reputation for virtue' (*MOW,* 28).

Fenton's poetry thus revisits the Western anti-Stalinist Left's dilemma in the 1960s and 1970s concerning Indochina's problematic amalgam of Marxism and Nationalism. As a member of the Trotskyist International Socialists, Fenton was anti-nationalistic, but pragmatically in favour of movements of national liberation against American imperialism. He supported but did not idealize the VietCong and Khmer Rouge, claiming to have learnt a lesson from the 1930s in seeking not to 'invent victories for the comrades'. But although Fenton admired the disciplined way in which the VietCong took Saigon at the time, he later accuses himself of 'political opportunism' in seeking to 'hitch a ride on the winning tank, just a few yards before the palace gates,' and admits that he later 'gr[ew] to loathe the *apparatchiks* who were arriving everyday with their cardboard suitcases from Hanoi'.[15] If Fenton retrospectively qualifies his sympathy for the Vietcong, he comes to regret even more deeply his support for the Khmer Rouge. In his introduction to the autobiography of one of his Cambodian friends, Someth May, Fenton states that the foreign press card held by his Cambodian colleagues became 'a death certificate' after the fall of Phnom Penh. But Fenton himself, along with other Western journalists, had dissuaded them from leaving Cambodia, perhaps partly because many on the political left feared the news of atrocities perpetrated by the Khmer Rouge were a propagandistic tool: 'Some people indeed foresaw utter disaster, but a large body of opinion held that the end of the war would be a relief. For one reason or another, many of us mourn friends whom we could well have saved.'[16] This comment seems to suggest that Fenton himself might be the 'one man' mentioned in **'Cambodia'**:

> One man shall smile one day and say goodbye.
> Two shall be left, two shall be left to die.
>
> One man shall give his best advice.
> Three men shall pay the price.
>
> One man shall live, live to regret.
> Four men shall meet the debt.
>
> One man shall wake from terror to his bed.
> Five men shall be dead.
>
> (*MOW,* 23)

This process of re-examination is continued in other poems in the collection. The first half of **'In a Notebook,'** written within the conventions of pastoral, represents the notebook entries of the title. These italicized stanzas paint a lyrical portrait of a pre-Year Zero Cambodia, remembering a village on the banks of 'a river overhung with trees,' where young boys fished, women washed and families cooked Chinese soup on charcoal stoves in houseboats. The 'pleasant war' intrudes only momentarily, as 'shy soldiers setting out for battle / Asked for a cigarette and laughed a little.' (*MOW,* 24). The poem ends, however, with a two-stanza reappraisal in normal type which repeats but inverts many of the phrases in the first part of the poem, and in which a present-tense narrator appears to be looking over these notebook entries and reflecting on the Khmer Rouge's destruction of the village:

> And the tide turned and brought me to my senses.
> The pleasant war brought the unpleasant answers.
>
> The villages are burnt, the cities void;
> The morning light has left the river view
> And I'm afraid, reading this passage now,
> That everything I knew has been destroyed
> By those whom I admired but never knew;
> The laughing soldiers fought to their defeat
> And I'm afraid most of my friends are dead.

> (*MOW,* 25)

'**Children in Exile,**' the longest and most ambitious of Fenton's Cambodian poems, is an account of young refugees from Pol Pot's regime after their arrival in Italy. The poem echoes '**A German Requiem**' in its concern with the unavoidable working through of historical trauma, which happens irrespective of geographical location:

> They have found out: it is hard to escape from
>   Cambodia,
>   Hard to escape the justice of Pol Pot,
> When they are called to report in dreams to their
>   tormentors.
>   One night is merciful, the next is not.

> (*MOW,* 30)

The narrator of this poem, who befriends the refugees and takes them to the Leaning Tower and the Campo Santo at Pisa, is more than a mere neutral observer. His 'enlightened' Western eyes blame the West (and more specifically, the US) for their suffering, and he pities their naive faith in 'Mother America,' claiming bitterly that they have been released on parole 'from five years of punishment for an offence / It took America five years to commit.' (*MOW,* 35, 30). But however much he tries to encompass imaginatively these children's experiences, he also comes to realize that his sense of righteousness is the luxury of the outsider, since the complexities of international power politics are beyond its victims. After all that they have been through, they only know 'what they do not want. / Better the owl before dawn than the devil by day.' (*MOW,* 36). In fact, it is the narrator, as well as these children, who must begin to let go of the experience of war by learning to accept their trust in the West: 'it is we, not they, who cannot forgive America, / And it is we who travel, they

who flee.' (*MOW,* 35). The poem ends on an accommodating note, the narrator reconciled to the 'negative ambition' of the children to escape to the US: 'Let them dream as they wish to dream. Let them dream / Of Jesus, America, Maths, lego, music and dance.' (*MOW,* 35, 37).

It is notable that, in *The Memory of War,* Fenton tends to favour the use of closed forms which means that, as Ian Gregson puts it, there is a 'gap between the manner and register of his war poems on the one hand and their violent content on the other'.[17] For example, as befits a writer whose favourite poem is Gray's 'Elegy in a Country Churchyard,' '**Children in Exile**' and '**In a Notebook**' are both written in slightly varying iambic pentameter. As Antony Easthope points out, the 'syntagmatic closure promoted by the pentameter can approximate to a poise and self-consistency that seems absolute'.[18] It is true that there is a sense in these poems of horror recollected in tranquillity which is more than simply an effect of their content as memories of war. There is a risk that, as Stan Smith puts it in a different context, the poem might thus appear to 'reconcile the historical anxiety of its genesis with the utopian bliss of its reading,' giving us a false sense that the nightmarish historical world might be somehow salvaged and rehabilitated through the individual sensibility of the poet.[19] What, I think, saves these poems from such a notion is their strenuous avoidance of any kind of autobiographical sentimentality. Although it is possible to piece together a continuous Fenton-like narrator in his poetry from his own comments about the war, the poems themselves, when read without these external clues, make few concessions to the reader and are more ambiguous and unsettling. In '**A German Requiem,**' for example, a disembodied and anonymous narrator addresses an equally unspecified 'they' and 'you,' and other characters in the poem tend to be referred to collectively and identified indistinctly as 'boiled shirts' or 'leering waistcoats' (*MOW,* 13). In fact, it is only really the title which gives the subject away—when the poem was first published as '**Elegy,**' it generally baffled readers. In part, this may be an effect of Fenton's writing technique, which tends to pare down an initial experience to its bare essentials—he describes his poems as 'more rooted in specific experience than would be apparent,' because 'there's been an editing technique to make the experience seem strange'.[20] In producing this confusion in the reader, Fenton creates a sense of historical and psychoanalytical complexity which disrupts the sometimes elegiac effect of the verse forms he employs.

Fenton returns to the subject of Cambodia in '**Out of the East,**' a long middle-section on Far and Middle Eastern Politics in his latest collection, *Out of Danger,* which includes poems on the Tiananmen Square massacre, the *Intifada* in the Israeli-occupied territories in

1987 and the Fundamentalist revolution in Iran. These poems are as pessimistic as those in *The Memory of War,* but here they seem to screen the historical turmoil they describe behind a range of verbal effects—insistent rhythms, inventive rhymes and word play. (In fact, the musicality has a specific purpose: these verses form the words to a 'pocket musical' performed in Paris in 1990.) The title poem in **'Out of the East'** is a ballad, with the verses narrated by a teenage Khmer Rouge soldier who describes the rebel army's long journey along the 'paddy track' from the jungles in the Thai border region to Phnom Penh. These verses are interrupted by a repetitive chorus:

> Out of the South came Famine.
> Out of the West came Strife.
> Out of the North came a storm cone
> And out of the East came a warrior wind
> And it struck you like a knife.[21]

As this chorus is modified ('Out of the North came an army . . . out of the South came a gun crew . . . Out of the West came Napalm' (**OOD,** [**Out of Danger**] 30)), it becomes clear that the poem is discussing the different factions at war in Cambodia—Lon Nol's troops, the Khmer Rouge, the North and South Vietnamese and the US, which invaded in 1970 and engaged in sporadic bombing between 1969 and 1973. But the use of compass points rather than specific regions means that there are few clues here as to what exactly is being referred to, an inscrutability which pervades the whole poem. This, for example, is the economical way in which Fenton describes the Khmer Rouge's installation of Prince Sihanouk (its former enemy) as a puppet for the ruthless regime led by Pol Pot:

> We have brought the king home to his palace.
> We shall leave him there to weep
> And we'll go back along the paddy track
> For we have promises to keep.
>
> For the promise made in the foxhole,
> For the oath in the temple yard,
> For the friend I killed on the battlefield
> I shall make that punishment hard.

> (**OOD,** 32)

Because the poem is narrated by one of the perpetrators of these atrocities—a Khmer Rouge soldier who is driven by the persuasiveness of his superiors and the exigencies of war to kill his former friends and allies—there is little opportunity for moral outrage here, just a general sense of violence as breeding violence and the desire for revenge. In the end, all the poem can urge the reader to do is 'cry for the war that can do this thing' (**OOD,** 29).

Another poem in the form of a story, **'The Ballad of the Imam and the Shah,'** recounts the Ayatollah Khomeini's life from his exile from Iran in 1964 up to the Iran-Iraq war. The poem's subtitle, however, is 'An Old Persian Legend' and it begins with the caveat that

> All this was many centuries ago—
> The kind of thing that couldn't happen now—
> When Persia was the empire of the Shah
> And many were the furrows on his brow.

> (**OOD,** 35)

The language used here (as throughout the poem) is deceptively simple and child-like, almost as though it is covering up a brutal truth which would be too hard to bear if related in more conventional vocabulary. The archaic references to Persia, Babylon and Persepolis in the poem also seem to function as a device which distances the reader from the historical immediacy of the Iranian Revolution and the Iran-Iraq war, although they may also be designed to point to the enduring nature of these conflicts. The poem ends:

> The song is yours. Arrange it as you will.
> Remember where each word fits in the line
> And every combination will be true
> And every permutation will be fine:
>
> *From policy to felony to fear*
> *From litany to heresy to fire*
> *From villainy to tyranny to war*
> *From tyranny to dynasty to shame*

> (**OOD,** 37-38)

The expiatory tone of Fenton's earlier Cambodian poems has given way here to a kind of nihilism. Either these lines (the italicized ones functioning as a chorus throughout the poem) suggest the complete absence of meaning—every interpretation of the poem is true—or they imply that the overthrow of despotism only ever succeeds in producing tyranny of a different kind. Again, the emphasis is on the way that violence reproduces itself: 'The child who saw his father's killer killed / Has slaughtered half the children in the land.' (**OOD,** 37).

This deep historical cynicism recurs in **'Jerusalem,'** a poem dated December 1988, placing it exactly a year after the beginning of the Palestinian riots in the Gaza strip and West Bank which produced an armed response from Israeli forces claiming nearly a thousand lives. Puzzlingly, though, having placed itself so precisely, the poem does not refer explicitly to these events. It is made up of a cacophony of opposing voices of different factions of 'warrior archaeologists,' each claiming the city as theirs: 'This is us and that is them. / This is Jerusalem.' (**OOD,** 21). Who 'us' and 'them' are is never precisely spelled out, although the references to Golgotha, Gethsemane, the Emperor Hadrian and the Holy Sepulchre seem to place the tension between Israel and its Arab neighbours in the wider context of the conflict between Muslims, Christians and Jews over the last two millennia. It is clear that Jerusalem's symbolic meaning is more significant than the geographical reality of the city itself:

> Jerusalem itself is on the move.
> It leaps and leaps from hill to hill
> And as it makes it way it also makes it will.
>
> (*OOD*, 19)

The misunderstandings described in the poem are cumulative, the result of arguments embedded deep in history and the refusal on both sides to recognize the discrete histories of their enemies:

> My history is proud.
> Mine is not allowed.
> This is the cistern where all wars begin,
> The laughter from the armoured car.
> This is the man who won't believe you're what you
>   are.
>
> (*OOD*, 18)

If there is a connecting theme in Fenton's poetry, then, it is his suspicion of any kind of fanaticism, either religious or political, which supposes the achievement of a perfectible world, and indeed his general distrust of progressivist views of history. Although Fenton may have been initially motivated by Marxism, a more relevant link might thus be made here with the work of Walter Benjamin, whose angel of history has his face forever 'turned toward the past. Where we perceive a chain of events, he sees one single catastrophe which keeps piling wreckage upon wreckage and hurls it in front of his feet.'[22] Fenton's reassessment of his own teleological conception of Third World revolution in his poetry, in fact, anticipates a critique of orthodox Marxist views of decolonization by certain post-colonial critics. Edward Said, for example, has criticized Marx's analysis of British rule in India for being 'Romantic and even messianic: as human material the Orient is less important than as an element in a Romantic redemptive project'.[23] Robert Young agrees that 'Marxism's universalizing narrative of the unfolding of a rational system of world history is simply a negative form of the history of European imperialism,' representing a kind of 'neo-colonialism'.[24]

Whether or not one agrees with these arguments, they provide a useful insight into Fenton's poetry, much of which is concerned with the problems of imposing a Western dialectic on a uniquely non-Western situation. A similar change of direction is evident, of course, in Auden's war poetry in the 1930s. In the Spanish Civil War, he appeared to have found an arena in which poetry could help to 'make action more urgent and its nature more clear,'[25] most obviously demonstrated in the exhortations of 'Spain,' with its refrain, 'to-day the struggle'.[26] By the time of his journey to the Sino-

Japanese war in 1938, however, these historical certainties had deserted Auden. His sonnet sequence and verse commentary 'In Time of War' is anything but a call to arms, despite his sympathy for the Chinese after the invasion of Manchuria. Here 'history opposes its grief to our buoyant song,' continually reaffirming the survival of tyranny: 'The mountains cannot judge us when we lie: / We dwell upon the earth; the earth obeys / The intelligent and evil till they die.'[27]

Although Auden can hardly be said to be innocent of the charge of political tourism (one of his reasons for going to China, he told Christopher Isherwood, was that it wouldn't be 'crowded with star literary observers . . . we'll have a war all of our very own'[28]), there is at least a sense in 'In Time of War,' as Samuel Hynes points out, of China forming the breeding-ground for a wider conflict of which Europe is also a part.[29] Fenton's war poetry, though, never suggests this kind of involvement of the poet or the reader in the conflicts described, because it remains exclusively foreign. Indeed, apart from the early, satirical **'Letter to Richard Crossman'** written for a *New Statesman* competition, Fenton's homegrown poems are confined to love poetry, light verse or other poems on domestic themes. In presenting the past and present of Asia and the Middle East as one of perpetual bloodshed, chaos and despotism, then, he risks reproducing what Said calls 'the imaginative demonology of "the mysterious Orient".'[30]

This is partly reinforced by the fact that his poetry gives away so little—the sheer lack of information can seem like a refusal to interrogate specific contexts. Arjuna Parakrama picks up on one example in **'Jerusalem,'** where the obliqueness of the poem means that an apparent reference to the *Intifada* ('Ill stone you. I shall break your every limb. / Oh I am not afraid of you / But maybe I should fear the things you make me do' (*OOD*, 19)) misrepresents the riots, implicitly referring to the stonethrowing of the Palestinians but not to the use of guns by Israeli troops. The events on the ground are thus

> completely obliterated by a poem that places the writer as one who has the luxury of being uninvolved, or, worse still, involved in an entirely different (touristic?) enterprise . . . the poet's ability to literally divorce and isolate Jerusalem from the urgent and catastrophic political realities of the area is symptomatic of the unquestioned privilege that he enjoys as classed-gendered-raced-regioned outsider.[31]

I am not sure, however, if the poem 'means' anything definite enough to be described as openly anti-Palestinian. The nub of the issue might be that in the later poems from *Out of Danger*, Fenton combines his historical and political concerns with another area of interest, the nonsense verse and verbal pyrotechnics exemplified in the co-authored *Partingtime Hall* (1987).

When dealing with tragic events in this way, he leaves himself open to the charge of lack of seriousness and 'dandyism, which I know is my besetting sin'.[32]

I am reluctant to dismiss so readily, though, a contemporary poet who has done much to undermine the popular idea of poetry as being 'of all literary genres the most apparently sealed from history, the one where "sensibility" may play in its purest, least socially tainted form'.[33] Fenton's problem is partly the sheer difficulty of representing at all the horrific events he describes in his poetry. Theodor Adorno notoriously declared that 'to write poetry after Auschwitz is barbaric,' although it is worth noting that he was referring to a particular kind of poetry, one of 'self-satisfied contemplation' which could never be equal to the challenge of the 'absolute reification' of totalitarian society.[34] (Adorno also later qualified his original statement by saying that *'literature must resist this verdict. . . .* It is now virtually in art alone that suffering can still find its own voice, consolation, without immediately being betrayed by it . . . it is to works of art that has fallen the burden of wordlessly asserting what is barred to politics.'[35]) In its subject matter, Fenton's poetry clearly does resist such a verdict, and his comments on poetry as a whole—his declared commitment to the narrative function of verse, 'obviousness' and 'extrinsic interest'[36]—make it clear that his aim is far from self-satisfied contemplation. However, he also says that he 'never believed in *agitprop* . . . There are certain things you can say in poetry but what you can't do with poetry is allow political ends to dictate your aesthetics.'[37] In the **'Manila Manifesto,'** a statement of intent in verse which concludes *Out of Danger,* Fenton seems to favour the idea of the poem *as a poem,* a verbal contraption to be read, spoken and heard: 'the wisdom of our age has forbidden us the use of our lips and our limbs. This wisdom is the enemy of poetry.' (*OOD,* 82).

These statements clearly point to a tension in Fenton's poetry between its historical groundedness and its overt literariness, its borrowing of a whole range of poetic styles and genres. As I have attempted to show in this article, this tension raises a number of issues about the representation of traumatic historical events in poetry which is dense and technically sophisticated. In Fenton's work, in particular, this means that he sometimes fails to interrogate adequately his own position as a First World observer of post-colonial conflict. But when his poetry is taken as a whole, the accusation of dilettantish posturing and voyeurism which has been levelled against him seems unfair. He has clearly thought deeply about his own changing relationship to the events he describes, while the 'difficulty' of the poems and their avoidance of any obvious position-taking stems partly from his refusal to provide easy answers to recalcitrant historical problems, dramatizing the difficulties of political commitment in relation to the complicated after-effects of colonialism. The problems of historical representation thus function as productive tensions within Fenton's work, allowing him to combine technical inventiveness with a historically informed subject matter in a way which is rare in contemporary poetry.

Notes

1. James Fenton, *All the Wrong Places: Adrift in the Politics of the Pacific Rim* (New York, 1988), p. 6.

2. Mark Wormald, 'Journey without Maps: An Interview with James Fenton,' *Oxford Poetry,* 6:1 (1991), p. 13.

3. James Fenton, *Terminal Moraine* (London, 1972), p. 29. All subsequent quotations are taken from this edition. Hereafter *TM*, with page numbers in brackets.

4. Tony Bennett, *The Birth of the Museum: History, Theory, Politics* (London, 1995), p. 186.

5. Benedict Anderson, 'James Fenton's Slideshow,' *New Left Review,* 158 (1986), 81-82.

6. Douglas Kerr, 'Orientations: James Fenton and Indochina,' *Contemporary Literature,* 35:3 (1994), 484.

7. Fenton, *All the Wrong Places,* p. 206.

8. Redmond O'Hanlon, *Into the Heart of Borneo: An Account of a Journey Made in 1983 to the Mountains of Batu Tiban with James Fenton* (Harmondsworth, 1985).

9. See, for example, Al Alvarez, 'Beyond the Gentility Principle,' in Al Alvarez (ed.), *The New Poetry* (Harmondsworth, revised ed., 1966), pp. 21-32, and Al Alvarez, *The Savage God: A Study of Suicide* (London, 1971).

10. Fenton, *All the Wrong Places,* p. 86.

11. James Fenton, *The Memory of War and Children in Exile: Poems, 1968-1983* (Harmondsworth, 1983), p. 11. All subsequent quotations are taken from this edition. Hereafter *MOW*, with page numbers in brackets.

12. Benedict Anderson, *Imagined Communities: Reflections on the Origin and Spread of Nationalism* (London, revised ed., 1991), p. xv.

13. Fenton, *All the Wrong Places,* pp. 3, 11, 6.

14. Hannah Arendt, *Eichmann in Jerusalem: A Report on the Banality of Evil* (London, 1963).

15. Fenton, *All the Wrong Places,* pp. 106, 104.

16. James Fenton, 'Introduction' in Someth May, *Cambodian Witness: The Autobiography of Someth May,* ed. James Fenton (London, 1986), p. 12.

17. Ian Gregson, 'James Fenton: Expert at Cross-Fertilization' in *idem, Contemporary Poetry and Postmodernism: Dialogue and Estrangement* (Basingstoke, 1996), p. 75.

18. Antony Easthope, *Poetry as Discourse* (London, 1983), p. 72.

19. Stan Smith, *W. H. Auden* (Oxford, 1985), p. 5.

20. Andrew Motion, 'An Interview with James Fenton,' *Poetry Review,* 72:2 (1982), 20-21.

21. James Fenton, *Out of Danger* (Harmondsworth, 1993), p. 27. All subsequent quotations are taken from this edition. Hereafter *OOD,* with page numbers in brackets.

22. Walter Benjamin, 'Theses on the Philosophy of History,' in *idem, Illuminations,* ed. Hannah Arendt, tr. Harry Zohn (London, 1973), p. 259.

23. Edward Said, *Orientalism* (Harmondsworth, revised ed., 1985), p. 154.

24. Robert Young, *White Mythologies: Writing History and the West* (London, 1990), pp. 2, 112.

25. W. H. Auden, 'Introduction,' in W. H. Auden and John Garrett (eds), *The Poet's Tongue* (London, 1935), p. ix.

26. W. H. Auden, 'Spain,' in *Selected Poems,* ed. Edward Mendelson (London, 1979), pp. 51-55.

27. W. H. Auden, 'In Time of War,' in W. H. Auden and Christopher Isherwood, *Journey to a War* (London, 1939), pp. 271-72, 293.

28. Christopher Isherwood, *Christopher and His Kind* (New York, 1976), p. 289, cited in Douglas Kerr, 'Disorientations: Auden and Isherwood's China,' *Literature and History,* 3rd ser., 5:2 (1996), 53.

29. Samuel Hynes, *The Auden Generation: Literature and Politics in England in the 1930s* (Princeton, 1976), p. 347.

30. Said, *Orientalism,* p. 26.

31. Arjuna Parakrama, 'The Art of (W)riting Oneself Out of Danger: Review of *Out of Danger,*' *Critical Quarterly,* 36:2 (1994), 112-13.

32. Fenton quoted in Ian Parker, 'Auden's Heir,' *New Yorker,* 25 July 1994, p. 65.

33. Terry Eagleton, *Literary Theory: An Introduction* (Oxford, 2nd edition, 1996), p. 44.

34. Theodor Adorno, *Prisms,* tr. Samuel and Sherry Weber (Cambridge, MA, 1981), p. 34.

35. Theodor Adorno, 'Commitment,' in Andrew Arato and Eike Gebhart (eds), *The Essential Frankfurt Reader* (New York, 1982), pp. 312, 318, cited in Shoshana Felman and Dori Laub, *Testimony: Crises of Witnessing in Literature, Psychoanalysis, and History* (London, 1992), p. 34.

36. See, for example, James Fenton, 'The Manifesto against Manifestos,' *Poetry Review,* 73:3 (1983), p. 14; James Fenton, 'Ars Poetica 12: Extrinsic Interest', *Independent on Sunday,* 15 April 1990, Sunday Review, p. 19.

37. Grevel Lindop, 'James Fenton in Conversation,' *PN Review,* 11:2 (1984), p. 31.

Lloyd Evans (review date 24 February 2001)

SOURCE: Evans, Lloyd. "A Side Dish for the Gourmet." *Spectator* 286, no. 9003 (24 February 2001): 38-9.

[*In the following review, Evans assesses* The Strength of Poetry *as "an amusing compendium of soundbites and snapshots from the lives of the twentieth century's leading poets."*]

Poets are an infuriating bunch. In ***The Strength of Poetry*** James Fenton draws together an amusing compendium of soundbites and snapshots from the lives of the 20th century's leading poets.

At home with Mr and Mrs D. H. Lawrence, for example, we learn that fisticuffs were a regular domestic pastime, both partners weighing in against each other. Writing was often the catalyst. Frieda was outraged to discover an early draft of the 1916 poem 'The Virgin Mother', in which her husband refers to his mother in blatantly sexual terms.

> My little love, my darling / You were a door-way to me . . . / You sweet love, my mother / Twice you have blooded me / Once with your blood at birth-time / Once with your misery.

Anyone who finds Lawrence's mawkish and mascara-caked verse beyond parody will recognise this as a typically ludicrous gem. Frieda took it personally, scrawling 'Good God!!!!! I hate it' in the margin. She then picked up an earthenware plate and smashed it over Lawrence's skull. Well, who wouldn't? He was fortunate she hit him with something breakable. I'd have chosen a piece of well-seasoned oak or perhaps just some concrete.

Fenton recalls spats of the past, notably Orwell's withering attack on Auden for his poem 'Spain', which he considered callow and opportunistic. 'So much of left-wing thought,' Orwell wrote in 1938, 'is a kind of playing with fire by people who don't know that fire is hot.' Orwell was further incensed by a request from the *Left Review* for authors 'to take sides on Spain'. Having recently been shot in the neck doing precisely that in Catalonia, he was less than delighted by this invitation. 'Stop sending me this bloody rubbish,' he fires back angrily,

> I'm not one of your fashionable pansies like Auden and Spender . . . By the way tell your pansy friend Spender that I am preserving specimens of his war-heroics and that when the time comes when he squirms for shame at having written it . . . I shall rub it in good and hard.

What's surprising here is the note of hysterical shrillness. Orwell's greatest weapon was his meticulously controlled anger, but in this unguarded outburst he sounds strangely petulant, vindictive and almost camp.

Fenton devotes three chapters to Auden, reminding us of his gift for prose and his aphoristic table-talk. 'Yeats spent the first half of his life writing minor poetry', said Auden, 'and the second half writing major poetry about what it had been like to be a minor poet.' Auden often postured for effect. Lecturing in America he loved to provoke his audience by flippantly declaring that Iago is the only honest character in *Othello*. He proved this by drawing diagrams on a blackboard and evidently relished the sight of senior academics stalking out of his lectures in disgust. Of *Hamlet* he says:

> When a director seeks an actor for the role . . . he may as well take the first person who comes along . . . The role doesn't require an actor. One has only to recite Hamlet's speeches, which are instructions and arguments to himself on how to act the roles he decides to play.

As with the remark about Yeats, this is not strictly true, yet it carries something valuable, a sly and sardonic freshness which opens up an unusual view of a subject that has grown overfamiliar.

While his admiration for Auden is undisguised, Fenton's attitude towards Seamus Heaney is less clear-cut. He lambasts the atrocious versification of 'An Open Letter' (Heaney's fit of pique at being referred to as a 'British' poet). Nor does he mince his words with, 'I don't much care for what he fishes out of bogs.' And yet he chooses to entitle the chapter on Heaney 'The Orpheus of Ulster'. Isn't that going a bit far? The much-praised Heaney is an entertaining provincial sentimentalist but hailing him as an Orpheus is rather like calling John Prescott 'the Pericles of Hull'.

The publisher's claim that *The Strength of Poetry* is 'a major account of modern poetry' suggests that it may stand as a definitive survey. It is no such thing, merely a diverting accompaniment, a side-dish for the gourmet but none the less tasty for that.

Charles Simic (review date 19 July 2001)

SOURCE: Simic, Charles. "That Elusive Something." *New York Review of Books* 48, no. 12 (19 July 2001): 34-6.

[*In the following review, Simic asserts that* The Strength of Poetry *is a "fine book, one that any general reader of literature would have absolutely no difficulty understanding and enjoying."*]

If nobody reads poetry anymore, as even people who ought to know better seem to believe, who then bothers to read books about poetry? The answer is, someone obviously must since they do get published and our publishers are not known for being sentimental fools. For those skeptical of any claims made on behalf of poetry, especially of the modern variety, the probable assumption is that these books are even more obscure, even more irrelevant than the poems themselves.

Like most widespread beliefs about poetry, this one is also wrong. Not only is much contemporary verse readable and worth anybody's time, the same can be said of some writing about poetry. This collection of lectures James Fenton delivered at Oxford, most of which were first published in these pages [*The Strength of Poetry*], demonstrates that to be the case. Notwithstanding what one thinks about Fenton's treatment of various poets under discussion, he has written a fine book, one that any general reader of literature would have absolutely no difficulty understanding and enjoying.

Fenton's writing is conspicuously free of contemporary scholarly jargon that has made most academic writing on poetry an ordeal to read. There are no trendy terms such as "logocentricism," "signification," "slippage," "code," "textuality," "patriarchy," "hegemony," or "post-individualism" in these lectures. Academic critics, working on the premise that the issues they are dealing with are of such complexity that ordinary words simply won't do, use these concepts repeatedly to give the impression that they have reached an advanced, more radical stage of thinking about literature. At their worst, they remind me of the way literary critics in Communist Russia peppered their pieces with all-purpose catch phrases of Marx, Lenin, and Stalin even when they came to write about Homer and Shakespeare. Of course, they were obliged to do so, often at the point of a gun, and our critics are not. Nonetheless, like their Marxist counterparts, others have some legitimate questions about literary works. For instance, who is the real author of a poem? Is it the poet's social class, gender, or race that writes the poem? Schools of literary criticism and the writings of poets themselves can be divided, by how they answer that question. Here are just a few possible ways:

1. The poet and no one else writes the poem.

2. The unconscious of the poet writes the poem.

3. All of past poetry writes the poem.

4. Language itself writes the poem.

5. Some higher power, angelic or demonic, writes the poem.

6. The spirit of the times writes the poem.

Probably all of these have a role in any work, but dogmatic criticism likes to pretend that there is only one correct viewpoint, be it linguistic, semantic, rhetorical, formal, structural, archetypal, or ideological. Instead of engaging the work at hand from various standpoints, it concentrates on one of these aspects of the poem to the exclusion of all the others. A critic like Fenton, who works on the assumption that any single, overall theory of poetry cannot succeed, is bound to be regarded as a relic of an earlier, unenlightened age when literary interpretation was not a science but merely the intuitive findings of an attentive reader who is not ashamed to admit that he mostly reads for pleasure.

Not surprisingly, with all is latest tools of exegesis, academic criticism has a difficult time with the lyric poem, which in most cases tends to be either unparaphrasable or completely transparent, making it difficult to erect a theoretical frame around it. In other words, it seems to resist interpretation. It won't reveal to us the secret of how it came about or how it seduces the reader. As Fenton puts it succinctly:

> There must *be* such a thing as causality, we assume; but we cannot expect to understand its workings. In the writing of poetry we may say that the thing we predict will not happen. If we can predict it, it is not poetry. We have to surprise ourselves. We have to outpace our colder calculations.

This is the crux of the problem. If there's no clear relationship between cause and effect—goodbye theory. And if there's no theory, how is the intellect going to revenge itself against the imagination by locking it up in some conceptual cage? It is worth emphasizing that the poet is not in control of his poems. He is like someone who imagines he is driving from New York to Boston only to find himself in Tuscaloosa, Alabama. The point being, we cannot turn to our imagination and say, give me an original description of what the moon looks like tonight because I need it for the poem I'm writing. An image like Rimbaud's famous "Madame X installed a piano in the Alps" literally pops out of nowhere. Our intellect wants to understand how poetry works, but it has no ability to cough up a single poetic image worth making a fuss about.

Here's a poem by Seamus Heaney that Fenton says went straight into his personal anthology:

"The Butter-Print"

Who carved on the butter-print's
   round open face
A cross-hatched head of rye, all
   jags and bristles?
Why should soft butter bear that
   sharp device
As if its breast were scored with
   slivered glass?

When I was small I swallowed an
   awn of rye.
My throat was like standing crop
   probed by a scythe.
I felt the edge slide and the point
   stick deep
Until, when I coughed and
   coughed and coughed it up,

My breathing came dawn-cold, so
   clear and sudden
I might have been inhaling airs
   from heaven
Where healed and martyred
   Agatha stares down
At the relic knife as I stared at the
   awn.

His explanation why he admires it so much will further explain what I have in mind:

> "The pleasure and surprise of poetry," says Heaney, is "a matter of angelic potential" and "a motion of the soul." When I look at a poem like this for the first time, I ask myself: How did it do that? How did we get from the butter-print to heaven and back down to the "awn" so quickly? It's like watching the three-card trick in Oxford Street. Suddenly the table is folded up under the arm and the trickster vanishes in the crowd—excepting that, when you tap your pocket, you find you have something valuable you could have sworn wasn't there just a moment before.

How one deals with these methodological issues depends on what one believes poetry to be in the first place. Is poetry a state of mind anyone may have from time to time or a gift only a rare few are blessed with? Should our readings and interpretations of poetry follow the same ground rules as our interpretations of deeply felt experiences or do we need experts? Is the work of a true poet an original creation that sets its own rules or the product of socially constructed reality? Does poetry take place on the deepest level of being or in that part of consciousness where our ideas and opinions are formed? Finally, is poetry more at home at the town dump or in the town library?

When one writes about a poet, one's primary effort involves trying to locate some quality of the imagination or voice—that one-of-a-kind aspect—that is present regardless of whatever purpose it has been put to. Note that I say nothing of the subject matter, nor is Fenton overly concerned with it in his lectures. How he brings to light that unique quality in the poets he is discussing. I find most interesting. What he does is not unlike what a novelist strives to do in conveying the peculiarities of his characters. Obviously, we have to see them, hear them, and feel their singularity if they are going to make an impact on us in the story. Fenton achieves that effect in his book by a kind of collage of different approaches. He does not shy away from literary ideas and very close reading of poems, but he combines them with close scrutiny of poets' biographies in search of small, revelatory details that not only bring the individual to life but also make us recall their poems.

He loves a good anecdote. For example, he tells about Marianne Moore's father, who went mad briefly after losing his fortune in the development of the smokeless furnace, and how, when he recovered sufficiently, he got employment at the same mental institution where he had been committed. Then there's the one about Elizabeth Bishop as a college student going to hear Edna St. Vincent Millay read her poetry. On that solemn occasion, for which Millay wore a long artistic robe and clutched a curtain while she recited her poems, Bishop and her friends sat doubled up with laughter. These lady poets, she thought, were always boasting about how "nice" they were. They had to make quite sure the reader was not going to misplace them socially. Of course, that kind of anxiety interfered with what they wrote. This is what she called "our beautiful old silver" school of female writing, and this little tableau of Millay tells it all.

The Strength of Poetry has chapters on Wilfred Owen, Philip Larkin, Seamus Heaney, Marianne Moore, Elizabeth Bishop, Sylvia Plath, D. H. Lawrence, three chapters on Auden, and separate chapters on poets' vicious rivalries and on poetry that celebrates imperialism. Fenton is both a debunker and defender of various claims made by poets. If it is true that poets do not really know how their poems came about, it is best to take both the statements they make about their work and the persona that emerges from their poetry with a grain of salt. Larkin's poems, as Fenton reminds us, seem to say:

> I detest dishonesty in writing; I detest self-mythologizing; if nothing of note happened in my childhood, I'm the kind of guy who's prepared to say so, rather than dress up non-events as events. Taken as lyric, the poem asserts its own right. It stands alone, as any lyric stands alone, to convince us, or not, on its own terms.

It sounds as if Larkin's telling the truth, but he is not. Behind his pose, there are many evasions. When he wrote in the famous poem of his, "They fuck you up, your mum and dad. / They may not mean to, but they do," he may have expressed something true of us all, but he got the idea at home. His father was an admirer of Hitler and even attended Nuremberg rallies. He didn't alter his views during the war and continued to praise the efficiency of Germans even during the blitzing of Coventry, where the family lived. As Fenton says, having his father call down a curse on the city must have made quite an impact on young Larkin. His other concealment was his wartime rejection from military service for medical reasons. Under his air of indiffer-ence, he was a troubled man, so perhaps cause and effect do operate after all in the creative process, however sneakily? Isn't this also the case with Moore, Plath, Bishop, Auden, and so many other poets with their complicated personal histories?

Fenton for the most part, is an astute psychologist. He knows that there are times when biography helps unlock the poetry. Certainly, if in one's youth one's parents paraded naked around the house and chased the mailman down the block in that condition, that just may turn out to make a difference. He also knows that luckily for poets, poems often end up by having a more wholehearted vision than their authors have. Nor does he believe that there's such a thing as an artistic personality. The genius of poetry makes house calls, but he or she is not picky and may often seek out some worthless human being.

As for women poets, Fenton has this to say:

> Something held women back when it came to the writing of poetry, and since whatever it was that held them back failed to hold women back from writing novels, we must suppose that the inhibition had something, at least, to do with the antiquity and prestige of the art.

This doubtlessly is historically true. He goes on to quote Germaine Greer to the effect that it was women who deified the poet, who fainted when Byron came into the room, and yet because of that adoration they were not able to write poetry. What's missing from this account is Sappho, who did originate a type of intimate lyric that after twenty-six centuries still sounds fresh. Not only that. It is still in my view the most radical invention in all of poetry. Thanks to that kind of lyric poem, ordinary mortals make their appearance in literature for the first time. Instead of myths, with their gods and heroes larger than life, we get the first breath of realism, someone's solitary voice speaking to us directly about what concerns her at that moment.

We know the fate of Sappho's poems, how thoroughly they were censored and destroyed, first by antiquity and thereafter by the Christian zealots. They knew what she had committed was an outrage. She made the lyric self into the sacred center, if not sacred cow, of poetry while the tribe with its beloved epics was relegated to the background. Subsequently, it was all right for a man to write like that, to be a Catullus or Propertius, but no woman could get away with it until modernism made scandal a part of its bag of tricks.

I bring this up to amplify Fenton's point that neither Moore nor Bishop seems to have traced her ancestry back through the line of women poets. True enough. On the other hand, one can imagine Sappho understanding where many of Plath's poems were coming from. I doubt there were elms in ancient Lesbos, but this great twentieth-century poem by Plath would have sounded familiar to her.

"Elm"

I know the bottom, she says. I
    know it with my great tap root:
It is what you fear.
I do not fear it: I have been there.

Is it the sea you hear in me,
Its dissatisfactions?
Or the voice of nothing, that was
    your madness?

Love is a shadow.
How you lie and cry after it
Listen: these are its hooves: it has
    gone off, like a horse.

All night I shall gallop thus,
    impetuously,
Till your head is a stone, your
    pillow a little turf,
Echoing, echoing.

Or shall I bring you the sound of
    poisons?
This rain now, this big hush.
And this is the fruit of it:
    tin-white, like arsenic.

I have suffered the atrocity of
    sunsets.
Scorched to the root
My red filaments burn and stand,
    a hand of wires.

Now I break up in pieces that fly
    about like clubs.
A wind of such violence
Will tolerate no bystanding: I
    must shriek. . . .

Moore and Bishop would have been unintelligible to Sappho for numerous reasons. Fenton reminds us that every line of Moore's "went first past her mother's censorship and was later offered to her minister brother, who considered each of her poems as a spiritual event." Women unquestionably had a tradition which men helped themselves to for centuries, but from which women stayed away because their upbringing would not allow them to acknowledge something so disrespectful. Bishop herself was extremely shy. She did not like intimate sexual details spelled out and was upset when her friend Robert Lowell started confessing them in his poems. It was not gushiness but the power of reticence that she valued in a poem. Still, one suspects that occasionally she would have preferred to write more freely about personal matters, as some of the posthumously published poems show. As for Moore, who, too, was a rebel against poetic conventions, even without her

mother peeking over her shoulder as she wrote, it is hard to imagine that her oddly sexless poem "Marriage" would have turned, out any differently.

The concluding three lectures in *The Strength of Poetry* deal with W. H. Auden, his writings on Shakespeare's sonnets, the influences on him of Blake and Henry James, and the final moving chapter on the poet's peripatetic life and melancholy old age. In Fenton's account, Auden experienced firsthand the political and moral crisis of the age, the conflict between reason and heart, individual and collective, as he clung to impossible ideals, failed, turned on himself, kept his integrity, only to find himself hated and have his greatest moment of courage taken for cowardice when he remained in the United States while England was at war. At the end, in his homelessness, he comes across as a tragic figure:

> Blake sat at Auden's left when he wrote, urging concision, definite views, plain language. He was not the Blake of the long line, of the interminable prophetic books, but the fiery Blake of *The Marriage of Heaven and Hell,* the Blake of the notebooks.
>
> Henry James sat on Auden's right, suggesting fascinating syntaxes and ways of prolonging a sentence, giving a nuance to a nuance.

Auden needed influences, Fenton writes—and who doesn't? "We steal from our masters. We steal from our friends, from our enemies even," he says elsewhere. I would also reiterate that men steal from women and women from men. Poets have always been thieves. In the last hundred years, with the proliferation of translations, it got even worse. Everybody was reading everybody else and being influenced by someone from another culture. That's why anthologies based on race and gender are suspect. Reading the poems by Auden that Fenton quotes. I was struck again by how inbred poetry is, how many echoes of our long lyrical tradition are to be found in them.

Dear, though the night is gone.
The dream still haunts to-day
That brought us to a room
Cavernous, lofty as
A railway terminus,
And crowded in that gloom
Were beds, and we in one
In a far corner lay.

Our whisper woke no clocks.
We kissed and I was glad
At everything you did.
Indifferent to those
Who sat with hostile eyes
In pairs on every bed,
Arms round each other's necks.
Inert and vaguely sad.

What hidden worm of guilt
Or what malignant doubt

Am I the victim of,
That you then, unabashed,
Did what I never wished,
Confessed another love;
And I, submissive, felt
Unwanted and went out?

Poets seek that elusive something called poetry, and so do those who write about them. Fenton is very much aware of that in his lectures, and that is part of their strength. Paradoxically, what is most important in a poem, that *something* for which we go back to it again and again, cannot be articulated. The best one can do under the circumstances is to give the reader a hint of what one has experienced reading the poem, but was unable to name. And when that fails, one can quote the poem itself in full, because only poems can trap the "poetic"—whatever that is. Poetry's strength lies in its endless elusiveness to the intellect. This is the reason why poems continue to be written everywhere in the world and why there are still people trying to convince others that reading them will not only give pleasure but also remind the reader of poetry's strange ability to safeguard the power of our most ordinary words.

Alexander Urquhart (review date 15 February 2002)

SOURCE: Urquhart, Alexander. "Breaking New Ground." *Times Literary Supplement,* no. 5159 (15 February 2002): 36.

[*In the following excerpted review, Urquhart applauds Fenton's botanical knowledge and his mix of playful and serious narrative in* A Garden from a Hundred Packets of Seed.]

James Fenton's *A Garden from a Hundred Packets of Seed* could easily be mistaken for a postmodern prayer book; hardly larger than a seed packet, it has a brightly painted dust jacket and pages coloured orange, mauve and navy blue with misty botanical imprints drifting across them. This is all part of the message that gardeners should lighten up, liberate themselves from the weighty considerations of design and recognize that the heart of a garden is in its flowers. Fenton is not talking about landmark shrubs or dependable herbaceous perennials; he means the flowers of the flighty annuals and biennials which can be raised cheaply from seed, and he proposes that you should make your garden from nothing else. These are provocative suggestions, since Fenton is an accomplished gardener, and knows that a garden also depends on well-sorted spaces and attention to the form and texture of its trees and shrubs. But his point is that there is an affordable and desirable alternative to the half-acre of decking and handful of architectural plants that feature in the current spate of media-driven garden makeovers. The hottest place in Fenton's hell is reserved for garden designers. Though he concedes in his introduction that "[the design] approach to gardening would never have become plausible or popular if it did not reflect a certain wisdom", once up to speed he is ready to condemn the practice of design as "a terrible and expensive tyrant". Designers have, of course, been crucial in the development of garden styles, but it is not difficult to see, in the context of Fenton's counter-proposals, why he affords them the status of bogeymen; even the owner of a small town garden can find that he owes thousands of pounds to a designer before he has bought a single delphinium. And the result is too often characterized by a sterility that invites no further input.

Mention annuals and most people think of bedding plants or flowers for a child's allotment. Fenton, however, demonstrates that the range of available seed is diverse enough to provide a plant for every situation. He groups his selection of one hundred species according to size, colour, exoticism, flowers for cutting, etc, and most importantly, species that "hop around"—those that self-seed and provide the ineffable satisfaction of knowing that at least some of the plants in your garden are there because they want to be. Fenton's botanical knowledge is impressive and includes much entertaining anecdote. His list is idiosyncratic, a bit like a horticultural version of *Desert Island Discs*: he favours orange, has a passion for poppies and a proper appreciation for the Umbellifer family. Whether or not one accepts Fenton's proposal that a satisfactory garden can be made entirely from annual and biennial species, he makes a convincing case for them, and this tiny volume is a milestone in their rehabilitation. It is an engaging mix of the serious and the playful, and Fenton writes with a lightness of touch perfectly suited to the subject.

Virginia Quarterly Review (review date spring 2002)

SOURCE: Review of *The Strength of Poetry,* by James Fenton. *Virginia Quarterly Review* 78, no. 2 (spring 2002): 68.

[*In the following review, the critic offers a laudatory assessment of* The Strength of Poetry.]

There is intelligent and compelling intimacy in Fenton's analyses of the life and work of some of our best modern British and American poets [in *The Strength of Poetry*], almost as if one is privileged to have their great secrets whispered into one's ear. Odd angles of view are enriched with a mixture of sympathy and criticism, as if the whisperer is the tolerant best friend of each. With such *tour-de-force* there is always the danger that beguiling solutions to complex problems are not entirely correct, but much of this has the ring of truth. Fenton gracefully considers the paradoxes of substance and appearance, community and individuality of poetry, and all of the ways in which the desire and genius of the poet may go right or wrong in life. He also gets us a good way down another road as he reminds us to appreciate the fact that good poets give us—"something valuable you could have sworn wasn't there just a moment before." He exemplifies that mystical gift in these lovely essays. Strong arguments fall away suddenly to intriguing surmises, apt guesses. Whether seeming delicacy of such points is natural beauty or a contrivance is for the reader to figure out. Fenton's additional and greater magic is that his whispering engenders a keen desire to look again at the poets and poems in order to confirm or deny what he has said of them.

Alberto Manguel (review date 18 May 2002)

SOURCE: Manguel, Alberto. "Ti-Tum, Ti-Tum, Ti-Tum, Ti-Tum, Ti-Tum." *Spectator* 288, no. 9067 (18 May 2002): 44.

[*In the following unfavorable review, Manguel deems* An Introduction to English Poetry *a dry, condescending book that lacks intimacy and passion.*]

After labouring through the 137 pages (index included) of James Fenton's **Introduction to English Poetry,** I emerged grateful to be left at the threshold of what might have been, *horresco referens,* a full-blown book. How is it possible, I asked myself, to bleed such a subject of every ounce of passion and sense of enjoyment? How can someone who is a poet himself be so surgically unfeeling about his craft?

From the very beginning the tone is set, wholesome as an oatmeal biscuit, dry as dust. Line after line, Professor Fenton addresses his class (because surely this text was not intended for any common reader) in a voice that is, in turn, arbitrary ('English poetry begins whenever we decide to say the modern language begins, and it extends as far as we decide to say that the English Language extends'), haughty ('We cannot expect everyone to agree with us when we make a decision in either case'), dismissive ('Some people, for instance, think that English poetry begins with the Anglo-Saxons') and arrogant ('I don't.'). These are the book's first four sentences.

Most of the introduction is concerned with technicalities. That is all very well, since technicalities are essential knowledge for the poet who must become familiar with the clockwork of his craft. But is it right for Professor Fenton to assume that his students are slightly retarded? Consider the first sentence of his chapter on 'The Iambic Pentameter': 'A line of five feet, each of which is an iamb, that is to say each of which is a ti-tum. As opposed to a tum-ti. Ti-tum, ti-tum, ti-tum, ti-tum, ti-tum.'

Without in any way dismissing 'the analytic study of metric', T. S. Eliot, not the most passionate of speakers (after a reading the Queen Mother referred to him as 'this rather lugubrious man in a suit'), has this to say about such things as iambic pentameters: 'But certainly, when it came to applying rules of scansion to English verse, with its very different stresses and variable syllabic values, I wanted to know why one line was good and another bad; and this, scansion could not tell me.'

Exactly. There are things that scansion won't tell us, and in a book that purports to be *An Introduction to English Poetry* some room must be made for the mysteries of taste, for questions of emotion, of pleasure, of that which makes poetry perhaps the most intimate, the most personal of our dealings with the world through language.

But even when Professor Fenton deigns to tell his class a possibly amusing anecdote out of his own experience, the tone he employs is equally forbidding:

> One night I found myself reading at a technical college, next door to a rugby club dinner. There was nothing for it but to raise the voice, to raise it as loud as I dared. Competing with a drinking song, I turned what I had imagined to be a meditative poem into a full-volume declaration of identity: this is who I am, I seemed to be saying; here I stand, I can do no other! Somewhat, but only somewhat, to my horror, the poem appeared to go down very well. I was no stranger to showing off, but I would never normally have shown off in that particular way. One read, or one recited, in the way Auden recited his poems: the proper style was self-deflation.

And yet, I wish Professor Fenton would show off in that particular way—a style not evident perhaps in Auden's recitals but certainly clear in his anthologies and writings about poetry. A little loudness, rashness, red-blooded enthusiasm surely would have done his book's audience no damage. On every page of his *Introduction* I wanted to hear what were the English poems that he really likes, what moving metaphors he has discovered and is willing to share with his audience, what lines have made him weep or smile or think of impending death. Instead, the cautionary selection he offers us to illustrate his poetry course is unfettered by any whimsy and is trite to the point of tears: a song from the *Book of Negro Folklore,* Henley's banal 'Villanelle', Dylan Thomas's over-exposed 'Do not go gentle into that good night', selections from Tennyson's 'Tithonus' and 'Locksley Hall', a few lines from Longfellow's 'Hiawatha', bits of Shakespeare, bits of Blake.

I am, however, grateful to Professor Fenton for two revelations. Kit Wright's 'George Herbert's Other Self in Africa' and (I agree with Professor Fenton's judgment) 'the only beautiful poem' consisting entirely of three letters, John Fuller's 'The Kiss'. In these two selections, something other than the stern professor is stirring. For a fraction of a paragraph, the reader can catch a glimpse of the poet Fenton, and he is neither purse-lipped, humourless nor deaf and (had the Professor not stood in the way) might have written a useful and sensitive ***Introduction to English Poetry.***

Adam Newey (review date 24 June 2002)

SOURCE: Newey, Adam. "Waxing Lyrical." *New Statesman* 131, no. 4592 (24 June 2002): 54-5.

[*In the following review, Newey considers Fenton's poetic theory in* An Introduction to English Poetry, *particularly his definition of English poetry.*]

Here is a book with a simple title [***An Introduction to English Poetry***] that conceals great ambiguities within its two baldly associated terms: what is English poetry? What, for that matter, is poetry? The first question is dealt with in chapter one, grandiloquently entitled "The History and Scope of English Poetry" (it occupies pages 1 to 9). As a former professor of poetry at Oxford, Fenton must know a thing or two about this. English poetry, he asserts, begins "some time around the reign of Henry VIII". Chaucer, let alone the *Gawain* or *Beowulf* poets, are excluded, as they are not readily comprehensible to us today as English. No matter that most anthologies of English poetry tend to start around 1300, or that there is such a thing as *The Oxford Book of Medieval English Verse.*

As for scope, that's as broad as the global spread of the language itself. "When a North American, an Australian, an Indian or a Jamaican writes a poem in English, that poem enters the corpus of English poetry." Fenton does not stop to consider whether the English that is spoken in, say, the Bronx or Port of Spain is readily comprehensible as such to a reader in Aberdeen or Delhi.

The other question—what is poetry?—is one of life's great imponderables. Fenton (who has written libretti for operas, as well as poetry) wants as broad a definition as possible. The roots of song and poetry, after all, are intertwined, so why not allow rap and other popular, music-based forms to be called poetry? (Whether they are good poetry is another question altogether.)

In order for the term to be meaningful, however, we have to decide on some criteria for delimiting poetry from other kinds of writing, or vocalising. This is where

poets themselves oft wax grandiose: they talk about poetry as "language in orbit" (Seamus Heaney), as "a zoo in which you keep demons and angels" (Les Murray), as being "born of speech and silence" (Paul Durcan). All very nice, but it doesn't help us with the strict issue of taxonomy. "The voice is raised, and that is where poetry begins," Fenton tells us. Well, if you ask me, that's where football chants begin. And much as one admires the wit and technical finesse in such terrace anthems as "If I had the wings of an angel / and the arse of a big black cow, / I'd fly over Burnley tomorrow / and shit on the bastards below", it's, well, not quite Milton.

These discussions are confined to the first two chapters. The rest of the book is mainly taken up with prosody, which is fine for those who take an interest in such things (I do, as it happens, and anyone who writes poetry should, too). Fenton explains the various elements of English metre clearly and effectively, with well-chosen examples. The trouble is, there isn't really anything new to say on the subject. And even then, the balance is a little odd. I mean, the trochee is without doubt a fascinating animal; I'm as big a fan as the next chap. But two whole chapters on it? There is, to be fair, a brief but interesting discursus on some obscure classical measures, the mollosus and the dochmiac, which you won't readily come across elsewhere but, as Fenton admits, their application is limited, their relevance disputable. Not unlike his book.

Ray Olson (review date 1 January 2003)

SOURCE: Olson, Ray. Review of *An Introduction to English Poetry*, by James Fenton. *Booklist* (1 January 2003): 832.

[*In the following review, Olson offers a positive assessment of* An Introduction to English Poetry.]

Fenton is primarily concerned with the whys of English verse [in his ***An Introduction to English Poetry***]. Why is iambic pentameter the standard line in English? Why do modern poets recite as they do (flatly)? Why are some poetic forms more versatile in English than others? Why has poetic drama in English been moribund since the seventeenth century? If he doesn't have definitive or original answers to such questions, he always speaks authoritatively about them as a poet and broad-ranging student of poetry. He knows and practices what he talks about. He gets history into the discussion by discriminating between what can and can't now be read comprehensibly—that is, between later-than-fifteenth-century verse and earlier poetry, even Chaucer's, which is pronounced very differently—and in the chronological range, from Elizabethan lyrics to a contemporary experimental sonnet, of the poems he quotes to exemplify different forms, meters, and rhythmic variations within the verse line. John Hollander's *Rhyme's Reason* (3d ed., 2001) remains the best primer on poetic forms per se, but to understand form in English verse, Fenton's your man.

Harriet Zinnes (review date October 2003)

SOURCE: Zinnes, Harriet. Review of *The Strength of Poetry,* by James Fenton. *Hollins Critic* 40, no. 4 (October 2003): 14.

[*In the following review, Zinnes finds* The Strength of Poetry *to be an enjoyable and interesting book.*]

To read the poet, journalist, and critic James Fenton on poetry is beyond pleasure. Here is no flaunting of literary terms from academia or elsewhere that seems to scorn the ordinary reader. This [*The Strength of Poetry*] is a book for readers who want to enjoy the word, to fit it into no scheme but into a world created by someone who may be a poet but who is as real as the reader. That these essays were delivered by Fenton when he was the Professor of Poetry at Oxford from 1994 to 1999, succeeding the Irish Nobel Prize winning poet Seamus Heaney, makes for a kind of irony. The international glories of a Heaney are not Fenton's though he is a prize-winning poet. In 1994 his book of poetry, *Out of Danger,* won the prestigious British Whitbread Prize, and in the States his essays appearing in the *New York Review of Books* (in fact, some of those included in this collection appeared there too) have made his name well known in literary circles. What is perhaps ironic is that Fenton does consider Heaney among the poets he discusses here, and his discussion, as has been true of late among critics, raises questions about the unanimity of rave interpretations of the Irish poet.

But Fenton begins with a story about Michelangelo (a story that most of us would not usually associate with the great Michelangelo), namely, a story about his treatment of the artist Giambologna, for Fenton wants to emphasize the normal competitive nature of artists (and poets!) and their craving for success. Even among the best of poets there is a competitiveness as Fenton reminds us. There was, after all, Byron's attack on Coleridge and above all Wordsworth's mean-spirited attack on that same poet's Kubla Khan.

So it is that Fenton in his conversational manner seems to urge poets to understand that whether the events in their lives are commonplace or dramatic—and as in everyone else's they are both—becoming a poet is learning the special ways of poetry in much the same

manner as learning the special ways of any other work. Fenton discusses leading poets of Britain and the United States with an emphasis that is neither entirely biographical nor critical. Fenton writes about the English Wilfrid Owen, who even before his tragic death at war, was able to emerge from his juvenilia, and about Philip Larkin, whose wounds from which this unpleasant English poet suffered were not from war but from "unshrapnel." The poet's discussion of Seamus Heaney, whom he calls "the Orpheus of Ulster," as has been suggested, provides some of the most fascinating pages (did Heaney start conventionally and now, through all his successes, is he ending conventionally in his own Ulster way?). There are interesting chapters on Marianne Moore, Elizabeth Bishop, and of course "Lady Lazarus." Fenton tries to be fair to this American poet and to discover the significant Plath from the chiefly insignificant and agrees that "the question when Plath begins to sound like Plath will divide people." It is not unfair to think that Fenton himself is not so sure about the certainty of her successful poems because of her terribly curtailed life.

I must say that to this reader Fenton's discussion of T. S. Eliot holds the greatest interest. There is no question that Eliot's reputation today has been hurt in many quarters, and what Fenton brings to the discussion is his contempt for Eliot's "imperialistic" politics, a "treachery" far beyond his leaving the States to become Anglicized. As Fenton notes about W. H. Auden, in contrast to Eliot, and a poet he clearly favors, "as for his turning his verse out for the sake of the Empire, nothing could have struck Auden—or his generation—as more ludicrous." What is fascinating in Fenton's discussion about Auden is Auden's concern with Shakespeare's sonnets. Fenton writes that Auden "thought of the Sonnets as a private record of Shakespeare's humiliation at the hands of both the young man and the Dark Lady, for the sonnets addressed to her are 'concerned with that most humiliating of all erotic experiences, sexual infatuation.'" And I must end this review with Fenton's quotation from Auden, who, in explaining Shakespeare's "humiliation," states that

> Simple lust is impersonal, that is to say the pursuer regards himself as a person but the object of his pursuit as a thing, to whose personal qualities if she has any, he is indifferent, and, if he succeeds, he expects to be able to make a safe getaway as soon as he becomes bored. Sometimes, however, he becomes trapped. Instead of becoming bored, he becomes sexually obsessed, and the girl, instead of conveniently remaining an object, becomes a real person to him, but a person whom he not only does not love, but actively dislikes.

Perhaps this explains Shakespeare's attitudes in the sonnets (or Auden?) but significantly Auden adds that "No other poet, not even Catullus, has described the anguish, self-contempt and rage produced by this unfortunate condition so well as Shakespeare in some of these sonnets."

FURTHER READING

Criticism

Bogen, Don. "Muses of History." *Nation* 209, no. 13 (24 October 1994): 464-68.

> Finds parallels between the lives and works of Fenton and W. H. Auden and offers a mixed assessment of the poems in *Out of Danger.*

"Only If It Hurts." *Economist* 359, no. 8218 (21 April 2001): 82.

> Review contrasting Fenton's *The Strength of Poetry* with Seamus Heaney's *The Redress of Poetry.*

Kendall, Tim. "Auden—The Sequel." *Times Literary Supplement,* no. 5115 (13 April 2001): 25.

> Views the nature of influence as the unifying theme of the essays collected in *The Strength of Poetry.*

Morrison, Blake. "This, and This, and That Too." *Times Literary Supplement,* no. 4500 (30 June-6 July 1989): 715.

> Describes *Manila Envelope* as a diverse and impressive collection and discusses Fenton's commentary on the state of contemporary poetry.

Additional coverage of Fenton's life and career is contained in the following sources published by Thomson Gale: *Contemporary Authors,* **Vol. 102;** *Contemporary Authors New Revision Series,* **Vol. 108;** *Contemporary Literary Criticism,* **Vol. 32;** *Contemporary Poets,* **Ed. 7;** *Dictionary of Literary Biography,* **Vol. 40;** *Literature Resource Center;* **and** *Poetry for Students,* **Vol. 11.**

P. J. O'Rourke
1947-

(Full name Patrick Jake O'Rourke) American essayist, poet, nonfiction writer, and editor.

The following entry presents an overview of O'Rourke's career through 2004.

INTRODUCTION

O'Rourke is recognized as one of America's top humorists. Often discussed within the tradition of New Journalism, a genre in which journalists abandon any pretense of objectivity, O'Rourke applies his conservative-libertarian leanings to such political subjects as the American presidential elections, military conflicts, the differences between liberals and conservatives, and the impact of economic and foreign policy on individuals and society. He also explores a wide variety of other topics, such as popular culture, foreign travel and customs, and domestic life. Rejecting the stereotype of conservatives as sober, dictatorial types, O'Rourke strives to inject his work with a sense of outrage, wit, and cynicism. Several of his works have been best-sellers and are viewed as provocative and entertaining reading.

BIOGRAPHICAL INFORMATION

O'Rourke was born on November 14, 1947, in Toledo, Ohio. He has identified his middle-class upbringing in suburban Toledo as the basis for his conservative perspective on American culture and politics. After receiving his B.A. from Miami University of Ohio in 1969, he became a Woodrow Wilson fellow and earned an M.A. from Johns Hopkins University in 1970. First a writer and editor for underground newspapers, O'Rourke began his journalism career with the *Baltimore Harry* in the late 1960s writing humor pieces. Around that time, O'Rourke began to embrace conservative ideology, which quickly became the basis of his writing. He moved to New York, eventually writing for the *Village Other, New York Herald,* and the notorious humor magazine *National Lampoon*. In 1973 he was hired as a junior editor for *National Lampoon,* and was elevated to managing editor in 1978. He left the magazine in 1981 and became head of the international affairs desk for *Rolling Stone*. He also moved to Hollywood and collaborated with the late comedian Rodney

Dangerfield, among others, on the film script *Easy Money* (1983). That same year, O'Rourke's humorous guidebook on etiquette, *Modern Manners,* was published. He has published several best-selling collections of his essays, most of which have appeared in *Rolling Stone* and other publications, such as *Harper's, Vanity Fair, Esquire,* and *Playboy*. He left *Rolling Stone* in 2001 and became a correspondent for *Atlantic Monthly*. O'Rourke resides in New Hampshire and Washington, D.C.

MAJOR WORKS

O'Rourke skewers a wide-ranging group of political and cultural topics in his humorous essays. His first two major publications, *Modern Manners* and *The Bachelor's Home Companion* (1987), are parodies of old-fashioned behavioral guidebooks, yet manage to comment on the lack of civilized standards of behavior in contemporary society. O'Rourke's first collection of essays, *Republican Party Reptile* (1987), includes twenty-one previously published pieces that introduce and expound on his conservative-libertarian philosophy. Dismissing the prevailing stereotype of conservatives as stuffy and oppressive on social issues, O'Rourke argues that one can be hip, outrageous, and fun while still believing in conservative values such as fiscal responsibility and limited government. As such, he believes that Republicans are capable of breaking laws and supporting such non-conservative behavior as smoking, illicit drug use and engaging in premarital sex. He skewers the American Left as inane and self-important. *Holidays in Hell* (1988) is a collection of his reports from such locations as Korea, Lebanon, the Philippines, South Africa, Nicaragua, and the Soviet Union and asserts the superiority of American idealism. In "Among the Euro-Weenies," he reveals contemptuousness toward European tradition and habits, and also targets such events as the Olympics in Seoul and the America's Cup race in Australia. In his next book, *Parliament of Whores* (1991), he turns his attention to U.S. politics. Revealing moral outrage at the waste, stupidity, power, and greed of the American government, O'Rourke argues that the main responsibility of the government toward its citizens is to leave them alone. He also attacks large federal programs, such as farm subsidies, housing policy, and Social Security.

O'Rourke's 1992 book, *Give War a Chance*, once again skewers liberal ideology and reflects on his experiences reporting on civil unrest around the globe as well as his eyewitness accounts of the Gulf War. *All the Trouble in the World* (1994) traces O'Rourke's travels to such places as Haiti, Vietnam, Somalia, Bangladesh, and the former Yugoslavia. He also takes on big government, environmentalists, population control theory, and eco-tourism and praises the virtues of a free-market economy. In 1998 *Eat the Rich* was published. The essays in this collection focus on economic systems around the world as well as the distribution of global wealth; O'Rourke traveled to Cuba, Albania, Tanzania, Hong Kong, Sweden, and other destinations to examine how economic policy impacts the quality of life of individuals. He concludes that factors such as the prevalence of private property, limited government, free markets, and personal freedom are integral to a nation's success. Told in a series of one-sided monologues, like Oliver Wendell Holmes's *The Autocrat of the Breakfast Table*, the essays in *The CEO of the Sofa* (2001) provide an armchair perspective on such topics as cell phones, wine tasting, the 2000 presidential election, and fatherhood. O'Rourke's latest collection, *Peace Kills* (2004), reflects on the events of September 11, 2001 and American policy in the run-up to the Iraq War. He also reports on his visits to Israel, Kosovo, Kuwait, and Egypt and his experiences in Iraq on the eve of hostilities.

CRITICAL RECEPTION

Although O'Rourke is considered one of America's best-known and most highly regarded political humorists, his work has met with mixed critical reviews. Most commentators regard him as an unapologetic and commonsense conservative whose acerbic views on American politics, economics, and the rest of the world provide hilarious and worthwhile reading. O'Rourke has been compared with such well-respected writers as Tom Wolfe, Norman Mailer, H. L. Mencken, and Hunter S. Thompson. However, some commentators deride O'Rourke's humor as stale and his insights as lazy, and believe his pose as a right-wing outlaw is tired and phony. Such detractors contend that he too often rails against foreigners, women, gays, and other minorities, and tends to rewrite conservative ideology to meet his own needs. Finding his essays biting and inflammatory, these reviewers argue that O'Rourke is an ego-driven and petulant writer who falls back on stereotypes and well-worn comic premises in order to make a point. Recent reviews have traced O'Rourke's stylistic and thematic development, noting that his recent collections have focused more on family and domestic issues.

PRINCIPAL WORKS

Our Friend the Vowel (poetry) 1975

Easy Money [screenwriter; with Rodney Dangerfield, Michael Endler, and David Blain] (film) 1983

Modern Manners: An Etiquette Book for Rude People (nonfiction) 1983

The Bachelor's Home Companion: A Practical Guide to Keeping House like a Pig (nonfiction) 1987

Republican Party Reptile: Essays and Outrages (essays) 1987

Holidays in Hell (essays) 1988

Parliament of Whores: A Lone Humorist Attempts to Explain the Entire U.S. Government (essays) 1991

Everybody Had His Own Gringo: The CIA and the Contras (essays) 1992

Give War a Chance: Eyewitness Accounts of Mankind's Struggle against Tyranny, Injustice, and Alcohol-free Beer (essays) 1992

All the Trouble in the World: The Lighter Side of Overpopulation, Famine, Ecological Disaster, Ethnic Hatred, Plague, and Poverty (essays) 1994; also published as *All the Trouble in the World: The Lighter Side of Famine, Pestilence, Destruction, and Death,* 1994

Age and Guile Beat Youth, Innocence, and a Bad Haircut: Twenty-five Years of P. J. O'Rourke (essays) 1995

The "American Spectator" Enemies List: A Vigilant Journalist's Plea for a Renewed Red Scare (essays) 1996

Eat the Rich: A Treatise on Economics (essays) 1998
The CEO of the Sofa (essays) 2001
Peace Kills (essays) 2004

CRITICISM

Bob Mack (review date 5 June 1987)

SOURCE: Mack, Bob. "Party Animal." *National Review* 39, no. 10 (5 June 1987): 47-8.

[*In the following favorable review of* Republican Party Reptile, *Mack views O'Rourke as a daring, provocative, and hilarious political commentator.*]

P. J. O'Rourke is a conservative for the future. As a former editor of *National Lampoon* and a frequent contributor to all the trendy glossies, he is a part of and yet apart from the East Coast Media Establishment. O'Rourke is funny, cool, hip, and sexy. He's everything Tom Shales says conservatives are not. And he is skillful enough to smuggle his cockamamie conservatism into any magazine he wants. (By the way, he's not a well-connected Harvard grad, but a Midwesterner who infiltrated the *Lampoon* hierarchy and went on from there.)

O'Rourke is infuriating, but also disarming. Who can suppress a snicker when confronted with the belligerent brand of social dissection that characterizes his new collection of 21 essays, *Republican Party Reptile*?

> We are the Republican Party Reptiles . . . I think our agenda is clear. We are opposed to: government spending, Kennedy kids, seatbelt laws . . . busing our kids anywhere other than Yale, trailer courts near our vacation homes, Gary Hart, all tiny Third World countries that don't have banking secrecy laws, aerobics, the UN, taxation without tax loopholes, and jewelry on men . . .
>
> There are thousands of people in America who feel this way, especially after three or four drinks. If all of us could unite and work together, we could give this country . . . well, a real big hangover.

There's an element of danger in O'Rourke. For one thing, he flaunts a Dionysian disposition that is largely charming but still a potential turnoff to traditional conservatives—as well as an easy stick for envious liberals to thwack him with. The former publisher of *Lampoon* told *NR* [*National Review*] that O'Rourke is a "flaming a——," while an ex-editor added, "The last time I saw P.J., I threw a drink in his face."

Left-wingers understandably see him as a pragmatic traitor who cashed in on the Reagan Revolution. But it's not as if O'Rourke can be sure of help from the Right. Many serious conservatives consider him a trendy lightweight, forgetting that he has reported from Beirut, Russia, Poland, El Salvador, and the Philippines (during Marcos's final days).

They also fail to notice that beneath a flippant surface and a frequently vulgar brand of humor, O'Rourke is remarkably concerned with mores and morals. For example, his earlier book, *Modern Manners,* was a farcical slap at what passes for etiquette in our bankrupt culture. But it was also a subtle declaration of disgust with today's self-righteous depravity. O'Rourke cleverly—and correctly—linked the disappearance of manners to the general decline of Western civilization.

In turn, the best essay in *Republican Party Reptile* is entitled **"Ferrari Refutes the Decline of the West."** And even in apparent bits of froth like **"Horrible Protestant Hats,"** O'Rourke slips in an eyebrow-raising insight:

> Until the last years of the Eisenhower era, WASPs wore wonderful haberdashery . . . Then something happened . . . Maybe it's no accident that the rise of the silly hat coincides with the disappearance of a coherent American foreign policy, the decay of business ethics, the increase in functional illiteracy, and the general decline of the United States as a world power. The head is symbolic of reason, discipline, good sense, and self-mastery. Putting a fuzzy green Tyrolean hat decorated with a tuft of deer behind on top of it means trouble.

O'Rourke himself always wears a suit and tie, is often mistaken for a CIA agent while traveling, and has this advice for youngsters (from his **"Alphabet for Schoolboys"**):

> *N is for Nike. It's a missile, not*
> *a shoe.*
> *Get yourself an oxford in cordovan,*
> *not blue.*

Conservatism needs P. J. O'Rourke. His audacity brings to mind the image of a vintage Jude Wanniski showing up for his first day at the *Wall Street Journal* behind the wheel of a convertible, in a gold lamé suit, with a Las Vegas showgirl on his arm. Christopher Buckley says that P. J. equals S. J. (Perelman) on LSD. But I see him more as Hunter Thompson minus the idiocies, or as Tom Wolfe with his white suit soiled and shredded after a catfight with Ayn Rand. Whatever else he is, O'Rourke is a party animal whose "be square or beware" attitude could teach timid conservatives to take a bogus accusation and cram it back down the accuser's throat—with a whisky chaser.

When it comes to political philosophy, however, O'Rourke, like many Republicans, unfortunately thinks "neither conservatives nor humorists believe man is good. But left-wingers do." This view mistakenly sets up Hobbes as the paradigmatic conservative antidote to the liberal god, Rousseau. Liberals are allegedly optimistic because they believe people are "perfectible" and can someday be molded into a kind of egalitarian Gumby. Conservatives are thus supposed to be pessimistic because they realize men are inherently evil and unequal, and that capitalism isn't perfect—it's just the best we can hope for.

Thomas Sowell sets up the same false alternative of "unconstrained" liberal versus "constrained" conservative in his latest book, *A Conflict of Visions.* Other apologists, like George Gilder, have felt compelled to defend capitalism by the *ethical* standard of compassion rather than by the *political* standard of competition.

There is, however, no need to shoulder the type of guilt that led to Gilder's "capitalism *is* altruism" equivocation. This form of appeasement—even if O'Rourke himself is tempted to succumb to it—is rendered laughable by P. J. O'Rourke's very existence.

Jack Shafer (review date September 1987)

SOURCE: Shafer, Jack. Review of *Republican Party Reptile,* by P. J. O'Rourke. *American Spectator* 20, no. 9 (September 1987): 45-7.

[*In the following review, Shafer considers O'Rourke's humorous and fun approach to political ideology in* Republican Party Reptile *in light of stereotypes of Republican political thought as severe and unexciting.*]

If P. J. O'Rourke was born a conservative Republican, as he claims, his new collection of essays and journalism, *Republican Party Reptile,* proves that the birth was rectal. To be sure, the former editor of *National Lampoon* barks like an orthodox conservative, with a hate list that maps neatly onto that of Pat Buchanan's: Commies, Ralph Nader, health food, child-proof aspirin bottle-tops, Senator John Kerry, no-nukers, and Roosevelt ("the Roosevelt in the wheelchair, and not . . . the good one who killed bears"). Throughout *Republican Party Reptile,* O'Rourke blasts the liberal agenda with a shower of ridicule, proclaiming that if liberty means anything, it means that we should be able to smoke, shoot guns, drive Corvairs, swallow saccharin, get in fistfights, and start barbecue fires with gasoline without interference from mom or OSHA.

O'Rourke's love of conservative orthodoxy is deep. It is so deep, in fact, that he doesn't mind rewriting it, bending it, even perverting it to make it meet his ends. "We are the Republican Party Reptiles," he brags in the book's introduction. "We look like Republicans, and

think like conservatives, but we drive a lot faster and keep vibrators and baby oil and a video camera behind the stack of sweaters on the bedroom closet shelf." O'Rourke's Reptiles are for a cleaner environment ("poor people should cut it out with the graffiti"), free love ("if our wives don't find out"), and Star Wars or anything else that makes the Russkies nervous. They oppose busing their children ("anywhere other than Yale"), trailer courts near their vacation homes, all tiny Third World countries that don't have banking secrecy laws, and Gary Hart—although the Gary and Donna episode has made O'Rourke rethink that stand.

Now, O'Rourke's conservatism was not learned at Bill Buckley's Yale, taught at Ben Hart's Dartmouth, or speechified by Ronald Reagan on the GE rubber-chicken lecture circuit. It's absorbed by osmosis with a cold one in the frat houses of the land-grant diploma mills of the Midwest—Miami University in Ohio, in O'Rourke's case. In the Midwest the most urgent debate has never been whether capitalism is superior to Communism, or authoritarianism preferable to totalitarianism, but which is better—fun or its antagonist, seriousness. O'Rourke's conservative breakthrough is that fun is better, and that conservatives can have fun.

O'Rourke says conservatives are actually *predisposed* to humor in a way that radicals and liberals cannot be. "People who worry themselves sick over sexism in language and think the government sneaks into their houses at night and puts atomic waste in the kitchen dispose-all cannot be expected to have a sense of humor. And they don't," he writes.

> Radicals and liberals and such want all jokes to have a "meaning," to "make a point." But laughter is involuntary and points are not. A conservative may tell you that you shouldn't make fun of something. "You shouldn't make fun of cripples," he might say. And he may be right. But a liberal will tell you, "You *can't* make fun of cripples." And he's wrong—as anyone who's heard the one about Helen Keller falling into a well and breaking three fingers calling for help can tell you.

Here, O'Rourke is spewing heresy. Historically, conservatism has been about as fun as watching your carpet get shampooed—as you know if you've ever attended a YAF rally, spent a day in ROTC, or dated a nice girl. Not only do most right-wingers hate fun themselves, they hate it when anybody else has fun. Consequently, the only way to have fun and be a conservative at the same time is to avoid all other conservatives. With each generation, this has made conservatism more like the sex act: satisfying if done alone, tolerable if practiced with a partner, but disgusting in higher concentrations. Liberalism, on the other hand, inverts this maxim. A solitary liberal can't have fun, because there is nobody to tax. But pair off a couple liberals and give them an intoxicant and suddenly you've got legislation *and* a party.

All that stands between conservatives and a good time (and perhaps world domination), O'Rourke argues, are a few broken laws, and in *Republican Party Reptile* he illustrates this idea repeatedly. In **"Ferrari Refutes the Decline of the West,"** he celebrates the sin of speed, slaloming down Interstate 10 at 140 mph in a Ferrari 308GTS. In **"How to Drive Fast on Drugs While Getting Your Wing-Wang Squeezed and Not Spill Your Drink"** he extends automotive pleasures with illicit drugs, alcohol, and vehicular sex. (If a Drunks Against Mad Mothers [DAMM] movement is ever launched, this lizard king of comedy would be the perfect poster-child.) Alcohol, O'Rourke learned while peering at the Soviet Union through the bottom of a vodka glass, is not only the way to make driving more fun, but also the great maker of brotherhood. It is also the only thing that makes the workers' paradise tolerable.

The fun paradigm is further bifurcated in **"A Cool and Logical Analysis of the Bicycle."** O'Rourke contends that fun danger is superior to unfun danger, and complains that bicycles are "dangerous without being any fun. You can't shoot pheasants with a bicycle or water-ski behind it or go 150 miles an hour or even mix it with soda and ice. Being dangerous without being fun puts bicycles in a category with open-heart surgery, the war in Vietnam, the South Bronx, and divorce. . . . Bicycles are too slow and impuissant for a country like ours. They belong in Czechoslovakia." Better to ban them and their riders, "organic-gardening zealots who advocate federal regulation of bedtime and want American foreign policy to be dictated by UNICEF."

The social graces fall into the Republican Party Reptile's purview as well, with an entire section devoted to "Manners and Mores." One piece anthologized here from *House and Garden* explains the dos and don'ts of dinner table conversation. "Mix good talkers with good listeners. And don't confuse good listeners with people who are simply quiet," he advises. "Furniture is quiet." But for the final word on the subject, I refer you to the complete volume O'Rourke wrote on this subject a couple years ago, *Modern Manners.* He describes it as the book that settles once and for all how much money a woman has to make before you can slug her without feeling ashamed.

Ultimately, though, the slitheriness of a Republican Party Reptile is best judged by his willingness to break the law. If a few broken laws are fun, a lot of broken laws are a lot more fun, and a place with no laws at all is a perpetual Mardi Gras. In Lebanon, where chaos reigns and drugs are abundant and cheap, O'Rourke found his paradise. But lest the reader think his voyage was all ideology, fun, and pharmaceuticals, listen to his brilliant descriptions of Beirut from **"With Hostage and Hijacker in Sunny Beirut"**:

> Beirut doesn't match any mental picture of anything. After ten years of polygonal civil war and invasions and air strikes by Syrians, Israelis, and multilateral peace-keeping forces, the place still isn't as squalid as some cities that have never been hit by anything but government social programs. There are zones of manic destruction, of course. The Green Line looks like an antinuke-benefit-concert album cover. The Bois de Pins, planted in the 1600s, has taken so many rocket attacks that it's a forest of phone poles. Hotel Row along the Corniche was destroyed in the first year of warfare. The best hotel, the St. George, is a burned hulk. But its bar is still open and people water-ski from the beach there in all but the worst of the fighting. "What about the sniper?" I once asked someone. He said, "Oh, most of the snipers have automatic weapons. They aren't very accurate."

As wonderful as *Republican Party Reptile* is, let's not pretend that the scaly beast has written a complete conservative treatise. For example, he is silent on the subject of immigration. What about the Snow-Mexicans, people like Mortimer Zuckerman, Peter Jennings, and Lorne Greene, who smuggle themselves down from the 49th Parallel to take jobs away from Americans? He is also silent on monetary reform, but one guesses that he would advocate the return to the gold standard in the same breath as a return to the Acapulco gold standard.

Already there is evidence that other prominent conservatives, like Lt. Col. Oliver North, have embraced the reptile agenda. Impatient with Congress's double-nickel speed on approving aid for the contras, he hot-wired American foreign policy and jetted around the world, collecting a gazillion dollars for the freedom fighters. When quizzed on his doings by a grand-standing Congress, he lied about it with reptilian charm. (I am pleased that North had a drop-dead gorgeous blonde in his employ all the while, but am disappointed that there have been no congressional revelations about vibrators or baby oil or video cameras.)

The small-minded may think of O'Rourke as an incubus sent by Gus Hall and black nationalists to pollute the conservative youth of today. Based on the vision presented in *Republican Party Reptile,* I prefer to think of him as that and more. He is our generation's moral compass—pointing straight to hell.

Jonathan Yardley (review date 14 September 1988)

SOURCE: Yardley, Jonathan. "Travels to the Infernal." *Washington Post Book World* (14 September 1988): C2.

[*In the following review, Yardley finds the essays collected in* Holidays in Hell *humorous, outrageous, and insightful.*]

If those airline tickets to the Olympic Games in Seoul are burning a hole in your pocket, you'll be relieved to know that there's still time to get a refund—which is precisely what you'll want to do after reading **"Seoul Brothers,"** P. J. O'Rourke's hilarious and devastating portrait of a city [in *Holidays in Hell*] in which "spontaneous regimentation" is the order of the day. Here's how O'Rourke describes a political rally there:

> When a Korean political candidate does a little stump-ing, a little flesh pressing, a little baby kissing, he puts on a sour face, mounts a platform and stares at the crowd. He's surrounded by Samoan-size bodyguards, his *chap-sae*, or goons (literally "trapped birds"). A couple of the goons hold an inch-thick plexiglass shield in front of the candidate's face. The shield has handles bolted on both ends like a see-through tea tray. The crowd shouts the candidate's name for half an hour, then the candidate yells at the crowd. Korean sounds like ack-ack fire, every syllable has a primary accent: *YO-YO CAMP STOVE HAM HOCK DIP STICK DUCK SOUP HAT RACK PING-PONG LIP SYNC!!!* If the candidate pauses, the crowd responds in unison with a rhymed slogan or with a precise fifteen seconds of wav-ing little paper Korean flags. There's no frenzy in this, no mob hysteria, and it's not a drill or an exercise.

In that paragraph as throughout the pages of *Holidays in Hell*, O'Rourke is here to tell us that whatever else it may be out there in the great wide world, it certainly is *different*. As a correspondent for numerous publications, chief among them *Rolling Stone*, O'Rourke has roamed the world's sore and troubled spots—Lebanon, El Salvador, the Philippines, Nicaragua, South Africa, Panama—and has learned that, although "people are all exactly alike," their similarities take startlingly diverse forms depending on the extent of deprivation they suf-fer, the nature of the wars they wage and the distance of their remove from the amenities of Western civiliza-tion.

For this last O'Rourke is an unabashed apologist. "So-called Western civilization," he writes, "as practiced in half of Europe, some of Asia and a few parts of North America, is better than anything else available. Western civilization not only provides a bit of life, a pinch of liberty and the occasional pursuit of a happiness, it's also the only thing that's ever tried to." In the rest of the world, by contrast, O'Rourke finds little except war, starvation, death and waste; he may be a humorist, but his laughter has a hollow ring.

His pose—his journalistic persona—is that of the tough, cynical man of the world: the *echt* foreign cor-respondent. "Personally," he writes, "I like the kind of research you can get your hands on, the kind you can heft. That is, I like to do my principal research in bars, where people are more likely to tell the truth or, at least, lie less convincingly than they do in briefings and books." As he tries (unsuccessfully) to get into Libya, he says: "I just figured, what with guns going off and things blowing up, there'd be plenty of deep truths and penetrating insights. Tragedy and strife produce these

things in boxcar lots, as any good reporter knows. Also, I wanted a chance to wear my new safari jacket. You really look like a twink if it isn't adequately dirty and sweat-stained."

Thus armed with cynicism and the obligatory apparel, O'Rourke ventures forth to fathom different societies, in each trying "to figure its contradictions, measure its attitudes, see it in its underpants." At this he is extremely good. He wastes little or no time talking with leaders or "spokespersons" but instead seeks out soldiers and bartenders, journalists and shopkeepers, laborers and itinerants. "This book is written from the worm's viewpoint," he says, "and the things I've asked my fel-low blind, spineless members of the phylum *Annelida* are things like, 'What's for dinner?' and 'Please don't kill me'—the stuff of mankind's real-life interviews."

The result is a number of superb pieces. On Warsaw, for example, which "sounds and smells more like a lonely freight yard than a capital city" and where O'Rourke concludes that life behind the Iron Curtain is "Boy Scout Camp-dusty; dilapidated; crummy food; lousy accommodations; and . . . counselors with whistles." On Paris, where he finds that French rock 'n' roll "sounds like somebody's chasing Edith Piaf around the old Peppermint Lounge with an electric hedge trim-mer." Or on the Philippines, where he delights in a cockfight: "my idea of a great sport—two armed entrees battling to see who'll be dinner."

This is funny, outrageous, perceptive stuff, written with brio. But there's another side to O'Rourke. In the Philip-pines the sight of a dead girl, the victim of random gunfire, brings him up short. "What ideology has that oozing face for a price?" he asks. "What abstraction is worth that smell?" In Nicaragua he is aroused to sorrow and anger by the wives of political prisoners. And in El Salvador he visits a dumping ground for the bodies of death-squad victims:

"The bones weren't hard to look at. They were clean from the birds and the sun—theatrical, really. But walk-ing back to the car, I saw matted clothes by the path, a sport shirt and jeans—teenage clothes, slim fit and nar-row in the hips. And then I was sick and shocked."

Patrick Skene Catling (review date 21 January 1989)

SOURCE: Catling, Patrick Skene. "Why, Oh Why, Did He Ever Leave Ohio?" *Spectator* 262, no. 8375 (21 January 1989): 38-9.

[*In the following unfavorable review of* Holidays in Hell, *Catling derides O'Rourke's humor as xenophobic and self-indulgent.*]

The *Wall Street Journal* is partly to blame. They called P. J. O'Rourke 'the funniest writer in America', a title which obviously imposes terrible pressure. It was once borne by Art Buchwald, and consider what it did to him, now a pitiable burnt-out case of humorous formularisation. Mr O'Rourke is the International Affairs Desk Chief at *Rolling Stone,* a position of responsibility that could be equalled only if *Private Eye* were to appoint a Vice President in charge of Ethics and Etiquette. Whenever he writes for his paper Mr O'Rourke is compelled to try to be continuously funny. He doesn't always succeed.

He was born 41 years ago in Toledo, Ohio, where the more intelligent young often feel frustrated by Middle Western provincialism and angry, until they join the Rotary Club or Kiwanis or the Elks and become smug and lethargic. The local newspaper is the *Toledo Blade,* which is as sharp as corn on the cob.

Having escaped early, with his indignation in good working order, he spent the Seventies as an editor of the *National Lampoon* and the early Eighties writing comic screenplays and comic articles for magazines. In the introduction to this collection **Holidays in Hell** of domestic and foreign dispatches, he says he became a foreign correspondent because he was 'tired of making bad jokes,' and yet

> I thought maybe I could use the techniques of humour to report on real news events. Or, at least, I thought I could use the phrase to convince editors and publishers to pay my way to Lebanon, El Salvador and so forth. Actually, I was just curious. I wanted to know where trouble came from and why the world was such a lousy place. . . . I wanted to know why life, which ought to be an only moderately miserable thing, is such a frightful, disgusting, horrid thing for so many people in so many places.

His apparently most influential antecedents have been Tom Wolfe, whose pioneering New Journalism encouraged its practitioners to exercise the subjective licence of fiction, often reporting what imaginary persons should have thought and might have said, and Dr Hunter S. Thompson, *Rolling Stone*'s inventor of 'Gonzo journalism', the very funny chronicles of the drug culture which twist, bend and discolour reality, as it is perceived through a blood-red haze of chemical mind-transformers. It was Dr Thompson who wrote the wonderfully appalling *Fear and Loathing in Las Vegas,* as long ago as 1971. Time flies when you're rolling stoned.

Mr O'Rourke is neither as elegantly imaginative as Wolfe nor as daringly savage as Thompson, but he is as lazily self-indulgent as both of them as reporters. Bringing his Ohioan xenophobia and facetiousness to bear on some of the most agonised places in the world, he has written of his own fear and loathing in the Lebanon, South Korea, Panama, the Philippines, El Salvador, South Africa, Nicaragua, Israel and Northern Ireland.

Like many other foreign correspondents, especially the majority nowadays who only undertake hit-and-run forays abroad rather than residing there, Mr O'Rourke is contemptuous of foreignness. In the manner of a first-time American trans-Atlantic tourist, he jeers at all amenities that deviate from the standards of Hilton hotels. In a catalogue of complaints entitled **'Among the Euro-Weenies,'** he says:

> Our forebears moved to the United States because they were sick to death of lukewarm beer—and lukewarm coffee and lukewarm bath water and lukewarm mystery cutlets with mucky-coloured mushroom cheese junk on them. Everything in Europe is lukewarm except the radiators. You could use the radiators to make party ice.

Analysing the ideology of an anti-Aquino sect in **'The Post-Marcos Philippines,'** he calls them 'red as a baboon's ass,' and adds: 'I've been to your communist countries. They are crap-your-pants-ugly, dull-as-church, dead-from-the-dick-up places . . .'. His prose lacks subtlety and charm.

He portrays Poland in terms of Polish jokes, which the Poles themselves tell better. Some of the jokes are old ones, such as: 'If the borders of Poland are ever opened, will the last out please turn off the lights and close the windows.'

In **'A Ramble Through Lebanon'**, he objects typically to Beirut's smog: 'Air pollution probably approaches a million parts per million. This, however, dulls the sense of smell.' Describing ruined buildings, he observes: 'There's a terrible lack of unreality to this part of the city.' On the people of Belfast, in **'The Piece of Ireland That Passeth All Understanding,'** he writes that 'they're so thoroughly journalised that urchins in the street ask, "Will you be needing a sound bite?" and criticise your choice of shutter speeds.'

Though he boasts a lot about his own boozing in the field, he can assume an attitude of Puritanism. He asks **'In Whitest Africa'** 'what's their [the white South Africans'] response to the quagmire of apartheid?' After spending a month in South Africa, travelling 5000 kilometres and talking to 'hundreds of people', he answers his own question: 'They're drunk.'

The Old City of Jerusalem (**'The Holy Land—God's Monkey House'**) is scornfully dismissed as 'the original for every game of Dungeons and Dragons,' 'a scene from an Indiana Jones movie'.

'Australia is not very exclusive', he discovered on his way to write **'At Sea with the America's Cup'** in Perth.

On the visa application they still ask if you've been convicted of a felony—although they are willing to give you a visa even if you haven't been . . . The Australian language, has more synonyms for vomit than any other non-slavic language. For example: 'liquid laughter,' 'technicolour yawn,' 'growling in the grass' and 'planting beets'. These came in handy for the would-be boat reporter or the would-be Yacht Club Ball society columnist, for that matter.

In **'Christmas in El Salvador,'** he notes that

> the wealthiest 20 per cent of the population gobbles up 66.4 per cent of El Salvador's personal income . . . Maybe this is unfair, but it still didn't look like any oligarch had enough worldly goods to scare Barry Manilow's accountant.

Mr O'Rourke evidently regards the whole world as his straight man. No situation is too frightful to inspire the riposte of a nightclub stand-up comic's one-liner. His wise-cracks about human suffering are breathtakingly vulgar.

Having transcribed unlikely quotations from anonymous taxi-drivers and interpreters in some exotic trouble-spot, he feels he has earned the right to a bit of blackmarket-currency, expense-account 'fun'. '. . . if I can't subtract from the world's sum of misery, do I have to add to it personally?' he demands. 'It's one of the questions I mean to take up if I ever get religion.'

He does not entirely evade responsibility. He has witnessed many a crisis overseas and believes he has a solution. It's the sort of solution frequently offered by American Veterans of Foreign Wars in their clubhouse bars late on Saturday nights—'Clobber the bastards'. Or, as Mr O'Rourke puts it, 'To extend civilisation, even with guns, isn't the worst thing in the world. War will exist as long as there's a food chain.'

'The hell with the bunch of them,' he said of the Sandinistas to a deputy assistant political officer who sat next to him at dinner at the American ambassador's house in Managua. 'Let's invade.' This, Mr O'Rourke admits, is called '*Double Foreign Policy on the Rocks*'.

"That's what the Sandys [Sandinistas] say we're going to do," I explained. "And that's what the peace creeps back home say we're going to do, too. So what the hell? Sure, there'll be a worldwide outbreak of anti-Americanism. But how much *more* anti-Americanism can there be than we've got already?"

Mr O'Rourke's only achievement as a print journalist has been to enhance the prestige of television. 'The funniest writer in America'? He's almost as funny as *Mein Kampf,* but not nearly as thoughtful.

Lawrence Person (review date June 1989)

SOURCE: Person, Lawrence. "The New King of Gonzo Journalism." *Reason* 21, no. 2 (June 1989): 52-4.

[*In the following review, Person favorably compares* Holidays in Hell *to Hunter S. Thompson's* Generation of Swine.]

And now let us speak of gonzo journalists. You might remember their heyday, in the late '60s and early '70s, when the likes of Tom Wolfe were busy stripping away the myth of the "objective journalist." To them, such a posture was all artifice, an unnecessary and artificial barrier between reporter and story. They viewed their own participation as part of the story.

Of their ranks, perhaps the most famous and celebrated was Hunter S. Thompson. When his style worked, it worked brilliantly. With the insightful and lucid *Hell's Angels,* he established himself firmly on the journalistic map, astutely capturing the Angels' free-wheeling lifestyle while scaling their reputation as sadistic monsters down to human proportions. He expanded this approach to journalism with *Fear and Loathing in Las Vegas,* a "savage journey into the heart of the American Dream" that left readers wondering what was real and what was drug-induced hallucination.

It was in *Fear and Loathing: On the Campaign Trail '72,* however, that Thompson found the perfect subject for his gonzo style. With acid commentary and outrageous verve, he relayed the white heat of a presidential campaign like a mad war correspondent, sending back twisted but accurate dispatches from the front. The man could *write,* damn it, and you could forgive his excesses and partisanship for his sheer panache.

But that was long ago. Fifteen years is a long time in the news business. And now, faced with *Generation of Swine,* a new collection of essays, we must ask ourselves: Has Hunter still got it?

The answer is, alas, no.

True, we must admit at the outset that the format of the book is not best suited to Thompson's talents. All the entries are culled from his biweekly newspaper column, despite the fact that Thompson has always worked better at longer lengths. Even so, he seems a shadow of his former self. Where he once became part of the story, he now seems content to watch it from a distance, dispensing high-octane scorn from his retreat in the Colorado Rockies. Thompson no longer weighs and evaluates, he merely slams (condemning any Republican in view). He is still occasionally interesting, but no longer insightful.

Thompson's antiquated worldview is hopelessly stuck in 1974. Indeed, Patrick Buchanan and Richard Nixon play far more important roles in these essays than do Jeanne Kirkpatrick, Mario Cuomo, or even Ronald Reagan. It is as if History As We Know It ended the day Nixon resigned, and all that has followed since is anticlimax. You see nary a mention of Afghanistan, unemployment, Gramm-Rudman, or Mikhail Gorbachev. He seems to regain interest around election time and during the Iran hearings, but only because they provide him an echo of his Watergate-era glory.

Perhaps the worst thing about Thompson is that he has become an unapologetic hack for the Democratic Party. Despite the likes of Mario Biaggi and Jim Wright, Thompson (save for an occasional shot at Gary Hart or Julian Bond) hasn't noticed a single crooked Democrat since the era of Hubert Humphrey. Indeed, he expresses open admiration for all the party's 1988 presidential candidates.

Thompson's apparent blindness on several topics is most puzzling. Although he decries the presence of crooks and jackals in public office, he never writes about the causes of their corruption. Not once does he consider the possibility that this so-called generation of swine might be the direct spawn of the lumbering monstrosity that our government has become. He slams those guzzling at the public trough but never seems to wonder about the size of the trough itself.

Thompson can still write like a crazed hyena on speed, but he no longer has anything to say. His writing is, like Macbeth's world, full of sound and fury, but signifies nothing.

On the other hand, there is another, younger gonzo journalist who has quite a good deal to say and says it brilliantly in his new book, *Holidays in Hell.* An unabashed (if slightly twisted) conservative, as well as a former editor at *National Lampoon,* O'Rourke turned in a hilarious performance in 1986 with *Republican Party Reptile.* In *Holidays,* O'Rourke, like Thompson in his prime, wants to be a part of the world going by, and to that end he reports on events from the globe's most-troubled sites. As an official "Roving Humorist" for *Rolling Stone,* O'Rourke travels to such vacation spots as Lebanon, Managua, and Warsaw, giving us the straight dope from the depths of the world's worst hellholes. Despite a propensity to view these locales through the bottom of a whiskey glass, O'Rourke's observations are on-target, insightful, and very, *very* funny.

He has a master's eye for the telling details of everyday existence. Such as changing currency in Managua: "Jim Denton went to the exchange window with $480 for our group [and] came back with 4,080,000 cordobas, which filled an entire Adidas gym bag. . . . you probably have to take economics over and over again two or three times at Moscow U. before you can make cash worth this little."

On life in Warsaw: "Communism doesn't really starve or execute that many people. Mostly it just bores them to death. Life behind the Iron Curtain is like living with your parents forever."

But, foreign countries are not the only locales that O'Rourke manages to visit. Indeed, he finds at least one equally frightening spot inside our very own nation: "My friend Dorothy and I spent a weekend at Heritage USA. . . . [We] came to scoff—but went away converted. Unfortunately, we were converted to Satanism."

O'Rourke is not afraid to take on anyone's sacred cow. El Salvador and Israel get their fair share of (justified) abuse. Take, for example, his observation that South Africans "don't say, like the Israelis, 'Arabs have a legal right to live in West Jerusalem, but they're afraid to.' They don't say, like the Americans, 'Indians have a legal right to live in Ohio, but, oops, we killed them all.' The South Africans just say, 'Fuck you.' I believe it's right there in their constitution—'Article IV: Fuck you. We're bigots.'"

Just as Thompson has a conclusion linking his essays (we're living in a generation of swine), so does O'Rourke. As he says in his introduction, "So-called Western Civilization, as practiced by half of Europe, some of Asia, and a few parts of North America, is better than anything else available. Western Civilization not only provides a bit of life, a pinch of liberty, and the occasional pursuance of happiness, it's the only thing that's ever tried to." It is O'Rourke's willingness to show us proof of that statement that makes his book more interesting, relevant, and amusing than Thompson's.

The King Is Dead. Long Live the New King.

T. Keating Holland (review date October 1989)

SOURCE: Holland, T. Keating. "Postmodern Emily Post." *Reason* 21, no. 5 (October 1989): 53-4.

[*In the following review, Holland regards* Modern Manners *to be a postmodern etiquette handbook that details "how Americans really behave rather than how they should."*]

P. J. O'Rourke's latest book, *Modern Manners,* does not describe the behavior of polite people. It deals instead with people who want to appear polite while doing whatever they damned well please—in a word, Americans.

"For most of the twentieth century," O'Rourke writes, "we Americans have preferred to ignore conventional social rites, dispense with pomp and circumstance, and set our highball glasses right on the George II sideboard without using coasters. Complex rituals, formalities, and taboos are the hallmark of civilization, and we don't have one, so what the heck."

If no modern American knows which fork to use, why bother learning? Far better, in modern times, to know the polite method of inviting people into the restroom to snort cocaine with you, or the most graceful way to vomit. "Every authority on etiquette discusses how to put things into your stomach," the author notes, "but very few discuss how to get them back out in a hurry." O'Rourke obliges.

The modern advice in **Modern Manners** is targeted at the part of society that styles itself postmodern, the crowd that started the traditional *fin-de-siècle* binge about a dozen years early. The crises facing us as the millennium approaches are different from the social situations described by Emily Post.

Take marriage. A well-mannered women's trousseau used to contain towels, linen, and the like. But in these modern times, a woman brings a different set of items to her marriage, including three cats, a Conran's sofa bed with Azuma bedspread, the complete works of Barbara Cartland, three framed drawings of unicorns, a Jane Fonda workout tape, and a bill from her psychoanalyst.

What about the wedding rehearsal dinner? "These days the honeymoon is rehearsed much more often than the wedding," O'Rourke succinctly notes. "It's not necessary to give a dinner every time you do that."

And for purely modern reasons, brides should still be given away, but only because it's illegal to sell them.

The word *manners,* of course, refers to people's customs and normal behavior as well as their rules of politeness. Accordingly, **Modern Manners** spends most of its time dryly detailing how Americans really behave rather than how they should.

Since we already know, for example, what polite hosts *should* stock their bars with, O'Rourke has much more fun describing what has become customary at the typical '80s party. Does this sound familiar?

2 sixpacks of Miller Lite

1 warm keg of extremely foamy Stroh's

150 half-gallon bottles of screw-top jug wine

40 bottles of gin

60 bottles of vodka

1 bottle of tonic

3 ice cubes

1 lime

Given his emphasis on alcohol, drugs, sex, and vomiting, O'Rourke's target is easy to define—the nouveau generation of wingtips, or pearls, or both. As a former editor of *National Lampoon* as well as a roving reporter for *Rolling Stone,* O'Rourke knows his readers and can be forgiven for making the assumption that they are burned-out, drug-frenzied, power-mad divorcees with bad home lives and bad haircuts. After all, most of them are.

O'Rourke's best work (short pieces compiled in **Republican Party Reptile** and **Holidays in Hell**) has a jaded, sarcastic attitude toward whatever subject matter happens to be on his plate, from designer drugs to pissant Third World countries with bad revolutions and bad hotels. Most of his writing is first-person, free-form, and terribly snide.

Modern Manners retains that worldview but suffers slightly from O'Rourke's insistence on writing in a mock-Emily Post tone of voice rather than his own. The book reads something like an extended *Mad* magazine satire and is best taken in small snippets rather than read at one sitting.

But even if this is his third-best book, that is saying a lot. His hints about how to chat up celebrities like Cornelia Guest ("Gosh, Cornelia, you really make liposuction come alive!") are a scream. And God bless the man for explaining why the drug Ecstasy went out of fashion so quickly: "It made you love everybody. Loving even one '80s person was repulsive enough; loving more than one was actually medically dangerous."

In an era—or at least a book—in which dating can be described as "a social engagement with the threat of sex at its conclusion," the reigning sentiment is apocalyptic. O'Rourke's only real advice is one his readers know he takes to heart: "The world is going to hell. All we can do is look good on the trip."

James Fallows (review date July-August 1991)

SOURCE: Fallows, James. "Rational Lampoon: Finally, P. J. O'Rourke Breaks from the Right-Wing Bad Boys." *Washington Monthly* 23, nos. 7-8 (July-August 1991): 54-7.

[*In the following review, Fallows surveys the strengths and weaknesses of* Parliament of Whores.]

This [*Parliament of Whores*] is a much better book than I would ever have expected. Its strengths reflect well on the author himself. Its weaknesses are mainly those of a genre O'Rourke has let himself fall into, one he should begin crawling out of as soon as he can.

The genre in question, that of the Right-Wing Outlaw, didn't even exist 15 years ago. During the generation or two before that, to be a cultural outlaw was to be a left-winger. Gore Vidal and Norman Mailer, Allen Ginsburg and Jack Kerouac, Hunter S. Thompson and Michael Herr, John Lennon and Mick Jagger and the music world in general, they all implied that to be sexy and clever you also had to be on the left. The Young Republicans of those days were the overearnest strivers who wore neckties to college classes and later got hauled up before the Watergate committees. Right-wing activists tended to resemble Ayn Rand or Pat Buchanan or Jeane Kirkpatrick or Jack Kemp. That is, they were forceful and tireless but not exactly blessed with the light touch.

Hollywood still seems to operate on the liberalism-equals-sex-appeal principle. Warren Beatty, Madonna, Spike Lee, and Jack Nicholson are all flashy. Charlton Heston, he of the NRA ads, is not. But things have certainly changed in the journalistic and political worlds. Tom Wolfe came out of the closet as a right-winger in the early eighties to become the first flashy conservative. *The American Spectator* made fun of, rather than moralized about, Jimmy Carter and Walter Mondale. College newspapers like the *Dartmouth Review* and overaged collegians like the editorial writers of *The Wall Street Journal* specialized in being wiseguys. Lee Atwater playing blues guitar represented Right-Wing Outlaw style at its peak.

BUFFALO SOLDIER

P. J. O'Rourke, who started out being a general-purpose outlaw as editor of the *National Lampoon,* has positioned himself as a right-winger for the past few years. He uses drugs but is against welfare. He loves it when the Republicans win but loves to make fun of them. (He says in this book that at the 1989 inaugural ball, Marilyn Quayle's chignon hairdo made her "look considerably less like a Cape buffalo than usual. . . . I have an idea that—like the Cape buffalo—if Marilyn gets furious and charges, you've got only one shot at the skull. You wouldn't want to just wound her.") The notion behind *Parliament of Whores,* apart from the idea that O'Rourke might combine some of his old magazine pieces with new reporting, is that the book will give a tour of the government and public policy that is conservative and funny at the same time.

The book is, indeed, very funny. What's more surprising is that so much of it is smart. Perhaps I'm over-reacting, as with Samuel Johnson and the talking dog.

It is so amazing to find that O'Rourke is serious and sophisticated about any governmental issue that it's tempting to forget the countless other issues about which he makes cheap-shot jokes. Still, the half or so of this book that is very strong shows that O'Rourke's main literary virtue is like Tom Wolfe's. That virtue is not showy writing nor glee in ridiculing leftist poseurs but a willingness to go out and look at things rather than sit home and work out bons mots. The most annoying trait of Right-Wing Outlaws in general is a lazy incuriosity about the real world. They know their lines, they're sure who the good guys and bad guys are. Therefore they view the passing world as a kind of animated *Bartlett's Quotations*—that is, as handy source material with which to illustrate, rather than challenge, preconceived views. Yes, everybody acts this way sometimes. But the very success of conservatism has made it quite complacent. When you read editorials in *The Wall Street Journal,* you sense, as with the Vatican Curia, that no conceivable event in the factual world could shake the cardinals' faith in their doctrine. One of the most successful (and funniest) current conservative outlaws, the radio talk-show host Rush Limbaugh, is happy to admit that his "research" consists of taking items off the newswire to fit his pat theories about animal rights, the Kennedy family, and so on.

P. J. O'Rourke, on the other hand, has spent a lot of time watching, listening, and apparently developing his views on the basis of what he sees and hears. The book is full of anthropological observations about the realities of daily life that make bureaucrats and reporters behave the way they do. "Numerous demonstrations, marches, PR stunts, and other staged events are held in Washington to give journalists an excuse for not covering real events, which are much harder to explain," he says. "Being in the White House press corps is essentially ceremonial. It entails—as all ceremonial roles do—ceaseless repetition, stultifying dullness, and swollen self-regard." This is not the first time such ideas have appeared in print—it's more like the 1,000th time, if you count the previous 999 mentions in this very magazine. Nonetheless, O'Rourke's view is an improvement over the usual right-wing moaning about pinko reporters.

In the same press-critic vein, O'Rourke says that "Peshawar was the principal Afghan war 'listening post,' which is journalese for 'place that's close, but not too close, to the action and has bottled water.'" This is imprecise; in reality, "listening post" means "place where at least one hotel has a bar, a swimming pool, and a staff that speaks English." Even in the inexact form, the concept will be familiar to *Washington Monthly* readers. But it is nice to see the lights going on in other parts of the political world.

FLOORED

O'Rourke's most intriguing excursion into political realities, and the one that shows most clearly how his experience as a reporter can shape his views, concerns Congress. The official conservative line about Congress, of course, is that it's a craven and unprincipled body, afraid to do anything except spend other people's money. It is easy to imagine O'Rourke writing just such a screed, especially since he includes a few of them in this book. But he also decided to see how a congressman actually spends his day. He accompanied one, whom he does not name, through a typical midweek schedule: two breakfast meetings; a hearing at 9:30 and another at 10; a baffling session on the floor; rushed meetings with constituents; cram-session briefings on a dozen issues the congressman has never heard of before but on which he must cast a vote. O'Rourke writes:

> Myself, I was completely exhausted by 7:00 and went home, leaving the congressman, 20 years my senior, looking as animated and energetic as a full school bus—shaking hands and trading chat with governors, firemen, ambulance drivers, other congressmen, and even, at one point, his own wife.

This is part of the human comedy of politics, as anyone who has seen it knows. Even those who have not seen it first hand may recognize it from James Boyd's famous "'Legislate? Who, Me?' What Happens to a Senator's Day," published in these pages 22 years ago. O'Rourke's description of Congress is impressive in several ways. He has focused on the main problem: the tyranny of the politician's schedule that barely leaves anyone time for two consecutive thoughts. He responds to and conveys the basic likability of the typical politician, however unlikable they may be as a class. While the official right-wing line, partly true, is that Congress sucks endless amounts of money into its own preservation and expansion, O'Rourke offers this semi-idealistic view:

> We Americans have struck a remarkable bargain. We pay $566,220 a year—less than a dollar apiece—for a congressman and his staff, and in return they listen to us carp and moan and fume and gripe and ask to be given things for free. Because this is, in the end, what legislators do. They listen to us. Not an enviable task.

Apart from all this, O'Rourke manages to explain the S&L fiasco with clarity, describes what it is like to go with the police on a drug raid, makes the right points about why farm programs and Social Security waste so much money, and inveighs against the American Association of Retired Persons for its greedy opposition to Medicare reform. I ended up with the wholly unanticipated feeling that, if O'Rourke went out and seriously boned up on a subject, he'd react with insight and, relatively speaking, good sense.

So what's the problem with this book? O'Rourke hasn't been as thorough in reporting every subject as he has with Social Security or the daily grind of a congressman's life. When he lacks reporting, he falls back on wisecracks and pat attitudes, and when forced to choose between making a joke and conveying a less snappy truth, he usually goes for the laugh.

A minor illustration is his relentless mockery of environmentalism. Yes, there is a pencil-neck, elitist side to the movement, but O'Rourke is pandering to Right-Wing Outlaw doctrine in sneering at the entire concept. He says:

> The average Juan and the average Mobutu out there in the parts of the world where every day is Earth Day, or Dirt and Squalor Day, anyhow, would like to have a color television, too. . . . I wouldn't care to be the skinny health-food nut waving a copy of *Fifty Simple Things You Can Do to Save the Earth* who tries to stand in Juan's way.

This sounds very hard-headed and Wolfe-like, piercing the delusions of the high-minded elite. But O'Rourke has traveled enough in the Third World to know that the average Juan and the average Mobutu are the ones whose lives are really being ruined by environmental problems. The most immediate effect of tropical deforestation, for example, is on the people in Borneo and Thailand who lose their homes and jobs and children when floods roar off denuded hills. The people who have the greatest reason to worry about air pollution are not the residents of Los Angeles but those of Mexico City and Bangkok. The average Juan does want a television and a car and name-brand tennis shoes. But environmental protection affects him in something more than the tooty-frooty way O'Rourke suggests.

The "skinny health-food nut" line represents the way O'Rourke approaches almost any issue that he hasn't gone out of his way to study. His natural instinct is to portray everyone except right-wing wiseguys as being ludicrous members of the Rainbow Coalition. The result is as fair and illuminating as if, say, Alexander Cockburn purported to describe modern Republicanism by profiling David Duke supporters in some Louisiana bayou. O'Rourke can be jolted out of the stereotypes by reporting, which is something. But he falls back into them when there's nothing else to go on.

A larger problem involves the two great pillars of right-wing orthodoxy: welfare, which is to say race, and defense. O'Rourke does not spend a lot of time on welfare, but what he does say is predictable and unconvincing. He takes the post-Charles Murray view that it's all been a mistake and that welfare, by trying too hard to "help" people, actually gives them incentives to fail. The significant point is that he seems to *take* this theory, donning it like a stylish suit, rather than developing it or testing it as he does some other concepts. His distinctive contribution to the welfare debate is to claim that he's been there himself and knows how corrupting charity can be:

My own family was poor when I was a kid, though I didn't know it; I just thought we were broke. My father died, and my mother married a drunken bum who shortly thereafter died himself. Then my mother got cancer. . . . But I honestly didn't know we were poor until just now, when I was researching poverty levels. . . . What we managed to escape in 1966 in Squaresville, Ohio, was not poverty. We had that. What we managed to escape was help.

O'Rourke goes on to say that he was saved by the stuffiness and intolerance of neighborhood values in the bad old unprogressive days. No one coddled or "understood" this distressed family. Everyone was expected simply to shut up and behave. So should it be today. Maybe I'm being unfair, but O'Rourke's recounting of this experience, which is out of character with almost everything else in the book, sounds fishy to me. It seems like a convenient, Reaganesque rendering of family history, drawn to neatly fit the current right-wing line. At the same time, it's an attempt (like Peggy Noonan's in her autobiography) to mau-mau his fellow Republicans and many Democrats: Look, don't tell me about the culture of poverty; I was part of it while you were summering in Maine. Perhaps O'Rourke is being completely sincere, and I'm the one who's being too cynical. But when Russell Baker described a very similar childhood predicament in *Growing Up,* it was impossible to doubt that it affected Baker just the way he said it did. Without announcing it directly, Baker showed that his family's misfortune in the Depression permanently altered his view of the chanciness of life. He saw some families survive and some sink for reasons that were more or less accidental. In one family, the father got sick or was laid off. In another, the father kept his health and, even more luckily in those years, kept his job. After an experience like that, it was hard for Baker to view the world with a steely, moralistic sense that people high and low fully "deserved" their stations in life.

It is possible to have such an experience and not reflect on it. Ronald Reagan, who had a truly hard-luck childhood, seemed to be more affected by his own fantasized versions of his past. But if P. J. O'Rourke, who unlike Reagan responds very acutely to experience, grew up poor, as he says, it is strange that it had no apparent effect other than to make him embrace right-wing orthodoxy about welfare programs. On the basis of this book, it did not shake his complacency about the deserving rich and undeserving poor.

MILD AT HEART

There is something more than fishy in his view of defense. If O'Rourke really wanted to be an outlaw, he'd make fun of the unending victory parades and We're-Number-One celebrations that followed the Gulf war. He takes just the opposite approach. The only budget he really likes is for the Pentagon, and he makes a little joke about it this way:

The best and final argument against cutting defense spending cannot be put into words. It's visceral, hormonal. It is that excitement in the gut, the swelling of the chest, the involuntary smile that comes across the face of every male when he has a weapon to hand.

This is a nice, roguish-sounding line. The strange thing is, as Lloyd Grove pointed out in *The Washington Post,* it was written by a man who, when he had a chance to put "weapon to hand" in Vietnam, avoided service by producing a doctor's letter saying that he used marijuana, mescaline, and LSD too often to be draftable.

P. J. O'Rourke is not the only male who is intrigued by weapons, or the only one who didn't want to go to Vietnam, or the only one for whom both statements are true. He is far from the only one, especially among the right-wing "chickenhawks," who finds the juxtaposition of these facts inconvenient now. But it is, well, shameful for O'Rourke to wisecrack his way around this subject, especially in a book saying that Americans don't take actions and their consequences seriously enough, that we live in a "well-padded little universe, a world with no sharp edges or hard surfaces."

Wisecracks and conventional wisdom are ways of avoiding the hard surfaces. In the many parts of this book that are good, O'Rourke has shown that he doesn't need to rely on these devices anymore.

Allen Randolph (review date 26 August 1991)

SOURCE: Randolph, Allen. "Right Books." *National Review* 43, no. 15 (26 August 1991): 41.

[*In the following review, Randolph asserts that* Parliament of Whores *is a provocative, insightful, and witty book.*]

Tom Wolfe, Gay Talese, Terry Southern, Joan Didion, Truman Capote, Hunter Thompson . . . P. J. O'Rourke? "New journalism" is a style popular among budding journalists because it allows the writer and his opinions to be part of whatever story he happens to be reporting. The danger is obvious: Will the author's sensibility become the whole subject of the report? Miss Didion, one feels, would find Hawaii arid and sinister. The worst excesses of this approach can be seen in the later Hunter Thompson, a psycho-babble cynicism lacking direction or credibility which inundates the reality it claims to report. At its best (early Thompson, O'Rourke) it is sharp, bold, entertaining, and even true in that it accurately depicts the intrusion of the author into a foreign situation and his reactions to it.

In Mr. O'Rourke's earlier book *Holidays in Hell,* he played the part of the U.S. tourist in the Peter Arno cartoon asking a scandalized Moslem in prayer: "Eh,

Mac, is this the way to Mecca?" In *Parliament of Whores: A Lone Humorist Attempts to Explain the Entire U.S. Government* he bursts into the Beltway with the same cheerful appallingness. The tone is set early: "The government is huge, stupid, greedy, and makes nosy, officious, and dangerous intrusions into the smallest corners of life . . ." But Mr. O'Rourke reminds us throughout that as long as we the people are munching prime pork, we had just better keep a sense of humor about things.

Mr. O'Rourke's standpoint, as the title of his first book admitted, is that of a Republican Reptile. Witness his contrasting Santa Claus and God, with the former being a Democrat and the Latter a Republican. "God," the author confides, "is an elderly or, at any rate, middle-aged male, a stern fellow, patriarchal rather than paternal and a great believer in rules and regulations. He holds men strictly accountable for their actions. . . . It is extremely difficult to get into God's heavenly club."

Santa Claus, on the other hand, is "nonthreatening. He's always cheerful. And he loves animals. He may know who has been naughty and nice, but he never does anything about it. . . . He works hard for charities, and he's famously generous to the poor. Santa Claus is preferable to God in every way but one: There is no such thing as Santa Claus."

From this unillusioned standpoint, the author gives periodic reports from two worlds: inside the Beltway, where he lived for an eternity of two years, and the real world, where he ventured to observe the consequences of government.

Take, for instance, the principle of "parity" which the U.S. Government adopted in the 1920s to ensure that farmers' goods would receive the same price in inflation-adjusted dollars as they had in 1910-1914. Sounds reasonable, even compassionate. But how does it work outside the Beltway? "If we applied the logic of parity to automobiles instead of feed and grain, a typical economy car would cost forty grand. $43,987 is what a 1910 Nash Rambler cost in 1990 dollars. And for that you got a car with 34 horsepower, no heat, no A/C, no tape deck or radio, and no windows around the front seat. If farm parity were a guiding principle of human existence we'd not only have lousy, high-priced economy cars, we'd have a total lack of civilization. When there isn't enough food, everybody has to spend all his time getting fed and nobody has a minute to invent law, architecture, or big clubs to hit cave bears over the head with. Agricultural prices have been falling, relative to the prices of other goods and services, not since the 1920s, but since the Paleolithic age. And it's a good thing. Otherwise we wouldn't grow food, we'd be food."

It would be hard to come up with sharper truths so well expressed, and in so economical a style. No congressional committee has managed even the first.

Parliament of Whores is being touted as a belly-aching good time by publicists; the very subtitle makes light of Mr. O'Rourke's efforts. Which is fine, and will probably put the book on the best-seller list. But don't expect brain candy. The author has asked too many questions and seen too much of the world to be shrugged off as a mere entertainer. The fizzing cynicism is as much a reflection of experience as a literary style.

Consider his description of a federally funded housing project: "The stairwell was a cascade of filth, a spilling of human urine and unidentifiable putrefying matter. . . . It would have cheered me up to see anything as vibrant as a rat. . . . I've been to Beirut, where people were living in holes scooped out of rubble. I've been to the Manila city dump, where people were living in holes scooped out of garbage. And I've been to villages in El Salvador where people weren't living any more because they had been shot. I've been to rioting Soweto shantytowns and besieged Gaza Strip refugee camps, and half-starved Contra outposts in the jungles of Honduras, and I've never been to a place I would less rather live than this housing project in New Jersey."

Does the truth hurt? Only when we laugh.

Daniel Wattenberg (review date September 1991)

SOURCE: Wattenberg, Daniel. Review of *Parliament of Whores,* by P. J. O'Rourke. *American Spectator* 24, no. 9 (September 1991): 36-8.

[*In the following review, Wattenberg praises O'Rourke's ability to appeal to both conservative and liberal readers, particularly with the essays in* Parliament of Whores.]

P. J. O'Rourke is taking conservatism into the exclusive after-hours clubs of American culture, places conservatives used to get turned away from because they looked too straight: the pages of *Rolling Stone* and *Vanity Fair,* the top of the bestseller lists, and the late-night talk shows. The left would love to stop this guy quick, but they haven't quite figured out how: his writing talent makes him virtually review-proof. His new book *Parliament of Whores* emerged virtually unscathed from the *New York Times Book Review* and the *Washington Post Book World,* usually killing fields for conservative intellectuals. But if his adversaries have despaired of making a dent in his literary reputation, they have tried everything else. First they tried to dismiss him. He was derided as "the Nazi jokester" in the *Nation* by Alexander Cockburn, a guy who thinks like a Stalinist and dresses like a hippie, making him a rare double anachronism. Then they tried character assassination: a year ago, *New Republic* deputy editor Andrew Sullivan excoriated him in *Esquire* as a racist and an opportunist. Of course, O'Rourke is no racist. His marriage alone is more integrated than any *New Republic* editorial meeting.

The latest challenge to O'Rourke's intellectual integrity and reputation is potentially the most dangerous: co-optation. Writing in the *Washington Monthly,* neoliberal pundit James Fallows, Washington editor of the *Atlantic Monthly,* offers a *quid pro quo*—O'Rourke can have a respectable niche in Washington, D.C., as a thorough and open-minded reporter, if only he will just stop being so funny and so conservative:

> When he lacks reporting, [O'Rourke] falls back on wisecracks and pat attitudes, and when forced to choose between making a joke and conveying a less snappy truth, he usually goes for the laugh.

While I, too, respect O'Rourke's reportorial abilities, this is a deeply retarded statement. It is like saying, "Because Doc Gooden has never perfected his pickoff move, he has to fall back on 95-mile-an-hour sternum-high fastballs and knee-buckling curves in order to get batters out."

Happily, O'Rourke has not succumbed to the siren song of co-optation. In *Parliament of Whores,* he is very funny and very conservative—more pro-military than Ed Crane and more pro-sex and -drugs and -rock 'n' roll than Pat Buchanan. (On drugs, his libertarian and conservative impulses are in conflict. Unable for now to synthesize them, he has arrived at a compromise: use drugs, conservatively.)

In the congressional chapter of *Parliament of Whores,* entitled **"National Busybodies,"** O'Rourke follows an unnamed congressman on his daily rounds. It is a grueling thirteen hours: strategy sessions, hearings, mark-ups, constituent visits, a frantic run-through of legislation with staff, a hurried perusal of outgoing mail, and, finally, two dinners on opposite sides of town. O'Rourke marvels at the politician's stamina and buoyancy:

> Myself, I was completely exhausted by 7:00 and went home, leaving the congressman, 20 years my senior, looking as animated and energetic as a full school bus—shaking hands and trading chat with governors, firemen, ambulance drivers, other congressmen, and even, at one point, his own wife.

Weekends, the congressman is back in his district doing more of the same. His staff—nine people—is not large, and his pay—$125,100 a year—is fair compensation for his exertions, "less than what a shortstop hitting .197

makes." Public outrage at the congressional pay grab and the size and cost of their staffs is unfounded. A congressman and his staff are a steal at the price:

> We Americans have struck a remarkable bargain. We pay $566,220 a year—less than a dollar apiece—for a congressman and his staff, and in return they listen to us carp and moan and fume and gripe and ask to be given things for free. Because this is, in the end, what legislators do. They listen to us. Not an enviable task.

Fallows praised this passage as an example of O'Rourke at his reportorial best. In his view, when O'Rourke takes the trouble to report a story, he confronts realities that clash with his conservative assumptions (perhaps this is why there are so few conservative reporters?). Here, according to Fallows, O'Rourke repudiates "the official conservative line" that Congress is a "craven and unprincipled body, afraid to do anything except spend other people's money." And, having left that Heritage Foundation "Backgrounder" on Congress at home, O'Rourke has successfully "focused on the main problem: the tyranny of the politician's schedule that barely leaves anyone time for two consecutive thoughts."

Interesting: when O'Rourke brings the notebook along, he not only rejects conservative doctrine, he embraces Common Causey/good government/neoliberal doctrine. If only congressmen didn't have to spend so much time politicking and raising money and schmoozing lobbyists and mixing with the masses, they would have the repose necessary for the rational, no-preconceptions, *Washington Monthly*-style policy analysis that is sure to produce wise legislation.

Neoliberals, of course, are the salon painters of public policy. Technique is everything for them, and if they've contrived to give a congressman more time to commune with himself, they figure they've done enough reforming for one day. But in trying to claim this O'Rourke piece for neoliberalism, Fallows is barking up the wrong decision tree. The piece isn't about over-scheduling; it's about over-legislating. O'Rourke writes:

> Congress meddles in every part of American life and then some. Congressional legislation reaches beyond the grave with estate taxes and back into those clouds of glory Wordsworth says we trail when it touches upon abortion issues.

O'Rourke then provides a list of the pieces of legislation that were wending through Congress the week he reported the piece. This list of twenty-five disparate items just about reaches "the limit of the human capacity for expertise," he says. "However, it is less than 10% of what we ask of a congressman." Then he gives a list of some of the 250 other items on the congressional calendar for that week.

What O'Rourke wants is not a congressman with more time to think about legislation. He wants a congressman with less legislation to think about. For neoliberals like Fallows, the size of government is of little importance; for them the key question is, "How do we make government work?" But as a limited-government conservative, O'Rourke recognizes that beyond a certain level—long since exceeded by Congress—it's hopeless. You can't make government work. So for him the question becomes, "How do you make it stop?"

In my opinion, O'Rourke overdramatizes the burdens of a congressman. A congressman has more help than the nine members of his personal staff. He has committee staff. He has subcommittee staff. He has the bureaucrats in the executive branch, whom he bosses around as if they were his staff. Re-election rates being what they are, he enjoys enviable job security. True, he makes less than the shortstop hitting .197. But congressmen crave power above money, and power they have: no shortstop, not even Ozzie Smith, has the power to subpoena me and then berate me on network TV.

But if he lets the congressman off easy, he does so for good reasons. The first is that's just the kind of guy O'Rourke is: he genuinely felt the man was overworked and underappreciated. But more importantly, he wanted to make a point that recurs throughout the book: that limited government depends on self-government. We have only ourselves to blame if government is too big. We demand way too much from our leaders and do way too little for ourselves. That's expensive and inefficient and—what's more—it's stealing. This book exposes all of us as thieves. The old steal from the young, farmers steal from urbanites, the poor steal from the rich (and the not-so-rich), consumers steal from producers (and ultimately other consumers), and, if that doesn't cover everybody, all of us who are alive are stealing from those who haven't yet been born. O'Rourke is a non-pandering populist. Because he has developed a persona that is down-to-earth and self-effacing, he is able to castigate us for our selfishness and indolence without coming across as a high-hatting policy wonk.

In **"Doing the Most Important Kind of Nothing,"** O'Rourke plays straight man to those incorrigible cut-ups: the Supreme Court justices. The piece is about how the Court defused the momentarily explosive debate about anti-flag burning laws. "I can't even remember what my own opinion was on the flag-burning issue, though I remember I had a strong one," O'Rourke writes.

There was an irony at the center of that debate. If you wanted to protect flag-burners, you had to argue that flag-burning was a meaningful, purposeful (and thus truly despicable) expression of hatred for America. If, on the other hand, you wanted to throw the book at flag-burners, you had to argue that flag-burning was kind of imprecise, didn't really mean much of anything, and hence was not constitutionally protected expression. O'Rourke exploits this irony to good effect, making the point that we Americans are a particularly faddish and emotional people, and we're damn lucky to have a Supreme Court to stop us from going off half-cocked and outlawing every form of thought and behavior we decide, for a fleeting moment, we don't like:

> There wouldn't even be any democracy to defend if our every national whim were put into law. We'd sacrifice the whole Constitution for those lost kids on milk cartons one week, and the next week we'd toss the Rights of Man out the window to help victims of date rape. That's why we—and the solicitor general and William Kunstler—have to take this guff from the Supreme Court.

"Poverty Policy: How to Endow Privation" unfolds a familiar argument—that poverty is culturally determined—in a dazzlingly original way, and comes to a conclusion that defies not only liberal orthodoxy about poverty but also two different strands of conservative orthodoxy. It's the best piece in the book. It's probably the best thing I've ever read on poverty. O'Rourke is a writer of exceptionally varied literary gifts, and all of them are on display here: aphoristic wit, a keen eye for detail, a narrative sixth gear, a foolish disregard for his own personal safety, a Menckenesque bullshit-detector, and a heartfelt kind of Dreiser-goes-to-the-South Bronx kind of urban poetry.

O'Rourke starts by "proving" statistically that there is no poverty in America: the amount of federal anti-poverty expenditure far exceeds the amount of money it would take to lift every poor person in the country above the poverty line. Of course, there *is* poverty, but (and here he follows the conservative line) you can't solve it by throwing money at it. Then, leafing through some old and yellowed poverty statistics, he learns that his own family was officially "poor" when he was a teenager in Ohio in the mid-sixties. Funny, they never *felt* poor. They lived in a four-bedroom house, had a power mower and a Buick, and his sisters spent their time frugging to the Dave Clark Five. And, while it would be overstating the case to say the O'Rourke family was "Glad All Over," their tidy surroundings were a far cry from the squalor O'Rourke glimpsed on the staircase of a Newark housing project. How do you have an income below the poverty line and a life above it? O'Rourke identifies the *x* factor:

> It was a narrow, stuffy, priggish world and deaf to excuses. . . . And it was a world that punished not only anti-social behavior but any deviation from the norm. My mom was not guaranteed housing by being a single mother; it almost lost her the house. A live-in boyfriend would have been out of the question for a

woman who worked as a secretary at the board of education and was a member of the Monroe Street Methodist Church. . . . I wasn't given counseling for my drug use or put in a therapy program with sympathetic peers. I was threatened with loss of my scholarship, expulsion from college, arrest, and maybe even having to find a job. . . . Where I grew up you didn't have a chance to live in poverty; you couldn't afford it.

What's missing in the housing projects and the crackhouses is the Harper Valley PTA. Hunt's Point is the nadir of O'Rourke's crack-house tour of New York:

There are parts of Hunt's Point where the actual majority of the residents are drugged to the eyes. Hunt's Point doesn't look much worse than other lousy neighborhoods, but the people do—dirty, skinny, disordered base-heads yelling at each other and us and people who aren't there. American slums are usually stylish. . . . But in the crack neighborhoods people are still wearing whatever they happened to have on at the moment the crack craze hit.

It's beyond bleak, because conventional answers, even conventional conservative answers, won't work. Jack Kemp won't get you there (O'Rourke expounds on the virtues of tenant management and ownership to a tenant in a New Jersey project, and the lady just keeps repeating, "I'm not going for any of that"). Neither will Bill Bennett (O'Rourke not only doubts the efficacy of arrests—he even questions whether certain drugs should be illegal). Neither will Nancy Reagan (O'Rourke quotes Guardian Angels leader Curtis Sliwa: "There's plenty of education. Everybody knows drugs are bad").

Social mores have to be enforced, and in the slums that means the Guardian Angels and "slamming and jamming." Introducing his informative and hair-raising account of a Guardian Angels raid, he explains that the Angels are more than bodyguards for little old ladies:

What Sliwa and his men intended to do was wreck the crack house—break everything breakable, rough up the patrons and take their drugs and money. The Guardian Angels call it slamming and jamming. The purpose is to show the flag of decency, to destroy the permissive atmosphere of the inner city and to provide, by main strength of hand, the social opprobrium missing in the slums. The Guardian Angels are trying to enforce the kind of propriety, the mores, that were usual in American society, at every income level, twenty-five years ago. . . . But modern society has become so lawless and screwy that the Guardian Angels have had to start a street gang to teach people decorum.

Since O'Rourke has been criticized (Fallows again) for falling back on pat conservative remedies, it's worth asking whether the Angels are a "conservative" answer. Law-and-order conservatives generally rely on police powers (more arrests, tougher sentences, walking the due-process cat back to 1965) for answers to the drugs/poverty/crime tangle. While they aren't opposed to Angels-style community-based action, they have been slow to grasp its importance. So it's unfair to say O'Rourke is a prisoner of conservative doctrine in this area—I think he's in its vanguard.

The account of the Angels is an example of the high-adventure reporting on wild, violent, unfathomably different places that O'Rourke has made his own. There is less of that in this book than in his *Holidays in Hell,* and I found myself missing it. But a book about Washington and public policy and ideas will inevitably be more sedate than one about murder and mayhem in the Third World. His humor, too, is evolving into something more cerebral and sophisticated. Books like *Modern Manners* and *Republican Party Reptile* bore some traces of *National Lampoon* humor (O'Rourke used to edit it)—stuff one rung up the humor ladder from barf-and-booger jokes. These vestiges have largely disappeared, and O'Rourke seems to have found a balance that will win him *Public Interest* readers without alienating his *Rolling Stone* faithful.

Anthony Quinn (review date 13 September 1991)

SOURCE: Quinn, Anthony. "Gas Guzzlers." *New Statesman and Society* 120, no. 4050 (13 September 1991): 37-8.

[*In the following review, Quinn offers a laudatory review of* Parliament of Whores.]

P J O'Rourke's last book of raving reportage, *Holidays in Hell,* constituted one of the most persuasive arguments on record for not living abroad. In his new treatise, the one-time Republican Party reptile fixes a hard basilisk stare on home, and presents an equally persuasive argument for not living in America. *Parliament of Whores* takes government as its theme, and if you're flummoxed by the Byzantine complexities of the American political system, don't worry—so is P J. As he warns in the preface, he will venture any enquiry into all that is wrong with it: "But I do so in the full knowledge that, if I go down in the basement and start fooling around with the gas furnace, I may blow up the house."

As O'Rourke likes to remind us, America is the richest and most powerful nation on earth, so how did it end up in such a goddawful mess? The book looks no further for an answer than to that moronic, incompetent, interfering, greedy and perfidious behemoth known as democracy, and it is the reader's privilege to ride shotgun as P J goes on the road to watch it in action.

First stop is the presidential election of 1988, and the dispiriting sight of Bush slugging it out with Dukakis: "How, in God's name, did we wind up with these two quibbledicks vying for helicopter rides on the South

Lawn?" Certainly not through either's oratorical gifts or personal dynamism, qualities notably absent in just about every other senator and congressman P J encounters. Then we're back on the trail to an inaugural jamboree at the White House, the sudden and mysterious apotheosis of George Bush, and an outbreak of flag-waving optimism not seen since, well, since the last presidential inauguration.

Optimism about government, unfortunately, has the approximate shelf-life of a pint of milk. Once the Bush administration grinds into action, P J is on hand to examine all the ways in which democracy makes life as tedious, difficult and unsatisfactory as possible. Take bureaucracy, for example, and the Traffic Administration's handling of the "unintended acceleration" controversy. For years, people had been claiming that their automobiles took off at high speed for no reason. Now, to you, me and P J this sounds like some klutz stepping on the gas instead of the brake—speeding, in a word; but no, the government commissions a huge report on "sudden-acceleration incidents", the findings of which point not to the culpability of an Audi 5000 but—hey!—"drive pedal misapplication". The report is funded, of course, by the taxpayer, and P J is one taxpayer who's pretty annoyed at forking out for this sort of idiocy.

A great many things annoy P J. The Federal Budget, welfare sponging, agricultural policy, defence, drug control, the ecology movement—these things don't just get up his nose, they pinch from his wallet too. O'Rourke enjoys notoriety as a Republican tub-thumper, but the only party he really cares for is the sort that goes on all night. His line is essentially *laissez-faire,* a libertarian credo that might run, "As long as no one interferes with my enjoyment of drugs and drink and doing what I like, then government can go hang (and stop squeezing me for taxes)."

Should you require a serious inquisition into US governance, give yourself a break and read this terrifically unserious one. I became a laughter-stricken pest who quoted paragraphs to anyone who would listen. You have to admire a man for the way he disposes of US$500 billion. "Five hundred billion dollars is enough money to pay for a New York City cab ride from Earth to the planet Uranus and back ten times, including tip (unless the driver spots you for a tourist and takes you via New York City's Belt Parkway)."

James Bowman (review date 27 September 1991)

SOURCE: Bowman, James. "The Politicians They Deserve." *Times Literary Supplement,* no. 4617 (27 September 1991): 31.

[*In the following review, Bowman contrasts* Parliament of Whores *with Alan Ehrenhalt's* The United States of Ambition.]

Alan Ehrenhalt in *The United States of Ambition* and P. J. O'Rourke in **Parliament of Whores** have set out to explain, in unorthodox fashion, how politics in the United States works. It happens that they are exact contemporaries (both were born in 1947); and in each book we see a political science born of a sense of alienation from the political process which was felt by so many of the "baby-boom" generation in the late 1960s and early 70s, and which has been fermenting for more than twenty years now. Although Ehrenhalt's book is meant to be serious, and O'Rourke's funny and satirical, both are concerned to advertise the consequences for democracy of Americans' appointing professionals to do their governing for them. The native democratic tradition which did so much to energize the protests of the 1960s is now being heard from again.

Its message, however, is ambiguous. Ehrenhalt and O'Rourke are now too individualistic to be 1960s-style protesters, and the progress of individualism is part of what each records. Ehrenhalt discovers that in the twenty years or so since he came of age, the political process in America, even at state and local levels, has come to be dominated by a class of careerist politicians, who have never held any other jobs and whose loyalties are to themselves and their ambitions rather than to a political party or an agenda. O'Rourke's 1960s-style anarcho-hippyism has given way to a more considered libertarian mistrust of all government, but his targets are primarily the same politicians whose generic make-up it is Ehrenhalt's purpose to describe.

They are, principally, Democrats, and it is one of the virtues of Ehrenhalt's book that he offers such a convincing explanation of why Americans persist in electing Republicans to the presidency and Democrats to everything else. It is because the presidential elections are so highly visible to the electorate. In a nation whose appetite for public affairs is limited both by romantic ideology and by bad education, it takes the massive exposure associated with the quadrennial election of the great priest-king to break through, however feebly, the massive opacity of American thinking about political issues.

Such a breakthrough is necessary for ideology (among the more sophisticated) and symbolism (among the less sophisticated) really to come into play. And ideologically and symbolically, the Republicans tend to have the advantage. At the local level, however, people have little to judge by except the personal plausibility of the candidate. In state and local elections, what counts is professionalism. According to Ehrenhalt:

> Once we drop beneath the level of presidential politics, there is no reason to believe that voters are trying to tell us much of anything. They are responding in an essentially passive way to the choices placed in front of them. The best candidates and the best campaigns win.

It is not really a matter of demand. It is a matter of supply. Over the past two decades, in most constituencies in America, Democrats have generated the best supply of talent, energy, and sheer political ambition. Under those circumstances it has not been crucial for them to match the opinions of the electorate on most of the important national issues of the day.

This supply-side theory of American politics is one with which O'Rourke, who really is very funny, is instinctively in sympathy. Temperamentally radical himself, he is both attracted and repelled by the fate of romantic radicalism in the contemporary United States. As he says of Jesse Jackson:

> Here was this firebrand, this radical, this leader of an alienated and angry minority. And was he in jail? Was he in exile? Was he dead? He certainly would have been one of the three in any other nation-state in history. But, no. He was being absorbed whole—daft notions, vexed supporters and all—by the largest political organization in the United States. He was turning into a pol, another spoils-mongering highbinder and wire-puller, one more bum on the plush. And this was heartwarming.

Of course, he is wrong about the uniqueness of "our orthodoxy of co-option", but his view of it makes the romantic nostalgia for a purer sort of native radicalism coexist with a love for the "heartwarming" blandness of democracy's domestication of ambition.

Something of the same ambivalence is to be found in Ehrenhalt. There is a kind of nostalgia for the old days of citizen legislators, and even for machine politics, in his descriptions of their supersession by what he rather confusingly calls the politics of ambition. In the days—only a few years ago—when state legislatures met for a few weeks annually, the representatives of the people were part-time public servants. Now in most of the larger states they are not only full-time professionals themselves, but they also employ one or two unelected professional assistants each. Congressmen in Washington have whole staffs of assistants.

No one, except perhaps the congressmen, can be very happy about this state of affairs, but it is also difficult to feel terribly indignant about it. Even O'Rourke has kind words to say about congressional staffs, pointing out that a congressman and nine assistants to service a constituency of, on average, 600,000 is not exorbitant. In fact, it is "a remarkable bargain".

> We pay $566,220 a year—less than a dollar apiece—for a congressman and his staff, and in return they listen to us carp and moan and fume and gripe and ask to be given things for free. Because this is, in the end, what legislators do. They listen to us. Not an enviable task.

As an example, he tells us of one congressman who kept getting letters from a constituent claiming that the CIA was using microwave radiation to read his mind.

At last he wrote back suggesting that the man line his hat with tinfoil. This seemed to satisfy him, and he has not been heard from since.

Ehrenhalt's interest in the legislative assistants is that it is from their ranks, and not from the laity, that new political candidates are now being recruited. The business of being a candidate is a complicated one and a hard trade to learn. This political professionalism has naturally been much harder on the Republicans, the party of limited government, than the more politically activist Democrats. People who believe in the power of government to do good are those most likely to make politics a profession and, as Ehrenhalt shows, a sort of political Gresham's Law has been in operation for the past forty years, by which the professional politician has driven the amateur out.

But neither Ehrenhalt nor the voters can bring themselves to miss the amateur very much. The latter, uninterested in ideology and too busy getting on with life to acquaint themselves with "the issues", will vote for the most plausible and well-packaged candidate, who is nearly always the most professional and experienced in modern techniques of vote-getting. Such a candidate is most likely a Democrat who has never had a non-political job; Republicans of the same age and education tend to have sought the rewards of business or private law practice, which afford a much better living.

It seems a fair trade-off: you get to choose money or power, but not both. O'Rourke, again, notices the same phenomenon:

> When you looked at the Republicans, you saw the scum off the top of business. When you looked at the Democrats, you saw the scum off the top of politics. Personally, I prefer business. A businessman will steal from you directly instead of getting the IRS to do it for him. And when Republicans ruin the environment, destroy the supply of affordable housing and wreck the industrial infrastructure, at least they make a buck off it. The Democrats just do these things for fun.

Except that it is not much fun for anyone else. O'Rourke, no less than Ehrenhalt, points to the real reason for the success of the professional politician:

> The government is huge, stupid, greedy and makes nosy, officious and dangerous intrusions into the smallest corners of life—this much we can stand. But the real problem is that government is boring. We could cure or mitigate the other ills Washington visits on us if we could only bring ourselves to pay attention to Washington itself. But we cannot.

So we hire the professionals who look as if they know what the arcana of government are all about to look after an institution we dislike but despair of reforming—which is essentially Ehrenhalt's conclusion. In his final chapter, O'Rourke develops this idea further to conclude that the boredom is a kind of camouflage for the invariably immoral political enterprise of forging a majority to vote in favour of dispossessing some minority. Even in that most democratic of institutions, a New Hampshire town meeting, this is what is going on: robbery masked by tedium: "It is the opposite of a mob or a riot, the flip side of human collective behaviour. Taking part in a New England town meeting is like being a cell in a plant."

It is this observation which leads him on to the conclusion that although "government is a parliament of whores" who will do anything for power, "in a democracy the whores are us". The characteristically libertarian view meshes surprisingly easily with Ehrenhalt's that "It does not make very much difference to the outcome of elections . . . what either of the two major parties thinks about the vital issues of the day. What matters most, as I have argued throughout this book, is ambition." But it is the ambition of those who share the values of their generation, which are, according to Ehrenhalt, equality, individualism and openness. "For all our ignorance as voters and inattentiveness as citizens we have a politics that is, in the end, appropriate to its time and place."

Both Ehrenhalt's and O'Rourke's conclusions strike me as banalities. But the banalities are of their generation as much as the politics. The love of individualism and openness that they share (O'Rourke is not so happy about equality) seems to give them few choices between revolutionary nihilism and complacency. Both choose complacency with easy appeals to "appropriateness" or the universally acknowledged shortcomings of human nature (or democracy). It is a characteristic pose. Nobody much likes the system we've got, but everybody is thankful for the relative peace and prosperity it has brought us.

Tom Wolfe has said that the appeal of Andy Warhol to those who came of age in the 1960s was that he allowed them to carry on their love-affair with consumerism while at the same time mocking and feeling superior to it. That state of emotional paralysis seems to me to be also a good description of these two authors' approaches to American politics. For both the pursuit and exercise of power are something to be watched like a television programme which both entertains them with its bizarre hypocrisies and depresses them with its vulgarity. Either way, they might as well enjoy it because there is nothing they can do about it.

Chris Goodrich (essay date 16 March 1992)

SOURCE: Goodrich, Chris. "P. J. O'Rourke: Shrewd Observation of the Contemporary Scene Informs His Irreverent Humor." *Publishers Weekly* 239, no. 14 (16 March 1992): 60-1.

[*In the following essay, Goodrich discusses O'Rourke's background, political ideology, and major themes.*]

P. J. O'Rourke, the man who once said he likes to "get drunk and drive like a fool," who described Walt Whitman as "a self-obsessed ratchet-jaw with an ear like a tin cookie sheet," who believes U.S. culture is "a spectacular triumph of the blah," who has called for a "new McCarthyism" and created a personal "enemies list" that includes Casey Kasem, Berkeley, Sting, the *Nation,* the Maryknoll order of nuns and Salman Rushdie ("Kick 'em when they're down is what I say"), is a typical American. Really. "I'm a quarter Irish, a quarter English, a quarter German, and a quarter French Canadian," O'Rourke tells us, "which happens to be the absolutely typical mix of an American. It's not a majority, but it's the statistically most likely mix for an American to have."

O'Rourke has mentioned his lineage in the course of explaining both his growing popularity—**Parliament of Whores,** his last book, was still on *PW*'s [*Publishers Weekly*'s] bestseller list after 30-odd weeks, far outstripping his previous titles—and the genesis of his political conservatism. And he's quite serious about being a typical American, for although O'Rourke may be quicker to find humor in a situation than the average citizen, regardless of political leanings, he believes his background provides a perspective on current affairs with which many Americans agree. His father was a car salesman in Toledo, Ohio, O'Rourke explains, "and we lived in the '50s version of suburbia—houses with lawns inside the city limits, like a working-class *Leave It to Beaver.* It was an utterly ordinary, middle-America sort of upbringing, and one with no regionalism other than the tendency to put an intrusive *r* into 'Washington, D.C.' And I also come at the very crest of the baby boom, so in terms of age, ethnic background, geographical background, my reference points are likely to be shared by a lot of Americans, probably even a majority. All that gives me a sense of confidence that when I refer to something, a lot of people are going to understand that reference."

And O'Rourke does seem confident this day, though hardly the vulgar, brash jingoist that he sometimes presents himself to be in his writing. He is wearing a white shirt, patterned red tie, yellow-striped suspenders, and the slacks from a dark, conservative suit, and the ensemble—complete with the occasional Nobel Petit cigarillo, "a knock-off of the far more expensive Davidoff"—seems more appropriate to Wall Street than a self-proclaimed Republican Party Reptile. But then O'Rourke is a writer in transition, at 44 less interested in guns, drugs and alcohol ("I only had two martinis last night," he says) than he was during the 1970s, when he served as a principal editor of the *National Lampoon,* and the early '80s, when he began to freelance and, for a time, write screenplays. He is no longer the right wing's answer to Hunter S. Thompson, in short, but a serious reporter who happens to be funny, a political commentator less dependent on gags and more astute in observation as time goes by.

O'Rourke denies, however, that there have been substantive changes in his conservative outlook on life—a credible self-assessment, considering that in recent years the world has changed in ways that leave O'Rourke smiling. Although he still travels the globe chronicling civil unrest for *Rolling Stone,* which first published most of the articles in his forthcoming Atlantic Monthly title, *Give War a Chance: Eyewitness Accounts of Mankind's Struggle Against Tyranny, Injustice, and Alcohol-Free Beer* (Nonfiction Forecasts, Feb. 17), O'Rourke has found himself writing with unexpected regularity about the triumph of Western ideals. Yes, O'Rourke admits, he really did cry upon seeing an East German border guard reach through the Berlin Wall as it was being dismantled in 1989 to ask for a chip as a souvenir. "I was very affected," O'Rourke says. "You know, any time you scratch a humorist you find sentimental mush."

O'Rourke—the P. J. stands for Patrick Jake—has come a long way from Toledo, now dividing his time between an apartment in Washington, D.C., and a 60-acre property in New Hampshire, both of which he shares with his wife, Amy Lumet (daughter of movie director Sidney Lumet and granddaughter of singer Lena Horne), whom he married in 1990. The trajectory of his career has not been particularly unusual, but it hasn't been ordinary, either: he graduated from Miami University of Ohio, then earned an M.A. at Johns Hopkins while on a writing fellowship. He joined *National Lampoon* in 1973, not long after the offices of the left-wing Baltimore paper for which he had been writing were occupied by a radical group calling itself the Balto Cong, planting second thoughts about liberal politics in O'Rourke's mind. O'Rourke says now that between the '50s and the '80s he went from Republican to Maoist and back again.

O'Rourke is in New York to speak at a PEN/AAP seminar concerning midlist writers who have "broken out" to a mass audience, but *PW* is most interested in hearing him talk about *Give War a Chance,* one of the first books to contain an eyewitness account of the Gulf war. It's the fourth book O'Rourke has written for the Atlantic Monthly Press. (The previous titles are *Holidays in Hell* [1988], *Republican Party Reptile* [1987] and *Parliament of Whores*—and soon all of his titles will be available from the press.) In 1989 Atlantic Monthly publisher Morgan Entrekin reissued an updated version of O'Rourke's first book, *Modern Manners*—"the bad etiquette book," says O'Rourke, "you can take that as you will"—which Entrekin initially published at Dell in 1983, and last year he acquired the rights to *The Bachelor Home Companion,* first published by Pocket in 1987.

O'Rourke started writing for *Rolling Stone* in 1981, soon after leaving *National Lampoon,* and he now bears the distinguished title of foreign affairs desk chief. *Rolling Stone* has become a happy base of operations, O'Rourke says, because it has given him "the freedom to write in my own style, to be able to express all those emotions, and never have to pretend to a journalistic omniscience—that great lie of objectivity." It doesn't hurt, either, that the magazine has long published Tom Wolfe and Hunter Thompson, whom O'Rourke counts as major influences . . . though he is careful to distinguish himself from the latter, to whom he is frequently compared. "Hunter and I are almost diametrically opposed in what we do," says O'Rourke. "He takes a unique sensibility and uses it with very ordinary events—a police convention in Las Vegas, interviews with sports figures. I'm just the opposite: I take a very conventional, middle-aged, Midwestern sensibility to very peculiar places—busting crack dens, strange countries where people are shooting each other for semi-unintelligible reasons." A further difference, O'Rourke says, thinking of the drug and alcohol consumption for which Thompson is still known, is that "Hunter's got an amazing constitution. I do not."

Violence and other forms of civil strife may seem odd grist for a humorist's mill, but O'Rourke resolves the apparent contradiction. "Humor is a terrific tool for explaining things," he says, "especially when what you're explaining is frightening or dull and complicated." "Frightening" clearly applies to most of O'Rourke's foreign-affairs topics, and "dull and complicated" to the entangled bureaucracies of Washington—a place O'Rourke still regards as something of a foreign country—depicted in *Parliament of Whores.* "All humor really is," he continues, "is distance on something; anything's funny from afar, and everything's pretty sad close up. All a humorist does is try to put things in perspective, and say, 'Well, look, in the long run, we're all dead.'" Humor, he says, is "just what I'm good at, and I'm not even that good at it."

Through humor, moreover, O'Rourke can write about subjects that border on the unspeakable, often by taking on a persona that's only a slight exaggeration of his everyday self. "When I'm doing these stories where people are getting hurt, murdered, where there's actual tragedy," he says, "it's important to have comic relief, and a fool is very useful for that. And I use myself as that fool—not that I'm not a fool, it's certainly an accurate persona in that respect—by making myself seem a little more ignorant of the situation than I actually am." O'Rourke has sometimes gotten in trouble for that sort of facetiousness: covering election riots in South Korea in 1987, he wrote that he found himself thinking, "Oh no, they *really do* look alike." O'Rourke says now that "Martians probably wouldn't be able to distinguish among races" on this planet, adding, "Packs of people called and said, '[Koreans] look more alike even than that!'"

O'Rourke, who covered the conflict in the Persian Gulf for both *Rolling Stone* and ABC Radio, found the experience to be at once more difficult and less frightening than previous assignments in such hot spots as Korea, the Philippines and Lebanon. What made it difficult was the fact that the recent war, as O'Rourke puts it, "was not a terribly absurd situation. I thought what we did was necessary and wise and good, and that made it perhaps a bit harder for me to use some of my usual tricks. Some of the stuff I did is really heartfelt, and I'm a little embarrassed. For instance, I was really upset when that Scud missile hit the barracks in Dhahran, and I haven't written many serious things in my life. You can get very emotionally involved in something like this, which is the exact opposite of the distance of humor, and there's an awful lot of writing about war—even by the very best people, A. J. Liebling, Ernie Pyle—that is kind of cornball when you read it now. I'm not sure I'm very good at that sort of thing; it worries me."

Eventually, needless to say, O'Rourke did discover a full complement of absurdities in the Gulf. The lack of alcohol, for one thing, which O'Rourke says caused him to lose 10 pounds and meant a complete absence of male bonding in the press corps. For another, the greater competition for news—no doubt one side effect of sobriety, but more directly linked, O'Rourke says, to "the incredible restrictions the Army put on access to information. People were constantly fighting each other to be in on this or that circumvention of the rules, keeping secrets from each other even within organizations. It was an ugly atmosphere, as always when you've got more reporters on hand than news. It was a positive relief to get into Kuwait, where everything was a total mess and you could do what you wanted."

And in Kuwait the Gulf war finally became frightening. "That was hazardous," says O'Rourke of the initial ground assault, "more probably because of accidents than land mines. And when we got into Kuwait City, in the middle of the night, the Kuwaiti resistance was running around—mostly kids with guns. I did nearly get blown up in a booby trap on the top of the hotel"—by a box of rocket-propelled grenades that had been wired. "But I'd say the most nervous time was when I drove up to cover the carnage on Mutlaa Ridge, where the American airplanes had blown up all those people," O'Rourke says. "Getting there and back you had to go through mine fields, and though a path had been swept, it had been poorly marked, and there were shifting sands. People are forever using that metaphor—'like walking through a mine field'? Well, walking, or in this case driving, through a mine field really does concentrate the mind."

O'Rourke punctuates all his stories with a loud guffaw, and he reserves the largest of these for what proved to be his most dangerous task during the Gulf war, right at

its conclusion—broadcasting radio spots from Kuwait City. "We had to go up on the hotel roof because that's where the satellite dishes were," he recalls, "and there was happy fire slamming down"—bullets coming to earth at terminal velocity after being shot skyward by the joyful victors. "That was scary. That was the only time in the whole war I wore a helmet and a flak jacket—up on the fucking roof of the hotel when the war was over!" Is it any wonder, given this particular experience with the outbreak of peace, that O'Rourke wants to give war a chance?

Danny Goldberg (review date 22 June 1992)

SOURCE: Goldberg, Danny. "Hip Con." *Nation* 259, no. 24 (22 June 1992): 866-68.

[*In the following review, Goldberg rejects the notion that O'Rourke is both hip and conservative (finding the two things mutually exclusive) and calls him a juvenile yet effective propagandist for the conservative movement.*]

The day John Lennon died he gave a radio interview in which he ridiculed a type of sixties activist who had turned sour on activism a decade later: "We're just gonna play rock and roll and not do anything else," said Lennon, impersonating a disillusioned hippie, whining like a spoiled child. "We're gonna stay in our rooms, and the world is a nasty horrible place 'cause it didn't give us everything we cried for." P. J. O'Rourke has fashioned a successful career pandering to the selfishness and alienation of the kind of people Lennon was describing. What Norman Podhoretz was to fiftysomething Jewish intellectuals who wanted a rationale for their romance with the Reagan Administration, O'Rourke has become for baby boomers in search of justification for apathy or Republicanism.

The title of O'Rourke's *Give War a Chance* (which reached number one on the *New York Times* nonfiction best-seller list for several weeks in May) mocks Lennon's famous antiwar anthem. As a stylist O'Rourke is a Hunter Thompson wannabe who uses four-letter words, rock and roll references, first-person wisecracks and pseudo-free association as packaging for stark Social Darwinism. Much of *Give War a Chance* and last year's best seller, *Parliament of Whores*, originally appeared as articles in *Rolling Stone*.

A typical chapter is titled: **"Our Government: What the Fuck Do They Do All Day and Why Does It Cost So Goddamned Much Money?"** Although his *Give War a Chance* book jacket describes him portentously as "the preeminent political humorist of our time," O'Rourke's favorite form of "satire" is name-calling.

Homeless activists are "angry black poverty pests." Liberals are the "giveaway and guilt bunch" or "the kind of creepy misfits who join mass movements." Social Security recipients are "fuddy-duddies and mossbacks." Environmentalists are "neo-hippie-dips . . ., sentimentality-crazed iguana anthropomorphizers" and "Chicken Littles." William Kunstler has "eyebrows the size of squirrels . . . [and is] wearing a hobo literature-professor-type suit no doubt carefully pre-rumpled at the special Pinko Dry Cleaner and Valet." O'Rourke refers to meeting a "dandruffy waiter" in Kiev and describes Americans in Nicaragua as "big, homely . . . American girls in stained T-shirts and dweeby little chicken-necked American boys in ripped jeans."

Juvenile though he is, O'Rourke is an effective propagandist with astute insight into the dark side of the id of the sixties generation. Like his hero, the late Republican chairman Lee Atwater, O'Rourke has a passion for the negative. His style becomes dry and dull when he describes his purported enthusiasms such as the Gulf War, to which he devotes several chapters written from Saudi Arabia. His writing comes alive only when de-legitimizing liberalism. In his latest book he actually compiles an "enemies" list of liberals who he says represent what is worst in America, under the rubric **"A Call for a New McCarthyism"** (the list includes, needless to say, *The Nation*).

Baby-boom neocons do not want to feel guilty, so propagandists like O'Rourke cannot brazenly suggest enrichment of 1 percent at the expense of the other 99 percent, or comfort for the middle-aged at the expense of their children and parents. His pitch, like that of conservative talk-radio superstar Rush Limbaugh, is that nothing else works except an unobstructed free market. Government doesn't work, liberalism doesn't work, compassion doesn't work. He "proves" this by attending a session of Congress, spending an hour at the Supreme Court, going to an Earth Day march and to a march for the homeless, to a housing project in Newark and to other "left" events and quoting the shallowest and most inane remarks he can hear. This is the intellectual equivalent of judging modern conservatism by the people who attend David Duke and Pat Buchanan rallies, but O'Rourke's faux-gonzo style has led some critics to excuse his distortions as mere "irreverence."

If yuppies actually believe O'Rourke's caricature of liberalism, they can delude themselves into believing they are decent citizens even as they contribute to the deterioration of society. This philosophy is summarized in the preface to *Parliament of Whores* in his glib distinction between the major parties, **"Why God Is a Republican and Santa Claus Is a Democrat."** God, according to O'Rourke, "holds men strictly accountable

for their actions" and "has little apparent concern for the material well-being of the disadvantaged." Santa Claus, on the other hand, "gives everyone everything they want without thought of a quid pro quo" and "is preferable to God in every way but one: There is no such thing as Santa Claus." Evidently O'Rourke would have his readers believe that there are also no such things as interstate highways, Medicare, post offices, police departments, etc. The God that O'Rourke believes in will rely on the "free market" to restrain polluters and is totally unconcerned about teaching children to read if they are unable to afford private school. The Santa Claus metaphor makes O'Rourke more of a mutant neo-Calvinist than a neoconservative. His logic should reject George Bush's "thousand points of light" as a privatized version of fairy tales. His readers, in other words, are encouraged to believe that not only are taxes counterproductive but so is charity. As the Church Lady says on *Saturday Night Live,* how convenient.

In *Give War a Chance,* O'Rourke directly confronts the source of all baby-boomer liberal evil under the title **"What I Believed in the Sixties."** In the list that follows he begins with the word: "Everything," followed by a litany of absurdities that no one actually believed: that "Mao was cute. . . . [that] Lyndon Johnson was plotting to murder all the Negroes. . . . [that] wearing my hair long would end poverty and injustice. . . . [that] my parents were Nazi space monsters." He follows this by disclosing **"What Caused Me to Have Second Thoughts."** O'Rourke worked for an underground newspaper in Baltimore and a Maoist group attacked the paper and held the staff hostage overnight. He ends with **"What I Believe Now: Nothing."** He hastens to reassure the reader that he does in fact believe in "Western civilization," and then quotes the opening lines of the Declaration of Independence as if they somehow contradicted the civil rights and antiwar movements of the sixties.

Of course this is really an elaborate rationalization for the kind of narcissism spoofed by the comedian who determines his politics based on "what's good for me—Al Franken." The truth about O'Rourke is that he was probably attracted to liberal ideas in the sixties when mouthing progressive phrases was the best way to meet girls and to work your way into the media through the alternative press. His second thoughts probably came around the time that Ronald Reagan was elected and conservatism represented access to power and money. His current beliefs are designed to get more access to more power and more money.

Ultimately, however, it is a stretch to be both hip and conservative. O'Rourke sycophantically rhapsodizes about the r&b music at George Bush's inaugural ball: "The president of the United States—a Republican president—is going to be pulled up on stage by Sam Moore of Sam and Dave." O'Rourke climaxes: "When President Bush entered the auditorium, no one played 'Hail to the Chief.' Instead, the 1967 Bar-Keys instrumental 'Soul Finger' had been chosen as the presidential theme." (As it happens, the name of the group is the Bar-Kays.) O'Rourke inadvertently reveals how much ass he must kiss when he calls Lee Atwater's guitar playing "excellent." One listen to Atwater's vanity album will convince even the most casual *Rolling Stone* reader that the guy couldn't have gotten a job in a bar band unless his father owned the bar.

For progressive to thrive in the nineties, it is not enough to despise O'Rourke as much as he despises us. The reasons his books sell so well include the fact that few political thinkers on the left bother to speak the language of popular culture, or speak to the distinctive set of cultural and political dramas that baby-boomers have experienced. The image of George Bush and Lee Atwater posing with electric guitars next to real musicians was designed to do the same thing that O'Rourke is trying to do: make conservatism palatable to rock fans. Forget that if George Bush's vote on the 1964 Civil Rights Act had prevailed, Sam Moore still wouldn't be allowed in the same bathroom as P. J. Forget that Bush was head of the Republican Party when Richard Nixon's Justice Department tried to get John Lennon thrown out of the country. Forget that Bush's first "drug czar," William Bennett, said the Woodstock festival was one of the most evil events in modern history, and that the new drug czar, Bob Martinez, is the guy who as Governor of Florida boasted that his policies caused Luther Campbell of 2 Live Crew to be taken to jail in handcuffs, while white pornographers in the same neighborhood went untouched. Forget all these things and everything you ever believed in, because caring about them is for losers and suckers. Smoke pot if you want to, take care of your own and to hell with everybody else. This is O'Rourke's not very subtle subtext, and he is as hip as Jesse Helms.

Charles H. Zwicker (review date summer 1992)

SOURCE: Zwicker, Charles H. Review of *Parliament of Whores,* by P. J. O'Rourke. *Presidential Studies Quarterly* 22, no. 3 (summer 1992): 581.

[*In the following review, Zwicker provides a mixed assessment of* Parliament of Whores.]

This [*Parliament of Whores*] is a humorous book about a very serious subject. It would be even more amusing if the subject were not quite so serious. However, even though the writer legitimately hits some raw nerves, more often than not he tends to overkill.

Exhibiting conservative libertarian views, O'Rourke nevertheless mirrors the attitude of the Woodstock Generation, the unlamented Sixties and a style of writing he has used as a correspondent for Rolling Stone magazine. It is this combination which reflects his opinion of the current economic and government dilemma.

He covers the whole gamut of government from the primaries and the political conventions through to the Congress, the Presidency and the Supreme Court. He applies his jaundiced (although funny) pen to the drug, agricultural and foreign policies, the plight of the farmers, the old, and even the savings and loan crisis. There is little the reader can disagree with to too great a degree because we are aware of the deficiencies, but again he carries it in many instances too far, although this is muted by an enveloping humor. Criticism is everywhere, but few recommendations for improvements are suggested.

Calling President Jimmy Carter a "pathetic coot" is irresponsible and downright sophomoric. Carter is considered by friends and foes alike to have been one of the brainiest and hardest-working men in the White House. Other public figures, holding responsible jobs, are personally described in an unflattering manner beyond the usual restraints of professional criticism. Calling an ex-President's wife a "tomato", a wife of a Vice President a "Cape Buffalo" and referring gleefully to the harmless foibles of others in or near public life is unnecessary, especially since in his preface he promised to keep the book "reasonably" free of personalities.

He writes very well, keeps his audience interested and amused, but too frequently his language becomes course to a degree unbecoming a writer of his linguistic abilities. At best it is excessive but it may titillate the readers and surely it has helped it become a best seller in the popular market. The book is not enhanced by its inclusion.

Yet, despite this criticism, this book is a worthwhile effort which can be recommended to the serious student of government who possibly may even benefit from the humor.

The gist of his message is that the non-voting, and especially the voting, public is responsible for this "Parliament of Whores", O'Rourke characterizes as our government. He concludes the book with "Every government is a Parliament of Whores. The trouble is, in a democracy, the whores are us."

It is recommended reading, but should be preceded, especially for younger readers, with a standard civics textbook (something he unfavorably criticizes) which cites what good government is or should be.

Marek Kohn (review date 4 September 1992)

SOURCE: Kohn, Marek. "Gulfs between Us." *New Statesman and Society* 5, no. 218 (4 September 1992): 37-8.

[*In the following review, Kohn examines coverage of the Gulf War in three works: O'Rourke's* Give War a Chance, *James Der Derian's* Antidiplomacy, *and Alex Thomson's* Smokescreen.]

P. J. O'Rourke, demonstrating his anti-credentials as a correspondent [in **Give War a Chance**], speculates that one of the cardinal journalistic W questions might be "What the fuck?" This is funny and contains a truth; or at least some comfort for those of us prone to find ourselves still shuffling notes an hour off deadline. Jean Baudrillard, turning *reductio ad absurdum* into an intellectual pole position, is merely fatuous when he claims that practical knowledge of the Gulf war is "out of question". But the two of them would agree that reality is for nerds.

While O'Rourke constructs a persona—more artfully than is immediately obvious—around not bothering to establish the facts, Baudrillard claims there is no point in anybody else trying to do so. But you don't have to swallow his Strawberry Fields philosophy—nothing is real, nothing to get hung up about—to accept that the Gulf War entailed the creation of a unique "hyperreal" spectacle. Even Christopher Norris acknowledged as much while kicking Baudrillard's ass, to use the Gulf idiom, in his essay *Uncritical Theory* (Lawrence & Wishart).

This leaves an opening for James Der Derian, who claims that contemporary modes of conflict cannot be addressed by traditional approaches to international relations and require a poststructuralist perspective. Out go assumptions about rational choice and game theory; in come simulation and cyberspace. But despite a title bristling like an arsenal, *Antidiplomacy* is not a counter-counterblast to Norris. Scratch Der Derian's poststructuralist skin, and you find a traditional liberal underneath. Even in hyperreality, he worries about right and wrong.

Affirming that cybernauts need not be nihilists is one thing, though. A tendency to doodle, lapsing into coyness, is another. Der Derian includes his journal of a "Baltic Peace and Freedom Cruise" in 1985, and observations on a Billy Bragg concert in Prague. He also prefaces the text with an allegorical dream in which a dog asks him, "Where's the beef?" By the end, I too was left pushing the food bowl around with my nose.

Der Derian's theme is that terror and surveillance distinguish "late-modern" (or "neomedieval") conflict. Some forms of terror are undoubtedly unique to the age, owing their *raison d'être* to the mass media. But repackaging ethnic violence as "ethno-terrorism" is an unpersuasive way to pad out the theory. Apart from anything else, Bosnia is not happening in cyberspace.

The reason is implicit in Der Derian's observation that "we eagerly found in cyberspace what we could no longer find in the new global disorder—comfort and security in a superior technostrategy". Technological power substitutes, in simulation, for political power. Where there is no strategic requirement—no oil in Sarajevo—there is no need for technostrategy. Either way, out in the real world, the bad guys stay in the saddle.

Der Derian looks to popular culture for what he cannot find in the traditions of his discipline. It is the journalists and the MTV generation who are in tune with the video-game war; who put the image first. As well as emulating home entertainment, the smart bomb videos encouraged analogous thinking. Targets vanish when hit, leaving neither wreckage nor corpses. The viewing public is less inclined to enquire after the debris.

It remains a puzzle, even to a journalist like Alex Thomson, whose book is all about the old-fashioned impulse to find out what happened, where, when and to whom. Where were the bodies? Thomson saw few as he travelled across Kuwait. Albeit sceptically, he quotes Robert Fox, who spoke of looking inside tanks and seeing nothing but piles of ash. Fox speculated that modern munitions simply obliterated people—almost as utterly as video game targets.

Thomson is disturbed by the unfilled vacuum of information about Iraqi casualties. One report estimated that 40,000 troops and 13,000 civilians were killed during the war, though Thomson feels this is on the high side. Other sources have put the total death toll nearer a quarter of a million. To add to the sinister eeriness of the Kuwait Theatre of Operations, the current view is that far fewer Iraqis were deployed than originally claimed. They really were a simulation.

Thomson's book is a detailed account, thoughtful and concerned, about what it was like to do a journalist's job in the desert. The media were constantly in danger of being colonised by the military, or of disappearing into cyberspace. O'Rourke puts this dilemma neatly: "Well, we spend all day broadcasting on the radio and TV telling people back home what's happening over here. And we learn what's happening over here by spending all day monitoring the radio and TV broadcasts from home. You may also wonder how any actual information gets into this loop. If you find out, please call."

Thomson describes how some journalists resisted pressure to wear military uniform, and thus to identify with the troops—but then donned it as disguise to move freely without their minders. Chemical protection suits were used as substitutes, though Thomson ruefully admits that, being blue, the ITN-issue outfits made him and his colleagues look like incompetent gas fitters wandering around the desert.

P J O'Rourke was troubled by no such considerations. If there was nothing going on, he would knock out a wisecracking piece on Saudi drivers. Then he got to use his traffic jokes again at the site of the Mutla convoy massacre, where, Thomson recounts, American troops were at pains to bury the bodies as fast as possible. P J arrived four days later, when only the odd corpse was left lying around. On the strength of the Iraqi loot, he pronounced it the "My Lai of consumer goods". "I caught myself giggling at the carnage," he recalled.

Unfortunately, I found myself giggling a lot less at this O'Rourke miscellany than at **Republican Party Reptile,** which was also far funnier than **Holidays in Hell** and **Parliament Of Whores.** None of the gags are as memorable as his final image of buzzing a Bedouin camp in a giant Hercules transport, striking awe into the soul of a boy looking up from below. This isn't the ecstasy of simulation. This is the power-surge of triumphalism induced by contact with the "sky-blackening, air-mauling, the thunder-engined" material reality of Western might—"*our* civilisation's mastery of *this* world". If you're looking for your ideal image of yourself in the gaze of the Other, swooping over a small boy in 20 monstrous tons of warplane is the American way to do it.

One of these days, that boy will have a slingshot.

Richard Cook (review date 18 September 1992)

SOURCE: Cook, Richard. "The Gonzo's Self-Love." *Times Literary Supplement,* no. 4668 (18 September 1992): 28.

[*In the following review, Cook finds* Give War a Chance *uneven, and contends that "we want to see the full range of [O'Rourke's] talents, rather than preening and petulance."*]

P. J. O'Rourke is the man who gave the world **"How to Drive Fast on Drugs While Getting Your Wing-Wang Squeezed and Not Spill Your Drink."** This essay, and others like it, **"Tune In, Turn On, Go to the Office Late on Monday"**, **"A Cool and Logical Analysis of the Bicycle Menace"**, made his name and established his credentials. A humorist certainly, and especially a gonzo journalist (a writer determined to explore a triumphant solipsism through the fog of too many whiskeys or a little sanitized drug abuse), O'Rourke is a Hunter S. Thompson who remembered to set his alarm clock.

Unlike so many who followed Thompson, though, this lurid chronicler of his very own American excess story has a unique selling point: a stridently right-wing view of the world. The about-turn in his own biography—a graduate-school-educated 1960s hippy and Vietnam draft-dodger who became a besuited Reagan voter—merely helps the jokes along. And it was jokes that helped an anti-establishment, establishment-party humorist leap from the pages of *National Lampoon* and *Car and Driver* magazine to hard covers and a job as International Affairs Desk Chief of another 60s rebel that had grown up respectable, the music magazine *Rolling Stone.*

There is a piece in **Give War a Chance,** O'Rourke's latest collection of articles, called **"Second Thoughts about the 60s"**, that showcases an ability to subvert this personal history for laughs. A grand rhetorical opening catalogues all the views that the author then held dear. A majestic anaphora, "I believed", re-coins the intellectual currency of the day: "I believed private property was tyranny. I believed I would live forever or until twenty-one, whichever came first", and so on till the punchline, "With the exception of anything my mom and dad said, I believed everything." This essay is the most successful in a wildly uneven book because the subject matter best falls in with what O'Rourke best writes about: himself.

The ostensible subjects of most of the collection—elections in Paraguay and Nicaragua, Eastern Europe following the collapse of communism, even diaries from the Gulf War—merely seem to get in the way of the author's relentless egotism, which often expresses itself in a kind of heavy-handed chauvinism:

> Many of the commercial signs in Saudi Arabia are printed in English—more or less. I've seen the "Decent Barber Shop" and the "Meat Cow Fresh Butcher Shop", also "Wow" brand toilet paper, a fast food restaurant advertising "Humburgers" (ham being illegal) and a fancy model of running shoe called, in all innocence, the "Crack".

Rejoicing at the rout completed against retreating Iraqis on the road to Basra, O'Rourke concludes: "Of course I didn't do this personally, but my tax dollars helped."

In fact, O'Rourke and a kind of idealized Norman Rockwell America, without poverty or drugs, are cast as the heroes of all the foreign reporting in this book. Abroad is not only where they speak funny English, but also a place difficult to find a good meal or a drink mixed right. A trip to Berlin before the Wall came down is remembered chiefly for a pizza that tasted like dog food. The overthrow of communism was notable for helping that city's restaurateurs produce "food you could swallow". Communist Hanoi provides a solitary exception to prove this rule. Here "the cooking was good", but then Hanoi is not really a communist capital, O'Rourke explains: instead "it seemed like 60s America—not pot, war and hirsute aggravation 60s America, but the madras-clad, record hop, beach-bumming nation of my high school days".

Closer to home, the selection includes a half-serious call for a modern McCarthyism, **"Notes towards a Blacklist for the 1990s,"** a series of book reviews, and an essay, **"An Argument in favour of Automobiles vs Pedestrians"**:

> Think how much less evil Central America would have experienced if, for example, all the Sandinistas had been in cars. They would have been stuck in the jungle, axle-deep in mud, and would never have been able to enslave peasants, kill Contras or get any Russian weapons into El Salvador.

In one scathing review—of the autobiography of former Chrysler chief, Lee Iacocca—O'Rourke is astute enough to note that "self-love cannot be displayed in full bloom without a leafy green background of hatred for others". Unfortunately for O'Rourke, the reasons behind his own hatred for others—for foreigners because they don't speak very good English, their cooking is disappointing or their plumbing poor, for the Kennedys because they were too good looking—constantly fail to ring true. And for a gonzo journalist, an inability to show off self-love to full advantage is disastrous. We want to see the full range of his talents, rather than preening and petulance.

Charles Glass (review date 9 December 1994)

SOURCE: Glass, Charles. "It's a Wonderful World." *Times Literary Supplement* (9 December 1994): 29.

[*In the following review, Glass deems* All the Trouble in the World *a funny and worthwhile read.*]

This [*All the Trouble in the World*] is a book for the smug and content, and it is very funny. In his six previous books, P. J. O'Rourke satirized American manners, the pretensions of liberation fighters, the politics of liberalism and the United States government. In his new work, he takes on the ecology movement, "multiculturalism", the Third World and other people's wars. Of Bosnia, he writes, "The unspellables were shooting the unpronounceables". O'Rourke is as innocent as any American teenager, bemused by foreigners and their strange ways, but the earnestness in his book nearly overwhelms the humour.

For O'Rourke, there is no population problem, no pollution problem, no nuclear waste problem. Using statistics without sources, he writes that the world's population—if living at Manhattan's density—could fit into former Yugoslavia. *The Times Atlas,* however, puts it another way: the 1975 population of the world left every person nine and a half acres, if all the land surface of the earth were habitable, which it isn't. Only 30 per cent of the land can sustain human life and the current world population is nearly 5 billion, leaving little over two acres per person. It's not much, and it is decreasing. In his population chapter, subtitled "Too Little of Me, Way Too Much of You", he accuses those who want to control human numbers of racism.

With everything so wonderful, O'Rourke complains that everyone else is complaining—particularly the conservationists and the poor in the Third World. He goes to the Amazon on an eco-tour and admits he hates nature, although he probably hates the eco-tourists more. He visits Haiti and falls in love with its people. But his summary of Haiti's history omits the hundreds of invasions by the British, French, Germans and Americans that bled the country in the nineteenth century. In Bangladesh, he blames the government for all the country's woes. He castigates the World Bank for its failed projects, but he neglects to mention that American corporations threatened to leave Bangladesh when workers attempted to form trade unions to raise wages above six pence an hour. Acknowledging that English colonization of India began in Bengal in 1650, he doesn't notice that the longest colonized parts of the non-white world, like Bangladesh, are the poorest, while Japan, the richest, is the only Asian state that avoided being eaten by a white empire.

While he is good at exposing pomposity, O'Rourke himself can be guilty of tiresome earnestness. "A politician is anyone who asks individuals to surrender part of their liberty—their power and privilege—to State, Masses, Mankind, Planet Earth or whatever." "Property rights, rule of law, responsible government, and universal education: that's all we need." "*Advocating the expansion of the powers of the state is treason to mankind, goddamnit!*" (O'Rourke says this to a woman who favoured President Clinton's health-care proposals.)

I would urge O'Rourke's publishers to let P. J. be P. J. (I would also urge them to put an index in the next printing.) O'Rourke is a comedian, not an economist or politician. His book is worth reading, both for the good travel writing and the laughs. In answer to a ludicrous Student Handbook at his *alma mater,* which is a paradigm of loony political correctness, instructing boys how to talk to girls, he writes "Jest, ignorance, or substance abuse have been the excuse, reason, or rationale for my entire existence." In Bosnia, he notes that, "As the war repels a certain number of Yugoslavs, so it attracts a certain number of foreigners. War is a great asshole magnet", and advises "You mustn't ever ask the Yugoslavs why they're fighting. They'll tell you."

O'Rourke is conservative without much of a conscience, but he does have a heart. He hates the UN, but he praises a UN body, the World Health Organization, for bringing measles vaccines to 70 per cent of the world's children. And he insists governments must protect children from their main enemy, diarrhoea. This disease kills about two and a half million children each year but has yet to become a fashionable cause in New York and Hollywood. "Diarrhoea is spread by contaminated water", he writes. "Public sanitation is, like personal security, national defence, and rule of law, one of the valid reasons for politics to exist." He may not realize that Britain has made public sanitation another source of privatized wealth and that the quality of water is declining accordingly.

The world beyond Uncle Sam's shores is dreadful, and O'Rourke saves the rose tint on his spectacles for the homeland: "Right now, at the end of the second millennium, is the best moment of all time, and right here, in the United States, is the best place to be." This is the same America of which Pete Hamill, a respected American journalist, wrote in the latest *Esquire,* "As this dreadful century winds down, its history heavy with gulags and concentration camps and atom bombs, the country that was its brightest hope seems to be breaking apart." Unlike O'Rourke, Hamill fears for a country where intellectual degradation has accompanied industrial decline: "We live in a country that has never made a movie about Leonardo da Vinci and has produced three about Joey Buttafuoco." (Buttafuoco is famous only for having had a teenage lover, Amy Fisher, who shot his wife.)

O'Rourke redeems himself, as always, with self-deprecation and humour: "Things are better now than things have been since men began keeping track of things. Things are better than they were only a few years ago. Things are better in fact, than they were at 9:30 this morning, thanks to Tylenol and two Bloody Marys."

Douglas Kennedy (review date 16 December 1994)

SOURCE: Kennedy, Douglas. "Shocking Pinks." *New Statesman and Society* 7, no. 333 (16 December 1994): 68.

[*In the following review, Kennedy asserts that although* All the Trouble in the World *is full of silly jingoism and chauvinism, it is humorous and sometimes perceptive writing.*]

> Famine is too close to dieting. We snap at our spouses, jiggle on the scale, and finish other people's cheesecake. If we've turned into angry, lying thieves by a mere foregoing of dessert, what must real hunger be like?

> Imagine a weight-loss programme at the end of which, instead of better health, good looks and hot romantic prospects, you die. Somalia had become just this kind of spa.

P J O'Rourke's fame as a "Republican Party Reptile" rests on smartass observations like that one. They are calculated to provoke, infuriate and exasperate the so-called "socially concerned classes"—ie, those (cliché! cliché!) muesli-munching, rainforest-obsessive, gender-conscious folk who subscribe to magazines like this one.

However, unlike such conservative *agents provocateurs* as Richard Littlejohn or Rush Limbaugh (the circumferentially challenged, Clinton-bashing talk show host), O'Rourke doesn't playact the low-rent grunt with predictable potshots at "*Guardian* readers" or "Feminazis". Rather, he casts himself in the role of a latter-day H L Mencken, his obvious literary hero and mentor. He sees his journalistic role in life as a libertarian "disturber of the peace".

But if you browse through any edition of Mencken's essays and broadsides, you will notice that—though he was deeply mistrustful of Roosevelt's New Deal policies—the primary focus of his contempt was the narrow-minded philistinism of mid-America: that silent majority whose "literary standards derived from the *Ladies Home Journal*".

O'Rourke, on the other hand, came to fame during the Reaganite revolution. Though certainly no knee-jerk New Right ideologue, he still plays to the conservative gallery when it comes to hating "big government" ("Advocating the expansion of the powers of the state is treason to mankind, goddamit") and waving the flag ("Right now, at the end of the second millennium, is the best moment of all time, and right here, in the United States, is the best place to be at the moment").

O'Rourke's writing is peppered with such silly jingoism. Yet whenever he tosses out this sort of comment, it's a bit like a comedian who believes he has to toss the yobbos a bone. But if you can ignore these flashes of chauvinism, his brand of satire has much to recommend it—especially as he is an avowed enemy of cant, hypocrisy and polyester fabrics. "Why do eco-tourists have neon-blue hiking shorts? And fluorescent-purple windbreakers? Caution-signal-yellow sweat socks? Crap-table-toned fanny packs? Hojo-tinted luggage? T-shirts the hue of sex dolls? What is the connection between love of nature and colours not found in ditto?"

All the Trouble in the World is the latest collection of despatches from in-the-news hotspots: Haiti, Somalia, Bangladesh, Prague, Sarajevo, Vietnam, and Ohio. Yes, they do display his trigger-happy penchant for one-liners ("Bangladesh has some 118,000,000 people, nearly half the citizenry of the United States, all in a nation the size of Iowa. It's crowded"). But at heart, they show O'Rourke as simply an old-fashioned libertarian—who, for all his mannered jadedness, remains appalled by the way corrupt regimes and inane ideologies manage to wreak human destruction: "Haitians aren't screwed up, but everything political, intellectual, and material around them is."

His opening essay on the new-fangled American culture of complaint—**"Fashionable Worries: If Meat Is Murder, Are Eggs Rape?"**—scores the biggest bullseye. This is one of the most incisive analyses of US self-absorption I have ever stumbled across. O'Rourke may like to portray himself as a hedonistic patriot—but he's also shrewd enough to know that his is a society where "tragedy is better than comedy for self-dramatisation".

It will be interesting to see how his libertarian brand of Republicanism will withstand the moral-majority type now preached by Newt Gingrich and his merry band of ultra-Christian patriots. Even right-wing hedonists tend to run for cover when faced with folks who believe that they've got a direct line to Jesus.

Stephen Dunstan (review date 14 January 1995)

SOURCE: Dunstan, Stephen. "Not Very Funny Ha Ha." *Spectator* 274, no. 8688 (14 January 1995): 27.

[*In the following mixed review, Dunstan derides* All the Troubles in the World *as unfunny and unsatisfying.*]

Humour is notoriously relative. Different cultures, different ages of man and different states of inebriation can all render the best joke flat or the most banal comment hilarious. For instance, I can record the funniest joke I have ever heard, *measured in terms of how much I laughed at the time,* went as follows. What goes 'Ha Ha Ha—Bonk!'? Answer: someone laughing his head off.

I also have to say I approach with caution any book whose flyleaf advertises it as bringing us 'the lighter side of famine, pestilence, destruction and death'—those things simply not having a lighter side. Fortunately Mr O'Rourke doesn't think so either; like all true satirists, he is motivated by anger, at the human folly, greed and stupidity which lie behind our collective failure to deal with problems, like those he refers to, all of which should be perfectly capable of solution.

Still, despite the author plainly being on the right side, about halfway through this volume [*All the Trouble in the World*] one begins to feel swizzed on two counts.

Firstly, by the claim that this is a book, and secondly, that it is a funny book (funny ha-ha-bonk! that is). In fact it is a collection of foreign correspondent pieces sewn together by not a very thick thread, i.e. the idea that together they summarise current 'fashionable worries'. The claim to being a sort of *tour d'horizon* is valid in a geographical rather than any intellectual sense as the idea licenses the author to visit Haiti, Somalia, Bangladesh, Bosnia, Brazil and Vietnam (to name but a few). Were it a proper book, one would expect more Argument, and certainly some views on What Must Be Done a bit more solid than what we are offered on the penultimate page as the sum of Mr O'Rourke's wisdom:

> I don't have any answers. Use your common sense. Be nice. This is the best I can do.

The frankness is appealing, and were it not for that exhortatory 'Be nice' it might have won me over as refreshingly unpompous. The tone of the writing here as elsewhere is designed to seduce: this is above all an honest fellow, we keep thinking, and deuced likeable to boot. Mr O'Rourke's chosen nonsenses are ones many of us would choose, his gut feelings are (mostly) ones we would all share, and his self-mocking commentary something we can all relate to. But it isn't a 'book' in the sense of contributing much to improving our understanding of the problems it describes. No doubt that wasn't the aim. Yet something is missing: if only the occasional straight-faced Swiftian prescription, such as arming all three sides in Bosnia with short range nuclear weapons so they can jolly well get on with it and stop monopolising Headline News.

Nor is the writing that funny. Set against five minutes of Rowan Atkinson it's as comic as the average *Financial Times* editorial. I laughed out loud three times in 340 pages, which is not that much for a book promoted as 'hilariously outrageous'. But then, please note disclaimer above. Several chapters give themselves theoretical cover by discussing a particular 'topic', before packing their bags and setting off to country X or Y to examine an example of the case. Thus **'Multiculturalism'** introduces a piece of reportage on Bosnia; and **'Famine'** gets us on the first flight to Somalia (not that easy). With the exception of a few passages of dreadful waffle, it is on the whole excellent journalism: serious subjects treated with wit (rather than comedy) and the occasional passing wise observation.

The last chapter, on Vietnam, is the best as well as the most amusing. Maybe because he likes the subject, money, we find the author really getting into his stride. It gives this otherwise staunch, declared Republican a chance to parade his own draft-dodging, substance-abusing background (a combination with a deliberate message, no doubt, but one which, nevertheless, I find hard to follow). The chapter also contains most of the (otherwise fairly scarce) thoughts in the collection. For instance, the suggestion that the depth of America's continuing problem with Vietnam is due to the fact that they collectively fell in love: with the place (which is beautiful), with its atmosphere (as mysteriously 'other' from Philadelphia as you can get), and of course with its women, on whose attractions O'Rourke cannot resist giving some personal commentary.

In discussing the resurgence of capitalism in Vietnam, O'Rourke also makes one of the most worthwhile comments I have read on a subject of some importance, and about which we have all suffered much heavy, inconclusive analysis: that is, who is winning and who is losing. O'Rourke's verdict:

> All we can really do in the study of poverty and wealth is watch carefully when one is turning into the other.

Having lived for the last 12 years in the region of the world where Vietnam finds itself, and during all that time returning to Europe, and more specifically Britain, at least once or twice a year, I know just how apposite this comment is. You really only have to look to see.

Perhaps because this is a compilation of separate pieces, one concludes with a slightly unsatisfied feeling. As a satirist, Mr O'Rourke is clearly not just trying to make us hoot and giggle at the troubles of the world. There is a serious core to all this, one supposes, especially as its pure entertainment value is not that great. The catch is, after we've all had a good smirk over our fellow man's foolishness, what do we do next? Something tells me I can guess what Mr O'Rourke's answer would be.

Scott Walter (review date March-April 1995)

SOURCE: Walter, Scott. "Pistol-Packin' Comics." *American Enterprise* 6, no. 2 (March-April 1995): 86-9.

[*In the following review, Walter finds parallels between* All the Trouble in the World *and Florence King's* The Florence King Reader.]

Don't mess with Florence King. True, she's gleaming on the dustjacket of one of her books—but so is the barrel of her Ruger automatic pistol, one of several weapons she keeps handy. Her last book was entitled, *With Charity Toward None: A Fond Look at Misanthropy.* It's not even safe to praise her, as one hapless reviewer at the *New York Times* discovered when King responded to the favorable review he'd given her: "You do not know how to write a review. I do. Here are your faults. . . ."

Her latest work, *The Florence King Reader,* has an affectionate introduction by her editor, but he admits that around the office they call her the Queen of Spleen.

"I've met her," he reassures us, "and she wouldn't hurt a piranha." Not many folks do meet Miss King, who treasures her solitude in Fredericksburg, Virginia. Fewer still dare to edit her. Her book contracts state that she will do her own copyediting, and her present editor admits, "I may not be the brightest deer in the forest, but I know how to keep out of sights."

Miss King is not easy to characterize. Perhaps the best term for her is the old-fashioned *belletrist,* but that makes her sound too serious to be funny and not serious enough to be enduring. As this 400-page overview of her last two decades' work reveals, King's serious humor is enduring. The *Reader* contains all of her comic novel, *When Sisterhood Was in Flower,* as well as generous excerpts from her essay collections; her hilarious studies of Southern ladies and gentlemen, WASPs, the American male, and misanthropy; her memoir, *Confessions of a Failed Southern Lady*; numerous articles and reviews; and even a chapter from her pseudonymous historical romance, *The Barbarian Princess.* Throughout her varied career, she has striven to be a craftsman, and she has re-edited her work before including it here, all the while inserting frank editorial asides describing the flaws she sees in the originals. Throughout, the prose is lean and sinewy, the organization taut, the wit eviscerating.

Within the right-wing humor brigade, P. J. O'Rourke is one of Miss King's few peers. He has written a book [*All the Trouble in the World*] that will surprise his devotees, for it is not his usual assemblage of wisecracking magazine pieces but a unified opus whose seams are reinforced with scholarly quotations, think-tank data, and sustained political argument. Of course, all this deep thinking is interlaced with his usual mordant asides, but even in these O'Rourke keeps his tongue gentler than usual, with the exception of a few ferocious lashings of his nemesis, Al Gore. As his subtitle explains, O'Rourke takes on "overpopulation, famine, ecological disaster, ethnic hatred, plague, and poverty." He seeks their "lighter side"; which is to say, he refuses to accede to the gloom-and-doom crowd's cries that the sky is falling, the earth crumbling.

The book has three parts: an opening chapter that attacks the do-gooder ideology underlying the fashionable worries of the subtitle; seven chapters that explore (and demolish) the explanations professional worriers give for what worries them; and a concluding chapter that offers O'Rourke's alternative to the worry-wart philosophy.

Why are there so many worriers running around, he asks, when by any standard measure "life is better than it ever has been"? (Or in P. J. prose, "History is on a roll, a toot, a bender," yet "I hear America whining, crybaby to the world.") O'Rourke's answer: "We whine because it works. We used to be shunned for weeping in our beer. Now we go on *Oprah*." Moreover, "worrying is less work than doing something to fix the worry. . . . everybody wants to save the earth; nobody wants to help Mom do the dishes."

O'Rourke might have ignored today's trendy lamentations and retreated to his Scotches (which are "older than the White House staff"), but he counterattacks instead because if somebody doesn't, the "professional worriers [will] put our fears to use." Whether the sob sisters are on the Left or Right matters not, for "there is really only one political goal in the world. Politics is the business of getting power and privilege without possessing merit." Not that O'Rourke doesn't have a political agenda himself, but it's limited to "property rights, rule of law, responsible government, and universal education: That's all we need." In short, O'Rourke prefers the sort of self-government championed by the classical liberals of the eighteenth century.

After thrashing the politics of anxiety, O'Rourke concludes with a chapter on **"Economic Justice"**: "There are better ways to solve life's problems than by holding voodoo ceremonies or shooting your neighbors or sending twits-of-all-nations to [an environmentalist conference in] Rio. Politics won't do it. And politicians surely won't. The best method of existential improvement is making money." To prove this assertion, he pens a paean to Vietnam, which despite the burden of a Communist regime began dramatically advancing its quality of life the moment its apparatchiks ended price controls, "put the privacy back into private property, and told everybody to go make a living."

Yet O'Rourke is not drunk on dreams of earthly paradise. His first chapter ends soberly with the recognition that the world's worries require us "to accept the undramatic and often extremely boring duties of working hard, exercising self-control, taking care of ourselves, our families, and our neighbors, being kind, and practicing as much private morality as we can stand without popping." Similarly, the book closes with O'Rourke's confession that "in the end, Vietnam was a bit depressing, too. Hard to believe that the thrilling idea of human liberty always results in people acting so . . . human."

You might say that O'Rourke has discovered the ancient truths of original sin, moral virtue, and philosophic moderation. In this discovery, he has a soulmate in Florence King and, as the sales of their books how, in much of the American public. Humor is the revenge of the normal, as a wise man once quipped.

The norms produced by Athens and Jerusalem, the taproots of the West, have been anti-utopian political philosophy and Judaeo-Christian religion, respectively.

Continuing this tradition, both King and O'Rourke moderate their expectations of the politically possible and acknowledge an objective moral order that they might less ostentatiously call "reality." On the Athens side, for example, both attack the upstart philosopher Rousseau.

Both authors take the Jerusalem strand seriously too. Admittedly, their rhetoric is far from evangelical, and Lord knows neither author is a saint. But readers who think religion and "social issues" should never be discussed in public ought to note that these two whisky-drinkers are popular precisely because of their blunt moral judgments. Neither shies away from abortion, for example. O'Rourke eschews pro-life fanaticism, but after giving Bangladesh's infant mortality rate of 108 deaths per 1,000 live births, he mischievously adds that in the U.S. "the rate of abortions per 1,000 live births is 404, if dead babies happen to be what you worry about." For her part, King includes an entire essay on abortion and decides that "Molly Yard is such a little old tennis shoe among ladies that anything she says has got to be wrong." King even views organ transplants with her famous jaundiced eye.

Whether or not a reader agrees with King and O'Rourke on these and other questions, there's a deeper lesson being taught: Don't worry about being loved, especially by your enemies. Rush Limbaugh recently gave that advice to the House freshmen, and it may be a secret of the success enjoyed not only by pundits like himself and King and O'Rourke, but also by politicians like Newt Gingrich and Virginia Gov. George Allen. Ordinary citizens take it for granted that the moral world has laws no more avoidable than the law of gravity is in the physical world, and they also crave plainspokenness. As a result, advocates who combine straightforward moral judgment with humor will command public respect. Aristotle said, "you should kill your opponents' earnestness with jesting." He also recognized that the capacity to call some things good and other things bad is central to human nature. Of course citizens will sometimes disagree about the good and the bad, but those arguments are what self-government is all about. Democracy is supposed to lead to civil argument. And "civil," as King and O'Rourke make clear, does not necessarily mean "dainty."

Deirdre McMurdy (review date 16 November 1998)

SOURCE: McMurdy, Deirdre. "Finding the Yuks in Bucks." *Maclean's* 111, no. 46 (16 November 1998): 86.

[*In the following review, McMurdy delineates the strengths and weaknesses of* Eat the Rich, *concluding that O'Rourke fails to pull together the disparate subjects of the essays.*]

Reading P. J. O'Rourke's new book is a lot like gorging on a bag of potato chips: they taste great at the time, but they leave you feeling still hungry, slightly guilty and with a peculiar taste in your mouth. *Eat the Rich* is essentially a series of stand-alone essays, a travelogue focused on economic conditions in various countries. A self-described "economic idiot," O'Rourke has set out to explore why some places "prosper and thrive, while others just suck." The American writer neatly bisects the world into examples of "good" and "bad" socialism and capitalism, with a clear bias in favor of free, unfettered markets. This odyssey, recounted in his distinctive, sardonic style, takes O'Rourke from Russia to Tanzania, from Cuba to Sweden, in search of answers—and excuses for brittle one-liners at the expense of the locals.

O'Rourke's first stop is Wall Street, which he upholds as the purest example of free-market capitalism. Visiting the floor of the New York Stock Exchange, he makes the requisite quips about the littering, the ugly outfits and bad language. He also provides a cleverly simplistic synopsis of the recent Asian crisis in financial markets. But lack of analysis and insight leave the reader with such clichéd conclusions as, "The investment industry creates panic and euphoria." As with subsequent chapters, this one relies too much on clustered numbers and facts, the sort one finds in official publicity packages and data searches. "The New York Stock Exchange does $23 billion in business on an average day," he reports. "There are 207 billion shares registered on the New York Stock Exchange . . . More than $1 trillion of international currency changes hands every day."

He fares much better in his take on Hong Kong-style capitalism, a "stewing pandemonium" that is "socialism's perfect opposite." An accomplished travel writer, O'Rourke captures the manic energy of the city-state and its laissez-faire system, which offers "hardly enough welfare to keep one U.S. trailer park in satellite dishes and Marlboro Lights." While lamenting the 1997 handover of Hong Kong to China's Communist regime, O'Rourke remains sanguine about the impact of the Asian crisis. He observes that "a mere continent-wide financial collapse is unlikely to faze the people of Hong Kong."

He does, however, have grave reservations about the effect of China's rule. O'Rourke has a scathing view of China's hybrid version of capitalism, specifically its manifestation in Shanghai. He compares the squalid tenements with the city's rabid commercialization,

pronouncing, "A free market is a natural evolution of freedom. There's a missing link in Shanghai." Unlike the Darwinian economy of Hong Kong, Shanghai is creationist, its prosperity bestowed by—and subject to—a higher power: the state.

For someone who claims to be an economic neophyte, O'Rourke has strong views about such matters as state intervention in economic affairs. He uses his travels to Cuba and Sweden to bolster his case against government-run economies, although Sweden's "good socialism" is depicted as more bumbling and less inherently evil than Castro's regime.

In fact, O'Rourke's take on Sweden is especially resonant for Canadians because it examines a parallel, albeit more extreme, socio-economic model. It is a snapshot of what Canada was poised to become before the deficit crisis of the early 1990s curtailed government spending and brought many of its programs to an abrupt end. Among other similarities, Sweden has a national sales tax on goods and services—25 per cent, as compared with Canada's seven-per-cent GST—and a high unemployment rate of 13 per cent compared with Canada's 8.3-per-cent rate. It also has an exceptionally polite population and a full-fledged identity crisis, both of which have been attributed to Canada as well.

The chapter on Sweden is one of the few in which O'Rourke breaks away from smart-mouth commentary and cribbed statistics to offer some fresh context. He observes, for example, that dating back to the time of the Vikings, Swedes have had a deeply-ingrained tradition of communal decision-making. As a result, a dominant role for government is an accepted part of community life.

A piece about modern Russia's version of community life is perhaps the most vivid and instructive part of O'Rourke's book. It is particularly relevant in light of that country's recent economic collapse—which is foreshadowed in the author's depiction of a newly-liberated economy run amok. While cataloging the damage done by decades of central planning and consumer deprivation, O'Rourke's portrait of inadequate infrastructure and weakly-rooted reforms overlaid by hyperbolic growth and expectations is simultaneously amusing and alarming.

In the end, however, O'Rourke fails to pull together all the disparate pieces of *Eat the Rich.* And he never really does resolve the reasons for the ups and downs of the global economy. In the book's banal conclusion, he declares that the modern industrial economy works, although it works better in some places than others. O'Rourke also offers up the obvious insight that hard work, education, responsibility, rule-of-law democracy and property rights are imperative for economic success. Pass the chips.

Dave Shiflett (review date January 1999)

SOURCE: Shiflett, Dave. "P. J. Peaking on the Laughter Curve." *American Spectator* 32, no. 1 (January 1999): 68-9.

[*In the following review, Shiflett lauds* Eat the Rich *as a noble and enjoyable book.*]

The ongoing CNN series on the Cold War has drawn its share of right-wing criticism, as one would expect of a series so clearly orchestrated by Hanoi Jane herself. But for some of us the series has inspired deep longings for the good old days, when we sprang from bed, lambasted the Soviet nomenklatura (or however we spelled it), made fun of their fat wives, taunted the sissies in Congress, ridiculed a few college professors, called for a tax cut, mooned the liberal media, cashed a check from the Moon media—then beat it over to a nonprofit think tank for a complimentary banquet and an address on the perils of the free lunch.

Then the unimaginable happened: The Soviets went belly up, Congress went Republican, and many a Cold War thunderhead now finds himself writing articles on the ruinous influence of situation comedies, the political habits of single women who live with cats, and Bill Clinton's imperialistic gonads, with the remainder of the day spent calculating how many conservative blondes know how to change a light bulb. History has brought us very low indeed.

Yet there are exceptions, the most notable being P. J. O'Rourke, now soundly into middle age but still in possession of the old spirit, the old edge, and the timeless ability to root out a commie and give him a swift kick in the teeth. These talents are on brilliant display in P. J.'s latest book, *Eat the Rich,* on page 132 of which the author observes:

> The New Russians are an amazing bunch. The men wear three-piece suits with stripes the width and color used to indicate no passing on two-lane highways. Shoulder pads are as high and far apart as tractor fenders, and lapel points stick out even farther, waving in the air like baseball pennants. The neckties are as wide as the wives. The wives have, I think, covered their bodies in Elmer's Glue and run the boutiques of Palm Springs, buying whatever stuck. Their dresses certainly appear to be glued on—flesh tight, no matter how vast the expanses of flesh involved.

This is heart-quickening prose, especially in this day when calling a hog a hog is a rare literary event and calling members of the National Organization for

Women "cows" (footnote, page 25) is far too honest an observation for most editors to allow. These passages are all the more remarkable because this book is subtitled *A Treatise on Economics* and really is about the dismal science, sort of. The author has set himself the task of trying to discover why some societies are rich, while others, such as Tanzania, generate 90 percent of their energy by lighting cooking fires. This is a noble and highly readable undertaking, though a warning or two may be in order.

First off, this is not a book for egalitarians, save for those who enjoy a good thumb-jab to the eye: "Fairness is a good thing in marriage and at the day-care center," the author observes. "It's a nice little domestic virtue. But a liking for fairness is not that noble a sentiment. Fairness doesn't rank with charity, love, duty, or self-sacrifice. And there's always a tinge of self-seeking in making sure that things are fair. Don't you go trying to get one up on me."

Nor is this a book for those who spend their days wondering whether or not Massa Greenspan will tune the interest rate by a quarter point or so, for it is clearly written for those of us who avoid treatises on economics with the same level of commitment we avoid articles on "national renewal." We are tipped off early on that the author is one of us. Only a fool, he asserts, takes economics very seriously, offering as Exhibit A Mr. Paul Samuelson, co-author of the famed text *Economics.* Samuelson is shamed in the traditional way an expert is shamed—he is quoted: "Marx was wrong about many things, but that does not diminish his stature as an important economist."

"Well, what would?" P. J. responds. "If Marx was wrong about many things and screwed the baby-sitter?" Few writers have ever so subtly woven a sexual theme into an economics treatise. Many readers will find themselves hooked from this point on.

Having put the experts in their place, the author turns to his presentation of a pleasantly proportioned body (246 pages) of insightful reporting on the way economic beings live and operate in Sweden, Hong Kong, Cuba, China, Wall Street, Russia, Tanzania, and Albania, where post-Communist profiteers have raised entrepreneurship to dramatic levels: "The National Commercial Bank in the city of Gjirokaster was robbed with a tank." His eye for the telling detail, his élan, and his talent for the inspired wise-crack will make most readers forget that they probably have better things to do than sit around reading an economic treatise. Indeed, only the least generous will begrudge him the $24 he is asking for this spiffed-up collection of old magazine articles.

Each chapter is entertaining and informative and reflects a huge amount of expense account spending. For this reader the chapter on Tanzania was the most rewarding, probably because over the past decade the entire continent of Africa has received less media attention than the spot on Monica's dress. As elsewhere, a statistical overview introduces the reader to the subject nation, and in this case the numbers paint a very grim picture. Tanzania "is poorer than Uganda, poorer than Chad, poorer than godforsaken Burundi. Haiti is 80 percent wealthier than Tanzania. Papua New Guinea is almost ten times more prosperous, never mind that some of its citizens have just discovered the wheel." Those with wheels find that "Tanzania has a population slightly less than California's and is slightly more than twice California's size, and Tanzania has 1,403 miles of paved roads. The District of Columbia has 1,104 miles (although, to be fair, our capital has worse potholes than their capital does)."

Then P. J. heads into the bush, where he finds that Mother Nature operates a highly disreputable empire. "The guidebooks will not tell you this," his guide announces, "but giraffes are homosexual." The heteros don't look much better. "One of the lions got up, walked a couple of steps away, took a leak, and—with no thought for the grace and style that Western-educated people so admire in African wildlife—lay down again in the piss."

These are images that undermine the idealized view of nature with which we are constantly bombarded, thus making this book a vital teaching tool for parents whose children have begun reflecting neopagan tendencies. At the same time, the author has a great deal of empathy for those who suffer under economic and political oppression. The death of a friend's child in Tanzania due to that nation's hideous medical system is a case in point, nor does he laugh too much at this exhibition label found in a Tanzanian museum:

> The Soda Bottle (ancient) The soda bottle which in use up to 1959. This bottle contain a marble and rubbering which jointly (wished) as stopper for the gas.

In fact, the author criticizes shortcomings close to home—"China's One Child program has succeeded (though whether at greater social costs than the success of America's One Parent program, I can't say)"—and even takes a swipe at his own tribe. "We baby boomers have caused everything since 1946. We'll keep buying stocks until we retire. But when we hit sixty-five, we're going to sell stocks. And the stock market is going to go down. And we're going to wet ourselves. The math is simple: 1946 + 65 = 2011. Buy stocks until 2011, then buy Depends."

Yet there is precious little even-handedness here. As *TAS* [*The American Spectator*] readers well know, O'Rourke is a man of strong and sometimes outlaw opinions. No MSNBC job for him. Or, for that matter,

no CBN job either, for the author nips a bit, sometimes starting out at four in the morning; sometimes not corking the jug until a bit after three. Nor does he confine himself to traditional cocktails, as revealed during a visit to Shanghai:

> One of the more expendable waiters opened the hinged front of the cobra case and pinned a four-foot serpent with a forked stick. He pried the critter out of its home, grabbed it beneath the head, and scuttled off to the kitchen, holding the thrashing reptile aloft as though it were a living string of furious bratwurst. A few minutes later, the fellow emerged with a tray of brandy snifters, each filled with bright, gory liquid, plus an extra glass holding the content of the snake's gallbladder.

Yet if drinking cobra blood disqualifies him from a teaching position at Regent University, P. J. does quote Scripture effectively in his concluding chapter. The lesson is taken from the biblical warning against coveting your neighbor's wife and ass: "The Tenth Commandment sends a message to socialists, to egalitarians, to people obsessed with fairness, to American presidential candidates in the year 2000—to everyone who believes that wealth should be redistributed. And that message is clear and concise: Go to hell."

Such is the core argument of *Eat the Rich*: That without property rights and the rule of law, people should expect to generate 90 percent of their energy with cooking fires and may, in lean years, face the prospect of eating second cousins. A simple lesson, to be sure, and surely an ancient one, but also one that continues to be contested in large parts of the world, even in places where they accept Visa and MasterCard from wandering journalists.

Max Schulz (review date February 1999)

SOURCE: Schulz, Max. "Tasty Economics." *Reason* 30, no. 9 (February 1999): 71-2.

[*In the following review, Schulz commends O'Rourke's grasp of economics in* Eat the Rich.]

Those whose exposure to economics is limited to collegiate readings of Paul Samuelson's popular textbook would likely second Thomas Carlyle's characterization of the subject as "the Dismal Science." Economics can indeed be dismal when confined to bewildering graphs, stupefying charts, mind-numbing (and often wrong) theories, and classroom discussions led by tenured careerists who may have never worked outside academia.

But economics is really the study of how people live and act day to day. Economics isn't the study of graphs and currency flows and GNP numbers as much as it is the study of human interaction.

Now comes *Eat the Rich,* a refreshing look at economics by someone who grasps this point and runs with it. The question P. J. O'Rourke, irreverent author of books such as *Parliament of Whores* and a contributor to *Rolling Stone,* seeks to answer is simple: "Why do some places prosper, and others just suck?" Not too different from the question Jude Wanniski, in slightly more elegant form, claimed to answer 20 years ago in his classic *The Way the World Works.* But O'Rourke has one thing over Jude Wanniski: His book is a hell of a lot funnier.

Open *Eat the Rich* and the one-liners jump out. On page 46, the "heart-surgery-colored" Albanian flag bears "the image of what's either a two-headed eagle or a very angry freak-show chicken." On page 149: "Measuring the current Russian economic situation against the old Soviet economy is like trying to do arithmetic by tasting the numbers." On page 178, discussing whether the stated reasons for the West's giving Tanzania so much foreign aid—to keep it from going communist— were sensible or not: "The ugly truth is that we care about Tanzanians because they have cool animals."

Credit O'Rourke with seeking empirical evidence to answer his grand question. Or at least credit whoever signs off on his expense account. In preparation for *Eat the Rich,* he traveled the globe, from Wall Street to Tiranë (capital of Albania), from Sweden to its "evil twin," Cuba. He explored locales such as Russia, Hong Kong, and Shanghai.

The charming conceit of this text is that its author has no formal economic training, that he is an idiot on the subject. He just traipses about, poking around and seeing what other peoples around the world do to get by each day. Those familiar with O'Rourke's previous writings will know this to be something of a pose. I recall a hilarious piece he wrote nearly a decade ago lambasting America's skewed agricultural price support system. It was among the most concise and on-the-mark treatments the subject has received. O'Rourke knows more than he lets on, even if he did blow off Econ 101.

He notes that governments don't cause affluence, that citizens of totalitarian countries have had lots of government for decades and nothing of anything else. At the same time, making his point that complete absence of government doesn't work either, he remarks that "for a million years mankind had no government at all, and *everyone*'s relatives were naked in trees."

So O'Rourke sees what works (or, more often, what doesn't work) in various countries, and his observations can be fascinating. His study of the **"Good Socialism"** of Sweden would seem to present one rather large ideological problem: The country works. Detailing the evils of, say, Cuba is not hard. Far from living in a socialist paradise, Castro's serfs are impoverished and the country is broken down. But in Sweden, people are affluent and relatively contented; the country is peaceful. Is this the real socialist paradise?

O'Rourke describes a society whose redistributive mania has been fully endorsed by the mass of citizens. People happily tax themselves to the gills and voluntarily restrict their personal freedoms as a means to achieve equalized prosperity. Which leads O'Rourke to remark, once it dawns on him that the Swedish Stepford streets contain no loons or nuts, "The last time I walked through Gamla Stan, I didn't wonder where the crazy people were. In Sweden the craziness is redistributed fairly. They're all a little crazy."

Those who advocate Swedish-style socialism are in fact a little bit crazy, at least in thinking it could have any sort of universal application. It can't. Swedes may be willing to shell out most of their income in taxes, but most people aren't. And even those high taxes don't cover the lavish benefits of Sweden's fabled "middle way." And while one country can get away with that, at least for a while, you don't need Kant to tell you that such a system can't work everywhere.

This may sound a bit serious or stuffy. But O'Rourke's charm is that he's not one of the self-serious types found haunting the low-rent neighborhood of cable television networks sponsored by NBC, pompously holding forth on the affairs of the day. None of which means this isn't a serious book. It is. Very much so. It just happens to be slap-ass funny, too. That kind of combination hasn't really occurred since, well, since O'Rourke's last book, *Age and Guile Beat Youth, Innocence and a Bad Haircut.*

Consider his foul three-day trip on the Trans-Siberian Railroad, one of many unholy relics of the old Soviet system. The hardships he records I can only hint at, but they involve disgusting and sweaty Russians cramped together, nasty overflowing restrooms, stiflingly hot cars, and (worst of all) a shortage of vodka. The lesson learned can be reprinted in full: The train is "reeking, grubby, airless, and clamorously loud," he writes. "This is central planning. And anybody who advocates central planning—from Gennady Zyuganov to Sidney Blumenthal—should be made to get down on his hands and knees and lick the Irkutsk-to-Vladivostock train." Somehow, I can't quite picture Hayek saying it the same way.

O'Rourke goes from countries that don't work to one that does—er, *did*—Hong Kong. Why did the former colony work? Because it was essentially unplanned. Its British overlords made Hong Kong successful, if those are the right words, by doing little or nothing.

Such laissez faire "isn't Tanzanian administrative sloth or Albanian popular anarchy. Quite a bit of government is required to create a system in which the government leaves people alone." "Doing nothing" is a relative term, O'Rourke explains. It really means keeping taxes and regulation to a minimum, maintaining the rule of law, and ensuring the currency is sound.

O'Rourke does us all a great service by providing a little history lesson on Hong Kong and giving appropriate credit to Britain's postwar administrator, John Cowperthwaite, who served there from 1945 until the early '70s. Histories tend to exalt government leaders who *do* and *act* and *build* and generally expand the state, whether it is Teddy Roosevelt or FDR, Mao or Stalin. Cowperthwaite, however, accomplished more good than those grandiose and arrogant dreamers ever could. Naturally, he is virtually unknown.

When he first arrived in Hong Kong to implement the recovery, Cowperthwaite wisely recognized that the island was recovering nicely without him. He thus inflicted as little government as possible on the island, leaving it to prosper of its own accord. That sensible ethic reigned until the communist takeover in 1997.

By the end of his journeys O'Rourke has a pretty good idea why some countries prosper and why others just suck. And it boils down to some simple things: the rule of law, private property, limited government, sound money, personal freedom.

He waxes philosophical on these points, and even a little theological, as in his hilarious reflection on the 10th Commandment and what God thinks about the politics of envy: "If you want a donkey, if you want a pot roast, if you want a cleaning lady, don't bitch about what the people across the street have. *Go get your own.*" The message to all wealth redistributors "is clear and concise: Go to hell."

Eat the Rich is a book written for people who might want to know more about economics "but have never gotten further into the subject than figuring out a trifecta at Belmont." Now, if O'Rourke would only write a book about handicapping. I have no illusions that he could help me decipher the Rosetta Stone of the *Racing Form* or figure a way to hit a daily double, but at least I'd be laughing while losing my shirt.

Et cetera **(review date spring 1999)**

SOURCE: Review of *Eat the Rich*, by P. J. O'Rourke. *Et cetera* 56, no. 1 (spring 1999): 106-07.

[*In the following review, the critic offers a favorable assessment of* Eat the Rich.]

Political humorist P. J. O'Rourke, whose best-seller *Parliament of Whores* attempted to explain the entire United States government, seeks to answer in this book [*Eat the Rich*] a fundamental economic question that he phrases as, "Why do some places prosper and thrive, while others just suck?"

To figure this out, O'Rourke pays a visit to the New York Stock Exchange, explaining along the way stocks, bonds, debentures, and other financial instruments—and he concludes that the stock market is for many reasons a source of "good capitalism" as well as a place that generates a terrific amount of litter. He then goes off on a world tour to investigate world economies.

In Albania he views "bad capitalism," in Sweden he finds "good socialism," and in Cuba he suffers "bad socialism." Then, after admitting that he avoided Econ 101 in college, O'Rourke proceeds to demonstrate that an intelligent autodidact doesn't need formal course work by presenting an astute, comprehensive, and concise explanation of the basic principles of economics that, unlike that Econ 101 course, will make you laugh as you learn.

Armed with economic theory the author travels to Russia described in a chapter titled **"How (Or How Not) to Reform (Maybe) an Economy (If There Is One)"** and reveals that this nation is somewhat of a disaster in progress. When he goes to Tanzania he discovers a land of abundant resources and maximum poverty which is a far cry from his experience of Hong Kong—a shining example of how unfettered economic activity can "Make everything from nothing." Shanghai is his last stop and he concludes that its system of top-down capitalism is no way to run a railroad or a country.

O'Rourke has a wonderful way with words and he so enlivens the "dismal science" that you may want to actually have a look at some serious economic texts. In case you do, the author obligingly provides a list of recommendations in his acknowledgments.

David R. Henderson (review date May-June 1999)

SOURCE: Henderson, David R. "The Wit of Nations." *American Enterprise* 10, no. 3 (May-June 1999): 81-2.

[*In the following positive review of* Eat the Rich, *Henderson contends that O'Rourke explores economic concepts in "humorous, understandable ways."*]

Since 1776, when Adam Smith published *The Wealth of Nations,* countless volumes have been written by people who call themselves economists, but in those 200-plus years, no one has tried to write books about economics that are purposely funny. Finally, however, there is such a book. It is **Eat the Rich** (I guess that title beats *Steal This Book*) by P. J. O'Rourke, the humorist and columnist for *Rolling Stone*.

O'Rourke addresses the most important question in economics: "Why do some places prosper and thrive while others just suck?" Adam Smith dealt with that same question. So think of O'Rourke as a modern Adam Smith, with these two differences: O'Rourke's data are more recent, and you'll get side-splitting laughs on every page.

O'Rourke leads off by junking the notion that a brilliant mind is sufficient, or even necessary, to generate wealth. "No part of the earth (with the possible exception of Brentwood) is dumber than Beverly Hills," he says, "and the residents are wading in gravy. In Russia, meanwhile, where chess is a spectator sport, they're boiling stones for soup." Nor is education the answer. "Fourth graders in the American school system know what a condom is but aren't sure about 9 × 7."

Why not figure out what makes economies rich by reading an economics textbook? O'Rourke lists a number of reasons, one of which is the prose style of the typical economics text: "puerile and impenetrable, *Goodnight Moon* rewritten by Henry James."

Style isn't O'Rourke's only objection to economics textbooks; he says the content is typically questionable, too. O'Rourke quotes famous MIT economist Paul Samuelson: "Marx was wrong about many things . . . but that does not diminish his stature as an important economist." Asks O'Rourke: "Well, what would? If Marx was wrong about many things and screwed the baby-sitter?"

Always, O'Rourke expresses economic ideas in humorous, understandable ways. Here he is on bond ratings. "A D-rated bond is like money lent to a younger brother. An AAA-rated bond is like money lent to a younger brother by the Gambino family."

To explain what kinds of economic systems work and what ones don't, he takes you on his travels—to Sweden, Cuba, Albania, Tanzania, Hong Kong, Russia, and Shanghai. O'Rourke notes that in Sweden, which practices **"Good Socialism,"** workers get unlimited sick leave with no reduction in pay rate. He writes: "During a brief period of nonsocialist rule in 1991, a one-day waiting period for sick-leave benefits was instituted. An enormous drop in Monday and Friday worker illnesses resulted—one of the medical miracles of the twentieth century."

O'Rourke is less funny when he discusses Cuba (**"Bad Socialism"**)—understandable, given that Cuba keeps a higher proportion of the population as political prison-

ers than any other country on earth. But even in discussing Cuba, O'Rourke launches some great lines. Pointing out that private restaurants are allowed so long as they employ only family members, O'Rourke writes: "It will be interesting to see how this model works if it's applied to other free enterprise undertakings, such as airlines. Mom will begin beverage service as soon as Junior gets the landing gear up."

O'Rourke's ruminations on the Russian economy are dead-on funny. How about this for a succinct statement of the problems with Communism:

> If a shoe factory was told to produce 1,000 shoes, it produced 1,000 baby shoes, because these were the cheapest and easiest to make. If it was told to produce 1,000 men's shoes, it made them all in one size. If it was told to produce 1,000 shoes in a variety for men, women, and children, it produced 998 baby shoes, one pump, and one wing tip. If it was told to produce 3,000 pounds of shoes, it produced one enormous pair of concrete sneakers.

When the Russian government allowed people to bring back $2,000 in duty-free imports, Russians reacted. "Clothing, toys, and small appliances were packed into enormous burlap sacks so that the baggage-claim area of any Russian airport with international flights seemed to be populated by hundreds of Santa Clauses in their off-duty clothes." During O'Rourke's four-day trip on the famed Trans-Siberian Railroad across Russia, he sat on the south side of the train, with no fan, no ventilation, no window shade, and a window that didn't open. So he got relief by sticking his head out of a window in the corridor and letting his jaw hang open in the breeze. "I saw most of Siberia the way your dog sees I-95."

So what does cause economic growth? O'Rourke reaches pretty much the same conclusions Adam Smith reached, namely that clearly enforced property rights, free markets, free trade, and small government create wealth. What keeps people poor, writes O'Rourke, are large governments doing too much, and almost all of it badly.

In a passage unusual for its serious passion, O'Rourke writes, "Poverty is hard, wretched, and humiliating. Poverty is schoolgirl prostitutes trying to feed their parents in Cuba. . . . But what poverty is not is sad. Poverty is infuriating."

P. J. O'Rourke and Steven Zeitchik (interview date 13 August 2001)

SOURCE: O'Rourke, P. J., and Steven Zeitchik. "*PW* Talks with P. J. O'Rourke." *Publishers Weekly* 248, no. 33 (13 August 2001): 302.

[In the following interview, O'Rourke discusses the current state of American politics.]

Sure he coos, "Are you the cutest thing on earth or what?" to his one-year-old. Yes, he can hold forth intelligently on the virtues of Disney's *Tarzan*. And seeing him carry a basket of toys from F.A.O. Schwarz does seem a little like watching Colin Powell play with Pokeman cards.

But P. J. O'Rourke's newest book [*The CEO of the Sofa*] doesn't show his softer side. The man who over the years has proven that "funny conservative" doesn't need to be an oxymoron, still knocks boy bands and NATO in the same breath. Yet we wondered about P. J. the man. On a recent Saturday, *PW* [*Publishers Weekly*] made the trip to his New Hampshire home, where, after a family picnic and an emergency outing to "The Velveteen Rabbit," O'Rourke tried to put our concerns to rest.

[Zeitchik]: There's talk in this book of bedtime stories and proper childhood nutrition. Readers want to know: Is P. J. O'Rourke jumping to the other side?

[O'Rourke]: Well, the book looks like it's about family, but it's not. It's a very cheap device to throw together a bunch of stuff that was sitting in my files. I owed Morgan Entrekin a book. And then I came across *The Autocrat of the Breakfast-Table* by Oliver Wendell Holmes and was charmed by it. He had discovered a way to cobble together all sorts of crap that he'd been writing for years. And I thought, "I've got to steal this."

As usual, you write a lot about Washington. What bothers you most about the current state of politics?

Politics sees itself as a panacea, and it's not. I'm very antiabortion. But the abortion question will not be solved in the courts or the legislatures. People will stop having abortions when they think it's wrong.

So you'd still call yourself a libertarian?

Yes, but not with a capital L. The capital L libertarian is the high school calculus teacher backing you into a corner over some warm white wine and explaining why the sidewalks should be privatized. Lovely guy, really nice person and for all I know he's right about the sidewalks. But it makes for a damn uninteresting hour-and-a-half.

You've been pretty hard on Bush. Not as hard as you were on Clinton, but hard.

Bush is a guy whom I think I would personally like, and yet I'm ticked off at him for all sorts of things he's doing, like starting all these entitlement programs. What

happened during the Clinton era was that, as a pundit, you end up turning on the American people, and there's little profit in that. You think: you idiots, you go for the WWF, *People* magazine and now Bill Clinton. But then, wait a minute, where does this line of thinking run?

Not to many freelance checks.

Right. And next thing you know, you've got a talk-radio show that's worse than Rush Limbaugh—it's Ezra Pound. The original bad talk-radio host.

You're pretty curmudgeonly on technology.

I hate cell phones. They take all the fun out of being far away. I hate computers. I'm a mechanical creature. I just threw up my hands at the e-mail thing. I think there should be a law that says that one month every year people can communicate only in person or in ink on nice paper, by post office.

How does that square with your libertarianism?

Not very well. But isn't consistency the bugbear of little minds.

Speaking of little minds . . .

Yeah, I don't know how Hillary Clinton is doing in the Senate. She doesn't seem to be doing much. But as I say in the book, the Senate is a tar pit. Nobody does much of anything.

There are critics who would say you go for the punch line first and ideology second.

Point well taken. I'll go for a punch line no matter how much it violates what I think, and explain later. Same goes for a good story. There are some things that are much too good to subject to the discourtesies of investigative journalism.

Andrew Anthony (review date 9 September 2001)

SOURCE: Anthony, Andrew. "Sitting Too Comfortably: Has Domesticity Finally Tamed P. J. O'Rourke?" *Observer* (9 September 2001): 15.

[In the following mixed review of The CEO of the Sofa, *Anthony traces O'Rourke's stylistic and thematic development as a humorist and essayist.]*

There is an American form of humour that no longer has an equivalent on this side of the water. The tradition of the comic essay died in Britain about the same time as *Punch* magazine. The cause of death, of course, was incurable tedium.

In the States, though, the names of James Thurber, S. J. Perelman and Wolcott Gibbs are still spoken of with something close to awe, and the role of the humorist is no joke. The writer who has done most to maintain its cultural importance is P. J. O'Rourke, author of such catchy titles as *Holidays in Hell* and *Give War a Chance.*

As Christopher Hitchens observed, O'Rourke's stock character is 'that of a crazed Sixties refugee who has renounced everything but the craziness'. Like many draft-aged men of his generation, O'Rourke waited until the end of the Vietnam War to cut his hair and make his peace with the good old-fashioned American values of militarism and materialism.

What set him apart from traditional conservatives (at least overtly) was a continuing interest in a libertarian lifestyle—his most celebrated essay was called **'How to Drive Fast on Drugs While Getting Your Wing-Wang Squeezed and Not Spill Your Drink'**.

That was back in the Eighties, when O'Rourke was already approaching 40. Thereafter, he furthered his reputation by being naughty abroad, writing the kind of unsayable things about Third World countries that make liberals guffaw with guilty laughter (conservatives don't read about the Third World).

Now 54, and perhaps keen to lose his long-time companion epithet 'sophomoric', he has written a book rooted in the middle-aged setting of a family house. *The CEO of the Sofa* is a rather mannered bow to Oliver Wendell Holmes, the nineteenth-century American author of *The Autocrat of the Breakfast Table.*

Perhaps in an effort to demonstrate his erudition, O'Rourke has adopted Holmes's folksy conceit of one-sided conversations with silent family members as a means of covering unrelated topics such as the New Economy, Leonardo DiCaprio and almost anything else that crosses his mind.

The digressive monologue is a natural progression for O'Rourke. He has always been a bit of a dinner-party bore, bombarding you with his wit and opinions. He even wrote an essay on dinner-table conversation in which he described the qualities of the good talker—'an ability to hold forth at length: to tell a fully rounded anecdote, make an elaborate jest, convey news in piquant detail, or give an unexpected coif to the feathers of reason.' Guess who he had in mind?

The point about O'Rourke is that he is funny. He memorably described the USA for Africa performers (the people who sang the dismal 'We Are the World')

as having 'that self-satisfied look of toddlers on a pot'. The other point about O'Rourke is that he's not that funny. One moment he'll come up with a piece of inspired absurdism that jumps off the page. Musing on the possibility of America becoming so rich that everyone is a billionaire, he writes: 'Nobody will care about money any more—just sex. I'll have to sleep with the guys at the car wash to get the interior vacuumed.'

Too often he is unable to resist a joke, no matter how lame. Take, for example, this sentence: 'People over 50 always think things are going to heck in a handbasket, or in one of those Prada backpacks, or in something.' There's a lot of this filler stuff in *The CEO of the Sofa*: not funny, not true, not needed. A ratio of one good joke for every three is very high. He may, sentence for sentence, be the funniest man in the English language. But he's also one of the most tiring.

Nearly as much as O'Rourke wants us to laugh at his every word, he wants us to take him seriously. If he is a humorist by talent, he's a polemicist by nature. You can make what you want of his politics, but, boy, does he need some new targets. His skewering here of Hillary Clinton's book *It Takes a Village* is savage, richly entertaining (including a joke about breastfeeding Chelsea that is the book's funniest) and at least three years out of date.

Like the Japanese soldier still fighting on a South Pacific island, O'Rourke doesn't seem to have noticed that no one believes in the Third Way or that the Clintons have left the White House, still less that Dubya has moved in. And for even the most devout Republican, it must be a full-time occupation not making fun of the Bush boy.

The datedness of O'Rourke's subjects is further pronounced by the datedness of O'Rourke. When he was younger (well, 39), there appeared to be a winning unorthodoxy about taking up reactionary positions more normally associated with ageing squares. But what's so radical or unusual about a fat guy in his mid-fifties holding forth on the evils of the United Nations?

There's much to enjoy in *The CEO of the Sofa*—a fine riff on why drugs should and should not be legalised; an amusing comparison between Venice and the Venetian hotel in Las Vegas; and welcome attacks on people such as Moby—'like something the guinea pig just gave birth to'—and Matt Damon. But, ultimately, the tone is smug and complacent. It's the sound of a well-fed, middle-aged humorist wielding a giant Havana like an award, sinking into a freshly plumped cushion.

John Dugdale (review date 7 December 2002)

SOURCE: Dugdale, John. Review of *The CEO of the Sofa,* by P. J. O'Rourke. *Guardian* (7 December 2002): 39.

[*In the following review, Dugdale regards the essays collected in* The CEO of the Sofa *as dated and stale.*]

As a "devotee of recycling", O'Rourke hates the idea of his one-off travel articles, book reviews and rants against the Clintons being consigned to oblivion, but his literary conscience makes him honourably reluctant simply to dump these old columns, unrevised and unlinked, in the reader's lap [in *The CEO of the Sofa.*] So he reworks a ruse used by the 19th-century writer Oliver Wendell Holmes and presents them as monologues or letters to his immediate circle. The result is probably not what he intended. Engagingly self-mocking and comparatively timeless, the connecting dialogues are fresh and fun; whereas his patchy, disparate writings from 2000-01 unappetisingly tackle bygone books and such musty topics as the presidential poll and the collapse of dotcom optimism. Only a few pieces—an anti-UN satire, an essay on summer and an ingenious guide to using childcare manuals to understand how women manage men—escape the sense of staleness.

Kirkus Reviews (review date 15 April 2004)

SOURCE: Review of *Peace Kills,* by P. J. O'Rourke. *Kirkus Reviews* 72, no. 8 (15 April 2004): 380-81.

[*In the following review, the critic finds* Peace Kills *less sour and barbed than O'Rourke's earlier work.*]

The senior satirist of the right returns to dissect foreign policy and—Lord help us—he seems to have moments of distinct sanity. Never mind the purposefully Orwellian title.

Because Americans are foreigners, Americans hate foreign policy, says the libertarian comedian. He doesn't seem too fond of foreign policy either. With less of his accustomed spleen [in *Peace Kills*], his points seem sometimes less barbed than might be expected. The pundit offers no puns; he is less sour and presents fewer ad hominem attacks than in his earlier texts (*The CEO of the Sofa,* 2001, etc.). He's not nearly as fractious as the Sunday morning talking heads. With less embroidery, our comedian seems to be maturing, citing eminent greybeards like Fouad Ajami and Bernard Lewis anent the inscrutable Middle East. O'Rourke lands in Israel in

time for Passover and in Egypt in time for Ramadan, 2001, and has a few cogent comments about what he sees, admittedly as a tourist. In Kuwait at the start of the most recent hostilities, he becomes a "unilateral" war correspondent amid Humvees, Bradley fighting vehicles, and Patriot missile launchers, embedded in a hotel full of TV producers. Checking out ravaged Iraq, his backgrounder journalism is first-rate and, reviewing a Washington Mall political demonstration, his color reportage is smartly selective and funny. We will never catch O'Rourke, ever the professional reporter, wearing a kaffiyeh to make an obscure point. Effectively ruining his chances for a Nobel, he bravely sasses the prize committee; with heavy sarcasm he deconstructs a surely well-meant, albeit fatuous, commemorative statement by a committee of laureates. Included is an obligatory September 11th essay and effective musings on warfare from the sands of Iwo Jima.

Publishers Weekly (review date 10 May 2004)

SOURCE: Review of *Peace Kills,* by P. J. O'Rourke. *Publishers Weekly* 251, no. 19 (10 May 2004): 47.

[*In the following review, the critic describes* Peace Kills *as less humorous and more sober than O'Rourke's earlier essays on American foreign policy.*]

O'Rourke has made a career out of telling people off. As a foreign correspondent for the *Atlantic Monthly* and *Rolling Stone,* he has demonstrated a flair for sarcasm and an aptitude for making people laugh. In his 11th book [*Peace Kills*], however, this provocateur par excellence presents a more sober and, alas, less funny, take than usual, this time in essays on American foreign policy, including visits to several important countries on the international scene. Starting with Kosovo, he comments on the Serbian-Albanian conflict, then makes his way to Israel, Egypt, Kuwait and Iraq. Other entries look at the effects of September 11 on the U.S. home front, which includes poking fun at airport search techniques and a clever deconstruction of a 2001 statement on peace and social justice signed by 103 Nobelists. O'Rourke's book does many of the things a conservative bestseller is supposed to do: it's irreverent, in-your-face and often offensive (Hillary Clinton: "the furious harridan on the White House third floor"). Yet O'Rourke, the funny man of foreign politics, seems less interested in humor here than in slightly skewed reporting. His articles on Israel and Egypt, for example, are basically descriptive, a diary account of where he went, what he saw, the hotels he stayed in, the food he ate, interrupted every so often by O'Rourke's trademark non sequitur humor. The author's fans probably won't mind the slight shift in direction, though they will wish for more laughs; O'Rourke is one of the most popular conservative authors around and this book, like his others, should find a happy nest on national bestseller lists.

FURTHER READING

Criticism

Boyer, Allen D. Review of *The CEO of the Sofa,* by P. J. O'Rourke. *New York Times Book Review* (16 September 2001): 28.

> Brief review of *The CEO of the Sofa.*

Chapman, Stephen. "P. J. O'Rourke Wields Humor to Shake Politics to Its Hoots." *Chicago Tribune Books* (10 May 1987): 4.

> Contends that although a few of the humorous essays in *Republican Party Reptile* don't work, the book as a whole is entertaining.

Conniff, Ruth. "Our Best Reading of 1992." *Progressive* 56, no. 12 (December 1992): 34.

> Deems *Parliament of Whores* the funniest book she read in 1992.

Friedman, Paula. Review of *Peace Kills,* by P. J. O'Rourke. *New York Times Book Review* (27 June 2004): 16.

> Mixed review of *Peace Kills.*

Greider, William. "Why I Don't Believe What He Believes." *Rolling Stone* (13 July 1995): 60-6.

> Finds weaknesses in O'Rourke's conservative agenda.

Parvin, Landon. "With Malice Towards All." *Washington Post Book World* 21, no. 22 (2 June 1991): 6.

> Deems *Parliament of Whores* "insulting, inflammatory, profane and absolutely great reading."

Quinn, Anthony. "Unpleasant Laughter." *Sunday Times* (11 December 1994): n.p.

> Review of *All the Trouble in the World,* calling O'Rourke "America's greatest prose comedian."

Welch, Colin. "Then America Mocks Itself." *Spectator* 267, no. 8511 (24 August 1991): 22-3.

> Review of *Parliament of Whores*; applauds O'Rourke's "ruthlessly iconoclastic conservatism" as well as his bold humor.

Witte, Griff. "It's Time to Leave the Sofa: O'Rourke a Victim of His Own Success?" *Denver Post* (9 September 2001): 1-5.

> Criticizes *The CEO of the Sofa* for stale humor and lazy observations.

Additional coverage of O'Rourke's life and career is contained in the following sources published by Thomson Gale: *Contemporary Authors,* **Vols. 77-80;** *Contemporary Authors New Revision Series,* **Vols. 13, 41, 67, 111;** *Contemporary Popular Writers*; *Dictionary of Literary Biography,* **Vol. 185;** *DISCovering Authors Modules: Popular Fiction and Genre Authors*; **and** *Literature Resource Center.*

How to Use This Index

The main references

> **Calvino, Italo**
> 1923-1985 .... **CLC 5, 8, 11, 22, 33, 39,**
> **73; SSC 3, 48**

list all author entries in the following Gale Literary Criticism series:

AAL = Asian American Literature
BG = The Beat Generation: A Gale Critical Companion
BLC = Black Literature Criticism
BLCS = Black Literature Criticism Supplement
CLC = Contemporary Literary Criticism
CLR = Children's Literature Review
CMLC = Classical and Medieval Literature Criticism
DC = Drama Criticism
HLC = Hispanic Literature Criticism
HLCS = Hispanic Literature Criticism Supplement
HR = Harlem Renaissance: A Gale Critical Companion
LC = Literature Criticism from 1400 to 1800
NCLC = Nineteenth-Century Literature Criticism
NNAL = Native North American Literature
PC = Poetry Criticism
SSC = Short Story Criticism
TCLC = Twentieth-Century Literary Criticism
WLC = World Literature Criticism, 1500 to the Present
WLCS = World Literature Criticism Supplement

The cross-references

> See also CA 85-88, 116; CANR 23, 61;
> DAM NOV; DLB 196; EW 13; MTCW 1, 2;
> RGSF 2; RGWL 2; SFW 4; SSFS 12

list all author entries in the following Gale biographical and literary sources:

AAYA = Authors & Artists for Young Adults
AFAW = African American Writers
AFW = African Writers
AITN = Authors in the News
AMW = American Writers
AMWR = American Writers Retrospective Supplement
AMWS = American Writers Supplement
ANW = American Nature Writers
AW = Ancient Writers
BEST = Bestsellers
BPFB = Beacham's Encyclopedia of Popular Fiction: Biography and Resources
BRW = British Writers
BRWS = British Writers Supplement
BW = Black Writers
BYA = Beacham's Guide to Literature for Young Adults
CA = Contemporary Authors
CAAS = Contemporary Authors Autobiography Series
CABS = Contemporary Authors Bibliographical Series
CAD = Contemporary American Dramatists
CANR = Contemporary Authors New Revision Series
CAP = Contemporary Authors Permanent Series
CBD = Contemporary British Dramatists
CCA = Contemporary Canadian Authors
CD = Contemporary Dramatists
CDALB = Concise Dictionary of American Literary Biography
CDALBS = Concise Dictionary of American Literary Biography Supplement
CDBLB = Concise Dictionary of British Literary Biography

CMW = *St. James Guide to Crime & Mystery Writers*
CN = *Contemporary Novelists*
CP = *Contemporary Poets*
CPW = *Contemporary Popular Writers*
CSW = *Contemporary Southern Writers*
CWD = *Contemporary Women Dramatists*
CWP = *Contemporary Women Poets*
CWRI = *St. James Guide to Children's Writers*
CWW = *Contemporary World Writers*
DA = *DISCovering Authors*
DA3 = *DISCovering Authors 3.0*
DAB = *DISCovering Authors: British Edition*
DAC = *DISCovering Authors: Canadian Edition*
DAM = *DISCovering Authors: Modules*
   DRAM: *Dramatists Module;* **MST:** *Most-studied Authors Module;*
   MULT: *Multicultural Authors Module;* **NOV:** *Novelists Module;*
   POET: *Poets Module;* **POP:** *Popular Fiction and Genre Authors Module*
DFS = *Drama for Students*
DLB = *Dictionary of Literary Biography*
DLBD = *Dictionary of Literary Biography Documentary Series*
DLBY = *Dictionary of Literary Biography Yearbook*
DNFS = *Literature of Developing Nations for Students*
EFS = *Epics for Students*
EXPN = *Exploring Novels*
EXPP = *Exploring Poetry*
EXPS = *Exploring Short Stories*
EW = *European Writers*
FANT = *St. James Guide to Fantasy Writers*
FW = *Feminist Writers*
GFL = *Guide to French Literature,* Beginnings to 1789, 1798 to the Present
GLL = *Gay and Lesbian Literature*
HGG = *St. James Guide to Horror, Ghost & Gothic Writers*
HW = *Hispanic Writers*
IDFW = *International Dictionary of Films and Filmmakers: Writers and Production Artists*
IDTP = *International Dictionary of Theatre: Playwrights*
LAIT = *Literature and Its Times*
LAW = *Latin American Writers*
JRDA = *Junior DISCovering Authors*
MAICYA = *Major Authors and Illustrators for Children and Young Adults*
MAICYAS = *Major Authors and Illustrators for Children and Young Adults Supplement*
MAWW = *Modern American Women Writers*
MJW = *Modern Japanese Writers*
MTCW = *Major 20th-Century Writers*
NCFS = *Nonfiction Classics for Students*
NFS = *Novels for Students*
PAB = *Poets: American and British*
PFS = *Poetry for Students*
RGAL = *Reference Guide to American Literature*
RGEL = *Reference Guide to English Literature*
RGSF = *Reference Guide to Short Fiction*
RGWL = *Reference Guide to World Literature*
RHW = *Twentieth-Century Romance and Historical Writers*
SAAS = *Something about the Author Autobiography Series*
SATA = *Something about the Author*
SFW = *St. James Guide to Science Fiction Writers*
SSFS = *Short Stories for Students*
TCWW = *Twentieth-Century Western Writers*
WLIT = *World Literature and Its Times*
WP = *World Poets*
YABC = *Yesterday's Authors of Books for Children*
YAW = *St. James Guide to Young Adult Writers*

Literary Criticism Series
Cumulative Author Index

Armah, Ayi Kwei 1939- . **BLC 1; CLC 5, 33, 136**
　　See also AFW; BRWS 10; BW 1; CA 61-64; CANR 21, 64; CDWLB 3; CN 7; DAM MULT, POET; DLB 117; EWL 3; MTCW 1; WLIT 2

Armatrading, Joan 1950- .... **CLC 17**
　　See also CA 114; 186

Armitage, Frank
　　See Carpenter, John (Howard)

Armstrong, Jeannette (C.) 1948- .... **NNAL**
　　See also CA 149; CCA 1; CN 7; DAC; SATA 102

Arnette, Robert
　　See Silverberg, Robert

Arnim, Achim von (Ludwig Joachim von Arnim) 1781-1831 ..... **NCLC 5; SSC 29**
　　See also DLB 90

Arnim, Bettina von 1785-1859 ...... **NCLC 38, 123**
　　See also DLB 90; RGWL 2, 3

Arnold, Matthew 1822-1888 ..... **NCLC 6, 29, 89, 126; PC 5; WLC**
　　See also BRW 5; CDBLB 1832-1890; DA; DAB; DAC; DAM MST, POET; DLB 32, 57; EXPP; PAB; PFS 2; TEA; WP

Arnold, Thomas 1795-1842 .... **NCLC 18**
　　See also DLB 55

Arnow, Harriette (Louisa) Simpson 1908-1986 .... **CLC 2, 7, 18**
　　See also BPFB 1; CA 9-12R; 118; CANR 14; DLB 6; FW; MTCW 1, 2; RHW; SATA 42; SATA-Obit 47

Arouet, Francois-Marie
　　See Voltaire

Arp, Hans
　　See Arp, Jean

Arp, Jean 1887-1966 .... **CLC 5; TCLC 115**
　　See also CA 81-84; 25-28R; CANR 42, 77; EW 10

Arrabal
　　See Arrabal, Fernando

Arrabal, Fernando 1932- ... **CLC 2, 9, 18, 58**
　　See Arrabal (Teran), Fernando
　　See also CA 9-12R; CANR 15; EWL 3; LMFS 2

Arrabal (Teran), Fernando 1932-
　　See Arrabal, Fernando
　　See also CWW 2

Arreola, Juan Jose 1918-2001 .... **CLC 147; HLC 1; SSC 38**
　　See also CA 113; 131; 200; CANR 81; CWW 2; DAM MULT; DLB 113; DNFS 2; EWL 3; HW 1, 2; LAW; RGSF 2

Arrian c. 89(?)-c. 155(?) .... **CMLC 43**
　　See also DLB 176

Arrick, Fran .... **CLC 30**
　　See Gaberman, Judie Angell
　　See also BYA 6

Arrley, Richmond
　　See Delany, Samuel R(ay), Jr.

Artaud, Antonin (Marie Joseph) 1896-1948 .... **DC 14; TCLC 3, 36**
　　See also CA 104; 149; DA3; DAM DRAM; DLB 258; EW 11; EWL 3; GFL 1789 to the Present; MTCW 1; RGWL 2, 3

Arthur, Ruth M(abel) 1905-1979 .... **CLC 12**
　　See also CA 9-12R; 85-88; CANR 4; CWRI 5; SATA 7, 26

Artsybashev, Mikhail (Petrovich) 1878-1927 .... **TCLC 31**
　　See also CA 170; DLB 295

Arundel, Honor (Morfydd) 1919-1973 .... **CLC 17**
　　See also CA 21-22; 41-44R; CAP 2; CLR 35; CWRI 5; SATA 4; SATA-Obit 24

Arzner, Dorothy 1900-1979 .... **CLC 98**

Asch, Sholem 1880-1957 .... **TCLC 3**
　　See also CA 105; EWL 3; GLL 2

Ascham, Roger 1516(?)-1568 .... **LC 101**
　　See also DLB 236

Ash, Shalom
　　See Asch, Sholem

Ashbery, John (Lawrence) 1927- .. **CLC 2, 3, 4, 6, 9, 13, 15, 25, 41, 77, 125; PC 26**
　　See Berry, Jonas
　　See also AMWS 3; CA 5-8R; CANR 9, 37, 66, 102, 132; CP 7; DA3; DAM POET; DLB 5, 165; DLBY 1981; EWL 3; INT CANR-9; MTCW 1, 2; PAB; PFS 11; RGAL 4; WP

Ashdown, Clifford
　　See Freeman, R(ichard) Austin

Ashe, Gordon
　　See Creasey, John

Ashton-Warner, Sylvia (Constance) 1908-1984 .... **CLC 19**
　　See also CA 69-72; 112; CANR 29; MTCW 1, 2

Asimov, Isaac 1920-1992 ..... **CLC 1, 3, 9, 19, 26, 76, 92**
　　See also AAYA 13; BEST 90:2; BPFB 1; BYA 4, 6, 7, 9; CA 1-4R; 137; CANR 2, 19, 36, 60, 125; CLR 12, 79; CMW 4; CPW; DA3; DAM POP; DLB 8; DLBY 1992; INT CANR-19; JRDA; LAIT 5; LMFS 2; MAICYA 1, 2; MTCW 1, 2; RGAL 4; SATA 1, 26, 74; SCFW 2; SFW 4; SSFS 17; TUS; YAW

Askew, Anne 1521(?)-1546 .... **LC 81**
　　See also DLB 136

Assis, Joaquim Maria Machado de
　　See Machado de Assis, Joaquim Maria

Astell, Mary 1666-1731 .... **LC 68**
　　See also DLB 252; FW

Astley, Thea (Beatrice May) 1925-2004 .... **CLC 41**
　　See also CA 65-68; 229; CANR 11, 43, 78; CN 7; DLB 289; EWL 3

Astley, William 1855-1911
　　See Warung, Price

Aston, James
　　See White, T(erence) H(anbury)

Asturias, Miguel Angel 1899-1974 .... **CLC 3, 8, 13; HLC 1**
　　See also CA 25-28; 49-52; CANR 32; CAP 2; CDWLB 3; DA3; DAM MULT, NOV; DLB 113, 290; EWL 3; HW 1; LAW; LMFS 2; MTCW 1, 2; RGWL 2, 3; WLIT 1

Atares, Carlos Saura
　　See Saura (Atares), Carlos

Athanasius c. 295-c. 373 .... **CMLC 48**

Atheling, William
　　See Pound, Ezra (Weston Loomis)

Atheling, William, Jr.
　　See Blish, James (Benjamin)

Atherton, Gertrude (Franklin Horn) 1857-1948 .... **TCLC 2**
　　See also CA 104; 155; DLB 9, 78, 186; HGG; RGAL 4; SUFW 1; TCWW 2

Atherton, Lucius
　　See Masters, Edgar Lee

Atkins, Jack
　　See Harris, Mark

Atkinson, Kate 1951- .... **CLC 99**
　　See also CA 166; CANR 101; DLB 267

Attaway, William (Alexander) 1911-1986 .... **BLC 1; CLC 92**
　　See also BW 2, 3; CA 143; CANR 82; DAM MULT; DLB 76

Atticus
　　See Fleming, Ian (Lancaster); Wilson, (Thomas) Woodrow

Atwood, Margaret (Eleanor) 1939- ... **CLC 2, 3, 4, 8, 13, 15, 25, 44, 84, 135; PC 8; SSC 2, 46; WLC**
　　See also AAYA 12, 47; AMWS 13; BEST 89:2; BPFB 1; CA 49-52; CANR 3, 24, 33, 59, 95, 133; CN 7; CP 7; CPW; CWP; DA; DA3; DAB; DAC; DAM MST, NOV, POET; DLB 53, 251; EWL 3; EXPN; FW; INT CANR-24; LAIT 5; MTCW 1, 2; NFS 4, 12, 13, 14, 19; PFS 7; RGSF 2; SATA 50; SSFS 3, 13; TWA; WWE 1; YAW

Aubigny, Pierre d'
　　See Mencken, H(enry) L(ouis)

Aubin, Penelope 1685-1731(?) .... **LC 9**
　　See also DLB 39

Auchincloss, Louis (Stanton) 1917- .. **CLC 4, 6, 9, 18, 45; SSC 22**
　　See also AMWS 4; CA 1-4R; CANR 6, 29, 55, 87, 130; CN 7; DAM NOV; DLB 2, 244; DLBY 1980; EWL 3; INT CANR-29; MTCW 1; RGAL 4

Auden, W(ystan) H(ugh) 1907-1973 . **CLC 1, 2, 3, 4, 6, 9, 11, 14, 43, 123; PC 1; WLC**
　　See also AAYA 18; AMWS 2; BRW 7; BRWR 1; CA 9-12R; 45-48; CANR 5, 61, 105; CDBLB 1914-1945; DA; DA3; DAB; DAC; DAM DRAM, MST, POET; DLB 10, 20; EWL 3; EXPP; MTCW 1, 2; PAB; PFS 1, 3, 4, 10; TUS; WP

Audiberti, Jacques 1899-1965 .... **CLC 38**
　　See also CA 25-28R; DAM DRAM; EWL 3

Audubon, John James 1785-1851 . **NCLC 47**
　　See also ANW; DLB 248

Auel, Jean M(arie) 1936- .... **CLC 31, 107**
　　See also AAYA 7, 51; BEST 90:4; BPFB 1; CA 103; CANR 21, 64, 115; CPW; DA3; DAM POP; INT CANR-21; NFS 11; RHW; SATA 91

Auerbach, Erich 1892-1957 .... **TCLC 43**
　　See also CA 118; 155; EWL 3

Augier, Emile 1820-1889 .... **NCLC 31**
　　See also DLB 192; GFL 1789 to the Present

August, John
　　See De Voto, Bernard (Augustine)

Augustine, St. 354-430 .... **CMLC 6; WLCS**
　　See also DA; DA3; DAB; DAC; DAM MST; DLB 115; EW 1; RGWL 2, 3

Aunt Belinda
　　See Braddon, Mary Elizabeth

Aunt Weedy
　　See Alcott, Louisa May

Aurelius
　　See Bourne, Randolph S(illiman)

Aurelius, Marcus 121-180 .... **CMLC 45**
　　See Marcus Aurelius
　　See also RGWL 2, 3

Aurobindo, Sri
　　See Ghose, Aurabinda

Aurobindo Ghose
　　See Ghose, Aurabinda

Austen, Jane 1775-1817 ...... **NCLC 1, 13, 19, 33, 51, 81, 95, 119, 150; WLC**
　　See also AAYA 19; BRW 4; BRWC 1; BRWR 2; BYA 3; CDBLB 1789-1832; DA; DA3; DAB; DAC; DAM MST, NOV; DLB 116; EXPN; LAIT 2; LATS 1:1; LMFS 1; NFS 1, 14, 18, 20; TEA; WLIT 3; WYAS 1

Auster, Paul 1947- .... **CLC 47, 131**
　　See also AMWS 12; CA 69-72; CANR 23, 52, 75, 129; CMW 4; CN 7; DA3; DLB 227; MTCW 1; SUFW 2

Austin, Frank
　　See Faust, Frederick (Schiller)
　　See also TCWW 2

Baraka, Amiri 1934- .... **BLC 1; CLC 1, 2, 3, 5, 10, 14, 33, 115; DC 6; PC 4; WLCS**
See Jones, LeRoi
See also AFAW 1, 2; AMWS 2; BW 2, 3; CA 21-24R; CABS 3; CAD; CANR 27, 38, 61, 133; CD 5; CDALB 1941-1968; CP 7; CPW; DA; DA3; DAC; DAM MST, MULT, POET, POP; DFS 3, 11, 16; DLB 5, 7, 16, 38; DLBD 8; EWL 3; MTCW 1, 2; PFS 9; RGAL 4; TUS; WP

Baratynsky, Evgenii Abramovich 1800-1844 .... **NCLC 103**
See also DLB 205

Barbauld, Anna Laetitia 1743-1825 .... **NCLC 50**
See also DLB 107, 109, 142, 158; RGEL 2

Barbellion, W. N. P. .... **TCLC 24**
See Cummings, Bruce F(rederick)

Barber, Benjamin R. 1939- .... **CLC 141**
See also CA 29-32R; CANR 12, 32, 64, 119

Barbera, Jack (Vincent) 1945- .... **CLC 44**
See also CA 110; CANR 45

Barbey d'Aurevilly, Jules-Amedee 1808-1889 .... **NCLC 1; SSC 17**
See also DLB 119; GFL 1789 to the Present

Barbour, John c. 1316-1395 .... **CMLC 33**
See also DLB 146

Barbusse, Henri 1873-1935 .... **TCLC 5**
See also CA 105; 154; DLB 65; EWL 3; RGWL 2, 3

Barclay, Alexander c. 1475-1552 .... **LC 109**
See also DLB 132

Barclay, Bill
See Moorcock, Michael (John)

Barclay, William Ewert
See Moorcock, Michael (John)

Barea, Arturo 1897-1957 .... **TCLC 14**
See also CA 111; 201

Barfoot, Joan 1946- .... **CLC 18**
See also CA 105

Barham, Richard Harris 1788-1845 .... **NCLC 77**
See also DLB 159

Baring, Maurice 1874-1945 .... **TCLC 8**
See also CA 105; 168; DLB 34; HGG

Baring-Gould, Sabine 1834-1924 ... **TCLC 88**
See also DLB 156, 190

Barker, Clive 1952- .... **CLC 52, 205; SSC 53**
See also AAYA 10, 54; BEST 90:3; BPFB 1; CA 121; 129; CANR 71, 111, 133; CPW; DA3; DAM POP; DLB 261; HGG; INT CA-129; MTCW 1, 2; SUFW 2

Barker, George Granville 1913-1991 .... **CLC 8, 48**
See also CA 9-12R; 135; CANR 7, 38; DAM POET; DLB 20; EWL 3; MTCW 1

Barker, Harley Granville
See Granville-Barker, Harley
See also DLB 10

Barker, Howard 1946- .... **CLC 37**
See also CA 102; CBD; CD 5; DLB 13, 233

Barker, Jane 1652-1732 .... **LC 42, 82**
See also DLB 39, 131

Barker, Pat(ricia) 1943- ...... **CLC 32, 94, 146**
See also BRWS 4; CA 117; 122; CANR 50, 101; CN 7; DLB 271; INT CA-122

Barlach, Ernst (Heinrich) 1870-1938 .... **TCLC 84**
See also CA 178; DLB 56, 118; EWL 3

Barlow, Joel 1754-1812 .... **NCLC 23**
See also AMWS 2; DLB 37; RGAL 4

Barnard, Mary (Ethel) 1909- .... **CLC 48**
See also CA 21-22; CAP 2

Barnes, Djuna 1892-1982 .... **CLC 3, 4, 8, 11, 29, 127; SSC 3**
See Steptoe, Lydia
See also AMWS 3; CA 9-12R; 107; CAD; CANR 16, 55; CWD; DLB 4, 9, 45; EWL 3; GLL 1; MTCW 1, 2; RGAL 4; TUS

Barnes, Jim 1933- .... **NNAL**
See also CA 108, 175; CAAE 175; CAAS 28; DLB 175

Barnes, Julian (Patrick) 1946- . **CLC 42, 141**
See also BRWS 4; CA 102; CANR 19, 54, 115; CN 7; DAB; DLB 194; DLBY 1993; EWL 3; MTCW 1

Barnes, Peter 1931-2004 .... **CLC 5, 56**
See also CA 65-68; CAAS 12; CANR 33, 34, 64, 113; CBD; CD 5; DFS 6; DLB 13, 233; MTCW 1

Barnes, William 1801-1886 .... **NCLC 75**
See also DLB 32

Baroja (y Nessi), Pio 1872-1956 .... **HLC 1; TCLC 8**
See also CA 104; EW 9

Baron, David
See Pinter, Harold

Baron Corvo
See Rolfe, Frederick (William Serafino Austin Lewis Mary)

Barondess, Sue K(aufman) 1926-1977 .... **CLC 8**
See Kaufman, Sue
See also CA 1-4R; 69-72; CANR 1

Baron de Teive
See Pessoa, Fernando (Antonio Nogueira)

Baroness Von S.
See Zangwill, Israel

Barres, (Auguste-)Maurice 1862-1923 .... **TCLC 47**
See also CA 164; DLB 123; GFL 1789 to the Present

Barreto, Afonso Henrique de Lima
See Lima Barreto, Afonso Henrique de

Barrett, Andrea 1954- .... **CLC 150**
See also CA 156; CANR 92

Barrett, Michele .... **CLC 65**

Barrett, (Roger) Syd 1946- .... **CLC 35**

Barrett, William (Christopher) 1913-1992 .... **CLC 27**
See also CA 13-16R; 139; CANR 11, 67; INT CANR-11

Barrett Browning, Elizabeth 1806-1861 ... **NCLC 1, 16, 61, 66; PC 6, 62; WLC**
See also BRW 4; CDBLB 1832-1890; DA; DA3; DAB; DAC; DAM MST, POET; DLB 32, 199; EXPP; PAB; PFS 2, 16; TEA; WLIT 4; WP

Barrie, J(ames) M(atthew) 1860-1937 .... **TCLC 2, 164**
See also BRWS 3; BYA 4, 5; CA 104; 136; CANR 77; CDBLB 1890-1914; CLR 16; CWRI 5; DA3; DAB; DAM DRAM; DFS 7; DLB 10, 141, 156; EWL 3; FANT; MAICYA 1, 2; MTCW 1; SATA 100; SUFW; WCH; WLIT 4; YABC 1

Barrington, Michael
See Moorcock, Michael (John)

Barrol, Grady
See Bograd, Larry

Barry, Mike
See Malzberg, Barry N(athaniel)

Barry, Philip 1896-1949 .... **TCLC 11**
See also CA 109; 199; DFS 9; DLB 7, 228; RGAL 4

Bart, Andre Schwarz
See Schwarz-Bart, Andre

Barth, John (Simmons) 1930- ... **CLC 1, 2, 3, 5, 7, 9, 10, 14, 27, 51, 89; SSC 10**
See also AITN 1, 2; AMW; BPFB 1; CA 1-4R; CABS 1; CANR 5, 23, 49, 64, 113;

CN 7; DAM NOV; DLB 2, 227; EWL 3; FANT; MTCW 1; RGAL 4; RGSF 2; RHW; SSFS 6; TUS

Barthelme, Donald 1931-1989 ... **CLC 1, 2, 3, 5, 6, 8, 13, 23, 46, 59, 115; SSC 2, 55**
See also AMWS 4; BPFB 1; CA 21-24R; 129; CANR 20, 58; DA3; DAM NOV; DLB 2, 234; DLBY 1980, 1989; EWL 3; FANT; LMFS 2; MTCW 1, 2; RGAL 4; RGSF 2; SATA 7; SATA-Obit 62; SSFS 17

Barthelme, Frederick 1943- ...... **CLC 36, 117**
See also AMWS 11; CA 114; 122; CANR 77; CN 7; CSW; DLB 244; DLBY 1985; EWL 3; INT CA-122

Barthes, Roland (Gerard) 1915-1980 .... **CLC 24, 83; TCLC 135**
See also CA 130; 97-100; CANR 66; DLB 296; EW 13; EWL 3; GFL 1789 to the Present; MTCW 1, 2; TWA

Bartram, William 1739-1823 .... **NCLC 145**
See also ANW; DLB 37

Barzun, Jacques (Martin) 1907- ..... **CLC 51, 145**
See also CA 61-64; CANR 22, 95

Bashevis, Isaac
See Singer, Isaac Bashevis

Bashkirtseff, Marie 1859-1884 .... **NCLC 27**

Basho, Matsuo
See Matsuo Basho
See also PFS 18; RGWL 2, 3; WP

Basil of Caesaria c. 330-379 .... **CMLC 35**

Basket, Raney
See Edgerton, Clyde (Carlyle)

Bass, Kingsley B., Jr.
See Bullins, Ed

Bass, Rick 1958- .... **CLC 79, 143; SSC 60**
See also ANW; CA 126; CANR 53, 93; CSW; DLB 212, 275

Bassani, Giorgio 1916-2000 .... **CLC 9**
See also CA 65-68; 190; CANR 33; CWW 2; DLB 128, 177, 299; EWL 3; MTCW 1; RGWL 2, 3

Bastian, Ann .... **CLC 70**

Bastos, Augusto (Antonio) Roa
See Roa Bastos, Augusto (Antonio)

Bataille, Georges 1897-1962 .... **CLC 29; TCLC 155**
See also CA 101; 89-92; EWL 3

Bates, H(erbert) E(rnest) 1905-1974 .... **CLC 46; SSC 10**
See also CA 93-96; 45-48; CANR 34; DA3; DAB; DAM POP; DLB 162, 191; EWL 3; EXPS; MTCW 1, 2; RGSF 2; SSFS 7

Bauchart
See Camus, Albert

Baudelaire, Charles 1821-1867 . **NCLC 6, 29, 55, 155; PC 1; SSC 18; WLC**
See also DA; DA3; DAB; DAC; DAM MST, POET; DLB 217; EW 7; GFL 1789 to the Present; LMFS 2; PFS 21; RGWL 2, 3; TWA

Baudouin, Marcel
See Peguy, Charles (Pierre)

Baudouin, Pierre
See Peguy, Charles (Pierre)

Baudrillard, Jean 1929- .... **CLC 60**
See also DLB 296

Baum, L(yman) Frank 1856-1919 .. **TCLC 7, 132**
See also AAYA 46; BYA 16; CA 108; 133; CLR 15; CWRI 5; DLB 22; FANT; JRDA; MAICYA 1, 2; MTCW 1, 2; NFS 13; RGAL 4; SATA 18, 100; WCH

Baum, Louis F.
See Baum, L(yman) Frank

Benary-Isbert, Margot 1889-1979 .... **CLC 12**
See also CA 5-8R; 89-92; CANR 4, 72;
CLR 12; MAICYA 1, 2; SATA 2; SATA-
Obit 21

Benavente (y Martinez), Jacinto
1866-1954 .... **HLCS 1; TCLC 3**
See also CA 106; 131; CANR 81; DAM
DRAM, MULT; EWL 3; GLL 2; HW 1,
2; MTCW 1, 2

Benchley, Peter (Bradford) 1940- .. **CLC 4, 8**
See also AAYA 14; AITN 2; BPFB 1; CA
17-20R; CANR 12, 35, 66, 115; CPW;
DAM NOV, POP; HGG; MTCW 1, 2;
SATA 3, 89

Benchley, Robert (Charles)
1889-1945 .... **TCLC 1, 55**
See also CA 105; 153; DLB 11; RGAL 4

Benda, Julien 1867-1956 .... **TCLC 60**
See also CA 120; 154; GFL 1789 to the
Present

Benedict, Ruth (Fulton)
1887-1948 .... **TCLC 60**
See also CA 158; DLB 246

Benedikt, Michael 1935- .... **CLC 4, 14**
See also CA 13-16R; CANR 7; CP 7; DLB
5

Benet, Juan 1927-1993 .... **CLC 28**
See also CA 143; EWL 3

Benet, Stephen Vincent 1898-1943 ..... **PC 64;**
SSC 10; TCLC 7
See also AMWS 11; CA 104; 152; DA3;
DAM POET; DLB 4, 48, 102, 249, 284;
DLBY 1997; EWL 3; HGG; MTCW 1;
RGAL 4; RGSF 2; SUFW; WP; YABC 1

Benet, William Rose 1886-1950 ..... **TCLC 28**
See also CA 118; 152; DAM POET; DLB
45; RGAL 4

Benford, Gregory (Albert) 1941- ..... **CLC 52**
See also BPFB 1; CA 69-72, 175; CAAE
175; CAAS 27; CANR 12, 24, 49, 95,
134; CSW; DLBY 1982; SCFW 2; SFW
4

Bengtsson, Frans (Gunnar)
1894-1954 .... **TCLC 48**
See also CA 170; EWL 3

Benjamin, David
See Slavitt, David R(ytman)

Benjamin, Lois
See Gould, Lois

Benjamin, Walter 1892-1940 .... **TCLC 39**
See also CA 164; DLB 242; EW 11; EWL
3

Ben Jelloun, Tahar 1944-
See Jelloun, Tahar ben
See also CA 135; CWW 2; EWL 3; RGWL
3; WLIT 2

Benn, Gottfried 1886-1956 .. **PC 35; TCLC 3**
See also CA 106; 153; DLB 56; EWL 3;
RGWL 2, 3

Bennett, Alan 1934- .... **CLC 45, 77**
See also BRWS 8; CA 103; CANR 35, 55,
106; CBD; CD 5; DAB; DAM MST;
MTCW 1, 2

Bennett, (Enoch) Arnold
1867-1931 .... **TCLC 5, 20**
See also BRW 6; CA 106; 155; CDBLB
1890-1914; DLB 10, 34, 98, 135; EWL 3;
MTCW 2

Bennett, Elizabeth
See Mitchell, Margaret (Munnerlyn)

Bennett, George Harold 1930-
See Bennett, Hal
See also BW 1; CA 97-100; CANR 87

Bennett, Gwendolyn B. 1902-1981 .... **HR 2**
See also BW 1; CA 125; DLB 51; WP

Bennett, Hal .... **CLC 5**
See Bennett, George Harold
See also DLB 33

Bennett, Jay 1912- .... **CLC 35**
See also AAYA 10; CA 69-72; CANR 11,
42, 79; JRDA; SAAS 4; SATA 41, 87;
SATA-Brief 27; WYA; YAW

Bennett, Louise (Simone) 1919- .... **BLC 1;**
CLC 28
See also BW 2, 3; CA 151; CDWLB 3; CP
7; DAM MULT; DLB 117; EWL 3

Benson, A. C. 1862-1925 .... **TCLC 123**
See also DLB 98

Benson, E(dward) F(rederic)
1867-1940 .... **TCLC 27**
See also CA 114; 157; DLB 135, 153;
HGG; SUFW 1

Benson, Jackson J. 1930- .... **CLC 34**
See also CA 25-28R; DLB 111

Benson, Sally 1900-1972 .... **CLC 17**
See also CA 19-20; 37-40R; CAP 1; SATA
1, 35; SATA-Obit 27

Benson, Stella 1892-1933 .... **TCLC 17**
See also CA 117; 154, 155; DLB 36, 162;
FANT; TEA

Bentham, Jeremy 1748-1832 .... **NCLC 38**
See also DLB 107, 158, 252

Bentley, E(dmund) C(lerihew)
1875-1956 .... **TCLC 12**
See also CA 108; DLB 70; MSW

Bentley, Eric (Russell) 1916- .... **CLC 24**
See also CA 5-8R; CANR 6, 67;
CBD; CD 5; INT CANR-6

ben Uzair, Salem
See Horne, Richard Henry Hengist

Beranger, Pierre Jean de
1780-1857 .... **NCLC 34**

Berdyaev, Nicolas
See Berdyaev, Nikolai (Aleksandrovich)

Berdyaev, Nikolai (Aleksandrovich)
1874-1948 .... **TCLC 67**
See also CA 120; 157

Berdyayev, Nikolai (Aleksandrovich)
See Berdyaev, Nikolai (Aleksandrovich)

Berendt, John (Lawrence) 1939- ...... **CLC 86**
See also CA 146; CANR 75, 93; DA3;
MTCW 1

Beresford, J(ohn) D(avys)
1873-1947 .... **TCLC 81**
See also CA 112; 155; DLB 162, 178, 197;
SFW 4; SUFW 1

Bergelson, David (Rafailovich)
1884-1952 .... **TCLC 81**
See Bergelson, Dovid
See also CA 220

Bergelson, Dovid
See Bergelson, David (Rafailovich)
See also EWL 3

Berger, Colonel
See Malraux, (Georges-)Andre

Berger, John (Peter) 1926- .... **CLC 2, 19**
See also BRWS 4; CA 81-84; CANR 51,
78, 117; CN 7; DLB 14, 207

Berger, Melvin H. 1927- .... **CLC 12**
See also CA 5-8R; CANR 4; CLR 32;
SAAS 2; SATA 5, 88; SATA-Essay 124

Berger, Thomas (Louis) 1924- .. **CLC 3, 5, 8,**
11, 18, 38
See also BPFB 1; CA 1-4R; CANR 5, 28,
51, 128; CN 7; DAM NOV; DLB 2;
DLBY 1980; EWL 3; FANT; INT CANR-
28; MTCW 1, 2; RHW; TCWW 2

Bergman, (Ernst) Ingmar 1918- ...... **CLC 16,**
72
See also CA 81-84; CANR 33, 70; CWW
2; DLB 257; MTCW 2

Bergson, Henri(-Louis) 1859-1941 . **TCLC 32**
See also CA 164; EW 8; EWL 3; GFL 1789
to the Present

Bergstein, Eleanor 1938- .... **CLC 4**
See also CA 53-56; CANR 5

Berkeley, George 1685-1753 .... **LC 65**
See also DLB 31, 101, 252

Berkoff, Steven 1937- .... **CLC 56**
See also CA 104; CANR 72; CBD; CD 5

Berlin, Isaiah 1909-1997 .... **TCLC 105**
See also CA 85-88; 162

Bermant, Chaim (Icyk) 1929-1998 ... **CLC 40**
See also CA 57-60; CANR 6, 31, 57, 105;
CN 7

Bern, Victoria
See Fisher, M(ary) F(rances) K(ennedy)

Bernanos, (Paul Louis) Georges
1888-1948 .... **TCLC 3**
See also CA 104; 130; CANR 94; DLB 72;
EWL 3; GFL 1789 to the Present; RGWL
2, 3

Bernard, April 1956- .... **CLC 59**
See also CA 131

Bernard of Clairvaux 1090-1153 .. **CMLC 71**
See also DLB 208

Berne, Victoria
See Fisher, M(ary) F(rances) K(ennedy)

Bernhard, Thomas 1931-1989 ..... **CLC 3, 32,**
61; DC 14; TCLC 165
See also CA 85-88; 127; CANR 32, 57; CD-
WLB 2; DLB 85, 124; EWL 3; MTCW 1;
RGWL 2, 3

Bernhardt, Sarah (Henriette Rosine)
1844-1923 .... **TCLC 75**
See also CA 157

Bernstein, Charles 1950- .... **CLC 142,**
See also CA 129; CAAS 24; CANR 90; CP
7; DLB 169

Bernstein, Ingrid
See Kirsch, Sarah

Beroul fl. c. 1150- .... **CMLC 75**

Berriault, Gina 1926-1999 .... **CLC 54, 109;**
SSC 30
See also CA 116; 129; 185; CANR 66; DLB
130; SSFS 7,11

Berrigan, Daniel 1921- .... **CLC 4**
See also CA 33-36R, 187; CAAE 187;
CAAS 1; CANR 11, 43, 78; CP 7; DLB 5

Berrigan, Edmund Joseph Michael, Jr.
1934-1983
See Berrigan, Ted
See also CA 61-64; 110; CANR 14, 102

Berrigan, Ted .... **CLC 37**
See Berrigan, Edmund Joseph Michael, Jr.
See also DLB 5, 169; WP

Berry, Charles Edward Anderson 1931-
See Berry, Chuck
See also CA 115

Berry, Chuck .... **CLC 17**
See Berry, Charles Edward Anderson

Berry, Jonas
See Ashbery, John (Lawrence)
See also GLL 1

Berry, Wendell (Erdman) 1934- ... **CLC 4, 6,**
8, 27, 46; PC 28
See also AITN 1; AMWS 10; ANW; CA
73-76; CANR 50, 73, 101, 132; CP 7;
CSW; DAM POET; DLB 5, 6, 234, 275;
MTCW 1

Berryman, John 1914-1972 ... **CLC 1, 2, 3, 4,**
6, 8, 10, 13, 25, 62; PC 64
See also AMW; CA 13-16; 33-36R; CABS
2; CANR 35; CAP 1; CDALB 1941-1968;
DAM POET; DLB 48; EWL 3; MTCW 1,
2; PAB; RGAL 4; WP

Bertolucci, Bernardo 1940- ...... **CLC 16, 157**
See also CA 106; CANR 125

Berton, Pierre (Francis Demarigny)
1920-2004 .... **CLC 104**
See also CA 1-4R; CANR 2, 56; CPW;
DLB 68; SATA 99

Bertrand, Aloysius 1807-1841 .... **NCLC 31**
See Bertrand, Louis oAloysiusc

Blom, Jan
See Breytenbach, Breyten
Bloom, Harold 1930- .... **CLC 24, 103**
See also CA 13-16R; CANR 39, 75, 92, 133; DLB 67; EWL 3; MTCW 1; RGAL 4
Bloomfield, Aurelius
See Bourne, Randolph S(illiman)
Bloomfield, Robert 1766-1823 ..... **NCLC 145**
See also DLB 93
Blount, Roy (Alton), Jr. 1941- .... **CLC 38**
See also CA 53-56; CANR 10, 28, 61, 125; CSW; INT CANR-28; MTCW 1, 2
Blowsnake, Sam 1875-(?) .... **NNAL**
Bloy, Leon 1846-1917 .... **TCLC 22**
See also CA 121; 183; DLB 123; GFL 1789 to the Present
Blue Cloud, Peter (Aroniawenrate)
1933- .... **NNAL**
See also CA 117; CANR 40; DAM MULT
Bluggage, Oranthy
See Alcott, Louisa May
Blume, Judy (Sussman) 1938- .... **CLC 12, 30**
See also AAYA 3, 26; BYA 1, 8, 12; CA 29-32R; CANR 13, 37, 66, 124; CLR 2, 15, 69; CPW; DA3; DAM NOV, POP; DLB 52; JRDA; MAICYA 1, 2; MAICYAS 1; MTCW 1, 2; SATA 2, 31, 79, 142; WYA; YAW
Blunden, Edmund (Charles)
1896-1974 .... **CLC 2, 56**
See also BRW 6; CA 17-18; 45-48; CANR 54; CAP 2; DLB 20, 100, 155; MTCW 1; PAB
Bly, Robert (Elwood) 1926- .... **CLC 1, 2, 5, 10, 15, 38, 128; PC 39**
See also AMWS 4; CA 5-8R; CANR 41, 73, 125; CP 7; DA3; DAM POET; DLB 5; EWL 3; MTCW 1, 2; PFS 6, 17; RGAL 4
Boas, Franz 1858-1942 .... **TCLC 56**
See also CA 115; 181
Bobette
See Simenon, Georges (Jacques Christian)
Boccaccio, Giovanni 1313-1375 ... **CMLC 13, 57; SSC 10**
See also EW 2; RGSF 2; RGWL 2, 3; TWA
Bochco, Steven 1943- .... **CLC 35**
See also AAYA 11; CA 124; 138
Bode, Sigmund
See O'Doherty, Brian
Bodel, Jean 1167(?)-1210 .... **CMLC 28**
Bodenheim, Maxwell 1892-1954 .... **TCLC 44**
See also CA 110; 187; DLB 9, 45; RGAL 4
Bodenheimer, Maxwell
See Bodenheim, Maxwell
Bodker, Cecil 1927-
See Bodker, Cecil
Bodker, Cecil 1927- .... **CLC 21**
See also CA 73-76; CANR 13, 44, 111; CLR 23; MAICYA 1, 2; SATA 14, 133
Boell, Heinrich (Theodor)
1917-1985 ..... **CLC 2, 3, 6, 9, 11, 15, 27, 32, 72; SSC 23; WLC**
See Boll, Heinrich
See also CA 21-24R; 116; CANR 24; DA; DA3; DAB; DAC; DAM MST, NOV; DLB 69; DLBY 1985; MTCW 1, 2; SSFS 20; TWA
Boerne, Alfred
See Doeblin, Alfred
Boethius c. 480-c. 524 .... **CMLC 15**
See also DLB 115; RGWL 2, 3
Boff, Leonardo (Genezio Darci)
1938- .... **CLC 70; HLC 1**
See also CA 150; DAM MULT; HW 2

Bogan, Louise 1897-1970 .... **CLC 4, 39, 46, 93; PC 12**
See also AMWS 3; CA 73-76; 25-28R; CANR 33, 82; DAM POET; DLB 45, 169; EWL 3; MAWW; MTCW 1, 2; PFS 21; RGAL 4
Bogarde, Dirk
See Van Den Bogarde, Derek Jules Gaspard Ulric Niven
See also DLB 14
Bogosian, Eric 1953- .... **CLC 45, 141**
See also CA 138; CAD; CANR 102; CD 5
Bograd, Larry 1953- .... **CLC 35**
See also CA 93-96; CANR 57; SAAS 21; SATA 33, 89; WYA
Boiardo, Matteo Maria 1441-1494 .... **LC 6**
Boileau-Despreaux, Nicolas 1636-1711 . **LC 3**
See also DLB 268; EW 3; GFL Beginnings to 1789; RGWL 2, 3
Boissard, Maurice
See Leautaud, Paul
Bojer, Johan 1872-1959 .... **TCLC 64**
See also CA 189; EWL 3
Bok, Edward W(illiam)
1863-1930 .... **TCLC 101**
See also CA 217; DLB 91; DLBD 16
Boker, George Henry 1823-1890 . **NCLC 125**
See also RGAL 4
Boland, Eavan (Aisling) 1944- .. **CLC 40, 67, 113; PC 58**
See also BRWS 5; CA 143, 207; CAAE 207; CANR 61; CP 7; CWP; DAM POET; DLB 40; FW; MTCW 2; PFS 12
Boll, Heinrich
See Boell, Heinrich (Theodor)
See also BPFB 1; CDWLB 2; EW 13; EWL 3; RGSF 2; RGWL 2, 3
Bolt, Lee
See Faust, Frederick (Schiller)
Bolt, Robert (Oxton) 1924-1995 .... **CLC 14**
See also CA 17-20R; 147; CANR 35, 67; CBD; DAM DRAM; DFS 2; DLB 13, 233; EWL 3; LAIT 1; MTCW 1
Bombal, Maria Luisa 1910-1980 .... **HLCS 1; SSC 37**
See also CA 127; CANR 72; EWL 3; HW 1; LAW; RGSF 2
Bombet, Louis-Alexandre-Cesar
See Stendhal
Bomkauf
See Kaufman, Bob (Garnell)
Bonaventura .... **NCLC 35**
See also DLB 90
Bond, Edward 1934- .... **CLC 4, 6, 13, 23**
See also AAYA 50; BRWS 1; CA 25-28R; CANR 38, 67, 106; CBD; CD 5; DAM DRAM; DFS 3, 8; DLB 13; EWL 3; MTCW 1
Bonham, Frank 1914-1989 .... **CLC 12**
See also AAYA 1; BYA 1, 3; CA 9-12R; CANR 4, 36; JRDA; MAICYA 1, 2; SAAS 3; SATA 1, 49; SATA-Obit 62; TCWW 2; YAW
Bonnefoy, Yves 1923- . **CLC 9, 15, 58; PC 58**
See also CA 85-88; CANR 33, 75, 97; CWW 2; DAM MST, POET; DLB 258; EWL 3; GFL 1789 to the Present; MTCW 1, 2
Bonner, Marita .... **HR 2**
See Occomy, Marita (Odette) Bonner
Bonnin, Gertrude 1876-1938 .... **NNAL**
See Zitkala-Sa
See also CA 150; DAM MULT
Bontemps, Arna(ud Wendell)
1902-1973 ..... **BLC 1; CLC 1, 18; HR 2**
See also BW 1; CA 1-4R; 41-44R; CANR 4, 35; CLR 6; CWRI 5; DA3; DAM MULT, NOV, POET; DLB 48, 51; JRDA;

MAICYA 1, 2; MTCW 1, 2; SATA 2, 44; SATA-Obit 24; WCH; WP
Boot, William
See Stoppard, Tom
Booth, Martin 1944-2004 .... **CLC 13**
See also CA 93-96, 188; 223; CAAE 188; CAAS 2; CANR 92
Booth, Philip 1925- .... **CLC 23**
See also CA 5-8R; CANR 5, 88; CP 7; DLBY 1982
Booth, Wayne C(layson) 1921- .... **CLC 24**
See also CA 1-4R; CAAS 5; CANR 3, 43, 117; DLB 67
Borchert, Wolfgang 1921-1947 .... **TCLC 5**
See also CA 104; 188; DLB 69, 124; EWL 3
Borel, Petrus 1809-1859 .... **NCLC 41**
See also DLB 119; GFL 1789 to the Present
Borges, Jorge Luis 1899-1986 ... **CLC 1, 2, 3, 4, 6, 8, 9, 10, 13, 19, 44, 48, 83; HLC 1; PC 22, 32; SSC 4, 41; TCLC 109; WLC**
See also AAYA 26; BPFB 1; CA 21-24R; CANR 19, 33, 75, 105, 133; CDWLB 3; DA; DA3; DAB; DAC; DAM MST, MULT; DLB 113, 283; DLBY 1986; DNFS 1, 2; EWL 3; HW 1, 2; LAW; LMFS 2; MSW; MTCW 1, 2; RGSF 2; RGWL 2, 3; SFW 4; SSFS 17; TWA; WLIT 1
Borowski, Tadeusz 1922-1951 .... **SSC 48; TCLC 9**
See also CA 106; 154; CDWLB 4; DLB 215; EWL 3; RGSF 2; RGWL 3; SSFS 13
Borrow, George (Henry)
1803-1881 .... **NCLC 9**
See also DLB 21, 55, 166
Bosch (Gavino), Juan 1909-2001 ..... **HLCS 1**
See also CA 151; 204; DAM MST, MULT; DLB 145; HW 1, 2
Bosman, Herman Charles
1905-1951 .... **TCLC 49**
See Malan, Herman
See also CA 160; DLB 225; RGSF 2
Bosschere, Jean de 1878(?)-1953 ... **TCLC 19**
See also CA 115; 186
Boswell, James 1740-1795 ... **LC 4, 50; WLC**
See also BRW 3; CDBLB 1660-1789; DA; DAB; DAC; DAM MST; DLB 104, 142; TEA; WLIT 3
Bottomley, Gordon 1874-1948 ..... **TCLC 107**
See also CA 120; 192; DLB 10
Bottoms, David 1949- .... **CLC 53**
See also CA 105; CANR 22; CSW; DLB 120; DLBY 1983
Boucicault, Dion 1820-1890 .... **NCLC 41**
Boucolon, Maryse
See Conde, Maryse
Bourdieu, Pierre 1930-2002 .... **CLC 198**
See also CA 130; 204
Bourget, Paul (Charles Joseph)
1852-1935 .... **TCLC 12**
See also CA 107; 196; DLB 123; GFL 1789 to the Present
Bourjaily, Vance (Nye) 1922- .... **CLC 8, 62**
See also CA 1-4R; CAAS 1; CANR 2, 72; CN 7; DLB 2, 143
Bourne, Randolph S(illiman)
1886-1918 .... **TCLC 16**
See also AMW; CA 117; 155; DLB 63
Bova, Ben(jamin William) 1932- ...... **CLC 45**
See also AAYA 16; CA 5-8R; CAAS 18; CANR 11, 56, 94, 111; CLR 3, 96; DLBY 1981; INT CANR-11; MAICYA 1, 2; MTCW 1; SATA 6, 68, 133; SFW 4

Bowen, Elizabeth (Dorothea Cole)
1899-1973 . **CLC 1, 3, 6, 11, 15, 22, 118; SSC 3, 28, 66; TCLC 148**
See also BRWS 2; CA 17-18; 41-44R; CANR 35, 105; CAP 2; CDBLB 1945-1960; DA3; DAM NOV; DLB 15, 162; EWL 3; EXPS; FW; HGG; MTCW 1, 2; NFS 13; RGSF 2; SSFS 5; SUFW 1; TEA; WLIT 4

Bowering, George 1935- .... **CLC 15, 47**
See also CA 21-24R; CAAS 16; CANR 10; CP 7; DLB 53

Bowering, Marilyn R(uthe) 1949- .... **CLC 32**
See also CA 101; CANR 49; CP 7; CWP

Bowers, Edgar 1924-2000 .... **CLC 9**
See also CA 5-8R; 188; CANR 24; CP 7; CSW; DLB 5

Bowers, Mrs. J. Milton 1842-1914
See Bierce, Ambrose (Gwinett)

Bowie, David .... **CLC 17**
See Jones, David Robert

Bowles, Jane (Sydney) 1917-1973 ..... **CLC 3, 68**
See Bowles, Jane Auer
See also CA 19-20; 41-44R; CAP 2

Bowles, Jane Auer
See Bowles, Jane (Sydney)
See also EWL 3

Bowles, Paul (Frederick) 1910-1999 . **CLC 1, 2, 19, 53; SSC 3**
See also AMWS 4; CA 1-4R; 186; CAAS 1; CANR 1, 19, 50, 75; CN 7; DA3; DLB 5, 6, 218; EWL 3; MTCW 1, 2; RGAL 4; SSFS 17

Bowles, William Lisle 1762-1850 . **NCLC 103**
See also DLB 93

Box, Edgar
See Vidal, (Eugene Luther) Gore
See also GLL 1

Boyd, James 1888-1944 .... **TCLC 115**
See also CA 186; DLB 9; DLBD 16; RGAL 4; RHW

Boyd, Nancy
See Millay, Edna St. Vincent
See also GLL 1

Boyd, Thomas (Alexander)
1898-1935 .... **TCLC 111**
See also CA 111; 183; DLB 9; DLBD 16

Boyd, William 1952- .... **CLC 28, 53, 70**
See also CA 114; 120; CANR 51, 71, 131; CN 7; DLB 231

Boyesen, Hjalmar Hjorth
1848-1895 .... **NCLC 135**
See also DLB 12, 71; DLBD 13; RGAL 4

Boyle, Kay 1902-1992 .... **CLC 1, 5, 19, 58, 121; SSC 5**
See also CA 13-16R; 140; CAAS 1; CANR 29, 61, 110; DLB 4, 9, 48, 86; DLBY 1993; EWL 3; MTCW 1, 2; RGAL 4; RGSF 2; SSFS 10, 13, 14

Boyle, Mark
See Kienzle, William X(avier)

Boyle, Patrick 1905-1982 .... **CLC 19**
See also CA 127

Boyle, T. C.
See Boyle, T(homas) Coraghessan
See also AMWS 8

Boyle, T(homas) Coraghessan
1948- .... **CLC 36, 55, 90; SSC 16**
See Boyle, T. C.
See also AAYA 47; BEST 90:4; BPFB 1; CA 120; CANR 44, 76, 89, 132; CN 7; CPW; DA3; DAM POP; DLB 218, 278; DLBY 1986; EWL 3; MTCW 2; SSFS 13, 19

Boz
See Dickens, Charles (John Huffam)

Brackenridge, Hugh Henry
1748-1816 .... **NCLC 7**
See also DLB 11, 37; RGAL 4

Bradbury, Edward P.
See Moorcock, Michael (John)
See also MTCW 2

Bradbury, Malcolm (Stanley)
1932-2000 .... **CLC 32, 61**
See also CA 1-4R; CANR 1, 33, 91, 98; CN 7; DA3; DAM NOV; DLB 14, 207; EWL 3; MTCW 1, 2

Bradbury, Ray (Douglas) 1920- .... **CLC 1, 3, 10, 15, 42, 98; SSC 29, 53; WLC**
See also AAYA 15; AITN 1, 2; AMWS 4; BPFB 1; BYA 4, 5, 11; CA 1-4R; CANR 2, 30, 75, 125; CDALB 1968-1988; CN 7; CPW; DA; DA3; DAB; DAC; DAM MST, NOV, POP; DLB 2, 8; EXPN; EXPS; HGG; LAIT 3, 5; LATS 1:2; LMFS 2; MTCW 1, 2; NFS 1; RGAL 4; RGSF 2; SATA 11, 64, 123; SCFW 2; SFW 4; SSFS 1, 20; SUFW 1, 2; TUS; YAW

Braddon, Mary Elizabeth
1837-1915 .... **TCLC 111**
See also BRWS 8; CA 108; 179; CMW 4; DLB 18, 70, 156; HGG

Bradfield, Scott (Michael) 1955- .... **SSC 65**
See also CA 147; CANR 90; HGG; SUFW 2

Bradford, Gamaliel 1863-1932 .... **TCLC 36**
See also CA 160; DLB 17

Bradford, William 1590-1657 .... **LC 64**
See also DLB 24, 30; RGAL 4

Bradley, David (Henry), Jr. 1950- .... **BLC 1; CLC 23, 118**
See also BW 1, 3; CA 104; CANR 26, 81; CN 7; DAM MULT; DLB 33

Bradley, John Ed(mund, Jr.) 1958- . **CLC 55**
See also CA 139; CANR 99; CN 7; CSW

Bradley, Marion Zimmer
1930-1999 .... **CLC 30**
See Chapman, Lee; Dexter, John; Gardner, Miriam; Ives, Morgan; Rivers, Elfrida
See also AAYA 40; BPFB 1; CA 57-60; 185; CAAS 10; CANR 7, 31, 51, 75, 107; CPW; DA3; DAM POP; DLB 8; FANT; FW; MTCW 1, 2; SATA 90, 139; SATA-Obit 116; SFW 4; SUFW 2; YAW

Bradshaw, John 1933- .... **CLC 70**
See also CA 138; CANR 61

Bradstreet, Anne 1612(?)-1672 ...... **LC 4, 30; PC 10**
See also AMWS 1; CDALB 1640-1865; DA; DA3; DAC; DAM MST, POET; DLB 24; EXPP; FW; PFS 6; RGAL 4; TUS; WP

Brady, Joan 1939- .... **CLC 86**
See also CA 141

Bragg, Melvyn 1939- .... **CLC 10**
See also BEST 89:3; CA 57-60; CANR 10, 48, 89; CN 7; DLB 14, 271; RHW

Brahe, Tycho 1546-1601 .... **LC 45**
See also DLB 300

Braine, John (Gerard) 1922-1986 . **CLC 1, 3, 41**
See also CA 1-4R; 120; CANR 1, 33; CDBLB 1945-1960; DLB 15; DLBY 1986; EWL 3; MTCW 1

Braithwaite, William Stanley (Beaumont)
1878-1962 .... **BLC 1; HR 2; PC 52**
See also BW 1; CA 125; DAM MULT; DLB 50, 54

Bramah, Ernest 1868-1942 .... **TCLC 72**
See also CA 156; CMW 4; DLB 70; FANT

Brammer, William 1930(?)-1978 ...... **CLC 31**
See also CA 77-80

Brancati, Vitaliano 1907-1954 .... **TCLC 12**
See also CA 109; DLB 264; EWL 3

Brancato, Robin F(idler) 1936- .... **CLC 35**
See also AAYA 9; BYA 6; CA 69-72; CANR 11, 45; CLR 32; JRDA; MAICYA 2; MAICYAS 1; SAAS 9; SATA 97; WYA; YAW

Brand, Dionne 1953- .... **CLC 192**
See also BW 2; CA 143; CWP

Brand, Max
See Faust, Frederick (Schiller)
See also BPFB 1; TCWW 2

Brand, Millen 1906-1980 .... **CLC 7**
See also CA 21-24R; 97-100; CANR 72

Branden, Barbara .... **CLC 44**
See also CA 148

Brandes, Georg (Morris Cohen)
1842-1927 .... **TCLC 10**
See also CA 105; 189; DLB 300

Brandys, Kazimierz 1916-2000 .... **CLC 62**
See also EWL 3

Branley, Franklyn M(ansfield)
1915-2002 .... **CLC 21**
See also CA 33-36R; 207; CANR 14, 39; CLR 13; MAICYA 1, 2; SAAS 16; SATA 4, 68, 136

Brant, Beth (E.) 1941- .... **NNAL**
See also CA 144; FW

Brant, Sebastian 1457-1521 .... **LC 112**
See also DLB 179; RGWL 2, 3

Brathwaite, Edward Kamau
1930- .... **BLCS; CLC 11; PC 56**
See also BW 2, 3; CA 25-28R; CANR 11, 26, 47, 107; CDWLB 3; CP 7; DAM POET; DLB 125; EWL 3

Brathwaite, Kamau
See Brathwaite, Edward Kamau

Brautigan, Richard (Gary)
1935-1984 .... **CLC 1, 3, 5, 9, 12, 34, 42; TCLC 133**
See also BPFB 1; CA 53-56; 113; CANR 34; DA3; DAM NOV; DLB 2, 5, 206; DLBY 1980, 1984; FANT; MTCW 1; RGAL 4; SATA 56

Brave Bird, Mary .... **NNAL**
See Crow Dog, Mary (Ellen)

Braverman, Kate 1950- .... **CLC 67**
See also CA 89-92

Brecht, (Eugen) Bertolt (Friedrich)
1898-1956 ..... **DC 3; TCLC 1, 6, 13, 35; WLC**
See also CA 104; 133; CANR 62; CDWLB 2; DA; DA3; DAB; DAC; DAM DRAM, MST; DFS 4, 5, 9; DLB 56, 124; EW 11; EWL 3; IDTP; MTCW 1, 2; RGWL 2, 3; TWA

Brecht, Eugen Berthold Friedrich
See Brecht, (Eugen) Bertolt (Friedrich)

Bremer, Fredrika 1801-1865 .... **NCLC 11**
See also DLB 254

Brennan, Christopher John
1870-1932 .... **TCLC 17**
See also CA 117; 188; DLB 230; EWL 3

Brennan, Maeve 1917-1993 ... **CLC 5; TCLC 124**
See also CA 81-84; CANR 72, 100

Brent, Linda
See Jacobs, Harriet A(nn)

Brentano, Clemens (Maria)
1778-1842 .... **NCLC 1**
See also DLB 90; RGWL 2, 3

Brent of Bin Bin
See Franklin, (Stella Maria Sarah) Miles (Lampe)

Brenton, Howard 1942- .... **CLC 31**
See also CA 69-72; CANR 33, 67; CBD; CD 5; DLB 13; MTCW 1

Breslin, James 1930-
See Breslin, Jimmy
See also CA 73-76; CANR 31, 75; DAM NOV; MTCW 1, 2

Burroughs, Edgar Rice 1875-1950 . **TCLC 2, 32**
See also AAYA 11; BPFB 1; BYA 4, 9; CA 104; 132; CANR 131; DA3; DAM NOV; DLB 8; FANT; MTCW 1, 2; RGAL 4; SATA 41; SCFW 2; SFW 4; TUS; YAW

Burroughs, William S(eward) 1914-1997 .. **CLC 1, 2, 5, 15, 22, 42, 75, 109; TCLC 121; WLC**
See Lee, William; Lee, Willy
See also AAYA 60; AITN 2; AMWS 3; BG 2; BPFB 1; CA 9-12R; 160; CANR 20, 52, 104; CN 7; CPW; DA; DA3; DAB; DAC; DAM MST, NOV, POP; DLB 2, 8, 16, 152, 237; DLBY 1981, 1997; EWL 3; HGG; LMFS 2; MTCW 1, 2; RGAL 4; SFW 4

Burton, Sir Richard F(rancis) 1821-1890 .... **NCLC 42**
See also DLB 55, 166, 184

Burton, Robert 1577-1640 .... **LC 74**
See also DLB 151; RGEL 2

Buruma, Ian 1951- .... **CLC 163**
See also CA 128; CANR 65

Busch, Frederick 1941- ... **CLC 7, 10, 18, 47, 166**
See also CA 33-36R; CAAS 1; CANR 45, 73, 92; CN 7; DLB 6, 218

Bush, Barney (Furman) 1946- .... **NNAL**
See also CA 145

Bush, Ronald 1946- .... **CLC 34**
See also CA 136

Bustos, F(rancisco)
See Borges, Jorge Luis

Bustos Domecq, H(onorio)
See Bioy Casares, Adolfo; Borges, Jorge Luis

Butler, Octavia E(stelle) 1947- .. **BLCS; CLC 38, 121**
See also AAYA 18, 48; AFAW 2; AMWS 13; BPFB 1; BW 2, 3; CA 73-76; CANR 12, 24, 38, 73; CLR 65; CPW; DA3; DAM MULT, POP; DLB 33; LATS 1:2; MTCW 1, 2; NFS 8; SATA 84; SCFW 2; SFW 4; SSFS 6; YAW

Butler, Robert Olen, (Jr.) 1945- ...... **CLC 81, 162**
See also AMWS 12; BPFB 1; CA 112; CANR 66; CSW; DAM POP; DLB 173; INT CA-112; MTCW 1; SSFS 11

Butler, Samuel 1612-1680 .... **LC 16, 43**
See also DLB 101, 126; RGEL 2

Butler, Samuel 1835-1902 .... **TCLC 1, 33; WLC**
See also BRWS 2; CA 143; CDBLB 1890-1914; DA; DA3; DAB; DAC; DAM MST, NOV; DLB 18, 57, 174; RGEL 2; SFW 4; TEA

Butler, Walter C.
See Faust, Frederick (Schiller)

Butor, Michel (Marie Francois) 1926- .... **CLC 1, 3, 8, 11, 15, 161**
See also CA 9-12R; CANR 33, 66; CWW 2; DLB 83; EW 13; EWL 3; GFL 1789 to the Present; MTCW 1, 2

Butts, Mary 1890(?)-1937 .... **TCLC 77**
See also CA 148; DLB 240

Buxton, Ralph
See Silverstein, Alvin; Silverstein, Virginia B(arbara Opshelor)

Buzo, Alex
See Buzo, Alexander (John)
See also DLB 289

Buzo, Alexander (John) 1944- .... **CLC 61**
See also CA 97-100; CANR 17, 39, 69; CD 5

Buzzati, Dino 1906-1972 .... **CLC 36**
See also CA 160; 33-36R; DLB 177; RGWL 2, 3; SFW 4

Byars, Betsy (Cromer) 1928- .... **CLC 35**
See also AAYA 19; BYA 3; CA 33-36R, 183; CAAE 183; CANR 18, 36, 57, 102; CLR 1, 16, 72; DLB 52; INT CANR-18; JRDA; MAICYA 1, 2; MAICYAS 1; MTCW 1; SAAS 1; SATA 4, 46, 80; SATA-Essay 108; WYA; YAW

Byatt, A(ntonia) S(usan Drabble) 1936- .... **CLC 19, 65, 136**
See also BPFB 1; BRWC 2; BRWS 4; CA 13-16R; CANR 13, 33, 50, 75, 96, 133; DA3; DAM NOV, POP; DLB 14, 194; EWL 3; MTCW 1, 2; RGSF 2; RHW; TEA

Byrd, Willam II 1674-1744 .... **LC 112**
See also DLB 24, 140; RGAL 4

Byrne, David 1952- .... **CLC 26**
See also CA 127

Byrne, John Keyes 1926-
See Leonard, Hugh
See also CA 102; CANR 78; INT CA-102

Byron, George Gordon (Noel) 1788-1824 ...... **DC 24; NCLC 2, 12, 109, 149; PC 16; WLC**
See also BRW 4; BRWC 2; CDBLB 1789-1832; DA; DA3; DAB; DAC; DAM MST, POET; DLB 96, 110; EXPP; LMFS 1; PAB; PFS 1, 14; RGEL 2; TEA; WLIT 3; WP

Byron, Robert 1905-1941 .... **TCLC 67**
See also CA 160; DLB 195

C. 3. 3.
See Wilde, Oscar (Fingal O'Flahertie Wills)

Caballero, Fernan 1796-1877 .... **NCLC 10**

Cabell, Branch
See Cabell, James Branch

Cabell, James Branch 1879-1958 .... **TCLC 6**
See also CA 105; 152; DLB 9, 78; FANT; MTCW 1; RGAL 4; SUFW 1

Cabeza de Vaca, Alvar Nunez 1490-1557(?) .... **LC 61**

Cable, George Washington 1844-1925 .... **SSC 4; TCLC 4**
See also CA 104; 155; DLB 12, 74; DLBD 13; RGAL 4; TUS

Cabral de Melo Neto, Joao 1920-1999 .... **CLC 76**
See Melo Neto, Joao Cabral de
See also CA 151; DAM MULT; DLB 307; LAW; LAWS 1

Cabrera Infante, G(uillermo) 1929- . **CLC 5, 25, 45, 120; HLC 1; SSC 39**
See also CA 85-88; CANR 29, 65, 110; CD-WLB 3; CWW 2; DA3; DAM MULT; DLB 113; EWL 3; HW 1, 2; LAW; LAWS 1; MTCW 1, 2; RGSF 2; WLIT 1

Cade, Toni
See Bambara, Toni Cade

Cadmus and Harmonia
See Buchan, John

Caedmon fl. 658-680 .... **CMLC 7**
See also DLB 146

Caeiro, Alberto
See Pessoa, Fernando (Antonio Nogueira)

Caesar, Julius .... **CMLC 47**
See Julius Caesar
See also AW 1; RGWL 2, 3

Cage, John (Milton, Jr.) 1912-1992 .... **CLC 41; PC 58**
See also CA 13-16R; 169; CANR 9, 78; DLB 193; INT CANR-9

Cahan, Abraham 1860-1951 .... **TCLC 71**
See also CA 108; 154; DLB 9, 25, 28; RGAL 4

Cain, G.
See Cabrera Infante, G(uillermo)

Cain, Guillermo
See Cabrera Infante, G(uillermo)

Cain, James M(allahan) 1892-1977 .. **CLC 3, 11, 28**
See also AITN 1; BPFB 1; CA 17-20R; 73-76; CANR 8, 34, 61; CMW 4; DLB 226; EWL 3; MSW; MTCW 1; RGAL 4

Caine, Hall 1853-1931 .... **TCLC 97**
See also RHW

Caine, Mark
See Raphael, Frederic (Michael)

Calasso, Roberto 1941- .... **CLC 81**
See also CA 143; CANR 89

Calderon de la Barca, Pedro 1600-1681 .... **DC 3; HLCS 1; LC 23**
See also EW 2; RGWL 2, 3; TWA

Caldwell, Erskine (Preston) 1903-1987 .... **CLC 1, 8, 14, 50, 60; SSC 19; TCLC 117**
See also AITN 1; AMW; BPFB 1; CA 1-4R; 121; CAAS 1; CANR 2, 33; DA3; DAM NOV; DLB 9, 86; EWL 3; MTCW 1, 2; RGAL 4; RGSF 2; TUS

Caldwell, (Janet Miriam) Taylor (Holland) 1900-1985 .... **CLC 2, 28, 39**
See also BPFB 1; CA 5-8R; 116; CANR 5; DA3; DAM NOV, POP; DLBD 17; RHW

Calhoun, John Caldwell 1782-1850 .... **NCLC 15**
See also DLB 3, 248

Calisher, Hortense 1911- ..... **CLC 2, 4, 8, 38, 134; SSC 15**
See also CA 1-4R; CANR 1, 22, 117; CN 7; DA3; DAM NOV; DLB 2, 218; INT CANR-22; MTCW 1, 2; RGAL 4; RGSF 2

Callaghan, Morley Edward 1903-1990 ..... **CLC 3, 14, 41, 65; TCLC 145**
See also CA 9-12R; 132; CANR 33, 73; DAC; DAM MST; DLB 68; EWL 3; MTCW 1, 2; RGEL 2; RGSF 2; SSFS 19

Callimachus c. 305B.C.-c. 240B.C. .... **CMLC 18**
See also AW 1; DLB 176; RGWL 2, 3

Calvin, Jean
See Calvin, John
See also GFL Beginnings to 1789

Calvin, John 1509-1564 .... **LC 37**
See Calvin, Jean

Calvino, Italo 1923-1985 .... **CLC 5, 8, 11, 22, 33, 39, 73; SSC 3, 48**
See also CA 85-88; 116; CANR 23, 61, 132; DAM NOV; DLB 196; EW 13; EWL 3; MTCW 1, 2; RGSF 2; RGWL 2, 3; SFW 4; SSFS 12

Camara Laye
See Laye, Camara
See also EWL 3

Camden, William 1551-1623 .... **LC 77**
See also DLB 172

Cameron, Carey 1952- .... **CLC 59**
See also CA 135

Cameron, Peter 1959- .... **CLC 44**
See also AMWS 12; CA 125; CANR 50, 117; DLB 234; GLL 2

Camoens, Luis Vaz de 1524(?)-1580
See Camoes, Luis de
See also EW 2

Camoes, Luis de 1524(?)-1580 . **HLCS 1; LC 62; PC 31**
See Camoens, Luis Vaz de
See also DLB 287; RGWL 2, 3

Campana, Dino 1885-1932 .... **TCLC 20**
See also CA 117; DLB 114; EWL 3

Campanella, Tommaso 1568-1639 .... **LC 32**
See also RGWL 2, 3

Campbell, John W(ood, Jr.) 1910-1971 .... **CLC 32**
See also CA 21-22; 29-32R; CANR 34; CAP 2; DLB 8; MTCW 1; SCFW; SFW 4

Casanova de Seingalt, Giovanni Jacopo
1725-1798 .... **LC 13**
Casares, Adolfo Bioy
See Bioy Casares, Adolfo
See also RGSF 2
Casas, Bartolome de las 1474-1566
See Las Casas, Bartolome de
See also WLIT 1
Casely-Hayford, J(oseph) E(phraim)
1866-1903 .... **BLC 1; TCLC 24**
See also BW 2; CA 123; 152; DAM MULT
Casey, John (Dudley) 1939- .... **CLC 59**
See also BEST 90:2; CA 69-72; CANR 23,
100
Casey, Michael 1947- .... **CLC 2**
See also CA 65-68; CANR 109; DLB 5
Casey, Patrick
See Thurman, Wallace (Henry)
Casey, Warren (Peter) 1935-1988 .... **CLC 12**
See also CA 101; 127; INT CA-101
Casona, Alejandro .... **CLC 49**
See Alvarez, Alejandro Rodriguez
See also EWL 3
Cassavetes, John 1929-1989 .... **CLC 20**
See also CA 85-88; 127; CANR 82
Cassian, Nina 1924- .... **PC 17**
See also CWP; CWW 2
Cassill, R(onald) V(erlin)
1919-2002 .... **CLC 4, 23**
See also CA 9-12R; 208; CAAS 1; CANR
7, 45; CN 7; DLB 6, 218; DLBY 2002
Cassiodorus, Flavius Magnus c. 490(?)-c.
583(?) .... **CMLC 43**
Cassirer, Ernst 1874-1945 .... **TCLC 61**
See also CA 157
Cassity, (Allen) Turner 1929- .... **CLC 6, 42**
See also CA 17-20R; 223; CAAE 223;
CAAS 8; CANR 11; CSW; DLB 105
Castaneda, Carlos (Cesar Aranha)
1931(?)-1998 .... **CLC 12, 119**
See also CA 25-28R; CANR 32, 66, 105;
DNFS 1; HW 1; MTCW 1
Castedo, Elena 1937- .... **CLC 65**
See also CA 132
Castedo-Ellerman, Elena
See Castedo, Elena
Castellanos, Rosario 1925-1974 .... **CLC 66;
HLC 1; SSC 39, 68**
See also CA 131; 53-56; CANR 58; CD-
WLB 3; DAM MULT; DLB 113, 290;
EWL 3; FW; HW 1; LAW; MTCW 1;
RGSF 2; RGWL 2, 3
Castelvetro, Lodovico 1505-1571 .... **LC 12**
Castiglione, Baldassare 1478-1529 ...... **LC 12**
See Castiglione, Baldesar
See also LMFS 1; RGWL 2, 3
Castiglione, Baldesar
See Castiglione, Baldassare
See also EW 2
Castillo, Ana (Hernandez Del)
1953- .... **CLC 151**
See also AAYA 42; CA 131; CANR 51, 86,
128; CWP; DLB 122, 227; DNFS 2; FW;
HW 1; LLW 1; PFS 21
Castle, Robert
See Hamilton, Edmond
Castro (Ruz), Fidel 1926(?)- .... **HLC 1**
See also CA 110; 129; CANR 81; DAM
MULT; HW 2
Castro, Guillen de 1569-1631 .... **LC 19**
Castro, Rosalia de 1837-1885 ... **NCLC 3, 78;
PC 41**
See also DAM MULT
Cather, Willa (Sibert) 1873-1947 . **SSC 2, 50;
TCLC 1, 11, 31, 99, 132, 152; WLC**
See also AAYA 24; AMW; AMWC 1;
AMWR 1; BPFB 1; CA 104; 128; CDALB
1865-1917; CLR 98; DA; DA3; DAB;
DAC; DAM MST, NOV; DLB 9, 54, 78,

256; DLBD 1; EWL 3; EXPN; EXPS;
LAIT 3; LATS 1:1; MAWW; MTCW 1,
2; NFS 2, 19; RGAL 4; RGSF 2; RHW;
SATA 30; SSFS 2, 7, 16; TCWW 2; TUS
Catherine II
See Catherine the Great
See also DLB 150
Catherine the Great 1729-1796 .... **LC 69**
See Catherine II
Cato, Marcus Porcius
234B.C.-149B.C. .... **CMLC 21**
See Cato the Elder
Cato, Marcus Porcius, the Elder
See Cato, Marcus Porcius
Cato the Elder
See Cato, Marcus Porcius
See also DLB 211
Catton, (Charles) Bruce 1899-1978 . **CLC 35**
See also AITN 1; CA 5-8R; 81-84; CANR
7, 74; DLB 17; SATA 2; SATA-Obit 24
Catullus c. 84B.C.-54B.C. .... **CMLC 18**
See also AW 2; CDWLB 1; DLB 211;
RGWL 2, 3
Cauldwell, Frank
See King, Francis (Henry)
Caunitz, William J. 1933-1996 .... **CLC 34**
See also BEST 89:3; CA 125; 130; 152;
CANR 73; INT CA-130
Causley, Charles (Stanley)
1917-2003 .... **CLC 7**
See also CA 9-12R; 223; CANR 5, 35, 94;
CLR 30; CWRI 5; DLB 27; MTCW 1;
SATA 3, 66; SATA-Obit 149
Caute, (John) David 1936- .... **CLC 29**
See also CA 1-4R; CAAS 4; CANR 1, 33,
64, 120; CBD; CD 5; CN 7; DAM NOV;
DLB 14, 231
Cavafy, C(onstantine) P(eter) .... **PC 36;
TCLC 2, 7**
See Kavafis, Konstantinos Petrou
See also CA 148; DA3; DAM POET; EW
8; EWL 3; MTCW 1; PFS 19; RGWL 2,
3; WP
Cavalcanti, Guido c. 1250-c.
1300 .... **CMLC 54**
See also RGWL 2, 3
Cavallo, Evelyn
See Spark, Muriel (Sarah)
Cavanna, Betty .... **CLC 12**
See Harrison, Elizabeth (Allen) Cavanna
See also JRDA; MAICYA 1; SAAS 4;
SATA 1, 30
Cavendish, Margaret Lucas
1623-1673 .... **LC 30**
See also DLB 131, 252, 281; RGEL 2
Caxton, William 1421(?)-1491(?) .... **LC 17**
See also DLB 170
Cayer, D. M.
See Duffy, Maureen
Cayrol, Jean 1911- .... **CLC 11**
See also CA 89-92; DLB 83; EWL 3
Cela (y Trulock), Camilo Jose
See Cela, Camilo Jose
See also CWW 2
Cela, Camilo Jose 1916-2002 .... **CLC 4, 13,
59, 122; HLC 1; SSC 71**
See Cela (y Trulock), Camilo Jose
See also BEST 90:2; CA 21-24R; 206;
CAAS 10; CANR 21, 32, 76; DAM
MULT; DLBY 1989; EW 13; EWL 3; HW
1; MTCW 1, 2; RGSF 2; RGWL 2, 3
Celan, Paul .... **CLC 10, 19, 53, 82; PC 10**
See Antschel, Paul
See also CDWLB 2; DLB 69; EWL 3;
RGWL 2, 3

Celine, Louis-Ferdinand .. **CLC 1, 3, 4, 7, 9,
15, 47, 124**
See Destouches, Louis-Ferdinand
See also DLB 72; EWL 3; GFL
1789 to the Present; RGWL 2, 3
Cellini, Benvenuto 1500-1571 .... **LC 7**
Cendrars, Blaise .... **CLC 18, 106**
See Sauser-Hall, Frederic
See also DLB 258; EWL 3; GFL 1789 to
the Present; RGWL 2, 3; WP
Centlivre, Susanna 1669(?)-1723 .... **DC 25;
LC 65**
See also DLB 84; RGEL 2
Cernuda (y Bidon), Luis
1902-1963 .... **CLC 54; PC 62**
See also CA 131; 89-92; DAM POET; DLB
134; EWL 3; GLL 1; HW 1; RGWL 2, 3
Cervantes, Lorna Dee 1954- ..... **HLCS 1; PC
35**
See also CA 131; CANR 80; CWP; DLB
82; EXPP; HW 1; LLW 1
Cervantes (Saavedra), Miguel de
1547-1616 .... **HLCS; LC 6, 23, 93; SSC
12; WLC**
See also AAYA 56; BYA 1, 14; DA; DAB;
DAC; DAM MST, NOV; EW 2; LAIT 1;
LATS 1:1; LMFS 1; NFS 8; RGSF 2;
RGWL 2, 3; TWA
Cesaire, Aime (Fernand) 1913- .... **BLC 1;
CLC 19, 32, 112; DC 22; PC 25**
See also BW 2, 3; CA 65-68; CANR 24,
43, 81; CWW 2; DA3; DAM MULT,
POET; EWL 3; GFL 1789 to the Present;
MTCW 1, 2; WP
Chabon, Michael 1963- ... **CLC 55, 149; SSC
59**
See also AAYA 45; AMWS 11; CA 139;
CANR 57, 96, 127; DLB 278; SATA 145
Chabrol, Claude 1930- .... **CLC 16**
See also CA 110
Chairil Anwar
See Anwar, Chairil
See also EWL 3
Challans, Mary 1905-1983
See Renault, Mary
See also CA 81-84; 111; CANR 74; DA3;
MTCW 2; SATA 23; SATA-Obit 36; TEA
Challis, George
See Faust, Frederick (Schiller)
See also TCWW 2
Chambers, Aidan 1934- .... **CLC 35**
See also AAYA 27; CA 25-28R; CANR 12,
31, 58, 116; JRDA; MAICYA 1, 2; SAAS
12; SATA 1, 69, 108; WYA; YAW
Chambers, James 1948-
See Cliff, Jimmy
See also CA 124
Chambers, Jessie
See Lawrence, D(avid) H(erbert Richards)
See also GLL 1
Chambers, Robert W(illiam)
1865-1933 .... **TCLC 41**
See also CA 165; DLB 202; HGG; SATA
107; SUFW 1
Chambers, (David) Whittaker
1901-1961 .... **TCLC 129**
See also CA 89-92; DLB 303
Chamisso, Adelbert von
1781-1838 .... **NCLC 82**
See also DLB 90; RGWL 2, 3; SUFW 1
Chance, James T.
See Carpenter, John (Howard)
Chance, John T.
See Carpenter, John (Howard)
Chandler, Raymond (Thornton)
1888-1959 .... **SSC 23; TCLC 1, 7**
See also AAYA 25; AMWC 2; AMWS 4;
BPFB 1; CA 104; 129; CANR 60, 107;
CDALB 1929-1941; CMW 4; DA3; DLB

Chomette, Rene Lucien 1898-1981
See Clair, Rene
See also CA 103

Chomsky, (Avram) Noam 1928- ..... **CLC 132**
See also CA 17-20R; CANR 28, 62, 110, 132; DA3; DLB 246; MTCW 1, 2

Chona, Maria 1845(?)-1936 .... **NNAL**
See also CA 144

Chopin, Kate .... **SSC 8, 68; TCLC 127; WLCS**
See Chopin, Katherine
See also AAYA 33; AMWR 2; AMWS 1; BYA 11, 15; CDALB 1865-1917; DA; DAB; DLB 12, 78; EXPN; EXPS; FW; LAIT 3; MAWW; NFS 3; RGAL 4; RGSF 2; SSFS 17; TUS

Chopin, Katherine 1851-1904
See Chopin, Kate
See also CA 104; 122; DA3; DAC; DAM MST, NOV

Chretien de Troyes c. 12th cent. - . **CMLC 10**
See also DLB 208; EW 1; RGWL 2, 3; TWA

Christie
See Ichikawa, Kon

Christie, Agatha (Mary Clarissa)
1890-1976 .. **CLC 1, 6, 8, 12, 39, 48, 110**
See also AAYA 9; AITN 1, 2; BPFB 1; BRWS 2; CA 17-20R; 61-64; CANR 10, 37, 108; CBD; CDBLB 1914-1945; CMW 4; CPW; CWD; DA3; DAB; DAC; DAM NOV; DFS 2; DLB 13, 77, 245; MSW; MTCW 1, 2; NFS 8; RGEL 2; RHW; SATA 36; TEA; YAW

Christie, Philippa .... **CLC 21**
See Pearce, Philippa
See also BYA 5; CANR 109; CLR 9; DLB 161; MAICYA 1; SATA 1, 67, 129

Christine de Pizan 1365(?)-1431(?) .... **LC 9**
See also DLB 208; RGWL 2, 3

Chuang Tzu c. 369B.C.-c.
286B.C. .... **CMLC 57**

Chubb, Elmer
See Masters, Edgar Lee

Chulkov, Mikhail Dmitrievich
1743-1792 .... **LC 2**
See also DLB 150

Churchill, Caryl 1938- .... **CLC 31, 55, 157; DC 5**
See Churchill, Chick
See also BRWS 4; CA 102; CANR 22, 46, 108; CBD; CWD; DFS 12, 16; DLB 13; EWL 3; FW; MTCW 1; RGEL 2

Churchill, Charles 1731-1764 .... **LC 3**
See also DLB 109; RGEL 2

Churchill, Chick
See Churchill, Caryl
See also CD 5

Churchill, Sir Winston (Leonard Spencer)
1874-1965 .... **TCLC 113**
See also BRW 6; CA 97-100; CDBLB 1890-1914; DA3; DLB 100; DLBD 16; LAIT 4; MTCW 1, 2

Chute, Carolyn 1947- .... **CLC 39**
See also CA 123; CANR 135

Ciardi, John (Anthony) 1916-1986 . **CLC 10, 40, 44, 129**
See also CA 5-8R; 118; CAAS 2; CANR 5, 33; CLR 19; CWRI 5; DAM POET; DLB 5; DLBY 1986; INT CANR-5; MAICYA 1, 2; MTCW 1, 2; RGAL 4; SAAS 26; SATA 1, 65; SATA-Obit 46

Cibber, Colley 1671-1757 .... **LC 66**
See also DLB 84; RGEL 2

Cicero, Marcus Tullius
106B.C.-43B.C. .... **CMLC 3**
See also AW 1; CDWLB 1; DLB 211; RGWL 2, 3

Cimino, Michael 1943- .... **CLC 16**
See also CA 105

Cioran, E(mil) M. 1911-1995 .... **CLC 64**
See also CA 25-28R; 149; CANR 91; DLB 220; EWL 3

Cisneros, Sandra 1954- .... **CLC 69, 118, 193; HLC 1; PC 52; SSC 32, 72**
See also AAYA 9, 53; AMWS 7; CA 131; CANR 64, 118; CWP; DA3; DAM MULT; DLB 122, 152; EWL 3; EXPN; FW; HW 1, 2; LAIT 5; LATS 1:2; LLW 1; MAICYA 2; MTCW 2; NFS 2; PFS 19; RGAL 4; RGSF 2; SSFS 3, 13; WLIT 1; YAW

Cixous, Helene 1937- .... **CLC 92**
See also CA 126; CANR 55, 123; CWW 2; DLB 83, 242; EWL 3; FW; GLL 2; MTCW 1, 2; TWA

Clair, Rene .... **CLC 20**
See Chomette, Rene Lucien

Clampitt, Amy 1920-1994 .... **CLC 32; PC 19**
See also AMWS 9; CA 110; 146; CANR 29, 79; DLB 105

Clancy, Thomas L., Jr. 1947-
See Clancy, Tom
See also CA 125; 131; CANR 62, 105; DA3; INT CA-131; MTCW 1, 2

Clancy, Tom .... **CLC 45, 112**
See Clancy, Thomas L., Jr.
See also AAYA 9, 51; BEST 89:1, 90:1; BPFB 1; BYA 10, 11; CANR 132; CMW 4; CPW; DAM NOV, POP; DLB 227

Clare, John 1793-1864 .. **NCLC 9, 86; PC 23**
See also DAB; DAM POET; DLB 55, 96; RGEL 2

Clarin
See Alas (y Urena), Leopoldo (Enrique Garcia)

Clark, Al C.
See Goines, Donald

Clark, (Robert) Brian 1932- .... **CLC 29**
See also CA 41-44R; CANR 67; CBD; CD 5

Clark, Curt
See Westlake, Donald E(dwin)

Clark, Eleanor 1913-1996 .... **CLC 5, 19**
See also CA 9-12R; 151; CANR 41; CN 7; DLB 6

Clark, J. P.
See Clark Bekederemo, J(ohnson) P(epper)
See also CDWLB 3; DLB 117

Clark, John Pepper
See Clark Bekederemo, J(ohnson) P(epper)
See also AFW; CD 5; CP 7; RGEL 2

Clark, Kenneth (Mackenzie)
1903-1983 .... **TCLC 147**
See also CA 93-96; 109; CANR 36; MTCW 1, 2

Clark, M. R.
See Clark, Mavis Thorpe

Clark, Mavis Thorpe 1909-1999 ...... **CLC 12**
See also CA 57-60; CANR 8, 37, 107; CLR 30; CWRI 5; MAICYA 1, 2; SAAS 5; SATA 8, 74

Clark, Walter Van Tilburg
1909-1971 .... **CLC 28**
See also CA 9-12R; 33-36R; CANR 63, 113; DLB 9, 206; LAIT 2; RGAL 4; SATA 8

Clark Bekederemo, J(ohnson) P(epper)
1935- .... **BLC 1; CLC 38; DC 5**
See Clark, J. P.; Clark, John Pepper
See also BW 1; CA 65-68; CANR 16, 72; DAM DRAM, MULT; DFS 13; EWL 3; MTCW 1

Clarke, Arthur C(harles) 1917- .... **CLC 1, 4, 13, 18, 35, 136; SSC 3**
See also AAYA 4, 33; BPFB 1; BYA 13; CA 1-4R; CANR 2, 28, 55, 74, 130; CN 7; CPW; DA3; DAM POP; DLB 261;
JRDA; LAIT 5; MAICYA 1, 2; MTCW 1, 2; SATA 13, 70, 115; SCFW; SFW 4; SSFS 4, 18; YAW

Clarke, Austin 1896-1974 .... **CLC 6, 9**
See also CA 29-32; 49-52; CAP 2; DAM POET; DLB 10, 20; EWL 3; RGEL 2

Clarke, Austin C(hesterfield) 1934- .. **BLC 1; CLC 8, 53; SSC 45**
See also BW 1; CA 25-28R; CAAS 16; CANR 14, 32, 68; CN 7; DAC; DAM MULT; DLB 53, 125; DNFS 2; RGSF 2

Clarke, Gillian 1937- .... **CLC 61**
See also CA 106; CP 7; CWP; DLB 40

Clarke, Marcus (Andrew Hislop)
1846-1881 .... **NCLC 19**
See also DLB 230; RGEL 2; RGSF 2

Clarke, Shirley 1925-1997 .... **CLC 16**
See also CA 189

Clash, The
See Headon, (Nicky) Topper; Jones, Mick; Simonon, Paul; Strummer, Joe

Claudel, Paul (Louis Charles Marie)
1868-1955 .... **TCLC 2, 10**
See also CA 104; 165; DLB 192, 258; EW 8; EWL 3; GFL 1789 to the Present; RGWL 2, 3; TWA

Claudian 370(?)-404(?) .... **CMLC 46**
See also RGWL 2, 3

Claudius, Matthias 1740-1815 .... **NCLC 75**
See also DLB 97

Clavell, James (duMaresq)
1925-1994 .... **CLC 6, 25, 87**
See also BPFB 1; CA 25-28R; 146; CANR 26, 48; CPW; DA3; DAM NOV, POP; MTCW 1, 2; NFS 10; RHW

Clayman, Gregory .... **CLC 65**

Cleaver, (Leroy) Eldridge
1935-1998 .... **BLC 1; CLC 30, 119**
See also BW 1, 3; CA 21-24R; 167; CANR 16, 75; DA3; DAM MULT; MTCW 2; YAW

Cleese, John (Marwood) 1939- .... **CLC 21**
See Monty Python
See also CA 112; 116; CANR 35; MTCW 1

Cleishbotham, Jebediah
See Scott, Sir Walter

Cleland, John 1710-1789 .... **LC 2, 48**
See also DLB 39; RGEL 2

Clemens, Samuel Langhorne 1835-1910
See Twain, Mark
See also CA 104; 135; CDALB 1865-1917; DA; DA3; DAB; DAC; DAM MST, NOV; DLB 12, 23, 64, 74, 186, 189; JRDA; LMFS 1; MAICYA 1, 2; NCFS 4; NFS 20; SATA 100; SSFS 16; YABC 2

Clement of Alexandria
150(?)-215(?) .... **CMLC 41**

Cleophil
See Congreve, William

Clerihew, E.
See Bentley, E(dmund) C(lerihew)

Clerk, N. W.
See Lewis, C(live) S(taples)

Cleveland, John 1613-1658 .... **LC 106**
See also DLB 126; RGEL 2

Cliff, Jimmy .... **CLC 21**
See Chambers, James
See also CA 193

Cliff, Michelle 1946- .... **BLCS; CLC 120**
See also BW 2; CA 116; CANR 39, 72; CD-WLB 3; DLB 157; FW; GLL 2

Clifford, Lady Anne 1590-1676 .... **LC 76**
See also DLB 151

Clifton, (Thelma) Lucille 1936- .... **BLC 1; CLC 19, 66, 162; PC 17**
See also AFAW 2; BW 2, 3; CA 49-52; CANR 2, 24, 42, 76, 97; CLR 5; CP 7; CSW; CWP; CWRI 5; DA3; DAM MULT,

POET; DLB 5, 41; EXPP; MAICYA 1, 2;
MTCW 1, 2; PFS 1, 14; SATA 20, 69,
128; WP

Clinton, Dirk
See Silverberg, Robert

Clough, Arthur Hugh 1819-1861 ... **NCLC 27**
See also BRW 5; DLB 32; RGEL 2

Clutha, Janet Paterson Frame 1924-2004
See Frame, Janet
See also CA 1-4R; 224; CANR 2, 36, 76,
135; MTCW 1, 2; SATA 119

Clyne, Terence
See Blatty, William Peter

Cobalt, Martin
See Mayne, William (James Carter)

Cobb, Irvin S(hrewsbury)
1876-1944 .... **TCLC 77**
See also CA 175; DLB 11, 25, 86

Cobbett, William 1763-1835 .... **NCLC 49**
See also DLB 43, 107, 158; RGEL 2

Coburn, D(onald) L(ee) 1938- .... **CLC 10**
See also CA 89-92

Cocteau, Jean (Maurice Eugene Clement)
1889-1963 ...... **CLC 1, 8, 15, 16, 43; DC
17; TCLC 119; WLC**
See also CA 25-28; CANR 40; CAP 2; DA;
DA3; DAB; DAC; DAM DRAM, MST,
NOV; DLB 65, 258; EW 10; EWL 3; GFL
1789 to the Present; MTCW 1, 2; RGWL
2, 3; TWA

Codrescu, Andrei 1946- .... **CLC 46, 121**
See also CA 33-36R; CAAS 19; CANR 13,
34, 53, 76, 125; DA3; DAM POET;
MTCW 2

Coe, Max
See Bourne, Randolph S(illiman)

Coe, Tucker
See Westlake, Donald E(dwin)

Coen, Ethan 1958- .... **CLC 108**
See also AAYA 54; CA 126; CANR 85

Coen, Joel 1955- .... **CLC 108**
See also AAYA 54; CA 126; CANR 119

The Coen Brothers
See Coen, Ethan; Coen, Joel

Coetzee, J(ohn) M(axwell) 1940- ..... **CLC 23,
33, 66, 117, 161, 162**
See also AAYA 37; AFW; BRWS 6; CA 77-
80; CANR 41, 54, 74, 114, 133; CN 7;
DA3; DAM NOV; DLB 225; EWL 3;
LMFS 2; MTCW 1, 2; WLIT 2; WWE 1

Coffey, Brian
See Koontz, Dean R(ay)

Coffin, Robert P(eter) Tristram
1892-1955 .... **TCLC 95**
See also CA 123; 169; DLB 45

Cohan, George M(ichael)
1878-1942 .... **TCLC 60**
See also CA 157; DLB 249; RGAL 4

Cohen, Arthur A(llen) 1928-1986 ...... **CLC 7,
31**
See also CA 1-4R; 120; CANR 1, 17, 42;
DLB 28

Cohen, Leonard (Norman) 1934- ...... **CLC 3,
38**
See also CA 21-24R; CANR 14, 69; CN 7;
CP 7; DAC; DAM MST; DLB 53; EWL
3; MTCW 1

Cohen, Matt(hew) 1942-1999 .... **CLC 19**
See also CA 61-64; 187; CAAS 18; CANR
40; CN 7; DAC; DLB 53

Cohen-Solal, Annie 19(?)- .... **CLC 50**

Colegate, Isabel 1931- .... **CLC 36**
See also CA 17-20R; CANR 8, 22, 74; CN
7; DLB 14, 231; INT CANR-22; MTCW
1

Coleman, Emmett
See Reed, Ishmael

Coleridge, Hartley 1796-1849 .... **NCLC 90**
See also DLB 96

Coleridge, M. E.
See Coleridge, Mary E(lizabeth)

Coleridge, Mary E(lizabeth)
1861-1907 .... **TCLC 73**
See also CA 116; 166; DLB 19, 98

Coleridge, Samuel Taylor
1772-1834 ...... **NCLC 9, 54, 99, 111; PC
11, 39; WLC**
See also BRW 4; BRWR 2; BYA 4; CD-
BLB 1789-1832; DA; DA3; DAB; DAC;
DAM MST, POET; DLB 93, 107; EXPP;
LATS 1:1; LMFS 1; PAB; PFS 4, 5;
RGEL 2; TEA; WLIT 3; WP

Coleridge, Sara 1802-1852 .... **NCLC 31**
See also DLB 199

Coles, Don 1928- .... **CLC 46**
See also CA 115; CANR 38; CP 7

Coles, Robert (Martin) 1929- .... **CLC 108**
See also CA 45-48; CANR 3, 32, 66, 70,
135; INT CANR-32; SATA 23

Colette, (Sidonie-Gabrielle)
1873-1954 .... **SSC 10; TCLC 1, 5, 16**
See Willy, Colette
See also CA 104; 131; DA3; DAM NOV;
DLB 65; EW 9; EWL 3; GFL 1789 to the
Present; MTCW 1, 2; RGWL 2, 3; TWA

Collett, (Jacobine) Camilla (Wergeland)
1813-1895 .... **NCLC 22**

Collier, Christopher 1930- .... **CLC 30**
See also AAYA 13; BYA 2; CA 33-36R;
CANR 13, 33, 102; JRDA; MAICYA 1,
2; SATA 16, 70; WYA; YAW 1

Collier, James Lincoln 1928- .... **CLC 30**
See also AAYA 13; BYA 2; CA 9-12R;
CANR 4, 33, 60, 102; CLR 3; DAM POP;
JRDA; MAICYA 1, 2; SAAS 21; SATA 8,
70; WYA; YAW 1

Collier, Jeremy 1650-1726 .... **LC 6**

Collier, John 1901-1980 . **SSC 19; TCLC 127**
See also CA 65-68; 97-100; CANR 10;
DLB 77, 255; FANT; SUFW 1

Collier, Mary 1690-1762 .... **LC 86**
See also DLB 95

Collingwood, R(obin) G(eorge)
1889(?)-1943 .... **TCLC 67**
See also CA 117; 155; DLB 262

Collins, Hunt
See Hunter, Evan

Collins, Linda 1931- .... **CLC 44**
See also CA 125

Collins, Tom
See Furphy, Joseph
See also RGEL 2

Collins, (William) Wilkie
1824-1889 .... **NCLC 1, 18, 93**
See also BRWS 6; CDBLB 1832-1890;
CMW 4; DLB 18, 70, 159; MSW; RGEL
2; RGSF 2; SUFW 1; WLIT 4

Collins, William 1721-1759 .... **LC 4, 40**
See also BRW 3; DAM POET; DLB 109;
RGEL 2

Collodi, Carlo .... **NCLC 54**
See Lorenzini, Carlo
See also CLR 5; WCH

Colman, George
See Glassco, John

Colman, George, the Elder
1732-1794 .... **LC 98**
See also RGEL 2

Colonna, Vittoria 1492-1547 .... **LC 71**
See also RGWL 2, 3

Colt, Winchester Remington
See Hubbard, L(afayette) Ron(ald)

Colter, Cyrus J. 1910-2002 .... **CLC 58**
See also BW 1; CA 65-68; 205; CANR 10,
66; CN 7; DLB 33

Colton, James
See Hansen, Joseph
See also GLL 1

Colum, Padraic 1881-1972 .... **CLC 28**
See also BYA 4; CA 73-76; 33-36R; CANR
35; CLR 36; CWRI 5; DLB 19; MAICYA
1, 2; MTCW 1; RGEL 2; SATA 15; WCH

Colvin, James
See Moorcock, Michael (John)

Colwin, Laurie (E.) 1944-1992 .... **CLC 5, 13,
23, 84**
See also CA 89-92; 139; CANR 20, 46;
DLB 218; DLBY 1980; MTCW 1

Comfort, Alex(ander) 1920-2000 .... **CLC 7**
See also CA 1-4R; 190; CANR 1, 45; CP 7;
DAM POP; MTCW 1

Comfort, Montgomery
See Campbell, (John) Ramsey

Compton-Burnett, I(vy)
1892(?)-1969 .... **CLC 1, 3, 10, 15, 34**
See also BRW 7; CA 1-4R; 25-28R; CANR
4; DAM NOV; DLB 36; EWL 3; MTCW
1; RGEL 2

Comstock, Anthony 1844-1915 ...... **TCLC 13**
See also CA 110; 169

Comte, Auguste 1798-1857 .... **NCLC 54**

Conan Doyle, Arthur
See Doyle, Sir Arthur Conan
See also BPFB 1; BYA 4, 5, 11

Conde (Abellan), Carmen
1901-1996 .... **HLCS 1**
See also CA 177; CWW 2; DLB 108; EWL
3; HW 2

Conde, Maryse 1937- ..... **BLCS; CLC 52, 92**
See also BW 2, 3; CA 110; 190; CAAE 190;
CANR 30, 53, 76; CWW 2; DAM MULT;
EWL 3; MTCW 1

Condillac, Etienne Bonnot de
1714-1780 .... **LC 26**

Condon, Richard (Thomas)
1915-1996 .... **CLC 4, 6, 8, 10, 45, 100**
See also BEST 90:3; BPFB 1; CA 1-4R;
151; CAAS 1; CANR 2, 23; CMW 4; CN
7; DAM NOV; INT CANR-23; MTCW 1,
2

Condorcet 1743-1794 .... **LC 104**
See also GFL Beginnings to 1789

Confucius 551B.C.-479B.C. .... **CMLC 19, 65;
WLCS**
See also DA; DA3; DAB; DAC; DAM
MST

Congreve, William 1670-1729 ... **DC 2; LC 5,
21; WLC**
See also BRW 2; CDBLB 1660-1789; DA;
DAB; DAC; DAM DRAM, MST, POET;
DFS 15; DLB 39, 84; RGEL 2; WLIT 3

Conley, Robert J(ackson) 1940- .... **NNAL**
See also CA 41-44R; CANR 15, 34, 45, 96;
DAM MULT

Connell, Evan S(helby), Jr. 1924- . **CLC 4, 6,
45**
See also AAYA 7; AMWS 14; CA 1-4R;
CAAS 2; CANR 2, 39, 76, 97; CN 7;
DAM NOV; DLB 2; DLBY 1981; MTCW
1, 2

Connelly, Marc(us Cook) 1890-1980 . **CLC 7**
See also CA 85-88; 102; CANR 30; DFS
12; DLB 7; DLBY 1980; RGAL 4; SATA-
Obit 25

Connor, Ralph .... **TCLC 31**
See Gordon, Charles William
See also DLB 92; TCWW 2

Conrad, Joseph 1857-1924 ..... **SSC 9, 67, 69,
71; TCLC 1, 6, 13, 25, 43, 57; WLC**
See also AAYA 26; BPFB 1; BRW 6;
BRWC 1; BRWR 2; BYA 2; CA 104; 131;
CANR 60; CDBLB 1890-1914; DA; DA3;
DAB; DAC; DAM MST, NOV; DLB 10,
34, 98, 156; EWL 3; EXPN; EXPS; LAIT
2; LATS 1:1; LMFS 1; MTCW 1, 2; NFS
2, 16; RGEL 2; RGSF 2; SATA 27; SSFS
1, 12; TEA; WLIT 4

Denmark, Harrison
See Zelazny, Roger (Joseph)
Dennis, John 1658-1734 .... **LC 11**
See also DLB 101; RGEL 2
Dennis, Nigel (Forbes) 1912-1989 ...... **CLC 8**
See also CA 25-28R; 129; DLB 13, 15, 233;
EWL 3; MTCW 1
Dent, Lester 1904-1959 .... **TCLC 72**
See also CA 112; 161; CMW 4; DLB 306;
SFW 4
De Palma, Brian (Russell) 1940- ...... **CLC 20**
See also CA 109
De Quincey, Thomas 1785-1859 ..... **NCLC 4,
87**
See also BRW 4; CDBLB 1789-1832; DLB
110, 144; RGEL 2
Deren, Eleanora 1908(?)-1961
See Deren, Maya
See also CA 192; 111
Deren, Maya .... **CLC 16, 102**
See Deren, Eleanora
Derleth, August (William)
1909-1971 .... **CLC 31**
See also BPFB 1; BYA 9, 10; CA 1-4R; 29-
32R; CANR 4; CMW 4; DLB 9; DLBD
17; HGG; SATA 5; SUFW 1
Der Nister 1884-1950 .... **TCLC 56**
See Nister, Der
Der Stricker c. 1190-c. 1250 .... **CMLC 75**
de Routisie, Albert
See Aragon, Louis
Derrida, Jacques 1930-2004 .... **CLC 24, 87**
See also CA 124; 127; CANR 76, 98, 133;
DLB 242; EWL 3; LMFS 2; MTCW 1;
TWA
Derry Down Derry
See Lear, Edward
Dersonnes, Jacques
See Simenon, Georges (Jacques Christian)
Desai, Anita 1937- .... **CLC 19, 37, 97, 175**
See also BRWS 5; CA 81-84; CANR 33,
53, 95, 133; CN 7; CWRI 5; DA3; DAB;
DAM NOV; DLB 271; DNFS 2; EWL 3;
FW; MTCW 1, 2; SATA 63, 126
Desai, Kiran 1971- .... **CLC 119**
See also BYA 16; CA 171; CANR 127
de Saint-Luc, Jean
See Glassco, John
de Saint Roman, Arnaud
See Aragon, Louis
Desbordes-Valmore, Marceline
1786-1859 .... **NCLC 97**
See also DLB 217
Descartes, Rene 1596-1650 .... **LC 20, 35**
See also DLB 268; EW 3; GFL Beginnings
to 1789
Deschamps, Eustache 1340(?)-1404 .. **LC 103**
See also DLB 208
De Sica, Vittorio 1901(?)-1974 .... **CLC 20**
See also CA 117
Desnos, Robert 1900-1945 .... **TCLC 22**
See also CA 121; 151; CANR 107; DLB
258; EWL 3; LMFS 2
Destouches, Louis-Ferdinand
1894-1961 .... **CLC 9, 15**
See Celine, Louis-Ferdinand
See also CA 85-88; CANR 28; MTCW 1
de Tolignac, Gaston
See Griffith, D(avid Lewelyn) W(ark)
Deutsch, Babette 1895-1982 .... **CLC 18**
See also BYA 3; CA 1-4R; 108; CANR 4,
79; DLB 45; SATA 1; SATA-Obit 33
Devenant, William 1606-1649 .... **LC 13**
Devkota, Laxmiprasad 1909-1959 . **TCLC 23**
See also CA 123
De Voto, Bernard (Augustine)
1897-1955 .... **TCLC 29**
See also CA 113; 160; DLB 9, 256

De Vries, Peter 1910-1993 ..... **CLC 1, 2, 3, 7,
10, 28, 46**
See also CA 17-20R; 142; CANR 41; DAM
NOV; DLB 6; DLBY 1982; MTCW 1, 2
Dewey, John 1859-1952 .... **TCLC 95**
See also CA 114; 170; DLB 246, 270;
RGAL 4
Dexter, John
See Bradley, Marion Zimmer
See also GLL 1
Dexter, Martin
See Faust, Frederick (Schiller)
See also TCWW 2
Dexter, Pete 1943- .... **CLC 34, 55**
See also BEST 89:2; CA 127; 131; CANR
129; CPW; DAM POP; INT CA-131;
MTCW 1
Diamano, Silmang
See Senghor, Leopold Sedar
Diamond, Neil 1941- .... **CLC 30**
See also CA 108
Diaz del Castillo, Bernal
1496-1584 .... **HLCS 1; LC 31**
See also LAW
di Bassetto, Corno
See Shaw, George Bernard
Dick, Philip K(indred) 1928-1982 ... **CLC 10,
30, 72; SSC 57**
See also AAYA 24; BPFB 1; BYA 11; CA
49-52; 106; CANR 2, 16, 132; CPW;
DA3; DAM NOV, POP; DLB 8; MTCW
1, 2; NFS 5; SCFW; SFW 4
Dickens, Charles (John Huffam)
1812-1870 .... **NCLC 3, 8, 18, 26, 37, 50,
86, 105, 113; SSC 17, 49; WLC**
See also AAYA 23; BRW 5; BRWC 1, 2;
BYA 1, 2, 3, 13, 14; CDBLB 1832-1890;
CLR 95; CMW 4; DA; DA3; DAB; DAC;
DAM MST, NOV; DLB 21, 55, 70, 159,
166; EXPN; HGG; JRDA; LAIT 1, 2;
LATS 1:1; LMFS 1; MAICYA 1, 2; NFS
4, 5, 10, 14, 20; RGEL 2; RGSF 2; SATA
15; SUFW 1; TEA; WCH; WLIT 4; WYA
Dickey, James (Lafayette)
1923-1997 .... **CLC 1, 2, 4, 7, 10, 15, 47,
109; PC 40; TCLC 151**
See also AAYA 50; AITN 1, 2; AMWS 4;
BPFB 1; CA 9-12R; 156; CABS 2; CANR
10, 48, 61, 105; CDALB 1968-1988; CP
7; CSW; DA3; DAM NOV, POET,
POP; DLB 5, 193; DLBD 7; DLBY 1982,
1993, 1996, 1997, 1998; EWL 3; INT
CANR-10; MTCW 1, 2; NFS 9; PFS 6,
11; RGAL 4; TUS
Dickey, William 1928-1994 .... **CLC 3, 28**
See also CA 9-12R; 145; CANR 24, 79;
DLB 5
Dickinson, Charles 1951- .... **CLC 49**
See also CA 128
Dickinson, Emily (Elizabeth)
1830-1886 ... **NCLC 21, 77; PC 1; WLC**
See also AAYA 22; AMW; AMWR 1;
CDALB 1865-1917; DA; DA3; DAB;
DAC; DAM MST, POET; DLB 1, 243;
EXPP; MAWW; PAB; PFS 1, 2, 3, 4, 5,
6, 8, 10, 11, 13, 16; RGAL 4; SATA 29;
TUS; WP; WYA
Dickinson, Mrs. Herbert Ward
See Phelps, Elizabeth Stuart
Dickinson, Peter (Malcolm de Brissac)
1927- .... **CLC 12, 35**
See also AAYA 9, 49; BYA 5; CA 41-44R;
CANR 31, 58, 88, 134; CLR 29; CMW 4;
DLB 87, 161, 276; JRDA; MAICYA 1, 2;
SATA 5, 62, 95, 150; SFW 4; WYA; YAW
Dickson, Carr
See Carr, John Dickson
Dickson, Carter
See Carr, John Dickson

Diderot, Denis 1713-1784 .... **LC 26**
See also EW 4; GFL Beginnings to 1789;
LMFS 1; RGWL 2, 3
Didion, Joan 1934- . **CLC 1, 3, 8, 14, 32, 129**
See also AITN 1; AMWS 4; CA 5-8R;
CANR 14, 52, 76, 125; CDALB 1968-
1988; CN 7; DA3; DAM NOV; DLB 2,
173, 185; DLBY 1981, 1986; EWL 3;
MAWW; MTCW 1, 2; NFS 3; RGAL 4;
TCWW 2; TUS
di Donato, Pietro 1911-1992 .... **TCLC 159**
See also CA 101; 136; DLB 9
Dietrich, Robert
See Hunt, E(verette) Howard, (Jr.)
Difusa, Pati
See Almodovar, Pedro
Dillard, Annie 1945- .... **CLC 9, 60, 115**
See also AAYA 6, 43; AMWS 6; ANW; CA
49-52; CANR 3, 43, 62, 90, 125; DA3;
DAM NOV; DLB 275, 278; DLBY 1980;
LAIT 4, 5; MTCW 1, 2; NCFS 1; RGAL
4; SATA 10, 140; TUS
Dillard, R(ichard) H(enry) W(ilde)
1937- .... **CLC 5**
See also CA 21-24R; CAAS 7; CANR 10;
CP 7; CSW; DLB 5, 244
Dillon, Eilis 1920-1994 .... **CLC 17**
See also CA 9-12R, 182; 147; CAAE 182;
CAAS 3; CANR 4, 38, 78; CLR 26; MAI-
CYA 1, 2; MAICYAS 1; SATA 2, 74;
SATA-Essay 105; SATA-Obit 83; YAW
Dimont, Penelope
See Mortimer, Penelope (Ruth)
Dinesen, Isak ..... **CLC 10, 29, 95; SSC 7, 75**
See Blixen, Karen (Christentze Dinesen)
See also EW 10; EWL 3; EXPS; FW; HGG;
LAIT 3; MTCW 1; NCFS 7; NFS 9;
RGSF 2; RGWL 2, 3; SSFS 3, 6, 13;
WLIT 2
Ding Ling .... **CLC 68**
See Chiang, Pin-chin
See also RGWL 3
Diphusa, Patty
See Almodovar, Pedro
Disch, Thomas M(ichael) 1940- ... **CLC 7, 36**
See Disch, Tom
See also AAYA 17; BPFB 1; CA 21-24R;
CAAS 4; CANR 17, 36, 54, 89; CLR 18;
CP 7; DA3; DLB 8; HGG; MAICYA 1, 2;
MTCW 1, 2; SAAS 15; SATA 92; SCFW;
SFW 4; SUFW 2
Disch, Tom
See Disch, Thomas M(ichael)
See also DLB 282
d'Isly, Georges
See Simenon, Georges (Jacques Christian)
Disraeli, Benjamin 1804-1881 ... **NCLC 2, 39,
79**
See also BRW 4; DLB 21, 55; RGEL 2
Ditcum, Steve
See Crumb, R(obert)
Dixon, Paige
See Corcoran, Barbara (Asenath)
Dixon, Stephen 1936- .... **CLC 52; SSC 16**
See also AMWS 12; CA 89-92; CANR 17,
40, 54, 91; CN 7; DLB 130
Dixon, Thomas 1864-1946 .... **TCLC 163**
See also RHW
Djebar, Assia 1936- .... **CLC 182**
See also CA 188; EWL 3; RGWL 3; WLIT
2
Doak, Annie
See Dillard, Annie
Dobell, Sydney Thompson
1824-1874 .... **NCLC 43**
See also DLB 32; RGEL 2
Doblin, Alfred .... **TCLC 13**
See Doeblin, Alfred
See also CDWLB 2; EWL 3; RGWL 2, 3

Author Index

Faust, Frederick (Schiller)
1892-1944(?) .... **TCLC 49**
See Austin, Frank; Brand, Max; Challis,
George; Dawson, Peter; Dexter, Martin;
Evans, Evan; Frederick, John; Frost, Fred-
erick; Manning, David; Silver, Nicholas
See also CA 108; 152; DAM POP; DLB
256; TUS
Faust, Irvin 1924- .... **CLC 8**
See also CA 33-36R; CANR 28, 67; CN 7;
DLB 2, 28, 218, 278; DLBY 1980
Faustino, Domingo 1811-1888 ...... **NCLC 123**
Fawkes, Guy
See Benchley, Robert (Charles)
Fearing, Kenneth (Flexner)
1902-1961 .... **CLC 51**
See also CA 93-96; CANR 59; CMW 4;
DLB 9; RGAL 4
Fecamps, Elise
See Creasey, John
Federman, Raymond 1928- .... **CLC 6, 47**
See also CA 17-20R, 208; CAAE 208;
CAAS 8; CANR 10, 43, 83, 108; CN 7;
DLBY 1980
Federspiel, J(uerg) F. 1931- .... **CLC 42**
See also CA 146
Feiffer, Jules (Ralph) 1929- ...... **CLC 2, 8, 64**
See also AAYA 3; CA 17-20R; CAD; CANR
30, 59, 129; CD 5; DAM DRAM; DLB 7,
44; INT CANR-30; MTCW 1; SATA 8,
61, 111
Feige, Hermann Albert Otto Maximilian
See Traven, B.
Feinberg, David B. 1956-1994 .... **CLC 59**
See also CA 135; 147
Feinstein, Elaine 1930- .... **CLC 36**
See also CA 69-72; CAAS 1; CANR 31,
68, 121; CN 7; CP 7; CWP; DLB 14, 40;
MTCW 1
Feke, Gilbert David .... **CLC 65**
Feldman, Irving (Mordecai) 1928- ..... **CLC 7**
See also CA 1-4R; CANR 1; CP 7; DLB
169
Felix-Tchicaya, Gerald
See Tchicaya, Gerald Felix
Fellini, Federico 1920-1993 .... **CLC 16, 85**
See also CA 65-68; 143; CANR 33
Felltham, Owen 1602(?)-1668 .... **LC 92**
See also DLB 126, 151
Felsen, Henry Gregor 1916-1995 ..... **CLC 17**
See also CA 1-4R; 180; CANR 1; SAAS 2;
SATA 1
Felski, Rita .... **CLC 65**
Fenno, Jack
See Calisher, Hortense
Fenollosa, Ernest (Francisco)
1853-1908 .... **TCLC 91**
Fenton, James Martin 1949- .... **CLC 32, 209**
See also CA 102; CANR 108; CP 7; DLB
40; PFS 11
Ferber, Edna 1887-1968 .... **CLC 18, 93**
See also AITN 1; CA 5-8R; 25-28R; CANR
68, 105; DLB 9, 28, 86, 266; MTCW 1,
2; RGAL 4; RHW; SATA 7; TCWW 2
Ferdowsi, Abu'l Qasem 940-1020 . **CMLC 43**
See also RGWL 2, 3
Ferguson, Helen
See Kavan, Anna
Ferguson, Niall 1964- .... **CLC 134**
See also CA 190
Ferguson, Samuel 1810-1886 .... **NCLC 33**
See also DLB 32; RGEL 2
Fergusson, Robert 1750-1774 .... **LC 29**
See also DLB 109; RGEL 2
Ferling, Lawrence
See Ferlinghetti, Lawrence (Monsanto)

Ferlinghetti, Lawrence (Monsanto)
1919(?)- ..... **CLC 2, 6, 10, 27, 111; PC 1**
See also CA 5-8R; CANR 3, 41, 73, 125;
CDALB 1941-1968; CP 7; DA3; DAM
POET; DLB 5, 16; MTCW 1, 2; RGAL 4;
WP
Fern, Fanny
See Parton, Sara Payson Willis
Fernandez, Vicente Garcia Huidobro
See Huidobro Fernandez, Vicente Garcia
Fernandez-Armesto, Felipe .... **CLC 70**
Fernandez de Lizardi, Jose Joaquin
See Lizardi, Jose Joaquin Fernandez de
Ferre, Rosario 1938- ...... **CLC 139; HLCS 1;**
SSC 36
See also CA 131; CANR 55, 81, 134; CWW
2; DLB 145; EWL 3; HW 1, 2; LAWS 1;
MTCW 1; WLIT 1
Ferrer, Gabriel (Francisco Victor) Miro
See Miro (Ferrer), Gabriel (Francisco
Victor)
Ferrier, Susan (Edmonstone)
1782-1854 .... **NCLC 8**
See also DLB 116; RGEL 2
Ferrigno, Robert 1948(?)- .... **CLC 65**
See also CA 140; CANR 125
Ferron, Jacques 1921-1985 .... **CLC 94**
See also CA 117; 129; CCA 1; DAC; DLB
60; EWL 3
Feuchtwanger, Lion 1884-1958 .... **TCLC 3**
See also CA 104; 187; DLB 66; EWL 3
Feuerbach, Ludwig 1804-1872 ..... **NCLC 139**
See also DLB 133
Feuillet, Octave 1821-1890 .... **NCLC 45**
See also DLB 192
Feydeau, Georges (Leon Jules Marie)
1862-1921 .... **TCLC 22**
See also CA 113; 152; CANR 84; DAM
DRAM; DLB 192; EWL 3; GFL 1789 to
the Present; RGWL 2, 3
Fichte, Johann Gottlieb
1762-1814 .... **NCLC 62**
See also DLB 90
Ficino, Marsilio 1433-1499 .... **LC 12**
See also LMFS 1
Fiedeler, Hans
See Doeblin, Alfred
Fiedler, Leslie A(aron) 1917-2003 ..... **CLC 4,**
13, 24
See also AMWS 13; CA 9-12R; 212; CANR
7, 63; CN 7; DLB 28, 67; EWL 3; MTCW
1, 2; RGAL 4; TUS
Field, Andrew 1938- .... **CLC 44**
See also CA 97-100; CANR 25
Field, Eugene 1850-1895 .... **NCLC 3**
See also DLB 23, 42, 140; DLBD 13; MAI-
CYA 1, 2; RGAL 4; SATA 16
Field, Gans T.
See Wellman, Manly Wade
Field, Michael 1915-1971 .... **TCLC 43**
See also CA 29-32R
Field, Peter
See Hobson, Laura Z(ametkin)
See also TCWW 2
Fielding, Helen 1958- .... **CLC 146**
See also CA 172; CANR 127; DLB 231
Fielding, Henry 1707-1754 .... **LC 1, 46, 85;**
WLC
See also BRW 3; BRWR 1; CDBLB 1660-
1789; DA; DA3; DAB; DAC; DAM
DRAM, MST, NOV; DLB 39, 84, 101;
NFS 18; RGEL 2; TEA; WLIT 3
Fielding, Sarah 1710-1768 .... **LC 1, 44**
See also DLB 39; RGEL 2; TEA
Fields, W. C. 1880-1946 .... **TCLC 80**
See also DLB 44

Fierstein, Harvey (Forbes) 1954- ..... **CLC 33**
See also CA 123; 129; CAD; CD 5; CPW;
DA3; DAM DRAM, POP; DFS 6; DLB
266; GLL
Figes, Eva 1932- .... **CLC 31**
See also CA 53-56; CANR 4, 44, 83; CN 7;
DLB 14, 271; FW
Filippo, Eduardo de
See de Filippo, Eduardo
Finch, Anne 1661-1720 .... **LC 3; PC 21**
See also BRWS 9; DLB 95
Finch, Robert (Duer Claydon)
1900-1995 .... **CLC 18**
See also CA 57-60; CANR 9, 24, 49; CP 7;
DLB 88
Findley, Timothy (Irving Frederick)
1930-2002 .... **CLC 27, 102**
See also CA 25-28R; 206; CANR 12, 42,
69, 109; CCA 1; CN 7; DAC; DAM MST;
DLB 53; FANT; RHW
Fink, William
See Mencken, H(enry) L(ouis)
Firbank, Louis 1942-
See Reed, Lou
See also CA 117
Firbank, (Arthur Annesley) Ronald
1886-1926 .... **TCLC 1**
See also BRWS 2; CA 104; 177; DLB 36;
EWL 3; RGEL 2
Fish, Stanley
See Fish, Stanley Eugene
Fish, Stanley E.
See Fish, Stanley Eugene
Fish, Stanley Eugene 1938- .... **CLC 142**
See also CA 112; 132; CANR 90; DLB 67
Fisher, Dorothy (Frances) Canfield
1879-1958 .... **TCLC 87**
See also CA 114; 136; CANR 80; CLR 71,;
CWRI 5; DLB 9, 102, 284; MAICYA 1,
2; YABC 1
Fisher, M(ary) F(rances) K(ennedy)
1908-1992 .... **CLC 76, 87**
See also CA 77-80; 138; CANR 44; MTCW
1
Fisher, Roy 1930- .... **CLC 25**
See also CA 81-84; CAAS 10; CANR 16;
CP 7; DLB 40
Fisher, Rudolph 1897-1934 .... **BLC 2; HR 2;**
SSC 25; TCLC 11
See also BW 1, 3; CA 107; 124; CANR 80;
DAM MULT; DLB 51, 102
Fisher, Vardis (Alvero) 1895-1968 .... **CLC 7;**
TCLC 140
See also CA 5-8R; 25-28R; CANR 68; DLB
9, 206; RGAL 4; TCWW 2
Fiske, Tarleton
See Bloch, Robert (Albert)
Fitch, Clarke
See Sinclair, Upton (Beall)
Fitch, John IV
See Cormier, Robert (Edmund)
Fitzgerald, Captain Hugh
See Baum, L(yman) Frank
FitzGerald, Edward 1809-1883 ...... **NCLC 9,**
153
See also BRW 4; DLB 32; RGEL 2
Fitzgerald, F(rancis) Scott (Key)
1896-1940 ... **SSC 6, 31, 75; TCLC 1, 6,**
14, 28, 55, 157; WLC
See also AAYA 24; AITN 1; AMW; AMWC
2; AMWR 1; BPFB 1; CA 110; 123;
CDALB 1917-1929; DA; DA3; DAB;
DAC; DAM MST, NOV; DLB 4, 9, 86,
219, 273; DLBD 1, 15, 16; DLBY 1981,
1996; EWL 3; EXPN; EXPS; LAIT 3;
MTCW 1, 2; NFS 2, 19, 20; RGAL 4;
RGSF 2; SSFS 4, 15; TUS

Garro, Elena 1920(?)-1998 .. **HLCS 1; TCLC 153**
See also CA 131; 169; CWW 2; DLB 145; EWL 3; HW 1; LAWS 1; WLIT 1
Garth, Will
See Hamilton, Edmond; Kuttner, Henry
Garvey, Marcus (Moziah, Jr.)
1887-1940 .... **BLC 2; HR 2; TCLC 41**
See also BW 1; CA 120; 124; CANR 79; DAM MULT
Gary, Romain .... **CLC 25**
See Kacew, Romain
See also DLB 83, 299
Gascar, Pierre .... **CLC 11**
See Fournier, Pierre
See also EWL 3
Gascoigne, George 1539-1577 .... **LC 108**
See also DLB 136; RGEL 2
Gascoyne, David (Emery)
1916-2001 .... **CLC 45**
See also CA 65-68; 200; CANR 10, 28, 54; CP 7; DLB 20; MTCW 1; RGEL 2
Gaskell, Elizabeth Cleghorn
1810-1865 .... **NCLC 5, 70, 97, 137; SSC 25**
See also BRW 5; CDBLB 1832-1890; DAB; DAM MST; DLB 21, 144, 159; RGEL 2; RGSF 2; TEA
Gass, William H(oward) 1924- . **CLC 1, 2, 8, 11, 15, 39, 132; SSC 12**
See also AMWS 6; CA 17-20R; CANR 30, 71, 100; CN 7; DLB 2, 227; EWL 3; MTCW 1, 2; RGAL 4
Gassendi, Pierre 1592-1655 .... **LC 54**
See also GFL Beginnings to 1789
Gasset, Jose Ortega y
See Ortega y Gasset, Jose
Gates, Henry Louis, Jr. 1950- ... **BLCS; CLC 65**
See also BW 2, 3; CA 109; CANR 25, 53, 75, 125; CSW; DA3; DAM MULT; DLB 67; EWL 3; MTCW 1; RGAL 4
Gautier, Theophile 1811-1872 .. **NCLC 1, 59; PC 18; SSC 20**
See also DAM POET; DLB 119; EW 6; GFL 1789 to the Present; RGWL 2, 3; SUFW; TWA
Gawsworth, John
See Bates, H(erbert) E(rnest)
Gay, John 1685-1732 .... **LC 49**
See also BRW 3; DAM DRAM; DLB 84, 95; RGEL 2; WLIT 3
Gay, Oliver
See Gogarty, Oliver St. John
Gay, Peter (Jack) 1923- .... **CLC 158**
See also CA 13-16R; CANR 18, 41, 77; INT CANR-18
Gaye, Marvin (Pentz, Jr.)
1939-1984 .... **CLC 26**
See also CA 195; 112
Gebler, Carlo (Ernest) 1954- .... **CLC 39**
See also CA 119; 133; CANR 96; DLB 271
Gee, Maggie (Mary) 1948- .... **CLC 57**
See also CA 130; CANR 125; CN 7; DLB 207
Gee, Maurice (Gough) 1931- .... **CLC 29**
See also AAYA 42; CA 97-100; CANR 67, 123; CLR 56; CN 7; CWRI 5; EWL 3; MAICYA 2; RGSF 2; SATA 46, 101
Geiogamah, Hanay 1945- .... **NNAL**
See also CA 153; DAM MULT; DLB 175
Gelbart, Larry (Simon) 1928- .... **CLC 21, 61**
See Gelbart, Larry
See also CA 73-76; CANR 45, 94
Gelbart, Larry 1928-
See Gelbart, Larry (Simon)
See also CAD; CD 5

Gelber, Jack 1932-2003 ...... **CLC 1, 6, 14, 79**
See also CA 1-4R; 216; CAD; CANR 2; DLB 7, 228
Gellhorn, Martha (Ellis)
1908-1998 .... **CLC 14, 60**
See also CA 77-80; 164; CANR 44; CN 7; DLBY 1982, 1998
Genet, Jean 1910-1986 . **DC 25; CLC 1, 2, 5, 10, 14, 44, 46; TCLC 128**
See also CA 13-16R; CANR 18; DA3; DAM DRAM; DFS 10; DLB 72; DLBY 1986; EW 13; EWL 3; GFL 1789 to the Present; GLL 1; LMFS 2; MTCW 1, 2; RGWL 2, 3; TWA
Gent, Peter 1942- .... **CLC 29**
See also AITN 1; CA 89-92; DLBY 1982
Gentile, Giovanni 1875-1944 .... **TCLC 96**
See also CA 119
Gentlewoman in New England, A
See Bradstreet, Anne
Gentlewoman in Those Parts, A
See Bradstreet, Anne
Geoffrey of Monmouth c.
1100-1155 .... **CMLC 44**
See also DLB 146; TEA
George, Jean
See George, Jean Craighead
George, Jean Craighead 1919- .... **CLC 35**
See also AAYA 8; BYA 2, 4; CA 5-8R; CANR 25; CLR 1; 80; DLB 52; JRDA; MAICYA 1, 2; SATA 2, 68, 124; WYA; YAW
George, Stefan (Anton) 1868-1933 . **TCLC 2, 14**
See also CA 104; 193; EW 8; EWL 3
Georges, Georges Martin
See Simenon, Georges (Jacques Christian)
Gerald of Wales c. 1146-c. 1223 ... **CMLC 60**
Gerhardi, William Alexander
See Gerhardie, William Alexander
Gerhardie, William Alexander
1895-1977 .... **CLC 5**
See also CA 25-28R; 73-76; CANR 18; DLB 36; RGEL 2
Gerson, Jean 1363-1429 .... **LC 77**
See also DLB 208
Gersonides 1288-1344 .... **CMLC 49**
See also DLB 115
Gerstler, Amy 1956- .... **CLC 70**
See also CA 146; CANR 99
Gertler, T. .... **CLC 34**
See also CA 116; 121
Gertsen, Aleksandr Ivanovich
See Herzen, Aleksandr Ivanovich
Ghalib .... **NCLC 39, 78**
See Ghalib, Asadullah Khan
Ghalib, Asadullah Khan 1797-1869
See Ghalib
See also DAM POET; RGWL 2, 3
Ghelderode, Michel de 1898-1962 ..... **CLC 6, 11; DC 15**
See also CA 85-88; CANR 40, 77; DAM DRAM; EW 11; EWL 3; TWA
Ghiselin, Brewster 1903-2001 .... **CLC 23**
See also CA 13-16R; CAAS 10; CANR 13; CP 7
Ghose, Aurabinda 1872-1950 .... **TCLC 63**
See Ghose, Aurobindo
See also CA 163
Ghose, Aurobindo
See Ghose, Aurabinda
See also EWL 3
Ghose, Zulfikar 1935- .... **CLC 42, 200**
See also CA 65-68; CANR 67; CN 7; CP 7; EWL 3
Ghosh, Amitav 1956- .... **CLC 44, 153**
See also CA 147; CANR 80; CN 7; WWE 1

Giacosa, Giuseppe 1847-1906 .... **TCLC 7**
See also CA 104
Gibb, Lee
See Waterhouse, Keith (Spencer)
Gibbon, Edward 1737-1794 .... **LC 97**
See also BRW 3; DLB 104; RGEL 2
Gibbon, Lewis Grassic .... **TCLC 4**
See Mitchell, James Leslie
See also RGEL 2
Gibbons, Kaye 1960- .... **CLC 50, 88, 145**
See also AAYA 34; AMWS 10; CA 151; CANR 75, 127; CSW; DA3; DAM POP; DLB 292; MTCW 1; NFS 3; RGAL 4; SATA 117
Gibran, Kahlil 1883-1931 . **PC 9; TCLC 1, 9**
See also CA 104; 150; DA3; DAM POET, POP; EWL 3; MTCW 2
Gibran, Khalil
See Gibran, Kahlil
Gibson, William 1914- .... **CLC 23**
See also CA 9-12R; CAD 2; CANR 9, 42, 75, 125; CD 5; DA; DAB; DAC; DAM DRAM, MST; DFS 2; DLB 7; LAIT 2; MTCW 2; SATA 66; YAW
Gibson, William (Ford) 1948- ... **CLC 39, 63, 186, 192; SSC 52**
See also AAYA 12, 59; BPFB 2; CA 126; 133; CANR 52, 90, 106; CN 7; CPW; DA3; DAM POP; DLB 251; MTCW 2; SCFW 2; SFW 4
Gide, Andre (Paul Guillaume)
1869-1951 ..... **SSC 13; TCLC 5, 12, 36; WLC**
See also CA 104; 124; DA; DA3; DAB; DAC; DAM MST, NOV; DLB 65; EW 8; EWL 3; GFL 1789 to the Present; MTCW 1, 2; RGSF 2; RGWL 2, 3; TWA
Gifford, Barry (Colby) 1946- .... **CLC 34**
See also CA 65-68; CANR 9, 30, 40, 90
Gilbert, Frank
See De Voto, Bernard (Augustine)
Gilbert, W(illiam) S(chwenck)
1836-1911 .... **TCLC 3**
See also CA 104; 173; DAM DRAM, POET; RGEL 2; SATA 36
Gilbreth, Frank B(unker), Jr.
1911-2001 .... **CLC 17**
See also CA 9-12R; SATA 2
Gilchrist, Ellen (Louise) 1935- .. **CLC 34, 48, 143; SSC 14, 63**
See also BPFB 2; CA 113; 116; CANR 41, 61, 104; CN 7; CPW; CSW; DAM POP; DLB 130; EWL 3; EXPS; MTCW 1, 2; RGAL 4; RGSF 2; SSFS 9
Giles, Molly 1942- .... **CLC 39**
See also CA 126; CANR 98
Gill, Eric 1882-1940 .... **TCLC 85**
See Gill, (Arthur) Eric (Rowton Peter Joseph)
Gill, (Arthur) Eric (Rowton Peter Joseph)
1882-1940
See Gill, Eric
See also CA 120; DLB 98
Gill, Patrick
See Creasey, John
Gillette, Douglas .... **CLC 70**
Gilliam, Terry (Vance) 1940- .... **CLC 21, 141**
See Monty Python
See also AAYA 19, 59; CA 108; 113; CANR 35; INT CA-113
Gillian, Jerry
See Gilliam, Terry (Vance)
Gilliatt, Penelope (Ann Douglass)
1932-1993 .... **CLC 2, 10, 13, 53**
See also AITN 2; CA 13-16R; 141; CANR 49; DLB 14
Gilligan, Carol 1936- .... **CLC 208**
See also CA 142; CANR 121; FW

Gomez de Avellaneda, Gertrudis
1814-1873 .... **NCLC 111**
See also LAW

Gomez de la Serna, Ramon
1888-1963 .... **CLC 9**
See also CA 153; 116; CANR 79; EWL 3;
HW 1, 2

Goncharov, Ivan Alexandrovich
1812-1891 .... **NCLC 1, 63**
See also DLB 238; EW 6; RGWL 2, 3

Goncourt, Edmond (Louis Antoine Huot) de
1822-1896 .... **NCLC 7**
See also DLB 123; EW 7; GFL 1789 to the
Present; RGWL 2, 3

Goncourt, Jules (Alfred Huot) de
1830-1870 .... **NCLC 7**
See also DLB 123; EW 7; GFL 1789 to the
Present; RGWL 2, 3

Gongora (y Argote), Luis de
1561-1627 .... **LC 72**
See also RGWL 2, 3

Gontier, Fernande 19(?)- .... **CLC 50**

Gonzalez Martinez, Enrique
See Gonzalez Martinez, Enrique
See also DLB 290

Gonzalez Martinez, Enrique
1871-1952 .... **TCLC 72**
See Gonzalez Martinez, Enrique
See also CA 166; CANR 81; EWL 3; HW
1, 2

Goodison, Lorna 1947- .... **PC 36**
See also CA 142; CANR 88; CP 7; CWP;
DLB 157; EWL 3

Goodman, Paul 1911-1972 ..... **CLC 1, 2, 4, 7**
See also CA 19-20; 37-40R; CAD; CANR
34; CAP 2; DLB 130, 246; MTCW 1;
RGAL 4

GoodWeather, Harley
See King, Thomas

Googe, Barnabe 1540-1594 .... **LC 94**
See also DLB 132; RGEL 2

Gordimer, Nadine 1923- ...... **CLC 3, 5, 7, 10,
18, 33, 51, 70, 123, 160, 161; SSC 17,
80; WLCS**
See also AAYA 39; AFW; BRWS 2; CA
5-8R; CANR 3, 28, 56, 88, 131; CN 7;
DA; DA3; DAB; DAC; DAM MST, NOV;
DLB 225; EWL 3; EXPS; INT CANR-28;
LATS 1:2; MTCW 1, 2; NFS 4; RGEL 2;
RGSF 2; SSFS 2, 14, 19; TWA; WLIT 2;
YAW

Gordon, Adam Lindsay
1833-1870 .... **NCLC 21**
See also DLB 230

Gordon, Caroline 1895-1981 . **CLC 6, 13, 29,
83; SSC 15**
See also AMW; CA 11-12; 103; CANR 36;
CAP 1; DLB 4, 9, 102; DLBD 17; DLBY
1981; EWL 3; MTCW 1, 2; RGAL 4;
RGSF 2

Gordon, Charles William 1860-1937
See Connor, Ralph
See also CA 109

Gordon, Mary (Catherine) 1949- .... **CLC 13,
22, 128; SSC 59**
See also AMWS 4; BPFB 2; CA 102;
CANR 44, 92; CN 7; DLB 6; DLBY
1981; FW; INT CA-102; MTCW 1

Gordon, N. J.
See Bosman, Herman Charles

Gordon, Sol 1923- .... **CLC 26**
See also CA 53-56; CANR 4; SATA 11

Gordone, Charles 1925-1995 .. **CLC 1, 4; DC
8**
See also BW 1, 3; CA 93-96, 180; 150;
CAAE 180; CAD; CANR 55; DAM
DRAM; DLB 7; INT CA-93-96; MTCW
1

Gore, Catherine 1800-1861 .... **NCLC 65**
See also DLB 116; RGEL 2

Gorenko, Anna Andreevna
See Akhmatova, Anna

Gorky, Maxim .... **SSC 28; TCLC 8; WLC**
See Peshkov, Alexei Maximovich
See also DAB; DFS 9; DLB 295; EW 8;
EWL 3; MTCW 2; TWA

Goryan, Sirak
See Saroyan, William

Gosse, Edmund (William)
1849-1928 .... **TCLC 28**
See also CA 117; DLB 57, 144, 184; RGEL
2

Gotlieb, Phyllis (Fay Bloom) 1926- .. **CLC 18**
See also CA 13-16R; CANR 7, 135; DLB
88, 251; SFW 4

Gottesman, S. D.
See Kornbluth, C(yril) M.; Pohl, Frederik

Gottfried von Strassburg fl. c.
1170-1215 .... **CMLC 10**
See also CDWLB 2; DLB 138; EW 1;
RGWL 2, 3

Gotthelf, Jeremias 1797-1854 .... **NCLC 117**
See also DLB 133; RGWL 2, 3

Gottschalk, Laura Riding
See Jackson, Laura (Riding)

Gould, Lois 1932(?)-2002 .... **CLC 4, 10**
See also CA 77-80; 208; CANR 29; MTCW
1

Gould, Stephen Jay 1941-2002 .... **CLC 163**
See also AAYA 26; BEST 90:2; CA 77-80;
205; CANR 10, 27, 56, 75, 125; CPW;
INT CANR-27; MTCW 1, 2

Gourmont, Remy(-Marie-Charles) de
1858-1915 .... **TCLC 17**
See also CA 109; 150; GFL 1789 to the
Present; MTCW 2

Gournay, Marie le Jars de
See de Gournay, Marie le Jars

Govier, Katherine 1948- .... **CLC 51**
See also CA 101; CANR 18, 40, 128; CCA
1

Gower, John c. 1330-1408 .... **LC 76; PC 59**
See also BRW 1; DLB 146; RGEL 2

Goyen, (Charles) William
1915-1983 .... **CLC 5, 8, 14, 40**
See also AITN 2; CA 5-8R; 110; CANR 6,
71; DLB 2, 218; DLBY 1983; EWL 3;
INT CANR-6

Goytisolo, Juan 1931- .... **CLC 5, 10, 23, 133;
HLC 1**
See also CA 85-88; CANR 32, 61, 131;
CWW 2; DAM MULT; EWL 3; GLL 2;
HW 1, 2; MTCW 1, 2

Gozzano, Guido 1883-1916 .... **PC 10**
See also CA 154; DLB 114; EWL 3

Gozzi, (Conte) Carlo 1720-1806 .... **NCLC 23**

Grabbe, Christian Dietrich
1801-1836 .... **NCLC 2**
See also DLB 133; RGWL 2, 3

Grace, Patricia Frances 1937- .... **CLC 56**
See also CA 176; CANR 118; CN 7; EWL
3; RGSF 2

Gracian y Morales, Baltasar
1601-1658 .... **LC 15**

Gracq, Julien .... **CLC 11, 48**
See Poirier, Louis
See also CWW 2; DLB 83; GFL 1789 to
the Present

Grade, Chaim 1910-1982 .... **CLC 10**
See also CA 93-96; 107; EWL 3

Graduate of Oxford, A
See Ruskin, John

Grafton, Garth
See Duncan, Sara Jeannette

Grafton, Sue 1940- .... **CLC 163**
See also AAYA 11, 49; BEST 90:3; CA 108;
CANR 31, 55, 111, 134; CMW 4; CPW;
CSW; DA3; DAM POP; DLB 226; FW;
MSW

Graham, John
See Phillips, David Graham

Graham, Jorie 1951- .... **CLC 48, 118; PC 59**
See also CA 111; CANR 63, 118; CP 7;
CWP; DLB 120; EWL 3; PFS 10, 17

Graham, R(obert) B(ontine) Cunninghame
See Cunninghame Graham, Robert
(Gallnigad) Bontine
See also DLB 98, 135, 174; RGEL 2; RGSF
2

Graham, Robert
See Haldeman, Joe (William)

Graham, Tom
See Lewis, (Harry) Sinclair

Graham, W(illiam) S(idney)
1918-1986 .... **CLC 29**
See also BRWS 7; CA 73-76; 118; DLB 20;
RGEL 2

Graham, Winston (Mawdsley)
1910-2003 .... **CLC 23**
See also CA 49-52; 218; CANR 2, 22, 45,
66; CMW 4; CN 7; DLB 77; RHW

Grahame, Kenneth 1859-1932 ...... **TCLC 64,
136**
See also BYA 5; CA 108; 136; CANR 80;
CLR 5; CWRI 5; DA3; DAB; DLB 34,
141, 178; FANT; MAICYA 1, 2; MTCW
2; NFS 20; RGEL 2; SATA 100; TEA;
WCH; YABC 1

Granger, Darius John
See Marlowe, Stephen

Granin, Daniil 1918- .... **CLC 59**
See also DLB 302

Granovsky, Timofei Nikolaevich
1813-1855 .... **NCLC 75**
See also DLB 198

Grant, Skeeter
See Spiegelman, Art

Granville-Barker, Harley
1877-1946 .... **TCLC 2**
See Barker, Harley Granville
See also CA 104; 204; DAM DRAM;
RGEL 2

Granzotto, Gianni
See Granzotto, Giovanni Battista

Granzotto, Giovanni Battista
1914-1985 .... **CLC 70**
See also CA 166

Grass, Günter (Wilhelm) 1927- .... **CLC 1, 2,
4, 6, 11, 15, 22, 32, 49, 88, 207; WLC**
See Grass, Guenter (Wilhelm)
See also BPFB 2; CA 13-16R; CANR 20,
75, 93, 133; CDWLB 2; CWW 2; DA;
DA3; DAB; DAC; DAM MST, NOV;
DLB 75, 124; EW 13; EWL 3; MTCW 1,
2; RGWL 2, 3; TWA

Gratton, Thomas
See Hulme, T(homas) E(rnest)

Grau, Shirley Ann 1929- .... **CLC 4, 9, 146;
SSC 15**
See also CA 89-92; CANR 22, 69; CN 7;
CSW; DLB 2, 218; INT CA-89-92,
CANR-22; MTCW 1

Gravel, Fern
See Hall, James Norman

Graver, Elizabeth 1964- .... **CLC 70**
See also CA 135; CANR 71, 129

Graves, Richard Perceval
1895-1985 .... **CLC 44**
See also CA 65-68; CANR 9, 26, 51

Graves, Robert (von Ranke)
1895-1985 .. **CLC 1, 2, 6, 11, 39, 44, 45;**
PC 6
See also BPFB 2; BRW 7; BYA 4; CA 5-8R;
117; CANR 5, 36; CDBLB 1914-1945;
DA3; DAB; DAC; DAM MST, POET;
DLB 20, 100, 191; DLBD 18; DLBY
1985; EWL 3; LATS 1:1; MTCW 1, 2;
NCFS 2; RGEL 2; RHW; SATA 45; TEA
Graves, Valerie
See Bradley, Marion Zimmer
Gray, Alasdair (James) 1934- .... **CLC 41**
See also BRWS 9; CA 126; CANR 47, 69,
106; CN 7; DLB 194, 261; HGG; INT
CA-126; MTCW 1, 2; RGSF 2; SUFW 2
Gray, Amlin 1946- .... **CLC 29**
See also CA 138
Gray, Francine du Plessix 1930- ..... **CLC 22,**
153
See also BEST 90:3; CA 61-64; CAAS 2;
CANR 11, 33, 75, 81; DAM NOV; INT
CANR-11; MTCW 1, 2
Gray, John (Henry) 1866-1934 ...... **TCLC 19**
See also CA 119; 162; RGEL 2
Gray, Simon (James Holliday)
1936- .... **CLC 9, 14, 36**
See also AITN 1; CA 21-24R; CAAS 3;
CANR 32, 69; CD 5; DLB 13; EWL 3;
MTCW 1; RGEL 2
Gray, Spalding 1941-2004 .... **CLC 49, 112;**
DC 7
See also CA 128; 225; CAD; CANR 74;
CD 5; CPW; DAM POP; MTCW 2
Gray, Thomas 1716-1771 .... **LC 4, 40; PC 2;**
WLC
See also BRW 3; CDBLB 1660-1789; DA;
DA3; DAB; DAC; DAM MST; DLB 109;
EXPP; PAB; PFS 9; RGEL 2; TEA; WP
Grayson, David
See Baker, Ray Stannard
Grayson, Richard (A.) 1951- .... **CLC 38**
See also CA 85-88, 210; CAAE 210; CANR
14, 31, 57; DLB 234
Greeley, Andrew M(oran) 1928- ...... **CLC 28**
See also BPFB 2; CA 5-8R; CAAS 7;
CANR 7, 43, 69, 104; CMW 4; CPW;
DA3; DAM POP; MTCW 1, 2
Green, Anna Katharine
1846-1935 .... **TCLC 63**
See also CA 112; 159; CMW 4; DLB 202,
221; MSW
Green, Brian
See Card, Orson Scott
Green, Hannah
See Greenberg, Joanne (Goldenberg)
Green, Hannah 1927(?)-1996 .... **CLC 3**
See also CA 73-76; CANR 59, 93; NFS 10
Green, Henry .... **CLC 2, 13, 97**
See Yorke, Henry Vincent
See also BRWS 2; CA 175; DLB 15; EWL
3; RGEL 2
Green, Julien (Hartridge) 1900-1998
See Green, Julian
See also CA 21-24R; 169; CANR 33, 87;
CWW 2; DLB 4, 72; MTCW 1
Green, Julian .... **CLC 3, 11, 77**
See Green, Julien (Hartridge)
See also EWL 3; GFL 1789 to the Present;
MTCW 2
Green, Paul (Eliot) 1894-1981 .... **CLC 25**
See also AITN 1; CA 5-8R; 103; CANR 3;
DAM DRAM; DLB 7, 9, 249; DLBY
1981; RGAL 4
Greenaway, Peter 1942- .... **CLC 159**
See also CA 127
Greenberg, Ivan 1908-1973
See Rahv, Philip
See also CA 85-88

Greenberg, Joanne (Goldenberg)
1932- .... **CLC 7, 30**
See also AAYA 12; CA 5-8R; CANR 14,
32, 69; CN 7; SATA 25; YAW
Greenberg, Richard 1959(?)- .... **CLC 57**
See also CA 138; CAD; CD 5
Greenblatt, Stephen J(ay) 1943- ...... **CLC 70**
See also CA 49-52; CANR 115
Greene, Bette 1934- .... **CLC 30**
See also AAYA 7; BYA 3; CA 53-56; CANR
4; CLR 2; CWRI 5; JRDA; LAIT 4; MAI-
CYA 1, 2; NFS 10; SAAS 16; SATA 8,
102; WYA; YAW
Greene, Gael .... **CLC 8**
See also CA 13-16R; CANR 10
Greene, Graham (Henry)
1904-1991 .... **CLC 1, 3, 6, 9, 14, 18, 27,**
37, 70, 72, 125; SSC 29; WLC
See also AITN 2; BPFB 2; BRWR 2; BRWS
1; BYA 3; CA 13-16R; 133; CANR 35,
61, 131; CBD; CDBLB 1945-1960; CMW
4; DA; DA3; DAB; DAC; DAM MST,
NOV; DLB 13, 15, 77, 100, 162, 201,
204; DLBY 1991; EWL 3; MSW; MTCW
1, 2; NFS 16; RGEL 2; SATA 20; SSFS
14; TEA; WLIT 4
Greene, Robert 1558-1592 .... **LC 41**
See also BRWS 8; DLB 62, 167; IDTP;
RGEL 2; TEA
Greer, Germaine 1939- .... **CLC 131**
See also AITN 1; CA 81-84; CANR 33, 70,
115, 133; FW; MTCW 1, 2
Greer, Richard
See Silverberg, Robert
Gregor, Arthur 1923- .... **CLC 9**
See also CA 25-28R; CAAS 10; CANR 11;
CP 7; SATA 36
Gregor, Lee
See Pohl, Frederik
Gregory, Lady Isabella Augusta (Persse)
1852-1932 .... **TCLC 1**
See also BRW 6; CA 104; 184; DLB 10;
IDTP; RGEL 2
Gregory, J. Dennis
See Williams, John A(lfred)
Grekova, I. .... **CLC 59**
See Ventsel, Elena Sergeevna
See also CWW 2
Grendon, Stephen
See Derleth, August (William)
Grenville, Kate 1950- .... **CLC 61**
See also CA 118; CANR 53, 93
Grenville, Pelham
See Wodehouse, P(elham) G(renville)
Greve, Felix Paul (Berthold Friedrich)
1879-1948
See Grove, Frederick Philip
See also CA 104; 141, 175; CANR 79;
DAC; DAM MST
Greville, Fulke 1554-1628 .... **LC 79**
See also DLB 62, 172; RGEL 2
Grey, Lady Jane 1537-1554 .... **LC 93**
See also DLB 132
Grey, Zane 1872-1939 .... **TCLC 6**
See also BPFB 2; CA 104; 132; DA3; DAM
POP; DLB 9, 212; MTCW 1, 2; RGAL 4;
TCWW 2; TUS
Griboedov, Aleksandr Sergeevich
1795(?)-1829 .... **NCLC 129**
See also DLB 205; RGWL 2, 3
Grieg, (Johan) Nordahl (Brun)
1902-1943 .... **TCLC 10**
See also CA 107; 189; EWL 3
Grieve, C(hristopher) M(urray)
1892-1978 .... **CLC 11, 19**
See MacDiarmid, Hugh; Pteleon
See also CA 5-8R; 85-88; CANR 33, 107;
DAM POET; MTCW 1; RGEL 2

Griffin, Gerald 1803-1840 .... **NCLC 7**
See also DLB 159; RGEL 2
Griffin, John Howard 1920-1980 ..... **CLC 68**
See also AITN 1; CA 1-4R; 101; CANR 2
Griffin, Peter 1942- .... **CLC 39**
See also CA 136
Griffith, D(avid Lewelyn) W(ark)
1875(?)-1948 .... **TCLC 68**
See also CA 119; 150; CANR 80
Griffith, Lawrence
See Griffith, D(avid Lewelyn) W(ark)
Griffiths, Trevor 1935- .... **CLC 13, 52**
See also CA 97-100; CANR 45; CBD; CD
5; DLB 13, 245
Griggs, Sutton (Elbert)
1872-1930 .... **TCLC 77**
See also CA 123; 186; DLB 50
Grigson, Geoffrey (Edward Harvey)
1905-1985 .... **CLC 7, 39**
See also CA 25-28R; 118; CANR 20, 33;
DLB 27; MTCW 1, 2
Grile, Dod
See Bierce, Ambrose (Gwinett)
Grillparzer, Franz 1791-1872 .... **DC 14;**
NCLC 1, 102; SSC 37
See also CDWLB 2; DLB 133; EW 5;
RGWL 2, 3; TWA
Grimble, Reverend Charles James
See Eliot, T(homas) S(tearns)
Grimke, Angelina (Emily) Weld
1880-1958 .... **HR 2**
See Weld, Angelina (Emily) Grimke
See also BW 1; CA 124; DAM POET; DLB
50, 54
Grimke, Charlotte L(ottie) Forten
1837(?)-1914
See Forten, Charlotte L.
See also BW 1; CA 117; 124; DAM MULT,
POET
Grimm, Jacob Ludwig Karl
1785-1863 .... **NCLC 3, 77; SSC 36**
See also DLB 90; MAICYA 1, 2; RGSF 2;
RGWL 2, 3; SATA 22; WCH
Grimm, Wilhelm Karl 1786-1859 .. **NCLC 3,**
77; SSC 36
See also CDWLB 2; DLB 90; MAICYA 1,
2; RGSF 2; RGWL 2, 3; SATA 22; WCH
Grimmelshausen, Hans Jakob Christoffel
von
See Grimmelshausen, Johann Jakob Christ-
offel von
See also RGWL 2, 3
Grimmelshausen, Johann Jakob Christoffel
von 1621-1676 .... **LC 6**
See Grimmelshausen, Hans Jakob Christof-
fel von
See also CDWLB 2; DLB 168
Grindel, Eugene 1895-1952
See Eluard, Paul
See also CA 104; 193; LMFS 2
Grisham, John 1955- .... **CLC 84**
See also AAYA 14, 47; BPFB 2; CA 138;
CANR 47, 69, 114, 133; CMW 4; CN 7;
CPW; CSW; DA3; DAM POP; MSW;
MTCW 2
Grosseteste, Robert 1175(?)-1253 . **CMLC 62**
See also DLB 115
Grossman, David 1954- .... **CLC 67**
See also CA 138; CANR 114; CWW 2;
DLB 299; EWL 3
Grossman, Vasilii Semenovich
See Grossman, Vasily (Semenovich)
See also DLB 272
Grossman, Vasily (Semenovich)
1905-1964 .... **CLC 41**
See Grossman, Vasilii Semenovich
See also CA 124; 130; MTCW 1

Harris, George Washington
1814-1869 .... **NCLC 23**
See also DLB 3, 11, 248; RGAL 4
Harris, Joel Chandler 1848-1908 ..... **SSC 19;
TCLC 2**
See also CA 104; 137; CANR 80; CLR 49;
DLB 11, 23, 42, 78, 91; LAIT 2; MAI-
CYA 1, 2; RGSF 2; SATA 100; WCH;
YABC 1
**Harris, John (Wyndham Parkes Lucas)
Beynon** 1903-1969
See Wyndham, John
See also CA 102; 89-92; CANR 84; SATA
118; SFW 4
Harris, MacDonald .... **CLC 9**
See Heiney, Donald (William)
Harris, Mark 1922- .... **CLC 19**
See also CA 5-8R; CAAS 3; CANR 2, 55,
83; CN 7; DLB 2; DLBY 1980
Harris, Norman .... **CLC 65**
Harris, (Theodore) Wilson 1921- .... **CLC 25,
159**
See also BRWS 5; BW 2, 3; CA 65-68;
CAAS 16; CANR 11, 27, 69, 114; CD-
WLB 3; CN 7; CP 7; DLB 117; EWL 3;
MTCW 1; RGEL 2
Harrison, Barbara Grizzuti
1934-2002 .... **CLC 144**
See also CA 77-80; 205; CANR 15, 48; INT
CANR-15
Harrison, Elizabeth (Allen) Cavanna
1909-2001
See Cavanna, Betty
See also CA 9-12R; 200; CANR 6, 27, 85,
104, 121; MAICYA 2; SATA 142; YAW
Harrison, Harry (Max) 1925- .... **CLC 42**
See also CA 1-4R; CANR 5, 21, 84; DLB
8; SATA 4; SCFW 2; SFW 4
Harrison, James (Thomas) 1937- ...... **CLC 6,
14, 33, 66, 143; SSC 19**
See Harrison, Jim
See also CA 13-16R; CANR 8, 51, 79; CN
7; CP 7; DLBY 1982; INT CANR-8
Harrison, Jim
See Harrison, James (Thomas)
See also AMWS 8; RGAL 4; TCWW 2;
TUS
Harrison, Kathryn 1961- .... **CLC 70, 151**
See also CA 144; CANR 68, 122
Harrison, Tony 1937- .... **CLC 43, 129**
See also BRWS 5; CA 65-68; CANR 44,
98; CBD; CD 5; CP 7; DLB 40, 245;
MTCW 1; RGEL 2
Harriss, Will(ard Irvin) 1922- .... **CLC 34**
See also CA 111
Hart, Ellis
See Ellison, Harlan (Jay)
Hart, Josephine 1942(?)- .... **CLC 70**
See also CA 138; CANR 70; CPW; DAM
POP
Hart, Moss 1904-1961 .... **CLC 66**
See also CA 109; 89-92; CANR 84; DAM
DRAM; DFS 1; DLB 7, 266; RGAL 4
Harte, (Francis) Bret(t)
1836(?)-1902 ... **SSC 8, 59; TCLC 1, 25;
WLC**
See also AMWS 2; CA 104; 140; CANR
80; CDALB 1865-1917; DA; DA3; DAC;
DAM MST; DLB 12, 64, 74, 79, 186;
EXPS; LAIT 2; RGAL 4; RGSF 2; SATA
26; SSFS 3; TUS
Hartley, L(eslie) P(oles) 1895-1972 ... **CLC 2,
22**
See also BRWS 7; CA 45-48; 37-40R;
CANR 33; DLB 15, 139; EWL 3; HGG;
MTCW 1, 2; RGEL 2; RGSF 2; SUFW 1
Hartman, Geoffrey H. 1929- .... **CLC 27**
See also CA 117; 125; CANR 79; DLB 67

Hartmann, Sadakichi 1869-1944 ... **TCLC 73**
See also CA 157; DLB 54
Hartmann von Aue c. 1170-c.
1210 .... **CMLC 15**
See also CDWLB 2; DLB 138; RGWL 2, 3
Hartog, Jan de
See de Hartog, Jan
Haruf, Kent 1943- .... **CLC 34**
See also AAYA 44; CA 149; CANR 91, 131
Harvey, Caroline
See Trollope, Joanna
Harvey, Gabriel 1550(?)-1631 .... **LC 88**
See also DLB 167, 213, 281
Harwood, Ronald 1934- .... **CLC 32**
See also CA 1-4R; CANR 4, 55; CBD; CD
5; DAM DRAM, MST; DLB 13
Hasegawa Tatsunosuke
See Futabatei, Shimei
Hasek, Jaroslav (Matej Frantisek)
1883-1923 .... **SSC 69; TCLC 4**
See also CA 104; 129; CDWLB 4; DLB
215; EW 9; EWL 3; MTCW 1, 2; RGSF
2; RGWL 2, 3
Hass, Robert 1941- ... **CLC 18, 39, 99; PC 16**
See also AMWS 6; CA 111; CANR 30, 50,
71; CP 7; DLB 105, 206; EWL 3; RGAL
4; SATA 94
Hastings, Hudson
See Kuttner, Henry
Hastings, Selina .... **CLC 44**
Hathorne, John 1641-1717 .... **LC 38**
Hatteras, Amelia
See Mencken, H(enry) L(ouis)
Hatteras, Owen .... **TCLC 18**
See Mencken, H(enry) L(ouis); Nathan,
George Jean
Hauptmann, Gerhart (Johann Robert)
1862-1946 .... **SSC 37; TCLC 4**
See also CA 104; 153; CDWLB 2; DAM
DRAM; DLB 66, 118; EW 8; EWL 3;
RGSF 2; RGWL 2, 3; TWA
Havel, Vaclav 1936- ..... **CLC 25, 58, 65, 123;
DC 6**
See also CA 104; CANR 36, 63, 124; CD-
WLB 4; CWW 2; DA3; DAM DRAM;
DFS 10; DLB 232; EWL 3; LMFS 2;
MTCW 1, 2; RGWL 3
Haviaras, Stratis .... **CLC 33**
See Chaviaras, Strates
Hawes, Stephen 1475(?)-1529(?) .... **LC 17**
See also DLB 132; RGEL 2
Hawkes, John (Clendennin Burne, Jr.)
1925-1998 .. **CLC 1, 2, 3, 4, 7, 9, 14, 15,
27, 49**
See also BPFB 2; CA 1-4R; 167; CANR 2,
47, 64; CN 7; DLB 2, 7, 227; DLBY
1980, 1998; EWL 3; MTCW 1, 2; RGAL
4
Hawking, S. W.
See Hawking, Stephen W(illiam)
Hawking, Stephen W(illiam) 1942- . **CLC 63,
105**
See also AAYA 13; BEST 89:1; CA 126;
129; CANR 48, 115; CPW; DA3; MTCW
2
Hawkins, Anthony Hope
See Hope, Anthony
Hawthorne, Julian 1846-1934 .... **TCLC 25**
See also CA 165; HGG
Hawthorne, Nathaniel 1804-1864 ... **NCLC 2,
10, 17, 23, 39, 79, 95; SSC 3, 29, 39;
WLC**
See also AAYA 18; AMW; AMWC 1;
AMWR 1; BPFB 2; BYA 3; CDALB
1640-1865; DA; DA3; DAB; DAC; DAM
MST, NOV; DLB 1, 74, 183, 223, 269;
EXPN; EXPS; HGG; LAIT 1; NFS 1, 20;
RGAL 4; RGSF 2; SSFS 1, 7, 11, 15;
SUFW 1; TUS; WCH; YABC 2

Hawthorne, Sophia Peabody
1809-1871 .... **NCLC 150**
See also DLB 183, 239
Haxton, Josephine Ayres 1921-
See Douglas, Ellen
See also CA 115; CANR 41, 83
Hayaseca y Eizaguirre, Jorge
See Echegaray (y Eizaguirre), Jose (Maria
Waldo)
Hayashi, Fumiko 1904-1951 .... **TCLC 27**
See Hayashi Fumiko
See also CA 161
Hayashi Fumiko
See Hayashi, Fumiko
See also DLB 180; EWL 3
Haycraft, Anna (Margaret) 1932-
See Ellis, Alice Thomas
See also CA 122; CANR 85, 90; MTCW 2
Hayden, Robert E(arl) 1913-1980 ..... **BLC 2;
CLC 5, 9, 14, 37; PC 6**
See also AFAW 1, 2; AMWS 2; BW 1, 3;
CA 69-72; 97-100; CABS 2; CANR 24,
75, 82; CDALB 1941-1968; DA; DAC;
DAM MST, MULT, POET; DLB 5, 76;
EWL 3; EXPP; MTCW 1, 2; PFS 1;
RGAL 4; SATA 19; SATA-Obit 26; WP
Haydon, Benjamin Robert
1786-1846 .... **NCLC 146**
See also DLB 110
Hayek, F(riedrich) A(ugust von)
1899-1992 .... **TCLC 109**
See also CA 93-96; 137; CANR 20; MTCW
1, 2
Hayford, J(oseph) E(phraim) Casely
See Casely-Hayford, J(oseph) E(phraim)
Hayman, Ronald 1932- .... **CLC 44**
See also CA 25-28R; CANR 18, 50, 88; CD
5; DLB 155
Hayne, Paul Hamilton 1830-1886 . **NCLC 94**
See also DLB 3, 64, 79, 248; RGAL 4
Hays, Mary 1760-1843 .... **NCLC 114**
See also DLB 142, 158; RGEL 2
Haywood, Eliza (Fowler)
1693(?)-1756 .... **LC 1, 44**
See also DLB 39; RGEL 2
Hazlitt, William 1778-1830 ...... **NCLC 29, 82**
See also BRW 4; DLB 110, 158; RGEL 2;
TEA
Hazzard, Shirley 1931- .... **CLC 18**
See also CA 9-12R; CANR 4, 70, 127; CN
7; DLB 289; DLBY 1982; MTCW 1
Head, Bessie 1937-1986 ...... **BLC 2; CLC 25,
67; SSC 52**
See also AFW; BW 2, 3; CA 29-32R; 119;
CANR 25, 82; CDWLB 3; DA3; DAM
MULT; DLB 117, 225; EWL 3; EXPS;
FW; MTCW 1, 2; RGSF 2; SSFS 5, 13;
WLIT 2; WWE 1
Headon, (Nicky) Topper 1956(?)- ..... **CLC 30**
Heaney, Seamus (Justin) 1939- ..... **CLC 5, 7,
14, 25, 37, 74, 91, 171; PC 18; WLCS**
See also BRWR 1; BRWS 5; CA 85-88;
CANR 25, 48, 75, 91, 128; CDBLB 1960
to Present; CP 7; DA3; DAB; DAM
POET; DLB 40; DLBY 1995; EWL 3;
EXPP; MTCW 1, 2; PAB; PFS 2, 5, 8,
17; RGEL 2; TEA; WLIT 4
Hearn, (Patricio) Lafcadio (Tessima Carlos)
1850-1904 .... **TCLC 9**
See also CA 105; 166; DLB 12, 78, 189;
HGG; RGAL 4
Hearne, Samuel 1745-1792 .... **LC 95**
See also DLB 99
Hearne, Vicki 1946-2001 .... **CLC 56**
See also CA 139; 201
Hearon, Shelby 1931- .... **CLC 63**
See also AITN 2; AMWS 8; CA 25-28R;
CANR 18, 48, 103; CSW

Heat-Moon, William Least .... **CLC 29**
See Trogdon, William (Lewis)
See also AAYA 9

Hebbel, Friedrich 1813-1863 . **DC 21; NCLC 43**
See also CDWLB 2; DAM DRAM; DLB 129; EW 6; RGWL 2, 3

Hebert, Anne 1916-2000 .... **CLC 4, 13, 29**
See also CA 85-88; 187; CANR 69, 126; CCA 1; CWP; CWW 2; DA3; DAC; DAM MST, POET; DLB 68; EWL 3; GFL 1789 to the Present; MTCW 1, 2; PFS 20

Hecht, Anthony (Evan) 1923-2004 .... **CLC 8, 13, 19**
See also AMWS 10; CA 9-12R; CANR 6, 108; CP 7; DAM POET; DLB 5, 169; EWL 3; PFS 6; WP

Hecht, Ben 1894-1964 ..... **CLC 8; TCLC 101**
See also CA 85-88; DFS 9; DLB 7, 9, 25, 26, 28, 86; FANT; IDFW 3, 4; RGAL 4

Hedayat, Sadeq 1903-1951 .... **TCLC 21**
See also CA 120; EWL 3; RGSF 2

Hegel, Georg Wilhelm Friedrich
1770-1831 .... **NCLC 46, 151**
See also DLB 90; TWA

Heidegger, Martin 1889-1976 .... **CLC 24**
See also CA 81-84; 65-68; CANR 34; DLB 296; MTCW 1, 2

Heidenstam, (Carl Gustaf) Verner von
1859-1940 .... **TCLC 5**
See also CA 104

Heidi Louise
See Erdrich, Louise

Heifner, Jack 1946- .... **CLC 11**
See also CA 105; CANR 47

Heijermans, Herman 1864-1924 .... **TCLC 24**
See also CA 123; EWL 3

Heilbrun, Carolyn G(old)
1926-2003 .... **CLC 25, 173**
See Cross, Amanda
See also CA 45-48; 220; CANR 1, 28, 58, 94; FW

Hein, Christoph 1944- .... **CLC 154**
See also CA 158; CANR 108; CDWLB 2; CWW 2; DLB 124

Heine, Heinrich 1797-1856 .... **NCLC 4, 54, 147; PC 25**
See also CDWLB 2; DLB 90; EW 5; RGWL 2, 3; TWA

Heinemann, Larry (Curtiss) 1944- .. **CLC 50**
See also CA 110; CAAS 21; CANR 31, 81; DLBD 9; INT CANR-31

Heiney, Donald (William) 1921-1993
See Harris, MacDonald
See also CA 1-4R; 142; CANR 3, 58; FANT

Heinlein, Robert A(nson) 1907-1988 . **CLC 1, 3, 8, 14, 26, 55; SSC 55**
See also AAYA 17; BPFB 2; BYA 4, 13; CA 1-4R; 125; CANR 1, 20, 53; CLR 75; CPW; DA3; DAM POP; DLB 8; EXPS; JRDA; LAIT 5; LMFS 2; MAICYA 1, 2; MTCW 1, 2; RGAL 4; SATA 9, 69; SATA-Obit 56; SCFW; SFW 4; SSFS 7; YAW

Helforth, John
See Doolittle, Hilda

Heliodorus fl. 3rd cent. - .... **CMLC 52**

Hellenhofferu, Vojtech Kapristian z
See Hasek, Jaroslav (Matej Frantisek)

Heller, Joseph 1923-1999 . **CLC 1, 3, 5, 8, 11, 36, 63; TCLC 131, 151; WLC**
See also AAYA 24; AITN 1; AMWS 4; BPFB 2; BYA 1; CA 5-8R; 187; CABS 1; CANR 8, 42, 66, 126; CN 7; CPW; DA; DA3; DAB; DAC; DAM MST, NOV, POP; DLB 2, 28, 227; DLBY 1980, 2002; EWL 3; EXPN; INT CANR-8; LAIT 4; MTCW 1, 2; NFS 1; RGAL 4; TUS; YAW

Hellman, Lillian (Florence)
1906-1984 .. **CLC 2, 4, 8, 14, 18, 34, 44, 52; DC 1; TCLC 119**
See also AAYA 47; AITN 1, 2; AMWS 1; CA 13-16R; 112; CAD; CANR 33; CWD; DA3; DAM DRAM; DFS 1, 3, 14; DLB 7, 228; DLBY 1984; EWL 3; FW; LAIT 3; MAWW; MTCW 1, 2; RGAL 4; TUS

Helprin, Mark 1947- .... **CLC 7, 10, 22, 32**
See also CA 81-84; CANR 47, 64, 124; CDALBS; CPW; DA3; DAM NOV, POP; DLBY 1985; FANT; MTCW 1, 2; SUFW 2

Helvetius, Claude-Adrien 1715-1771 .. **LC 26**

Helyar, Jane Penelope Josephine 1933-
See Poole, Josephine
See also CA 21-24R; CANR 10, 26; CWRI 5; SATA 82, 138; SATA-Essay 138

Hemans, Felicia 1793-1835 ...... **NCLC 29, 71**
See also DLB 96; RGEL 2

Hemingway, Ernest (Miller)
1899-1961 .... **CLC 1, 3, 6, 8, 10, 13, 19, 30, 34, 39, 41, 44, 50, 61, 80; SSC 1, 25, 36, 40, 63; TCLC 115; WLC**
See also AAYA 19; AMW; AMWC 1; AMWR 1; BPFB 2; BYA 2, 3, 13, 15; CA 77-80; CANR 34; CDALB 1917-1929; DA; DA3; DAB; DAC; DAM MST, NOV; DLB 4, 9, 102, 210, 308; DLBD 1, 15, 16; DLBY 1981, 1987, 1996, 1998; EWL 3; EXPN; EXPS; LAIT 3, 4; LATS 1:1; MTCW 1, 2; NFS 1, 5, 6, 14; RGAL 4; RGSF 2; SSFS 17; TUS; WYA

Hempel, Amy 1951- .... **CLC 39**
See also CA 118; 137; CANR 70; DA3; DLB 218; EXPS; MTCW 2; SSFS 2

Henderson, F. C.
See Mencken, H(enry) L(ouis)

Henderson, Sylvia
See Ashton-Warner, Sylvia (Constance)

Henderson, Zenna (Chlarson)
1917-1983 .... **SSC 29**
See also CA 1-4R; 133; CANR 1, 84; DLB 8; SATA 5; SFW 4

Henkin, Joshua .... **CLC 119**
See also CA 161

Henley, Beth .... **CLC 23; DC 6, 14**
See Henley, Elizabeth Becker
See also CABS 3; CAD; CD 5; CSW; CWD; DFS 2; DLBY 1986; FW

Henley, Elizabeth Becker 1952-
See Henley, Beth
See also CA 107; CANR 32, 73; DA3; DAM DRAM, MST; MTCW 1, 2

Henley, William Ernest 1849-1903 .. **TCLC 8**
See also CA 105; DLB 19; RGEL 2

Hennissart, Martha 1929-
See Lathen, Emma
See also CA 85-88; CANR 64

Henry VIII 1491-1547 .... **LC 10**
See also DLB 132

Henry, O. ..... **SSC 5, 49; TCLC 1, 19; WLC**
See Porter, William Sydney
See also AAYA 41; AMWS 2; EXPS; RGAL 4; RGSF 2; SSFS 2, 18

Henry, Patrick 1736-1799 .... **LC 25**
See also LAIT 1

Henryson, Robert 1430(?)-1506(?) ..... **LC 20, 110**
See also BRWS 7; DLB 146; RGEL 2

Henschke, Alfred
See Klabund

Henson, Lance 1944- .... **NNAL**
See also CA 146; DLB 175

Hentoff, Nat(han Irving) 1925- .... **CLC 26**
See also AAYA 4, 42; BYA 6; CA 1-4R; CAAS 6; CANR 5, 25, 77, 114; CLR 1,

52; INT CANR-25; JRDA; MAICYA 1, 2; SATA 42, 69, 133; SATA-Brief 27; WYA; YAW

Heppenstall, (John) Rayner
1911-1981 .... **CLC 10**
See also CA 1-4R; 103; CANR 29; EWL 3

Heraclitus c. 540B.C.-c. 450B.C. ... **CMLC 22**
See also DLB 176

Herbert, Frank (Patrick)
1920-1986 .... **CLC 12, 23, 35, 44, 85**
See also AAYA 21; BPFB 2; BYA 4, 14; CA 53-56; 118; CANR 5, 43; CDALBS; CPW; DAM POP; DLB 8; INT CANR-5; LAIT 5; MTCW 1, 2; NFS 17; SATA 9, 37; SATA-Obit 47; SCFW 2; SFW 4; YAW

Herbert, George 1593-1633 ...... **LC 24; PC 4**
See also BRW 2; BRWR 2; CDBLB Before 1660; DAB; DAM POET; DLB 126; EXPP; RGEL 2; TEA; WP

Herbert, Zbigniew 1924-1998 ..... **CLC 9, 43; PC 50**
See also CA 89-92; 169; CANR 36, 74; CDWLB 4; CWW 2; DAM POET; DLB 232; EWL 3; MTCW 1

Herbst, Josephine (Frey)
1897-1969 .... **CLC 34**
See also CA 5-8R; 25-28R; DLB 9

Herder, Johann Gottfried von
1744-1803 .... **NCLC 8**
See also DLB 97; EW 4; TWA

Heredia, Jose Maria 1803-1839 .... **HLCS 2**
See also LAW

Hergesheimer, Joseph 1880-1954 ... **TCLC 11**
See also CA 109; 194; DLB 102, 9; RGAL 4

Herlihy, James Leo 1927-1993 .... **CLC 6**
See also CA 1-4R; 143; CAD; CANR 2

Herman, William
See Bierce, Ambrose (Gwinett)

Hermogenes fl. c. 175- .... **CMLC 6**

Hernandez, Jose 1834-1886 .... **NCLC 17**
See also LAW; RGWL 2, 3; WLIT 1

Herodotus c. 484B.C.-c. 420B.C. .. **CMLC 17**
See also AW 1; CDWLB 1; DLB 176; RGWL 2, 3; TWA

Herrick, Robert 1591-1674 .... **LC 13; PC 9**
See also BRW 2; BRWC 2; DA; DAB; DAC; DAM MST, POP; DLB 126; EXPP; PFS 13; RGAL 4; RGEL 2; TEA; WP

Herring, Guilles
See Somerville, Edith Oenone

Herriot, James 1916-1995 .... **CLC 12**
See Wight, James Alfred
See also AAYA 1, 54; BPFB 2; CA 148; CANR 40; CLR 80; CPW; DAM POP; LAIT 3; MAICYA 2; MAICYAS 1; MTCW 2; SATA 86, 135; TEA; YAW

Herris, Violet
See Hunt, Violet

Herrmann, Dorothy 1941- .... **CLC 44**
See also CA 107

Herrmann, Taffy
See Herrmann, Dorothy

Hersey, John (Richard) 1914-1993 .... **CLC 1, 2, 7, 9, 40, 81, 97**
See also AAYA 29; BPFB 2; CA 17-20R; 140; CANR 33; CDALBS; CPW; DAM POP; DLB 6, 185, 278, 299; MTCW 1, 2; SATA 25; SATA-Obit 76; TUS

Herzen, Aleksandr Ivanovich
1812-1870 .... **NCLC 10, 61**
See Herzen, Alexander

Herzen, Alexander
See Herzen, Aleksandr Ivanovich
See also DLB 277

Herzl, Theodor 1860-1904 .... **TCLC 36**
See also CA 168

Author Index

Author Index

Juana Inez de La Cruz, Sor
See Juana Ines de la Cruz, Sor
Judd, Cyril
See Kornbluth, C(yril) M.; Pohl, Frederik
Juenger, Ernst 1895-1998 .... **CLC 125**
See Junger, Ernst
See also CA 101; 167; CANR 21, 47, 106;
DLB 56
Julian of Norwich 1342(?)-1416(?) . **LC 6, 52**
See also DLB 146; LMFS 1
Julius Caesar 100B.C.-44B.C.
See Caesar, Julius
See also CDWLB 1; DLB 211
Junger, Ernst
See Juenger, Ernst
See also CDWLB 2; EWL 3; RGWL 2, 3
Junger, Sebastian 1962- .... **CLC 109**
See also AAYA 28; CA 165; CANR 130
Juniper, Alex
See Hospital, Janette Turner
Junius
See Luxemburg, Rosa
Just, Ward (Swift) 1935- .... **CLC 4, 27**
See also CA 25-28R; CANR 32, 87; CN 7;
INT CANR-32
Justice, Donald (Rodney)
1925-2004 .... **CLC 6, 19, 102; PC 64**
See also AMWS 7; CA 5-8R; CANR 26,
54, 74, 121, 122; CP 7; CSW; DAM
POET; DLBY 1983; EWL 3; INT CANR-
26; MTCW 2; PFS 14
Juvenal c. 60-c. 130 .... **CMLC 8**
See also AW 2; CDWLB 1; DLB 211;
RGWL 2, 3
Juvenis
See Bourne, Randolph S(illiman)
K., Alice
See Knapp, Caroline
Kabakov, Sasha .... **CLC 59**
Kabir 1398(?)-1448(?) .... **LC 109; PC 56**
See also RGWL 2, 3
Kacew, Romain 1914-1980
See Gary, Romain
See also CA 108; 102
Kadare, Ismail 1936- .... **CLC 52, 190**
See also CA 161; EWL 3; RGWL 3
Kadohata, Cynthia 1956(?)- ..... **CLC 59, 122**
See also CA 140; CANR 124
Kafka, Franz 1883-1924 ... **SSC 5, 29, 35, 60;**
TCLC 2, 6, 13, 29, 47, 53, 112; WLC
See also AAYA 31; BPFB 2; CA 105; 126;
CDWLB 2; DA; DA3; DAB; DAC; DAM
MST, NOV; DLB 81; EW 9; EWL 3;
EXPS; LATS 1:1; LMFS 2; MTCW 1, 2;
NFS 7; RGSF 2; RGWL 2, 3; SFW 4;
SSFS 3, 7, 12; TWA
Kahanovitsch, Pinkhes
See Der Nister
Kahn, Roger 1927- .... **CLC 30**
See also CA 25-28R; CANR 44, 69; DLB
171; SATA 37
Kain, Saul
See Sassoon, Siegfried (Lorraine)
Kaiser, Georg 1878-1945 .... **TCLC 9**
See also CA 106; 190; CDWLB 2; DLB
124; EWL 3; LMFS 2; RGWL 2, 3
Kaledin, Sergei .... **CLC 59**
Kaletski, Alexander 1946- .... **CLC 39**
See also CA 118; 143
Kalidasa fl. c. 400-455 .... **CMLC 9; PC 22**
See also RGWL 2, 3
Kallman, Chester (Simon)
1921-1975 .... **CLC 2**
See also CA 45-48; 53-56; CANR 3
Kaminsky, Melvin 1926-
See Brooks, Mel
See also CA 65-68; CANR 16

Kaminsky, Stuart M(elvin) 1934- ..... **CLC 59**
See also CA 73-76; CANR 29, 53, 89;
CMW 4
Kamo no Chomei 1153(?)-1216 .... **CMLC 66**
See also DLB 203
Kamo no Nagaakira
See Kamo no Chomei
Kandinsky, Wassily 1866-1944 .... **TCLC 92**
See also CA 118; 155
Kane, Francis
See Robbins, Harold
Kane, Henry 1918-
See Queen, Ellery
See also CA 156; CMW 4
Kane, Paul
See Simon, Paul (Frederick)
Kanin, Garson 1912-1999 .... **CLC 22**
See also AITN 1; CA 5-8R; 177; CAD;
CANR 7, 78; DLB 7; IDFW 3, 4
Kaniuk, Yoram 1930- .... **CLC 19**
See also CA 134; DLB 299
Kant, Immanuel 1724-1804 ..... **NCLC 27, 67**
See also DLB 94
Kantor, MacKinlay 1904-1977 .... **CLC 7**
See also CA 61-64; 73-76; CANR 60, 63;
DLB 9, 102; MTCW 2; RHW; TCWW 2
Kanze Motokiyo
See Zeami
Kaplan, David Michael 1946- .... **CLC 50**
See also CA 187
Kaplan, James 1951- .... **CLC 59**
See also CA 135; CANR 121
Karadzic, Vuk Stefanovic
1787-1864 .... **NCLC 115**
See also CDWLB 4; DLB 147
Karageorge, Michael
See Anderson, Poul (William)
Karamzin, Nikolai Mikhailovich
1766-1826 .... **NCLC 3**
See also DLB 150; RGSF 2
Karapanou, Margarita 1946- .... **CLC 13**
See also CA 101
Karinthy, Frigyes 1887-1938 .... **TCLC 47**
See also CA 170; DLB 215; EWL 3
Karl, Frederick R(obert)
1927-2004 .... **CLC 34**
See also CA 5-8R; 226; CANR 3, 44
Karr, Mary 1955- .... **CLC 188**
See also AMWS 11; CA 151; CANR 100;
NCFS 5
Kastel, Warren
See Silverberg, Robert
Kataev, Evgeny Petrovich 1903-1942
See Petrov, Evgeny
See also CA 120
Kataphusin
See Ruskin, John
Katz, Steve 1935- .... **CLC 47**
See also CA 25-28R; CAAS 14, 64; CANR
12; CN 7; DLBY 1983
Kauffman, Janet 1945- .... **CLC 42**
See also CA 117; CANR 43, 84; DLB 218;
DLBY 1986
Kaufman, Bob (Garnell) 1925-1986 . **CLC 49**
See also BG 3; BW 1; CA 41-44R; 118;
CANR 22; DLB 16, 41
Kaufman, George S. 1889-1961 ...... **CLC 38;**
DC 17
See also CA 108; 93-96; DAM DRAM;
DFS 1, 10; DLB 7; INT CA-108; MTCW
2; RGAL 4; TUS
Kaufman, Sue .... **CLC 3, 8**
See Barondess, Sue K(aufman)
Kavafis, Konstantinos Petrou 1863-1933
See Cavafy, C(onstantine) P(eter)
See also CA 104

Kavan, Anna 1901-1968 .... **CLC 5, 13, 82**
See also BRWS 7; CA 5-8R; CANR 6, 57;
DLB 255; MTCW 1; RGEL 2; SFW 4
Kavanagh, Dan
See Barnes, Julian (Patrick)
Kavanagh, Julie 1952- .... **CLC 119**
See also CA 163
Kavanagh, Patrick (Joseph)
1904-1967 .... **CLC 22; PC 33**
See also BRWS 7; CA 123; 25-28R; DLB
15, 20; EWL 3; MTCW 1; RGEL 2
Kawabata, Yasunari 1899-1972 ..... **CLC 2, 5,**
9, 18, 107; SSC 17
See Kawabata Yasunari
See also CA 93-96; 33-36R; CANR 88;
DAM MULT; MJW; MTCW 2; RGSF 2;
RGWL 2, 3
Kawabata Yasunari
See Kawabata, Yasunari
See also DLB 180; EWL 3
Kaye, M(ary) M(argaret)
1908-2004 .... **CLC 28**
See also CA 89-92; 223; CANR 24, 60, 102;
MTCW 1, 2; RHW; SATA 62; SATA-Obit
152
Kaye, Mollie
See Kaye, M(ary) M(argaret)
Kaye-Smith, Sheila 1887-1956 .... **TCLC 20**
See also CA 118; 203; DLB 36
Kaymor, Patrice Maguilene
See Senghor, Leopold Sedar
Kazakov, Iurii Pavlovich
See Kazakov, Yuri Pavlovich
See also DLB 302
Kazakov, Yuri Pavlovich 1927-1982 . **SSC 43**
See Kazakov, Iurii Pavlovich; Kazakov,
Yury
See also CA 5-8R; CANR 36; MTCW 1;
RGSF 2
Kazakov, Yury
See Kazakov, Yuri Pavlovich
See also EWL 3
Kazan, Elia 1909-2003 .... **CLC 6, 16, 63**
See also CA 21-24R; 220; CANR 32, 78
Kazantzakis, Nikos 1883(?)-1957 .... **TCLC 2,**
5, 33
See also BPFB 2; CA 105; 132; DA3; EW
9; EWL 3; MTCW 1, 2; RGWL 2, 3
Kazin, Alfred 1915-1998 ..... **CLC 34, 38, 119**
See also AMWS 8; CA 1-4R; CAAS 7;
CANR 1, 45, 79; DLB 67; EWL 3
Keane, Mary Nesta (Skrine) 1904-1996
See Keane, Molly
See also CA 108; 114; 151; CN 7; RHW
Keane, Molly .... **CLC 31**
See Keane, Mary Nesta (Skrine)
See also INT CA-114
Keates, Jonathan 1946(?)- .... **CLC 34**
See also CA 163; CANR 126
Keaton, Buster 1895-1966 .... **CLC 20**
See also CA 194
Keats, John 1795-1821 ...... **NCLC 8, 73, 121;**
PC 1; WLC
See also AAYA 58; BRW 4; BRWR 1; CD-
BLB 1789-1832; DA; DA3; DAB; DAC;
DAM MST, POET; DLB 96, 110; EXPP;
LMFS 1; PAB; PFS 1, 2, 3, 9, 17; RGEL
2; TEA; WLIT 3; WP
Keble, John 1792-1866 .... **NCLC 87**
See also DLB 32, 55; RGEL 2
Keene, Donald 1922- .... **CLC 34**
See also CA 1-4R; CANR 5, 119
Keillor, Garrison .... **CLC 40, 115**
See Keillor, Gary (Edward)
See also AAYA 2; BEST 89:3; BPFB 2;
DLBY 1987; EWL 3; SATA 58; TUS

King, Steve
See King, Stephen (Edwin)

King, Thomas 1943- .... **CLC 89, 171; NNAL**
See also CA 144; CANR 95; CCA 1; CN 7;
DAC; DAM MULT; DLB 175; SATA 96

Kingman, Lee .... **CLC 17**
See Natti, (Mary) Lee
See also CWRI 5; SAAS 3; SATA 1, 67

Kingsley, Charles 1819-1875 .... **NCLC 35**
See also CLR 77; DLB 21, 32, 163, 178,
190; FANT; MAICYA 2; MAICYAS 1;
RGEL 2; WCH; YABC 2

Kingsley, Henry 1830-1876 .... **NCLC 107**
See also DLB 21, 230; RGEL 2

Kingsley, Sidney 1906-1995 .... **CLC 44**
See also CA 85-88; 147; CAD; DFS 14, 19;
DLB 7; RGAL 4

Kingsolver, Barbara 1955- . **CLC 55, 81, 130**
See also AAYA 15; AMWS 7; CA 129; 134;
CANR 60, 96, 133; CDALBS; CPW;
CSW; DA3; DAM POP; DLB 206; INT
CA-134; LAIT 5; MTCW 2; NFS 5, 10,
12; RGAL 4

Kingston, Maxine (Ting Ting) Hong
1940- .... **AAL; CLC 12, 19, 58, 121;
WLCS**
See also AAYA 8, 55; AMWS 5; BPFB 2;
CA 69-72; CANR 13, 38, 74, 87, 128;
CDALBS; CN 7; DA3; DAM MULT,
NOV; DLB 173, 212; DLBY 1980; EWL
3; FW; INT CANR-13; LAIT 5; MAWW;
MTCW 1, 2; NFS 6; RGAL 4; SATA 53;
SSFS 3

Kinnell, Galway 1927- ..... **CLC 1, 2, 3, 5, 13,
29, 129; PC 26**
See also AMWS 3; CA 9-12R; CANR 10,
34, 66, 116; CP 7; DLB 5; DLBY 1987;
EWL 3; INT CANR-34; MTCW 1, 2;
PAB; PFS 9; RGAL 4; WP

Kinsella, Thomas 1928- .... **CLC 4, 19, 138**
See also BRWS 5; CA 17-20R; CANR 15,
122; CP 7; DLB 27; EWL 3; MTCW 1, 2;
RGEL 2; TEA

Kinsella, W(illiam) P(atrick) 1935- . **CLC 27,
43, 166**
See also AAYA 7, 60; BPFB 2; CA 97-100,
222; CAAE 222; CAAS 7; CANR 21, 35,
66, 75, 129; CN 7; CPW; DAC; DAM
NOV, POP; FANT; INT CANR-21; LAIT
5; MTCW 1, 2; NFS 15; RGSF 2

Kinsey, Alfred C(harles)
1894-1956 .... **TCLC 91**
See also CA 115; 170; MTCW 2

Kipling, (Joseph) Rudyard 1865-1936 . **PC 3;
SSC 5, 54; TCLC 8, 17; WLC**
See also AAYA 32; BRW 6; BRWC 1, 2;
BYA 4; CA 105; 120; CANR 33; CDBLB
1890-1914; CLR 39, 65; CWRI 5; DA;
DA3; DAB; DAC; DAM MST, POET;
DLB 19, 34, 141, 156; EWL 3; EXPS;
FANT; LAIT 3; LMFS 1; MAICYA 1, 2;
MTCW 1, 2; RGEL 2; RGSF 2; SATA
100; SFW 4; SSFS 8; SUFW 1; TEA;
WCH; WLIT 4; YABC 2

Kirk, Russell (Amos) 1918-1994 .. **TCLC 119**
See also AITN 1; CA 1-4R; 145; CAAS 9;
CANR 1, 20, 60; HGG; INT CANR-20;
MTCW 1, 2

Kirkham, Dinah
See Card, Orson Scott

Kirkland, Caroline M. 1801-1864 . **NCLC 85**
See also DLB 3, 73, 74, 250, 254; DLBD
13

Kirkup, James 1918- .... **CLC 1**
See also CA 1-4R; CAAS 4; CANR 2; CP
7; DLB 27; SATA 12

Kirkwood, James 1930(?)-1989 .... **CLC 9**
See also AITN 2; CA 1-4R; 128; CANR 6,
40; GLL 2

Kirsch, Sarah 1935- .... **CLC 176**
See also CA 178; CWW 2; DLB 75; EWL
3

Kirshner, Sidney
See Kingsley, Sidney

Kis, Danilo 1935-1989 .... **CLC 57**
See also CA 109; 118; 129; CANR 61; CD-
WLB 4; DLB 181; EWL 3; MTCW 1;
RGSF 2; RGWL 2, 3

Kissinger, Henry A(lfred) 1923- ..... **CLC 137**
See also CA 1-4R; CANR 2, 33, 66, 109;
MTCW 1

Kivi, Aleksis 1834-1872 .... **NCLC 30**

Kizer, Carolyn (Ashley) 1925- ... **CLC 15, 39,
80**
See also CA 65-68; CAAS 5; CANR 24,
70, 134; CP 7; CWP; DAM POET; DLB
5, 169; EWL 3; MTCW 2; PFS 18

Klabund 1890-1928 .... **TCLC 44**
See also CA 162; DLB 66

Klappert, Peter 1942- .... **CLC 57**
See also CA 33-36R; CSW; DLB 5

Klein, A(braham) M(oses)
1909-1972 .... **CLC 19**
See also CA 101; 37-40R; DAB; DAC;
DAM MST; DLB 68; EWL 3; RGEL 2

Klein, Joe
See Klein, Joseph

Klein, Joseph 1946- .... **CLC 154**
See also CA 85-88; CANR 55

Klein, Norma 1938-1989 .... **CLC 30**
See also AAYA 2, 35; BPFB 2; BYA 6, 7,
8; CA 41-44R; 128; CANR 15, 37; CLR
2, 19; INT CANR-15; JRDA; MAICYA
1, 2; SAAS 1; SATA 7, 57; WYA; YAW

Klein, T(heodore) E(ibon) D(onald)
1947- .... **CLC 34**
See also CA 119; CANR 44, 75; HGG

Kleist, Heinrich von 1777-1811 ...... **NCLC 2,
37; SSC 22**
See also CDWLB 2; DAM DRAM; DLB
90; EW 5; RGSF 2; RGWL 2, 3

Klima, Ivan 1931- .... **CLC 56, 172**
See also CA 25-28R; CANR 17, 50, 91;
CDWLB 4; CWW 2; DAM NOV; DLB
232; EWL 3; RGWL 3

Klimentev, Andrei Platonovich
See Klimentov, Andrei Platonovich

Klimentov, Andrei Platonovich
1899-1951 .... **SSC 42; TCLC 14**
See Platonov, Andrei Platonovich; Platonov,
Andrey Platonovich
See also CA 108

Klinger, Friedrich Maximilian von
1752-1831 .... **NCLC 1**
See also DLB 94

Klingsor the Magician
See Hartmann, Sadakichi

Klopstock, Friedrich Gottlieb
1724-1803 .... **NCLC 11**
See also DLB 97; EW 4; RGWL 2, 3

Kluge, Alexander 1932- .... **SSC 61**
See also CA 81-84; DLB 75

Knapp, Caroline 1959-2002 .... **CLC 99**
See also CA 154; 207

Knebel, Fletcher 1911-1993 .... **CLC 14**
See also AITN 1; CA 1-4R; 140; CAAS 3;
CANR 1, 36; SATA 36; SATA-Obit 75

Knickerbocker, Diedrich
See Irving, Washington

Knight, Etheridge 1931-1991 ... **BLC 2; CLC
40; PC 14**
See also BW 1, 3; CA 21-24R; 133; CANR
23, 82; DAM POET; DLB 41; MTCW 2;
RGAL 4

Knight, Sarah Kemble 1666-1727 .... **LC 7**
See also DLB 24, 200

Knister, Raymond 1899-1932 .... **TCLC 56**
See also CA 186; DLB 68; RGEL 2

Knowles, John 1926-2001 ... **CLC 1, 4, 10, 26**
See also AAYA 10; AMWS 12; BPFB 2;
BYA 3; CA 17-20R; 203; CANR 40, 74,
76, 132; CDALB 1968-1988; CLR 98; CN
7; DA; DAC; DAM MST, NOV; DLB 6;
EXPN; MTCW 1, 2; NFS 2; RGAL 4;
SATA 8, 89; SATA-Obit 134; YAW

Knox, Calvin M.
See Silverberg, Robert

Knox, John c. 1505-1572 .... **LC 37**
See also DLB 132

Knye, Cassandra
See Disch, Thomas M(ichael)

Koch, C(hristopher) J(ohn) 1932- .... **CLC 42**
See also CA 127; CANR 84; CN 7; DLB
289

Koch, Christopher
See Koch, C(hristopher) J(ohn)

Koch, Kenneth (Jay) 1925-2002 .... **CLC 5, 8,
44**
See also CA 1-4R; 207; CAD; CANR 6,
36, 57, 97, 131; CD 5; CP 7; DAM POET;
DLB 5; INT CANR-36; MTCW 2; PFS
20; SATA 65; WP

Kochanowski, Jan 1530-1584 .... **LC 10**
See also RGWL 2, 3

Kock, Charles Paul de 1794-1871 . **NCLC 16**

Koda Rohan
See Koda Shigeyuki

Koda Rohan
See Koda Shigeyuki
See also DLB 180

Koda Shigeyuki 1867-1947 .... **TCLC 22**
See Koda Rohan
See also CA 121; 183

Koestler, Arthur 1905-1983 ... **CLC 1, 3, 6, 8,
15, 33**
See also BRWS 1; CA 1-4R; 109; CANR 1,
33; CDBLB 1945-1960; DLBY 1983;
EWL 3; MTCW 1, 2; NFS 19; RGEL 2

Kogawa, Joy Nozomi 1935- ...... **CLC 78, 129**
See also AAYA 47; CA 101; CANR 19, 62,
126; CN 7; CWP; DAC; DAM MST,
MULT; FW; MTCW 2; NFS 3; SATA 99

Kohout, Pavel 1928- .... **CLC 13**
See also CA 45-48; CANR 3

Koizumi, Yakumo
See Hearn, (Patricio) Lafcadio (Tessima
Carlos)

Kolmar, Gertrud 1894-1943 .... **TCLC 40**
See also CA 167; EWL 3

Komunyakaa, Yusef 1947- .. **BLCS; CLC 86,
94, 207; PC 51**
See also AFAW 2; AMWS 13; CA 147;
CANR 83; CP 7; CSW; DLB 120; EWL
3; PFS 5, 20; RGAL 4

Konrad, George
See Konrad, Gyorgy

Konrad, Gyorgy 1933- .... **CLC 4, 10, 73**
See also CA 85-88; CANR 97; CDWLB 4;
CWW 2; DLB 232; EWL 3

Konwicki, Tadeusz 1926- .... **CLC 8, 28, 54,
117**
See also CA 101; CAAS 9; CANR 39, 59;
CWW 2; DLB 232; EWL 3; IDFW 3;
MTCW 1

Koontz, Dean R(ay) 1945- .... **CLC 78, 206**
See also AAYA 9, 31; BEST 89:3, 90:2; CA
108; CANR 19, 36, 52, 95; CMW 4;
CPW; DA3; DAM NOV, POP; DLB 292;
HGG; MTCW 1; SATA 92; SFW 4;
SUFW 2; YAW

Kopernik, Mikolaj
See Copernicus, Nicolaus

Kopit, Arthur (Lee) 1937- ...... **CLC 1, 18, 33**
See also AITN 1; CA 81-84; CABS 3; CD
5; DAM DRAM; DFS 7, 14; DLB 7;
MTCW 1; RGAL 4

Lautreamont, Isidore Lucien Ducasse
  See Lautreamont
  See also DLB 217
Lavater, Johann Kaspar
  1741-1801 .... **NCLC 142**
  See also DLB 97
Laverty, Donald
  See Blish, James (Benjamin)
Lavin, Mary 1912-1996 . **CLC 4, 18, 99; SSC 4, 67**
  See also CA 9-12R; 151; CANR 33; CN 7;
  DLB 15; FW; MTCW 1; RGEL 2; RGSF 2
Lavond, Paul Dennis
  See Kornbluth, C(yril) M.; Pohl, Frederik
Lawes Henry 1596-1662 .... **LC 113**
  See also DLB 126
Lawler, Ray
  See Lawler, Raymond Evenor
  See also DLB 289
Lawler, Raymond Evenor 1922- .... **CLC 58**
  See Lawler, Ray
  See also CA 103; CD 5; RGEL 2
Lawrence, D(avid) H(erbert Richards)
  1885-1930 .... **PC 54; SSC 4, 19, 73; TCLC 2, 9, 16, 33, 48, 61, 93; WLC**
  See Chambers, Jessie
  See also BPFB 2; BRW 7; BRWR 2; CA
  104; 121; CANR 131; CDBLB 1914-
  1945; DA; DA3; DAB; DAC; DAM MST,
  NOV, POET; DLB 10, 19, 36, 98, 162,
  195; EWL 3; EXPP; EXPS; LAIT 2, 3;
  MTCW 1, 2; NFS 18; PFS 6; RGEL 2;
  RGSF 2; SSFS 2, 6; TEA; WLIT 4; WP
Lawrence, T(homas) E(dward)
  1888-1935 .... **TCLC 18**
  See Dale, Colin
  See also BRWS 2; CA 115; 167; DLB 195
Lawrence of Arabia
  See Lawrence, T(homas) E(dward)
Lawson, Henry (Archibald Hertzberg)
  1867-1922 .... **SSC 18; TCLC 27**
  See also CA 120; 181; DLB 230; RGEL 2;
  RGSF 2
Lawton, Dennis
  See Faust, Frederick (Schiller)
Layamon fl. c. 1200- .... **CMLC 10**
  See Laȝamon
  See also DLB 146; RGEL 2
Laye, Camara 1928-1980 ..... **BLC 2; CLC 4, 38**
  See Camara Laye
  See also AFW; BW 1; CA 85-88; 97-100;
  CANR 25; DAM MULT; MTCW 1, 2;
  WLIT 2
Layton, Irving (Peter) 1912- .... **CLC 2, 15, 164**
  See also CA 1-4R; CANR 2, 33, 43, 66,
  129; CP 7; DAC; DAM MST, POET;
  DLB 88; EWL 3; MTCW 1, 2; PFS 12;
  RGEL 2
Lazarus, Emma 1849-1887 ...... **NCLC 8, 109**
Lazarus, Felix
  See Cable, George Washington
Lazarus, Henry
  See Slavitt, David R(ytman)
Lea, Joan
  See Neufeld, John (Arthur)
Leacock, Stephen (Butler)
  1869-1944 .... **SSC 39; TCLC 2**
  See also CA 104; 141; CANR 80; DAC;
  DAM MST; DLB 92; EWL 3; MTCW 2;
  RGEL 2; RGSF 2
Lead, Jane Ward 1623-1704 .... **LC 72**
  See also DLB 131
Leapor, Mary 1722-1746 .... **LC 80**
  See also DLB 109

Lear, Edward 1812-1888 .... **NCLC 3**
  See also AAYA 48; BRW 5; CLR 1, 75;
  DLB 32, 163, 166; MAICYA 1, 2; RGEL
  2; SATA 18, 100; WCH; WP
Lear, Norman (Milton) 1922- .... **CLC 12**
  See also CA 73-76
Leautaud, Paul 1872-1956 .... **TCLC 83**
  See also CA 203; DLB 65; GFL 1789 to the
  Present
Leavis, F(rank) R(aymond)
  1895-1978 .... **CLC 24**
  See also BRW 7; CA 21-24R; 77-80; CANR
  44; DLB 242; EWL 3; MTCW 1, 2;
  RGEL 2
Leavitt, David 1961- .... **CLC 34**
  See also CA 116; 122; CANR 50, 62, 101,
  134; CPW; DA3; DAM POP; DLB 130;
  GLL 1; INT CA-122; MTCW 2
Leblanc, Maurice (Marie Emile)
  1864-1941 .... **TCLC 49**
  See also CA 110; CMW 4
Lebowitz, Fran(ces Ann) 1951(?)- ... **CLC 11, 36**
  See also CA 81-84; CANR 14, 60, 70; INT
  CANR-14; MTCW 1
Lebrecht, Peter
  See Tieck, (Johann) Ludwig
le Carre, John .... **CLC 3, 5, 9, 15, 28**
  See Cornwell, David (John Moore)
  See also AAYA 42; BEST 89:4; BPFB 2;
  BRWS 2; CDBLB 1960 to Present; CMW
  4; CN 7; CPW; DLB 87; EWL 3; MSW;
  MTCW 2; RGEL 2; TEA
Le Clezio, J(ean) M(arie) G(ustave)
  1940- .... **CLC 31, 155**
  See also CA 116; 128; CWW 2; DLB 83;
  EWL 3; GFL 1789 to the Present; RGSF
  2
Leconte de Lisle, Charles-Marie-Rene
  1818-1894 .... **NCLC 29**
  See also DLB 217; EW 6; GFL 1789 to the
  Present
Le Coq, Monsieur
  See Simenon, Georges (Jacques Christian)
Leduc, Violette 1907-1972 .... **CLC 22**
  See also CA 13-14; 33-36R; CANR 69;
  CAP 1; EWL 3; GFL 1789 to the Present;
  GLL 1
Ledwidge, Francis 1887(?)-1917 .... **TCLC 23**
  See also CA 123; 203; DLB 20
Lee, Andrea 1953- .... **BLC 2; CLC 36**
  See also BW 1, 3; CA 125; CANR 82;
  DAM MULT
Lee, Andrew
  See Auchincloss, Louis (Stanton)
Lee, Chang-rae 1965- .... **CLC 91**
  See also CA 148; CANR 89; LATS 1:2
Lee, Don L. .... **CLC 2**
  See Madhubuti, Haki R.
Lee, George W(ashington)
  1894-1976 .... **BLC 2; CLC 52**
  See also BW 1; CA 125; CANR 83; DAM
  MULT; DLB 51
Lee, (Nelle) Harper 1926- . **CLC 12, 60, 194; WLC**
  See also AAYA 13; AMWS 8; BPFB 2;
  BYA 3; CA 13-16R; CANR 51, 128;
  CDALB 1941-1968; CSW; DA; DA3;
  DAB; DAC; DAM MST, NOV; DLB 6;
  EXPN; LAIT 3; MTCW 1, 2; NFS 2;
  SATA 11; WYA; YAW
Lee, Helen Elaine 1959(?)- .... **CLC 86**
  See also CA 148
Lee, John .... **CLC 70**
Lee, Julian
  See Latham, Jean Lee
Lee, Larry
  See Lee, Lawrence

Lee, Laurie 1914-1997 .... **CLC 90**
  See also CA 77-80; 158; CANR 33, 73; CP
  7; CPW; DAB; DAM POP; DLB 27;
  MTCW 1; RGEL 2
Lee, Lawrence 1941-1990 .... **CLC 34**
  See also CA 131; CANR 43
Lee, Li-Young 1957- .... **CLC 164; PC 24**
  See also CA 153; CANR 118; CP 7; DLB
  165; LMFS 2; PFS 11, 15, 17
Lee, Manfred B(ennington)
  1905-1971 .... **CLC 11**
  See Queen, Ellery
  See also CA 1-4R; 29-32R; CANR 2; CMW
  4; DLB 137
Lee, Nathaniel 1645(?)-1692 .... **LC 103**
  See also DLB 80; RGEL 2
Lee, Shelton Jackson 1957(?)- .. **BLCS; CLC 105**
  See Lee, Spike
  See also BW 2, 3; CA 125; CANR 42;
  DAM MULT
Lee, Spike
  See Lee, Shelton Jackson
  See also AAYA 4, 29
Lee, Stan 1922- .... **CLC 17**
  See also AAYA 5, 49; CA 108; 111; CANR
  129; INT CA-111
Lee, Tanith 1947- .... **CLC 46**
  See also AAYA 15; CA 37-40R; CANR 53,
  102; DLB 261; FANT; SATA 8, 88, 134;
  SFW 4; SUFW 1, 2; YAW
Lee, Vernon .... **SSC 33; TCLC 5**
  See Paget, Violet
  See also DLB 57, 153, 156, 174, 178; GLL
  1; SUFW 1
Lee, William
  See Burroughs, William S(eward)
  See also GLL 1
Lee, Willy
  See Burroughs, William S(eward)
  See also GLL 1
Lee-Hamilton, Eugene (Jacob)
  1845-1907 .... **TCLC 22**
  See also CA 117
Leet, Judith 1935- .... **CLC 11**
  See also CA 187
Le Fanu, Joseph Sheridan
  1814-1873 .... **NCLC 9, 58; SSC 14**
  See also CMW 4; DA3; DAM POP; DLB
  21, 70, 159, 178; HGG; RGEL 2; RGSF
  2; SUFW 1
Leffland, Ella 1931- .... **CLC 19**
  See also CA 29-32R; CANR 35, 78, 82;
  DLBY 1984; INT CANR-35; SATA 65
Leger, Alexis
  See Leger, (Marie-Rene Auguste) Alexis
  Saint-Leger
Leger, (Marie-Rene Auguste) Alexis
  Saint-Leger 1887-1975 .. **CLC 4, 11, 46; PC 23**
  See Perse, Saint-John; Saint-John Perse
  See also CA 13-16R; 61-64; CANR 43;
  DAM POET; MTCW 1
Leger, Saintleger
  See Leger, (Marie-Rene Auguste) Alexis
  Saint-Leger
Le Guin, Ursula K(roeber) 1929- ..... **CLC 8, 13, 22, 45, 71, 136; SSC 12, 69**
  See also AAYA 9, 27; AITN 1; BPFB 2;
  BYA 5, 8, 11, 14; CA 21-24R; CANR 9,
  32, 52, 74, 132; CDALB 1968-1988; CLR
  3, 28, 91; CN 7; CPW; DA3; DAB; DAC;
  DAM MST, POP; DLB 8, 52, 256, 275;
  EXPS; FANT; FW; INT CANR-32;
  JRDA; LAIT 5; MAICYA 1, 2; MTCW 1,
  2; NFS 6, 9; SATA 4, 52, 99, 149; SCFW;
  SFW 4; SSFS 2; SUFW 1, 2; WYA; YAW

Longfellow, Henry Wadsworth
1807-1882 .... **NCLC 2, 45, 101, 103; PC 30; WLCS**
See also AMW; AMWR 2; CDALB 1640-1865; CLR 99; DA; DA3; DAB; DAC; DAM MST, POET; DLB 1, 59, 235; EXPP; PAB; PFS 2, 7, 17; RGAL 4; SATA 19; TUS; WP

Longinus c. 1st cent. - .... **CMLC 27**
See also AW 2; DLB 176

Longley, Michael 1939- .... **CLC 29**
See also BRWS 8; CA 102; CP 7; DLB 40

Longus fl. c. 2nd cent. - .... **CMLC 7**

Longway, A. Hugh
See Lang, Andrew

Lonnbohm, Armas Eino Leopold 1878-1926
See Leino, Eino
See also CA 123

Lonnrot, Elias 1802-1884 .... **NCLC 53**
See also EFS 1

Lonsdale, Roger ed. .... **CLC 65**

Lopate, Phillip 1943- .... **CLC 29**
See also CA 97-100; CANR 88; DLBY 1980; INT CA-97-100

Lopez, Barry (Holstun) 1945- .... **CLC 70**
See also AAYA 9; ANW; CA 65-68; CANR 7, 23, 47, 68, 92; DLB 256, 275; INT CANR-7, -23; MTCW 1; RGAL 4; SATA 67

Lopez Portillo (y Pacheco), Jose
1920-2004 .... **CLC 46**
See also CA 129; 224; HW 1

Lopez y Fuentes, Gregorio
1897(?)-1966 .... **CLC 32**
See also CA 131; EWL 3; HW 1

Lorca, Federico Garcia
See Garcia Lorca, Federico
See also DFS 4; EW 11; PFS 20; RGWL 2, 3; WP

Lord, Audre
See Lorde, Audre (Geraldine)
See also EWL 3

Lord, Bette Bao 1938- .... **AAL; CLC 23**
See also BEST 90:3; BPFB 2; CA 107; CANR 41, 79; INT CA-107; SATA 58

Lord Auch
See Bataille, Georges

Lord Brooke
See Greville, Fulke

Lord Byron
See Byron, George Gordon (Noel)

Lorde, Audre (Geraldine)
1934-1992 .. **BLC 2; CLC 18, 71; PC 12**
See Domini, Rey; Lord, Audre
See also AFAW 1, 2; BW 1, 3; CA 25-28R; 142; CANR 16, 26, 46, 82; DA3; DAM MULT, POET; DLB 41; FW; MTCW 1, 2; PFS 16; RGAL 4

Lord Houghton
See Milnes, Richard Monckton

Lord Jeffrey
See Jeffrey, Francis

Loreaux, Nichol .... **CLC 65**

Lorenzini, Carlo 1826-1890
See Collodi, Carlo
See also MAICYA 1, 2; SATA 29, 100

Lorenzo, Heberto Padilla
See Padilla (Lorenzo), Heberto

Loris
See Hofmannsthal, Hugo von

Loti, Pierre .... **TCLC 11**
See Viaud, (Louis Marie) Julien
See also DLB 123; GFL 1789 to the Present

Lou, Henri
See Andreas-Salome, Lou

Louie, David Wong 1954- .... **CLC 70**
See also CA 139; CANR 120

Louis, Adrian C. .... **NNAL**
See also CA 223

Louis, Father M.
See Merton, Thomas (James)

Louise, Heidi
See Erdrich, Louise

Lovecraft, H(oward) P(hillips)
1890-1937 .... **SSC 3, 52; TCLC 4, 22**
See also AAYA 14; BPFB 2; CA 104; 133; CANR 106; DA3; DAM POP; HGG; MTCW 1, 2; RGAL 4; SCFW; SFW 4; SUFW

Lovelace, Earl 1935- .... **CLC 51**
See also BW 2; CA 77-80; CANR 41, 72, 114; CD 5; CDWLB 3; CN 7; DLB 125; EWL 3; MTCW 1

Lovelace, Richard 1618-1657 .... **LC 24**
See also BRW 2; DLB 131; EXPP; PAB; RGEL 2

Lowe, Pardee 1904- .... **AAL**

Lowell, Amy 1874-1925 ... **PC 13; TCLC 1, 8**
See also AAYA 57; AMW; CA 104; 151; DAM POET; DLB 54, 140; EWL 3; EXPP; LMFS 2; MAWW; MTCW 2; RGAL 4; TUS

Lowell, James Russell 1819-1891 ... **NCLC 2, 90**
See also AMWS 1; CDALB 1640-1865; DLB 1, 11, 64, 79, 189, 235; RGAL 4

Lowell, Robert (Traill Spence, Jr.)
1917-1977 .... **CLC 1, 2, 3, 4, 5, 8, 9, 11, 15, 37, 124; PC 3; WLC**
See also AMW; AMWC 2; AMWR 2; CA 9-12R; 73-76; CABS 2; CANR 26, 60; CDALBS; DA; DA3; DAB; DAC; DAM MST, NOV; DLB 5, 169; EWL 3; MTCW 1, 2; PAB; PFS 6, 7; RGAL 4; WP

Lowenthal, Michael (Francis)
1969- .... **CLC 119**
See also CA 150; CANR 115

Lowndes, Marie Adelaide (Belloc)
1868-1947 .... **TCLC 12**
See also CA 107; CMW 4; DLB 70; RHW

Lowry, (Clarence) Malcolm
1909-1957 .... **SSC 31; TCLC 6, 40**
See also BPFB 2; BRWS 3; CA 105; 131; CANR 62, 105; CDBLB 1945-1960; DLB 15; EWL 3; MTCW 1, 2; RGEL 2

Lowry, Mina Gertrude 1882-1966
See Loy, Mina
See also CA 113

Loxsmith, John
See Brunner, John (Kilian Houston)

Loy, Mina .... **CLC 28; PC 16**
See Lowry, Mina Gertrude
See also DAM POET; DLB 4, 54; PFS 20

Loyson-Bridet
See Schwob, Marcel (Mayer Andre)

Lucan 39-65 .... **CMLC 33**
See also AW 2; DLB 211; EFS 2; RGWL 2, 3

Lucas, Craig 1951- .... **CLC 64**
See also CA 137; CAD; CANR 71, 109; CD 5; GLL 2

Lucas, E(dward) V(errall)
1868-1938 .... **TCLC 73**
See also CA 176; DLB 98, 149, 153; SATA 20

Lucas, George 1944- .... **CLC 16**
See also AAYA 1, 23; CA 77-80; CANR 30; SATA 56

Lucas, Hans
See Godard, Jean-Luc

Lucas, Victoria
See Plath, Sylvia

Lucian c. 125-c. 180 .... **CMLC 32**
See also AW 2; DLB 176; RGWL 2, 3

Lucretius c. 94B.C.-c. 49B.C. .... **CMLC 48**
See also AW 2; CDWLB 1; DLB 211; EFS 2; RGWL 2, 3

Ludlam, Charles 1943-1987 .... **CLC 46, 50**
See also CA 85-88; 122; CAD; CANR 72, 86; DLB 266

Ludlum, Robert 1927-2001 .... **CLC 22, 43**
See also AAYA 10, 59; BEST 89:1, 90:3; BPFB 2; CA 33-36R; 195; CANR 25, 41, 68, 105, 131; CMW 4; CPW; DA3; DAM NOV, POP; DLBY 1982; MSW; MTCW 1, 2

Ludwig, Ken .... **CLC 60**
See also CA 195; CAD

Ludwig, Otto 1813-1865 .... **NCLC 4**
See also DLB 129

Lugones, Leopoldo 1874-1938 .... **HLCS 2; TCLC 15**
See also CA 116; 131; CANR 104; DLB 283; EWL 3; HW 1; LAW

Lu Hsun .... **SSC 20; TCLC 3**
See Shu-Jen, Chou
See also EWL 3

Lukacs, George .... **CLC 24**
See Lukacs, Gyorgy (Szegeny von)

Lukacs, Gyorgy (Szegeny von) 1885-1971
See Lukacs, George
See also CA 101; 29-32R; CANR 62; CDWLB 4; DLB 215, 242; EW 10; EWL 3; MTCW 2

Luke, Peter (Ambrose Cyprian)
1919-1995 .... **CLC 38**
See also CA 81-84; 147; CANR 72; CBD; CD 5; DLB 13

Lunar, Dennis
See Mungo, Raymond

Lurie, Alison 1926- ..... **CLC 4, 5, 18, 39, 175**
See also BPFB 2; CA 1-4R; CANR 2, 17, 50, 88; CN 7; DLB 2; MTCW 1; SATA 46, 112

Lustig, Arnost 1926- .... **CLC 56**
See also AAYA 3; CA 69-72; CANR 47, 102; CWW 2; DLB 232, 299; EWL 3; SATA 56

Luther, Martin 1483-1546 .... **LC 9, 37**
See also CDWLB 2; DLB 179; EW 2; RGWL 2, 3

Luxemburg, Rosa 1870(?)-1919 ..... **TCLC 63**
See also CA 118

Luzi, Mario 1914- .... **CLC 13**
See also CA 61-64; CANR 9, 70; CWW 2; DLB 128; EWL 3

L'vov, Arkady .... **CLC 59**

Lydgate, John c. 1370-1450(?) .... **LC 81**
See also BRW 1; DLB 146; RGEL 2

Lyly, John 1554(?)-1606 .... **DC 7; LC 41**
See also BRW 1; DAM DRAM; DLB 62, 167; RGEL 2

L'Ymagier
See Gourmont, Remy(-Marie-Charles) de

Lynch, B. Suarez
See Borges, Jorge Luis

Lynch, David (Keith) 1946- ...... **CLC 66, 162**
See also AAYA 55; CA 124; 129; CANR 111

Lynch, James
See Andreyev, Leonid (Nikolaevich)

Lyndsay, Sir David 1485-1555 .... **LC 20**
See also RGEL 2

Lynn, Kenneth S(chuyler)
1923-2001 .... **CLC 50**
See also CA 1-4R; 196; CANR 3, 27, 65

Lynx
See West, Rebecca

Lyons, Marcus
See Blish, James (Benjamin)

Lyotard, Jean-Francois
1924-1998 .... **TCLC 103**
See also DLB 242; EWL 3

Lyre, Pinchbeck
See Sassoon, Siegfried (Lorraine)

Maillet, Antonine 1929- .... **CLC 54, 118**
    See also CA 115; 120; CANR 46, 74, 77,
      134; CCA 1; CWW 2; DAC; DLB 60;
      INT CA-120; MTCW 2
Maimonides 1135-1204 .... **CMLC 76**
    See also DLB 115
Mais, Roger 1905-1955 .... **TCLC 8**
    See also BW 1, 3; CA 105; 124; CANR 82;
      CDWLB 3; DLB 125; EWL 3; MTCW 1;
      RGEL 2
Maistre, Joseph 1753-1821 .... **NCLC 37**
    See also GFL 1789 to the Present
Maitland, Frederic William
    1850-1906 .... **TCLC 65**
Maitland, Sara (Louise) 1950- .... **CLC 49**
    See also CA 69-72; CANR 13, 59; DLB
      271; FW
Major, Clarence 1936- ... **BLC 2; CLC 3, 19,**
      48
    See also AFAW 2; BW 2, 3; CA 21-24R;
      CAAS 6; CANR 13, 25, 53, 82; CN 7;
      CP 7; CSW; DAM MULT; DLB 33; EWL
      3; MSW
Major, Kevin (Gerald) 1949- .... **CLC 26**
    See also AAYA 16; CA 97-100; CANR 21,
      38, 112; CLR 11; DAC; DLB 60; INT
      CANR-21; JRDA; MAICYA 1, 2; MAIC-
      YAS 1; SATA 32, 82, 134; WYA; YAW
Maki, James
    See Ozu, Yasujiro
Makine, Andrei 1957- .... **CLC 198**
    See also CA 176; CANR 103
Malabaila, Damiano
    See Levi, Primo
Malamud, Bernard 1914-1986 .. **CLC 1, 2, 3,**
      5, 8, 9, 11, 18, 27, 44, 78, 85; SSC 15;
      TCLC 129; WLC
    See also AAYA 16; AMWS 1; BPFB 2;
      BYA 15; CA 5-8R; 118; CABS 1; CANR
      28, 62, 114; CDALB 1941-1968; CPW;
      DA; DA3; DAB; DAC; DAM MST, NOV,
      POP; DLB 2, 28, 152; DLBY 1980, 1986;
      EWL 3; EXPS; LAIT 4; LATS 1:1;
      MTCW 1, 2; NFS 4, 9; RGAL 4; RGSF
      2; SSFS 8, 13, 16; TUS
Malan, Herman
    See Bosman, Herman Charles; Bosman,
      Herman Charles
Malaparte, Curzio 1898-1957 .... **TCLC 52**
    See also DLB 264
Malcolm, Dan
    See Silverberg, Robert
Malcolm, Janet 1934- .... **CLC 201**
    See also CA 123; CANR 89; NCFS 1
Malcolm X .... **BLC 2; CLC 82, 117; WLCS**
    See Little, Malcolm
    See also LAIT 5; NCFS 3
Malherbe, Francois de 1555-1628 .... **LC 5**
    See also GFL Beginnings to 1789
Mallarme, Stephane 1842-1898 ...... **NCLC 4,**
      41; PC 4
    See also DAM POET; DLB 217; EW 7;
      GFL 1789 to the Present; LMFS 2; RGWL
      2, 3; TWA
Mallet-Joris, Francoise 1930- .... **CLC 11**
    See also CA 65-68; CANR 17; CWW 2;
      DLB 83; EWL 3; GFL 1789 to the Present
Malley, Ern
    See McAuley, James Phillip
Mallon, Thomas 1951- .... **CLC 172**
    See also CA 110; CANR 29, 57, 92
Mallowan, Agatha Christie
    See Christie, Agatha (Mary Clarissa)
Maloff, Saul 1922- .... **CLC 5**
    See also CA 33-36R
Malone, Louis
    See MacNeice, (Frederick) Louis

Malone, Michael (Christopher)
    1942- .... **CLC 43**
    See also CA 77-80; CANR 14, 32, 57, 114
Malory, Sir Thomas 1410(?)-1471(?) . **LC 11,**
      88; WLCS
    See also BRW 1; BRWR 2; CDBLB Before
      1660; DA; DAB; DAC; DAM MST; DLB
      146; EFS 2; RGEL 2; SATA 59; SATA-
      Brief 33; TEA; WLIT 3
Malouf, (George Joseph) David
    1934- .... **CLC 28, 86**
    See also CA 124; CANR 50, 76; CN 7; CP
      7; DLB 289; EWL 3; MTCW 2
Malraux, (Georges-)Andre
    1901-1976 .... **CLC 1, 4, 9, 13, 15, 57**
    See also BPFB 2; CA 21-22; 69-72; CANR
      34, 58; CAP 2; DA3; DAM NOV; DLB
      72; EW 12; EWL 3; GFL 1789 to the
      Present; MTCW 1, 2; RGWL 2, 3; TWA
Malthus, Thomas Robert
    1766-1834 .... **NCLC 145**
    See also DLB 107, 158; RGEL 2
Malzberg, Barry N(athaniel) 1939- ... **CLC 7**
    See also CA 61-64; CAAS 4; CANR 16;
      CMW 4; DLB 8; SFW 4
Mamet, David (Alan) 1947- .. **CLC 9, 15, 34,**
      46, 91, 166; DC 4, 24
    See also AAYA 3, 60; AMWS 14; CA 81-
      84; CABS 3; CANR 15, 41, 67, 72, 129;
      CD 5; DA3; DAM DRAM; DFS 2, 3, 6,
      12, 15; DLB 7; EWL 3; IDFW 4; MTCW
      1, 2; RGAL 4
Mamoulian, Rouben (Zachary)
    1897-1987 .... **CLC 16**
    See also CA 25-28R; 124; CANR 85
Mandelstam, Osip
    See Mandelstam, Osip (Emilievich)
    See also EW 10; EWL 3; RGWL 2, 3
Mandelstam, Osip (Emilievich)
    1891(?)-1943(?) .... **PC 14; TCLC 2, 6**
    See Mandelshtam, Osip
    See also CA 104; 150; MTCW 2; TWA
Mander, (Mary) Jane 1877-1949 ... **TCLC 31**
    See also CA 162; RGEL 2
Mandeville, Bernard 1670-1733 .... **LC 82**
    See also DLB 101
Mandeville, Sir John fl. 1350- ...... **CMLC 19**
    See also DLB 146
Mandiargues, Andre Pieyre de .... **CLC 41**
    See Pieyre de Mandiargues, Andre
    See also DLB 83
Mandrake, Ethel Belle
    See Thurman, Wallace (Henry)
Mangan, James Clarence
    1803-1849 .... **NCLC 27**
    See also RGEL 2
Maniere, J.-E.
    See Giraudoux, Jean(-Hippolyte)
Mankiewicz, Herman (Jacob)
    1897-1953 .... **TCLC 85**
    See also CA 120; 169; DLB 26; IDFW 3, 4
Manley, (Mary) Delariviere
    1672(?)-1724 .... **LC 1, 42**
    See also DLB 39, 80; RGEL 2
Mann, Abel
    See Creasey, John
Mann, Emily 1952- .... **DC 7**
    See also CA 130; CAD; CANR 55; CD 5;
      CWD; DLB 266
Mann, (Luiz) Heinrich 1871-1950 ... **TCLC 9**
    See also CA 106; 164, 181; DLB 66, 118;
      EW 8; EWL 3; RGWL 2, 3
Mann, (Paul) Thomas 1875-1955 . **SSC 5, 80,**
      82; TCLC 2, 8, 14, 21, 35, 44, 60;
      WLC
    See also BPFB 2; CA 104; 128; CANR 133;
      CDWLB 2; DA; DA3; DAB; DAC; DAM
      MST, NOV; DLB 66; EW 9; EWL 3; GLL

      1; LATS 1:1; LMFS 1; MTCW 1, 2; NFS
      17; RGSF 2; RGWL 2, 3; SSFS 4, 9;
      TWA
Mannheim, Karl 1893-1947 .... **TCLC 65**
    See also CA 204
Manning, David
    See Faust, Frederick (Schiller)
    See also TCWW 2
Manning, Frederic 1882-1935 .... **TCLC 25**
    See also CA 124; 216; DLB 260
Manning, Olivia 1915-1980 .... **CLC 5, 19**
    See also CA 5-8R; 101; CANR 29; EWL 3;
      FW; MTCW 1; RGEL 2
Mano, D. Keith 1942- .... **CLC 2, 10**
    See also CA 25-28R; CAAS 6; CANR 26,
      57; DLB 6
Mansfield, Katherine .... **SSC 9, 23, 38, 81;**
      TCLC 2, 8, 39, 164; WLC
    See Beauchamp, Kathleen Mansfield
    See also BPFB 2; BRW 7; DAB; DLB 162;
      EWL 3; EXPS; FW; GLL 1; RGEL 2;
      RGSF 2; SSFS 2, 8, 10, 11; WWE 1
Manso, Peter 1940- .... **CLC 39**
    See also CA 29-32R; CANR 44
Mantecon, Juan Jimenez
    See Jimenez (Mantecon), Juan Ramon
Mantel, Hilary (Mary) 1952- .... **CLC 144**
    See also CA 125; CANR 54, 101; CN 7;
      DLB 271; RHW
Manton, Peter
    See Creasey, John
Man Without a Spleen, A
    See Chekhov, Anton (Pavlovich)
Manzano, Juan Francisco
    1797(?)-1854 .... **NCLC 155**
Manzoni, Alessandro 1785-1873 ... **NCLC 29,**
      98
    See also EW 5; RGWL 2, 3; TWA
Map, Walter 1140-1209 .... **CMLC 32**
Mapu, Abraham (ben Jekutiel)
    1808-1867 .... **NCLC 18**
Mara, Sally
    See Queneau, Raymond
Maracle, Lee 1950- .... **NNAL**
    See also CA 149
Marat, Jean Paul 1743-1793 .... **LC 10**
Marcel, Gabriel Honore 1889-1973 . **CLC 15**
    See also CA 102; 45-48; EWL 3; MTCW 1,
      2
March, William 1893-1954 .... **TCLC 96**
    See also CA 216
Marchbanks, Samuel
    See Davies, (William) Robertson
    See also CCA 1
Marchi, Giacomo
    See Bassani, Giorgio
Marcus Aurelius
    See Aurelius, Marcus
    See also AW 2
Marguerite
    See de Navarre, Marguerite
Marguerite d'Angouleme
    See de Navarre, Marguerite
    See also GFL Beginnings to 1789
Marguerite de Navarre
    See de Navarre, Marguerite
    See also RGWL 2, 3
Margulies, Donald 1954- .... **CLC 76**
    See also AAYA 57; CA 200; DFS 13; DLB
      228
Marie de France c. 12th cent. - ..... **CMLC 8;**
      PC 22
    See also DLB 208; FW; RGWL 2, 3
Marie de l'Incarnation 1599-1672 ...... **LC 10**
Marier, Captain Victor
    See Griffith, D(avid Lewelyn) W(ark)
Mariner, Scott
    See Pohl, Frederik

Merimee, Prosper 1803-1870 ... **NCLC 6, 65; SSC 7, 77**
See also DLB 119, 192; EW 6; EXPS; GFL 1789 to the Present; RGSF 2; RGWL 2, 3; SSFS 8; SUFW

Merkin, Daphne 1954- .... **CLC 44**
See also CA 123

Merleau-Ponty, Maurice
1908-1961 .... **TCLC 156**
See also CA 114; 89-92; DLB 296; GFL 1789 to the Present

Merlin, Arthur
See Blish, James (Benjamin)

Mernissi, Fatima 1940- .... **CLC 171**
See also CA 152; FW

Merrill, James (Ingram) 1926-1995 .. **CLC 2, 3, 6, 8, 13, 18, 34, 91; PC 28**
See also AMWS 3; CA 13-16R; 147; CANR 10, 49, 63, 108; DA3; DAM POET; DLB 5, 165; DLBY 1985; EWL 3; INT CANR-10; MTCW 1, 2; PAB; RGAL 4

Merriman, Alex
See Silverberg, Robert

Merriman, Brian 1747-1805 .... **NCLC 70**

Merritt, E. B.
See Waddington, Miriam

Merton, Thomas (James)
1915-1968 . **CLC 1, 3, 11, 34, 83; PC 10**
See also AMWS 8; CA 5-8R; 25-28R; CANR 22, 53, 111, 131; DA3; DLB 48; DLBY 1981; MTCW 1, 2

Merwin, W(illiam) S(tanley) 1927- ... **CLC 1, 2, 3, 5, 8, 13, 18, 45, 88; PC 45**
See also AMWS 3; CA 13-16R; CANR 15, 51, 112; CP 7; DA3; DAM POET; DLB 5, 169; EWL 3; INT CANR-15; MTCW 1, 2; PAB; PFS 5, 15; RGAL 4

Metastasio, Pietro 1698-1782 .... **LC 115**
See also RGWL 2, 3

Metcalf, John 1938- .... **CLC 37; SSC 43**
See also CA 113; CN 7; DLB 60; RGSF 2; TWA

Metcalf, Suzanne
See Baum, L(yman) Frank

Mew, Charlotte (Mary) 1870-1928 .. **TCLC 8**
See also CA 105; 189; DLB 19, 135; RGEL 2

Mewshaw, Michael 1943- .... **CLC 9**
See also CA 53-56; CANR 7, 47; DLBY 1980

Meyer, Conrad Ferdinand
1825-1898 .... **NCLC 81; SSC 30**
See also DLB 129; EW; RGWL 2, 3

Meyer, Gustav 1868-1932
See Meyrink, Gustav
See also CA 117; 190

Meyer, June
See Jordan, June (Meyer)

Meyer, Lynn
See Slavitt, David R(ytman)

Meyers, Jeffrey 1939- .... **CLC 39**
See also CA 73-76, 186; CAAE 186; CANR 54, 102; DLB 111

Meynell, Alice (Christina Gertrude Thompson) 1847-1922 .... **TCLC 6**
See also CA 104; 177; DLB 19, 98; RGEL 2

Meyrink, Gustav .... **TCLC 21**
See Meyer, Gustav
See also DLB 81; EWL 3

Michaels, Leonard 1933-2003 ..... **CLC 6, 25; SSC 16**
See also CA 61-64; 216; CANR 21, 62, 119; CN 7; DLB 130; MTCW 1

Michaux, Henri 1899-1984 .... **CLC 8, 19**
See also CA 85-88; 114; DLB 258; EWL 3; GFL 1789 to the Present; RGWL 2, 3

Micheaux, Oscar (Devereaux)
1884-1951 .... **TCLC 76**
See also BW 3; CA 174; DLB 50; TCWW 2

Michelangelo 1475-1564 .... **LC 12**
See also AAYA 43

Michelet, Jules 1798-1874 .... **NCLC 31**
See also EW 5; GFL 1789 to the Present

Michels, Robert 1876-1936 .... **TCLC 88**
See also CA 212

Michener, James A(lbert)
1907(?)-1997 .. **CLC 1, 5, 11, 29, 60, 109**
See also AAYA 27; AITN 1; BEST 90:1; BPFB 2; CA 5-8R; 161; CANR 21, 45, 68; CN 7; CPW; DA3; DAM NOV, POP; DLB 6; MTCW 1, 2; RHW

Mickiewicz, Adam 1798-1855 . **NCLC 3, 101; PC 38**
See also EW 5; RGWL 2, 3

Middleton, (John) Christopher
1926- .... **CLC 13**
See also CA 13-16R; CANR 29, 54, 117; CP 7; DLB 40

Middleton, Richard (Barham)
1882-1911 .... **TCLC 56**
See also CA 187; DLB 156; HGG

Middleton, Stanley 1919- .... **CLC 7, 38**
See also CA 25-28R; CAAS 23; CANR 21, 46, 81; CN 7; DLB 14

Middleton, Thomas 1580-1627 ...... **DC 5; LC 33**
See also BRW 2; DAM DRAM, MST; DFS 18; DLB 58; RGEL 2

Migueis, Jose Rodrigues 1901-1980 . **CLC 10**
See also DLB 287

Mikszath, Kalman 1847-1910 .... **TCLC 31**
See also CA 170

Miles, Jack .... **CLC 100**
See also CA 200

Miles, John Russiano
See Miles, Jack

Miles, Josephine (Louise)
1911-1985 .... **CLC 1, 2, 14, 34, 39**
See also CA 1-4R; 116; CANR 2, 55; DAM POET; DLB 48

Militant
See Sandburg, Carl (August)

Mill, Harriet (Hardy) Taylor
1807-1858 .... **NCLC 102**
See also FW

Mill, John Stuart 1806-1873 .... **NCLC 11, 58**
See also CDBLB 1832-1890; DLB 55, 190, 262; FW 1; RGEL 2; TEA

Millar, Kenneth 1915-1983 .... **CLC 14**
See Macdonald, Ross
See also CA 9-12R; 110; CANR 16, 63, 107; CMW 4; CPW; DA3; DAM POP; DLB 2, 226; DLBD 6; DLBY 1983; MTCW 1, 2

Millay, E. Vincent
See Millay, Edna St. Vincent

Millay, Edna St. Vincent 1892-1950 ..... **PC 6, 61; TCLC 4, 49; WLCS**
See Boyd, Nancy
See also AMW; CA 104; 130; CDALB 1917-1929; DA; DA3; DAB; DAC; DAM MST, POET; DLB 45, 249; EWL 3; EXPP; MAWW; MTCW 1, 2; PAB; PFS 3, 17; RGAL 4; TUS; WP

Miller, Arthur 1915- ...... **CLC 1, 2, 6, 10, 15, 26, 47, 78, 179; DC 1; WLC**
See also AAYA 15; AITN 1; AMW; AMWC 1; CA 1-4R; CABS 3; CAD; CANR 2, 30, 54, 76, 132; CD 5; CDALB 1941-1968; DA; DA3; DAB; DAC; DAM DRAM, MST; DFS 1, 3, 8; DLB 7, 266; EWL 3; LAIT 1, 4; LATS 1:2; MTCW 1, 2; RGAL 4; TUS; WYAS 1

Miller, Henry (Valentine)
1891-1980 .... **CLC 1, 2, 4, 9, 14, 43, 84; WLC**
See also AMW; BPFB 2; CA 9-12R; 97-100; CANR 33, 64; CDALB 1929-1941; DA; DA3; DAB; DAC; DAM MST, NOV; DLB 4, 9; DLBY 1980; EWL 3; MTCW 1, 2; RGAL 4; TUS

Miller, Hugh 1802-1856 .... **NCLC 143**
See also DLB 190

Miller, Jason 1939(?)-2001 .... **CLC 2**
See also AITN 1; CA 73-76; 197; CAD; CANR 130; DFS 12; DLB 7

Miller, Sue 1943- .... **CLC 44**
See also AMWS 12; BEST 90:3; CA 139; CANR 59, 91, 128; DA3; DAM POP; DLB 143

Miller, Walter M(ichael, Jr.)
1923-1996 .... **CLC 4, 30**
See also BPFB 2; CA 85-88; CANR 108; DLB 8; SCFW; SFW 4

Millett, Kate 1934- .... **CLC 67**
See also AITN 1; CA 73-76; CANR 32, 53, 76, 110; DA3; DLB 246; FW; GLL 1; MTCW 1, 2

Millhauser, Steven (Lewis) 1943- .... **CLC 21, 54, 109; SSC 57**
See also CA 110; 111; CANR 63, 114, 133; CN 7; DA3; DLB 2; FANT; INT CA-111; MTCW 2

Millin, Sarah Gertrude 1889-1968 ... **CLC 49**
See also CA 102; 93-96; DLB 225; EWL 3

Milne, A(lan) A(lexander)
1882-1956 .... **TCLC 6, 88**
See also BRWS 5; CA 104; 133; CLR 1, 26; CMW 4; CWRI 5; DA3; DAB; DAC; DAM MST; DLB 10, 77, 100, 160; FANT; MAICYA 1, 2; MTCW 1, 2; RGEL 2; SATA 100; WCH; YABC 1

Milner, Ron(ald) 1938-2004 ..... **BLC 3; CLC 56**
See also AITN 1; BW 1; CA 73-76; CAD; CANR 24, 81; CD 5; DAM MULT; DLB 38; MTCW 1

Milnes, Richard Monckton
1809-1885 .... **NCLC 61**
See also DLB 32, 184

Milosz, Czeslaw 1911- ...... **CLC 5, 11, 22, 31, 56, 82; PC 8; WLCS**
See also CA 81-84; CANR 23, 51, 91, 126; CDWLB 4; CWW 2; DA3; DAM MST, POET; DLB 215; EW 13; EWL 3; MTCW 1, 2; PFS 16; RGWL 2, 3

Milton, John 1608-1674 ..... **LC 9, 43, 92; PC 19, 29; WLC**
See also BRW 2; BRWR 2; CDBLB 1660-1789; DA; DA3; DAB; DAC; DAM MST, POET; DLB 131, 151, 281; EFS 1; EXPP; LAIT 1; PAB; PFS 3, 17; RGEL 2; TEA; WLIT 3; WP

Min, Anchee 1957- .... **CLC 86**
See also CA 146; CANR 94

Minehaha, Cornelius
See Wedekind, (Benjamin) Frank(lin)

Miner, Valerie 1947- .... **CLC 40**
See also CA 97-100; CANR 59; FW; GLL 2

Minimo, Duca
See D'Annunzio, Gabriele

Minot, Susan 1956- .... **CLC 44, 159**
See also AMWS 6; CA 134; CANR 118; CN 7

Minus, Ed 1938- .... **CLC 39**
See also CA 185

Mirabai 1498(?)-1550(?) .... **PC 48**

Miranda, Javier
See Bioy Casares, Adolfo
See also CWW 2

Moore, Marianne (Craig)
1887-1972 .... **CLC 1, 2, 4, 8, 10, 13, 19, 47; PC 4, 49; WLCS**
See also AMW; CA 1-4R; 33-36R; CANR 3, 61; CDALB 1929-1941; DA; DA3; DAB; DAC; DAM MST, POET; DLB 45; DLBD 7; EWL 3; EXPP; MAWW; MTCW 1, 2; PAB; PFS 14, 17; RGAL 4; SATA 20; TUS; WP

Moore, Marie Lorena 1957- .... **CLC 165**
See Moore, Lorrie
See also CA 116; CANR 39, 83; CN 7; DLB 234

Moore, Thomas 1779-1852 .... **NCLC 6, 110**
See also DLB 96, 144; RGEL 2

Moorhouse, Frank 1938- .... **SSC 40**
See also CA 118; CANR 92; CN 7; DLB 289; RGSF 2

Mora, Pat(ricia) 1942- .... **HLC 2**
See also AMWS 13; CA 129; CANR 57, 81, 112; CLR 58; DAM MULT; DLB 209; HW 1, 2; LLW 1; MAICYA 2; SATA 92, 134

Moraga, Cherrie 1952- ...... **CLC 126; DC 22**
See also CA 131; CANR 66; DAM MULT; DLB 82, 249; FW; GLL 1; HW 1, 2; LLW 1

Morand, Paul 1888-1976 .... **CLC 41; SSC 22**
See also CA 184; 69-72; DLB 65; EWL 3

Morante, Elsa 1918-1985 .... **CLC 8, 47**
See also CA 85-88; 117; CANR 35; DLB 177; EWL 3; MTCW 1, 2; RGWL 2, 3

Moravia, Alberto .... **CLC 2, 7, 11, 27, 46; SSC 26**
See Pincherle, Alberto
See also DLB 177; EW 12; EWL 3; MTCW 2; RGSF 2; RGWL 2, 3

More, Hannah 1745-1833 ...... **NCLC 27, 141**
See also DLB 107, 109, 116, 158; RGEL 2

More, Henry 1614-1687 .... **LC 9**
See also DLB 126, 252

More, Sir Thomas 1478(?)-1535 .... **LC 10, 32**
See also BRWC 1; BRWS 7; DLB 136, 281; LMFS 1; RGEL 2; TEA

Moreas, Jean .... **TCLC 18**
See Papadiamantopoulos, Johannes
See also GFL 1789 to the Present

Moreton, Andrew Esq.
See Defoe, Daniel

Morgan, Berry 1919-2002 .... **CLC 6**
See also CA 49-52; 208; DLB 6

Morgan, Claire
See Highsmith, (Mary) Patricia
See also GLL 1

Morgan, Edwin (George) 1920- .... **CLC 31**
See also BRWS 9; CA 5-8R; CANR 3, 43, 90; CP 7; DLB 27

Morgan, (George) Frederick
1922-2004 .... **CLC 23**
See also CA 17-20R; 224; CANR 21; CP 7

Morgan, Harriet
See Mencken, H(enry) L(ouis)

Morgan, Jane
See Cooper, James Fenimore

Morgan, Janet 1945- .... **CLC 39**
See also CA 65-68

Morgan, Lady 1776(?)-1859 .... **NCLC 29**
See also DLB 116, 158; RGEL 2

Morgan, Robin (Evonne) 1941- .... **CLC 2**
See also CA 69-72; CANR 29, 68; FW; GLL 2; MTCW 1; SATA 80

Morgan, Scott
See Kuttner, Henry

Morgan, Seth 1949(?)-1990 .... **CLC 65**
See also CA 185; 132

Morgenstern, Christian (Otto Josef Wolfgang) 1871-1914 .... **TCLC 8**
See also CA 105; 191; EWL 3

Morgenstern, S.
See Goldman, William (W.)

Mori, Rintaro
See Mori Ogai
See also CA 110

Mori, Toshio 1910-1980 .... **SSC 83**
See also AAL; CA 116; DLB 312; RGSF 2

Moricz, Zsigmond 1879-1942 .... **TCLC 33**
See also CA 165; DLB 215; EWL 3

Morike, Eduard (Friedrich)
1804-1875 .... **NCLC 10**
See also DLB 133; RGWL 2, 3

Mori Ogai 1862-1922 .... **TCLC 14**
See Ogai
See also CA 164; DLB 180; EWL 3; RGWL 3; TWA

Moritz, Karl Philipp 1756-1793 .... **LC 2**
See also DLB 94

Morland, Peter Henry
See Faust, Frederick (Schiller)

Morley, Christopher (Darlington)
1890-1957 .... **TCLC 87**
See also CA 112; 213; DLB 9; RGAL 4

Morren, Theophil
See Hofmannsthal, Hugo von

Morris, Bill 1952- .... **CLC 76**
See also CA 225

Morris, Julian
See West, Morris L(anglo)

Morris, Steveland Judkins 1950(?)-
See Wonder, Stevie
See also CA 111

Morris, William 1834-1896 . **NCLC 4; PC 55**
See also BRW 5; CDBLB 1832-1890; DLB 18, 35, 57, 156, 178, 184; FANT; RGEL 2; SFW 4; SUFW

Morris, Wright 1910-1998 .. **CLC 1, 3, 7, 18, 37; TCLC 107**
See also AMW; CA 9-12R; 167; CANR 21, 81; CN 7; DLB 2, 206, 218; DLBY 1981; EWL 3; MTCW 1, 2; RGAL 4; TCWW 2

Morrison, Arthur 1863-1945 .... **SSC 40; TCLC 72**
See also CA 120; 157; CMW 4; DLB 70, 135, 197; RGEL 2

Morrison, Chloe Anthony Wofford
See Morrison, Toni

Morrison, James Douglas 1943-1971
See Morrison, Jim
See also CA 73-76; CANR 40

Morrison, Jim .... **CLC 17**
See Morrison, James Douglas

Morrison, Toni 1931- .... **BLC 3; CLC 4, 10, 22, 55, 81, 87, 173, 194**
See also AAYA 1, 22; AFAW 1, 2; AMWC 1; AMWS 3; BPFB 2; BW 2, 3; CA 29-32R; CANR 27, 42, 67, 113, 124; CDALB 1968-1988; CLR 99; CN 7; CPW; DA; DA3; DAB; DAC; DAM MST, MULT, NOV, POP; DLB 6, 33, 143; DLBY 1981; EWL 3; EXPN; FW; LAIT 2, 4; LATS 1:2; LMFS 2; MAWW; MTCW 1, 2; NFS 1, 6, 8, 14; RGAL 4; RHW; SATA 57, 144; SSFS 5; TUS; YAW

Morrison, Van 1945- .... **CLC 21**
See also CA 116; 168

Morrissy, Mary 1957- .... **CLC 99**
See also CA 205; DLB 267

Mortimer, John (Clifford) 1923- ..... **CLC 28, 43**
See also CA 13-16R; CANR 21, 69, 109; CD 5; CDBLB 1960 to Present; CMW 4; CN 7; CPW; DA3; DAM DRAM, POP; DLB 13, 245, 271; INT CANR-21; MSW; MTCW 1, 2; RGEL 2

Mortimer, Penelope (Ruth)
1918-1999 .... **CLC 5**
See also CA 57-60; 187; CANR 45, 88; CN 7

Mortimer, Sir John
See Mortimer, John (Clifford)

Morton, Anthony
See Creasey, John

Morton, Thomas 1579(?)-1647(?) .... **LC 72**
See also DLB 24; RGEL 2

Mosca, Gaetano 1858-1941 .... **TCLC 75**

Moses, Daniel David 1952- .... **NNAL**
See also CA 186

Mosher, Howard Frank 1943- .... **CLC 62**
See also CA 139; CANR 65, 115

Mosley, Nicholas 1923- .... **CLC 43, 70**
See also CA 69-72; CANR 41, 60, 108; CN 7; DLB 14, 207

Mosley, Walter 1952- .... **BLCS; CLC 97, 184**
See also AAYA 57; AMWS 13; BPFB 2; BW 2; CA 142; CANR 57, 92; CMW 4; CPW; DA3; DAM MULT, POP; DLB 306; MSW; MTCW 2

Moss, Howard 1922-1987 . **CLC 7, 14, 45, 50**
See also CA 1-4R; 123; CANR 1, 44; DAM POET; DLB 5

Mossgiel, Rab
See Burns, Robert

Motion, Andrew (Peter) 1952- .... **CLC 47**
See also BRWS 7; CA 146; CANR 90; CP 7; DLB 40

Motley, Willard (Francis)
1909-1965 .... **CLC 18**
See also BW 1; CA 117; 106; CANR 88; DLB 76, 143

Motoori, Norinaga 1730-1801 .... **NCLC 45**

Mott, Michael (Charles Alston)
1930- .... **CLC 15, 34**
See also CA 5-8R; CAAS 7; CANR 7, 29

Mountain Wolf Woman 1884-1960 . **CLC 92; NNAL**
See also CA 144; CANR 90

Moure, Erin 1955- .... **CLC 88**
See also CA 113; CP 7; CWP; DLB 60

Mourning Dove 1885(?)-1936 .... **NNAL**
See also CA 144; CANR 90; DAM MULT; DLB 175, 221

Mowat, Farley (McGill) 1921- .... **CLC 26**
See also AAYA 1, 50; BYA 2; CA 1-4R; CANR 4, 24, 42, 68, 108; CLR 20; CPW; DAC; DAM MST; DLB 68; INT CANR-24; JRDA; MAICYA 1, 2; MTCW 1, 2; SATA 3, 55; YAW

Mowatt, Anna Cora 1819-1870 ..... **NCLC 74**
See also RGAL 4

Moyers, Bill 1934- .... **CLC 74**
See also AITN 2; CA 61-64; CANR 31, 52

Mphahlele, Es'kia
See Mphahlele, Ezekiel
See also AFW; CDWLB 3; DLB 125, 225; RGSF 2; SSFS 11

Mphahlele, Ezekiel 1919- ... **BLC 3; CLC 25, 133**
See Mphahlele, Es'kia
See also BW 2, 3; CA 81-84; CANR 26, 76; CN 7; DA3; DAM MULT; EWL 3; MTCW 2; SATA 119

Mqhayi, S(amuel) E(dward) K(rune Loliwe)
1875-1945 .... **BLC 3; TCLC 25**
See also CA 153; CANR 87; DAM MULT

Mrozek, Slawomir 1930- .... **CLC 3, 13**
See also CA 13-16R; CAAS 10; CANR 29; CDWLB 4; CWW 2; DLB 232; EWL 3; MTCW 1

Mrs. Belloc-Lowndes
See Lowndes, Marie Adelaide (Belloc)

Mrs. Fairstar
See Horne, Richard Henry Hengist

M'Taggart, John M'Taggart Ellis
See McTaggart, John McTaggart Ellis

MST, MULT, NOV, POP; DLB 173; EWL 3; FW; MTCW 1, 2; NFS 4, 7; RGAL 4; TUS

Neff, Debra .... **CLC 59**

Neihardt, John Gneisenau
1881-1973 .... **CLC 32**
See also CA 13-14; CANR 65; CAP 1; DLB 9, 54, 256; LAIT 2

Nekrasov, Nikolai Alekseevich
1821-1878 .... **NCLC 11**
See also DLB 277

Nelligan, Emile 1879-1941 .... **TCLC 14**
See also CA 114; 204; DLB 92; EWL 3

Nelson, Willie 1933- .... **CLC 17**
See also CA 107; CANR 114

Nemerov, Howard (Stanley)
1920-1991 .... **CLC 2, 6, 9, 36; PC 24; TCLC 124**
See also AMW; CA 1-4R; 134; CABS 2; CANR 1, 27, 53; DAM POET; DLB 5, 6; DLBY 1983; EWL 3; INT CANR-27; MTCW 1, 2; PFS 10, 14; RGAL 4

Neruda, Pablo 1904-1973 .. **CLC 1, 2, 5, 7, 9, 28, 62; HLC 2; PC 4, 64; WLC**
See also CA 19-20; 45-48; CANR 131; CAP 2; DA; DA3; DAB; DAC; DAM MST, MULT, POET; DLB 283; DNFS 2; EWL 3; HW 1; LAW; MTCW 1, 2; PFS 11; RGWL 2, 3; TWA; WLIT 1; WP

Nerval, Gerard de 1808-1855 ... **NCLC 1, 67; PC 13; SSC 18**
See also DLB 217; EW 6; GFL 1789 to the Present; RGSF 2; RGWL 2, 3

Nervo, (Jose) Amado (Ruiz de)
1870-1919 .... **HLCS 2; TCLC 11**
See also CA 109; 131; DLB 290; EWL 3; HW 1; LAW

Nesbit, Malcolm
See Chester, Alfred

Nessi, Pio Baroja y
See Baroja (y Nessi), Pio

Nestroy, Johann 1801-1862 .... **NCLC 42**
See also DLB 133; RGWL 2, 3

Netterville, Luke
See O'Grady, Standish (James)

Neufeld, John (Arthur) 1938- .... **CLC 17**
See also AAYA 11; CA 25-28R; CANR 11, 37, 56; CLR 52; MAICYA 1, 2; SAAS 3; SATA 6, 81, 131; SATA-Essay 131; YAW

Neumann, Alfred 1895-1952 .... **TCLC 100**
See also CA 183; DLB 56

Neumann, Ferenc
See Molnar, Ferenc

Neville, Emily Cheney 1919- .... **CLC 12**
See also BYA 2; CA 5-8R; CANR 3, 37, 85; JRDA; MAICYA 1, 2; SAAS 2; SATA 1; YAW

Newbound, Bernard Slade 1930-
See Slade, Bernard
See also CA 81-84; CANR 49; CD 5; DAM DRAM

Newby, P(ercy) H(oward)
1918-1997 .... **CLC 2, 13**
See also CA 5-8R; 161; CANR 32, 67; CN 7; DAM NOV; DLB 15; MTCW 1; RGEL 2

Newcastle
See Cavendish, Margaret Lucas

Newlove, Donald 1928- .... **CLC 6**
See also CA 29-32R; CANR 25

Newlove, John (Herbert) 1938- .... **CLC 14**
See also CA 21-24R; CANR 9, 25; CP 7

Newman, Charles 1938- .... **CLC 2, 8**
See also CA 21-24R; CANR 84; CN 7

Newman, Edwin (Harold) 1919- ...... **CLC 14**
See also AITN 1; CA 69-72; CANR 5

Newman, John Henry 1801-1890 . **NCLC 38, 99**
See also BRWS 7; DLB 18, 32, 55; RGEL 2

Newton, (Sir) Isaac 1642-1727 ...... **LC 35, 53**
See also DLB 252

Newton, Suzanne 1936- .... **CLC 35**
See also BYA 7; CA 41-44R; CANR 14; JRDA; SATA 5, 77

New York Dept. of Ed. .... **CLC 70**

Nexo, Martin Andersen
1869-1954 .... **TCLC 43**
See also CA 202; DLB 214; EWL 3

Nezval, Vitezslav 1900-1958 .... **TCLC 44**
See also CA 123; CDWLB 4; DLB 215; EWL 3

Ng, Fae Myenne 1957(?)- .... **CLC 81**
See also BYA 11; CA 146

Ngema, Mbongeni 1955- .... **CLC 57**
See also BW 2; CA 143; CANR 84; CD 5

Ngugi, James T(hiong'o) . **CLC 3, 7, 13, 182**
See Ngugi wa Thiong'o

Ngugi wa Thiong'o
See Ngugi wa Thiong'o
See also DLB 125; EWL 3

Ngugi wa Thiong'o 1938- ... **BLC 3; CLC 36, 182**
See also Ngugi, James T(hiong'o); Ngugi wa Thiong'o
See also AFW; BRWS 8; BW 2; CA 81-84; CANR 27, 58; CDWLB 3; DAM MULT, NOV; DNFS 2; MTCW 1, 2; RGEL 2; WWE 1

Niatum, Duane 1938- .... **NNAL**
See also CA 41-44R; CANR 21, 45, 83; DLB 175

Nichol, B(arrie) P(hillip) 1944-1988 . **CLC 18**
See also CA 53-56; DLB 53; SATA 66

Nicholas of Cusa 1401-1464 .... **LC 80**
See also DLB 115

Nichols, John (Treadwell) 1940- .... **CLC 38**
See also AMWS 13; CA 9-12R, 190; CAAE 190; CAAS 2; CANR 6, 70, 121; DLBY 1982; LATS 1:2; TCWW 2

Nichols, Leigh
See Koontz, Dean R(ay)

Nichols, Peter (Richard) 1927- .... **CLC 5, 36, 65**
See also CA 104; CANR 33, 86; CBD; CD 5; DLB 13, 245; MTCW 1

Nicholson, Linda ed. .... **CLC 65**

Ni Chuilleanain, Eilean 1942- .... **PC 34**
See also CA 126; CANR 53, 83; CP 7; CWP; DLB 40

Nicolas, F. R. E.
See Freeling, Nicolas

Niedecker, Lorine 1903-1970 ..... **CLC 10, 42; PC 42**
See also CA 25-28; CAP 2; DAM POET; DLB 48

Nietzsche, Friedrich (Wilhelm)
1844-1900 .... **TCLC 10, 18, 55**
See also CA 107; 121; CDWLB 2; DLB 129; EW 7; RGWL 2, 3; TWA

Nievo, Ippolito 1831-1861 .... **NCLC 22**

Nightingale, Anne Redmon 1943-
See Redmon, Anne
See also CA 103

Nightingale, Florence 1820-1910 ... **TCLC 85**
See also CA 188; DLB 166

Nijo Yoshimoto 1320-1388 .... **CMLC 49**
See also DLB 203

Nik. T. O.
See Annensky, Innokenty (Fyodorovich)

Nin, Anais 1903-1977 ..... **CLC 1, 4, 8, 11, 14, 60, 127; SSC 10**
See also AITN 2; AMWS 10; BPFB 2; CA 13-16R; 69-72; CANR 22, 53; DAM

NOV, POP; DLB 2, 4, 152; EWL 3; GLL 2; MAWW; MTCW 1, 2; RGAL 4; RGSF 2

Nisbet, Robert A(lexander)
1913-1996 .... **TCLC 117**
See also CA 25-28R; 153; CANR 17; INT CANR-17

Nishida, Kitaro 1870-1945 .... **TCLC 83**

Nishiwaki, Junzaburo
See Nishiwaki, Junzaburo
See also CA 194

Nishiwaki, Junzaburo 1894-1982 .... **PC 15**
See Nishiwaki, Junzaburo; Nishiwaki Junzaburo
See also CA 194; 107; MJW; RGWL 3

Nishiwaki Junzaburo
See Nishiwaki, Junzaburo
See also EWL 3

Nissenson, Hugh 1933- .... **CLC 4, 9**
See also CA 17-20R; CANR 27, 108; CN 7; DLB 28

Nister, Der
See Der Nister
See also EWL 3

Niven, Larry .... **CLC 8**
See Niven, Laurence Van Cott
See also AAYA 27; BPFB 2; BYA 10; DLB 8; SCFW 2

Niven, Laurence Van Cott 1938-
See Niven, Larry
See also CA 21-24R, 207; CAAE 207; CAAS 12; CANR 14, 44, 66, 113; CPW; DAM POP; MTCW 1, 2; SATA 95; SFW 4

Nixon, Agnes Eckhardt 1927- .... **CLC 21**
See also CA 110

Nizan, Paul 1905-1940 .... **TCLC 40**
See also CA 161; DLB 72; EWL 3; GFL 1789 to the Present

Nkosi, Lewis 1936- .... **BLC 3; CLC 45**
See also BW 1, 3; CA 65-68; CANR 27, 81; CBD; CD 5; DAM MULT; DLB 157, 225; WWE 1

Nodier, (Jean) Charles (Emmanuel)
1780-1844 .... **NCLC 19**
See also DLB 119; GFL 1789 to the Present

Noguchi, Yone 1875-1947 .... **TCLC 80**

Nolan, Christopher 1965- .... **CLC 58**
See also CA 111; CANR 88

Noon, Jeff 1957- .... **CLC 91**
See also CA 148; CANR 83; DLB 267; SFW 4

Norden, Charles
See Durrell, Lawrence (George)

Nordhoff, Charles Bernard
1887-1947 .... **TCLC 23**
See also CA 108; 211; DLB 9; LAIT 1; RHW 1; SATA 23

Norfolk, Lawrence 1963- .... **CLC 76**
See also CA 144; CANR 85; CN 7; DLB 267

Norman, Marsha 1947- . **CLC 28, 186; DC 8**
See also CA 105; CABS 3; CAD; CANR 41, 131; CD 5; CSW; CWD; DAM DRAM; DFS 2; DLB 266; DLBY 1984; FW

Normyx
See Douglas, (George) Norman

Norris, (Benjamin) Frank(lin, Jr.)
1870-1902 .... **SSC 28; TCLC 24, 155**
See also AAYA 57; AMW; AMWC 2; BPFB 2; CA 110; 160; CDALB 1865-1917; DLB 12, 71, 186; LMFS 2; NFS 12; RGAL 4; TCWW 2; TUS

Norris, Leslie 1921- .... **CLC 14**
See also CA 11-12; CANR 14, 117; CAP 1; CP 7; DLB 27, 256

North, Andrew
See Norton, Andre

Pabst, G. W. 1885-1967 .... **TCLC 127**
Pacheco, C.
　See Pessoa, Fernando (Antonio Nogueira)
Pacheco, Jose Emilio 1939- .... **HLC 2**
　See also CA 111; 131; CANR 65; CWW 2;
　DAM MULT; DLB 290; EWL 3; HW 1,
　2; RGSF 2
Pa Chin .... **CLC 18**
　See Li Fei-kan
　See also EWL 3
Pack, Robert 1929- .... **CLC 13**
　See also CA 1-4R; CANR 3, 44, 82; CP 7;
　DLB 5; SATA 118
Padgett, Lewis
　See Kuttner, Henry
Padilla (Lorenzo), Heberto
　1932-2000 .... **CLC 38**
　See also AITN 1; CA 123; 131; 189; CWW
　2; EWL 3; HW 1
Page, James Patrick 1944-
　See Page, Jimmy
　See also CA 204
Page, Jimmy 1944- .... **CLC 12**
　See Page, James Patrick
Page, Louise 1955- .... **CLC 40**
　See also CA 140; CANR 76; CBD; CD 5;
　CWD; DLB 233
Page, P(atricia) K(athleen) 1916- ...... **CLC 7,**
　18; PC 12
　See Cape, Judith
　See also CA 53-56; CANR 4, 22, 65; CP 7;
　DAC; DAM MST; DLB 68; MTCW 1;
　RGEL 2
Page, Stanton
　See Fuller, Henry Blake
Page, Stanton
　See Fuller, Henry Blake
Page, Thomas Nelson 1853-1922 .... **SSC 23**
　See also CA 118; 177; DLB 12, 78; DLBD
　13; RGAL 4
Pagels, Elaine Hiesey 1943- .... **CLC 104**
　See also CA 45-48; CANR 2, 24, 51; FW;
　NCFS 4
Paget, Violet 1856-1935
　See Lee, Vernon
　See also CA 104; 166; GLL 1; HGG
Paget-Lowe, Henry
　See Lovecraft, H(oward) P(hillips)
Paglia, Camille (Anna) 1947- .... **CLC 68**
　See also CA 140; CANR 72; CPW; FW;
　GLL 2; MTCW 2
Paige, Richard
　See Koontz, Dean R(ay)
Paine, Thomas 1737-1809 .... **NCLC 62**
　See also AMWS 1; CDALB 1640-1865;
　DLB 31, 43, 73, 158; LAIT 1; RGAL 4;
　RGEL 2; TUS
Pakenham, Antonia
　See Fraser, Antonia (Pakenham)
Palamas, Costis
　See Palamas, Kostes
Palamas, Kostes 1859-1943 .... **TCLC 5**
　See Palamas, Kostis
　See also CA 105; 190; RGWL 2, 3
Palamas, Kostis
　See Palamas, Kostes
　See also EWL 3
Palazzeschi, Aldo 1885-1974 .... **CLC 11**
　See also CA 89-92; 53-56; DLB 114, 264;
　EWL 3
Pales Matos, Luis 1898-1959 .... **HLCS 2**
　See Pales Matos, Luis
　See also DLB 290; HW 1; LAW
Paley, Grace 1922- .. **CLC 4, 6, 37, 140; SSC**
　8
　See also AMWS 6; CA 25-28R; CANR 13,
　46, 74, 118; CN 7; CPW; DA3; DAM
　POP; DLB 28, 218; EWL 3; EXPS; FW;

INT CANR-13; MAWW; MTCW 1, 2;
　RGAL 4; RGSF 2; SSFS 3, 20
Palin, Michael (Edward) 1943- .... **CLC 21**
　See Monty Python
　See also CA 107; CANR 35, 109; SATA 67
Palliser, Charles 1947- .... **CLC 65**
　See also CA 136; CANR 76; CN 7
Palma, Ricardo 1833-1919 .... **TCLC 29**
　See also CA 168; LAW
Pamuk, Orhan 1952- .... **CLC 185**
　See also CA 142; CANR 75, 127; CWW 2
Pancake, Breece Dexter 1952-1979
　See Pancake, Breece D'J
　See also CA 123; 109
Pancake, Breece D'J .... **CLC 29; SSC 61**
　See Pancake, Breece Dexter
　See also DLB 130
Panchenko, Nikolai .... **CLC 59**
Pankhurst, Emmeline (Goulden)
　1858-1928 .... **TCLC 100**
　See also CA 116; FW
Panko, Rudy
　See Gogol, Nikolai (Vasilyevich)
Papadiamantis, Alexandros
　1851-1911 .... **TCLC 29**
　See also CA 168; EWL 3
Papadiamantopoulos, Johannes 1856-1910
　See Moreas, Jean
　See also CA 117
Papini, Giovanni 1881-1956 .... **TCLC 22**
　See also CA 121; 180; DLB 264
Paracelsus 1493-1541 .... **LC 14**
　See also DLB 179
Parasol, Peter
　See Stevens, Wallace
Pardo Bazan, Emilia 1851-1921 .... **SSC 30**
　See also EWL 3; FW; RGSF 2; RGWL 2, 3
Pareto, Vilfredo 1848-1923 .... **TCLC 69**
　See also CA 175
Paretsky, Sara 1947- .... **CLC 135**
　See also AAYA 30; BEST 90:3; CA 125;
　129; CANR 59, 95; CMW 4; CPW; DA3;
　DAM POP; DLB 306; INT CA-129;
　MSW; RGAL 4
Parfenie, Maria
　See Codrescu, Andrei
Parini, Jay (Lee) 1948- .... **CLC 54, 133**
　See also CA 97-100, 229; CAAE 229;
　CAAS 16; CANR 32, 87
Park, Jordan
　See Kornbluth, C(yril) M.; Pohl, Frederik
Park, Robert E(zra) 1864-1944 ..... **TCLC 73**
　See also CA 122; 165
Parker, Bert
　See Ellison, Harlan (Jay)
Parker, Dorothy (Rothschild)
　1893-1967 . **CLC 15, 68; PC 28; SSC 2;**
　TCLC 143
　See also AMWS 9; CA 19-20; 25-28R; CAP
　2; DA3; DAM POET; DLB 11, 45, 86;
　EXPP; FW; MAWW; MTCW 1, 2; PFS
　18; RGAL 4; RGSF 2; TUS
Parker, Robert B(rown) 1932- .... **CLC 27**
　See also AAYA 28; BEST 89:4; BPFB 3;
　CA 49-52; CANR 1, 26, 52, 89, 128;
　CMW 4; CPW; DAM NOV, POP; DLB
　306; INT CANR-26; MSW; MTCW 1
Parkin, Frank 1940- .... **CLC 43**
　See also CA 147
Parkman, Francis, Jr. 1823-1893 .. **NCLC 12**
　See also AMWS 2; DLB 1, 30, 183, 186,
　235; RGAL 4
Parks, Gordon (Alexander Buchanan)
　1912- .... **BLC 3; CLC 1, 16**
　See also AAYA 36; AITN 2; BW 2, 3; CA
　41-44R; CANR 26, 66; DA3; DAM
　MULT; DLB 33; MTCW 2; SATA 8, 108

Parks, Suzan-Lori 1964(?)- .... **DC 23**
　See also AAYA 55; CA 201; CAD; CD 5;
　CWD; RGAL 4
Parks, Tim(othy Harold) 1954- ...... **CLC 147**
　See also CA 126; 131; CANR 77; DLB 231;
　INT CA-131
Parmenides c. 515B.C.-c.
　450B.C. .... **CMLC 22**
　See also DLB 176
Parnell, Thomas 1679-1718 .... **LC 3**
　See also DLB 95; RGEL 2
Parr, Catherine c. 1513(?)-1548 .... **LC 86**
　See also DLB 136
Parra, Nicanor 1914- ... **CLC 2, 102; HLC 2;**
　PC 39
　See also CA 85-88; CANR 32; CWW 2;
　DAM MULT; DLB 283; EWL 3; HW 1;
　LAW; MTCW 1
Parra Sanojo, Ana Teresa de la
　1890-1936 .... **HLCS 2**
　See de la Parra, (Ana) Teresa (Sonojo)
　See also LAW
Parrish, Mary Frances
　See Fisher, M(ary) F(rances) K(ennedy)
Parshchikov, Aleksei 1954- .... **CLC 59**
　See Parshchikov, Aleksei Maksimovich
Parshchikov, Aleksei Maksimovich
　See Parshchikov, Aleksei
　See also DLB 285
Parson, Professor
　See Coleridge, Samuel Taylor
Parson Lot
　See Kingsley, Charles
Parton, Sara Payson Willis
　1811-1872 .... **NCLC 86**
　See also DLB 43, 74, 239
Partridge, Anthony
　See Oppenheim, E(dward) Phillips
Pascal, Blaise 1623-1662 .... **LC 35**
　See also DLB 268; EW 3; GFL Beginnings
　to 1789; RGWL 2, 3; TWA
Pascoli, Giovanni 1855-1912 .... **TCLC 45**
　See also CA 170; EW 7; EWL 3
Pasolini, Pier Paolo 1922-1975 .. **CLC 20, 37,**
　106; PC 17
　See also CA 93-96; 61-64; CANR 63; DLB
　128, 177; EWL 3; MTCW 1; RGWL 2, 3
Pasquini
　See Silone, Ignazio
Pastan, Linda (Olenik) 1932- .... **CLC 27**
　See also CA 61-64; CANR 18, 40, 61, 113;
　CP 7; CSW; CWP; DAM POET; DLB 5;
　PFS 8
Pasternak, Boris (Leonidovich)
　1890-1960 ...... **CLC 7, 10, 18, 63; PC 6;**
　SSC 31; WLC
　See also BPFB 3; CA 127; 116; DA; DA3;
　DAB; DAC; DAM MST, NOV, POET;
　DLB 302; EW 10; MTCW 1, 2; RGSF 2;
　RGWL 2, 3; TWA; WP
Patchen, Kenneth 1911-1972 .... **CLC 1, 2, 18**
　See also BG 3; CA 1-4R; 33-36R; CANR
　3, 35; DAM POET; DLB 16, 48; EWL 3;
　MTCW 1; RGAL 4
Pater, Walter (Horatio) 1839-1894 . **NCLC 7,**
　90
　See also BRW 5; CDBLB 1832-1890; DLB
　57, 156; RGEL 2; TEA
Paterson, A(ndrew) B(arton)
　1864-1941 .... **TCLC 32**
　See also CA 155; DLB 230; RGEL 2; SATA
　97
Paterson, Banjo
　See Paterson, A(ndrew) B(arton)
Paterson, Katherine (Womeldorf)
　1932- .... **CLC 12, 30**
　See also AAYA 1, 31; BYA 1, 2, 7; CA 21-
　24R; CANR 28, 59, 111; CLR 7, 50;
　CWRI 5; DLB 52; JRDA; LAIT 4; MAI-

CYA 1, 2; MAICYAS 1; MTCW 1; SATA
13, 53, 92, 133; WYA; YAW

Patmore, Coventry Kersey Dighton
1823-1896 .... **NCLC 9; PC 59**
See also DLB 35, 98; RGEL 2; TEA

Paton, Alan (Stewart) 1903-1988 ...... **CLC 4,
10, 25, 55, 106; TCLC 165; WLC**
See also AAYA 26; AFW; BPFB 3; BRWS
2; BYA 1; CA 13-16; 125; CANR 22;
CAP 1; DA; DA3; DAB; DAC; DAM
MST, NOV; DLB 225; DLBD 17; EWL
3; EXPN; LAIT 4; MTCW 1, 2; NFS 3,
12; RGEL 2; SATA 11; SATA-Obit 56;
TWA; WLIT 2; WWE 1

Paton Walsh, Gillian 1937- .... **CLC 35**
See Paton Walsh, Jill; Walsh, Jill Paton
See also AAYA 11; CANR 38, 83; CLR 2,
65; DLB 161; JRDA; MAICYA 1, 2;
SAAS 3; SATA 4, 72, 109; YAW

Paton Walsh, Jill
See Paton Walsh, Gillian
See also AAYA 47; BYA 1, 8

Patterson, (Horace) Orlando (Lloyd)
1940- .... **BLCS**
See also BW 1; CA 65-68; CANR 27, 84;
CN 7

Patton, George S(mith), Jr.
1885-1945 .... **TCLC 79**
See also CA 189

Paulding, James Kirke 1778-1860 ... **NCLC 2**
See also DLB 3, 59, 74, 250; RGAL 4

Paulin, Thomas Neilson 1949-
See Paulin, Tom
See also CA 123; 128; CANR 98; CP 7

Paulin, Tom .... **CLC 37, 177**
See Paulin, Thomas Neilson
See also DLB 40

Pausanias c. 1st cent. - .... **CMLC 36**

Paustovsky, Konstantin (Georgievich)
1892-1968 .... **CLC 40**
See also CA 93-96; 25-28R; DLB 272;
EWL 3

Pavese, Cesare 1908-1950 .... **PC 13; SSC 19;
TCLC 3**
See also CA 104; 169; DLB 128, 177; EW
12; EWL 3; PFS 20; RGSF 2; RGWL 2,
3; TWA

Pavic, Milorad 1929- .... **CLC 60**
See also CA 136; CDWLB 4; CWW 2; DLB
181; EWL 3; RGWL 3

Pavlov, Ivan Petrovich 1849-1936 . **TCLC 91**
See also CA 118; 180

Pavlova, Karolina Karlovna
1807-1893 .... **NCLC 138**
See also DLB 205

Payne, Alan
See Jakes, John (William)

Paz, Gil
See Lugones, Leopoldo

Paz, Octavio 1914-1998 . **CLC 3, 4, 6, 10, 19,
51, 65, 119; HLC 2; PC 1, 48; WLC**
See also AAYA 50; CA 73-76; 165; CANR
32, 65, 104; CWW 2; DA; DA3; DAB;
DAC; DAM MST, MULT, POET; DLB
290; DLBY 1990, 1998; DNFS 1; EWL
3; HW 1, 2; LAW; LAWS 1; MTCW 1, 2;
PFS 18; RGWL 2, 3; SSFS 13; TWA;
WLIT 1

p'Bitek, Okot 1931-1982 .... **BLC 3; CLC 96;
TCLC 149**
See also AFW; BW 2, 3; CA 124; 107;
CANR 82; DAM MULT; DLB 125; EWL
3; MTCW 1, 2; RGEL 2; WLIT 2

Peacock, Molly 1947- .... **CLC 60**
See also CA 103; CAAS 21; CANR 52, 84;
CP 7; CWP; DLB 120, 282

Peacock, Thomas Love
1785-1866 .... **NCLC 22**
See also BRW 4; DLB 96, 116; RGEL 2;
RGSF 2

Peake, Mervyn 1911-1968 .... **CLC 7, 54**
See also CA 5-8R; 25-28R; CANR 3; DLB
15, 160, 255; FANT; MTCW 1; RGEL 2;
SATA 23; SFW 4

Pearce, Philippa
See Christie, Philippa
See also CA 5-8R; CANR 4, 109; CWRI 5;
FANT; MAICYA 2

Pearl, Eric
See Elman, Richard (Martin)

Pearson, T(homas) R(eid) 1956- .... **CLC 39**
See also CA 120; 130; CANR 97; CSW;
INT CA-130

Peck, Dale 1967- .... **CLC 81**
See also CA 146; CANR 72, 127; GLL 2

Peck, John (Frederick) 1941- .... **CLC 3**
See also CA 49-52; CANR 3, 100; CP 7

Peck, Richard (Wayne) 1934- .... **CLC 21**
See also AAYA 1, 24; BYA 1, 6, 8, 11; CA
85-88; CANR 19, 38, 129; CLR 15; INT
CANR-19; JRDA; MAICYA 1, 2; SAAS
2; SATA 18, 55, 97; SATA-Essay 110;
WYA; YAW

Peck, Robert Newton 1928- .... **CLC 17**
See also AAYA 3, 43; BYA 1, 6; CA 81-84,
182; CAAE 182; CANR 31, 63, 127; CLR
45; DA; DAC; DAM MST; JRDA; LAIT
3; MAICYA 1, 2; SAAS 1; SATA 21, 62,
111; SATA-Essay 108; WYA; YAW

Peckinpah, (David) Sam(uel)
1925-1984 .... **CLC 20**
See also CA 109; 114; CANR 82

Pedersen, Knut 1859-1952
See Hamsun, Knut
See also CA 104; 119; CANR 63; MTCW
1, 2

Peele, George .... **LC 115**
See also BW 1; DLB 62, 167; RGEL 2

Peeslake, Gaffer
See Durrell, Lawrence (George)

Peguy, Charles (Pierre)
1873-1914 .... **TCLC 10**
See also CA 107; 193; DLB 258; EWL 3;
GFL 1789 to the Present

Peirce, Charles Sanders
1839-1914 .... **TCLC 81**
See also CA 194; DLB 270

Pellicer, Carlos 1897(?)-1977 .... **HLCS 2**
See also CA 153; 69-72; DLB 290; EWL 3;
HW 1

Pena, Ramon del Valle y
See Valle-Inclan, Ramon (Maria) del

Pendennis, Arthur Esquir
See Thackeray, William Makepeace

Penn, Arthur
See Matthews, (James) Brander

Penn, William 1644-1718 .... **LC 25**
See also DLB 24

PEPECE
See Prado (Calvo), Pedro

Pepys, Samuel 1633-1703 ... **LC 11, 58; WLC**
See also BRW 2; CDBLB 1660-1789; DA;
DA3; DAB; DAC; DAM MST; DLB 101,
213; NCFS 4; RGEL 2; TEA; WLIT 3

Percy, Thomas 1729-1811 .... **NCLC 95**
See also DLB 104

Percy, Walker 1916-1990 .... **CLC 2, 3, 6, 8,
14, 18, 47, 65**
See also AMWS 3; BPFB 3; CA 1-4R; 131;
CANR 1, 23, 64; CPW; CSW; DA3;
DAM NOV, POP; DLB 2; DLBY 1980,
1990; EWL 3; MTCW 1, 2; RGAL 4;
TUS

Percy, William Alexander
1885-1942 .... **TCLC 84**
See also CA 163; MTCW 2

Perec, Georges 1936-1982 .... **CLC 56, 116**
See also CA 141; DLB 83, 299; EWL 3;
GFL 1789 to the Present; RGWL 3

**Pereda (y Sanchez de Porrua), Jose Maria
de** 1833-1906 .... **TCLC 16**
See also CA 117

Pereda y Porrua, Jose Maria de
See Pereda (y Sanchez de Porrua), Jose
Maria de

Peregoy, George Weems
See Mencken, H(enry) L(ouis)

Perelman, S(idney) J(oseph)
1904-1979 .. **CLC 3, 5, 9, 15, 23, 44, 49;
SSC 32**
See also AITN 1, 2; BPFB 3; CA 73-76;
89-92; CANR 18; DAM DRAM; DLB 11,
44; MTCW 1, 2; RGAL 4

Peret, Benjamin 1899-1959 .... **PC 33; TCLC
20**
See also CA 117; 186; GFL 1789 to the
Present

Peretz, Isaac Leib
See Peretz, Isaac Loeb
See also CA 201

Peretz, Isaac Loeb 1851(?)-1915 ...... **SSC 26;
TCLC 16**
See Peretz, Isaac Leib
See also CA 109

Peretz, Yitzkhok Leibush
See Peretz, Isaac Loeb

Perez Galdos, Benito 1843-1920 ..... **HLCS 2;
TCLC 27**
See Galdos, Benito Perez
See also CA 125; 153; EWL 3; HW 1;
RGWL 2, 3

Peri Rossi, Cristina 1941- .. **CLC 156; HLCS
2**
See also CA 131; CANR 59, 81; CWW 2;
DLB 145, 290; EWL 3; HW 1, 2

Perlata
See Peret, Benjamin

Perloff, Marjorie G(abrielle)
1931- .... **CLC 137**
See also CA 57-60; CANR 7, 22, 49, 104

Perrault, Charles 1628-1703 .... **LC 2, 56**
See also BYA 4; CLR 79; DLB 268; GFL
Beginnings to 1789; MAICYA 1, 2;
RGWL 2, 3; SATA 25; WCH

Perry, Anne 1938- .... **CLC 126**
See also CA 101; CANR 22, 50, 84; CMW
4; CN 7; CPW; DLB 276

Perry, Brighton
See Sherwood, Robert E(mmet)

Perse, St.-John
See Leger, (Marie-Rene Auguste) Alexis
Saint-Leger

Perse, Saint-John
See Leger, (Marie-Rene Auguste) Alexis
Saint-Leger
See also DLB 258; RGWL 3

Persius 34-62 .... **CMLC 74**
See also AW 2; DLB 211; RGWL 2, 3

Perutz, Leo(pold) 1882-1957 .... **TCLC 60**
See also CA 147; DLB 81

Peseenz, Tulio F.
See Lopez y Fuentes, Gregorio

Pesetsky, Bette 1932- .... **CLC 28**
See also CA 133; DLB 130

Peshkov, Alexei Maximovich 1868-1936
See Gorky, Maxim
See also CA 105; 141; CANR 83; DA;
DAC; DAM DRAM, MST, NOV; MTCW
2

Pessoa, Fernando (Antonio Nogueira)
1888-1935 ..... **HLC 2; PC 20; TCLC 27**
See also CA 125; 183; DAM MULT; DLB 287; EW 10; EWL 3; RGWL 2, 3; WP

Peterkin, Julia Mood 1880-1961 ...... **CLC 31**
See also CA 102; DLB 9

Peters, Joan K(aren) 1945- .... **CLC 39**
See also CA 158; CANR 109

Peters, Robert L(ouis) 1924- .... **CLC 7**
See also CA 13-16R; CAAS 8; CP 7; DLB 105

Petofi, Sandor 1823-1849 .... **NCLC 21**
See also RGWL 2, 3

Petrakis, Harry Mark 1923- .... **CLC 3**
See also CA 9-12R; CANR 4, 30, 85; CN 7

Petrarch 1304-1374 .... **CMLC 20; PC 8**
See also DA3; DAM POET; EW 2; LMFS 1; RGWL 2. 3

Petronius c. 20-66 .... **CMLC 34**
See also AW 2; CDWLB 1; DLB 211; RGWL 2, 3

Petrov, Evgeny .... **TCLC 21**
See Kataev, Evgeny Petrovich

Petry, Ann (Lane) 1908-1997 .. **CLC 1, 7, 18; TCLC 112**
See also AFAW 1, 2; BPFB 3; BW 1, 3; BYA 2; CA 5-8R; 157; CAAS 6; CANR 4, 46; CLR 12; CN 7; DLB 76; EWL 3; JRDA; LAIT 1; MAICYA 1, 2; MAIC-YAS 1; MTCW 1; RGAL 4; SATA 5; SATA-Obit 94; TUS

Petursson, Halligrimur 1614-1674 .... **LC 8**

Peychinovich
See Vazov, Ivan (Minchov)

Phaedrus c. 15B.C.-c. 50 .... **CMLC 25**
See also DLB 211

Phelps (Ward), Elizabeth Stuart
See Phelps, Elizabeth Stuart
See also FW

Phelps, Elizabeth Stuart
1844-1911 .... **TCLC 113**
See Phelps (Ward), Elizabeth Stuart
See also DLB 74

Philips, Katherine 1632-1664 . **LC 30; PC 40**
See also DLB 131; RGEL 2

Philipson, Morris H. 1926- .... **CLC 53**
See also CA 1-4R; CANR 4

Phillips, Caryl 1958- .... **BLCS; CLC 96**
See also BRWS 5; BW 2; CA 141; CANR 63, 104; CBD; CD 5; CN 7; DA3; DAM MULT; DLB 157; EWL 3; MTCW 2; WLIT 4; WWE 1

Phillips, David Graham
1867-1911 .... **TCLC 44**
See also CA 108; 176; DLB 9, 12, 303; RGAL 4

Phillips, Jack
See Sandburg, Carl (August)

Phillips, Jayne Anne 1952- .... **CLC 15, 33, 139; SSC 16**
See also AAYA 57; BPFB 3; CA 101; CANR 24, 50, 96; CN 7; CSW; DLBY 1980; INT CANR-24; MTCW 1, 2; RGAL 4; RGSF 2; SSFS 4

Phillips, Richard
See Dick, Philip K(indred)

Phillips, Robert (Schaeffer) 1938- .... **CLC 28**
See also CA 17-20R; CAAS 13; CANR 8; DLB 105

Phillips, Ward
See Lovecraft, H(oward) P(hillips)

Philostratus, Flavius c. 179-c.
244 .... **CMLC 62**

Piccolo, Lucio 1901-1969 .... **CLC 13**
See also CA 97-100; DLB 114; EWL 3

Pickthall, Marjorie L(owry) C(hristie)
1883-1922 .... **TCLC 21**
See also CA 107; DLB 92

Pico della Mirandola, Giovanni
1463-1494 .... **LC 15**
See also LMFS 1

Piercy, Marge 1936- .... **CLC 3, 6, 14, 18, 27, 62, 128; PC 29**
See also BPFB 3; CA 21-24R, 187; CAAE 187; CAAS 1; CANR 13, 43, 66, 111; CN 7; CP 7; CWP; DLB 120, 227; EXPP; FW; MTCW 1, 2; PFS 9; SFW 4

Piers, Robert
See Anthony, Piers

Pieyre de Mandiargues, Andre 1909-1991
See Mandiargues, Andre Pieyre de
See also CA 103; 136; CANR 22, 82; EWL 3; GFL 1789 to the Present

Pilnyak, Boris 1894-1938 . **SSC 48; TCLC 23**
See Vogau, Boris Andreyevich
See also EWL 3

Pinchback, Eugene
See Toomer, Jean

Pincherle, Alberto 1907-1990 ...... **CLC 11, 18**
See Moravia, Alberto
See also CA 25-28R; 132; CANR 33, 63; DAM NOV; MTCW 1

Pinckney, Darryl 1953- .... **CLC 76**
See also BW 2, 3; CA 143; CANR 79

Pindar 518(?)B.C.-438(?)B.C. .... **CMLC 12; PC 19**
See also AW 1; CDWLB 1; DLB 176; RGWL 2

Pineda, Cecile 1942- .... **CLC 39**
See also CA 118; DLB 209

Pinero, Arthur Wing 1855-1934 .... **TCLC 32**
See also CA 110; 153; DAM DRAM; DLB 10; RGEL 2

Pinero, Miguel (Antonio Gomez)
1946-1988 .... **CLC 4, 55**
See also CA 61-64; 125; CAD; CANR 29, 90; DLB 266; HW 1; LLW 1

Pinget, Robert 1919-1997 .... **CLC 7, 13, 37**
See also CA 85-88; 160; CWW 2; DLB 83; EWL 3; GFL 1789 to the Present

Pink Floyd
See Barrett, (Roger) Syd; Gilmour, David; Mason, Nick; Waters, Roger; Wright, Rick

Pinkney, Edward 1802-1828 .... **NCLC 31**
See also DLB 248

Pinkwater, Daniel
See Pinkwater, Daniel Manus

Pinkwater, Daniel Manus 1941- .... **CLC 35**
See also AAYA 1, 46; BYA 9; CA 29-32R; CANR 12, 38, 89; CLR 4; CSW; FANT; JRDA; MAICYA 1, 2; SAAS 3; SATA 8, 46, 76, 114; SFW 4; YAW

Pinkwater, Manus
See Pinkwater, Daniel Manus

Pinsky, Robert 1940- .... **CLC 9, 19, 38, 94, 121; PC 27**
See also AMWS 6; CA 29-32R; CAAS 4; CANR 58, 97; CP 7; DA3; DAM POET; DLBY 1982, 1998; MTCW 2; PFS 18; RGAL 4

Pinta, Harold
See Pinter, Harold

Pinter, Harold 1930- .. **CLC 1, 3, 6, 9, 11, 15, 27, 58, 73, 199; DC 15; WLC**
See also BRWR 1; BRWS 1; CA 5-8R; CANR 33, 65, 112; CBD; CD 5; CDBLB 1960 to Present; DA; DA3; DAB; DAC; DAM DRAM, MST; DFS 3, 5, 7, 14; DLB 13; EWL 3; IDFW 3, 4; LMFS 2; MTCW 1, 2; RGEL 2; TEA

Piozzi, Hester Lynch (Thrale)
1741-1821 .... **NCLC 57**
See also DLB 104, 142

Pirandello, Luigi 1867-1936 .. **DC 5; SSC 22; TCLC 4, 29; WLC**
See also CA 104; 153; CANR 103; DA; DA3; DAB; DAC; DAM DRAM, MST;

DFS 4, 9; DLB 264; EW 8; EWL 3; MTCW 2; RGSF 2; RGWL 2, 3

Pirsig, Robert M(aynard) 1928- ... **CLC 4, 6, 73**
See also CA 53-56; CANR 42, 74; CPW 1; DA3; DAM POP; MTCW 1, 2; SATA 39

Pisarev, Dmitrii Ivanovich
See Pisarev, Dmitry Ivanovich
See also DLB 277

Pisarev, Dmitry Ivanovich
1840-1868 .... **NCLC 25**
See Pisarev, Dmitrii Ivanovich

Pix, Mary (Griffith) 1666-1709 .... **LC 8**
See also DLB 80

Pixerecourt, (Rene Charles) Guilbert de
1773-1844 .... **NCLC 39**
See also DLB 192; GFL 1789 to the Present

Plaatje, Sol(omon) T(shekisho)
1878-1932 .... **BLCS; TCLC 73**
See also BW 2, 3; CA 141; CANR 79; DLB 125, 225

Plaidy, Jean
See Hibbert, Eleanor Alice Burford

Planche, James Robinson
1796-1880 .... **NCLC 42**
See also RGEL 2

Plant, Robert 1948- .... **CLC 12**

Plante, David (Robert) 1940- . **CLC 7, 23, 38**
See also CA 37-40R; CANR 12, 36, 58, 82; CN 7; DAM NOV; DLBY 1983; INT CANR-12; MTCW 1

Plath, Sylvia 1932-1963 ..... **CLC 1, 2, 3, 5, 9, 11, 14, 17, 50, 51, 62, 111; PC 1, 37; WLC**
See also AAYA 13; AMWR 2; AMWS 1; BPFB 3; CA 19-20; CANR 34, 101; CAP 2; CDALB 1941-1968; DA; DA3; DAB; DAC; DAM MST, POET; DLB 5, 6, 152; EWL 3; EXPN; EXPP; FW; LAIT 4; MAWW; MTCW 1, 2; NFS 1; PAB; PFS 1, 15; RGAL 4; SATA 96; TUS; WP; YAW

Plato c. 428B.C.-347B.C. .... **CMLC 8, 75; WLCS**
See also AW 1; CDWLB 1; DA; DA3; DAB; DAC; DAM MST; DLB 176; LAIT 1; LATS 1:1; RGWL 2, 3

Platonov, Andrei
See Klimentov, Andrei Platonovich

Platonov, Andrei Platonovich
See Klimentov, Andrei Platonovich
See also DLB 272

Platonov, Andrey Platonovich
See Klimentov, Andrei Platonovich
See also EWL 3

Platt, Kin 1911- .... **CLC 26**
See also AAYA 11; CA 17-20R; CANR 11; JRDA; SAAS 17; SATA 21, 86; WYA

Plautus c. 254B.C.-c. 184B.C. ...... **CMLC 24; DC 6**
See also AW 1; CDWLB 1; DLB 211; RGWL 2, 3

Plick et Plock
See Simenon, Georges (Jacques Christian)

Plieksans, Janis
See Rainis, Janis

Plimpton, George (Ames)
1927-2003 .... **CLC 36**
See also AITN 1; CA 21-24R; 224; CANR 32, 70, 103, 133; DLB 185, 241; MTCW 1, 2; SATA 10; SATA-Obit 150

Pliny the Elder c. 23-79 .... **CMLC 23**
See also DLB 211

Pliny the Younger c. 61-c. 112 ...... **CMLC 62**
See also AW 2; DLB 211

Quevedo, Francisco de 1580-1645 .... **LC 23**

Quiller-Couch, Sir Arthur (Thomas)
  1863-1944 .... **TCLC 53**
  See also CA 118; 166; DLB 135, 153, 190;
  HGG; RGEL 2; SUFW 1

Quin, Ann (Marie) 1936-1973 .... **CLC 6**
  See also CA 9-12R; 45-48; DLB 14, 231

Quincey, Thomas de
  See De Quincey, Thomas

Quindlen, Anna 1953- .... **CLC 191**
  See also AAYA 35; CA 138; CANR 73, 126;
  DA3; DLB 292; MTCW 2

Quinn, Martin
  See Smith, Martin Cruz

Quinn, Peter 1947- .... **CLC 91**
  See also CA 197

Quinn, Simon
  See Smith, Martin Cruz

Quintana, Leroy V. 1944- ...... **HLC 2; PC 36**
  See also CA 131; CANR 65; DAM MULT;
  DLB 82; HW 1, 2

Quintilian c. 35-40-c. 96. .... **CMLC 77**
  See also AW 2; DLB 211; RGWL 2, 3

Quiroga, Horacio (Sylvestre)
  1878-1937 .... **HLC 2; TCLC 20**
  See also CA 117; 131; DAM MULT; EWL
  3; HW 1; LAW; MTCW 1; RGSF 2;
  WLIT 1

Quoirez, Françoise 1935- .... **CLC 9**
  See Sagan, Françoise
  See also CA 49-52; CANR 6, 39, 73;
  MTCW 1, 2; TWA

Raabe, Wilhelm (Karl) 1831-1910 . **TCLC 45**
  See also CA 167; DLB 129

Rabe, David (William) 1940- .. **CLC 4, 8, 33, 200; DC 16**
  See also CA 85-88; CABS 3; CAD; CANR
  59, 129; CD 5; DAM DRAM; DFS 3, 8,
  13; DLB 7, 228; EWL 3

Rabelais, Francois 1494-1553 .... **LC 5, 60; WLC**
  See also DA; DAB; DAC; DAM MST; EW
  2; GFL Beginnings to 1789; LMFS 1;
  RGWL 2, 3; TWA

Rabinovitch, Sholem 1859-1916
  See Aleichem, Sholom
  See also CA 104

Rabinyan, Dorit 1972- .... **CLC 119**
  See also CA 170

Rachilde
  See Vallette, Marguerite Eymery; Vallette,
  Marguerite Eymery
  See also EWL 3

Racine, Jean 1639-1699 .... **LC 28, 113**
  See also DA3; DAB; DAM MST; DLB 268;
  EW 3; GFL Beginnings to 1789; LMFS
  1; RGWL 2, 3; TWA

Radcliffe, Ann (Ward) 1764-1823 ... **NCLC 6, 55, 106**
  See also DLB 39, 178; HGG; LMFS 1;
  RGEL 2; SUFW; WLIT 3

Radclyffe-Hall, Marguerite
  See Hall, (Marguerite) Radclyffe

Radiguet, Raymond 1903-1923 ...... **TCLC 29**
  See also CA 162; DLB 65; EWL 3; GFL
  1789 to the Present; RGWL 2, 3

Radnoti, Miklos 1909-1944 .... **TCLC 16**
  See also CA 118; 212; CDWLB 4; DLB
  215; EWL 3; RGWL 2, 3

Rado, James 1939- .... **CLC 17**
  See also CA 105

Radvanyi, Netty 1900-1983
  See Seghers, Anna
  See also CA 85-88; 110; CANR 82

Rae, Ben
  See Griffiths, Trevor

Raeburn, John (Hay) 1941- .... **CLC 34**
  See also CA 57-60

Ragni, Gerome 1942-1991 .... **CLC 17**
  See also CA 105; 134

Rahv, Philip .... **CLC 24**
  See Greenberg, Ivan
  See also DLB 137

Raimund, Ferdinand Jakob
  1790-1836 .... **NCLC 69**
  See also DLB 90

Raine, Craig (Anthony) 1944- .. **CLC 32, 103**
  See also CA 108; CANR 29, 51, 103; CP 7;
  DLB 40; PFS 7

Raine, Kathleen (Jessie) 1908-2003 .. **CLC 7, 45**
  See also CA 85-88; 218; CANR 46, 109;
  CP 7; DLB 20; EWL 3; MTCW 1; RGEL
  2

Rainis, Janis 1865-1929 .... **TCLC 29**
  See also CA 170; CDWLB 4; DLB 220;
  EWL 3

Rakosi, Carl .... **CLC 47**
  See Rawley, Callman
  See also CA 228; CAAS 5; CP 7; DLB 193

Ralegh, Sir Walter
  See Raleigh, Sir Walter
  See also BRW 1; RGEL 2; WP

Raleigh, Richard
  See Lovecraft, H(oward) P(hillips)

Raleigh, Sir Walter 1554(?)-1618 .... **LC 31, 39; PC 31**
  See Ralegh, Sir Walter
  See also CDBLB Before 1660; DLB 172;
  EXPP; PFS 14; TEA

Rallentando, H. P.
  See Sayers, Dorothy L(eigh)

Ramal, Walter
  See de la Mare, Walter (John)

Ramana Maharshi 1879-1950 .... **TCLC 84**

Ramoacn y Cajal, Santiago
  1852-1934 .... **TCLC 93**

Ramon, Juan
  See Jimenez (Mantecon), Juan Ramon

Ramos, Graciliano 1892-1953 .... **TCLC 32**
  See also CA 167; DLB 307; EWL 3; HW 2;
  LAW; WLIT 1

Rampersad, Arnold 1941- .... **CLC 44**
  See also BW 2, 3; CA 127; 133; CANR 81;
  DLB 111; INT CA-133

Rampling, Anne
  See Rice, Anne
  See also GLL 2

Ramsay, Allan 1686(?)-1758 .... **LC 29**
  See also DLB 95; RGEL 2

Ramsay, Jay
  See Campbell, (John) Ramsey

Ramuz, Charles-Ferdinand
  1878-1947 .... **TCLC 33**
  See also CA 165; EWL 3

Rand, Ayn 1905-1982 ...... **CLC 3, 30, 44, 79; WLC**
  See also AAYA 10; AMWS 4; BPFB 3;
  BYA 12; CA 13-16R; 105; CANR 27, 73;
  CDALBS; CPW; DA; DA3; DAC; DAM
  MST, NOV, POP; DLB 227, 279; MTCW
  1, 2; NFS 10, 16; RGAL 4; SFW 4; TUS;
  YAW

Randall, Dudley (Felker) 1914-2000 . **BLC 3; CLC 1, 135**
  See also BW 1, 3; CA 25-28R; 189; CANR
  23, 82; DAM MULT; DLB 41; PFS 5

Randall, Robert
  See Silverberg, Robert

Ranger, Ken
  See Creasey, John

Rank, Otto 1884-1939 .... **TCLC 115**

Ransom, John Crowe 1888-1974 .. **CLC 2, 4, 5, 11, 24; PC 61**
  See also AMW; CA 5-8R; 49-52; CANR 6,
  34; CDALBS; DA3; DAM POET; DLB
  45, 63; EWL 3; EXPP; MTCW 1, 2;
  RGAL 4; TUS

Rao, Raja 1909- .... **CLC 25, 56**
  See also CA 73-76; CANR 51; CN 7; DAM
  NOV; EWL 3; MTCW 1, 2; RGEL 2;
  RGSF 2

Raphael, Frederic (Michael) 1931- ... **CLC 2, 14**
  See also CA 1-4R; CANR 1, 86; CN 7;
  DLB 14

Ratcliffe, James P.
  See Mencken, H(enry) L(ouis)

Rathbone, Julian 1935- .... **CLC 41**
  See also CA 101; CANR 34, 73

Rattigan, Terence (Mervyn)
  1911-1977 .... **CLC 7; DC 18**
  See also BRWS 7; CA 85-88; 73-76; CBD;
  CDBLB 1945-1960; DAM DRAM; DFS
  8; DLB 13; IDFW 3, 4; MTCW 1, 2;
  RGEL 2

Ratushinskaya, Irina 1954- .... **CLC 54**
  See also CA 129; CANR 68; CWW 2

Raven, Simon (Arthur Noel)
  1927-2001 .... **CLC 14**
  See also CA 81-84; 197; CANR 86; CN 7;
  DLB 271

Ravenna, Michael
  See Welty, Eudora (Alice)

Rawley, Callman 1903-2004
  See Rakosi, Carl
  See also CA 21-24R; CANR 12, 32, 91

Rawlings, Marjorie Kinnan
  1896-1953 .... **TCLC 4**
  See also AAYA 20; AMWS 10; ANW;
  BPFB 3; BYA 3; CA 104; 137; CANR 74;
  CLR 63; DLB 9, 22, 102; DLBD 17;
  JRDA; MAICYA 1, 2; MTCW 2; RGAL
  4; SATA 100; WCH; YABC 1; YAW

Ray, Satyajit 1921-1992 .... **CLC 16, 76**
  See also CA 114; 137; DAM MULT

Read, Herbert Edward 1893-1968 ..... **CLC 4**
  See also BRW 6; CA 85-88; 25-28R; DLB
  20, 149; EWL 3; PAB; RGEL 2

Read, Piers Paul 1941- .... **CLC 4, 10, 25**
  See also CA 21-24R; CANR 38, 86; CN 7;
  DLB 14; SATA 21

Reade, Charles 1814-1884 .... **NCLC 2, 74**
  See also DLB 21; RGEL 2

Reade, Hamish
  See Gray, Simon (James Holliday)

Reading, Peter 1946- .... **CLC 47**
  See also BRWS 8; CA 103; CANR 46, 96;
  CP 7; DLB 40

Reaney, James 1926- .... **CLC 13**
  See also CA 41-44R; CAAS 15; CANR 42;
  CD 5; CP 7; DAC; DAM MST; DLB 68;
  RGEL 2; SATA 43

Rebreanu, Liviu 1885-1944 .... **TCLC 28**
  See also CA 165; DLB 220; EWL 3

Rechy, John (Francisco) 1934- ...... **CLC 1, 7, 14, 18, 107; HLC 2**
  See also CA 5-8R, 195; CAAE 195; CAAS
  4; CANR 6, 32, 64; CN 7; DAM MULT;
  DLB 122, 278; DLBY 1982; HW 1, 2;
  INT CANR-6; LLW 1; RGAL 4

Redcam, Tom 1870-1933 .... **TCLC 25**

Reddin, Keith .... **CLC 67**
  See also CAD

Redgrove, Peter (William)
  1932-2003 .... **CLC 6, 41**
  See also BRWS 6; CA 1-4R; 217; CANR 3,
  39, 77; CP 7; DLB 40

Redmon, Anne .... **CLC 22**
  See Nightingale, Anne Redmon
  See also DLBY 1986

Reed, Eliot
  See Ambler, Eric

Reed, Ishmael 1938- ..... **BLC 3; CLC 2, 3, 5, 6, 13, 32, 60, 174**
  See also AFAW 1, 2; AMWS 10; BPFB 3;
  BW 2, 3; CA 21-24R; CANR 25, 48, 74,

Riggs, (Rolla) Lynn
1899-1954 .... **NNAL; TCLC 56**
See also CA 144; DAM MULT; DLB 175

Riis, Jacob A(ugust) 1849-1914 ..... **TCLC 80**
See also CA 113; 168; DLB 23

Riley, James Whitcomb 1849-1916 .... **PC 48; TCLC 51**
See also CA 118; 137; DAM POET; MAI-CYA 1, 2; RGAL 4; SATA 17

Riley, Tex
See Creasey, John

Rilke, Rainer Maria 1875-1926 .... **PC 2; TCLC 1, 6, 19**
See also CA 104; 132; CANR 62, 99; CD-WLB 2; DA3; DAM POET; DLB 81; EW 9; EWL 3; MTCW 1, 2; PFS 19; RGWL 2, 3; TWA; WP

Rimbaud, (Jean Nicolas) Arthur
1854-1891 ... **NCLC 4, 35, 82; PC 3, 57; WLC**
See also DA; DA3; DAB; DAC; DAM MST, POET; DLB 217; EW 7; GFL 1789 to the Present; LMFS 2; RGWL 2, 3; TWA; WP

Rinehart, Mary Roberts
1876-1958 .... **TCLC 52**
See also BPFB 3; CA 108; 166; RGAL 4; RHW

Ringmaster, The
See Mencken, H(enry) L(ouis)

Ringwood, Gwen(dolyn Margaret) Pharis
1910-1984 .... **CLC 48**
See also CA 148; 112; DLB 88

Rio, Michel 1945(?)- .... **CLC 43**
See also CA 201

Rios, Alberto (Alvaro) 1952- .... **PC 57**
See also AMWS 4; CA 113; CANR 34, 79; CP 7; DLB 122; HW 2; PFS 11

Ritsos, Giannes
See Ritsos, Yannis

Ritsos, Yannis 1909-1990 .... **CLC 6, 13, 31**
See also CA 77-80; 133; CANR 39, 61; EW 12; EWL 3; MTCW 1; RGWL 2, 3

Ritter, Erika 1948(?)- .... **CLC 52**
See also CD 5; CWD

Rivera, Jose Eustasio 1889-1928 ... **TCLC 35**
See also CA 162; EWL 3; HW 1, 2; LAW

Rivera, Tomas 1935-1984 .... **HLCS 2**
See also CA 49-52; CANR 32; DLB 82; HW 1; LLW 1; RGAL 4; SSFS 15; TCWW 2; WLIT 1

Rivers, Conrad Kent 1933-1968 .... **CLC 1**
See also BW 1; CA 85-88; DLB 41

Rivers, Elfrida
See Bradley, Marion Zimmer
See also GLL 1

Riverside, John
See Heinlein, Robert A(nson)

Rizal, Jose 1861-1896 .... **NCLC 27**

Roa Bastos, Augusto (Antonio)
1917- .... **CLC 45; HLC 2**
See also CA 131; CWW 2; DAM MULT; DLB 113; EWL 3; HW 1; LAW; RGSF 2; WLIT 1

Robbe-Grillet, Alain 1922- .... **CLC 1, 2, 4, 6, 8, 10, 14, 43, 128**
See also BPFB 3; CA 9-12R; CANR 33, 65, 115; CWW 2; DLB 83; EW 13; EWL 3; GFL 1789 to the Present; IDFW 3, 4; MTCW 1, 2; RGWL 2, 3; SSFS 15

Robbins, Harold 1916-1997 .... **CLC 5**
See also BPFB 3; CA 73-76; 162; CANR 26, 54, 112; DA3; DAM NOV; MTCW 1, 2

Robbins, Thomas Eugene 1936-
See Robbins, Tom
See also CA 81-84; CANR 29, 59, 95; CN 7; CPW; CSW; DA3; DAM NOV, POP; MTCW 1, 2

Robbins, Tom .... **CLC 9, 32, 64**
See Robbins, Thomas Eugene
See also AAYA 32; AMWS 10; BEST 90:3; BPFB 3; DLBY 1980; MTCW 2

Robbins, Trina 1938- .... **CLC 21**
See also CA 128

Roberts, Charles G(eorge) D(ouglas)
1860-1943 .... **TCLC 8**
See also CA 105; 188; CLR 33; CWRI 5; DLB 92; RGEL 2; RGSF 2; SATA 88; SATA-Brief 29

Roberts, Elizabeth Madox
1886-1941 .... **TCLC 68**
See also CA 111; 166; CLR 100; CWRI 5; DLB 9, 54, 102; RGAL 4; RHW; SATA 33; SATA-Brief 27; WCH

Roberts, Kate 1891-1985 .... **CLC 15**
See also CA 107; 116

Roberts, Keith (John Kingston)
1935-2000 .... **CLC 14**
See also BRWS 10; CA 25-28R; CANR 46; DLB 261; SFW 4

Roberts, Kenneth (Lewis)
1885-1957 .... **TCLC 23**
See also CA 109; 199; DLB 9; RGAL 4; RHW

Roberts, Michele (Brigitte) 1949- .... **CLC 48, 178**
See also CA 115; CANR 58, 120; CN 7; DLB 231; FW

Robertson, Ellis
See Ellison, Harlan (Jay); Silverberg, Robert

Robertson, Thomas William
1829-1871 .... **NCLC 35**
See Robertson, Tom
See also DAM DRAM

Robertson, Tom
See Robertson, Thomas William
See also RGEL 2

Robeson, Kenneth
See Dent, Lester

Robinson, Edwin Arlington
1869-1935 .... **PC 1, 35; TCLC 5, 101**
See also AMW; CA 104; 133; CDALB 1865-1917; DA; DAC; DAM MST, POET; DLB 54; EWL 3; EXPP; MTCW 1, 2; PAB; PFS 4; RGAL 4; WP

Robinson, Henry Crabb
1775-1867 .... **NCLC 15**
See also DLB 107

Robinson, Jill 1936- .... **CLC 10**
See also CA 102; CANR 120; INT CA-102

Robinson, Kim Stanley 1952- .... **CLC 34**
See also AAYA 26; CA 126; CANR 113; CN 7; SATA 109; SCFW 2; SFW 4

Robinson, Lloyd
See Silverberg, Robert

Robinson, Marilynne 1944- ...... **CLC 25, 180**
See also CA 116; CANR 80; CN 7; DLB 206

Robinson, Mary 1758-1800 .... **NCLC 142**
See also DLB 158; FW

Robinson, Smokey .... **CLC 21**
See Robinson, William, Jr.

Robinson, William, Jr. 1940-
See Robinson, Smokey
See also CA 116

Robison, Mary 1949- .... **CLC 42, 98**
See also CA 113; 116; CANR 87; CN 7; DLB 130; INT CA-116; RGSF 2

Rochester
See Wilmot, John
See also RGEL 2

Rod, Edouard 1857-1910 .... **TCLC 52**

Roddenberry, Eugene Wesley 1921-1991
See Roddenberry, Gene
See also CA 110; 135; CANR 37; SATA 45; SATA-Obit 69

Roddenberry, Gene .... **CLC 17**
See Roddenberry, Eugene Wesley
See also AAYA 5; SATA-Obit 69

Rodgers, Mary 1931- .... **CLC 12**
See also BYA 5; CA 49-52; CANR 8, 55, 90; CLR 20; CWRI 5; INT CANR-8; JRDA; MAICYA 1, 2; SATA 8, 130

Rodgers, W(illiam) R(obert)
1909-1969 .... **CLC 7**
See also CA 85-88; DLB 20; RGEL 2

Rodman, Eric
See Silverberg, Robert

Rodman, Howard 1920(?)-1985 .... **CLC 65**
See also CA 118

Rodman, Maia
See Wojciechowska, Maia (Teresa)

Rodo, Jose Enrique 1871(?)-1917 .... **HLCS 2**
See also CA 178; EWL 3; HW 2; LAW

Rodolph, Utto
See Ouologuem, Yambo

Rodriguez, Claudio 1934-1999 .... **CLC 10**
See also CA 188; DLB 134

Rodriguez, Richard 1944- .... **CLC 155; HLC 2**
See also AMWS 14; CA 110; CANR 66, 116; DAM MULT; DLB 82, 256; HW 1, 2; LAIT 5; LLW 1; NCFS 3; WLIT 1

Roelvaag, O(le) E(dvart) 1876-1931
See Rolvaag, O(le) E(dvart)
See also CA 117; 171

Roethke, Theodore (Huebner)
1908-1963 .... **CLC 1, 3, 8, 11, 19, 46, 101; PC 15**
See also AMW; CA 81-84; CABS 2; CDALB 1941-1968; DA3; DAM POET; DLB 5, 206; EWL 3; EXPP; MTCW 1, 2; PAB; PFS 3; RGAL 4; WP

Rogers, Carl R(ansom)
1902-1987 .... **TCLC 125**
See also CA 1-4R; 121; CANR 1, 18; MTCW 1

Rogers, Samuel 1763-1855 .... **NCLC 69**
See also DLB 93; RGEL 2

Rogers, Thomas Hunton 1927- .... **CLC 57**
See also CA 89-92; INT CA-89-92

Rogers, Will(iam Penn Adair)
1879-1935 .... **NNAL; TCLC 8, 71**
See also CA 105; 144; DA3; DAM MULT; DLB 11; MTCW 2

Rogin, Gilbert 1929- .... **CLC 18**
See also CA 65-68; CANR 15

Rohan, Koda
See Koda Shigeyuki

Rohlfs, Anna Katharine Green
See Green, Anna Katharine

Rohmer, Eric .... **CLC 16**
See Scherer, Jean-Marie Maurice

Rohmer, Sax .... **TCLC 28**
See Ward, Arthur Henry Sarsfield
See also DLB 70; MSW; SUFW

Roiphe, Anne (Richardson) 1935- .. **CLC 3, 9**
See also CA 89-92; CANR 45, 73; DLBY 1980; INT CA-89-92

Rojas, Fernando de 1475-1541 ... **HLCS 1, 2; LC 23**
See also DLB 286; RGWL 2, 3

Rojas, Gonzalo 1917- .... **HLCS 2**
See also CA 178; HW 2; LAWS 1

Roland, Marie-Jeanne 1754-1793 .... **LC 98**

Rolfe, Frederick (William Serafino Austin Lewis Mary) 1860-1913 .... **TCLC 12**
See Al Siddik
See also CA 107; 210; DLB 34, 156; RGEL 2

Rolland, Romain 1866-1944 .... **TCLC 23**
See also CA 118; 197; DLB 65, 284; EWL 3; GFL 1789 to the Present; RGWL 2, 3

Rolle, Richard c. 1300-c. 1349 ...... **CMLC 21**
See also DLB 146; LMFS 1; RGEL 2

Sanchez, Florencio 1875-1910 .... **TCLC 37**
    See also CA 153; DLB 305; EWL 3; HW 1;
    LAW
Sanchez, Luis Rafael 1936- .... **CLC 23**
    See also CA 128; DLB 305; EWL 3; HW 1;
    WLIT 1
Sanchez, Sonia 1934- .... **BLC 3; CLC 5, 116;**
    PC 9
    See also BW 2, 3; CA 33-36R; CANR 24,
    49, 74, 115; CLR 18; CP 7; CSW; CWP;
    DA3; DAM MULT; DLB 41; DLBD 8;
    EWL 3; MAICYA 1, 2; MTCW 1, 2;
    SATA 22, 136; WP
Sancho, Ignatius 1729-1780 .... **LC 84**
Sand, George 1804-1876 ..... **NCLC 2, 42, 57;**
    WLC
    See also DA; DA3; DAB; DAC; DAM
    MST, NOV; DLB 119, 192; EW 6; FW;
    GFL 1789 to the Present; RGWL 2, 3;
    TWA
Sandburg, Carl (August) 1878-1967 . **CLC 1,**
    4, 10, 15, 35; PC 2, 41; WLC
    See also AAYA 24; AMW; BYA 1, 3; CA
    5-8R; 25-28R; CANR 35; CDALB 1865-
    1917; CLR 67; DA; DA3; DAB; DAC;
    DAM MST, POET; DLB 17, 54, 284;
    EWL 3; EXPP; LAIT 2; MAICYA 1, 2;
    MTCW 1, 2; PAB; PFS 3, 6, 12; RGAL
    4; SATA 8; TUS; WCH; WP; WYA
Sandburg, Charles
    See Sandburg, Carl (August)
Sandburg, Charles A.
    See Sandburg, Carl (August)
Sanders, (James) Ed(ward) 1939- .... **CLC 53**
    See Sanders, Edward
    See also BG 3; CA 13-16R; CAAS 21;
    CANR 13, 44, 78; CP 7; DAM POET;
    DLB 16, 244
Sanders, Edward
    See Sanders, (James) Ed(ward)
    See also DLB 244
Sanders, Lawrence 1920-1998 .... **CLC 41**
    See also BEST 89:4; BPFB 3; CA 81-84;
    165; CANR 33, 62; CMW 4; CPW; DA3;
    DAM POP; MTCW 1
Sanders, Noah
    See Blount, Roy (Alton), Jr.
Sanders, Winston P.
    See Anderson, Poul (William)
Sandoz, Mari(e Susette) 1900-1966 .. **CLC 28**
    See also CA 1-4R; 25-28R; CANR 17, 64;
    DLB 9, 212; LAIT 2; MTCW 1, 2; SATA
    5; TCWW 2
Sandys, George 1578-1644 .... **LC 80**
    See also DLB 24, 121
Saner, Reg(inald Anthony) 1931- .... **CLC 9**
    See also CA 65-68; CP 7
Sankara 788-820 .... **CMLC 32**
Sannazaro, Jacopo 1456(?)-1530 .... **LC 8**
    See also RGWL 2, 3
Sansom, William 1912-1976 . **CLC 2, 6; SSC**
    21
    See also CA 5-8R; 65-68; CANR 42; DAM
    NOV; DLB 139; EWL 3; MTCW 1;
    RGEL 2; RGSF 2
Santayana, George 1863-1952 .... **TCLC 40**
    See also AMW; CA 115; 194; DLB 54, 71,
    246, 270; DLBD 13; EWL 3; RGAL 4;
    TUS
Santiago, Danny .... **CLC 33**
    See James, Daniel (Lewis)
    See also DLB 122
Santillana, Íñigo López de Mendoza,
    Marqués de 1398-1458 .... **LC 111**
    See also DLB 286
Santmyer, Helen Hooven
    1895-1986 .... **CLC 33; TCLC 133**
    See also CA 1-4R; 118; CANR 15, 33;
    DLBY 1984; MTCW 1; RHW

Santoka, Taneda 1882-1940 .... **TCLC 72**
Santos, Bienvenido N(uqui)
    1911-1996 ... **AAL; CLC 22; TCLC 156**
    See also CA 101; 151; CANR 19, 46; DAM
    MULT; EWL; RGAL 4; SSFS 19
Sapir, Edward 1884-1939 .... **TCLC 108**
    See also CA 211; DLB 92
Sapper .... **TCLC 44**
    See McNeile, Herman Cyril
Sapphire
    See Sapphire, Brenda
Sapphire, Brenda 1950- .... **CLC 99**
Sappho fl. 6th cent. B.C.- ... **CMLC 3, 67; PC**
    5
    See also CDWLB 1; DA3; DAM POET;
    DLB 176; PFS 20; RGWL 2, 3; WP
Saramago, Jose 1922- ..... **CLC 119; HLCS 1**
    See also CA 153; CANR 96; CWW 2; DLB
    287; EWL 3; LATS 1:2
Sarduy, Severo 1937-1993 .... **CLC 6, 97;**
    HLCS 2
    See also CA 89-92; 142; CANR 58, 81;
    CWW 2; DLB 113; EWL 3; HW 1, 2;
    LAW
Sargeson, Frank 1903-1982 .... **CLC 31**
    See also CA 25-28R; 106; CANR 38, 79;
    EWL 3; GLL 2; RGEL 2; RGSF 2; SSFS
    20
Sarmiento, Domingo Faustino
    1811-1888 .... **HLCS 2**
    See also LAW; WLIT 1
Sarmiento, Felix Ruben Garcia
    See Dario, Ruben
Saro-Wiwa, Ken(ule Beeson)
    1941-1995 .... **CLC 114**
    See also BW 2; CA 142; 150; CANR 60;
    DLB 157
Saroyan, William 1908-1981 ... **CLC 1, 8, 10,**
    29, 34, 56; SSC 21; TCLC 137; WLC
    See also CA 5-8R; 103; CAD; CANR 30;
    CDALBS; DA; DA3; DAB; DAC; DAM
    DRAM, MST, NOV; DFS 17; DLB 7, 9,
    86; DLBY 1981; EWL 3; LAIT 4; MTCW
    1, 2; RGAL 4; RGSF 2; SATA 23; SATA-
    Obit 24; SSFS 14; TUS
Sarraute, Nathalie 1900-1999 .... **CLC 1, 2, 4,**
    8, 10, 31, 80; TCLC 145
    See also BPFB 3; CA 9-12R; 187; CANR
    23, 66, 134; CWW 2; DLB 83; EW 12;
    EWL 3; GFL 1789 to the Present; MTCW
    1, 2; RGWL 2, 3
Sarton, (Eleanor) May 1912-1995 ..... **CLC 4,**
    14, 49, 91; PC 39; TCLC 120
    See also AMWS 8; CA 1-4R; 149; CANR
    1, 34, 55, 116; CN 7; CP 7; DAM POET;
    DLB 48; DLBY 1981; EWL 3; FW; INT
    CANR-34; MTCW 1, 2; RGAL 4; SATA
    36; SATA-Obit 86; TUS
Sartre, Jean-Paul 1905-1980 . **CLC 1, 4, 7, 9,**
    13, 18, 24, 44, 50, 52; DC 3; SSC 32;
    WLC
    See also CA 9-12R; 97-100; CANR 21; DA;
    DA3; DAB; DAC; DAM DRAM, MST,
    NOV; DFS 5; DLB 72, 296; EW 12; EWL
    3; GFL 1789 to the Present; LMFS 2;
    MTCW 1, 2; RGSF 2; RGWL 2, 3; SSFS
    9; TWA
Sassoon, Siegfried (Lorraine)
    1886-1967 .... **CLC 36, 130; PC 12**
    See also BRW 6; CA 104; 25-28R; CANR
    36; DAB; DAM MST, NOV, POET; DLB
    20, 191; DLBD 18; EWL 3; MTCW 1, 2;
    PAB; RGEL 2; TEA
Satterfield, Charles
    See Pohl, Frederik
Satyremont
    See Peret, Benjamin

Saul, John (W. III) 1942- .... **CLC 46**
    See also AAYA 10; BEST 90:4; CA 81-84;
    CANR 16, 40, 81; CPW; DAM NOV,
    POP; HGG; SATA 98
Saunders, Caleb
    See Heinlein, Robert A(nson)
Saura (Atares), Carlos 1932-1998 .... **CLC 20**
    See also CA 114; 131; CANR 79; HW 1
Sauser, Frederic Louis
    See Sauser-Hall, Frederic
Sauser-Hall, Frederic 1887-1961 ...... **CLC 18**
    See Cendrars, Blaise
    See also CA 102; 93-96; CANR 36, 62;
    MTCW 1
Saussure, Ferdinand de
    1857-1913 .... **TCLC 49**
    See also DLB 242
Savage, Catharine
    See Brosman, Catharine Savage
Savage, Richard 1697(?)-1743 .... **LC 96**
    See also DLB 95; RGEL 2
Savage, Thomas 1915-2003 .... **CLC 40**
    See also CA 126; 132; 218; CAAS 15; CN
    7; INT CA-132; SATA-Obit 147; TCWW
    2
Savan, Glenn 1953-2003 .... **CLC 50**
    See also CA 225
Sax, Robert
    See Johnson, Robert
Saxo Grammaticus c. 1150-c.
    1222 .... **CMLC 58**
Saxton, Robert
    See Johnson, Robert
Sayers, Dorothy L(eigh) 1893-1957 . **SSC 71;**
    TCLC 2, 15
    See also BPFB 3; BRWS 3; CA 104; 119;
    CANR 60; CDBLB 1914-1945; CMW 4;
    DAM POP; DLB 10, 36, 77, 100; MSW;
    MTCW 1, 2; RGEL 2; SSFS 12; TEA
Sayers, Valerie 1952- .... **CLC 50, 122**
    See also CA 134; CANR 61; CSW
Sayles, John (Thomas) 1950- .... **CLC 7, 10,**
    14, 198
    See also CA 57-60; CANR 41, 84; DLB 44
Scammell, Michael 1935- .... **CLC 34**
    See also CA 156
Scannell, Vernon 1922- .... **CLC 49**
    See also CA 5-8R; CANR 8, 24, 57; CP 7;
    CWRI 5; DLB 27; SATA 59
Scarlett, Susan
    See Streatfeild, (Mary) Noel
Scarron, Paul 1610-1660 .... **LC 116**
    See also GFL Beginnings to 1789; RGWL
    2, 3
Scarron 1847-1910
    See Mikszath, Kalman
Schaeffer, Susan Fromberg 1941- ..... **CLC 6,**
    11, 22
    See also CA 49-52; CANR 18, 65; CN 7;
    DLB 28, 299; MTCW 1, 2; SATA 22
Schama, Simon (Michael) 1945- ..... **CLC 150**
    See also BEST 89:4; CA 105; CANR 39,
    91
Schary, Jill
    See Robinson, Jill
Schell, Jonathan 1943- .... **CLC 35**
    See also CA 73-76; CANR 12, 117
Schelling, Friedrich Wilhelm Joseph von
    1775-1854 .... **NCLC 30**
    See also DLB 90
Scherer, Jean-Marie Maurice 1920-
    See Rohmer, Eric
    See also CA 110
Schevill, James (Erwin) 1920- .... **CLC 7**
    See also CA 5-8R; CAAS 12; CAD; CD 5
Schiller, Friedrich von 1759-1805 ...... **DC 12;**
    NCLC 39, 69
    See also CDWLB 2; DAM DRAM; DLB
    94; EW 5; RGWL 2, 3; TWA

POET; DLB 96, 110, 158; EXPP; LMFS 1; PAB; PFS 2; RGEL 2; TEA; WLIT 3; WP

Shepard, Jim 1956- .... **CLC 36**
See also CA 137; CANR 59, 104; SATA 90

Shepard, Lucius 1947- .... **CLC 34**
See also CA 128; 141; CANR 81, 124; HGG; SCFW 2; SFW 4; SUFW 2

Shepard, Sam 1943- .... **CLC 4, 6, 17, 34, 41, 44, 169; DC 5**
See also AAYA 1, 58; AMWS 3; CA 69-72; CABS 3; CAD; CANR 22, 120; CD 5; DA3; DAM DRAM; DFS 3, 6, 7, 14; DLB 7, 212; EWL 3; IDFW 3, 4; MTCW 1, 2; RGAL 4

Shepherd, Michael
See Ludlum, Robert

Sherburne, Zoa (Lillian Morin)
1912-1995 .... **CLC 30**
See also AAYA 13; CA 1-4R; 176; CANR 3, 37; MAICYA 1, 2; SAAS 18; SATA 3; YAW

Sheridan, Frances 1724-1766 .... **LC 7**
See also DLB 39, 84

Sheridan, Richard Brinsley
1751-1816 .... **DC 1; NCLC 5, 91; WLC**
See also BRW 3; CDBLB 1660-1789; DA; DAB; DAC; DAM DRAM, MST; DFS 15; DLB 89; WLIT 3

Sherman, Jonathan Marc .... **CLC 55**

Sherman, Martin 1941(?)- .... **CLC 19**
See also CA 116; 123; CAD; CANR 86; CD 5; DFS 20; DLB 228; GLL 1; IDTP

Sherwin, Judith Johnson
See Johnson, Judith (Emlyn)
See also CANR 85; CP 7; CWP

Sherwood, Frances 1940- .... **CLC 81**
See also CA 146; 220; CAAE 220

Sherwood, Robert E(mmet)
1896-1955 .... **TCLC 3**
See also CA 104; 153; CANR 86; DAM DRAM; DFS 11, 15, 17; DLB 7, 26, 249; IDFW 3, 4; RGAL 4

Shestov, Lev 1866-1938 .... **TCLC 56**

Shevchenko, Taras 1814-1861 .... **NCLC 54**

Shiel, M(atthew) P(hipps)
1865-1947 .... **TCLC 8**
See Holmes, Gordon
See also CA 106; 160; DLB 153; HGG; MTCW 2; SFW 4; SUFW

Shields, Carol (Ann) 1935-2003 ...... **CLC 91, 113, 193**
See also AMWS 7; CA 81-84; 218; CANR 51, 74, 98, 133; CCA 1; CN 7; CPW; DA3; DAC; MTCW 2

Shields, David (Jonathan) 1956- ...... **CLC 97**
See also CA 124; CANR 48, 99, 112

Shiga, Naoya 1883-1971 **CLC 33; SSC 23**
See Shiga Naoya
See also CA 101; 33-36R; MJW; RGWL 3

Shiga Naoya
See Shiga, Naoya
See also DLB 180; EWL 3; RGWL 3

Shilts, Randy 1951-1994 .... **CLC 85**
See also AAYA 19; CA 115; 127; 144; CANR 45; DA3; GLL 1; INT CA-127; MTCW 2

Shimazaki, Haruki 1872-1943
See Shimazaki Toson
See also CA 105; 134; CANR 84; RGWL 3

Shimazaki Toson .... **TCLC 5**
See Shimazaki, Haruki
See also DLB 180; EWL 3

Shirley, James 1596-1666 .... **DC 25; LC 96**
See also DLB 58; RGEL 2

Sholokhov, Mikhail (Aleksandrovich)
1905-1984 .... **CLC 7, 15**
See also CA 101; 112; DLB 272; EWL 3; MTCW 1, 2; RGWL 2, 3; SATA-Obit 36

Shone, Patric
See Hanley, James

Showalter, Elaine 1941- .... **CLC 169**
See also CA 57-60; CANR 58, 106; DLB 67; FW; GLL 2

Shreve, Susan
See Shreve, Susan Richards

Shreve, Susan Richards 1939- .... **CLC 23**
See also CA 49-52; CAAS 5; CANR 5, 38, 69, 100; MAICYA 1, 2; SATA 46, 95, 152; SATA-Brief 41

Shue, Larry 1946-1985 .... **CLC 52**
See also CA 145; 117; DAM DRAM; DFS 7

Shu-Jen, Chou 1881-1936
See Lu Hsun
See also CA 104

Shulman, Alix Kates 1932- .... **CLC 2, 10**
See also CA 29-32R; CANR 43; FW; SATA 7

Shuster, Joe 1914-1992 .... **CLC 21**
See also AAYA 50

Shute, Nevil .... **CLC 30**
See Norway, Nevil Shute
See also BPFB 3; DLB 255; NFS 9; RHW; SFW 4

Shuttle, Penelope (Diane) 1947- .... **CLC 7**
See also CA 93-96; CANR 39, 84, 92, 108; CP 7; CWP; DLB 14, 40

Shvarts, Elena 1948- .... **PC 50**
See also CA 147

Sidhwa, Bapsy (N.) 1938- .... **CLC 168**
See also CA 108; CANR 25, 57; CN 7; FW

Sidney, Mary 1561-1621 .... **LC 19, 39**
See Sidney Herbert, Mary

Sidney, Sir Philip 1554-1586 . **LC 19, 39; PC 32**
See also BRW 1; BRWR 2; CDBLB Before 1660; DA; DA3; DAB; DAC; DAM MST, POET; DLB 167; EXPP; PAB; RGEL 2; TEA; WP

Sidney Herbert, Mary
See Sidney, Mary
See also DLB 167

Siegel, Jerome 1914-1996 .... **CLC 21**
See Siegel, Jerry
See also CA 116; 169; 151

Siegel, Jerry
See Siegel, Jerome
See also AAYA 50

Sienkiewicz, Henryk (Adam Alexander Pius)
1846-1916 .... **TCLC 3**
See also CA 104; 134; CANR 84; EWL 3; RGSF 2; RGWL 2, 3

Sierra, Gregorio Martinez
See Martinez Sierra, Gregorio

Sierra, Maria (de la O'LeJarraga) Martinez
See Martinez Sierra, Maria (de la O'LeJarraga)

Sigal, Clancy 1926- .... **CLC 7**
See also CA 1-4R; CANR 85; CN 7

Siger of Brabant 1240(?)-1284(?) . **CMLC 69**
See also DLB 115

Sigourney, Lydia H.
See Sigourney, Lydia Howard (Huntley)
See also DLB 73, 183

Sigourney, Lydia Howard (Huntley)
1791-1865 .... **NCLC 21, 87**
See Sigourney, Lydia H.; Sigourney, Lydia Huntley
See also DLB 1

Sigourney, Lydia Huntley
See Sigourney, Lydia Howard (Huntley)
See also DLB 42, 239, 243

Siguenza y Gongora, Carlos de
1645-1700 .... **HLCS 2; LC 8**
See also LAW

Sigurjonsson, Johann
See Sigurjonsson, Johann

Sigurjonsson, Johann 1880-1919 ... **TCLC 27**
See also CA 170; DLB 293; EWL 3

Sikelianos, Angelos 1884-1951 .... **PC 29; TCLC 39**
See also EWL 3; RGWL 2, 3

Silkin, Jon 1930-1997 .... **CLC 2, 6, 43**
See also CA 5-8R; CAAS 5; CANR 89; CP 7; DLB 27

Silko, Leslie (Marmon) 1948- .... **CLC 23, 74, 114; NNAL; SSC 37, 66; WLCS**
See also AAYA 14; AMWS 4; ANW; BYA 12; CA 115; 122; CANR 45, 65, 118; CN 7; CP 7; CPW; DA; DA3; DAC; DAM MST, MULT, POP; DLB 143, 175, 256, 275; EWL 3; EXPP; EXPS; LAIT 4; MTCW 2; NFS 4; PFS 9, 16; RGAL 4; RGSF 2; SSFS 4, 8, 10, 11

Sillanpaa, Frans Eemil 1888-1964 ... **CLC 19**
See also CA 129; 93-96; EWL 3; MTCW 1

Sillitoe, Alan 1928- .. **CLC 1, 3, 6, 10, 19, 57, 148**
See also AITN 1; BRWS 5; CA 9-12R, 191; CAAE 191; CAAS 2; CANR 8, 26, 55; CDBLB 1960 to Present; CN 7; DLB 14, 139; EWL 3; MTCW 1, 2; RGEL 2; RGSF 2; SATA 61

Silone, Ignazio 1900-1978 .... **CLC 4**
See also CA 25-28; 81-84; CANR 34; CAP 2; DLB 264; EW 12; EWL 3; MTCW 1; RGSF 2; RGWL 2, 3

Silone, Ignazione
See Silone, Ignazio

Silver, Joan Micklin 1935- .... **CLC 20**
See also CA 114; 121; INT CA-121

Silver, Nicholas
See Faust, Frederick (Schiller)
See also TCWW 2

Silverberg, Robert 1935- .... **CLC 7, 140**
See also AAYA 24; BPFB 3; BYA 7, 9; CA 1-4R, 186; CAAE 186; CAAS 3; CANR 1, 20, 36, 85; CLR 59; CN 7; CPW; DAM POP; DLB 8; INT CANR-20; MAICYA 1, 2; MTCW 1, 2; SATA 13, 91; SATA-Essay 104; SCFW 2; SFW 4; SUFW 2

Silverstein, Alvin 1933- .... **CLC 17**
See also CA 49-52; CANR 2; CLR 25; JRDA; MAICYA 1, 2; SATA 8, 69, 124

Silverstein, Shel(don Allan)
1932-1999 .... **PC 49**
See also AAYA 40; BW 3; CA 107; 179; CANR 47, 74, 81; CLR 5, 96; CWRI 5; JRDA; MAICYA 1, 2; MTCW 2; SATA 33, 92; SATA-Brief 27; SATA-Obit 116

Silverstein, Virginia B(arbara Opshelor)
1937- .... **CLC 17**
See also CA 49-52; CANR 2; CLR 25; JRDA; MAICYA 1, 2; SATA 8, 69, 124

Sim, Georges
See Simenon, Georges (Jacques Christian)

Simak, Clifford D(onald) 1904-1988 . **CLC 1, 55**
See also CA 1-4R; 125; CANR 1, 35; DLB 8; MTCW 1; SATA-Obit 56; SFW 4

Simenon, Georges (Jacques Christian)
1903-1989 .... **CLC 1, 2, 3, 8, 18, 47**
See also BPFB 3; CA 85-88; 129; CANR 35; CMW 4; DA3; DAM POP; DLB 72; DLBY 1989; EW 12; EWL 3; GFL 1789 to the Present; MSW; MTCW 1, 2; RGWL 2, 3

Simic, Charles 1938- .... **CLC 6, 9, 22, 49, 68, 130**
See also AMWS 8; CA 29-32R; CAAS 4; CANR 12, 33, 52, 61, 96; CP 7; DA3; DAM POET; DLB 105; MTCW 2; PFS 7; RGAL 4; WP

Simmel, Georg 1858-1918 .... **TCLC 64**
See also CA 157; DLB 296

Simmons, Charles (Paul) 1924- .... **CLC 57**
See also CA 89-92; INT CA-89-92

Smith, Patti 1946- .... **CLC 12**
See also CA 93-96; CANR 63
Smith, Pauline (Urmson)
1882-1959 .... **TCLC 25**
See also DLB 225; EWL 3
Smith, Rosamond
See Oates, Joyce Carol
Smith, Sheila Kaye
See Kaye-Smith, Sheila
Smith, Stevie .... **CLC 3, 8, 25, 44; PC 12**
See Smith, Florence Margaret
See also BRWS 2; DLB 20; EWL 3; MTCW
2; PAB; PFS 3; RGEL 2
Smith, Wilbur (Addison) 1933- .... **CLC 33**
See also CA 13-16R; CANR 7, 46, 66, 134;
CPW; MTCW 1, 2
Smith, William Jay 1918- .... **CLC 6**
See also AMWS 13; CA 5-8R; CANR 44,
106; CP 7; CSW; CWRI 5; DLB 5; MAI-
CYA 1, 2; SAAS 22; SATA 2, 68, 154;
SATA-Essay 154
Smith, Woodrow Wilson
See Kuttner, Henry
Smith, Zadie 1976- .... **CLC 158**
See also AAYA 50; CA 193
Smolenskin, Peretz 1842-1885 .... **NCLC 30**
Smollett, Tobias (George) 1721-1771 ... **LC 2,
46**
See also BRW 3; CDBLB 1660-1789; DLB
39, 104; RGEL 2; TEA
Snodgrass, W(illiam) D(e Witt)
1926- .... **CLC 2, 6, 10, 18, 68**
See also AMWS 6; CA 1-4R; CANR 6, 36,
65, 85; CP 7; DAM POET; DLB 5;
MTCW 1, 2; RGAL 4
Snorri Sturluson 1179-1241 .... **CMLC 56**
See also RGWL 2, 3
Snow, C(harles) P(ercy) 1905-1980 ... **CLC 1,
4, 6, 9, 13, 19**
See also BRW 7; CA 5-8R; 101; CANR 28;
CDBLB 1945-1960; DAM NOV; DLB 15,
77; DLBD 17; EWL 3; MTCW 1, 2;
RGEL 2; TEA
Snow, Frances Compton
See Adams, Henry (Brooks)
Snyder, Gary (Sherman) 1930- . **CLC 1, 2, 5,
9, 32, 120; PC 21**
See also AMWS 8; ANW; BG 3; CA 17-
20R; CANR 30, 60, 125; CP 7; DA3;
DAM POET; DLB 5, 16, 165, 212, 237,
275; EWL 3; MTCW 2; PFS 9, 19; RGAL
4; WP
Snyder, Zilpha Keatley 1927- .... **CLC 17**
See also AAYA 15; BYA 1; CA 9-12R;
CANR 38; CLR 31; JRDA; MAICYA 1,
2; SAAS 2; SATA 1, 28, 75, 110; SATA-
Essay 112; YAW
Soares, Bernardo
See Pessoa, Fernando (Antonio Nogueira)
Sobh, A.
See Shamlu, Ahmad
Sobh, Alef
See Shamlu, Ahmad
Sobol, Joshua 1939- .... **CLC 60**
See Sobol, Yehoshua
See also CA 200
Sobol, Yehoshua 1939-
See Sobol, Joshua
See also CWW 2
Socrates 470B.C.-399B.C. .... **CMLC 27**
Soderberg, Hjalmar 1869-1941 ...... **TCLC 39**
See also DLB 259; EWL 3; RGSF 2
Soderbergh, Steven 1963- .... **CLC 154**
See also AAYA 43
Sodergran, Edith (Irene) 1892-1923
See Soedergran, Edith (Irene)
See also CA 202; DLB 259; EW 11; EWL
3; RGWL 2, 3

Soedergran, Edith (Irene)
1892-1923 .... **TCLC 31**
See Sodergran, Edith (Irene)
Softly, Edgar
See Lovecraft, H(oward) P(hillips)
Softly, Edward
See Lovecraft, H(oward) P(hillips)
Sokolov, Alexander V(sevolodovich) 1943-
See Sokolov, Sasha
See also CA 73-76
Sokolov, Raymond 1941- .... **CLC 7**
See also CA 85-88
Sokolov, Sasha .... **CLC 59**
See Sokolov, Alexander V(sevolodovich)
See also CWW 2; DLB 285; EWL 3; RGWL
2, 3
Solo, Jay
See Ellison, Harlan (Jay)
Sologub, Fyodor .... **TCLC 9**
See Teternikov, Fyodor Kuzmich
See also EWL 3
Solomons, Ikey Esquir
See Thackeray, William Makepeace
Solomos, Dionysios 1798-1857 .... **NCLC 15**
Solwoska, Mara
See French, Marilyn
Solzhenitsyn, Aleksandr I(sayevich)
1918- .. **CLC 1, 2, 4, 7, 9, 10, 18, 26, 34,
78, 134; SSC 32; WLC**
See Solzhenitsyn, Aleksandr Isaevich
See also AAYA 49; AITN 1; BPFB 3; CA
69-72; CANR 40, 65, 116; DA; DA3;
DAB; DAC; DAM MST, NOV; DLB 302;
EW 13; EXPS; LAIT 4; MTCW 1, 2; NFS
6; RGSF 2; RGWL 2, 3; SSFS 9; TWA
Solzhenitsyn, Aleksandr Isaevich
See Solzhenitsyn, Aleksandr I(sayevich)
See also CWW 2; EWL 3
Somers, Jane
See Lessing, Doris (May)
Somerville, Edith Oenone
1858-1949 .... **SSC 56; TCLC 51**
See also CA 196; DLB 135; RGEL 2; RGSF
2
Somerville & Ross
See Martin, Violet Florence; Somerville,
Edith Oenone
Sommer, Scott 1951- .... **CLC 25**
See also CA 106
Sommers, Christina Hoff 1950- ...... **CLC 197**
See also CA 153; CANR 95
Sondheim, Stephen (Joshua) 1930- . **CLC 30,
39, 147; DC 22**
See also AAYA 11; CA 103; CANR 47, 67,
125; DAM DRAM; LAIT 4
Sone, Monica 1919- .... **AAL**
Song, Cathy 1955- .... **AAL; PC 21**
See also CA 154; CANR 118; CWP; DLB
169; EXPP; FW; PFS 5
Sontag, Susan 1933- .... **CLC 1, 2, 10, 13, 31,
105, 195**
See also AMWS 3; CA 17-20R; CANR 25,
51, 74, 97; CN 7; CPW; DA3; DAM POP;
DLB 2, 67; EWL 3; MAWW; MTCW 1,
2; RGAL 4; RHW; SSFS 10
Sophocles 496(?)B.C.-406(?)B.C. .... **CMLC 2,
47, 51; DC 1; WLCS**
See also AW 1; CDWLB 1; DA; DA3;
DAB; DAC; DAM DRAM, MST; DFS 1,
4, 8; DLB 176; LAIT 1; LATS 1:1; LMFS
1; RGWL 2, 3; TWA
Sordello 1189-1269 .... **CMLC 15**
Sorel, Georges 1847-1922 .... **TCLC 91**
See also CA 118; 188
Sorel, Julia
See Drexler, Rosalyn
Sorokin, Vladimir .... **CLC 59**
See Sorokin, Vladimir Georgievich

Sorokin, Vladimir Georgievich
See Sorokin, Vladimir
See also DLB 285
Sorrentino, Gilbert 1929- .. **CLC 3, 7, 14, 22,
40**
See also CA 77-80; CANR 14, 33, 115; CN
7; CP 7; DLB 5, 173; DLBY 1980; INT
CANR-14
Soseki
See Natsume, Soseki
See also MJW
Soto, Gary 1952- ... **CLC 32, 80; HLC 2; PC
28**
See also AAYA 10, 37; BYA 11; CA 119;
125; CANR 50, 74, 107; CLR 38; CP 7;
DAM MULT; DLB 82; EWL 3; EXPP;
HW 1, 2; INT CA-125; JRDA; LLW 1;
MAICYA 2; MAICYAS 1; MTCW 2; PFS
7; RGAL 4; SATA 80, 120; WYA; YAW
Soupault, Philippe 1897-1990 .... **CLC 68**
See also CA 116; 147; 131; EWL 3; GFL
1789 to the Present; LMFS 2
Souster, (Holmes) Raymond 1921- .... **CLC 5,
14**
See also CA 13-16R; CAAS 14; CANR 13,
29, 53; CP 7; DA3; DAC; DAM POET;
DLB 88; RGEL 2; SATA 63
Southern, Terry 1924(?)-1995 .... **CLC 7**
See also AMWS 11; BPFB 3; CA 1-4R;
150; CANR 1, 55, 107; CN 7; DLB 2;
IDFW 3, 4
Southerne, Thomas 1660-1746 .... **LC 99**
See also DLB 80; RGEL 2
Southey, Robert 1774-1843 .... **NCLC 8, 97**
See also BRW 4; DLB 93, 107, 142; RGEL
2; SATA 54
Southwell, Robert 1561(?)-1595 .... **LC 108**
See also DLB 167; RGEL 2; TEA
Southworth, Emma Dorothy Eliza Nevitte
1819-1899 .... **NCLC 26**
See also DLB 239
Souza, Ernest
See Scott, Evelyn
Soyinka, Wole 1934- .. **BLC 3; CLC 3, 5, 14,
36, 44, 179; DC 2; WLC**
See also AFW; BW 2, 3; CA 13-16R;
CANR 27, 39, 82; CD 5; CDWLB 3; CN
7; CP 7; DA; DA3; DAB; DAC; DAM
DRAM, MST, MULT; DFS 10; DLB 125;
EWL 3; MTCW 1, 2; RGEL 2; TWA;
WLIT 2; WWE 1
Spackman, W(illiam) M(ode)
1905-1990 .... **CLC 46**
See also CA 81-84; 132
Spacks, Barry (Bernard) 1931- .... **CLC 14**
See also CA 154; CANR 33, 109; CP 7;
DLB 105
Spanidou, Irini 1946- .... **CLC 44**
See also CA 185
Spark, Muriel (Sarah) 1918- ..... **CLC 2, 3, 5,
8, 13, 18, 40, 94; SSC 10**
See also BRWS 1; CA 5-8R; CANR 12, 36,
76, 89, 131; CDBLB 1945-1960; CN 7;
CP 7; DA3; DAB; DAC; DAM MST,
NOV; DLB 15, 139; EWL 3; FW; INT
CANR-12; LAIT 4; MTCW 1, 2; RGEL
2; TEA; WLIT 4; YAW
Spaulding, Douglas
See Bradbury, Ray (Douglas)
Spaulding, Leonard
See Bradbury, Ray (Douglas)
Speght, Rachel 1597-c. 1630 .... **LC 97**
See also DLB 126
Spelman, Elizabeth .... **CLC 65**
Spence, J. A. D.
See Eliot, T(homas) S(tearns)
Spencer, Anne 1882-1975 .... **HR 3**
See also BW 2; CA 161; DLB 51, 54

Spencer, Elizabeth 1921- .... **CLC 22; SSC 57**
See also CA 13-16R; CANR 32, 65, 87; CN 7; CSW; DLB 6, 218; EWL 3; MTCW 1; RGAL 4; SATA 14

Spencer, Leonard G.
See Silverberg, Robert

Spencer, Scott 1945- .... **CLC 30**
See also CA 113; CANR 51; DLBY 1986

Spender, Stephen (Harold)
1909-1995 .... **CLC 1, 2, 5, 10, 41, 91**
See also BRWS 2; CA 9-12R; 149; CANR 31, 54; CDBLB 1945-1960; CP 7; DA3; DAM POET; DLB 20; EWL 3; MTCW 1, 2; PAB; RGEL 2; TEA

Spengler, Oswald (Arnold Gottfried)
1880-1936 .... **TCLC 25**
See also CA 118; 189

Spenser, Edmund 1552(?)-1599 ..... **LC 5, 39; PC 8, 42; WLC**
See also AAYA 60; BRW 1; CDBLB Before 1660; DA; DA3; DAB; DAC; DAM MST, POET; DLB 167; EFS 2; EXPP; PAB; RGEL 2; TEA; WLIT 3; WP

Spicer, Jack 1925-1965 .... **CLC 8, 18, 72**
See also BG 3; CA 85-88; DAM POET; DLB 5, 16, 193; GLL 1; WP

Spiegelman, Art 1948- .... **CLC 76, 178**
See also AAYA 10, 46; CA 125; CANR 41, 55, 74, 124; DLB 299; MTCW 2; SATA 109; YAW

Spielberg, Peter 1929- .... **CLC 6**
See also CA 5-8R; CANR 4, 48; DLBY 1981

Spielberg, Steven 1947- .... **CLC 20, 188**
See also AAYA 8, 24; CA 77-80; CANR 32; SATA 32

Spillane, Frank Morrison 1918-
See Spillane, Mickey
See also CA 25-28R; CANR 28, 63, 125; DA3; MTCW 1, 2; SATA 66

Spillane, Mickey .... **CLC 3, 13**
See Spillane, Frank Morrison
See also BPFB 3; CMW 4; DLB 226; MSW; MTCW 2

Spinoza, Benedictus de 1632-1677 .. **LC 9, 58**

Spinrad, Norman (Richard) 1940- ... **CLC 46**
See also BPFB 3; CA 37-40R; CAAS 19; CANR 20, 91; DLB 8; INT CANR-20; SFW 4

Spitteler, Carl (Friedrich Georg)
1845-1924 .... **TCLC 12**
See also CA 109; DLB 129; EWL 3

Spivack, Kathleen (Romola Drucker)
1938- .... **CLC 6**
See also CA 49-52

Spoto, Donald 1941- .... **CLC 39**
See also CA 65-68; CANR 11, 57, 93

Springsteen, Bruce (F.) 1949- .... **CLC 17**
See also CA 111

Spurling, (Susan) Hilary 1940- .... **CLC 34**
See also CA 104; CANR 25, 52, 94

Spyker, John Howland
See Elman, Richard (Martin)

Squared, A.
See Abbott, Edwin A.

Squires, (James) Radcliffe
1917-1993 .... **CLC 51**
See also CA 1-4R; 140; CANR 6, 21

Srivastava, Dhanpat Rai 1880(?)-1936
See Premchand
See also CA 118; 197

Stacy, Donald
See Pohl, Frederik

Stael
See Stael-Holstein, Anne Louise Germaine Necker
See also EW 5; RGWL 2, 3

Stael, Germaine de
See Stael-Holstein, Anne Louise Germaine Necker
See also DLB 119, 192; FW; GFL 1789 to the Present; TWA

Stael-Holstein, Anne Louise Germaine Necker 1766-1817 .... **NCLC 3, 91**
See Stael; Stael, Germaine de

Stafford, Jean 1915-1979 .. **CLC 4, 7, 19, 68; SSC 26**
See also CA 1-4R; 85-88; CANR 3, 65; DLB 2, 173; MTCW 1, 2; RGAL 4; RGSF 2; SATA-Obit 22; TCWW 2; TUS

Stafford, William (Edgar)
1914-1993 .... **CLC 4, 7, 29**
See also AMWS 11; CA 5-8R; 142; CAAS 3; CANR 5, 22; DAM POET; DLB 5, 206; EXPP; INT CANR-22; PFS 2, 8, 16; RGAL 4; WP

Stagnelius, Eric Johan 1793-1823 . **NCLC 61**

Staines, Trevor
See Brunner, John (Kilian Houston)

Stairs, Gordon
See Austin, Mary (Hunter)
See also TCWW 2

Stalin, Joseph 1879-1953 .... **TCLC 92**

Stampa, Gaspara c. 1524-1554 .... **PC 43; LC 114**
See also RGWL 2, 3

Stampflinger, K. A.
See Benjamin, Walter

Stancykowna
See Szymborska, Wislawa

Standing Bear, Luther
1868(?)-1939(?) .... **NNAL**
See also CA 113; 144; DAM MULT

Stannard, Martin 1947- .... **CLC 44**
See also CA 142; DLB 155

Stanton, Elizabeth Cady
1815-1902 .... **TCLC 73**
See also CA 171; DLB 79; FW

Stanton, Maura 1946- .... **CLC 9**
See also CA 89-92; CANR 15, 123; DLB 120

Stanton, Schuyler
See Baum, L(yman) Frank

Stapledon, (William) Olaf
1886-1950 .... **TCLC 22**
See also CA 111; 162; DLB 15, 255; SFW 4

Starbuck, George (Edwin)
1931-1996 .... **CLC 53**
See also CA 21-24R; 153; CANR 23; DAM POET

Stark, Richard
See Westlake, Donald E(dwin)

Staunton, Schuyler
See Baum, L(yman) Frank

Stead, Christina (Ellen) 1902-1983 ... **CLC 2, 5, 8, 32, 80**
See also BRWS 4; CA 13-16R; 109; CANR 33, 40; DLB 260; EWL 3; FW; MTCW 1, 2; RGEL 2; RGSF 2; WWE 1

Stead, William Thomas
1849-1912 .... **TCLC 48**
See also CA 167

Stebnitsky, M.
See Leskov, Nikolai (Semyonovich)

Steele, Sir Richard 1672-1729 .... **LC 18**
See also BRW 3; CDBLB 1660-1789; DLB 84, 101; RGEL 2; WLIT 3

Steele, Timothy (Reid) 1948- .... **CLC 45**
See also CA 93-96; CANR 16, 50, 92; CP 7; DLB 120, 282

Steffens, (Joseph) Lincoln
1866-1936 .... **TCLC 20**
See also CA 117; 198; DLB 303

Stegner, Wallace (Earle) 1909-1993 .. **CLC 9, 49, 81; SSC 27**
See also AITN 1; AMWS 4; ANW; BEST 90:3; BPFB 3; CA 1-4R; 141; CAAS 9; CANR 1, 21, 46; DAM NOV; DLB 9, 206, 275; DLBY 1993; EWL 3; MTCW 1, 2; RGAL 4; TCWW 2; TUS

Stein, Gertrude 1874-1946 .... **DC 19; PC 18; SSC 42; TCLC 1, 6, 28, 48; WLC**
See also AMW; AMWC 2; CA 104; 132; CANR 108; CDALB 1917-1929; DA; DA3; DAB; DAC; DAM MST, NOV, POET; DLB 4, 54, 86, 228; DLBD 15; EWL 3; EXPS; GLL 1; MAWW; MTCW 1, 2; NCFS 4; RGAL 4; RGSF 2; SSFS 5; TUS; WP

Steinbeck, John (Ernst) 1902-1968 ... **CLC 1, 5, 9, 13, 21, 34, 45, 75, 124; SSC 11, 37, 77; TCLC 135; WLC**
See also AAYA 12; AMW; BPFB 3; BYA 2, 3, 13; CA 1-4R; 25-28R; CANR 1, 35; CDALB 1929-1941; DA; DA3; DAB; DAC; DAM DRAM, MST, NOV; DLB 7, 9, 212, 275, 309; DLBD 2; EWL 3; EXPS; LAIT 3; MTCW 1, 2; NFS 1, 5, 7, 17, 19; RGAL 4; RGSF 2; RHW; SATA 9; SSFS 3, 6; TCWW 2; TUS; WYA; YAW

Steinem, Gloria 1934- .... **CLC 63**
See also CA 53-56; CANR 28, 51; DLB 246; FW; MTCW 1, 2

Steiner, George 1929- .... **CLC 24**
See also CA 73-76; CANR 31, 67, 108; DAM NOV; DLB 67, 299; EWL 3; MTCW 1, 2; SATA 62

Steiner, K. Leslie
See Delany, Samuel R(ay), Jr.

Steiner, Rudolf 1861-1925 .... **TCLC 13**
See also CA 107

Stendhal 1783-1842 .. **NCLC 23, 46; SSC 27; WLC**
See also DA; DA3; DAB; DAC; DAM MST, NOV; DLB 119; EW 5; GFL 1789 to the Present; RGWL 2, 3; TWA

Stephen, Adeline Virginia
See Woolf, (Adeline) Virginia

Stephen, Sir Leslie 1832-1904 .... **TCLC 23**
See also BRW 5; CA 123; DLB 57, 144, 190

Stephen, Sir Leslie
See Stephen, Sir Leslie

Stephen, Virginia
See Woolf, (Adeline) Virginia

Stephens, James 1882(?)-1950 .... **SSC 50; TCLC 4**
See also CA 104; 192; DLB 19, 153, 162; EWL 3; FANT; RGEL 2; SUFW

Stephens, Reed
See Donaldson, Stephen R(eeder)

Steptoe, Lydia
See Barnes, Djuna
See also GLL 1

Sterchi, Beat 1949- .... **CLC 65**
See also CA 203

Sterling, Brett
See Bradbury, Ray (Douglas); Hamilton, Edmond

Sterling, Bruce 1954- .... **CLC 72**
See also CA 119; CANR 44, 135; SCFW 2; SFW 4

Sterling, George 1869-1926 .... **TCLC 20**
See also CA 117; 165; DLB 54

Stern, Gerald 1925- .... **CLC 40, 100**
See also AMWS 9; CA 81-84; CANR 28, 94; CP 7; DLB 105; RGAL 4

Stern, Richard (Gustave) 1928- ... **CLC 4, 39**
See also CA 1-4R; CANR 1, 25, 52, 120; CN 7; DLB 218; DLBY 1987; INT CANR-25

Tanizaki, Jun'ichiro 1886-1965 ... **CLC 8, 14, 28; SSC 21**
See Tanizaki Jun'ichiro
See also CA 93-96; 25-28R; MJW; MTCW 2; RGSF 2; RGWL 2

Tanizaki Jun'ichiro
See Tanizaki, Jun'ichiro
See also DLB 180; EWL 3

Tannen, Deborah F. 1945- .... **CLC 206**
See also CA 118; CANR 95

Tanner, William
See Amis, Kingsley (William)

Tao Lao
See Storni, Alfonsina

Tapahonso, Luci 1953- .... **NNAL**
See also CA 145; CANR 72, 127; DLB 175

Tarantino, Quentin (Jerome)
1963- .... **CLC 125**
See also AAYA 58; CA 171; CANR 125

Tarassoff, Lev
See Troyat, Henri

Tarbell, Ida M(inerva) 1857-1944 . **TCLC 40**
See also CA 122; 181; DLB 47

Tarkington, (Newton) Booth
1869-1946 .... **TCLC 9**
See also BPFB 3; BYA 3; CA 110; 143; CWRI 5; DLB 9, 102; MTCW 2; RGAL 4; SATA 17

Tarkovskii, Andrei Arsen'evich
See Tarkovsky, Andrei (Arsenyevich)

Tarkovsky, Andrei (Arsenyevich)
1932-1986 .... **CLC 75**
See also CA 127

Tartt, Donna 1963- .... **CLC 76**
See also AAYA 56; CA 142

Tasso, Torquato 1544-1595 .... **LC 5, 94**
See also EFS 2; EW 2; RGWL 2, 3

Tate, (John Orley) Allen 1899-1979 .. **CLC 2, 4, 6, 9, 11, 14, 24; PC 50**
See also AMW; CA 5-8R; 85-88; CANR 32, 108; DLB 4, 45, 63; DLBD 17; EWL 3; MTCW 1, 2; RGAL 4; RHW

Tate, Ellalice
See Hibbert, Eleanor Alice Burford

Tate, James (Vincent) 1943- ..... **CLC 2, 6, 25**
See also CA 21-24R; CANR 29, 57, 114; CP 7; DLB 5, 169; EWL 3; PFS 10, 15; RGAL 4; WP

Tate, Nahum 1652(?)-1715 .... **LC 109**
See also DLB 80; RGEL 2

Tauler, Johannes c. 1300-1361 ...... **CMLC 37**
See also DLB 179; LMFS 1

Tavel, Ronald 1940- .... **CLC 6**
See also CA 21-24R; CAD; CANR 33; CD 5

Taviani, Paolo 1931- .... **CLC 70**
See also CA 153

Taylor, Bayard 1825-1878 .... **NCLC 89**
See also DLB 3, 189, 250, 254; RGAL 4

Taylor, C(ecil) P(hilip) 1929-1981 ... **CLC 27**
See also CA 25-28R; 105; CANR 47; CBD

Taylor, Edward 1642(?)-1729 . **LC 11; PC 63**
See also AMW; DA; DAB; DAC; DAM MST, POET; DLB 24; EXPP; RGAL 4; TUS

Taylor, Eleanor Ross 1920- .... **CLC 5**
See also CA 81-84; CANR 70

Taylor, Elizabeth 1932-1975 ..... **CLC 2, 4, 29**
See also CA 13-16R; CANR 9, 70; DLB 139; MTCW 1; RGEL 2; SATA 13

Taylor, Frederick Winslow
1856-1915 .... **TCLC 76**
See also CA 188

Taylor, Henry (Splawn) 1942- .... **CLC 44**
See also CA 33-36R; CAAS 7; CANR 31; CP 7; DLB 5; PFS 10

Taylor, Kamala (Purnaiya) 1924-2004
See Markandaya, Kamala
See also CA 77-80; 227; NFS 13

Taylor, Mildred D(elois) 1943- .... **CLC 21**
See also AAYA 10, 47; BW 1; BYA 3, 8; CA 85-88; CANR 25, 115; CLR 9, 59, 90; CSW; DLB 52; JRDA; LAIT 3; MAICYA 1, 2; SAAS 5; SATA 135; WYA; YAW

Taylor, Peter (Hillsman) 1917-1994 .. **CLC 1, 4, 18, 37, 44, 50, 71; SSC 10**
See also AMWS 5; BPFB 3; CA 13-16R; 147; CANR 9, 50; CSW; DLB 218, 278; DLBY 1981, 1994; EWL 3; EXPS; INT CANR-9; MTCW 1, 2; RGSF 2; SSFS 9; TUS

Taylor, Robert Lewis 1912-1998 .... **CLC 14**
See also CA 1-4R; 170; CANR 3, 64; SATA 10

Tchekhov, Anton
See Chekhov, Anton (Pavlovich)

Tchicaya, Gerald Felix 1931-1988 .. **CLC 101**
See Tchicaya U Tam'si
See also CA 129; 125; CANR 81

Tchicaya U Tam'si
See Tchicaya, Gerald Felix
See also EWL 3

Teasdale, Sara 1884-1933 .... **PC 31; TCLC 4**
See also CA 104; 163; DLB 45; GLL 1; PFS 14; RGAL 4; SATA 32; TUS

Tecumseh 1768-1813 .... **NNAL**
See also DAM MULT

Tegner, Esaias 1782-1846 .... **NCLC 2**

Fujiwara no Teika 1162-1241 .... **CMLC 73**
See also DLB 203

Teilhard de Chardin, (Marie Joseph) Pierre
1881-1955 .... **TCLC 9**
See also CA 105; 210; GFL 1789 to the Present

Temple, Ann
See Mortimer, Penelope (Ruth)

Tennant, Emma (Christina) 1937- .. **CLC 13, 52**
See also BRWS 9; CA 65-68; CAAS 9; CANR 10, 38, 59, 88; CN 7; DLB 14; EWL 3; SFW 4

Tenneshaw, S. M.
See Silverberg, Robert

Tenney, Tabitha Gilman
1762-1837 .... **NCLC 122**
See also DLB 37, 200

Tennyson, Alfred 1809-1892 ... **NCLC 30, 65, 115; PC 6; WLC**
See also AAYA 50; BRW 4; CDBLB 1832-1890; DA; DA3; DAB; DAC; DAM MST, POET; DLB 32; EXPP; PAB; PFS 1, 2, 4, 11, 15, 19; RGEL 2; TEA; WLIT 4; WP

Teran, Lisa St. Aubin de .... **CLC 36**
See St. Aubin de Teran, Lisa

Terence c. 184B.C.-c. 159B.C. ...... **CMLC 14; DC 7**
See also AW 1; CDWLB 1; DLB 211; RGWL 2, 3; TWA

Teresa de Jesus, St. 1515-1582 .... **LC 18**

Terkel, Louis 1912-
See Terkel, Studs
See also CA 57-60; CANR 18, 45, 67, 132; DA3; MTCW 1, 2

Terkel, Studs .... **CLC 38**
See Terkel, Louis
See also AAYA 32; AITN 1; MTCW 2; TUS

Terry, C. V.
See Slaughter, Frank G(ill)

Terry, Megan 1932- .... **CLC 19; DC 13**
See also CA 77-80; CABS 3; CAD; CANR 43; CD 5; CWD; DFS 18; DLB 7, 249; GLL 2

Tertullian c. 155-c. 245 .... **CMLC 29**

Tertz, Abram
See Sinyavsky, Andrei (Donatevich)
See also RGSF 2

Tesich, Steve 1943(?)-1996 .... **CLC 40, 69**
See also CA 105; 152; CAD; DLBY 1983

Tesla, Nikola 1856-1943 .... **TCLC 88**

Teternikov, Fyodor Kuzmich 1863-1927
See Sologub, Fyodor
See also CA 104

Tevis, Walter 1928-1984 .... **CLC 42**
See also CA 113; SFW 4

Tey, Josephine .... **TCLC 14**
See Mackintosh, Elizabeth
See also DLB 77; MSW

Thackeray, William Makepeace
1811-1863 .... **NCLC 5, 14, 22, 43; WLC**
See also BRW 5; BRWC 2; CDBLB 1832-1890; DA; DA3; DAB; DAC; DAM MST, NOV; DLB 21, 55, 159, 163; NFS 13; RGEL 2; SATA 23; TEA; WLIT 3

Thakura, Ravindranatha
See Tagore, Rabindranath

Thames, C. H.
See Marlowe, Stephen

Tharoor, Shashi 1956- .... **CLC 70**
See also CA 141; CANR 91; CN 7

Thelwell, Michael Miles 1939- .... **CLC 22**
See also BW 2; CA 101

Theobald, Lewis, Jr.
See Lovecraft, H(oward) P(hillips)

Theocritus c. 310B.C.- .... **CMLC 45**
See also AW 1; DLB 176; RGWL 2, 3

Theodorescu, Ion N. 1880-1967
See Arghezi, Tudor
See also CA 116

Theriault, Yves 1915-1983 .... **CLC 79**
See also CA 102; CCA 1; DAC; DAM MST; DLB 88; EWL 3

Theroux, Alexander (Louis) 1939- .... **CLC 2, 25**
See also CA 85-88; CANR 20, 63; CN 7

Theroux, Paul (Edward) 1941- ..... **CLC 5, 8, 11, 15, 28, 46**
See also AAYA 28; AMWS 8; BEST 89:4; BPFB 3; CA 33-36R; CANR 20, 45, 74, 133; CDALBS; CN 7; CPW 1; DA3; DAM POP; DLB 2, 218; EWL 3; HGG; MTCW 1, 2; RGAL 4; SATA 44, 109; TUS

Thesen, Sharon 1946- .... **CLC 56**
See also CA 163; CANR 125; CP 7; CWP

Thespis fl. 6th cent. B.C.- .... **CMLC 51**
See also LMFS 1

Thevenin, Denis
See Duhamel, Georges

Thibault, Jacques Anatole Francois
1844-1924
See France, Anatole
See also CA 106; 127; DA3; DAM NOV; MTCW 1, 2; TWA

Thiele, Colin (Milton) 1920- .... **CLC 17**
See also CA 29-32R; CANR 12, 53, 105; CLR 27; DLB 289; MAICYA 1, 2; SAAS 2; SATA 14, 72, 125; YAW

Thistlethwaite, Bel
See Wetherald, Agnes Ethelwyn

Thomas, Audrey (Callahan) 1935- .... **CLC 7, 13, 37, 107; SSC 20**
See also AITN 2; CA 21-24R; CAAS 19; CANR 36, 58; CN 7; DLB 60; MTCW 1; RGSF 2

Thomas, Augustus 1857-1934 .... **TCLC 97**

Thomas, D(onald) M(ichael) 1935- . **CLC 13, 22, 31, 132**
See also BPFB 3; BRWS 4; CA 61-64; CAAS 11; CANR 17, 45, 75; CDBLB 1960 to Present; CN 7; CP 7; DA3; DLB 40, 207, 299; HGG; INT CANR-17; MTCW 1, 2; SFW 4

Toomer, Eugene Pinchback
See Toomer, Jean
Toomer, Jean 1894-1967 .. **BLC 3; CLC 1, 4, 13, 22; HR 3; PC 7; SSC 1, 45; WLCS**
See also AFAW 1, 2; AMWS 3, 9; BW 1; CA 85-88; CDALB 1917-1929; DA3; DAM MULT; DLB 45, 51; EWL 3; EXPP; EXPS; LMFS 2; MTCW 1, 2; NFS 11; RGAL 4; RGSF 2; SSFS 5
Toomer, Nathan Jean
See Toomer, Jean
Toomer, Nathan Pinchback
See Toomer, Jean
Torley, Luke
See Blish, James (Benjamin)
Tornimparte, Alessandra
See Ginzburg, Natalia
Torre, Raoul della
See Mencken, H(enry) L(ouis)
Torrence, Ridgely 1874-1950 .... **TCLC 97**
See also DLB 54, 249
Torrey, E(dwin) Fuller 1937- .... **CLC 34**
See also CA 119; CANR 71
Torsvan, Ben Traven
See Traven, B.
Torsvan, Benno Traven
See Traven, B.
Torsvan, Berick Traven
See Traven, B.
Torsvan, Berwick Traven
See Traven, B.
Torsvan, Bruno Traven
See Traven, B.
Torsvan, Traven
See Traven, B.
Tourneur, Cyril 1575(?)-1626 .... **LC 66**
See also BRW 2; DAM DRAM; DLB 58; RGEL 2
Tournier, Michel (Edouard) 1924- .... **CLC 6, 23, 36, 95**
See also CA 49-52; CANR 3, 36, 74; CWW 2; DLB 83; EWL 3; GFL 1789 to the Present; MTCW 1, 2; SATA 23
Tournimparte, Alessandra
See Ginzburg, Natalia
Towers, Ivar
See Kornbluth, C(yril) M.
Towne, Robert (Burton) 1936(?)- ..... **CLC 87**
See also CA 108; DLB 44; IDFW 3, 4
Townsend, Sue .... **CLC 61**
See Townsend, Susan Lilian
See also AAYA 28; CA 119; 127; CANR 65, 107; CBD; CD 5; CPW; CWD; DAB; DAC; DAM MST; DLB 271; INT CA-127; SATA 55, 93; SATA-Brief 48; YAW
Townsend, Susan Lilian 1946-
See Townsend, Sue
Townshend, Pete
See Townshend, Peter (Dennis Blandford)
Townshend, Peter (Dennis Blandford) 1945- .... **CLC 17, 42**
See also CA 107
Tozzi, Federigo 1883-1920 .... **TCLC 31**
See also CA 160; CANR 110; DLB 264; EWL 3
Tracy, Don(ald Fiske) 1905-1970(?)
See Queen, Ellery
See also CA 1-4R; 176; CANR 2
Trafford, F. G.
See Riddell, Charlotte
Traherne, Thomas 1637(?)-1674 .... **LC 99**
See also BRW 2; DLB 131; PAB; RGEL 2
Traill, Catharine Parr 1802-1899 .. **NCLC 31**
See also DLB 99
Trakl, Georg 1887-1914 .... **PC 20; TCLC 5**
See also CA 104; 165; EW 10; EWL 3; LMFS 2; MTCW 2; RGWL 2, 3

Tranquilli, Secondino
See Silone, Ignazio
Transtroemer, Tomas Gosta
See Transtromer, Tomas (Goesta)
Transtromer, Tomas (Gosta)
See Transtromer, Tomas (Goesta)
See also CWW 2
Transtromer, Tomas (Goesta) 1931- .... **CLC 52, 65**
See Transtromer, Tomas (Gosta)
See also CA 117; 129; CAAS 17; CANR 115; DAM POET; DLB 257; EWL 3; PFS 21
Transtromer, Tomas Gosta
See Transtromer, Tomas (Goesta)
Traven, B. 1882(?)-1969 .... **CLC 8, 11**
See also CA 19-20; 25-28R; CAP 2; DLB 9, 56; EWL 3; MTCW 1; RGAL 4
Trediakovsky, Vasilii Kirillovich 1703-1769 .... **LC 68**
See also DLB 150
Treitel, Jonathan 1959- .... **CLC 70**
See also CA 210; DLB 267
Trelawny, Edward John 1792-1881 .... **NCLC 85**
See also DLB 110, 116, 144
Tremain, Rose 1943- .... **CLC 42**
See also CA 97-100; CANR 44, 95; CN 7; DLB 14, 271; RGSF 2; RHW
Tremblay, Michel 1942- .... **CLC 29, 102**
See also CA 116; 128; CCA 1; CWW 2; DAC; DAM MST; DLB 60; EWL 3; GLL 1; MTCW 1, 2
Trevanian .... **CLC 29**
See Whitaker, Rod(ney)
Trevor, Glen
See Hilton, James
Trevor, William .. **CLC 7, 9, 14, 25, 71, 116; SSC 21, 58**
See Cox, William Trevor
See also BRWS 4; CBD; CD 5; CN 7; DLB 14, 139; EWL 3; LATS 1:2; MTCW 2; RGEL 2; RGSF 2; SSFS 10
Trifonov, Iurii (Valentinovich)
See Trifonov, Yuri (Valentinovich)
See also DLB 302; RGWL 2, 3
Trifonov, Yuri (Valentinovich) 1925-1981 .... **CLC 45**
See Trifonov, Iurii (Valentinovich); Trifonov, Yury Valentinovich
See also CA 126; 103; MTCW 1
Trifonov, Yury Valentinovich
See Trifonov, Yuri (Valentinovich)
See also EWL 3
Trilling, Diana (Rubin) 1905-1996 . **CLC 129**
See also CA 5-8R; 154; CANR 10, 46; INT CANR-10; MTCW 1, 2
Trilling, Lionel 1905-1975 ..... **CLC 9, 11, 24; SSC 75**
See also AMWS 3; CA 9-12R; 61-64; CANR 10, 105; DLB 28, 63; EWL 3; INT CANR-10; MTCW 1, 2; RGAL 4; TUS
Trimball, W. H.
See Mencken, H(enry) L(ouis)
Tristan
See Gomez de la Serna, Ramon
Tristram
See Housman, A(lfred) E(dward)
Trogdon, William (Lewis) 1939-
See Heat-Moon, William Least
See also CA 115; 119; CANR 47, 89; CPW; INT CA-119
Trollope, Anthony 1815-1882 .... **NCLC 6, 33, 101; SSC 28; WLC**
See also BRW 5; CDBLB 1832-1890; DA; DA3; DAB; DAC; DAM MST, NOV; DLB 21, 57, 159; RGEL 2; RGSF 2; SATA 22

Trollope, Frances 1779-1863 .... **NCLC 30**
See also DLB 21, 166
Trollope, Joanna 1943- .... **CLC 186**
See also CA 101; CANR 58, 95; CPW; DLB 207; RHW
Trotsky, Leon 1879-1940 .... **TCLC 22**
See also CA 118; 167
Trotter (Cockburn), Catharine 1679-1749 .... **LC 8**
See also DLB 84, 252
Trotter, Wilfred 1872-1939 .... **TCLC 97**
Trout, Kilgore
See Farmer, Philip Jose
Trow, George W. S. 1943- .... **CLC 52**
See also CA 126; CANR 91
Troyat, Henri 1911- .... **CLC 23**
See also CA 45-48; CANR 2, 33, 67, 117; GFL 1789 to the Present; MTCW 1
Trudeau, G(arretson) B(eekman) 1948-
See Trudeau, Garry B.
See also AAYA 60; CA 81-84; CANR 31; SATA 35
Trudeau, Garry B. .... **CLC 12**
See Trudeau, G(arretson) B(eekman)
See also AAYA 10; AITN 2
Truffaut, Francois 1932-1984 ... **CLC 20, 101**
See also CA 81-84; 113; CANR 34
Trumbo, Dalton 1905-1976 .... **CLC 19**
See also CA 21-24R; 69-72; CANR 10; DLB 26; IDFW 3, 4; YAW
Trumbull, John 1750-1831 .... **NCLC 30**
See also DLB 31; RGAL 4
Trundlett, Helen B.
See Eliot, T(homas) S(tearns)
Truth, Sojourner 1797(?)-1883 ...... **NCLC 94**
See also DLB 239; FW; LAIT 2
Tryon, Thomas 1926-1991 .... **CLC 3, 11**
See also AITN 1; BPFB 3; CA 29-32R; 135; CANR 32, 77; CPW; DA3; DAM POP; HGG; MTCW 1
Tryon, Tom
See Tryon, Thomas
Ts'ao Hsueh-ch'in 1715(?)-1763 .... **LC 1**
Tsushima, Shuji 1909-1948
See Dazai Osamu
See also CA 107
Tsvetaeva (Efron), Marina (Ivanovna) 1892-1941 .... **PC 14; TCLC 7, 35**
See also CA 104; 128; CANR 73; DLB 295; EW 11; MTCW 1, 2; RGWL 2, 3
Tuck, Lily 1938- .... **CLC 70**
See also CA 139; CANR 90
Tu Fu 712-770 .... **PC 9**
See Du Fu
See also DAM MULT; TWA; WP
Tunis, John R(oberts) 1889-1975 ..... **CLC 12**
See also BYA 1; CA 61-64; CANR 62; DLB 22, 171; JRDA; MAICYA 1, 2; SATA 37; SATA-Brief 30; YAW
Tuohy, Frank .... **CLC 37**
See Tuohy, John Francis
See also DLB 14, 139
Tuohy, John Francis 1925-
See Tuohy, Frank
See also CA 5-8R; 178; CANR 3, 47; CN 7
Turco, Lewis (Putnam) 1934- ..... **CLC 11, 63**
See also CA 13-16R; CAAS 22; CANR 24, 51; CP 7; DLBY 1984
Turgenev, Ivan (Sergeevich) 1818-1883 ..... **DC 7; NCLC 21, 37, 122; SSC 7, 57; WLC**
See also AAYA 58; DA; DAB; DAC; DAM MST, NOV; DFS 6; DLB 238, 284; EW 6; LATS 1:1; NFS 16; RGSF 2; RGWL 2, 3; TWA

Walther von der Vogelweide c.
1170-1228 .... **CMLC 56**

Walton, Izaak 1593-1683 .... **LC 72**
See also BRW 2; CDBLB Before 1660;
DLB 151, 213; RGEL 2

Wambaugh, Joseph (Aloysius), Jr.
1937- .... **CLC 3, 18**
See also AITN 1; BEST 89:3; BPFB 3; CA
33-36R; CANR 42, 65, 115; CMW 4;
CPW 1; DA3; DAM NOV, POP; DLB 6;
DLBY 1983; MSW; MTCW 1, 2

Wang Wei 699(?)-761(?) .... **PC 18**
See also TWA

Warburton, William 1698-1779 .... **LC 97**
See also DLB 104

Ward, Arthur Henry Sarsfield 1883-1959
See Rohmer, Sax
See also CA 108; 173; CMW 4; HGG

Ward, Douglas Turner 1930- .... **CLC 19**
See also BW 1; CA 81-84; CAD; CANR
27; CD 5; DLB 7, 38

Ward, E. D.
See Lucas, E(dward) V(errall)

Ward, Mrs. Humphry 1851-1920
See Ward, Mary Augusta
See also RGEL 2

Ward, Mary Augusta 1851-1920 ... **TCLC 55**
See Ward, Mrs. Humphry
See also DLB 18

Ward, Nathaniel 1578(?)-1652 .... **LC 114**
See also DLB 24

Ward, Peter
See Faust, Frederick (Schiller)

Warhol, Andy 1928(?)-1987 .... **CLC 20**
See also AAYA 12; BEST 89:4; CA 89-92;
121; CANR 34

Warner, Francis (Robert le Plastrier)
1937- .... **CLC 14**
See also CA 53-56; CANR 11

Warner, Marina 1946- .... **CLC 59**
See also CA 65-68; CANR 21, 55, 118; CN
7; DLB 194

Warner, Rex (Ernest) 1905-1986 ...... **CLC 45**
See also CA 89-92; 119; DLB 15; RGEL 2;
RHW

Warner, Susan (Bogert)
1819-1885 .... **NCLC 31, 146**
See also DLB 3, 42, 239, 250, 254

Warner, Sylvia (Constance) Ashton
See Ashton-Warner, Sylvia (Constance)

Warner, Sylvia Townsend
1893-1978 .. **CLC 7, 19; SSC 23; TCLC
131**
See also BRWS 7; CA 61-64; 77-80; CANR
16, 60, 104; DLB 34, 139; EWL 3; FANT;
FW; MTCW 1, 2; RGEL 2; RGSF 2;
RHW

Warren, Mercy Otis 1728-1814 ..... **NCLC 13**
See also DLB 31, 200; RGAL 4; TUS

Warren, Robert Penn 1905-1989 .. **CLC 1, 4,
6, 8, 10, 13, 18, 39, 53, 59; PC 37; SSC
4, 58; WLC**
See also AITN 1; AMW; AMWC 2; BPFB
3; BYA 1; CA 13-16R; 129; CANR 10,
47; CDALB 1968-1988; DA; DA3; DAB;
DAC; DAM MST, NOV, POET; DLB 2,
48, 152; DLBY 1980, 1989; EWL 3; INT
CANR-10; MTCW 1, 2; NFS 13; RGAL
4; RGSF 2; RHW; SATA 46; SATA-Obit
63; SSFS 8; TUS

Warrigal, Jack
See Furphy, Joseph

Warshofsky, Isaac
See Singer, Isaac Bashevis

Warton, Joseph 1722-1800 .... **NCLC 118**
See also DLB 104, 109; RGEL 2

Warton, Thomas 1728-1790 .... **LC 15, 82**
See also DAM POET; DLB 104, 109;
RGEL 2

Waruk, Kona
See Harris, (Theodore) Wilson

Warung, Price .... **TCLC 45**
See Astley, William
See also DLB 230; RGEL 2

Warwick, Jarvis
See Garner, Hugh
See also CCA 1

Washington, Alex
See Harris, Mark

Washington, Booker T(aliaferro)
1856-1915 .... **BLC 3; TCLC 10**
See also BW 1; CA 114; 125; DA3; DAM
MULT; LAIT 2; RGAL 4; SATA 28

Washington, George 1732-1799 .... **LC 25**
See also DLB 31

Wassermann, (Karl) Jakob
1873-1934 .... **TCLC 6**
See also CA 104; 163; DLB 66; EWL 3

Wasserstein, Wendy 1950- ... **CLC 32, 59, 90,
183; DC 4**
See also CA 121; 129; CABS 3; CAD;
CANR 53, 75, 128; CD 5; CWD; DA3;
DAM DRAM; DFS 5, 17; DLB 228;
EWL 3; FW; INT CA-129; MTCW 2;
SATA 94

Waterhouse, Keith (Spencer) 1929- . **CLC 47**
See also CA 5-8R; CANR 38, 67, 109;
CBD; CN 7; DLB 13, 15; MTCW 1, 2

Waters, Frank (Joseph) 1902-1995 .. **CLC 88**
See also CA 5-8R; 149; CAAS 13; CANR
3, 18, 63, 121; DLB 212; DLBY 1986;
RGAL 4; TCWW 2

Waters, Mary C. .... **CLC 70**

Waters, Roger 1944- .... **CLC 35**

Watkins, Frances Ellen
See Harper, Frances Ellen Watkins

Watkins, Gerrold
See Malzberg, Barry N(athaniel)

Watkins, Gloria Jean 1952(?)- .... **CLC 94**
See also BW 2; CA 143; CANR 87, 126;
DLB 246; MTCW 2; SATA 115

Watkins, Paul 1964- .... **CLC 55**
See also CA 132; CANR 62, 98

Watkins, Vernon Phillips
1906-1967 .... **CLC 43**
See also CA 9-10; 25-28R; CAP 1; DLB
20; EWL 3; RGEL 2

Watson, Irving S.
See Mencken, H(enry) L(ouis)

Watson, John H.
See Farmer, Philip Jose

Watson, Richard F.
See Silverberg, Robert

Watts, Ephraim
See Horne, Richard Henry Hengist

Watts, Isaac 1674-1748 .... **LC 98**
See also DLB 95; RGEL 2; SATA 52

Waugh, Auberon (Alexander)
1939-2001 .... **CLC 7**
See also CA 45-48; 192; CANR 6, 22, 92;
DLB 14, 194

Waugh, Evelyn (Arthur St. John)
1903-1966 .. **CLC 1, 3, 8, 13, 19, 27, 44,
107; SSC 41; WLC**
See also BPFB 3; BRW 7; CA 85-88; 25-
28R; CANR 22; CDBLB 1914-1945; DA;
DA3; DAB; DAC; DAM MST, NOV,
POP; DLB 15, 162, 195; EWL 3; MTCW
1, 2; NFS 13, 17; RGEL 2; RGSF 2; TEA;
WLIT 4

Waugh, Harriet 1944- .... **CLC 6**
See also CA 85-88; CANR 22

Ways, C. R.
See Blount, Roy (Alton), Jr.

Waystaff, Simon
See Swift, Jonathan

Webb, Beatrice (Martha Potter)
1858-1943 .... **TCLC 22**
See also CA 117; 162; DLB 190; FW

Webb, Charles (Richard) 1939- .... **CLC 7**
See also CA 25-28R; CANR 114

Webb, Frank J. .... **NCLC 143**
See also DLB 50

Webb, James H(enry), Jr. 1946- ...... **CLC 22**
See also CA 81-84

Webb, Mary Gladys (Meredith)
1881-1927 .... **TCLC 24**
See also CA 182; 123; DLB 34; FW

Webb, Mrs. Sidney
See Webb, Beatrice (Martha Potter)

Webb, Phyllis 1927- .... **CLC 18**
See also CA 104; CANR 23; CCA 1; CP 7;
CWP; DLB 53

Webb, Sidney (James) 1859-1947 .. **TCLC 22**
See also CA 117; 163; DLB 190

Webber, Andrew Lloyd .... **CLC 21**
See Lloyd Webber, Andrew
See also DFS 7

Weber, Lenora Mattingly
1895-1971 .... **CLC 12**
See also CA 19-20; 29-32R; CAP 1; SATA
2; SATA-Obit 26

Weber, Max 1864-1920 .... **TCLC 69**
See also CA 109; 189; DLB 296

Webster, John 1580(?)-1634(?) ...... **DC 2; LC
33, 84; WLC**
See also BRW 2; CDBLB Before 1660; DA;
DAB; DAC; DAM DRAM, MST; DFS
17, 19; DLB 58; IDTP; RGEL 2; WLIT 3

Webster, Noah 1758-1843 .... **NCLC 30**
See also DLB 1, 37, 42, 43, 73, 243

Wedekind, (Benjamin) Frank(lin)
1864-1918 .... **TCLC 7**
See also CA 104; 153; CANR 121, 122;
CDWLB 2; DAM DRAM; DLB 118; EW
8; EWL 3; LMFS 2; RGWL 2, 3

Wehr, Demaris .... **CLC 65**

Weidman, Jerome 1913-1998 .... **CLC 7**
See also AITN 2; CA 1-4R; 171; CAD;
CANR 1; DLB 28

Weil, Simone (Adolphine)
1909-1943 .... **TCLC 23**
See also CA 117; 159; EW 12; EWL 3; FW;
GFL 1789 to the Present; MTCW 2

Weininger, Otto 1880-1903 .... **TCLC 84**

Weinstein, Nathan
See West, Nathanael

Weinstein, Nathan von Wallenstein
See West, Nathanael

Weir, Peter (Lindsay) 1944- .... **CLC 20**
See also CA 113; 123

Weiss, Peter (Ulrich) 1916-1982 .. **CLC 3, 15,
51; TCLC 152**
See also CA 45-48; 106; CANR 3; DAM
DRAM; DFS 3; DLB 69, 124; EWL 3;
RGWL 2, 3

Weiss, Theodore (Russell)
1916-2003 .... **CLC 3, 8, 14**
See also CA 9-12R; 189; 216; CAAE 189;
CAAS 2; CANR 46, 94; CP 7; DLB 5

Welch, (Maurice) Denton
1915-1948 .... **TCLC 22**
See also BRWS 8, 9; CA 121; 148; RGEL
2

Welch, James (Phillip) 1940-2003 ..... **CLC 6,
14, 52; NNAL; PC 62**
See also CA 85-88; 219; CANR 42, 66, 107;
CN 7; CP 7; CPW; DAM MULT, POP;
DLB 175, 256; LATS 1:1; RGAL 4;
TCWW 2

Weldon, Fay 1931- . **CLC 6, 9, 11, 19, 36, 59,
122**
See also BRWS 4; CA 21-24R; CANR 16,
46, 63, 97; CDBLB 1960 to Present; CN

White, Walter F(rancis) 1893-1955 ... **BLC 3; HR 3; TCLC 15**
See also BW 1; CA 115; 124; DAM MULT; DLB 51

White, William Hale 1831-1913
See Rutherford, Mark
See also CA 121; 189

Whitehead, Alfred North
1861-1947 .... **TCLC 97**
See also CA 117; 165; DLB 100, 262

Whitehead, E(dward) A(nthony)
1933- .... **CLC 5**
See also CA 65-68; CANR 58, 118; CBD; CD 5

Whitehead, Ted
See Whitehead, E(dward) A(nthony)

Whiteman, Roberta J. Hill 1947- ...... **NNAL**
See also CA 146

Whitemore, Hugh (John) 1936- .... **CLC 37**
See also CA 132; CANR 77; CBD; CD 5; INT CA-132

Whitman, Sarah Helen (Power)
1803-1878 .... **NCLC 19**
See also DLB 1, 243

Whitman, Walt(er) 1819-1892 .. **NCLC 4, 31, 81; PC 3; WLC**
See also AAYA 42; AMW; AMWR 1; CDALB 1640-1865; DA; DA3; DAB; DAC; DAM MST, POET; DLB 3, 64, 224, 250; EXPP; LAIT 2; LMFS 1; PAB; PFS 2, 3, 13; RGAL 4; SATA 20; TUS; WP; WYAS 1

Whitney, Phyllis A(yame) 1903- .... **CLC 42**
See also AAYA 36; AITN 2; BEST 90:3; CA 1-4R; CANR 3, 25, 38, 60; CLR 59; CMW 4; CPW; DA3; DAM POP; JRDA; MAICYA 1, 2; MTCW 2; RHW; SATA 1, 30; YAW

Whittemore, (Edward) Reed, Jr.
1919- .... **CLC 4**
See also CA 9-12R, 219; CAAE 219; CAAS 8; CANR 4, 119; CP 7; DLB 5

Whittier, John Greenleaf
1807-1892 .... **NCLC 8, 59**
See also AMWS 1; DLB 1, 243; RGAL 4

Whittlebot, Hernia
See Coward, Noel (Peirce)

Wicker, Thomas Grey 1926-
See Wicker, Tom
See also CA 65-68; CANR 21, 46

Wicker, Tom .... **CLC 7**
See Wicker, Thomas Grey

Wideman, John Edgar 1941- ... **BLC 3; CLC 5, 34, 36, 67, 122; SSC 62**
See also AFAW 1, 2; AMWS 10; BPFB 4; BW 2, 3; CA 85-88; CANR 14, 42, 67, 109; CN 7; DAM MULT; DLB 33, 143; MTCW 2; RGAL 4; RGSF 2; SSFS 6, 12

Wiebe, Rudy (Henry) 1934- .. **CLC 6, 11, 14, 138**
See also CA 37-40R; CANR 42, 67, 123; CN 7; DAC; DAM MST; DLB 60; RHW

Wieland, Christoph Martin
1733-1813 .... **NCLC 17**
See also DLB 97; EW 4; LMFS 1; RGWL 2, 3

Wiene, Robert 1881-1938 .... **TCLC 56**

Wieners, John 1934- .... **CLC 7**
See also BG 3; CA 13-16R; CP 7; DLB 16; WP

Wiesel, Elie(zer) 1928- .... **CLC 3, 5, 11, 37, 165; WLCS**
See also AAYA 7, 54; AITN 1; CA 5-8R; CAAS 4; CANR 8, 40, 65, 125; CDALBS; CWW 2; DA; DA3; DAB; DAC; DAM MST, NOV; DLB 83, 299; DLBY 1987; EWL 3; INT CANR-8; LAIT 4; MTCW 1, 2; NCFS 4; NFS 4; RGWL 3; SATA 56; YAW

Wiggins, Marianne 1947- .... **CLC 57**
See also BEST 89:3; CA 130; CANR 60

Wigglesworth, Michael 1631-1705 .... **LC 106**
See also DLB 24; RGAL 4

Wiggs, Susan .... **CLC 70**
See also CA 201

Wight, James Alfred 1916-1995
See Herriot, James
See also CA 77-80; SATA 55; SATA-Brief 44

Wilbur, Richard (Purdy) 1921- ..... **CLC 3, 6, 9, 14, 53, 110; PC 51**
See also AMWS 3; CA 1-4R; CABS 2; CANR 2, 29, 76, 93; CDALBS; CP 7; DA; DAB; DAC; DAM MST, POET; DLB 5, 169; EWL 3; EXPP; INT CANR-29; MTCW 1, 2; PAB; PFS 11, 12, 16; RGAL 4; SATA 9, 108; WP

Wild, Peter 1940- .... **CLC 14**
See also CA 37-40R; CP 7; DLB 5

Wilde, Oscar (Fingal O'Flahertie Wills)
1854(?)-1900 .... **DC 17; SSC 11, 77; TCLC 1, 8, 23, 41; WLC**
See also AAYA 49; BRW 5; BRWC 1, 2; BRWR 2; BYA 15; CA 104; 119; CANR 112; CDBLB 1890-1914; DA; DA3; DAB; DAC; DAM DRAM, MST, NOV; DFS 4, 8, 9; DLB 10, 19, 34, 57, 141, 156, 190; EXPS; FANT; LATS 1:1; NFS 20; RGEL 2; RGSF 2; SATA 24; SSFS 7; SUFW; TEA; WCH; WLIT 4

Wilder, Billy .... **CLC 20**
See Wilder, Samuel
See also DLB 26

Wilder, Samuel 1906-2002
See Wilder, Billy
See also CA 89-92; 205

Wilder, Stephen
See Marlowe, Stephen

Wilder, Thornton (Niven)
1897-1975 .. **CLC 1, 5, 6, 10, 15, 35, 82; DC 1, 24; WLC**
See also AAYA 29; AITN 2; AMW; CA 13-16R; 61-64; CAD; CANR 40, 132; CDALBS; DA; DA3; DAB; DAC; DAM DRAM, MST, NOV; DFS 1, 4, 16; DLB 4, 7, 9, 228; DLBY 1997; EWL 3; LAIT 3; MTCW 1, 2; RGAL 4; RHW; WYAS 1

Wilding, Michael 1942- ...... **CLC 73; SSC 50**
See also CA 104; CANR 24, 49, 106; CN 7; RGSF 2

Wiley, Richard 1944- .... **CLC 44**
See also CA 121; 129; CANR 71

Wilhelm, Kate .... **CLC 7**
See Wilhelm, Katie (Gertrude)
See also AAYA 20; BYA 16; CAAS 5; DLB 8; INT CANR-17; SCFW 2

Wilhelm, Katie (Gertrude) 1928-
See Wilhelm, Kate
See also CA 37-40R; CANR 17, 36, 60, 94; MTCW 1; SFW 4

Wilkins, Mary
See Freeman, Mary E(leanor) Wilkins

Willard, Nancy 1936- .... **CLC 7, 37**
See also BYA 5; CA 89-92; CANR 10, 39, 68, 107; CLR 5; CWP; CWRI 5; DLB 5, 52; FANT; MAICYA 1, 2; MTCW 1; SATA 37, 71, 127; SATA-Brief 30; SUFW 2

William of Malmesbury c. 1090B.C.-c.
1140B.C. .... **CMLC 57**

William of Ockham 1290-1349 ..... **CMLC 32**

Williams, Ben Ames 1889-1953 ..... **TCLC 89**
See also CA 183; DLB 102

Williams, C(harles) K(enneth)
1936- .... **CLC 33, 56, 148**
See also CA 37-40R; CAAS 26; CANR 57, 106; CP 7; DAM POET; DLB 5

Williams, Charles
See Collier, James Lincoln

Williams, Charles (Walter Stansby)
1886-1945 .... **TCLC 1, 11**
See also BRWS 9; CA 104; 163; DLB 100, 153, 255; FANT; RGEL 2; SUFW 1

Williams, Ella Gwendolen Rees
See Rhys, Jean

Williams, (George) Emlyn
1905-1987 .... **CLC 15**
See also CA 104; 123; CANR 36; DAM DRAM; DLB 10, 77; IDTP; MTCW 1

Williams, Hank 1923-1953 .... **TCLC 81**
See Williams, Hiram King

Williams, Helen Maria
1761-1827 .... **NCLC 135**
See also DLB 158

Williams, Hiram Hank
See Williams, Hank

Williams, Hiram King
See Williams, Hank
See also CA 188

Williams, Hugo (Mordaunt) 1942- ... **CLC 42**
See also CA 17-20R; CANR 45, 119; CP 7; DLB 40

Williams, J. Walker
See Wodehouse, P(elham) G(renville)

Williams, John A(lfred) 1925- . **BLC 3; CLC 5, 13**
See also AFAW 2; BW 2, 3; CA 53-56, 195; CAAE 195; CAAS 3; CANR 6, 26, 51, 118; CN 7; CSW; DAM MULT; DLB 2, 33; EWL 3; INT CANR-6; RGAL 4; SFW 4

Williams, Jonathan (Chamberlain)
1929- .... **CLC 13**
See also CA 9-12R; CAAS 12; CANR 8, 108; CP 7; DLB 5

Williams, Joy 1944- .... **CLC 31**
See also CA 41-44R; CANR 22, 48, 97

Williams, Norman 1952- .... **CLC 39**
See also CA 118

Williams, Sherley Anne 1944-1999 ... **BLC 3; CLC 89**
See also AFAW 2; BW 2, 3; CA 73-76; 185; CANR 25, 82; DAM MULT, POET; DLB 41; INT CANR-25; SATA 78; SATA-Obit 116

Williams, Shirley
See Williams, Sherley Anne

Williams, Tennessee 1911-1983 . **CLC 1, 2, 5, 7, 8, 11, 15, 19, 30, 39, 45, 71, 111; DC 4; SSC 81; WLC**
See also AAYA 31; AITN 1, 2; AMW; AMWC 1; CA 5-8R; 108; CABS 3; CAD; CANR 31, 132; CDALB 1941-1968; DA; DA3; DAB; DAC; DAM DRAM, MST; DFS 17; DLB 7; DLBD 4; DLBY 1983; EWL 3; GLL 1; LAIT 4; LATS 1:2; MTCW 1, 2; RGAL 4; TUS

Williams, Thomas (Alonzo)
1926-1990 .... **CLC 14**
See also CA 1-4R; 132; CANR 2

Williams, William C.
See Williams, William Carlos

Williams, William Carlos
1883-1963 .... **CLC 1, 2, 5, 9, 13, 22, 42, 67; PC 7; SSC 31**
See also AAYA 46; AMW; AMWR 1; CA 89-92; CANR 34; CDALB 1917-1929; DA; DA3; DAB; DAC; DAM MST, POET; DLB 4, 16, 54, 86; EWL 3; EXPP; MTCW 1, 2; NCFS 4; PAB; PFS 1, 6, 11; RGAL 4; RGSF 2; TUS; WP

Williamson, David (Keith) 1942- ..... **CLC 56**
See also CA 103; CANR 41; CD 5; DLB 289

Woolf, (Adeline) Virginia 1882-1941 .. **SSC 7, 79; TCLC 1, 5, 20, 43, 56, 101, 123, 128; WLC**
See also AAYA 44; BPFB 3; BRW 7; BRWC 2; BRWR 1; CA 104; 130; CANR 64, 132; CDBLB 1914-1945; DA; DA3; DAB; DAC; DAM MST, NOV; DLB 36, 100, 162; DLBD 10; EWL 3; EXPS; FW; LAIT 3; LATS 1:1; LMFS 2; MTCW 1, 2; NCFS 8, 12; RGEL 2; RGSF 2; SSFS 4, 12; TEA; WLIT 4

Woollcott, Alexander (Humphreys)
1887-1943 .... **TCLC 5**
See also CA 105; 161; DLB 29

Woolrich, Cornell .... **CLC 77**
See Hopley-Woolrich, Cornell George
See also MSW

Woolson, Constance Fenimore
1840-1894 .... **NCLC 82**
See also DLB 12, 74, 189, 221; RGAL 4

Wordsworth, Dorothy 1771-1855 . **NCLC 25, 138**
See also DLB 107

Wordsworth, William 1770-1850 .. **NCLC 12, 38, 111; PC 4; WLC**
See also BRW 4; BRWC 1; CDBLB 1789-1832; DA; DA3; DAB; DAC; DAM MST, POET; DLB 93, 107; EXPP; LATS 1:1; LMFS 1; PAB; PFS 2; RGEL 2; TEA; WLIT 3; WP

Wotton, Sir Henry 1568-1639 .... **LC 68**
See also DLB 121; RGEL 2

Wouk, Herman 1915- .... **CLC 1, 9, 38**
See also BPFB 2, 3; CA 5-8R; CANR 6, 33, 67; CDALBS; CN 7; CPW; DA3; DAM NOV, POP; DLBY 1982; INT CANR-6; LAIT 4; MTCW 1, 2; NFS 7; TUS

Wright, Charles (Penzel, Jr.) 1935- .. **CLC 6, 13, 28, 119, 146**
See also AMWS 5; CA 29-32R; CAAS 7; CANR 23, 36, 62, 88, 135; CP 7; DLB 165; DLBY 1982; EWL 3; MTCW 1, 2; PFS 10

Wright, Charles Stevenson 1932- ..... **BLC 3; CLC 49**
See also BW 1; CA 9-12R; CANR 26; CN 7; DAM MULT, POET; DLB 33

Wright, Frances 1795-1852 .... **NCLC 74**
See also DLB 73

Wright, Frank Lloyd 1867-1959 .... **TCLC 95**
See also AAYA 33; CA 174

Wright, Jack R.
See Harris, Mark

Wright, James (Arlington)
1927-1980 ..... **CLC 3, 5, 10, 28; PC 36**
See also AITN 2; AMWS 3; CA 49-52; 97-100; CANR 4, 34, 64; CDALBS; DAM POET; DLB 5, 169; EWL 3; EXPP; MTCW 1, 2; PFS 7, 8; RGAL 4; TUS; WP

Wright, Judith (Arundell)
1915-2000 .... **CLC 11, 53; PC 14**
See also CA 13-16R; 188; CANR 31, 76, 93; CP 7; CWP; DLB 260; EWL 3; MTCW 1, 2; PFS 8; RGEL 2; SATA 14; SATA-Obit 121

Wright, L(aurali) R. 1939- .... **CLC 44**
See also CA 138; CMW 4

Wright, Richard (Nathaniel)
1908-1960 ... **BLC 3; CLC 1, 3, 4, 9, 14, 21, 48, 74; SSC 2; TCLC 136; WLC**
See also AAYA 5, 42; AFAW 1, 2; AMW; BPFB 3; BW 1; BYA 2; CA 108; CANR 64; CDALB 1929-1941; DA; DA3; DAC; DAM MST, MULT, NOV; DLB 76, 102; DLBD 2; EWL 3; EXPN; LAIT 3, 4; MTCW 1, 2; NCFS 1; NFS 1, 7; RGAL 4; RGSF 2; SSFS 3, 9, 15, 20; TUS; YAW

Wright, Richard B(ruce) 1937- .... **CLC 6**
See also CA 85-88; CANR 120; DLB 53

Wright, Rick 1945- .... **CLC 35**

Wright, Rowland
See Wells, Carolyn

Wright, Stephen 1946- .... **CLC 33**

Wright, Willard Huntington 1888-1939
See Van Dine, S. S.
See also CA 115; 189; CMW 4; DLBD 16

Wright, William 1930- .... **CLC 44**
See also CA 53-56; CANR 7, 23

Wroth, Lady Mary 1587-1653(?) .... **LC 30; PC 38**
See also DLB 121

Wu Ch'eng-en 1500(?)-1582(?) .... **LC 7**

Wu Ching-tzu 1701-1754 .... **LC 2**

Wulfstan c. 10th cent. -1023 .... **CMLC 59**

Wurlitzer, Rudolph 1938(?)- .... **CLC 2, 4, 15**
See also CA 85-88; CN 7; DLB 173

Wyatt, Sir Thomas c. 1503-1542 . **LC 70; PC 27**
See also BRW 1; DLB 132; EXPP; RGEL 2; TEA

Wycherley, William 1640-1716 .... **LC 8, 21, 102**
See also BRW 2; CDBLB 1660-1789; DAM DRAM; DLB 80; RGEL 2

Wyclif, John c. 1330-1384 .... **CMLC 70**
See also DLB 146

Wylie, Elinor (Morton Hoyt)
1885-1928 .... **PC 23; TCLC 8**
See also AMWS 1; CA 105; 162; DLB 9, 45; EXPP; RGAL 4

Wylie, Philip (Gordon) 1902-1971 ... **CLC 43**
See also CA 21-22; 33-36R; CAP 2; DLB 9; SFW 4

Wyndham, John .... **CLC 19**
See Harris, John (Wyndham Parkes Lucas) Beynon
See also DLB 255; SCFW 2

Wyss, Johann David Von
1743-1818 .... **NCLC 10**
See also CLR 92; JRDA; MAICYA 1, 2; SATA 29; SATA-Brief 27

Xenophon c. 430B.C.-c. 354B.C. ... **CMLC 17**
See also AW 1; DLB 176; RGWL 2, 3

Xingjian, Gao 1940-
See Gao Xingjian
See also CA 193; RGWL 3

Yakamochi 718-785 .... **CMLC 45; PC 48**

Yakumo Koizumi
See Hearn, (Patricio) Lafcadio (Tessima Carlos)

Yamada, Mitsuye (May) 1923- .... **PC 44**
See also CA 77-80

Yamamoto, Hisaye 1921- .... **AAL; SSC 34**
See also CA 214; DAM MULT; LAIT 4; SSFS 14

Yamauchi, Wakako 1924- .... **AAL**
See also CA 214

Yanez, Jose Donoso
See Donoso (Yanez), Jose

Yanovsky, Basile S.
See Yanovsky, V(assily) S(emenovich)

Yanovsky, V(assily) S(emenovich)
1906-1989 .... **CLC 2, 18**
See also CA 97-100; 129

Yates, Richard 1926-1992 .... **CLC 7, 8, 23**
See also AMWS 11; CA 5-8R; 139; CANR 10, 43; DLB 2, 234; DLBY 1981, 1992; INT CANR-10

Yau, John 1950- .... **PC 61**
See also CA 154; CANR 89; CP 7; DLB 234

Yeats, W. B.
See Yeats, William Butler

Yeats, William Butler 1865-1939 . **PC 20, 51; TCLC 1, 11, 18, 31, 93, 116; WLC**
See also AAYA 48; BRW 6; BRWR 1; CA 104; 127; CANR 45; CDBLB 1890-1914; DA; DA3; DAB; DAC; DAM DRAM, MST, POET; DLB 10, 19, 98, 156; EWL 3; EXPP; MTCW 1, 2; NCFS 3; PAB; PFS 1, 2, 5, 7, 13, 15; RGEL 2; TEA; WLIT 4; WP

Yehoshua, A(braham) B. 1936- .. **CLC 13, 31**
See also CA 33-36R; CANR 43, 90; CWW 2; EWL 3; RGSF 2; RGWL 3

Yellow Bird
See Ridge, John Rollin

Yep, Laurence Michael 1948- .... **CLC 35**
See also AAYA 5, 31; BYA 7; CA 49-52; CANR 1, 46, 92; CLR 3, 17, 54; DLB 52; FANT; JRDA; MAICYA 1, 2; MAICYAS 1; SATA 7, 69, 123; WYA; YAW

Yerby, Frank G(arvin) 1916-1991 ..... **BLC 3; CLC 1, 7, 22**
See also BPFB 3; BW 1, 3; CA 9-12R; 136; CANR 16, 52; DAM MULT; DLB 76; INT CANR-16; MTCW 1; RGAL 4; RHW

Yesenin, Sergei Alexandrovich
See Esenin, Sergei (Alexandrovich)

Yesenin, Sergey
See Esenin, Sergei (Alexandrovich)
See also EWL 3

Yevtushenko, Yevgeny (Alexandrovich)
1933- ...... **CLC 1, 3, 13, 26, 51, 126; PC 40**
See Evtushenko, Evgenii Aleksandrovich
See also CA 81-84; CANR 33, 54; DAM POET; EWL 3; MTCW 1

Yezierska, Anzia 1885(?)-1970 .... **CLC 46**
See also CA 126; 89-92; DLB 28, 221; FW; MTCW 1; RGAL 4; SSFS 15

Yglesias, Helen 1915- .... **CLC 7, 22**
See also CA 37-40R; CAAS 20; CANR 15, 65, 95; CN 7; INT CANR-15; MTCW 1

Yokomitsu, Riichi 1898-1947 .... **TCLC 47**
See also CA 170; EWL 3

Yonge, Charlotte (Mary)
1823-1901 .... **TCLC 48**
See also CA 109; 163; DLB 18, 163; RGEL 2; SATA 17; WCH

York, Jeremy
See Creasey, John

York, Simon
See Heinlein, Robert A(nson)

Yorke, Henry Vincent 1905-1974 ..... **CLC 13**
See Green, Henry
See also CA 85-88; 49-52

Yosano Akiko 1878-1942 .... **PC 11; TCLC 59**
See also CA 161; EWL 3; RGWL 3

Yoshimoto, Banana .... **CLC 84**
See Yoshimoto, Mahoko
See also AAYA 50; NFS 7

Yoshimoto, Mahoko 1964-
See Yoshimoto, Banana
See also CA 144; CANR 98; SSFS 16

Young, Al(bert James) 1939- ... **BLC 3; CLC 19**
See also BW 2, 3; CA 29-32R; CANR 26, 65, 109; CN 7; CP 7; DAM MULT; DLB 33

Young, Andrew (John) 1885-1971 ...... **CLC 5**
See also CA 5-8R; CANR 7, 29; RGEL 2

Young, Collier
See Bloch, Robert (Albert)

Young, Edward 1683-1765 .... **LC 3, 40**
See also DLB 95; RGEL 2

Young, Marguerite (Vivian)
1909-1995 .... **CLC 82**
See also CA 13-16; 150; CAP 1; CN 7

Young, Neil 1945- .... **CLC 17**
See also CA 110; CCA 1

445

Literary Criticism Series
Cumulative Topic Index

This index lists all topic entries in Gale's *Children's Literature Review* (CLR), *Classical and Medieval Literature Criticism* (CMLC), *Contemporary Literary Criticism* (CLC), *Drama Criticism* (DC), *Literature Criticism from 1400 to 1800* (LC), *Nineteenth-Century Literature Criticism* (NCLC), *Short Story Criticism* (SSC), and *Twentieth-Century Literary Criticism* (TCLC). The index also lists topic entries in the Gale Critical Companion Collection, which includes the following publications: *The Beat Generation* (BG), and *Harlem Renaissance* (HR).

Topic Index

Topic Index

Topic Index

CLC Cumulative Nationality Index

CLC-209 Title Index

ISBN 0-7876-7979-8

90000